Film Theory and Criticism

FILM THEORY
AND
CRITICISM
Introductory Readings

FOURTH EDITION

GERALD MAST
MARSHALL COHEN
LEO BRAUDY

New York   Oxford
OXFORD UNIVERSITY PRESS
1992

Oxford University Press

Oxford   New York   Toronto
Delhi   Bombay   Calcutta   Madras   Karachi
Kuala Lumpur   Singapore   Hong Kong   Tokyo
Nairobi   Dar es Salaam   Cape Town
Melbourne   Auckland

and associated companies in
Berlin   Ibadan

Published by Oxford University Press, Inc.,
200 Madison Avenue, New York, New York 10016

Oxford is a registered trademark of Oxford University Press

Library of Congress Cataloging-in-Publication Data
Mast, Gerald, 1940–1990
Film theory and criticism : introductory readings
Gerald Mast, Marshall Cohen, Leo Braudy.—4th ed.
p. cm.   Includes bibliographical references.
ISBN 0-19-506398-8
1. Motion pictures.
I. Cohen, Marshall.   II. Braudy, Leo.
III. Title.
PN1994.M364   1992   791.43—dc20
91-15995

2 4 6 8 9 7 5 3 1

Printed in the United States of America
on acid-free paper

PREFACE

In the years since the first edition of this collection appeared in 1974, the academic study of film in America has changed enormously and the journalistic and popular criticism of film has been deeply affected as well. Many of the same issues that pre-occupied and stimulated writers from the very beginning of film theory and criticism are still puzzling later generations: Is the filmed world realistic or artificial? Does it use a special language? Is its vision best expressed in silence? in sound? in black and white? in color? in live action? in animation? in two dimensions? in three? on a wide screeen? on a narrow screen? through stories that may be derived from other arts? through stories that can only be told on film?

Many of these questions about film were first formulated in critical language that owed an important debt to the methods and terminology of such humanistic disciplines as literary criticism, art history, and aesthetics. Meanwhile, beginning in the 1970s and continuing to the present, at the same time that film study was achieving an academic status separate from the departments of language and art where it had often first flourished, interpretive approaches derived from the social sciences began to have a tremendous influence.

In this fertile and energetic period—perhaps the richest in new explorations of the nature of film since the invention of the medium itself—the most salient avenues of interpretation first followed semiotic and structuralist imperatives, derived from linguistics and anthropology and often augmented with Marxist historical and Freudian psychoanalytic analysis. Somewhat later came Lacan's revisionary view of Freud (itself responsive to linguistic issues), the feminist interrogation of the power structures of vision (in which Marx and Freud were often married), and the deconstructive views of Jacques Derrida (where efforts to pierce the surface of the text and discover its "contradictions" often employed Marxist and psychoanalytic tools).

None of these new approaches has appeared without controversy or has maintained its relevance without polemic. Each in its own way has contributed to such classical issues of film theory as the relation of film to reality and how film may (or may not) be considered a language. In addition, they have introduced such new considerations as the way that films reveal the underlying social attitudes and ideologies of the cultures that produce them, the ways films manipulate audience beliefs, and the ways they raise, exploit, and seek to satisfy the audience's desires.

In the light both of continuing issues and new approaches, we might roughly divide the history of film theory into three somewhat overlapping phases. The first, which generally corresponds to the silent period, was formalist. From about 1916 (the year in which the earliest essay in this volume was published) to the mid-1930s, theorists such as Hugo Munsterberg, Rudolf Arnheim, and Sergei Eisenstein attempted to demonstrate that film was indeed an art, not just a direct recording of nature. The coming of synchronized sound and a nostalgia for the achievements of silent film then brought on a realist reaction to the formalist argument. Erwin Panofsky, Siegfried Kracauer, and André Bazin among others argued that film was not an art in opposition to nature but somehow, in a rich paradox, an art *of* nature.

In the 1960s and 1970s, this classical phase of film theory was challenged by writers responding both to historical conditions (the Vietnam War, the student riots in France and America) and to new developments in the academic concept of "knowledge," as defined by literature and the social sciences. These writers questioned the confidence with which classical film theory had used such terms as art, nature, society, reality, illusion, self, performance, work, author, and artist. The study of linguistics—drawing on the work of C. S. Peirce, Ferdinand de Saussure, Roman Jakobson, Louis Hjelmslev, and Noam Chomsky—explored the systems of meaning that allow communication itself to exist. Along with Lacan's psychoanalytic approach and Derrida's philosophic inquisition of textual meaning, the structural anthropology of Claude Lévi-Strauss and the demystified cultural history of Roland Barthes and Michel Foucault exerted a powerful influence on film study.

Now, as we begin the 1990s, there is a continuing concern with discovering the general terms and assumptions required for understanding film. However, since the mid-1980s, a complementary trend has begun to gather strength. One significant aspect of this trend seeks to merge insights owed to history, psychology, and linguistics into a synthesis suitable for understanding individual films as well as film in general. This potential synthesis is sometimes proposed under the general sponsorship of feminism, neoformalism, cognitive psychology, empiricism, or phenomenology. It often emphasizes the audience's active contribution to the creation of film meaning (as opposed to the passivity usually postulated in earlier cultural approaches). It may also emphasize the resistance of the performer, especially the star, to the meaning imposed by the film narrative; the ability of the independent filmmaker to construct a personal statement despite the supposedly totalitarian necessities of the medium; or the web of financial, political, and artistic decisions that constitute film production.

With this new phase as yet only beginning to demonstrate its potential, we have maintained the historical perspective of this collection as a broad survey of thinking about film over the past eight decades. Surveys of how the earlier editions of this collection were being used in the classroom showed us how often courses were structured around an interplay between classical and contemporary answers to the basic questions of film theory, along with an acute awareness of the new avenues that have been opened by the willingness to venture beyond disciplinary barriers. In rethinking the selections, we have therefore retained a good number of "classical" works that have set the agenda of even much of the most advanced recent theory and criticism. At the same time we have tried to illustrate the crucial new directions theory has taken over the last twenty-five years. In the process of opening space for new essays, we have regretted the need to drop old favorites, if only to keep the collection to a manageable size (and price).

Perhaps because so many of these questions about film have turned out to be perennially interwoven, our division of the complexity of theory into seven prime topics now also seems more a question of emphasis than of exclusivity. Especially when they consider the more recent essays, readers will discover connections that go beyond the confines of a particular section. As before, the final section, "Film: Psychology, Society, and Ideology," most obviously carries the banners of the new approaches: how film shapes or reflects cultural attitudes, reinforces or rejects the dominant modes of cultural thinking, stimulates or frustrates the needs and drives of the psyche. But the impact of new thinking is visible in each section. The title of the second section has been changed from "Film Image and Film Language" to "Film Language" to correspond to its concern with that question. Section III has accordingly been retitled "The Film Medium: Image and Sound" to register the inclusion of essays that deal with both the visual and the aural components of the medium. In addition to other changes, essays on the question of adaptation have been added to the section on "Film, Theater, and Literature." The "Film Genres" section has been extensively redone, as has the section on "The Film Artist"—an area brushed aside by contemporary theory that is now beginning to receive acute new attention.

Our deep thanks to those whose suggestions and criticism helped us formulate this new edition, especially Ernest Callenbach, Allan Casebier, Marsha Kinder, and the many (anonymous) teachers of film who took the time to respond to Oxford's queries about their use of the third edition.

We are also grateful to Angel Shekerdjian and Valentina Stoicescu for their great help in the complicated task of re-editing and reorganization.

Finally, we dedicate this edition to the memory of Gerald Mast, scholar, critic, and friend, whose contributions to film studies were at once so comprehensive and so insightful.

Los Angeles   L. B.
June 1991   M. C.

CONTENTS

IV ❑ Film, Theater, and Literature 351

Film Theory and Criticism

I

Film and Reality

The main tradition of Western aesthetics, deriving fom Aristotle's *Poetics,* adopts
the view that art "imitates" nature or, in Hamlet's phrase, holds "the mirror up to
nature." Painting, from the early Renaissance to the late nineteenth century, from
Giotto to Manet and the Impressionists, pursued this ideal with ever-increasing success. Later the novels of Balzac and Tolstoy provided a more detailed representation of nature and society than anything literature had previously known, and the
plays of Ibsen and Chekhov seemed to carry Hamlet's ideal of the theater to its limit.
All these achievements were eclipsed, however, by the invention of photography.
For the camera, and especially the motion picture camera, was unique in its ability
to represent nature. If the ideal of art is to create an illusion of reality, the motion
picture made it possible to achieve this ideal in an unprecedented way.

But is the aim of art to imitate nature at all? And if it is, what role remains for
the other arts when film achieves it so simply and perfectly? An anti-realist tradition
therefore denies that the goal of art is the imitation of nature. Some anti-realists
have argued that to create a work of art is not simply to copy the world but to add
another, and very special, object to the world. This object may be valuable because
it offers an interpretation or idealization of the world, or even because it creates
another, wholly autonomous, world. Others in this anti-realist tradition argue that
the value of such an object may be that it expresses the feelings and emotions of its
creator, or that the artist manages to impose a beautiful or a significant form on the
materials with which he works. The artist's feelings may be expressed abstractly,
and the resulting form may be purely imaginative. The work of art may not allude
to nature at all.

For example, theorists of modern painting have argued that painting should not
even attempt to provide a three-dimensional representation of reality but acknowledge, instead, that it is essentially the application of pigments to a two-dimensional

3

surface. This modernist view assumes that painting cannot and should not compete with film in attempting to mirror reality. Painting must renounce that task altogether. Other critics have countered, however, that film cannot reproduce reality either. And, even if it could, it ought not to try. According to this anti-realist view, film, like any other art form, must offer an interpretation of the world or, by the manipulation of the camera, create an alternative world. Just as painting must acknowledge that it is not really a mirror but pigments on canvas, cinema must acknowledge that it is simply projected images on a screen. To claim that these images ought to be images of physical reality—as opposed to any other kinds of images—is pure dogma. Why should these images not liberate the imagination from the tedium of reality, introducing us to the world of abstractions or of dreams instead?

Siegfried Kracauer is a leading exponent of the realist view of cinema. In his book, *Theory of Film*, Kracauer argues that because film literally photographs reality it alone is capable of holding the mirror up to nature. Film actually reproduces the raw material of the physical world within the work of art. This makes it impossible for a film to be a "pure" expression of the artist's formative intentions or an abstract, imaginative expression of his emotions. Kracauer insists that it is the clear obligation and the special privilege of film (a descendant of still photography) to record and reveal, and thereby redeem, physical reality.

Kracauer's attitude is a response to the common complaint that the abstractions and categorizations of modern science and technology make it impossible for us to appreciate the concrete world in which we live—what John Crowe Ransom called "the world's body." The distinct function of art (especially of poetic imagery) might therefore well be to help us possess the concrete world once more. Kracauer believes that film art actually does this; it "literally redeems this world from its dormant state, its state of virtual nonexistence, by endeavoring to experience it through the camera." For Kracauer film delivers us from technology by technology.

In his earlier work, *From Caligari to Hitler,* a study of the German cinema from 1919 to 1933, Kracauer traces the decline of German political culture as reflected in the history of its cinema. By representing its story as a tale told by a madman, Caligari reflects the general retreat from the facts of German life as well as the abuse of power and authority characteristic of German political institutions. The total organization of Caligari's landscapes within studio walls, its scenery of the soul, reveal the German cinema turning away from a reality which is haphazard, incalculable, and uncontrollable. In doing so, says Kracauer, German cinema helped prepare the way for Hitler's rise by subtly diverting the audience from a serious appraisal of social realities. This era of German film, usually considered one of the great periods in the history of cinema, is for Kracauer an example of all that cinema must avoid. By ignoring the claims of camera reality the German cinema achieved the damnation, not the redemption, of German life.

André Bazin, who also insists on the unique realism of cinema, does so, however, from a markedly different viewpoint. Bazin, a French critic who founded the influential journal, *Cahiers du Cinéma,* in the late 1940s and whose practicing disciples include Jean-Luc Godard, François Truffaut, and Claude Chabrol, is perhaps the most important theorist of the "second" film generation, a generation for whom the experience of the silent film was no longer decisive. Unlike Kracauer, Bazin views the film's realism as an expression of the mythic, not the scientific, spirit and believes that its function is not to redeem physical reality but to exempt us from our physical destiny. This magical aim finds expression in the "myth of total cinema," the ideal of a complete recreation of the world in its own image. Bazin welcomes the sound film as a necessary step toward this ideal in which Italian neorealism constitutes one of the greatest achievements.

In contrast both to the chief schools of realism that preceded it and to Soviet cinema, neorealism never makes reality the servant of some pre-existing point of view. And in contrast to expressionism it asks the actor, often the man in the street rather than the professional actor, to *be* rather than to act or pretend to be; it prefers an open, natural setting to an expressionistic mise-en-scène that imposes meaning on action; and, above all, it requires the narrative to respect the actual qualities and duration of the event in preference to the artificial, abstract, or dramatic duration favored in classic montage. Bazin's admiration for these characteristics of neorealism manifest an ontological position rather than a stylistic preference and, in the films of Vittorio de Sica, manifest a love for the creation itself.

But Bazin's conception of total cinema also leads to interesting questions—particularly in view of more recent advances in film technology and film style. Would he have welcomed the widespread use of color and the advent of holography and of three-dimensional cinema, as his principles seem to indicate? And what would his attitude have been to the self-consciousness and self-referential tendencies of the film in the last decades? Devices such as slow motion, the freeze frame, the split screen, and color tinting call attention to the screen itself, rather than treating it as a simple window on the world. Although Bazin put his trust in the representation of uninterpreted reality, many of his followers have insisted on the artifice of the cinematic image.

Rudolf Arnheim, who has also written extensively on the psychology of perception, is a leading "first generation" exponent of the anti-realist tradition in film theory. For Arnheim, if cinema were the mere mechanical reproduction of real life it could not be an art at all. Arnheim acknowledges the existence of a primitive desire to get material objects into one's power by creating them afresh, but he believes that this primitive impulse must be distinguished from the impulse to create art. The "wax museum" ideal may satisfy our primitive impulse, but it fails to satisfy the true artistic urge—not simply to copy, but to originate, to interpret, and to mold. The very properties that keep photography from reproducing reality perfectly must be exploited by the film artist, for they alone provide the possibilities for a film art. Bazin's myth of "total" cinema is nothing more than Arnheim's fallacy of the "complete" film. The pursuit of an ever more complete realism through the use of sound, color, and stereoscopic vision is simply a prescription for undermining the achievement of film art, which must respect, even welcome, the inherent limitations of the art.

V. F. Perkins attempts to incorporate the insights of both the realist and the antirealist traditions. For him the film medium is capable of both documentation and fantasy, of copying as well as creation. But the central achievement of film is to be found in fictional narration, and this type of movie achieves a synthesis of film's two tendencies. Cinema obscures the distinction between authentic and staged events, making us feel like eyewitnesses at what are in fact fictional events. The credibility that photography and movement confer on films' images encourages us to place an inaccurate construction on an accurate series of images. Film thereby achieves its unique blend of photographic realism and dramatic illusion.

As Perkins suggests, the consideration of film's relationship to reality has powerfully influenced evaluations of fictional, narrative films; however, these considerations are also important to an alternative film tradition, one called, variously, independent, experimental, or avant garde cinema. Two of the most important American contributors to that tradition are Maya Deren and Stan Brakhage. Deren accepted the inherent realism of the photographic image, beginning with her very first film, *Meshes of the Afternoon,* in 1943. For Deren, as for Kracauer and Bazin, "the photographic image as reality . . . is the building block for the creative use of the medium." But Deren's program for the "creative use" of this photographic reality synthesizes the opposing views of the realist theorists and Rudolf Arnheim: the filmmaker creatively alters photographic reality by distorting the anticipated and familiar spatio-temporal relationships within the sequential flow of images. Deren suggests ways to alter what Arnheim called reality's "space-time continuum"—by using slow motion, reverse motion, and the freeze frame.

However, Deren also depends on our recognizing and understanding the perceptual reality which the photographic image presents and represents. Her films can then creatively exploit the "various attributes of the photographic image"—its fidelity, reality, and authority—by effectively undermining what we know about these realistic spaces.

Stan Brakhage, who began making his highly personal films just after the Second World War, takes an exactly opposite position. For Brakhage, the supposed reality of the photographic image is itself a conventionalized illusion, imposed by rules of perspective, compositional logic, and "lenses grounded to achieve 19th century Western compositional perspective." Brakhage's argument thus looks forward to those of the post-structuralist theorists who similarly attack the ideology of perspective and the cinema apparatus (see especially Section VII of this volume). But its fundamental purpose is to propose that the goal of cinema is the liberation of the eye itself, the creation of an act of seeing previously unimagined and undefined by conventions of representation, an eye as natural and unprejudiced as that of a cat, a bee, or an infant. Brakhage hopes to replace the absolute realism of the motion picture, which he calls "a contemporary mechanical myth," with a new "unrealized, therefore potential, magic." If there is one clear link between Deren and Brakhage it is that, whatever their opposing views, their films and writings represent reflexive, modernist meditations on the act and art of cinema itself.

Colin McCabe introduces concerns of political ideology, gender perspective, and psychoanalytic theory in a manner characteristic of much film scholarship in the past decade or more. These perspectives appear throughout the anthology but are explored most elaborately in Section VII. From these perspectives McCabe rejects the assumptions of classical realist cinema, which remains the dominant force within commercial cinema, as well as the realist theories of André Bazin. In McCabe's view Bazin thinks that the revelation of reality is the prime task of cinema: all aesthetic devices are present to unmake themselves so that we can experience, as the artist has experienced, that moment in which reality presents itself whole. For MacCabe, however, film does not reveal reality in a moment of transparency or establish an omnicompetent point of view. Rather, in his Althusserian Marxist view film is constituted by a set of contradictory discourses, which are themselves the production of a set of socially and politically defined positions. None of these discourses is normative and there is no possibility of verification, no correspondence between sound and image, which enables the spectator to enter a Bazinian realm of truth. In terms adopted from Lacanian psychoanalysis MacCabe argues that it is impossible for the spectator to maintain the world of plenitude in which there are no traces of lack, of castration. The spectator must emerge from this imaginary order, and enter the symbolic order, in which the look is related, not to the object, but only to other looks. Realism is no longer a question of an exterior reality nor of the relation of the reader to the text: It is simply one of the ways in which they interact amid specific social and political circumstances.

Finally, in "Recent Developments in Feminist Criticism," Christine Gledhill rejects the anti-realist epistemology implicit in much neo-Marxist and neo-Freudian thought, along with the assumption that feminism must ally itself with an anti-realist cinema. Under the influence of Althusser, some feminists have thought that, since lived experience is the inevitable materialization of the dominant ideology, a realist cinema lacks the resources to escape that ideology. Under the influence of Lacan, many have also thought that the threat of castration is necessary to the production of the speaking subjects and for entrance into the paternalistically dominated symbolic order. But for the subject to speak, the possibility of castration must be overcome or concealed. For this reason female sexuality cannot be expressed. This mechanism of suppression is at play in the voyeurism and fetishism that govern the presentation of women in the narrative film, and it is this feature that leads Laura Mulvey to endorse an alternative cinema (see Section VII below). For Gledhill, however, it is a mistake to make language and the signifying process so exclusively central to social analysis. By concentrating exclusively on the semiotic production of meaning, theorists create a cultural condition in which the effectiveness of social, economic, and political practice threatens to disappear altogether. To say that language has a determining effect on society is a different matter from saying that society is nothing but its languages and signifying practices (as French theorists like Roland Barthes, Jacques Derrida, and Louis Althusser have tended to do). In the end, it is difficult for Gledhill to see how, if a radical ideology such as feminism is to be defined as a basis for practical political action, it is going to be possible to avoid some kind of realist epistemology.

SIEGFRIED KRACAUER
FROM THEORY OF FILM

BASIC CONCEPTS

Like the embryo in the womb, photographic film developed from distinctly separate components. Its birth came about from a combination of instantaneous photography, as used by Muybridge and Marey, with the older devices of the magic lantern and the phenakistoscope. Added to this later were the contributions of other nonphotographic elements, such as editing and sound. Nevertheless photography, especially instantaneous photography, has a legitimate claim to top priority among these elements, for it undeniably is and remains the decisive factor in establishing film content. The nature of photography survives in that of film.

Originally, film was expected to bring the evolution of photography to an end—satisfying at last the age-old desire to picture things moving. This desire already accounted for major developments within the photographic medium itself. As far back as 1839, when the first daguerreotypes and talbotypes appeared, admiration mingled with disappointment about their deserted streets and blurred landscapes. And in the 'fifties, long before the innovation of the hand camera, successful attempts were made to photograph subjects in motion. The very impulses which thus led from time exposure to snapshot engendered dreams of a further extension of photography in the same direction—dreams, that is, of film. Abut 1860, Cook and Bonnelli, who had developed a device called a photobioscope, predicted a "complete revolution of photographic art. . . . We will see . . . landscapes," they announced, "in which the trees bow to the whims of the wind, the leaves ripple and glitter in the rays of the sun."

Along with the familiar photographic leitmotif of the leaves, such kindred subjects as undulating waves, moving clouds, and changing facial expressions ranked high in early prophecies. All of them conveyed the longing for an instrument which would capture the slightest incidents of the world about us—scenes that often would involve crowds, whose incalculable movements resemble, somehow, those of waves or leaves. In a memorable statement published before the emergence of instantaneous photography, Sir John Herschel not only predicted the basic features of the film camera but assigned to it a task which it has never since disowned: "the vivid and lifelike reproduction and handing down to the latest posterity of any transaction in real life—a battle, a debate, a public solemnity, a pugilistic conflict." Ducos du Hauron and other forerunners also looked forward to what we have come to label newsreels and documentaries—films devoted to the rendering of real-life events. This insistence on recording went hand in hand with the expectation that motion pictures could acquaint us with normally imperceptible or otherwise induplicable movements—flashlike transformations of matter, the slow growth of plants, etc. All in all, it was taken for granted that film would continue along the lines of photography. . . .

PROPERTIES OF THE MEDIUM

The properties of film can be divided into basic and technical properties.

The basic properties are identical with the properties of photography. Film, in other words, is uniquely equipped to record and reveal physical reality and, hence, gravitates toward it.

Now there are different visible worlds. Take a stage performance or a painting: they too are real and can be perceived. But the only reality we are concerned with is actually existing physical reality—the transitory world we live in. (Physical reality will also be called "material reality," or "physical existence," or "actuality," or loosely just "nature." Another fitting term might be "camera-reality.") . . . The other visible worlds reach into this world without, however, really forming a part of it. A theatrical play, for instance, suggests a universe of its own which would immediately crumble were it related to its real-life environment.

As a reproductive medium, film is of course justified in reproducing memorable ballets, operas, and the like. Yet even assuming that such reproductions try to do justice to the specific requirements of the screen, they basically amount to little more than "canning," and are of no interest to us here. Preservation of performances which lie outside physical reality proper is at best a sideline of a medium so particularly suited to explore that reality. This is not to deny that reproductions, say, of stage production numbers may be put to good cinematic use in certain feature films and film genres.

Of all the technical properties of film the most general and indispensable is editing. It serves to establish a meaningful continuity of shots and is therefore unthinkable in photography. (Photomontage is a graphic art rather than a specifically photographic genre.) Among the more special cinematic techniques are some which have been taken over from photography—e.g. the close-up, soft-focus pictures, the use of negatives, double or multiple exposure, etc. Others, such as the lap-dissolve, slow and quick motion, the reversal of time, certain "special effects," and so forth, are for obvious reasons exclusively peculiar to film.

These scanty hints will suffice. It is not necessary to elaborate on technical matters which have been dealt with in most previous theoretical writings on film. Unlike these, which invariably devote a great deal of space to editing devices, modes of lighting, various effects of the close-up, etc., the present book concerns itself with cinematic techniques only to the extent to which they bear on the nature of film, as defined by its basic properties and their various implications. The interest lies not with editing in itself, regardless of the purposes it serves, but with editing as a means of implementing—or defying, which amounts to the same—such potentialities of the medium as are in accordance with its substantive characteristics. In other words, the task is not to survey all possible methods of editing for their own sake; rather, it is to determine the contributions which editing may make to cinematically significant achievements. Problems of film technique will not be neglected; however, they will be discussed only if issues going beyond technical considerations call for their investigation.

This remark on procedures implies what is fairly obvious anyway: that the basic and technical properties differ substantially from each other. As a rule the former take precedence over the latter in the sense that they are responsible for the cinematic quality of a film. Imagine a film which, in keeping with the basic properties, records interesting aspects of physcal reality but does so in a technically imperfect manner; perhaps the lighting is awkward or the editing uninspired. Nevertheless such a film is more specifically a film than one which utilizes brilliantly all the cinematic devices and tricks to produce a statement disregarding camera-reality. Yet this should not lead one to underestimate the influence of the technical properties. It will be seen that in certain cases the knowing use of a variety of techniques may endow otherwise nonrealistic films with a cinematic flavor.

THE TWO MAIN TENDENCIES

If film grows out of photography, the realistic and formative tendencies must be operative in it also. Is it by sheer accident that the two tendencies manifested themselves side by side immediately after the rise of the medium? As if to encompass the whole range of cinematic endeavors at the outset, each went the limit in exhausting its own possibilities. Their prototypes were Lumière, a strict realist, and Méliès, who gave free rein to his artistic imagination. The films they made embody, so to speak, thesis and antithesis in a Hegelian sense.

Lumière and Méliès

Lumiére's films contained a true innovation, as compared with the repertoire of the zootropes or Edison's peep boxes: they pictured everyday life after the manner of photographs. Some of his early pictures, such as *Baby's Breakfast (Le Déjeuner de bébé)* or *The Card Players (La Partie d'écarté)*, testify to the amateur photographer's delight in family idyls and genre scenes. And there was *Teasing the Gardener (L'Arroseur arrosé)*, which enjoyed immense popularity because it elicited from the flow of everyday life a proper story with a funny climax to boot. A gardener is watering flowers and, as he unsuspectingly proceeds, an impish boy steps on the hose, releasing it at the very moment when his perplexed victim examines the dried-up nozzle. Water squirts out and hits the gardener smack in the face. The denouement is true to style, with the gardener chasing and spanking the boy. This film, the germ cell and archetype of all film comedies to come, represented an imaginative attempt on the part of Lumière to develop photography into a means of story telling. Yet the story was just a real-life incident. And it was precisely its photographic veracity which made Maxim Gorki undergo a shock-like experience. "You think," he wrote about *Teasing the Gardener,* "the spray is going to hit you too, and instinctively shrink back."

On the whole, Lumière seems to have realized that story telling was none of his business; it involved problems with which he apparently did not care to cope. Whatever story-telling films he, or his company, made—some more comedies in the vein of his first one, tiny historical scenes, etc.—are not characeristic of his production. The bulk of his films recorded the world about us for no other purpsoe than to present it. This is in any case what Mesguich, one of Lumière's "ace" cameramen, felt to be their message. At a time when the talkies were already in full swing he epitomized the work of the master as follows: "As I see it, the Lumière Brothers had established the true domain of the cinema in the right manner. The novel, the theater, suffice for the study of the human heart. The cinema is the dynamism of life, of nature and its manifestations, of the crowd and its eddies. All that asserts itself through movement depends on it. Its lens opens on the world."

Lumière's lens did open on the world in this sense. Take his immortal first reels *Lunch Hour at the Lumière Factory (Sortie des usines Lumière), Arrival of a Train (L'Arrivée d'un train), La Place des Cordeliers à Lyon:* their themes were public places, with throngs of people moving in diverse directions. The crowded streets captured by the stereographic photographs of the late 'fifties thus reappeared on the primitive screen. It was life at its least controllable and most unconscious moments, a jumble of transient, forever dissolving patterns accessible only to the camera. The much-imitated shot of the railway station, with its emphasis on the confusion of arrival and departure, effectively illustrated the fortuity of these patterns; and their fragmentary character was exemplifed by the clouds of smoke which leisurely drifted upward. Significantly, Lumière used the motif of smoke on several occasions. And he seemd anxious to avoid any personal interference with the given data. Detached records, his shots resembled the imaginary shot of the grandmother which Proust contrasts with the memory image of her.

Contemporaries praised these films for the very qualities which the prophets and forerunners had singled out in their visions of the medium. It is inevitable that, in the comments on Lumière, "the ripple of leaves stirred by the wind" should be referred to enthusiastically. The Paris journalist Henri de Parville, who used the image of the trembling leaves, also identified Lumière's over-all theme as "nature caught in the act." Others pointed to the benefits which science would derive from Lumière's invention. In America his camera-realism defeated Edison's kinetoscope with its staged subjects.

Lumière's hold on the masses was ephemeral. In 1897, not more than two years after he had begun to make films, his popularity subsided. The sensation had worn off; the heyday was over. Lack of interest caused Lumière to reduce his production.

Georges Méliès took over where Lumière left off, renewing and intensifying the medium's waning appeal. This is not to say that he did not occasionally follow the latter's example. In his beginnings he too treated the audience to sightseeing tours;

The Two Tendencies: Lumière's *Workers Leaving the Lumière Factory* (1895) and Méliès' *The Witch* (1900). "Lumière's lens did open on the world . . . Méliès ignored the workings of nature out of the artist's delight in sheer fantasy" (KRACAUER, pages 12, 14).

or he dramatized, in the fashion of the period, realistically staged topical events. But his main contribution to the cinema lay in substituting staged illusion for unstaged reality, and contrived plots for everyday incidents.

The two pioneers were aware of the radical differences in their approach. Lumière told Méliès that he considered film nothing more than a "scientific curiosity," thereby implying that his cinematograph could not possibly serve artistic purposes. In 1897, Méliès on his part published a prospectus which took issue with Lumière: "Messrs. Méliès and Reulos specialize mainly in fantastic or artistic scenes, reproductions of theatrical scenes, etc. . . . thus creating a special genre which differs entirely from the customary views supplied by the cinematograph—street scenes or scenes of everyday life."

Méliès's tremendous success would seem to indicate that he catered to demands left unsatisfied by Lumière's photographic realism. Lumière appealed to the sense of observation, the curiosity about "nature caught in the act"; Méliès ignored the workings of nature out of the artist's delight in sheer fantasy. The train in *Arrival of a Train* is the real thing, whereas its counterpart in Méliès's *An Impossible Voyage (Voyage à travers l'impossible)* is a toy train as unreal as the scenery through which it is moving. Instead of picturing the random movements of phenomena, Méliès freely interlinked imagined events according to the requirements of his charming fairy-tale plots. Had not media very close to film offered similar gratifications? The artist-photographers preferred what they considered aesthetically attractive compositions to searching explorations of nature. And immediately before the arrival of the motion picture camera, magic lantern performances indulged in the projection of religious themes, Walter Scott novels, and Shakespearean dramas.

Yet even though Méliès did not take advantage of the camera's ability to record and reveal the physical world, he increasingly created his illusions with the aid of techniques peculiar to the medium. Some he found by accident. When taking shots of the Paris Place de l'Opéra, he had to discontinue the shooting because the celluloid strip did not move as it should; the surprising result was a film in which, for no reason at all, a bus abruptly transformed itself into a hearse. True, Lumière also was not disinclined to have a sequence of events unfold in reverse, but Méliès was the first to exploit cinematic devices systematically. Drawing on both photography and the stage, he innovated many techniques which were to play an enormous rôle in the future—among them the use of masks, multiple exposure, superimposition as a means of summoning ghosts, the lap-dissolve, etc. And through his ingenuity in using these techniques he added a touch of cinema to his playful narratives and magic tricks. Stage traps ceased to be indispensable; sleights-of-hand yielded to incredible metamorphoses which film alone was able to accomplish. Illusion produced in this climate depended on another kind of craftsmanship than the magician's. It was cinematic illusion, and as such went far beyond theatrical make-believe. Méliès's *The Haunted Castle (Le Manoir du diable)* "is conceivable only in the cinema and due to the cinema," says Henri Langlois, one of the best connoisseurs of the primitive era.

Notwithstanding his film sense, however, Méliès still remained the theater director he had been. He used photography in a pre-photographic spirit—for the reproduction of a papier-maché universe inspired by stage traditions. In one of his great-est films, *A Trip to the Moon (Le Voyage dans la lune),* the moon harbors a grimacing man in the moon and the stars are bull's-eyes studded with the pretty faces of music hall girls. By the same token, his actors bowed to the audience, as if they performed on the stage. Much as his films differed from the theater on a tech-nical plane, they failed to transcend its scope by incorporating genuinely cinematic subjects. This also explains why Méliès, for all his inventiveness, never thought of moving his camera; the stationary camera perpetuated the spectator's relation to the stage. His ideal spectator was the traditional theatergoer, child or adult. There seems to be some truth in the observation that, as people grow older, they instinc-tively withdraw to the positions from which they set out to struggle and conquer. In his later years Méliès more and more turned from theatrical film to filmed the-ater, producing *féeries* which recalled the Paris Châtelet pageants.

The Realistic Tendency

In following the realistic tendency, films go beyond photography in two respects. First, they picture movement itself, not only one or another of its phases. But what kinds of movements do they picture? In the primitive era when the camera was fixed to the ground, it was natural for film makers to concentrate on moving mate-rial phenomena; life on the screen was life only if it manifested itself through exter-nal, or "objective," motion. As cinematic techniques developed, films increasingly drew on camera mobility and editing devices to deliver their messages. Although their strength still lay in the rendering of movements inaccessible to other media, these movements were no longer necessarily objective. In the technically mature film "subjective" movements—movements, that is, which the spectator is invited to execute—constantly compete with objective ones. The spectator may have to identify himself with a tilting, panning, or traveling camera which insists on bring-ing motionless as well as moving objects to his attention. Or an appropriate arrange-ment of shots may rush the audience through vast expanses of time and/or space so as to make it witness, almost simultaneously, events in different periods and places.

Nevertheless the emphasis is now as before on objective movement; the medium seems to be partial to it. As René Clair puts it: "If there is an aesthetics of the cinema . . . it can be summarized in one word: 'movement.' The external movement of the objects perceived by the eye, to which we are today adding the inner movement of the action." The fact that he assigns a dominant role to external movement reflects, on a theoretical plane, a marked feature of his own earlier films—the ballet-like evolutions of their characters.

Second, films may seize upon physical reality with all its manifold movements by means of an intermediary procedure which would seem to be less indispensable in photography—staging. In order to narrate an intrigue, the film maker is often obliged to stage not only the action but the surroundings as well. Now this recourse to staging is most certainly legitimate if the staged world is made to appear as a faithful reproduction of the real one. The important thing is that studio-built settings convey the impression of actuality, so that the spectator feels he is watching events which might have occurred in real life and have been photographed on the spot.

Falling prey to an interesting misconception, Emile Vuillermoz champions, for the sake of "realism," settings which represent reality as seen by a perceptive painter. To his mind they are more real than real-life shots because they impart the essence of what such shots are showing. Yet from the cinematic point of view these allegedly realistic settings are no less stagy than would be, say, a cubist or abstract composition. Instead of staging the given raw material itself, they offer, so to speak, the gist of it. In other words, they suppress the very camera-reality which film aims at incorporating. For this reason, the sensitive moviegoer will feel disturbed by them. (The problems posed by films of fantasy which, as such, show little concern for physical reality will be considered later on.)

Strangely enough, it is entirely possible that a staged real-life event evokes a stronger illusion of reality on the screen than would the original event if it had been captured directly by the camera. The late Ernö Metzner who devised the settings for the studio-made mining disaster in Pabst's *Kameradschaft*—an episode with the ring of stark authenticity—insisted that candid shots of a real mining disaster would hardly have produced the same convincing effect.

One may ask, on the other hand, whether reality can be staged so accurately that the camera-eye will not detect any difference between the original and the copy. Blaise Cendrars touches on this issue in a neat hypothetical experiment. He imagines two film scenes which are completely identical except for the fact that one has been shot on the Mont Blanc (the highest mountain of Europe) while the other was staged in the studio. His contention is that the former has a quality not found in the latter. There are on the mountain, says he, certain "emanations, luminous or otherwise, which have worked on the film and given it a soul." Presumably large parts of our environment, natural or man-made, resist duplication.

The Formative Tendency

The film maker's formative faculties are offered opportunities far exceeding those offered the photographer. The reason is that film extends into dimensions which photography does not cover. These differ from each other according to area and composition. With respect to areas, film makers have never confined themselves to exploring only physical reality in front of the camera but, from the outset, persistently tried to penetrate the realms of history and fantasy. Remember Méliès. Even the realistic-minded Lumière yielded to the popular demand for historical scenes. As for composition, the two most general types are the story film and the nonstory film. The latter can be broken down into the experimental film and the film of fact, which on its part comprises, partially or totally, such subgenres as the film on art, the newsreel, and the documentary proper.

It is easy to see that some of these dimensions are more likely than others to prompt the film maker to express his formative aspirations at the expense of the realistic tendency. As for areas, consider that of fantasy: movie directors have at all times rendered dreams or visions with the aid of settings which are anything but realistic. Thus in *Red Shoes* Moira Shearer dances, in a somnambulistic trance, through fantastic worlds avowedly intended to project her conscious mind—agglomerates of landscape-like forms, near-abstract shapes, and luscious color schemes which have all the traits of stage imagery. Disengaged creativity thus drifts away from the basic concerns of the medium. Several dimensions of composition favor the same preferences. Most experimental films are not even designed to focus on physical existence; and practically all films following the lines of a theatrical story evolve narratives whose significance overshadows that of the raw material of nature used for their implementation. For the rest, the film maker's formative endeavors may also impinge on his realistic loyalties in dimensions which, because of their emphasis on physical reality, do not normally invite such encroachments; there are enough documentaries with real-life shots which merely serve to illustrate some self-contained oral commentary.

Clashes Between the Two Tendencies

Films which combine two or more dimensions are very frequent; for instance, many a movie featuring an everyday-life incident includes a dream sequence or a documentary passage. Some such combinations may lead to overt clashes between the realistic and formative tendencies. This happens whenever a film maker bent on creating an imaginary universe from freely staged material also feels under an obligation to draw on camera-reality. In his *Hamlet* Laurence Olivier has the cast move about in a studio-built, conspicuously stagy Elsinore, whose labyrinthine architecture seems calculated to reflect Hamlet's unfathomable being. Shut off from our real-life environment, this bizarre structure would spread over the whole of the film were it not for a small, otherwise insignificant scene in which the real ocean outside that dream orbit is shown. But no sooner does the photographed ocean appear than the spectator experiences something like a shock. He cannot help recognizing that this little scene is an outright intrusion; that it abruptly introduces an element incompatible with the rest of the imagery. How he then reacts to it depends upon his sensibilities. Those indifferent to the peculiarities of the medium, and therefore unquestioningly accepting the staged Elsinore, are likely to resent the unexpected emergence of crude nature as a letdown, while those more sensitive to the properties of film will in a flash realize the make-believe character of the castle's mythical splendor. Another case in point is Renato Castellani's *Romeo and Juliet*. This attempt to stage Shakespeare in natural surroundings obviously rests upon the belief that camera-reality and the poetic reality of Shakespeare verse can be made to fuse into each other. Yet the dialogue as well as the intrigue establish a universe so remote from the chance world of real Verona streets and ramparts that all the scenes in which the two disparate worlds are seen merging tend to affect one as an unnatural alliance between conflicting forces.

Actually collisions of this kind are by no means the rule. Rather, there is ample evidence to suggest that the two tendencies which sway the medium may be interrelated in various other ways. Since some of these relationships between realistic and formative efforts can be assumed to be aesthetically more gratifying than the rest, the next step is to try to define them.

THE CINEMATIC APPROACH

It follows from what has been said . . . that films may claim aesthetic validity if they build from their basic properties; like photographs, that is, they must record and reveal physical reality. . . . One might argue that too exclusive an emphasis on the medium's primary relation to physical reality tends to put film in a strait jacket. This objection finds support in the many existing films which are completely unconcerned about the representation of nature. There is the abstract experimental film. There is an unending succession of "photoplays" or theatrical films which do not picture real-life material for its own sake but use it to build up action after the manner of the stage. And there are the many films of fantasy which neglect the external world in freely composed dreams or visions. The old German expressionist films went far in this direction; one of their champions, the German art critic Herman G. Scheffauer, even eulogizes expressionism on the screen for its remoteness from photographic life.

Why, then, should these genres be called less "cinematic" than films concentrating on physical existence? The answer is of course that it is the latter alone which afford insight and enjoyment otherwise unattainable. True, in view of all the genres which do not cultivate outer reality and yet are here to stay, this answer sounds somewhat dogmatic. But perhaps it will be found more justifiable in the light of the following two considerations.

First, favorable response to a genre need not depend upon its adequacy to the medium from which it issues. As a matter of fact, many a genre has a hold on the audience because it caters to widespread social and cultural demands; it is and remains popular for reasons which do not involve questions of aesthetic legitimacy. Thus the photoplay has succeeded in perpetuating itself even though most responsible critics are agreed that it goes against the grain of film. Yet the public which feels attracted, for instance, by the screen version of *Death of a Salesman,* likes this version for the very virtues which made the Broadway play a hit and does not in the least care whether or not it has any specifically cinematic merits.

Second, let us for the sake of argument assume that my definition of aesthetic validity is actually one-sided; that it results from a bias for one particular, if important, type of cinematic activities and hence is unlikely to take into account, say, the possibility of hybrid genres or the influence of the medium's nonphotographic components. But this does not necessarily speak against the propriety of that definition. In a strategic interest it is often more advisable to loosen up initial one-sidedness— provided it is well founded—than to start from all too catholic premises and then try to make them specific. The latter alternative runs the risk of blurring differences between the media because it rarely leads far enough away from the generalities postulated at the outset; its danger is that it tends to entail a confusion of the arts. When Eisenstein, the theoretician, began to stress the similarities between the cinema and the traditional art media, identifying film as their ultimate fulfillment, Eisenstein, the artist, increasingly trespassed the boundaries that separate film from elaborate theatrical spectacles: think of his *Alexander Nevsky* and the operatic aspects of his *Ivan the Terrible.*

In strict analogy to the term "photographic approach" the film maker's approach is called "cinematic" if it acknowledges the basic aesthetic principle. It is evident that the cinematic approach materializes in all films which follow the realistic tendency. This implies that even films almost devoid of creative aspirations, such as newsreels, scientific or educational films, artless documentaries, etc., are tenable propositions from an aesthetic point of view—presumably more so than films which for all their artistry pay little attention to the given outer world. But as with photographic reportage, newsreels and the like meet only the minimum requirement.

What is of the essence in film no less than photography is the intervention of the film maker's formative energies in all the dimensions which the medium has come to cover. He may feature his impressions of this or that segment of physical existence in documentary fashion, transfer hallucinations and mental images to the screen, indulge in the rendering of rhythmical patterns, narrate a human-interest story, etc. All these creative efforts are in keeping with the cinematic approach as long as they benefit, in some way or other, the medium's substantive concern with our visible world. As in photography, everything depends on the "right" balance between the realistic tendency and the formative tendency; and the two tendencies are well balanced if the latter does not try to overwhelm the former but eventually follows its lead.

THE ISSUE OF ART

When calling the cinema an art medium, people usually think of films which resemble the traditional works of art in that they are free creations rather than explorations of nature. These films organize the raw material to which they resort into some self-sufficient composition instead of accepting it as an element in its own right. In other words, their underlying formative impulses are so strong that they defeat the cinematic approach with its concern for camera-reality. Among the film types customarily considered art are, for instance, the above-mentioned German expressionist films of the years after World War I; conceived in a painterly spirit, they seem to implement the formula of Hermann Warm, one of the designers of *The Cabinet of Dr. Caligari* settings, who claimed that "films must be drawings brought to life." Here also belongs many an experimental film; all in all, films of this type are not only intended as autonomous wholes but frequently ignore physical reality or exploit it for purposes alien to photographic veracity. By the same token, there is an inclination to classify as works of art feature films which combine forceful artistic composition with devotion to significant subjects and values. This would apply to a number of adaptations of great stage plays and other literary works.

Yet such a usage of the term "art" in the traditional sense is misleading. It lends support to the belief that artistic qualities must be attributed precisely to films which neglect the medium's recording obligations in an attempt to rival achievements in the fields of the fine arts, the theater, or literature. In consequence, this usage tends to obscure the aesthetic value of films which are really true to the medium. If the term "art" is reserved for productions like *Hamlet* or *Death of a Salesman,* one will find it difficult indeed to appreciate properly the large amount of creativity that goes into many a documentary capturing material phenomena for their own sake. Take Ivens's *Rain* or Flaherty's *Nanook,* documentaries saturated with formative intentions: like any selective photographer, their creators have all the traits of the imaginative reader and curious explorer; and their readings and discoveries result from full absorption in the given material and significant choices. Add to this that some of the crafts needed in the cinematic process—especially editing—represent tasks with which the photographer is not confronted. And they too lay claim to the film maker's creative powers.

This leads straight to a terminological dilemma. Due to its fixed meaning, the concept of art does not, and cannot, cover truly "cinematic" films—films, that is, which incorporate aspects of physical reality with a view to making us experience them. And yet it is they, not the films reminiscent of traditional art works, which are valid aesthetically. If film is an art at all, it certainly should not be confused with the established arts. There may be some justification in loosely applying this fragile concept to such films as *Nanook,* or *Paisan,* or *Potemkin* which are deeply steeped in camera-life. But in defining them as art, it must always be kept in mind that even the most creative film maker is much less independent of nature in the raw than the painter or poet; that his creativity manifests itself in letting nature in and penetrating it.

1960

SIEGFRIED KRACAUER
FROM FROM CALIGARI TO HITLER

THE CABINET OF DR. CALIGARI

The Czech Hans Janowitz, one of the two authors of the film *Das Cabinet des Dr. Caligari (The Cabinet of Dr. Caligari),* was brought up in Prague—that city where reality fuses with dreams, and dreams turn into visions of horror.* One evening in October 1913 this young poet was strolling through a fair at Hamburg, trying to find a girl whose beauty and manner had attracted him. The tents of the fair covered the Reeperbahn, known to any sailor as one of the world's chief pleasure spots. Nearby, on the Holstenwall, Lederer's gigantic Bismarck monument stood sentinel over the ships in the harbor. In search of the girl, Janowitz followed the fragile trail of a laugh which he thought hers into a dim park bordering the Holstenwall. The laugh, which apparently served to lure a young man, vanished somewhere in the shrubbery. When, a short time later, the young man departed, another shadow, hidden until then in the bushes, suddenly emerged and moved along—as if on the scent of that laugh. Passing this uncanny shadow, Janowitz caught a glimpse of him: he looked like an average bourgeois. Darkness reabsorbed the man, and made further pursuit impossible. The following day big headlines in the local press announced: "Horrible sex crime on the Holstenwall! Young Gertrude . . . murdered." An obscure feeling that Gertrude might have been the girl of the fair impelled Janowitz to attend the victim's funeral. During the ceremony he suddenly had the sensation of discovering the murderer, who had not yet been captured. The man he suspected seemed to recognize him, too. It was the bourgeois—the shadow in the bushes.

---

*The following episode, along with other data appearing in my pages on *Caligari,* is drawn from an interesting manuscript Mr. Hans Janowitz has written about the genesis of this film. I feel greatly indebted to him for having put his material at my disposal. I am thus in a position to base my interpretation of *Caligari* on the true inside story, up to now unknown.

21

Carl Mayer, co-author with Janowitz of *Caligari,* was born in the Austrian provincial capital of Graz, where his father, a wealthy businessman, would have prospered had he not been obsessed by the idea of becoming a "scientific" gambler. In the prime of life he sold his property, went, armed with an infallible "system," to Monte Carlo, and reappeared a few months later in Graz, broke. Under the stress of this catastrophe, the monomaniac father turned the sixteen-year-old Carl and his three younger brothers out into the street and finally committed suicide. A mere boy, Carl Mayer was responsible for the three children. While he toured through Austria, peddling barometers, singing in choirs, and playing extras in peasant theaters, he became increasingly interested in the stage. There was no branch of theatrical production which he did not explore during those years of nomadic life—years full of experiences that were to be of immense use in his future career as a film poet. At the beginning of the war, the adolescent made his living by sketching Hindenburg portraits on postcards in Munich cafés. Later in the war, Janowitz reports, he had to undergo repeated examinations of his mental condition. Mayer seems to have been very embittered against the high-ranking military psychiatrist in charge of his case.

The war was over. Janowitz, who from its outbreak had been an officer in an infantry regiment, returned as a convinced pacifist, animated by hatred of an authority which had sent millions of men to death. He felt that absolute authority was bad in itself. He settled in Berlin, met Carl Mayer there, and soon found out that this eccentric young man, who had never before written a line, shared his revolutionary moods and views. Why not express them on the screen? Intoxicated with Wegener's films, Janowitz believed that this new medium might lend itself to powerful poetic revelations. As youth will, the two friends embarked on endless discussions that hovered around Janowitz' Holstenwall adventure as well as Mayer's mental duel with the psychiatrist. These stories seemed to evoke and supplement each other. After such discussions the pair would stroll through the night, irresistibly attracted by a dazzling and clamorous fair on Kantstrasse. It was a bright jungle, more hell than paradise, but a paradise to those who had exchanged the horror of war for the terror of want. One evening, Mayer dragged his companion to a sideshow by which he had been impressed. Under the title "Man or Machine" it presented a strong man who achieved miracles of strength in an apparent stupor. He acted as if he were hypnotized. The strangest thing was that he accomanied his feats with utterances which affected the spellbound spectators as pregnant forebodings.

Any creative process approaches a moment when only one additional experience is needed to integrate all elements into a whole. The mysterious figure of the strong man supplied such an experience. On the night of this show the friends first visualized the original story of *Caligari.* They wrote the manuscript in the following six weeks. Defining the part each took in the work, Janowitz calls himself "the father who planted the seed, and Mayer the mother who conceived and ripened it." At the end, one small problem arose: the authors were at a loss as to what to christen their main character, a psychiatrist shaped after Mayer's archenemy during the war. A rare volume, *Unknown Letters of Stendhal,* offered the solution. While Janowitz was skimming through this find of his, he happened to notice that Stendhal, just come from the battlefield, met at La Scala in Milan an officer named Caligari. The name clicked with both authors.

Their story is located in a fictitious North German town near the Dutch border, significantly called Holstenwall. One day a fair moves into the town, with merry-go-rounds and sideshows—among the latter that of Dr. Caligari, a weird, bespectacled man advertising the somnambulist Cesare. To procure a license, Caligari goes to the town hall, where he is treated haughtily by an arrogant official. The following morning this official is found murdered in his room, which does not prevent the townspeople from enjoying the fair's pleasures. Along with numerous onlookers, Francis and Alan—two students in love with Jane, a medical man's daughter—enter the tent of Dr. Caligari, and watch Cesare slowly stepping out of an upright, coffinlike box. Caligari tells the thrilled audience that the somnambulist will answer questions about the future. Alan, in an excited state, asks how long he has to live. Cesare opens his mouth; he seems to be dominated by a terrific, hypnotic power emanating from his master. "Until dawn," he answers. At dawn Francis learns that his friend has been stabbed in exactly the same manner as the official. The student, suspicious of Caligari, persuades Jane's father to assist him in an investigation. With a search warrant the two force their way into the showman's wagon, and demand that he end the trance of his medium. However, at this very moment they are called away to the police station to attend the examination of a criminal who has been caught in the act of killing a woman, and who now frantically denies that he is the pursued serial murderer.

Francis continues spying on Caligari, and, after nightfall, secretly peers through a window of the wagon. But while he imagines he sees Cesare lying in his box, Cesare in reality breaks into Jane's bedroom, lifts a dagger to pierce the sleeping girl, gazes at her, puts the dagger away and flees, with the screaming Jane in his arms, over roofs and roads. Chased by her father, he drops the girl, who is then escorted home, whereas the lonely kidnaper dies of exhaustion. As Jane, in flagrant contradiction of what Francis believes to be the truth, insists on having recognized Cesare, Francis approaches Caligari a second time to solve the torturing riddle. The two policemen in his company seize the coffinlike box, and Francis draws out of it—a dummy representing the somnambulist. Profiting by the investigators' carelessness, Caligari himself manages to escape. He seeks shelter in a lunatic asylum. The student follows him, calls on the director of the asylum to inquire about the fugitive, and recoils horror-struck: the director and Caligari are one and the same person.

The following night—the director has fallen asleep—Francis and three members of the medical staff whom he has initiated into the case search the director's office and discover material fully establishing the guilt of this authority in psychiatric matters. Among a pile of books they find an old volume about a showman named Caligari who, in the eighteenth century, traveled through North Italy, hypnotized his medium Cesare into murdering sundry people, and, during Cesare's absence, substituted a wax figure to deceive the police. The main exhibit is the director's clinical records; they are evidence that he desired to verify the account of Caligari's hypnotic faculties, that his desire grew into an obsession, and that, when a somnambulist was entrusted to his care, he could not resist the temptation of repeating with him those terrible games. He had adopted the identity of Caligari. To make him admit his crimes, Francis confronts the director with the corpse of his tool, the somnambulist. No sooner does the monster realize Cesare is dead than he begins to rave. Trained attendants put him into a straitjacket.

This horror tale in the spirit of E.T.A. Hoffmann was an outspoken revolutionary story. In it, as Janowitz indicates, he and Carl Mayer half-intentionally stigmatized the omnipotence of a state authority manifesting itself in universal conscription and declarations of war. The German war government seemed to the authors the prototype of such voracious authority. Subjects of the Austro-Hungarian monarchy, they were in a better position than most citizens of the Reich to penetrate the fatal tendencies inherent in the German system. The character of Caligari embodies these tendencies; he stands for an unlimited authority that idolizes power as such, and, to satisfy its lust for domination, ruthlessly violates all human rights and values. Functioning as a mere instrument, Cesare is not so much a guilty murderer as Caligari's innocent victim. This is how the authors themselves understood him. According to the pacifist-minded Janowitz, they had created Cesare with the dim design of portraying the common man who, under the pressure of compulsory military service, is drilled to kill and to be killed. The revolutionary meaning of the story reveals itself unmistakably at the end, with the disclosure of the psychiatrist as Caligari: reason overpowers unreasonable power, insane authority is symbolically abolished. Similar ideas were also being expressed on the contemporary stage, but the authors of *Caligari* transferred them to the screen without including any of those eulogies of the authority-freed "New Man" in which many expressionist plays indulged.

A miracle occurred: Erich Pommer, chief executive of Decla-Bioscop, accepted this unusual, if not subversive, script. Was it a miracle? Since in those early postwar days the conviction prevailed that foreign markets could only be conquered by artistic achievements, the German film industry was of course anxious to experiment in the field of aesthetically qualified entertainment.[1] Art assured export, and export meant salvation. An ardent partisan of this doctrine, Pommer had moreover an incomparable flair for cinematic values and popular demands. Regardless of whether he grasped the significance of the strange story Mayer and Janowitz submitted to him, he certainly sensed its timely atmosphere and interesting scenic potentialities. He was a born promoter who handled screen and business affairs with equal facility, and, above all, excelled in stimulating the creative energies of directors and players. In 1923, Ufa was to make him chief of its entire production.[2] His behind-the-scenes activities were to leave their imprint on the pre-Hitler screen.

Pommer assigned Fritz Lang to direct *Caligari,* but in the middle of the preliminary discussions Lang was ordered to finish his serial *The Spiders;* the distributors

---

[1] Vincent, *Histoire de l'Art Cinématographique,* p. 140.
[2] *Jahrbuch der Filmindustrie,* 1922/3, pp. 35, 46. For an appraisal of Pommer, see Lejeune, *Cinema,* pp. 125–31.

of this film urged its completion.[1] Lang's successor was Dr. Robert Wiene. Since his father, a once-famous Dresden actor, had become slightly insane toward the end of his life, Wiene was not entirely unprepared to tackle the case of Dr. Caligari. He suggested, in complete harmony with what Lang had planned, an essential change of the original story—a change against which the two authors violently protested. But no one heeded them.[2]

The original story was an account of real horrors; Wiene's version transforms that account into a chimera concocted and narrated by the mentally deranged Francis. To effect this transformation the body of the original story is put into a framing story which introduces Francis as a madman. The film *Caligari* opens with the first of the two episodes composing the frame. Francis is shown sitting on a bench in the park of the lunatic asylum, listening to the confused babble of a fellow sufferer. Moving slowly, like an apparition, a female inmate of the asylum passes by: it is Jane. Francis says to his companion: "What I have experienced with her is still stranger than what you have encountered. I will tell it to you."[3] Fade-out. Then a view of Holstenwall fades in, and the original story unfolds, ending, as has been seen, with the identification of Caligari. After a new fade-out the second and final episode of the framing story begins. Francis, having finished the narration, follows his companion back to the asylum, where he mingles with a crowd of sad figures— among them Cesare, who absentmindedly caresses a little flower. The director of the asylum, a mild and understanding-looking person, joins the crowd. Lost in the maze of his hallucinations, Francis takes the director for the nightmarish character he himself has created, and accuses this imaginary fiend of being a dangerous madman. He screams, he fights the attendants in a frenzy. The scene is switched over to a sickroom, with the director putting on horn-rimmed spectacles which immediately change his appearance: it seems to be Caligari who examines the exhausted Francis. After this he removes his spectacles and, all mildness, tells his assistants that Francis believes him to be Caligari. Now that he understands the case of his patient, the director concludes, he will be able to heal him. With this cheerful message the audience is dismissed.

Janowitz and Mayer knew why they raged against the framing story: it perverted, if not reversed, their intrinsic intentions. While the original story exposed the madness inherent in authority, Wiene's *Caligari* glorified authority and convicted its antagonist of madness. A revolutionary film was thus turned into a conformist one—following the much-used pattern of declaring some normal but troublesome individual insane and sending him to a lunatic asylum. This change undoubtedly resulted not so much from Wiene's personal predilections as from his instinctive submission to the necessities of the screen; films, at least commercial films, are forced to answer to mass desires. In its changed form *Caligari* was no longer a

---

[1] Information offered by Mr. Lang.
[2] Extracted from Mr. Janowitz's manuscript. See also Vincent, Histoire de l'Art Cinématographique, pp. 140, 143–44.
[3] Film license, issued by Board of Censors, Berlin, 1921 and 1925 (Museum of Modern Art Library, clipping files); *Film Society Programme,* March 14, 1926.

product expressing, at best, sentiments characteristic of the intelligentsia, but a film supposed equally to be in harmony with what the less educated felt and liked.

If it holds true that during the postwar yeras most Germans eagerly tended to withdraw from a harsh outer world into the intangible realm of the soul, Wiene's version was certainly more consistent with their attitude than the original story; for, by putting the original into a box, this version faithfully mirrored the general retreat into a shell. In *Caligari* (and several other films of the time) the device of a framing story was not only an aesthetic form, but also had symbolic content. Significantly, Wiene avoided mutilating the original story itself. Even though *Caligari* had become a conformist film, it preserved and emphasized this revolutionary story— as a madman's fantasy. Caligari's defeat now belonged among psychological experiences. In this way Wiene's film does suggest that during their retreat into themselves the Germans were stirred to reconsider their traditional belief in authority. Down to the bulk of social democratic workers they refrained from revolutionary action; yet at the same time a psychological revolution seems to have prepared itself in the depths of the collective soul. The film reflects this double aspect of German life by coupling a reality in which Caligari's authority triumphs with a hallucination in which the same authority is overthrown. There could be no better configuration of symbols for that uprising against the authoritarian dispositions which apparently occurred under the cover of a behavior rejecting uprising.

Janowitz suggested that the settings for *Caligari* be designed by the painter and illustrator Alfred Kubin, who, a forerunner of the surrealists, made eerie phantoms invade harmless scenery and visions of torture emerge from the subconscious. Wiene took to the idea of painted canvases, but preferred to Kubin three expressionist artists: Hermann Warm, Walter Röhrig and Walter Reimann. They were affiliated with the Berlin Sturm group, which, through Herwarth Walden's magazine *Sturm,* promoted expressionism in every field of art.[1]

Although expressionist painting and literature had evolved years before the war, they acquired a public only after 1918. In this respect the case of Germany somewhat resembled that of Soviet Russia where, during the short period of war communism, diverse currents of abstract art enjoyed a veritable heyday.[2] To a revolutionized people expressionism seemed to combine the denial of bourgeois traditions with faith in man's power freely to shape society and nature. On account of such virtues it may have cast a spell over many Germans upset by the breakdown of their universe.[3]

"Films must be drawings brought to life": this was Hermann Warm's formula at

---

[1] Mr. Janowitz's manuscript; Vincent, *Histoire de l'Art Cinématographique,* p. 144; Rotha, *Film Till Now,* p. 43.

[2] Kurtz, *Expressionismus,* p. 61.

[3] In Berlin, immediately after the war, Karl Heinz Martin staged two little dramas by Ernst Toller and Walter Hasenclever within expressionist settings. Cf. Kurtz, ibid., p. 48; Vincent, *Histoire de l'Art Cinématographique,* pp. 142–43; Schapiro, "Nature of Abstract Art," *Marxist Quarterly,* Jan–March 1937, p. 97.

the time that he and his two fellow designers were constructing the *Caligari* world.[1] In accordance with his beliefs, the canvases and draperies of *Caligari* abounded in complexes of jagged, sharp-pointed forms strongly reminiscent of gothic patterns. Products of a style which by then had become almost a mannerism, these complexes suggested houses, walls, landscapes. Except for a few slips or concessions— some backgrounds opposed the pictorial convention in too direct a manner, while others all but preserved them—the settings amounted to a perfect transformation of material objects into emotional ornaments. With its oblique chimneys on pell- mell roofs, its windows in the form of arrows or kites and its treelike arabesques that were threats rather than trees, Holstenwall resembled those visions of unheard- of cities which the painter Lyonel Feininger evoked through his edgy, crystalline compositions.[2] In addition, the ornamental system in *Caligari* expanded through space, annuling its conventional aspect by means of painted shadows in dishar- mony with the lighting effects, and zigzag delineations designed to efface all rules of perspective. Space now dwindled to a flat plane, now augmented its dimensions to become what one writer called a "stereoscopic universe."[3]

Lettering was introduced as an essential element of the settings—appropriately

---

[1]Quotation from Kurtz, *Expressionismus,* p.66. Warm's views, which implied a verdict on films as photographed reality, harmonized with those of Viking Eggeling, an abstract Swedish painter living in Germany. Having eliminated all objects from his canvases, Eggeling deemed it logical to involve the surviving geometrical compositions in rhythmic movements. He and his painter friend Hans Richter submitted this idea to Ufa, and Ufa, guided as ever by the maxim that art is good business or, at least, good propaganda, enabled the two artists to go ahead with their experiments. The first abstract films appeared in 1921. While Eggeling—he died in 1925—orchestrated spiral lines and comblike figures in a short he called *Diagonal Symphony,* Richter composed his *Rhythm 21* of squares in black, gray and white. One year later, Walter Ruttmann, also a painter, joined in the trend with *Opus I,* which was a dynamic display of spots vaguely recalling X-ray photographs. As the titles reveal, the authors themselves considered their products a sort of optical music. It was a music that, whatever else it tried to impart, marked an utter withdrawal from the outer world. This esoteric *avantgarde* movement soon spread over other countries. From about 1924, such advanced French artists as Fernand Léger and René Clair made films which, less abstract than the German ones, showed an affinity for the formal beauty of machine parts, and molded all kinds of objects and motions into surrealistic dreams.—I feel indebted to Mr. Hans Richter for having per- mitted me to use his unpublished manuscript, "Avantgarde, History and Dates of the Only Inde- pendent Artistic Film Movement, 1921–1931." See also *Film Society Programme,* Oct. 16, 1927; Kurtz, *Expressionismus,* pp. 86, 94; Vincent, *Histoire de l'Art Cinématographique,* pp. 159–61; Man Ray, "Answer to a Questionnaire," *Film Art,* no. 7, 1936, p. 9; Kraszna-Krauss, "Exhibition in Stuttgart, June 1929, and Its Effects," *Close Up,* Dec. 1929, pp. 461–62.

[2]Mr. Feininger wrote to me about his relation to *Caligari* on Sept. 13, 1944: "Thank you for your . . . letter of Sept. 8. But if there has been anything I never had a part in nor the slightest knowl- edge of at the time, it is the film Caligari. I have never even seen the film . . . I never met nor knew the artists you name (Warm, Röhrig and Reimann) who devised the settings. Some time about 1911 I made, for my own edification, a series of drawings which I entitled: 'Die Stadt am Ende der Welt.' Some of these drawings were printed, some were exhibited. Later, after the birth of *Caligari,* I was frequently asked whether I had had a hand in its devising. This is all I can tell you. . . ."

[3]Cited by Carter, *The New Spirit,* p. 250, from H. G. Scheffauer, *The New Spirit in the German Arts.*—For the *Caligari* décor, see also Kurtz, *Expressionismus,* p. 66; Rotha, *Film Till Now,* p. 46; Jahier, "42 Ans de Cinéma," *Le Rôle intellecutal du Cinéma,* pp. 60–61; "The Cabinet of Dr. Caligari," *Exceptional Photoplays,* March 1921, p. 4; Amiguet, *Cinéma! Cinéma!,* p. 50. For the beginnings of Werner Krauss and Conrad Veldt, see Kalbus, *Deutsche Filmkunst,* I, 28, 30, and Veidt, "Mein Leben," *Ufa-Magazin,* Jan. 14–20, 1927.

enough, considering the close relationship between lettering and drawing. In one scene the mad psychiatrist's desire to imitate Caligari materializes in jittery characters composing the words "I must become Caligari"—words that loom before his eyes on the road, in the clouds, in the treetops. The incorporation of human beings and their movements into the texture of these surroundings was tremendously difficult. Of all the players only the two protagonists seemed actually to be created by a draftman's imagination. Werner Krauss as Caligari had the appearance of a phantom magician himself weaving the lines and shades through which he paced, and when Conrad Veidt's Cesare prowled along a wall, it was as if the wall had exuded him. The figure of an old dwarf and the crowd's antiquated costumes helped to remove the throng on the fair's tent-street from reality and make it share the bizarre life of abstract forms.

If Decla had chosen to leave the original story of Mayer and Janowitz as it was, these "drawings brought to life" would have told it perfectly. As expressionist abstractions they were animated by the same revolutionary spirit that impelled the two scriptwriters to accuse authority—the kind of authority revered in Germany— of inhuman excesses. However, Wiene's version disavowed this revolutionary meaning of expressionist staging, or, at least, put it, like the original story itself, in brackets. In the film *Caligari* expressionism seems to be nothing more than the adequate translation of a madman's fantasy into pictorial terms. This was how many contemporary German reviewers understood, and relished, the settings and gestures. One of the critics stated with self-assured ignorance: "The idea of rendering the notions of sick brains . . . through expressionist pictures is not only well conceived but also well realized. Here this style has a right to exist, proves an outcome of solid logic."[1]

In their triumph the philistines overlooked one significant fact: even though *Caligari* stigmatized the oblique chimneys as crazy, it never restored the perpendicular ones as normal. Expressionist ornaments also overrun the film's concluding episode, in which, from the philistines' viewpoint, perpendiculars should have been expected to characterize the revival of conventional reality. In consequence, the *Caligari* style was as far from depicting madness as it was from transmitting revolutionary messages. What function did it really assume?

During the postwar years expressionism was frequently considered a shaping of primitive sensations and experiences. Gerhart Hauptmann's brother Carl—a distinguished writer and poet with expressionist inclinations—adopted this definition, and then asked how the spontaneous manifestations of a profoundly agitated soul might best be formulated. While modern language, he contended, is too perverted to serve this purpose, the film—or the bioscop, as he termed it—offers a unique opportunity to externalize the fermentation of inner life. Of course, he said, the bioscop must feature only those gestures of things and of human beings which are truly soulful. . . .[2]

---

[1]Review in *8 Uhr Abendblatt*, cited in *Caligari-Heft*, p. 8
[2]Carl Hauptmann, "Film und Theater," *Der Film von Morgen*, p. 20. See also Alten, "Die Kunst in Deutschland," *Ganymed*, 1920, p. 146; Kurtz, *Expressionismus*, p. 14.

Carl Hauptmann's views elucidate the expressionist style of *Caligari*. It had the function of characterizing the phenomena on the screen as phenomena of the soul—a function which overshadowed its revolutionary meaning. By making the film an outward projection of psychological events, expressionist staging symbolized—much more strikingly than did the device of a framing story—that general retreat into a shell which occurred in postwar Germany. It is not accidental that, as long as this collective process was effective, odd gestures and settings in a expressionist or similar style marked many a conspicuous film. *Variety*, of 1925, showed the final traces of them. Owing to their stereotyped character, these settings and gestures were like some familiar street sign—"Men at Work," for instance. Only here the lettering was different. The sign read: "Soul at Work."

After a thorough propaganda campaign culminating in the puzzling poster "You must become Caligari," Decla released the film in February 1920 in the Berlin Marmorhaus.[1] Among the press reviews—they were unanimous in praising *Caligari* as the first work of art on the screen—that of *Vorwärts*, the leading Social Democratic Party organ, distinguished itself by utter absurdity. It commented upon the film's final scene, in which the director of the asylum promises to heal Francis, with the words: "This film is also morally invulnerable inasmuch as it evokes sympathy for the mentally diseased, and comprehension for the self-sacrificing activity of the psychiatrists and attendants."[2] Instead of recognizing that Francis' attack against an odious authority harmonized with the Party's own antiauthoritarian doctrine, *Vorwärts* prefered to pass off authority itself as a paragon of progressive virtues. It was always the same psychological mechanism: the rationalized middle-class propensities of the Social Democrats interfering with their rational socialist designs. While the Germans were too close to *Caligari* to appraise its symptomatic value, the French realized that this film was more than just an exceptional film. They coined the term *"Caligarisme"* and applied it to a postwar world seemingly all upside down; which, at any rate, proves that they sensed the film's bearing on the structure of society. The New York première of *Caligari,* in April 1921, firmly established its world fame. But apart from giving rise to stray imitations and serving as a yardstick for artistic endeavors, this "most widely discussed film of the time" never seriously influenced the course of the American or French cinema.[3] It stood out lonely, like a monolith.

Caligari shows the "Soul at Work." On what adventures does the revolutionized soul embark? The narrative and pictorial elements of the film gravitate toward two opposite poles. One can be labeled "Authority," or, more explicitly, "Tyranny." The theme of tyranny, with which the authors were obsessed, pervades the screen from beginning to end. Swivel chairs of enormous height symbolize the superiority of the city officials turning on them, and, similarly, the gigantic back of the chair in Alan's attic testifies to the invisible presence of powers that have their grip on him. Staircases reinforce the effect of the furniture: numerous steps ascend to police

[1] *Jahrbuch der Filmindustrie*, 1922/3, p. 81.
[2] Quoted from *Caligari-Heft*, p. 23.
[3] Quotation from Jacobs, *American Film*, p. 303; see also pp. 304–5.

headquarters, and in the lunatic asylum itself no less than three parallel flights of stairs are called upon to mark Dr. Caligari's position at the top of the hierarchy. That the film succeeds in picturing him as a tyrant figure of the stamp of Homunculus and Lubitsch's Henry VIII is substantiated by a most illuminating statement in Joseph Freeman's novel, *Never Call Retreat.* Its hero, a Viennese professor of history, tells of his life in a German concentration camp where, after being tortured, he is thrown into a cell: "Lying alone in that cell, I thought of Dr. Caligari; then, without transition, of the Emperor Valentinian, master of the Roman world, who took great delight in imposing the death sentence for slight or imaginary offenses. This Caesar's favorite expressions were: 'Strike off his head!'—'Burn him alive!'— 'Let him be beaten with clubs till he expires!' I thought what a genuine twentieth century ruler the emperor was, and promptly fell asleep."[1] This dreamlike reasoning penetrates Dr. Caligari to the core by conceiving him as a counterpart of Valentinian and a premonition of Hitler. Caligari is a very specific premonition in the sense that he uses hypnotic power to force his will upon his tool—a technique foreshadowing, in content and purpose, that manipulation of the soul which Hitler was the first to practice on a gigantic scale. Even though, at the time of *Caligari,* the motif of the masterful hypnotizer was not unknown on the screen—it played a prominent role in the American film *Trilby,* shown in Berlin during the war —nothing in their environment invited the two authors to feature it.[2] They must have been driven by one of those dark impulses which, stemming from the slowly moving foundations of a people's life, sometimes engender true visions.

One should expect the pole opposing that of tyranny to be the pole of freedom; for it was doubtless their love of freedom which made Janowitz and Mayer disclose the nature of tyranny. Now this counterpole is the rallying point of elements pertaining to the fair—the fair with its rows of tents, its confused crowds besieging them, and its diversity of thrilling amusements. Here Francis and Alan happily join the swarm of onlookers; here, on the scene of his triumphs, Dr. Caligari is finally trapped. In their attempts to define the character of a fair, literary sources repeatedly evoke the memory of Babel and Babylon alike. A seventeenth-century pamphlet describes the noise typical of a fair as "such a distracted noise that you would think Babel not comparable to it," and, almost two hundred years later, a young English poet feels enthusiastic about "that Babylon of booths—the Fair."[3] The manner in which such biblical images insert themselves unmistakably characterizes the fair as an enclave of anarchy in the sphere of entertainment. This accounts for its eternal attractiveness. People of all classes and ages enjoy losing themselves in a wilderness of glaring colors and shrill sounds, which is populated with monsters and abounding in bodily sensations—from violent shocks to tastes of incredible sweetness. For adults it is a regression into childhood days, in which games and serious affairs are identical, real and imagined things mingle, and anarchical desires aimlessly test infi-

---

[1] Freeman, *Never Call Retreat,* p. 528.
[2] Kalbus, *Deutsche Filmkunst,* I, 95.
[3] McKechnie, *Popular Entertainments,* pp. 33, 47.

nite possibilities. By means of this regression the adult escapes a civilization which tends to overgrow and starve out the chaos of instincts—escapes it to restore that chaos upon which civilization nevertheless rests. The fair is not freedom, but anarchy entailing chaos.

Significantly, most fair scenes in *Caligari* open with a small iris-in exhibiting an organ-grinder whose arm constantly rotates, and, behind him, the top of a merry-go-round which never ceases its circular movement.* The circle here becomes a symbol of chaos. While freedom resembles a river, chaos resembles a whirlpool. Forgetful of self, one may plunge into chaos; one cannot move on in it. That the two authors selected a fair with its liberties as contrast to the oppressions of Caligari betrays the flaw in their revolutionary aspirations. Much as they longed for freedom, they were apparently incapable of imagining its contours. There is something Bohemian in their conception; it seems the product of naïve idealism rather than true insight. But it might be said that the fair faithfully reflected the chaotic condition of postwar Germany.

Whether intentionally or not, *Caligari* exposes the soul wavering between tyranny and chaos, and facing a desperate situation: any escape from tyranny seems to throw it into a state of utter confusion. Quite logically, the film spreads an all-pervading atmosphere of horror. Like the Nazi world, that of *Caligari* overflows with sinister portents, acts of terror and outbursts of panic. The equation of horror and hopelessness comes to a climax in the final episode which pretends to re-establish normal life. Except for the ambiguous figure of the director and the shadowy members of his staff, normality realizes itself through the crowd of insane moving in their bizarre surroundings. The normal as a madhouse: frustration could not be pictured more finally. And in this film, as well as in *Homunculus,* is unleashed a strong sadism and an appetite for destruction. The reappearance of these traits on the screen once more testifies to their prominence in the German collective soul.

Technical peculiarities betray peculiarities of meaning. In *Caligari* methods begin to assert themselves which belong among the special properties of German film technique. *Caligari* initiates a long procession of 100 percent studio-made films. Whereas, for instance, the Swedes at that time went to great pains to capture the actual appearance of a snowstorm or a wood, the German directors, at least until 1924, were so infatuated with indoor effects that they built up whole landscapes within the studio walls. They preferred the command of an artificial universe to dependence upon a haphazard outer world. Their withdrawal into the studio was part of the general retreat into a shell. Once the Germans had determined to seek shelter within the soul, they could not well allow the screen to explore that very reality which they abandoned. This explains the conspicuous role of architecture

---

*Rotha, *Film Till Now,* p. 285. For the role of fairs in films, see E. W. and M. M. Robson, *The Film Answers Back,* pp. 196–97—An iris-in is a technical term for opening up the scene from a small circle of light in a dark screen until the whole frame is revealed.

after *Caligari*—a role that has struck many an observer. "It is of the utmost importance," Paul Rotha remarks in a survey of the postwar period, "to grasp the significant part played by the architect in the development of the German cinema."[1] How could it be otherwise? The architect's façades and rooms were not merely backgrounds, but hieroglyphs. They expressed the structure of the soul in terms of space.

Caligari also mobilizes light. It is a lighting device which enables the spectators to watch the murder of Alan without seeing it; what they see, on the wall of the student's attic, is the shadow of Cesare stabbing that of Alan. Such devices developed into a specialty of the German studios. Jean Cassou credits the Germans with having invented a "laboratory-made fairy illumination,"[2] and Harry Alan Potamkin considers the handling of the light in the German film its "major contribution to the cinema."[3] This emphasis upon light can be traced to an experiment Max Reinhardt made on the stage shortly before *Caligari*. In his *mise-en-scène* of Sorge's prewar drama *The Beggar (Der Bettler)*—one of the earliest and most vigorous manifestations of expressionism—he substituted for normal settings imaginary ones created by means of lighting effects.[4] Reinhardt doubtless introduced these effects to be true to the drama's style. The analogy to the films of the postwar period is obvious: it was their expressionist nature which impelled many a German director of photography to breed shadows as rampant as weeds and associate ethereal phantoms with strangely lit arabesques or faces. These efforts were designed to bathe all scenery in an unearthly illumination marking it as scenery of the soul. "Light has breathed soul into the expressionist films," Rudolph Kurtz states in his book on the expressionist cinema. Exactly the reverse holds true: in those films the soul was the virtual source of the light. The task of switching on this inner illumination was somewhat facilitated by powerful romantic traditions.

The attempt made in *Caligari* to coordinate settings, players, lighting, and action is symptomatic of the sense of structural organization which, from this film on, manifests itself on the German screen. Rotha coins the term "studio constructivism" to characterize "that curious air of completeness, of finality, that surrounds each product of the German studios."[5] But organizational completeness can be achieved only if the material to be organized does not object to it. (The ability of the Germans to organize themselves owes much to their longing for submission.) Since reality is essentially incalculable and therefore demands to be observed rather than commanded, realism on the screen and total organization exclude each other. Through their "studio constructivism" no less than their lighting the German films

---

[1]Rotha, *Film Till Now,* p. 180. Cf. Potamkin, "Kino and Lichtspiel," *Close Up,* Nov. 1929, p. 387.

[2]Cited in Leprohon, "Le Cinéma Allemand," *Le Rouge et le Noir,* July 1928, p. 135.

[3]Potamkin, "The Rise and Fall of the German Film," *Cinema,* April 1980, p.24.

[4]Kurtz, *Expressionismus,* p. 59.

[5]Rotha, *Film Till Now,* pp. 107–8. Cf. Potamkin, "Kino and Lichtspiel," *Close Up,* Nov. 1929, p. 388, and "The Rise and Fall of the German Film," *Cinema,* April 1930, p. 24.

revealed that they dealt with unreal events displayed in a sphere basically controllable.[1]

In the course of a visit to Paris about six years after the première of *Caligari,* Janowitz called on Count Etienne de Beaumont in his old city residence, where he lived among Louis Seize furniture and Picassos. The Count voiced his admiration of *Caligari,* terming it "as fascinating and abstruse as the German soul." He continued: "Now the time has come for the German soul to speak, Monsieur. The French soul spoke more than a century ago, in the Revolution, and you have been mute. . . . Now we are waiting for what you have to impart to us, to the world."[2]

The Count did not have long to wait.

1947

---

[1]Film connoisseurs have repeatedly criticized *Caligari* for being a stage imitation. This aspect of the film partly results from its genuinely theatrical action. It is action of a well-constructed dramatic conflict in stationary surroundings—action which does not depend upon screen representaion for significance. Like *Caligari,* all "indoor" films of the postwar period showed affinity for the stage in that they favored inner-life dramas at the expense of conflicts involving outer reality. However, this did not necessarily prevent them from growing into true films. When, in the wake of *Caligari,* film technique steadily progressed, the psychological screen dramas increasingly exhibited an imagery that elaborated the significance of their action. *Caligari's* theatrical affinity was also due to technical backwardness. An immovable camera focused upon the painted décor; no cutting device added a meaning of its own to that of the pictures. One should, of course, not forget the reciprocal influence *Caligari* and kindred films exerted, for their part, on the German stage. Stimulated by the use they made of the iris-in, stage lighting took to singling out a lone player, or some important sector of the scene. Cf. Barry, *Program Notes,* Series III, program 1; Gregor, *Zeitalter des Films,* pp. 134, 144–45; Rotha, *Film Till Now,* p. 275; Vincent, *Histoire de l'Art Cinématographique,* p. 189.

[2]From Janowitz's manuscript.

ANDRÉ BAZIN
FROM WHAT IS CINEMA?

THE MYTH OF TOTAL CINEMA

Paradoxically enough, the impression left on the reader by Georges Sadoul's admirable book on the origins of the cinema is of a reversal, in spite of the author's Marxist views, of the relations between an economic and technical evolution and the imagination of those carrying on the search. The way things happened seems to call for a reversal of the historical order of causality, which goes from the economic infrastructure to the ideological superstructure, and for us to consider the basic technical discoveries as fortunate accidents but essentially second in importance to the preconceived ideas of the inventors. The cinema is an idealistic phenomenon. The concept men had of it existed so to speak fully armed in their minds, as if in some platonic heaven, and what strikes us most of all is the obstinate resistance of matter to ideas rather than of any help offered by techniques to the imagination of the researchers.

Furthermore, the cinema owes virtually nothing to the scientific spirit. Its begetters are in no sense savants, except for Marey, but it is significant that he was only interested in analyzing movement and not in reconstructing it. Even Edison is basically only a do-it-yourself man of genius, a giant of the *concours Lépine*. Niepce, Muybridge, Leroy, Joly, Demeny, even Louis Lumière himself, are all monomaniacs, men driven by an impulse, do-it-yourself men or at best ingenious industrialists. As for the wonderful, the sublime E. Reynaud, who can deny that his animated drawings are the result of an unremitting pursuit of an *idée fixe?* Any account of the cinema that was drawn merely from the technical inventions that made it possible would be a poor one indeed. On the contrary, an approximate and complicated visualization of an idea invariably precedes the industrial discovery which alone can open the way to its practical use. Thus if it is evident to us today that the cinema even at its most elementary stage needed a transparent, flexible, and resistant base and a dry sensitive emulsion capable of receiving an image instantly—

34

everything else being a matter of setting in order a mechanism far less complicated than an eighteenth-century clock—it is clear that all the definitive stages of the invention of the cinema had been reached before the requisite conditions had been fulfilled. In 1877 and 1880, Muybridge, thanks to the imaginative generosity of a horse-lover, managed to construct a large complex device which enabled him to make from the image of a galloping horse the first series of cinematographic pictures. However to get this result he had to be satisfied with wet collodion on a glass plate, that is to say, with just one of the three necessary elements—namely instantaneity, dry emulsion, flexible base. After the discovery of gelatino-bromide of silver but before the appearance on the market of the first celluloid reels, Marey had made a genuine camera which used glass plates. Even after the appearance of celluloid strips Lumière tried to use paper film.

Once more let us consider here only the final and complete form of the photographic cinema. The synthesis of simple movements studied scientifically by Plateau had no need to wait upon the industrial and economic developments of the nineteenth century. As Sadoul correctly points out, nothing had stood in the way, from antiquity, of the manufacture of a phenakistoscope or a zoötrope. It is true that here the labors of that genuine savant Plateau were at the origin of the many inventions that made the popular use of his discovery possible. But while, with the photographic cinema, we have cause for some astonishment that the discovery somehow precedes the technical conditions necessary to its existence, we must here explain, on the other hand, how it was that the invention took so long to emerge, since all the prerequisites had been assembled and the persistence of the image on the retina had been known for a long time. It might be of some use to point out that although the two were not necessarily connected scientifically, the efforts of Plateau are pretty well contemporary with those of Nicéphore Niepce, as if the attention of researchers had waited to concern itself with synthesizing movement until chemistry quite independently of optics had become concerned, on its part, with the automatic fixing of the image.

I emphasize the fact that this historical coincidence can apparently in no way be explained on grounds of scientific, economic, or industrial evolution. The photographic cinema could just as well have grafted itself onto a phenakistoscope foreseen as long ago as the sixteenth century. The delay in the invention of the latter is as disturbing a phenomenon as the existence of the precursors of the former.

But if we examine their work more closely, the direction of their research is manifest in the instruments themselves, and, even more undeniably, in their writings and commentaries we see that these precursors were indeed more like prophets. Hurrying past the various stopping places, the very first of which materially speaking should have halted them, it was at the very height and summit that most of them were aiming. In their imaginations they saw the cinema as a total and complete representation of reality; they saw in a trice the reconstruction of a perfect illusion of the the outside world in sound, color, and relief.

As for the latter, the film historian P. Potoniée has even felt justified in maintaining that it was not the discovery of photography but of stereoscopy, which came onto the market just slightly before the first attempts at animated photography in 1851, that opened the eyes of the researchers. Seeing people immobile in space, the photographers realized that what they needed was movement if their photographs were to become a picture of life and a faithful copy of nature. In any case, there was not a single inventor who did not try to combine sound and relief with animation of the image—whether it be Edison with his kinetoscope made to be attached to a phonograph, or Demenay and his talking portraits, or even Nadar who shortly before producing the first photographic interview, on Chevreul, had written, "My dream is to see the photograph register the bodily movements and the facial expressions of a speaker while the phonograph is recording his speech" (February, 1887). If color had not yet appeared it was because the first experiments with the three-color process were slower in coming. But E. Reynaud had been painting his little figurines for some time and the first films of Méliès are colored by stencilling. There are numberless writings, all of them more or less wildly enthusiastic, in which inventors conjure up nothing less than a total cinema that is to provide that complete illusion of life which is still a long way away. Many are familiar with that passage from *L'Éve Future* in which Villiers de l'Isle-Adam, two years before Edison had begun his researches on animated photography, puts into the inventor's mouth the following description of a fantastic achievement: ". . . the vision, its transparent flesh miraculously photographed in color and wearing a spangled costume, danced a kind of popular Mexican dance. Her movements had the flow of life itself, thanks to the process of successive photography which can retain six minutes of movement on microscopic glass, which is subsequently reflected by means of a powerful lampascope. Suddenly was heard a flat and unnatural voice, dull-sounding and harsh. The dancer was singing the *alza* and the *olé* that went with her *fandango.*"

The guiding myth, then, inspiring the invention of cinema, is the accomplishment of that which dominated in a more or less vague fashion all the techniques of the mechanical reproduction of reality in the nineteenth century, from photography to the phonograph, namely an integral realism, a recreation of the world in its own image, an image unburdened by the freedom of interpretation of the artist or the irreversibilty of time. If cinema in its cradle lacked all the attributes of the cinema to come, it was with reluctance and because its fairy guardians were unable to provide them however much they would have liked to.

If the origins of an art reveal something of its nature, then one may legitimately consider the silent and the sound film as stages of a technical development that little by little made a reality out of the original "myth." It is understandable from this point of view that it would be absurd to take the silent film as a state of primal perfection which has gradually been forsaken by the realism of sound and color. The primacy of the image is both historically and technically accidental. The nostalgia that some still feel for the silent screen does not go far enough back into the childhood of the seventh art. The real primitives of the cinema, existing only in the imaginations of a few men of the nineteenth century, are in complete imitation of nature. Every new development added to the cinema must, paradoxically, take it nearer and nearer to its origins. In short, cinema has not yet been invented!

It would be a reversal then of the concrete order of causality, at least psychologically, to place the scientific discoveries or the industrial techniques that have loomed so large in its development at the source of the cinema's invention. Those who had the least confidence in the future of the cinema were precisely the two industrialists Edison and Lumière. Edison was satisfied with just his kinetoscope and if Lumière judiciously refused to sell his patent to Méliès it was undoubtedly because he hoped to make a large profit out of it for himself, but only as a plaything of which the public would soon tire. As for the real savants such as Marey, they were only of indirect assistance to the cinema. They had a specific purpose in mind and were satisfied when they had accomplished it. The fanatics, the madmen, the disinterested pioneers, capable, as was Berard Palissy, of burning their furniture for a few seconds of shaky images, are neither industrialists nor savants, just men obsessed by their own imaginings. The cinema was born from the converging of these various obsessions, that is to say, out of a myth, the myth of total cinema. This likewise adequately explains the delay of Plateau in applying the optical principle of the persistence of the image on the retina, as also the continuous progress of the syntheses of movement as compared with the state of photographic techniques. The fact is that each alike was dominated by the imagination of the century. Undoubtedly there are other examples in the history of techniques and inventions of the convergence of research, but one must distinguish between those which come as a result precisely of scientific evolution and industrial or military requirements and those which quite clearly precede them. Thus, the myth of Icarus had to wait on the internal combustion engine before descending from the platonic heavens. But it had dwelt in the soul of everyman since he first thought about birds. To some extent one could say the same thing about the myth of cinema, but its forerunners prior to the nineteenth century have only a remote connection with the myth which we share today and which has prompted the appearance of the mechanical arts that characterize today's world.

1946

ANDRÉ BAZIN
FROM WHAT IS CINEMA

DE SICA: METTEUR EN SCÈNE

. . . It is by way of its poetry that the realism of De Sica takes on its meaning, for in art, at the source of all realism, there is an aesthetic paradox that must be resolved. The faithful reproduction of reality is not art. We are repeatedly told that it consists in selection and interpretation. That is why up to now the "realist" trends in cinema, as in other arts, consisted simply in introducing a greater measure of reality into the work: but this additional measure of reality was still only an effective way of serving an abstract purpose, whether dramatic, moral, or ideological. In France, "naturalism" goes hand in hand with the multiplication of novels and plays *à thèse*. The originality of Italian neorealism as compared with the chief schools of realism that preceded it and with the Soviet cinema, lies in never making reality the servant of some *à priori* point of view. Even the Dziga-Vertov theory of the "Kino-eye" only employed the crude reality of everyday events so as to give it a place on the dialectic spectrum of montage. From another point of view, theater (even realist theater) used reality in the service of dramatic and spectacular structure. Whether in the service of the interests of an ideological thesis, of a moral idea, or of a dramatic action, realism subordinates what it borrows from reality to its transcendent needs. Neorealism knows only immanence. It is from appearance only, the simple appearance of beings and of the world, that it knows how to deduce the ideas that it unearths. It is a phenomenology.

In the realm of means of expression, neorealism runs counter to the traditional categories of spectacle—above all, as regards acting. According to the classic understanding of this function, inherited from the theater, the actor expresses something: a feeling, a passion, a desire, an idea. From his attitude and his miming the spectator can read his face like an open book. In this perspective, it is agreed implicitly between spectator and actor that the same psychological causes produce the same

38

physical effect and that one can without any ambiguity pass backward and forward from one to the other. This is, strictly speaking, what is called acting.

The structures of the *mise-en-scène* flow from it: decor, lighting, the angle and framing of the shots, will be more or less expressionistic in their relation to the behavior of the actor. They contribute their part to confirm the meaning of the action. Finally, the breaking up of the scenes into shots and their assemblage is the equivalent of an expressionism in time, a reconstruction of the event according to an artificial and abstract duration: dramatic duration. There is not a single one of these commonly accepted assumptions of the film spectacle that is not challenged by neorealism.

First, the performance: it calls upon the actor to *be* before expressing himself. This requirement does not necessarily imply doing away with the professional actor but it normally tends to substitute the man in the street, chosen uniquely for his general comportment, his ignorance of theatrical technique being less a positively required condition than a guarantee against the expressionism of traditional acting. For De Sica, Bruno was a silhouette, a face, a way of walking.

Second, the setting and the photography: the natural setting is to the artificial set what the amateur actor is to the professional. It has, however, the effect of at least partly limiting the opportunity for plastic compositions available with artificial studio lighting.

But it is perhaps especially the structure of the narrative which is most radically turned upside down. It must now respect the actual duration of the event. The cuts that logic demands can only be, at best, descriptive. The assemblage of the film must never add anything to the existing reality. If it is part of the meaning of the film as with Rossellini, it is because the empty gaps, the white spaces, the parts of the event that we are not given, are themselves of a concrete nature: stones which are missing from the building. It is the same in life: we do not know everything that happens to others. Ellipsis in classic montage is an effect of style. In Rossellini's films it is a lacuna in reality, or rather in the knowledge we have of it, which is by its nature limited.

Thus, neorealism is more an ontological position than an aesthetic one. That is why the employment of its technical attributes, like a recipe, do not necessarily produce it, as the rapid decline of American neorealism proves. In Italy itself not all films without actors, based on a news item, and filmed in real exteriors, are better than the traditional melodramas and spectacles. On the contrary, a film like *Cronaca di un Amore* by Michelangelo Antonioni can be described as neorealist (in spite of the professional actors, of the detective-storylike arbitrariness of the plot, of expensive settings, and the baroque dress of the heroine) because the director has not relied on an expressionism outside the characters; he builds all his effects on their way of life, their way of crying, of walking, of laughing. They are caught in the maze of the plot like laboratory rats being sent through a labyrinth.

The diversity of styles among the best Italian directors might be advanced as a counter argument and I know how much they dislike the word neorealist. Zavattini is the only one who shamelessly admits to the title. The majority protest against the existence of a new Italian school of realism that would include them all. But that is a reflex reaction of the creator to the critic. The director as artist is more aware of his differences than his resemblances. The word neorealist was thrown like a fishing net over the postwar Italian cinema and each director on his own is doing his best to break the toils in which, it is claimed, he has been caught. However, in spite of this normal reaction, which has the added advantage of forcing us to review a perhaps too easy critical classification, I think there are good reasons for staying with it, even against the views of those most concerned.

Certainly the succinct definition I have just given of neorealism might appear on the surface to be given the lie by the work of Lattuada with its calculated, subtly architectural vision, or by the baroque exuberance, the romantic eloquence of De Santis, or by the refined theatrical sense of Visconti, who makes compositions of the most down-to-earth reality as if they were scenes from an opera or a classical tragedy. These terms are summary and debatable, but can serve for other possible epithets which consequently would confirm the existence of formal differences, of oppositions in style. These three directors are as different from one another as each is from De Sica, yet their common origin is evident if one takes a more general view and especially if one stops comparing them with one another and instead looks at the American, French, and Soviet cinema.

Neorealism does not necessarily exist in a pure state and one can conceive of it being combined with other aesthetic tendencies. Biologists distinguish, in genetics, characteristics derived from different parents, so-called dominant factors. It is the same with neorealism. The exacerbated theatricality of Malaparte's *Cristo Proibito* may owe a lot to German expressionism, but the film is nonetheless neorealist, radically different from the realist expressionism of a Fritz Lang.

But I seem to have strayed a long way from De Sica. This was simply that I might be better able to situate him in contemporary Italian production. The difficulty of taking a critical stand about the director of *Miracolo a Milano* might indeed be precisely the real indication of his style. Does not our inability to analyze its formal characteristics derive from the fact that it represents the purest form of neorealism, from the fact that *Ladri di Biciclette* is the ideal center around which gravitate, each in his own orbit, the works of the other great directors? It could be this very purity which makes it impossible to define, for it has as its paradoxical intention not to produce a spectacle which appears real, but rather to turn reality into a spectacle: a man is walking along the street and the onlooker is amazed at the beauty of the man walking.

Until further information is available, until the realization of Zavattini's dream of filming eighty minutes in the life of a man without a cut, *Ladri di Biciclette* is without a doubt the ultimate expression of neorealism.

Though this *mise-en-scène* aims at negating itself, at being transparent to the reality it reveals, it would be naïve to conclude that it does not exist. Few films have been more carefully put together, more pondered over, more meticulously elaborated, but all this labor by De Sica tends to give the illusion of chance, to result in giving dramatic necessity the character of something contingent. Better still, he has succeeded in making dramatic contingency the very stuff of drama. Nothing happens in *Ladri di Biciclette* that might just as well not have happened. The worker could have chanced upon his bicycle in the middle of the film, the lights in the auditorium would have gone up and De Sica would have apologized for having disturbed us, but after all, we would be happy for the worker's sake. The marvelous aesthetic paradox of this film is that it has the relentless quality of tragedy while nothing happens in it except by chance. But it is precisely from the dialectical synthesis of contrary values, namely artistic order and the amorphous disorder of reality, that it derives its originality. There is not one image that is not charged with meaning, that does not drive home into the mind the sharp end of an unforgettable moral truth, and not one that to this end is false to the ontological ambiguity of reality. Not one gesture, not one incident, not a single object in the film is given a prior significance derived from the ideology of the director.

If they are set in order with an undeniable clarity on the spectrum of social tragedy, it is after the manner of the particles of iron filings on the spectrum of a magnet—that is to say, individually; but the result of this art in which nothing is necessary, where nothing has lost the fortuitous character of chance, is in effect to be doubly convincing and conclusive. For, after all, it is not surprising that the novelist, the playwright, or the filmmaker should make it possible for us to hit on this or that idea, since they put them there beforehand, and have seeded their work with them. Put salt into water, let the water evaporate in the fire of reflection, and you will get back the salt. But if you find salt in water drawn directly from a stream, it is because the water is salty by nature. The workman, Bruno, might have found his bike just as he might have won the lottery—even poor people win lotteries. But this potential capacity only serves to bring out more forcefully the terrible powerlessness of the poor fellow. If he found his bike, then the enormous extent of his good luck would be an even greater condemnation of society, since it would make a priceless miracle, an exorbitant favor, out of the return to a human order, to a natural state of happiness, since it would signify his good fortune at not still being poor.

It is clear to what an extent this neorealism differs from the formal concept which consists of decking out a formal story with touches of reality. As for the technique, properly so called, *Ladri di Biciclette,* like a lot of other films, was shot in the street with nonprofessional actors but its true merit lies elsewhere: in not betraying the essence of things, in allowing them first of all to exist for their own sakes, freely; it is in loving them in their singular individuality. "My little sister reality," says De Sica, and she circles about him like the birds around Saint Francis. Others put her in a cage or teach her to talk, but De Sica talks with her and it is the true language of reality that we hear, the word that cannot be denied, that only love can utter.

To explain De Sica, we must go back to the source of his art, namely to his tenderness, his love. The quality shared in common by *Miracolo a Milano* and *Ladri di Biciclette,* in spite of differences more apparent than real, is De Sica's inexhaustible affection for his characters. It is significant then in *Miracolo a Milano,* that none of the bad people, even the proud or treacherous ones, are antipathetic. The junkyard Judas who sells his companion's hovels to the vulgar Mobbi does not stir the least anger in the onlookers. Rather he amuses us in the tawdry costume of the "villain" of melodrama, which he wears awkwardly and clumsily: he is a good traitor. In the same way the new poor, who in their decline still retain the proud ways of their former fine neighborhoods, are simply a special variety of that human fauna and are not therefore excluded from the vagabond community—even if they charge

In Vittorio de Sica's *The Bicycle Thief* (1948) Father (Lamberto Maggiorani) and son (Enzo Staiola) search for the father's stolen bicycle, without which he will lose his job. ". . . *Ladri di Biciclette*, like a lot of other films, was shot in the street with nonprofessional actors but its true merit lies elsewhere: in not betraying the essence of things, in allowing them first of all to exist for their own sakes, freely; it is in loving them in their singular individuality" (BAZIN, page 41).

people a lira a sunset. And a man must love the sunset with all his heart to come up with the idea of making people pay for the sight of it, and to suffer this market of dupes.

Besides, none of the principal characters in *Ladri di Biciclette* is unsympathetic. Not even the thief. When Bruno finally manages to get his hands on him, the public would be morally disposed to lynch him, as the crowd could have done earlier to Bruno. But the spark of genius in this film is to force us to swallow his hatred the moment it is born and to renounce judgment, just as Bruno will refuse to bring charges.

The only unsympathetic characters in *Miracolo a Milano* are Mobbi and his acolytes, but basically they do not exist. They are only conventional symbols. The moment De Sica shows them to us at slightly closer quarters, we almost feel a tender curiosity stirring inside us. "Poor rich people," we are tempted to say, "how deceived they are." There are many ways of loving, even including the way of the inquisitor. The ethics and politics of love are threatened by the worst heresies. From this point of view, hate is often more tender, but the affection De Sica feels for his creatures is no threat to them, there is nothing threatening or abusive about it. It is courtly and discreet gentleness, a liberal generosity, and it demands nothing in return. There is no admixture of pity in it even for the poorest or the most wretched, because pity does violence to the dignity of the man who is its object. It is a burden on his conscience.

The tenderness of De Sica is of a special kind and for this reason does not easily lend itself to any moral, religious, or political generalization. The ambiguities of *Miracolo a Milano* and *Ladri di Biciclette* have been used by the Christian Democrats and by the Communists. So much the better: a true parable should have something for everyone. I do not think De Sica and Zavattini were trying to argue anybody out of anything. I would not dream of saying that the kindness of De Sica is of greater value than the third theological virtue* or than class consciousness, but I see in the modesty of his position a definite artistic advantage. It is a guarantee of its authenticity while, at the same time, assuring it a universal quality. This penchant for love is less a moral question than one of personal and ethnic temperament. As for its authenticity, this can be explained in terms of a naturally happy disposition developed in a Neapolitan atmosphere. But these psychological roots reach down to deeper layers than the consciousness cultivated by partisan ideologies. Paradoxically and in virtue of their unique quality, of their inimitable flavor, since they have not been classified in the categories of either morals or politics, they escape the latter's censure, and the Neapolitan charm of De Sica becomes, thanks to the cinema, the most sweeping message of love that our times have heard since Chaplin.

To anyone who doubted the importance of this, it is enough to point out how quick partisan critics were to lay claim to it. What party indeed could afford to leave love to the other? In our day there is no longer a place for unattached love but since

---

*The first two theological virtues, according to 1st Corinthians, are faith and hope. The third is ἀγάπη (agape), translated in the King James Bible as "charity" and in the Revised Version as "love," in Bazin's French "amour."—Eds.

each party can with equal plausibility lay claim to being the proprietor of it, it means that much authentic and naïve love scales the walls and penetrates the stronghold of ideologies and social theory.

Let us be thankful to Zavattini and De Sica for the ambiguity of their position— and let us take care not to see it as just intellectual astuteness in the land of Don Camillo, a completely negative concern to give pledges on all sides in return for an all-around censorship clearance. On the contrary it is a positive striving after poetry, the stratagem of a person in love, expressing himself in the metaphors of his time, while at the same time making sure to choose such of them as will open the hearts of everyone. The reason why there have been so many attempts to give a political exegesis to *Miracolo a Milano* is that Zavattini's social allegories are not the final examples of this symbolism, these symbols themselves being simply the allegory of love. Psychoanalysts explain to us that our dreams are the very opposite of a free flow of images. When these express some fundamental desire, it is in order perforce to cross the threshold of the superego, hiding behind the mark of a twofold symbolism, one general, the other individual. But this censorship is not something negative. Without it, without the resistance it offers to the imagination, dreams would not exist.

There is only one way to think of *Miracolo a Milano,* namely as a reflection, on the level of a film dream, and through the medium of the social symbolism of contemporary Italy, of the warm heart of Vittorio De Sica. This would explain what seems bizarre and inorganic in this strange film: otherwise it is hard to understand the gaps in its dramatic continuity and its indifference to all narrative logic.

In passing, we might note how much the cinema owes to a love for living creatures. There is no way of completely understanding the art of Flaherty, Renoir, Vigo, and especially Chaplin unless we try to discover beforehand what particular kind of tenderness, of sensual or sentimental affection, they reflect. In my opinion, the cinema more than any other art is particularly bound up with love. The novelist in his relations to his characters needs intelligence more than love; understanding is his form of loving. If the art of a Chaplin were transposed into literature, it would tend to lapse into sentimentality; that is why a man like André Suarès, a man of letters *par excellence,* and evidently impervious to the poetry of the cinema, can talk about the "ignoble heart" of Chaplin when this heart brings to the cinema the nobility of myth. Every art and every stage in the evolution of each art has its specific scale of values. The tender, amused sensuality of Renoir, the more heartrending tenderness of Vigo, achieve on the screen a tone and an accent which no other medium of expression could give them. Between such feelings and the cinema there exists a mysterious affinity which is sometimes denied even to the greatest of men. No one better than De Sica can lay claim to being the successor to Chaplin. We have already remarked how as an actor he has a quality of presence, a light which subtly transforms both the scenario and the other actors to such an extent that no one can pretend to play opposite De Sica as he would opposite someone else. We in France have not hitherto known the brilliant actor who appeared in Camerini's films. He had to become famous as a director before he was noticed by the public. By then he no longer had the physique of a young leading man, but his charm survived, the more remarkable for being the less easy to explain. Even when appearing as just a simple actor in the films of other directors, De Sica was already himself a director since his presence modified the film and influenced its style. Chaplin concentrates on himself and within himself the radiation of his tenderness, which means that cruelty is not always excluded from his world; on the contrary, it has a necessary and dialectic relationship to love, as is evident from *Monsieur Verdoux.* Charlie is goodness itself, projected onto the world. He is ready to love everything, but the world does not always respond. On the other hand, De Sica the director infuses into his actors the power to love that he himself possesses as an actor. Chaplin also chooses his cast carefully but always with an eye to himself and to putting his character in a better light. We find in De Sica the humanity of Chaplin, but shared with the world at large. De Sica possesses the gift of being able to convey an intense sense of the human presence, a disarming grace of expression and of gesture which, in their unique way, are an irresistible testimony to man. Ricci *(Ladri di Biciclette),* Toto *(Miracolo a Milano),* and *Umberto D,* although greatly differing in physique from Chaplin and De Sica, make us think of them.

It would be a mistake to believe that the love De Sica bears for man, and forces us to bear witness to, is a form of optimism. If no one is really bad, if face to face with each individual human being we are forced to drop our accusation, as was Ricci when he caught up with the thief, we are obliged to say that the evil which undeniably does exist in the world is elsewhere than in the heart of man, that it is somewhere in the order of things. One could say it is in society and be partly right. In one way *Ladri di Biciclette, Miracolo a Milano,* and *Umberto D* are indictments of a revolutionary nature. If there were no unemployment it would not be a tragedy to lose one's bicycle. However, this political explanation does not cover the whole drama. De Sica protests the comparison that has been made between *Ladri di Biciclette* and the works of Kafka on the grounds that his hero's alienation is social and not metaphysical. True enough, but Kafka's myths are no less valid if one accepts them as allegories of social alienation, and one does not have to believe in a cruel God to feel the guilt of which Joseph K. is culpable. On the contrary, the drama lies in this: God does not exist, the last office in the castle is empty. Perhaps we have here the particular tragedy of today's world, the raising of a self-deifying social reality to a transcendental state.

The troubles of Bruno and Umberto D have their immediate and evident causes but we also observe that there is an insoluable residue comprised of the psychological and material complexities of our social relationships, which neither the high quality of an institution nor the good will of our neighbors can dispose of. The nature of the latter is positive and social, but its action proceeds always from a necessity that is at once absurd and imperative. This is, in my opinion, what makes this film so great and so rich. It renders a twofold justice: one by way of an irrefutable description of the wretched condition of the proletariat, another by way of the implicit and constant appeal of a human need that any society whatsoever must respect. It condemns a world in which the poor are obliged to steal from one another to survive (the police protect the rich only too well) but this imposed condemnation is not enough, because it is not only a given historical institution that is in question or a particular economic setup, but the congenital indifference of our social organization, as such, to the fortuitousness of individual happiness. Otherwise Sweden could be the earthly paradise, where bikes are left along the sidewalk both day and night. De Sica loves mankind, his brothers, too much not to want to remove every conceivable cause of their unhappiness, but he also reminds us that every man's happiness is a miracle of love whether in Milan or anywhere else. A society which does not take every opportunity to smother happiness is already better than one which sows hate, but the most perfect still would not create love, for love remains a private matter between man and man. In what country in the world would they keep rabbit hutches in an oil field? In what other would the loss of an administrative document not be as agonizing as the theft of a bicycle? It is part of the realm of politics to think up and promote the objective conditions necessary for human happiness, but it is not part of its essential function to respect its subjective conditions. In the universe of De Sica, there lies a latent pessimism, an unavoidable pessimism we can never be grateful enough to him for, because in it resides the appeal of the potential of man, the witness to his final and irrefutable humanity.

I have used the word love. I should rather have said poetry. These two words are synonymous or at least complementary. Poetry is but the active and creative form of love, its projection into the world. Although spoiled and laid waste by social upheaval, the childhood of the shoeshine boy has retained the power to transform his wretchedness in a dream. In France, in the primary schools, the children are taught to say "Who steals an egg, steals a bull." De Sica's formula is "Who steal an egg is dreaming of a horse." Toto's miraculous gift which was handed on to him by his adopted grandmother is to have retained from childhood an inexhaustible capacity for defense by way of poetry; the piece of business I find most significant in *Miracolo a Milano* is that of Emma Grammatica rushing toward the spilled milk. It does not matter who else scolds Toto for his lack of initiative and wipes up the milk with a cloth, so long as the quick gesture of the old woman has as its purpose to turn the little catastrophe into a marvelous game, a stream in the middle of a landscape of the same proportion. And so on to the multiplication tables, another profound terror of one's childhood, which, thanks to the little old woman, turns into a dream. City dweller Toto names the streets and the squares "four times four is sixteen" or "nine times nine is eighty-one," for these cold mathematical symbols are more beautiful in his eyes than the names of the characters of mythology. Here again we think of Charlie; he also owes to his childhood spirit his remarkable power of transforming the world to a better purpose. When reality resists him and he cannot materially change it—he switches its meaning. Take for example, the dance of the rolls, in *The Gold Rush,* or the shoes in the soup pot, with this proviso that, always on the defensive, Charlie reserves his power of metamorphosis for his own advantage, or, at most, for the benefit of the woman he loves. Toto on the other hand goes out to others. He does not give a moment's thought to any benefit the dove can bring him, his joy lies in his being able to spread joy. When he can no longer do anything for his neighbor he takes it on himself to assume various shapes, now limping for the lame man, making himself small for the dwarf, blind for the one-eyed man. The dove is just an arbitrarily added possibility, to give poetry a material form, because most people need something to assist their imaginations. But Toto does not know what to do with himself unless it is for someone else's benefit.

Zavattini told me once: "I am like a painter standing before a field, who asks himself which blade of grass he should begin with." De Sica is the ideal director for a declaration of faith such as this. There is also the art of the playwright who divides the moments of life into episodes which, in respect of the moments lived, are what the blades of grass are to the field. To paint every blade of grass one must be the Douanier Rousseau. In the world of cinema one must have the love of a De Sica for creation itself.

1953

RUDOLF ARNHEIM
FROM FILM AS ART

THE COMPLETE FILM

The technical development of the motion picture will soon carry the mechanical imitation of nature to an extreme. The addition of sound was the first obvious step in this direction. The introduction of sound film must be considered as the imposition of a technical novelty that did not lie on the path the best film artists were pursuing. They were engaged in working out an explicit and pure style of silent film, using its restrictions to transform the peep show into an art. The introduction of sound film smashed many of the forms that the film artists were using in favor of the inartistic demand for the greatest possible "naturalness" (in the most superficial sense of the word). By sheer good luck, sound film is not only destructive but also offers artistic potentialities of its own. Owing to this accident alone the majority of art-lovers still do not realize the pitfalls in the road pursued by the movie producers. They do not see that the film is on its way to the victory of wax museum ideals over creative art.

The development of the silent film was arrested possibly forever when it had hardly begun to produce good results; but it has left us with a few splendidly mature films. In the future, no doubt, "progress" will be faster. We shall have color films and stereoscopic films, and the artistic potentialities of the sound film will be crushed at an even earlier stage of their development.

What will the color film have to offer when it reaches technical perfection? We know what we shall lose artistically by abandoning the black-and-white film. Will color ever allow us to achieve a similar compositional precision, a similar independence of "reality"?

The masterpieces of painting prove that color provides wider possibilities than black-and-white and at the same time permits of a very exact and genuine style. But can painting and color photography be compared? Whereas the painter has a perfectly free hand with color and form in presenting nature, photography is obliged to record mechanically the light values of physical reality. In achromatic photography the reduction of everything to the gray scale resulted in an art medium that was sufficiently independent and divergent from nature. There is not much likelihood of any such transposition of reality into a qualitatively different range of colors in color film. To be sure, one can eliminate individual colors—one may, for example, cut out all blues, or, vice versa, one may cut out everything except the blues. Probably it is possible also to change one or more color tones qualitatively—for example, give all reds a cast of orange or make all the yellows greenish—or let colors change places with one another—turn all blues to red and all reds to blue—but all this would be, so to speak, only transposition of reality, mechanical shifts, whose usefulness as a formative medium may be doubted. Hence there remains only the possibility of controlling the color by clever choice of what is to be photographed. All kinds of fine procedures are conceivable, especially in the montage of colored pictures, but it must not be overlooked that in this way the subjective formative virtues of the camera, which are so distinctive a characteristic of film, will be more and more restricted, and the artistic part of the work will be more and more focused upon what is set up and enacted *before* the camera. The camera is thereby increasingly related to the position of a mere mechanical recording machine.

Above all, it is hardly realistic to speculate on the artistic possibilities of the color film without keeping in mind that at the same time we are likely to be presented with the three-dimensional film and the wide screen. Efforts in these directions are in progress. The illusion of reality will thereby have been increased to such a degree that the spectator will not be able to appreciate certain artistic color effects even if they should be feasible technically. It is quite conceivable that by a careful choice and arrangement of objects it might be possible to use the color on the projection surface artistically and harmoniously. But if the film image becomes stereoscopic there is no longer a plane surface within the confines of the screen, and therefore there can be no composition of that surface; what remains will be effects that are also possible on the stage. The increased size of the screen will render any two-dimensional or three-dimensional composition less compelling; and formative devices such as montage and changing camera angles will become unusable if the illusion of reality is so enormously strengthened. Obviously, montage will seem an intolerable accumulation of heterogeneous settings if the illusion of reality is very strong. Obviously also a change in the position of the camera will now be felt as an actual displacement within the space of the picture. The camera will have to become an immobile recording machine, every cut in the film strip will be mutilation. Scenes will have to be taken in their entire length and with a stationary camera, and they will have to be shown as they are. The artistic potentialities of this form of film will be exactly those of the stage. Film will no longer be able in any sense to be considered as a separate art. It will be thrown back to before its first beginnings—for it was with a fixed camera and an uncut strip that film started. The only difference will be that instead of having all before it film will have nothing to look forward to.

This curious development signifies to some extent the climax of that striving after likeness to nature which has hitherto permeated the whole history of the visual arts. Among the strivings that make human beings create faithful images is the primitive desire to get material objects into one's power by creating them afresh. Imitation also permits people to cope with significant experiences; it provides release, and makes for a kind of reciprocity between the self and the world. At the same time a reproduction that is true to nature provides the thrill that by the hand of man an image has been created which is astoundingly like some natural object. Nevertheless, various countertendencies—some of them purely perceptual—have prevented mechanically faithful imitation from being achieved hundreds of years ago. Apart from rare exceptions, only our modern age has succeeded in approaching this dangerous goal. In practice, there has always been the artistic urge not simply to copy but to originate, to interpret, to mold. We may, however, say that aesthetic theory has rarely sanctioned such activities. Even for artists like Leonardo da Vinci the demand for being as true to nature as possible was a matter of course when he talked theory, and Plato's attack on artists, in which he charged them with achieving nothing but reproductions of physical objects, is far from the general attitude.

To this very day some artists cherish this doctrine, and the general public does so to an even greater extent. In painting and sculpture it is only in recent decades that works have been appearing which show that their creators have broken with this principle intellectually and not merely practically. If a man considers that the artist should imitate nature, he may possibly paint like Van Gogh, but certainly not like Paul Klee. We know that the very powerful and widespread rejection of modern art is almost entirely supported by the argument that it is not true to nature. The development of film shows clearly how all-powerful this ideal still is.

Photography and its offspring, film, are art media so near to nature that the general public looks upon them as superior to such old-fashioned and imperfect imitative techniques as drawing and painting. Since on economic grounds film is much more dependent on the general public than any other form of art, the "artistic" preferences of the public sweep everything before them. Some work of good quality can be smuggled in but it does not compensate for the more fundamental defeats of film art. The complete film is the fulfillment of the age-old striving for the complete illusion. The attempt to make the two-dimensional picture as nearly as possible like its old model succeeds; original and copy become practically indistinguishable. Thereby all formative potentialities which were based on the differences between model and copy are eliminated and only what is inherent in the original in the way of significant form remains to art.

H. Baer in a remarkable little essay in the *Kunstblatt* has pointed out that color film represents the accomplishment of tendencies which have long been present in graphic art.

"Graphic art (he says)—of which photography is one branch—has always striven after color. The oldest woodcuts, the blockbooks, were finished off by being hand-painted. Later, a second, colored, plate was added to the black-and-white—as in Dürer's portrait of 'Ulrich Varnbühler.' A magnificent picture of a knight in armor in black, silver, and gold, exists by Burgmair. In the eighteenth century multicolored etchings were produced. In the nineteenth the lithographs of Daumier and Gavarni are colored in mass production. . . . Color invaded the graphic arts as an increased attraction for the eye. Uncivilized man is not as a rule satisfied with black-and-white. Children, peasants and primitive peoples demand the highest degree of bright coloring. It is the primitives of the great cities who congregate before the film screen. Therefore film calls in the aid of bright colors. It is a fresh stimulus."

In itself, the perfection of the "complete" film need not be a catastrophe—if silent film, sound film, and colored sound film were allowed to exist alongside it. There is no objection to the "complete" film as an alternative to the stage—it might help to take into remote places fine performances of good works, as also of operas, musical comedies, ballets, the dance. Moreover, by its very existence it would probably have an excellent influence on the other—the real—film forms, by forcing them to advance along their own lines. Silent film, for example, would no longer provide dialogue in its titles, because then the absence of the spoken word would be felt as artificial and disturbing. In sound film, too, any vague intermediate form between it and the stage would be avoided. Just as the stage will feel itself obliged by the very existence of film to emphasize its own characteristic—the predominance of dramatic speech—so the "complete" film could relegate the true film forms to their own sphere.

The fact is, however, that whereas aesthetically these categories of film could and should exist along with mechanically complete reproduction, they are inferior to it in the capacity to imitate nature. Therefore the "complete" film is certain to be considered an advance upon the preceding film forms, and will supplant them all.

1933

V. F. PERKINS
FROM FILM AS FILM

FORM AND DISCIPLINE

I do not believe that the film (or any other medium) has an essence which we can usefully invoke to justify our criteria. We do not deduce the standards relevant to Rembrandt from the essence of paint; nor does the nature of words impose a method of judging ballads and novels. Standards of judgment cannot be appropriate to a medium as such but only to particular ways of exploiting its opportunities. That is why the concept of the cinematic, presented in terms of demands, has stunted the useful growth of film theory. Helpful criteria are more likely to be based on positive statements of value than on prohibitions. To regard criticism positively, as a search for the most satisfactory definitions of function and value, allows an escape from academic systems of rules and requirements. Criteria then relate to claims which the critic can sustain rather than to demands which he must make. The clarification of standards should help to develop the disciplines of criticism without seeking to lay obligations on the film-maker. Criticism and its theory are concerned with the interplay of available resources and desirable functions. They attempt to establish what the medium is good for. They cannot determine what is good for the medium, because the question is senseless. The search for appropriate criteria leads us to observe limitations; it does not allow us to prescribe them. Anything possible is also permissible, but we still have to establish its value. We cannot assess worth without indicating function.

Hence we can evolve useful criteria only for specific types of film, not for the cinema. Our standards of judgement will have to follow from definitions of types in terms of both their possibilities and their limitations. We have to discover what values we can claim for, what functions it makes sense to assign to, particular applications of the moving picture's resources. Our major concern will be with the different opportunities which can be realized within the various forms of cinema. A theory of film which claims universal validity must provide either an exhaustive catalogue of film forms or a description of the medium in such general terms as to offer minimal guidance to the appreciation of any movie. The problem arises from the embarrassing richness of the cinema's aptitudes.

The movie offers two forms of magic, since its conquest of the visible world extends in two opposite directions. The first, on which the realist theory concentrates, gives it the power to "possess" the real world by capturing its appearance. The second, focus of the traditional aesthetic, permits the presentation of an ideal image, ordered by the film-maker's will and imagination. Since the cinema's mechanism incorporates both these tendencies, neither of them can be condemned on rational, technical or aesthetic grounds. A useful film theory must acknowledge the range and diversity of the film-maker's achievements. At one end of the scale we find the most rigorous forms of documentary, which aim to present the truth about an event with the minimum of human intervention between the real object and its film image; at the other end lies the abstract, cartoon or fantasy film which presents a totally controlled vision. This diversity of methods might be attributed to the movies' mixed parentage, the "objective," factual elements being derived from the camera and the "subjective," magical ones from the Phenakistascope and its relations.

Within the first few years of the cinema's existence the polarities were firmly established. The Lumière brothers' first movie-show presented short "actualities"—a train entering a station, baby eating breakfast and so on. In the earliest days the fact that a machine could present real situations in recognizable form was sufficient sensation to draw enthusiastic audiences throughout Europe and the United States. As soon as that magic lost its appeal, Georges Méliès was ready to step in with the other kind. A professional magician, Méliès took up film-making in 1896 and devoted himself to exploiting the cinema as a medium for fantasy. Using every form of camera trickery he could invent, he told a series of amusing and amazing stories. His two most famous pictures, *A Trip to the Moon* (1902) and *The Impossible Voyage* (1904), presented fantastic situations in fantastic settings. They are packed with magical appearances, disappearances and transformations. The arrival of Méliès and the subsequent development of the narrative film revived the public's waning interest in motion pictures.

Lumière's actualities represent one extreme of the cinema and Méliès's fantasies are quite near to the other. But few films confine themselves to either a purely reproductive or a purely imaginative technique. The cinema extends across the whole of the area between the two extremes. The photographic narrative film occupies a compromise position where a fictional "reality" is *created* in order to be *recorded*. Here the relationship between reality and illusion, object and image, becomes extremely complex; any attempt to isolate either in a "pure" state becomes correspondingly inept.

The fiction movie exploits the possibilities of synthesis between photographic realism and dramatic illusion. That synthesis, its value and implications, will be the major subject of this study. Unless a wider relevance is explicitly claimed, the reader should assume that arguments are meant to apply only to the cinema of photographic fiction. I hope to present criteria which will aid discussion of various kinds and degrees of excellence within this form. I shall offer no case about the usefulness of other forms, nor will my remarks be relevant to the qualities of works outside the range of my definitions. The chosen field to some extent reflects the limits of my familiarity and enthusiasm, but that is all. It would clearly be possible and useful to argue claims and criteria for cartoon, documentary, instructional and many other kinds of film which lie beyond the scope of this study. Nonetheless the fiction movie presents the most urgent claim to attention for two reasons: by almost any reasonable method of calculation, it must be granted the central role in the cinema's development; but it is also precisely the fictional element which existing film theories have most difficulty in accommodating.

A necessary consequence of adopting positive criteria is that we are better equipped to praise than to condemn. Discriminations will be possible within the type, in so far as we see one film as a more complete or skilful realization of its opportunities than another. But the claims we can make for a comedy by Howard Hawks will not yield ammunition for use against an Ingmar Bergman allegory, because they belong to types almost as distinct as cartoon and documentary. Even within the field of cine-fiction the range of possibilities remains enormous. The critical problem is to arrive at descriptions which are both specific and comprehensive enough to be useful. The critic cannot require a movie to fit his definitions; it's his task to find the description which best fits the movie. The most he can "demand" from a film is coherence: a structure which points consistently towards the performance of comprehensible functions. Without that, judgement becomes impossible. From this viewpoint the most significant limitations are those of the form rather than of the medium, the disciplines which the film-maker obeys in order to pursue a particular range of opportunities. For if there are no rules by which every movie can be bound, there are forms which, once adopted by the film-maker, impose their own logic both on him and on the intelligent spectator, since the opportunities of the form may be realized only at the expense of other, attractive but incompatible, possibilities. Yet the central issue remains: not what the film-maker may not do, but the value we can find in what he has done.

In a hybrid form the quest for purity is much less important than the achievement of an ideal compromise, a meaningful resolution of inherent conflict. The fictional film exploits, where purer forms attempt to negate, the conflict between reality and illusion. Instead of trying exclusively either to create or to record, the story film attempts a synthesis: it both records what has been created and creates by its manner of recording. At its most powerful it achieves a credibility which consummates the cinema's blend of actuality and fantasy.

The credibility of the movies comes, I believe, from our habit of placing more trust in the evidence of our eyes than in any other form of sense data: a film makes us feel like eye-witnesses of the events which it portrays. Moreover, our belief extends even to the least realistic forms of movie because movement so strongly connotes life. The source meaning of the term "animation" indicates that we regard a moving picture, even a cartoon, as a picture *brought to life*. In the early days of movies words like cinematograph and kinetoscope, which meant *moving* picture, were interchangeable with words meaning *living* picture (vitascope, biograph, bioscope, etc.). The powerful combination of picture and movement tempts us to disregard the involvement of our imaginations in what we see. . . .

The most "realistic" films are the ones which convey the most complete illusion. The most obviously imaginative films, the "pure works of man"—cartoons and fantasies— lean heavily upon the cinema's realistic resources in order to make us see the impossible and believe the incredible. When the cartoon cat walks confidently off the edge of a skyscraper and stands paralyzed for a couple of fearful seconds before falling, it is precisely our habit of believing our eyes that makes a piece of anti-Newtonian nonsense amusing.

Some abstract films make no use of the cinema's realism (the spectator's credulity). They do not pretend to show real objects but are an extension of non-representational painting. Yet even films in this genre—like Norman McLaren's "caprice in colour," *Begone, Dull Care*—seem to rely on our anthropomorphic tendencies. Whenever the opportunity arises movement becomes action (a round blob "bumps into" a vertical line: accident or aggression?) and shape becomes object (a coloured circle: a ball, a wheel, the sun?). Ernest Pintoff's cartoon *The Critic* comments joyfully on the abstract film's tendency to shed its abstract quality. The screen is filled with coloured shapes which apparently defy interpretation. After a few seconds we hear a Bronx-accented voice demanding "what the hell is this?" the question is momentarily resolved: "Must be a cartoon." Pause. Small blob emerges from "inside" larger blob and the interpretation begins: "Must be Birth." The shapes are rearranged and the spectator becomes confused again: "This is cute. This is cute. This is nice. What the hell *is* it?" Two black shapes converge from opposite sides of the screen: "Two Things! . . . They like each other." (Rhythmic movement of black shapes.) "Could this be the sex life of two Things?" As the commentary progresses (spikey black oval: "Uh-uh! It's a cockroach") it becomes increasingly contemptuous of the movie's imagined content ("Dirt! Dirt and filth!") until, after four minutes of "pure" abstraction the critic reaches his conclusion: "I don't know much about psychoanalysis, but I'd say this is a dirty picture." Pintoff's movie is funny because it is accurate. With any luck actual spectators can be heard commenting and interpreting before "the critic" starts to speak; the two sets of remarks are often very similar.

If abstract shapes in movement attract "realistic" interpretation as objects and actions, it is hardly surprising that the moving photograph carries such conviction. Photographic subjects, says Newhall, "can be misrepresented, distorted, faked . . . and [we] even delight in it occasionally, but the knowledge still cannot shake our implicit faith in the truth of a photographic record."*

In 1895 the Lumières' audience believed completely in the reality of a soundless, colourless, two-dimensional and rigidly enclosed image: the spectators feared for their lives when shown an oncoming train. Sixty years later, engulfed in Cinerama's huge screen and surrounded by a battery of realistic sound effects, people reacted to film taken from the front of a roller-coaster just as they would react to a ride on a real switchback. They gripped the arms of their seats, screamed and even felt the authentic stomach-tumbling effect. Still, we can hardly claim that *This Is Cinerama*

---

*Beaumont Newhall, *The History of Photography from 1839 to the Present Day,* Museum of Modern Art, New York, 1949, p. 91.

offered a perfect illusion. Its picture, while not exactly flat, was less than three-dimensional. The joins between its three images were clearly visible. We were subject to none of the physical effects essential to a total illusion: no wind disturbed the spectator's hair as he rode the switchback, no smell reached his nostrils as he was conducted along the canals of Venice.

But although Cinerama provided only a partial illusion, it imposed the only sort of belief which we can regard as truly complete: the audience was made to react to the image as it would to the event. The trick here is just the same as it was with the Lumières' presentation and with the 3-D films whose audiences dived for cover under a barrage of arrows, axes and ping-pong balls: not to provide a perfect illusion, that is an integral reproduction of reality, but to offer enough of reality to make the spectator disregard what is missing.

This kind and degree of belief is inevitably short-lived since "enough" means "more than ever before." Audiences rapidly adjust to an extension of the cinema's realism. The primitive magic which creates belief in the real presence of the object shown soon loses its power. "Illusion wears off once . . . expectation is stepped up; we take it for granted and want more."* After less than ten minutes of *This Is Cinerama* the sense of being transported around the world began to be replaced by a more conscious appreciation of the techniques by which the world was so convincingly brought into the cinema. The illusory environment of the roller-coaster or the Venetian canal is too inconsistent with what we know about our actual situation for a lasting deception.

But even if we do not believe in the actual presence of the things we see, a film remains credible so long as we are not led to question the *reality* of the objects and events presented. Verbal statements and propositions are seen as either true or false: if we believe them, we believe them; if not, not. Sights, sounds and, particularly, stories—the things which we believe *in*—present a much more complex problem. Belief here can occur in so many ways and at so many levels.

Films are often described as existing in the present tense. Like most direct linguistic analogies this one promotes confusion rather than enlightenment. It implies that we see a film as a series of events taking place for the first time. Usually we are well aware that this is not the case, just as we know that the conjurer has not magically transformed the queen of hearts into the king of spades. If films were really seen in the present tense cinema managers would have always to protect their screens against assault by gallant spectators rushing to the aid of embattled heroines. If we can describe the movie as existing in any tense at all then the nearest equivalent is probably the historic present which evokes the vividness of memory or fantasy: "There I am walking along the street, and there's this old man standing on the corner. And then he steps out into the road just as this lorry comes around . . ."

Our reaction to the cinema, when we are not caught unawares by some new development like Cinerama or 3-D, is conditioned by our awareness that the camera is a recording instrument and the projected film a method of reproduction. Just

---

*E. H. Gombrich, *Art and Illusion*, Phaidon Press, London, 1962, pp. 52–4.

as we can talk of hearing Bessie Smith on a gramophone record despite our knowledge that the singer is long dead, so we can watch events taking place on the screen *now* while remaining aware that they actually occurred some time ago. In both cases we accept the accuracy of the illusion.

Ideally the sounds coming from the gramophone's loudspeaker are indistinguishable from the sounds which first went into the microphone. Even when a recorded performance falls spectacularly short of this ideal we have great difficulty in disentangling the sounds made by the artist from the noises made by the recording: it is impossible to be certain how much our concept of what Bessie Smith sounded like is derived from tones which should be attributed to primitive recording mechanisms, not to the singer. Our belief in the recording is not shaken by our knowledge that the "Bessie Smith sound" may not be a very faithful reproduction of the voice of Bessie Smith. It is hard not to feel, against reason, that the recording renders accurately the sounds made by the jazz-singer and her accompanists: if I ask myself to describe Bessie Smith's vocal quality, "scratchy" is one of the words which most immediately comes to mind.

Similarly I find it hard to form a mental picture of life in the first decade of this century which does not include people walking faster and more jauntily than they do nowadays. The image offered by accelerated projection of early films takes mental precedence over the recognized unlikelihood of an evolution towards slower walking.

It is the belief in the actual (if past) existence of the objects on the screen which enables us to discuss movies in terms of credibility. Clearly, one cannot record something which has never existed. Everything that happens on the screen in a live-action picture has happened in front of the camera. The particular magic of the narrative film is to make us put an inaccurate construction on an accurate series of images. The camera neither lies nor tells the truth, because the camera does not make statements. It is we who convert images into assertions. The cinema shows us a man holding a pistol at his head, squeezing the trigger and falling to the floor. This is precisely what happened. But we fictionalize this documentary image when we claim to have seen a man committing suicide. . . .

The camera does not discriminate between real events (which would have taken place even if it had not been on the spot to record them) and action created specifically in order to be recorded. In this respect, the movie simply extends the ambiguity present in any credible image; so long as it looks correct we have no way of telling whether a picture portrays an actual or an imagined subject. The blurred distinction between authentic and staged events helps to make the cinema a peculiarly vivid medium. It is absurd to claim that movies are like life; but it is certain that they can impress us as being more lifelike than any other form of narrative.

The moving image lends its immediacy and conviction, its concreteness of credible detail, to the fictional world. But at this point the film-maker confronts the limitation that accompanies opportunity. If he chooses to exploit the credibility of the recording, he thereby sacrifices some of the freedom to invent and arrange which is offered by the celluloid strip. The discipline is inherent in the attempt to create from a succession of images an apparently solid world which exists in its own right.

In the fiction movie, reality becomes malleable but remains (or continues to seem) solid. The world is shaped by the filmmaker to reveal an order beyond chronology, in a system of time and space which is both natural and synthetic. The movie offers its reality in a sequence of privileged moments during which actions achieve a clarity and intensity seldom found in everyday life. Motive and gesture, action and reaction, cause and effect, are brought into a more immediate, dynamic and revealing relationship. The filmmaker fashions a world more concentrated and more shaped than that of our usual experience.

Movies are not distinguished from other forms of narrative by the fact that they isolate and mould aspects of experience in order to intensify our perception. But films are peculiar in performing this work primarily in the sphere of action and appearance rather than of reflection or debate.

The story-teller's freedom to create is inhibited by his two first requirements: clarity and credibility. In movies, the most direct and concrete method of narration, these aims impose a greater restraint than on any other medium. The audience has to know what is happening, of course, but it must also be convinced by what it sees. The organization of image and sound must usually defer to these interests. The narrative picture, in most of its forms, submits to the twin criteria of order and credibility. The movie itself creates these criteria whenever it proposes to be at the same time significant and convincing. The impurity of the medium is consummated by a decision to project a world which is both reproduced and imagined, a creation and a copy. Committed to this impurity, the film-maker is also committed to maintaining a balance between its elements. His aim is to organize the world to the point where it becomes most meaningful but to resist ordering it out of all resemblance to the real world which it attempts to evoke. . . .

1972

MAYA DEREN
CINEMATOGRAPHY: THE CREATIVE USE OF REALITY

The motion-picture camera is perhaps the most paradoxical of all machines, in that it can be at once independently active and infinitely passive. Kodak's early slogan, "You push the button, it does the rest," was not an exaggerated advertising claim, and, connected to any simple trigger device, a camera can even take pictures all by itself. At the same time, while a comparable development and refinement of other mechanisms has usually resulted in an increased specialization, the advances in the scope and sensitivity of lenses and emulsions have made the camera capable of infinite receptivity and indiscriminate fidelity. To this must be added the fact that the medium deals, or can deal, in terms of the most elemental actuality. In sum, it can produce maximum results for virtually minimal effort: it requires of its operator only a modicum of aptitude and energy; of its subject matter, only that it exist; and of its audience, only that they can see. On this elementary level it functions ideally as a mass medium for communicating equally elementary ideas.

The photographic medium is, as a matter of fact, so amorphous that it is not merely unobtrusive but virtually transparent, and so becomes, more than any other medium, susceptible of servitude to any and all the others. The enormous value of such servitude suffices to justify the medium and to be generally accepted as its function. This has been a major obstacle to the definition and development of motion pictures as a creative fine-art form—capable of creative action in its own terms—for its own character is as a latent image which can become manifest only if no other image is imposed upon it to obscure it.

Those concerned with the emergence of this latent form must therefore assume a partially protective role, one which recalls the advice of an art instructor who said, "If you have trouble drawing the vase, try drawing the space around the vase." Indeed, for the time being, the definition of the creative form of film involves as careful attention to what it is not as to what it is.

ANIMATED PAINTINGS

In recent years, perceptible first on the experimental fringes of the film world and now in general evidence at the commercial art theaters, there has been an accelerated development of what might be called the "graphic arts school of animated film." Such films, which combine abstract backgrounds with recognizable but not realistic figures, are designed and painted by trained and talented graphic artists who make use of a sophisticated, fluent knowledge of the rich resources of plastic media, including even collage. A major factor in the emergence of this school has been the enormous technical and laboratory advance in color film and color processing, so that it is now possible for these artists to approach the two-dimensional, rectangular screen with all the graphic freedom they bring to a canvas.

The similarity between screen and canvas had long ago been recognized by artists such as Hans Richter, Oskar Fischinger, and others, who were attracted not by its graphic possibilities (so limited at that time) but rather by the excitements of the film medium, particularly the exploitation of its time dimension—rhythm, spatial depth created by a diminishing square, the three-dimensional illusion created by the revolutions of a spiral figure, etc. They put their graphic skills at the service of the film medium, as a means of extending film expression.*

The new graphic-arts school does not so much advance those early efforts as reverse them, for here the artists make use of the film medium as an extension of the plastic media. This is particularly clear when one analyzes the principle of movement employed, for it is usually no more than a sequential articulation—a kind of spelling out in time—of the dynamic ordinarily implicit in the design of an individual composition. The most appropriate term to describe such works, which are often interesting and witty, and which certainly have their place among visual arts, is "animated paintings."

This entry of painting into the film medium presents certain parallels with the introduction of sound. The silent film had attracted to it persons who had talent for and were inspired by the exploration and development of a new and unique form of visual expression. The addition of sound opened the doors for the verbalists and dramatists. Armed with the authority, power, laws, techniques, skills, and crafts which the venerable literary arts had accumulated over centuries, the writers hardly even paused to recognize the small resistance of the "indigenous" film-maker, who had had barely a decade in which to explore and evolve the creative potential of his medium.

The rapid success of the "animated painting" is similarly due to the fact that it comes armed with all the plastic traditions and techniques which are its impressive heritage. And just as the sound film interrupted the development of film form on the commercial level by providing a more finished substitute, so the "animated

---

*It is significant that Hans Richter, a pioneer in such a use of film, soon abandoned this approach. All his later films, along with the films of Léger, Man Ray, Dali, and the painters who participated in Richter's later films (Ernst, Duchamp, etc.) indicate a profound appreciation of the distinction between the plastic and the photographic image and make enthusiastic and creative use of photographic reality.

painting" is already being accepted as a form of film art in the few areas (the distribution of 16 mm. film shorts of film series and societies) where experiments in film form can still find an audience.

The motion-picture medium has an extraordinary range of expression. It has in common with the plastic arts the fact that it is a visual composition projected on a two dimensional surface; with dance, that it can deal in the arrangement of movement; with theater, that it can create a dramatic intensity of events; with music, that it can compose in the rhythms and phrases of time and can be attended by song and instrument; with poetry, that it can juxtapose images; with literature generally, that it can encompass in its sound track the abstractions available only to language.

This very profusion of potentialities seems to create confusion in the minds of most film-makers, a confusion which is diminished by eliminating a major portion of those potentialities in favor of one or two, upon which the film is subsequently structured. An artist, however, should not seek security in a tidy mastery over the simplifications of deliberate poverty; he should, instead, have the creative courage to face the danger of being overwhelmed by fecundity in the effort to resolve it into simplicity and economy.

While the "animated painting" film has limited itself to a small area of film potential, it has gained acceptance on the basis of the fact that it *does* use an art form—the graphic art form—and that it does seem to meet the general condition of film: it makes its statement as an image in movement. This opens the entire question of whether a photograph is of the same order of image as all others. If not, is there a correspondingly different approach to it in a creative context? Although the photographic process is the basic building block of the motion-picture medium, it is a tribute to its self-effacement as a servant that virtually no consideration has been given to its own character and the creative implications thereof.

THE CLOSED CIRCUIT OF THE PHOTOGRAPHIC PROCESS

The term "image" (originally based on "imitation") means in its first sense the visual likeness of a real object or person, and in the very act of specifying resemblance it distinguishes and establishes the entire category of visual experience which is *not* a real object or person. In this specifically negative sense—in the sense that the photograph of a horse is not the horse itself—a photograph is an image.

But the term "image" also has positive implications: it presumes a mental activity, whether in its most passive form (the "mental images" of perception and memory) or, as in the arts, the creative action of the imagination realized by the art instrument. Here reality is first filtered by the selectivity of individual interests and modified by prejudicial perception to become experience; as such it is combined with similar, contrasting or modifying experiences, both forgotten and remembered, to become assimilated into a conceptual image; this in turn is subject to the manipulations of the art instrument; and what finally emerges is a plastic image which is a reality in its own right. A painting is not, fundamentally, a likeness or image of a horse; it is a likeness of a mental concept which may resemble a horse or which may, as in abstract painting, bear no visible relation to any real object.

Photography, however, is a process by which an object creates its own image by the action of its light or light-sensitive material. It thus presents a closed circuit precisely at the point where, in the traditional art forms, the creative process takes place as reality passes through the artist. This exclusion of the artist at that point is responsible both for the absolute fidelity of the photographic process and for the widespread conviction that a photographic medium cannot be, itself, a creative form. From these observations it is but a step to the conclusion that its use as a visual printing press or as an extension of another creative form represents a full realization of the potential of the medium. It is precisely in this manner that the photographic process is used in "animated paintings."

But in so far as the camera is applied to objects which are already accomplished images, is this really a more creative use of the instrument than when, in scientific films, its fidelity is applied to reality in conjunction with the revelatory functions of telescopic or microscopic lenses and a comparable use of the motor?

Just as the magnification of a lens trained upon matter shows us a mountainous, craggy landscape in an apparently smooth surface, so slow-motion can reveal the actual structure of movements or changes which either cannot be slowed down in actuality or whose nature would be changed by a change in tempo of performance. Applied to the flight of a bird, for example, slow-motion reveals the hitherto unseen sequence of the many separate strains and small movements of which it is compounded.

By a telescopic use of the motor, I mean the telescoping of time achieved by triggering a camera to take pictures of a vine at ten-minute intervals. When projected at regular speed, the film reveals the actual integrity, almost the intelligence, of the movement of the vine as it grows and turns with the sun. Such telescoped-time photography has been applied to chemical changes and to physical metamorphoses whose tempo is so slow as to be virtually imperceptible.

Although the motion-picture camera here functions as an instrument of discovery rather than of creativity, it does yield a kind of image which, unlike the images of "animated paintings" (animation itself is a use of the telescoped-time principle), is unique to the motion-picture medium. It may therefore be regarded as an even more valid basic element in a creative film form based on the singular properties of the medium.

REALITY AND RECOGNITION

The application of the photographic process to reality results in an image which is unique in several respects. For one thing, since a specific reality is the prior condition of the existence of a photograph, the photograph not only testifies to the existence of that reality (just as drawing testifies to the existence of an artist) but is, to all intents and purposes, its equivalent. This equivalence is not at all a matter of fidelity but is of a different order altogether. If realism is the term of a graphic image which precisely simulates some real object, then a photograph must be differentiated from it as *a form of reality itself.*

This distinction plays an extremely important role in the address of these respective images. The intent of the plastic arts is to make meaning manifest. In creating an image for the express purpose of communicating, the artist primarily undertakes to create the most effective aspect possible out of the total resources of his medium. Photography, however, deals in a living reality which is structured primarily to endure, and whose configurations are designed to serve that purpose, not to communicate its meaning; they may even serve to conceal that purpose as a protective measure. In a photograph, then, we begin by recognizing a reality, and our attendant knowledges and attitudes are brought into play; only then does the aspect become meaningful in reference to it. The abstract shadow shape in a night scene is not understood at all until revealed and identified as a person; the bright red shape on a pale ground which might, in an abstract, graphic context, communicate a sense of gaiety, conveys something altogether different when recognized as a wound. As we watch a film, the continuous act of recognition in which we are involved is like a strip of memory unrolling beneath the images of the film itself, to form the invisible underlayer of an implicit double exposure.

The process by which we understand an abstract, graphic image is almost directly opposite, then, to that by which we understand a photograph. In the first case, the aspect leads us to meaning; in the second case the understanding which results from recognition is the key to our evaluation of the aspect.

PHOTOGRAPHIC AUTHORITY AND THE "CONTROLLED ACCIDENT"

As a reality, the photographic image confronts us with the innocent arrogance of an objective fact, one which exists as an independent presence, indifferent to our response. We may in turn view it with an indifference and detachment we do not have toward the man-made images of other arts, which invite and require our perception and demand our response in order to consummate the communication they initiate and which is their *raison d'être*. At the same time precisely because we are aware that our personal detachment does not in any way diminish the verity of the photographic image, it exercises an authority comparable in weight only to the authority of reality itself.

It is upon this authority that the entire school of the social documentary film is based. Although expert in the selection of the most effective reality and in the use of camera placement and angle to accentuate the pertinent and effective features of it, the documentarists operate on a principle of minimal intervention, in the interests of bringing the authority of reality to the support of the moral purpose of the film.

Obviously, the interest of a documentary film corresponds closely to the interest inherent in its subject matter. Such films enjoyed a period of particular pre-eminence during the war. This popularity served to make fiction-film producers more keenly aware of the effectiveness and authority of reality, an awareness which gave rise to the "neo-realist" style of film and contributed to the still growing trend toward location filming.

In the theater, the physical presence of the performers provides a sense of reality which induces us to accept the symbols of geography, the intermissions which represent the passage of time, and the other conventions which are part of the form. Films cannot include this physical presence of the performers. They can, however, replace the artifice of theater by the actuality of landscape, distances, and place; the interruptions of intermissions can be transposed into transitions which sustain and even intensify the momentum of dramatic development; while events and episodes which, within the context of theatrical artifice, might not have been convincing in their logic or aspect can be clothed in the verity which emanates from the reality of the surrounding landscape, the sun, the streets and buildings.

In certain respects, the very absence in motion pictures of the physical presence of the performer, which is so important to the theater, can even contribute to our sense of reality. We can, for example, believe in the existence of a monster if we are not asked to believe that it is present in the room with us. The intimacy imposed upon us by the physical reality of other art works presents us with alternative choices: either to identify with or to deny the experience they propose, or to withdraw altogether to a detached awareness of that reality as merely a metaphor. But the film image—whose intangible reality consists of lights and shadows beamed through the air and caught on the surface of a silver screen—comes to us as the reflection of another world. At that distance we can accept the reality of the most monumental and extreme of images, and from that perspective we can perceive and comprehend them in their full dimension.

The authority of reality is available even to the most artificial constructs if photography is understood as an art of the "controlled accident." By "controlled accident" I mean the maintenance of a delicate balance between what is there spontaneously and naturally as evidence of the independent life of actuality, and the persons and activities which are deliberately introduced into the scene. A painter, relying primarily upon aspect as the means of communicating his intent, would take enormous care in the arrangement of every detail of, for example, a beach scene. The cinematographer, on the other hand, having selected a beach which, in general, has the desired aspect—whether grim or happy, deserted or crowded— must on the contrary refrain from overcontrolling the aspect if he is to retain the authority of reality. The filming of such a scene should be planned and framed so as to create a context of limits within which anything that occurs is compatible with the intent of the scene.

The invented event which is then introduced, though itself an artifice, borrows reality from the reality of the scene—from the natural blowing of the hair, the irregularity of the waves, the very texture of the stones and sand—in short, from all the uncontrolled, spontaneous elements which are the property of actuality itself. Only in photography—by the delicate manipulation which I call controlled accident— can natural phenomena be incorporated into our own creativity, to yield an image where the reality of a tree confers its truth upon the events we cause to transpire beneath it.

ABSTRACTIONS AND ARCHETYPES

Inasmuch as the other art forms are not constituted of reality itself, they create metaphors for reality. But photography, being itself the reality or the equivalent thereof, can use its own reality as a metaphor for ideas and abstractions. In painting, the image is an abstraction of the aspect; in photography, the abstraction of an idea produces the archetypal image.

This concept is not new to motion pictures, but its development was interrupted by the intrusions of theatrical traditions into the film medium. The early history of film is studded with archetypal figures: Theda Bara, Mary Pickford, Marlene Dietrich, Greta Garbo, Charles Chaplin, Buster Keaton, etc. These appeared as personages, not as people or personalities, and the films which were structured around them were like monumental myths which celebrated cosmic truths.

The invasion of the motion-picture medium by modern playwrights and actors introduced the concept of realism, which is at the root of theatrical metaphor and which, in the a priori reality of photography, is an absurd redundancy which has served merely to deprive the motion-picture medium of its creative dimension. It is significant that, despite every effort of pretentious producers, directors and film critics who seek to raise their professional status by adopting the methods, attitudes, and criteria of the established and respected art of theater, the major figures—both the most popular stars and the most creative directors (such as Orson Welles)—continue to operate in the earlier archetypal tradition. It was even possible, as Marlon Brando demonstrated, to transcend realism and to become an archetypal realist, but it would appear that his early intuition has been subsequently crushed under the pressures of the repertory complex, another carry-over from theater, where it functioned as the means by which a single company could offer a remunerative variety of plays to an audience while providing consistent employment for its members. There is no justification whatsoever for insisting on a repertory variety of roles for actors involved in the totally different circumstances of motion pictures.

PHOTOGRAPHY'S UNIQUE IMAGES

In all that I have said so far, the fidelity, reality, and authority of the photographic image serve primarily to modify and to support. Actually, however, the sequence in which we perceive photography—an initial identification followed by an interpretation of the aspect according to that identification (rather than in primarily aspectual terms)—becomes irreversible and confers meaning upon aspect in a manner unique to the photographic medium.

I have previously referred to slow-motion as a time microscope, but it has its expressive uses as well as its revelatory ones. Depending upon the subject and the context, it can be a statement of either ideal ease or nagging frustration, a kind of intimate and loving meditation on a movement or a solemnity which adds ritual weight to an action; or it can bring into reality that dramatic image of anguished helplessness, otherwise experienced only in the nightmares of childhood, when our legs refused to move while the terror which pursues us comes ever closer.

Yet, slow-motion is not simply slowness of speed. It is, in fact, something which exists in our minds, not on the screen, and can be created only in conjunction with the identifiable reality of the photographic image. When we see a man in the attitudes of running and identify the activity as a run, one of the knowledges which is part of that identification is the pulse normal to that activity. It is because we are aware of the known pulse of the identified action while we watch it occur at a slower rate of speed that we experience the double-exposure of time which we know as slow-motion. It cannot occur in an abstract film, where a triangle, for instance, may go fast or slow, but, having no necessary pulse, cannot go in slow-motion.

Another unique image which the camera can yield is reverse motion. When used meaningfully, it does not convey so much a sense of a backward movement spatially, but rather an undoing of time. One of the most memorable uses of this occurs in Cocteau's *Blood of a Poet,* where the peasant is executed by a volley of fire which also shatters the crucifix hanging on the wall behind him. This scene is followed by a reverse motion of the action—the dead peasant rising from the ground and the crucifix reassembling on the wall; then again the volley of fire, the peasant falling, the crucifix shattering; and again the filmic resurrection. Reverse motion also, for obvious reasons, does not exist in abstract films.

The photographic negative image is still another striking case in point. This is not a direct white-on-black statement but is understood as an inversion of values. When applied to a recognizable person or scene, it conveys a sense of a critically qualitative change, as in its use for the landscape on the other side of death in Cocteau's *Orpheus.*

Both such extreme images and the more familiar kind which I referred to earlier make use of the motion-picture medium as a form in which the meaning of the image originates in our recognition of a known reality and derives its authority from the direct relationship between reality and image in the photographic process. While the process permits some intrusion by the artist as a modifier of that image, the limits of its tolerance can be defined as that point at which the original reality becomes unrecognizable or is irrelevant (as when a red reflection in a pond is used for its shape and color only and without contextual concern for the water or the pond).

In such cases the camera itself has been conceived of as the artist, with distorting lenses, multiple superpositions, etc. used to simulate the creative action of the eye, the memory, etc. Such well-intentioned efforts to use the medium creatively, by forcibly inserting the creative act in the position it traditionally occupies in the visual arts, accomplish, instead, the destruction of the photographic image as reality. This image, with its unique ability to engage us simultaneously on several levels—by the objective authority of reality, by the knowledges and values which we attach to that reality, by the direct address of its aspect, and by a manipulated relationship between these—is the building block for the creative use of the medium.

THE PLACEMENT OF THE CREATIVE ACT AND TIME-SPACE MANIPULATIONS

Where does the film-maker then undertake his major creative action if, in the interests of preserving these qualities of the image, he restricts himself to the control of accident in the pre-photographic stage and accepts almost complete exclusion from the photographic process as well?

Once we abandon the concept of the image as the end product and consummation of the creative process (which it is in both the visual arts and the theater), we can take a larger view of the total medium and can see that the motion-picture instrument actually consists of two parts, which flank the artist on either side. The images with which the camera provides him are like fragments of a permanent, incorruptible memory; their individual reality is in no way dependent upon their sequence in actuality, and they can be assembled to compose any of several statements. In film, the image can and should be only the beginning, the basic material of the creative action.

All invention and creation consist primarily of a new relationship between known parts. The images of film deal in realities which, as I pointed out earlier, are structured to fulfill their various functions, not to communicate a specific meaning. Therefore they have several attributes simultaneously, as when a table may be, at once, old, red, and high. Seeing it as a separate entity, an antique dealer would appraise its age, an artist its color, and a child its inaccessible height. But in a film such a shot might be followed by one in which the table falls apart, and thus a particular aspect of its age would constitute its meaning and function in the sequence, with all other attributes becoming irrelevant. The editing of a film creates the sequential relationship which gives particular or new meaning to the images *according to their function;* it establishes a context, a form which transfigures them without distorting their aspect, diminishing their reality and authority, or impoverishing that variety of potential functions which is the characteristic dimension of reality.

Whether the images are related in terms of common or contrasting qualities, in the causal logic of events which is narrative, or in the logic of ideas and emotions which is the poetic mode, the structure of a film is sequential. The creative action in film, then, takes place in its time dimension; and for this reason the motion picture, though composed of spatial images, is primarily *a time form.*

A major portion of the creative action consists of a manipulation of time and space. By this I do not mean only such established filmic techniques as flashback, condensation of time, parallel action etc. These affect not the action itself but the method of revealing it. In a flashback there is no implication that the usual chronological integrity of the action itself is in any way affected by the process, however disrupted, of memory. Parallel action, as when we see alternately the hero who rushes to the rescue and the heroine whose situation becomes increasingly critical, is an omnipresence on the part of the camera as a witness of action, not as a creator of it.

The kind of manipulation of time and space to which I refer becomes itself part of the organic structure of a film. There is, for example, the extension of space by time and of time by space. The length of a stairway can be enormously extended if three different shots of the person ascending it (filmed from different angles so that it is not apparent that the identical area is being covered each time) are so edited together that the action is continuous and results in an image of enduring labor toward some elevated goal. A leap in the air can be extended by the same technique, but in this case, since the film action is sustained far beyond the normal duration of the real action itself, the effect is one of tension as we wait for the figure to return, finally, to earth.

Time may be extended by the reprinting of a single frame, which has the effect of freezing the figure in mid-action; here the frozen frame becomes a moment of suspended animation which, according to its contextual position, may convey either the sense of critical hesitation (as in the turning back of Lot's wife) or may constitute a comment on stillness and movement as the opposition of life and death. The reprinting of scenes of a casual situation involving several persons may be used either in a prophetic context, as a *déjà-vu;* or, again, precise reiteration, by inter-cutting reprints, of those spontaneous movements, expressions, and exchanges, can change the quality of the scene from one of informality to that of a stylization akin to dance; in so doing it confers dance upon non-dancers, by shifting emphasis from the purpose of the movement to the movement itself, and an informal social encounter then assumes the solemnity and dimension of ritual.

Similarly, it is possible to confer the movement of the camera upon the figures in the scene, for the large movement of a figure in a film is conveyed by the changing relationship between that figure and the frame of the screen. If, as I have done in my recent film *The Very Eye of Night,* one eliminates the horizon line and any background which would reveal the movement of the total field, then the eye accepts the frame as stable and ascribes all movement to the figure within it. The hand-held camera, moving and revolving over the white figures on a totally black ground, produces images in which their movement is as gravity-free and as three-dimensional as that of birds in air or fish in water. In the absence of any absolute orientation, the push and pull of their interrelationships becomes the major dialogue.

By manipulation of time and space, I mean also the creation of a relationship between separate times, places, and persons. A swing-pan—whereby a shot of one person is terminated by a rapid swing away and a shot of another person or place begins with a rapid swing of the camera, the two shots being subsequently joined in the blurred area of both swings—brings into dramatic proximity people, places, and actions which in actuality might be widely separated. One can film different people at different times and even in different places performing approximately the same gesture or movement, and, by a judicious joining of the shots in such a manner as to preserve the continuity of the movement, the action itself becomes the dominant dynamic which unifies all separateness.

Separate and distant places not only can be related but can be made continuous by a continuity of identity and of movement, as when a person begins a gesture in one setting, this shot being immediately followed by the hand entering another setting altogether to complete the gesture there. I have used this technique to make a dancer step from woods to apartment in a single stride, and similarly to transport him from location to location so that the world itself became his stage. In my *At Land,* it has been the technique by which the dynamic of the *Odyssey* is reversed and the protagonist, instead of undertaking the long voyage of search for adventure, finds instead that the universe itself has usurped the dynamic action which was once the prerogative of human will, and confronts her with a volatile and relentless metamorphosis in which her personal identity is the sole constancy.

These are but several indications of the variety of creative timespace relationships which can be accomplished by a meaningful manipulation of the sequence of film images. It is an order of creative action available only to the motion-picture medium because it is a photographic medium. The ideas of condensation and of extension, of separateness and continuity, in which it deals, exploit to the fullest degree the various attributes of the photographic image: its fidelity (which establishes the identity of the person who serves as a transcendent unifying force between all separate times and places), its reality (the basis of the recognition which activates our knowledges and values and without which the geography of location and dislocation could not exist), and its authority (which transcends the impersonality and intangibility of the image and endows it with independent and objective consequence).

THE TWENTIETH-CENTURY ART FORM

I initiated this discussion by referring to the effort to determine what creative film form is not, as a means by which we can arrive eventually at a determination of what it is. I recommend this as the only valid point of departure for all custodians of classifications, to the keepers of catalogues, and in particular to the harassed librarians, who, in their effort to force film into one or another of the performing or the plastic arts, are engaged in an endless Procrustean operation.

A radio is not a louder voice, an airplane is not a faster car, and the motion picture (an invention of the same period of history) should not be thought of as a faster painting or a more real play.

All of these forms are qualitatively different from those which preceded them. They must not be understood as unrelated developments, bound merely by coincidence, but as diverse aspects of a new way of thought and a new way of life—one in which an appreciation of time, movement, energy, and dynamics is more immediately meaningful than the familiar concept of matter as a static solid anchored to a stable cosmos. It is a change reflected in every field of human endeavor, for example, architecture, in which the notion of mass-upon-mass structure has given way to the lean strength of steel and the dynamics of cantilever balances.

It is almost as if the new age, fearful that whatever was there already would not be adequate, had undertaken to arrive completely equipped, even to the motion-picture medium, which, structured expressly to deal in movement and time-space relationships, would be the most propitious and appropriate art form for expressing, in terms of its own paradoxically intangible reality, the moral and metaphysical concepts of the citizen of this new age.

This is not to say that cinema should or could replace the other art forms, any more than flight is a substitute for the pleasures of walking or for the leisurely panorama of landscapes seen from a car or train window. Only when new things serve the same purpose better do they replace old things. Art, however, deals in ideas; time does not deny them, but may merely make them irrelevant. The truths of the Egyptians are no less true for failing to answer questions which they never raised. Culture is cumulative, and to it each age should make its proper contribution.

How can we justify the fact that it is the art instrument, among all that fraternity of twentieth-century inventions, which is still the least explored and exploited; and that it is the artist—of whom, traditionally, the culture expects the most prophetic and visionary statements—who is the most laggard in recognizing that the formal and philosophical concepts of his age are implicit in the actual structure of his instrument and the techniques of his medium?

If cinema is to take its place beside the others as a full-fledged art form, it must cease merely to record realities that owe nothing of their actual existence to the film instrument. Instead, it must create a total experience so much out of the very nature of the instrument as to be inseparable from its means. It must relinquish the narrative disciplines it has borrowed from literature and its timid imitation of the causal logic of narrative plots, a form which flowered as a celebration of the earthbound, step-by-step concept of time, space and relationship which was part of the primitive materialism of the nineteenth century. Instead, it must develop the vocabulary of filmic images and evolve the syntax of filmic techniques which relate those. It must determine the disciplines inherent in the medium, discover its own structural modes, explore the new realms and dimensions accessible to it and so enrich our culture artistically as science has done in its own province.

1960

STAN BRAKHAGE
FROM METAPHORS ON VISION

Imagine an eye unruled by man-made laws of perspective, an eye unprejudiced by compositional logic, an eye which does not respond to the name of everything but which must know each object encountered in life through an adventure of perception. How many colors are there in a field of grass to the crawling baby unaware of "Green?" How many rainbows can light create for the untutored eye? How aware of variations in heat waves can that eye be? Imagine a world alive with incomprehensible objects and shimmering with an endless variety of movement and innumerable gradations of color. Imagine a world before the "beginning was the word."

To see is to retain—to behold. Elimination of all fear is in sight—which must be aimed for. Once vision may have been given—that which seems inherent in the infant's eye, an eye which reflects the loss of innocence more eloquently than any other human feature, an eye which soon learns to classify sights, an eye which mirrors the movement of the individual toward death by its increasing inability to see.

But one can never go back, not even in imagination. After the loss of innocence, only the ultimate of knowledge can balance the wobbling pivot. Yet I suggest that there is a pursuit of knowledge foreign to language and founded upon visual communication, demanding a development of the optical mind, and dependent upon perception in the original and deepest sense of the word.

Suppose the Vision of the saint and the artist to be an increased ability to see—vision. Allow so-called hallucination to enter the realm of perception, allowing that mankind always finds derogatory terminology for that which doesn't appear to be readily usable, accept dream visions, day-dreams or night-dreams, as you would so-called real scenes, even allowing that the abstractions which move so dynamically when closed eyelids are pressed are actually perceived. Become aware of the fact that you are not only influenced by the visual phenomenon which you are focused upon and attempt to sound the depths of all visual influence. There is no need for the mind's eye to be deadened after infancy, yet in these times the development of visual understanding is almost universally forsaken.

This is an age which has no symbol for death other than the skull and bones of one stage of decomposition . . . and it is an age which lives in fear of total annihilation. It is a time haunted by sexual sterility yet almost universally incapable of perceiving the phallic nature of every destructive manifestation of itself. It is an age which artificially seeks to project itself materialistically into abstract space and to fulfill itself mechanically because it has blinded itself to almost all external reality within eyesight and to the organic awareness of even the physical movement properties of its own perceptibility. The earliest cave paintings discovered demonstrate that primitive man had a greater understanding than we do that the object of fear must be objectified. The entire history of erotic magic is one of possession of fear thru the beholding of it. The ultimate searching visualization has been directed toward God out of the deepest possible human understanding that there can be no ultimate love where there is fear. Yet in this contemporary time how many of us even struggle to deeply perceive our own children?

The artist has carried the tradition of vision and visualization down through the ages. In the present time a very few have continued the process of visual perception in its deepest sense and transformed their inspirations into cinematic experiences. They create a new language made possible by the moving picture image. They create where fear before them has created the greatest necessity. They are essentially preoccupied by and deal imagistically with—birth, sex, death, and the search for God.

CAMERA EYE

Oh transparent hallucination, superimposition of image on image, mirage of movement, heroine of a thousand and one nights (Scheherazade must surely be the muse of this art), you obstruct the light, muddie the pure white beaded screen (it perspires) with your shuffling patterns. Only the spectators (the unbelievers who attend the carpeted temples where coffee and paintings are served) think your spirit is in the illuminated occasion (mistaking your sweaty, flaring, rectangular body for more than it is). The devout, who break popcorn together in your humblest double-feature services, know that you are still being born, search for your spirit in their dreams, and dare only dream when in contact with your electrical reflection. Unknowingly, as innocent, they await the priests of this new religion, those who can stir cinematic entrails divinely. They await the prophets who can cast (with the precision of Confucian sticks) the characters of this new order across filmic mud. Being innocent, they do not consciously know that this church too is corrupt; but they react with counter hallucinations, believing in the stars, and cast themselves among these Los Angelic orders. Of themselves, they will never recognize what they are awaiting. Their footsteps, the dumb drum which destroys cinema. They are having the dream piped into their homes, the destruction of the romance thru marriage, etc.

So the money vendors have been at it again. To the catacombs then, or rather plant this seed deeper in the undergrounds beyond false nourishing of sewage waters. Let it draw nourishment from hidden uprising springs channeled by gods. Let there be no cavernous congregation but only the network of individual channels, that narrowed vision which splits beams beyond rainbow and into the unknown dimensions. (To those who think this is waxing poetic, squint, give the visual objects at hand their freedom, and allow the distant to come to you; and when mountains are moving, you will find no fat in this prose). Forget ideology, for film unborn as it has no language and speaks like an aborigine—monotonous rhetoric. Abandon aesthetics—the moving picture image without religious foundations, let alone the cathedral, the art form, starts its search for God with only the danger of accepting an architectural inheritance from the categorized "seven," other arts its sins, and closing its circle, stylistic circle, therefore zero. Negate technique, for film, like America, has not been discovered yet, and mechanization, in the deepest possible sense of the word, traps both beyond measuring even chances—chances are these twined searches may someday orbit about the same central negation. Let film be. It is something . . . becoming. (The above being for creator and spectator alike in searching, an ideal of anarchic religion where all are priests both giving and receiving, or rather witch doctors, or better witches, or . . . O, for the unnamable).

And here, somewhere, we have an eye (I'll speak for myself) capable of any imagining (the only reality). And there (right there) we have the camera eye (the limitation, the original liar); yet lyre sings to the mind so immediately (the exalted selectivity one wants to forget that its strings can so easily make puppetry of human motivation (for form as finality) dependent upon attunation, what it's turned to (ultimately death) or turned from (birth) or the way to get out of it (transformation). I'm not just speaking of that bird on fire (not thinking of circles) or of Spengler (spirals neither) or of any known progression (nor straight lines) logical formation (charted levels) or ideological formation (mapped for scenic points of interest); but I am speaking for possibilities (myself), infinite possibilites (preferring chaos).

And here, somewhere, we have an eye capable of any imagining. And then we have the camera eye, its lenses grounded to achieve 19th century Western compositional perspective (as best exemplified by the 19th century architectural conglomeration of details of the "classic" ruin) in bending the light and limiting the frame of the image just so, its standard camera and projector speed for recording movement geared to the feeling of the ideal slow Viennese waltz, and even its tripod head, being the neck it swings on, balled with bearings to permit it that Les Sylphides motion (ideal to the contemplative romantic) and virtually restricted to horizontal and vertical movements (pillars and horizon lines) a diagonal requiring a major adjustment, its lenses coated or provided with filters, its light meters balanced, and its color film manufactured, to produce that picture post card effect (salon painting) exemplifed by those oh so blue skies and peachy skins.

By deliberately spitting on the lens or wrecking its focal intention, one can achieve the early stages of impressionism. One can make this prima donna heavy in performance of image movement by speeding up the motor, or one can break up movement, in a way that approaches a more direct inspiration of contemporary human eye perceptibility of movement, by slowing the motion while recording the image. One may hand hold the camera and inherit worlds of space. One may over or under-expose the film. One may use the filters of the world, fog, downpours, unbalanced lights, neons with neurotic color temperatures, glass which was never designed for a camera, or even glass which was but which can be used against specifications, or one may photograph an hour after sunrise or an hour before sunset, those marvelous taboo hours when the film labs will guarantee nothing, or one may go into the night with a specified daylight film or vice versa. One may become the supreme trickster, with hatfuls of all the rabbits listed above breeding madly. One may, out of incredible courage, become Méliès, that marvelous man who gave even the "art of the film" its beginning in magic. Yet Méliès was not witch, witch doctor, priest, or even sorcerer. He was a 19th-century stage magician. His films *are* rabbits.

What about the hat? the camera? or if you will, the stage, the page, the ink, the hieroglyphic itself, the pigment shaping that original drawing, the musical and/or all other instruments for copula-and-then-procreation? Kurt Sachs talks sex (which fits the hat neatly) in originating musical instruments, and Freud's revitalization of symbol charges all contemporary content in art. Yet possession thru visualization speaks for fear-of-death as motivating force—the tomb art of the Egyptian, etc. And then there's "In the beginning," "Once upon a time," or the very concept of a work of art being a "Creation." Religious motivation only reaches us thru the anthropologist these days—viz., Frazer on a golden bough. And so it goes—ring around the rosary, beating about the bush, describing. One thread runs clean thru the entire fabric of expression—the trick-and-effect. And between those two words, somewhere, magic . . . the brush of angel wings, even rabbits leaping heavenwards and, given some direction, language corresponding. Dante looks upon the face of God and Rilke is heard among the angelic orders. Still the Night Watch was tricked by Rembrandt and Pollack was out to produce an effect. The original word was a trick, and so were all the rules of the game that followed in its wake. Whether the instrument be musical or otherwise, it's still a hat with more rabbits yet inside the head wearing it—i.e., thought's a trick, etc. Even The Brains for whom thought's the world, and the word and visi-or-audibility of it, eventually end with a ferris wheel of a solar system in the middle of the amusement park of the universe. They know it without experiencing it, screw it lovelessly, find "trick" or "effect" derogatory terminology, too close for comfort, are utterly unable to comprehend "magic." We are either experiencing (copulating) or conceiving (procreating) or very rarely both are balancing in that moment of living, loving, and creating, giving and receiving, which is so close to the imagined divine as to be more unmentionable than "magic."

In the event you didn't know, "magic" is realmed in "the imaginable," the moment of it being when that which is imagined dies, is penetrated by mind and known rather than believed in. Thus "reality" extends its picketing fence and each is encouraged to sharpen his wits. The artist is one who leaps that fence at night, scatters his seeds among the cabbages, hybrid seeds inspired by both the garden and wits-end forest where only fools and madmen wander, seeds needing several generations to be . . . finally proven edible. Until then they remain invisible, to those with both feet on the ground, yet prominent enough to be tripped over. Yes, those unsightly bulges between those oh so even rows will find their flowering moment . . . and then be farmed. Are you really thrilled at the sight of a critic tentatively munching artichokes? Wouldn't you rather throw overalls in the eventual collegic chowder? Realize the garden as you will—the growing is mostly underground. Whatever daily care you may give it—all is planted only by moonlight. However you remember it—everything in it originates elsewhere. As for the unquotable magic—it's as indescribable as the unbound woods it comes from.

(A foot-on-the-ground-note: The sketches of T. E. Lawrence's "realist" artist companion were scratches to Lawrence's Arab friends. Flaherty's motion picture projection of NANOOK OF THE NORTH was only a play of lights and silhouettes to the Aleutian Islander Nanook himself. The schizophrenic does see symmetrically, does believe in the reality of Rorschach, yet he will not yield to the suggestion that a pinpoint light in a darkened room will move, being the only one capable of perceiving its stasis correctly. Question any child as to his drawing and he will defend the "reality" of what you claim "scribbles." Answer any child's question and he will shun whatever quest he'd been beginning.)

Light, lens concentrated, either burns negative films to a chemical crisp which, when lab washed, exhibits the blackened pattern of its ruin or, reversal film, scratches the emulsion to eventually bleed it white. Light, again lens concentrated, pierces white and casts its shadow patterned self to reflect upon the spectator. When light strikes a color emulsion, multiple chemical layers restrict its various wave lengths, restrain its bruises to eventually produce a phenomenon unknown to dogs. Don't think of creatures of uncolored vision as restricted, but wonder, rather, and marvel at the known internal mirrors of the cat which catch each spark of light in the darkness and reflect it to an intensification. Speculate as to insect vision, such as the bee's sense of scent thru ultraviolet perceptiblity. To search for human visual realities, man must, as in all other homo motivation, transcend the original physical restrictions and inherit worlds of eyes. The very narrow contemporary moving visual reality is exhausted. The belief in the sacredness of any man-achievement sets concrete about it, statues becoming statutes, needing both explosives, and earthquakes for disruption. As to the permanency of the present or any established reality, consider in this light and thru most individual eyes that without either illumination or photographic lens, any ideal animal might claw the black off a strip of film or walk ink-footed across transparent celluloid and produce an effect for projection identical to a photographed image. As to color, the earliest color films were entirely hand painted a frame at a time. The "absolute realism" of the motion picture image is a human invention.

What reflects from the screen is shadow play. Look, there's no real rabbit. Those ears are index fingers and the nose a knuckle interfering with the light. If the eye were more perceptive it would see the sleight of 24 individual pictures and an equal number of utter blacknesses every second of the show. What incredible films might ultimately be made for such an eye. But the machine has already been fashioned to outwit even that perceptibility, a projector which flashes advertisement at subliminal speed to up the sale of popcorn. Oh, slow-eyed spectator, this machine is grinding you out of existence. Its electrical storms are manufactured by pure white frames interrupting the flow of the photographed images, its real tensions are a dynamic interplay of two-dimensional shapes and lines, the horizon line and background shapes battering the form of the horseback rider as the camera moves with it, the curves of the tunnel exploding away from the pursued, camera following, and tunnel perspective converging on the pursuer, camera preceding, the dream of the close-up kiss being due to the linear purity of facial features after cluttersome background, the entire film's soothing syrup being the depressant of imagistic repetition, a feeling akin to counting sheep to sleep. Believe in it blindly, and it will fool you— mind wise, instead of sequins on cheesecloth or max-manu-factured make-up, you'll see stars. Believe in it eye-wise, and the very comet of its overhead throw from projector to screen will intrigue you so deeply that its fingering play will move integrally with what's reflected, a comet-tail integrity which would lead back finally to the film's creator. I am meaning, simply, that the rhythms of change in the beam of illumination which now goes entirely over the heads of the audience would, in the work of art, contain in itself some quality of a spiritual experience. As is, and at best, that hand spreading its touch toward the screen taps a neurotic chaos comparable to the doodles it produces for reflection. The "absolute realism" of the motion picture image is a 20th-century, essentially Western, illusion.

Nowhere in its mechanical process does the camera hold either mirror or candle to nature. Consider its history. Being machine, it has always been manufacturer of the medium, mass-producer of stilled abstract images, its virtue—related variance, the result—movement. Essentially, it remains fabricator of a visual language, no less a linguist than the typewriter. Yet in the beginning, each of an audience thought himself the camera, attending a play or, toward the end of the purely camera career, being run over by the unedited filmic image of a locomotive which had once rushed straight at the lens, screaming when a revolver seemed fired straight out of the screen, motion of picture being the original magic of the medium. Méliès is credited with the first splice. Since then, the strip of celluloid has increasingly revealed itself suited to transformations beyond those conditioned by the camera. Originally Méliès' trickery was dependent upon starting and stopping the photographic mechanism and between-times creating, adding objects to its field of vision, transformations, substituting one object for another, and disappearances, removing the objectionable. Once the celluloid could be cut, the editing of filmic images began its development toward Eisensteinian montage, the principle of 1 plus 2 making 3 in moving imagery as anywhere else. Meantime labs came into the picture, playing with the illumination of original film, balancing color temperature, juggling double imagery in superimposition, adding all the acrobatic grammar of the film inspired by D. W. Griffith's dance; fades to mark the montage sentenced motion picture paragraph, dissolves to indicate lapse of time between interrelated subject matter, variations in the framing for the epic horizontal composition, origin of Cinemascope, and vertical picture delineating character, or the circle exclamating a pictorial detail, etc. The camera itself taken off the pedestal, began to move, threading its way, in and around its source of material for the eventual intricately patterned fabric of the edited film. Yet editing is still in its 1, 2, 3 infancy, and the labs are essentially still just developing film, no less trapped by the standards they're bearing than the camera by its original mechanical determination. No very great effort has ever been made to interrelate these two or three processes, and already another is appearing possible, the projector as creative instrument with the film show a kind of performance, celluloid or tape merely source of material to the projectioning interpreter, this expression finding its origins in the color, or the scent, or even the musical organ, its most recent manifestations—the increased programming potential of the IBM and other electronic machines now capable of inventing imagery from scratch. Considering then the camera eye as almost obsolete, it can at last be viewed objectively and, perhaps, viewpointed with subjective depth as never before. Its life is truly all before it. The future fabricating machine in performance will invent images as patterned after cliché vision as those of the camera, and its results will suffer a similar claim to "realism," IBM being no more God nor even a "Thinking machine" than the camera eye all-seeing or capable of creative selectivity, both essentially restricted to "yes-no," "stop-go," "on-off," and instrumentally dedicated to communication of the simplest sort. Yet increased human intervention and control renders any process more capable of a balance between sub-and-objective expression, and between those two concepts, somewhere, soul . . . The second stage of transformation of image editing revealed the magic of the movement. Even though each in the audience then proceeded to believe himself part of the screen reflection, taking two-dimension visual characters as his being within the drama, he could not become every celluloid sight running thru the projector, therefore allowance of another viewpoint, and no attempt to make him believe his eye to be where the camera eye once was has ever since proven successful—excepting the novelty of three-dimension, audiences jumping when rocks seemed to avalanche out of the screen and into the theatre. Most still imagine, however, the camera a recording mechanism, a lunatic mirroring, now full of sound and fury presenting its half of a symmetrical pattern, a kaleidoscope with the original pieces of glass missing and their movement removed in time. And the instrument is still capable of winning Stanford's bet about horse-hooves never all leaving the ground in galloping, though Stanford significantly enough used a number of still cameras with strings across the track and thus inaugurated the flip-pic of the penny arcade, Hollywood still racing after the horse. Only when the fans move on to another track can the course be cleared for this eye to interpret the very ground, perhaps to discover its non-solidity, to create a contemporary Pegasus, without wings, to fly with its hooves, beyond any imagining, to become gallop, a creation. It can then inherit the freedom to agree or disagree with 2000 years of Western equine painting and attain some comparable aesthetic stature. As is, the "absolute realism" of the motion picture image is a contemporary mechanical myth. Consider this prodigy for its virtually untapped talents, viewpoints it possesses more readily recognizable as visually non-human yet within the realm of the humanly imaginable. I am speaking of its speed for receptivity which can slow the fastest motion for detailed study, or its ability to create a continuity for time compression, increasing the slowest motion to a comprehensibility. I am praising its cyclopean penetration of haze, its infra-red visual ability in darkness, its just-developed 360 degree view, its prismatic revelation of rainbows, its zooming potential for exploding space and its telephotic compression of same to flatten perspective, its micro- and macroscopic revelations. I am marvelling at its Schlaeran self capable of representing heat waves and the most invisible air pressures, and appraising its other still camera developments which may grow into motion, its rendering visible the illumination of bodily heat, its transformation of ultraviolets to human cognizance, its penetrating X-ray. I am dreaming of the mystery camera capable of graphically representing the form of an object after it's been removed from the photographic scene, etc. The "absolute realism" of the motion picture is unrealized, therefore potential, magic.

1963

COLIN MACCABE
THEORY AND FILM: PRINCIPLES OF REALISM AND PLEASURE

Film theory has undergone an extraordinary expansion and mutation in the last few years. Without wishing to specify either their relative importance or their interdependence, one could indicate three factors which have contributed to this growth: increasingly heterogenous developments within filmic practice; an enlarged educational investment; and a growing concern with the general theoretical problems of signification. The result of these complex determinants is that, while developing its own specific area of analysis, film theory has come in recent years to have more and more to contribute to many of the most important and central cultural debates. *Screen* has participated actively in this process and it is through a consideration of one crucial area of discussion, namely realism, that we can attempt to understand the impetus and direction of *Screen's* work in the recent past. Brecht remarked that realism was not simply a matter for aesthetic debate but was one of the crucial questions of our age.[1] The problems of realism occur in an acute and critical form in the cinema, and perhaps no single topic concentrates so many of the developments that have taken place in film theory.

If we say that realism is, and has been, the dominant aesthetic in film, it is important to realize that this dominance does not date from film's inception. At the moment of its invention, various possibilities remained upon to film; possibilities which were closed down by a set of ideological choices, and the manner of this closure is of great interest to the study of ideology.[2] But if we recognize the extent to

---

[1]"Realism is an issue not only for literature: it is a major political, philosophical and practical issue and must be handled and explained as such," Bertolt Brecht, "Against George Lukacs," *New Left Review* (March–April 1974), no. 84, p. 45.

[2]This should not be taken to imply that the cinematic apparatus is ideologically neutral, but that its ideological effects are only one of the determinants of what became the dominant cinema and its ideological effects. Stephen Heath has begun the investigation of this inscription in "On Screen, in Frame," *Quarterly Review of Film Studies* (Autumn 1976), vol. 1, no. 3.

which realism became dominant in film only after the development of sound, and after film production throughout the world had been hegemonized in Hollywood, it is still the case that realism has been the dominant aesthetic since the Second World War. Whether we look to Hollywood, where realism is purchased at almost any price, or to the Italian neorealist cinema, we find that the struggle is to represent reality as effectively as possible; in both cinemas the possibility as such of the representational relation is taken for granted. If cinéma-vérité opposed Hollywood, this opposition was in terms of the effacement of style, where a pristine representation, an authentic relation between film and fact, was contaminated by arrangement and conscious intervention. Only in the early 1960s do we begin to find filmic practices which question the very validity of the representational relation. Within the Continental tradition, and owing an explicit debt to neorealism and particularly to Rossellini, the films of Godard began an investigation of film which took as its object the very processes of representation as well as the problem of what was represented. At the same time, in America, the development of cheaper filmmaking technology allowed many of the theoretical concerns of modern American painting to find a practical application in film. The name of Warhol can serve as an index of this development. But if these practices can best be articulated outside any representational problematic, the theoretical debates around them have constantly lagged behind those practices, and very often, the most important factor contributing to this backwardness has been difficulties with the problem of realism. At the same time a traditional realism remains the dominant force within the commercial cinema, where, if many of the tricks and effects of other cinemas are constantly borrowed, films like *Nashville* or *American Graffiti* reproduce the major strategies and procedures of films like *Giant* or *The Chase*. Finally, realism poses a constant problem within the Marxist theoretical and political tradition as a legacy of the primacy attached to it in the Soviet Union in the 1930s. It is thus difficult in any field of cinema to avoid the term, and indeed it is vitally necessary to examine it and its consequences in some detail.

REALISM AND EMPIRICISM

As a starting point one could take the objection that realism cannot be dominant in the cinema because Hollywood cinema is not realistic. By the criteria of one of the great realist critics, André Bazin, for a film to be realistic, it must locate its characters and action in a determinate social and historical setting. Most Hollywood films, it could be argued, fail to do this and are, therefore, unrealistic. But Bazin's characterization of realism is much more centrally concerned with a transparency of form which is reduplicated within Hollywood filmic practice. Bazin's criteria for distinguishing between films can only be based on nonfilmic concerns. (It should be said in advance that although these considerations will tend to collapse Hollywood and neorealist cinema together, there is a different reading of Bazin that could disengage from his text a set of incoherences which can be articulated so as to produce distinctions between neorealism and much Hollywood cinema such that the value judgments Bazin wished to confer on the postwar Italian cinema could be retained without a commitment to Bazin's theory of representation.)[1]

For Bazin, as for almost all realist theorists, what is in question is not just a rendering of reality but the rendering of a reality made more real by the use of aesthetic device. Talking of the use of convention within the cinema, Bazin writes that such a use may be made "at the service or at the disservice of realism, it may increase or neutralize the efficacy of the elements of reality captured by the camera. . . . One can class, if not hierarchize, the cinematographic styles as a function of the gain of reality that they represent. We shall thus call *realist* any system of expression, any narrative procedure which tends to make more reality appear on the screen."[2] This "more" is not quantitative but qualitative: it measures the extent to which the essence of the object represented is grasped. For Bazin the essence is attained through globality and totality; it is understood as coherence. Rossellini's vision is assessed in terms of the globality of the real that it represents: this globality

> does not signify, completely the contrary, that neorealism can be reduced to some objective documentaryism. Rossellini likes to say that the basis of his conception of mise-en-scène lies in a love not only of his characters but also of reality just as it is, and it is exactly this love which forbids him to dissociate that which reality has united; the character and the decor. Neorealism is defined neither by a refusal to take up a position with regard to the world nor by a refusal to judge it but it supposes in fact a mental attitude; it is always reality seen through an artist, refracted by his consciousness, but by all his consciousness, and not by his reason or his passion or his belief and reconstituted from dissociated elements.[3]

The central nature of the artistic activity becomes the presentation of a reality more real than that which could be achieved by a simple recording. The play on the notions of "real" and "reality" which is involved in Bazin's conception (the artist produces a reality more real than reality) is also the central feature of empiricism. In *Reading Capital,* Louis Althusser locates the specific feature of empiricism not in the confrontation between subject and object which is postulated as anterior to any knowledge (though to be sure empiricism relies on this), but rather in its characterization of the knowledge to be obtained as defined by the object of which it is knowledge. Althusser writes: "The whole empiricist process of knowledge lies in that operation of the subject named abstraction. To know is to abstract from the real object its essence, the possession of which by the subject is then called knowledge."[4] The whole empiricist conception thus depends on two notions of real and ultimately two notions of object, and this play suppresses the process at work in the production of knowledge. Bazin too starts out with the reality of everyday life and ends up with the greater reality of the filmmaker's representation of it. What must be hidden by the "author" is the process by which this "greater reality" is arrived

---

[1]A good survey of Bazin's comments on realism can be found in Christopher Williams, "Bazin on Neo-Realism," *Screen* (Winter 1973–74), 14(4):61–68.

[2]André Bazin, *Qu' est-ce que le cinéma?* (Paris: Ed, du Cerf, 1962), 4:22.

[3]*Ibid.* p. 154.

[4]Louis Althusser, *Reading Capital,* trans. Ben Brewster (London: New Left Books, 1970), pp. 35–36.

at, for, of course, on this account the "greater reality" is there all along just waiting to be seen. Thus, for Bazin, any concept of process which would call both subject and object into play instead of positing them as constitutive moments is eliminated. This finds clear expression in his discussion of de Sica's *Bicycle Thieves:*

> As the disappearance of the actor is the result of an overcoming of the style of acting, the disappearance of the mise-en-scène is equally the fruit of a dialectical process of the style of narration. If the event is sufficient unto itself without the director having need to illuminate it by angles or the special position of the camera, it is true that it has come to that perfect luminosity which permits art to unmask a nature which finally resembles it.[1]

All interference by the subject must be reduced to a minimum because such interference involves subject and object in a process which destroys their full and punctual autonomy. The triumph of *Bicycle Thieves* is that it completely does away with the cinematic process. Bazin writes: "*Bicycle Thieves* is one of the first examples of pure cinema. There are no more actors, no more story, no more mise-en-scène, that is to say finally in the aesthetic illusion of reality—no more cinema."[2] The revelation of reality is the prime task of the cinema, and all aesthetic devices are simply there to unmake themselves so that we too can experience, as the artist experienced before us, that moment at which reality presents itself as whole.

CONTRADICTION AND THE REAL

Against this traditional analysis, I argue that film does not reveal the real in a moment of transparency, but rather that film is constituted by a set of discourses which (in the positions allowed to subject and object) produce a certain reality. The emphasis on production must be accompanied by one on another crucial Marxist term, that of contradiction. There is no one discourse that produces a certain reality—to believe so is to fall into the idealism complementary to the empiricism already discussed. A film analysis is dealing with a set of contradictory discourses transformed by specific practices. Within a film text these may be different "views" of reality which are articulated together in different ways. Most documentaries . . . bind the images together by the verbal interpretation of the voiceover commentary. Classical fictional cinema, on the other hand, has the crucial opposition between spoken discourses that may be mistaken and a visual discourse that guarantees truth—which reveals all. For this opposition to be set up, the spectator must be placed in a position from which the image is regarded as primary. The movement of this placing can be grasped by considering a third group of films which find their constitutive principle in the refusal so to place the spectator. In a film such as the Dziga-Vertov Group's *Wind from the East* a set of political discourses and images are juxtaposed so that, although what the Second Female Voice says is what the filmmakers regard as politically correct, it neither subdues the images, as in the documentary, nor is judged by them. None of the discourses can be read off one against the other. There is no possibility of verification, no correspondence between sound

---

[1] Bazin, *Qu'est-ce que le cinéma?* p. 57.
[2] *Ibid.,* p. 59.

and image enabling the spectator to enter the realm of truth. This dislocation between sound and image focuses attention on the position of the spectator—both in the cinema and politically. These juxtapositions make the spectator constantly aware of the discourses that confront him as discourses—as, that is, the production of sets of positions—rather than allowing him to ignore the process of articulation by entering a world of correspondence in which the only activity required is to match one discourse against the realm of truth.

It might here be objected that "filmic discourse" has not been defined with sufficient precision. Rather than giving an exact definition, one must indicate the range of application of the term. Within language studies, from at least the Renaissance onward, "discourse" is the term used to indicate a shifting of attention from the formal oppositions, which the linguist attempts to define and articulate, to the way in which these formal oppositions relate to the speaking subject. When we talk of "discourse" we move away from a conception of language as a set of significant oppositions independent of the speaking subject (Saussure's *langue*) to focus on the position of the speaking subject within the utterance. With discourse we become interested in the dialectical relation between speaker and language in which language always already offers a position to the speaker, and yet, at the same time, the act of speaking may itself displace that position. In filmic terms this means the kinds of combinations of words and images which can be differentiated in terms of different positions allocated to the viewer. I hope to make clear the kinds of elements involved in this combination later in my examination of *American Graffiti.* For the moment it can be stated that it is neither a question of the filmmaker using a transparent discourse to render the real nor of her or him inventing a discourse which produces a real. Instead the production of a film must be understood as involving a work, a practice, a transformation on and of the discourses available. One such practice, which I have called classical realism,* and shall analyze in *American Graffiti,* involves the homogenization of different discourses by their relation to one dominant discourse—assured of its domination by the security and transparency of the image. The fact that one such practice involves this homogenization is a matter of ideological and political but not normative interest. My aim in this article is to demonstrate how the practices which articulate the different elements in the discourses which constitute a filmic text have certain political effects. For the moment, and against a traditional realist emphasis, one could say that, at any given time, it is the contradictory positions available discursively to the subject, together with the positions made available by nonlinguistic practices, that constitute the reality of the social situation.

It is contradiction that Bazin wishes at all costs to conceal and coherence that furnishes him with his crucial emphasis. The coherence and the totality of the artist's vision provide the final criterion of reality—subject and object confront one another in full luminosity. This luminosity draws attention to the fact that the relation is visual—that all we have to do in the cinema is look. It is here that we begin to analyze the practices of classical realist cinema, for the distinguishing feature of

---

*In Colin MacCabe, "Realism and the Cinema: Notes on Some Brechtian Theses," *Screen* (Summer 1974), 15(2):7–27. For a criticism of the positions put forward in that article, see below.

these practices is the production of a perfect point of view for the audience—a point of vision.

THE POINT OF VIEW AND THE LOOK

Jacques Lacan has offered an analysis of vision which is of great relevance to any attempt to understand the reality of film. For Lacan, vision offers a peculiarly privileged basis to an *imaginary* relation of the individual to the world.[1] This imaginary relationship is characterized by the plenitude it confers on both subject and object, caught as they are outside any definition in terms of difference—given in a full substantial unity. The imaginary is central to the operations of the human psyche and is constituted as such in early infancy. Somewhere between the sixth and eighteenth month, the small human infant discovers its reflection in the mirror; an apprehension of unity all the more surprising in that it normally occurs before motor control has ensured that unity in practice. The specular relation thus established in this, the mirror phase, provides the basis for primary narcissism, and is then transferred onto the rest of the human world where the other is simply seen as another version of the same—of the "I" which is the center of the world. It is only with the apprehension of genital difference that the child leaves the comfortable world of the imaginary to enter into the world of the symbolic. The symbolic is understood by Lacan (after Lévi-Strauss) not as a set of one-to-one relationships but as a tissue of differences which articulate the crucial elements within the child's world. It is the acceptance of a potential lack (castration) which marks the child's access to the symbolic and to language. Language in the realm of the imaginary is understood in terms of some full relation between word and thing: a mysterious unity of sign and referent. In the symbolic, language is understood in terms of lack and absence—the sign finds its definition diacritically through the absent syntagmatic and paradigmatic chains it enters into. As speaking subjects we constantly oscillate between the symbolic and the imaginary—constantly imagining ourselves granting some full meaning to the words we speak, and constantly being surprised to find them determined by relations outside our control. But if it is the phallus which is the determining factor for the entry into difference, difference has already troubled the full world of the infant. The imaginary unity has already been disrupted by the cruel separation from those objects originally understood as part of the subject—the breast and the feces. The phallus becomes the dominating metaphor for all these previous lacks. Lacan defines the centrality of the phallus for the entry into the symbolic and language when he describes the phallus as "the signifier destined to designate the effects, taken as a set, of signified, insofar as the signifier conditions these effects by its presence as signifier."[2] The signified here is exactly the imaginary full meaning con-

[1] The analysis of a Holbein painting which is discussed in this section can be found in "Du regard comme objet petit a" in Jacques Lacan, *Le Séminaire XI* (Paris: Ed. du Seuil, 1973), pp. 65–109. My understanding of the issues has benefited from Christian Metz's "The Imaginary Signifier," *Screen* (Summer 1975), 16(2):14–76, and Jacqueline Rose's British Film Institute Educational Advisory Service seminar paper "The Imaginary, the Insufficient Signifier," mimeographed.

[2] Jacques Lacan, *Ecrits* (Paris: Ed. du Seuil, 1966), p. 690.

stantly contaminated by the signifier's organization along constitutive and absent chains.

In *Le Séminaire XI,* Lacan attempts to demonstrate the relation between the symbolic and the imaginary at the level of vision and to demonstrate the existence of lack within the scopic field (this lack being the condition of the existence of desire within the visual field—a desire which can find satisfaction in a variety of forms). Taking the Holbein picture *The Ambassadors* (National Gallery, London), Lacan comments on the death's-head hidden in the picture by a trick of perspective and only visible from one particular angle. The rest of the picture is caught in the world of the imaginary—the spectator is the all-seeing subject and, as if to emphasize the narcissistic nature of the relation, Holbein fills the picture with Renaissance emblems of vanity. However, the death's-head, perceived when we leave the field of the picture, reintroduces the symbolic. For the death's-head draws attention to the fact that we see the picture at a distance and from a particular angle (if we think back to Bazin's quotation about *Bicycle Thieves,* it is clear that for him cinema must obliterate distance and angles). With the introduction of the spectator's position the objects simply and substantially there are transformed into a set of differential relationships; a set of traces left by a paint brush; an organized area of space which, from one particular point, can be read as an object. That the object thus seen is a skull is in no way surprising when we consider that the entry into the symbolic can be most simply described as the recognition of the world independently of my consciousness—as the recognition, that is, of the possibility of my own death. Holbein's picture demonstrates a congruence between the organization of language and the organization of the visual field. Just as the constitutive elements of language must be absent in the moment of speaking, so the constitutive nature of the distance and position of the viewing subject must be absent from the all-embracing world of vision. *The Ambassadors* reintroduces the look into vision. As such it bears witness to the separation (castration) on which vision is based, but which it endlessly attempts to ignore.

The intervention of the symbolic in the imaginary is already in evidence at the very opening of the mirror phase. For the infant verifies its reflection by looking to the mother who holds it in front of the mirror. It is the mother's look that confirms the validity of the infant's image, and with this look we find that at the very foundation of the dual imaginary relationship there is a third term already unsettling it. The mother verifies the relationship for the child, but at the cost of introducing a look, a difference where there should be only similitude. The fact that this look which both sets up and potentially destroys the full visual field is felt as castration explains why, traditionally, the eye is always evil. We are now in a position to grasp Lacan's claim that the visual is organized in terms of the look *(le regard)*—defined by the others' look that it is not—and of the blot *(la tache),* the fact that any visual field is already structured so that certain effects will be seen, Lacan writes:

> The function of the blot and the look is, at one and the same time, that which commands the most secretly, and that which always escapes the grip of, that form of vision which finds its contentment in imagining itself as consciousness.*

---

*Lacan, *Le Séminaire XI,* p. 71.

Bazin wishes to do away with the camera because it constantly threatens the world of imaginary plenitude and must therefore be repressed at all costs. In its place a visual world is instituted from which the look, any trace of castration, has been expelled. The distinction between the symbolic and the imaginary can be understood in cinematic terms by contrasting the look and the point of view. The point of view is always related to an object.[1] But insofar as the object is a given unity there is always the possibility of seeing it together with all the possible points of view—there is always the possibility of a point of overview. The point of view preserves the primacy of vision, for what is left out of one point-of-view shot can always be supplied by another. The look, however, is radically defective. Where the point of view is related to an object, the look is related to other looks. The look's field is not defined by a science of optics in which the eye features as a geometrical point but by the fact that the object we are looking at offers a position from which we can be looked at—and this look is not punctual but shifts over the surface. It is important that it is a head that looks back at us from Holbein's painting.

From this account of the pleasure involved in vision it might seem that the ideal film would show us a static perspective. But this is to ignore the dialectic of pleasure and desire revealed to us by Freud.[2] If, on the one hand, there is a tendency toward stasis, toward a normalization of excitation within the psyche, there is also a compulsion to repeat those moments at which the stasis is set in motion, at which the level of excitation rises to unbearable heights. The small boy in *Beyond the Pleasure Principle* in his endless game of *fort-da* ceaselessly throws away the object at the end of the string only to draw it back and start again. This action, which Freud tells us reproduces the experience of separation from the mother, shows that it is exactly the moment of anxiety, of heightened tension, the moment of coming which is relived in a constant cycle, which threatens itself. What lies beyond the pleasure principle is not a threatening and exterior reality but a reality whose virulence knows no cessation, the reality of those constitutive moments at which we experience ourselves in the very moment of separation; which moments we are compelled to repeat in that endless movement which can find satisfaction only in death. Desire is set up only by absence, by the possibility of return to a former state—the field of vision becomes invested libidinally only after it has been robbed of its unity by the gaze of the other. The charm of classical realism is that it introduces the gaze of the other but this introduction is always accompanied by the guarantee of the supremacy of the point of view; the threat appears so that it can be smoothed over, and it is in that smoothing that we can locate pleasure—in a plenitude which is fractured but only on condition that it will be reset. Here the stock terms demonstrate what is at stake: the motion pictures, the movies, the flicks; it is the threat of motion, of displacement that is in question, but this threat is overcome from the start.

The logic of this contradictory movement can be understood on the basis of the set of interchanges that take place between screen and viewer—that complicated

---

[1] See Edward Branigan, "Formal Permutations of the Point-of-View Shot," *Screen* (Autumn 1975), 16(3):54–64.

[2] For a summary of Freud's argument in its Lacanian reformulation, see Colin MacCabe, "Presentation of 'The Imaginary Signifier'," *Screen* (Summer 1975), 16(2):7–13.

circulation which ensures that I am not only a spectator in the cinema but also, by a process of identification, a character on the screen. The cinema constantly poses me as the constant point of a fixed triangle and it constantly obscures and effaces the complicated progress of the shots, the impossible movements of that point by the logic of events on the screen. To analyze this process we need the concepts elaborated by Benveniste to distinguish between the *sujet de l'énonciation* and the *sujet de l'énoncé.** Benveniste suggests that to arrive at a logical understanding of tenses and to understand fully the importance of language for subjectivity, the speaker as the producer of the discursive chain, *le sujet de l'énonciation,* must be distinguished from the speaker as the grammatical subject, *le sujet de l'énoncé.* The distance between these two subjects gives us a formal linguistic account of the distance between the philosophical subject, *le sujet de l'énoncé,* the "I," judge of the correspondence between world and language, and the psychoanalytic subject, *le sujet de l'énonciation,* the "it," unable to distinguish between word and world and constantly threatening and unmasking the stability of the "I." Applied to film this is the distinction between the spectator as viewer, the comforting "I," the fixed point, and the spectator as he or she is caught up in the play of events on the screen, as he or she "utters," "enounces" the film. Hollywood cinema is largely concerned to make these two coincide so that we can ignore what is at risk. But this coincidence can never be perfect because it is exactly in the divorce between the two that the film's existence is possible. This bringing into play of the process of the text's production takes us out of the classical field of semiotics, the field of the *énoncé* in which the text is treated as the assertion of a set of disjunctions permuted to produce actions, and into the question of the production of these very disjunctions. The subject is neither the full presence of traditional "auteur" criticism nor the effect of the structure of traditional structuralism; it is divided in the movement between the two. The contradiction between *énonciation* and *énoncé* is also the contradiction between narrative and discourse. Narrative is always propelled by both a heterogeneity and a surplus—a heterogeneity which must be *both* overcome *and* prolonged. The narrative begins with an incoherence but already promises the resolution of that incoherence. The story is the passage from ignorance to knowledge, but this passage is denied as process—the knowledge is always already there as the comforting resolution of the broken coherence (every narration is always a suspense story). Narrative must deny the time of its own telling—it must refuse its status as discourse (as articulation), in favor of its self-presentation as simply identity, complete knowledge.

AMERICAN GRAFFITI: AN EXAMPLE

To understand a film like *American Graffiti,* its reality and its pleasure—the reality of its pleasure—it is necessary to consider the logic of that contradiction which produces a position for the viewer but denies that production. To admit that production would be to admit a position, and the position that has been produced is

---

*See Emile Benveniste, *Problems of General Linguistics* (Coral Gables, Fl: University of Miami Press: 1971), part 5.

the position of the point of view, promising, as Bazin wished, that the event is sufficient to itself and needs no illumination from angles or the special position of the camera—promising, in short, a suprapositional omniscience, the full imaginary relation. In *American Graffiti* this contradiction of a process of production and the denial of that process take form around the fact that we know, from the beginning of the narrative, that Curt Henderson will leave the town and yet that we hover, in suspense, over a decision which, once resolved, is obvious. The question, as always in classical realism, is one of identity. This identity may be questioned and suspended, but it is, in a deferred moment, asserted and read back over the text. Nor is this reading back an optional extra. Without it the very concept of identity and truth, the very concept of character, on which classical realism rests would disintegrate. If the hero were not really good (or bad or whatever) all along then there would be no point to the story—the narrative would become merely the retailing of successive states of affairs. The resolution of the identity of Curt Henderson is also the production for the viewer of that point of view from which he can watch the film, but the pleasure of this production is provided by two looks which threaten to disturb that point of view, to displace an identity. These looks are each of a different order and I want to consider them separately, for one remains within the order of pleasure guaranteed by the point of view while the other threatens a disruption of a very different order.

The first look that introduces the moment of heterogeneity and surplus which is the impetus of the narrative comes from the girl in the white T-bird.* Securely placed within a point-of-view shot (Curt Henderson's) it nevertheless troubles a full imaginary identity—throwing open an uncertainty about Curt and his future on the night he has to decide whether to leave town. It is explicitly a gaze of sexuality and introduces the unsettling evidence of woman's desire as the girl mouths "I love you." *American Graffiti* thus traverses the classical path of narrative in that it is a desperate attempt to deny sexuality, the knowledge of which provides its first impetus. The girl's glance introduces a look into our point of view and calls attention to our position as we become separated from our full being in the world (as Curt becomes an other for someone he does not know, so he becomes aware of his position, loses the full security of the imaginary). In order to replace ourselves fully in the world it is necessary to refind an origin which can function as a guarantee of identity. In order to overcome the unsettling gaze of the mother we must find a father, someone who will figure as that moment of originating identity and power which will deny the possibility of the interplay of looks. It is this search that Curt Henderson undertakes. His progress from the schoolteacher to the Pharaohs to Wolfman Jack is the search for a father who will confirm him in his identity and expunge the possibility of difference; who will reassert the point of view over the look. In the scene in the radio studio we have another very heavily marked point-of-view sequence (three shots of Curt watching, two of Wolfman Jack performing,

---

*The analysis of the interplay of identification and vision leans heavily on two earlier articles in *Screen*—Stephen Heath's "Film and System, Terms of Analysis" (Spring 1975), 16(1):7–77 and (Summer 1975), 16(2):91–113; and Laura Mulvey, "Visual Pleasure and Narrative Cinema" (Autumn 1975), 16(3):6–18.

in exactly the same sequence as we had earlier seen the blonde at the traffic lights), which provides the knowledge to overcome the earlier threat.

It might be objected that this approach ignores the complicated intercrossing of the stories of the four boys. But not only can one find the same logic at play in two of the other three (Milner constitutes a special case), it would also be a mistake to think they are on the same level. *Nashville* and *American Graffiti* are two of a set of films which, although they have borrowed tricks and devices from other cinemas, remain within a traditional Hollywood practice. The two most obvious tricks are the refusal to weight the sound track in the traditional manner, a development drawing on such different sources as Welles, Godard, and cinéma-vérité, and, on the other hand, a proliferation of characters such that the dominance of narrative has been replaced by the freedom of the "slice of life." Both these novelties function as noise rather than structure. A close analysis of the sound shows that a traditional weighting is given to those elements necessary for the development of the narrative. Equally, the proliferation of characters does not affect the traditional movement of narrative. Rivette's *Out One: Spectre* is an example of a film which does break down narrative by proliferation of character, but at the cost of an enormous extension of the duration of the film and a genuine inability to find it an *end.*

It is Curt Henderson's point of view which offers within the narrative that knowledge and security we enjoy as we sit in the cinema, and it is this visual primacy which indicates his traditional centrality to the narrative. For Curt accomplishes the final imaginary task—he discovers the father. For everyone else Wolfman Jack is a name which finds its reality only in the differential world of sound, but Curt is able to reunite name and bearer so that a full presence can provide the certainty of what he is and what he must do—he is a *seer* and must leave town in order to see the world. The girl's gaze troubled this identity, but in the final shots of the film Curt is in a position where that gaze cannot trouble him. Before she knew who and where he was—now the positions are reversed. And it is from the point of view of the plane that the film accomplishes the progress toward the knowledge implicit in it from the beginning. The primacy of Curt's progress for an understanding of the film is underlined when the final titles tell us that he is now a writer living in Canada. The implication is that it is he who has written the story, he has conferred on us his point of view.

The other look within the film is of a different order and radically displaces the point of view, introducing a far more threatening moment of separation for the spectator. This look does not occur within the diegetic space between characters but in the space between screen and audience. John Milner and Carol attack a car whose occupants have been so foolish as to throw something at them, racing around it, letting out its tires, and covering it in foam. As this happens, changes of camera position are no longer motivated either by point-of-view shots or by diegetic considerations—for a moment we have lost our position and point of view as the camera breaks the 180-degree rule, though this losing of position has a certain diegetic motivation in the actions of John and Carol. Most significantly, we see the film lights appear beside the car. The diegetic space is broken up as the film looks back at us. This encounter with the real, this movement into the symbolic is the moment of ecstasy in which Carol squirts foam all over the car and Milner lets out all the tires (a sexual symbolism obvious enough), showing us that the pleasure involved here is of a more radical nature—a pleasure of tension and its release. If Curt provides the pleasure of security and position, John Milner functions as that threatening repetition which can only end in death and which offers no position but rather ceaseless motion. This is not to suggest that Milner offers any real alternative in the film; if he did it would contaminate the pleasure provided by Curt more significantly. But as the representative of an element which finds its definition outside the synchronic space of the other characters, he introduces time in a potentially threatening way. The political nature of the film, as will be argued later, depends on a repression of time outside a process of natural growth. Milner introduces, admittedly in a minimal way, a time which is not reducible to this natural cycle—his attitude to the culture is different from that of the other boys, because he is older than they.

THE QUESTION OF THE AUDIENCE

What has been said so far may seem to have removed all questions of realism and film from any consideration of their social conditions of production and reception. Concentration on the organization of the text has proposed a viewer caught only within an atemporal movement between the symbolic and the imaginary and confronted only by the reality of difference. It might seem from this that film and, by implication, art in general are caught in an eternal battle between the imaginary fullness of ideology and the real emptiness of the symbolic. Nothing could be further from my intentions in this article. My aim is to introduce certain general concepts that can be used to analyze film in a determinate social moment. That the breaking of the imaginary relation between text and viewer is that first prerequisite of political questions in art has, I would hold, been evident since Brecht. That the breaking of the imaginary relationship can constitute a political goal in itself is the ultraleftist fantasy of the surrealists and of much of the avant-garde work now being undertaken in the cinema. In certain of their formulations this position is given a theoretical backing by the writers of the *Tel Quel* group.

I hope that my analysis of *American Graffiti* has sketched in outline how the process of the production of a point of view for the spectator is effaced by mechanisms of identification. What is politically important about this textual organization is that it removes the spectator from the realm of contradiction. But it is not just contradiction in general that is avoided but a specific set of contradictions—those raised by the impact of the Vietnam War on American society. Portrait of a pre-Vietnam America, the film presents to us the children of the Kennedy Generation in the age of innocence—an innocence that we can regard from our position of knowledge. But this knowledge presupposes us outside politics now, outside contradiction. Indeed, Curt Henderson is a writer living in Canada, reflecting on an earlier reality of America that could not be sustained. (The fact that the writer is living in Canada is a further index of the repression of Vietnam—he has presumably dodged the draft, but this remains unspoken: to interrogate that decision would introduce contradiction.) The passing of innocence is reduced in the film to the process of growing up—there is no way in which external forces could be introduced into the homogenous society of small-town California. Toad grows up and goes off to die at An Loc, but this is simply part of a human cycle. The position of the viewer after the Vietnam War is simply held to be the same but different—the position of the imaginary. The Vietnam War is repressed and smoothed over.

However, if this is our criticism of the film it is clear that what we object to is not the fact that bits of reality have somehow got left out, but rather the whole relation of the film to its audience. The audience and their representations are the terms of the "realism" of any film or work of art—not some preexistent reality which it merely conveys. . . . [W]hat is at issue is not simply the reality external to the text but the reality of the text itself. We must understand the text's effectivity within the social process, which is to say we have to consider the relation between reader and text in its historical specificity.

CONCLUSIONS AND CONSEQUENCES

In an earlier article,* I argued for a typology of texts classified according to the organization of discourses within them. What was crucial was not the content of the text but the relations inscribed for the reader. The real was not an external object represented in the text but the relation between text and reader which reduplicated or cut across the subject's relation to his or her experience. Classically, realism depended on obscuring the relation between text and reader in favor of a dominance accorded to a supposedly given reality; but this dominance, far from sustaining a "natural" relation, was the product of a definite organization which, of necessity, effaced its own workings. In so far as the "reality" thus granted dominance was in contradiction with the ideologically dominant determinations of reality, then a text could be deemed progressive, but nevertheless such an organization was fundamentally reactionary; for it posed a reality which existed independently of both the text's and the reader's activity, a reality which was essentially noncontradictory and unchangeable. Alternatively, one could have an organization of discourses which broke with any dominance and which, as such, remained essentially subversive of any ideological order. At the end of the article I raised the question as to whether there could be a revolutionary film which would subvert the traditional position of the spectator in a more positive fashion than the simple deconstruction of the subversive film or whether any such positivity inevitably replaced one in a position of imaginary dominance.

Although I think that the earlier article can be read in a more favorable light, there is no doubt that it is contaminated by formalism; by a structuralism that it claimed to have left behind. Traditional criticism holds text and author/reader separate, with the author able to inject meaning which is then passed on to the reader. The position outlined in my article made the subject the effect of the structure (the subject is simply the sum of positions allocated to it) but it preserved the inviolability and separateness of the text—no longer given as an immutable content fixed in its determinations by reality through the author, but rather as immutable struc-

---

*MacCabe, "Realism and the Cinema."

ture determining reality and author/reader in their positions. But the text has no such separate existence. If we dissolve the reader into the text in the system of identification which I have outlined in this article, it is impossible to hold text and reader (or author as first reader) separate. Rather it is a question of analyzing a film within a determinate social moment so that it is possible to determine what identifications will be made and by whom. . . .[1] The text has no separate existence, and for this reason it is impossible to demand a typology of texts such as I proposed in my earlier article. Rather each reading must be a specific analysis which may use certain general concepts but these concepts will find their articulation within the specific analyses and not within an already defined combinatory.

Realism is no longer a question of an exterior reality nor of the relation of reader to text, but one of the ways in which these two interact. The filmmaker must draw the viewer's attention to his or her relation to the screen in order to make him or her "realize" the social relations that are being portrayed. Inversely one could say that it is the "strangeness" of the social relations displayed which draws the viewer's attention to the fact of watching a film. It is at the moment that an identification is broken, becomes difficult to hold, that we grasp in one and the same moment both the relations that determine that identity and our relation to its representation.[2] . . .

1976

---

[1]Such an analysis, it must be emphasized, has nothing to do with a counting of heads but is a class analysis. Its validity will be determined in its relations to practice, both political and cinematic.

[2]This is the burden of the argument in Colin MacCabe, "The Politics of Separation," *Screen* (Winter 1975–76), 16(4):46–61.

CHRISTINE GLEDHILL
RECENT DEVELOPMENTS IN
FEMINIST CRITICISM

WOMEN AND REPRESENTATION

A crucial issue of Feminist film criticism is the examination of the fact that "women as women" are not represented in the cinema, that they do not have a voice, that the female point of view is not heard. Recognition of this fact unites all attempts at a Feminist critique of the cinema. Sharon Smith, in the first issue of *Women and Film,* writes:

> Women, in any fully human form, have almost completely been left out of film. . . . That is, from its very beginning they were present, but not in characterizations any self-respecting person could identify with. (p. 13)

The introductory "overview" locates the female image in terms of stereotypes:

> These roles—child/woman, whore, bitch, wife, mother, secretary or girl Friday, frigid career woman, vamp, etc.—were all portrayed falsely and one dimensionally.

Naome Gilbert in the second issue of *Women and Film* develops a notion of the female image as representing the male "other":

> The female is portrayed with an archetypal ambivalence. The "Eternal Feminine" has been aesthetically more a principle for realizing male objectives than a person in her own right. Thus the dynamic of myth and reality when converging upon a female aesthetic has been quintessentially objectifying. . . . the terms of the female aesthetic have been imposed on the basis of man's fears and desires.

Claire Johnston in "Women's Cinema as Counter-Cinema" introduces the notion of fetishism into this argument:

> Within a sexist ideology and a male-dominated cinema, woman is presented as what she represents for man. . . . The fetishistic image portrayed relates only to male narcissism. Woman represents not herself, but by a process of displacement, the male phallus.

It is probably true to say that despite the enormous emphasis placed on woman as spectacle in the cinema, woman as woman is largely absent. (p. 26)

And in "The Place of Women in the Cinema of Raoul Walsh," Pam Cook and Claire Johnston develop this analysis:

In the tradition of classic cinema and 19th century realism, characters are presented as "autonomous individuals". . . . but the construction of the discourse contradicts this convention by reducing these "real" women to images and tokens functioning in a circuit of signs the values of which have been determined by and for men. (p. 93)

The crucial question (which would be answered in very different ways by these different writers) is *why "women as women" are not represented in the media, and whether this is always and must be the case in cinematic representation.* Further if this is the case, *how is it* (seeing that female roles and stars are not absent, from films), *that images of concrete women end up signifying a male discourse, and women are drawn to the cinema to consume such images. What does it mean to pass from the "real" experiences of concrete women to their representation in film?*

Recent Feminist work on film has sought to utilize a theoretical approach to such questions that breaks with the dominant assumptions of the literary tradition taught in schools and of journalistic critical practice, which treat film as an expressive medium revealing in the story of a character's experiences and development truths about the human condition that can be judged according to their depth, maturity, etc. Thus against traditional concern with characters and stereotypes, this critical "break" confronts Feminists with the semiotic/structuralist notion of textual production. The *Camera Obscura* editorial spells out the implications of this shift for Feminist analysis as involving:

a process of investigation and theoretical reflection on the mechanisms by which meaning is produced in film. (p. 3)

In other words, we cannot understand or change sexist images of women for progressive ones without considering how the operations of narrative, genre, lighting, *mise en scène,* etc. work to construct such images and their meanings.

More complexly we have to consider the relationship between these formal mechanisms and ideology. The crucial shift from interpretation of meaning to an investigation of the means of its production locates the identification of ideology in aesthetic structures and film-making practices themselves, which as organizing principles produce their own ideological effect in the material they organize.

The value of this semiotic redefinition of film as text for Feminist analysis is that it enables us to escape the simple enumeration of sexist stereotypes (to which there is a limit) and the discussion of characters as to the degrees of liberation they represent, which often depends more on the critic's personal point of view than anything that can be determined by a reading of the film.* Elizabeth Cowie has sum-

---

*Julia Lesage comments on *Women and Their Sexuality in the New Film* that Mellen rejects characters she finds "unpleasant." Thus Chloe in Rohmer's *Chloe in the Afternoon* is "plain, with shaggy, unwashed hair falling in her eyes. Her complexion is sallow and unaided by makeup. Her sloppiness is intensified by a decrepit raincoat without style." "Whose Heroines?" *Jump Cut,* No. 1 (May–June 1974), pp. 22–24.

moned up the problems with the still prevalent tendency in Feminist film criticism to identify the absence of women in films in terms of their failure to reflect the social reality of women:

> Films are criticised for not showing "women as women", or "as fully human." It (sic) is criticised as inadequate, as partial and one-sided in relation to a possible definition of women elsewhere, or else it is seen as a negation of that definition. Film is therefore precisely denied as a process of production when it comes to definitions of women, of woman as signifier and signified in the system of the film. ("Woman as Sign," in *M/F* No. 1, 1978, p. 50)

Nevertheless there is a danger that, once the object of Feminist criticism is defined solely in terms of the cinematic production of meaning, we lose the ability to deal with its relationship to women as defined in society altogether. Ann Kaplan has noted, for instance, how the concern in Claire Johnston's early "Women's Cinema as Counter-Cinema" to assert an economic determination on films as products of a particular set of socioeconomic relations disappears in her later essays.[1] *Camera Obscura 1* makes a number of acknowledgments of the social context of film production:

> A theoretical examination. . . . locates analysis at the intersection of the process of construction of the text and the social context which determines and is represented in that text. (p. 3)

However, this interaction is not pursued in any detail in this issue of the journal.[2] What is also missing from this formulation, and from much recent Feminist film theory, is any sense of the reading process performed by the audience and of how this may both *be determined by* and *determine* the effectivity of a film's ideological impact.

Although it is necessary to move away from concrete women in society in order to grapple with the social and aesthetic specificity of cinematic practices, the current concern with how meaning is produced tends to stop at producing readings of films that are illuminating to Feminist film theorists, or at a film-making practice whose first aim is to produce knowledge of its own production; the problem facing Feminist work on the cinema now is what knowledge can be derived from film theory that can make an intervention into both the production and distribution of films and the way they are understood and used by women at large. This problem appears to be felt in the recent work of Feminist film-makers who have also been concerned to reflect on and change the dominant modes of representation—for instance Laura Mulvey and Peter Wollen's venture into a modified narrative mode in *Riddles of the Sphinx* or the London Women's Film Group's use of intercut narrative and documentary interviews in *Whose Choice?*, a film intended to introduce the abortion issue to schoolgirls. What is at issue, then, is the possibility of radical representation for women's cinema. And this invokes the thorny theoretical issues of the rejection of realism and the adoption of psychoanalysis in recent Feminist film theory.

---

[1]Kaplan, "Aspects of British Feminist Film Theory." (See note 1 above.)
[2]The new issue that has just appeared has not yet arrived in England so I have been unable to follow how the collective is proceeding.

REPRESENTATION, VERISIMILITUDE, REALISM, NATURALISM, ILLUSIONISM

Feminist film theory must inevitably encounter and do battle with the hybrid phenomenon of realism as a dominant expectation of cultural production in the late 19th and 20th centuries, which embraces both hegemonic and radical aspirations. As the subtitle to this section indicates, realism is discussed through a wide range of terms and concepts with different shades of reference and indicating different relations to ideology. For instance in Claire Johnston's "Women's Cinema as Counter-Cinema," a variety of different concepts are used: Barthes's notion of myth as a process of naturalization (describing a mechanism specific to bourgeois ideology); representation (a cultural activity not necessarily tied to realism, e.g., medieval painting); the laws of verisimilitude (implying consonance with what is generally accepted by a particular society to be true as opposed to what a "progressive" realism might want to reveal); the camera developed "to safeguard the bourgeois notion of realism" (a construct belonging to an anti-realist position) and which grasps only "the natural world of the dominant ideology" (referring to the world of phenomenal forms it is the aim of naturalism, as distinct from realism, to reflect). To this array of terms *Camera Obscura* adds a view of mainstream cinema as "illusionist," thereby introducing a modernist inflection which rescues the materials and processes of art production from vulgar, bourgeois utilitarian ends; and by reprinting the piece by Jean-Louis Baudry on the cinematic apparatus, the collective shifts the meaning of realism from the deployment of a specific set of aesthetic techniques with more or less ideological effects to the capacity of a technological apparatus to reproduce in the subject the psychoanalytic structure now termed the "reality effect."

First I want to examine in what ways the current critique of realism shows that its dominance as a general cultural attitude constitute a problem for Feminist cinema. Realism in this general sense is the first recourse of any oppressed group wishing to combat the ideology promulgated by the media in the interests of hegemonic power. Once an oppressed group becomes aware of its cultural as well as political oppression, and identifies oppressive myths and stereotypes—and in the case of women, female images that simply express male fantasies—it becomes the concern of that group to expose the oppression of such images and replace their falsity, lies, deceptions and escapist illusions with reality and the truth.

The problems of a simplistic use of the notion of cinematic realism are threefold. The first has to do with defining the "reality" of women and the fact that it is not self-evidently given. There clearly will be contradictions between what the condition of women is, what their struggles for change aim to achieve, and how these realities are recognized and understood by Feminists on the one hand, and non-Feminists on the other. So while it is certainly possible to point to what is absent from media screens—women at work, home as a workplace, struggles to change legal and economic structures, the issues of sexual politics, expressions of women's sexuality and so on—there is no simple alternative reality to fill the gap and displace the stereotypes, which will be instantly recognized and accepted by women at large. On the one hand the reality of women can only be grasped through a Socialist-Feminist analysis, the terms of which are not immediately available in phenomenal appearances. On the other, as has already been suggested, the mass media produce their own definitions of women which also have a concrete existence and determining effect on social reality. Stereotypes do not vanish on the production of an image of real women, or of Feminist aspiration. They are materialized in the way society is structured and the way we live our lives; they are part of our reality. Clearly then, as Roman Jakobson pointed out long ago, the claim to realism can be invoked by forces seeking to preserve or to challenge the status quo.[1] This means Feminist cultural analysis needs to question the power and role of recognition. On the one hand a female audience will not necessarily make a Feminist reading of what they see. On the other hand, recognition of a powerfully evoked woman's dilemma, as for instance in *Klute* or *Alice Doesn't Live Here Any More,* may lead us to accept the recuperative ideology through which this dilemma is resolved. Diane Giddis, for instance, in an article on *Klute,* makes a convincing case for the authenticity with which Pakula has grasped the dilemma of the would-be independent woman faced with both the need to love and the threat of assimilation by the male.[2] But this account is then recuperated into a commonplace of traditional criticism that a divided self is a bad thing, which any mature person must seek to unify, rather than the product of the social and psychic contradictions women live under which are amenable to political not personal solutions. The psychologism of this approach leads Giddis to validate Pakula's profoundly un-Feminist, though no doubt "true" ending, that the woman must accept her vulnerability and expose herself to assimilation in the relationship with the man.

This said, it seems to me that these problems need not, as they do in the thinking of many anti-realist theorists, lead to an equation between 1) concrete reality, 2) its ideological configuration, the status quo, and 3) realism as a political goal in cultural production. Nor does it mean that recognition and identification cannot under certain conditions be utilized (or indeed done without). As I shall argue, for women to take up a Feminist position requires precisely an act of identification— with women as a group and of our oppressed place in society.

The second problem with a naive recourse to reality as a counter to stereotyping is that it ignores the need to engage with the multiple function of the cinema as entertainment/ritual/art/fiction, which, although it must exist politically, does not exist alone, or even predominantly, for politics. Hans Magnus Enzensberger has suggested that mass consumerism invokes real needs and desires which capitalism orchestrates commercially in order to exploit.[3] And Claire Johnston argues the inherent puritanism of narrowly realist attitudes, suggesting the necessity of engaging the "collective fantasies of women" in a Feminist cinema.[4] Women are crucially located in this consumerist culture and its utopian elaboration in entertainment,

[1]Roman Jakobson, "On Artistic Realism," in *Readings in Russian Poetics,* eds. Ladislav Matejka and Krystyna Ponovska (MIT Press, 1971).

[2]Diane Giddis, "The Divided Woman: Bree Daniels in *Klute,*" *Women and Film,* 1, Nos. 3/4 (1973), 57–61. Anthologized in *Movies and Methods,* ed. Bill Nichols. (U. Cal. Press, 1976).

[3]"Constituents of a Theory of the Media," *New Left Review,* 64 (Nov.–Dec. 1970).

[4]Claire Johnston, "Nelly Kaplan, An Introduction," *Notes on Women's Cinema, Screen* Pamphlet No. 2, p. 15.

both in terms of our social-economic role and in terms of our image, which is used to materialize its appeal. Realism narrowly defined in terms of actuality is not a powerful enough weapon to disengage women's fantasy from its imbrication in consumerist structures; the relation of propaganda and consciousness-raising films to the utopian, consumerist thrust of entertainment has yet to be worked through.

The third problem of a simple realist approach to the media is that it ignores the fact that "realism" as a mode of cinematic production involves a complex interplay of techniques and devices—that it has to be produced and is not simply evoked by the intention to be real or true. The value of semiology for *Camera Obscura* is that it "attempts to deconstruct the assumption of the naturalness of the iconic image" (p. 6). The issue here is a naturalism which subsumes cinema and film within the operation of the camera lens under the ideological propositions that reality equals what we can see, that perception equals cognition, and that the camera offers a window on the world and does not lie. What such propositions do is deny the existence of those material socioeconomic forces which, though not immediately perceptible in phenomenal appearances, are responsible for their production. Thus reality figures not as a product of society, amenable to human control and change, but of nature, a notion much exploited by bourgeois ideology.* By constituting the whole of cinematic production in the visual image, naturalism not only ignores the film-making apparatus but also that the iconic sign is caught up in other signifying systems—linguistic, aesthetic, social, fictional, etc.—which together structure the film.

The view generated by the media of their own practices reproduces this ideology in that it refuses acknowledgment of the mediating intervention of the film-making process. This is supported by a technology and aesthetic system developed and improved in the service of a naturalist practice, which works precisely to substantiate the claim of the media to reveal the world in an unmediated fashion—for example, lightweight camera, synchronous sound, and all the devices of direct cinema. It is important to show that this is an ideology that the media strive to perpetuate. However, I think it highly questionable whether a theory of realism should equate all varieties of realist practice with the goal of naturalism and so with the operation of bourgeois ideology; or the socioeconomic conditions of the production of a technology with the ultimate aesthetic/ideological effect it produces in the audience who inhabit a different set of conditions.

That "realism" is dominant as an epistemology and aesthetic goal since the Renaissance seems to be an inevitable part of materialist history in so far as we are seeking to free ourselves from superstition, religion, idealism in order to gain control over our material, social, and psychological world. Thus in the days of the revolutionary bourgeoisie, visual and fictional techniques were developed, aimed at grasping the concrete world of human practice rather than the spiritual hierarchy of feudalism. Certain forms of the realist practice have in the 20th century been

---

*The account of bourgeois ideology which I draw on in this article is that given by Stuart Hall, "Culture, the Media, and the 'Ideological Effect,'" *Mass Communication and Society,* eds. James Curran et al. (Arnold, 1977).

theorized in different ways (e.g., Lukacs, Brecht) as the means of reflecting on and analyzing the socially constructed world, in order to produce an understanding of its constitutive forces, and underlying contradictions. However, the problem of hegemonic bourgeois ideology is to try to disguise the fact of reality as a social and historical production and to return it to the world of nature. So the realist endeavor is frequently dehistoricized and reduced to the reflection of the surface appearances of phenomenal reality under the new ethic of naturalism, which becomes the ideology of the media.

It seems important to stress these distinctions because the current anti-realist position has produced a monolithic construct which collapses realism into naturalism and invalidates the fact that different media forms—say a classic Hollywood revival, a modern blockbusting spectacular, the "Play for Today," or a TV documentary—refer to and construct reality in very different ways. To take this argument further, however, requires looking in more detail at the different positions used against realism. These arguments turn about the epistemological status of reality itself, or representation of reality in aesthetic discourse, and of signification as the production of meaning.

BARTHES'S CONCEPT OF MYTH

In "Myth Today," Barthes describes how bourgeois ideology inserts itself into modern semiotic cultural phenomena.[1] His concern is with how the fabric of bourgeois cultural life divests reality of its material, historical specificity and returns it to an eternal, unchanging world of nature which reflects the world of bourgeois values but disguises its name. In "Rhetoric of the Image," he concentrates on how this happens specifically in the photographic image,[2] which has an existential relation to the person or object it represents in a way that the world does not. For a totally hypothetical and, in practice, unrealizable instant, he suggests the photographic image is purely denotative—it is what it means and what it is. Similarly the social world is full of objects which have a purely utilitarian function—clothes exist to be worn, food to be eaten, houses to protect us from the weather and so on. The issue for Barthes is what happens when these objects or photographic images are caught up in a semiotic system and enter the processes of signification.

At this point in bourgeois culture, the denotative image ceases to have as its referent the person, object, or function as these exist materially and historically. The denotative sign becomes a signifier in the second order of signification—connotation. Within bourgeois culture this process constitutes a kind of semiotic vampirism. The connotative signifier drains the original purely denotative sign of its historical and material reference—what Barthes rather suspectly calls its meaning—and turns it into a support for a new bourgeois signifier, the naturalized concept of eternal truths or the "human condition."

---

[1] Roland Barthes, *Mythologies* (Jonathan Cape, 1972).
[2] Roland Barthes, "The Rhetoric of the Image," *Working Papers in Cultural Studies No. 1* (Spring 1971).

I am at the barber's, and a copy of *Paris-Match* is offered to me. On the cover, a young Negro in a French uniform is saluting, with his eyes uplifted, probably fixed on a fold of the tricolour. All this is the *meaning* of the picture. But, whether naively or not, I see very well what it signifies to me: that France is a great Empire, that all her sons, without colour discrimination, faithfully serve under her flag, and that there is no better answer to the detractors of an alleged colonialism than the zeal shown by this Negro in serving his so-called oppressors.

As meaning, the signifier already postulates a reading, I grasp it through my eyes, it has a sensory reality.... there is a richness in it.... it belongs to history, that of the... Negro: in the meaning, a signification is already built.... it postulates a kind of knowledge, a past, a memory, a comparative order of facts, ideas, decisions.

When it becomes form, the meaning leaves its contingency behind; it empties itself, it becomes impoverished, history evaporates, only the latter remains. ("Myth Today," pp. 116–117)

For feminism this theoretical construct has a great attraction. As I have noted, it has long been a common-place of Feminist analysis that women are culturally located outside history—the world that is made and remade by the activity of real material men—and placed in an idealist sphere of nature, eternal values etc. It is also commonplace that women exist in cultural production as "the other," or the "eternal feminine," the necessary complement to the male, the opposite against which men struggle for self-definition and manhood.

For Pam Cook and Claire Johnston, Barthes's concept of the naturalized connotation offers an analysis of how the photographic image of woman becomes a signifier in patriarchal discourse without any sense of violence being done to it. In their study of *The Revolt of Mamie Stover* the image of woman is a sign emptied of its hypothetical denotation referring to the concrete individual woman photographed, meaning "this is a woman" of "woman so-and-so," to become the dehistoricized signifier of the patriarchal connotation—"non-male."

For the moment I want to hold in abeyance the question as to whether the iconic image of woman must always produce a patriarchal connotation, to look at a slightly different appropriation of Barthes for feminism made by Eileen McGarry. In an article on "Documentary, Realism and Women's Cinema" (*Women and Film*, Vol. 2, No. 7, Summer 1975) she takes up Barthes's analysis of cultural objects and practices—such as clothing, eating, etc.—as having first a pure function and then a semiotic signification to elaborate the theory that reality itself is coded, and that within a patriarchal social structure everything to do with women is coded in a sexist way. In a film these social codes are overlaid with the codes of appearance for the actress or film star. She makes a convincing critique of Wiseman's *High School* in terms of the way he photographs and organizes the image of an elderly schoolteacher according to the stereotype "crabby old spinster," just as if he were organizing an actress in a role. Following this line of reasoning, what the audience recognizes as real is not an unmediated reality but the product of socially formed codes. Accepting that the world is perceived through such codes, the issue is whether reality is so monolithically coded in terms of bourgeois and sexist ideology as McGarry suggests. The argument as she presents it does not exclude the codings of dress, appearance, and gesture that connote, for instance, women's liberation *(The Woman's Film)*, the oppression of women *(Women of the Rhondda)*, or the struggle of women *(Women Against the Bill.)*[1] Yet her view of the coding of reality appears to leave no room for the contradictions in the social formation which make Marxist-Feminist analysis and struggle possible.

It is not only reality which is monolithically conceived in this argument but also the audience. Eileen McGarry does suggest that an audience's class position may modify the operation of the codes, but her argument seems to imply that this is at the level of selective perception. Stuart Hall is one of the few cultural analysts who has tried to give the decoding process an active rather than passive dimension in a model of different possible reading processes—hegemonic, negotiated, and oppositional.[2] And Elizabeth Cowie has convincingly argued that a Feminist reading of particular films or filmic processes in general is not an inevitable consequence of the film itself:

> Sexism in an image cannot be designated materially as a content in the way that denotative elements such as colours or objects in the image can be pointed to. Rather it is the development of new or different definitions and understandings of what men and women are and their roles in society which produces readings of images as sexist; the political perspective of feminism produces a further level of connotative reading. ("Women, Representation and the Image," *Screen Education,* Summer 1977)

This argument suggests that the fact that we are able to see the school teacher in Wiseman's *High School* as a sexist stereotype at all is not because sexism resides inside the image itself, but because the Women's Liberation Movement has produced a Feminist perspective which enables us to read the connotation of the teacher in other than naturalized patriarchal terms. In this respect no artistic practice, realist or otherwise, can ensure either a conservative or radical reading on the part of the audience.

There is a further problem in the contribution of semiotics to cultural analysis, which compounds the question of realism in film. As I have already suggested, Barthes tries to take account of the existential relation between photographic image and person or object photographed by hypothesizing a purely denotative moment when phenomenal meaning and existence unite. So the fact that the iconic image can then be caught up into other signifying systems constitutes a kind of cheat on the premise of an original pure denotation. Eileen McGarry takes up this aspect of Barthes's semiology:

> When reality becomes a pro-filmic event it becomes the first stage in a process of signification—i.e., the functional element of human existence which makes it *more* than

---

[1] *Woman's Film* by the Newsreel Group, USA 1971; *Women of the Rhondda* by the London Women's Film Group 1973; *Women Against the Bill* by Esther Ronay and members of the Notting Hill Women's Liberation Group.

[2] Stuart Hall, "Encoding and Decoding in the TV Discourse," paper available from Centre for Contemporary Cultural Studies, University of Birmingham, England. The *hegemonic* decoding is one that takes the reading preferred by the dominant ideology; the *negotiated* decoding attempts to maintain the preferred reading in tandem with understandings drawn from a class position which is in contradiction (though disguised contradiction) to the dominant ideology; and the *oppositional* decoding transforms the readings offered by the dominant ideology into what they mean for an oppositional discourse.

signification is eliminated. People and objects are abstracted to the level of pure sign. ("Documentary, Realism and Women's Cinema," p. 52)

Her earlier insistence, along with Barthes, that reality is not transparently given but is itself a coded social construct and that images similarly produce meaning according to a system of semiotic codes is important as an intervention against naturalist ideologies. However, the route she takes from here into the anti-realist position suggests that this acknowledgment involves one also in renouncing the goal of a realist representation aimed at probing that production in terms that can make a connection with the experience people gain through their social and political practices. In other words, if the iconic image is unable to deliver us images of women in our pure "function" and "meaning," it does not seem to me the logical next step to assert that our reality cannot be signified so as to be better understood; if the functional elements of human existence are suppressed in the process of semiotic signification, may they not be spoken about in the organized message? This tendency to critique the realist endeavour for not rendering the "real" in its full immediacy does seem to stem in part from Barthes's nostalgia for the hypothesized and fleeting moment of pure denotation.[1]

ALTHUSSER AND IDEOLOGY

My appeal to experience and understanding at the end of the last section introduces a different strand in the anti-realist position, which turns on the problematic relation of individual consciousness and experience to a materialist understanding of reality and derives from a theory of ideology propounded by Louis Althusser. How far can the acts of recognition daily performed in the practical activity of women and men be informed by or produce an understanding of the nature of the social process in which they are caught up? To a large extent the possibility or otherwise of a cognitive artistic practice which can aim to produce understanding about the world stands or falls on the answer to this question.

Whereas many Marxist theorists—Lukacs and Brecht as two major and often opposed exponents of Marxist aesthetics—have sought to develop the terms of a realist practice capable of producing an understanding of the real world in its social practices and historical production, the Althusserian position claims that the attempt to represent the social formation can produce only "the natural world of the dominant ideology."[2] Behind this view lie two crucial concepts developed by Althusser, first, "ideology in general," and second, the ideological category of the subject. Althusser proposes a distinction between "ideology in general," which is necessary to the functioning of any society, and specific ideologies belonging to particular social formations at particular points in their history—bourgeois ideology, for instance. "Ideology in general" is theorized as a material force rather than

---

[1]Terry Lovell has critiqued Barthes in these terms in "Cultural Studies," *Screen,* 14, No. 3 (Autumn 1973).

[2]Claire Johnston, "Women's Cinema as Counter-Cinema," *Notes on Women's Cinema, Screen* Pamphlet No. 2 (Sept. 1972), p. 28.

merely a set of false ideas circulating in people's heads that should by now have been changed by Socialist teaching and example. It acts as a material support to specific ideologies, and is a structure providing the necessary mediation between (1) the forces and relations of production, (2) the social institutions they give rise to, and (3) the individuals who have to live through them. Ideology enables men and women to make sense of their world and feel in control of it. However, it is in their practical activity rather than in their ideas that ideology materializes itself; in fact it provides the terms of such activity.

> Ideology is indeed a system of representations, but in the majority of cases these representations have nothing to do with "consciousness": they are usually images, and occasionally concepts, but it is above all as *structures* that they impose on the vast majority of men (sic), not via their "consciousness". They are perceived accepted-suffered cultural objects and they act functionally on men (sic) via a process that escapes them. Men (sic) "live" their ideologies . . . as their *"world"* itself. . . . the "lived" relation between men (sic) and the world, including History (in political action or inaction), passes through ideology, or better, is ideology itself. ("Marxism and Humanism," p. 233)

As such, ideology is a necessary component of human society; "it . . . is not an aberration or a contingent excrescence of History; it is a structure essential to the historical life of societies" (p. 232).

Ideology is able to materialize itself in the activities of women and men precisely because they operate under the illusion of being concrete individuals at the center of and to a measure initiating their lived experience, because they perform the daily acts of recognition which maintain and perpetuate the structures and institutions of the social formation. Althusser theorizes the ideological nature of identity and recognition through the psychoanalytic category of the subject developed by Lacan (which I will come to later):

> You and I are *always already* subjects, and as such constantly practice the rituals of ideological recognition, which guarantee for us that we are indeed concrete, individual, distinguishable and (naturally) irreplaceable subjects. (pp. 161–62)

> All ideology hails or interpellates concrete individuals as concrete subjects, by the functioning of the category of the subject. (p. 162)

This attack on the dominant discourse of Western philosophy since the Renaissance, aimed at irrevocably shifting humanist Man from the scene of history and women and men from the scene of their daily lives, also puts the "real" back a stage, not simply beyond the reach of phenomenal appearances, but making it inaccessible to the conscious social practice of men and women. Everyday life and its struggles can only be experienced in ideological terms; knowledge about the causes and nature of these struggles is produced only by theoretical practice:

> Ideology . . . is identical with the "lived" experience of human existence itself. This "lived" experience is not a given, given by a pure "reality," but the spontaneous "lived experience" of the ideology in its peculiar relationship to the real. (Althusser, "A Letter on Art," p. 205)

This position clearly has grave consequences for an artistic practice seeking to represent the real world. The problem is compounded by the fact that in capitalism it is bourgeois ideology that uses "ideology in general" for a material support. For the work of bourgeois ideology is understood to be aimed at dissolving class membership with its resulting contradictions into individuals, producing and maintaining them in the illusion of their non-contradictory discreteness, autonomy, freedom, and centrality. To do this it has to reorganize sociality into forms that obscure the fact of society as a historical social production and an interrelated totality grounded in contradiction. This requires the masking, displacing, or imaginary unifying of contradiction in terms of such myths as "nature" or the unchangeable "human condition." Thus in bourgeois ideology the members of the social formation find themselves isolated individuals who confront over and against them society as a preconstituted given appearing to derive from nature.*

In these terms the mechanisms of recognition and identification are complicit at the level both of "ideology in general" and bourgeois ideology. The former would appear to provide a sound support system for the latter in the inaccessibility to conscious experience of "the real" and in the formation of the subject. Thus in analyses of realist aesthetics, this distinction between "ideology in general" and "bourgeois ideology" often appears to get lost, so that bourgeois ideology becomes monolithic and inescapable to the point that the room for manoeuver available to social practices such as artistic production is very limited.

For Feminist culture practice this position constitutes a serious problem. The Women's Liberation Movement, for instance, has set great store on the interrogation of personal experience and consciousness-raising as a form of work aimed at uncovering the political in the personal and creating new identifications for individual women where the recognition of a gender position in terms of the category *women,* as opposed to the patriarchal abstractions "women," the "eternal feminine," etc., is precisely to leave behind an individual identification and begin to recast the self in terms of a group membership. The first issue of *Camera Obscura* can be seen as attempting to negotiate this contradiction between women's movement politics, their corresponding demands of Feminist film-making, and the anti-representational emphasis of recent film theory. Stating their allegiance to neo-Marxist structural theory developed in terms of feminism by Claire Johnston, Pam Cook, Laura Mulvey and others, the collective claims a break with the classic (Hollywood) text and the dominant "realist" mode of film production. Accounting for their interest in the avant-garde work of Yvonne Rainer, they state:

> We felt that the Feminist problematic—the complex and ambiguous permutations of male dominance/female submission—could not be presented as a political and therefore changeable, problem using the conventional modes of representation. (p. 59)

In consequence *Camera Obscura* rejects "identification" as a mechanism in the classic text or documentary for making a political intervention and this means taking a distance from much of the early film-making of the Women's Liberation Movement. The problem with *Janie's Janie,* for instance, is that "we can rather easily imagine *not* identifying with Janie, the subject." In Yvonne Rainer's films,

---

*See note 8.

on the other hand, their "formal construction . . . forces the audience to analyze the problems which the films demonstrate." (p. 59). . . .

If we have a certain freedom not to identify with Janie, it is unclear how Yvonne Rainer's films can "force" an audience into an appropriate analytical activity. This problem is the subject of an interesting debate between the collective and Rainer over the relation between the function of mainstream and avant-garde practices:

> CO: In *The Mother and the Whore* you *are* provided with situations that you can iden- tify with, that you can see yourself in, but you've given no conceptual tools to analyze the situation. It has to do with questions of perception, with the way we see things. . . . these films provide you with a ready-made experience. Once you're inside that fictional world, you may see situations you can identify with, but when you come back out of that world, out of the theater, it's hard to transfer that filmed situation outside because it's so much tied to the characters and the emotional situations inside the film. When you watch a film that you have to think about in order to determine its coherence or relevance, you are engaging in an active process which is exactly the same inside and outside the film. You don't have to rethink the milieu of the film in order to examine the situation it presents.

> YR: I couldn't agree more. However, I think one of the problems in talking about what films do is, you start talking about some kind of Everyperson. . . . Perhaps it is a mistake to compare narrative films from the standpoint of those which use distancing devices and those which do not. How can we say which type of film will make "people" think, or make them active, and which will not? A friend of mine thought that *The Mother and the Whore* summed up the male-female predicament in a nutshell. I got bogged down in the talkiness, the actors, my difficulty with Leaud, a thousand and one details . . . As she talked about it I had to agree with her. What other film has so explicitly dealt with the child-man's expectations of women? She, my friend, came out of that movie critical and objective. I, poor soul, was adrift in that other tradition. It is very difficult to cross over to the other shore. (pp. 83–84)

The issue raised here is whether the audience is as automatically taken over by the identificatory mechanisms of mainstream cinema as the antirealist position sug- gests, or whether there is not a considerable degree of work required on the part of the audience in negotiating what a particular fictional world offers according to where they are placed in society. Similarly, although it is clear that the view of the media as "a window on the world" must be firmly resisted, it is not clear that the audience, even while accepting that view as a general proposition, automatically accept it on any and every occasion. It seems more likely that the audience will be as contradictory in its utilization of media products as any other aspect of society— though not necessarily consciously so. Disproving the epistemological claims of a particular medium or artistic practice is a different thing from analyzing its ideo- logical effects in a particular concrete conjuncture. Thus, I would argue that *Cam- era Obscura's* rejection of early women's film-making is both right and wrong:

> We feel that most of these filmmakers fell into the trap of trying to employ an essentially male-oriented bourgeois notion of film—the notion of film as a window on the world, and have simply chosen to shoot out of other windows than did most filmmakers before the women's movement. (p. 60)

It is not clear that "shooting out of other windows" could not be a very illuminating and subversive activity. For instance, Ann Kaplan has suggested that although the movement films do not demystify the system of representation, they can "reorder the signs within the convention, giving us unfamiliar images of women; we make unfamiliar identifications, sympathies and alliances and are given new perceptions" ("Aspects of British Feminist Film Theory," p. 52).

There seems to be a danger in the current critique of realism of taking the claims for the media at their face values and so ignoring the fact that phenomenal appearances rendered in film have nevertheless to be read through a variety of signifying and social codes which are distributed differently among audiences. In the end what continually eludes attempts to confront the realist text is the question: at what level we are to understand its realism to be constituted and so available for interrogation. Are we dealing with an aesthetic form, an epistemological construct, a political practice, or an ideological claim surrounding media production?

More recently the technology of the cinema has been critiqued from the antirealist perspective on psychoanalytic grounds. The ideological realism of the cinema is not now only a matter of the deployment of techniques of verisimilitude; rather the "reality effect" is ensured through the apparatus of cinematic projection, by the production of the individual spectator in the place of the subject—unified outside contradiction. Crucial to this production is the psychoanalytic representation of woman and her fetishized cinematic counterpart.*

PSYCHOANALYSIS AND FEMINIST FILM THEORY

In "The Place of Women in the Cinema of Raoul Walsh," Pam Cook and Claire Johnston move from Barthes's "myth" to Lacanian psychoanalysis. Thus reasons are found why the iconic image of woman must produce a patriarchal meaning, and why "women as women" are silent in our culture. At the same time the grounds for the rejection of a possible radical realism are shifted to a concern with iconic representation which now subsumes all forms of realism. In these terms, representation has less the force of a purposive cultural activity than of a compulsive psychoanalytic mechanism centering on the female figure. Laura Mulvey gives an unequivocal statement of this in "Visual Pleasure and Narrative Cinema":

> The paradox of phallocentrism in all its manifestations is that it depends on the image of the castrated woman to give order and meaning to its world. (p. 6)

In Pam Cook and Claire Johnston's account, the cinematic image presents the body of woman as a spectacle for the erotic male gaze, at the same time rendering her as "non-male," so that her image may become the substitute phallus necessary to counter the castration threat to men posed by woman's lack of a penis. Thus the very act of representation ipso facto involves the objectification of women and the repression of female sexuality.

---

*For accounts of the anti-realist polemic, see: Paul Willamen, "On Realism in the Cinema," *Screen,* 13, No. 1 (Spring 1972); Colin MacCabe, "Realism in the Cinema: Notes on some Brechtian Theses," *Screen,* 15, No. 2; Peter Wollen, "*Vent d'Est:* Counter Cinema," *Afterimages* No. 4 (Autumn 1972). And for Feminist applications of these positions, see: Eileen McGarry, "Documentary, Realism and Women's Cinema," *Women and Film,* 2, No. 7 (Summer 1975); "Feminism and Film: Critical Approaches," editorial, *Camera Obscura* 1 (Fall 1976).

THE PLACE OF THE WOMAN IN THE LACANIAN CINEMA[1] PLENITUDE AND IDENTITY/BREAST AND "MIRROR PHASE"

The article in *Camera Obscura* by Jean-Louis Baudry and the most recent writings of Claire Johnston[2] cite the reality effect not in techniques of verisimilitude, but in the construction in the spectator of a certain position in relation to the film. This position produces a highly desired state of being termed "plenitude" or "unity." There are several aspects to this notion of unity: the desire to be united with reality, with the others who confer on one a sense of identity with one's own self, with one's words and their meanings. What is terrifying to us is the notion of separation, difference, and lack. An intimation of this desired state of being is first experienced by the baby at the breast, but this illusion of plenitude in unity with the mother is soon thrown into question by the experience of separation and loss when the mother leaves the baby to go about her own affairs. The pleasure of the cinema lies in its reconstruction in the spectator of an illusory sense of this imagined early experience of unity.

As the baby develops, however, it enters a second phase of illusory unity described as the "mirror phase," in which the baby's emerging subjectivity achieves an *imaginary* unity with its own idealized image reflected in a mirror—a fragmentation first indicated in the return look of the mother/"other" that confirms for the baby the identity between itself and its reflection. This forms the basis of the fragmentation through which the ego is formed to become conscious of self. In "Towards a Feminist Film Practice: Some Theses,"[3] Claire Johnston describes how the filmic text constructs a place for the spectator, which reproduces this illusory identification. This is achieved by an identification with the imaginary spectator implied in the presentation of a shot ("this scene is being looked at by someone") which in the reverse shot is then transferred to a fictional character, so denying the return look of the image and the separateness of the concrete viewer in the auditorium and stitching her or him into the fiction (suture) and into the subject place where the filmic text constructs.

DIFFERENCE: CASTRATION AND LANGUAGE

If unity and identity are illusions, then the crucial reality is difference, the master concept of psychoanalysis. The splitting of self which takes place when the ego separates out from the imaginary unity of image and self-image during the mirror phase is coincident with the beginnings of language. With the ego and language begins the differentiation in the world of objects and others from each other and

---

[1] The account of Lacanian psychoanalysis given here is largely drawn from: Steve Burniston and Chris Weedon, "Ideology, Subjectivity and the Artistic Text," *Working Papers in Cultural Studies* No. 10 (1977); Laura Mulvey, "Visual Pleasure and Narrative Cinema," *Screen,* 16, No. 3 (Autumn 1975); Colin MacCabe, "Principles of Realism and Pleasure," *Screen,* 17, No. 3.

[2] Claire Johnston, "Towards a Feminist Film Practice: Some Theses," in *Edinburgh '76 Magazine* No. 1, *Psychoanalysis/Cinema/Avant-Garde.*

[3] See note 18.

from the self, and at the same time the gradual establishment of an individual subject in the place marked out for it through a series of prohibitions and approbia-
tions. The child gradually finds out who it is, who it has to become. Finally and most
crucially for an analysis of patriarchy, the child acquires the sexed place indicated
by the pronoun positions of "he" and "she" and everything that is predicated
socially and culturally on them.

The crucial role of difference in this process arises from the structural linguistics
of Ferdinand Saussure. He argued that there are no positive terms in language—
single words united and full with their single meanings and their referents in the
real world—but only a system of related differences or oppositions. For instance,
the meaning of the word "sheep" in English is not the meaning of "mouton" in
French because English also has "mutton," which French does not. "Sheep" only
has meaning in terms of its difference from "mutton" (and from a whole series of
other interconnected differences, to pursue which would mean reading the dictionary of the English language). According to the logic of psychoanalysis, the starting
place in this relay of differences is the first perception of sexual difference in the
woman's lack of a penis.

DIFFERENCE, LACK, AND THE PHALLUS

In this instance the term difference becomes highly loaded. It is not a matter of
functional oppositions as in the difference of "t" and "d" or "sheep" and "mutton."
Sexual difference is said to be the key opposition in which presence (the phallus
symbolized by the penis) is faced with absence (no penis).* Here for the emerging
human subject a bitter paradox enters. Plenitude is only experienced in terms of the
mother; for a short time, she "is the phallus" (symbol of plenitude) for the child—
retrospectively, that is, for the mother offers that plenitude the possibility of which
the phallus will later come to represent as a memory. But then the child is faced,
not only with the fact of the mother's necessary absences, but also with her betrayal
of her exclusive relation to the child in that she is possessed also by the father. Thus
the maternal identification is broken by the entry of "the father"—the third term
representing the look of "the other" suppressed during the mirror phase—whose
prohibition against incest turns the perception of sexual difference into the threat
of castration. The traumatic experience of this oppositional difference sets in
motion the acquisition of the organized relay of linguistic differences which constitute language and so the human subject.

The drive which will impel the child onward from the realization of castration
into culture and the resolution of the Oedipus complex will be haunted by the memory of his original illusory experience of plenitude when baby and world were at
one. As this subject is constructed through language, so desire is constituted as the
attempt to recapture these illusions, through language, which is its only means of
knowing the world and so of gaining control over it. But the language user has to

*Penis and phallus should not be confused. While the penis refers to the anatomical organ, the
phallus, which the penis is able to symbolize, represents the object of desire as it is structured under
patriarchy.

submit to the rules of a language he or she has not made; moreover there is an unbridgeable gap between the uttering ego, the moment of utterance, and reception of the utterance by the other. The desire of the subject is doomed to failure. Hence the double importance of the iconic media which appear to promise an escape from the constraints of language and a return to the pleasure of an achieved unity between subject and reality.

MALE ENTRY INTO THE SYMBOLIC

At this point we can examine the differential entry of the male and female child into the patriarchal order, a difference that turns on the crucial role of the penis/no penis opposition in the institution of language. The mother originally represents the place of the phallus but then with the entry of the third term betrays the child by her lack. For the boy, the father's penis demonstrates a comforting and recuperative presence. Thus the penis stands in for the phallus, the key signifier, the importance of which is that it is a kind of end-stop to the otherwise endless chain of signifiers. It represents the possibility of arriving back where one wants to be, a kind of finality which makes the production of meaning possible from the play of difference. The patriarchal fact that the penis can be the signifier of the phallus is paralleled by the boy's reassuring expectation that one day he will himself wield such a penis, taking the place of his father, and once more gain symbolic possession of his mother in the person of his wife. The terror of castration and lack can be evaded at the same time as the fact of difference facilitates entry into the symbolic order of human culture. Thus through the correspondence between his anatomy and the possibility of wielding language the boy can escape from the illusory unity of the imaginary and enter the symbolic, the sphere of articulation, of signification, and the expression of desire.

WOMEN AND THE SYMBOLIC ORDER

If the boy enters into a position of command within the patriarchal symbolic order, what is the girl's position in patriarchy? For our purposes there are two questions: What is the relation of women to language as speaking subject? What is the role of the representation of women in cultural artifacts? Put simply: *Can women speak, and can images of women speak for women?* The answers seem negative. First, women anatomically play a key part in the production of the symbolic (language and culture), but by virtue of this role (castration) women can only have a negative relation to language; they cannot wield control over the symbolic; they do not carry in themselves the symbol of the signifier, the phallic authority for signification, only the absence which sets the signifier in place. Thus their entry into human discourse must be tentative, highly negotiated, and ambiguous. Second, though the threat of castration is necessary to the production of the speaking subject, in order for the subject to speak, the possibility of castration must not have taken place or has to be concealed. Thus female sexuality cannot be expressed; the symbolic activity of language and culture is set into motion in an attempt to liquidate the very lack that women represent. For women themselves to attain mastery within this system they would have to want to liquidate themselves. Hence the enigmatic silence of women.

So the answer to the first question (can women speak?) is no, or only in a highly negotiated fashion, because the subject position from which mastery of language is possible is a male construct—one which women help to form but which we cannot operate.

> Woman's desire is subjected to her image as bearer of the bleeding wound, she can exist only in relation to castration and cannot transcend it. She turns her child into the signifier of her own desire to possess a penis (the condition, she images, of entry into the symbolic). Either she must gracefully give way to the word, the Name of the Father and the Law, or else struggle to keep her child down with her in the half-light of the imaginary. Woman then stands in patriarchal culture as signifier for the male other, bound by a symbolic order in which men can live out his phantasies and obsessions through linguistic command by imposing them on the silent image of woman still tied to her place as bearer of meaning, not maker of meaning. (Laura Mulvey, "Visual Pleasure and Narrative Cinema." p. 7)

Not only can women not speak, but fully realized femininity is an unknown condition:

> Because under patriarchy we are condemned to live by our sexed identities, the ideological definitions of the "masculine" and the "feminine," Juliet Mitchell makes a strong case for seeing femininity in patriarchal culture as to some extent a repressed condition, which can only be acquired partially and in a distorted form. Perhaps it can only be fully understood in its symptoms, as in the case of hysteria ("a disorder with feminine characteristics"—Freud which embodies both the representation of desire and its prohibition. It would seem to me that within patriarchal culture there is a "definitely defined male sexuality" which can find expression (the fetishization of woman as spectacle is one example) while female sexuality is indeed repressed, its real nature only fully knowable with the overthrow of patriarchal culture itself. (Claire Johnston,[*] "Femininity and the Masquerade: *Anne of the Indies*," p. 43)

WOMEN AND REPRESENTATION

In these terms, then, the answer to the second question is similarly negative: images of women cannot speak for women. Because of the role played by the image of woman in the formation of the (masculine) subject, representations of women in cultural artifacts are bound to return to and play on the regressive desire to reestablish for the viewer the desired unity with the real—thrown into question by the possibility of castration—difference. So "woman as woman" can be presented in classic film representation, only as a fetishized image constituting a denial of female sexuality and desire. Claire Johnston describes how this fetishization is achieved cinematically and at the same time reverses the claims usually made for Mae West.

> Many women have read into her parody of the star system and her verbal aggression an attempt at the subversion of male domination in the cinema. If we look more closely there are many traces of phallic replacement in her persona which suggest quite the opposite. The voice itself is strongly masculine, suggesting the absence of the male, and

---

[*]*Jacques Tourneur,* eds. Claire Johnston and Paul Willamen (Edinburgh Film Festival, 1975).

establishes the male/non-male dichotomy. The characteristic phallic dress possesses elements of the fetish. The female element which is introduced, the mother image, expresses male oedipal fantasy. In other words, at the unconscious level, the persona of Mae West is entirely consistent with sexist ideology; it in no way subverts existing myths, but reinforces them. ("Women's Cinema as Counter-Cinema," p. 26)

The connotation "non-male" or "substitute phallus" required by patriarchal ideology is imposed through a system of iconic rather than fictional or narrative codes, so that women are realized filmically as "to-be-looked-at" images rather than in speech or action.

Lighting, camera angles, the cutting between actors and use of close shot v. long shot—all the techniques of filming are used to differentiate radically the presentation of men and women on the screen . . . techniques normally used . . . for women in films . . . essentially produce a specularity in relation to the character in a way which places her role in the film as iconic rather than diegetic; i.e., the classical sexual objectification of women in films. (Elizabeth Cowie, "Feminist Film Criticism: A Reply," *Screen,* Vol. 16, No. 1, p. 138)

Laura Mulvey in "Visual Pleasure and Narrative Cinema" uses the Lacanian interpretation of this visual objectification of women to argue that because the super-abundant iconicity of the female image also threatens an eruption of extreme unpleasure—castration—classic Hollywood cinema has developed various devices and structures to give the male hero and, by proxy, the male spectator, control over her enchanting and threatening image. Given the crucial role of the female representation in patriarchal culture, these forms control the material of any film.

Patriarchal ideology is an effect of the form of the film text itself, and may even in isolated cases be at variance with the beliefs of the author. . . . This domain of form imposes itself on the film-maker whether or not he or she likes it, defining the limits and meanings of the work of art itself. (Claire Johnston, "Feminist Politics and Film History," *Screen,* Vol. 16, no. 3, p. 122)

A Feminist film-maker, then, finds the root of patriarchy in the very tools she wishes to employ to speak about women. So what is required of her is the development of a counter-cinema that will deconstruct the language and techniques of "classic cinema" at the point where the patriarchal subject is formed and female desire repressed: *castration.*

In her article on *Anne of the Indies,* Claire Johnston sees the girl child's masquerade, her disguise as a pirate, as a destructive refusal of the feminine position within the symbolic order. In so doing she asserts sexual difference in the face of the male fear of castration. Johnston defines this in terms of the Barthesian notion developed in *The Pleasure of the Text* and *S/Z,* of "radical heterogeneity." In these terms, the means of attack on patriarchy consists in the assertion of castration and the fundamental difference it opens up. In "Towards a Feminist Film Practice: Some Theses" she argues that the union of signifier and signified in patriarchal and classic filmic discourse ipso facto represses the feminine because it constitutes a denial of difference. Thus Woman is "the unnameable, the unsaid." Feminist practice must work toward dislocating and restructuring the symbolic order in order to change the function, in the moment of perception of sexual difference, of the entry of the third term in the production of the symbolic signifier; thus a new subject will be created and a new order of language that will assert rather than repress sexual difference.

PSYCHOANALYSIS AND IDEOLOGY

It is important for Feminist analysis of patriarchal culture to understand how psychoanalysis affects our understanding of the nature of reality, for in changing this it changes our point of attack. In this respect the impact of Lacanian psychoanalysis has to be understood in its conjunction with Althusser's theory of ideology. The chief issue for feminism is the patriarchal construction of the subject (to which both women and men have to conform). This construct is both the origin and support of ideology in general, in the sense that the illusions of identity, personal experience, and language use that are necessary to social life offer, as it were, the soil in which specific ideologies can seed and naturalize themselves; and simultaneously constitute the point at which the "feminine" is repressed. The first question that arises is the problematic relation of the patriarchal symbolic order to the material existence of men and women and their social practices, which in orthodox Marxist terms constitute the reality it is the struggle of human beings to transform. The problem with orthodox Marxism, it is claimed, is that socioeconomic determinants are seen as operating within already constituted and therefore potentially autonomous subjects.* Thus the recourse to Lacan seeks a "materialist" theory of the subject in the discovery of the so-called primary processes that construct the true subject. The problem here is that the theoretical juncture of Lacan and Althusser in the de-centering of individuals from their consciousness seems to remove them from much else as well, for although the Lacanian subject accounts for different sexual locations in the symbolic order, it says little about class; the constitutive force of language, primary in both a chronological and formative sense, appears to displace the effectivity of the forces and relations of production in the social formation. Sexual difference is made homologous to the Marxist concept of contradiction, the driving force of history. Desire, the motivation of human endeavor, is seen as the compulsive wish to overcome this contradiction—if such it is—in order to regain the original unity experienced in babyhood. It is difficult to see how the dialectical process of history and class struggle is to be articulated in relation to this. Moreover the construction of the subject construct *individuals;* it is unclear what effectivity class or racial location has on the production of individuals or in what sense individuals can be said to belong to *social groups.*

For women this has grave consequences. On the one hand we are faced with almost total repression of femininity within patriarchal culture; on the other with the intensification in the 20th century of struggles around the economic and political emancipation of women. The issue then, is the relation of the construction of the subject to the social structure; for Feminists this could be posed as a question about the relation of the penis to the phallus. For if the trauma of castration is

---

*For a discussion of this problem see the collective article by the editorial board of *Ideology and Consciousness* No. 1 (1977).

relieved by the phallus, what needs explaining is why the penis is able to escape the linguistic rule of negativity and signify it. *Unless patriarchy is a product of chance, the role of the penis as support for the symbolic signifier seems to be predicated on patriarchal dominance as an already constituted fact.* This seems to be implicitly acknowledged in the account Steve Burniston and Chris Weedon give of the Lacanian system and of the moment of entry of the "third term" into the castration complex. Explaining that the Father in this system is symbolic of patriarchal law and not necessarily coincident with a real father, they say:

> In the situation with which the child is faced at the moment of the intervention of the Father in the pre-Oedipal relation, the paternal authority is inseparable from maleness. The penis, the distinguishing mark of maleness and thus the possibility of direct identification with the Father (if only *in prospect*), thus becomes the crux of the complex. ("Ideology, Subjectivity and the Artistic Text," in *Working Papers in Cultural Studies,* No. 10, p. 220)

The hiatus between women as constructed in language and women as produced by historical, social, and economic forces is more marked if we try to envisage the relation of patriarchy to capitalism and bourgeois ideology. In these terms patriarchy is coincident with ideology in general and would appear to precede, even be a condition of, any other form of oppression. This raises two general problems. First, a Feminist theory and cultural practice that seeks practical political effectivity must be able to take account of the intersection of gender with class and racial difference among others. In political terms it would seem essential to have recourse to some form of recognition through which women can make a first identification with themselves as women and as an oppressed group and at the same time relate this identification to their class experience. The second problem is the magnitude of the task facing Feminists if patriarchy can be shifted only by an assault on the structure of the subject and ideology in general. Our understanding of this task has been given us in terms of psycholinguistic representational structure to which fictional and cinematic forms of representation are understood as being homologous. But we are clearly in a very weak political position if rupturing the place of the subject in representation is our chief point of entry.

There clearly is a danger in posing the question in chicken-and-egg terms. But the problem remains if we are to locate an effective point of Feminist attack; how are the socioeconomic structures of power and subordination articulated with the repression of femininity in the psycholinguistic construction of the subject? and how can one level effect changes in the other? . . .

CONCLUSION

Recent developments in Feminist film theory rest on the meeting of three different strands in neo-Marxist analysis: 1) the Althusserian designation of lived experience, empirical reality, as the materialization of ideology; 2) the Lacanian theory of the primacy of language in the construction of the subject in which visual representation of woman plays a key role; and 3) the designation of cinema as an iconic medium ideologically complicit with an epistemology of vision based on the self-evident character of phenomenal appearances, and devoted to re-playing the process of the construction of the subject in order to reconfirm the ideological unity of the patriarchal subject outside contradiction.

The ultimate problem, it seems to me, lies in the attempt to make language and the signifying process so exclusively central to the production of the social formation. Under the insistence on the semiotic production of meaning, the effectivity of social, economic, and political practice threatens to disappear altogether. There is a danger of conflating the social structure of reality with its signification, by virtue of the fact that social processes and relations have to be mediated through language, and the evidence that the mediating power of language reflects back on the social process. But to say that language has a determining effect on society is a different matter from saying that society is nothing but its languages and signifying practices.

Once the social construction of reality and women is defined in terms of psychoanalytic signifying practice alone, the process of realist representation can only be ideologically complicit, for it is itself based on an imaginary unity between signifier and signified and the suppression of difference from which originates our illusory sense of the real world in the first place. Thus in Barthes's *The Pleasure of the Text* and *S/Z,* part of his rejection of realism is that it demands that writers make a choice between meanings; for within the anti-realist epistemology, the only way to avoid ideology is to put off the signified—the moment of closure, of ideological fixity—for as long as possible, to stay within process, the infinite play of meanings. From the point of view of the Women's Liberation Movement, or any other political grouping, this demand has serious implications; there are some meanings associated with the image of women that have to be rejected forcibly. In the end it is difficult to see how if a radical ideology, such as feminism, is to be defined as a means of providing a framework for political action, one is not going to put one's finger on the scales, enter some kind of realist epistemology.

                                                                              1978

II

Film Language

The art of music did not arise as soon as man learned how to create pleasing sounds. It was necessary to arrange those sounds into scales, to organize them into harmonic systems, and to devise appropriate musical forms for them. Similarly, the art of poetry required more than the mere existence of a list of words. These words had to be arranged according to rules of grammar and organized into intelligible literary structures. When the poet writes an epic, his words must be capable of telling a story, and when he writes a sonnet, they must fall into specific rhyme schemes and structural patterns.

The great Soviet filmmakers Sergei Eisenstein and Vsevolod Pudovkin thought about the art of the cinema in a similar way. This art required more than the mere ability to make moving pictures of reality, and, therefore, it required more than the discovery of photography. But what more? What is it that transformed a new technical ability into a great new art? Their answer was montage, the art of combining pieces of film or shots (film's "sounds" or "words") into larger units—first, the scene, then the sequence, and, finally the complete film. D. W. Griffith, the great American director of *The Birth of a Nation* and *Intolerance,* to whom the Soviet directors acknowledged a great debt, was not important because he took better pictures than anybody else. He was important for having discovered montage, the fluid integration of the camera's total range of shots, from extreme close-up to distant panorama, so as to produce the most coherent narrative sequence, the most systematic meaning, and the most effective rhythmic pattern. In doing so, Griffith had, they thought, contributed to the development of a cinematic language and invented the distinctive art of the film.

Sergei M. Eisenstein, the most brilliant figure in Soviet cinema, began his career as a stage director. The youthful Eisenstein then made four films in five years: *Strike* (1924), *Potemkin* (1925), *October* (1927), and *Old and New* (1928). In the 1930s and 1940s (until his death in 1948) he worked primarily as a theorist and teacher, completing only *Alexander Nevsky* and *Ivan the Terrible, Parts I and II*. Eisenstein's conversion from an artist to a theorist is to be explained in part by political realities, for his emphasis on cinematic "form" was uncongenial to his government's official aesthetics. But it is equally true that his conception of montage did not easily accommodate itself to the use of synchronized dialogue and, therefore, to the kind of film which had prevailed by the 1930s.

Eisenstein viewed montage as a kind of collision or conflict, especially between a shot and its successor. He sees each shot as having a kind of potential energy—in purely visual terms of its direction of movement, its volumes of shapes, its intensity of light, and so forth. This potential energy becomes kinetic when the first shot collides with the succeeding one. The two shots can produce a conflict in their emotional content (happy versus sad), in their use of illumination (dark versus light), in their rhythms (slow versus fast), in their objects (large versus small), in their directions of movement (right versus left), in their distances (close-up versus far shot) or in any combination thereof. In his films, this conflict produced the tense, violent rhythms that became an Eisenstein trademark. Conflict was also important to Eisenstein because he took it to be an expression, in the realm of images, of the Marxist dialectical principle. Indeed, Eisenstein maintained that just as the meaning of a sentence arises from the interaction of its individual words, cinematic meaning is the result of the dialectical interplay of shots. His emphasis on the conflict of shots, as distinct from a mere linking of shots, distinguishes his concept from that of his colleague, Pudovkin. Pudovkin's view of montage as a method of building, of adding one thing to another, is not merely of theoretical interest. His theory produced more realistic narratives *(Mother, Storm over Asia),* with their more deliberate, calmer pace.

Eisenstein, like most of the "first" generation theorists, was uncomfortable with the addition of synchronized dialogue. Because "silent" films had always used asynchronous sound effects and music, Eisenstein believed that the sound film could use these tools with even greater precision and complexity. But he rejected dialogue as being incompatible with the proper use of montage. (See Section III). By contrast André Bazin, a theorist of the "second" generation, while assenting to the incompatibility of dialogue and montage, regards synchronized speech as a necessary and proper development. For Bazin, dialogue returns film to the rightful path from which montage and silence diverted it. According to him, the film image ought to reveal reality whole, not by cutting it into tiny bits. The cinematic method Bazin endorses, which combines composing with the camera and staging an action in front of it, has, like montage, come to be known by a French term, mise-en-scène.

In Bazin's view the montage theorists did not in fact speak for all of the silent film. He discerns in the work of von Stroheim, Murnau, and Flaherty an alternative, mise-en-scène tradition, which emphasizes not the ordering, but the content of images. The film's effect and meaning is not the product of a juxtaposition of images, but is inherent in the visual images themselves. For Bazin, the montage theorists' emphasis on the analogy between word and shot is false, and he rejects it along with their reluctance to employ sound as a source of cinematic meaning. Bazin argues that the mise-en-scène tradition within silent film actually looked toward the incorporation of synchronous sound as a fulfillment, not as a violation, of the film's destiny.

Bazin considers German expressionism and Russian symbolism to have been superseded in the 1930s and 1940s by a form of editing more appropriate to the dialogue film. This "analytic" editing, which characteristically manifests itself in the dramatic technique of shot/reverse shot, was an important innovation. Still more important, however, was the development of the shot-in-depth by Orson Welles and William Wyler in the early 1940s (anticipated in the 1930s by Jean Renoir), which made even the use of "analytic" montage unnecessary. Entire scenes could now be covered in one take, the camera remaining motionless. For Bazin, the shot-in-depth, like the use of synchronous sound, constituted a crucial advance toward total cinema.

Many contemporary film theorists wish to put film theory and criticism on a firmer scientific basis. To consider film as a semiological system would permit film study—which suffers (in the opinion of many besides semiologists) from impressionism, subjectivity, and vagueness—to attain a scientific precision and rigor. In what is in part a revival of Eisenstein's analogy between word and shot, an important development in recent film theory therefore investigates the way images are understood and the way sequences of images can be called a "language." Christian Metz is the most influential spokesman for the view that film does not simply reveal reality. Rather, it constitutes a mode of discourse whose signifying processes must nevertheless be carefully distinguished from those of verbal languages. Using the linguistic science as a model, Metz's goal is to discover and establish the semiotics of the cinema—a theory of cinema as a system of signs.

Metz argues that the concept of a "code," of encoded signs whose meanings we have learned to translate, is central to the development of a theory of film language. In the beginning, film was purely iconic—it signified exclusively by means of the resemblance of its imagery to objects in the visible world. But the development of narrative techniques required the development of various codes to denote the narrative progression. These rules and conventions, which were more or less complete by the time of D. W. Griffith, constitute the essence of film language and permit us to explain the procedures by which cinema denotes such narrative phenomena as successivity, priority, temporal breaks, and spatial continuity. As he shows in his analysis of what he calls the alternating *syntagma,* the order in which the signifying images occur may or may not be the same as that in which the realities they signify occur. The student of the language of cinema must therefore account for the processes and mechanisms which make it possible for the viewer to interpret them correctly. For Metz, film describes reality in a language whose features we are only beginning to understand.

Daniel Dayan views film language from a post-structuralist perspective which goes beyond Metz's earlier, structuralist concept. Using a term drawn from the psychoanalytic theories of Jacques Lacan, Dayan describes the system of the suture which negotiates the viewer's access to the film. In Dayan's view this system, which relates to classical narrative cinema as verbal language does to literature, is ideologically charged. Essential to the system is the shot/reverse shot sequence. The viewer's pleasurable possession of the image, his seeing of the image in shot one, is disrupted by his discovery of the frame and his sense of being dispossessed of what he is prevented from seeing. In the first step of reading the film he discovers that he is authorized to see only what happens to be in the axis of the glance of another spectator, called by Jean-Pierre Oudart "the absent-one." The second shot, the reverse shot of the first, represents the fictional owner of the glance corresponding to the first shot. The reverse shot "sutures" the hole opened in the spectator's imaginary relationship with the filmic field by the perception of the absent one.

The absent one stands for that which any shot necessarily lacks if it is to attain meaning—another shot. For, within the system of the suture, the meaning of a shot depends on the next shot and the pair constitute a cinematic statement. The meaning of the shot is given retrospectively and only in the memory of the spectator. Thus, the system encroaches on the spectator's freedom by interpreting, indeed, by remodeling his memory. According to this deconstructive analysis, the system imposes an ideology and the spectator loses his access to the present. The system of the suture is not, however, the only cinematographic system and Dayan describes how Godard has explored an alternative in his later films.

William Rothman rejects Dayan's assumption of a prior relation in which the viewer "sees" the film image as an unmediated image of reality. He also questions the assumption that classical narrative continuity is illusionistic or necessarily the vehicle of bourgeois ideology. Rothman's critique of Dayan proceeds, however, by a detailed examination of the contention that the "system of the suture" is based on a two-shot (view/viewer) figure: a pair of shots that together constitute a complete cinematographic statement. In Rothman's conception the point-of-view shot is ordinarily part of a three shot (viewer/view/viewer) sequence, typically initiated when, within an "objective" shot, a character visibly attends to something outside the borders of the frame. Accordingly, no ghostly sovereign is invoked by the point-of-view sequence as authorizing the shot. The point-of-view sequence ordinarily manifests the film's power by appropriating a character's gaze without authorization. It does *not* then present a figure and force the viewer to accept it as the source of that power. Thus, the point-of-view sequence in itself does not constitute a lying statement about its own real origin. Indeed, the point-of-view sequence in itself makes no statement about reality—because it makes no statement at all. The sequence is analogous to a sentence, not a statement, and makes no claim that it is true or false. It is the film not the sequence that constitutes the statement—if, indeed, the film makes a statement. According to Rothman what we need is a critical history of the use of cinematic forms, not an a priori demonstration that certain cinematic forms are destined by their nature to serve bourgeois ideology.

According to Kaja Silverman the system of suture should not be too closely identified with the shot/reverse shot formation in which the function of looking is firmly associated with a fictional character. The shot/reverse shot formation is merely one device for encoding anticipation into a film, for directing our attention and our desire beyond the limits of one shot to the next. Narrative represents a much more indispensable part of the system of suture, transforming cinematic into dramatic space and thereby providing the viewer not just with a vantage but with a subject position. In her analysis of Hitchcock's *Psycho* she attempts to show how, by violating the shot/reverse shot convention, Hitchcock throws a much wider net over his audience. He forces the viewing subject to take up residence not only within one of the film's discursive positions (that of victim) but a second (that of sadistic and legalistic voyeur). She contends that the whole operation of suture can be made even more irresistible when the field of the speaking subject is continually implied.

Nick Browne also rejects the adequacy of the shot/reverse shot sequence to account for the operation and effects of classic film style and his more complex rhetorical analysis is meant to contribute to the semiotic study of filmic texts. According to him the system of suture establishes the origin of film imagery by reference to the agency of character (the absent-one) but, surprisingly, does not consider the final agency, the authority of the narrator. The traces of the narrator's action may seem to be effaced by the system as the suture theorists suggest but, in Browne's opinion, such an effect can only be the result of a more general rhetoric. He therefore proposes an account in which the structure of the imagery, whatever its apparent forms of presentation, refers jointly to the action of an implied narrator (who defines his position with respect to the tale by his judgments, including his moral judgments) as well as to the imaginative action occasioned by his placing or being placed by the spectator. The point-of-view of the spectator, in turn, and contrary to the views of Comolli and Baudry, is not centered at a single point of view or at the center of any simply optical system. The way in which we, as spectators, are implicated in the action is as much a matter of our position with respect to the unfolding of events as it is in their representation from a point in space. In Browne's analysis of Ford's *Stagecoach* he shows that, although we see the action with Lucy's eyes and are invited by a set of structures to experience the force and character of that view, we are put in a position finally of having to reject it as a view either that is right or that we must assent to. Even though we have been sutured into that point of view, we are not thereby committed to the ideology enforced by the system of the suture.

VSEVOLOD PUDOVKIN
FROM FILM TECHNIQUE

[ON EDITING]

METHODS OF TREATMENT OF THE MATERIAL
(Structural Editing)

A cinematograph film, and consequently also a scenario, is always divided into a great number of separate pieces (more correctly, it is built out of these pieces). The sum of the shooting-script is divided into sequences, each sequence into scenes, and, finally, the scenes themselves are constructed from a whole series of pieces (script-scenes) shot from various angles. An actual scenario, ready for use in shooting, must take into account this basic property of the film. The scenarist must be able to write his material on paper exactly as it will appear upon the screen, thus giving exactly the content of each shot as well as its position in sequence. The construction of a scene from pieces, a sequence from scenes, and reel from sequences, and so forth, is called *editing*. Editing is one of the most significant instruments of effect possessed by the film technician and, therefore, by the scenarist also. Let us now become acquainted with its methods one by one.

Editing of the Scene

Everyone familiar with a film is familiar with the expression "close-up." The alternating representation of the faces of the characters during a dialogue; the representation of hands, or feet, filling the whole screen—all this is familiar to everyone. But in order to know how properly to use the close-up, one must understand its significance, which is as follows: the close-up directs the attention of the spectator to that detail which is, at the moment, important to the course of the action. For instance, three persons are taking part in a scene. Suppose the significance of this scene consist in the *general* course of the action (if, for example, all three are lifting some heavy object), then they are taken simultaneously in a *general* view, the so-called long-shot. But suppose any one of them change to an independent action having significance in the scenario (for example, separating himself from the others, he draws a revolver cautiously from his pocket), then the camera is directed on him alone. His action is recorded separately.

What is said above applies not only to persons, but also to separate parts of a person, and objects. Let us suppose a man is to be taken apparently listening calmly to the conversation of someone else, but actually restraining his anger with difficulty. The man crushes the cigarette he holds in his hand, a gesture unnoticed by the other. This hand will always be shown on the screen separately, in close-up, otherwise the spectator will not notice it and a characteristic detail will be missed. The view formerly obtained (and is still held by some) that the close-up is an "interruption" of the long-shot. This idea is entirely false. It is no sort of interruption. It represents a proper form of construction.

In order to make clear to oneself the nature of the process of editing a scene, one may draw the following analogy. Imagine yourself observing a scene unfolded in front of you, thus: a man stands near the wall of a house and turns his head to the left; there appears another man slinking cautiously through the gate. The two are fairly widely distant from one another—they stop. The first takes some object and shows it to the other, mocking him. The latter clenches his fists in a rage and throws himself at the former. At this moment a woman looks out of a window on the third floor and calls, "Police!" The antagonists run off in opposite directions. Now, how would this have been observed?

1. The observer looks at the first man. He turns his head.

2. What is he looking at? The observer turns his glance in the same direction and sees the man entering the gate. The latter stops.

3. How does the first react to the appearance on the scene of the second? A new turn by the observer; the first takes out an object and mocks the second.

4. How does the second react? Another turn; he clenches his fists and throws himself on his opponent.

5. The observer draws aside to watch how both opponents roll about fighting.

6. A shout from above. The observer raises his head and sees the woman shouting at the window.

7. The observer lowers his head and sees the result of her warning—the antagonists running off in opposite directions.

The observer happened to be standing near and saw every detail, saw it clearly, but to do so he had to turn his head, first left, then right, then upwards, whithersoever his attention was attracted by the interest of observation and the sequence of the developing scene. Suppose he had been standing farther away from the action, taking in the two persons and the window on the third floor simultaneously, he would have received only a general impression, without being able to look separately at the first, the second, or the woman. Here we have approached closely the basic significance of editing. Its object is the showing of the development of the scene in relief, as it were, by guiding the attention of the spectator now to one, now to the other separate element. The lens of the camera replaces the eye of the observer, and the changes of angle of the camera—directed now on one person, now on another, now on one detail, now on another—must be subject to the same conditions as those of the eyes of the observer. The film technician, in order to secure the greatest clarity, emphasis, and vividness, shoots the scene in separate pieces and, joining them and showing them, directs the attention of the spectator to the separate elements, compelling him to see as the attentive observer saw. From the above is clear the manner in which editing can even work upon the emotions. Imagine to yourself the excited observer of some rapidly developing scene. His agitated glance is thrown rapidly from one spot to another. If we imitate this glance with the camera we get a series of pictures, rapidly alternating pieces, creating a *stirring scenario editing-construction.* The reverse would be long pieces changing by mixes, conditioning a calm and slow editing-construction (as one may shoot, for example, a herd of cattle wandering along a road, taken from the viewpoint of a pedestrian on the same road).

We have established, by these instances, the basic significance of the constructive editing of scenes. It builds the scenes from separate pieces, of which each concentrates the attention of the spectator only on that element important to the action. The sequence of these pieces must not be uncontrolled, but must correspond to the natural transference of attention of an imaginary observer (who, in the end, is represented by the spectator). In this sequence must be expressed a special logic that will be apparent only if each shot contain an impulse towards transference of the attention to the next. For example (1) A man turns his head and looks; (2) What he looks at is shown.

Editing of the Sequence

The guidance of the attention of the spectator to different elements of the developing action in succession is, in general, characteristic of the film. It is its basic method. We have seen that the separate scene, and often even the movement of one man, is built up upon the screen from separate pieces. Now, the film is not simply a collection of different scenes. Just as the pieces are built up into scenes endowed, as it were, with a connected action, so the separate scenes are assembled into groups forming whole sequences. The sequence is constructed (edited) from scenes. Let us suppose ourselves faced with the task of constructing the following sequence: two spies are creeping forward to blow up a powder magazine; on the way one of them loses a letter with instructions. Someone else finds the letter and warns the guard, who appears in time to arrest the spies and save the magazine. Here the scenarist has to deal with simultaneity of various actions in several different places. While the spies are crawling towards the magazine, someone else finds the letter and hastens to warn the guard. The spies have nearly reached their objective; the guards are warned and rushing towards the magazine. The spies have completed their preparations; the guard arrives in time. If we pursue the previous analogy between the camera and an observer, we now not only have to turn it from side to side, but also to move it from place to place. The observer (the camera) is now on the road shadowing the spies, now in the guardroom recording the confusion, now back at the magazine showing the spies at work, and so forth. But, in combination of the separate scenes (editing), the former law of sequence succession remains in force. A consecutive sequence will appear upon the screen only if the attention of the spec-

tator be transferred correctly from scene to scene. And this correctness is conditioned as follows: the spectator sees the creeping spies, the loss of the letter, and
finally the person who finds the letter. The person with the letter rushes for help.
The spectator is seized with inevitable excitement—Will the man who found the
letter be able to forestall the explosion? The scenarist immediately answers by showing the spies nearing the magazine—his answer has the effect of a warning "Time
is short." The excitement of the spectator—Will they be in time?—continues; the
scenarist shows the guard turning out. Time is very short—the spies are shown
beginning their work. Thus, transferring attention now to the rescuers, now to the
spies, the scenarist answers with actual impulses to increase of the spectator's interest, and the construction (editing) of the sequence is correctly achieved.

There is a law in psychology that lays it down that if an emotion give birth to a
certain movement, by imitation of this movement the corresponding emotion can
be called forth. If the scenarist can effect in even rhythm the transference of interest
of the intent spectator, if he can so construct the elements of increasing interest that
the question, "What is happening at the other place?" arises and at the same
moment the spectator is transferred whither he wishes to go, then the editing thus
created can really excite the spectator. One must learn to understand that editing is
in actual fact a compulsory and deliberate guidance of the thoughts and associations of the spectator. If the editing be merely an uncontrolled combination of the
various pieces, the spectator will understand (apprehend) nothing from it; but if it
be co-ordinated according to a definitely selected course of events or conceptual
line, either agitated or calm, it will either excite or soothe the spectator.

Editing of the Scenario

The film is divided into reels. The reels are usually equal in length, on an average
from 900 to 1,200 feet long. The combination of the reels forms the picture. The
usual length of a picture should not be more than from 6,500 to 7,500 feet. This
length, as yet, involves no unnecessary exhaustion of the spectator. The film is usually divided into from six to eight reels. It should be noted here, as a practical hint,
that the average length of a piece (remember the editing of scenes) is from 6 to 10
feet, and consequently from 100 to 150 pieces go to a reel. By orientating himself
on these figures, the scenarist can visualise how much material can be fitted into the
scenario. The scenario is composed of a series of sequences. In discussing the construction (editing) of the scenario from sequences, we introduce a new element into
the scenarist's work—the element of so-called dramatic continuity of action that
was discussed at the beginning of this sketch. The continuity of the separate
sequences when joined together depends not merely upon the simple transference
of attention from one place to another, but is conditioned by the development of
the action forming the foundation of the scenario. It is important, however, to
remind the scenarist of the following point: a scenario has always in its development
a moment of greatest tension, found nearly always at the end of the film. To prepare
the spectator, or, more correctly, preserve him, for this final tension, it is especially
important to see that he is not affected by unnecessary exhaustion during the course
of the film. A method . . . that the scenarist can employ to this end is the careful
distribution of the titles (which always distract the spectator), securing compression

of the greater quantity of them into the first reels, and leaving the last one for uninterrupted action.

Thus, first is worked out the action of the scenario, the action is then worked out into sequences, the sequences into scenes, and these constructed by editing from the pieces, each corresponding to a camera angle.

EDITING AS AN INSTRUMENT OF IMPRESSION
(Relational Editing)

We have already mentioned, in the section on editing of sequences, that editing is not merely a method of the junction of separate scenes or pieces, but is a method that controls the "psychological guidance" of the spectator. We should now acquaint ourselves with the main special editing methods having as their aim the impression of the spectator.

Contrast.—Suppose it be our task to tell of the miserable situation of a starving man; the story will impress the more vividly if associated with mention of the senseless gluttony of a well-to-do man.

On just such a simple contrast relation is based the corresponding editing method. On the screen the impression of this contrast is yet increased, for it is possible not only to relate the starving sequence to the gluttony sequence, but also to relate separate scenes and even separate shots of the scenes to one another, thus, as it were, forcing the spectator to compare the two actions all the time, one strengthening the other. The editing of contrast is one of the most effective, but also one of the commonest and most standardised, of methods, and so care should be taken not to overdo it.

Parallelism.—This method resembles contrast, but is considerably wider. Its substance can be explained more clearly by an example. In a scenario as yet unproduced a section occurs as follows: a working man, one of the leaders of a strike, is condemned to death; the execution is fixed for 5 a.m. The sequence is edited thus: a factory-owner, employer of the condemned man, is leaving a restaurant drunk, he looks at his wrist-watch: 4 o'clock. The accused is shown—he is being made ready to be led out. Again the manufacturer, he rings a door-bell to ask the time: 4.30. The prison waggon drives along the street under heavy guard. The maid who opens the door—the wife of the condemned—is subjected to a sudden senseless assault. The drunken factory-owner snores on a bed, his leg with trouser-end upturned, his hand hanging down with wrist-watch visible, the hands of the watch crawl slowly to 5 o'clock. The workman is being hanged. In this instance two thematically unconnected incidents develop in parallel by means of the watch that tells of the approaching execution. The watch on the wrist of the callous brute, as it were connects him with the chief protagonist of the approaching tragic *dénouement,* thus ever present in the consciousness of the spectator. This is undoubtedly an interesting method, capable of considerable development.

Symbolism.—In the final scenes of the film *Strike* the shooting down of workmen is punctuated by shots of the slaughter of a bull in a stockyard. The scenarist, as it were, desires to say: just as a butcher fells a bull with the swing of a pole-axe, so, cruelly and in cold blood, were shot down the workers. This method is especially interesting because, by means of editing, it introduces an abstract concept into the consciousness of the spectator without use of a title.

Simultaneity.—In American films the final section is constructed from the simultaneous rapid development of two actions, in which the outcome of one depends on the outcome of the other. The end of the present-day section of *Intolerance* . . . is thus constructed. The whole aim of this method is to create in the spectator a maximum tension of excitement by the constant forcing of a question, such as, in this case: Will they be in time?—will they be in time?

The method is a purely emotional one, and nowadays overdone almost to the point of boredom, but it cannot be denied that of all the methods of constructing the end hitherto devised it is the most effective.

Leit-motif (reiteration of theme).—Often it is interesting for the scenarist especially to emphasise the basic theme of the scenario. For this purpose exists the method of reiteration. Its nature can easily be demonstrated by an example. In an anti-religious scenario that aimed at exposing the cruelty and hypocrisy of the Church in employ of the Tsarist régime the same shot was several times repeated: a church-bell slowly ringing and, superimposed on it, the title: "The sound of bells sends into the world a message of patience and love." This piece appeared whenever the scenarist desired to emphasise the stupidity of patience, or the hypocrisy of the love thus preached.

The little that has been said above of relational editing naturally by no means exhausts the whole abundance of its methods. It has merely been important to show that constructional editing, a method specifically and peculiarly filmic, is, in the hands of the scenarist, an important instrument of impression. Careful study of its use in pictures, combined with talent, will undoubtedly lead to the discovery of new possibilities and, in conjunction with them, to the creation of new forms.

1926

SERGEI EISENSTEIN
FROM FILM FORM

THE CINEMATOGRAPHIC PRINCIPLE AND
THE IDEOGRAM

It is a weird and wonderful feat to have written a pamphlet on something that in reality does not exist. There is, for example, no such thing as a cinema without cinematography. And yet the author of the pamphlet preceding this essay* has contrived to write a book about the *cinema* of a country that has no *cinematography*. About the cinema of a country that has, in its culture, an infinite number of cinematographic traits, strewn everywhere with the sole exception of—its cinema.

This essay is on the cinematographic traits of Japanese culture that lie outside the Japanese cinema, and is itself as apart from the preceding pamphlet as these traits are apart from the Japanese cinema.

Cinema is: so many corporations, such and such turnovers of capital, so and so many stars, such and such dramas.

Cinematography is, first and foremost, montage.

The Japanese cinema is excellently equipped with corporations, actors, and stories. But the Japanese cinema is completely unaware of montage. Nevertheless the principle of montage can be identified as the basic element of Japanese representational culture.

Writing—for their writing is primarily representational.

The hieroglyph.

The naturalistic image of an object, as portrayed by the skilful Chinese hand of Ts'ang Chieh 2650 years before our era, becomes slightly formalized and, with its 539 fellows, forms the first "contingent" of hieroglyphs. Scratched out with a stylus

---

*Eisenstein's essay was originally published as an "afterword" to N. Kaufman's pamphlet, *Japanese Cinema* (Moscow, 1929).

on a slip of bamboo, the portrait of an object maintained a resemblance to its original in every respect.

But then, by the end of the third century, the brush is invented. In the first century after the "joyous event" (A.D.)—paper. And, lastly, in the year 220—India ink.

A complete upheaval. A revolution in draughtsmanship. And, after having undergone in the course of history no fewer than fourteen different styles of handwriting, the hieroglyph crystallized in its present form. The means of production (brush and India ink) determined the form.

The fourteen reforms had their way. As a result:

In the fierily cavorting hieroglyph *ma* (a horse) it is already impossible to recognize the features of the dear little horse sagging pathetically in its hindquarters, in the writing style of Ts'ang Chieh, so well-known from ancient Chinese bronzes.

But let it rest in the Lord, this dear little horse, together with the other 607 remaining *hsiang cheng* symbols—the earliest extant category of hieroglyphs.

The real interest begins with the second category of hieroglyphs—the *huei-i,* i.e., "copulative."

The point is that the copulation (perhaps we had better say, the combination) of two hieroglyphs of the simplest series is to be regarded not as their sum, but as their product, i.e., as a value of another dimension, another degree; each, separately, corresponds to an *object,* to a fact, but their combination corresponds to a *concept.* From separate hieroglyphs has been fused—the ideogram. By the combination of two "depictables" is achieved the representation of something that is graphically undepictable.

For example: the picture for water and the picture of an eye signifies "to weep"; the picture of an ear nearing the drawing of

a dog = "to listen";
a dog + a mouth = "to bark";
a mouth + a child = "to scream";
a mouth + a bird = "to sing";
a knife + a heart = "sorrow," and so on.

But this is—montage!

Yes. It is exactly what we do in the cinema, combining shots that are *depictive, single in meaning, neutral in content*—into *intellectual* contexts and series.

This is a means and method inevitable in any cinematographic exposition. And, in a condensed and purified form, the starting point for the "intellectual cinema."

For a cinema seeking a maximum laconism for the visual representation of abstract concepts.

And we hail the method of the long-lamented Ts'ang Chieh as a first step along these paths.

We have mentioned laconism. Laconism furnishes us a transition to another point. Japan possesses the most laconic form of poetry: the *haikai* (appearing at the beginning of the thirteenth century and known today as "haiku" or "hokku") and the even earlier *tanka* (mythologically assumed to have been created along with heaven and earth).

Both are little more than hieroglyphs transposed into phrases. So much so that half their quality is appraised by their calligraphy. The method of their resolution is completely analogous to the structure of the ideogram.

As the ideogram provides a means for the laconic imprinting of an abstract concept, the same method, when transposed into literary exposition, gives rise to an identical laconism of pointed imagery.

Applied to the collision of an austere combination of symbols this method results in a dry definition of abstract concepts. The same method, expanded into the luxury of a group of already formed verbal combinations, swells into a splendor of *imagist* effect.

The concept is a bare formula; its adornment (an expansion by additional material) transforms the formula into an image—a finished form.

Exactly, though in reverse, as a primitive thought process—imagist thinking, displaced to a definite degree, becomes transformed to conceptual thinking.

But let us turn to examples.

The *haiku* is a concentrated impressionist sketch:

> A lonely crow
>   On leafless bough,
>   One autumn eve.
> > > BASHO

> What a resplendent moon!
>   It casts the shadow of pine boughs
>   Upon the mats.
> > > KIKAKU

> An evening breeze blows.
>   The water ripples
>   Against the blue heron's legs.
> > > BUSON

> It is early dawn.
> The castle is surrounded
> By the cries of wild ducks.
>
> KYOROKU

The earlier *tanka* is slightly longer (by two lines):

> O mountain pheasant
> long are the feathers trail'st thou
> on the wooded hill-side—
> as long the nights seem to me
> on lonely couch sleep seeking.
>
> HITOMARO[?]

From our point of view, these are montage phrases. Shot lists. The simple combination of two or three details of a material kind yields a perfectly finished representation of another kind—psychological.

And if the finely ground edges of the intellectually defined concepts formed by the combined ideograms are blurred in these poems, yet, in *emotional quality,* the concepts have blossomed forth immeasurably. We should observe that the emotion is directed towards the reader, for, as Yone Nobuchi has said, "it is the readers who make the *haiku's* imperfection a perfection of art."

It is uncertain in Japanese writing whether its predominating aspect is as a system of characters (denotative), or as an independent creation of graphics (depictive). In any case, born of the dual mating of the depictive by method, and the denotative by purpose, the ideogram continued both these lines (not consecutive historically but consecutive in principle in the minds of those developing the method).

Not only did the denotative line continue into literature, in the *tanka*, as we have shown, but exactly the same method (in its depictive aspect) operates also in the most perfect examples of Japanese pictorial art.

Sharaku—creator of the finest prints of the eighteenth century, and especially of an immortal gallery of actors' portraits. The Japanese Daumier. Despite this, almost unknown to us. The characteristic traits of his work have been analyzed only in our century. One of these critics, Julius Kurth, in discussing the question of the influence on Sharaku of sculpture, draws a parallel between his wood-cut portrait of the actor Nakayama Tomisaburō and an antique mask of the semi-religious Nō theater, the mask of a Rozo.

The faces of both the print and the mask wear an *identical expression*. . . . Features and masses are similarly arranged although the mask represents an old priest, and the print a young woman. This relationship is striking, yet these two works are otherwise totally dissimilar; this in itself is a demonstration of Sharaku's originality. While the carved mask was constructed according to fairly accurate anatomical proportions, the proportions of the portrait print are simply impossible. The space between the eyes comprises a width that makes mock of all good sense. The nose is almost twice as long in relation to the eyes as any normal nose would dare to be, and the chin stands in no sort of relation to the mouth; the brows, the mouth, and every feature—is hopelessly misrelated. *This observation may be made in all the large heads by Sharaku.* That the artist was unaware that all these proportions are false is, of course, out of the question. It was with a full awareness that he repudiated normalcy, and, while the drawing of the separate features depends on severely concentrated naturalism, their proportions have been subordinated to purely intellectual considerations. *He set up the essence of the psychic expression as the norm for the proportions of the single features.*

Is not this process that of the ideogram, combining the independent "mouth" and the dissociated symbol of "child" to form the significance of "scream"?

Is this not exactly what we of the cinema do temporally, just as Sharaku in simultaneity, when we cause a monstrous disproportion of the parts of a normally flowing event, and suddenly dismember the event into "close-up" of clutching hands," "medium shots of the struggle," and "extreme close-up of bulging eyes," in making a montage disintegration of the event in various planes? In making an eye twice as large as a man's full figure?! By combining these monstrous incongruities we newly collect the disintegrated event into one whole, but in *our* aspect. According to the treatment of our relation to the event.

The disproportionate depiction of an event is organically natural to us from the beginning. Professor Luriya, of the Psychological Institute in Moscow, has shown me a drawing by a child of "lighting a stove." Everything is represented in passably accurate relationship and with great care. Firewood. Stove. Chimney. But what are those zigzags in that huge central rectangle? They turn out to be—matches. Taking into account the crucial importance of these matches for the depicted process, the child provides a proper scale for them.*

The representation of objects in the actual (absolute) proportions proper to them is, of course, merely a tribute to orthodox formal logic. A subordination to an inviolable order of things.

Both in painting and sculpture there is a periodic and invariable return to periods

---

*It is possible to trace this particular tendency from its ancient, almost prehistorical source (". . . in all ideational art, objects are given size according to their importance, the king being twice as large as his subjects, or a tree half the size of a man when it merely informs us that the scene is out-of-doors. Something of this principle of size according to significance persisted in the Chinese tradition. The favorite disciple of Confucius looked like a little boy beside him and the most important figure in any group was usually the largest." [George Rowley, *Principles of Chinese Painting*. Princeton University Press, 1947, p. 56.]) through the highest development of Chinese art, parent of Japanese graphic arts: ". . . natural scale always had to bow to pictorial scale . . . size according to distance never followed the laws of geometric perspective but the needs of the design. Foreground features might be diminished to avoid obstruction and overemphasis, and far distant objects, which were too minute to count pictorially, might be enlarged to act as a counterpoint to the middle distance or foreground." [Rowley, p. 66.]

of the establishment of absolutism. Displacing the expressiveness of archaic dispro-portion for regulated "stone tables" of officially decreed harmony.

Absolute realism is by no means the correct form of perception. It is simply the function of a certain form of social structure. Following a state monarchy, a state uniformity of thought is implanted. Ideological uniformity of a sort that can be developed pictorially in the ranks of colors and designs of the Guards regiments . . .

Thus we have seen how the principle of the hieroglyph—"denotation by depic-tion"—split in two: along the line of its purpose (the principle of "denotation"), into the principles of creating literary imagery; along the line of its method of real-izing this purpose (the principle of "depiction"), into the striking methods of expressiveness used by Sharaku.*

And, just as the two outspreading wings of a hyperbola meet, as we say, at infinity (though no one has visited so distant a region!), so the principle of hieroglyphics, infinitely splitting into two parts (in accordance with the function of symbols), unexpectedly unites again from this dual estrangement, in yet a fourth sphere—in the theater.

Estranged for so long, they are once again—in the cradle period of the drama—present in a *parallel* form, in a curious dualism.

The *significance* (denotation) of the action is effected by the reciting of the *Jōruri* by a voice behind the stage—the *representation* (depiction) of the action is effected by silent marionettes on the stage. Along with a specific manner of movement this archaism migrated into the early Kabuki theater, as well. To this day it is preserved, as a partial method, in the classical repertory (where certain parts of the action are narrated from behind the stage while the actor mimes).

But this is not the point. The most important fact is that into the technique of acting itself the ideographic (montage) method has been wedged in the most inter-esting ways.

However, before discussing this, let us be allowed the luxury of a digression—on the matter of the shot, to settle the debated question of its nature, once and for all.

A shot. A single piece of celluloid. A tiny rectangular frame in which there is, organized in some way, a piece of an event.

"Cemented together, these shots form montage. When this is done in an appro-priate rhythm, *of course!"*

This, roughly, is what is taught by the old, old school of film-making, that sang:

> "Screw by screw,
> Brick by brick . . ."

Kuleshov, for example, even writes with a brick:

If you have an idea-phrase, a particle of the story, a link in the whole dramatic chain, then that idea is to be expressed and accumulated from shot-ciphers, just like bricks.

"The shot is an element of montage. Montage is an assembly of these elements."
This is a most pernicious make-shift analysis.

---

*It has been left to James Joyce to develop in *literature* the depictive line of the Japanese hier-oglyph. Every word of Kurth's analysis of Sharaku may be applied, neatly and easily, to Joyce.

Here the understanding of the process as a whole (connection, shot-montage) derives only from the external indications of its flow (a piece cemented to another piece). Thus it would be possible, for instance, to arrive at the well-known conclusion that street-cars exist in order to be laid across streets. An entirely logical deduction, if one limits oneself to the external indications of the functions they performed during the street-fighting of February 1917, here in Russia. But the materialist conception of history interprets it otherwise.

The worst of it is that an approach of this kind does actually lie, like an insurmountable street-car, across the potentialities of formal development. Such an approach overrules dialectical development, and dooms one to mere evolutionary "perfecting," in so far as it gives no bite into the dialectical substance of events.

In the long run, such evolutionizing leads either through refinement to decadence or, on the other hand, to a simple withering away due to stagnation of the blood.

Strange as it may seem, a melodious witness to both these distressing eventualities, simultaneously, is Kuleshov's latest film, *The Gay Canary* [1929].

The shot is by no means an *element* of montage.

The shot is a montage *cell.*

Just as cells in their division form a phenomenon of another order, the organism or embryo, so, on the other side of the dialectical leap from the shot, there is montage.

By what, then, is montage characterized and, consequently, its cell—the shot?

By collision. By the conflict of two pieces in opposition to each other. By conflict. By collision.

In front of me lies a crumpled yellowed sheet of paper. On it is a mysterious note: "Linkage—P" and "Collision—E."

This is a substantial trace of a heated bout on the subject of montage between P (Pudovkin) and E (myself).

This has become a habit. At regular intervals he visits me late at night and behind closed doors we wrangle over matters of principle. A graduate of the Kuleshov school, he loudly defends an understanding of montage as a *linkage* of pieces. Into a chain. Again, "bricks." Bricks, arranged in series to *expound* an idea.

I confronted him with my viewpoint on montage as a *collision.* A view that from the collision of two given factors *arises* a concept.

From my point of view, linkage is merely a possible *special* case.

Recall what an infinite number of combinations is known in physics to be capable of arising from the impact (collision) of spheres. Depending on whether the spheres be resilient, non-resilient, or mingled. Amongst all these combinations there is one in which the impact is so weak that the collision is degraded to an even movement of both in the same direction.

This is the one combination which would correspond with Pudovkin's view.

Not long ago we had another talk. Today he agrees with my point of view. True, during the interval he took the opportunity to acquaint himself with the series of lectures I gave during that period at the State Cinema Institute. . . .

So, montage is conflict.

As the basis of every art is conflict (an "imagist" transformation of the dialectical principle). The shot appears as the *cell* of montage. Therefore it also must be considered from the viewpoint of *conflict.*

Conflict within the shot is potential montage, in the development of its intensity shattering the quadrilateral cage of the shot and exploding its conflict into montage impulses *between* the montage pieces. As, in a zigzag of mimicry, the *mise-en-scéne* splashes out into a spatial zigzag with the *same* shattering. As the slogan, "All obstacles are vain before Russians," bursts out in the multitude of incident of *War and Peace.*

If montage is to be compared with something, then a phalanx of montage pieces, of shots, should be compared to the series of explosions of an internal combustion engine, driving forward its automobile or tractor: for, similarly, the dynamics of montage serve as impulses driving forward the total film.

Conflict within the frame. This can be very varied in character: it even can be a conflict in—the story. As in that "prehistoric" period in films (although there are plenty of instances in the present, as well), when entire scenes would be photographed in a single, uncut shot. This, however, is outside the strict jurisdiction of the film-form.

These are the "cinematographic" conflicts within the frame: *Conflict of graphic directions.*

(Lines—either static or dynamic)

Conflict of scales.
Conflict of volumes.
Conflict of masses.

(Volumes filled with various intensities of light)

Conflict of depths.

And the following conflicts, requiring only one further impulse of intensification before flying into antagonistic pairs of pieces:

Close shots and long shots.

Pieces of graphically varied directions. Pieces resolved in volume, with pieces resolved in area.

Pieces of darkness and pieces of lightness.

And, lastly, there are such unexpected conflicts as:

Conflicts between an object and its dimension—and conflicts between an event and its duration.

These may sound strange, but both are familiar to us. The first is accomplished by an optically distorted lens, and the second by stop-motion or slow-motion.

The compression of all cinematographic factors and properties within a single dialectical formula of conflict is no empty rhetorical diversion.

We are now seeking a unified system for methods of cinematographic expressiveness that shall hold good for all its elements. The assembly of these into series of common indications will solve the task as a whole.

Experience in the separate elements of the cinema cannot be absolutely measured.

Whereas we know a good deal about montage, in the theory of the shot we are still floundering about amidst the most academic attitudes, some vague tentatives, and the sort of harsh radicalism that sets one's teeth on edge.

To regard the frame as a particular, as it were, molecular case of montage makes possible the direct application of montage practice to the theory of the shot.

And similarly with the theory of lighting. To sense this as a collision between a stream of light and an obstacle, like the impact of a stream from a fire-hose striking a concrete object, or of the wind buffeting a human figure, must result in a usage of light entirely different in comprehension from that employed in playing with various combinations of "gauzes" and "spots."

Thus far we have one such significant principle of conflict: *the principle of optical counterpoint.*

And let us not now forget that soon we shall face another and less simple problem in counterpoint: *the conflict in the sound film of acoustics and optics.*

Let us return to one of the most fascinating of optical conflicts: the conflict between the frame of the shot and the object!

The camera position, as a materialization of the conflict between organizing logic of the director and the inert logic of the object, in collision, reflects the dialectic of the camera-angle.

In this matter we are still impressionistic and lacking in principle to a sickening degree. Nevertheless, a sharpness of principle can be had in the technique of this, too. The dry quadrilateral, plunging into the hazards of nature's diffuseness . . .

And once again we are in Japan! For the cinematographic method is used in teaching drawing in Japanese schools.

What is our method of teaching drawing? Take any piece of white paper with four corners to it. Then cram onto it, usually even without using the edges (mostly greasy from the long drudgery!), some bored caryatid, some conceited Corinthian capital, or a plaster Dante (not the magician performing at the Moscow Hermitage, but the other one—Alighieri, the comedy writer).

The Japanese approach this from a quite different direction: Here's the branch of a cherry-tree. And the pupils cuts out from this whole, with a square, and a circle, and a rectangle—compositional units:

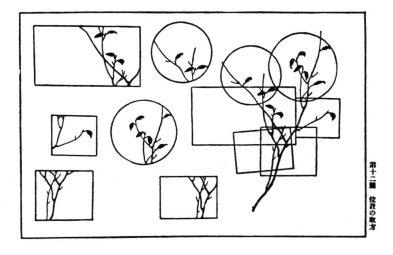

He frames a shot!

These two ways of teaching drawing can characterize the two basic tendencies struggling within the cinema of today. One—the expiring method of artificial spatial organization of an event in front of the lens. From the "direction" of a sequence, to the erection of a Tower of Babel in front of the lens. The other—a "picking-out" by the camera: organization by means of the camera. Hewing out a piece of actuality with the ax of the lens.

However, at the present moment, when the center of attention of finally beginning, in the intellectual cinema, to be transferred from the materials of cinema, as such, to "deductions and conclusions," to "slogans" based on the material, both schools of thought are losing distinction in their differences and can quickly blend into a synthesis.

Several pages back we lost, like an overshoe in a street-car, the question of the theater. Let us turn back to the question of methods of montage in the Japanese theater, particularly in acting.

The first and most striking example, of course, is the purely cinematographic method of "acting without transitions." Along with mimic transitions carried to a limit of refinement, the Japanese actor uses an exactly contrary method as well. At a certain moment of his performance he halts; the black-shrouded *kurogo* obligingly conceals him from the spectators. And lo!—he is resurrected in a new make-up. And in a new wig. Now characterizing another stage (degree) of his emotional state.

Thus, for example, in the Kabuki play *Narukami,* the actor Sadanji must change from drunkenness to madness. This transition is solved by a mechanical cut. And a change in the arsenal of grease-paint colors on his face, emphasizing those streaks whose duty it is to fulfill the expression of a higher intensity than those used in his previous make-up.

This method is organic to the film. The forced introduction into the film, by European acting traditions, of pieces of "emotional transitions" is yet another influence forcing the cinema to mark time. Whereas the method of "cut" acting makes possible the construction of entirely new methods. Replacing one changing face with a whole scale of facial types of varying moods affords a far more acutely expressive result than does the changing surface, too receptive and devoid of organic resistance, of any single professional actor's face.

In our new film [*Old and New*] I have eliminated the intervals between the sharply contrasting polar stages of a face's expression. Thus is achieved a greater sharpness in the "play of doubts" around the new cream separator. Will the milk thicken or no? Wealth? Here the psychological process of mingled faith and doubt is broken up into its two extreme states of joy (confidence) and gloom (disillusionment). Furthermore, this is sharply emphasized by light—illumination in no wise conforming to actual light conditions. This brings a distinct strengthening of the tension.

Another remarkable characteristic of the Kabuki theater is the principle of "disintegrated" acting. Shocho, who played the leading female rôles in the Kabuki theater that visited Moscow, in depicting the dying daughter in *Yashaō (The Mask-Maker)*, performed his rôle in pieces of acting completely detached from each other: Acting with only the right arm. Acting with one leg. Acting with the neck and head only. (The whole process of the death agony was disintegrated into solo performances of each member playing its own rôle: the rôle of the leg, the rôle of the arms, the rôle of the head.) A breaking-up into shots. With a gradual shortening of these separate, successive pieces of acting as the tragic end approached.

Freed from the yoke of primitive naturalism, the actor is enabled by this method to fully grip the spectator by "rhythms," making not only acceptable, but definitely attractive, a stage built on the most consecutive and detailed flesh and blood of naturalism.

Since we no longer distinguish in principle between questions of shot-content and montage, we may here cite a third example:

The Japanese theater makes use of a slow tempo to a degree unknown to our stage. The famous scene of hara-kiri in *Chushingura* is based on an unprecedented slowing down of all movement—beyond any point we have ever seen. Whereas, in the previous example, we observed a disintegration of the transitions between movements, here we see disintegration of the process of movement, viz., slow-motion. I have heard of only one example of a thorough application of this method, using the technical possibility of the film with a compositionally reasoned plan. It is usually employed with some purely pictorial aim, such as the "submarine kingdom" in *The Thief of Bagdad,* or to represent a dream, as in *Zvenigora.* Or, more often, it is used simply for formalist jackstraws and unmotivated camera mischief as in Vertov's *Man with the Movie-Camera.* The more commendable example appears to be in Jean Epstein's *La chute de la Maison Usher*—at least according to the press reports. In this film, normally acted emotions filmed with a speeded-up camera are said to give unusual emotional pressure by their unrealistic slowness on the screen. If it be borne in mind that the effect of an actor's performance on the audience is based on its identification by each spectator, it will be easy to relate both examples (the Kabuki play and the Epstein film) to an identical causal explanation. The intensity of perception increases as the didactic process of identification proceeds more easily along a disintegrated action.

Even instruction in handling a rifle can be hammered into the tightest motor-mentality among a group of raw recruits if the instructor uses a "break-down" method.

The most interesting link of the Japanese theater is, of course, its link with the sound film, which can and must learn its fundamentals from the Japanese—the reduction of visual and aural sensations to a common physiological denominator.

So, it has been possible to establish (cursorily) the permeation of the most varied branches of Japanese culture by a pure cinematographic element—its basic nerve, montage.

And it is only the Japanese cinema that falls into the same error as the "leftward drifting" Kabuki. Instead of learning how to extract the principles and technique of their remarkable acting from the traditional feudal forms of their materials, the most progressive leaders of the Japanese theater throw their energies into an adaptation of the spongy shapelessness of our own "inner" naturalism. The results are tearful and saddening. In its cinema Japan similarly pursues imitations of the most revolting examples of American and European entries in the international commercial film race.

To understand and apply her cultural peculiarities to the cinema, this is the task of Japan! Colleagues of Japan, are you really going to leave this for us to do?

1929

A DIALECTIC APPROACH TO FILM FORM

In nature we never see anything isolated, but everything in connection with something else which is before it, beside it, under it, and over it.

GOETHE

According to Marx and Engels the dialectic system is only the conscious reproduction of the dialectic course (substance) of the external events of the world.

Thus:

The projection of the dialectic system of things
into the brain
into creating abstractly
into the process of thinking
yields: dialectic methods of thinking;
dialectic materialism—   PHILOSOPHY.

And also:

The projection of the same system of things
while creating concretely
while giving form
yields: ART.

The foundation for this philosophy is a *dynamic* concept of things:

Being—as a constant evolution from the interaction of two contradictory opposites.

Synthesis—arising from the opposition between thesis and antithesis.

A dynamic comprehension of things is also basic to the same degree, for a correct understanding of art and of all art-forms. In the realm of art this dialectic principle of dynamics is embodied in

CONFLICT

as the fundamental principle for the existence of every artwork and every art-form.
For art is always conflict:
(1) according to its social mission,
(2) according to its nature,
(3) according to its methodology.

According to its social mission *because:* It is art's task to make manifest the contradictions of Being. To form equitable views by stirring up contradictions within the spectator's mind, and to forge accurate intellectual concepts from the dynamic clash of opposing passions.

According to its nature *because:* Its nature is a conflict between natural existence and creative tendency. Between organic inertia and purposeful initiative. Hypertrophy of the purposive initiative—the principles of rational logic—ossifies art into mathematical technicalism. (A painted landscape becomes a topographical map, a painted Saint Sebastian becomes an anatomical chart.) Hypertrophy of organic naturalness—of organic logic— dilutes art into formlessness. (A Malevich becomes a Kaulbach, an Archipenko becomes a wax-works side-show.)

Because the limit of organic form (the passive principle of being) is *Nature.* The limit of rational form (the active principle of production) is *Industry.* At the intersection of Nature and Industry stands *Art.*

The logic of organic form *vs.* the logic of rational form yields, in collision,

the dialectic of the art-form.

The interaction of the two produces and determines Dynamism. (Not only in the sense of a space-time continuum, but also in the field of absolute thinking. I also regard the inception of new concepts and viewpoints in the conflict between customary conception and particular representation as dynamic—as a dynamization of the inertia of perception—as a dynamization of the "traditional view" into a new one.)

The quantity of interval determines the pressure of the tension. (See in music, for example, the concept of intervals. There can be cases where the distance of separation is so wide that it leads to a break—to a collapse of the homogeneous concept of art. For instance, the "inaudibility" of certain intervals.)

The spatial form of this dynamism is expression.
The phrases of its tension: rhythm.

This is true for every art-form, and, indeed, for every kind of expression.

Similarly, human expression is a conflict between conditioned and unconditioned reflexes. (In this I cannot agree with Klages, who, *a*) does not consider human expression dynamically as a process, but statically as a result, and who, *b*) attributes everything in motion to the field of the "soul," and only the hindering element to "reason." ["Reason" and "Soul" of the idealistic concept here correspond remotely with the ideas of conditioned and unconditioned reflexes.])

This is true in every field that can be understood as an art. For example, logical thought, considered as an art, shows the same dynamic mechanism:

... the intellectual lives of Plato or Dante or Spinoza or Newton were largely guided and sustained by their delight in the sheer beauty of the rhythmic relation between law and instance, species and individual, or cause and effect.

This holds in other fields, as well, e.g., in speech, where all its sap, vitality, and dynamism arise from the irregularity of the part in relation to the laws of the system as a whole.

In contrast we can observe the sterility of expression in such artificial, totally regulated languages as Esperanto.

It is from this principle that the whole charm of poetry derives. Its rhythm arises as a conflict between the metric measure employed and the distribution of accents, over-riding this measure.

The concept of a formally static phenomenon as a dynamic function is dialectically imaged in the wise words of Goethe:

> *Die Baukunst ist eine ertarrte Musik.*
> (Architecture is frozen music.)

Just as in the case of a homogeneous ideology (a monistic viewpoint), the whole, as well as the least detail, must be penetrated by a sole principle. So, ranged alongside the conflict of *social conditionality,* and the conflict of *existing nature,* the *methodology* of an art reveals this same principle of conflict. As the basic principle of the rhythm to be created and the inception of the art-form.

Art is always conflict, according to its methodology.

Here we shall consider the general problem of art in the specific example of its highest form—film.

Shot and montage are the basic elements of cinema.

Montage

has been established by the Soviet film as the nerve of cinema.

To determine the nature of montage is to solve the specific problem of cinema. The earliest conscious film-makers, and our first film theoreticians, regarded montage as a means of description by placing single shots one after the other like building-blocks. The movement within these building-block shots, and the consequent length of the component pieces, was then considered as rhythm.

A completely false concept!

This would mean the defining of a given object solely in relation to the nature of its external course. The mechanical process of splicing would be made a principle. We cannot describe such a relationship of lengths as rhythm. From this comes metric rather than rhythmic relationships, as opposed to one another as the mechanical-metric system of Mensendieck is to the organic-rhythmic school of Bode in matters of body exercise.

According to this definition, shared even by Pudovkin as a theoretician, montage is the means of *unrolling* an idea with the help of single shots: the "epic" principle.

In my opinion, however, montage is an idea that arises from the collision of independent shots—shots even opposite to one another: the "dramatic" principle.*

A sophism? Certainly not. For we are seeking a definition of the whole nature, the principal style and spirit of cinema from its technical (optical) basis.

We know that the phenomenon of movement in film resides in the fact that two

---

* "Epic" and "dramatic" are used here in regard to methodology of form—not to *content* or *plot!*

motionless images of a moving body, following one another, blend into an appearance of motion by showing them sequentially at a required speed.

This popularized description of what happens as a *blending* has its share of responsibility for the popular miscomprehension of the nature of montage that we have quoted above.

Let us examine more exactly the course of the phenomenon we are discussing—how it really occurs—and draw our conclusion from this. Placed next to each other, two photographed immobile images result in the appearance of movement. Is this accurate? Pictorially—and phraseologically, yes.

But mechanically, it is not. For, in fact, each sequential element is perceived not *next* to the other, but on *top* of the other. For the idea (or sensation) of movement arises from the process of superimposing on the retained impression of the object's first position, a newly visible further position of the object. This is, by the way, the reason for the phenomenon of spatial depth, in the optical superimposition of two planes in stereoscopy. From the superimposition of two elements of the same dimension always arises a new, higher dimension. In the case of stereoscopy the superimposition of two nonidentical two-dimensionalities results in stereoscopic three-dimensionality.

In another field; a concrete word (a denotation) set beside a concrete word yields an abstract concept—as in the Chinese and Japanese languages,* where a material ideogram can indicate a transcendental (conceptual) result.

The incongruence in contour of the first picture—already impressed on the mind—with the subsequently perceived second picture engenders, in conflict, the feeling of motion. Degree of incongruence determines intensity of impression, and determines that tension which becomes the real element of authentic rhythm.

Here we have, temporally, what we see arising spatially on a graphic or painted plane.

What comprises the dynamic effect of a painting? The eye follows the direction of an element in the painting. It retains a visual impression, which then collides with the impression derived from following the direction of a second element. The conflict of these directions forms the dynamic effect in apprehending the whole.

I. It may be purely linear: Fernand Léger, or Suprematism.

II. It may be "anecdotal." The secret of the marvelous mobility of Daumier's and Lautrec's figures dwells in the fact that the various anatomical parts of a body are represented in spatial circumstances (positions) that are temporally various, disjunctive. For example, in Toulouse-Lautrec's lithograph of Miss Cissy Loftus, if one logically develops position A of the foot, one builds a body in position A corresponding to it. But the body is represented from knee up already in position A + a. The cinematic effect of joined motionless pictures is already established here! From hips to shoulders we can see A + a + a. The figures comes alive and kicking!

III. Between I and II lies primitive Italian futurism—such as in Balla's "Man with Six Legs in Six Positions"—for II obtains its effect by retaining natural unity and

---

*See discussion in preceding essay.

anatomical correctness, while I, on the other hand, does this with purely elementary elements. III, although destroying naturalness, has not yet pressed forward to abstraction.

IV. The conflict of directions may also be of an ideographic kind. It was in this way that we have gained the pregnant characterizations of a Sharaku, for example. The secret of his extremely perfected strength of expression lies in the anatomical and *spatial disproportion* of the parts—in comparison with which, our I might be termed *temporal disproportion.*

Generally termed "irregularity," this *spatial disproportion* has been a constant attraction and instrument for artists. In writing of Rodin's drawings, Camille Mauclair indicated one explanation for this search:

> The greatest artists, Michelangelo, Rembrandt, Delacroix, all, at a certain moment of the upthrusting of their genius, threw aside, as it were, the ballast of exactitude as conceived by our simplifying reason and our ordinary eyes, in order to attain the fixation of ideas, the synthesis, the *pictorial handwriting* of their dreams.

Two experimental artists of the nineteenth century—a painter and a poet— attempted esthetic formulations of this "irregularity." Renoir advanced this thesis:

> Beauty of every description finds its charm in variety. Nature abhors both vacuum and regularity. For the same reason, no work of art can really be called such if it has not been created by an artist who believes in irregularity and rejects any set form. Regularity, order, desire for perfection (which is always a false perfection) destroy art. The only possibility of maintaining taste in art is to impress on artists and the public the importance of irregularity. Irregularity is the basis of all art.

And Baudelaire wrote in his journal:

> That which is not slightly distorted lacks sensible appeal; from which it follows that irregularity—that is to say, the unexpected, surprise and astonishment, are an essential part and characteristic of beauty.

Upon closer examination of the particular beauty of irregularity as employed in painting, whether by Grünewald or by Renoir, it will be seen that it is a disproportion in the relation of a detail in one dimension to another detail in a different dimension.

The spatial development of the relative size of one detail in correspondence with another, and the consequent collision between the proportions designed by the artist for that purpose, result in a characterization—a definition of the represented matter.

Finally, color. Any shade of a color imparts to our vision a given rhythm of vibration. This is not said figuratively, but purely physiologically, for colors are distinguished from one another by their number of light vibrations.

The adjacent shade or tone of color is in another rate of vibration. The counterpoint (conflict) of the two—the retained rate of vibration against the newly perceived one—yields the dynamism of our apprehension of the interplay of color.

Hence, with only one step from visual vibrations to acoustic vibrations, we find ourselves in the field of music. From the domain of the spatial-pictorial—to the domain of the temporal-pictorial—where the same law rules. For counterpoint is to music not only a form of composition, but is altogether the basic factor for the possibility of tone perception and tone differentiation.

It may almost be said that in every case we have cited we have seen in operation the same *Principle of Comparison* that makes possible for us perception and definition in every field.

In the moving image (cinema) we have, so to speak, a synthesis of two counterpoints—the spatial counterpoint of graphic art, and the temporal counterpoint of music.

Within cinema, and characterizing it, occurs what may be described as:

visual counterpoint

In applying this concept to the film, we gain several leads to the problem of film grammar. As well as a *syntax* of film manifestations, in which visual counterpoint may determine a whole new system of forms of manifestation.

For all this, the *basic premise* is:

The shot is by no means an element of montage.
The shot is a montage cell (molecule).

In this formulation the dualistic division of

Sub-title and shot
and
Shot and montage

leaps forward in analysis to a dialectic consideration as three different phases of one homogeneous task of expression, its homogeneous characteristics determining the homogeneity of their structural laws.

Inter-relation of the three phases:

Conflict within a thesis (an abstract idea)—*formulates* itself in the dialectics of the sub-title—*forms* itself spatially in the conflict within the shot—and *explodes* with increasing intensity in montage-conflict among the separate shots.

This is fully analogous to human, psychological expression. This is a conflict of motives, which can also be comprehended in three phases:

1. Purely verbal utterance. Without intonation—expression in speech.

2. Gesticulatory (mimic-intonational) expression. Projection of the conflict onto the whole expressive bodily system of man. Gesture of bodily movement and gesture of intonation.

3. Projection of the conflict into space. With an intensification of motives, the zigzag of mimic expression is propelled into the surrounding space following the same formula of distortion. A zigzag of expression arising from the spatial division caused by man moving in space. *Mise-en-scène.*

This gives us the basis for an entirely new understanding of the problem of film form.

We can list, as examples of types of conflicts within the form—characteristic for the conflict within the shot, as well as for the conflict between colliding shots, or, montage:

1. Graphic conflict.
2. Conflict of planes.
3. Conflict of volumes.
4. Spatial conflict.
5. Light conflict.
6. Tempo conflict, and so on.

Nota bene: This list of principal features, of *dominants.* It is naturally understood that they occur chiefly as complexes.

For a transition to montage, it will be sufficient to divide any example into two independent primary pieces, as in the case of graphic conflict, although all other cases can be similarly divided:

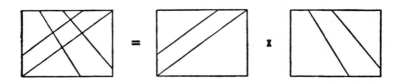

Some further examples:

7. Conflict between matter and viewpoint (achieved by spatial distortion through camera-angle).
8. Conflict between matter and its spatial nature (achieved by *optical distortion* by the lens).
9. Conflict between an event and its temporal nature (achieved by *slow-motion* and *stop-motion*)

and finally

10. Conflict between the whole *optical* complex and a quite different sphere.

Thus does conflict between optical an acoustical experience produce:
sound-film,

which is capable of being realized as
audio-visual counterpoint.

Formulation and investigation of the phenomenon of cinema as forms of conflict yield the first possibility of devising a homogeneous system of *visual dramaturgy* for all general and particular cases of the film problem.

Of devising a *dramaturgy of the visual film-form* as regulated and precise as the existing *dramaturgy of the film-story.*

From this viewpoint on the film medium, the following forms and potentialities of style may be summed up as a film syntax, or it may be more exact to describe the following as:
a tentative film-syntax.

We shall list here a number of potentialities of dialectical development to be derived from this proposition: The concept of the moving (time-consuming) image arises from the superimposition—or counterpoint—of two differing immobile images.

I. Each *moving fragment of montage*. Each photographed piece. Technical definition of the phenomenon of movement. *No composition as yet.* (A running man. A rifle fired. A splash of water.)

II. *An artificially produced image of motion.* The basic optical element is used for deliberate compositions:

   A. Logical

   Example 1 (from *October*): a montage rendition of a machine-gun being fired, by cross-cutting details of the firing.
   Combination A: a brightly lit machine-gun. A different shot in a low key. Double burst: graphic burst + light burst. Closeup of machine-gunner.
   Combination B: Effect almost of double exposure achieved by *clatter* montage effect. Length of montage pieces—two frames each.

Example 2 (from *Potemkin*): an illustration of instantaneous action. Woman with pince-nez. Followed immediately—without transition—by the same woman with shattered pince-nez and bleeding eye: impression of a shot hitting the eye.

B. Illogical

Example 3 (from *Potemkin*): the same devise used for pictorial symbolism. In the thunder of the *Potemkin's* guns, a marble lion leaps up, in protest against the bloodshed on the Odessa steps. Composed of three shots of three stationary marble lions at the Alupka Palace in the Crimea: a sleeping lion, an awakening lion, a rising lion. The effect is achieved by a correct calculation of the length of the second shot. Its superimposition on the first shot produces the first action. This establishes time to impress the second position on the mind. Superimposition of the third position on the second produces the second action: the lion finally rises.

Example 4 (from *October*): Example 1 showed how the firing was manufactured symbolically from elements outside the process of firing itself. In illustrating the monarchist *putsch* attempted by General Kornilov, it occurred to me that his militarist *tendency* could be shown in a montage that would employ religious details for its material. For Kornilov had revealed his intention in the guise of a peculiar "Crusade" of Moslems (!), his Caucasian "Wild Division," together with some Christians, against the Bolsheviki. So we intercut shots of a Baroque Christ (apparently exploding in the radiant beams of his halo) with shots of an egg-shaped mask of Uzume, Goddess of Mirth, completely self-contained. The temporal conflict between the closed egg-form and the graphic star-form produced the effect of an instantaneous *burst*—of a bomb, or shrapnel. . . .

Thus far the examples have shown *primitive-physiological* cases—employing superimposition of optical motion *exclusively.*

III. *Emotional* combinations, not only with the visible elements of the shots, but chiefly with chains of psychological associations. *Association montage.* As a means for pointing up a situation emotionally.

From *Potemkin* (1925). "An illustration of instantaneous action. Woman with pince-nez. Followed immediately—without transition—by the same woman with shattered pince-nez and bleeding eye: impression of a shot hitting the eye" (EISENSTEIN, page 145).

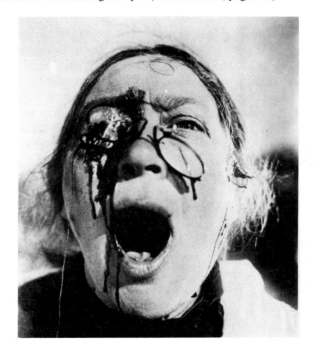

In Example 1, we had two successive shots A and B, identical in subject. However, they were not identical in respect to the position of the subject within the frame:

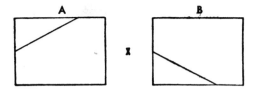

producing *dynamization in space*—an impression of spatial dynamics:

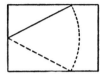

The degree of difference between the positions A and B determines the tension of the movement.

For a new case, let us suppose that the subjects of Shots A and B are not *identical.* Although the associations of the two shots are identical, that is, associatively identical.

This *dynamization of the subject,* not in the field of space but of psychology, i.e., *emotion,* thus produces:

emotional dynamization.

Example 1 (in *Strike*): the montage of the killing of the workers is actually a cross montage of this carnage with the butchering of a bull in an abattoir. Though the subjects are different, "butchering" is the associative link. This made for a powerful emotional intensification of the scene. As a matter of fact, homogeneity of gesture plays an important part in this case in achieving the effect—both the movement of the dynamic gesture within the frame, and the static gesture dividing the frame graphically.

This is a principle subsequently used by Pudovkin in *The End of St. Petersburg,* in his powerful sequence intercutting shots of stock exchange and battlefield. His previous film, *Mother,* had a similar sequence: the ice-break on the river, paralleled with the workers' demonstration.

Such a means may decay pathologiclly if the essential viewpoint—emotional dynamization of the subject—is lost. As soon as the film-maker loses sight of this essence the means ossifies into lifeless literary symbolism and stylistic mannerism. Two examples of such hollow use of this means occur to me:

Example 2 (in *October*): the sugary chants of compromise by the Mensheviki at the Second Congress of Soviets—during the storming of the Winter Palace— are intercut with hands playing harps. This was a purely literary parallelism that by no means dynamized the subject matter. Similarly in Otzep's *Living Corpse,* church spires (in imitation of those in *October*) and lyrical landscapes are intercut with the courtroom speeches of the prosecutor and defense lawyer. This error was the same as in the "harp" sequence.

On the other hand, a majority of *purely dynamic* effects can produce positive results:

> Example 3 (in *October*): The dramatic moment of the union of the Motorcycle Battalion with the Congress of Soviets was dynamized by shots of abstractly spinning bicycle wheels, in association with the entrance of the new delegates. In this way the large-scale emotional content of the event was transformed into actual dynamics.

This same principle—giving birth to concepts, to emotions, by juxtaposing two disparate events—led to:

IV. *Liberation of the whole action from the definition of time and space.* My first attempts at this were in *October*.

> Example 1: a trench crowded with soldiers appears to be crushed by an enormous gun-base that comes down inexorably. As an anti-militarist symbol seen from the viewpoint of subject alone, the effect is achieved by an apparent bringing together of an independently existing trench and an overwhelming military product, just as physically independent.
>
> Example 2: in the scene of Kornilov's *putsch,* which puts an end to Kerensky's Bonapartist dreams. Here one of Kornilov's tanks climbs up and crushes a plaster-of-Paris Napoleon standing on Kerensky's desk in the Winter Palace, a juxtaposition of purely symbolic significance.
>
> This method has now been used by Dovzhenko in *Arsenal* to shape whole sequences, as well as by Esther Schub in her use of library footage in *The Russia of Nikolai II and Lev Tolstoy.*

I wish to offer another example of this method, to upset the traditional ways of handling plot—although it has not yet been put into practice.

In 1924–1925 I was mulling over the idea of a filmic portrait of *actual* man. At that time, there prevailed a tendency to show actual man in films only in *long* uncut dramatic scenes. It was believed that cutting (montage) would destroy the idea of actual man. Abram Room established something of a record in this respect when he used in *The Death Ship* uncut dramatic shots as long as 40 meters or 135 feet. I considered (and still do) such a concept to be utterly unfilmic.

Very well—what would be a linguistically accurate characterization of a man?

> His raven-black hair . . .
> The waves of his hair . . .
> His eyes radiating azure beams . . .
> His steely muscles . . .

Even in a less exaggerated description, any verbal account of a person is bound to find itself employing an assortment of waterfalls, lightning-rods, landscapes, birds, etc.

Now why should the cinema follow the forms of theater and painting rather than the methodology of language, which allows wholly new concepts of ideas to arise from the combination of two concrete denotations of two concrete objects? Language is much closer to film than painting is. For example, in painting the form arises from *abstract* elements of line and color, while in cinema the material *concreteness* of the image within the frame presents—as an element— the greatest difficulty in manipulation. So why not rather lean towards the system of language, which is forced to use the same mechanics in inventing words and word-complexes?

On the other hand, why is it that montage cannot be dispensed with in orthodox films?

The differentiation in montage-pieces lies in their lack of existence as single units. Each piece can evoke no more than a certain association. The accumulation of such associations can achieve the same effect as is provided for the spectator by purely physiological means in the plot of a realistically produced play.

For instance, murder on the stage has a purely physiological effect. Photographed in *one* montage-piece, it can function simply as *information,* as a sub-title. *Emotional* effect begins only with the reconstruction of the event in montage fragments, each of which will summon a certain association—the sum of which will be an all-embracing complex of emotional feeling. Traditionally:

1. A hand lifts a knife.
2. The eyes of the victim open suddenly.
3. His hands clutch the table.
4. The knife is jerked up.
5. The eye blink involuntarily.
6. Blood gushes.
7. A mouth shrieks.
8. Something drips onto a shoe . . .

and similar film clichés. Nevertheless, in regard to the *action as a whole, each fragment-piece* is almost *abstract.* The more differentiated they are the more abstract they become, provoking no more than a certain association.

Quite logically the thought occurs: could not the same thing be accomplished more productively by not following the plot so slavishly, but by materializing the idea, the impression, of *Murder* through a free accumulation of association matter? For the most important task is still to reestablish the idea of murder—the feeling of murder, as such. The plot is no more than a device without which one isn't yet capable of telling something to the spectator! In any case, effort in this direction would certainly produce the most interesting variety of forms.

Someone should try, at least! Since this thought occurred to me, I have not had time to make this experiment. And today I am more concerned with quite different problems. But, returning to the main line of our syntax, something there may bring us closer to these tasks.

While, with I, II, and III, tension was calculated for purely physiological effect—from the purely optical to the emotional, we must mention here also the case of the same conflict-tension serving the ends of new concepts—of new attitudes, that is, of purely intellectual aims.

Ten shots from the montage sequence on the "Odessa Steps" from *Potemkin* (1925). "Step by step, by a process of comparing each new image with the common denotation, power is accumulated behind a process that can be formally identified with that of logical deduction" (EISENSTEIN, page 154). "The creation of a sense or meaning not proper to the images themselves but derived exclusively from their juxtaposition" (BAZIN, page 156).

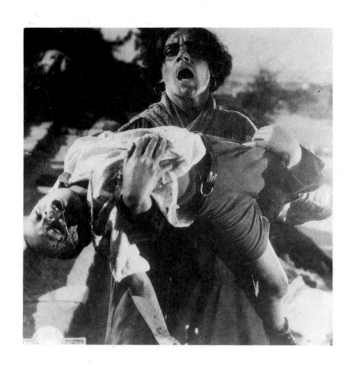

Example 1 (in *October*): Kerensky's rise to power and dictatorship after the July uprising of 1917. A comic effect was gained by sub-titles indicating regular ascending ranks (*"Dictator"*—*"Generalissimo"*—*"Minister of Navy*—*and of Army"*—etc.) climbing higher and higher—cut into five or six shots of Kerensky, climbing the stairs of the Winter Palace, all with exactly the *same* pace. Here a conflict between the flummery of the ascending ranks and the "hero's" trotting up the same unchanging flight of stairs yields an intellectual result: Kerensky's essential nonentity is shown satirically. We have the counterpoint of a literally expressed conventional idea with the *pictured* action of a particular person who is unequal to his swiftly increasing duties. The incongruence of these two factors results in the spectator's purely *intellectual* decision at the expense of this particular person. Intellectual dynamization.

Example 2 (in *October*): Kornilov's march on Petrograd was under the banner of "In the Name of God and Country." Here we attempted to reveal the religious significance of this episode in a rationalistic way. A number of religious images, from a magnificent Baroque Christ to an Eskimo idol, were cut together. The conflict in this case was between the concept and the symbolization of God. While idea and image appear to accord completely in the first statue shown, the two elements move further from each other with each successive image. Maintaining the denotation of "God," the images increasingly disagree with our concept of God, inevitably leading to individual conclusions about the true nature of all deities. In this case, too, a chain of images attempted to achieve a purely intellectual resolution, resulting from a conflict between a preconception and a *gradual discrediting of it in purposeful steps.*

Step by step, by a process of comparing each new image with the common denotation, power is accumulated behind a process that can be formally identified with that of logical deduction. The decision to release these ideas, as well as the method used, is already *intellectually* conceived.

The conventional *descriptive* form for film leads to the formal possibility of a kind of filmic reasoning. While the conventional film directs the *emotions,* this suggests an opportunity to encourage and direct the whole *thought process,* as well.

1929

ANDRÉ BAZIN
FROM WHAT IS CINEMA?

THE EVOLUTION OF THE LANGUAGE OF CINEMA

By 1928 the silent film had reached its artistic peak. The despair of its elite as they witnessed the dismantling of this ideal city, while it may not have been justified, is at least understandable. As they followed their chosen aesthetic path it seemed to them that the cinema had developed into an art most perfectly accommodated to the "exquisite embarrassment" of silence and that the realism that sound would bring could only mean a surrender to chaos.

In point of fact, now that sound has given proof that it came not to destroy but to fulfill the Old Testament of the cinema, we may most properly ask if the technical revolution created by the sound track was in any sense an aesthetic revolution. In other words, did the years from 1928 to 1930 actually witness the birth of a new cinema? Certainly, as regards editing, history does not actually show as wide a breach as might be expected between the silent and the sound film. On the contrary there is discernible evidence of a close relationship between certain directors of 1925 and 1935 and especially of the 1940's through the 1950's. Compare for example Erich von Stroheim and Jean Renoir or Orson Welles, or again Carl Theodore Dreyer and Robert Bresson. These more or less clear-cut affinities demonstrate first of all that the gap separating the 1920's and the 1930's can be bridged, and secondly that certain cinematic values actually carry over from the silent to the sound film and, above all, that it is less a matter of setting silence over against sound than of contrasting certain families of styles, certain basically different concepts of cinematographic expression.

Aware as I am that the limitations imposed on this study restrict me to a simplified and to that extent enfeebled presentation of my argument, and holding it to be less an objective statement than a working hypothesis, I will distinguish, in the cinema between 1920 and 1940, between two broad and opposing trends: those directors who put their faith in the image and those who put their faith in reality. By "image" I here mean, very broadly speaking, everything that the representation on the screen adds to the object there represented. This is a complex inheritance but it can be reduced essentially to two categories: those that relate to the plastics of the image and those that relate to the resources of montage, which after all, is simply the ordering of images in time.

Under the heading "plastics" must be included the style of the sets, of the make-up, and, up to a point, even of the performance, to which we naturally add the lighting and, finally, the framing of the shot which gives us its composition. As regards montage, derived initially as we all know from the masterpieces of Griffith, we have the statement of Malraux in his *Psychologie du cinéma* that it was montage that gave birth to film as an art, setting it apart from mere animated photography, in short, creating a language.

The use of montage can be "invisible" and this was generally the case in the pre-war classics of the American screen. Scenes were broken down just for one purpose, namely, to analyze an episode according to the material or dramatic logic of the scene. It is this logic which conceals the fact of the analysis, the mind of the spectator quite naturally accepting the viewpoints of the director which are justified by the geography of the action or the shifting emphasis of dramatic interest.

But the neutral quality of this "invisible" editing fails to make use of the full potential of montage. On the other hand these potentialities are clearly evident from the three processes generally known as parallel montage, accelerated montage, montage by attraction. In creating parallel montage, Griffith succeeded in conveying a sense of the simultaneity of two actions taking place at a geographical distance by means of alternating shots from each. In *La Roue* Abel Gance created the illusion of the steadily increasing speed of a locomotive without actually using any images of speed (indeed the wheel could have been turning on one spot) simply by a multiplicity of shots of ever-decreasing length.

Finally there is "montage by attraction," the creation of S. M. Eisenstein, and not so easily described as the others, but which may be roughly defined as the reenforcing of the meaning of one image by association with another image not necessarily part of the same episode—for example the fireworks display in *The General Line* following the image of the bull. In this extreme form, montage by attraction was rarely used even by its creator but one may consider as very near to it in principle the more commonly used ellipsis, comparison, or metaphor, examples of which are the throwing of stockings onto a chair at the foot of a bed, or the milk overflowing in H.G. Clouzot's *Quai des orfèvres*. There are of course a variety of possible combinations of these three processes.

Whatever these may be, one can say that they share that trait in common which constitutes the very definition of montage, namely, the creation of a sense or meaning not proper to the images themselves but derived exclusively from their juxtaposition. The well-known experiment of Kuleshov with the shot of Mozhukhin in which a smile was seen to change its significance according to the image that preceded it, sums up perfectly the properties of montage.

Montage as used by Kuleshov, Eisenstein, or Gance did not give us the event; it alluded to it. Undoubtedly they derived at least the greater part of the constituent

McTeague (Gibson Gowland) confronting Marcus Schouler (Jean Hersholt) in the wastes of Death Valley in *Greed* (1923); Nanook building his igloo in *Nanook of the North* (1922). Von Stroheim and Flaherty were two of "those who put their faith in reality" (BAZIN, page 155).

elements from the reality they were describing but the final significance of the film was found to reside in the ordering of these elements much more than in their objective content.

The matter under recital, whatever the realism of the individual image, is born essentially from these relationships—Mozhukhin plus dead child equal pity—that is to say an abstract result, none of the concrete elements of which are to be found in the premises; maidens plus appletrees in bloom equal hope. The combinations are infinite. But the only thing they have in common is the fact that they suggest an idea by means of a metaphor or by an association of ideas. Thus between the scenario properly so-called, the ultimate object of the recital, and the image pure and simple, there is a relay station, a sort of aesthetic "transformer." The meaning is not in the image, it is in the shadow of the image projected by montage onto the field of consciousness of the spectator.

Let us sum up. Through the contents of the image and the resources of montage, the cinema has at its disposal a whole arsenal of means whereby to impose its interpretation of an event on the spectator. By the end of the silent film we can consider this arsenal to have been full. On the one side the Soviet cinema carried to its ultimate consequences the theory and practice of montage while the German school did every kind of violence to the plastics of the image by way of sets and lighting. Other cinemas count too besides the Russian and German, but whether in France or Sweden or the United States, it does not appear that the language of cinema was at a loss for ways of saying what it wanted to say.

If the art of cinema consists in everything that plastics and montage can add to a given reality, the silent film was an art on its own. Sound could only play at best a subordinate and supplementary role: a counterpoint to the visual image. But this possible enhancement—at best only a minor one—is likely not to weigh much in comparison with the additional bargain-rate reality introduced at the same time by sound.

Thus far we have put forward the view that expressionism of montage and image constitute the essence of cinema. And it is precisely on this generally accepted notion that directors from silent days, such as Erich von Stroheim, F.W. Murnau, and Robert Flaherty, have by implication cast a doubt. In their films, montage plays no part, unless it be the negative one of inevitable elimination where reality superabounds. The camera cannot see everything at once but it makes sure not to lose any part of what it chooses to see. What matters to Flaherty, confronted with Nanook hunting the seal, is the relation between Nanook and the animal; the actual length of the waiting period. Montage could suggest the time involved. Flaherty however confines himself to showing the actual waiting period; the length of the hunt is the very substance of the image, its true object. Thus in the film this episode requires one set-up. Will anyone deny that it is thereby much more moving than a montage by attraction?

Murnau is interested not so much in time as in the reality of dramatic space. Montage plays no more of a decisive part in *Nosferatu* than in *Sunrise*. One might be inclined to think that the plastics of his image are impressionistic. But this would be a superficial view. The composition of his image is in no sense pictorial. It adds nothing to the reality, it does not deform it, it forces it to reveal its structural depth, to bring out the preexisting relations which become constitutive of the drama. For example, in *Tabu,* the arrival of a ship from left screen gives an immediate sense of destiny at work so that Murnau has no need to cheat in any way on the uncompromising realism of a film whose settings are completely natural.

But it is most of all Stroheim who rejects photographic expressionism and the tricks of montage. In his films reality lays itself bare like a suspect confessing under the relentless examination of the commissioner of police. He has one simple rule for direction. Take a close look at the world, keep on doing so, and in the end it will lay bare for you all its cruelty and its ugliness. One could easily imagine as a matter of fact a film by Stroheim composed of a single shot as long-lasting and as close-up as you like. These three directors do not exhaust the possibilities. We would undoubtedly find scattered among the works of others elements of nonexpressionistic cinema in which montage plays no part—even including Griffith. But these examples suffice to reveal, at the very heart of the silent film, a cinematographic art the very opposite of that which has been identified as *"cinéma par excellence,"* a language the semantic and syntactical unit of which is in no sense the Shot; in which the image is evaluated not according to what it adds to reality but what it reveals of it. In the latter art the silence of the screen was a drawback, that is to say, it deprived reality of one of its elements. *Greed,* like Dreyer's *Jeanne d' Arc,* is already virtually a talking film. The moment that you cease to maintain that montage and the plastic composition of the image are the very essence of the language of cinema, sound is no longer the aesthetic crevasse dividing two radically different aspects of the seventh art. The cinema that is believed to have died of the soundtrack is in no sense *"the* cinema." The real dividing line is elsewhere. It was operative in the past and continues to be through thirty-five years of the history of the language of the film.

Having challenged the aesthetic unity of the silent film and divided it off into two opposing tendencies, now let us take a look at the history of the last twenty years.

From 1930 to 1940 there seems to have grown up in the world, originating largely in the United States, a common form of cinematic language. It was the triumph in Hollywood, during that time, of five or six major kinds of film that gave it its overwhelming superiority: (1) American comedy (*Mr. Smith Goes to Washington,* 1936); (2) The burlesque film (The Marx Brothers); (3) The dance and vaudeville film (Fred Astaire and Ginger Rogers and the Ziegfield Follies); (4) The crime and gangster film *(Scarface, I Am a Fugitive from a Chain Gang, The Informer);* (5) Psychological and social dramas. *(Back Street, Jezebel);* (6) Horror or fantasy films *(Dr. Jekyll and Mr. Hyde, The Invisible Man, Frankenstein);* (7) The western (*Stagecoach,* 1939). During that time the French cinema undoubtedly ranked next. Its superiority was gradually manifested by way of a trend towards what might be roughly called stark somber realism, or poetic realism, in which four names stand out: Jacques Feyder, Jean Renoir, Marcel Carné, and Julien Duvivier. My intention not being to draw up a list of prize-winners, there is little use in dwelling on the Soviet, British, German, or Italian films for which these years were less significant than the ten that were to follow. In any case, American and French production sufficiently clearly indicate that the sound film, prior to World War II, had reached a well-balanced stage of maturity.

First as to content: Major varieties with clearly defined rules capable of pleasing a worldwide public, as well as a cultured elite, provided it was not inherently hostile to the cinema.

Secondly as to form: well-defined styles of photography and editing perfectly adapted to their subject matter; a complete harmony of image and sound. In seeing again today such films as *Jezebel* by Willian Wyler, *Stagecoach* by John Ford, or *Le Jour se lève* by Marcel Carné, one has the feeling that in them an art has found its perfect balance, its ideal form of expression, and reciprocally one admires them for dramatic and moral themes to which the cinema, while it may not have created them, has given a grandeur, an artistic effectiveness, that they would not otherwise have had. In short, here are all the characteristics of the ripeness of a classical art.

I am quite aware that one can justifiably argue that the originality of the postwar cinema as compared with that of 1938 derives from the growth of certain national schools, in particular the dazzling display of the Italian cinema and of a native English cinema freed from the influence of Hollywood. From this one might conclude that the really important phenomenon of the years 1940–1950 is the introduction of new blood, of hitherto unexplored themes. That is to say, the real revolution took place more on the level of subject matter than of style. Is not neorealism primarily a kind of humanism and only secondarily a style of film-making? Then as to the style itself, is it not essentially a form of self-effacement before reality?

Our intention is certainly not to preach the glory of form over content. Art for art's sake is just as heretical in cinema as elsewhere, probably more so. On the other hand, a new subject matter demands new form, and as good a way as any towards understanding what a film is trying to say to us is to know how it is saying it.

Thus by 1938 or 1939 the talking film, particularly in France and in the United States, had reached a level of classical perfection as a result, on the one hand, of the maturing of different kinds of drama developed in part over the past ten years and in part inherited from the silent film, and, on the other, of the stabilization of technical progress. The 1930's were the years, at once, of sound and of panchromatic film. Undoubtedly studio equipment had continued to improve but only in matters of detail, none of them opening up new, radical possibilities for direction. The only changes in this situation since 1940 have been in photography, thanks to the increased sensitivity of the film stock. Panchromatic stock turned visual values upside down, ultrasensitive emulsions have made a modification in their structure possible. Free to shoot in the studio with a much smaller aperture, the operator could, when necessary, eliminate the soft-focus background once considered essential. Still there are a number of examples of the prior use of deep focus, for example in the work of Jean Renoir. This had always been possible on exteriors, and given a measure of skill, even in the studios. Anyone could do it who really wanted to. So that it is less a question basically of a technical problem, the solution of which has admittedly been made easier, than of a search after a style—a point to which we will come back. In short, with panchromatic stock in common use, with an understanding of the potentials of the microphone, and with the crane as standard studio equipment, one can really say that since 1930 all the technical requirements for the art of cinema have been available.

Since the determining technical factors were practically eliminated, we must look elsewhere for the signs and principles of the evolution of film language, that is to say by challenging the subject matter and as a consequence the styles necessary for its expression.

By 1939 the cinema had arrived at what geographers call the equilibrium-profile of a river. By this is meant that ideal mathematical curve which results from the requisite amount of erosion. Having reached this equilibrium-profile, the river flows effortlessly from its source to its mouth without further deepening of its bed. But if any geological movement occurs which raises the erosion level and modifies the height of the source, the water sets to work again, seeps into the surrounding land, goes deeper, burrowing and digging. Sometimes when it is a chalk bed, a new pattern is dug across the plain, almost invisible but found to be complex and winding, if one follows the flow of the water.

THE EVOLUTION OF EDITING SINCE THE ADVENT OF SOUND

In 1938 there was an almost universal standard pattern of editing. If, somewhat conventionally, we call the kind of silent films based on the plastics of the image and the artifices of montage, "expressionist" or "symbolistic," we can describe the new form of storytelling "analytic" and "dramatic." Let us suppose, by way of reviewing one of the elements of the experiment of Kuleshov, that we have a table covered with food and a hungry tramp. One can imagine that in 1936 it would have been edited as follows:

(1) Full shot of the actor and the table.
(2) Camera moves forward into a close-up of a face expressing a mixture of amazement and longing.
(3) Series of close-ups of food.
(4) Back to full shot of person who starts slowly towards the camera.
(5) Camera pulls slowly back to a three-quarter shot of the actor seizing a chicken wing.

Whatever variants one could think of for this scene, they would all have certain points in common:

(1) The verisimilitude of space in which the position of the actor is always determined, even when a close-up eliminates the decor.
(2) The purpose and the effects of the cutting are exclusively dramatic or psychological.

In other words, if the scene were played on a stage and seen from a seat in the orchestra, it would have the same meaning, the episode would continue to exist objectively. The changes of point of view provided by the camera would add nothing. They would present the reality a little more forcefully, first by allowing a better view and then by putting the emphasis where it belongs.

It is true that the stage director like the film director has at his disposal a margin within which he is free to vary the interpretation of the action but it is only a margin and allows for no modification of the inner logic of the event. Now, by way of contrast, let us take the montage of the stone lions in *The End of St. Petersburg*. By skillful juxtaposition a group of sculptured lions are made to look like a single lion getting to its feet, a symbol of the aroused masses. This clever device would be unthinkable in any film after 1932. As late as 1935 Fritz Lang, in *Fury,* followed a series of shots of women dancing the can-can with shots of clucking chickens in a farmyard. This relic of associative montage came as a shock even at the time, and today seems entirely out of keeping with the rest of the film. However decisive the art of Marcel Carné, for example, in our estimate of the respective values of *Quai des Brumes* or of *Le Jour se lève* his editing remains on the level of the reality he is analyzing. There is only one proper way of looking at it. That is why we are witnessing the almost complete disappearance of optical effects such as superimpositions, and even, especially in the United States, of the close-up, the too violent impact of which would make the audience conscious of the cutting. In the typical American comedy the director returns as often as he can to a shot of the characters from the knees up, which is said to be best suited to catch the spontaneous attention of the viewer—the natural point of balance of his mental adjustment.

Actually this use of montage originated with the silent movies. This is more or less the part it plays in Griffith's films, for example in *Broken Blossoms,* because with *Intolerance* he had already introduced that synthetic concept of montage which the Soviet cinema was to carry to its ultimate conclusion and which is to be found again, although less exclusively, at the end of the silent era. It is understandable, as a matter of fact, that the sound image, far less flexible than the visual image, would carry montage in the direction of realism, increasingly eliminating both plastic impressionism and the symbolic relation between images.

Thus around 1938 films were edited, almost without exception, according to the same principle. The story was unfolded in a series of set-ups numbering as a rule about 600. The characteristic procedure was by shot-reverse-shot, that is to say, in a dialogue scene, the camera followed the order of the text, alternating the character shown with each speech.

It was this fashion of editing, so admirably suitable for the best films made between 1930 and 1939, that was challenged by the shot in depth introduced by Orson Welles and William Wyler. *Citizen Kane* can never be too highly praised. Thanks to the depth of field, whole scenes are covered in one take, the camera remaining motionless. Dramatic effects for which we had formerly relied on montage were created out of the movements of the actors within a fixed framework. Of course Welles did not invent the in-depth shot any more than Griffith invented the close-up. All the pioneers used it and for a very good reason. Soft focus only appeared with montage. It was not only a technical must consequent upon the use of images in juxtaposition, it was a logical consequence of montage, its plastic equivalent. If at a given moment in the action the director, as in the scene imagined above, goes to a close-up of a bowl of fruit, it follows naturally that he also isolates it in space through the focusing of the lens. The soft focus of the background confirms therefore the effect of montage, that is to say, while it is of the essence of the storytelling, it is only an accessory of the style of the photography. Jean Renoir had already clearly understood this, as we see from a statement of his made in 1938 just after he had made *La Bête humaine* and *La Grande illusion* and just prior to *La Règle du jeu:* "The more I learn about my trade the more I incline to direction in depth relative to the screen. The better it works, the less I use the kind of set-up that shows two actors facing the camera, like two well-behaved subjects posing for a still portrait." The truth of the matter is, that if you are looking for the precursor of Orson Welles, it is not Louis Lumière or Zecca, but rather Jean Renoir. In his films, the search after composition in depth is, in effect, a partial replacement of montage by frequent panning shots and entrances. It is based on a respect for the continuity of dramatic space and, of course, of its duration.

To anybody with eyes in his head, it is quite evident that the sequence of shots used by Welles in *The Magnificent Ambersons* is in no sense the purely passive recording of an action shot within the same framing. On the contrary, his refusal to break up the action, to analyze the dramatic field in time, is a positive action the results of which are far superior to anything that could be achieved by the classical "cut."

All you need to do is compare two frames shot in depth, one from 1910, the other from a film by Wyler or Welles, to understand just by looking at the image, even apart from the context of the film, how different their functions are. The framing in the 1910 film is intended, to all intents and purposes, as a substitute for the missing fourth wall of the theatrical stage, or at least in exterior shots, for the best vantage point to view the action, whereas in the second case the setting, the lighting, and the camera angles give an entirely different reading. Between them, director and cameraman have converted the screen into a dramatic checkerboard, planned down to the last detail. The clearest if not the most original examples of this are to be found in *The Little Foxes* where the mise-en-scène takes on the severity of a working drawing. Welles' pictures are more difficult to analyze because of his overfondness for the baroque. Objects and characters are related in such a fashion that it is impossible for the spectator to miss the significance of the scene. To get the same results by way of montage would have necessitated a detailed succession of shots.

What we are saying then is that the sequence of shots "in depth" of the contemporary director does not exclude the use of montage—how could he, without reverting to a primitive babbling?—he makes it an integral part of his "plastic." The storytelling of Welles or Wyler is no less explicit than John Ford's but theirs has the advantage over his that it does not sacrifice the specific effects that can be derived from unity of image in space and time. Whether an episode is analyzed bit by bit or presented in its physical entirety cannot surely remain a matter of indifference, at least in a work with some pretensions to style. It would obviously be absurd to deny that montage had added considerably to the progress of film language, but this has happened at the cost of other values, no less definitely cinematic.

This is why depth of field is not just a stock in trade of the cameraman like the use of a series of filters or of such-and-such style of lighting, it is a capital gain in the field of direction—a dialectical step forward in the history of film language.

Nor is it just a formal step forward. Well used, shooting in depth is not just a more economical, a simpler, and at the same time a more subtle way of getting the most out of a scene. In addition to affecting the structure of film language, it also affects the relationships of the minds of the spectators to the image, and in consequence it influences the interpretation of the spectacle.

It would lie outside the scope of this article to analyze the psychological modal-

The shot-in-depth from *Citizen Kane* (1941). "Thanks to the depth of field, whole scenes are covered in one take, the camera remaining motionless . . . . Director and cameraman have converted the screen into a dramatic checkerboard, planned down to the last detail" (BAZIN, pages 162, 163).

ities of these relations, as also their aesthetic consequences, but it might be enough here to note, in general terms:

(1) That depth of focus brings the spectator into a relation with the image closer to that which he enjoys with reality. Therefore it is correct to say that, independently of the contents of the image, its structure is more realistic;

(2) That it implies, consequently, both a more active mental attitude on the part of the spectator and a more positive contribution on his part to the action in progress. While analytical montage only calls for him to follow his guide, to let his attention follow along smoothly with that of the director who will choose what he should see, here he is called upon to exercise at least a minimum of personal choice. It is from his attention and his will that the meaning of the image in part derives.

(3) From the two preceding propositions, which belong to the realm of psychology, there follows a third which may be described as metaphysical. In analyzing reality, montage presupposes of its very nature the unity of meaning of the dramatic event. Some other form of analysis is undoubtedly possible but then it would be another film. In short, montage by its very nature rules out ambiguity of expression. Kuleshov's experiment proves this *per absurdum* in giving on each occasion a precise meaning to the expression on a face, the ambiguity of which alone makes the three successively exclusive expressions possible.

On the other hand, depth of focus reintroduced ambiguity into the structure of the image if not of necessity—Wyler's films are never ambiguous—at least as a possibility. Hence it is no exaggeration to say that *Citizen Kane* is unthinkable shot in any other way but in depth. The uncertainty in which we find ourselves as to the spiritual key or the interpretation we should put on the film is built into the very design of the image.

It is not that Welles denies himself any recourse whatsoever to the expressionistic procedures of montage, but just that their use from time to time in between sequences of shots in depth gives them a new meaning. Formerly montage was the very stuff of cinema, the texture of the scenario. In *Citizen Kane* a series of superimpositions is contrasted with a scene presented in a single take, constituting another and deliberately abstract mode of story-telling. Accelerated montage played tricks with time and space while that of Welles, on the other hand, is not trying to deceive us; it offers us a contrast, condensing time, and hence is the equivalent for example of the French imperfect or the English frequentative tense. Like accelerated montage and montage of attractions these superimpositions, which the talking film had not used for ten years, rediscovered a possible use related to temporal realism in a film without montage.

If we have dwelt at some length on Orson Welles it is because the date of his appearance in the filmic firmament (1941) marks more or less the beginning of a new period and also because his case is the most spectacular and, by virtue of his very excesses, the most significant.

Yet *Citizen Kane* is part of a general movement, of a vast stirring of the geological bed of cinema, confirming that everywhere up to a point there had been a revolution in the language of the screen.

I could show the same to be true, although by different methods, of the Italian cinema. In Roberto Rossellini's *Paisà* and *Allemania Anno Zero* and Vittorio de

Sica's *Ladri de Biciclette,* Italian neorealism contrasts with previous forms of film realism in its stripping away of all expressionism and in particular in the total absence of the effects of montage. As in the films of Welles and in spite of conflicts of style, neorealism tends to give back to the cinema a sense of the ambiguity of reality. The preoccupation of Rossellini when dealing with the face of the child in *Allemania Anno Zero* is the exact opposite of that of Kuleshov with the close-up of Mozhukhin. Rossellini is concerned to preserve its mystery. We should not be misled by the fact that the evolution of neorealism is not manifest, as in the United States, in any form of revolution in editing. They are both aiming at the same results by different methods. The means used by Rossellini and de Sica are less spectacular but they are no less determined to do away with montage and to transfer to the screen the *continuum* of reality. The dream of Zavattini is just to make a ninety-minute film of the life of a man to whom nothing ever happens. The most "aesthetic" of the neorealists, Luchino Visconti, gives just as clear a picture as Welles of the basic aim of his directorial art in *La Terra Trema,* a film almost entirely composed of one-shot sequences, thus clearly showing his concern to cover the entire action in interminable deep-focus panning shots.

However we cannot pass in review all the films that have shared in this revolution in film language since 1940. Now is the moment to attempt a synthesis of our reflections on the subject.

It seems to us that the decade from 1940 to 1950 marks a decisive step forward in the development of the language of the film. If we have appeared since 1930 to have lost sight of the trend of the silent film as illustrated particularly by Stroheim, F. W. Murnau, Robert Flaherty, and Dreyer, it is for a purpose. It is not that this trend seems to us to have been halted by the talking film. On the contrary, we believe that it represented the richest vein of the so-called silent film and, precisely because it was not aesthetically tied to montage, but was indeed the only tendency that looked to the realism of sound as a natural development. On the other hand it is a fact that the talking film between 1930 and 1940 owes it virtually nothing save for the glorious and retrospectively prophetic exception of Jean Renoir. He alone in his searchings as a director prior to *La Règle du jeu* forced himself to look back beyond the resources provided by montage and so uncovered the secret of a film form that would permit everything to be said without chopping the world up into little fragments, that would reveal the hidden meanings in people and things without disturbing the unity natural to them.

It is not a question of thereby belittling the films of 1930 to 1940, a criticism that would not stand up in the face of the number of masterpieces, it is simply an attempt to establish the notion of a dialectic progress, the highest expression of which was found in the films of the 1940's. Undoubtedly, the talkie sounded the knell of a certain aesthetic of the language of film, but only wherever it had turned its back on its vocation in the service of realism. The sound film nevertheless did preserve the essentials of montage, namely discontinuous description and the dramatic analysis of action. What it turned its back on was metaphor and symbol in exchange for the illusion of objective presentation. The expressionism of montage has virtually disppeared but the relative realism of the kind of cutting that flourished around 1937 implied a congenital limitation which escaped us so long as it was perfectly suited to its subject matter. Thus American comedy reached its peak within the framework of a form of editing in which the realism of the time played no part. Dependent on logic for its effects, like vaudeville and plays on words, entirely conventional in its moral and sociological content, American comedy had everything to gain, in strict line-by-line progression, from the rhythmic resources of classical editing.

Undoubtedly it is primarily with the Stroheim-Murnau trend—almost totally eclipsed from 1930 to 1940—that the cinema has more or less consciously linked up once more over the last ten years. But it has no intention of limiting itself simply to keeping this trend alive. It draws from it the secret of the regeneration of realism in storytelling and thus of becoming capable once more of bringing together real time, in which things exist, along with the duration of the action, for which classical editing had insidiously substituted mental and abstract time. On the other hand, so far from wiping out once and for all the conquests of montage, this reborn realism gives them a body of reference and a meaning. It is only an increased realism of the image that can support the abstraction of montage. The stylistic repertory of a director such as Hitchcock, for example, ranged from the power inherent in the basic document as such, to superimpositions, to large close-ups. But the close-ups of Hitchcock are not the same as those of C. B. de Mille in *The Cheat* [1915]. They are just one type of figure, among others, of his style. In other words, in the silent days, montage evoked what the director wanted to say; in the editing of 1938, it described it. Today we can say that at last the director writes in film. The image—its plastic composition and the way it is set in time, because it is founded on a much higher degree of realism—has at its disposal more means of manipulating reality and of modifying it from within. The film-maker is no longer the competitor of the painter and the playwright, he is, at last, the equal of the novelist.

1950–55

CHRISTIAN METZ
FROM FILM LANGUAGE

SOME POINTS IN THE SEMIOTICS OF THE CINEMA

The purpose of this text is to examine some of the problems and difficulties confronting the person who wants to begin undertaking, in the field of "cinematographic language," de Saussure's project of a general semiotics: to study the ordering and functionings of the main signifying units used in the filmic message. Semiotics, as de Saussure conceived it, is still in its childhood, but any work bearing on one of the nonverbal "languages," provided that it assumes a resolutely semiological relevance and does not remain satisfied with vague considerations of "substance," brings its contribution, whether modest or important, to that great enterprise, the general study of significations.

The very term "cinematographic *language*" already poses the whole problem of the semiotics of film. It would require a long justification, and strictly speaking it should be used only after the indepth study of the semiological mechanisms at work in the filmic message had been fairly well advanced. Convenience, however, makes us retain, right from the start, that frozen syntagma—"language—which has gradually assumed a place in the special vocabulary of film theoreticians and aestheticians. Even from a strictly semiological point of view, one can perhaps at this time give a preliminary justification for the expression "cinematographic language" (not to be confused with "cinematographic *langue*" (language system), which does not seem to me acceptable)—a justification that, in the present state of semiological investigations, can only be very general. I hope to outline it in this essay. . . .

CINEMA AND NARRATIVITY

A first choice confronts the "film semiologist": Is the corpus to be made up of feature films *(narrative films)* or, on the contrary, of short films, documentaries, technological, pedagogical, or advertising films, etc.? It could be answered that it depends simply on what one wants to study—that the cinema possesses various "dialects," and that each one of these "dialects" can become the subject of a specific analysis. This is undoubtedly true. Nevertheless, there is a hierarchy of concerns (or, better yet, a methodological urgency) that favors—in the beginning at least— the study of the narrative film. We know that, in the few years immediately before and after the Lumière brothers' invention in 1895, critics, journalists, and the pioneer cinematographers disagreed considerably among themselves as to the *social function* that they attributed to, or predicted for, the new machine: whether it was a means of preservation or of making archives, whether it was an auxiliary technography for research and teaching in sciences like botany or surgery, whether it was a new form of journalism, or an instrument of sentimental devotion, either private or public, which could perpetuate the living image of the dear departed one, and so on. That, over all these possibilities, the cinema could evolve into a machine for telling stories had never been really considered. From the very beginnings of the cinematograph there were various indications and statements that suggested such an evolution, but they had no common measure with the magnitude that the narrative phenomenon was to assume. The merging of the cinema and of narrativity was a great fact, which was by no means predestined—nor was it strictly fortuitous. It was a historical and social fact, a fact of civilization (to use a formula dear to the sociologist Marcel Mauss), a fact that in turn conditioned the later evolution of the film as a semiological reality, somewhat in the same way—indirect and general,[1] though effective—that "external" linguistic events (conquests, colonizations, transformations of language) influence the "internal" functioning of idioms. In the realm of the cinema, all nonnarrative genres—the documentary, the technical film, etc.—have become marginal provinces, border regions so to speak, while the *feature-length film of novelistic fiction,* which is simply called a "film"—the usage is significant[2]—has traced more and more clearly the king's highway of filmic expression.

This purely numerical and social superiority is not the only fact concerned. Added to it is a more "internal" consideration: Nonnarrative films for the most part are distinguished from "real" films by their social purpose and by their content much more than by their "language processes." The basic figures of the semiotics of the cinema—montage, camera movements, scale of the shots, relationships between the image and speech, sequences, and other large syntagmatic units—are on the whole the same in "small" films and in "big" films. It is by no means certain that an independent semiotics of the various nonnarrative genres is possible other than in the form of a series of discontinuous remarks on the points of difference between these films and "ordinary" films. To examine fiction films is to proceed more directly and more rapidly to the heart of the problem.

There is, moreover, an encouraging diachronic consideration. We know, since

---

[1]Except, of course, for specific lexical facts.

[2]As in statements like "The short was terrible, but the film was great" or "What are they showing tonight? a series of shorts or a film?"etc.

the observations of Béla Balázs, André Malraux, Edgar Morin, Jean Mitry, and many others, that the cinema was not a specific "language" from its inception. Before becoming the means of expression familiar to us, it was a simple means of mechanical recording, preserving, and reproducing moving visual spectacles— whether of life, of the theater, or even of small *mises-en-scène,* which were specially prepared and which, in the final analysis, remained theatrical—in short, a "means of reproduction," to use André Malraux's term. Now, *it was precisely to the extent that the cinema confronted the problems of narration* that, in the course of successive groupings, it came to produce a body of specific signifying procedures. Historians of the cinema generally agree in dating the beginning of the "cinema" as we know it in the period 1910–15. Films like *Enoch Arden, Life for the Czar, Quo Vadis?, Fantômas, Cabria, The Golem, The Battle of Gettysburg,* and above all *Birth of a Nation* were among the first films, in the acceptation we now give this word when we use it without a determinant: Narration of a certain magnitude based on procedures that are supposed to be specifically cinematographic. It so happens that these procedures were perfected in the wake of the narrative endeavor. The pioneers of "cinematographic language"—Méliès, Porter, Griffith—couldn't care less about "formal" research conducted for its own sake; what is more (except for occasional naïve and confused attempts), they cared little about the symbolic, philosophical or human "message" of their films. Men of denotation rather than of connotation, they wanted above all to tell a story; they were not content unless they could subject the continuous, analogical material of photographic duplication to the *articulations*—however rudimentary—of a narrative discourse. Georges Sadoul has indeed shown how Méliès, in his story-teller's naïveté, was led to invent double exposure, the device of multiple exposures with a mask and a dark backdrop, the dissolve and the fade-in, and the pan shot. Jean Mitry, who has written a very precise synthesis of these problems, examines the first occurrences of a certain number of procedures of filmic language—the close-up, the pan shot, the tracking shot, parallel montage, and interlaced, or alternative, montage—among the film primitives. I will summarize the conclusions he reaches: The principal "inventions" are credited to the Frenchmen Méliès and Promio, to the Englishmen G. A. Smith and J. Williamson, and to the American E. S. Porter; it was Griffith's role to define and to stabilize— we would say, to codify—the *function* of these different procedures in relation to the filmic *narrative,* and thereby unify them up to a certain point in a coherent "syntax" (note that it would be better to use the term *syntagmatic category;* Jean Mitry himself avoids the word syntax). Between 1911 and 1915, Griffith made a whole series of films having, more or less consciously, the value of experimental probings, and *Birth of a Nation,* released in 1915, appears as the crowning work, the sum and the public demonstration of investigations that, however naïve they may have been, were nonetheless systematic and fundamental. Thus, it was in a single motion that the cinema became narrative and took over some of the attributes of a language.

Today, still, the so-called filmic procedures are in fact filmic-narrative. This, to my mind, justifies the priority of the narrative film in the filmosemiological enterprise—a priority that must not of course become an exclusivity.

STUDIES OF DENOTATION AND STUDIES OF CONNOTATION IN THE SEMIOTICS OF THE CINEMA

The facts I have just reviewed lead to another consequence. The semiotics of the cinema can be conceived of either as a semiotics of connotation or as a semiotics of denotation. Both directions are interesting, and it is obvious that on the day when the semiological study of film makes some progress and begins to form a body of knowledge, it will have considered connotative and denotative significations together. The study of connotation brings us closer to the notion of the cinema as an art (the "seventh art"). As I have indicated elsewhere in more detail, the art of film is located on the same semiological "plane" as literary art: The properly aesthetic orderings and constraints—versification, composition, and tropes in the first case; framing, camera movements, and light "effects" in the second—serve as the connoted instance, which is superimposed over the denoted meaning. In literature, the latter appears as the purely linguistic singification, which is linked, in the employed idiom, to the units used by the author. In the cinema, it is represented by the literal (that is, perceptual) meaning of the spectacle reproduced in the image, or of the sounds duplicated by the soundtrack. As for connotation, which plays a major role in all aesthetic languages,* its significate is the literay or cinematographic "style," "genre" (the epic, the western, etc.), "symbol" (philosophical, humanitarian, ideological, and so on), or "poetic atmosphere"—and its signifier is the whole denotated semiological material, whether signified or signifying. In American gangster movies, where, for example, the slick pavement of the waterfront distills an impression of anxiety and hardness (significate of the connotation), the scene represented (dimly lit, deserted wharves, with stacks of crates and overhead cranes, the significate of denotation), and the technique of the shooting, which is dependent on the effects of lighting in order to produce a certain *picture* of the docks (signifier of denotation), converge to form the signifier of connotation. The same scene filmed in a different light would produce a different impression; and so would the same technique used on a different subject (for example, a child's smiling face). Film aestheticians have often remarked that filmic effects must not be "gratuitous," but must remain "subordinate to the plot." This is another way of saying that the significate of connotation can establish itself only when the corresponding signifier brings into play *both* the signifier and the significate of denotation.

The study of the cinema as an art—the study of cinematographic expressiveness—can therefore be conducted according to methods derived from linguistics. For instance, there is no doubt that films are amenable to analyses comparable *(mutatis mutandis)* to those Thomas A. Sebeok has applied to Cheremis songs, or to those Samuel R. Levin has proposed. But there is another task that requires the careful attention of the film semiologist. For also, and even first of all, through its procedures of *denotation,* the cinema is a specific language. The concept of *diegesis*

---

*Aesthetic language practices a kind of promotion of connotation, but connotation occurs as well in various phenomena of expressiveness proper to ordinary language, like those studied by Charles Bally (*Le Langage et la vie,* Geneva, Payot, 1926).

is as important for the film semiologist as the idea of art. The word is derived from the Greek διηγησις, "narration" and was used particularly to designate one of the obligatory parts of judiciary discourse, the recital of facts. The term was introduced into the framework of the cinema by Étienne Souriau. It designates the film's *represented* instance (which Mikel Dufrenne contrasts to the expressed, properly aesthetic, instance)—that is to say, the sum of a film's denotation: the narration itself, but also the fictional space and time dimensions implied in and by the narrative, and consequently the characters, the landscapes, the events, and other narrative elements, in so far as they are considered in their denoted aspect. How does the cinema indicate successivity, precession, temporal breaks, causality, adversative relationships, consequence, spatial proximity, or distance, etc.? These are central questions to the semiotics of the cinema.

One must not indeed forget that, from the semiological point of view, the cinema is very different from still photography whence its technique is derived. In photography, as Roland Barthes has clearly shown, the denoted meaning is secured entirely through the automatic process of photochemical reproduction; denotation is a visual transfer,[1] which is not codified and has no inherent organization. Human intervention, which carries some elements of a proper semiotics, affects only the level of connotation (lighting, camera angle, "photographic effects," and so on). And, in point of fact, there is no specifically photographic procedure for designating the significate "house" in its denotated aspect, unless it is by showing a house. In the cinema, on the other hand, a whole semiotics of denotation is possible and necessary, for a film is composed of *many* photographs (the concept of montage, with its myriad consequences)—photographs that give us mostly only partial views of the diegetic referent. In film a "house" would be shot of a staircase, a shot of one of the walls taken from the outside, a close-up of a window, a brief establishing shot of the building,[2] etc. Thus a kind of filmic *articulation* appears, which has no equivalent in photography: It is the denotation itself that is being constructed, organized, and to a certain extent codified (*codified,* not necessarily *encoded*). Lacking absolute laws, filmic intelligibility nevertheless depends on a certain number of dominant habits: A film put together haphazardly would not be understood.

I return to my initial observations: "Cinematographic language" is first of all the literalness of a plot. Artistic effects, even when they are substantially inseparable from the semic act by which the film tells us its story, nevertheless constitute

---

[1] I am speaking here as a semiologist and not as a psychologist. Comparative studies of visual perception, both in "real" and in filmic conditions, have indeed isolated all the optical distortions that differentiate between the photograph and the object. But these transformations, which obey the laws of optical physics, of the chemistry of emulsions and of retinal physiology, do not constitute a signifying system.

[2] Even if this over-all view is the only one shown us in the film, it is still the result of a choice. We know that the modern cinema has partially abandoned the practices of visual fragmentation and excessive montage in favor of the continuous shot (cf. the famous "shot-sequence" controversy). This conditon *modifies* to the same extent the semiotics of filmic denotation, but it in no way dismisses it. Simply, cinematographic language, like other languages, has a diachronic side. A single "shot" itself contains several elements (example: switching from one view to another through a camera movement, and without montage).

another level of signification, which from the methodological point of view must come "later."

PARADIGMATIC AND SYNTAGMATIC CATEGORIES

There is a danger that the semiotics of the cinema will tend to develop along the syntagmatic rather than along the paradigmatic axis. It is not that there is no filmic paradigm: At specific points along the chain of images the number of units liable to occur is limited, so that, in these circumstances, the unit that does appear derives its meaning in relation to the other members of the paradigm. This is the case with the "fade-dissolve" duality within the framework of the "conjunction of two sequences":[1] a simple commutation, which the users—that is to say, the spectators—perform spontaneously, makes it possible to isolate the corresponding significates: a spatiotemporal break with the establishing of an underlying transitive link (dissolve), and a straightforward spatiotemporal break (fade). But in most of the *positions* of the filmic chain, the number of units liable to appear is very much open (though not infinite). Much more open, in any case, than the series of lexemes that, by their nonfinite nature, are nonetheless opposed to the series of grammatical monemes in linguistics. For, despite the difficulty, already emphasized by Joseph Vendryes in *Le Langage,* of accurately enumerating the words of an idiom, it is at least possible to indicate the maximum and minimum limits, thus arriving at the approximate order of magnitude (for example, in French the lexeme "*lav-*" exists, but the lexeme *"patouf"* does not[2]). The case is different in the cinema, where the number of images is indefinite. Several times indefinite, one should say. For the "pro-filmic" spectacles[3] are themselves unlimited in number; the exact nature of lighting can be varied infinitely and by quantities that are nondiscrete; the same applies to the axial distance between the subject and the camera (in variations which are said to be scalar—that is, scale of the shot),[4] to the camera angle, to the properties of the film and the focal length of the lens, and to the exact trajectory of the camera movements (including the stationary shot, which represents zero degree in this case). It suffices to vary one of these elements by a perceptible quantity to obtain *another* image. The shot is therefore not comparable to the word in a lexicon; rather it resembles a complete statement (of one or more sentences), in that it is already the result of an essentially free combination, a "speech" arrangement. On

---

[1]Fades, or dissolves, can also occur in other settings, especially at the center of sequences. In such cases, their value is different.

[2]The lexemic unit *"lav-"* corresponds to *"wash-"* in English; *"patouf"* is no more of a lexeme in English than it is in French.—TRANSLATOR.

[3]As defined by Étienne Souriau. The "profilmic" spectacle is whatever is placed in front of the camera, or whatever one places the camera in front of, in order to "shoot" it.

[4]In *Le Langage cinématographique* (Paris, 1962), Francois Chevassu maintains (p. 14) that the "scale of shots" is coded. I would say instead that it is the technical terminology ("close-up," "thirty-degree angle shot," "medium shot," etc.) that is coded. The actual scale of the shots constitutes a continuous gradation, from the closest to the furthest shot. Codification intervenes at the metalinguistic level (studio jargon) in this case, and not on that of the language object (that is, cinematographic language).

the other hand the word is a syntagma that is precast by code—a "vertical" syntagma, as R. F. Mikus would say. Let us note in this connection that there is another similarity between the image and the statement: Both are actualized units, whereas the word in itself is a purely potential unit of code. The image is almost always assertive—and assertion is one of the great "modalities" of actualization, of the semic act. It apepars therefore that the paradigmatic category in film is condemned to remain partial and fragmentary, at least as long as one tries to isolate it on the level of the *image*. This is naturally derived from the fact that *creation* plays a larger role in cinematographic language than it does in the handling of idioms: To "speak" a language is to use it, but to "speak" cinematographic language is to a certain extent to invent it. The speakers of ordinary language consitute a group of users; film-makers are a group of creators. On the other hand, movie *spectators* in turn constitute a group of users. That is why the semiotics of the cinema must frequently consider things from the point of view of spectator rather than of the film-maker. Étienne Souriau's distinction between the filmic point of view and the *"cinéastique,"* of filmmaking, point of view is a very useful concept; film semiotics is mainly a *filmic* study. The situation has a rough equivalent in linguistics: Some linguists connect the speaker with the message, while the listener in some way "represents" the code, since he requires it to understand what is being said to him, while the speaker is presumed to know beforehand what he wants to say.

But, more than paradigmatic studies, it is the syntagmatic considerations that are at the center of the problems of filmic denotation. Although each image is a free creation, the arrangement of these images into an intelligible sequence—cutting and montage—brings us to the heart of the semiological dimension of film. It is a rather paradoxical situation: Those proliferating (and not very discrete!) units—the *images*—when it is a matter of composing a film, suddenly accept with reasonably good grace the constraint of a few large syntagmatic structures. While no image ever entirely resembles another image, the great majority of narrative films resemble each other in their principal syntagmatic figures. *Filmic narrativity*—since it has again crossed our path—by becoming stable through convention and repetition over innumerable films, has gradually shaped itself into forms that are more or less fixed, but certainly not immutable. These forms represent a synchronic "state" (that of the present cinema), but if they were to change, it could only be through a complete positive evolution, liable to be challenged—like those that, in spoken languages, produce diachronic transformations in the distribution of aspects and tenses. Applying de Saussure's thought to the cinema, one could say that the large syntagmatic category of the narrative film *can change,* but that no single person can make it change over night.* A failure of intellection among the viewers would be the automatic sanctioning of a purely individual innovation, which the system would refuse to confirm. The originality of creative artists consists, here as elsewhere, in tricking the code, or at least in *using* it ingeniously, rather than in attacking it directly or in violating it—and still less in ignoring it.

---

*But then, I should have added, by the same token, that this syntagmatic category contains a paradigmatic category, and consequently I should have shown less skepticism as to the possibilities of a paradigmatic category in the cinema.

AN EXAMPLE: THE ALTERNATING SYNTAGMA

It is not within the scope of this paper to analyze the principal types of *large* filmic *syntagma*. Instead, as an example, I will simply indicate some of the characteristics of one type, the *alternating syntagma* (for example, image of a mother-image of her daughter-image of the mother, etc.). The alternating syntagma rests on the principle of alternating distribution of two or more diegetic elements. The images thus fall into two or more *series,* each one of which, if shown continuously, would constitute a normal sequence. The alternating syntagma is, precisely, a rejection of the grouping by continuous series (which remains potential), for reasons of connotation—the search for a certain "construction" or a certain "effect." This type of syntagma apparently made its first appearance in 1901 in England, in a film by Williamson, *Attack on a Mission in China,* one of those "re-enacted news reels" that were popular at the time. In it, one saw images of a mission surrounded by Boxers (during the rebellion of that name) alternating with shots of marines coming to the rescue.*
Subsequently the procedure becomes more or less usual.

The alternation defines the form of the signifier, but not necessarily, as we shall see, that of the significate—which amounts to saying that the relationship between the signifier and the significate is not always analogous in the alternating syntagma. If one takes the nature of the *significate of temporal denotation* as a relevant basis, one can distinguish three cases of alternating syntagma. In the first case (which might be called the *alternator*), the alternation of the signifiers refers to a parallel alternation of the significates (analogous relationship). Example: two tennis players framed alternately, at the moment each one is returning the ball. In the second case (which would be the *alternate syntagma*), the alternating of the signifiers corresponds to a simultaneity of the significates. Example: the pursuers and the pursued. Every spectator understands that he is seeing two chronological series which are contemporaneous at each instant, and that, while he is seeing the pursued galloping away (locus of the signifier, on the screen), the pursuers are nonetheless continuing the chase (locus of the signifier, in the diegesis). Thus the semiotic *nexus*—alternating simultaneity—is no longer analogous. But it does not become "arbitrary" because of that: It remains motivated (remember that analogy is one of the forms of motivation), and the understanding of this kind of syntagma by the viewer is relatively "natural." The motivation must be explained by the spontaneous psychological mechanisms of filmic perception. Anne Souriau has shown that sequences of the "pursued-pursuing" variety are readily understood, with little previous exposure, by the spectator (on the condition, only, that the rhythm of the alternation not be too slow), for he "interpolates spontaneously" the visual material that the film presents. He guesses that series 1 continues to unfold in the plot while he is seeing series 2 in the image. The third case could be called *parallel syntagma:* Two series of events are mixed together through montage without having any relevant temporal relationships on the level of the significate (diegesis), at least with respect to denotation. It is this variety of syntagma that film theoreticians some-

---

*"Alternation" means simultaneity here. It pertains therefore to the alternate *syntagma,* as I am about to define that term.

times refer to with expressions like "neutral temporal relationships." Example: a sinister urban landscape at night, alternating with a sunny pastoral view. There is nothing to indicate whether the two scenes are simultaneous or not (and if not, which precedes and which follows). It is simply a matter of two motifs brought together for "symbolic" reasons by montage (the rich and the poor, life and death, reaction and revolution, etc.) and without their literal location in time as a pertinent factor. It is as if the denoted temporal relationship had yielded to the rich, multiple values of connotation, which depend on the context as well as on the substance of the significate.

The three varieties of alternating syntagma constitute a small system whose internal configuration recalls somewhat the structure of verbal grammatical persons as conceived by Émile Benveniste. A first correlation (presence or absence of relevant temporal denotation) allows us to distribute parallel montage to one side (absence), and alternate and alternator montage to the other (presence). Within the second term, another correlation (nature of the significate of temporal denotation) distinguishes between the alternate (significate equals simultaneity) and the alternator (significate equals alternation).*

OTHER PROBLEMS

These very brief remarks provided an example of what the syntagmatic study of filmic denotation could be. There are important differences between the semiotics of the cinema and linguistics itself. Without repeating those mentioned elsewhere, let me recall some of the main points: Film contains nothing corresponding to the purely distinctive units of the second articulation; all of its units—even the simplest, like the dissolve and the wipe—are directly significant (and moreover, as I have already pointed out, they only occur in the actualized state). The commutations and other manipulations by which the semiotics of the cinema proceeds therefore affect the large significatory units. The "laws" of cinematographic language call

---

*I have retained this passage because it gives a simple example of what commutation can be in the filmic corpus, but the factual conclusions presented here no longer correspond to the current state of my investigations of the considered point. First of all, the study of various passages of films has made it appear that the "alternator" cannot always be distinguished from the "alternate" syntagma (or, in rarer cases, from the parallel syntagma) by any really probing difference: In the example of the tennis players, it can also be considered that the two partners are both supposed to be engaged in action continuously and simultaneously (i.e., alternate syntagma). Thus—and although certain cases seem to subsist where the alternate syntagma appears, more clearly than in other cases, as a *variant* similar to what I have called here the "alternator"—I have not retained the alternator as a separate type or subtype. Then, there are cases where the alternating of images on the screen corresponds to temporal relationships not mentioned in this article: For example, one finds "alternating syntagmas" that interweave a "present" series with a "past" series (a kind of alternating flashback), and in which consequently the relationship of the two series can be defined neither by simultaneity nor by the term "neutral temporal relationship." One will note also that the concept of "alternating syntagma" has a certain obscure correspondence to that of the "frequentative syntagma." . . . In the final analysis, however, the reason I have dropped the "alternator" *as a general category of classification* is less because of the drawbacks I have just pointed out (and which various adjustments could suppress) than because of an over-all *reformulation of* the table of the main types of filmic arrangement. Taken separately, the analysis developed above remains partially valid.

for *statements* within a narrative, and not monemes within a statement, or still less phonemes within a moneme.

Contrary to what many of the theoreticians of the silent film declared or suggested (*Ciné langue,"* "visual Esperanto," etc.), the cinema is certainly not a language system *(langue)*. It can, however, be considered as a *language,* to the extent that it orders signifying elements within ordered arrangements different from those of spoken idioms—and to the extent that these elements are not traced on the perceptual configurations of reality itself (which does not tell sotries). Filmic manipulation transforms what might have been a mere visual transfer of reality into discourse. Derived from a kind of signification that is purely analogous and continuous—animated photography, cinematography—the cinema gradually shaped, in the course of its diachronic maturation, some elements of a proper semiotics, which remain scattered and fragmentary within the open field of simple visual duplication.[1]

The "shot"—an already complex unit, which must be studied—remains an indispensable reference for the time being, in somewhat the same way that the "word" was during a period of linguistic research. It might be somewhat adventurous to compare the shot to the *taxeme,* in Louis Hjelmslev's sense, but one can consider that it constitutes the largest *minimum segment* (the expression is borrowed from André Martinet), since at least one shot is required to make a film, or part of a film—in the same way, a linguistic statement must be made up of at least one phoneme. To isolate several shots from a sequence is still, perhaps, to analyze the sequence; to remove several frames from a shot is to destroy the shot. If the shot is not the smallest unit of filmic *signification* (for a single shot may convey several informational elements), it is at least the smallest unit of the filmic chain.[2]

One cannot conclude, however, that every minimum filmic segment is a shot. Besides shots, there are other minimum segments, *optical devices*—various dissolves, wipes, and so on—that can be defined as visual but not photographic elements. Whereas images have the objects of reality as referents, optical procedures, which do not represent anything, have images as referents (those contiguous in the syntagma). The relationship of these procedures to the actual shooting of the film is somewhat like that of morphemes to lexemes; depending on the context, they have two main functions: as "trick" devices (in this instance, they are sorts of semiological exponents influencing contiguous images), or as "punctuaction." The expression "filmic punctuation," which use has ratified, must not make us forget that optical procedures separate large, complex statements and thus correspond to the articulations of the literary narrative (with its pages and paragraphs, for example), whereas actual punctuation—that is to say, typographical punctuation—sep-

---

[1]But I should have added here that the significations that analogy and mechanical duplication yield—although they do not pertain to *cinematographic* language as a specific system—nevertheless do have the effect of bringing structures and elements that belong to *other* systems which are also cultural, which also carry meaning and which are also more or less organized, into the cinema (as a whole).

[2]Similarly, the phoneme is not the minimum distinctive unit, since the latter is the "feature," but it is the minimum element of the spoken *sequence,* the threshold below which an order of consecutiveness yields to an order of simultaneity.

arates sentences (period, exclamation mark, question mark, semicolon), and clauses (comma, semicolon, dash), possibly even "verbal bases," with or without characteristics (apostrophe, or dash, between two "words," and so on).

IN CONCLUSION

The concepts of linguistics can be applied to the semiotics of the cinema only with the greatest caution. On the other hand, the methods of linguistics—commutation, analytical breakdown, strict distinction between the significate and the signifier, between substance and form, between the relevant and the irrelevant, etc.—provide the semiotics of the cinema with a constant and precious aid in establishing units that, though they are still very approximate, are liable over time (and, one hopes, through the work of many scholars) to become progressively refined. . . .

1968

DANIEL DAYAN
THE TUTOR-CODE OF CLASSICAL CINEMA

Semiology deals with film in two ways.* On the one hand it studies the level of fiction, that is, the organization of film content. On the other hand, it studies the problem of "film language," the level of enunciation. Structuralist critics such as Barthes and the *Cahiers du Cinéma* of *"Young Mr. Lincoln"* have shown that the level of fiction is organized into a language of sorts, a mythical organization through which ideology is produced and expressed. Equally important, however, and far less studied, is filmic enunciation, the system that negotiates the viewer's access to the film—the system that "speaks" the fiction. This study argues that this level is itself far from ideology-free. It does not merely convey neutrally the ideology of the fictional level. As we will see, it is built so as to mask the ideological origin and nature of cinematographic statements. Fundamentally, the enunciation system analyzed below—the system of the *suture*—functions as a "tutor-code." It speaks the codes on which the fiction depends. It is the necessary intermediary between them and us. The system of the suture is to classical cinema what verbal language is to literature. Linguistic studies stop when one reaches the level of the sentence. In the same way, the system analyzed below leads only from the shot to the cinematographic statement. Beyond the statement, the level of enunciation stops. The level of fiction begins.

Our inquiry is rooted in the theoretical work of a particular time and place, which must be specified. The political events of May 1968 transformed reflection on cinema in France. After an idealist period dominated by André Bazin, a phenomenologist period influenced by Cohen-Séat and Jean Mitry, and a structuralist period initiated by the writings of Christian Metz, several film critics and theorists adopted

---

*Brian Henderson collaborated in writing this article from a previous text.

a perspective bringing together semiology and Marxism. This tendency is best represented by three groups, strongly influenced by the literary review *Tel Quel;* the cinematographic collective *Dziga Vertov,* headed by Jean-Pierre Gorin and Jean-Luc Godard: the review *Cinéthique;* the new and profoundly transformed *Cahiers du Cinéma.*

After a relatively short period of hesitation and polemics, *Cahiers* established a sort of common front with *Tel Quel* and *Cinéthique.* Their program, during the period which culminated between 1969 and 1971, was to establish the foundations of a science of cinema. Defined by Althusser, this required an "epistemological break" with previous, ideological discourses on cinema. In the post-1968 view of *Cahiers,* ideological discourses included structuralist systems of an empiricist sort. In seeking to effect such a break within discourse on cinema, *Cahiers* concentrated on authors of the second structuralist generation (Kristeva, Derrida, Schefer) and on those of the first generation who opposed any empiricist interpretation of Lévi-Strauss's work.

The point was to avoid any interpretion of a structure that would make it appear as its own cause, thus liberating it from the determinations of the *subject* and of *history.* As Alain Badiou put it,

> The structuralist activity was defined a few years ago as the construction of a "simulacrum of the object," this simulacrum being in itself nothing but intellect added to the object. Recent theoretical work conducted both in the Marxist field and in the psychoanalytic field shows that such a conception of structure should be completely rejected. Such a conception pretends to find inside of the real, a knowledge of which the real can only be the object. Supposedly, this knowledge is already there, just waiting to be revealed.*

Unable to understand the causes of a structure, what they are and how they function, such a conception considers the structure as a cause in itself. The effect is substituted for the cause; the cause remains unknown or becomes mythical (the "theological" author). The structuralism of *Cahiers* holds, on the other hand, that there is more to the whole than to the sum of its parts. The structure is not only a result to be described, but the trace of a structuring *function.* The critic's task is to locate the invisible agent of this function. The whole of the structure thus becomes the sum of its parts plus the cause of the structure plus the relationship betwen them, through which the structure is linked to the context that produced it. To study a structure is therefore *not* to search for latent meanings, but to look for that which causes or determines the structure.

Given the *Cahiers* project of a search for causes, what means were available to realize it? As Badiou points out, two systems of thought propose a structural conception of causality, Louis Althusser's Marxism and Jacques Lacan's psychoanalysis. Althusser's theses massively influenced the *Cahiers* theoretical production during the period in question. His influence was constantly commented on and made explicit, both within the *Cahiers* texts and by those who commented on them.

---

*Cited by Jean Narboni in an article on Jancsó *Cahiers du Cinéma,* no. 219. (April, 1970).

Less well understood is the influence on *Cahiers* of Lacanian psychoanalysis, that *other* system from which a science of cinema could be expected to emerge by means of a critique of empiricist structuralism.

For Lacan, psychoanalysis is a science.

> Lacan's first word is to say: in principle, Freud founded a *science.* A new science which was the science of a new object: the unconscious. . . . If psychoanalysis is a science because it is the science of a distinct object, it is also a science with the structure of all sciences: it has a *theory* and a *technique* (method) that makes possible the knowledge and transformation of its object in a specific *practice.* As in every authentically consti-tuted science, the practice is not the absolute of the science but a theoretically subor-dinate moment; the moment in which the theory, having become method (technique), comes into theoretical contact (knowledge) or practical contact (cure) with its specific object (the unconscious).*

Like Claude Lévi-Strauss, Lacan distinguishes three levels within human reality. The first level is nature, the third is culture. The intermediate is that in which nature is transformed into culture. This particular level gives its structure to human real-ity—it is the level of the symbolic. The symbolic level, or order, includes both lan-guage and other systems which produce signification, but it is fundamentally struc-tured by language.

Lacanian psychoanalysis is a theory of intersubjectivity, in the sense that it addresses the relationship(s) between "self" and "other" independently of the sub-jects who finally occupy these places. The symbolic order is a net of relationships. Any "self" is definable by its position within this net. From the moment a "self" belongs to culture its fundamental relationships to the "other" are taken in charge by this net. In this way, the laws of the symbolic order give their shape to originally physical drives by assigning the compulsory itineraries through which they can be satisfied. The symbolic order is in turn structured by language. This structuring power of language explains the therapeutic function of speech in psychoanalysis. The psychoanlyst's task is, through the patient's speech, to re-link the patient to the symbolic order, from which he has received his particular mental configuration.

Thus for Lacan, unlike Descartes, the subject is *not* the fundamental basis of cog-nitive processes. First, it is only one of many psychological functions. Second, it is not an innate function. It appears at a certain time in the development of the child and has to be constituted in a certain way. It can also be altered, stop functioning, and disappear. Being at the very center of what we perceive as our self, this function is invisible and unquestioned. To avoid the encrusted connotations of the term "subjectivity," Lacan calls this function "the imaginary." It must be understood in a literal way—it is the domain of images.

The imaginary can be characterized through the circumstances of its genesis or through the consequences of its disappearance.

The imaginary is constituted through a process which Lacan calls the mirror-phase. It occurs when the infant is six to eighteen months old and occupies a con-

---

*Louis Althusser, *Lenin and Philosophy* (New York: Monthly Review Press, 1971), pp. 198–199.

tradictory situation. On the one hand, it does not possess mastery of its body; the various segments of the nervous system are not coordinated yet. The child cannot move or control the whole of its body, but only isolated discrete parts. On the other hand, the child enjoys from its first days a precocious visual maturity. During this stage, the child identifies itself with the visual image of the mother or the person playing the part of the mother. Through this identification, the child perceives its own body as a unified whole by analogy with the mother's body. The notion of a unified body is thus fantasy before being a reality. It is an image that the child receives from outside.

Through the imaginary function, the respective parts of the body are united so as to constitute one body, and therefore to constitute somebody: one self. Identity is thus a formal structure which fundamentally depends upon an identification. Identity is one effect, among others, of the structure through which images are formed: the imaginary. Lacan thus operates a radical desacralization of the subject: the "I," the "ego," the "subject" are nothing but images, reflections. The imaginary constitutes the subject through a "speculary" effect common to the constitution of all images. A mirror on a wall organizes the various objects of a room into a unified, finite image. So also the "subject" is no more than a unifying reflection.

The disappearance of the imaginary results in schizophrenia. On the one hand, the schizophrenic loses the notion of his "ego" and, more generally, the very notion of ego, of person. He loses both the notion of his identity and the faculty of identification. On the other hand, he loses the notion of the unity of his body. His fantasies are inhabited by horrible visions of dismantled bodies, as in the paintings of Hieronymus Bosch. Finally, the schizophrenic loses his mastery of language. The instance of schizophrenia illuminates the role of language in the functioning of the imaginary in general. Because this relationship language-imaginary is highly important for our subject, the role of the imaginary in cinema, we will puruse this point in some detail.

The role of the imaginary in the utilization of language points to an entire realm of inadequacy, indeed absence, in traditional accounts of language. Saussure merely repressed or avoided the problem of the role of the subject in language utilization. The subject is eliminated from the whole field of Saussurian linguistics. This elimination commands the famous oppositions between code and message, paradigm and syntagm, language system and speech. In each case, Saussure grants linguistic relevance to one of the terms and denies it to the other. (The syntagm term is not eliminated, but is put under the paradigms of syntagms, i.e., syntax). In this way, Saussure distinguishes a deep level of linguistic structures from a superficial one where these structures empirically manifest themselves. The superficial level belongs to the domain of subjectivity, that is, to psychology. "The language system equals language less speech." Speech, however, represents the utilization of language. The entity which Saussure defines is language less its utilization. In the converse way, traditional psychology ignores language by defining thought as prior to it. Despite this mutual exclusion, however, the world of the subject and the universe of language do meet. The subject speaks, understands what he is told, reads, and so on.

To be complete, the structuralist discourse must explain the relationship language/subject. (Note the relevance of Badiou's critique of empiricist structuralism to Saussure.) Here Lacan's definition of the subject as an imaginary function is useful. Schizophrenic regression shows that language cannot function without a subject. This is not the subject of traditional psychology: what Lacan shows is that language cannot function outside of the imaginary. The conjunction of the language system and the imaginary produces the effect of reality: the referential dimension of language. What we perceive as "reality" is definable as the intersection of two functions, either of which may be lacking. In that language is a system of differences, the meaning of a statement is produced negatively, that is, by elimination of the other possibilities formally allowed by the system. The domain of the imaginary translates this negative meaning into a positive one. By organizing the statement into a whole, by giving limits to it, the imaginary transforms the statement into an image, a reflection. By conferring its own unity and continuity upon the statement, the subject organizes it into a body, giving it a fantasmatic identity. This identity, which may be called the "being" or the "ego" of the statement, is its meaning, in the same way that "I" am the meaning of my body's unity.

The imaginary function is not limited to the syntagmatic aspect of language utilization. It commands the paradigms also. A famous passage by Borges, quoted by Foucault in *The Order of Things,* illustrates this point. An imaginary Chinese encyclopedia classified animals by this scheme: (a) belonging to the emperor; (b) embalmed; (c) tamed; (d) guinea-pigs; (e) sirens; (f) fabulous; (g) dogs without a leash; (h) included in the present classification. According to Foucault, such a scheme is "impossible to think" because the sites where things are laid are so different from each other that it becomes impossible to find any surface that would accept all the things mentioned. It is impossible to find a space common to all the animals, a common ground under them. The common place lacking here is that which holds together words and things. The paradigms of language and culture hold together thanks to the perception of a common place, of a "topos" common to its elements. This common place can be defined at the level of history or society as "episteme" or "ideology." This common place is what the schizophrenic lacks.

Thus, in summary, the specular, unifying, imaginary function constitutes, on the one hand, the proper body of the subject and, on the other, the limits and the common ground without which linguistic syntagms and paradigms would be dissolved in an infinite sea of differences. Without the imaginary and the limit it imposes on any statement, statements would not function as mirrors of the referent.

The imaginary is an essential consitutent in the functioning of language. What is its role in the functioning of language? What is its role in *other* semiotic systems? Semiotic systems do not follow the same patterns. Each makes a specific use of the imaginary; that is, each confers a distinctive function upon the subject. We move now from the role of the subject in language use to the role of the subject in classical painting and in classical cinema. Here the writings of Jean-Pierre Oudart, Jean-

Louis Schefer, and others will serve as a guide in establishing the foundations of our inquiry.[1]

We meet at the outset a fundamental difference between language and other semiotic systems. A famous Stalinian judgment established the theoretical status of language: language is neither part of science nor part of ideology. It represents some sort of a third power, appearing to function—to some extent—free of historical influences. The functioning of semiotic systems such as painting and cinema, however, clearly manifests a direct dependency upon ideology and history. Cinema and painting are historical products of human activity. If their functioning assigns certain roles to the imaginary, one must consider these roles as resulting from choices (conscious or unconscious) and seek to determine the rationale of such choices. Oudart therefore asks a double question: What is the semiological functioning of the classical painting? Why did the classical painters develop it?

Oudart advances the following answers. (1) Classical figurative painting is a discourse. This discourse is produced according to figurative codes. These codes are directly produced by ideology and are therefore subjected to historical transformations. (2) This discourse defines in advance the role of the subject, and therefore predetermines the reading of the painting. The imaginary (the subject) is used by the painting to mask the presence of the figurative codes. Functioning without being perceived, the codes reinforce the ideology which they embody while the painting produces "an impression of reality" *(effet-de-réel)*. This invisible functioning of the figurative codes can be defined as a "naturalization": the impression of reality produced testifies that the figurative codes are "natural" (instead of being ideological products). It imposes as "truth" the vision of the world entertained by a certain class. (3) This exploitation of the imaginary, this utilization of the subject is made possibly by the presence of a system which Oudart calls "representation." This system englobes the painting, the subject, and their relationship upon which it exerts a tight control.

Oudart's position here is largely influenced by Schefer's *Scénographie d'un tableau*. For Schefer, the image of an object must be understood to be the pretext that the painter uses to illustrate the system through which he translates ideology into perceptual schemes. The object represented is a "pretext" for the painting as a "text" to be produced. The object hides the painting's textuality by preventing the viewer from focusing on it. However, the text of the painting is totally offered to view. It is, as it were, hidden *outside* the object. It is here but we do not see it. We see through it to the imaginary object. Ideology is hidden in our very eyes.

How this codification and its hiding process work Oudart explains by analyzing *Las Meninas* by Velasquez.[2] In this painting, members of the court and the painter himself look out at the spectator. By virtue of a mirror in the back of the room

---

[1]See Jean-Louis Schefer, *Scénographie d'un tableau* (Paris: Seuil, 1969); and articles by Jean-Pierre Oudart, "La Suture, I and II," *Cahiers du Cinéma*, nos. 211, 212 (April–May, 1969), "Travail, Lecture, Jouissance," *Cahiers du Cinéma*, no. 222 (with S. Daney, July 1970), "Un discours en defaut," *Cahiers du Cinéma*, no. 232 (October 1971).

[2]Oudart borrows here from ch. 1 of Michel Foucault's *The Order of Things* (London: Tavistock, 1970).

(depicted at the center of the painting), we see what they are looking at: the king and queen, whose portrait Velasquez is painting. Foucault calls this the representation of classical representation, because the spectator—usually invisible—is here inscribed into the painting itself. Thus the painting represents its own functioning, but in a paradoxical, contradictory way. The painter is staring at *us,* the spectators who pass in front of the canvas; but the mirror reflects only one, unchanging thing, the royal couple. Through this contradiction, the system of "representation" points toward its own functioning. In cinematographic terms the mirror represents the reverse shot of the painting. In theatrical terms, the painting represents the stage while the mirror represents its audience. Oudart concludes that the text of the painting must be be reduced to its visible part; it does not stop where the canvas stops. The text of the painting is a system which Oudart defines as a double-stage. On one stage, the show is enacted; on the other, the spectator looks at it. In classical representation, the visible is only the first part of a system which always includes an invisible second part (the "reverse shot").

Historically speaking, the system of classical representation may be placed in the following way. The figurative techniques of the quattrocento constituted a figurative system which permitted a certain type of pictorial utterance. Classical representation produces the same type of utterances but submits them to a characteristic transformation—by presenting them as the embodiment of the glance of a subject. The pictorial discourse is not only a discourse which uses figurative codes. It is that which somebody sees.

Thus, even without the mirror in *Las Meninas,* the other stage would be part of the text of the painting. One would still notice the attention in the eyes of the painting's figures, etc. But even such psychological clues only reinforce a structure which could function without them. Classical representation as a system does not depend upon the subject of the painting. The Romantic landscapes of the nineteenth century submit nature to a remodeling which imposes on them a monocular perspective, transforming the landscape into that which is seen by a given subject. This type of landscape is very different from the Japanese landscape with its multiple persepctive. The latter is *not* the visible part of a two-stage system.

While it uses figurative codes and techniques, the distinctive feature of representaiton as a semiological system is that it transforms the painted object into a sign. The object which is figured on the canvas in a certain way is the signifier of the presence of a subject who is looking at it. The paradox of *Las Meninas* proves that the presence of the subject must be signified but empty, defined but left free. Reading the signifers of the presence of the subject, the spectator occupies this place. His own subjectivity fills the empty spot predefined by the painting. Lacan stresses the unifying function of the imaginary, through which the act of reading is made possible. The representational painting is *already unified.* The painting proposes not only itself, but its own reading. The specator's imaginary can only coincide with the painting's built-in subjectivity. The receptive freedom of the spectator is reduced to the minimum—he has to accept or reject the painting as a whole. This has important consequences, ideologically speaking.

When I occupy the place of the subject, the codes which led me to occupy this place become invisible to me. The signifiers of the presence of the subject disappear from my consciousness because they are the signifiers of my presence. What I perceive is their signified: myself. If I want to understand the painting and not just be instrumental in it as a catalyst to its ideological operation, I must avoid the empirical relationship it imposes on me. To understand the ideology which the painting conveys, I must avoid providing my own imaginary as a support for that ideology. I must refuse that identification which the painting so imperiously proposes to me.

Oudart stresses that the initial relationship between a subject and any ideological object is set up by ideology as a trap which prevents any real knowledge concerning the object. This trap is built upon the properties of the imaginary and must be deconstructed through a critique of these properties. On this critique depends the possibility of a real knowledge. Oudart's study of classical painting provides the analyst of cinema with two important tools for such a critique: the concept of a double-stage and the concept of the entrapment of the subject.

We note first that the filmic image considered in isolation, the single frame or the perfectly static shot, is (for purposes of our analysis) equivalent to the classical painting. Its codes, even though "analogic" rather than figurative, are organized by the system of representation: it is an image designed and organized not merely as an object that is seen, but as the glance of a subject. Can there be a cinematography not based upon the system of representation? This is an interesting and important question which cannot be explored here. It would seem that there has not been such a cinematography. Certainly the classical narrative cinema, which is our present concern, is founded upon the representation system. The case for blanket assimilation of cinema to the system of representation is most strongly put by Jean-Louis Baudry, who argues that the perceptual system and ideology of representation are built into the cinematographic apparatus itself. (See "Ideological Effects of the Basic Cinematographic Apparatus," in *Cinéthique* #7–8.) [See Section III of this volume.] Camera lenses organize their visual field according to the laws of perspective, which thereby operate to render it as the perception of a subject. Baudry traces this system to the sixteenth and seventeenth centuries, during which the lens technology which still governs photography was developed.

Of course cinema cannot be reduced to its still frames and the semiotic system of cinema cannot be reduced to the systems of painting or of photography. Indeed, the cinematic succession of images threatens to interrupt or even to expose and to deconstruct the representation system which commands static paintings or photos. For its succession of shots is, by that very system, a succession of views. The viewer's identification with the subjective function proposed by the painting or photograph is broken again and again during the viewing of a film. Thus cinema regularly and systematically raises the question which is exceptional in painting *(Las Meninas):* "Who is watching this?" The point of attack of Oudart's analysis is precisely here— what happens to the spectator-image relation by virtue of the shot-change peculiar to cinema?

The ideological question is hardly less important than the semiological one and, indeed, is indispensable to its solution. From the standpoint of the imaginary and of ideology, the problem is that cinema threatens to expose its own functioning as a semiotic system, as well as that of painting and photography. If cinema consists in a series of shots which have been produced, selected, and ordered in a certain way, then these operations will serve, project, and realize a certain ideological position. The viewer's question, cued by the system of representation itself—"Who is watching this?" and "Who is ordering these images?"—tends, however, to expose this ideological operation and its mechanics. Thus the viewer will be aware (1) of the cinematographic system for producing ideology and (2) therefore of specific ideological messages produced by this system. We know that ideology cannot work in this way. It must hide its operations, "naturalizing" its functioning and its messages in some way. Specifically, the cinematographic system for producing ideology must be hidden and the relation of the filmic message to this system must be hidden. As with classical painting, the code must be hidden by the message. The message must appear to be complete in itself, coherent and readable entirely on its own terms. In order to do this, the filmic message must account *within itself* for those elements of the code which it seeks to hide—changes of shot and, above all, what lies behind these changes, the questions "Who is viewing this?" and "Who is ordering these images?" and "For what purpose are they doing so?" In this way, the viewer's attention will be restricted to the message itself and the codes will not be noticed. That system by which the filmic message provides answers to the viewer's questions—imaginary answers—is the object of Oudart's analysis.

Narrative cinema presents itself as a "subjective" cinema. Oudart refers here not to avant-garde experiments with subjective cameras, but to the vast majority of fiction films. These films propose images which are subtly designated and intuitively perceived as corresponding to the point of view of one character or another. The point of view varies. There are also moments when the image does not represent anyone's point of view; but in the classical narrative cinema, these are relatively exceptional. Soon enough, the image is reasserted as somebody's point of view. In this cinema, the image is only "objective" or "impersonal" during the intervals between its acting as the actors' glances. Structurally, this cinema passes constantly from the personal to the impersonal form. Note, however, that when this cinema adopts the personal form, it does so somewhat obliquely, rather like novelistic descriptions which use "he" rather than "I" for descriptions of the central character's experience. According to Oudart, this obliqueness is typical of the narrative cinema: it gives the impression of being subjective while never or almost never being strictly so. When the camera *does* occupy the very place of a protagonist, the normal functioning of the film is impeded. Here Oudart agrees with traditional film grammars. Unlike them, however, Oudart can justify this taboo, by showing that this necessary obliquity of the camera is part of a coherent system. This system is that of the suture. It has the function of transforming a vision or seeing of the film into a reading of it. It introduces the film (irreducible to its frames) into the realm of signification.

Oudart contrasts the seeing and the reading of a film by comparing the experiences associated with each. To *see* the film is *not* to perceive the frame, the camera angle and distance, etc. The space between planes or objects on the screen is perceived as real, hence the viewer may perceive himself (in relation to this space) as fluidity, expansion, elasticity.

When the viewer discovers the frame—the first step in reading the film—the triumph of his former *possession* of the image fades out. The viewer discovers that the camera is hiding things, and therefore distrusts it and the frame itself, which he now understands to be arbitrary. He wonders why the frame is what it is. This radically transforms his mode of participation—the unreal space between characters and/or objects is no longer perceived as pleasurable. It is now the space which separates the camera from the characters. The latter have lost their quality of presence. Space puts them between parentheses so as to assert its own presence. The spectator discovers that his possession of space was only partial, illusory. He feels dispossessed of what he is prevented from seeing. He discovers that he is only authorized to see what happens to be in the axis of the glance of another spectator, who is ghostly or absent. This ghost, who rules over the frame and robs the spectator of his pleasure, Oudart proposes to call "the absent-one" *(l'absent)*.

The description above is not contingent or impressionistic—the experiences outlined are the effects of a system. The system of the absent-one distinguishes cinematography, a system producing meaning, from any impressed strip of film (mere footage). This system depends, like that of classical painting, upon the fundamental opposition between two fields: (1) what I see on the screen, (2) that complementary field which can be defined as the place from which the absent-one is looking. Thus: any filmic field defined by the camera corresponds to *another* field from which an absence emanates.

So far we have remained at the level of the shot. Oudart now considers that common cinematographic utterance which is composed of a shot and a reverse shot. In the first, the missing field imposes itself upon our consciousness under the form of the absent-one who is looking at what we see. In the second shot, the reverse shot of the first, the missing field is abolished by the presence of somebody or something occupying the absent-one's field. The reverse shot represents the fictional owner of the glance corresponding to shot one.

This shot/reverse shot system orders the experience of the viewer in this way. The spectator's pleasure, dependent upon his identification with the visual field, is interrupted when he perceives the frame. From this perception he infers the presence of the absent-one and that other field from which the absent-one is looking. Shot two reveals a character who is presented as the owner of the glance corresponding to shot one. That is, the character in shot two occupies the place of the absent-one corresponding to shot one. This character retrospectively transforms the absence emanating from shot one's other stage into a presence.

What happens in *systemic* terms is this: the absent-one of shot one is an element of the code that is attracted into the message by means of shot two. When shot two replaces shot one, the absent-one is transferred from the level of enunciation to the level of fiction. As a result of this, the code effectively disappears and the ideological effect of the film is thereby secured. The code, which *produces* an imaginary, ideological effect, is hidden by the message. Unable to see the workings of the code, the spectator is at its mercy. His imaginary is sealed into the film; the spectator thus absorbs an ideological effect without being aware of it, as in the very different system of classical painting.

The consequences of this system deserve careful attention. The absent-one's glance is that of a nobody, which becomes (with the reverse shot) the glance of a somebody (a character present on the screen). Being on screen he can no longer compete with the spectator for the screen's possession. The spectator can resume his previous relationship with the film. The reverse shot has "sutured" the hole opened in the spectator's imaginary relationship with the filmic field by his perception of the absent-one. This effect and the system which produces it liberates the imaginary of the spectator, in order to manipulate if for its own ends.

Besides a *liberation of the imaginary,* the system of the suture also commands a *production of meaning.* The spectator's inference of the absent-one and the other field must be described more precisely: it is a *reading.* For the spectator who becomes frame-conscious, the visual field *means* the presence of the absent-one as the owner of the glance that constitutes the image. The filmic field thus simultaneously belongs to representation and to signification. Like the classical painting, on the one hand it represents objects or beings, on the other hand it signifies the presence of a spectator. When the spectator ceases to identify with the image, the image necessarily signifies to him the presence of another spectator. The filmic image presents itself here not as a simple image but as a show, that is, it structurally asserts the presence of an audience. The filmic field is then a signifier; the absent-one is its signified. Since it represents another field from which a fictional character looks at the field corresponding to shot one, the reverse shot is offered to the film audience as being the other field, the field of the absent-one. In this way, shot two establishes itself as the signified of shot one. By substituting for the other field, shot two becomes the meaning of shot one.

Within the system of the suture, the absent-one can therefore be defined as the intersubjective "trick" by means of which the second part of a given representative statement is no longer simply what comes after the first part, but what is *signified* by it. The absent-one makes the different parts of a given statement the signifiers of each other. His stratagem: Break the statement into shots. Occupy the space between shots.

Oudart thus defines the basic statement of classical cinematography as a unit composed of two terms: the filmic field and the field of the absent-one. The sum of these two terms, stages, and fields realizes the meaning of the statement. Robert Bresson once spoke of an exchange between shots. For Oudart such an exchange is impossible—the exchange between shot one and shot two cannot take place directly. Between shot one and shot two the other stage corresponding to shot one is a necessary intermediary. The absent-one represents the exchangability between shots. More precisely, within the system of the suture, the absent-one represents the fact that no shot can constitute by itself a complete statement. The absent-one stands for that which any shot necessarily lacks in order to attain meaning: another shot. This brings us to the dynamics of meaning in the system of the suture.

Within this system, the meaning of a shot depends on the next shot. At the level of the signifier, the absent-one continually destroys the balance of a filmic statement by making it the incomplete part of a whole yet to come. On the contrary, at the level of the signified, the effect of the suture system is a retroactive one. The character presented in shot two does not replace the absent-one corresponding to shot two, but the absent-one corresponding to shot one. The suture is always chrono-logically posterior to the corresponding shot, that is, when we finally know what the other field was, the filmic field is no longer on the screen. The meaning of a shot is given retrospectively, it does not meet the shot on the screen, but only in the memory of the spectator.

The process of reading the film (perceiving its meaning) is therefore a retroactive one, wherein the present modifies the past. The system of the suture systematically encroaches upon the spectator's freedom by interpreting, indeed by remodeling his memory. The spectator is torn to pieces, pulled in opposite directions. On the one hand, a retroactive process organizes the *signified*. On the other hand, an antici-patory process organizes the *signifier*. Falling under the control of the cinemato-graphic system, the spectator loses access to the present. When the absent-one points toward it, the signification belongs to the future. When the suture realizes it, the signification belongs to the past. Oudart insists on the brutality, on the tyranny with which this signification imposes itself on the spectator or, as he puts it, "transits through him."

Oudart's analysis of classical cinema is a deconstruction not a destruction of it. To deconstruct a system implies that one inhabits it, studies its functioning very carefully, and locates its basic articulations, both external and internal. Of course there are other cinematographic systems besides that of the suture.* One of many such others is that of Godard's late films such as *Wind from the East*. Within this system, (1) the shot tends to constitute a complete statement, and (2) the absent-one is continuously perceived by the spectator. Since the shot constitutes a whole statement, the reading of the film is no longer suspended. The spectator is not kept waiting for the remaining-part-of-the statement-which-is-yet-to-come. The reading of the shot is contemporary to the shot itself. It is immediate, its temporality is the present.

Thus the absent-one's functional definition does not change. Within the Godar-dian system as well as within the suture system the absent-one is what ties the shot (filmic level) to the statement (cinematographic level). However, in Godard's case, the two levels are not disjoined. Cinematography does not hide the filmicity of the shot. It stands in a clear relationship to it.

The system of the suture represents exactly the opposite choice. The absent-one is masked, replaced by a character, hence the real origin of the image—the condi-tions of its production represented by the absent-one—is replaced with a false origin and this false origin is situated inside the fiction. The cinematographic level fools the spectator by connecting him to the fictional level rather than to the filmic level.

But the difference between the two origins of the image is not only that one (filmic) is true and the other (fictional) false. The true origin represents the cause of the image. The false origin suppresses that cause and does not offer anything in exchange. The character whose glance takes possession of the image did not pro-

---

*Indeed, shot/reverse shot is itself merely one figure in the system(s) of classical cinema. In this initial moment of enunciation in film, we have chosen it as a privileged example of the way in which the origin of the glance is displaced in order to hide the film's production of meaning.

duce it. He is only somebody who sees, a spectator. The image therefore exists independently. It has no cause. It is.

In other terms, it is its own cause. By means of the suture, the film-discourse presents itself as a product without a producer, a discourse without an origin. It speaks.
Who speaks? Things speak for themselves and, of course, they tell the truth. Classical cinema establishes itself as the ventriloquist of ideology.

1974

WILLIAM ROTHMAN
AGAINST "THE SYSTEM OF THE SUTURE"

Dayan is interested in what he calls the "system of enunciation" basic to "classical" cinema.

He writes, "Structuralist critics such as Barthes and the *Cahiers du Cinéma* of *'Young Mr. Lincoln'* have shown that the level of fiction is organized into a language of sorts, a mythical organization through which ideology is produced and expressed. Equally important, however, and far less studied, is filmic enunciation, the system that negotiates the viewer's access to the film—the system that 'speaks' the fiction."

The system of enunciation of classical cinema, the "tutor-code" which "speaks the codes on which the fiction depends," is, according to Dayan (here as elsewhere in the article in large part summarizing the ideas of Jean-Pierre Oudart, who in turn draws on many sources) *the system of the suture.*

This is not the forum for a detailed criticism of Dayan's position from a theoretical point of view. Such a criticism might well systematically investigate his use of terms such as "ideology," "system," "codes," "classical cinema," "fiction," "enunciation," "de-construction" and so on—each of which is used in a way loaded with theoretical implications which could be challenged. Nor for a thorough analysis of the prose strategy of invoking—and assuming the authority of—a body of writing that is only partially explained and yet unavailable to the ordinary reader's independent criticism. Nor for a critical account of the interpenetration of structuralism, semiology, modernism, and Marxism which find expression in Oudart and the other writers Dayan cites.

I will rather concentrate on what I take to be clear-cut flaws in Dayan's argument.

According to Oudart/Dayan, the system of the suture is grounded in a two-shot figure. This figure causes the viewer's experience to conform to a certain scenario.

In the first shot, the viewer discovers the frame.

When the viewer discovers the frame—the first step in reading the film—the triumph of his former *possession* of the image fades out. The viewer discovers that the camera is hiding things, and therefore distrusts it and the frame itself, which he now understands to be arbitrary. He wonders why the frame is what it is. This radically transforms his mode of participation—the unreal space between characters and/or objects is no longer perceived as pleasurable. . . . He feels dispossessed of what he is prevented from seeing. He discovers that he is only authorized to see what happens to be in the axis of the glance of another spectator, who is ghostly or absent. This ghost, who rules over the frame and robs the spectator of his pleasure, Oudart proposed to call "the absent-one."

In the second shot, the reverse field shot of the first, "the missing field is abolished by the presence of somebody or something occupying the absent-one's field. The reverse shot represents the fictional owner of the glance corresponding to shot one."

The first shot as it were opens a hole in the spectator's imaginary relationship with the filmic field. This hole is "sutured" by the shot of the character presented as the absent-one of the preceding shot. Then "the spectator can resume his previous relationship with the film."

At the same time, the second shot constitutes the *meaning* of the first shot, and the system of the suture makes a "cinematographic statement" out of the pair of shots. The first shot presents, say, a view looking across Bodega Bay to the Brenner home, and as it were raises the question, "Whose view is this?"* The second shot presents itself as answering that question, thereby revealing the meaning of the first shot. It is *Melanie Daniels'* view.

It is Oudart's and Dayan's central contention that this system is an intrinsically tyrannical one. "It does not merely convey neutrally the ideology of the fictional level. . . . It is built so as to mask the ideological origin and nature of cinematographic statements." The first shot raises a question as to the source of the image. The second shot identifies that source as a character within the fiction. The two-shot figure constitutes a statement about itself. This statement is a *lie.*

Dayan argues that this sequence of "experiences" (the viewer's discomforting discovery of the frame; his uncertainty as to why the frame is what it is; his realization that he is only authorized to see what is contained in the glance of an "absent-one" who rules over that frame; his acceptance of the figure shown in the subsequent reverse shot *as* that sovereign "absent-one") is not contingent: it is the effect of a system.

But *what* is the "system" of which the above outlined experiences are effects? Studying Dayan's article, it becomes clear that he has not in fact described any mechanism which could cause a viewer to "discover the frame," and so on.

I see this failure as linked to a general uncertainty as to the actual role of the "system of the suture" in classical film. At times, Dayan writes as if it were *the* "system of enunciation" of classical cinema ("the system of the suture is to classical cinema what verbal language is to literature," etc.). But at other times (for example, in a footnote that appears added as an afterthought, despite the apparent centrality of

---

*Throughout, I will use this example from *The Birds.* The sequence is analyzed in detail, shot by shot, by Raymond Bellour in *Cahiers du Cinéma,* no. 216 (October 1969), pp 24–38.

the point it registers) he modifies the claim: it is *one* of the central enunciation systems of classical cinema (although still a "privileged" one).

The Oudart/Dayan scenario is predicted on a "previous" relationship which the viewer is said to enjoy with the film—an initial relationship that is supposedly disrupted by the viewer's discovery of the frame, and to which he returns when that disruption is "sutured." Dayan understands this to be a relationship in which the viewer "sees" rather than "reads" the film. This relationship is comparable to the relationship between spectator and representational painting, as Oudart analyses it.

Then how and why is this relationship disrupted?

Is it that film "naturally" disrupts this relationship? If that were the case, there would be no need for an explanation of the *means* by which classical cinema effects such a disruption, nor for an account of its (historical) motivation. Is it that this disruption is the necessary consequence of cutting from shot to shot in a film (as Dayan seems to suggest at one point)? But then it would need to be explained why shot changes were ever instituted.

In fact, the natural suggestion is that the strategies and "rules" of *continuity cutting* developed by Griffith and his contemporaries and followers (crystallized in the "30° rule," the "180° rule," and others) constituted precisely a system for sustaining *across shot changes* just that relationship between the viewer and the film that Dayan takes to be disrupted by the viewer's discovery of the frame. This means that the "system of the suture" was—for some reason, and in some manner—instituted despite the priority of a system which would appear to have satisfied the demands of *bourgeois* "illusionism." Given the system of continuity cutting (which would seem to have made film an extension of painting's system of representation), the viewer had to be *made* aware of the frame for the "system of the suture" to be instituted. How this awareness was effected, and what motivated the institution of this system, then become questions crucial to our understanding of "classical cinema" and its history.

Although I cannot argue this claim here, I would wish to assert that once the relationship between continuity cutting and the "system of the suture" (that is to say, *point-of-view cutting*)* is opened up to serious investigation, Dayan's assumption of a "previous relationship" in which the viewer "sees" the film image as an unmediated image of reality will have to be challenged. The time has come for a re-examination of the whole idea that classical narrative continuity is "illusionistic." I will here only suggest that Dayan's avoidance of a serious consideration of the historical

---

*Dayan avoids the term "point-of-view shot." I see no reason to follow him in this. The kind of shot whose frame is discovered in his scenario is what everyone knows is called a point-of-view shot. Dayan's terminology gives us no way of referring to the "figure" of which the point-of-view shot is part. If we call it a "shot/reverse shot pair," that does not differentiate it from the shot/reverse shot forms which do *not* contain point-of-view shots. In *The Birds,* the dialogue between Melanie and the mother is an example of this non-point-of-view shot/reverse shot form. Characteristically used in the filming of dialogues, it is logically and historically distinct from the kind of point-of-view sequence Dayan is describing. Then again, point-of-view sequences must also be differentiated from "subjective" sequences which attempt to render directly non-objective states of consciousness (rather than a view objectively seen by a fictional viewer). Hitchcock uses subjective rather than point-of-view form in *Notorious,* for example, to convey Ingrid Bergman's experience of poisoning.

motivation of the "system of the suture" and his avoidance of a serious consideration of continuity cutting, in general, are aspects of a single strategy.

Once we address ourselves to the question of how the viewer actually reads a point-of-view shot, a fundamental error in the Oudart/Dayan scenario becomes apparent.

The scenario presumes that the "system of the suture" is based on a two-shot [view/viewer] figure: a pair of shots which together constitute a complete cinematographic statement.

But in fact, the point-of-view shot is ordinarily (that is to say, *always,* except in special cases) part of a three shot [viewer/view/viewer] sequence.

Typically, such a sequence is initiated when, within an "objective" shot, a character visibly attends to something outside the borders of the frame. For example, Melanie looks out from her boat to something we cannot see. This constitutes a cue that the next shot may be a point-of-view shot presenting that "absent-view" to the viewer. Sure enough, we get the shot looking across the Bay, as if in response to the question, "What is she looking at?" (or "What does she see?"). Then we get a "reaction shot," which shows us Melanie's reaction to what she has seen, and at the same time confirms that the previous shot *was* from her point of view. (As is usual with Hitchcock, no particular identifiable emotion is registered in the reaction shot.)*

Thus the point-of-view shot is ordinarily introduced by a shot which calls attention to its own frame by indicating (by a *cue*) that there is something about to be shown that lies outside the boundaries of that frame. This cue is a condition of the viewer's discovery of the frame of the point-of-view shot itself. The viewer recognizes this as a point-of-view shot from Melanie's point of view in part because the cue establishes the significance of Melanie's absence from the following frame. The viewer perceives Melanie as significantly absented from that frame, and hence indirectly perceives the frame. This perception is a condition of the viewer's reading of the shot as one from Melanie's point of view.

Note that this specifically reverses the Oudart/Dayan scenario. It is not that the viewer discovers the frame of the shot looking out across Bodega Bay (unaccountably), infers a sovereign "absent-one," and falls prey to a tyrannical system, which makes him take Melanie, shown in the reverse shot, to be that absent-one. Rather, following on the first shot of the sequence with its conventional cue that asserts its

---

*Two points. (a) The third shot can double as the initial shot of a second point-of-view sequence. The shot that presents Melanie's reaction to what she has just seen also shows her continuing to look. Thus it contains a cue that prepares the viewer for another point-of-view shot. An extended series of telescoped point-of-view sequences can be constructed in this way. (This is in fact the case at this point in *The Birds.*) Dayan's model cannot easily accommodate this possibility. (b) A general distinction can be drawn between point-of-view sequences which attribute a particular (psychological) reaction to the character whose view is presented, and sequences which provide no psychologically unambiguous reaction shot. The Hitchcock point-of-view sequence ordinarily authorizes the viewer to accept with no possibility of doubt that the character has seen what the point-of-view shot has just shown. The meaning of that view is not revealed by the character's "reaction," but in the actions he proceeds to take which acknowledge, or withhold acknowledgment of, what he has witnessed.

frame, the viewer perceives Melanie's absence from the next frame. Perception of this specific absence is a condition of the viewer's reading of it as a shot from her point of view. This reading is confirmed by the third shot of the sequence, with its return to Melanie.

No ghostly sovereign is invoked by the point-of-view sequence.

According to the Oudart/Dayan scenario, the viewer discovers that he is "only authorized to see what happens to be in the axis of the glance of another spectator, who is ghostly or absent." *This ghost rules over the frame and robs the spectator of his pleasure.* The implication is that it is this ghost who "authorizes" the shot we are presented, who is *responsible* for the film, who *produces* the image. Thus when we accept as that "absent-one" the figure shown in the reverse shot, we are accepting what is in reality a fictional character created by the film as the creator of the film. We accept a lying statement as to the film's real source or production.

But when the viewer takes Melanie to be the "owner" of the glance corresponding to the point-of-view shot, he in no way regards Melanie as *authorizing* that shot. On the contrary, the point-of-view shot is read as an *appropriation* of her gaze. It is read as *unauthorized* by her.

The point-of-view sequence, then, ordinarily manifests the film's power of appropriating a character's gaze without authorization. It does *not* then present a figure and force the viewer to accept it as the source of that power.

Thus the point-of-view sequence in itself does not constitute a lying statement about its own real origin. Melanie is *not* presented as the real source of the image we read as "hers." The image of Melanie is manifestly derived from the same source as the image that we read as an appropriation of her gaze. Again, the sequence in itself does not constitute a statement about that source. (But the possiblity cannot be ruled out a priori that the film as a whole inscribes a statement about that source, which may truthfully acknowledge that this is a film and its world is not present.)

Dayan writes as if viewers did not know what point-of-view shots *were,* as if they did not possess the *category* of the point-of-view shot. But, of course, films that use point-of-view shots are designed for viewers who are familiar with their logic, who know how to recognize and read them.

I have spoken of the viewer's perception of "cues" that lead him to read the subsequent shot as a point-of-view shot. It is perfectly possible for a viewer to recognize such a cue and to read the point-of-view sequence correctly whether or not he has had any particular "experiences" at all. A point-of-view sequence does not depend for its reading on its "effects." It is an error to suppose that point-of-view sequences simply correspond to some "system" that can be defined by its "effects."

Not only is a point-of-view sequence not dependent for its reading on any particular effects, but its reading also does not depend on the viewer's acceptance of the *reality* of the world projected in the film. The viewer can "read" a point-of-view sequence whether or not he takes the film's world to correspond to "reality."

Dayan has given no argument that counters the commonsense position that the "effects" of a point-of-view sequence depend on the sequence, its context within the particular film, and also on the viewer's stance toward it. So, too, whether a point-of-view sequence is integral to an ideological project of a particular kind depends on the sequence and on the film. And whether a film's ideological project is *successful*—whether a viewer will actually submit to a film designed to tyrannize—depends in part on the attitude of the viewer.

Part of what I am saying is that the point-of-view sequence in itself makes no statement about reality—that is, makes no statement—at all.

Christian Metz erred in his supposition that a single shot in a "classical" film is equivalent to a *sentence*. As Dayan shows, a single shot is ordinarily incomplete ("grammatically"). But Dayan in turn is wrong in concluding that a "sutured" sequence of shots in itself constitutes a *statement*. The point-of-view sequence, with its syntactical structure, is analogous to a *sentence,* not a statement. In itself, it makes no claim that is true or false.

Films have been used in many ways. The making of various kinds of statements is, historically, among the uses of "classical" films. In order to make its statement, a film may require that a particular point-of-view sequence be placed in a specific setting within it.

Again, it seems to me that it is the film and not the sequence that constitutes the statement (if the film *makes* a statement). The statement thus made by a film may be, at one level, a statement—lying or truthful—about itself. Whether a film makes a false statement about itself, or about the world, cannot be settled merely by determining whether the film incorporates point-of-view sequences into its form.*

I think it is clear that Dayan has not succeeded in demonstrating that a point-of-view sequence as such, by its very nature, necessarily turns any film that depends on it (and thus the whole body of "classical" films) into a system of *bourgeois* ideology. *Distinctions have to be made,* grounded in serious acts of criticism, and integrated into a serious history.

But Dayan's argument was designed as a demonstration that such distinctions do not have to be made. If classical cinema depends on a system of enunciation that is by its very nature ideological *(bourgeois),* then criticism and history can be reduced to (replaced by) "de-construction."

Dayan begins from the assumption that he already knows what "'classical cinema" *is:* a *bourgeois* ideological system. Of course, he also assumes that he already knows what "*bourgeois* ideology" is. Dayan's writing reveals the attitude that "*bourgeois* ideology" and "classical cinema" are a-historical absolutes, linked by their essences which may be abstracted from history. Throughout Dayan's article, there is an unacknowledged tension between the Marxist trappings he adopts and the fundamentally anti-Marxist idea that point-of-view sequences and hence "clas-

---

*Dayan is clearly wrong as well in suggesting that the shot of the "owner" constitutes the *meaning* of the point-of-view shot. If that were so, what is contained within the frame of the point-of-view shot itself would be irrelevant to its meaning. That is hardly plausible. The point-of-view shot has significance within the film, which arises in part from the identity of the character whose view it is, in part from the occasion of his act of viewing, and in part from what is contained in the view itself. In the same way, the meaning of an utterance "in the real world" is determined by the identity of the person who utters it, by the specific circumstances of his act of uttering these words, and also by the meanings of the words he utters.

sical" films are *by their very nature* (regardless of history) reflections of a timeless *bourgeois* ideology.

The commonsense position would appear to be that "classical cinema" has through its complex history served a variety of masters. "Classical" films, to be sure, have in countless cases served many different forms of *bourgeois* ideology. But they have also been instrumental in concrete attacks on particular ideological forms. Nor has Dayan said anything which would rule out the possiblity that there have been "classical" films that were their *own* masters.

We ought not to let ourselves feel constrained from the outset to deny on a priori grounds that there are fundamental differences among point-of-view sequences and the films that use them.

Dayan argues that *Wind from the East* resorts to an alternative system of enunciation in formulating its anti-*bourgeois* acknowledgment of its own form and production. But *Man with a Movie Camera* would appear to be no less anti-*bourgeois* for its systematic use of point-of-view technique (Vertov can be said to use point-of-view sequences in this film as a tool for his de-construction of conventional narrative forms).* And I have been working on a critical analysis of late Hitchcock films which attempts to demonstrate that Hitchcock attacks conventional uses of point-of-view form by taking its logic absolutely seriously. Hitchcock does not "de-construct" the fundamental forms of "classical cinema": he acknowledges the meanings his films have accorded them.

Again: what we need is a serious history of cinematic forms, grounded in critical analyses of the sigificant uses to which these forms were put. Dayan proposes in place of such a concrete history an a priori demonstration that certain forms of cinema are destined by their nature to serve *bourgeois* ideology, and thus do not stand in need of serious critical acknowledgment.

1975

---

*Linda Podheiser has analyzed Vertov's use of point-of-view technique in an unpublished paper.

KAJA SILVERMAN
FROM THE SUBJECT OF SEMIOTICS

[ON SUTURE]

The concept of suture attempts to account for the means by which subjects emerge within discourse . . . although that concept has been most intensely theorized in relation to cinematic texts, its initial formulation comes from Jacques-Alain Miller, one of Lacan's disciples. We will look briefly at that formulation before turning to the cinematic one.

Miller defines suture as that moment when the subject inserts itself into the symbolic register in the guise of a signifier, and in so doing gains meaning at the expense of being. In "Suture (elements of the logic of the signifier)," he writes:

> Suture names the relation of the subject to the chain of its discourse . . . it figures there as the element which is lacking, in the form of a stand-in. For, while there lacking, it is not purely and simply absent. Suture, by extension—the general relation of lack to the structure of which it is an element, inasmuch as it implies the position of a taking-the-place-of.*

Miller's account of suture locates the emphasis in orthodox Lacanian places; the key terms in his definition of it are "lack" and "absence." Indeed, as Miller describes it, suture closely resembles the subject's inauguration into language, illustrated by Lacan with the *"fort"/ "da"* game. A given signifier (a pronoun, a personal name) grants the subject access to the symbolic order, but alienates it not only from its own needs but from its drives. That signifier stands in for the absent subject (i.e. absent in being) whose lack it can never stop signifying.

The French theoretician Jean-Pierre Oudart subsequently transported the concept of suture into film studies, where it has been used to probe the precise nature of cinematic signification—to answer the frequently pondered questions "What is

---

*Miller, "Suture (elements of the logic of the signifier)," *Screen* (1977–78), *18*(4): 25–26.

the cinematic equivalent for language in the literary text?" and "What is cinematic syntax?" These formal speculations have not pre-empted those about subjectivity but have been integrated into them. The theory of suture has been rendered more complex with each new statement about it, so that it now embraces a set of assumptions not only about cinematic signification, but about the viewing subject and the operations of ideology. Rather than retracing each argument in turn, we will here attempt to provide a synthesis of the contributions made by Jean-Pierre Oudart, Daniel Dayan, Stephen Heath, [and] Laura Mulvey. . . .

SUTURE: THE CINEMATIC MODEL

Theoreticians of cinematic suture agree that films are articulated and the viewing subject spoken by means of interlocking shots. They are thus in fundamental accord with Noel Burch's remark that "Although camera movements, entrances into and exits from frame, composition and so on can all function as devices aiding in the organization of the film object . . . the shot transition [remains] the basic element [of that organization]."* Shot relationships are seen as the equivalent of syntactic ones in linguistic discourse, as the agency whereby meaning emerges and a subject-position is constructed for the viewer.

However, some theoreticians conceptualize those relationships differently from others. Whereas Oudart and Dayan find the shot/reverse shot formation to be virtually synonymous with the operations of suture, Heath suggests that it is only one element in a much larger system, and emphasizes features of the editing process which are common to all shot transitions. We will begin by discussing the shot/reverse shot formation and then extend the theory of suture in the directions indicated by Heath.

The shot/reverse shot formation is a cinematic set in which the second shot shows the field from which the first shot is assumed to have been taken. The logic of this set is closely tied to certain "rules" of cinematic expression, in particular the 180° rule, which dictates that the camera not cover more than 180° in a single shot. This stricture means that the camera always leaves unexplored the other 180° of an implicit circle—the half of the circle which it in fact occupies. The 180° rule is predicated on the assumption that a complete camera revolution would be "unrealistic," defining a space larger than the "naked eye" would normally cover. Thus it derives from the imperative that the camera deny its own existence as much as possible, fostering the illusion that what is shown has an autonomous existence, independent of any technological interference, or any coercive gaze.

However, the viewing subject, unable to sustain for long its belief in the autonomy of the cinematic image, demands to know whose gaze controls what it sees. The shot/reverse shot formation is calculated to answer that question in such a manner that the cinematic illusion remains intact: Shot 1 shows a space which may or may not contain a human figure (e.g., the wall of a building, a view of the ocean, a room full of people), being careful not to violate the 180° rule. Shot 2 locates a

---

*Burch, *Theory of Film Practice,* trans. Helen R. Lane (New York: Praeger, 1973), p. 12.

spectator in the other 180° of the same circular field, thereby implying that the preceding shot was seen through the eyes of a figure in the cinematic narrative.[1] As a result, the level of enunciation remains veiled from the viewing subject's scrutiny, which is entirely absorbed within the level of the fiction; the subject of the speech seems to be the speaking subject, or to state it differently, the gaze which directs our look seems to belong to a fictional character rather than to the camera.

Theoretically, the filmmaker would be obliged to achieve an exact match between the two parts of the shot/reverse shot formation (i.e. shot 1 would delineate precisely half of a circle, and shot 2 the other half; moreover, in shot 1 the camera would take up a position identical with that of the spectator in shot 2). In practice, however, such precision is rarely observed. A simple display of a fictional character looking in shot 2 usually proves sufficient to maintain the illusion that shot 1 visually "belongs" to that character. The camera may even adopt an oblique position, slightly to one side of the actor, rather than directly facing him or her.

Filmmakers are generally no more literal with shot 1 of the shot/reverse shot formation. Often we are shown the shoulders or head of the character through whose eyes we are ostensibly looking. In fact, mathematical exactitude provides a much less successful approximation of "reality" than does the loose application of the shot/reverse shot convention.

In "Notes on Suture," Stephen Heath cautions against too restrictive an identification of suture with the shot/reverse shot formation, which statistical studies have shown to be symptomatic of only about one-third of the shots in a classical Hollywood film.[2] Actually, the suture argument relies much less centrally on the notion of syntagmatic progression, and the question of whether it is achieved through the shot/reverse shot formation or by some other means, than on the process of cinematic signification and its relationship to the viewing subject.

Consequently, the shot/reverse shot formation derives its real importance and interest for many of the theoreticians of suture because it demonstrates so lucidly the way in which cinema operates to reduplicate the history of the subject. The viewer of the cinematic spectacle experiences shot 1 as an imaginary plenitude, unbounded by any gaze, and unmarked by difference. Shot 1 is thus the site of a *jouissance* akin to that of the mirror stage prior to the child's discovery of its separation from the ideal image which it has discovered in the reflecting glass.

However, almost immediately the viewing subject becomes aware of the limitations on what it sees—aware, that is, of an absent field. At this point shot 1 becomes a signifier of that absent field, and *jouissance* gives way to unpleasure. Daniel Dayan offers a very clear summary of this transition in "The Tutor-Code of Classical Cinema":

> When the viewer discovers the frame—the first step in reading the film—the triumph of his former *possession* of the image fades out. The viewer discovers that the camera is hiding things, and therefore distrusts it and the frame itself which he now understands to be arbitrary. He wonders why the frame is what it is. This radically transforms his mode of participation—the unreal space between characters and/or objects is no longer

---

[1] This paradigm may be reversed.
[2] Heath, "Notes on Suture," *Screen* (1977–78), *18*(2): 65–66.

perceived as pleasurable. It is now the space which separates the camera from the characters. The latter have lost their quality of presence. The spectator discovers that his possession of space was only partial, illusory. He feels dispossessed of what he is prevented from seeing. He discovers that he is only authorized to see what happens to be in the axis of the gaze of another spectator, who is ghostly or absent.[1]

Jean-Pierre Oudart refers to the spectator who occupies the missing field as the "Absent One." The Absent One, also known as the Other, has all the attributes of the mythically potent symbolic father: potency, knowledge, transcendental vision, self-sufficiency, and discursive power. It is of course the speaking subject of the cinematic text, a subject which . . . finds its locus in a cluster of technological apparatuses (the camera, the tape-recorder, etc.) We will see that this speaking subject often finds its fictional correlative in an ideal paternal representation.

The speaking subject has everything which the viewing subject, suddenly cognizant of the limitations on its vision, understands itself to be lacking. This sense of lack inspires in that subject the desire for "something else," a desire to see more.

However, it is equally important that the presence of the speaking subject be hidden from the viewer. Oudart insists that the classic film text must at all costs conceal from the viewing subject the passivity of that subject's position, and this necessitates denying the fact that there is any reality outside of the fiction.

The shot/reverse shot formation is ideally suited for this dual purpose, since it alerts the spectator to that other field whose absence is experienced as unpleasurable while at the same time linking it to the gaze of a fictional character. Thus a gaze within the fiction serves to conceal the controlling gaze outside the fiction; a benign other steps in and obscures the presence of the coercive and castrating Other. In other words, the subject of the speech passes itself off as the speaking subject.

For Oudart, cinematic signification depends entirely upon the moment of unpleasure in which the viewing subject perceives that it is lacking something, that is, that there is an absent field. Only then, with the disruption of imaginary plenitude, does the shot become a signifier, speaking first and foremost of that thing about which the Lacanian signifier never stops speaking: castration. A complex signifying chain is introduced in place of the lack which can never be made good, suturing over the wound of castration with narrative. However, it is only by inflicting the wound to begin with that the viewing subject can be made to want the restorative of meaning and narrative.

Stephen Heath emphasizes the process of negation which occurs concurrently with a film's positive assertions—its structuring absences and losses. In "Narrative Space," he writes:

Film is the production not just of a negation but equally, simultaneously, of a negativity, the excessive foundation of the process itself, of the very movement of the spectator as subject in the film; which movement is stopped in the negation and its centering positions, the constant phasing in of subject vision ("this but not that" as the sense of the image in flow).[2]

---

[1]Dayan, "The Tutor-Code of Classical Cinema," in *Movies and Methods,* ed. Bill Nichols (Berkeley: Univ. of California Press, 1976), p. 448.
[2]Heath, "Narrative Space," *Screen* (1976), 17(3): 107.

The unseen apparatuses of enunciation represent one of these structuring losses, but there are others which are equally important. The classic cinematic organization depends upon the subject's willingness to become absent to itself by permitting a fictional character to "stand in" for it, or by allowing a particular point of view to define what it sees. The operation of suture is successful at the moment that the viewing subject says, "Yes, that's me," or "That's what I see."

Equally important to the cinematic organization are the operations of cutting and excluding. It is not merely that the camera is incapable of showing us everything at once, but that it does not wish to do so. We must be shown only enough to know that there is more, and to want that "more" to be disclosed. A prime agency of disclosure is the cut, which divides one shot from the next. The cut guarantees that both the preceding and the subsequent shots will function as structuring absences to the present shot. These absences make possible a signifying ensemble, convert one shot into a signifier of the next one, and the signified of the preceding one.

Thus cinematic coherence and plenitude emerge through multiple cuts and negations. Each image is defined through its differences from those that surround it syntagmatically and those it paradigmatically implies ("this but not that"), as well as through its denial of any discourse but its own. Each positive cinematic assertion represents an imaginary conversion of a whole series of negative ones. This castrating coherence, this definition of a discursive position for the viewing subject which necessitates not only its loss of being, but the repudiation of alternative discourses, is one of the chief aims of the system of suture.

Most classic cinematic texts go to great lengths to cover over these "cuts." Hitchcock's *Psycho,* on the other hand, deliberately exposes the negations upon which filmic plenitude is predicated. It unabashedly foregrounds the voyeuristic dimensions of the cinematic experience, making constant references to the speaking subject, and forcing the viewer into oblique and uncomfortable positions both *vis-à-vis* the cinematic apparatuses and the spectacle which they produce.

Psycho not only ruptures the Oedipal formation which provides the basis of the present symbolic order, but declines to put it back together at the end. The final shot of Norman/mother, which conspicuously lacks a reverse shot, makes clear that the coherence of that order proceeds from the institution of sexual difference, and the denial of bisexuality.

Finally, *Psycho* obliges the viewing subject to make abrupt shifts in identification. These identifications are often in binary opposition to each other; thus the viewing subject finds itself inscribed into the cinematic discourse at one juncture as victim, and at the next juncture as victimizer. These abrupt shifts would seem to thwart the process of identification, as would all the other strategies just enumerated. However, quite the reverse holds true. The more intense the threat of castration and loss, the more intense the viewing subject's desire for narrative closure.

Psycho's opening few shots take in the exterior of a group of city buildings, without a single reverse shot to anchor that spectacle to a fictional gaze. The transition from urban skyline to the interior of a hotel room is achieved by means of a trick shot: the camera appears to penetrate the space left at the bottom of a window whose venetian blind is three-quarters closed. The viewing subject is made acutely aware of the impossibility of this shot—not just the technical but the "moral" impossibility, since the shot in question effects a startling breach of privacy.

Our sense of intruding is accentuated by the first shot inside the hotel room, which shows us a woman (Marion), still in bed, and her lover (Sam) standing beside the bed, half-undressed, with a towel in his hands. His face is cropped by the frame, so that he preserves a certain anonymity denied to Marion, who will be the object of numerous coercive gazes during the film. From the very outset, the viewer is not permitted to forget that he or she participates in that visual coercion.

Marion and Sam exchange a series of embraces before leaving the hotel room. Their lovemaking is interrupted by a discussion about Sam's marital status, and the strain imposed by their clandestine meetings. Marion expresses an intense desire to have their relationship "normalized"—to be inserted through marriage into an acceptable discursive position. Sam comments bitterly on the economic obstacles in the way of such a union. Later in the same day when Marion is entrusted with $40,000 which is intended to buy someone else's marital bliss, and when the man who gives it to her announces that he never carries more money that he can afford to lose, Marion decides to achieve her culturally induced ambitions through culturally taboo means.

The sequence which follows is an extremely interesting one in terms of suture. In the first shot of that scene Marion stands in the doorway of her bedroom closet, her right side toward the camera, wearing a black brassiere and half-slip. A bed separates the camera from her, and in the left far corner there is a vanity-table and mirror. Suddenly the camera moves backward to reveal a corner of the bed not previously exposed, on which lies the envelope of stolen money. It zooms in on the money, then pans to the left and provides a close-up of an open suitcase, full of clothing. During all of this time, Marion is facing the closet, unable to see what we see.

There is a cut to Marion, who turns and looks toward the bed. Once again the camera pulls back to reveal the packet of money. In the next shot, Marion adjusts her hair and clothes in front of the vanity-table and mirror. She turns to look at the bed, and we are given a reverse shot of the stolen envelope. This particular shot/ reverse shot formation is repeated. Finally, Marion sits down on the bed, puts the money in her purse, picks up the suitcase, and leaves.

This sequence achieves a number of things: It establishes the fascination of the money, not only for Marion but for us (we can't help looking at it, even when Marion's back is turned). It delimits a claustral transactional area, an area from which all mediating objects (i.e., the bed) are eventually removed, from which Marion can no longer emerge. The film resorts more and more obsessively to shot/reverse shots in the following episodes, suggesting Marion's absolute entrapment within the position of a thief. Finally, it associates the money with a transcendental gaze, a gaze which exceeds Marion's, and that can see her without ever being seen—one which knows her better than she knows herself.

The privileged object in the shot/reverse shot formations which punctuate the second half of this episode is the packet of money, not Marion. Indeed, the entire spatial field is defined in relation to that spot on the bed where the $40,000 lies; positioned in front of it, we look for a long time at the contents of the room before its human inhabitant ever casts a significant glance at anything. By privileging the point of view of an inanimate object, Hitchcock makes us acutely aware of what Oudart would call the "Absent One"—that is, of the speaking subject. Our relationship with the camera remains unmediated, "unsoftened" by the intervention of a human gaze.

Far from attempting to erase our perception of the cinematic apparatus, the film exploits it, playing on the viewing subject's own paranoia and guilt. We enjoy our visual superiority to Marion, but at the same time we understand that the gaze of the camera—that gaze in which we participate—exceeds us, threatening not only Marion but anyone exposed to the film's spectacle.

It would appear that the system of suture cannot be too closely identified with that shot/reverse shot formation in which the function of looking is firmly associated with a fictional character, since by violating that convention Hitchcock throws a much wider net over his audience. He thereby forces the viewing subject to take up residence not only within one of the film's discursive positions (that of victim), but a second (that of sadistic and legalistic voyeur). The whole operation of suture can be made *more* rather than less irresistible when the field of the speaking subject is continually implied. Two other episodes in *Psycho* demonstrate the same point.

The earlier of these inscribes the law into the fictional level of the film through the figure of a highway patrolman. An opening long-shot shows Marion's car pulled over to the side of a deserted road. A police car pulls into frame and parks behind it. In the next shot the patrolman climbs out of his car, walks over to the driver's side of Marion's automobile, and looks through the window. A third shot shows us what he sees—a sleeping Marion. A succession of almost identical shot/reverse shot formations follow, by means of which the superiority of the legal point of view is dramatized. The patrolman knocks on Marion's window and at last she wakes up. We are now provided with a shot/reverse shot exchange between the two characters, but although Marion does in fact look back at the person who has intruded upon her, his eyes are concealed by a pair of dark glasses.

The policeman interrogates Marion about her reasons for sleeping in her car, and she explains that she pulled over because of fatigue. She asks: "Have I broken a law?" The conversation is as oblique as the exchange of looks—rather than answering her question, the patrolman asks: "Is there anything wrong?" His question is neither casual nor solicitous; it is a threat, backed up by a series of quick shot/reverse shots which expose Marion yet further to the scrutiny of a law which it seems impossible to evade, and impossible to decipher.

The police officer asks to see Marion's license. Again the question is far from innocent; "license" has as broadly existential a meaning as the word "wrong" in the earlier question. After she gives him her driver's license, the patrolman walks around to the front of the car to write down the license plate number. We see him through the windshield, still protected by his dark glasses from any personal recognition. The reverse shot discloses not Marion, but the license plate, which seems to speak for her with greater authority, and to do so through a legal discourse which renders her even more passive.

The policeman permits Marion to resume her journey, but he tails her for several miles. Her paranoia during this period is conveyed through a group of alternating frontal shots of her driving, and reverse shots of her rearview mirror. The patrol car is clearly visible in both—Marion is now doubly inscribed.

Several sequences later, as Marion continues on her journey in the rain and darkness, the voices of her boss, of the man whose money she has stolen, and of a female friend are superimposed on the sound track, speaking about Marion and defining her even more fully. This device is the acoustic equivalent of all those shots which we have seen, but which Marion has been unable to see because her back was turned, because she was looking in another direction, or because she was asleep. It serves, like those shots, to reinforce the viewing subject's consciousness of an Other whose transcendent and castrating gaze can never be returned, and which always sees one thing: guilt.

The famous shower sequence not only further disassociates the film's spectacle from any of its characters but suggests how much larger the system of suture is than any shot formation. The scene begins with Marion undressing in a motel bedroom, watched through a peephole by Norman, her eventual killer. She goes into the bathroom and flushes down the torn pieces of paper on which she has just taken stock of her financial situation (she has decided to return the stolen money, and wants to calculate how much of it she has spent). Marion then closes the bathroom door, effectively eliminating the possibility of Norman or anyone else within the fiction watching her while she showers. Once again the camera insists on the primacy of its own point of view.

Marion steps inside the bath, and we see her outline through the half-transparent curtain. Then, in a shot which parallels the earlier one in which we seem to slip through the bottom of the hotel window, we penetrate the curtain and find ourselves inside the shower with Marion. The film flaunts these trick shots, as if to suggest the futility of resisting the gaze of the speaking subject.

There are nine shots inside the shower before Marion's killer attacks. They are remarkable for their brevity, and for their violation of the 30° rule (the rule that at least 30° of space must separate the position of the camera in one shot from that which follows it in order to justify the intervening cut). Some of the theoreticians of suture argue that the narrative text attempts to conceal its discontinuities and ruptures, but the shower sequence repeatedly draws our attention to the fact of the cinematic cut. This episode also includes a number of obtrusive and disorienting shots—shots taken from the point of view of the shower head at which Marion looks. When the stabbing begins, there is a cinematic cut with almost every thrust of the knife. The implied equation is too striking to ignore: the cinematic machine is lethal; it too murders and dissects. The shower sequence would seem to validate Heath's point that the coherence and plenitude of narrative film are created through negation and loss.

We have no choice but to identify with Marion in the shower, to insert ourselves into the position of the wayward subject who has strayed from the highway of cultural acceptability, but who now wants to make amends. The vulnerability of her naked and suprisingly small body leaves us without anything to deflect that transaction. Marion's encounter with the warm water inside the shower not only suggests a ritual purification, but a contact so basic and primitive as to break down even such dividing lines as class or sexual difference. Finally, the whole process of identification is formally insisted upon by the brevity of the shots; the point of view shifts constantly within the extremely confined space of the shower, making Marion the only stable object, that thing to which we necessarily cling.

That identification is not even disrupted when the cutting activity is mirrored at the level of the fiction, and a bleeding, stumbling Marion struggles to avoid the next knife wound. It is sustained up until the moment when Marion is definitively dead, an inanimate eye now closed to all visual exchanges. At this point we find ourselves in the equally appalling position of the gaze which has negotiated Marion's murder, and the showing of the corners of the frame so as to simulate the perspective of a peephole insists that we acknowledge our own voyeuristic implication.

Relief comes with the resumption of narrative, a resumption which is effected through a tracking shot from the bathroom into the bedroom. That tracking shot comes to rest first upon the packet of money, then upon an open window through which Norman's house can be seen, and finally upon the figure of Norman himself, running toward the motel. When Norman emerges from his house, adjacent to the motel, the full extent of our complicity becomes evident, since we then realize that for the past five or ten minutes we have shared not his point of view, but that of a more potent and castrating Other. But the envelope of money rescues us from too prolonged a consideration of that fact.

The $40,000 assures us that there is more to follow, and that even though we have just lost our heroine, and our own discursive position, we can afford to finance others. What sutures us at this juncture is the fear of being cut off from narrative. Our investment in the fiction is made manifest through the packet of money which provides an imaginary bridge from Marion to the next protagonist.

Psycho is relentless in its treatment of the viewing subject, forcing upon it next an identification with Norman, who with sober face and professional skill disposes of the now affectless body of Marion, cleans the motel room, and sinks the incriminating car in quicksand. Marion is subsequently replaced in the narrative by her look-alike sister, and Norman's schizophrenia dramatizes the same vacillation from the position of victim to that of victimizer which the viewing subject is obliged to make in the shower sequence and elsewhere. *Psycho* runs through a whole series of culturally overdetermined narratives, showing the same cool willingness to substitute one for another that it adopts with its characters. Moreover, the manifest context of these narratives yields all too quickly to the latent, undergoing in the process a disquieting vulgarization. We understand perfectly the bourgeois inspiration of Marion's marital dreams, and the spuriousness of the redemptive scenario she hopes to enact by returning the money. Similarly, Norman's Oedipal crisis is played more as farce than melodrama, replete with stuffed birds and hackneyed quarrels in which he plays both parts.

The film terrorizes the viewing subject, refusing ever to let it off the hook. That hook is the system of suture, which is held up to our scrutiny even as we find ourselves thoroughly ensnared by it. What *Psycho* obliges us to understand is that we want suture so badly that we'll take it at any price, even with the fullest knowledge of what it entails—passive insertions into pre-existing discursive positions (both mythically potent and mythically impotent); threatened losses and false recoveries; and subordination to the castrating gaze of a symbolic Other.

In fact, the more the operations of enunciation are revealed to the viewing subject, the more tenancious is its desire for the comfort and closure of narrative—the more anxious it will be to seek refuge within the film's fiction. In so doing, the viewing subject submits to cinematic signification, permits itself to be spoken by the film's discourse. For the theoreticians of suture, the viewing subject thereby reenacts its entry into the symbolic order.

We have seen how central a role narrative plays in determining the viewer's relationship to *Psycho,* but we have not yet attempted a general formulation of the ways in which suture overlaps with story. It is once again Stephen Heath to whom we must turn for such a formulation.

Heath argues that narrative not only makes good the losses and negations which result from classic cinema's editing operations, but that its coherence is made possible through them. He points out that fragmentation is the basis of diegetic unity—that narrative integration is predicated not so much on long takes and invisible cuts as on short takes which somehow foreground their own partial and incomplete status. The narrative moves forward and acts upon the viewer only through the constant intimation of something which has not yet been fully seen, understood, revealed; in short, it relies upon the inscription of lack:

> . . . the work of classical continuity is not to hide or ignore off-screen space but, on the contrary, to contain it, to regularise its fluctuation in a constant movement of reappropriation. It is this movement that defines the rules of continuity and the fiction of space they serve to construct, the whole functioning according to a kind of metonymic lock in which off-screen space becomes on-screen space and is replaced in turn by the space it holds off, each joining over the next. The join is conventional and ruthlessly selective (it generally leaves out of account, for example, the space that might be supposed to be masked at the top and bottom of the frame, concentrating much more on the space at the sides of the frame or on that "in front," "behind the camera," as in variations of field/reverse field), and demands that the off-screen space recaptured must be "called for," must be "logically consequential," must arrive as "answer," "fulfilment of promise" or whatever (and not as difference or contradiction)—must be narrativised.*

Heath here suggests that the shot/reverse shot formation is merely one device among many for encoding anticipation into a film, and for regularizing the difference which might otherwise emerge as contradiction. Camera movement, movement within the frame, off-screen sound, and framing can all function in a similar indexical fashion to a fictional gaze, directing our attention and our desire beyond the limits of one shot to the next. Narrative, however, represents a much more indispensable part of the system of suture. It transforms cinematic space into dramatic place, thereby providing the viewer not just with a vantage but a subject position.

Cinematic suture is thus largely synonymous with the operations of classic narrative, operations which include a wide variety of editing, lighting, compositional, and other formal elements, but within which the values of absence and lack always play a center role. Those values not only activate the viewer's desire and transform one shot into a signifier for the next, but serve to deflect attention away from the

---

*Heath, "Narrative Space," pp. 91–92.

level of enunciation to that of the fiction, even when as in *Psycho* the cinematic apparatus is constantly implied. As Heath observes,

> The suturing operation is in the process, the give and take of presence and absence, the play of negativity and negation, flow and bind. Narrativisation, with its continuity, closes, and is that movement of closure that shifts the spectator as subject in its terms. . . .*

A closely adjacent passage from "Narrative Space" emphasizes the never ending nature of the suture process, the fact that the subject's "construction-reconstruction has always to be renewed." What seems to us a stable world is actually nothing more than the effect of this constant renewal, of the ceaselessness of the discursive activities which provide us with our subjectivity. . . .

1983

---

*Ibid., p. 99.

NICK BROWNE
THE SPECTATOR-IN-THE-TEXT: THE RHETORIC OF *STAGECOACH*

The sequence from John Ford's *Stagecoach,* shown in the accompanying stills, raises the problem of accounting for the organization of images in an instance of the "classical" fiction film and of proposing the critical terms appropriate for that account. The formal features of these images—the framing of shots and their sequencing, the repetition of setups, the position of characters, the direction of their glances—can be taken together as a complex structure and understood as a characteristic answer to the rhetorical problem of telling a story, of showing an action to a spectator. Because the significant relations have to do with seeing—both in the ways the characters "see" each other and the way those relations are shown to the spectator—and because their complexity and coherence can be considered as a matter of "point of view," I call the object of this study the "specular text."

Explanations of the imagery of the classical narrative film are offered by technical manuals and various theories of editing. Here, though, I wish to examine the connection between the act of narration and the imagery, specifically in the matter of the framing and the angle of view determined by setups, by characterizing the narrating agency or authority which can be taken to rationalize the presentation of shots. An explanation of this kind necessarily involves clarifying in some detail the notion of the "position of the spectator." Thus we must characterize the spectator's implied position with respect to the action, the way it is structured, and the specific features of the process of "reading" (though not in the sense of interpretation). Doing so entails a description (within the terms of the narrative) of the relation of literal and fictional space that comprehends what seems, ambiguously, like the double origin of the filmic images.

An inquiry into the forms of authority for the imagery and the corresponding strategies which implicate the viewer in the action has few precedents, yet it raises general but basic questions about filmic narration that begin to clarify existing

210

accounts of the relation of narrative to image. The sequence from *Stagecoach* is interesting as a structure precisely because, in spite of its simplicity (it has no narrative or formal eccentricity), it challenges the traditional premises of critical efforts to account for the operation and effects of "classical" film style.

The traditional rationale for the presentation of imagery is often stated by the camera's relation to the spectator. For instance, a basically dramatic account has it that the shots should show essentially what a spectator would see if the action were played on a stage, and if at each moment he had the best view of the action (thus the changing angles only supply "accents"). Editing would follow the spectator's natural course of attention as it is implied by the action of the *mise-en-scène*. In such a mode the question of agency—that is, who is "staging" and making these events appear in this way—is referred not to the author or narrator but to the action itself, fully embodied in the characters. Everything that happens must be exhibited clearly for the eye of the spectator. On this theory, all the structures of the presentation are directed to a place external to the scene of the action—to the final authority, the ideal spectator. Oudart's account (*Film Quarterly,* Fall 1974) proposes that imagery is paradigmatically referred to the authority of the glance of the "absent one," the offscreen character within the story who in the countershot is depicted within the frame; the spectator "identifies" with the visual field of the "owner" of the glance. The "system of the suture" is an explanation that establishes the origin of the imagery by reference to the agency of character, but, surprisingly, it does not consider (indeed it seems to deny) the final agency, the authority of the narrator. The traces of the action of the narrator may seem to be effaced by this sytem, but such an effect can only be the result of a certain more general rhetoric. Thus I am proposing an account in which the structure of the imagery, whatever its apparent forms of presentation, refers jointly to the action of an implied narrator (who defines his position with respect to the tale by his judgments) and to the imaginative action occasioned by his placing and being placed by the spectator. Neither the traditional nor the more recent theories seem fully adequate to this problematic.

Thus the problem that arises from *Stagecoach* is to explain the functioning of the narrator and the nature and effects of spectator placement; specifically, describing and accounting for in detail a filmic rhetoric in which the agency of the narrator in his relation to the spectator is enacted jointly by the characters and the particular sequence of shots that show them. To describe this rhetoric in a rigorous and illuminating way means clarifying in filmic terms the notions of "narrative authority," "point of view," and "reading," and showing that these concepts are of use precisely because they arise naturally from the effort to account for the concrete structures of the text.

The moment in the story that the sequence depicts is the taking of a meal at the Dry Fork station on the stage's way to Lordsburg. Earlier in the film, the prostitute Dallas (the woman in the dark hat) has been run out of town by the Ladies' Law and Order League and has been put aboard the stagecoach. There she joined, among others, a cavalry officer's wife named Lucy (in the white hat) and Hatfield, her chivalrous but distant escort. Just before the present scene, the Ringo Kid (John Wayne), who has broken out of jail to avenge his brother's murder, has been ordered aboard by the sheriff when discovered by the side of the road. The sequence begins immediately after a vote among the members of the group to decide whether to go on to Lordsburg and ends shortly before the end of the scene when the group exits the station. For purposes of convenience, I have called shots 4, 8, and 10, which are from the same setup, series A, and shots 3, 7, 9, and 11, series B.

One of the rationales that might be proposed to account for the setups, the spatial fields they show, the sequence of shots, is their relation to the "psychology" of the characters. How, if at all, are the setups linked to the visual attention, as with the glance, or say the interests of a character in the story? In the shot/reverse shot pattern which is sometimes, wrongly I think, taken as an exclusive paradigm of the "classical" style, the presence of the shot on the screen is "explained" or read as the depiction of the glance of the offscreen character, who, a moment later, is shown in the reverse shot. But because only a few shots of this sequence (or of most films) follow this pattern, we shall be pressed to a different formulation. The general question is how the two setups of the two major series of shots—series A from the head of the table and series B from the left side—are to be explained.

Series A is related to the visual attention of the woman at the head of the table, Lucy. The connection between the shots and her view, especially in the modulation of the force and meaning of that view, must, however, be established. These shots from A are readable as the depiction of Lucy's glance only retrospectively, after series B has shown her at the head of the table and after the animation conveyed in the dolly forward has implied its significance. The point remains, however, that the shots of series A are finally clearly authorized by a certain disposition of attention of one of the characters.

In contrast to series A, the series B shots from the left of the table are like the opening and closing shots (1, 12) in not being associated with or justified spatially as the depiction of anyone's glance. Can the placement of these shots be justified either as the "best angle" for the spectator or as the depiction of some other more complex conception of "psychology" of character than an act of attention in a glance? Persons to whom these shots might be attributed as mental disposition, ensemble of attitude, judgment and intention, is this framing significant of? Whose disposition? On what basis would such an attribution be effected? If establishing the interpretation of the framing depended on or was referred to as a character's "state of mind," which in fact changes significantly over the course of the sequence for each of the major characters (Dallas, Ringo, and Lucy), how would it be possible to accommodate those changing feelings to the fixity of setup? The fact of the fixity of setup denies that the explanation for camera placement can as a principle be referred to a psychology of character(s) based on the kind of emotional changes—surprise, repudiation, naiveté, humiliation—that eventuate in the sequence.

As another hypothesis we could say that the particular compositional features of series B are a presentation not of the "mind" of any single character but of a state of affairs within the group, a relationship among the parties. What is the state of affairs within this society that the framing depicts? There are two significant features of the compostion from setup B: the relation of Lucy in the immediate foreground to the group behind her, a group whose responsiveness to events repeats the direction of her own attention, and her relation, spatially, to Dallas and Ringo, who,

1

4a DALLAS: Thank you.

2 RINGO: Set down here, ma'am.

4b

3a

4c

3b

5

A sequence from John Ford's *Stagecoach* (1939). "The formal features of these images—the framing of shots and their sequencing, the repetition of setups, the position of characters, the direction of their glances—can be taken as a complex structure and understood as a characteristic answer to the rhetorical problem of telling a story, of showing an action to a spectator" (BROWNE, page 210).

6a

8a

6b

8b

7a

9 HATFIELD: May I find you another place, Mrs. Mallory? It's cooler by the window.

7b

10

11a LUCY: Thank you.

12a

11b

12b

11c

excluded by the left edge of the frame, are outside. The permanent and underlying fact about the mise-en-scène which justifies the fixity of camera placement is its status as a social drama of alliance and antagonism between two social roles—Lucy, an insider, a married woman and defender of custom; and Dallas, outsider and prostitute who violates the code of the table. The camera setups and the spatial fields they reveal, the compositional exclusion of the outlaw couple and their isolation in a separate space, with the implied assertion of Lucy's custodial relation to the body of legitimate society, respond to and depict in formal terms the social "positions" of the characters. In the kind of dramatic presentation they effect, the features of the framing are not justified as the depiction of personal psychology considered as changes of feeling; instead, by their emphasis on social positions, or types, they declare a psychology of intractable situations.

The framing of series B from the left of the table does not represent literally or figuratively any single person's view; rather, it might be said, it depicts, by what it excludes and includes, the interplay of social positions within a group. This asymmetry of social position of Lucy over Dallas extends as well to formal and compositional features of the sequence. Though setup B represents both positions, Dallas's negatively, it makes Lucy's position privileged in the formal mechanism of narrative exposition. The fundamental narrative feature of the sequence is a modification and inflection of the logic of shot/countershot. Here it is an alternation of series A and B around, not two characters, but either Lucy's eye or body. That is, in series A Lucy is present as an eye, as the formal beholder of the scene. Alternately, in B, Lucy is shown bodily dominating the foreground, and as the eye to which the views of series A are referred. Formally the narration proceeds by alternatingly shifting Lucy's presence from the level of the depicted action, as body (B), to the level of representation, as the invisible eye (A), making Lucy's presence the central point of spatial orientation and legibility. In shots 5 and 6, the closeup of the exchange of looks between the two women, the formal asymmetry is the difference of their frontality, and the shot of Lucy is from a place that Dallas could not literally occupy. Lucy's frontality (5) marks a dispossession, a displacement, that corresponds to Dallas's social "absence" in the entire sequence—to her exclusion from the frame in B, to her isolation as the object of Lucy's scornful glance in A. By contrast to Lucy's presence everywhere, as body and eye, Dallas's eye is never taken as the source of authority for a shot. Her eye is averted. She is always, in both A and B, the object of another's gaze—a condition that corresponds to the inferiority of her social position, and to her formal invisibility—she cannot authorize a view.

The shots of setup B, which might be called "objective," or perhaps "nobody's" shots, in fact refer to or are a representation of Lucy's social dominance and formal privilege. B shows a field of vision that closely matches Lucy's *conception* of her own place in that social world: its framing corresponds to her alliance with the group and to her intention to exclude the outsiders, to deny their claim to recognition. It is, in other words, not exactly a description of Lucy's subjectivity but an objectification of her social self-conception. Though Lucy is visible in the frame, series B might be said, metaphorically, to embody her point of view.

This explanation seems cogent as far as it goes. But there are some further issues that arise from the passage, in the way it is experienced, that suggests that the foregoing analysis of the justification of these formal features is incomplete as an account of the grounds for the effects the passage produces and theoretically limited in terms of explaining the strategies of framing and other premises of the narration.

Simply put, the experience of the passage is a feeling of empathy for Dallas's exclusion and humiliation, and a repudiation of Lucy's prejudice as unjust, two feelings brought together by a sense of inevitability of the conflict. There is, in other words, a curious opposition between the empathetic response of a spectator toward Dallas and the underlying premises of the mechanism of the narrative which are so closely related, formally, to Lucy's presence, point of view, and interests. It is this sense of incongruity between feeling and formal structure that occasions the following effort to consider the sequence in terms of the ways it produces its effects, that is, rhetorically.

One question about a formal matter which draws attention to the limitations of a structural account based on a conception of the social order is why the outsiders are seen from a position that is associated with Lucy's place at the table, her gaze. This fact, and the action of the audience within the film, casts doubt on two theories of agency. Our attention as spectators, in the shots of series B, does not follow the visual attention of any depicted characters. These shots might perhaps be read as statements of the "interests" of characters, the nature of their social positions, but that is already a kind of commentary or interpretation that needs explanation. The actions of the men at the bar, the audience within the film, disprove the traditional rationale for editing stated by reference to an ideal spectator: as "placed" spectators we anticipate, not follow, the movements of their attention (2, 3); the object of their attention is sometimes out of the frame we see (3b) and what they see is shown only from a view significantly different from any simply "accented" or "best view," indeed from a place they could not occupy; and sometimes (7b, 8) they have turned away, uninterested, but the screen doesn't go black. In general, an adequate account of the formal choices of the passage must be quite different from an account of the event as if it were staged for the natural attention of a spectator, depicted or real. To ask why the spectator sees in the way he does refers to a set of premises distinguishable from an account based on the attention of either a character or an ideal spectator. It refers to the concrete logic of the placement of the implied spectator and to the theory of presentation that accounts for the shaping of his response. Such an account makes the "position" of the spectator, the way in which he is implicated in the scene, the manner and location of his presence, his point of view, problematical.

It is this notion of the "position of the spectator" that I wish to clarify insofar as that notion illuminates the rhetorical strategies, particularly choice of setup (implying scale and framing) that depicts the action. In contemporary French film theory, particularly in the work of Comolli and Baudry, the notion of the "place" of the spectator is derived from the central position of the eye in perspective and photographic representation. By literally substituting the epistemological subject, the spectator, for the eye, in an argument about filmic representation, the filmic spectator is said to be "theological," and "centered" with respect to filmic images. Thus the theory of the filmic spectator is treated as if subject to the Derridean critique of center, presence, etc. French theory is wrong to enforce this analogy, based on the position of the eye in photographic perspective, because what is optical and literal in that case corresponds only to the literal palce of the spectator in the projection hall, and not at all to his figurative place in the film, nor to his place as subject to the rhetoric of the film, or reader or producer of the sense of the discourse. Outside of a French ideological project which fails to discriminate literal and figurative space, the notion of "place" of the spectator, and of "center," is an altogether problematic notion whose significance and function in critical discussion has yet to be explicated.

The sequence from *Stagecoach* provides the terms in which the notion of the position of the spectator might be clarified, provided we distinguish, without yet expecting full clarification, the different senses of "position." A spectator is (a) seated physically in the space of the projection hall and (b) placed by the camera in a certain fictional position with respect to the depicted action; moreover (c), insofar as we see from what we might take to be the eye of a character, we are invited to occupy the place allied to the place he holds, for example, in the social system; and finally (d), in another figurative sense of place, it is the only way that our response can be accounted for, that we can identify with a character's position in a certain situation.

In terms of the passage at hand, the question is then: how can I describe my "position" as spectator in identifying with the humiliated position of one of the depicted characters, Dallas, when my views of her belong to those of another, fictional character, Lucy, who is in the act of rejecting her? What is the spectator's "position" in identifying with Dallas in the role of the passive character? Dallas in averting her eyes from Lucy's in shot 6 accepts a view of herself in this encounter as "prostitute" and is shamed. However, in identifying with Dallas in the role of outcast, presumably the basis for the evocation of our sympathy and pity, our response as spectator is not one of shame, or anything even analogous. We do not suffer or repeat the humiliation. I understand Dallas's feeling but I am not so identified with her that I reenact it. One of the reasons for this restraint is that though I identify with Dallas's abject position of being seen as an unworthy object by someone whose judgment she accepts, I identify with her as the object of another's action. Indeed, in a remarkable strategy, I am asked to see Dallas through Lucy's eyes. That as spectator I am sharing Lucy's view and, just as important, her manner of viewing, is insisted on most emphatically by the dolly forward (4) and by disclosures effected by shot/countershot, thus placing me in a lively and implicated way in a position fully associated with Lucy's place at the head of the table.

Insofar as I identify with Dallas, it is not by repeating her shame, but by imagining myself in her position (situation). The early scenes of the film have carefully prepared us to believe that this exclusion is an unjust act. When the climactic moment arrives, our identification with Dallas as an object of view is simultaneously established as the ground for repudiating the one whose view we share and are implicated in. Though I share Lucy's literal geographical position of viewing at this moment in the film, I am not committed to her figurative point of view. I can, in other words, repudiate Lucy's view of or judgment on Dallas, without negating it as a view, in a way that Dallas herself, captive of the other's image, cannot.

Because our feelings as spectators are not "analogous" to their interests and feelings of the characters, we are not bound to accept their views either of themselves or of others. Our "position" as spectator then is very different from the previous senses of "position"; it is defined neither in terms of orientation within the constructed geography of the fiction nor in terms of social position of the viewing character. On the contrary, our point of view on the sequence is tied more closely to our attitude of approval or disapproval and is very different from any literal viewing angle or character's point of view.

Identification asks us as spectators to be two places at once, where the camera is and "with" the depicted person—thus its double structure of viewer/viewed. As a powerful emotional process it thus throws into question any account of the position of the spectator as centered at a single point or at the center of any simply optical system. Identification, this passage shows, necessarily has a double structure in the way it implicates the spectator in the position of both the one seeing and the one seen. This sequence, however, does establish a certain kind of "center" in the person of Lucy. Each of the shots is referred alternatingly to the scene before her eye or the scene of her body, but it is a "center" that functions as a principle of spatial legibility, and is associated with a literal point within the constructed space of the fiction. This center stands, though, as I have suggested, in a very complicated relation to our "position" as spectator. That is, the experience of the passage shows that our identification, in the Freudian sense of an emotional investment, is not with the center, either Lucy or the camera. Rather, if, cautiously, we can describe our figurative relation to a film in geographical terms, of "in," "there," "here," "distance" (and this sequence, as part of its strategy as a fiction, explicitly asks us to by presenting action to us from the literal view of a character), then as spectators, we might be said to formally occupy someone else's place, to be "in" the film, all the while being "outside" it in our seats. We can identify with a character and share her "point of view" even if the logic of the framing and selection of shots of the sequence deny that she has a view or a place within the society that the mise-en-scène depicts. There are significant differences between structures of shots, views, and identification: indeed, this sequence has shown, as a principle, that we do not "identify" with the camera but with the characters, and hence do not feel dispossessed by a change in shots. For a spectator, as distinct perhaps from a character, point of view is not definitively or summarily stated by any single shot or even set of shots from a given spatial location.

The way in which we as spectators are implicated in the action is as much a matter of our position with respect to the unfolding of those events in time as in their representation from a point in space. The effect of the mode of sequencing, the regular opposition of insiders and outsiders, is modulated in ways that shape the attitudes of the spectator/reader toward the action. This durational aspect emphasizes the process of inhabiting a text with its rhythms of involvement and disengagement in the action, and suggests that the spectator's position, his being in time, might appropriately be designated the "reader-in-the-text." His doubly structured position of identification with the features and force of the act of viewing and with the object in the field of vision are the visual terms of the dialectic of spectator placement. The rhetorical effort of shots 2–6 is directed to establishing the connection between shots and a "view," to endowing the position at the head of the table with a particular sense of a personalized glance. Shot 2, like 4, cannot at the moment it appears on the screen be associated with Lucy's glance. The shot/countershot sequencing discloses Lucy's location, and the turn of the head (3b) establishes a spatial relation between A and B; the animation, or gesture, implied by the dolly forward, combined with the emotional intensity implied by the choice of scale (5, 6) is read in terms of a personalized agency and clarified by what is shown in the visible field, Lucy's stern face (5). It is a rhetoric that unites the unfolding shots and gives meaning to this depicted glance—affront. It creates with the discrete shots (2, 3, 4) the impression of a coherent act of viewing, a mental unity whose meaning must make itself felt by the viewer at the moment of confrontation (5, 6) to effect the sense of repudiation of Lucy's view and the abjectness of Dallas. It takes time— a sequence of shots, in other words—to convey and specify the meaning of an act of viewing.

Reading, as this instance shows, is in part a process of retrospection, situating what could not be "placed" at the moment of its origin and bringing it forward to an interpretation of the meaning of the present moment. As such it has a complex relation to the action and to the spatial location of viewing. But the process of reading also depends on forgetting. After the climactic moment (5, 6) signaling Dallas's averting her eyes, a different temporal strategy is in effect. Lucy has looked away in 7b, and in subsequent shots from the head of the table, our attention is directed not so much to the act of showing, and what it means—unawareness (2), recognition (4), rejection (6)—but rather in 8 and 10 is directed at the action within the frame. The spectator's forgetting of what the dramatic impact depended on just a few moments before (here the personalized force that accompanied the act of showing the shot as a glance) is an effect of placement that depends on an experience of duration which occludes a previous significance and replaces it with another, a process we might call fading.

The modulation of the effects of fading is what, to take another example, is at issue in the interpretation of the shots of both series A and B. I have argued above that the setup and field of B correspond to Lucy's understanding of her place in the social system—to her point of view in the metaphorical sense. This interpretation corresponds to the general impression of the first six shots, taken together, as representing Lucy's manner of seeing. Shot 7 initiates a new line of dramatic action that poses the question of what Lucy will do now, and also begins a process not exactly of rereading, but a search for a new reading of the meaning of the setups. At this moment (7b), Lucy has turned her attention away from Dallas and is now turned toward Hatfield; and Ringo, previously occupied with his table etiquette (2, 4) is looking (8b, 10) intently out of frame right. The initial sense of the setup B is partially replaced by but coexists with another: that the depicted action in the frame is now being viewed by someone looking from outside the frame, namely Ringo, who is waiting expectantly for something to happen. The view from the left of the table is readable, not exactly as Lucy's self-conceptions as before, and not as a depiction of Ringo's glance, but as a representation of his interest in the scene, his point of view (again, in the metaphorical sense). Similarly, shots 8 and 10, showing Dallas and Ringo, no longer seem to characterize Lucy as the one doing the seeing, as in

4 and 6; they have become impersonal. The rigidity and opposition of setups A and B correspond to the rigidity of social position, but our reading of the changing secondary significances of the framing is an effect of fading that is responsive to acts of attention and seeing depicted within the frame.

Our anticipation, our waiting to see what will happen, is provoked and represented on the level of the action by the turning around of the audience-in-the-film (Billy and Doc Boone in 3b, 9). Our own feeling, because of our visual place to the left of the table, is closer to Ringo's than to theirs. Certainly the distention and delay of the climactic moment by a virtual repetition (9, 11a) of those shots of a hestitating Lucy (unnecessary for simple exposition) produce a sense of our temporal identification with Ringo (8b, 10), necessary for the success of the moment as drama—its uncertainty and resolution. The drama depends for the lesson it demonstrates not on Lucy's self-regard before a general public as previously, but on being watched by the parties to be affected. It is Ringo's increasingly involved presence as an authority for a view, even though he mistakenly thinks he is being ostracized, that makes the absent place left by Lucy's departure so evidently intended as a lesson in manners, so accusingly empty. By these strategies and effects of duration—retrospection, fading, delay, and anticipation—the reading of emphasis on the act of showing or what is shown, the significance of angle and framing, can be modulated. Together these means define features of a rhetoric which, though different from the placement effected by visual structures, also locate and implicate the reader/spectator in the text.

The spectator's place, the locus around which the spatiotemporal structures of presentation are organized, is a construction of the text which is ultimately the product of the narrator's disposition toward the tale. Such structures, which in shaping and presenting the action prompt a manner and indeed a path of reading, convey and are closely allied to the guiding moral commentary of the film. In this sequence the author has effaced himself, as in other instances of indirect discourse, for the sake of the characters and the action. Certainly he is nowhere visible in the same manner as the characters. Rather he is visible only through the materialization of the scene and in certain masked traces of his action. The indirect presence to his audience that the narrator enacts, the particular form of self-effacement, could be described as the masked displacement of his narrative authority as the producer of imagery from himself to the agency of his characters. That is, the film makes it appear as though it were the depicted characters to whom the authority for the presentation of shots can be referred—most evidently in the case of a depiction of a glance, but also, in more complex fashion, in the reading of shots as depictions of a "state of mind." The explanation of the presence of the imagery is referred by the film not to the originating authority who stands invisible, behind the action, but to his masks within the depicted space.

In accord with the narrator's efforts to direct attention away from his own activity, to mask and displace it, the narrator of *Stagecoach* has a visible persona, Lucy, perform a significant formal function in the narration: to constitute and to make legible and continuous the depicted space, by referring shots on the screen alternately to the authority of her eye or the place of her body. The literal place of the spectator in the projection hall, where in a sense all the shots are directed, is a "center" that has a figurative correspondence on the level of the discourse in the "place" that Lucy occupies in the depicted space. But because Lucy performs her integrative function not exactly by her being at a place, the head of the table, but by enacting a kind of central consciousness that corresponds to a social and formal role, a role which for narrative purposes can be exploited by shifting the views representing the manner of her presence, the notion of "center" might be thought of not as a geographical place but as a structure or function. As such, this locus makes it possible for the reader himself to occupy that role and himself to make the depicted space coherent and readable. For the spectator, the "center" is not just a point either in the projection hall or in the depicted geography, but is the result of the impression produced by the functioning of the narrative and of his being able to fictionally occupy the absent place.

Locating this function, "inscribing" the spectator's place on the level of the depicted action, has the effect of making the story seem to tell itself by reference not to an outside author but to a continuously visible, internal narrative authority. This governing strategy, of seeming to internalize the source of the exposition in characters, and thus of directing the spectator's attention to the depicted action, is supported by other features of the style: shot/countershot, matching of glances, continuity.

Consequently, the place of the spectator in his relation to the narrator is established by, though not limited to, identifications with characters and the views they have of each other. More specifically his "place" is defined through the variable force of identification with the one viewing and the one viewed—as illustrated in the encounter between Lucy and Dallas. Though the spectator may be placed in the "center" by the formal function Lucy performs, he is not committed to her view of things. On the contrary, in the context of the film, that view is instantly regarded as insupportable. Our response to Dallas supports the sense that the spectator's figurative position is not stated by a description of where the camera is in the geography of the scene. On the contrary, though the spectator's position is closely tied to the fortunes and views of characters, our analysis suggests that identification, in the original sense of an emotional bond, need not be with the character whose view he shares, even less with the disembodied camera. Evidently, a spectator is several places at once—with the fictional viewer, with the viewed, and at the same time in a position to evaluate and respond to the claims of each. This fact suggests that like the dreamer, the filmic spectator is a plural subject: in his reading he is and is not himself.

In a film, imagining ourselves in a character's place by identification, in respect to the actual sitaution, is a different process, indeed a different order of fiction than taking a shot as originating from a certain point within the fictional geography. The relation though between the literal space of the projection hall and the depicted space of the film image is continuously problematic for a definition of the "thatness" of the screen and for an account of the place of the spectator. If a discourse carries a certain impression of reality, it is an effect not exactly of the image but rather of the way the image is placed by the narrative or argument. My relation to an image on the screen is literal because it can be taken as being directed to a physical point, my seat (changing that seat doesn't alter my viewing angle on the action), as though I were the fixed origin of the view. On the other hand, the image can also be taken as originating from a point in a different kind of space, recognizably different in terms of habitability from that of the projection hall: it is from a fictional and changeable place implied by an origin contained in the image. The filmic image thus implies the ambiguity of a double origin—both from my literal place as spectator and from the place where the camera is within the imaginative space.

One structural result of the ambiguous relation of literal and depicted space and of the seemingly contradictory efforts of the text to both place and displace the spectator is the prohibition against the "meeting," though no such act is literally possible, of actor's and spectator's glances, a prohibition that is an integral feature of the sequence as a "specular text." In its effect on the spectator, the prohibition defines the different spaces he simultaneously inhabits before the screen. By denying his presence in one sense, the prohibition establishes a boundary at the screen that underscores the fact that the spectator can have no actual physical exchange with the depicted world, that he can do nothing relevant to change the course of the action. It places him irretrievably outside the action.

At the same time, the prohibition is the initial premise of a narrative system for the representation of fictional space and the means of introducing the spectator imaginatively into it. The prohibition effects this construction and engagement by creating an obliquity between our angle of viewing and that of the characters which works to make differences of angle and scale readable as representations of different points of view. As such it plays a central part in our process of identification or nonidentification with the camera and depicted characters. It provides the author an ensemble of narrative forms—an imaginary currency consisting of temporary exchange, substitution, and identification—that enables us, fictionally, to take the place of another, to inhabit the text as a reader.

Establishing agency by either the authority of character or of spectator corresponds in its alternative rhetorical forms to the articulation of the ambiguity of the double origin of the image. In a particular text it is the narration that establishes and arbitrates the spectator's placement between these two spaces. *Stagecoach* makes definite efforts to imply that not only is the spectator not there, not present in his seat, but that the film-object originates form an authority within the fictional space. The narration seems to insist that the film is a free-standing entity which a spectator, irrelevant finally to its construction, could only look on from the outside. On the other hand, in the ways that I have described, the film is directed in all its structures of presentation toward the narrator's construction of a commentary on the story and toward placing the spectator at a certain "angle" to it. The film has tried not just to direct the attention but to place the eye of the spectator inside the fictional space, to make his presence integral and constitutive of the structure of views. The explanation the film seems to give of the action of narrative authority is a denial of the existence of a narrator different from character and an affirmation of the dominating role of fictional space. It is a spatial mode not determined by the ontology of the image as such but is in the last instance an effect of the narration.

Masking and displacement of narrative authority are thus integral to establishing the sense of the spectator "in" the text, and the prohibition to establishing the film as an independent fiction, different from dream in being the product of another, that can nevertheless be inhabited. Fascination by identification with character is a way the integrity of fictional space is validated, and because the spectator occupies a fictional role, is a way too that the film can efface the specator's consciousness of his position. As a production of the spectator's reading, the sense of reality that the film enacts, the "impression of the real," protects the account the text seems to give of the absent narrator.

The cumulative effect of the narrator's strategy of placement of the spectator from moment to moment is his introduction into what might be called the moral order of the text. That is, the presentational structures which shape the action both convey a point of view and define the course of the reading, and are fundamental to the exposition of moral idea—specifically a discussion about the relation of insiders to outsiders. The effect of the distinction between pure and impure is the point of the sequence, though as a theme it is just a part of the total exposition. The sequence thus assists in the construction of attitudes toward law and custom and to those who live outside their strictures. It introduces the question of the exercise of social and customary (as distinguished from legal) authority. To the extent we identify with Ringo and Dallas—and the film continuously invites us to by providing multiple grounds: the couple's bravery, competence, and sincerity—the conventional order and the morality it enforces is put in doubt. Without offering a full interpretation of the theme of *Stagecoach,* which would I think be connected with the unorthodox nature of their love and the issue of Ringo's revenge and final exemption from the law by the sheriff, I can still characterize the spectator's position at this particular moment in the film.

It amounts to this: that though we see the action from Lucy's eyes and are invited by a set of structures and strategies to experience the force and character of that view, we are put in the position finally of having to reject it as a view that is right or that we could be committed to. The sequence engages us on this point through effecting an identification with a situation in which the outsider is wronged and thus that challenges Lucy's position as the agent of an intolerant authority. We are asked, by the manner in which we must read, by the posture we must adopt, to repudiate Lucy's view, to see behind the moral convention that supports intolerance, to break out of a role that may be confining us. As such, the importance of the sequence in the entire film is the way it allies us emotionally with the interests and fortunes of the outsiders as against social custom, an identification and theme that, modulated in subsequent events, continues to the end of the film. The passage, lifted out of its context, but drawing on dispositions established in prevous sequences, is an illustration of the process of constructing a spectator's attitudes in the film as a whole through the control of point of view. Whether or not the western genre can in general be characterized by a certain mode of identification, as, for example, in the disposition or wish to see the right done, and whether *Stagecoach* has a particularly significant place in the history of the genre by virtue of its treatment of outsiders, is an open question. In any case the reader's position is constituted by a set of views, identifications, and judgments that establish his place in the moral order of the text.

Like the absent narrator who discloses himself and makes his judgments from a position inseparable from the sequence of depicted events that constitute the narrative, the spectator, in following the story, in being subject of and to the spatial and temporal placement and effects of exposition, is in the process of realizing an identity we have called his position. Following the trajectory of identifications that establishes the structure of values of a text, "reading" as a temporal process could be said to continuously reconstruct the place of the narrator and his implied commentary on the scene. In this light, reading, as distinct from interpretation, might be characterized as a guided and prompted performance that (to the extent a text allows it, and I believe *Stagecoach* does) recreates the point of view enacted in a scene. As a correlative of narration, reading could be said to be the process of reenactment by fictionally occupying the place of the narrator.

Certain formal features of the imagery—framing, sequencing, the prohibition, and "invisibility" of the narrator—I have suggested, can be explained as the ensemble of ways authority implicitly positions the spectator/reader. As a method, this analysis of *Stagecoach* points to a largely unexplored body of critical problems associated with describing and accounting for narrative and rhetorical signifying structures. The "specular text" and the allied critical concepts of "authority," "reading," "point of view," and "position of the spectator," however provisional, might be taken then as a methodological initiative for a semiotic study of filmic texts.

1975

III

The Film Medium: Image and Sound

Film theory and film criticism have been largely concerned with one central issue: What is "cinematic?" Which paths should the cinema follow? Which should it reject? Attempts to answer this question inevitably take their lead from Lessing's classic essay, *Laocoön,* in which the eighteenth-century German dramatist and essayist attempted to demonstrate that the visual arts organize their materials spatially while the poetic arts organize their materials temporally. The materials, procedures, subjects, and effects of these two different forms (or "media") of artistic organization are therefore necessarily different. In this spirit, film theorists have attempted to discover the characteristics of the film medium, declaring those subjects, materials, procedures, and effects that "exploit" the characteristics of the medium proper, legitimate, and truly cinematic and those subjects, materials, procedures, and effects that "violate" the characteristics of the medium barren, misleading and fundamentally uncinematic.

The concept of a medium is, of course, a difficult one. Is the medium to be defined in purely physical terms (that is, the projection of images at twenty-four frames per second on a screen) or rather in terms of an artistic language (angle and distance of shots, rhythms and patterns of editing, and so forth)? Does it include the main structural features of the art (such as plot) and its main historical conventions (say, its genres)? And how are we to determine which possibilities of the medium are legitimate? Is it legitimate to pursue any possibility inherent in the medium, or only those for which the medium has a special affinity? And how are we to judge what those special affinities are? May two different artistic media share those affinities or must an art confine itself, as certain purists urge, to realizing only those possibilities that it shares with no other art?

Erwin Panofsky, an art historian who was a contemporary of both Arnheim and Kracauer, has written the most influential discussion of the subject. He argues that an art ought to exploit the "unique and specific" possibilities of its medium; and in the film medium these can be defined as the "dynamization of space" and the "spatialization of time." Both these features are visual ones, and Panofsky's primarily visual concept of the film medium is vulnerable to the objection that it accords an undue priority to the silent film, placing unwise restrictions on the use of speech in films. According to Panofsky's principle of "co-expressibility," "the sound, articulate or not, cannot express any more than is expressed, at the same time, by visible movement." Panofsky claims that the Shavian dialogue in the film version of Shaw's *Pygmalion* falls flat and suggests that Olivier's monologues in *Henry V* are successful only to the extent that Olivier's face becomes "a huge field of action" in oblique "close-up." But those who admire the brilliant Hollywood "dialogue" comedies of the 30s and early 40s and who recall that Olivier does not deliver the "St. Crispin's Day" speech in *Henry V* in close-up will receive these views with a measure of skepticism. Indeed, Panofsky modified them in the revised version of his essay that appears in this anthology.

Siegfried Kracauer acknowledges the difficulty of defining the film medium but also believes, nevertheless, that cinema has certain "inherent affinities." There are, in particular, certain subjects in the physical world that may be termed "cinematic" because they exert a peculiar attraction for the medium. Kracauer argues that cinema is predestined and even eager to exhibit them. Like Panofsky, Kracauer accepts the use of sound in films only under certain very restrictive conditions, and he especially dislikes the development of the "theatrical" film: "What even the most theatrical minded silent film could not incorporate—pointed controversies, Shavian witticisms, Hamlet's soliloquies—has been annexed to the screen." Kraucauer finds this annexation unfortunate; it in no way proves that such theatrical speeches are legitimate possibilities of the cinematic medium, for "popularity," in Kracauer's view, has no bearing on questions of aesthetic legitimacy.

Kracauer calls the comedies of Frank Capra and Preston Sturges borderline cases, but only on the ground that their witty dialogue is "complemented and compensated for" by "visuals of independent interest" (he means that they include slapstick sequences). Just as witty dialogue violates the visual requirements of the medium and requires "compensation," surrealistic projections of inner realities, expressionist dreams and visions, and experimental abstractions violate the realist requirements of the medium. On the other hand, certain types of movement—the chase and dancing—and certain types of objects—those that are normally too big or too small to be seen—are peculiarly appropriate subjects of cinema. But does the dance really have a greater affinity for the film than it does for the stage? Must the film avoid what is normally seen simply because it is the subject matter of other arts? One can agree with Kracauer that the close-up is a peculiarly cinematic technique, and even with the Hungarian filmmaker Béla Balázs, that the close-up is responsible for the "discovery of the human face," without supposing that the film must devote itself exclusively to the exploitation of these "unique" potentialities.

Rudolf Arnheim shares Panofsky's and Kracauer's view that the film ought to stress the specific possibilities of the cinematic medium. But he feels obligated to refute the view that cinema is a mere mechanical reproduction of physical reality. If it were, it would not be an art. Arnheim therefore emphasizes the various discrepancies between the film image and the standard perception of physical reality. The film image suffers a reduction of depth, a distortion of perspective, an accentuation of perspective overlapping, and, in the past, an absence of color and articulate speech. Arnheim asserts that the true task of cinema is to exploit these very "defects" and turn them to an advantage, just as painting exploits the fact that it is a two-dimensional, enclosed object. Perhaps a great art can be devised that confines itself to exploiting these defects (the silent film may have been such an art), but can we accept the suggestion that film must avoid exploiting the affinities with physical reality that Kracauer mentions, just because they conform to, rather than deviate from, reality? And should we regret the fact that we can remedy some of the "defects" of a medium rather than exploit them? Should we regret the development of sound, as all three of these theorists do?

Noël Carroll examines the logic underlying the specificity thesis that is assumed by all these theorists. He challenges the notion that what a medium does best will coincide with what differentiates it from other media. Indeed, he questions whether an art should confine itself either to doing what it does best or to what differentiates it from the other arts. In particular, Carroll's critique of Arnheim's *A New Laocoön* provides a very different view of the possibilities for combining language and visuals in the art of film.

Gerald Mast rejects the problem of defining the distinctively cinematic medium as any function of the method of recording moving images—photographic or otherwise. Instead, he regards the projection of images by light as the essential feature of any cinematic work. And the fact of projection permits him to distinguish the experience of cinema from that of theater, television, and painting. He also argues that a careful investigation of the characteristics of projected images undermines a number of commonly held opinions. Among them are the view that one must project photographic images—upon which Kracauer's theory (and that of all realist cinema theory) is founded, and the view that the projected image is two-dimensional and perceived as flat—claims upon which Arnheim's theory (and that of most puristic and modernistic cinema theory) is based.

Stanley Cavell does place great emphasis on the importance of projection and, more particularly, on the fact of projection onto a screen. The projected image is the image of a world, and of a world which, in contrast to the world of a painting, exists beyond the frame. Indeed, the only difference between the projected world and reality is that the projected world does not exist now. It is simultaneously absent and present. One function of the movie screen, then, is to screen that world from the audience. Another is to screen the audience from the projected world. Unlike the audience in a theater which is not present to the actors on stage by convention, the film medium renders the audience absent mechanically and automatically. By this enforced invisibility, movies give expression to our modern experience of privacy and anonymity. Man has longed for invisibility and the absence of responsibility it confers, and film satisfies precisely this wish. In watching a film we view a magically reproduced world while remaining invisible to it. This condition makes the experience of film essentially voyeuristic and even pornographic. It permits the audience a magical-sexual contact with the hypnotic Garbos, Dietrichs, and Gables of the screen.

However, unlike Panofsky and many other theorists, Cavell does not think that the aesthetic possibilities of the movie medium can be deduced from its physical or technical properties. A medium, in his unconventional construal, is simply something through which or by means of which something specific gets said or done in particular ways. In his view, only the art itself, and not a mere consideration of its physical medium, can discover its aesthetic possibilities.

Cavell argues that the issues of genre and of medium are inseparable, and that the classical Hollywood world was composed of three such media—stories or structures that revolve about the Military Man, the Dandy, and the Woman. The Military Man conquers evil for the sake of society (James Stewart in *The Man Who Shot Liberty Valance,* Gary Cooper in *Mr. Deeds Goes to Town*); the Dandy pursues his own interests, values, and self-respect (John Wayne in *Red River,* Cary Grant in anything); and the Woman attracts men as flames attract the moth (Garbo, Dietrich, Davis). With the loss of conviction in these genres, film reached (very belatedly in comparison to the other arts of the twentieth century) the condition of modernism, in which the self-conscious artist seeks to produce a new genre, a new medium, rather than simply producing more instances of a familiar one.

Jean-Louis Baudry concentrates his attention on the ideological effects of the cinematogrpahic apparatus. The camera records a series of static images. However, projection on a screen restores both the illusion of continuous movement and of temporal succession. In doing so, the cinematographic apparatus conceals work and imposes an idealistic ideology, rather than producing what Althusser calls a "knowledge effect." Limited by the framing, lined up, and put at the proper distance the world offers up an object endowed with meaning. This Husserlian intentional object implies the action of a transcendental subject or camera eye which views it. As the Lacanian mirror assembles the fragmented body in a sort of imaginary integration of the self, so the transcendental self unites the dislocated fragments of lived experienced into a metaphysic, a unified meaning. Thus, the cinema assumes the role played throughout Western history by various artistic formations. The ideology of representation and specularization form a singularly coherent system in the cinema. But the illusion they create is possible only if the instrumentation on which they depend is hidden and repressed. (The notion of the optically centered subject and of the ideological effects which attend this position are usefully questioned by Nick Browne in his "The Spectator-in-the-Text: The Rhetoric of *Stagecoach*" reprinted in Section II.)

As we have seen, many of the classic film theorists considered the cinema an essentially visual medium. Even those who admit the importance of the aural dimension of film have generally not paid as much attention to it as they have to the visual aspect of the medium. Christian Metz's essay suggests that this fact is to be explained by the primitive substantialism deeply rooted in our culture. This concept distinguishes sharply between primary qualities or substances and the attributes which characterize them. Visual qualities are regarded as primary or substantial while aural qualities are secondary or adjectival. (This assumption manifests itself in the incorrect description of some sound as "off-screen.") Metz suggests, however, that this phenomenological truth is socially constructed and in this sense ideological. The world as we apprehend it could be otherwise.

Even those who have welcomed, or at least endorsed, the exploitation of sound in cinema have had difficulty in agreeing on the terms of its admission to the film medium. Thus, in their "Statement" on sound, Eisenstein, Pudovkin, and Alexandrov acknowledge the use of sound as an important new resource for film. They believe, however, that the montage principle, to which they attribute the greatest achievement of film, would be undermined if sounds were synchronized with sights. As they see it, every adhesion of sound to a visual montage piece increases its inertia as a montage piece. They therefore endorse only the nonsynchronous use of sound, a use that would eschew "talking films" and propose that sound be used only in orchestral counterpoint to visual images. Avoiding the use of naturalistic "talk," films of this sort would strengthen the possibility of a truly international cinema.

By contrast, the more recent avant-garde theorists and filmmakers, Jean-Marie Straub and Danièle Huillet are committed to the faithful use of direct sound and believe, indeed, that the world of sound is far more vast than the visible world. (Those who employ direct sound not only film images but at the same time record the sounds accompanying those images.) Straub and Huillet recognize that fidelity to direct sound not only precludes the type of editing practiced by the montage theorists but even the types of editing characteristic of classical narrative film. (If you respect sound, you cannot cut even when the frame is empty, for you may still hear the character's footsteps.) Straub and Huillet are particularly offended by the practice of dubbing which violates the true relationship between what you see and what you hear and, indeed, renders visual space illusory. In their view the motivation for dubbing is commercial (you can use stars from different countries) and it creates a cinema of lies, mental laziness, and violence. Dubbed cinema is an expression of the bourgeois belief that all art is international. The contrast between the internationalist aspirations of the Soviet radicals and the anti-internationalism of later radicals such as Straub and Huillet is striking and reflects the very different implications of montage theory and direct realism both as techniques and as realizations of anti-bourgeois ideals.

As we have seen, Jean-Louis Baudry argues that the cinematic apparatus conceals work and presents as natural that which is in fact an ideological production. Recent writers such as Rick Altman and Mary Ann Doane have extended this argument to the evolution of sound technology. John Belton argues, however, that even though technological evolution performs an ideological function, the work of technology can never efface itself and disappear. It remains visible—or audible—in every film. For there is always present in the positioning of the camera or the microphones a consciousness that sees and hears and that coexists with that which is seen and heard.

Charles Affron provides a keen appreciation of the contribution of sound to classical narrative cinema and, indeed, challenges some prevailing assumptions. In his view, our ability to follow a narrative line and to make sense of a story, even in cinema, is primarily a verbal, not a visual, one and the presence of voice helps to power cinema's narrative thrust. In contrast to Balázs, Affron thinks it fruitless to distinguish the iconographic value of the star's face and the star's voice. The star's personality is as much dependent on the phonogenic "grain of the voice" as it is on the photogenic configuration of body and face. Similarly, the director's world is characterized vocally. Thus, in Capra's films the political, social, and ethical worlds of the protagonists are spatialized by the voices that resonate within them. In Affron's analysis the contribution of sound to the film medium is acknowledged fully and without reservation, either practical or theoretical.

According to John Ellis, television and cinema exploit image and sound in characteristically different ways and in a characteristically different balance. For Ellis the image remains the central reference for cinema. The cinema viewer is centered by the phyiscal arrangement of cinema seats and by the customs of film viewing (unlike the TV viewer, the moviegoer does not move about the house). Consequently, in cinema sound follows the image or diverges from it. For TV, however, sound is primary and carries the fiction or the documentary, with the image playing a more illustrative role. TV employs a type of vision less intense than cinema's. It is a regime of the glance not the gaze. In psychoanalytic terms, TV exemplifies a displacement of the scopophiliac regime from seeing to the closest related sense, hearing. The TV viewer is copresent with the image and it is familar and intimate. This contrasts with the voyeuristic mode of cinema that Cavell describes. TV is, in consequence, less concerned with the representation of the female body and of female sexuality and its narratives lack the forward thrust of entertainment cinema. Rather, the activity of the glance calls for variety and the accumulation of segments rather than the accumulation of sequences that characterize cinematic narration. Ellis's account of the differences between the media of cinema and TV draws on their physical, psychological, and social characteristics. It does not, however, mount an argument in the *Laocoön* tradition. Ellis does not try to determine which features of their respective media cinema and TV should exploit or eschew.

ERWIN PANOFSKY
STYLE AND MEDIUM IN THE
MOTION PICTURES

Film art is the only art the development of which men now living have witnessed from the very beginnings; and this development is all the more interesting as it took place under conditions contrary to precedent. It was not an artistic urge that gave rise to the discovery and gradual perfection of a new technique; it was a technical invention that gave rise to the discovery and gradual perfection of a new art.

From this we understand two fundamental facts. First, that the primordial basis of the enjoyment of moving pictures was not an objective interest in a specific subject matter, much less an aesthetic interest in the formal presentation of subject matter, but the sheer delight in the fact that things seemed to move, no matter what things they were. Second, that films—first exhibited in "kinetoscopes," viz., cinematographic peep shows, but projectable to a screen since as early as 1894—are, originally, a product of genuine folk art (whereas, as a rule, folk art derives from what is known as "higher art"). At the very beginning of things we find the simple recording of movements: galloping horses, railroad trains, fire engines, sporting events, street scenes. And when it had come to the making of narrative films these were produced by photographers who were anything but "producers" or "directors," performed by people who were anything but actors, and enjoyed by people who would have been much offended had anyone called them "art lovers."

The casts of these archaic films were usually collected in a "café" where unemployed supers or ordinary citizens possessed of a suitable exterior were wont to assemble at a given hour. An enterprising photographer would walk in, hire four or five convenient characters and make the picture while carefully instructing them what to do: "Now, you pretend to hit this lady over the head"; and (to the lady): "And you pretend to fall down in a heap." Productions like these were shown, together with those purely factual recordings of "movement for movement's sake," in a few small and dingy cinemas mostly frequented by the "lower classes" and a

233

sprinkling of youngsters in quest of adventure (about 1905, I happen to remember, there was only one obscure and faintly disreptuable *kino* in the whole city of Berlin, bearing, for some unfathomable reason, the English name of "The Meeting Room"). Small wonder that the "better classes," when they slowly began to venture into these early picture theaters, did so, not by way of seeking normal and possibly serious entertainment, but with that characteristic sensation of self-conscious condescension with which we may plunge, in gay company, into the folkloristic depths of Coney Island or a European kermis; even a few years ago it was the regulation attitude of the socially or intellectually prominent that one could confess to enjoying such austerely educational films as *The Sex Life of the Starfish* or films with "beautiful scenery," but never to a serious liking for narratives.

Today there is no denying that narrative films are not only "art"—not often good art, to be sure, but this applies to other media as well—but also, besides architecture, cartooning and "commercial design," the only visual art entirely alive. The "movies" have reestablished that dynamic contact between art production and art consumption which, for reasons too complex to be considered here, is sorely attenuated, if not entirely interrupted, in many other fields of artistic endeavor. Whether we like it or not, it is the movies that mold, more than any other single force, the opinions, the taste, the language, the dress, the behavior, and even the physical appearance of a public comprising more than 60 per cent of the population of the earth. If all the serious lyrical poets, composers, painters and sculptors were forced by law to stop their activities, a rather small fraction of the general public would become aware of the fact and a still smaller fraction would seriously regret it. If the same thing were to happen with the movies the social consequences would be catastrophic.

In the beginning, then, there were the straight recordings of movement no matter what moved, viz., the prehistoric ancestors of our "documentaries"; and, soon after, the early narratives, viz., the prehistoric ancestors of our "feature films." The craving for a narrative element could be satisfied only by borrowing from older arts, and one should expect that the natural thing would have been to borrow from the theater, a theater play being apparently the *genus proximum* to a narrative film in that it consists of a narrative enacted by persons that move. But in reality the imitation of stage performances was a comparatively late and thoroughly frustrated development. What happened at the start was a very different thing. Instead of imitating a theatrical performance already endowed with a certain amount of motion, the earliest films added movement to works of art originally stationary, so that the dazzling technical invention might achieve a triumph of its own without intruding upon the sphere of higher culture. The living language, which is always right, has endorsed this sensible choice when it still speaks of a "moving picture" or, simply, a "picture," instead of accepting the pretentious and fundamentally erroneous "screenplay."

The stationary works enlivened in the earliest movies were indeed pictures: bad nineteenth-century paintings and postcards (or waxworks à la Madame Tussaud's), supplemented by the comic strips—a most important root of cinematic art—and the subject matter of popular songs, pulp magazines and dime novels; and the films descending from this ancestry appealed directly and very intensely to a folk art mentality. They gratified—often simultaneously—first, a primitive sense of justice and decorum when virtue and industry were rewarded while vice and laziness were punished; second, plain sentimentality when "the thin trickle of a fictive love interest" took its course "through somewhat serpentine channels," or when Father, dear Father returned from the saloon to find his child dying of diphtheria; third, a primordial instinct for bloodshed and cruelty when Andreas Hofer faced the firing squad, or when (in a film of 1893–94) the head of Mary Queen of Scots actually came off; fourth, a taste for mild pornography (I remember with great pleasure a French film of *ca.* 1900 wherein a seemingly but not really well-rounded lady as well as a seemingly but not really slender one were shown changing to bathing suits—an honest, straightforward *porcheria* much less objectionable than the now extinct Betty Boop films and, I am sorry to say, some of the more recent Walt Disney productions); and, finally, that crude sense of humor, graphically described as "slapstick," which feeds upon the sadistic and the pornographic instinct, either singly or in combination.

Not until as late as *ca.* 1905 was a film adaptation of *Faust* ventured upon (cast still "unknown," characteristically enough), and not until 1911 did Sarah Bernhardt lend her prestige to an unbelievably funny film tragedy, *Queen Elizabeth of England.* These films represent the first conscious attempt at transplanting the movies from the folk art level to that of "real art"; but they also bear witness to the fact that this commendable goal could not be reached in so simple a manner. It was soon realized that the imitation of a theater performance with a set stage, fixed entries and exits, and distinctly literary ambitions is the one thing the film must avoid.

The legitimate paths of evolution were opened, not by running away from the folk art character of the primitive film but by developing it within the limits of its own possibilities. Those primordial archetypes of film productions on the folk art level—success or retribution, sentiment, sensation, pornography, and crude humor—could blossom forth into genuine history, tragedy and romance, crime and adventure, and comedy, as soon as it was realized that they could be transfigured—not by an artificial injection of literary values but by the exploitation of the unique and specific possibilities of the new medium. Significantly, the beginnings of this legitimate development antedate the attempts at endowing the film with higher values of a foreign order (the crucial period being the years from 1902 to *ca.* 1905), and the decisive steps were taken by people who were laymen or outsiders from the viewpoint of the serious stage.

These unique and specific possibilities can be defined as *dynamization of space* and, accordingly, *spatialization of time.* This statement is self-evident to the point of triviality but it belongs to that kind of truths which, just because of their triviality, are easily forgotten or neglected.

In a theater, space is static, that is, the space represented on the stage, as well as the spatial relation of the beholder to the spectacle, is unalterably fixed. The spectator cannot leave his seat, and the setting of the stage cannot change, during one act (except for such incidentals as rising moons or gathering clouds and such illegitimate reborrowings from the film as turning wings or gliding backdrops). But, in return for this restriction, the theater has the advantage that time, the medium of emotion and thought conveyable by speech, is free and independent of anything that may happen in visible space. Hamlet may deliver his famous monologue lying on a couch in the middle distance, doing nothing and only dimly discernible to the spectator and listener, and yet by his mere words enthrall him with a feeling of intensest emotional action.

With the movies the situation is reversed. Here, too, the spectator occupies a fixed seat, but only physically, not as the subject of an aesthetic experience. Aesthetically, he is in permanent motion as his eye identifies itself with the lens of the camera, which permanently shifts in distance and direction. And as movable as the spectator is, as movable is, for the same reason, the space presented to him. Not only bodies move in space, but space itself does, approaching, receding, turning, dissolving and recrystallizing as it appears through the controlled locomotion and focusing of the camera and through the cutting and editing of the various shots— not to mention such special effects as visions, transformations, disappearances, slow-motion and fast-motion shots, reversals and trick films. This opens up a world of possibilities of which the stage can never dream. Quite apart from such photographic tricks as the participation of disembodied spirits in the action of the *Topper* series, or the more effective wonders wrought by Roland Young in *The Man Who Could Work Miracles,* there is, on the purely factual level, an untold wealth of themes as inaccessible to the "legitimate" stage as a fog or a snowstorm is to the sculptor; all sorts of violent elemental phenomena and, conversely, events too microscopic to be visible under normal conditions (such as the life-saving injection with the serum flown in at the very last moment, or the fatal bite of the yellow-fever mosquito); full-scale battle scenes; all kinds of operations, not only in the surgical sense but also in the sense of any actual construction, destruction or experimentation, as in *Louis Pasteur* or *Madame Curie;* a really grand party, moving through many rooms of a mansion or a palace. Features like these, even the mere shifting of the scene from one place to another by means of a car perilously negotiating heavy traffic or a motorboat steered through a nocturnal harbor, will not only always retain their primitive cinematic appeal but also remain enormously effective as a means of stirring the emotions and creating suspense. In addition, the movies have the power, entirely denied to the theater, to convey psychological experiences by directly projecting their content to the screen, substituting, as it were, the eye of the beholder for the consciousness of the character (as when the imaginings and hallucinations of the drunkard in the otherwise overrated *Lost Weekend* appear as stark realities instead of being described by mere words). But any attempt to convey thought and feelings exclusively, or even primarily, by speech leaves us with a feeling of embarrassment, boredom, or both.

What I mean by thoughts and feelings "conveyed exclusively, or even primarily, by speech" is simply this: Contrary to naïve expectation, the invention of the sound track in 1928 has been unable to change the basic fact that a moving picture, even when it has learned to talk, remains a picture that moves and does not convert itself into a piece of writing that is enacted. Its substance remains a series of visual sequences held together by an uninterrupted flow of movement in space (except, of course, for such checks and pauses as have the same compositional value as a rest in music), and not a sustained study in human character and destiny transmitted by effective, let alone "beautiful," diction. I cannot remember a more misleading statement about the movies than Mr. Eric Russell Bentley's in the spring number of the *Kenyon Review,* 1945: "The potentialities of the talking screen differ from those of the silent screen in adding the dimension of dialogue—which could be poetry." I would suggest: "The potentialities of the talking screen differ form those of the silent screen in integrating visible movement with dialogue which, therefore, had better not be poetry."

All of us, if we are old enough to remember the period prior to 1928, recall the old-time pianist who, with his eyes glued on the screen, would accompany the events with music adapted to their mood and rhythm; and we also recall the weird and spectral feeling overtaking us when this pianist left his post for a few minutes and the film was allowed to run by itself, the darkness haunted by the monotonous rattle of the machinery. Even the silent film, then, was never mute. The visible spectacle always required, and received, an audible accompaniment which, from the very beginning, distinguished the film from simple pantomime and rather classed it—*mutatis mutandis*—with the ballet. The advent of the talkie meant not so much an "addition" as a transformation: the transformation of musical sound into articulate speech and, therefore, of quasi pantomime into an entirely new species of spectacle which differs from the ballet, and agrees with the stage play, in that its acoustic component consists of intelligible words, but differs from the stage play and agrees with the ballet in that this acoustic component is not detachable form the visual. In a film, that which we hear remains, for good or worse, inextricably fused with that which we see; the sound, articulate or not, cannot express any more than is expressed, at the same time, by visible movement; and in a good film it does not even attempt to do so. To put it briefly, the play—or, as it is very properly called, the "script"—of a moving picture is subject to what might be termed the *principle of coexpressibility.*

Empirical proof of this prnciple is furnished by the fact that, wherever the dialogical or monological element gains temporary prominence, there appears, with the inevitability of a natural law, the "close-up." What does the close-up achieve? In showing us, in magnification, either the face of the speaker or the face of the listeners or both in alternation, the camera transforms the human physiognomy into a huge field of action where—given the qualification of the performers—every subtle movement of the features, almost imperceptible from a natural distance, becomes an expressive event in visible space and thereby completely integrates itself with the expressive content of the spoken word; whereas, on the stage, the spoken word makes a stronger rather than a weaker impression if we are not permitted to count the hairs in Romeo's mustache.

This does not mean that the scenario is a negligible factor in the making of a moving picture. It only means that its artistic intention differs in kind from that of a stage play, and much more from that of a novel or a piece of poetry. As the success of a Gothic jamb figure depends not only upon its quality as a piece of sculpture but also, or even more so, upon its integrability with the architecture of the portal, so does the success of a movie script—not unlike that of an opera libretto—depend, not only upon its quality as a piece of literature but also, or even more so, upon its integrability with the events on the screen.

As a result—another empirical proof of the coexpressibility principle—good movie scripts are unlikely to make good reading and have seldom been published in book form; whereas, conversely, good stage plays have to be severely altered, cut, and, on the other hand, enriched by interpolations to make good movie scripts. In Shaw's *Pygmalion,* for instance, the actual process of Eliza's phonetic education and, still more important, her final triumph at the grand party, are wisely omitted; we see—or, rather, hear—some samples of her gradual linguistic improvement and finally encounter her, upon her return from the reception, victorious and splendidly arrayed but deeply hurt for want of recognition and sympathy. In the film adaptation, precisely these two scenes are not only supplied but also strongly emphasized; we witness the fascinating activities in the laboratory with its array of spinning disks and mirrors, organ pipes and dancing flames, and we participate in the ambassadorial party, with many moments of impending catastrophe and a little counter-intrigue thrown in for suspense. Unquestionably these two scenes, entirely absent from the play, and indeed unachievable upon the stage, were the highlights of the film; whereas the Shavian dialogue, however severely cut, turned out to fall a little flat in certain moments. And wherever, as in so many other films, a poetic emotion, a musical outburst, or a literary conceit (even, I am grieved to say, some of the wise-cracks of Groucho Marx) entirely lose contact with visible movement, they strike the sensitive spectator as, literally, out of place. It is certainly terrible when a soft-boiled he-man, after the suicide of his mistress, casts a twelve-foot glance upon her photograph and says something less-than-coexpressible to the effect that he will never forget her. But when he recites, instead, a piece of poetry as sublimely more-than-coexpressible as Romeo's monologue at the bier of Juliet, it is still worse. Reinhardt's *Midsummer Night's Dream* is probably the most unfortunate major film ever produced; and Olivier's *Henry V* owes its comparative success, apart from the all but providential adaptability of this particular play, to so many *tours de force* that it will, God willing, remain an exception rather than set a pattern. It combines "judicious pruning" with the interpolation of pageantry, nonverbal comedy and melodrama; it uses a device perhaps best designated as "oblique close-up" (Mr. Olivier's beautiful face inwardly listening to but not pronouncing the great soliloquy); and, most notably, it shifts between three levels of archaeological reality: a reconstruction of Elizabethan London, a reconstruction of the events of 1415 as laid down in Shakespeare's play, and the reconstruction of a performance of this play on Shakespeare's own stage. All this is perfectly legitimate; but, even so, the highest praise of the film will always come from those who, like the critic of the *New Yorker,* are not quite in sympathy with either the movies *au naturel* or Shakespeare *au naturel.*

As the writings of Conan Doyle potentially contain all modern mystery stories (except for the tough specimens of the Dashiell Hammett school), so do the films produced between 1900 and 1910 pre-establish the subject matter and methods of the moving picture as we know it. This period produced the incunabula of the Western and the crime film (Edwin S. Porter's amazing *Great Train Robbery* of 1903) from which developed the modern gangster, adventure, and mystery pictures (the latter, if well done, is still one of the most honest and genuine forms of film entertainment, space being doubly charged with time as the beholder asks himself not only "What is going to happen?" but also "What has happened before?"). The same period saw the emergence of the fantastically imaginative film (Méliès) which was to lead to the expressionist and surrealist experiments (*The Cabinet of Dr. Caligari, Sang d'un Poète,* etc.), on the one hand, and to the more superficial and spectacular fairy tales à la Arabian Nights, on the other. Comedy, later to triumph in Charlie Chaplin, the still insufficiently appreciated Buster Keaton, the Marx Brothers and the pre-Hollywood creations of René Clair, reached a respectable level in Max Linder and others. In historical and melodramatic films the foundations were laid for movie iconography and movie symbolism, and in the early work of D. W. Griffith we find, not only remarkable attempts at psychological analysis *(Edgar Allan Poe)* and social criticism *(A Corner in Wheat)* but also such basic technical innovations as the long shot, the flashback and the close-up. And modest trick films and cartoons paved the way to Felix the Cat, Popeye the Sailor, and Felix's prodigious offspring, Mickey Mouse.

Within their self-imposed limitations the earlier Disney films, and certain sequences in the later ones,* represent, as it were, a chemically pure distillation of cinematic possibilities. They retain the most important folkloristic elements—sadism, pornography, the humor engendered by both, and moral justice—almost without dilution and often fuse these elements into a variation on the primitive and inexhaustible David-and-Goliath motif, the triumph of the seemingly weak over the seemingly strong; and their fantastic independence of the natural laws gives them the power to integrate space with time to such perfection that the spatial and

---

*I make this distinction because it was, in my opinion, a fall from grace when *Snow White* introduced the human figure and when *Fantasia* attempted to picturalize The World's Great Music. The very virtue of the animated cartoon is to animate, that is to say endow lifeless things with life, or living things with a different kind of life. It effects a metamorphosis, and such a metamorphosis is wonderfully present in Disney's animals, plants, thunderclouds and railroad trains. Whereas his dwarfs, glamourized princesses, hillbillies, baseball players, rouged centaurs and *amigos* from South America are not transformations but caricatures at best, and fakes or vulgarities at worst. Concerning music, however, it should be borne in mind that its cinematic use is no less predicated upon the principle of coexpressibility than is the cinematic use of the spoken word. There is music permitting or even requiring the accompaniment of visible action (such as dances, ballet music and any kind of operatic compositions) and music of which the opposite is true; and this is, again, not a question of quality (most of us rightly prefer a waltz by Johann Strauss to a symphony by Sibelius) but one of intention. In *Fantasia* the hippopotamus ballet was wonderful, and the Pastoral Symphony and "Ave Maria" sequences were deplorable, not because the cartooning in the first case was infinitely better than in the two others (*cf.* above), and certainly not because Beethoven and Schubert are too sacred for picturalization, but simply because Ponchielli's "Dance of the Hours" is coexpressible while the Pastoral Symphony and the "Ave Maria" are not. In cases like these even the best imaginable music and the best imaginable cartoon will impair rather than enhance each other's effectiveness.

Experimental proof of all this was furnished by Disney's recent *Make Mine Music* where The World's Great Music was fortunately restricted to Prokofieff. Even among the other sequences the most successful ones were those in which the human element was either absent or reduced to a minimum; Willie the Whale, the Ballad of Johnny Fedora and Alice Blue-Bonnet, and, above all, the truly magnificent Goodman Quartet.

temporal experiences of sight and hearing come to be almost interconvertible. A series of soap bubbles, successively punctured, emits a series of sounds exactly corresponding in pitch and volume to the size of the bubbles; the three uvulae of Willie the Whale—small, large and medium—vibrate in consonance with tenor, bass and baritone notes; and the very concept of stationary existence is completely abolished. No object in creation, whether it be a house, a piano, a tree or an alarm clock, lacks the faculties of organic, in fact anthropomorphic, movement, facial expression and phonetic articulation. Incidentally, even in normal, "realistic" films the inanimate object, provided that it is dynamizable, can play the role of a leading character as do the ancient railroad engines in Buster Keaton's *General* and *Niagara Falls.* How the earlier Russian films exploited the possibility of heroizing all sorts of machinery lives in everybody's memory; and it is perhaps more than an accident that the two films which will go down in history as the great comical and the great serious masterpiece of the silent period bear the names and immortalize the personalities of two big ships: Keaton's *Navigator* (1924) and Eisenstein's *Potemkin* (1925).

The evolution from the jerky beginnings to this grand climax offers the fascinating spectacle of a new artistic medium gradually becoming conscious of its legitimate, that is, exclusive, possibilities and limitations—a spectacle not unlike the development of the mosaic, which started out with transposing illusionistic genre pictures into a more durable material and culminated in the hieratic supernaturalism of Ravenna; or the development of line engraving, which started out as a cheap and handy substitute for book illumination and culminated in the purely "graphic" style of Dürer.

Just so the silent movies developed a definite style of their own, adapted to the specific conditions of the medium. A hitherto unknown language was forced upon a public not yet capable of reading it, and the more proficient the public became the more refinement could develop in the language. For a Saxon peasant of around 800 it was not easy to understand the meaning of a picture showing a man as he pours water over the head of another man, and even later many people found it difficult to grasp the significance of two ladies standing behind the throne of an emperor. For the public of around 1910 it was no less difficult to understand the meaning of the speechless action in a moving picture, and the producers employed means of clarification similar to those we find in medieval art. One of these were printed titles or letters, striking equivalents of the medieval *tituli* and scrolls (at a still earlier date there even used to be explainers who would say, *viva voce,* "Now he thinks his wife is dead but she isn't" or "I don't wish to offend the ladies in the audience but I doubt that any of them would have done that much for her child"). Another, less obtrusive method of explanation was the introduction of a fixed iconography which from the outset informed the spectator about the basic facts and characters, much as the two ladies behind the emperor, when carrying a sword and a cross respectively, were uniquely determined as Fortitude and Faith. There arose, identifiable by standardized appearance, behavior and attributes, the well-remembered types of the Vamp and the Straight Girl (perhaps the most convincing modern equivalents of the medieval personifications of the Vices and Virtues), the Family Man, and the Villain, the latter marked by a black mustache and walking stick.

Nocturnal scenes were printed on blue or green film. A checkered tablecloth meant, once for all, a "poor but honest" milieu; a happy marriage, soon to be endangered by the shadows from the past, was symbolized by the young wife's pouring the breakfast coffee for her husband; the first kiss was invariably announced by the lady's gently playing with her partner's necktie and was invariably accompanied by her kicking out with her left foot. The conduct of the characters was predetemined accordingly. The poor but honest laborer who, after leaving his little house with the checkered tablecloth, came upon an abandoned baby could not but take it to his home and bring it up as best he could; the Family Man could not but yield, however temporarily, to the temptations of the Vamp. As a result these early melodramas had a highly gratifying and soothing quality in that events took shape, without the complications of individual psychology, according to a pure Aristotelian logic so badly missed in real life.

Devices like these became gradually less necessary as the public grew accustomed to interpret the action by itself and were virtually abolished by the invention of the talking film. But even now there survive—quite legitimately, I think—the remnants of a "fixed attitude and attribute" principle and, more basic, a primitive or folkloristic concept of plot construction. Even today we take it for granted that the diphtheria of a baby tends to occur when the parents are out and, having occurred, solves all their matrimonial problems. Even today we demand of a decent mystery film that the butler, though he may be anything from an agent of the British Secret Service to the real father of the daughter of the house, must not turn out to be the murderer. Even today we love to see Pasteur, Zola or Ehrlich win out against stupidity and wickedness, with their respective wives trusting and trusting all the time. Even today we much prefer a happy finale to a gloomy one and insist, at the very least, on the observance of the Aristotelian rule that the story have a beginning, a middle and an ending—a rule the abrogation of which has done so much to estrange the general public from the more elevated spheres of modern writing. Primitive symbolism, too, survives in such amusing details as the last sequence of *Casablanca* where the delightfully crooked and right-minded *préfet de police* casts an empty bottle of Vichy water into the wastepaper basket; and in such telling symbols of the supernatural as Sir Cedric Hardwicke's Death in the guise of a "gentleman in a dustcoat trying" *(On Borrowed Time)* or Claude Rains's Hermes Psychopompos in the striped trousers of an airline manager *(Here Comes Mister Jordan)*.

The most conspicuous advances were made in directing, lighting, camera work, cutting and acting proper. But while in most of these fields the evolution proceeded continuously—though, of course, not without detours, breakdowns and archaic relapses—the development of acting suffered a sudden interruption by the invention of the talking film; so that the style of acting in the silents can already be evaluated in retrospect, as a lost art not unlike the painting technique of Jan van Eyck or, to take up our previous simile, the burin technique of Dürer. It was soon realized that acting in a silent film neither meant a pantomimic exaggeration of stage acting (as was generally and erroneously assumed by professional stage actors who more and more frequently condescended to perform in the movies), nor could dispense with stylization altogether; a man photographed while walking down a gangway in ordinary, every-day-life fashion looked like anything but a man walking down a gangway when the result appeared on the screen. If the picture was to look both natural and meaningful the acting had to be done in a manner equally different from the style of the stage and the reality of ordinary life; speech had to be made dispensable by establishing an organic relation between the acting and the technical procedure of cinephotography—much as in Dürer's prints color had been made dispensable by establishing an organic relation between the design and the technical procedure of line engraving.

This was precisely what the great actors of the silent period accomplished, and it is a significant fact that the best of them did not come from the stage, whose crystallized tradition prevented Duse's only film, *Cenere,* from being more than a priceless record of Duse. They came instead from the circus or the variety, as was the case of Chaplin, Keaton and Will Rogers; from nothing in particular, as was the case of Theda Bara, of her greater European parallel, the Danish actress Asta Nielsen, and of Garbo; or from everything under the sun, as was the case of Douglas Fairbanks. The style of these "old masters" was indeed comparable to the style of line engraving in that it was, and had to be, exaggerated in comparison with stage acting (just as the sharply incised and vigorously curved *tailles* of the burin are exaggerated in comparison with pencil strokes or brushwork), but richer, subtler and infinitely more precise. The advent of the talkies, reducing if not abolishing this difference between screen acting and stage acting, thus confronted the actors and actresses of the silent screen with a serious problem. Buster Keaton yielded to temptation and fell. Chaplin first tried to stand his ground and to remain an exquisite archaist but finally gave in, with only moderate success *(The Great Dictator).* Only the glorious Harpo has thus far successfully refused to utter a single articulate sound; and only Greta Garbo succeeded, in a measure, in transforming her style in principle. But even in her case one cannot help feeling that her first talking picture, *Anna Christie,* where she could ensconce herself, most of the time, in mute or monosyllabic sullenness, was better than her later performances; and in the second, talking version of *Anna Karenina,* the weakest moment is certainly when she delivers a big Ibsenian speech to her husband, and the strongest when she silently moves along the platform of the railroad station while her despair takes shape in the consonance of her movement (and expression) with the movement of the nocturnal space around her, filled with the real noises of the trains and the imaginary sound of the "little men with the iron hammers" that drives her, relentlessly and almost without her realizing it, under the wheels.

Small wonder that there is sometimes felt a kind of nostalgia for the silent period and that devices have been worked out to combine the virtues of sound and speech with those of silent acting, such as the "oblique close-up" already mentioned in connection with *Henry V;* the dance behind glass doors in *Sous les Toits de Paris;* or, in the *Histoire d'un Tricheur,* Sacha Guitry's recital of the events of his youth while the events themselves are "silently" enacted on the screen. However, this nostalgic feeling is no argument against the talkies as such. Their evolution has shown that, in art, every gain entails a certain loss on the other side of the ledger; but that the gain remains a gain, provided that the basic nature of the medium is realized and respected. One can imagine that, when the cavemen of Altamira began to paint their buffaloes in natural colors instead of merely incising the contours, the more conservative cavemen foretold the end of paleolithic art. But paleolithic art went on, and so will the movies. New technical inventions always tend to dwarf the values already attained, especially in a medium that owes its very existence to technical experimentation. The earliest talkies were infinitely inferior to the then mature silents, and most of the present technicolor films are still inferior to the now mature talkies in black and white. But even if Aldous Huxley's nightmare should come true and the experiences of taste, smell and touch should be added to those of sight and hearing, even then we may say with the Apostle, as we have said when first confronted with the sound track and the technicolor film, "We are troubled on every side, yet not distressed; we are perplexed, but not in despair."

From the law of time-charged space and space-bound time, there follows the fact that the screenplay, in contrast to the theater play, *has no aesthetic existence independent of its performance, and that its characters have no aesthetic existence outside the actors.*

The playwright writes in the fond hope that his work will be an imperishable jewel in the treasure house of civilization and will be presented in hundreds of performances that are but transient variations on a "work" that is constant. The scriptwriter on the other hand, writes for one producer, one director and one cast. Their work achieves the same degree of permanence as does his; and should the same or a similar scenario ever be filmed by a different director and a different cast there will result in an altogether different "play."

Othello or Nora are definite, substantial figures created by the playwright. They can be played well or badly, and they can be "interpreted" in one way or another; but they most definitely exist, no matter who plays them or even whether they are played at all. The character in a film, however, lives and dies with the actor. It is not the entity "Othello" interpreted by Robeson or the entity "Nora" interpreted by Duse; it is the entity "Greta Garbo" incarnate in a figure called Anna Christie or the entity "Robert Montgomery" incarnate in a murderer who, for all we know or care to know, may forever remain anonymous but will never cease to haunt our memories. Even when the names of the characters happen to be Henry VIII or Anna Karenina, the king who ruled England from 1509 to 1547 and the woman created by Tolstoy, they do not exist outside the being of Garbo and Laughton. They are but empty and incorporeal outlines like the shadows in Homer's Hades, assuming the character of reality only when filled with the lifeblood of an actor. Conversely, if a movie role is badly played there remains literally nothing of it, no matter how interesting the character's psychology or how elaborate the words.

What applies to the actor applies, *mutatis mutandis,* to most of the other artists, or artisans, who contribute to the making of a film: the director, the soundman, the enormously important cameraman, even the make-up man. A stage production is rehearsed until everything is ready, and then it is repeatedly performed in three consecutive hours. At each performance everybody has to be on hand and does his work; and afterward he goes home and to bed. The work of the stage actor may thus be likened to that of a musician, and that of the stage director to that of a conductor. Like these, they have a certain repertoire which they have studied and present in a number of complete but transitory performances, be it *Hamlet* today and *Ghosts* tomorrow, or *Life with Father per saecula saeculorum*. The activites of the film actor and the film director, however, are comparable, respectively, to those of the plastic artist and the architect, rather than to those of the musician and the conductor. Stage work is continuous but transitory; film work is discontinuous but permanent. Individual sequences are done piecemeal and out of order according to the most efficient use of sets and personnel. Each bit is done over and over again until it stands; and when the whole has been cut and composed everyone is through with it forever. Needless to say that this very procedure cannot but emphasize the curious consubstantiality that exists between the person of the movie actor and his role. Coming into existence piece by piece, regardless of the natural sequence of events, the "character" can grow into a unified whole only if the actor manages to be, not merely to play, Henry VIII or Anna Karenina throughout the entire wearisome period of shooting. I have it on the best of authorities that Laughton was really difficult to live with in the particular six or eight weeks during which he was doing— or rather being—Captain Bligh.

It might be said that a film, called into being by a co-operative effort in which all contributions have the same degree of permanence, is the nearest modern equivalent of a medieval cathedral; the role of the producer corresponding, more or less, to that of the bishop or archbishop; that of the director to that of the architect in chief; that of the scenario writers to that of the scholastic advisers establishing the iconographical program; and that of the actors, cameramen, cutters, sound men, make-up men and the diverse technicians to that of those whose work provided the physical entity of the finished product, from the sculptors, glass painters, bronze casters, carpenters and skilled masons down to the quarry men and woodsmen. And if you speak to any one of these collaborators he will tell you, with perfect *bona fides,* that his is really the most important job—which is quite true to the extent that it is indispensable.

The comparison may seem sacrilegious, not only because there are, proportionally, fewer good films than there are good cathedrals, but also because the movies are commercial. However, if commercial art be defined as all art not primarily produced in order to gratify the creative urge of its maker but primarily intended to meet the requirements of a patron or a buying public, it must be said that noncommercial art is the exception rather than the rule, and a fairly recent and not always felicitous exception at that. While it is true that commercial art is always in danger of ending up as a prostitute, it is equally true that noncommercial art is always in danger of ending up as an old maid. Noncommercial art has given us Seurat's "Grande Jatte" and Shakespeare's sonnets, but also much that is esoteric to the point of incommunicability. Conversely, commercial art has given us much that is vulgar or snobbish (two aspects of the same thing) to the point of loathsomeness, but also Dürer's prints and Shakespeare's plays. For, we must not forget that Dürer's prints were partly made on commission and partly intended to be sold in the open market; and that Shakespeare's plays—in contrast to the earlier masques and intermezzi which were produced at court by aristocratic amateurs and could afford

Laurence Olivier in *Henry V* (1944). The film "uses a device perhaps best designated as 'oblique close-up' (Mr. Olivier's beautiful face inwardly listening to but not pronouncing the great soliloquy)." (PANOFSKY, page 238).

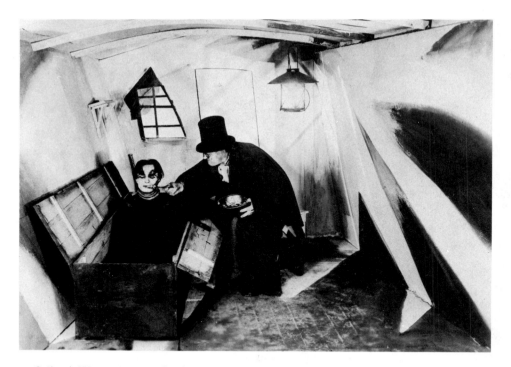

Caligari (Werner Krauss) feeding Cesare (Conrad Veidt) in *The Cabinet of Doctor Caligari* (1919). "The expressionist settings . . . could exert but little influence upon the general course of events. To prestylize reality prior to tackling it amounts to dodging the problem" (PANOFSKY, page 248). "Films of this type are not only intended as autonomous wholes but frequently ignore physical reality or exploit it for purposes alien to photographic veracity" (KRACAUER, page 19).

to be so incomprehensible that even those who described them in printed monographs occasionally failed to grasp their intended significance—were meant to appeal, and did appeal, not only to the select few but also to everyone who was prepared to pay a shilling for admission.

It is this requirement of communicabiilty that makes commercial art more vital than noncommercial, and therefore potentially much more effective for better or for worse. The commercial producer can both educate and pervert the general public, and can allow the general public—or rather his idea of the general public—both to educate and to pervert himself. As is demonstrated by a number of excellent films that proved to be great box office successes, the public does not refuse to accept good products if it gets them. That it does not get them very often is caused not so much by commercialism as such as by too little discernment and, paradoxical though it may seem, too much timidity in its application. Hollywood believes that it must produce "what the public wants" while the public would take whatever Hollywood produces. If Hollywood were to decide for itself what it wants it would get away with it—even if it should decide to "depart from evil and do good." For, to revert to whence we started, in modern life the movies are what most other forms of art have ceased to be, not an adornment but a necessity.

That this should be so is understandable, not only from a sociological but also from an art-historical point of view. The processes of all the earlier representational arts conform, in a higher or lesser degree, to an idealistic conception of the world. These arts operate from top to bottom, so to speak, and not from bottom to top; they start with an idea to be projected into shapeless matter and not with the objects that constitute the physical world. The painter works on a blank wall or canvas which he organizes into a likeness of things and persons according to his idea (however much this idea may have been nourished by reality); he does not work with the things and persons themselves even if he works "from the model." The same is true of the sculptor with his shapeless mass of clay or his untooled block of stone or wood; of the writer with his sheet of paper or his dictaphone; and even of the stage designer with his empty and sorely limited section of space. It is the movies, and only the movies, that do justice to that materialistic interpretation of the universe which, whether we like it or not, pervades contemporary civilization. Excepting the very special case of the animated cartoon, the movies organize material things and persons, not a neutral medium, into a composition that receives its style, and may even become fantastic or pretervoluntarily symbolic, not so much by an interpretation in the artist's mind as by the actual manipulation of physical objects and recording machinery. The medium of the movies is physcial reality as such: the physical reality of eighteenth-century Versailles—no matter whether it be the original or a Hollywood facsimile indistinguishable therefrom for all aesthetic intents and purposes—or of a suburban home in Westchester; the physical reality of the Rue de Lappe in Paris or of the Gobi Desert, of Paul Ehrlich's apartment in Frankfurt or of the streets of New York in the rain; the physical reality of engines and animals, of Edward G. Robinson and Jimmy Cagney. All these objects and persons must be organized into a work of art. They can be arranged in all sorts of ways ("arrangement" comprising, of course, such things as make-up, lighting and camera work); but there is no running away from them. From this point of view it becomes evident that an attempt at subjecting the world to artistic prestylization, as in the expressionist settings of *The Cabinet of Dr. Caligari* (1919), could be no more than an exciting experiment that could exert but little influence upon the general course of events. To prestylize reality prior to tackling it amounts to dodging the problem. The problem is to manipulate and shoot unstylized reality in such a way that the result has style. This is a proposition no less legitmate and no less difficult than any proposition in the older arts.

1934; revised 1947

SIEGFRIED KRACAUER
FROM THEORY OF FILM

THE ESTABLISHMENT OF PHYSICAL EXISTENCE

In establishing physical existence, films differ from photographs in two respects: they represent reality as it evolves in time; and they do so with the aid of cinematic techniques and devices.

Consequently, the recording and revealing duties of the two kindred media coincide only in part. And what do they imply for film in particular? The hunting ground of the motion picture camera is in principle unlimited; it is the external world expanding in all directions. Yet there are certain subjects within that world which may be termed "cinematic" because they seem to exert a peculiar attraction on the medium. It is as if the medium were predestined (and eager) to exhibit them. The following pages are devoted to a close examination of these cinematic subjects. Several lie, so to speak, on the surface; they will be dealt with under the title "recording functions." Others would hardly come to our attention or be perceptible were it not for the film camera and/or the intervention of cinematic techniques; they will be discussed in the subsequent section "revealing functions." To be sure, any camera revelation involves recording, but recording on its part need not be revealing.

RECORDING FUNCTIONS

Movement

At least two groups of quite common external phenomena are naturals for the screen. As might be expected, one is made up of all kinds of movements, these being cinematic because only the motion picture camera is able to record them. Among them are three types which can be considered cinematic subjects par excellence.

The Chase

"The chase," says Hitchcock, "seems to me the final expression of the motion picture medium." This complex of interrelated movements is motion at its extreme, one might almost say, motion as such—and of course it is immensely serviceable for establishing a continuity of suspenseful physical action. Hence the fascination the chase has held since the beginning of the century. The primitive French comedies availed themselves of it to frame their space-devouring adventures. Gendarmes pursued a dog who eventually turned the tables on them *(Course des sergeants de ville);* pumpkins gliding from a cart were chased by the grocer, his donkey, and passers-by through sewers and over roofs (*La Course des potirons, 1907;* English title: *The Pumpkin Race*). For any Keystone comedy to forgo the chase would have been an unpardonable crime. It was the climax of the whole, its orgiastic finale—a pandemonium, with onrushing trains telescoping into automobiles and narrow escapes down ropes that dangled above a lion's den.

But perhaps nothing reveals the cinematic significance of the reveling in speed more drastically than D. W. Griffith's determination to transfer, at the end of all his great films, the action from the ideological plane to that of his famous "last-minute rescue," which was a chase pure and simple. Or should one say, a race? In any case, the rescuers rush ahead to overwhelm the villains or free their victims at the very last moment, while simultaneously the inner emotion which the dramatic conflict has aroused yields to a state of acute physiological suspense called forth by exuberant physical motion and its immediate implications. Nor is a genuine Western imaginable without a pursuit or a race on horseback. As Flaherty put it, Westerns are popular "because people never get tired of seeing a horse gallop across the plains." Its gallop seems still to gain momentum by contrast with the immense tranquility of the far-away horizon.

Dancing

The second type of specifically cinematic movement is dancing. This does not apply, of course, to the stage ballet which evolves in a space-time outside actuality proper. Interestingly enough, all attempts at "canning" it adequately have so far failed. Screen reproductions of theatrical dancing either indulge in a completeness which is boring or offer a selection of attractive details which confuse in that they dismember rather than preserve the original. Dancing attains to cinematic eminence only if it is part and parcel of physical reality. René Clair's early sound films have judiciously been called ballets. True, they are, but the performers are real-life Parisians who just cannot help executing dance movements when going about their love adventures and minor quarrels. With infinite subtlety Clair guides them along the divide between the real and unreal. Sometimes it appears as though these delivery boys, taxi drivers, girls, clerks, shopkeepers, and nondescript figures are marionettes banding together and parting from each other according to designs as delicate as lacework; and then again they are made to look and behave like ordinary people in Paris streets and bistros. And the latter impression prevails. For, even granted that they are drawn into an imaginary universe, this universe itself reflects throughout our real world in stylizing it. What dancing there is, seems to occur on the spur of the moment; it is the vicissitudes of life from which these ballets issue.

Fred Astaire too prefers apparent impromptu performances to stage choreography; he is quite aware that this type of performance is appropriate to the medium. "Each dance," says he, "ought to spring somehow out of character or situation, otherwise it is simply a vaudeville act." This does not mean that he would dispense with theatrical production numbers. But no sooner does he perform in vaudeville fashion than he breaks out of the prison of prearranged stage patterns and, with a genius for improvisation, dances over tables and gravel paths into the everyday world. It is a one-way route which invariably leads from the footlights to the heart of camera-reality. Astaire's consummate dancing is meant to belong among the real-life events with which he toys in his musicals; and it is so organized that it imperceptibly emerges from, and disappears, in the flow of these happenings. . . .

Nascent Motion

The third type of motion which offers special interest cinematically is not just another group of interrelated movements but movement as contrasted with motionlessness. In focusing upon this contrast, films strikingly demonstrate that objective movement—any movement, for that matter—is one of their choice subjects. Alexander Dovzhenko in both *Arsenal* and *Earth* frequently stops the action to resume it after a short lull. The first phase of this procedure—characters or parts of them abruptly ceasing to move—produces a shock effect, as if all of a sudden we found ourselves in a vacuum. The immediate consequence is that we acutely realize the significance of movement as an integral element of the external world as well as film.

But this is only part of the story. Even though the moving images on the screen come to a standstill, the thrust of their movement is too powerful to be discontinued simultaneously. Accordingly, when the people in *Arsenal* or *Earth* are shown in the form of stills, the suspended movement nevertheless perpetuates itself by changing from outer motion into inner motion. Dovzhenko has known how to make this metamorphosis benefit his penetrations of reality. The immobile lovers in *Earth* become transparent; the deep happiness which is moving them turns inside out. And the spectator on his part grasps their inward agitation because the cessation of external motion moves him all the more intensely to commune with them. Yet despite these rewarding experiences he cannot help feeling a certain relief when eventually the characters take on life again—an event which marks the second and final phase of the procedure. It is a return to the world of film, whose inherent motion alone renders possible such excursions into the whirlpool of the motionless. . . .

Inanimate Objects

Since the inanimate is featured in many paintings, one might question the legitimacy of characterizing it as a cinematic subject. Yet it is a painter—Fernand Léger—who judiciously insists that only film is equipped to sensitize us, by way of big close-ups, to the possibilities that lie dormant in a hat, a chair, a hand, and a foot. Similarly Cohen-Séat: "And I? says the leaf which is falling.—And we? say the orange peel, the gust of wind. . . . Film, whether intentionally or not, is their mouthpiece." Nor should it be forgotten that the camera's ability to single out and record the orange peel or the hand marks a decisive difference between screen and stage, so close to each other in some respects. Stage imagery inevitably centers on the actor, whereas film is free to dwell on parts of his appearance and detail the objects about him. In using its freedom to bring the inanimate to the fore and make it a carrier of action, film only protests its peculiar requirement to explore all of physical existence, human or nonhuman. Within this context it is of interest that in the early 'twenties, when the French cinema was swamped with theatrical adaptations and stage-minded dramas, Louis Delluc tried to put the medium on its own feet by stressing the tremendous importance of objects. If they are assigned the role due to them, he argued, the actor too "is no more than a detail, a fragment of the matter of the world."

Actually, the urge to raise hats and chairs to the status of full-fledged actors has never completely atrophied. From the malicious escalators, the unruly Murphy beds, and the mad automobiles in silent comedy to the cruiser Potemkin, the oil derrick in *Louisiana Story* and the dilapidated kitchen in *Umberto D.*, a long procession of unforgettable objects has passed across the screen—objects which stand out as protagonists and all but overshadow the rest of the case. Or remember the powerful presence of environmental influences in *The Grapes of Wrath*, the part played by nocturnal Coney Island in *Little Fugitive*, the interaction between the marshland and the guerilla fighters in the last episode of *Paisan*. Of course, the reverse hold true also: films in which the inanimate merely serves as a background to self-contained dialogue and the closed circuit of human relationships are essentially uncinematic.

REVEALING FUNCTIONS

"I ask that a film *discover* something for me" declares Luis Buñuel, who is himself a fiery pathfinder of the screen. And what are films likely to discover? The evidence available suggests that they assume three kinds of revealing functions. They tend to reveal things normally unseen; phenomena overwhelming consciousness; and certain aspects of the outer world which may be called "special modes of reality."

Things Normally Unseen

The many material phenomena which elude observation under normal circumstances can be divided into three groups. The first includes objects too small to be readily noticed or even perceived by the naked eye and objects so big that they will not be fully taken in either.

The Small and the Big

The small. The small is conveyed in the form of close-ups. D. W. Griffith was among the first to realize that they are indispensable for cinematic narration. He initiated their use, as we now know it, in *After Many Years* (1908), an adaptation of Tennyson's *Enoch Arden*. There his memorable first close-up appeared within contexts which Lewis Jacobs describes as follows: "Going further than he had ventured before, in a scene showing Annie Lee brooding and waiting for her husband's return, Griffith daringly used a large close-up of her face. . . . He had another surprise, even more radical, to offer. Immediately following the close-up of Annie, he inserted a picture of the object of her thoughts—her husband cast away on a desert isle."

On the surface, this succession of shots seems simply designed to lure the spectator into the dimension of her intimate preoccupations. He first watches Annie from a distance and then approaches her so closely that he sees only her face; if he moves on in the same direction, as the film invites him to do, it is logical that he should penetrate Annie's appearance and land inside her mind. Granting the validity of this interpretation, the close-up of her face is not an end in itself; rather, along with the subsequent shots, it serves to suggest what is going on behind that face— Annie's longing for reunion with her husband. A knowingly chosen detail of her physique thus would help establish the whole of her being in a dramatic interest.

The same obviously holds true of another famous Griffith closeup: Mae Marsh's clasped hands in the trial episode of *Intolerance*. It almost looks as if her huge hands with the convulsively moving fingers were inserted for the sole purpose of illustrating eloquently her anguish at the most crucial moment of the trial; as if, generally speaking, the function of any such detail exhausted itself in intensifying our participation in the total situation. This is how Eisenstein conceives of the close-up. Its main function, says he, is "not so much to *show* or to *present* as to *signify, to give meaning, to designate.*" To designate what? Evidently something of importance to the narrative. And montage-minded as he is, he immediately adds that the significance of the close-up for the plot accrues to it less from its own content than from the manner in which it is juxtaposed with the surrounding shots. According to him, the close-up is primarily a montage unit.

But is this really its function? Consider again the combination of shots with the close-up of Annie's face: the place assigned to the latter in the sequence intimates that Griffith wanted us also to absorb the face for its own sake instead of just passing through and beyond it; the face appears before the desires and emotions to which it refers have been completely defined, thus tempting us to get lost in its puzzling indeterminacy. Annie's face is also an end in itself. An so is the image of Mae Marsh's hands. No doubt it is to impress upon us her inner condition, but besides making us experience what we would in a measure have experienced anyway because of our familiarity with the characters involved, this close-up contributes something momentous and unique—it reveals how her hands behave under the impact of utter despair.

Eisenstein criticizes the close-ups in Griffith films precisely for their relative independence of the contexts in which they occur. He calls them isolated units which tend "to show or to present"; and he insists that to the extent that they indulge in isolation they fail to yield the meanings which the interweaving processes of montage may elicit from them. Had Eisenstein been less possessed with the magic powers of montage he would certainly have acknowledged the cinematic superiority of the Griffith close-up. To Griffith such huge images of small material phenomena are not only integral components of the narrative but disclosures of new aspects of physical reality. In representing them the way he does, he seems to have been guided by the conviction that the cinema is all the more cinematic if it acquaints us with the physical origins, ramifications, and connotations of all the emotional and intellectual events which comprise the plot; that it cannot adequately account for these inner developments unless it leads us through the thicket of material life from which they emerge and in which they are embedded. . . .

The big. Among the large objects, such as vast plains or panoramas of any kind, one deserves special attention: the masses. No doubt imperial Rome already teemed with them. But masses of people in the modern sense entered the historical scene only in the wake of the industrial revolution. Then they became a social force of first magnitude. Warring nations resorted to levies on an unheard-of scale and identifiable groups yielded to the anonymous multitude which filled the big cities in the form of amorphous crowds. Walter Benjamin observes that in the period marked by the rise of photography the daily sight of moving crowds was still a spectacle to which eyes and nerves had to get adjusted. The testimony of sensitive contemporaries would seem to corroborate this sagacious observation: The Paris crowds omnipresent in Baudelaire's *Les Fleurs du mal* function as stimuli which call forth irritating kaleidoscopic sensations; the jostling and shoving passers-by who, in Poe's *Man of the Crowd,* throng gas-lit London provoke a succession of electric shocks.

At the time of its emergence the mass, this giant animal, was a new and upsetting experience. As might be expected, the traditional arts proved unable to encompass and render it. Where they failed, photography easily succeeded; it was technically equipped to portray crowds as the accidental agglomerations they are. Yet only film, the fulfillment of photography in a sense, was equal to the task of capturing them in motion. In this case the instrument of reproduction came into being almost simultaneously with one of its main subjects. Hence the attraction which masses exerted on still and motion picture cameras from the outset. It is certainly more than sheer coincidence that the very first Lumière films featured a crowd of workers and the confusion of arrival and departure at a railway station. Early Italian films elaborated upon the theme; and D. W. Griffith, inspired by them, showed how masses can be represented cinematically. The Russians absorbed his lesson, applying it in ways of their own. . . .

The Transient

The second group of things normally unseen comprises the transient. Here belong, first, fleeting impressions—"the shadow of a cloud passing across the plain, a leaf which yields to the wind." Evanescent, like dream elements, such impressions may haunt the moviegoer long after the story they are called upon to implement has sunk into oblivion. The manes of the galloping horses—flying threads or streamers rather than manes—in the chariot race episode of Fred Niblo's *Ben Hur* are as unforgettable as the fiery traces of the projectiles that tear the night in *Desert Victory.* The motion picture camera seems to be partial to the least permanent components of our environment. It may be anticipated that the street in the broadest sense of the word is a place where impressions of this kind are bound to occur. "The cinema," says Aragon, delighting in its snapshot-like predilection for the ephemeral, "has taught us more about man in a few years than centuries of painting have taught: fugitive expressions, attitudes scarcely credible yet real, charm and hideousness."

Second, there are movements of so transitory a nature that they would be imperceptible were it not for two cinematic techniques: accelerated-motion, which condenses extremely slow and, hence, unobservable developments, such as the growth of plants, and slow-motion, which expands movements too fast to be registered. Like the big close-up, these correlated techniques lead straight into "reality of another dimension." Pictures of stalks piercing the soil in the process of growing open up imaginary areas, and racing legs shown in slow-motion do not just slow down but change in appearance and perform bizarre evolutions—patterns remote from reality as we know it. Slow-motion shots parallel the regular close-ups; they are, so to speak, temporal close-ups achieving in time what the close-up proper is achieving in space. That, unlike the latter, they are used rather infrequently, may be traced to the fact that the enlargement of spatial phenomena, as effected by the close-up, seems more "natural" to us than the expansion of a given time interval. (On the other hand, it appears that film makers draw more readily on slow-motion than on the reverse technique—perhaps simply because it does not require so lengthy preparations.)

As contrived-reality pictures, the deviant images gained by both techniques, especially slow-motion, may well figure in nonrealistic experimental films. Yet they live up to the cinematic approach only if they are made to fulfill a revealing function within contexts focusing on physical existence. The late Jean Epstein, who felt so immensely attracted by "reality of another dimension," considered this their true destination. Referring to waves in slow-motion and clouds in accelerated-motion, he declared that for all their "startling physics and strange mechanics" they "are but a portrait—seen in a certain perspective—of the world in which we live."

Blind Spots of the Mind

The third and last group of things normally unseen consists of phenomena which figure among the blind spots of the mind; habit and prejudice prevent us from noticing them. The role which cultural standards and traditions may play in these processes of elimination is drastically illustrated by a report on the reactions of African natives to a film made on the spot. After the screening the spectators, all of them still unacquainted with the medium, talked volubly about a chicken they allegedly had seen picking food in the mud. The film maker himself, entirely unaware of its presence, attended several performances without being able to detect it. Had it been dreamed up by the natives? Only by scanning his film foot by foot did he eventually succeed in tracing the chicken: it appeared for a fleeting moment somewhere in a corner of a picture and then vanished forever.

The following types of objects are cinematic because they stubbornly escape our attention in everyday life.

Unconventional complexes. Film may bare real-life complexes which the conventional figure-ground patterns usually conceal from view. Imagine a man in a room: accustomed as we are to visualize the human figure as a whole, it would take us an enormous effort to perceive instead of the whole man a pictorial unit consisting, say, of his right shoulder and arm, fragments of furniture and a section of the wall. But this is exactly what photography and, more powerfully, film may make us see. The motion picture camera has a way of disintegrating familiar objects and bringing to the fore—often just in moving about—previously invisible interrelationships between parts of them. These newly arising complexes lurk behind the things known and cut across their easily identifiable contexts. *Jazz Dance,* for instance, abounds with shots of ensembles built from human torsos, clothes, scattered legs, and what not—shapes which are almost anonymous. In rendering physical existence, film tends to reveal configurations of semi-abstract phenomena. Sometimes these textures take on an ornamental character. In the Nazi propaganda film *Triumph of the Will* moving banners fuse into a very beautiful pattern at the moment when they begin to fill the screen.

The refuse. Many objects remain unnoticed simply because it never occurs to us to look their way. Most people turn their backs on garbage cans, the dirt underfoot, the waste they leave behind. Films have no such inhibitions; on the contrary, what we ordinarily prefer to ignore proves attractive to them precisely because of this common neglect. Ruttman's *Berlin* includes a wealth of sewer grates, gutters, and streets littered with rubbish; and Cavalcanti in his *Rein que les heures* is hardly less garbage-minded. To be sure, shots in this vein may be required by the action, but intrigues inspired by a sense of the medium are often so devised that they offer the camera ample opportunity to satisfy its inborn curiosity and function as a rag-picker; think of the old silent comedies—e.g. Chaplin's *A Dog's Life*—or pictures which involve crime, war, or misery. Since sights of refuse are particularly impressive after spectacles extolling the joy of living, film makers have repeatedly capitalized on the contrast between glamorous festivities and their dreary aftermath. You see a banquet on the screen and then, when everybody has gone, you are made to linger for a moment and stare at the crumpled tablecloth, the half-emptied glasses, and the unappetizing dishes. The classical American gangster films indulged in this effect. *Scarface* opens on a restaurant at dawn, with the remnants of the nocturnal orgy strewn over floors and tables; and after the gangster's ball in Sternberg's *Underworld* Bancroft totters through a maze of confetti and streamers left over from the feast.

The familiar. Nor do we perceive the familiar. It is not as if we shrank from it, as we do in the case of refuse; we just take it for granted without giving it a thought. Intimate faces, streets we walk day by day, the house we live in—all these things are part of us like our skin, and because we know them by heart we do not know them with the eye. Once integrated into our existence, they cease to be objects of perception, goals to be attained. In fact, we would be immobilized if we focused on them. This is confirmed by a common experience. A man entering his room will immediately feel disturbed if during his absence something has been changed in it. But in order to find out about the cause of his uneasiness he must discontinue his routine occupations; only in deliberately scrutinizing, and thus estranging, the room will be able to discover what it actually is that has been changed. Proust's narrator is acutely aware of this very estrangement when he suddenly sees his grandmother not as he always believed her to be but as she is or at least as she would appear to a stranger—a snapshot likeness severed from his dreams and memories.

Films make us undergo similar experiences a thousand times. They alienate our environment in exposing it. One ever-recurrent film scene runs as follows: Two or more people are conversing with each other. In the middle of their talk the camera, as if entirely indifferent to it, slowly pans through the room, inviting us to watch the faces of the listeners and various furniture pieces in a detached spirit. Whatever this may mean within the given context, it invariably dissolves a well-known total situation and thereby confronts the spectator with isolated phenomena which he previously neglected or overlooked as matter-of-course components of that situation. As the camera pans, curtains become eloquent and eyes tell a story of their own. The way leads toward the unfamiliar in the familiar. How often do we not come across shots of street corners, buildings, and landscapes with which we were acquainted all our life; we naturally recognize them and yet it is as if they were virgin impressions emerging from the abyss of nearness. The opening sequence of Vigo's *Zéro de conduite* shows two boys traveling back to school by train. Is it just an ordinarily night trip? Vigo manages to transform a familiar railway compartment into a magic wigwam in which the two, drunk from their boasts and pranks, are floating through the air.

This transformation is partly achieved with the aid of a device, both photographic and cinematic, which deserves some attention—the use of uncommon camera angles. Vigo occasionally represents the railway compartment slantwise and from below so that the whole room seems to drift along in the haze from the cigars which the high-strung schoolboys are smoking, while little toy balloons hover to and fro before their pale faces. Proust knew about the alienating effect of this device. After having mentioned that certain photographs of scenery and towns are called "admirable," he continues: "If we press for a definition of what their admirers mean by that epithet, we shall find that it is generally applied to some unusual picture of a familiar object, a picture different from those that we are accustomed to see, unusual and yet true to nature, and for that reason doubly impressive because it startles us, makes us emerge from our habits, and at the same time brings us back to ourselves by recalling to us an earlier impression." And to concretize this definition, he refers to the picture of a cathedral which does not render it as it is normally seen—namely, in the middle of the town—but is taken from a point of view from which the building "will appear thirty times the height of the houses." . . .

Phenomena Overwhelming Consciousness

Elemental catastrophes, the atrocities of war, acts of violence and terror, sexual debauchery, and death are events which tend to overwhelm consciousness. In any case, they call forth excitements and agonies bound to thwart detached observation. No one witnessing such an event, let alone playing an active part in it, should therefore be expected accurately to account for what he has seen. Since these manifestations of crude nature, human or otherwise, fall into the area of physical reality, they range all the more among the cinematic subjects. Only the camera is able to represent them without distortion.

Actually the medium has always shown a predilection for events of this type.

There is practically no newsreel that would not indulge in the ravages of an inundation, a hurricane, an airplane crash, or whatever catastrophe happens to be at hand. The same applies to feature films. One of the first film strips ever made was *The Execution of Mary Queen of Scots* (1895); the executioner cuts off her head and then holds it in his uplifted hand so that no spectator can possibly avoid looking at the frightful exhibit. Pornographic motifs also emerged at a very early date. The path of the cinema is beset with films reveling in disasters and nightmarish incidents. Suffice it to pick out, at random, the war horrors in Dovzhenko's *Arsenal* and Pabst's *Westfront 1918;* the terrible execution sequence at the end of *Thunder over Mexico,* a film based on Eisenstein's Mexican material; the earthquake in *San Francisco;* the torture episode in Rossellini's *Open City;* the depiction of a Polish Nazi concentration camp in *The Last Stop;* the scene with the young hoodlums wantonly mistreating a blind man in Buñuel's *Los Olvidados.*

Because of its sustained concern with all that is dreadful and off limits, the medium has frequently been accused of a penchant for cheap sensationalism. What lends support to this verdict is the indisputable fact that films have a habit of dwelling on the sensational much longer than any moral purpose would seem to justify; it often is as if that purpose served merely as a pretext for rendering a savage murder or the like.

In defense of the medium one might argue that it would not be the main medium it is if it failed to provide stunning sensations; and that, in offering them, it only follows a venerable tradition. Since time immemorial, people have craved spectacles permitting them vicariously to experience the fury of conflagrations, the excesses of cruelty and suffering, and unspeakable lusts—spectacles which shock the shuddering and delighted onlooker into unseeing participation.

Yet this argument misses the point. The point is, rather, that the cinema does not simply imitate and continue the ancient gladiator fights or the *Grand Guignol* but adds something new and momentous: it insists on rendering visible what is commonly drowned in inner agitation. Of course, such revelations conform all the more to the cinematic approach if they bear on actual catastrophes and horrors. In deliberately detailing feats of sadism in their films, Rossellini and Buñuel force the spectator to take in these appalling sights and at the same time impress them on him as real-life events recorded by the imperturbable camera. Similarly, besides trying to put across their propaganda messages, the Russian films of the 'twenties convey to us the paroxysmal upheavals of real masses which, because of their emotional *and* spatial enormity, depend doubly upon cinematic treatment to be perceptible.

The cinema, then, aims at transforming the agitated witness into a conscious observer. Nothing could be more legitimate than its lack of inhibitions in picturing spectacles which upset the mind. Thus it keeps us from shutting our eyes to the "blind drive of things."

Special Modes of Reality

Finally films may expose physical reality as it appears to individuals in extreme states of mind generated by such events as we have mentioned, mental disturbances, or any other external or internal causes. Supposing such a state of mind is provoked by an act of violence, then the camera often aspires to render the images which an emotionally upset witness or participant will from of it. These images also belong among the cinematic subjects. They are distorted from the viewpoint of a detached observer; and they differ from each other according to the varying states of mind in which they originate.

In his *Ten Days That Shook the World,* for instance, Eisenstein composes a physical universe reflecting exultation. This episode runs as follows: At the beginning of the October Revolution, worker delegates succeed in bringing a contingent of Cossacks over to their side; the Cossacks put their half-drawn swords with the ornamented pommels back into their sheaths, and then the two groups boisterously fraternize in a state of euphoria. The ensuing dance scene is represented in the form of an accelerated montage sequence which pictures the world as experienced by the overjoyed. In their great joy, dancers and onlookers who constantly mingle cannot help perceiving incoherent pieces of their immediate environment in motion. It is a whirling agglomerate of fragments that surrounds them. And Eisenstein captures this jumble to perfection by having follow each other—in a succession which becomes ever faster with the growing ecstasy—shots of Cossack boots executing the *krakoviak,* worker legs dancing through a puddle, clapping hands, and faces inordinately broadened by laughter.

In the world of a panic-stricken individual laughter yields to grimacing and dazzling confusion to fearful rigidity. At any rate, this is how Ernö Metzner conceived of that world in his *Ueberfall.* Its "hero" is a wretched little fellow who gets a lucky break thanks to a coin he furtively picks up in the street and then stakes in a crap game. As he walks away with his wallet stuffed, a thug follows him at a steadily diminishing distance. The man is scared. No sooner does he take to his heels than all the objects about him make common cause with his pursuer. The dark railway underpass turns into a sinister trap; frozen threats, the dilapidated slum houses close ranks and stare at him. (It is noteworthy that these effects are largely due to accomplished photography.) Temporarily saved by a streetwalker, who puts him up in her room, the man knows that the thug continues to lie in wait for him down in the street. The curtain moves, and he feels that the room itself harbors dangers. There is no escape wherever he looks. He looks into the mirror: what shines out of it are distorted reflections of his mask-like features.

1960

BÉLA BALÁZS
FROM THEORY OF THE FILM

THE CLOSE-UP

THE FACE OF THINGS

The first new world discovered by the film camera in the days of the silent film was the world of very small things visible only from very short distances, the hidden life of little things. By this the camera showed us not only hitherto unknown objects and events: the adventures of beetles in a wilderness of blades of grass, the tragedies of day-old chicks in a corner of the poultry-run, the erotic battles of flowers and the poetry of miniature landscapes. It brought us not only new themes. By means of the close-up the camera in the days of the silent film revealed also the hidden main-springs of a life which we had thought we already knew so well. Blurred outlines are mostly the result of our insensitive short-sightedness and superficiality. We skim over the teeming substance of life. The camera has uncovered that cell-life of the vital issues in which all great events are ultimately conceived; for the greatest land-slide is only the aggregate of the movements of single particles. A multitude of close-ups can show us the very instant in which the general is transformed into the par-ticular. The close-up has not only widened our vision of life, it has also deepened it. In the days of the silent film it not only revealed new things, but showed us the meaning of the old.

VISUAL LIFE

The close-up can show us a quality in a gesture of the hand we never noticed before when we saw that hand stroke or strike something, a quality which is often more expressive than any play of the features. The close-up shows your shadow on the wall with which you have lived all your life and which you scarcely knew; it

260

shows the speechless face and fate of the dumb objects that live with you in your room and whose fate is bound up with your own. Before this you looked at your life as a concert-goer ignorant of music listens to an orchestra playing a symphony. All he hears is the leading melody, all the rest is blurred into a general murmur. Only those can really understand and enjoy the music who can hear the contrapuntal architecture of each part in the score. This is how we see life: only its leading melody meets the eye. But a good film with its close-ups reveals the most hidden parts in our polyphonous life, and teaches us to see the intricate visual details of life as one reads an orchestral score.

LYRICAL CHARM OF THE CLOSE-UP

The close-up may sometimes give the impression of a mere naturalist preoccupation with detail. But good close-ups radiate a tender human attitude in the contemplation of hidden things, a delicate solicitude, a gentle bending over the intimacies of life-in-the-miniature, a warm sensibility. Good close-ups are lyrical; it is the heart, not the eye, that has perceived them.

Close-ups are often dramatic revelations of what is really happening under the surface of appearances. You may see a medium shot of someone sitting and conducting a conversation with icy calm. The close-up will show trembling fingers nervously fumbling a small object—sign of an internal storm. Among pictures of a comfortable house breathing a sunny security, we suddenly see the evil grin of a vicious head on the carved mantelpiece or the menacing grimace of a door opening into darkness. Like the *leitmotif* of impending fate in an opera, the shadow of some impending disaster falls across the cheerful scene.

Close-ups are the pictures expressing the poetic sensibility of the director. They show the faces of things and those expressions on them which are significant because they are reflected expressions of our own subconscious feeling. Herein lies the art of the true cameraman.

In a very old American film I saw this dramatic scene: the bride at the altar suddenly runs away from the bridegroom whom she detests, who is rich and who has been forced on her. As she rushes away she must pass through a large room full of wedding presents. Beautiful things, good things, useful things, things radiating plenty and security smile at her and lean towards her with expressive faces. And there are the presents given by the bridegroom: faces of things radiating touching attention, consideration, tenderness, love—and they all seem to be looking at the fleeing bride, because she looks at them; all seem to stretch out hands towards her, because she feels they do so. There are ever more of them—they crowd the room and block her path—her flight slows down more and more, then she stops and finally turns back. . . .

Having discovered the soul of things in the close-up, the silent film undeniably overrated their importance and sometimes succumbed to the temptation of showing "the hidden little life" as an end in itself, divorced from human destinies; it strayed away from the dramatic plot and presented the "poetry of things" instead of human beings. But what Lessing said in his *Laokoon* about Homer—that he never depicted anything but human actions and always described objects only inas-

much as they took part in the action—should to this day serve as a model for all
epic and dramatic art as long as it centers around the presentation of man.

THE FACE OF MAN

Every art deals with human beings, it is a human manifestation and presents
human beings. To paraphrase Marx: "The root of all art is man." When the film
close-up strips the veil of our imperceptiveness and insensitivity from the hidden
little things and shows us the face of objects, it still shows us man, for what makes
objects expressive are the human expressions projected on to them. The objects
only reflect our own selves, and this is what distinguished art from scientific knowledge (although even the latter is to a great extent subjectively determined). When
we see the face of things, we do what the ancients did in creating *gods* in man's
image and breathing a human soul into them. The close-ups of the film are the creative instruments of this mighty visual anthropomorphism.

What was more important, however, than the discovery of the physiognomy of
things, was the discovery of the human face. Facial expression is the most subjective
manifestation of man, more subjective even than speech, for vocabulary and grammar are subject to more or less universally valid rules and conventions, while the
play of features, as has already been said, is a manifestation not governed by objective canons, even though it is largely a matter of imitation. This most subjective
and individual of human manifestations is rendered objective in the close-up.

A NEW DIMENSION

If the close-up lifts some object or some part of an object out of its surroundings,
we nevertheless perceive it as existing in space; we do not for an instant forget that
the hand, say, which is shown by the close-up, belongs to some human being. It is
precisely this connection which lends meaning to its every movement. But when
Griffith's genius and daring first projected gigantic "severed heads" on to the cinema screen, he not only brought the human face closer to us in space, he also transposed it from space into another dimension. We do not mean, of course, the cinema
screen and the patches of light and shadow moving across it, which being visible
things, can be conceived only in space; we mean the expression on the face as
revealed by the close-up. We have said that the isolated hand would lose its meaning, its expression, if we did not know and imagine its connection with some human
being. The facial expression on a face is complete and comprehensible in itself and
therefore we need not think of it as existing in space and time. Even if we had just
seen the same face in the middle of a crowd and the close-up merely separated it
from the others, we would still feel that we have suddenly been left alone with this
one face to the exclusion of the rest of the world. Even if we have just seen the owner
of the face in a long shot, when we look into the eyes in a close-up, we no longer
think of that wide space, because the expression and significance of the face has no
relation to space and no connection with it. Facing an isolated face takes us out of
space, our consciousness of space is cut out and we find ourselves in another dimen-

sion: that of physiognomy. The fact that the features of the face can be seen side by side, i.e., in space—that the eyes are at the top, the ears at the sides and the mouth lower down—loses all reference to space when we see, not a figure of flesh and bone, but an expression, or in other words when we see emotions, moods, intentions and thoughts, things which although our eyes can see them, are not in space. For feelings, emotions, moods, intentions, thoughts are not themselves things pertaining to space, even if they are rendered visible by means which are.

MELODY AND PHYSIOGNOMY

We will be helped in understanding this peculiar dimension by Henri Bergson's analysis of time and duration. A melody, said Bergson, is composed of single notes which follow each other in sequence, i.e. in time. Nevertheless a melody has no dimension in time, because the first note is made an element of the melody only because it refers to the next note and because it stands in a definite relation to all other notes down to the last. Hence the last note, which may not be played for some time, is yet already present in the first note as a melody-creating element. And the last note completes the melody only because we hear the first note along with it. The notes sound one after the other in a time-sequence, hence they have a real duration, but the coherent line of melody has no dimension in time; the relation of the notes to each other is not a phenomenon occurring in time. The melody is not born gradually in the course of time but is already in existence as a complete entity as soon as the first note is played. How else would we know that a melody is begun? The single notes have duration in time, but their relation to each other, which gives meaning to the individual sounds, is outside time. A logical deduction also has its sequence, but premise and conclusion do not follow one another in time. The process of thinking as a psychological process may have duration; but the logical forms, like melodies, do not belong to the dimension of time.

Now facial expression, physiognomy, has a relation to space similar to the relation of melody to time. The single features, of course, appear in space; but the significance of their relation to one another is not a phenomenon pertaining to space, no more than are the emotions, thoughts and ideas which are manifested in the facial expressions we see. They are picture-like and yet they seem outside space; such is the psychological effect of facial expression.

SILENT SOLILOQUY

The modern stage no longer uses the spoken soliloquy, although without it the characters are silenced just when they are the most sincere, the least hampered by convention: when they are alone. The public of today will not tolerate the spoken soliloquy, allegedly because it is "unnatural." Now the film has brought us the silent soliloquy, in which a face can speak with the subtlest shades of meaning without appearing unnatural and arousing the distaste of the spectators. In this silent monologue the solitary human soul can find a tongue more candid and uninhibited than in any spoken soliloquy, for it speaks instinctively, subconsciously. The language of the face cannot be suppressed or controlled. However disciplined and practisedly hypocritical a face may be, in the enlarging close-up we see even that it is concealing something, that is looking a lie. For such things have their own specific expressions superimposed on the feigned one. It is much easier to lie in words than with the face and the film has proved it beyond doubt.

In the film the mute soliloquy of the face speaks even when the hero is not alone, and herein lies a new great opportunity for depicting man. The poetic significance of the soliloquy is that it is a manifestation of mental, not physical, loneliness. Nevertheless, on the stage a character can speak a monologue only when there is no one else there, even though a character might feel a thousand times more lonely if alone among a large crowd. The monologue of loneliness may raise its voice within him a hundred times even while he is audibly talking to someone. Hence the most deepfelt human soliloquies could not find such expression, for the close-up can lift a character out of the heart of the greatest crowd and show how solitary it is in reality and what it feels in this crowded solitude.

The film, especially the sound film, can separate the words of a character talking to others from the mute play of features by means of which, in the middle of such a conversation, we are made to overhear a mute soliloquy and realize the difference between this soliloquy and the audible conversation. What a flesh-and-blood actor can show on the real stage is at most that his words are insincere and it is a mere convention that the partner in such a conversation is blinded to what every spectator can see. But in the isolated close-up of the film we can see to the bottom of a soul by means of such tiny movements of facial muscles which even the most observant partner would never perceive.

A novelist can, of course, write a dialogue so as to weave into it what the speakers think to themselves while they are talking. But by so doing he splits up the sometimes comic, sometimes tragic, but always awe-inspiring, unity between spoken word and hidden thought with which this contradiction is rendered manifest in the human face and which the film was the first to show us in all its dazzling variety.

"POLYPHONIC" PLAY OF FEATURES

The film first made possible what, for lack of better description, I call the "polyphonic" play of features. By it I mean the appearance on the same face of contradictory expressions. In a sort of physiognomic chord a variety of feelings, passions and thoughts are synthesized in the play of the features as an adequate expression of the multiplicity of the human soul.

Asta Nielsen once played a woman hired to seduce a rich young man. The man who hired her is watching the results from behind a curtain. Knowing that she is under observation, Asta Nielsen feigns love. She does it convincingly: the whole gamut of appropriate emotion is displayed in her face. Nevertheless we are aware that it is only play-acting, that it is a sham, a mask. But in the course of the scene Asta Nielsen really falls in love with the young man. Her facial expression shows little change; she had been "registering" love all the time and done it well. How else could she now show that this time she was really in love? Her expression changes only by a scarcely perceptible and yet immediately obvious nuance—and what a few minutes before was a sham is now the sincere expression of a deep emotion.

Then Asta Nielsen suddenly remembers that she is under observation. The man behind the curtain must not be allowed to read her face and learn that she is now no longer feigning, but really feeling love. So Asta now pretends to be pretending. Her face shows a new, by this time threefold, change. First she feigns love, then she genuinely shows love, and as she is not permitted to be in love in good earnest, her face again registers a sham, a pretence of love. But now it is this pretence that is a lie. Now she is lying that she is lying. And we can see all this clearly in her face, over which she has drawn two different masks. At such times an invisible face appears in front of the real one, just as spoken words can by association of ideas conjure up things unspoken and unseen, perceived only by those to whom they are addressed.

In the early days of the silent film Griffith showed a scene of this character. The hero of the film is a Chinese merchant. Lillian Gish, playing a beggar-girl who is being pursued by enemies, collapses at his door. The Chinese merchant finds her, carries her into his house and looks after the sick girl. The girl slowly recovers, but her face remains stone-like in its sorrow. "Can't you smile?" the Chinese asks the frightened child who is only just beginning to trust him. "I'll try," says Lillian Gish, picks up a mirror and goes through the motions of a smile, aiding her face muscles with her fingers. The result is a painful, even horrible mask which the girl now turns towards the Chinese merchant. But his kindly friendly eyes bring a real smile to her face. The face itself does not change; but a warm emotion lights it up from inside and an intangible nuance turns the grimace into a real expression.

In the days of the silent film such a close-up provided an entire scene. A good idea of the director and a fine performance on the part of the actor gave as a result an interesting, moving, new experience for the audience.

MICROPHYSIOGNOMY

In the silent facial expression, isolated from its surroundings, seemed to penetrate to a strange new dimension of the soul. It revealed to us a new world—the world of microphysiognomy which could not otherwise be seen with the naked eye or in everyday life. In the sound film the part played by this 'microphysiognomy' has greatly diminished because it is now apparently possible to express in words much of what facial expression apparently showed. But it is never the same—many profound emotional experiences can never be expressed in words at all.

Not even the greatest writer, the most consummate artist of the pen, could tell in words what Asta Nielsen tells with her face in close-up as she sits down to her mirror and tries to make up for the last time her aged, wrinkled face, riddled with poverty, misery, disease and prostitution, when she is expecting her lover, released after ten years in jail; a lover who has retained his youth in captivity because life could not touch him there.

ASTA AT THE MIRROR

She looks into the mirror, her face pale and deadly earnest. It expresses anxiety and unspeakable horror. She is like a general who, hopelessly encircled with his whole army, bends once more, for the last time, over this maps to search for a way

The accusers and Joan (Falconetti) in *The Passion of Joan of Arc* (1928). In "Dreyer's film
. . . we move in the spiritual dimension of facial expression alone" (BALÁZS, page 267). "It
is a documentary of faces" (BAZIN, page 384).

out and finds there is no escape. Then she begins to work feverishly, attacking that disgustingly riddled face with a trembling hand. She holds her lipstick as Michelangelo might have held his chisel on the last night of his life. It is a life-and-death struggle. The spectator watches with bated breath as this woman paints her face in front of her mirror. The mirror is cracked and dull, and from it the last convulsions of a tortured soul look out on you. She tries to save her life with a little rouge! No good! She wipes it off with a dirty rag. She tries again. And again. Then she shrugs her shoulders and wipes it all off with a movement which clearly shows that she has now wiped off her life. She throws the rag away. A close-up shows the dirty rag falling on the floor and after it has fallen, sinking down a little more. This movement of the rag is also quite easy to understand—it is the last convulsion of a death agony.

In this close-up "microphysiognomy" showed a deeply moving human tragedy with the greatest economy of expression. It was a great new form of art. The sound film offers much fewer opportunities for this kind of thing, but by no means excludes it and it would be a pity if such opportunities were to be neglected, unnecessarily making us all the poorer. . . .

MUTE DIALOGUES

In the last years of the silent film the human face had grown more and more visible, that is, more and more expressive. Not only had "microphysiognomy" developed but together with it the faculty of understanding its meaning. In the last years of the silent film we saw not only masterpieces of silent monologue but of mute dialogue as well. We saw conversations between the facial expressions of two human beings who understood the movements of each others' faces better than each others' words and could perceive shades of meaning too subtle to be conveyed in words.

A necessary result of this was . . . that the more space and time in the film was taken up by the inner drama revealed in the "microphysiognomic" close-up, the less was left of the predetermined 8,000 feet of film for all the external happenings. The silent film could thus dive into the depths—it was given the possibility of presenting a passionate life-and-death struggle almost exclusively by close-ups of faces.

Dreyer's film *Jeanne d'Arc* provided a convincing example of this in the powerful, lengthy, moving scene of the Maid's examination. Fifty men are sitting in the same place all the time in this scene. Several hundred feet of film show nothing but big close-ups of heads, of faces. We move in the spiritual dimension of facial expression alone. We neither see nor feel the space in which the scene is in reality enacted. Here no riders gallop, no boxers exchange blows. Fierce passions, thoughts, emotions, convictions battle here, but their struggle is not in space. Nevertheless this series of duels between looks and frowns, duels in which eyes clash instead of swords, can hold the attention of an audience for ninety minutes without flagging. We can follow every attack and riposte of these duels on the faces of the combatants; the play of their features indicates every strategem, every sudden onslaught. The silent film has here brought an attempt to present a drama of the spirit closer to realization than any stage play has ever been able to do. . . .

1945

RUDOLF ARNHEIM
FROM FILM AS ART

FILM AND REALITY

Film resembles painting, music, literature, and the dance in this respect—it is a medium that may, but need not, be used to produce artistic results. Colored picture post cards, for instance, are not art and are not intended to be. Neither are a military march, a true confessions story, or a strip tease. And the movies are not necessarily film art.

There are still many educated people who stoutly deny the possibility that film might be art. They say, in effect: "Film cannot be art, for it does nothing but reproduce reality mechanically." Those who defend this point of view are reasoning from the analogy of painting. In painting, the way from reality to the picture lies via the artist's eye and nervous system, his hand and, finally, the brush that puts strokes on canvas. The process is not mechanical as that of photography, in which the light rays reflected from the object are collected by a system of lenses and are then directed onto a sensitive plate where they produce chemical changes. Does this state of affairs justify our denying photography and film a place in the temple of the Muses?

It is worth while to refute thoroughly and systematically the charge that photography and film are only mechanical reproductions and that they therefore have no connection with art—for this is an excellent method of getting to understand the nature of film art.

With this end in view, the basic elements of the film medium will be examined separately and compared with the corresponding characteristics of what we perceive "in reality." It will be seen how fundamentally different the two kinds of image are; and that it is just these differences that provide film with its artistic resources. We shall thus come at the same time to understand the working principles of film art.

268

THE PROJECTION OF SOLIDS UPON A PLANE SURFACE

Let us consider the visual reality of some definite object such as a cube. If this cube is standing on a table in front of me, its position determines whether I can realize its shape properly. If I see, for example, merely the four sides of a square, I have no means of knowing that a cube is before me, I see only a square surface. The human eye, and equally the photographic lens, acts from a particular position and from there can take in only such portions of the field of vision as are not hidden by things in front. As the cube is now placed, five of its faces are screened by the sixth, and therefore this last only is visible. But since this face might equally well conceal something quite different—since it might be the base of a pyramid or one side of a sheet of paper, for instance—our view of the cube has not been selected characteristically.

We have, therefore, already established one important principle: If I wish to photograph a cube, it is not enough for me to bring the object within range of my camera. It is rather a question of my position relative to the object, or of where I placed it. The aspect chosen above gives very little information as to the shape of the cube. One, however, that reveals three surfaces of the cube and their relation to one another, shows enough to make it fairly unmistakable what the object is supposed to be. Since our field of vision is full of solid objects, but our eye (like the camera) sees this field from only one station point at any given moment, and since the eye can perceive the rays of light that are reflected from the object only by projecting them onto a plane surface—the retina—the reproduction of even a perfectly simple object is not a mechanical process but can be set about well or badly.

The second aspect gives a much truer picture of the cube than the first. The reason for this is that the second shows more than the first—three faces instead of only one. As a rule, however, truth does not depend on quantity. If it were merely a matter of finding which aspect shows the greatest amount of surface, the best point of view could be arrived at by purely mechanical calculation. There is no formula to help one choose the most characteristic aspect: it is a question of feeling. Whether a particular person is "more himself" in profile than full face, whether the palm or the outside of the hand is more expressive, whether a particular mountain is better taken from the north or the west cannot be ascertained mathematically—they are matters of delicate sensibility.

Thus, as a preliminary, people who contemptuously refer to the camera as an automatic recording machine must be made to realize that even in the simplest photographic reproduction of a perfectly simple object, a feeling for its nature is required which is quite beyond any mechanical operation. We shall see later, by the way, that in artistic photography and film, those aspects that best show the characteristics of a particular object are not by any means always chosen; others are often selected deliberately for the sake of achieving specific effects.

REDUCTION OF DEPTH

How do our eyes succeed in giving us three-dimensional impressions even though the flat retinae can receive only two-dimensional images? Depth perception relies mainly on the distance between the two eyes, which makes for two slightly different images. The fusion of these two pictures into one image gives the three-dimensional impression. As is well known, the same principle is used in the stereo-scope, for which two photographs are taken at once, about the same distance apart as the human eyes. This process cannot be used for film without recourse to awkward devices, such as colored spectacles, when more than one person is to watch the projection. For a single spectator it would be easy to make a stereoscopic film. It would only mean taking two simultaneous shots of the same incident a couple of inches apart and then showing one of them to each eye. For display to a larger number of spectators, however, the problem of stereoscopic film has not yet been solved satisfactorily—and hence the sense of depth in film pictures is extraordinarily small. The movement of people or objects from front to back makes a certain depth evident—but it is only necessary to glance into a stereoscope, which makes everything stand out most realistically, to recognize how flat the film picture is. This is another example of the fundamental difference between visual reality and film.

The effect of film is neither absolutely two-dimensional nor absolutely three-dimensional, but something between. Film pictures are at once plane and solid. In Ruttmann's film *Berlin* there is a scene of two subway trains passing each other in opposite directions. The shot is taken looking down from above onto the two trains. Anyone watching this scene realizes, first of all, that one train is coming toward him and the other going away from him (three-dimensional image). He will then also see that one is moving from the lower margin of the screen toward the upper and the other from the upper toward the lower (plane image). This second impression results from the projection of the three-dimensional movement onto the screen surface, which, of course, gives different directions of motion.

The obliteration of the three-dimensional impression has as a second result a stronger accentuation of perspective overlapping. In real life or in a stereoscope, overlapping is accepted as due merely to the accidental arrangement of objects, but very marked cuts result from superimpositions in a plane image. If man is holding up a newspaper so that one corner comes across his face, this corner seems almost to have been cut out of his face, so sharp are the edges. Moreover, when the three-dimensional impression is lost, other phenomena, known to psychologists as the constancies of size and shape, disappear. Physically, the image thrown onto the retina of the eye by any object in the field of vision diminishes in proportion to the square of the distance. If an object a yard distant is moved away another yard, the area of the image on the retina is diminished to one-quarter of that of the first image. Every photographic plate reacts similarly. Hence in a photograph of someone sitting with his feet stretched out far in front of him the subject comes out with enormous feet and much too small a head. Curiously enough, however, we do not in real life get impressions to accord with the images on the retina. If a man is standing three feet away and another equally tall six feet away, the area of the image of the second does not appear to be only a quarter of that of the first. Nor if a man stretches out his hand toward one does it look disproportionately large. One sees the two men as equal in size and the hand as normal. This phenomenon is known as the constancy of size. It is impossible for most people—excepting those accustomed to drawing and painting, that is, artificially trained—to see according to the image on the retina. This fact, incidentally, is one of the reasons the average person has trouble copying things "correctly." Now an essential for the functioning of the constancy of size is a clear three-dimensional impression; it works excellently in a stereoscope with an ordinary photograph, but hardly at all in a film picture. Thus, in a film picture, if one man is twice as far from the camera as another, the one in front looks very considerably the taller and broader.

It is the same with the constancy of shape. The retinal image of a table top is like the photograph of it; the front edge, being nearer to the spectator, appears much wider than the back; the rectangular surface becomes a trapezoid in the image. As far as the average person is concerned, however, this again does not hold good in practice: he *sees* the surface as rectangular and draws it that way too. Thus the perspective changes taking place in any object that extends in depth are not observed but are compensated unconsciously. That is what is meant by the constancy of form. In a film picture it is hardly operative at all—a table top, especially if it is near the camera, looks very wide in front and very narrow at the back.

These phenomena, as a matter of fact, are due not only to the reduction of three-dimensionality but also to the unreality of the film picture altogether—an unreality due just as much to the absence of color, the delimitation of the screen, and so forth. The result of all this is that sizes and shapes do not appear on the screen in their true proportions but distorted in perspective. . . .

ABSENCE OF THE NONVISUAL WORLD OF THE SENSES

As regards the other senses: No one who went unprejudiced to watch a silent film missed the noises which would have been heard if the same events had been taking place in real life. No one missed the sound of walking feet, nor the rustling of leaves, nor the ticking of a clock. The lack of such sounds (speech, of course, is also one of them) was hardly ever apparent, although they would have been missed with a desperate shock in real life. People took the silence of the movies for granted because they never quite lost the feeling that what they saw was after all only pictures. This feeling alone, however, would not be sufficient to prevent the lack of sound being felt as an unpleasant violation of the illusion. That this did not happen is again connected with what was explained above: that in order to get a full impression it is not necessary for it to be complete in the naturalistic sense. All kinds of things may be left out which would be present in real life, so long as what is shown contains the essentials. Only after one has known talkies is the lack of sound conspicuous in a silent film. But that proves nothing and is not an argument against the potentialities of silent film, even since the introduction of sound.

It is much the same with the sense of smell. There may be people who if they see a Roman Catholic service on the screen imagine that they can smell incense; but no one will miss the stimulus. Sensations of smell, equilibrium, or touch are, of course, never conveyed in a film through direct stimuli, but are suggested indirectly through sight. Thence arises the important rule that it is improper to make films of occurrences whose central features cannot be expressed visually. Of course a revolver shot might occur as the central point of a silent film; a clever director could afford to dispense with the actual noise of the shot. It is enough for the spectator to see the revolver being fired and possibly to see the wounded man fall. In Josef von Sternberg's *The Docks of New York* a shot is very cleverly made visible by the sudden rising of a flock of scared birds.

THE MAKING OF A FILM

It has been shown above that the images we receive of the physical world differ from those on the movie screen. This was done in order to refute the assertion that film is nothing but the feeble mechanical reproduction of real life. The analysis has furnished us with the data from which we can hope to derive now the principles of film art.

By its very nature, of course, the motion picture tends to satisfy the desire for faithful reports about curious, characteristic, exciting things going on in this world of ours. The first sensation provided by film in its early music-hall days was to depict everyday things in a lifelike fashion on the screen. People were greatly thrilled by the sight of a locomotive approaching at top speed or the emperor in person riding down *Unter den Linden*. In those days, the pleasure given by film derived almost entirely from the subject matter. A film art developed only gradually when the movie makers began consciously or unconsciously to cultivate the peculiar possibilities of cinematographic technique and to apply them toward the creation of artistic productions. To what extent the use of these means of expression affects the large audiences remains a moot question. Certainly box-office success depends even now much more on what is shown than on whether it is shown artistically.

The film producer himself is influenced by the strong resemblance of his photographic material to reality. As distinguished from the tools of the sculptor and the painter, which by themselves produce nothing resembling nature, the camera starts to turn and a likeness of the real world results mechanically. There is serious danger that the filmmaker will rest content with such shapeless reproduction. In order that the film artist may create a work of art it is important that he consciously stress the peculiarities of his medium. This, however, should be done in such a manner that the character of the objects represented should not thereby be destroyed but rather strengthened, concentrated, and interpreted.

Our next task will be to bring examples to show how the various peculiarities of film material can be, and have been, used to achieve artistic effects.

ARTISTIC USE OF PROJECTIONS UPON A PLANE SURFACE

In an earlier section I showed what conditions arise from the fact that in a photographic representation three-dimensional bodies and spaces are projected on a two-dimensional plane, that is, the surface of the picture. It was first demonstrated that an object can be reproduced characteristically or otherwise according to what view of it is chosen. When film art was in its infancy, nobody paid much attention to the subtleties of these problems. The camera was stationed well in front of the people to be photographed in order that their faces and movements might be easily seen. If a house was to be shown, the cameraman placed himself straight in front of it at such a distance that nothing would be left out of the picture. It was only gradually that the particular effects that can be achieved by means of perspective projection were realized.

In Chaplin's film *The Immigrant* the opening scene shows a boat rolling horribly and all the passengers being seasick. They stagger to the side of the ship pressing their hands to their mouths. Then comes the first shot of Charlie Chaplin: he is seen hanging over the side with his back to the audience, his head well down, his legs kicking wildly—everyone thinks the poor devil is paying his toll to the sea. Suddenly Charlie pulls himself up, turns round and shows that he has hooked a large fish with his walking stick. The effect of surprise is achieved by making use of the fact that the spectator will be looking at the situation from a certain definite position. The idea underlying the scene is no longer "a man is doing such and such a thing, for example, he is fishing or being sick," but "a man is doing this and that, *and* at the same time the spectator is watching him from a particular station point." The element of surprise exists only when the scene is watched from one particular position. If the scene had been taken from the waterside, the audience would have realized at once that Charlie was not being sick but was fishing; and hence the wrong idea would not have first been implanted. The invention is no longer concerned merely with the subject matter but is cinematographic inasmuch as a definite feature of film technique is being used as a means to secure an effect.

ARTISTIC UTILIZATION OF REDUCED DEPTH

Every object reproduced in film appears solid and at the same time flat. This fact contributes greatly to the impressive results achieved by the clever shots discussed in the last section. The worm's-eye view of a man appears as such a great distortion of nature because the depth effect is reduced. The same view looked at in a stereoscope seems much less distorted. The contrast between the vast bulk of the trunk and the disproportionately small head is much less forcible when it is perceived as being due to foreshortening. But if there is only a slight feeling of space and if the three-dimensional volume of the pictured object is flattened out, a huge body and a little head are seen.

The purely formal qualities of the picture come into prominence only because of the lack of depth. Every good film shot is satisfying in a purely formal sense as a linear composition. The lines are harmoniously disposed with reference to one another as well as to the margins. The distribution of light and shade in the shot is evenly balanced. Only because the spatial effect is so slight, the spectator's attention is drawn to the two-dimensional pattern of lines and shadow masses. These, after all, are actually the components of three-dimensional bodies and become elements of the surface composition only through being projected onto a plane. It has already been mentioned above how the skirt of a dancer seen through a pane of glass seemed to open and close like the petals of a flower. This is an entirely antifunctional effect in that it is not a normally characteristic feature of the skirt as a material object. The curious expansion and contraction of the edge of the skirt results only when it is looked at from one particular viewpoint and then projected upon a flat surface. It would be less noticeable in a stereoscopic view. Only when the feeling of depth is reduced does the up-and-down movement of the skirt give the effect of being an in-and-out movement. It is one of the most important formal qualities of film that every object that is reproduced appears simultaneously in two entirely different frames of reference, namely, the two-dimensional and the three-dimensional, and that as one identical object it fulfills two different functions in the two contexts.

The reduction of depth serves, moreover, to emphasize the perspective super-position of objects. In a strongly stereoscopic picture of the manner in which these various objects are placed relative to one another does not impose itself any more than it does in real life. The concealing of certain parts of the various objects by others that come in front seems chance and unimportant. Indeed, the position of the camera in a stereoscopic picture seems itself to be a matter of indifference inas-much as it is obvious that there is a three-dimensional space which may just as eas-ily, and at the next moment probably will, be looked at from another point of view. If, however, the effect of depth is almost negligible, the perspective is conspicuous and compelling. What is visible and what is hidden strike one as being definitely intentional; one is forced to seek for a reason to be clear in one's own mind as to why the objects are arranged in this particular way and not in some other. There is no leeway between the objects: they are like flat surfaces stuck over one another, and seem almost to lie in the same plane.

Thus the lack of depth brings a very welcome element of unreality into the film picture. Formal qualities, such as the compositional and evocative significance of particular superimpositions, acquire the power to force themselves on the attention of the spectator. A shot like that described above where half of the girl's full face is cut off by the dark silhouette of the man's head, would possess only a fraction of its effectiveness if there were a strong feeling of space. In order to achieve the striking effect it is essential that the division across the face shall not seem accidental but intentional. The two faces must seem to be practically in one plane, with no leeway between them to show that they might easily be moved into different relative posi-tions.

The fact that the lack of depth perception also leads to the almost total disap-pearance of the phenomena which the psychologist calls the "constancies" of size and form has already been discussed. The film artist takes advantage of their absence to produce remarkable effects. Everyone has seen a railway engine rushing on the scene in a film. It seems to be coming straight at the audience. The effect is most vivid because the dynamic power of the forward-rushing movement is enhanced by another source of dynamics that has no inherent connection with the object itself, that is, with the locomotive, but depends on the position of the spec-tator, or—in other words—of the camera. The nearer the engine comes the larger it appears, the dark mass on the screen spreads in every direction at tremendous pace (a dynamic dilation toward the margins of the screen), and the actual objective movement of the engine is strengthened by this dilation. Thus the apparent alteration in the size of an object which in reality remains the same size enhances its actual activity, and thus helps the film artist to interpret the impact of that activity visually. . . .

ARTISTIC USE OF THE ABSENCE OF NONVISUAL SENSE EXPERIENCES

People who did not understand anything of the art of film used to cite silence as one of its most serious drawbacks. These people regard the introduction of sound as an improvement or completion of silent film. This opinion is just as senseless as if the invention of three-dimensional oil painting were hailed as an advance on the hitherto known principles of painting.

From its very silence film received the impetus as well as the power to achieve excellent artistic effects. Charles Chaplin wrote somewhere that in all his films there was not a single scene where he "spoke," that is, moved his lips. Hundreds of the most various situations in human relationships are shown in his films, and yet he did not feel the need to make use of such an ordinary faculty as speech. And nobody has missed it. The spoken word in Chaplin's films is as rule replaced by pantomime. He does not *say* that he is pleased that some pretty girls are coming to see him, but performs the silent dance, in which two bread rolls stuck on forks act as dancing feet on the table *(The Gold Rush)*. He does not argue, he fights. He avows his love by smiling, swaying his shoulders, and moving his hat. When he is in the pulpit he does not preach in words, but acts the story of David and Goliath *(The Pilgrim)*. When he is sorry for a poor girl, he stuffs money into her handbag. He shows renunciation by simply walking away (finale of *The Circus*). The incredible visual concreteness of every one of his scenes makes for a great part of Chaplin's art; and this should not be forgotten when it is said—as is often done and of course not without foundation—that his films are not really "filmic" (because his camera serves mainly as a recording machine).

Mention has already been made of the scene from Sternberg's *The Docks of New York* in which a revolver shot is illustrated by the rising of a flock of birds. Such an effect is not just a contrivance on the part of a director to deal with the evil of silence by using an indirect visual method of explaining to the audience that there has been a bang. On the contrary, a positive artistic effect results from the paraphrase. Such indirect representation of an event in a material that is strange to it, or giving not the action itself but only its consequences, is a favorite method in all art. To take an example at random: when Francesca da Rimini tells how she fell in love with the man with whom she was in the habit of reading, and only says "We read no more that day," Dante thereby indicates indirectly, simply by giving the consequences, that on this day they kissed each other. And this indirectness is shockingly impressive.

In the same way, the rising of the birds is particularly effective, and probably more so than if the actual sound of the pistol shot were heard. And then another factor comes in: the spectator does not simply *infer* that a shot has been fired, but he actually *sees* something of the quality of the noise—the suddenness, the abruptness of the rising birds, give visually the exact quality that the shot possess acoustically. In Jacques Feyder's *Les Nouveaux Messieurs* a political meeting becomes very uproarious, and in order to calm the rising emotions Suzanne puts a coin into a mechanical piano. Immediately the hall is lit up by hundreds of electric bulbs, and now the music chimes in with the agitative speech. The music is not heard: it is a silent film. But Feyder shows the audience excitedly listening to the speaker; and suddenly the faces soften and relax; all the heads begin quite gently to sway in time to the music. The rhythm grows more pronounced until at last the spirit of the dance has seized them all; and they swing their bodies gaily from side to side as if to an unheard word of command. The speaker has to give way to the music. Much more clearly than if the music were actually heard, this shows the power that suddenly unites all these discontented people, puts them into the same merry mood; and indicates as well the character of the music itself, its sway and rhythm. What is particularly noteworthy in such a scene is not merely how easily and cleverly the director makes visible something that is not visual, but by so doing, actually strengthens its effect. If the music were really heard, the spectator might simply realize that music was sounding, but by this indirect method, the particular point, the important part of this music—its rhythm, its power to unite and "move" men—is conspicuously brought out. Only these special attributes of the music are given, and appear as the music itself. Similarly the fact that a pistol shot is sudden, explosive, startling, becomes doubly impressive by transposition into the visible, because only these particular attributes and not the shot itself are given. Thus silent film derives definite artistic potentialities from its silence. What it wishes particularly to emphasize in an audible occurrence is transposed into something visual; and thus instead of giving the occurrence "itself," it gives only some of its telling characteristics, and thereby shapes and interprets it.

Owing to its insubstantiality silent film does not in any way give the effect of being dumb pantomime. Its silence is not noticed, unless the action happens to culminate in something acoustic for which nothing can be substituted, and which is therefore felt as missing—or unless one is accustomed to sound film. Because of sound film, in the future it will be possible only with great difficulty to show speech in a silent way. Yet this is a most effective artistic device. For if a man is heard speaking, his gestures and facial expression only appear as an accompaniment to underline the sense of what is said. But if one does not hear what is said, the meaning becomes indirectly clear and is artistically interpreted by muscles of the face, of the limbs, of the body. The emotional quality of the conversation is made obvious with a clarity and definiteness which are hardly possible in the medium of actual speech. Moreover, the divergence between reality and dumb show gives the actor and his director plenty of leeway for artistic invention. (The creative power of the artist can only come into play where reality and the medium of representation do not coincide.)

Dialogue in silent film is not simply the visible part of a real spoken dialogue. If a real dialogue is shown without the sound, the spectator will often fail to grasp what it is all about; he will find the facial expression and the gestures unintelligible. In silent film, the lips are no longer word-forming physical organs but a means of visual expression—the distortion of an excited mouth or the fast chatter of lips are not mere by-products of talking; they are communications in their own right. Silent laughter is often more effective than if the sound is actually heard. The gaping of the open mouth gives a vivid, highly artistic interpretation of the phenomenon "laughter." If, however, the sound is also heard, the opening of the mouth appears obvious and its value as a means of expression is almost entirely lost. This opportunity of the silent film was once used by the Russians in a most unusual and effective manner. A shot of a soldier who had gone mad in the course of a battle and was laughing hideously with his mouth wide open was joined with a shot of the body of a soldier who had died of poison gas, and whose mouth was fixed in death in a ghastly, rigid grin.

The absence of the spoken word concentrates the spectator's attention more closely on the visible aspect of behavior, and thus the whole event draws particular interest to itself. Hence it is that very ordinary shots are often so impressive in silent films—such as a documentary shot of an itinerant hawker crying his wares with grandiose gestures. If his words could be heard the effect of the gestures would not be half as great, and the whole episode might attract very little attention. If, however, the words are omitted, the spectator surrenders entirely to the expressive power of the gestures. Thus by merely robbing the real event of something—the sound—the appeal of such an episode is greatly heightened. . . .

1933

NOËL CARROLL
FROM PHILOSOPHICAL PROBLEMS
OF CLASSICAL FILM THEORY

THE SPECIFICITY THESIS

The notion that each art form has its own special subject matter that it of all the arts is best suited to represent is an eighteenth-century idea. The idea grew in reaction to an earlier style of art theorizing, represented by words such as Abbé Charles Batteux's 1746 treatise called *The Fine Arts Reduced to the Same Principle.*[1] For Batteux, all the arts were similar because they all had the same subject—the imitation of the beautiful in nature. This tendency to reduce the arts to their common denominator was the dominant trend in pre-Enlightenment art theory. During the eighteenth century, however, thinkers began to oppose this type of theorizing. They began to focus on what differentiated the arts from one another. An important work in this new tendency was Abbé Jean Baptiste Dubos's *Critical Reflections on Painting and Poetry.*[2] Dubos claimed that poetry and painting differ, in that painting imitates the single moment whereas poetry imitates process. Similar analyses were offered in the works of James Harris and Moses Mendelsohn.[3] The best known work of this revisionist sort, entitled *Laocoön,* was published in 1766 by Gotthold Ephraim Lessing. That book contains several important presumptions of Arnheim's *Materialtheorie:* that the arts (1) differ from each other in terms of (2) what each represents (imitates) best, due to (3) the peculiar (specific) structure of its formal/physical medium.

Comparing painting and poetry, Lessing writes:

> I argue thus. If it be true that painting employs wholly different signs or means of imitation from poetry—the one using forms and colors in space and the other articulate

---

[1] In Monroe Beardsley, *Aesthetics: From Classical Greece to the Present* (New York: Macmillan, 1966; Alabama: University of Alabama Press, 1975), 160.
[2] Ibid.
[3] Ibid.

sounds in time—and if signs must unquestionably stand in convenient relation with the thing signified, then signs arranged side by side can represent only objects existing side by side, or whose parts so exist, while consecutive signs can express only objects which succeed each other in time.

Objects which exist side by side, or whose parts so exist, are called bodies. Consequently, bodies with their visible properties are the peculiar subjects of painting.

Objects which succeed each other, or whose parts succeed each other in time, are actions. Consequently, actions are the peculiar subjects of poetry.*

Here we see Lessing attempting to extrapolate from the structure of the medium—the structure of what, in advance of semiotics, he calls "signs"—to the appropriate subject matter of the medium. Arnheim, as well, attempts to move from the structural peculiarities of the medium to injunctions about the proper direction of filmmaking.

Before examining the specificity thesis in terms of truth or falsity, I would like to note that although for many reasons the thesis no longer seems acceptable, in its day it performed a useful service. The specificity thesis served as a corrective to the vagueness of the tendency to reduce all the arts to a common denominator. As a result, theorists began to look more closely at the various art forms. The gain was one of rigor. This does not, of course, entail that the specificity thesis is true. However, theorists like Arnheim who adopt it do tend to give very close, precise accounts of artistic structures. Thus, even if the specificity thesis is false, it has beneficial side effects.

One difference between Lessing and Arnheim is that Lessing focuses on the physical medium, of painting for example, and teases out of that an analysis of what the medium can represent at its best—what is most convenient for its signs to depict—whereas Arnheim, in *Film as Art,* examines cinematic devices to find where they fall short of successful representation. Lessing is concerned to find where a medium excels in representation, whereas Arnheim is most interested in where a medium falters in terms of perfect representation. In and of itself, this contrast does not present a problem for Arnheim. Arnheim, like Lessing, wants to establish a special domain for each medium. Film, he tells us, is the realm of the animated image. But here is a lacuna in this New Laocoön. For how do the various peculiarities that Arnheim points to—the lack of constancy of size and of the spatiotemporal continuum, and so forth—ever add up to or imply that film is concerned with the animated image? The peculiarities or specificities of the medium that Arnheim points to constitute a list of things that cinematic representations do not have. How do these amount to a positive commitment to the animated image? If the peculiar structures of the medium are what entail the medium's commitment to the animated image, it is not clear how Arnheim's examples show this.

Another problem with the specificity thesis is that Arnheim seems to believe that, as a matter of fact, every medium diverges from the referents it represents because of its own peculiar formal/physical structure. Arnheim says "representation never produces a replica of the object but its structural equivalent in a *given* medium" (*Art and Visual Perception,* 162). But if each medium automatically, so to speak,

---

*Gotthold Ephraim Lessing, *Laocoön* (New York: Noonday Press, 1969), 91.

diverges not only from each referent but also from the depiction of such referents in other media, then what point is there to the specificity thesis stated as an injunction? That is, why urge artists to make certain that they exploit the peculiarities of their medium if this is unavoidable and bound to happen anyway? Moreover, how can Arnheim rail against sound films? Sound films will automatically be differentiated from theater because the media are physically different. If one believes that every medium is automatically unique in terms of the structure of its symbols, then why fear that media will illegitimately spill over each others' boundaries? It will be impossible.

Arnheim's specificity thesis is not a description; it is a recommendation. Were the specificity thesis a description, there could be no problems involving the trespassing of the sound film in the domain of theater. It would make no sense to use the specificity thesis to attempt to chide filmmakers if the specificity thesis were a description—filmmakers would necessarily employ the peculiar (specific) characteristics of their medium.

As a recommendation, the specificity thesis appears to have two components. One component is the idea that there is something that each medium does best. The other is that each of the arts should do what differentiates it from the other arts. These two components can be called the excellence requirement and the differentiation requirement. The two can be combined in the imperative that each art form should explore only those avenues of development in which it exclusively excels above all other arts. The incorporation of "exclusively" in this formula sounds the differentiation requirement while the rest of the formula states the excellence requirement. Applied to Arnheim's film theory, the specificity thesis states that filmmakers should stress the differentiating features (the limitations) that enable the medium to portray animated action (what cinema does best).

Some of the problems with the specificity thesis are the result of the combination of the differentiation and excellence requirements. The assumption is that what a medium does best will coincide with what differentiates it. But why should this be so? For example, many media narrate. Film, drama, prose, and epic poetry all tell stories. For argument's sake, let us say narration is what each does best—that is, best of all the things each of them does. However, this does not differentiate these art forms. What does the specificity thesis require in such a situation? If film and the novel both excel in narration, should (1) neither art form narrate since narration fails to differentiate them? or (2) should film not narrate since narration will fail to differentiate it from the novel and the novel claimed the domain of narration first? or (3) should the novel give up narration and let the newcomer have its chance?

The first alternative is simply absurd; it would sacrifice a magnificent cultural invention—narration—for whatever bizarre satisfaction that could be derived from adherence to the differentation requirement. I am assuming that excellence is more important to us than differentiation.

The second alternative is also unattractive. In this case the specificity thesis would seem to confuse history with ontology. That is, film is to forswear narrating just because literature already has that turf staked out. But surely this is only an accident of history. What if movies had arisen before writing? Then would literature have to find some other occupation? Clearly such accidents of history should not preclude a medium from pursuing an area in which it excels. Nor should accidents of history be palmed off as ontological necessities—another proclivity of the specificity thesis. The special subject matter of each medium supposedly follows from its nature. But the story is more complicated, since a medium specializes in what it excels in only if that area of special achievement differentiates it from other media. The question of differentiation is not simply a question about the nature of the medium; it is a question about the comparison of arts. And it is quite possible that a new art may be invented that excels in an area where an older art already excels. Awarding the domain to the older art just because it is already established seems arbitrary, as does the third alternative—awarding the domain to the younger art just because it is younger. If two arts both excel in domain, it seems natural to allow them both to explore it. That will enrich the culture by multiplying the number of excellent things. This is surely the case with narrative. The world is far richer for having novels *and* fiction films *and* epic poems *and* dramas *and* comic books *and* narrative paintings *and* operas, though the differentiation component of the specificity thesis would block this.

One point should be emphasized in the preceding discussion: narration does seem to be one instance where many arts do share the same pursuit. And yet specificity theorists, especially the major film theorists who champion the specificity thesis, rarely seem to be ruffled by this fact. It seems as though they are so concerned to differentiate film from theater that they fail to notice that film is similar to other narrative arts, such as the short story and the novel. These latter similarities or overlaps seem to be tolerable. Why? The only way I can account for this anomaly is that historical circumstances were such that only the canned theater argument against film vividly presented itself as so threatening that it had to be dealt with. For, of course, in the days when these arguments raged, theater and film could be thought of as directly competing for the same audience. They were locked in economic conflict as well as aesthetic struggle, which meant that more was at issue in the battle between them than in the relation between film and the other narrative arts. Thus, many film theorists who upheld the specificity thesis never noticed that they should have been exercised by the overlap with the other narrative arts, even though such an overlap should call into question the specificity thesis.

The specificity thesis has both an excellence component and a differentiation component. Perhaps one interpretation of the theory is that each art form should pursue those projects that fall in the area of intersection between what the art form excels in and what differentiates it from other art forms. But this does not seem to be an acceptable principle because, among other things, it entails that the reason an art form might not be employed to do what it does best is that some other art form also does it well. *The specificity thesis seems to urge us to sacrifice excellence on principle.* But excellence is, in fact, always the overriding consideration in deciding whether a particular practice or development is acceptable in art.

Indeed, I believe that what could be called the priority of excellence is the central telling point against the specificity thesis. To dramatize this, let us imagine that for some reason the only way that G. B. Shaw could get backing for *Pygmalion* was to make it as a talking picture—since in our possible world Shaw was known only as a successful screenwriter. Let us also suppose that in some sense it is true that theater is a better showcase for aesthetically crafted language. Would we decide that *Pygmalion* should not be made? I think our answer is "no," because our intuitions are that the specificity thesis should not be allowed to stand between us and excellence.

Nor need the excellence in question be a matter of the highest excellence achievable in a given medium. The specificity thesis seems to urge that a medium pursue only what it does best. But if a medium does something well and the occasion arises to do it, why should it be inhibited because there is something it does better? Certain magical transformations—turning weaklings into werewolves for example—can be most vividly executed in cinema. But they can also be done quite efficiently on stage. Should this minor excellence be foregone in a stage adaptation of *Dr. Jekyll and Mr. Hyde,* either because transformation is not what theater does best or because film can do it better?

Another disturbing feature of the specificity thesis is that it appears to envision each art form on the model of a highly specialized tool with a range of determinate functions. A film, play, poem, or painting is thought of, it seems, analogous to something like a Phillips screwdriver. If you wish to turn a screw with a cross-shaped groove on top, use a Phillips screwdriver. If you wish to explore the potentials of aesthetically crafted language, use theater. If your topic is animated action, use film. Likewise, just as you should not use a Phillips screwdriver as a church key (though it can open a beer can), you should not, all things being equal, use cinema to perform theater's task, and vice versa. But I think it is incumbent on us to question whether this underlying metaphor has any applicability when it comes to art forms. Are art forms highly specialized tools? I think not. If art forms are like tools at all, then they are more like sticks than like Phillips screwdrivers. That is, they can be used to do many things; they have not been designed to perform a specific task. In most cases art forms are not designed—that is, they are not invented with a specific task in mind. Moreover, even with self-consciously invented arts like film, it is soon discovered that the form can perform many more tasks than the one it was originally designed for. Indeed, interest in art forms is to a large measure interest in how artists learn or discover new ways of using their medium. The idea of the artist discovering new ways of using the medium would make no sense if the medium were designed for a single purpose.

An artistic medium, including a self-consciously invented one, is such that many of its potentials remain to be discovered. But discovery would not be a relevant expectation to have of artists nor would an interest in it be relevant to an art form, if the task of the art form were as fixed as that of a Phillips screwdriver. A correlative fact against the idea of the fixedness of function of art forms is the fact that they very often continue to exist over time, obviously because they are periodically reinvented and new uses are found for them. But if art forms were as determinately set in their functions as are Phillips screwdrivers, one would expect them, or at least many of them, to pass away as their function becomes archaic. That they are readapted, reinvented, and redirected bodes ill for the metaphor of the art form as a specialized tool—a view that seems strongly suggested by the specificity thesis.

One consideration offered in favor of the specificity thesis proceeds by asking why else there would be *different* media unless they were supposed to pursue different ends? That is, the specificity thesis is, in this light, an inference to the best explanation. Given the fact that we have a number of arts, we ask "Why?" The answer that seems most reasonable is that each art has, or should have, a different function.

This particular line of thought presupposes that it is legitimate to ask why we have different arts. It also supposes that it is legitimate to expect as an answer to this question something like a rational principle. Perhaps for idealists it is reasonable to expect a rationale or a rationalization here. But for others the issue appears to be a matter of historical accident. I believe that it was Wittgenstein who said that where there is no question, there is no answer. We can use this principle, I think, to rid ourselves of the preceding argument. For its question, when stated nonelliptically, is not "Why are there diverse arts?" but "What is the rationale that explains why we have exactly the diverse arts that we have?" Now there may be no single answer to this question. Rather we may have to settle for a series of answers to the former question—answers of a historical and anthropological variety. For example, we have film because Edison invented it to supplement the phonograph; we have painting because one day a Cro-Magnon splashed some adhesive victuals on a cave wall and it looked strikingly like a bison; and so on. But there is no answer to the second question: "What is the rationale for having exactly the several arts we do have?" Rather, each art arose due to a chain of events that led to its discovery or invention and to its popularization. The result is the *collection* of arts we have, which we only honorifically refer to as a *system*. There is no rationale for the system, for in truth it is only a collection. Thus, we have no need for the specificity thesis, for the question it answers—"Why is there a system of different arts?"—is really not an admissible question at all.*

Before concluding this section, some discussion of Arnheim's application of the specificity thesis to sound film is appropriate, for Arnheim's maledictions against the talking picture are undoubtedly the most notorious part of his film theory. Arnheim holds that if there is a truly composite art form, then none of the constituent media can be anything but fully developed. That is, in a truly composite art form none of the media combined would be subservient, nor would any be redundant, that is, merely repetitive of what is already conveyed by another, more dominant, medium. Each must function equally and be fully articulated on its own terms. For Arnheim, opera is not really a composite because music is the dominant constituent medium to which the language and the scenography are subservient. Nor are laconic talking films with functional dialogue acceptable composites, because such dialogue is subservient to the visuals and, for the most part, is redundant to the action. On the other hand, more fully developed dialogue tends to make the film medium subservient to speech, paralyzing the action and thwarting the medium's commitment to animated movement. Dialogue cannot be artistically

---

*For expanded and amplified arguments against the specificity thesis, see my "The Specificity of Media in the Arts," *The Journal of Aesthetic Education* 19 (Winter 1984), 5–20; and my "Medium Specificity Arguments and the Self-consciously Invented Arts: Film, Photography and Video." *Millennium Film Journal,* nos. 14/15 (1984–1985), 127–53.

expanded upon and articulated without interfering with the depiction of action, which will transform the work into a piece of theater, denying the camera the opportunity to represent what it alone portrays best (*FAA*, 228–30).

There are two sides to this argument. Either dialogue is made to facilitate action, in which case the medium of speech is short-changed, or dialogue is developed artistically, in which case the action of the film is paralyzed. In neither case is the art truly composite. Instead, the sound film is a mongrel.

Of course, one wonders whether Arnheim's ideal of a truly composite art form is a worthwhile one. Why must a legitimate composite abide by such inflexible standards of equality between the constituent media? Often in nineteenth-century ballet the music was not so distinguished as the dancing, since the point of this form was to direct attention to the movement. Does this imply that ballet, or at least ballet done in this format, is not a truly composite art? But if ballet is not a truly composite art and neither is opera, then one suspects that Arnheim is defining the category of composite art out of existence. Moreover, if the example of nineteenth-century ballet is taken seriously, one horn of Arnheim's dilemma can be neutralized. It may be perfectly acceptable to have composite art forms where one medium is subservient to another. Specifically, there may be many sound films that, although their scripts do not make edifying reading, have perfectly serviceable dialogue supporting the visuals. Films like *Citizen Kane, Psycho,* and *Rules of the Game* surely are examples of this sort. Thus, questioning Arnheim's criterion for a truly composite medium dispels half of the dilemma.*

The other half can be dispelled by questioning whether it is impossible to combine language and visuals so that each is given full honor. Surely the opening scene of Olivier's *Henry V* fully honors both action and poetry. Other examples also come to mind, Polonsky's *Force of Evil* for one—a film whose highly poetic script was rhythmically integrated with the action.

Furthermore, several objections raised against the specificity thesis in general can be applied to its use in the context of the sound film. Undoubtedly, great moments in dialogue film—for example, Groucho's speech to the ministers in *Duck Soup*—are not begrudged because they were seen on celluloid rather than on stage. If the specificity thesis entails cutting this scene, then so much the worse for the specificity thesis. Of course, it may be held that the specificity theorist is not committed to disparaging this scene. Rather, such a theorist might praise the scene, but as theater rather than film. But this seems wrong. For part of what is excellent about the scene is that it is delivered by that man, Groucho Marx, with that voice, at that period of time (the Depression). These things fit together in a powerful expressive ensemble. Indeed, part of what is valuable about the scene is that it is a *recording* of a performance, exactly the aspect of cinema Arnheim is most disposed to denounce. Moreover, the black and white photography, the cut of the actor's clothing, their diction,

---

*Interestingly, Arnheim differs from other specificity theorists like Panofsky who are willing to accept functional dialogue as the proper means of keeping cinema pure while at the same time using sound.

their bearing all conspire to evoke a powerful feeling of "thirties-ness" that could not be replicated today on stage or film—not only because many of the actors are dead but also because films don't look and sound that way any more, and, in all likelihood, theater never did. That that specific performance is on film—film of a certain technological vintage—is part and parcel of the scene's power, no matter that it is dominated by speech.

1988

GERALD MAST
FROM FILM/CINEMA/MOVIE

PROJECTION

An obvious assumption of the preceding chapter is that the *aesthetic event* of cinema is the projection of the finished work—analogous to the reading of the type that is a novel, the attending to the motion and conversation that are a play, the listening to the sound that is a piece of music, or the looking at the color on canvas that is a painting. The creative process of shooting and assembling film is certainly a worthy subject of study—as are the notebooks of Henry James or the Georges Seurat sketches for *A Sunday Afternoon on the Island of La Grande Jatte.* To study this process reveals both the artist's specific choices and the general way he viewed his art and his craft. But it nonetheless studies the means to the end, and that end is experiencing the work of art itself, which remains its own testament and as solid a piece of evidence as any. With the cinema art it is perhaps an even solider piece of evidence than its maker's recollections of the creative process, since the memories of moviemakers are at least as prone to error as any, since the movie business encourages self-congratulation, and since the creative process of moviemaking is such an admittedly collective one.*

This emphasis on projection necessarily excludes certain interesting kinds of questions, among them some of the classic problems of film, cinema, and movie

---

*Movie directors are notoriously unreliable. Frank Capra claims he watched Leo McCarey direct Laurel and Hardy at the Hal Roach studio in 1924 (L & H never worked together until 1927); Mack Sennett went to his grave claiming Buster Keaton was one of his Keystone Cops (never); Groucho Marx is under the impression that there are no musical numbers in *A Night at the Opera* (poor Kitty Carlisle and Allan Jones; or rather, poor us—because Groucho is unfortunately wrong). One of the consistent mistakes of film historians is to quote the recollections of moviemakers as gospel; the American Film Institute has invested both time and money in the recording of some four-hundred "oral histories" of their recollections. To preserve these thoughts and voices for posterity is undeniably valuable, but gospel it isn't.

theory. It denies the notion of "the cinematic" altogether, since it assumes that any finished piece of cinema is indisputably a piece of cinema. The precise meaning of "cinematic" is "of or pertaining to the cinema," and its essence is merely that a succession of frames moves forward through the projector. You can, of course, then discuss whether that succession of frames is interesting or boring, beautiful or ugly, good or bad. True, the primitive film strips of Edison, Lumière, and most of their pre-Griffith contemporaries might properly be called "uncinematic," simply because they had no notion at all of one of the three principles of temporal succession (imagistic succession) and a very clumsy and undeveloped notion of another (structural succession). One of today's experimental, minimal films is certainly not uncinematic in the same way, for its maker was aware of all the possible principles of succession, but deliberately tried to extend or eliminate the use of some of them.

The insistence on projection has certain theoretical advantages. First, it clearly distinguishes cinema from a live theatrical performance, on the one hand, and from television on the other. The fact that film is projected alters its tense (it must necessarily *have been* photographed and processed in the past), whereas the tense of a live theatrical performance (dance, drama, opera) is the now. The fact that film is projected also means that it will be perceived and received differently from a live performance, particularly since projections are perceived and received as a series of different kinds of successions. In a live performance, although plot might parallel structural succession, there are no equivalents to the literal and imagistic successions of cinema; the stage movement is continuous, not successive. The visual power and concentration of cinema's successiveness (coupled with the kinetic power of the individual images) give the force of the spoken word a different (and lighter) "weight" in the cinema than in the drama (as noted and developed by Bazin). Television transmission is not a projection at all; nor is its literal succession identical to cinema's. These differences produce the reduced clarity, sublety, luminosity, density, and (for the present anyway) size of the television image. This reduction also guarantees a different emotional response and reaction to our perception of the weakened kinesis of the television image.

Indeed, the emphasis on projection as the aesthetic event consistently forces our attention on how a work of cinema is received and perceived rather than on what cinema is. Arnheim gets into all kinds of trouble with this problem since he constantly explores the ways in which the cinema image differs physically from natural vision. What he never unscrambles, however, is whether the cinema makes us perceive its differences from nature or whether it fools us by erasing those physical differences so that we perceive the image as apparently quite natural. For example, Arnheim's first principle is that photography converts three-dimensional space into a two-dimensional plane. He then develops the ways that this "fact" can be exploited artistically, some of those exploitations based on the way that the focal lengths of various lenses can alter the way we perceive relative distances between objects. One of his examples is that a newspaper appears to be "cut out" of the face of the person reading it; the converse effect would be the way that a wide-angle lens can make a hand holding a gun in the foreground appear ten times larger than the assailant's face, only an arm's length away.

But do we perceive the projected image as two-dimensional at all? The very fact that we call one object in the projected image apparently close to or far away from another implies that there is some kind of mental translation of the two-dimensional image into three-dimensional terms. In the cinema, when we see large and small, we translate our perception either into close and far (based on our awareness of relative distances and the sizes of objects in life) or into not so close or far but deliberately distorted for some effect by the lens (as in that hand-face example, which we know is based on an impossible relationship of size and distance in nature). We perceive the projected image as a king of three-dimensional system, once we have learned to translate it (which means that we must learn to watch cinema, just as we must learn any system of translation—and just as we learn to translate sizes into distances in life).

The occasional 3-D movie (or the re-release of one from the Great Flurry of '52) proves that our perception of the projected three-dimensional image is nothing like that of the natural three-dimensional one either. The whole tendency of the 3-D image is to push the action and motion at us; not simply the deliberately hurled objects that sail toward our heads, but even the horizontal movement of walking from left to right feels as if it were thrusting toward us. Even the stationary walls seem to loom out at us, in a way that I do not usually perceive walls to do in life.

The projected cinema image does not appear to be flat; light on a screen is not perceived the same way as paint on canvas. Why not? First, paint is itself a hard, physical material that refracts light. That refraction is the physical stimulus that produces the effect of the painting (since light produces our perception of color by refraction); but it also reminds us of the flatness of the canvas and the material on it(because light bounces off the paint material itself, and that bouncing is perceived as a kind of surface refraction). Those painters who became self-conscious about the flatness of paint on canvas (for example, the evolving rough-textured brush strokes of Van Gogh) simply called attention to the essential flatness of the art by trying to avoid or exploit it. And what else was the development of perspective but a response to the flatness of canvas and paint? It was not the modernist response, however, as was Van Gogh's.

But the "material" of projected images is the immaterial operation of light itself; the images of cinema are produced by light's bouncing off the beaded surface of a screen, a refraction that is not, however, perceived as a refractive bouncing of light off a surface, but as the images themselves. The screen seems more to absorb the images (like a sponge) than to refract and bounce them, although such a refraction is literally what we see (but not perceive). The immateriality of light itself and the perception that the screen is a kind of translucent sponge (yet another cinema illusion) militate against the flatness of the projected image, convincing us that the image has a kind of depth (which it obviously does not).

Second, paintings are still and projected images are not. The two physical forms of cinema succession work upon the eye by keeping the photographed subjects constantly in motion. Not only is this motion a further diversion from any consciousness of the screen's flatness, but it is also a way of defining distance and dimensionality. The enlarging or shrinking of an object over a period of time or the length of time required to travel between two points are two familiar ways of defining terms like "close" and "far." One of the striking effects of halting the cinema's motion—of the "freeze frame"—is the sudden reduction of the screen's apparent depth. Only by freezing the movement that is the essence of cinema's succession does one convert the photographed image into a truly two-dimensional plane.

The projection of successive images does not convert three-dimensional nature into a two-dimensional pattern, but changes three-dimensional nature into a different three-dimensional system using two-dimensional symbols. As always, there are exceptional films that attempt to make the projected image appear as flat as possible (the Zagreb animation films, any experimental films that deliberately use the static flatness of lettering and title cards, the films of Len Lye, Norman McLaren, Robert Breer, or anyone else who uses drawn figures of any kind). Walt Disney's entire career in animation can be chronicled as a progressive war against the flatness of cinema cartooning, as a struggle to make the drawn image as apparently three-dimensional as the photographed one. Like so many valuable cinema experiments, these uses or denials of two-dimensionality are ironic reversals or revelations of traits that seem inherent to cinema.

The insistence on projection also addresses whether cinema is or is not an "automatic" art (is for Bazin, Kracauer, Cavell, and their followers; is not for Arnheim, Eisenstein, and theirs). Projection is obviously "automatic," but is the shooting of a film equally "automatic"? And these theories of film as "automatic" art are all based on the recording, not the projection, process. There is *something* about the shooting of a film that is certainly automatic—the precise moment of etching the light on the film material itself. Other than that moment of recording, however, almost nothing about the shooting of a film is automatic. The creators control the intensity and quality of the light; even outdoor sequences use key lights, floodlights, reflectors, and scrims, as well as selecting the precise type of time of day for shooting—as Antonioni did in *Red Desert* or Mizoguchi did in all his films). They control the action within the shot, the setting, the colors, the objects, the details of décor. They control the specific lens that will be used, and the filters for it (if any), and the speed and type of film itself. To reduce the question to the absurd, could you call the shooting of an animated film automatic? Yes, the film captures the light automatically when the single frame is exposed. But no, the entire world that is so captured is the project of a human imagination.

The primacy of projection also solves the nature-nurture controversy in the cinema, since that controversy is a corollary of considering the shooting process as automatic (i.e., cinema automatically records the integrity of nature) or not (i.e., cinema is the artificial project of human choices, not a mechanical recording of nature). Obviously, the projection of a reel of film has nothing to do with nature—no more than does the reading of a novel or the looking at a painting. There may be a good deal of nature (or human life, or natural experience) in the work's succession of frames, images, and events, but there may also be a good deal of this same kind of nature in the content of a novel or the subject of a painting. To emphasize projection is to reiterate that the work of cinema is necessarily as artifical as any work of any art.

To emphasize projection is also to reiterate that an essential condition of the cinema experience is viewing flickering light in an enveloping darkness. This piercing of darkness by projected light is the source of cinema's hypnotic power, paralleling the way that the professional hypnotist entrances a subject by focusing attention on a bright and rhythmically flickering source of light. This light-in-darkness also generates several paradoxes that infuse and influence our experiencing of cinema: we both sit in darkness and are bathed in light; the experience is both private and public at the same time; the projected images both speak to our personal dreams and fantasies and seem to depict the most public and familiar realities. Projection gives us both the concreteness of visual images and the abstract play of light itself.

1977

STANLEY CAVELL
FROM THE WORLD VIEWED

PHOTOGRAPH AND SCREEN

Let us notice the specific sense in which photographs are of the world, of reality as a whole. You can always ask, pointing to an object in a photograph—a building, say—what lies behind it, totally obscured by it. This only accidentally makes sense when asked of an object in a painting. You can always ask, of an area photographed, what lies adjacent to that area, beyond the frame. This generally makes no sense asked of a painting. You can ask these questions of objects in photographs because they have answers in reality. The world of a painting is not continuous with the world of its frame; at its frame, a world finds its limits. We might say: A painting *is* a world; a photograph is *of* the world. What happens in a photograph is that *it* comes to an end. A photograph is cropped, not necessarily by a paper cutter or by masking but by the camera itself. The camera crops it by predetermining the amount of view it will accept; cutting, masking, enlarging, predetermine the amount after the fact. (Something like this phenomenon shows up in recent painting. In this respect, these paintings have found, at the extremest negation of the photographic, media that achieve the condition of photographs.) The camera, being finite, crops a portion from an indefinitely larger field; continuous portions of that field could be included in the photograph in fact taken; in principle, it could all be taken. Hence objects in photographs that run past the edge do not feel cut; they are aimed at, shot, stopped live. When a photograph is cropped, the rest of the world is cut *out*. The implied presence of the rest of the world, and its explicit rejection, are as essential in the experience of a photograph as what it explicitly presents. A camera is an opening in a box: that is the best emblem of the fact that a camera holding on an object is holding the rest of the world away. The camera has been praised for extending the senses; it may, as the world goes, deserve more praise for confining them, leaving room for thought.

The world of a moving picture is screened. The screen is not a support, not like a canvas; there is nothing to support, that way. It holds a projection, as light as light. A screen is a barrier. What does the silver screen screen? It screens me from the world it holds—that is, makes me invisible. And it screens that world from me—that is, screens its existence from me. That the projected world does not exist (now) is its only difference from reality. (There is no feature, or set of features, in which it differs. Existence is not a predicate.) Because it is the field of a photograph, the screen has no frame; that is to say, no border. Its limits are not so much the edges of a given shape as they are the limitations, or capacity, of a container. The screen *is* a frame; the frame is the whole field of the screen—as a frame of film is the whole field of a photograph, like the framer of a loom or a house. In this sense, the screen-frame is a mold, or form.

The fact that in moving picture successive film frames are fit flush into the fixed screen frame results in a phenomenological frame that is indefinitely extendible and contractible, limited in the smallness of the object it can grasp only by the state of its technology, and in largeness only by the span of the world. Drawing the camera back, and panning it, are two ways of extending the frame; a close-up is of a part of the body, or of one object or small set of objects, supported by and reverberating the whole frame of nature. The altering frame is the image of perfect attention. Early in its history the cinema discovered the possibility of *calling* attention to persons and parts of persons and objects; but it is equally a possibility of the medium not to call attention to them but, rather, to let the world happen, to let its parts draw attention to themselves according to their natural weight. This possibility is less explored than its opposite. Dreyer, Flaherty, Vigo, Renoir, and Antonioni are masters of it.

AUDIENCE, ACTOR, AND STAR

The depth of the automatism of photography is to be read not alone in its mechanical production of an image of reality, but in its mechanical defeat of our presence to that reality. The audience in a theater can be defined as those to whom the actors are present while they are not present to the actors. But movies allow the audience to be mechanically absent. The fact that I am invisible and inaudible to the actors, and fixed in position, no longer needs accounting for; it is not part of a convention I have to comply with; the proceedings do not have to make good the fact that I do nothing in the face of tragedy, or that I laugh at the follies of others. In viewing a movie my helplessness is mechanically assured: I am present not at something happening, which I must confirm, but at something that has happened, which I absorb (like a memory). In this, movies resemble novels, a fact mirrored in the sound of narration itself, whose tense is the past.

It might be said: "But surely there is the obvious difference between a movie house and a theater that is not recorded by what has so far been said and that outweighs all this fiddle of differences. The obvious difference is that in a theater we are in the presence of an actor, in a movie house we are not. You have said that in both places the actor is in our presence and in neither are we in his, the difference lying in the mode of our absence. But there is also the plain fact that in a theater a real man is *there,* and in a movie no real man is there. That is obviously essential to the differences between our responses to a play and to a film." What that means must not be denied; but the fact remains to be understood. Bazin meets it head on by simply denying that "the screen is incapable of putting us 'in the presence of' the actor"; it, so to speak, relays his presence to us, as by mirrors. Bazin's idea here really fits the facts of live television, in which the thing we are presented with is happening simultaneously with its presentation. But in live television, what is present to us while it is happening is not the world, but an event standing out from the world. Its point is not to reveal, but to cover (as with a gun), to keep something on view.

It is an incontestable fact that in a motion picture no live human being is up there. But a human *something* is, and something unlike anything else we know. We can stick to our plain description of that human something as "in our presence while we are not in his" (present *at* him, because looking at him, but not present *to* him) and still account for the difference between his live presence and his photographed presence to us. We need to consider what is present or, rather, since the topic is the human being, *who* is present.

One's first impulse may be to say that in a play the character is present, whereas in a film the actor is. That sounds phony or false: one wants to say that both are present in both. But there is more to it, ontologically more. Here I think of a fine passage of Panofsky's:

> Othello or Nora are definite, substantial figures created by the playwright. They can be played well or badly, and they can be "interpreted" in one way or another; but they most definitely exist, no matter who plays them or even whether they are played at all. The character in a film, however, lives and dies with the actor. It is not the entity "Othello" interpreted by Robeson or the entity "Nora" interpreted by Duse, it is the entity "Greta Garbo" incarnate in a figure called Anna Christie or the entity "Robert Montgomery" incarnate in a murderer who, for all we know or care to know, may forever remain anonymous but will never cease to haunt our memories.

If the character lives and dies with the actor, that ought to mean that the actor lives and dies with the character. I think that is correct, but it needs clarification. Let us develop it slightly.

For the stage, an actor works himself into a role; for the screen, a performer takes the role onto himself. The stage actor explores his potentialities and the possibilities of his role simultaneously; in performance these meet at a point in spiritual space—the better the performance, the deeper the point. In this respect, a role in a play is like a position in a game, say, third base: various people can play it, but the great third baseman is a man who has accepted and trained his skills and instincts most perfectly and matches them most intimately with his discoveries of the possibilities and necessities of third base. The screen performer explores his role like an attic and takes stock of his physical and temperamental endowment; he lends his being to the role and accepts only what fits; the rest is nonexistent. On the stage there are two beings, and the being of the character assaults the being of the actor; the actor survives only by yielding. A screen performance requires not so much training as planning. Of course, both the actor and the performer require, or can make use of, experience. The actor's role is his subject for study, and there is no end to it. But the screen performer is essentially not an actor at all: he *is* the subject of study, and a study not his own. (That is what the content of a photograph is—its subject.) On a screen the study is projected; on a stage the actor is the projector. An exemplary stage performance is one which, for a time, most fully creates a character. After Paul Scofield's performance in *King Lear,* we know who King Lear is, we have seen him in the flesh. An exemplary screen performance is one in which, at a time, a star is born. After *The Maltese Falcon* we know a new star, only distantly a person. "Bogart" *means* "the figure created in a given set of films." His presence in those films is who he is, not merely in the sense in which a photograph of an event is that event; but in the sense that if those films did not exist, Bogart would not exist, the name "Bogart" would not mean what it does. The figure it names is not only in our presence, we are in his, in the only sense we could ever be. That is all the "presence" he has.

But it is complicated. A full development of all this would require us to place such facts as these: Humphrey Bogart was a man, and he appeared in movies both before and after the ones that created "Bogart." Some of them did not create a new star (say, the stable groom in *Dark Victory),* some of them defined stars—anyway meteors—that may be incompatible with Bogart (e.g., Duke Mantee and Fred C. Dobbs) but that are related to that figure and may enter into our later experience of it. And Humphrey Bogart was both an accomplished actor and a vivid subject for a camera. Some people are, just as some people are both good pitchers and good hitters; but there are so few that it is surprising that the word "actor" keeps on being used in place of the more beautiful and more accurate word "star"; the stars are only to gaze at, after the fact, and their actions divine our projects. Finally, we must note the sense in which the creation of a (screen) performer is also the creation of a character—not the kind of character an author creates, but the kind that certain real people are: a type.

TYPES; CYCLES AS GENRES

Our attention turns from the physical medium of cinema in general to the specific forms or genres the medium has taken in the course of its history.

Both Panofsky and Bazin begin at the beginning, noting and approving that early movies adapt popular or folk arts and themes and performers and characters: farce, melodrama, circus, music hall, romance, etc. And both are gratifyingly contemptuous of intellectuals who could not come to terms with those facts of life. (Such intellectuals are the alter egos of the film promoters they so heartily despise. Roxy once advertised a movie as "Art, in every sense of the word"; his better half declaims, "This is not art, in any sense of the word.") Our question is, why did such forms and themes and characters lend themselves to film? Bazin, in what I have read of him, is silent on the subject, except to express gratitude to film for revivifying these ancient forms, and to justify in general the legitimacy of adaptation from one art to another. Arnold Hauser, if I understand him, suggests wrong answers, in a passage that includes the remark "Only a young art can be popular," a remark that not only is in itself baffling (did Verdi and Dickens and Shakespeare and Chaplin and Frank Loesser work in young arts?) but suggests that it was only natural for the movies to pick up the forms they did. It *was* natural—anyway it happened fast enough—but not because movies were destined to popularity (they were at first no more popular than other forms of entertainment). In any case, popular arts are likely to pick up the forms and themes of high art for their material—popular theater naturally *burlesques*. And it means next to nothing to say that movies are young, because we do not know what the normal life span of an art is supposed to be, nor what would count as a unit of measure. Panofsky raises the question of the appropriateness of these original forms, but his answer is misleading.

> The legitimate paths of evolution [for the film] were opened, not by running away from the folk art character of the primitive film but by developing it within the limits of its own possibilities. Those primordial archetypes of film productions on the folk art level—success or retribution, sentiment, sensation, pornography, and crude humor— could blossom forth into genuine history, tragedy and romance, crime and adventure, and comedy, as soon as it was realized that they could be transfigured—not by an artifical injection of literary values but by the exploitation of the unique and specific possibilities of the new medium.

The instinct here is sound, but the region is full of traps. What are "the unique and specific possibilities of the new medium"? Panofsky defines them as dynamization of space and spatialization of time—that is, in a movie things move, and you can be moved instantaneously from anywhere to anywhere, and you can witness successively events happening at the same time. He speaks of these properties as "self-evident to the point of triviality" and, because of that, "easily forgotten or neglected." One hardly disputes this, or its importance. But we still do not understand what makes these properties "the possibilities of the medium." I am not now asking how one would know that these are *the* unique and specific possibilities (though I will soon get back to that); I am asking what it means to call them possibilities at all.

Why, for example, didn't the medium begin and remain in the condition of home movies, one shot just physically tacked on to another, cut and edited simply according to subject? (Newsreels essentially did, and they are nevertheless valuable, enough so to have justified the invention of moving pictures.) The answer seems obvious: narrative movies emerged because someone "saw the possibilities" of the medium—cutting and editing and taking shots at different distances from the subject. But again, these are mere actualities of film mechanics: every home movie and newsreel contains them. We could say: to make them "possibilities of the medium" is to realize what will give them *significance*—for example, the narrative and physical rhythms of melodrama, farce, American comedy of the 1930s. It is not as if film-makers saw these possibilities and then looked for something to apply them to. It is truer to say that someone with the wish to make a movie saw that certain established forms would give point to certain properties of film.

This perhaps sounds like quibbling, but what it means is that the aesthetic possibilities of a medium are not givens. You can no more tell what will give significance to the unique and specific aesthetic possibilities of projecting photographic images by thinking about them or seeing some, than you can tell what will give significance to the possibilities of paint by thinking about paint or by looking some over. You have to think about painting, and paintings; you have to think about motion pictures. What does this "thinking about them" consist in? Whatever the useful criticism of an art consists in. (Painters before Jackson Pollock had dripped paint, even deliberately. Pollock made dripping into a medium of painting.) I feel like saying: The first successful movies—i.e., the first moving pictures accepted as motion pictures—were not applications of a medium that was defined by given possibilities, but the *creation of a medium* by their giving significance to specific possibilities. Only the art itself can discover its possibilities, and the discovery of a new possibility is the discovery of a new medium. A medium is something through which or by means of which something specific gets done or said in particular ways. It provides, one might say, particular ways to get through to someone, to make sense; in art, they are forms, like forms of speech. To discover ways of making sense is always a matter of the relation of an artist to his art, each discovering the other.

Panofsky uncharacteristically skips a step when he describes the early silent films as an "unknown language . . . forced upon a public not yet capable of reading it." His notion is (with good reason, writing when he did) of a few industrialists forcing their productions upon an addicted multitude. But from the beginning the language was not "unknown"; it was known to its creators, those who found themselves speaking it; and in the beginning there was no "public" in question; there were just some curious people. There soon was a public, but that just proves how easy the thing was to know. If we are to say that there was an "unknown" something, it was less like a language than like a fact—in particular, the fact that something is intelligible. So while it may be true, as Panofsky says, that "for a Saxon peasant of around 800 it was not easy to understand the meaning of a picture showing a man as he pours water over the head of another man," this has nothing special to do with the problems of a moviegoer. The meaning of that act of pouring in certain communities is still not easy to understand; it was and is impossible to understand for anyone to whom the practice of baptism is unknown. Why did Panofsky suppose that comparable understanding is essential, or uniquely important, to the reading of movies? Apparently he needed an explanation for the persistence in movies of "fixed iconography"—"the well-remembered types of the Vamp and the Straight Girl . . . the Family Man, and the Villain," characters whose conduct was "predetermined accordingly"—an explanation for the persistence of an obviously primitive or folkloristic element in a rapidly developing medium. For he goes on, otherwise inexplicably, to say that "devices like these became gradually less necessary as the public grew accustomed to interpret the action by itself and were virtually abolished by the invention of the talking film." In fact such devices persist as long as there are still Westerns and gangster films and comedies and musicals and romances. *Which* specific iconography the Villain is given will alter with the times, but that his iconography remains specific (i.e., operates according to a "fixed attitude and attribute" principle) seems undeniable: if Jack Palance in *Shane* is not a Villain, no honest home was ever in danger. Films have changed, but that is not because we don't need such explanations any longer; it is because we can't *accept* them.

These facts are accounted for by the actualities of the film medium itself: types are exactly what carry the forms movies have relied upon. These media created new types, or combinations and ironic reversals of types; but there they were, and stayed. Does this mean that movies can never create individuals, only types? What it means is that this is the movies' way of creating individuals: they create *individualities.* For what makes someone a type is not his similarity with other members of that type but his striking separateness from other people.

Until recently, types of black human beings were not created in film: black people were stereotypes—mammies, shiftless servants, loyal retainers, entertainers. We were not given, and were not in a position to be given, individualities that projected particular *ways* of inhabiting a social role; we recognized only the role. Occasionally the humanity behind the role would manifest itself; and the result was a revelation not of a human individuality, but of an entire realm of humanity becoming visible. When in *Gone With the Wind* Vivien Leigh, having counted on Butterfly McQueen's professed knowledge of midwifery, and finding her as ignorant as herself, slaps her in rage and terror, the moment can stun us with a question: What was the white girl assuming about blackness when she believed the casual claim of a black girl, younger and duller and more ignorant than herself, to know all about the mysteries of childbirth? The assumption, though apparently complimentary, is dehumanizing—with such creatures knowledge of the body comes from nowhere, and in general they are to be trusted absolutely or not at all, like lions in a cage, with whom you either do or do not know how to deal. After the slap, we are left with two young girls equally frightened in a humanly desperate situation, one limited by a distraction which expects and forgets that it is to be bullied, the other by an energetic resourcefulness which knows only how to bully. At the end of Michael Curtiz' *Breaking Point,* as the wounded John Garfield is carried from his boat to the dock, awaited by his wife and children and, just outside the circle, by the other woman in his life (Patricia Neal), the camera pulls away, holding on the still waiting child of his black partner who only the unconscious Garfield knows has been killed. The poignance of the silent and unnoticed black child overwhelms the yarn we had been shown. Is he supposed to symbolize the fact of general human isolation and abandonment? Or the fact that every action has consequences for innocent bystanders? Or that children are the real sufferers from the entangled efforts of adults to straighten out their lives? The effect here is to rebuke Garfield for attaching so much importance to the loss of his arm, and generally to blot out attention to individual suffering by invoking a massive social evil about which this film has nothing to say.

The general difference between a film type and a stage type is that the individuality captured on film naturally takes precedence over the social role in which that individuality gets expressed. Because on film social role appears arbitrary or incidental, movies have an inherent tendency toward the democratic, or anyway the idea of human equality. (But because of film's equally natural attraction to crowds, it has opposite tendencies toward the fascistic or populistic.) This depends upon recognizing film types as inhabited by figures we have met or may well meet in other circumstances. The recognized recurrence of film performers will become a central idea as we proceed. At the moment I am emphasizing only that in the case of black performers there was until recently no other place for them to recur in, except just the role within which we have already met them. For example, we would not have expected to see them as parents or siblings. I cannot at the moment remember a black person in a film making an ordinary purchase—say of a newspaper, or a ticket to a movie or for a train, let alone writing a check. *(Pinky* and *A Raisin in the Sun* prove the rule: in the former, the making of a purchase is a climactic scene in the film; in the latter, it provides the whole subject and structure.)

One recalls the list of stars of every magnitude who have provided the movie camera with human subjects—individuals capable of filling its need for individualities, whose individualities in turn, whose inflections of demeanor and disposition were given full play in its projection. They provided, and still provide, staples for impersonators: one gesture or syllable of mood, two strides, or a passing mannerism was enough to single them out from all other creatures. They realized the myth of singularity—that we can still be found, behind our disguises of bravado and cowardice, by someone, perhaps a god, capable of defeating our self-defeats. This was always more important than their distinction by beauty. Their singularity made them more like us—anyway, made their difference from us less a matter of metaphysics, to which we must accede, than a matter of responsibility, to which we must bend. But then that made them even more glamorous. That they should be able to stand upon their singularity! If one did that, one might be found, and called out, too soon, or at an inconvenient moment.

What was wrong with type-casting in films was not that it displaced some other, better principle of casting, but that factors irrelevant to film-making often influenced the particular figures chosen. Similarly, the familiar historical fact that there are movie cycles, taken by certain movie theorists as in itself a mark of unscrupulous commercialism, is a possibility internal to the medium; one could even say, it is the best emblem of the fact that a medium had been created. For a cycle is a genre (prison movies, Civil War movies, horror movies, etc.); and a genre is a medium.

As Hollywood developed, the original types ramified into individualities as various and subtle, as far-reaching in their capacities to inflect mood and release fantasy, as any set of characters who inhabited the great theaters of our world. We do not know them by such names of Pulcinella, Crispin, Harlequin, Pantaloon, the Doctor, the Captain, Columbine; we call them the Public Enemy, the Priest, James Cagney, Pat O'Brien, the Confederate Spy, the Army Scout, Randolph Scott, Gary Cooper, Gable, Paul Muni, the Reporter, the Sergeant, the Sheriff, the Deputy, the D.A., the Quack, the Shyster, the Other Woman, the Fallen Woman, the Moll, the Dance Hall Hostess. Hollywood was the theater in which they appeared, because the films of Hollywood constituted a world, with recurrent faces more familiar to me than the faces of the neighbors of all the places I have lived.

The great movie comedians—Chaplin, Keaton, W. C. Fields—form a set of types that could not have been adapted from any other medium. Its creation depended upon two conditions of the film medium mentioned earlier. These conditions seem to be necessities, not merely possibilities, so I will say that two necessities of the medium were discovered or expanded in the creation of these types. First, movie performers cannot project, but are projected. Second, photographs are of the world, in which human beings are not ontologically favored over the rest of nature, in which objects are not props but natural allies (or enemies) of the human character. The first necessity—projected visibility—permits the sublime comprehensibility of Chaplin's natural choreography; the second—ontological equality—

permits his Proustian or Jamesian relationships with Murphy beds and flights of stairs and with vases on runners on tables on rollers: the heroism of momentary survival, Nietzsche's man as a tightrope across an abyss. These necessities permit not merely the locales of Keaton's extrications, but the philosophical mood of his countenance and the Olympic resourcefulness of his body; permit him to be perhaps the only constantly beautiful and continuously hilarious man ever seen, as though the ugliness in laughter should be redeemed. They permit Fields to mutter and suffer and curse obsessively, but heard and seen only by us; because his attributes are those of the gentleman (confident swagger and elegant manners, gloves, cane, outer heartiness), he can manifest continuously with the remorselessness of nature, the psychic brutalities of bourgeois civilization.

IDEAS OF ORIGIN

It is inevitable that in theorizing about film one at some point speculate about its origins, because despite its recentness, its origin remains obscure. The facts are well enough known about the invention and the inventors of the camera, and about improvements in fixing and then moving the image it captures. The problem is that the invention of the photographic picture is not the same thing as the creation of photography as a medium for making sense. The historical problem is like any other: a chronicle of the facts preceding the appearance of this technology does not explain why it happened when and as it did. Panofsky opens his study of film by remarking, "It was not an artistic urge that gave rise to the discovery and gradual perfection of a new technique; it was a technical invention that gave rise to the discovery and gradual perfection of a new art." We seem to understand this, but do we understand it? Panofsky assumes we know what it is that at any time has "given rise" to a "new art." He mentions an "artistic urge," but that is hardly a candidate to serve as an explanation; it would be about as useful as explaining the rise of modern science by appealing to "a scientific urge." There may be such urges, but they are themselves rather badly in need of explanation. Panofsky cites an artistic urge explicitly as the occasion for a new "technique." But the motion picture is not a new *technique,* any more than the airplane is. (What did we use to do that such a thing enables us to do better?) Yet some idea of flying, and an urge to do it, preceded the mechanical invention of the airplane. What is "given rise to" by such inventions as movable type or the microscope or the steam engine or the pianoforte?

It would be surprising if the history of the establishment of an artistic medium were less complex a problem for the historical understanding than (say) the rise of modern science. I take Bazin to be suggesting this when he reverses the apparent relation between the relevant technology and the idea of cinema, emphasizing that the idea preceded the technology, parts of it by centuries, and that parts of the technology preceded the invention of movies, some of it by centuries. So what has to be explained is not merely how the feat was technically accomplished but, for example, what stood in the way of its happening earlier. Surprisingly, Bazin, in the selection of essays I have read, does not include the contemporary condition of the related arts as a part of the ideological superstructure that elicited the new material basis of film. But it is certainly relevant that the burning issue during the latter half of the nineteenth century, in painting and in the novel and in the theater, was realism. And unless film captured possibilities opened up by the arts themselves, it is hard to imagine that its possibilities as an artistic medium would have shown up as, and as suddenly as, they did.

The idea of and wish for the world re-created in its own image was satisfied *at last* by cinema. Bazin calls this the myth of total cinema. But it had always been one of the myths of art; each of the arts had satisfied it in its own way. The mirror was in various hands held up to nature. In some ways it was more fully satisfied in theater. (Since theater is on the whole not now a major art for us, it on the whole no longer makes contact with its historical and psychological sources; so we are rarely gripped by the trauma we must once have suffered when the leader of the chorus stopped contributing to a narrative or song and turned to face the others, suffering incarnation.)

What is cinema's way of satisfying the myth? Automatically, we said. But what does that mean—mean mythically, as it were? It means satisfying it without *my* having to do anything, satisfying it *by* wishing. In a word, *magically*. I have found myself asking: How could film be art, since all the major arts arise in some way out of religion? Now I can answer: Because movies arise out of magic; from *below* the world.

The better a film, the more it makes contact with this source of its inspiration; it never wholly loses touch with the magic lantern behind it. This suggests why movies of the fantastic *(The Cabinet of Dr. Caligari, Blood of a Poet)* and filmed scenes of magic (say, materialization and dematerialization), while they have provided moods and devices, have never established themselves as cinematic media, however strongly this "possibility" is suggested by the physical medium of film: they are technically and psychologically trivial compared with the medium of magic itself. It is otherwise if the presented magic is itself made technically or physically interesting *(The Invisible Man, Dr. Jekyll and Mr. Hyde, Frankenstein, 2001: A Space Odyssey)*, but then that becomes another way of confirming the physicality of our world. Science presents itself, in movies, as magic, which was indeed one source of science. In particular, projected science retains magic's mystery and forbiddenness. Science-fiction films exploit not merely certain obvious aspects of adventure, and of a physicality that special effects specialize in, but also the terrific mumbo-jumbo of hearsay science: "My God, the thing is impervious to the negative beta ray! We must reverse the atom recalcitration spatter, before it's too late!" The dialogue has the surface of those tinbox-and-lever contraptions that were sufficiently convincing in prime *Flash Gordon*. These films are carried by the immediacy of the fantasy that motivates them (say, destruction by lower or higher forms of life, as though the precariousness of human life is due to its biological stage of development); together with the myth of the one way and last chance in which the (external) danger can be averted. And certainly the beauty of forms and motions in Frankenstein's laboratory is essential to the success of *Frankenstein;* computers seem primitive in comparison. It always made more sense to steal from God than to try to outwit him.

How do movies reproduce the world magically? Not by literally presenting us with the world, but by permitting us to view it unseen. This is not a wish for power over creation (as Pygmalion's was), but a wish not to need power, not to have to bear its burdens. It is, in this sense, the reverse of the myth of Faust. And the wish for invisibility is old enough. Gods have profited from it, and Plato tells it at the end of the *Republic* as the Myth of the Ring of Gyges. In viewing films, the sense of invisibility is an expression of modern privacy or anonymity. It is as though the world's projection explains our forms of unknownness and of our ability to know. The explanation is not so much that the world is passing us by, as that we are displaced from our natural habitation within it, placed at a distance from it. The screen overcomes our fixed distance; it makes displacement appear as our natural condition.

1971

JEAN-LOUIS BAUDRY
IDEOLOGICAL EFFECTS OF THE
BASIC CINEMATOGRAPHIC
APPARATUS

At the end of *The Interpretation of Dreams,* when he seeks to integrate dream elaboration and its particular "economy" with the psyche as a whole, Freud assigns to the latter an optical model: "Let us simply imagine the instrument which serves in psychic productions as a sort of complicated microscope or camera." But Freud does not seem to hold strongly to this optical model, which, as Derrida has pointed out,[1] brings out the shortcomings of graphic representation in the area earlier covered by his work on dreams. Moreover, he will later abandon the optical model in favor of a writing instrument, the "mystic writing pad." Nonetheless, this optical choice seems to prolong the tradition of Western science, whose birth coincides exactly with the development of the optical apparatus which will have as a consequence the decentering of the human universe, the end of geocentrism (Galileo).

But also, and paradoxically,the optical apparatus camera obscura will serve in the same period to elaborate in pictorial work a new mode of representation, *perspectiva artificalis.* This system, recentering or at least displacing the center (which settles itself in the eye), will ensure the setting up of the "subject"[2] as the active center and origin of meaning. One could doubtless question the privileged position which optical instruments seem to occupy on the line of intersection of science and ideological productions. Does the technical nature of optical instruments, directly attached to scientific practice, serve to conceal not only their use in ideological products but also the ideological effects which they may themselves provoke? Their

---

[1]See on this subject Derrida's work "La Scène de l'écriture" in *L'Ecriture et la différence* (Paris: Seuil, 1967).

[2][The term "subject" is used by Baudry and others to mean not the topic of discourse—though this is clearly involved—but rather the perceiving and ordering self, as in our term "subjective"— TRANS.]

scientific base would ensure them a sort of neutrality and help to avoid their being questioned.

But already a question: if we are to take account of the imperfections of these instruments, their limitations, by what criteria may these be defined? If, for example, one can speak of a restricted depth of field as a limitation, doesn't this term itself depend on a particular conception of reality for which such a limitation would not exist? Contemporary media are particularly in question here, to the extent that instrumentation plays a more and more important role in them and that their distribution is more and more extensive. It is strange (but is it so strange?) that emphasis has been placed almost exclusively on their influence, on the effects that they have as finished products, their content, the field of the signified if you like; the technical bases on which these effects depend and the specific characteristics of these bases have, however, been ignored. They have been protected by the inviolability that science is supposed to provide. We would like to establish for the cinema a few guidelines which will need to be completed, verified, improved.

We must first establish the place of the instrumental base in the set of operations which combine in the production of a film (we omit consideration of economic implications). Between "objective reality" and the camera, site of inscription, and between the inscription and the projection are situated certain operations, a *work* which has as its result a finished product. To the extent that it is cut off from the raw material ("objective reality") this product does not allow us to see the transformation which has taken place.

Equally distant from "objective reality" and the finished product, the camera occupies an intermediate position in the work process which leads from raw material to finished product. Though mutually dependent from other points of view, *découpage* [shot breakdown before shooting] and *montage* [editing, done afterward] must be distinguished because of the essential difference in the signifying raw material on which each operates: language (scenario) or image. Between the two complementary stages of production a mutation of signifying material takes place (neither translation nor transcription, obviously, for the image is not reducible to language) precisely in the place occupied by the camera. Finally, between the finished product (possessing exchange value, a commodity) and its consumption (use value) is introduced another operation effected by a set of instruments. Projector and screen restore the light lost in the shooting process, and transform a succession of separate images into an unrolling which also restores, but according to another scansion, the movement seized from "objective reality."

Cinematographic specificity thus refers to a *work,* that is, to a process of transformation. The question becomes: is the work made evident, does consumption of the product bring about a "knowledge effect" [Althusser], or is the work concealed? If the latter, consumption of the product will obviously be accompanied by ideological surplus value. On the practical level, this poses the question of by what procedures the work can in fact be made "readable" in its inscription. These procedures must of necessity call cinematographic technique into play. But, on the other hand, going back to the first question, one may ask, do the instruments (the technical base) produce specific ideological effects, and are these effects themselves determined by the dominant ideology? In which case, concealment of the technical base will also bring about an inevitable ideological effect. Its inscription, its manifestation as such, on the other hand, would produce a knowledge effect, as actualization of the work process, as denunciation of ideology, and as critique of idealism.

THE EYE OF THE SUBJECT

Central in the process of production[1] of the film, the camera—an assembly of optical and mechanical instrumentation—carries out a certain mode of inscription characterized by marking, by the recording of differences between the frames. Fabricated on the model of the camera obscura, it permits the construction of an image analogous to the perspective projections developed during the Italian Renaissance. Of course, the use of lenses of different focal lengths can alter the perspective of an image. But this much, at least, is clear in the history of cinema: it is the perspective construction of the Renaissance which originally served as a model. The use of different lenses, when not dictated by technical considerations aimed at restoring habitual perspective (such as shooting in limited or extended spaces which one wishes to expand or contract), does not destroy [traditional] perspective but rather makes it play the role of norm. Departure from the norm, by means of a wide-angle or telephoto lens, is clearly marked in comparison with so-called "normal" perspective. We will see in any case that the resulting ideological effect is still defined in relation to the ideology inherent in perspective. The dimensions of the image itself, the ratio between height and width, seem clearly taken from an average drawn from Western easel painting.

The conception of space which conditions the construction of perspective in the Renaissance differs from that of the Greeks. For the latter, space is discontinuous and heterogeneous (for Aristotle, but also for Democritus, for whom space is the location of an infinity of indivisible atoms), whereas with Nicholas of Cusa will be born a conception of space formed by the relation between elements which are equally near and distant from the "source of all life." In addition, the pictorial construction of the Greeks corresponded to the organization of their stage, based on a multiplicity of points of view, whereas the painting of the Renaissance will elaborate a centered space. ("Painting is nothing but the intersection of the visual pyramid following a given distance, a fixed center, and a certain lighting."—Alberti.) The center of this space coincides with the eye which Jean Pellerin Viator will so appropriately call the "subject." ("The principal point in perspective should be placed at eye level: this point is called fixed or subject.")[2] Monocular vision, which as Pleynet points out is what the camera has, calls forth a sort of play of "reflection." Based on the principle of a fixed point by reference to which the visualized objects are organized, it specifies in return the position of the "subject,"[3] the very spot it must necessarily occupy.

---

[1] Obviously we are not speaking here of investment of capital in the process.

[2] See L. Brion Guerry, *Jean Pellerin Viator* (Paris: Belles Lettres, 1962.)

[3] We understand the term "subject" here as a vehicle and as a place of intersection of the ideological implications which we are attempting progressively to make clear, and not as the structural function which analytic discourse attempts to locate. It would rather partially take the place of the *ego,* of which we know the deviations seen in the analytic field.

In focusing it, the optical construct appears to be truly the projection-reflection of a "virtual image" whose hallucinatory reality it creates. It lays out the space of an ideal vision and in this way assures the necessity of a transcendence—metaphorically (by the unknown to which it appeals—here we must recall the structural place occupied by the vanishing point) and metonymically (by the displacement that it seems to carry out: a subject is both "in place of" and "a part for the whole"). Contrary to Chinese and Japanese painting, Western easel painting, presenting as it does a motionless and continuous whole, elaborates a total vision which corresponds to the idealist conception of the fullness and homogenity of "being,"* and is, so to speak, representative of this conception. In this sense it contributes in a singularly emphatic way to the ideological function of art, which is to provide the tangible representation of metaphysics. The principle of transcendence which conditions and is conditioned by the perspective construction represented in painting and in the photographic image which copies from it seems to inspire all the idealist paeans to which the cinema has given rise:

> This strange mechanism, parodying man's spirit, seems better to accomplish the latter's own tasks. This mimetic play, brother and rival of the intelligence, is, finally, a means of the discovery of truth. (Cohen-Séat)

> Far from leading us down the path of determinism, as one could legitimately believe, this art—the most positive of all, insensible to all that is not brute fact, pure appearance—presents us on the contrary the idea of a hierarchical universe, ordered in terms of an ultimate end. Behind what film gives us to see, it is not the existence of atoms that we are led to seek, but rather the existence of an "other world" of phenomena, of a soul or of other spiritual principles. It is in this revelation, above all, of a spiritual presence, that I propose that we seek Poetry. (André Bazin)

PROJECTION: DIFFERENCE DENIED

Nevertheless, whatever the effects proper to optics generally, the movie camera differs from still photography by registering through its mechanical instrumentation a series of images. It might thus seem to counter the unifying and "substantializing" character of the single-perspective image, taking what would seem to be instants of time or slices from "reality" (but always a reality already worked upon, elaborated, selected). This might permit the supposition, especially since the camera moves, of a multiplicity of points of view which would neutralize the fixed position of the eye-subject and even nullify it. But here we must turn to the relation between the succession of images inscribed by the camera and their projection, bypassing momentarily the place occupied by editing, which plays a decisive role in the strategy of the ideology produced.

The projection operation (projector and screen) restores continuity of movement and the temporal dimension to the sequence of static images. The relation between the individual frames and the projection would resemble the relation between points and a curve in geometry. But it is precisely this relation and the restoration

---

*The perspective "frame" which will have such an influence on cinematographic shooting has as its role to intensify, to increase the effect of the spectacle, which no divergence may be allowed to split.

of continuity to discontinuous elements which poses a problem. The meaning effect produced does not depend only on the content of the images but also on the material procedures by which an illusion of continuity, dependent on persistence of vision, is restored from discontinuous elements. These separate frames have between them differences that are indispensible for the creation of an illusion of continuity, of a continuous passage (movement, time). But only on one condition can these differences create this illusion: they must be effaced as differences.*

Thus on the technical level the question becomes one of the adoption of a very small difference between images, such that each image, in consequence of an organic factor [presumably persistence of vision], is rendered incapable of being seen as such. In this sense we could say that film—and perhaps this instance is exemplary—lives on the denial of difference: difference is necessary for it to live, but it lives on its negation. This is indeed the paradox that emerges if we look directly at a strip of processed film: adjacent images are almost exactly repeated, their divergence being verifiable only by comparison of images at a sufficient distance from each other. We should remember, moreover, the disturbing effects which result during a projection from breakdowns in the recreation of movement, when the spectator is brought abruptly back to discontinuity—that is, to the body, to the technical apparatus which he had *forgotten*.

We might not be far from seeing what is in play on this material basis if we recall that the "language" of the unconscious, as it is found in dreams, slips of the tongue, or hysterical symptoms, manifests itself as continuity destroyed, broken and as the unexpected surging forth of a marked difference. Couldn't we thus say that cinema reconstructs and forms the mechanical model (with the simplifications that this can entail) of a system of writing [*écriture*] constituted by a material base and a countersystem (ideology, idealism) which uses this system while also concealing it? On the one hand, the optical apparatus and the film permit the marking of difference (but the marking is already negated, we have seen, in the constitution of the perspective image with its mirror effect). On the other hand, the mechanical apparatus both selects the minimal difference and represses it in projection, so that meaning can be constituted; it is at once direction, continuity, movement. The projection mechanism allows the differential elements (the discontinuity inscribed by the camera) to be suppressed, bringing only the relation into play. The individual images as such disappear so that movement and continuity can appear. But movement and continuity are the visible expression (one might even say, the projection) of their relations, derived from the tiny discontinuities between the images. Thus one may presume that what was already at work as the originating basis of the perspective

---

*We know that the spectator finds it impossible to notice that the images which succeed one another before his eyes were assembled end to end, because the projection of film on the screen offers an impression of continuity although the images which compose it are, in reality, distinct, and are differentiated, moreover, by variations in space and time.

"In a film, there can be hundreds, even thousands of cuts and intervals. But if in the hands of specialists who know the art, the spectacle will not be divulged as such. Only an error or lack of competence will permit them to seize, and this is a disagreeable sensation, the changes of time and place of action." (V.I. Pudovkin, "Le Montage," in *Cinéma d'aujourd'hui et de demain* [Moscow, 1956].

image, namely the eye, the "subject," is put forth, liberated (in the sense that a chemical reaction liberates a substance) by the operation which transforms successive, discrete images (as isolated images they have, strictly speaking, no meaning, or at least no unity of meaning) into continuity, movement, meaning. With continuity restored, both meaning and consciousness are restored.[1]

THE TRANSCENDENTAL SUBJECT

Meaning and consciousness, to be sure, at this point we must return to the camera. Its mechanical nature not only permits the shooting of differential images as rapidly as desired but also destines it to change position, to move. Film history shows that as a result of the combined inertia of painting, theater, and photography, it took a certain time to notice the inherent mobility of the cinematic mechanism. The ability to reconstitute movement is after all only a partial, elementary aspect of a more general capability. To seize movement is to become movement, to follow a trajectory is to become trajectory, to choose a direction is to have the possibility of choosing one, to determine a meaning is to give oneself a meaning. In this way the eye subject, the invisible base of artificial perspective (which in fact only represents a larger effort to produce an ordering, a regulated transcendence) becomes absorbed in, "elevated" to a vaster function, proportional to the movement which it can perform.

And if the eye which moves is no longer fettered by a body, by the laws of matter and time, if there are no more assignable limits to its displacement—conditions fulfilled by the possibilities of shooting and of film—the world will be constituted not only by this eye but for it.[2] The mobility of the camera seems to fulfill the most favorable conditions for the manifestation of the "transcendental subject." There is a phantasmatization of objective reality (images, sounds, colors)—but of an objective reality which, limiting its powers of constraint, seems equally to augment the possibilities or the power of the subject.[3] As it is said of consciousness—and in point of fact we are concerned with nothing less—the image *of* something; it must result from a deliberate act of consciousness [*visée intentionelle*]. "The word intentionality signifies nothing other than this peculiarity that consciousness has of being consciousness *of* something, of carrying in its quality of *ego* its *cogitatum* within itself."[4] In such a definition could perhaps be found the status of the cinematographic image, or rather of its operation, the mode of working which it carries out. For it to be an image of something, it has to constitute this something as meaning. The image seems to reflect the world but solely in the naive inversion of a founding

---

[1] It is thus first at the level of the apparatus that the cinema functions as a language: inscription of discontinuous elements whose effacement in the relationship instituted among them produces meaning.

[2] "In the cinema I am simultaneously in this action and *outside* it, in this space and out of this space. Having the power of ubiquity. I am everywhere and nowhere." Jean Mitry, *Esthétique et psychologie du cinéma* [Paris: Presses Universitaires de France, 1965), p. 179].

[3] The cinema manifests in a hallucinatory manner the belief in the omnipotence of thought, described by Freud, which plays so important a role in neurotic defense mechanisms.

[4] Husserl, *Les Méditations Cartésiennes* (Paris: Vrin, 1953), p. 28.

hierarchy: "The domain of natural existence thus has only an authority of the second order, and always presupposes the domain of the transcendental."[1]

The world is no longer only an "open and indeterminate horizon." Limited by the framing, lined up, put at the proper distance, the world offers up an object endowed with meaning, an intentional object, implied by and implying the action of the "subject" which sights it. At the same time that the world's transfer as image seems to accomplish this phenomenological reduction, this putting into parentheses of its real existence (a suspension necessary, we will see, to the formation of the impression of reality) provides a basis for the apodicity[2] of the ego. The multiplicity of aspects of the object in view refers to a synthesizing operation, to the unity of this constituting subject: Husserl speaks of

"aspects," sometimes of "proximity," sometimes of "distance," in variable modes of "here" and "there," as opposed to an absolute here (which is located—for me—in "my own body" which appears to me at the same time), the consciousness of which, though it remains *unperceived,* always accompanies them. [We will see moreover what happens with the body in the mise-en-scène of projection.—J.L.B.] Each "aspect" which the mind grasps, for example, this cube here in the sphere of proximity, is revealed in turn as a unity synthesized from a multiplicity of corresponding modes of presentation. The nearby object may present itself as the same, but under one or another "aspect." There may be variation of visual perspective, but also of "tacile," "acoustic" phenomena, or of other "modes of presentation"[3] as we can observe in directing our attention in the proper direction.[4]

For Husserl, "the original operation [of intentional analysis] is to *unmask the potentialities implied* in the present states of consciousness. And it is by this that will be carried out, from the noematic point of view, the eventual *explication, definition,* and *elucidation* of what is meant by consciousness, that is, its *objective meaning.*[5] And again in the *Cartesian Meditations:* "A second type of polarization now presents itself to us, another type of synthesis which embraces the particular multiplicities of *cogitationes,* which embraces them all and in a special manner, namely, as *cogitationes* of an identical self which, *active* or *passive,* lives in all the lived states of consciousness and which, through them, relates to all objects.[6]

Thus is articulated the relation between the continuity necessary to the constitution of meaning and the "subject" which constitutes this meaning: continuity is an attribute of the subject. It supposes the subject and it circumscribes its place. It appears in the cinema in the two complementary aspects of a "formal" continuity established through a system of negated differences and narrative continuity in the

[1]*Ibid,* p. 18.

[2]["Apodicity," in phenomenological terminology, indicates something of an irrefutable nature. See Husserl, *Les Méditations Cartesiennes.* Here, Baudry is using the term critically—in a sense *ironically.*—TRANS.]

[3]On this point it is true that the camera is revealed as incomplete. But this is only a technical imperfection which, since the birth of cinema, has already in large measure been remedied.

[4]*Ibid.,* p. 34, emphasis added.

[5]*Ibid.,* p. 40.

[6]*Ibid.,* p. 56.

filmic space. The latter, in any case, could not have been conquered without exercising violence to the instrumental base, as can be discovered from most of the texts by filmmakers and critics: the discontinuity that had been effaced at the level of the image could have reappeared on the narrative level, giving rise to effects of rupture disturbing to the spectator (to a *place* which ideology must both conquer and, in the degree that it already dominates it, must also satisfy: fill). "What is important in a film is the feeling of continuity which joins shots and sequences while maintaining unity and cohesion of movements. This continuity was one of the most difficult things to obtain.[1] Pudovkin defined montage as "the art of assembling pieces of film, shot separately, in such a way as to give the spectator the impression of continuous movement." The search for such narrative continuity, so difficult to obtain from the material base, can only be explained by an essential ideological stake projected in this point: it is a question of preserving at any cost the synthetic unity of the locus where meaning originates [the subject]—the constituting transcendental function to which narrative continuity points back as its natural secretion.[2]

THE SCREEN-MIRROR: SPECULARIZATION AND DOUBLE IDENTIFICATION

But another supplementary operation (made possible by a special technical arrangement) must be added in order that the mechanism thus described can play its role effectively as an ideological machine, so that not only the reworked "objective reality" but also the specific type of identification we have described can be represented.

No doubt the darkened room and the screen bordered with black like a letter of condolence already present privileged conditions of effectiveness—no exchange, no circulation, no communication with any outside. Projection and reflection take place in a closed space, and those who remain there, whether they know it or not (but they do not), find themselves chained, captured, or captivated. (What might one say of the function of the head in this captivation: it suffices to recall that for Bataille materialism makes itself headless—like a wound that bleeds and thus trans-

---

[1]Mitry, *Esthétique et psychologie*, p. 157.

[2]The lens, the "objective," is of course only a particular location of the "subjective," Marked by the idealist opposition interior/exterior, topologically situated at the meeting point of the two, it corresponds, one could say, to the empirical organ of the subjective, to the opening, the fault in the organs of meaning, by which the exterior world may penetrate the interior and assume meaning. "It is the interior which commands," says Bresson. "I know this may seem paradoxical in an art which is all exterior." Also the use of different lenses is already conditioned by camera movement as implication and trajectory of meaning, by this transcendental function which we are attempting to define: it is the possibility of choosing a field as accentuation or modification of the *visée intentionelle*.
No doubt this transcendental function fits without difficulty into the field of psychology. This, moreover, is insisted upon by Husserl himself, who indicates that Brentano's discovery, intentionality, "permits one truly to distinguish the method of a descriptive science of consciousness, as much philosophical and transcendental as psychological."

fuses.) And the mirror, as a reflecting surface, is framed, limited, circumscribed. *An infinite mirror would no longer be a mirror.* The paradoxical nature of the cinematic mirror-screen is without doubt that it reflects *images* but not "reality"; the word *reflect,* being transitive, leaves this ambiguity unresolved. In any case this "reality" comes from behind the spectator's head, and if he looked at it directly he would see nothing except the moving beams from an already veiled light source.

The arrangement of the different elements—projector, darkened hall, screen— in addition to reproducing in a striking way the mise-en-scène of Plato's cave (pro- totypical set for all transcendence and the topological model of idealism,)[1] recon- structs the situation necessary to the release of the "mirror stage" discovered by Lacan. This psychological phase, which occurs between six and eighteen months of age, generates via the mirror image of a unified body the constitution or at least the first sketches of the "I" as an imaginary function. "It is to this unreachable image in the mirror that the specular image gives its garments.[2] But for this imaginary constitution of the self to be possible, there must be—Lacan strongly emphasizes this point—two complementary conditions: immature powers of mobility and a precocious maturation of visual organization (apparent in the first few days of life). If one considers that these two conditions are repeated during cinematographic pro- jection—suspension of mobility and predominance of the visual function—per- haps one could suppose that this is more than a simple analogy. And possibly this very point explains the "impression of reality" so often invoked in connection with the cinema, for which the various explanations proposed seem only to skirt the real problem. In order for this impression to be produced, it would be necessary that the conditions of a formative scene be reproduced. This scene would be repeated and reenacted in such a manner that the imaginary order (activated by a specularization which takes place, everything considered, in reality) fulfills its particular function of occultation or of filling the gap, the split, of the subject on the order of the sig- nifier.[3]

On the other hand, it is to the extent that the child can sustain the look of another in the presence of a third party that he can find the assurance of an identification with the image of his own body. From the very fact that during the mirror stage a dual relationship is established, it constitutes, in conjunction with the formation of the self in the imaginary order, the nexus of secondary identification.[4] The origin of the self, as discovered by Lacan, in pertaining to the imaginary order effectively subverts the "optical machinery" of idealism which the projection room scrupu-

---

[1]The arrangement of the cave, except that in the cinema it is already doubled in a sort of enclo- sure in which the camera, the darkened chamber, is enclosed in another darkened chamber, the projection hall.

[2]Jacques Lacan, *Ecrits* (Paris: Seuil, 1966). See in particular "Le Stade du miroir comme for- mateur de la fonction du je."

[3]We see that what has been defined as impression of reality refers less to the "reality" than to the apparatus which, although of a hallucinatory order, nonetheless founds this possibility. Reality will never appear except as relative to the images which reflect it, in some way inaugurated by a reflec- tion anterior to itself.

[4]We refer here to what Lacan says of identifications in connection with the structure determined by an optical instrument (the mirror), as they are constituted, in the prevailing figuration of the ego, as lines of resistance to the advance of the analytic work.

lously reproduces.[1] But it is not as specifically "imaginary," nor as a reproduction of its first configuration, that the self finds a "place" in the cinema. This occurs, rather, as a sort of proof or verification of that function, a solidification through repetition.

The "reality" mimed by the cinema is thus first of all that of a "self." But because the reflected image is not that of the body itself but that of a world already given as meaning, one can distinguish two levels of identification. The first, attached to the image itself, derives from the character portrayed as a center of secondary identifications, carrying an identity which constantly must be seized and reestablished. The second level permits the appearance of the first and places it "in action"—this is the transcendental subject whose place is taken by the camera which constitutes and rules the objects in the "world." Thus the spectator identifies less with what is represented, the spectacle itself, than with what stages the spectacle, makes it seen, obliging him to see what it sees: this is exactly the function taken over by the camera as a sort of relay.[2] Just as the mirror assembles the fragmented body in a sort of imaginary integration of the self, the transcendental self unites the discontinuous fragments of phenomena, of lived experience into unifying meaning. Through it each fragment assumes meaning by being integrated into an "organic" unity. Between the imaginary gathering of the fragmented body into a unity and the transcendentality of the self, giver of unifying meaning, the current is indefinitely reversible.

The ideological mechanism at work in the cinema seems thus to be concentrated in the relationship between the camera and the subject. The question is whether the former will permit the latter to constitute and seize itself in a particular mode of specular reflection. Ultimately, the forms of narrative adopted, the "contents" of the image, are of little importance so long as an identification remains possible.[3] What emerges here (in outline) is the specific function fulfilled by the cinema as support and instrument of ideology. It constitutes the "subject" by the illusory delimitation of a central location—whether this be that of a god or of any other substitute. It is an apparatus destined to obtain a precise ideological effect, necessary to the dominant ideology: creating a phantasmatization of the subject, it collaborates with a marked efficacy in the maintenance of idealism.

Thus the cinema assumes the role played throughout Western history by various artistic formations. The ideology of representation (as a principal axis orienting the notion of aesthetic "creation") and specularization (which organizes the mise-en-scène required to constitute the transcendental function) form a singularly coherent system in the cinema. Everything happens as if, the subject himself being unable—and for a reason—to account for his own situation, it was necessary to substitute

---

[1]"That the ego be 'in the right' must be avowed, from experience, to be a function of misunderstanding" (Lacan, *Ecrits* p. 637).

[2]"That it sustains itself as 'subject' means that language permits it to consider itself as the stage-hand or even the director of all the imaginary capturings of which it would otherwise only be the living marionette" (*Ibid.*, p. 637).

[3]It is on this point and in terms of the elements which we are trying to put in place that a discussion of editing could be opened. We will at a later date attempt to make some remarks on this subject.

secondary organs, grafted on to replace his own defective ones, instruments or ideological formations capable of filling his function as subject. In fact, this substitution is only possible on the condition that the instrumentation itself be hidden or repressed. Thus disturbing cinematic elements—similar, precisely, to those elements indicating the return of the repressed—signify without fail the arrival of the instrument "in flesh and blood," as in Vertov's *Man With a Movie Camera*. Both specular tranquility and the assurance of one's own identity collapse simultaneously with the revealing of the mechanism, that is, of the inscription of the film work.

The cinema can thus appear as a sort of psychic apparatus of substitution, corresponding to the model defined by the dominant ideology. The system of repression (primarily economic) has as its goal the prevention of deviations and of the active exposure of this "model."* Analogously one could say that its "unconscious" is not recognized (we speak of the apparatus and not of the content of films, which have used the unconscious in ways we know all too well). to this unconscious would be attached the mode of production of film, the process of "work" in its multiple determinations, among which must be numbered those depending on instrumentation. This is why reflections on the basic apparatus ought to be possible to integrate into a general theory of the ideology of cinema.

1970

---

*J.-D. Pollet and Phillipe Sollers' *Mediterranée* (1963), which dismantles with exemplary efficiency the "transcendental specularization" which we have attempted to delineate, gives a manifest proof of this point. The film was never able to overcome the economic blockade.

CHRISTIAN METZ
AURAL OBJECTS

ON PRIMITIVE SUBSTANTIALISM

There is a kind of primitive substantialism which is profoundly rooted in our culture (and without a doubt in other cultures as well, though not necessarily in all cultures) which distinguishes fairly rigidly the primary qualities that determine the list of objects (substances) and the secondary qualities which correspond to attributes applicable to these objects. This conception is reflected in the entire Western philosophic tradition beginning with notions put forth by Descartes and Spinoza. It is also clear that this "world view" has something to do with the subject-predicate structure particularly prevalent in Indo-European languages.

For us, the primary qualities are in general visual and tactile. Tactile because touch is traditionally the very criterion of materiality.[1] Visual because the identification processes necessary to present-day life and to production techniques rely on the eye above all the other senses (it is only in language that the auditory order is "rehabilitated," as if by compensation). The subject is too vast for this study. Nevertheless, it is possible to begin to discern certain qualities which seem to be "secondary": sounds (evoked above), olfactory qualities (a "scent" is barely an object), and even certain subdimensions of the visual order such as color.[2]

---

[1] I had already been led to this remark via a completely different route in my article "A propos de l'impression de réalité au cinéma" (1965), taken from pp. 13–24 of vol. 1 of *Essais sur la signification au cinéma* (Paris: Klincksieck, 1968), notably pp. 18–19.

[2] There is a reason why film without color, the black-and-white film, was "possible" (culturally, in relation to demand) for many years, and still is to a large extent, that the odor-film has no past or future development, that the "sound talkie" (today's usual film) is almost always more talk than sound, the noises being so impoverished and stereotyped. In fact, the only cinematographic aspects that interest everyone, and not just some specialists, are the image and speech.

313

In a clothing store, if two articles of clothing have the same cut, and are only distinguishable by color, they are considered to be "the *same* sweater (or pair of pants) in two different colors." Culture depends on the permanence of the object, language reaffirms it: only the adjective has varied. But if the two articles of clothing are the same color but have different cuts, no one will say or think that the store was offering "the same color in two different articles of clothing" (an incorrect formula, and not by accident, since color is in the grammatical position of subject). One would be more likely to say that these were "two articles of clothing," this scarf and this skirt, for example, "of the same color." The utterance put color back in its place, that of predicate: these are two distinct objects which have an attribute in common.

"OFF-SCREEN SOUND" IN THE CINEMA

The division between primary and secondary qualities plays a large role in one of the classical problems of film theory, that of "off-screen sound." In a film a sound is considered "off" (literally off the screen) when in fact it is the sound's source that is off the screen; therefore an "off-screen voice" is defined as one which belongs to a character who does not appear (visually) on the screen. We tend to forget that a sound in itself in never "off": either it is audible or it doesn't exist. When it exists, it could not possibly be situated within the interior of the rectangle or outside of it, since the nature of sounds is to diffuse themselves more or less into the entire surrounding space: sound is simultaneously "in" the screen, in front, behind, around, and throughout the entire movie theater.*

On the contrary, when a visual element is said to be "off," it really is: it can be reconstructed by inference in relation to what is visible within the rectangle, but it is not seen. A well-known example would be "the lure": the presence of a person on a side of the screen is surmised when you can only see a hand or shoulder; the rest is out of the visual field.

The situation is clear: the language used by technicians and studios, without realizing it, conceptualizes sound in a way that makes sense only for the image. We claim that we are talking about sound, but we are actually thinking of the visual image of the sound's source.

This confusion is obviously reinforced by a characteristic of sound that is physical and not social: spatial anchoring of aural events is much more vague and uncer-

---

*This relates to another characteristic fact about present-day cinema. The visual events are only "reproduced" by means of certain distortions in perspective (absence of binocular depth, the rectangular screen which distorts real vision, etc.). But auditory aspects, providing that the recording is well done, undergo no appreciable loss in relation to the corresponding sound in the real world: in principle, nothing distinguishes a gunshot heard in a film from a gunshot heard on the street. Béla Baláza, the film theoretician, used to say that "sounds have no images." Thus the sounds of a film spread into space as do sounds in life, or almost. This difference in perceptual status between what is called "reproduction" in the case of the visible, and that to which the same name has been given in the case of the audible, already seemed important to me in "Problèmes actuels de théorie du cinéma," *Essais sur la signification au cinéma,* vol. 2, pp. 57–58 and in *Langage et cinéma* (Paris: Larousse, 1971), pp. 209–10.

tain than that of visual events. The two sensory orders don't have the same relationship to space, sound's relationship being much less precise, restrictive, even when it indicates a general direction (but it rarely indicates a really precise site, which on the contrary is the rule for the visible). It is perfectly understandable that film technicians should have based their classification on the less elusive of the two elements. (However, it should be remembered that the phylogenetic choice of a particular acoustic material, the sound of the voice, for the signifiers of human language, is probably due to similar reasons: phonic communication is not interrupted by darkness or by night. You can speak to someone who is in back of you, or who is behind something, or whose location is unknown. The relatively weak relation to space provides multiple advantages which the human race would not have benefited from had a visual language been chosen.)

But, to get back to off-screen sound, the laws of physics do not adequately explain this persistent confusion between the aural object itself and the visual image of its source (yet even the most literal definition of off-screen sound rests on this confusion). There is something else behind it, something cultural that we have already encountered in this study: the conception of sound as an attribute, as a nonobject, and therefore the tendency to neglect its own characteristics in favor of those of its corresponding "substance," which in this case is the visible object, which has emitted the sound.

SEMIOLOGY AND PHENOMENOLOGY

The above heading poses an epistemological question which is not new. It seems to me that the semiological project in its entirety, because of its initial anchoring in and so on, a concern for the perceptible signifier and its perceptible transformations, defines itself in a certain way as the continuation of phenomenological inspiration. I myself have "admitted" to this necessary stage (this debt, also) in the first chapter of my first book.*

Of course, these "continuations" are also always reversals, reactions. The phenomenologists wanted to "describe" the spontaneous apprehension of things (and they sometimes did that with a correctness which will become less quickly outmoded than certain semiological overstatements). They were not sufficiently aware of the fact that this "apprehension" is in itself a product, that therefore it could very well be "otherwise" in cultures not of the describer. But (and I'm not trying to create paradoxes) it remains true that these conclusions are also beginnings. It is a great illusion of positivistic scientism to blind itself to all that is nonscientific in science, or in the effort toward science, without which it could not even exist. We are all, at some time, phenomenologists, and those who declare themselves as such at least have the merit of admitting to a certain kind of relationship to the world, which is not the only possible relationship, nor the only desirable one, but one which exists in everybody, even if it is hidden or unknown.

When I think about my own field of research, cinematographic analysis, how

---

*Essais sur la signification au cinéma, published thanks to Mikel Dufrenne. . . .

could I hide from myself—and why would I—the fact that an entire body of pre-vious cultural knowledge, without which a "first viewing" of the film would not even be a *viewing* (nor would any of the subsequent "viewings," which become more fragmented, less descriptive, and, in another sense, more "semiological")—that an entire body of knowledge already present in my immediate perception is necessarily mobilized to make it possible for me to work? And how could I miss the fact that this body of knowledge is—that it is and isn't—the "perceptual *cogito*" of phenomenology? The content is the same, the status we grant it is not.

In this study, I wanted to show that the perceptual object is a constructed unity, *socially constructed,* and also (to some extent) a linguistic unity. We find ourselves quite far, you could say, from the "adverse spectacle" of subject and object, from the cosmological as well as existential (or at least transcendental) "there is" in which phenomenology wanted to place our presence in objects, and the presence of objects in us. I am not so sure, or else this "distance" is only along certain axes, and does not imply a complete rupture of the horizon. Obviously, I spoke of semes, of pertinent optical traits, etc., that is to say, of elements whose nature is to have no lived existence and which are on the contrary—on the contrary or for that very reason?—the conditions of possibility of the lives, the structures of production which create the lived and are abolished in it, which simultaneously find in it the site of their manifestation and their negation: the objective determinants of subjec-tive feeling. To concentrate interest on this latent stratum is to stray from the phe-nomenological path. But the manifest stratum, besides the fact that it has its own reality, authorizing potential, or completed studies, is the only stratum available to us in the beginning, even though we soon leave it behind.

I have tried to understand why perception proceeds by means of objects. But I first felt, and felt strongly, that it does in fact proceed this way: phenomenologists have always made the same claim. In order for me to have tried to dismantle the "objects" which so strike the native (and at first, even in order for me to have had that desire), it was necessary that I be that native myself, and that I be struck by the same things as he. Every psychoanalytic project begins by a "phenomenology," according to the analyst's own terminology. This is true not only for this domain. Every time something is to be explained, it is more prudent to begin by experiencing it.

1975

S. M. EISENSTEIN, V. I. PUDOVKIN, AND G. V. ALEXANDROV
A STATEMENT [ON SOUND]

The dream of a sound film has come true. With the invention of a practical sound film, the Americans have placed it on the first step of substantial and rapid realization. Germany is working intensively in the same direction. The whole world is talking about the silent thing that has learned to talk.

We who work in the U.S.S.R. are aware that with our technical potential we shall not move ahead to a practical realization of the sound film in the near future. At the same time we consider it opportune to state a number of principal premises of a theoretical nature, for in the accounts of the invention it appears that this advance in films is being employed in an incorrect direction. Meanwhile, a misconception of the potentialities within this new technical discovery may not only hinder the development and perfection of the cinema as an art but also threaten to destroy all its present formal achievements.

At present, the film, working with visual images, has a powerful effect on a person and has rightfully taken one of the first places among the arts.

It is known that the basic (and only) means that has brought the cinema to such a powerfully effective strength is MONTAGE. The affirmation of montage, as the chief means of effect, has become the indisputable axiom on which the worldwide culture of the cinema has been built.

The success of Soviet films on the world's screens is due, to a significant degree, to those methods of montage which they first revealed and consolidated.

Therefore, for the further development of the cinema, the important moments will be only those that strengthen and broaden the montage methods of affecting the spectator. Examining each new discovery from this viewpoint, it is easy to show the insignificance of the color and the stereoscopic film in comparison with the vast significance of SOUND.

317

Sound recording is a two-edged invention, and it is most probable that its use will proceed along the line of least resistance, for example, along the line of *satisfying simple curiosity.*

In the first place there will be commercial exploitation of the most salable merchandise, TALKING FILMS. Those in which sound recording will proceed on a naturalistic level, exactly corresponding with the movement on the screen, and providing a certain "illusion" of talking people, of audible objects, and so on.

A first period of sensations does not injure the development of a new art, but it is the second period that is fearful in this case, a second period that will take the place of the fading virginity and purity of this first perception of new technical possibilities, and will assert an epoch of its automatic utilization for "highly cultured dramas" and other photographed performances of a theatrical sort.

To use sound in this way will destroy the culture of montage, for every ADHESION of sound to a visual montage piece increases its inertia as a montage piece, and increases the independence of its meaning—and this will undoubtedly be to the detriment of montage, operating in the first place not on the montage pieces but on the JUXTAPOSITION.

ONLY A CONTRAPUNTAL USE of sound in relation to the visual montage piece will afford a new potentiality of montage development and perfection.

THE FIRST EXPERIMENTAL WORK WITH SOUND MUST BE DIRECTED ALONG THE LINE OF ITS DISTINCT NONSYNCHRONIZATION WITH THE VISUAL IMAGES. And only such an attack will give the necessary palpability which will later lead to the creation of an ORCHESTRAL COUNTERPOINT of visual and aural images.

This new technical discovery is not an accidental moment in film history but an organic way out of a whole series of impasses that have seemed hopeless to the cultured cinematic avant-garde.

The FIRST IMPASSE is the subtitle and all the unavailing attempts to tie it into the montage composition, as a montage piece (such as breaking it up into phrases and even words, increasing and decreasing the size of type used, employing camera movement, animation, and so on).

The SECOND IMPASSE is the EXPLANATORY pieces (for example, certain inserted close-ups) that burden the montage composition and retard the tempo,.

The tasks of theme and story grow more complicated every day; attempts to solve these by methods of "visual" montage alone either lead to unsolved problems or force the director to resort to fanciful montage structures, arousing the fearsome eventuality of meaninglessness and reactionary decadence.

Sound, treated as a new montage element (as a factor divorced from the visual image), will inevitably introduce new means of enormous power to the expression and solution of the most complicated tasks that now oppress us with the impossibility of overcoming them by means of an imperfect film method, working only with visual images.

The CONTRAPUNTAL METHOD of constructing the sound film will not only not weaken the INTERNATIONAL CINEMA but will bring its significance to unprecedented power and cultural height.

Such a method for constructing the sound film will not confine it to a national market, as must happen with the photographing of plays, but will give a greater possibility than ever before for the circulation throughout the world of a filmically expressed idea.

(signed by)

S. M. Eisenstein
V. I. Pudovkin
G. V. Alexandrov

1928

JEAN-MARIE STRAUB AND DANIÈLE HUILLET
DIRECT SOUND: AN INTERVIEW

Question: Italy has, to the rest of the world, the reputation of being the country that dubs "the best." The Italians don't just dub the foreign films, but Italian ones as well: they are shot without sound, or with an international sound track, then they are dubbed. You are members of that group—and they are few enough—who film directly with sound, that is, who film the images and record at the same time the sounds of those images.

Straub: Dubbing is not only a technique, it's also an ideology. In a dubbed film, there is not the least rapport between what you see and what you hear. The dubbed cinema is the cinema of lies, mental laziness, and violence, because it gives no space to the viewer and makes him still more deaf and insensitive. In Italy, every day the people are becoming more deaf at a terrifying rate.

Huillet: The thing is still sadder when you think that it's in Italy that, in a certain sense, Western music, polyphony, was born.

Straub: The world of sound is much more vast than the visual world. Dubbing, as it is practiced in Italy, does not work with the sound to enrich it, to give more to the viewer. The greatest part of the waves that a film contains come from the sound, and if in relation to the images the sound is lazy, greedy, and puritan, what sense does that make? But then, it takes courage to make silent films.

Huillet: The great silent films gives the viewers the freedom to imagine the sound. A dubbed film doesn't even do that.

Straub: The waves that a sound transmits are not just sound waves. The waves of ideas, movements, emotions, travel across the sound. The waves that we hear in a Pasolini film, for example, are restrictive. They do not enhance the image, they kill it.

Question: There are filmmakers like Robert Bresson or, better, Jacques Tati who use dubbing intelligently. Certain Tati films would be much less rich if they didn't have an artificial sound.

320

Straub: You can make a dubbed film, but it is necessary to use a hundred times more imagination and work to make a direct-sound film. In effect, the sonorous reality that you record is so rich that to erase it and replace it with another sonorous reality (to dub a film) would take three or four times the amount of time needed to shoot the film. On the contrary, the films are usually dubbed in three days, and sometimes in a day and a half: there is no work. It would make sense to shoot without sound and then make an effort with the sound, in counterpoint to the image. But filmmakers tend to paste the background noises to the silent images that give the impression of reality, the voices that don't belong to the faces we see. It's boring, vain, and a terrible parasitism.

Question: Filming with sound costs less than dubbing.

Straub: Yes, but that would kill the dubbing industry and it violates the local customs.

Huillet: Directors prefer to dub out of laziness: if you have decided to make a film with direct sound, the locations that you choose have to be right not only in terms of the images but also in terms of the sound.

Straub: And that is translated into a thorough analysis of the whole film. For example, our last film, *Moses and Aaron,* the Schoenberg opera, we shot in the Roman amphitheater of Alba Fucense, near Avezzano, in Abruzzi. But we weren't looking for an ancient theater. What we wanted was simply a high plateau, dominated, if possible, by a mountain. We started to look for this plateau four years ago, in a borrowed car, and we put 11,000 kilometers on it, driving more on back roads and country lanes than on paved roads, through all of southern Italy, down to the middle of Sicily. In the course of this research, we didn't see one high plateau, no matter how beautiful, that was good for the sound, because when we found ourselves on a plateau, everything was lost in the air and the wind. And, if there was a valley, we were assaulted by the noises from below. We were therefore obliged to reconsider our intentions and we discovered what we wanted, which was a basin or crater. And in the end, we saw that to film in a basin, in our case the amphitheater, was better for the images also, because we had a natural theatrical space in which the subject, instead of being dissolved, was concentrated. We followed the opposite course of the Taviani brothers of Pasolini, who look for pretty spots, postcards such as you see in magazines, in which the subject of the film is dissipated instead of being localized. For us, the necessity of filming with direct sound, of recording all the singers you see in the frame, of getting at the same time their songs and their bodies that sing, led us to discoveries and we arrived at an idea that we never would have had otherwise.

Question: Filming in direct sound means also editing in a certain way, rather than in another.

Straub: That's obvious. When you film in direct sound, you can't allow yourself to play with the images: you have blocks of a certain length and you can't use the scissors any way you want, for pleasure, for effect.

Huillet: It's exactly the impossibility of playing with the editing that is discouraging. You can't edit direct sound as you edit the films you are going to dub: each image has a sound and you're forced to respect it. Even when the frame is empty, when the character leaves the shot, you can't cut, because you continue to hear, off-camera, the sound of receding footsteps. In a dubbed film, you wait only for the last piece of the foot to leave the range of the camera to cut.

THE ART OF ILLUSION

Question: Many filmmakers don't believe in an empty frame with sound that continues off-camera, because they want cinema to be a frame: it should have nothing outside. They deny the existence of a world outside the frame. In your films, the off-screen space is something that exists and is materially felt.

Straub: That's another illusion of the dubbed film. Not only are the lips that move on the screen not the ones that say the words you hear, but the space itself becomes illusionary. Filming in direct sound you can't fool with the space, you have to respect it, and in doing so offer the viewer the chance to reconstruct it, because film is made up of "extracts" of time and space. It's possible not to respect the space you are filming, but then you have to give the viewer the possibility of understanding why it has not been respected and not, as is done in dubbed films, transform a real space into a confused labyrinth and put the viewer into the confusion, from which he can no longer escape. The viewer becomes a dog who can't find its young.

Question: In sum, direct sound is not merely a technical decision but a moral and ideological one: it changes the whole film and especially the rapport that is established between the film and the viewer.

Huillet: I must say this: when you arrive at the conclusion that you must do a film like that, you cut yourself off from the industry, more or less completely. If you refuse to film with just a general sound track, if you refuse to dub your film, if you refuse to use such and such an actor because he's been seen too much and it's absurd to always use the same faces, it's over. You cut yourself off completely. In fact, the main reason for dubbing is industrial: only by accepting the dictatorship of dubbing can you use two or three stars from different countries in the same film.

Straub: And the result is an international product, something stripped of words, onto which each country grafts its respective language. Languages that don't belong to the lips, words that don't belong to the faces. But it's a product that sells well. Everything becomes illusion. There is no longer any truth. In the end, even the ideas and emotions become false. For example, in *Allonsanfan,* and I mention this film because it's not worth talking about Petri's or Lizzani's, there is not a single moment, not one instant where there is a true, human emotion. Not even by accident, by chance. It's trash. It has only the illusion of a comic book.

Question: Many filmmakers identify the international aesthetic with the popular aesthetic, and accept dubbing, stars from different countries, and the rest, because they think it's the only way to make successful films

Straub: The international aesthetic is an invention and weapon of the bourgeoisie. The popular aesthetic is always a personal aesthetic.

Question: For the bourgeoisie, there is no art that is not universal. The international aesthetic is like Esperanto.

Straub: Exactly. Esperanto has always been the dream of the bourgeoisie.

1975

JOHN BELTON
TECHNOLOGY AND AESTHETICS
OF FILM SOUND

Contemporary Marxist and psychoanalytic film theory regards technology, the evolution of technology, and the evolution of technique as products of an ideological demand that is, in turn, constituted by socioeconomic determinants.[1] Neither techniques nor technologies are natural, nor do they evolve naturally. Contrary to André Bazin's idealist notions of the history of technology and of cinematic forms, their evolution is not natural but "cultural," responding to the pressures of ideology. These pressures suppress signs of technique and technology. For Jean-Louis Baudry, the technological apparatus of the cinema, for example, the camera, transforms what is set before it but conceals the *work* of that transformation by effacing all traces of it.[2] Thus the basic apparatus reflects the actions of bourgeois ideology in general, which seeks to mask its operations and to present as "natural" that which is a product of ideology.

Recent studies of film sound by Rick Altman and Mary Ann Doane extend this argument to the study of the evolution of sound technology, viewing it as an ideologically determined progression toward self-effacement. For Altman, technological innovations "derive from a felt need to reduce all traces of the sound-work from the soundtrack."[3] And Doane argues that "technical advances in sound recording (such as the Dolby system) are aimed at diminishing the noise of the system, concealing the work of the apparatus."[4] Even though technological evolution performs

---

[1]Jean-Louis Comolli, "Technique et ideologie (part 2: Depth of Field: The Double Scene)," *Cahiers du cinéma*, nos. 229–31 (1971): 2a.2, trans. Chistopher Williams.
[2]Jean-Louis Baudry, "Ideological Effects of the Basic Cinematographic Apparatus," *Film Quarterly* 28 (Winter 1974–75):40, trans. Alan Williams.
[3]Rick Altman, "Introduction," *Cinema Sound: Yale French Studies*, no. 60 (1980):4.
[4]Mary Ann Doane, "The Voice in the Cinema: The Articulation of Body and Space," *Cinema/ Sound: Yale French Studies*, no. 60 (1980):35.

an ideological function, I would argue that the work of technology can never quite become invisible. Work, even the work that seeks to efface itself, can never disappear. A fundamental law of physics tells us that energy, though it may change in form, can be neither created nor destroyed. Neither mass nor energy nor work is ever lost. Similarly, technology and the effects of technology—by which I mean the aesthetics and stylistic practices that grow out of it—remain visible, though to varying degrees, in every film. The work of sound technology, through its very efforts to remain inaudible, announces itself and, though concealed, becomes audible for those who choose to listen for it.

Russian formalist notions of the "laying bare" of devices, whereby the work announces itself, are rooted in theories that view art as a perceptual process that derives its effects from a prolongation of the processes of perception. Consideration of the perception of sound and of the prolongation of that process thus constitutes the first step in a study of the "audibility" of the sound track.

The perception of sound is necessarily bound up with perception of the image; the two are apprehended together, though sound is often perceived *through* or *in terms of* the image and, as a result, acquires a "secondary" status. For this reason, the psychology of the image differs from that of the sound track. The viewer perceives and regards the information presented on the sound track differently from that on the image "track," though in both cases the viewer, through his/her response to visual and aural cues, plays a decisive role in the realization of the events seen and heard on the screen.

Sound recording and mixing lack the psychology of the photographic image, which guarantees the authenticity of the reproduction.[1] The camera, recording the visible world set before it, produces images that—"no matter how distorted"—remain directly motivated by that world, the automatic and mechanical nature of the process of their production generating in viewers a "quality of credibility absent from all other picture-making."[2] At the same time, the image possesses a wholeness that serves as further testimony to its "integrity." The image, as Christian Metz points out, is a unity that cannot be broken down into smaller elements.[3] The microphone, however, records an invisible world—that of the audible—which consists of different categories of sound—dialogue, sound effects, and music—and which is regularly broken down into and experienced as separate elements. Not only does sound in general possess a different psychology from that of the image, but the psychology of each category of sound differs slightly. As Metz argues, sound is experienced not as a concrete object or thing but as an attribute or characteristic of it.[4] The voice (i.e., the dialogue category) is one of several attributes of the human body, which also produces noises and sounds that fall under the category of sound

---

[1]See André Bazin. "The Ontology of the Photographic Image," *What is Cinema?*, vol. 1, trans. Hugh Gray (Berkeley: University of California Press, 1967), pp. 13–14; and Christian Metz, "On the Impression of Reality in the Cinema," *Film Language: A Semiotics of the Cinema*, trans. Michael Taylor (New York: Oxford University Press, 1974), pp. 5–6.

[2]Bazin, "Ontology," p. 13.

[3]Metz, "The Cinema: Language or Language System," *Film Language,"* pp. 61–63.

[4]Christian Metz, "Aural Objects." *Cinema/Sound: Yale French Studies*, no. 60 (1980):26–27.

effects; sound effects, in turn, are the attributes of the world and of the objects within it (and include the body as object).

Sound lacks "objectivity" (thus authenticity) not only because it is invisible but because it is an attribute and is thus incomplete in itself. Sound achieves authenticity only as a consequence of its submission to tests imposed upon it by other senses—primarily by sight. One of the conventions of sound editing confirms this. In order to assure an audience that the dialogue and/or sound effects are genuine, the editor must, as soon as possible in a scene, establish synchronization between sound and image, usually through lip-sync. Once that has been done, the editor is free to do almost anything with the picture and sound, confident that the audience now trust what they hear, since it corresponds to (or is not overtly violated by) what they see.

By the same token, dubbing, and especially the dubbing of foreign films in which one language is seen spoken but another heard, is "read" by audiences as false. As early as 1930, the industry noted "a public reaction against . . . voice doubling," forcing a discontinuation of that practice.[1] More recently, Jean Renoir, an advocate of realistic sound practices, wrote that "if we were living in the twelfth century . . . , the practitioners of dubbing would be burnt in the marketplace for heresy. Dubbing is equivalent to a belief in the duality of the soul."[2] The rather obvious intervention of technology involved with dubbing severely circumscribes our faith in both sound and image, provoking a crisis in their credibility.

This perceptual process of testing or attempting to identify sound can, through a system of delays that postpone the synchronism of sound and source, be manipulated to create suspense, both in the area of voice/dialogue and in that of sound effects, calling attention to sound as a device by playing with our perception of it. The identification of a voice with a body can be delayed, as in the case, say, of *The Wizard of Oz* (1939), in which the Wizard's unmasking occurs at the precise moment that synchronization is established; the achievement of synchronization creates a unity whose completeness spells the end of a hermeneutic chain within which an enigma is introduced, developed, prolonged, and resolved. Or in the more complex case of *Psycho* (1960), in which off-screen sound is employed to create a nonexistent character (Mrs. Bates), the particular revelation of the sound's source carefully avoids synchronism: we never see Bates speak in his mother's voice; even at the end, his/her request for a blanket comes from off-screen and his/her final monologue is interiorized. Image and sound here produce a tenuous, almost schizophrenic "synchronization" of character and voice, which precisely articulates the fragmented nature of the enigma's "resolution" and completes an "incompletable" narrative.

As for sound effects, their separation from their source can produce suspense that ranges from the familiar off-screen footsteps that stalk central characters, such as the helpless L. B. Jeffries trapped in his darkened apartment at the end of *Rear Win-*

[1]Jack Alicoate, ed., *The 1930 Film Daily Year Book of Motion Pictures* (New York: The Film Daily, 1930), p. 857.

[2]Jean Renoir, *My Life and My Films,* trans. Norman Denny (New York: Atheneum, 1974), p. 106.

dow (1954), to the mysterious noises and screeches throughout *The Haunting* (1963), whose effects, unlike the earlier example from *The Wizard of Oz,* remain unexplained and unidentified. Though off-screen diegetic sound—whether dialogue or sound effects—will, with few exceptions, ultimately be tied to seen (or unseen) sources and thus be "explained" or "identified," we experience that sound through what we see on the screen. It is an extension or completion (or even denial) of the images, but it operates on a plane that is less concrete than that of the images. One could argue that even our experience of on-screen sound involves, though in a much less extreme form, a recognition of a reality of a different order, a reality one step removed from that of the images. The sound track corresponds not, like the image track, directly to "objective reality" but rather to a secondary representation of it, that is, to the images that, in turn, guarantee the objectivity of the sounds. The sound track, in other words, does not undergo the same tests of verisimilitude to which the images are subjected. Images attain credibility in the conformation to objective reality; sounds, in their conformation to the images of that reality, to a derivative reconstruction of objective reality. The rules the sound track obeys—for the spectator at least—are not those of the visible world or of external reality to which photographic images appear to correspond point by point but those of the audible world, which occupies part of the spectrum of phenomena that remain invisible. Paradoxically, the sound track can only duplicate the invisible by means of the visible. Thus sound defines itself in terms of the temporality and spatiality of the image, observing a synchronism and/or perspective dictated by the visuals. Its mimetic processes take as a model not the pro-filmic event but the recorded image of it. The sound track does not duplicate the world set before it; it realizes an imaginary world, endowing the space and objects within the story space with another dimension that complements their temporal and spatial existence as *representations.*

What the sound track seeks to duplicate is the sound of an image, not that of the world. The evolution of sound technology and, again, that of studio recording, editing, and mixing practice illustrate, to some degree, the quest for a sound track that captures an idealized reality, a world carefully filtered to eliminate sounds that fall outside of understanding or significance; every sound must signify. In other words, the goal of sound technology in reproducing sound is to eliminate any noise that interferes with the transmission of meaningful sound. As Mary Ann Doane points out, technical developments in sound recording, after the creation of the basic technology (which was in place by 1928–29), were inspired, in part, by attempts to improve the system's signal-to-noise ratio, to reduce noise and distortion introduced by recording, developing, printing, and projection or playback practices.* During 1929–30, blimps and "bungalows" are developed to encase and thus silence cameras. By 1930, electrical circuits for arc lighting systems are devised to eliminate hum, enabling cinematographers to return from incandescent to arc lighting. Mate-

---

*Mary Ann Doane, "Ideology and the Practice of Sound Editing and Mixing," *The Cinematic Apparatus,* ed. Teresa De Lauretis and Stephen Heath (New York: St. Martin's 1980), p. 55.

rials used in the construction of sets and the design of costumes are changed to reduce excessive reverberation and rustling. Condenser microphones, which tend to "go noisy" in wet weather, are supplanted (ca. 1931) by the quieter dynamic microphone. By 1939, unidirectional microphones are designed, achieving a 10:1 ratio of "desired to undesired pickup" and effectively reducing "camera noise, floor squeaks, dolly noises, and sounds reflected from walls and other reflecting surfaces."[1] Biased recording and printing (ca. 1930–31) and push-pull recording (ca. 1935) reduce ground noise and harmonic distortion.[2] Nonslip printers (ca. 1934) further help control noise: by ensuring a more precise registration between negative and print films, they reduce the loss of quality formerly observed in the printing process. And throughout the thirties special fine-grain negative, intermediate, and print film stocks are developed, along with ultraviolet recording and printing lights (ca. 1936), producing a sharper, distortionless image on the sound track. Meanwhile, the frequency characteristics of recording and playback systems are improved from a range of 100 to 4,000 cycles per second in 1928–30 to that of 30 to 10,000 in 1938, expanding the range of the signal while holding the noise level down.[3] The evolutionary process culminates in the Dolby noise reduction and stereo sound system introduced into the cinema in 1975 in such musical films as *Tommy* and *Lisztomania*. By flattening, during recording, the response to low frequencies and boosting the highs and by reversing this process in playback, the Dolby system effectively masks out surface noise, producing a sound that is clean and that permits louder playback in the theater without increasing noise.

Yet the Dolby system also changes the characteristics of whatever sound it records, albeit only slightly. It cuts the very tops and bottoms off the sounds, resulting in a sound that is somewhat "unnatural." At the same time, the nearly total elimination of noise—the goal toward which sound technology has evolved, like that of camera movement "noise" with the perfection of the Steadicam in 1976 (see *Bound for Glory, Marathon Man, Rocky*, etc.)—results in a final product that is too perfect, that is ideal to a fault. In watching Claude Lelouch's Steadicamed opus *Another Man, Another Chance* (1977) or listening to Steven Spielberg's postrecorded and Dolbyized *Raiders of the Lost Ark* (1981), one misses the rough, jittery camera movements, floor squeaks, and unmixed, ambient sound of films like Jean Renoir's

---

[1] G. R. Groves, "The Soundman," *JSMPTE* 48, no. 13 (March 1947):223.

[2] Biased recording effectively reduces the noise of film grain by reducing the amount of light that reaches the negative. As a result, the sound track on positive prints has a darker exposure. Thus less film-grain noise is reproduced during silent or low sound level passages. Push-pull recording involves doubling the width of the track, thereby increasing the useful area of modulated light and decibel output. One variety of push-pull recording splits the track into positive and negative parts of the sound waves. As a result, there is never any transparent or clear area on the track and, thus, ground noise is eliminated.

[3] The frequency range of the human ear extends from 16 to 20,00 cycles per second. Thus evolution in this area might be said to have as its goal the range of the human ear. Unless otherwise noted, technological data in this paragraph derive from material in Groves (see note 12); Edward W. Kellogg. "History of Sound Motion Pictures, Parts I-III," *JSMPTE* 48, nos. 6–8 (June-August 1955); Barry Salt, "Film Style and Technology in the Thirties," *Film Quarterly*, 30—31 (Fall 1976).

La Chienne (1931). A certain amount of noise has become necessary to signify realism; its absence betokens a sound that has returned to an ideal state of existence, to a point just before it enters into the world and acquires the imperfections inherent in its own realization. The sound track has become artificially quiet, pushing beyond the realism of the outside world into an inner, psychological realism. The sound track duplicates what sound recordist Mark Dichter and sound designer Walter Murch refer to as the sound one hears in one's head,[1] a sound that has not been marked by any system noise nor by transmission through any medium, such as air, that might alter its fidelity to an ideal.

The technology and practice devoted to the duplication of sound's spatial properties have undergone a similar evolution, becoming unreal in a quest for realism. With the abandonment in 1927–29 of radio-style recording such as that in *The Lights of New York* (1928), in which performers speak into a stationary microphone and depth is "suggested" by changes in volume (e.g., when doors leading onto a dance floor open and close in the background), sound recording strives to model sound the way a cameraman models figures with light. The industry seeks to produce a track that reflects the space of the original scene. Carefully positioning the microphone to blend direct and reflected sound, soundmen record not only the informational "content" of an actor's speech or sound effects but also its spatial presence. The soundman, in effect, duplicates through sound the space seen on the screen: the microphone mimics the angle and distance of the camera, creating a sound perspective that matches the visual perspective of the image. The advent of wide-screen cinematography—whether the Grandeur system (1929–30), Cinerama (1952), CinemaScope (1953), or Todd-AO/70mm (1955)—provides a wider visual field for the sound track to duplicate, necessitating multiple track, stereo sound. In Fox's CinemaScope process, for example, four different tracks play on three separate speakers behind the screen and on one "surround" speaker.[2] The footsteps (or speech) of a character walking across the screen from right to left would originate first from the right horn, then from the center, and finally from the left, the source of the sound matching, point for point, the character's various positions on the screen. The final effect, however, is that of three sound perspectives rather than one. No matter how many speakers or tracks film technology develops, it can never quite duplicate the spatial qualities of the sound of the event seen on the screen. Every square inch of the screen would require a separate speaker and track to reflect the nearly limitless number of potential sources for sounds, while an infinite number of speakers and tracks would be needed to duplicate sounds emanating from off-screen space. Stereo systems that establish two, three, four, or even five sound sources, rather than creating a more perfect illusion of depth on the screen, call

---

[1] Mark Dichter, interview with Elisabeth Weis (March 1975). Walter Murch, interview with F. Paine, *University Film Association Journal,* 33, no. 4 (1981):15—20.

[2] These tracks are narratively coded. The behind-the-screen tracks contain on-screen sound while the surround track contains off-screen sound and voice-over commentary. The authority of a voice-over track is partly the result of its spatial qualities. It occupies a space that is beyond or outside that of the film, thus it can be either privileged *(Apocalypse Now)* or disadvantaged *(Days of Heaven)* in terms of its knowledge of information on the picture "track."

attention to the arbitrariness of their choice of sources. Instead of becoming better able to approximate the real and to efface its own presence, stereo sound remains marked by the nature of the system(s) it uses to create the illusion of real space. The infinite supply of original information has been *channeled* into a handful of tracks. We experience stereo soundtracks as a limited (rather than limitless) number of distinct sound sources. No matter how "noiseless" it becomes, the system never quite disappears.

At the same time, perspective undergoes stylistic as well as technological evolution. The careful correlation of aural and visual spaces achieved by Hollywood in the thirties gives way in the postwar period to the violation of perspective. Influenced in part by television sound, which tends to maintain constant close-up levels, ignoring the nuances of perspective, contemporary cinema frequently "mismatches" long shots with close-up sound, as in *The Graduate* (1967) and any number of other films that combine long shots of a car on a highway with close-up sound of its occupants conversing. The current fondness for radio mikes, seen in the work of Robert Altman and others, involves a similar disruption of traditional spatial codes in sound recording. Radio microphones pick up speech (and body tone) *before* it is projected—that is, before it can acquire spatial properties. Though it can be given some perspective during the mixing process, the quality of the sound differs from that recorded by traditional microphones hung just beyond the camera's field of view. Though it permits more freedom in shooting and ensures good sound coverage, recording with radio microphones, like mismatched perspective, lends a surfacy quality to the image, which may suit certain modern stylists such as Altman but which plays havoc with more traditional, illusionistic notions of space. By the same token, contemporary sound editing, in which the sound cut often precedes the picture cut by six to eight frames or more (e.g., *Somebody Up There Likes Me,* 1956; *The Loneliness of the Long Distance Runner,* 1962; *Jaws,* 1975; any number of contemporary Hollywood films; and even recent Robert Bresson films like *L'Argent,* 1983), violates the invisible cutting of the thirties in which the picture cut often precedes the sound cut by a frame or two, the sound bridging and thus concealing the picture cut.

It is perhaps useful to distinguish at some point between technological and stylistic evolution, which do not always share a single goal, and to acknowledge the coexistence of disparate stylistic uses of a single technology. Theories of technological evolution are shaped by Darwinian notions of advancement and self-perfection; the tools that an artist (or culture) uses become more and more perfect, developing from lower into higher forms. But theories of stylistic evolution such as Bazin's are informed, in large part, by the "mimetic fallacy," and are clearly more problematical. As Heinrich Wolfflin argues, "It is a mistake [for art history] to work with the clumsy notion of the imitation of nature, as though it were merely a homogeneous process of increasing perfection."* For that matter, can art or even artists themselves be said to possess goals that it/they seek to realize? Is not that notion the height of idealistic thinking? As Jean-Louis-Comolli has shown, Bazinian theories

---

*Heinrich Wolfflin, *Principles of Art History* (New York: Dover, n.d.), 13.

of the evolution of cinematic forms are essentially idealistic reconstructions of film history that fail to account for delays, gaps, and contradictions in their development.[1] Given that cinematic forms do not necessarily evolve in the direction of qualities that enable "a recreation of the world in its own image,"[2] can they be said to improve, or to perfect themselves over time? Is the style of a Fassbinder better or even more evolved than that of a Griffith? Is that of Picasso better than that of Rembrandt? No; it is merely *different,* reflecting the different technological, socioeconomic, and cultural systems within which each artist worked. If development can be gauged at all, it is not to be found in the comparison of individual artists or works but in that of different schools, groups, or periods, as Wölfflin has demonstrated. It is only in the area of dominant practice—the point of intersection between the timeliness of technology and the timelessness of style, between tools and cultural/individual expression—that change can be charted and given a goal.

At each stage along the axis of technological development, recording, editing, and mixing practices change in response to linear changes in technology and to unpredictable shifts in stylistic concerns of a period, nation, or group of individuals. Thus dominant film practice conforms, more or less, to the direction taken by the technology that informs it, that is, toward self-perfection and invisibility, *and* to the attitudes of those who use that technology, attitudes that color its "invisibility."

Developments in the area of sound recording—especially in the use of radio microphones and Dolby—point, as we have seen, in the direction of the ideal: they culminate in the sounds one hears in one's head. Changes in editing and mixing practice reflect an increase in control over the sound track and in its ability to duplicate the sound not of the pro-filmic event but of that event's photographic image. The initial practice (ca. 1926–29) of mixing sound while it is being recorded and recording it (except for music that was often added later) at the same time that the image is recorded locks the sound indexically into the pro-filmic event of which it is the record, giving it an immediacy and integrity resembling that of the image. The introduction of rerecording and mixing in the early thirties breaks that indexical bond of sound to the pro-filmic event. Mixing now takes place *after* the film has been shot (and often even after it has been edited) during the phase of postproduction. At the same time, the sound track loses its wholeness: it is separated into dialogue, sound effects, and music tracks that are recorded at different times, dialogue and some sound effects being recorded during production, other sound effects, music, and even some dialogue during postproduction. Whereas initially the sound track was "recorded," now it is "built." Sound mixing no longer observes the integrity of any preexistent reality; it builds its own to match earlier recorded visual information. The growth of postproduction departments within the studio system institutionalizes the separation of sound and image that frees the former from its ties to the events that produced the latter. The building of the sound track, using the image rather than the pro-filmic event as a guide, now becomes a final stage in the "realization" of the image.

During the postwar period, even the recording of dialogue, which is traditionally

[1]Comolli, "Technique et ideologie," 1.7–1.17.
[2]Bazin, "The Myth of Total Cinema," *What Is Cinema?* vol. 1, p. 21.

tied, through concerns for synchronization, to the moment at which the image is recorded, is freed from its bonds to the pro-filmic event. The use of wide-angle lenses (which provide a wide field of view and thus force the microphone further away from its target, resulting in a less acceptable sound) and the practice of shooting on location (where ambient noise cannot be controlled as well as in the studio) result in the use of the "production" sound track as a guide track to cue the actor's dialogue during looping sessions back at the studio. The original track, at times, functions merely as a blueprint for an entirely new track created on the sound stage to match an image that has already been assembled in rough cut form. Again, changing practice reveals that it is the sound of the image that Hollywood strives to recreate.

Neither the cinematic institution, seen in its practices, nor the cinematic apparatus possesses a single identity. Practice seeks to produce a more realistic sound track by "unrealizing" its recording and rerecording methods. Its final product is thus marked as a product. Although Baudry and others argue to the contrary, the cinema never quite succeeds in masking the work that produces it. This is due, in large part, to the very nature of the apparatus itself. The recording aspects of motion picture technology possess dual characteristics: they both transmit and transform. Though the cinematic apparatus becomes, decade by decade, a more perfect transmitter, reducing signs of its own existence by eliminating its system's noise, it inevitably reproduces not only the light and sound waves reflected and emitted by objective reality but also its own presence, which is represented by the perspective from which these waves are seen or heard. In the cinema, there is always present, in the positioning of the camera and the microphone(s), a consciousness that sees and (in the sound film) hears and that coexists with what is seen or heard. Even in the silent cinema, someone is always speaking and something is always spoken. In the sound cinema, we always see and hear events *through* images and sounds of them. The cinema remains the phenomenological art par excellence, wedding, if indeed not collapsing, consciousness with the world.

1985

CHARLES AFFRON
FROM CINEMA AND SENTIMENT

VOICE AND SPACE

SPEAKING OUT

A viewer expects characters to speak in sound films, and that expectation is a strong element of affectivity in talkies whose protagonists are mute *(The Spiral Staircase, The Miracle Worker, The Heart Is a Lonely Hunter)* or for whom speech is problematic *(The Bride of Frankenstein,* the Tarzan series, Chaplin's first talkies).[1] Peter Brooks gives muteness a privileged position in his melodramaturgy. Accounting for different kinds of drama in terms of "their corresponding sense deprivations," he designates muteness as being appropriate for melodrama "since melodrama is about expression," the particular fullness of expression that accommodates the fullness of meaning, the "pure moral and psychological integers" that are the genre's concern.[2] This fullness, requiring a reading of texts oversaturated with codes, is exhibited in Jean Negulesco's *Johnny Belinda* when the deaf-mute Belinda (Jane Wyman) signs the Lord's Prayer over her dead father while the doctor (Lew Ayres) speaks the words. The magnified image filled with gestural and oral discourse fills us with the movies' silent and "talked" voices. Here, muteness and speech, in their emphatic juxtaposition, test each other's expressive power, their adequacy to articulate feelings for which most discourse is inadequate. Stanley Cavell describes the effect achieved when the wordless integrity of mime is breached by excesses of feeling in Marcel Carné's *Children of Paradise,* a sound film about

---

[1]Frank McConnell, *The Spoken Seen: Film and the Romantic Imagination,* (Baltimore: Johns Hopkins University Press, 1975), pp. 57–71. McConnell examines the affectivity of momentous utterance in these and other films.

[2]Peter Brooks, *The Melodramatic Imagination* (New York: Columbia University Press), 1985, 56–57.

theatrical registers ranging from tragedy to pantomime. "The speaking of the word in those times and at those places collects to itself the fantasies it expresses and shatters them against the reality it shatters."[1]

These plays of muteness exploit the virtuality of sound in a medium some of whose basic visual conventions emanate from speech and audition. The shot/countershot pattern of classic decoupage insistently propels locution from interlocutor to interlocutor. Meaning in sound films is often conveyed through the imaging of aural configurations: "talking" faces, conversational two-shots, shouting mobs, political forums, on-screen representations of theatrical performances. (I do not mean to suggest that silent films are less reverberant than sound films. Many viewers tend to forget that silent films were not really silent at all, and that the human presence of the piano player, or that of other agents, musical and narrational, during the projection of films prior to the talkies provided aural mediation and reverberation for the screen image.) Signs of audition are repeatedly pictured on film: telephones, telephone lines, radios, microphones, mass meetings, responsive audiences. These are signs of the power of sound and of sound being powered.

A voice must be powered so that it will be heard.[2] The relationship between power and voice is exemplified by the singing voice that fills a vast auditorium, projecting the individual performer through space to thousands of auditors. The voices of opera singers project presence through power, presence that deeply moves audiences, filling them with sound and feeling. Pleasure is often derived from perceiving what appears to be the effortless emission of a tone that simultaneously fills one's head and the yawning space of the theater. The voice of the "little" soprano resonates through the Metropolitan Opera House, passing over a hundred-piece orchestra; the sturdy-lunged and chested heroic tenor holds a high note in what seems as much an athletic feat as an artistic one.

The enthusiasm for voice is demonstrated near the conclusion of W. S. Van Dyke's *San Francisco*. Mary's (Jeanette MacDonald's) operatic voice lends itself to ragtime and other popular music styles, and inspires the in-film audience to join her in a joyous rendition of the film's title song. This is topped moments later by the spectacularly staged earthquake. At the film's climax, Blackie (Clark Gable) searches the ruined city for Mary. He witnesses scenes of despair, of happy reunion, of grief. When he finds her out of danger, singing hymns to console the disaster victims, he sinks to his knees in a prayer of thanks, his face streaming with tears. Others join their voices to Mary's, filling the sound track and filling the frame, marching ahead toward a new city rising from the ruins, made to rise from the ruins through the power of movie editing and of voice.

In the present era, whose popular music is a function of electronic amplification, the decibel level generated by the Rolling Stones and other groups in arenas and ball parks incites audiences to hysterical manifestations of approval. The affect of this phenomenon is repeatedly displayed in "performance" films *(Gimme Shelter, The Last Waltz)* and dramatized in *The Rose,* where the star singer (Bette Midler)

---

[1]Stanley Cavell, *The World Viewed* (New York: Viking, 1971), p. 152.
[2]Walter J. Ong, *The Presence of the Word* (New Haven: Yale University Press, 1967). Ong, p. 112, states, "Being powered projections, spoken words themselves have an aura of power."

is finally destroyed by the sound of her own voice. The frenzy of life she expresses in her songs accumulates in the screams of her public, and its repercussions overwhelm her in their violence. The megaphones of Greek tragedians, Jeanette MacDonald's high notes, and the loudspeakers of Mick Jagger, Janis Joplin, and Bette Midler increase an audience's hunger for the enthusiasm "carried" by the magnified voice.

The importance of powered sound among the codes of cinema has become a prime industrial consideration. Audiences are now dolbyized and sensurrounded; an enormous percentage of a film's production budget is allocated to the sound track. It is not too farfetched to suggest that the movie industry is putting its money where its mouth is because that is what the public wants to hear. But even without modern sound technology, film has employed fictional and visual magnifying systems to create a sense of rich vocal resonance. The opening of *How Green Was My Valley,* with its narrative voice-over, establishes a temporal echo that is almost immediately visualized in the hero's first recollection, that of his voice, as a little boy, echoing in answer to his sister's, reverberating across the once green valley. In this film about family links, the first is made when names are powered by lungs and throats, filling the space with identity and presence. These echoes are internalized by the film's fictional ploys, and literally so when Hew, searching for his father in the caved-in mine, "reaches" the trapped man through his echoing voice. In a medium whose primary means of expression is visual, voice serves when eyes fail.

VOICES IN CLOSE-UP

Magnification turns the mechanics of sound emission, of speech, into a highly visual act of expression. How then does this expressive medium preserve the ontological interiority of speech? If, as Ong asserts, "sound . . . reveals the interior without the necessity of physical invasion," and "to discover such things by sight we should have to open what we examine, making the inside an outside, destroying its interiority as such,"* does not the visualization of sound imperil its essential interiority? In fact, the levels and planes of depth that I have been attempting to locate in the processes of cinematic production and reception do provide for areas that can be characerized as interior to other areas, that provide the viewer's perception a dynamics that can be described as penetration, going toward the interior core of the mise-en-scène, the performer, the word. It is as if there were an interior within the expressed sound, behind the screen. The screen, in its utter superficiality, provides a jumping-off point, a readily identifiable locus of flatness that hovers above the various depths of which it is the illusory representation. We then perceive states of inwardness between the flat image on the flat screen and a wide range of utterance, vocality, reverberation.

In Elia Kazan's *A Tree Grows in Brooklyn,* Francie (Peggy Ann Garner), the mediator, generates the fiction through her coming of age, her ever-more urgent literary vocation, and her increasing ability to sort out the echoes of the said and

---

*Ong, p. 118.

the unsaid. The way we assimilate the film is posited on the paradox of a narrator whose own relationship to speech is problematic. Her mother, a hard-nosed pragmatist, says, "Francie, why don't you say what you mean?", her father lends an ear to the girl's whispered effusion, "My cup runneth over." Caught between her imprecisions and her clichés, Francie identifies a rhetorical crisis in which sentiment is challenged by vocal expression.

In this demonstrative medium, any effort to hide has the countereffect of disclosure, and this holds for speech as well as for action. Whatever a character's subterfuges, the cinema's power of exposure trumpets intimacy. Both the excessively sweet voice of fantasy and "soul," and the excessively hard one of necessity and money are tested in the stagings of *A Tree Grows in Brooklyn*. Francie's father, Johnny (James Dunn), is an alcoholic, often an unemployed singing waiter who habitually announces his arrival home with his voice resounding through the tenement staircase; the family's meager living is earned by Francie's hardworking mother, Katie (Dorothy McGuire), who scrubs that staircase. A moment of happy remembrance and hope that unites the couple on a window sill is shattered when the crescendo of the pipe-dreamer's fabrications snaps the pragmatist back to harsh reality. "Stop it—stop talking." The railroad flat, with its partitions and tight little compartments, becomes then a site for disunion. Later, the distance between Johnnie and Katie in yet a smaller flat is vocalized when he, angry at her cold response to the death of a neighbor's child, defiantly sits at their piano and sings "Annie Laurie" while she angrily nails the family's tin can bank to the floor.

After Johnny's sacrificial death Francie comes to disapprove of her mother's money-grubbing, critical ways. But in the pain preceding the birth of Johnny's posthumous child, it is Katie's voice that makes remarkable sense out of the film's rather pat distinctions. A series of shots brings the mother and daughter closer together in the darkened bedroom while Francie reads the story she has written about Johnny. Here, the casting of Dorothy McGuire is fully exploited. Her characteristic softness of voice and manner, subverted through the body of the film, is released by the pain of labor and her grief and loneliness. Katie, established in close-ups and in compositions that emphasize her stiffness of body and mind, her distance from a dreamy husband and an expansively loving sister (Joan Blondell), is now altered by the scrutiny of a daughter who sees her as she has never seen her before and by a camera that captures the intimacy of a bedside confession. The audience, previously denied the fey charm and lilting voice of the star of *Claudia,* is finally rewarded with McGuire's immediately identifiable aural persona, a softness of utterance that is the sum of other soft voices previously heard in the film, and that now relates the pain of confession to the pain of repression and need.

The relationship between the star's aural personality and the locus of confession is demonstrated near the climax of Richard Boleslawski's *The Garden of Allah.* Charles Boyer, identifiable for the richness of his voice, plays a man who has left a Trappist monastery and has broken his vow of silence. He finally confesses his secret to his wife (Marlene Dietrich) in the limitless expanse of desert sand and desert sky. Given the particular fictions of *A Tree Grows in Brooklyn* (family drama) and *The Garden of Allah* ("transcendental" romance), it is not remarkable that their respective confessions take place in a bedroom and on a sand dune. Yet it is significant that we should be privy to their enactments in a medium that extracts intimacy from both loci and from the mere fact that they are spoken by these particular performers.

The particularity of cinema voices, powered by the presence of the performer, the microphone, and the loudspeaker, is further magnified by a stylistics of display. In close-up, Garbos's sigh and Garland's tremulous high note exploit the medium's visual and aural power through the ironic disproportion between the intimacy of utterance and the expanse of revelation. This disproportion is heightened in telephone scenes, where voice is simultaneously directed to the single, private ear of the receiver and to the collective, public ear of the audience. Cinema has an affinity for the telephone and its figurations of intimate discourse. From the rat-tat-tat newspaper yarns to the opening sequence of Edmund Gouldings's *Grand Hotel,* where the narrative is literally plugged into a gigantic switchboard, the telephone conveys words from mouth to ear, apparently bypassing the reverberation of ambient space. Garbo in *Grand Hotel* (she transforms the receiver into a surrogate lover), Luise Rainer in *The Great Ziegfeld* (the scene won her an Oscar), Anna Magnani in *La voce umana* (for almost the whole of the film the actress is on the phone, an object that becomes all the fiction and all her life), Liza Minnelli in *The Sterile Cuckoo* (the actress's hysteria is generated by the uninterrupted trajectory of phone call and shot), Bette Midler in *The Rose* (the singer whose voice is habitually transmitted to thousands of screaming fans in the vast expanses of arenas is pathetically isolated in a phone booth, in front of a vast, empty football stadium) exploit the double standard of telephone scrutiny in cinema. The spectator has access to the face denied the listener at the other end of the line. Capra, with great virtuosity, uses a single telephone receiver to force two characters to express the depth of their feelings for each other. In *It's a Wonderful Life,* George and Mary (Donna Reed), who have just argued, violently embrace when the receiver they have been sharing brings them into the proximity they have been avoiding during the sequence. Here, and in more conventional situations, the receiver elicits secret utterance. We share in the secrets of this surrogate for the microphone, this object that concentrates the performer's presence in voice. The concentration is further projected in visual close-up onto the screen—a close-up that is a visual analogy for the aural close-up produced by the phone and microphone.

Roland Barthes, in his hedonics of art, declares:

> It suffices that the cinema capture the sound of speech *close up* . . . and make us hear in their materiality, their sensuality, the breath, the gutturals, the fleshiness of the lips, a whole presence of the human muzzle . . . to succeed in shifting the signified a great distance and in throwing, so to speak, the anonymous body of the actor into my ear: it granulates, it crackles, it caresses, it grates, it cuts, it comes: that is bliss.[1]

Basing his argument on Julia Kristeva's formulation of *geno-song,*[2] "the space where significations germinate 'from within the language and in its very materiality'

[1]Roland Barthes, *Pleasure of the Text,* (New York: Hill and Wang, 1975), p. 67.
[2]Julia Kristeva, *Sémiotike: Recherches pour une sémianalyse* (Paris: Seuil, 1969), pp. 278–89.

... that apex (or that depth) of production where the melody really works at the language."[1] Barthes locates pleasure in perceiving "the *grain* of the voice," a vocal physicality, the precise placing of the voice in the emitting body, "the language lined with flesh."[2] The close-up makes it difficult, perhaps fruitless, to distinguish between the iconographic value of the star's face and that of the star's voice, or to argue that performers become stars because their vocal and physical aspects match. The cinematic apparatus matches them for us. Yet the vocal/aural entity, the star's immediately identifiable personality, is as much dependent on the phonogenic "grain of the voice" as it is on the photogenic configuration of body and face. In the first years of talking film, the microphone was merciless to stage actors unable to rid themselves of the projective technique, the excessively refined diction, the pearl-shaped tones (satirized in the voice lesson sequences of *Singin' in the Rain*) necessary to make oneself heard in large theaters. In her second talkie, *Romance,* Garbo pitches her voice to the close-up ear of the microphone while her co-star, Gavin Gordon, does all he can to reach the last row of a hypothetical second balcony. At the movies, we are often closer to the speaker than are the other in-frame performers.

The apparatus of sound reproduction allows the screen performer to expose the particularities of voice at its source of emission, what Barthes calls "the human muzzle," that vulnerable and highly expressive area of the face adjacent to the eyes. Resonance becomes as palpable and luminous as the gleam in the eye. The stage actor, relying on the acoustics of the theater, breath support, enunciation, and pitch, exteriorizes voice over great distances. This factor counts less in films, where a speech defect (Kay Francis), a foreign accent (Dietrich, Garbo), a vocal tic (James Stewart) can, and often has, constituted a performer's memorable vocal personality. And what nuances those personalities impart to our experience of film: Irene Dunne's quasisung heroine of *Back Street* (1932), a model of evenness and control; Margaret Sullavan's version (1941) of the same role, high-strung, a bit neurotic, her voice always on the verge of breaking; Mae West's baritonal vamp; Marilyn Monroe, whose breathiness puts words right in the listener's ear; the depth of Charles Boyer's accented basso cantante, a range adequate to his desire to tell the deepest secrets to the woman he loves; the staccato rhythm of Jimmy Cagney's speech-punctuated gait.[3]

VOICE AND NARRATIVITY

The relationship between voice and the oral tradition of fiction has been widely discussed in recent narrative criticism, where it is traced to the sagas and the *chan-*

---

[1] Barthes, *Image—Music—Text,* p. 182.
[2] Barthes, *Pleasure of the Text,* p. 66.
[3] Gerald Mast, in *Film/Cinema/Movie: A Theory of Experience* (New York: Harper & Row, 1977), pp. 206–37, is particularly sensitive to movie voices. He is one of the few critics to have paid sustained attention to sound in cinema.

sons de geste.[1] The voice of the bard validated fiction: it served to establish a life-bearing presence in the fictional system. It was always *here,* reverberant as is sound in the movie theater, and it brought fictions *here* from *there,* from sources that were elsewhere temporally and often spatially. Today too our belief in fiction is promoted by the presence of the speaker's voice.

The presence of visualized sound is operant even in silent films, where the mere picturing of speaker and audience is enough to suggest much of what we *ought* to hear and to inspire in us the belief that silent speech can be heard. Lars Hansen moves his congregations in Stiller's *The Saga of Gösta Berling* and Seastrom's *The Scarlet Letter;* Brigitte Helm incites to prayer and to riot as the true and false Maria in Lang's *Metropolis.* The modes of vocalization that naturally manifest themselves in all talkies convey the "sound" of voice in "silent" films through gesticulation and audience expectation. But whether silent or sounded, both apparent and actual vocalizations animate the fictions of cinema through their visual/aural resonance. The presence of voice, whether seen or heard, helps power much of cinema's narrative thrust. Our ability to follow a narrative line and to make sense of a story is not primarily a visual process, but a verbal one. Verbality is made resonant by images that the words string together in a narrative.

Vocal persuasion is contiguous to storytelling in the work of Frank Capra, where the single speaker who engages the belief of a single auditor and eventually of an audience is a recurrent figure, where the fiction's obsessive enactments of persuasion serve as models for the spectator's belief in fiction. The director's concern with the status of the democratic man in the democratic community is echoed by the agent that produces echo—the sounded voice. Ong states that "voice has a kind of primacy in the formation of true communities of men, groups of individuals constituted by shared awareness. A common language is essential for a real community to form."[2] In the characteristic Capra narrative, the hero—Mr. Deeds, Mr. Smith, John Doe—speaks in order to be heeded by the diffuse body of listeners that becomes a community when it understands the hero's language and truly hears his voice. The community imaged on film and the audience in the movie theater are held in the thrall of vocal/fictional persuasion and of fictions ranging from the American Dream to the films of Frank Capra.

The parameters of cinematic space defined by the persuasive narrativity of voice are projected by an early Capra film, *The Miracle Woman* (1931). Florence, the protagonist (Barbara Stanwyck), reads the sermon prepared by her father, a text that she interrupts with the announcement that he died in her arms five minutes before. She goes on to harangue the heartless congregation that, unable to silence her, walks out of the church in protest. One man stays and applauds her ability to "move" her audience, a talent that will be put to the service of a highly emotive and lucrative faith-healing act. Florence becomes a fiction of miracle, a fiction that instills belief in her listeners. Her voice tests credulity in a variety of contexts; the

[1]See Robert Scholes and Robert Kellogg, *The Nature of Narrative* (London and New York: Oxford University Press, 1966), pp. 17–56 and bibliography.
[2]Ong, p. 24.

blind hero (a composer) is prevented from committing suicide when he hears her voice over the radio; she complains to her accomplice that her circuslike act will fail if she perceives the planted "cures" in the audience to be fakes; her voice is visualized in the cut-out letters of the alphabet with which she writes to the blind man. When Florence decides to speak the truth to her congregation, her accomplice tries to silence her by turning off the lights, causing a fire to break out in her tabernacle. Florence's voice then refills the space, transforms it, and calms the panicking crowd. In the darkness of the blind hero, in the hypocritical response of the first congregation, and in the various levels of belief to which she inspires her followers, Florence's voice defines its areas of aural and fictional resonance and engages us in the integrity of those definitions.

The sound of Stanwyck's voice is endowed with similar power in other films she made for Capra; a voice that transcends the words it utters to involve the warlord General Yen (Nils Asther) in the myth of Christian charity ("When you ask me like that I forget I am General Yen"), a voice, mimicking that of the director himself, that elicits from John Doe the required expression of anger for a press photograph. It is Walter Huston's voice, in *American Madness,* that quells a riot and restores order to the precisely delimited space of the bank. Claudette Colbert, the "poor little rich girl," finds her identity, her voice, and true love when she sings with "just plain folks" on a democratic bus ride in *It Happened One Night.* Mr. Deeds (Gary Cooper), the rhymster, remains silent at his sanity hearing. When finally he yields to the constant urgings that he speak to identify himself, his voice makes sense out of the courtroom and the community it presumably validates. *Meet John Doe* is the story of a man created by words, "a typical American who can keep his mouth shut." John's reticence at giving voice to words that are not his is intensified by the vocal persona of Gary Cooper, the prototypical "strong, silent" type of American films in the thirties (a persona no less operant for its failure to take into account Cooper's verbal epertise in the repartee of comedies such as *Design for Living, Desire,* and *Bluebeard's Eighth Wife*). In *Meet John Doe* it is the response of the studio audience that spurs him to eloquence during his first radio speech. The sound of that voice is intercut with shots of the writer (Barbara Stanwyck), who overflows with feeling at hearing her words (the words she drew from her dead father's diary) uttered with such sincerity. This spatial figure of voice and audition enacted in the confines of the radio studio is both amplified and shattered when John Doe, at last about to speak the truth to his credulous admirers (much like the Miracle Woman), is silenced when the wires to his microphone are cut. His single, unamplified voice is lost in the sea of umbrellas that fills the rain-drenched ball park. At the film's conclusion the power of voice is restored; the writer voices her own words, whose fervor prevents John's suicide. In their evocation of the original preacher/persuader/miracle man, Jesus, they are words that assert the basis of their own fictive power, the power of belief.

In Capra's films the political, social, and ethical systems that identify the protagonists are clearly spatialized by the voices that resonate within them, from the Miracle Woman's fake tabernacle to John Doe's ball park. The presidential candidate (Spencer Tracy) proclaims his political dishonesty and his love for his wife (Katherine Hepburn) over nationwide television *(State of the Union).* George Bailey, the hero of *It's a Wonderful Life* (a film that begins, quite literally, with voices in space), is made partially deaf, as a boy, when he speaks a "painful" truth; as a grown man he tries in vain to speak his life to his mother (Beulah Bondi), wife, and friends when they refuse to acknowledge that he has lived. At the conclusion of *It's a Wonderful Life* the quintessential American living room seems to be packed with the whole population of the quintessential American town. Centrifugal to the community at large, the tight enclosure radiates from the hero whose presence is both singular and plural and whose voice is the voice that sums those of "the man on the street." That individual voice, the primary locus, animates and makes resonant the space of the film and the other figures in the film. When George Bailey runs through is town, exulting over the recovery of his "wonderful life," he consecrates the streets and houses that are then resumed, crammed into, made to explode inside the living room, the ultimate home for the hero of family and community. Hero and community are voiced through the singing of the Christmas carols and "Auld Lang Syne."*

Much of our response to this particular sequence is elicited by Capra's invitations to us, the film audience, to "join in," just as the townspeople join their voices to celebrate George's presence. That is indeed what he is celebrating—the recovery of his presence after having been made to experience a fiction of his own absence, his deidentification to those he knows and loves. Everyone in the Bailey living room gives George money and voice, pays admission as it were, confers value on being there as witness to George's life, as we have paid our way into the theater and paid attention to the film. Even the skeptical sheriff and the man from the auditor's office (officials of the society that seems to threaten George) are moved to add their money and voices to the contributions and the songs, as we join in with our pleasure at watching the film.

1982

---

*Cavell, in *World Viewed*, p. 190, writes, "The sentiment in the scene is very deep. It has been constructed as cunningly as a Keaton gag; what caps it, finally bursting the dam of tears, is the crowding of this band of goodness into this hero's house, each member testifying indivdually to his or her affection for him; so that the good society, the good of society at large, is pictured as this man's family (personally sponsored, what's more, by a denizen of heaven)."

JOHN ELLIS
FROM VISIBLE FICTIONS

BROADCAST TV AS SOUND AND IMAGE

TV offers a radically different image from cinema, and a different relation between sound and image. The TV image is of a lower quality than the cinematic image in terms of its resolution of detail. It is far more apparent that the broadcast TV picture is composed of lines than it is that the cinema image is composed of particles of silver compounds. Not only this, but the TV image is virtually always substantially smaller than the cinema image. Characteristically, the size of TV sets ranges from the 12-inch portable to the 24-inch or sometimes 30-inch model: all these measurements refer to the distance across the screen diagonally. The TV image shows things smaller than they are, unless it is a close-up of a small object, or of a person in head and shoulders only, when they appear more or less their real size. Such simple observations have profound effects on the kind of representations and spectator attitudes that broadcast TV creates for itself.

First, it is a characteristic of broadcast TV that the viewer is larger than the image: the opposite of cinema. It seems to be a convention also that the TV image is looked down on, rather than up to as in cinema. TV sets that are produced with stands are about two feet off the floor, which gives the effect of being almost but not quite level with the eyes of an individual lounging in an easy chair (as indeed we are meant to watch TV according to the advertisements it screens for itself). TV takes place in domestic surroundings, and is usually viewed in normal light conditions, though direct sunlight reflects off the screen to an unacceptable degree. The regime of viewing TV is thus very different from the cinema: TV does not encourage the same degree of spectator concentration. There is no surrounding darkness, no anonymity of the fellow viewers, no large image, no lack of movement amongst the spectators, no rapt attention. TV is not usually the only thing going on, sometimes it is not even the principal thing. TV is treated casually rather than concentratedly. It is something of a last resort ('What's on TV tonight, then') rather than a special event.

It has a lower degree of sustained concentration from its viewers, but a more extended period of watching and more frequent use than cinema.

This has two major effects on the kind of regime of represenation that has developed for TV. First, the role that sound plays in TV is extremely imporant. Second, it engages the look and the glance rather than the gaze, and thus has a different relation to voyeurism from cinema's. Sound on TV is a strange paradox; although it is manifestly important, the manufacturers of TV sets provide speakers of dismal quality, even though the broadcast sound signal in many places has a wide tonal range. TV sets come with speakers that are massively geared towards the acceptable reproduction of speech. Music, especially rock music, does not reproduce at all well. This provides an alibi for broadcast TV to provide a minimum of rock music, and to provide the wasteful simultaneous stereo radio and TV transmissions of classical music on occasions.

The role played by sound stems from the fact that it radiates in all directions, whereas view of the TV image is sometimes restricted. Direct eye contact is needed with the TV screen. Sound can be heard where the screen cannot be seen. So sound is used to ensure a certain level of attention, to drag viewers back to looking at the set. Hence the importance of programme announcements and signature tunes and, to some extent, of music in various kinds of series. Sound holds attention more consistently than image, and provides a continuity that holds across momentary lapses of attention. The result is a slightly different balance between sound and image from that which is characeristic of cinema. Cinema is guaranteed a centred viewer by the physical arrangement of cinema seats and customs of film viewing. Sound therefore follows the image or diverges from it. The image is the central reference in cinema. But for TV, sound has a more centrally defining role. Sound carries the fiction or the documentary; the image has a more illustrative function. The TV image tends to be simple and straightforward, stripped of detail and excess of meanings. Sound tends to carry the details (background noises, music). This is a tendency towards a different sound/image balance than in cinema, rather than a marked and consistent difference. Broadcast TV has areas which tend towards the cinematic, especially the areas of serious drama or of various kinds of TV film. But many of TV's characteristic broadcast forms rely upon sound as the major carrier of information and the major means of ensuring continuity of attention. The news broadcast, the documentary with voice-over commentary, the bulk of TV comedy shows, all display a greater reliance on sound than any form that cinema has developed for itself. The image becomes illustration, and only occasionally provides material that is not covered by the sound track (e.g., comedy sight gags, news actuality footage). Sound tends to anchor meaning on TV, where the image tends to anchor it with cinema. In both, these are a matter of emphasis rather than any simple reliance one upon another. Sound and image exist in relation to each other in each medium rather than acting as separate entities. However, the difference of emphasis does exist between the two. It gives rise to two critical attitudes that are fundamental to the way in which newspaper critics and practitioners alike tend to conceive of the two media. Any film that contains a large amount of dialogue is open to the criticism that 'it could have been a radio play', as was Bergman's *From the Life of Marionettes (Aus dem Leben der Marionetten,* 1980). A similar accusation is never hurled at a TV play, however wordy. Instead, there are unwritten rules that govern the image for TV. Especially in British broadcast TV (possibly the most hide-bound in the world), the image is to be kept literal for almost all the time. There are licensed exceptions (science fiction, rock music programmes) where experimentation with the physical composition of the video image can take place; but the rule is that the image must show whatever is before the camera with the minimum of fuss and conscious technique. The image is to be kept in its place. Both these attitudes refer to occasions in which the subservient partner in the sound/image relationship tends to assert itself too much: for cinema, it is sound; for TV it is the image.

TV's lower level of sustained concentration on the image has had another effect upon its characteristic regime of representation. The image on broadcast TV, being a lower grade image than cinema's, has developed in a particular way. Contrasting with cinema's profusion (and sometimes excess) of detail, broadcast TV's image is stripped-down, lacking in detail. The visual effects of this are immediately apparent: the fussy detail of a film shown on TV compared to the visual bareness of a TV cop series, where cars chase each other through endless urban wastes of bare walls and near-deserted streets. The broadcast TV image has to be certain that its meaning is obvious: the streets are almost empty so that the movement of the car is all the more obvious. The walls are bare so that no writing distracts attention from the segmental event. This is not an effect of parsimony of production investment (rather, it enables it to happen). It is a more fundamental aspect of the broadcast TV image coming to terms with itself. Being small, low definition, subject to attention that will not be sustained, the TV image becomes jealous of its meaning. It is unwilling to waste it on details and inessentials. So background and context tend to be sketched rather than brought forward and subject to a certain fetishism of details that often occurs in cinema, especially art cinema. The narratively important detail is stressed by this lack of other detail. Sometimes, it is also stressed by music, producing an emphasis that seems entirely acceptable on TV, yet would seem ludicrously heavy-handed in cinema. This is particularly so with American crime series, where speed of action and transition from one segment to another dictates the concentration of resources on to single meanings. Where detail and background are used in TV programmes, for example the BBC historical serials, action tends to slow down as a result. The screen displays historical detail in and for itself; characters are inserted around it, carrying on their lengthy conversations as best they can. Segments are drawn out, their meanings unfolding gradually. For historical dramas, especially of the Victorian and Edwardian era, this tends to lend greater authenticity to the fiction: these are assumed to have been the decades of leisure and grace.

The stripped-down image that broadcast TV uses is a central feature of TV production. Its most characteristic result is the TV emphasis on close-ups of people, which are finely graded into types. The dramatic close-up is of a face virtually filling the screen; the current affairs close-up is more distant, head-and-shoulders are shown, providing a certain distance, even reticence. Close-ups are regularly used in TV, to a much greater extent than in cinema. They even have their own generic name: talking heads. The effect is very different from the cinema close-up. Whereas the cinema close-up accentuates the difference between screen-figure and any attainable human figure by drastically increasing its size, the broadcast TV close-up produces a face that approximates to normal size. Instead of an effect of distance and unattainability, the TV close-up generates an equality and even intimacy.

The broadcast TV image is gestural rather than detailed; variety and interest are provided by the rapid change of images rather than richness within one image. TV compensates for the simplicity of its single images by the techniques of rapid cutting. Again, the organisation of studios is designed for this style of work. The use of several cameras and the possibility of alternation between them produces a style of shooting that is specific to TV: the fragmentation of events that keeps strictly to the continuity of their performance. There is much less condensation of events in TV than in cinema. Events are shown in real time from a multiple of different points of camera view (all, normally, from the same side of the action). Cinema events are shot already fragmented and matched together in editing. Still today, video editing is expensive, and the use of the studio set-up (in which much is already invested: capital and skills alike) provides instantaneous editing as the images are being transferred to tape for later transmission. This enables a rapid alternation of images, a practice which also affects the editing of TV programmes made on film. The standard attitude is that an image should be held on screen only until its information value is exhausted. Since the information value of the TV image is deliberately honed-down, it is quickly exhausted. Variation is provided by changing the image shown rather than by introducing a complexity of elements into a single image. Hence the material nature of the broadcast TV image has two profound effects on the regime of representation and working practices that TV has adopted. It produces an emphasis on sound as the carrier of continuity of attention and therefore of meaning; it produces a lack of detail in the indivdual image that reduces the image to its information value and produces an aesthetic that emphasises the close-up and fast cutting with strict time continuity.

However, this is to compare the broadcast TV image with the cinema image. The TV image has further distinct qualities of its own, no doubt the result of a tenacious ideological operation, that mark it decisively as different from the cinema image with its photo effect. The broadcast TV image has the effect of immediacy. It is as though the TV image is a 'live' image, transmitted and received in the same moment that it is produced. For British broadcast TV, with its tight schedules and fear of controversy, this has not been true for a decade. Only news and sport are routinely live transmissions. However, the notion that broadcast TV is live still haunts the medium; even more so does the sense of immediacy of the image. The immediacy of the broadcast TV image does not just lie in the presumption that it is live, it lies more in the relations that the image sets up for itself. Immediacy is the effect of the directness of the TV image, the way in which it constitutes itself and its viewers as held in a relationship of co-present intimacy. Broadcast TV very often uses forms of direct address from an individual in close-up to individuals gathered around the set. This is very different from cinema's historic mode of narration, where events do not betray a knowledge that they are being watched. Broadcast TV is forever buttonholing, addressing its viewers as though holding a conversation with them. Announcers and newsreaders speak directly from the screen, simulating the eye contact of everyday conversation by looking directly out of the screen and occasionally looking down (a learned and constructed technique). Advertisements contain elements of direct address: questions, exhortations, warnings. Sometimes they go further, providing riddles and jokes that assume that their viewers share a common frame of reference with them. Hence advertisements for various staple commodities, beer for example, tend to make oblique and punning references to each other's advertising campaigns. The audience is expected to understand these references. This also is an operation of direct address: an ephemeral and immediate knowledge is assumed in the viewer, who otherwise would have no understanding of the reference or the joke. Hence these advertisements are addressing a viewer as an equal: 'we both know what we are talking about'.

Direct address is recognised as a powerful effect of TV. Its most obvious form, that of an individual speaking directly (saying 'I' and 'you'), is reserved for specific kinds of people. It can be used by those who are designated as politically neutral by TV itself (newsmen and women), or by those who have ultimate political power: heads of state. Otherwise, direct address is denied to individuals who appear on TV. Important personalities are interviewed in three-quarter face. Other strategies of address are open to them, that of recruiting the audience against the interviewer by appealing to a common sense that media persons do not share, for instance. Interviewers in their turn tend to construct themselves as asking questions on behalf of the viewers: 'what the public/the viewers/ordinary people *really* want to know is. . . .' This is also a form of highly motivated direct address. Again, it assumes an audience who is there simultaneously, for whom events are being played out.

Direct address is not the only form of construction of broadcast TV's effect of immediacy. Broadcast TV's own perpetual presence (there every night of the year), and its series formats, breed a sense of the perpetual present. Broadcast TV declares itself as being in the present tense, denying recording as effectively as cinema uses it. TV fictions take place to a very large extent as though they were transmitted directly from the place in which they were really happening. The soap opera is the most obvious example of this, where events in a particular milieu are everlastingly updated. Broadcast TV has a very marked sense of presence to its images and sounds which far outweighs any counterbalancing sense of absence, any sense of recording. The technical operation of the medium in its broadcast form strengthens this feeling. The tight scheduling that is favoured by most large broadcast operations means that an audience wanting to see a particular programme has to be present at a very precise time, or they miss it. This increases the sense that broadcast TV is of the specific present moment. In addition, unlike cinema, the signal comes from elsewhere, and can be sent live. The technical origin of the signal is not immediately apparent to the viewer, but all the apparatus of direct address and of contemporaneity of broadcast TV messages is very present. The broadcast signal is always available during almost all normal waking hours. It is ever-present.

The favoured dramatic forms of broadcast TV work within this framework of presence and immediacy. Besides the obvious forms of soap opera, entirely cast in a continuous present, the series format tends towards the creation of immediacy and presence. The open-ended series format of the situation comedy or the dramatic series tends to produce the sense of immediacy by the fact that it presents itself as having no definite end. Unlike the cinema narrative, the end of the episode and the end of the series alike leave events unresolved. They are presented as on-going, part of the texture of life. This sense even extends to the historical reconstruction dramas beloved of the BBC, through the operation of a further mechanism that produces the effect of immediacy.

Immediacy is also produced by the logical extension of the direct address form: by echoing the presumed form of the TV audience within the material of the TV fiction itself. The institution of broadcast TV assumes its audience to be the family; it massively centres its fictional representations around the question of the family. Hence TV produces its effect of immediacy even within dramas of historically remote periods by reproducing the audience's view of itself within its fictions. Hence TV dramas are concerned with romance and the family, both conceived of within certain basic kinds of definition. Broadcast TV's view of the family is one which is at variance with the domestic practices of the majority of domestic units and of individuals in Britain at the moment. Yet broadcast TV's definition has a strength in that it participates in the construction of an idea of the normal family/domestic unit, from which other forms are experienced and remembered as temporary aberrations.

Broadcast TV dramas are constructed around the heterosexual romance in its normal and perverse forms, and the perpetual construction of standard families: wage-earning husband, housekeeping wife, two children. Situation comedies play on the discrepancies between this assumed norm and other forms of existence: male and female students sharing a flat *(Man About the House)*, the childless, woman-dominated couple *(George and Mildred)*, the landlord and his variegated bedsit tenants *(Rising Damp)*, the rejuvenated divorced father *(Father Dear Father)*. Historical dramas found their sense of the historical on the never-changing patterns of romance and family life: Edward VIII's *amour fou (Edward and Mrs Simpson)*, the problems of the powerful career woman *(Elizabeth R)*, the problems of male lust breaking the confines of the family *(The Six Wives of Henry VIII)*, the consequences of one sexual transgression repercussing down the centuries (*The Forsyte Saga, Poldark*, etc.).

The centring of all kinds of broadcast TV drama upon the family (much as direct address assumes a family unit as its audience) produces a sense of intimacy, a bond between the viewers' conception of themselves (or how they ought to be) and the programme's central concerns. So a relationship of humanist sympathy is set up, along the lines of seeing how everyone is normal really, how much they really do desire the norm that our society has created for itself. But the intimacy that broadcast TV sets up is more than just this form of sympathy. It is made qualitatively different by the sense that the TV image carries of being a live event, which is intensified by the habit of shooting events in real time within any one segment, the self-contained nature of each segment, and the use of close-up and sound continuity. All of these factors contribute to an overall impression, that the broadcast TV image is providing an intimacy with events between couples and within families, an intimacy that gives the impression that these events are somehow co-present with the viewer, shared rather than witnessed from outside. The domestic nature of the characteristic use of broadcast TV certainly contributes here, but more important is the particular way in which TV has internalised this in its own representations. Broadcast TV has ingested the domestic and bases its dramas upon it. When it does not address its audience directly, it creates a sense of familiarity between its fictions and its audience, a familiarity based on a notion of the familial which is assumed to be shared by all.

Broadcast TV has a particular regime of representation that stresses the immediacy and co-presence of the TV representation. Its particular physical and social characteristics have created a very particular mode of representation that includes the image centred upon the significant at the cost of detail, and sound as carrier of continuity. It gives its audience a particular sense of intimacy with the events it portrays. All of these features of broadcast TV create and foster a form of looking by the TV viewer that is different from the kind of voyeurism (with fetishistic undertow) that cinema presents for its spectators.

TV's regime of vision is less intense than cinema's: it is a regime of the glance rather than the gaze. The gaze implies a concentration of the spectator's activity into that of looking, the glance implies that no extraordinary effort is being invested in the activity of looking. The very terms we habitually use to designate the person who watches TV or the cinema screen tend to indicate this difference. The cinema-looker is a spectator: caught by the projection yet separate from its illusion. The TV-looker is a viewer, casting a lazy eye over proceedings, keeping an eye on events, or, as the slightly archaic designation had it, 'looking in'. In psychoanalytic terms, when compared to cinema, TV demonstrates a displacement from the invocatory drive of scopophilia (looking) to the closest related of the invocatory drives, that of hearing. Hence the crucial role of sound in ensuring continuity of attention and producing the utterances of direct address ('I' to 'you').

The different balance between the activities of looking and listening produces a qualitatively different relation to the TV transmission. It is not that the experience is less intense than cinema; rather, it has a distinctive form of its own. In particular, there is far less separation between viewer and image than with cinema. Broadcast TV does not construct an image that is marked by present absence, its regime is one of co-presence of image and viewer. The image is therefore not an impossible one, defined by the separation of the viewer from it, but rather one that is familiar and intimate. The cost of this intimacy is that the voyeuristic mode cannot operate as intensely as in cinema. In particular, the broadcast TV viewer's look is not a controlling look in the same sense as that which operates in cinema. The cinema spectator is secure in the separation from the image that allows events to take place as though they were not watched. The broadcast TV image is quite often directly addressed to the viewer, in a simulation of everyday eye contact. In addition, the sense of cinema's consent to the act of being watched (implied in the event of the projection of a film for spectators) is radically absent from broadcast TV. TV continues whether a particular set is turned on or not. In this sense, it is not for the viewer in the way that the cinema projection is for the spectator. If no one turns up to a film screening, it can be cancelled, but if no one is watching a TV programme, it will be transmitted anyway in blithe ignorance of its lack of reception. The broadcast TV event is just there, it carries no sense with it of being for anyone as the cinema projection is for a definite group. This implies a lack of the consent by the representation to being watched that is vital to the construction of a regime of the voyeuristic gaze in cinema.

Broadcast TV can be left on with no one watching it, playing in the background of other activities in the home. This is perhaps a frequent event; certainly, it also makes impossible the construction of a voyeuristic contract between looker and representation. Instead, broadcast TV uses sound to appeal to its audience, using a large degree of direct address whose function is to attract the look and attention of the viewer, and to hold it. The separation that this practice implies is different from that of cinematic voyeurism. It makes explicit a relationship between viewer and broadcast TV image, designating a TV first person singular or plural ('I', 'we') and a viewing second person ('you', beautifully flexible in its lack of singular/plural difference). Together these first and second person designations can observe and speculate about third persons: 'he', 'she', 'they'. The practice of segmentalising TV broadcasting means that direct address is present regularly to reaffirm this relationship. It surrounds the segments of dramatic material and comic material so that they become constituted as 'they': the people whom we *and television* both look in upon. But drama's characters are not constituted as a totally separate 'they'. TV drama is constructed around the presumed self-image of the audience: the family. The mobilisation of this sense of intimacy, together with TV's effect of co-presence both tend to push even dramatic material into this sense of first and second person togetherness. Characters in drama series on broadcast TV tend to become familiar figures, loved, or excused with a tolerance that is quite remarkable: it is more than is normally extended to members of the family or to neighbours. The construction of a 'real monster' in a TV series is a difficult process: this is perhaps why J.R. Ewing in *Dallas* excited such attention.

The community of address that broadcast TV is able to set up excludes a fully developed regime of voyeurism as found in cinema. This is perhaps why films screened on TV do not quite achieve the same intensity of experience as they would in the cinema, and why broadcast TV's adoption of the cinematic mode has not been more widespread. The community of address sets up a different relation between viewer and representation. The distance between viewer and image is reduced; but a compensatory distance is constructed and separation/between the 'I' and 'you' of the community of address and the third person outside that it constructs. The 'they' that is always implied and often stated in direct address forms becomes an other, a grouping outside the consensus that confirms the consensus. Certain characteristic attitudes are taken towards these outsiders: patronisation, hate, wilful ignorance, pity, generalised concern, indifference. These are encouraged by the complicity that broadcast TV sets up between itself and its viewers; a series of categories of 'they' has begun to appear, often creating curious dislocations in the operation of TV representations when they are used in news and current affairs. . . .

Dramatic forms of various kinds occur regularly within TV's direct address context, and are inflected by it to some extent. Dramatic forms are not constructed in broadcast TV for the voyeuristic gaze in the same way as cinematic forms. There is a sense of complicity of the institution of TV in the process of looking at dramatic events which increases their sense of co-presence with the viewer. The effects of immediacy, of segmentation, and of the series rather than strong narrative development, and the concentration of TV drama on the family (as a presumed reflection of its audience) all intensify this sense of TV drama as part of the consensus between broadcast TV and its audience. Hence drama is crucial in revising and altering the effects of news and current affairs rather more brutal division of its world into a series of 'theys' beyond the consensus of viewer and TV first persons. . . .

The final effects of TV's low emphasis on the construction of the voyeuristic position lie in the representation of the female body and of female sexuality, and in its characteristic forms of narration of events. Cinematic voyeurism, with its fetishistic counterpart, is centrally concerned with the representation of the female body and of female sexuality as a problem, constructed from the security of a definition of the masculine as positive. TV's concerns are not so heavily centred towards the investigation of the female. This is not only the result of the different mechanisms of self-censorship and imposed censorship that prevail in the two media, nor only of the different sense of the viewing conditions that the two media have of themselves. After all, Hollywood's relentless investigation of the female was carried out under codes of censorship in the 1940s that were every bit as vigilant as those operating in broadcast TV today. TV does not have its equivalents of the *film noir* or of the 'love interest'. Different conditions prevail. Broadcast TV's lack of an intense voyeuristic appeal produces a lack of the strong investigatory drive that is needed alike for tightly organised narration and for intense concern with the 'problem' of the female. Similarly, the regime of broadcast TV does not demonstrate a particular drift towards a fetishistic activity of viewing. Its forms of narration are not particularly repetitive in the fetishistic manner of obsessive replaying of events. The series and the segmental form construct a different pattern of repetition that has much more to do with constructing a pattern of familiarity. The fetishistic regime does operate to some extent, however, as does voyeurism. Its characteristic attention in broadcast TV is not directed towards the whole body, but to the face. The display of the female body on TV, in dance sequences or in a series like *Charlie's Angels,* is gestural rather than fascinating. The techniques of rapid cutting prevent the access of the gaze at the body being displayed. Instead, TV's displays of the female body, frequent and depressing enough as they are, provide material for the glance only. Details and complete bodies are both presented only to the extent that they can be registered as 'a bit of a body/a whole body'. The exception to this is the face, and specifically the female face. In some sense, the female body is hidden, made obscure, by the heavy emphasis that broadcast TV gives to the various kinds of close-up. . . . The close-up of the face is the one moment where the average TV image is more or less life-sized rather than less than life-size, and the equality of scale between image and viewer contributes to a dramatic reduction of separation between image and viewer that is one aspect of the fetishistic regime. The fetishism is still concentrated upon women, because of the generalised culture of sexual difference under which we suffer.

Broadcast TV's level of investment in voyeuristic activity is generally not intense enough to produce the investigatory and forward-moving narratives that are characteristic of entertainment cinema. Instead, the form of narration that corresponds with the activity of the glance rather than the gaze is one of providing variety. Broadcast TV provides a variety of segments rather than the progressive accumulation of sequences that characterises cinematic narration. The segment form corresponds to the regime of the glance. It is relatively coherent and assumes an attention span of relatively limited duration. Broadcast TV's characteristic form of multi-camera editing tends to give the segment the strong coherence of proceeding in real time; TV's characteristic use of a small number of actors in any one situation also increases the coherence of individual segments. Segmentation has been developed in broadcast TV towards the provision of variety: segments of different kinds follow each other for most of TV's output. Hence the TV cop series will present successively the dramatic face-to-face confrontation, the comic routine, the chase sequence, the scene of pathos. Soap operas tend to present a variety of different moods across each episode by alternating between different kinds of segment. Broadcast TV's whole attitude to scheduling is nothing other than the provision of this variety on a grand scale. Scheduling ensures that programmes of the same kind are not bunched together, that a spread of different forms will be found over an evening's output. Such a conception has virtually disappeared from the entertainment cinema, which is more and more intent on presenting one film-text only.

Broadcast TV characteristically offers an image that is stripped down, with no unnecessary details. Cutting produces forms of variation of visual information, and sound has an important role in drawing the viewer's attention back to the screen. The image and sound both tend to create a sense of immediacy, which produces a kind of complicity between the viewer and the TV institution. This can provide a powerful form of consensus, since it tends to define the domestic place of the TV set as a kind of norm, against which the 'outside world' represented on TV can be measured. This regime of image and sound, together with the segment and series forms, has created a distinct form of narration in broadcast TV.

                                                                            1982

IV

Film, Theater, and Literature

Theorists have often attempted to discover the characteristics of the film medium by comparing it with other media. Panofsky, for example, contrasts the theater's static use of space and its independence of the principle of co-expressibility with cinema's more dynamic use of space and its rigorous subjection to that principle. For Panofsky, this difference explains why film adaptations of plays are so unlikely to succeed. Any attempt to transfer theater's essentially verbal resources to the cinema violates the principle that no more should be expressed verbally than can be expressed visually. The cinema's business is not the photographing of theatrical decor, a prestylized reality, but the photographing of actual physical reality so that is has style. Panofsky finds cinema the only medium that does justice to the materialistic interpretation of the universe which pervades contemporary civilization.

Like Panofsky, Hugo Münsterberg, a Harvard psychologist and philosopher who was a colleague of both William James and George Santayana, attempted in 1916 to delineate the features of the silent "photoplay" by contrasting it with the theater. For Münsterberg, the representation of physical reality is the concern not of cinema, but of theater. In true cinema, "the massive outer world has lost its weight, it has been freed from space, time and causality, and it has been clothed in the forms of our consciousness." Theater is bound by the same laws that govern nature, but the cinema is free to be shaped by the inner movements of the mind. Theater therefore trespasses on the realm of cinema when it employs any analogue of the close-up or the flash-back, and Münsterberg is as harsh a critic of "cinematified" theater as Panofsky is of "theatricalized" film.

For Münsterberg the true function of the close-up is not to provide a closer view of nature but to reproduce the mental act of attention. Similarly, the cut-back provides a cinematic equivalent of human memory and is alien to theater, which is bound by the laws of nature and the necessities of temporal succession. In the the-

351

ater, "men of flesh and blood with really plastic bodies stand before us. They move like any moving body in our surroundings. Moreover, those happenings on the stage, just like events in life, are independent of our subjective attention and memory and imagination. They go their objective course." If it were the object of cinema, then, to "imitate" nature, film could hardly compete with theater. "The color of the world has disappeared, the persons are dumb, no sound reaches our ears. The depth of the scene appears unreal, the motion has lost its natural character. Worst of all, the objective course of events is falsified. . . ." The genius of cinema is not, then, to "imitate" nature; rather it is to display the triumph of mind over matter.

The essay by Susan Sontag may be read as a critique of both Panofsky and Münsterberg. Despite their many and important differences, both "insist on a single model for film" and for theater, too. Their conception of the stage derives from notions of realism based on Ibsen and the French well-made play more than it does on the epic use of the stage by Shakespeare, the Russian constructivists, or Brecht. Similarly, their views of film display a strong prejudice in favor of the methods of the silent film. They are all too ready to confine cinema within rigid boundaries and to insist on maintaining artistic "purity," a separation of the various arts. Although Sontag understands the impulse to purity, she also understands a contrasting artistic ideal, one descending from Wagner rather than Lessing, which takes as its ideal a comprehensive "mixed-media" art form in the tradition of Greek theater and the Wagnerian music-drama. She does not choose between puristic and anti-puristic conceptions of the cinema or of the theater, but suggests awaiting future developments without prejudice.

Sontag accepts both the fact that many successful films have been "adapted" from plays and the fact that cinematic effects have been employed successfully in the theater. André Bazin, too, insists on the value of adaptations. He thinks that Cocteau's *Les Parents Terrible* and Olivier's *Henry V* are superb films. But he does not feel that one should "cinematify," simply "open up" the original play by moving around outdoors, in order to make a successful adaptation. Rather, "a good adaptation should result in a restoration of the essence and spirit" of the original play. Indeed, in films like Cocteau's and Olivier's, one is "no longer adapting, one is staging a play by means of cinema."

Bazin realizes that if the living actor's presence were essential to the effects of theater, the successful staging of a play by means of cinema would be impossible. He therefore argues that there is a sense in which the actor is present on the screen just as a person is "present" in a mirror. Although Bazin's refutation of the importance of presence is not very convincing (Stanley Cavell treats the issue much more systematically in *The World Viewed*), it allows him to assert that the primary difference between stage and screen is not one of living beings but of architecture. Bazin thinks that theatrical speech often fails in a film not because it was written for living speakers but because it was written to be uttered in a particular kind of world. The problem of filming a play is to find a decor that preserves the closed, microcosmic qualities of theatrical architecture for which the dialogue was written and which at the same time preserves the natural realism of the screen. The screen is not a world in itself but a window on the world which consistently dwarfs and dissipates theatrical speech. Bazin believes this problem is worth solving, for even if original film scripts are preferable to adaptations, truly distinguished ones are rare. The cinema cannot afford to ignore its theatrical heritage, any more than the drama can afford the loss of the audiences that film can bring it.

Like Bazin, Leo Braudy focuses the central issues of the interrelations of film, theater, and literature by emphasizing the varying ways that each has dealt with the human image and the question of characterization. He broadly distinguishes first between the visual and the verbal ways of presenting character and then defines the basic nature of film character as the omission of any explicit connection between appearances, of explicit explorations of inner life, or of anything about the character other than what we see before us. It is not merely the "presence" of the performer before us in the film that creates the character, but also the palpable absences and implications of that performance, particularly our basic knowledge that the performer is not really there. With a look back at historical styles of stage performance and conceptions of acting, he then explores this elusiveness of the film character in contrast with what he argues are the more patterned ways in which the novel and especially the stage construct character. Directly connected with these differing conceptions of character are very different demands made upon performers in the two visual media.

Similarly aware of the cultural inheritance of cinema, Sergei Eisenstein, as a filmmaker himself, emphasizes the question of the ease and effectiveness of adapting one medium to another. He argues that Griffith even learned montage, which Eisenstein considers the essence of film, from the pages of Dickens. Eisenstein plainly sees no theoretical bar to adapting novels successfully to the screen, as proved by his own attempt to adapt Drieser's *An American Tragedy*. Indeed, it is not implausible to argue, as Bazin and Sontag have, that the film's deepest affinities are with the novel, not with the play. The novel is "cinematic" in its fluid handling of time and space, in its "focused" narrative control, in its ability to alternate description with dialogue, and even in the privacy and isolation of its audiences. The film has adapted more fiction than drama.

Because of the commitment of many early writers to defining film in opposition to more traditional art-forms, the question of adaptation still remains a vexed one for most film theorists and in contemporary film criticism is perhaps the least theoretically considered. This attitude has even been reinforced among later theorists who wish to disentangle not only film but also film study from that of literature or theater. Yet there is some reason to think that adaptation is a way into the processes of creation, since a good number of important filmmakers, like Eisenstein, have not felt the same compunctions about "impurity" that have worried many critics. It may also be a way into understanding the different ways that different media tell stories.

Seymour Chatman, who has written extensively on narrative and narrative processes in fiction and film, takes up this question in his essay. His perspective is predicated, as he says, on the ways in which narrative theorists have explored the storytelling structures that they claim are independent of medium, especially the distinction between story and discourse. The mechanism of adaptation is an especially intriguing way to test the kinds of transformations that narrative undergoes in the two media. Chatman's analysis of Jean Renoir's version of Maupassant's short story "Une Partie de campagne" emphasizes the way in which story elements, description, and point of view, are changed in the metamorphosis from prose fiction to film, as Renoir creates a self-sufficient film that is yet clearly linked to its literary source.

Also beginning with some examples drawn from "Une Partie de campagne," Dudley Andrew expands the implications of Chatman's argument to a general consideration of the use of source material in the making of films. As Chatman concentrates on the underlying narrative similarities to illustrate differences, Andrew explores the points of contact between two artistic "signifying systems," the literary and the cinematic, that otherwise seem to achieve their effects in exactly reverse ways: film from perception to signification, literature from signification to perception. Rejecting those writers who therefore argue for sharp and unbridgeable distinctions between the media, Andrew moves the question of adaptation from the periphery of film study to its center: "the study of adaptation is logically tantamount to the study of cinema as a whole." What is needed, he concludes, is not a more refined set of medium-specific definitions but an effort to situate the transformations in a historical and sociological context of actual adaptors with their complex motivations.

HUGO MÜNSTERBERG
FROM THE FILM: A PSYCHOLOGICAL STUDY

THE MEANS OF THE PHOTOPLAY

We have now reached the point at which we can knot together all our threads, the psychological and the esthetic ones. If we do so, we come to the true thesis of this whole book. Our esthetic discussion showed us that it is the aim of art to isolate a significant part of our experience in such a way that it is separate from our practical life and is in complete agreement within itself. Our esthetic satisfaction results from this inner agreement and harmony, but in order that we may feel such agreement of the parts we must enter with our own impulses into the will of every element, into the meaning of every line and color and form, every word and tone and note. Only if everything is full of such inner movement can we really enjoy the harmonious cooperation of the parts. The means of the various arts, we saw, are the forms and methods by which this aim is fulfilled. They must be different for every material. Moreover the same material may allow very different methods of isolation and elimination of the insignificant and reënforcement of that which contributes to the harmony. If we ask now what are the characteristic means by which the photoplay succeeds in overcoming reality, in isolating a significant dramatic story and in presenting it so that we enter into it and yet keep it away from our practical life and enjoy the harmony of the parts, we must remember all the results to which our psychological discussion in the first part of the book has led us.

We recognized there that the photoplay, incomparable in this respect with the drama, gave us a view of dramatic events which was completely shaped by the inner movements of the mind. To be sure, the events in the photoplay happen in the real space with its depth. But the spectator feels that they are not presented in the three dimensions of the outer world, that they are flat pictures which only the mind molds into plastic things. Again the events are seen in continuous movement; and yet the pictures break up the movement into a rapid succession of instantaneous impressions. We do not see the objective reality, but a product of our own mind which

355

binds the pictures together. But much stronger differences came to light when we turned to the processes of attention, of memory, of imagination, of suggestion, of division of interest and of emotion. The attention turns to detailed points in the outer world and ignores everything else: the photoplay is doing exactly this when in the close-up a detail is enlarged and everything else disappears. Memory breaks into present events by bringing up pictures of the past: the photoplay is doing this by its frequent cutbacks, when pictures of events long past flit between those of the present. The imagination anticipates the future or overcomes reality by fancies and dreams; the photoplay is doing all this more richly than any chance imagination would succeed in doing. But chiefly, through our division of interest our mind is drawn hither and thither. We think of events which run parallel in different places. The photoplay can show in intertwined scenes everything which our mind embraces. Events in three or four or five regions of the world can be woven together into one complex action. Finally, we saw that every shade of feeling and emotion which fills the spectator's mind can mold the scenes in the photoplay until they appear the embodiment of our feelings. In every one of these aspects the photoplay succeeds in doing what the drama of the theater does not attempt.

If this is the outcome of esthetic analysis on the one side, of psychological research on the other, we need only combine the results of both into a unified principle: *the photoplay tells us the human story by overcoming the forms of the outer world, namely, space, time, and causality, and by adjusting the events to the forms of the inner world, namely, attention, memory, imagination, and emotion.*

We shall gain our orientation most directly if once more, under this point of view, we compare the photoplay with the performance on the theater stage. We shall not enter into a discussion of the character of the regular theater and its drama. We take this for granted. Everybody knows that highest art form which the Greeks created and which from Greece has spread over Asia, Europe, and America. In tragedy and in comedy from ancient times to Ibsen, Rostand, Hauptmann, and Shaw we recognize one common purpose and one common form for which no further commentary is needed. How does the photoplay differ from a theater performance? We insisted that every work of art must be somehow separated from our sphere of practical interests. The theater is no exception. The structure of the theater itself, the framelike form of the stage, the difference of light between stage and house, the stage setting and costuming, all inhibit in the audience the possibility of taking the action on the stage to be real life. Stage managers have sometimes tried the experiment of reducing those differences, for instance, keeping the audience also in a fully lighted hall, and they always had to discover how much the dramatic effect was reduced because the feeling of distance from reality was weakened. The photoplay and the theater in this respect are evidently alike. The screen too suggests from the very start the complete unreality of the events.

But each further step leads us to remarkable differences between the stage play and the film play. In every respect the film play is further away from the physical reality than the drama and in every respect this greater distance from the physical world brings it nearer to the mental world. The stage shows us living men. It is not the real Romeo and not the real Juliet; and yet the actor and the actress have the ringing voices of true people, breathe like them, have living colors like them, and fill physical space like them. What is left in the photoplay? The voice has been stilled: the photoplay is a dumb show. Yet we must not forget that this alone is a step away from reality which has often been taken in the midst of the dramatic world. Whoever knows the history of the theater is aware of the tremendous rôle which the pantomime has played in the development of mankind. From the old half-religious pantomimic and suggestive dances out of which the beginnings of the real drama grew to the fully religious pantomimes of medieval ages and, further on, to many silent mimic elements in modern performances, we find a continuity of conventions which make the pantomime almost the real background of all dramatic development. We know how popular the pantomimes were among the Greeks, and how they stood in the foreground in the imperial period of Rome. Old Rome cherished the mimic clowns, but still more the tragic pantomimics. "Their very nod speaks, their hands talk and their fingers have a voice." After the fall of the Roman empire the church used the pantomime for the portrayal of sacred history, and later centuries enjoyed very unsacred histories in the pantomimes of their ballets. Even complex artistic tragedies without words have triumphed on our present-day stage. *L'Enfant Prodigue* which came from Paris, *Sumurun* which came from Berlin, *Petroushka* which came from Petrograd, conquered the American stage; and surely the loss of speech, while it increased the remoteness from reality, by no means destroyed the continuous consciousness of the bodily existence of the actors.

Moreover the student of a modern pantomime cannot overlook a characteristic difference between the speechless performance on the stage and that of the actors of a photoplay. The expression of the inner states, the whole system of gestures, is decidedly different: and here we might say that the photoplay stands nearer to life than the pantomime. Of course, the photoplayer must somewhat exaggerate the natural expression. The whole rhythm and intensity of his gestures must be more marked than it would be with actors who accompany their movements by spoken words and who express the meaning of their thoughts and feelings by the content of what they say. Nevertheless the photoplayer uses the regular channels of mental discharge. He acts simply as a very emotional person might act. But the actor who plays in a pantomime cannot be satisfied with that. He is expected to add something which is entirely unnatural, namely a kind of artificial demonstration of his emotions. He must not only behave like an angry man, but he must behave like a man who is consciously interested in his anger and wants to demonstrate it to others. He exhibits his emotions for the spectators. He really acts theatrically for the benefit of the bystanders. If he did not try to do so, his means of conveying a rich story and a real conflict of human passions would be too meager. The photoplayer, with the rapid changes of scenes, has other possibilities of conveying his intentions. He must not yield to the temptation to play a pantomime on the screen, or he will seriously injure the artistic quality of the reel.

The really decisive distance from bodily reality, however, is created by the substitution of the actor's picture for the actor himself. Lights and shades replace the manifoldness of color effects and mere perspective must furnish the suggestion of depth. We traced it when we discussed the psychology of kinematoscopic perception. But we must not put the emphasis on the wrong point. The natural tendency might be to lay the chief stress on the fact that those people in the photoplay do not stand before us in flesh and blood. The essential point is rather that we are conscious of the flatness of the picture. If we were to see the actors of the stage in a mirror, it would also be a reflected image which we perceive. We should not really have the actors themselves in our straight line of vision; and yet this image would appear to us equivalent to the actors themselves, because it would contain all the depth of the real stage. The process which leads from the living men to the screen is more complex than a mere reflection in a mirror, but in spite of the complexity in the transmission we do, after all, see the real actor in the picture. The photograph is absolutely different from those pictures which a clever draughtsman has sketched. In the photoplay we see the actors themselves and the decisive factor which makes the impression different from seeing real men is not that we see the living persons through the medium of photographic reproduction but that this reproduction shows them in a flat form. The bodily space has been eliminated. We said once before that stereoscopic arrangements could reproduce somewhat this plastic form also. Yet this would seriously interfere with the character of the photoplay. We need there this overcoming of the depth, we want to have it as a picture only and yet as a picture which strongly suggests to us the actual depth of the real world. We want to keep the interest in the plastic world and want to be aware of the depth in which the persons move, but our direct object of perception must be without the depth. That idea of space which forces on us most strongly the idea of heaviness, solidity and substantiality must be replaced by the light flitting immateriality.

But the photoplay sacrifices not only the space values of the real theater; it disregards no less its order of time. The theater presents its plot in the time order of reality. It may interrupt the continuous flow of time without neglecting the conditions of the dramatic art. There may be twenty years between the third and the fourth act, inasmuch as the dramatic writer must select those elements spread over space and time which are significant for the development of his story. But he is bound by the fundamental principle of real time, that it can move only forward and not backward. Whatever the theater shows us now must come later in the story than that which it showed us in any previous moment. The strict classical demand for complete unity of time does not fit every drama, but a drama would give up its mission if it told us in the third act something which happened before the second act. Of course, there may be a play within a play, and the players on the stage which is set on the stage may play events of old Roman history before the king of France. But this is an enclosure of the past in the present, which corresponds exactly to the actual order of events. The photoplay, on the other hand, does not and must not respect this temporal structure of the physical universe. At any point the photoplay interrupts the series and brings us back to the past. We studied this unique feature of the film art when we spoke of the psychology of memory and imagination. With the full freedom of our fancy, with the whole mobility of our association of ideas, pictures of the past flit through the scenes of the present. Time is left behind. Man becomes boy; today is interwoven with the day before yesterday. The freedom of the mind has triumphed over the unalterable law of the outer world.

It is interesting to watch how playwrights nowadays try to steal the thunder of the photoplay and experiment with time reversals on the legitimate stage. We are esthetically on the borderland when a grandfather tells his grandchild the story of his own youth as a warning, and instead of the spoken words the events of his early years come before our eyes. This is, after all, quite similar to a play within a play. A very different experiment is tried in *Under Cover.* The third act, which plays on the second floor of the house, ends with an explosion. The fourth act, which plays downstairs, begins a quarter of an hour before the explosion. Here we have a real denial of a fundamental condition of the theater. Or if we stick to recent products of the American stage, we may think of *On Trial,* a play which perhaps comes nearest to a dramatic usurpation of the rights of the photoplay. We see the court scene and as one witness after another begins to give his testimony the courtroom is replaced by the scenes of the actions about which the witness is to report. Another clever play, *Between the Lines,* ends the first act with a postman bringing three letters from the three children of the house. The second, third, and fourth acts lead us to the three different homes from which the letters came and the action in the three places not only precedes the writing of the letters, but goes on at the same time. The last act, finally, begins with the arrival of the letters which tell the ending of those events in the three homes. Such experiments are very suggestive but they are not any longer pure dramatic art. It is always possible to mix arts. An Italian painter produces very striking effects by putting pieces of glass and stone and rope into his paintings, but they are no longer pure paintings. The drama in which the later event comes before the earlier is an esthetic barbarism which is entertaining as a clever trick in a graceful superficial play, but intolerable in ambitious dramatic art. It is not only tolerable but perfectly natural in any photoplay. The pictorial reflection of the world is not bound by the rigid mechanism of time. Our mind is here and there, our mind turns to the present and then to the past: the photoplay can equal it in its freedom from the bondage of the material world.

But the theater is bound not only by space and time. Whatever it shows is controlled by the same laws of causality which govern nature. This involves a complete continuity of the physical events: no cause without following effect, no effect without preceding cause. This whole natural course is left behind in the play on the screen. The deviation from reality begins with that resolution of the continuous movement which we studied in our psychological discussions. We saw that the impression of movement results from an activity of the mind which binds the separate pictures together. What we actually see is a composite; it is like the movement of a fountain in which every jet is resolved into numberless drops. We feel the play of those drops in their sparkling haste as one continuous stream of water, and yet are conscious of the myriads of drops, each one separate from the others. This fountainlike spray of pictures has completely overcome the causal world.

In an entirely different form this triumph over causality appears in the interruption of the events by pictures which belong to another series. We find this whenever the scene suddenly changes. The processes are not carried to their natural consequences. A movement is started, but before the cause brings its results another scene has taken its place. What this new scene brings may be an effect for which we saw no causes. But not only the processes are interrupted. The intertwining of the scenes which we have traced in detail is itself such a contrast to causality. It is as if different objects could fill the same space at the same time. It is as if the resistance of the material world had disappeared and the substances could penetrate one another. In the interlacing of our ideas we experience this superiority to all physical laws. The theater would not have even the technical means to give us such impressions, but if it had, it would have no right to make use of them, as it would destroy the basis on which the drama is built. We have only another case of the same type in those series of pictures which aim to force a suggestion on our mind. We have spoken of them. A certain effect is prepared by a chain of causes and yet when the causal result is to appear the film is cut off. We have the causes without the effect. The villain thrusts with his dagger—but a miracle has snatched away his victim.

While the moving pictures are lifted above the world of space and time and causality and are freed from its bounds, they are certainly not without law. We said before that the freedom with which the pictures replace one another is to a large degree comparable to the sparkling and streaming of the musical tones. The yielding to the play of the mental energies, to the attention and emotion, which is felt in the film pictures, is still more complete in the musical melodies and harmonies in which the tones themselves are merely the expressions of the ideas and feelings and will impulses of the mind. Their harmonies and disharmonies, their fusing and blending, is not controlled by any outer necessity, but by the inner agreement and disagreement of our free impulses. And yet in this world of musical freedom, everything is completely controlled by esthetic necessities. No sphere of practical life stands under such rigid rules as the realm of the composer. However bold the musical genius may be he cannot emancipate himself from the iron rule that his work must show complete unity in itself. All the separate prescriptions which the musical student has to learn are ultimately only the consequences of this central demand which music, the freest of the arts, shares with all the others. In the case of the film, too, the freedom from the physical forms of space, time, and causality does not mean any liberation from this esthetic bondage either. On the contrary, just as music is surrounded by more technical rules than literature, the photoplay must be held together by the esthetic demands still more firmly than is the drama. The arts which are subordinated to the conditions of space, time, and causality find a certain firmness of structure in these material forms which contain an element of outer connectedness. But where these forms are given up and where the freedom of mental play replaces their outer necessity, everything would fall asunder if the esthetic unity were disregarded.

This unity is, first of all, the unity of action. The demand for it is the same which we know from the drama. The temptation to neglect it is nowhere greater than in the photoplay where outside matter can so easily be introduced or independent interests developed. It is certainly true for the photoplay, as for every work of art, that nothing has the right to existence in its midst which is not internally needed for the unfolding of the unified action. Wherever two plots are given to us, we receive less by far than if we had only one plot. We leave the sphere of valuable art entirely when a unified action is ruined by mixing it with declamation, and propaganda which is not organically interwoven with the action itself. It may be still fresh in memory what an esthetically intolerable helter-skelter performance was offered to the public in *The Battlecry of Peace*. Nothing can be more injurious to the esthetic cultivation of the people than such performances which hold the attention of the spectators by ambitious detail and yet destroy their esthetic sensibility by a complete disregard of the fundamental principle of art, the demand for unity. But we recognized also that this unity involves complete isolation. We annihilate beauty when we link the artistic creation with practical interests and transform the spectator into a selfishly interested bystander. The scenic background of the play is not presented in order that we decide whether we want to spend our next vacation there. The interior decoration of the rooms is not exhibited as a display for a department store. The men and women who carry out the action of the plot must not be people whom we may meet tomorrow on the street. All the threads of the play must be knotted together in the play itself and none should be connected with our outside interests. A good photoplay must be isolated and complete in itself like a beautiful melody. It is not an advertisement for the newest fashions.

This unity of action involves unity of characters. It has too often been maintained by those who theorize on the photoplay that the development of character is the special task of the drama, while the photoplay, which lacks words, must be satisfied with types. Probably this is only a reflection of the crude state which most photoplays of today have not outgrown. Internally, there is no reason why the means of the photoplay should not allow a rather subtle depicting of complex character. But the chief demand is that the characters remain consistent, that the action be developed according to inner necessity and that the characters themselves be in harmony with the central idea of the plot. However, as soon as we insist on unity we have no right to think only of the action which gives the content of the play. We cannot make light of the form. As in music the melody and rhythms belong together, as in painting not every color combination suits every subject, and as in poetry not every stanza would agree with every idea, so the photoplay must bring action and pictorial expression into perfect harmony. But this demand repeats itself in every single picture. We take it for granted that the painter balances perfectly the forms in his painting, groups them so that an internal symmetry can be felt and that the lines and curves and colors blend into a unity. Every single picture of the sixteen thousand which are shown to us in one reel ought to be treated with this respect of the pictorial artist for the unity of the forms.

The photoplay shows us a significant conflict of human actions in moving pictures which, freed from the physical forms of space, time, and causality, are adjusted to the free play of our mental experiences and which reach complete isolation from the practical world through the perfect unity of plot and pictorial appearance.

1916

SUSAN SONTAG
FILM AND THEATRE

The big question is whether there is an unbridgeable division, even opposition, between the two arts. Is there something genuinely "cinematic"?

Almost all opinion holds that there is. A commonplace of discussion has it that film and theatre are distinct and even antithetical arts, each giving rise to its own standards of judgment and canons of form. Thus Erwin Panofsky argues, in his celebrated essay "Style and Medium in the Motion Pictures" (1934, rewritten in 1946), that one of the criteria for evaluating a movie is its freedom from the impurities of theatricality. To talk about film, one must first define "the basic nature of the medium." Those who think prescriptively about the nature of live drama, less confident in the future of their art than the *cinéphiles* in theirs, rarely take a comparable exclusivist line.

The history of cinema is often treated as the history of its emancipation from theatrical models. First of all from theatrical "frontality" (the unmoving camera reproducing the situation of the spectator of a play fixed in his seat), then from theatrical acting (gestures needlessly stylized, exaggerated—needlessly, because now the actor could be seen "close up"), then from theatrical furnishings (unnecessary "distancing" of the audience's emotions, disregarding the opportunity to immerse the audience in reality). Movies are regarded as advancing from theatrical stasis to cinematic fluidity, from theatrical artificiality to cinematic naturalness and immediacy. But this view is far too simple.

Such over-simplification testifies to the ambiguous scope of the camera eye. Because the camera *can* be used to project a relatively passive, unselective kind of vision—as well as the highly selective ("edited") vision generally associated with movies—cinema is a "medium" as well as an art, in the sense that it can encapsulate any of the performing arts and render it in a film transcription. (This "medium" or

362

non-art aspect of film attained its routine incarnation with the advent of television. There, movies themselves became another performing art to be transcribed, miniaturized on film.) One *can* film a play or ballet or opera or sporting event in such a way that film becomes, relatively speaking, a transparency, and it seems correct to say that one is seeing the event filmed. But theatre is never a "medium." Thus, because one can make a movie "of" a play but not a play "of" a movie, cinema had an early but, I should argue, fortuitous connection with the stage. Some of the earliest films were filmed plays. Duse and Bernhardt and Barrymore are on film—marooned in time, absurd, touching; there is a 1913 British film of Forbes-Robertson playing Hamlet, a 1923 German film of *Othello* starring Emil Jannings. More recently, the camera has "preserved" Helene Weigel's performance of *Mother Courage* with the Berliner Ensemble, the Living Theatre production of *The Brig* (filmed by the Mekas brothers), and Peter Brook's staging of Weiss's *Marat/Sade.*

But from the beginning, even within the confines of the notion of film as a "medium" and the camera as a "recording" instrument, a great deal other than what occurred in theatres was taken down. As with still photography, some of the events captured on moving photographs were staged but others were valued precisely because they were *not* staged—the camera being the witness, the invisible spectator, the invulnerable voyeuristic eye. (Perhaps public happenings, "news," constitute an intermediate case between staged and unstaged events; but film as "newsreel" generally amounts to using film as a "medium.") To create on film a *document* of a transient reality is a conception quite unrelated to the purposes of theatre. It only appears related when the "real event" being recorded is a theatrical performance. And the first use of the motion picture camera was to make a documentary record of unstaged, casual reality: Louis Lumière's films of crowd-scenes in Paris and New York made in the 1890's antedate any use of film in the service of plays.

The other paradigmatic non-theatrical use of film, which dates from the earliest activity of the motion-picture camera, is for the creation of *illusion,* the construction of fantasy. The pioneer figure here is, of course, Georges Méliès. To be sure, Méliès (like many directors after him) conceived of the rectangle of the screen on analogy with the proscenium stage. And not only were the events staged; they were the very stuff of invention: imaginary journeys, imaginary objects, physical metamorphoses. But this, even adding the fact that Méliès situated his camera "in front of" the action and hardly moved it, does not make his films theatrical in an invidious sense. In their treatment of persons as things (physical objects) and in their disjunctive presentation of time and space, Méliès' films are quintessentially "cinematic"—so far as there is such a thing.

The contrast between theatre and films is usually taken to lie in the materials represented or depicted. But exactly where does the difference lie? It's tempting to draw a crude boundary. Theatre deploys artifice while cinema is committed to reality, indeed to an ultimately physical reality which is "redeemed," to use Siegfried Kracauer's striking word, by the camera. The aesthetic judgment that follows this bit of intellectual map-making is that films shot in real-life settings are better (*i.e.,* more cinematic) than those shot in a studio (where one can detect the difference).

Obviously, if Flaherty and Italian neo-realism and the *cinema verité* of Vertov, Rouch, Marker, and Ruspoli are the preferred models, one would judge rather harshly the period of 100% studio-made films inaugurated around 1920 by *The Cabinet of Dr. Caligari,* films with ostentatiously artificial landscapes and decor, and deem the right direction to be that taken at the same period in Sweden, where many films with strenuous natural settings were being shot "on location." Thus, Panofsky attacks *Dr. Caligari* for "prestylizing reality," and urges upon cinema "the problem of manipulating and shooting unstylized reality in such a way that the result has style."

But there is no reason to insist on a single model for film. And it is helpful to notice that, for the most part, the apotheosis of realism, the prestige of "unstylized reality," in cinema is actually a covert political-moral position. Films have been rather too often acclaimed as the democratic art, the art of mass society. Once one takes this description very seriously, one tends (like Panofsky and Kracauer) to want movies to continue to reflect their origins in a vulgar level of the arts, to remain loyal to their vast uneducated audience. Thus, a vaguely Marxist orientation jibes with a fundamental tenet of romanticism. Cinema, at once high art and popular art, is cast as the art of the authentic. Theatre, by contrast, means dressing up, pretense, lies. It smacks of aristocratic taste and the class society. Behind the objection of critics to the stagy sets of *Dr. Caligari,* the improbable costumes and florid acting of Renoir's *Nana,* the talkiness of Dreyer's *Gertrud,* as "theatrical," lay the feeling that such films were false, that they exhibited a sensibility both pretentious and reactionary which was out-of-step with the democratic and more mundane sensibility of modern life.

Anyway, whether aesthetic defect or not in the particular case, the synthetic look in films is not necessarily a misplaced theatricalism. From the beginning of film history, there were painters and sculptors who claimed that cinema's true future resided in artifice, construction. It lay not in figurative narration or story-telling of any kind (either in a relatively realistic or in a "surrealistic" vein), but in abstraction. Thus, Theo van Doesburg in his essay of 1929, "Film as Pure Form," envisages film as the vehicle of "optical poetry," dynamic light architecture," "the creation of a moving ornament." Films will realize "Bach's dream of finding an optical equivalent for the temporal structure of a musical composition." Today, a few filmmakers—for example, Robert Breer—continue to pursue this conception of film, and who is to say it is not cinematic?

Could anything be farther from the scope of theatre than such a degree of abstraction? It's important not to answer that question too quickly.

Some locate the division between theatre and film as the difference between the play and the filmscript. Panofsky derives this difference from what he takes to be the most profound one: the difference between the *formal* conditions of seeing a play and those of seeing a movie. In the theatre, says Panofsky, "space is static, that is, the space represented on the stage, as well as the spatial relation of the beholder to the spectacle, is unalterably fixed," while in the cinema "the spectator occupies a fixed seat, but only physically, not as the subject of an aesthetic experience." In the cinema, the spectator is "aesthetically . . . in permanent motion as his eye identifies with the lens of the camera, which permanently shifts in distance and direction."

True enough. But the observation does not warrant a radical dissociation of theatre from film. Like many critics, Panofsky is assuming a "literary" conception of theatre. To a theatre which is conceived of basically as dramatized literature, texts, words, he contrasts cinema which is, according to the received phrase, primarily "a visual experience." In effect, we are being asked to acknowledge tacitly the period of silent films as definitive of cinematic art and to identify theatre with "plays," from Shakespeare to Tennessee Williams. But many of the most interesting movies today are not adequately described as images with sound added. And what if theatre is conceived of as more than, or something different from, plays?

Panofsky may be over-simplifying when he decries the theatrical taint in movies, but he is sound when he argues that, historically, theatre is only one of the arts that feeds into cinema. As he remarks, it is apt that films came to be known popularly as moving *pictures* rather than as "photoplays" or "screen plays." Movies derive less from the theatre, from a performance art, an art that already moves, than they do from works of art which were stationary. Bad nineteenth-century paintings and postcards, wax-works à la Madame Tussaud, and comic strips are the sources Panofsky cites. What is surprising is that he doesn't connect movies with earlier narrative uses of still photography—like the family photo-album. The narrative techniques developed by certain nineteenth-century novelists, as Eisenstein pointed out in his brilliant essay on Dickens, supplied still another prototype for cinema.

Movies are images (usually photographs) that move, to be sure. But the distinctive unit of films is not the image but the principle of connection between the images, the relation of a "shot" to the one that preceded it and the one that comes after. There is no peculiarly "cinematic" as opposed to "theatrical" mode of linking images.

Panofsky tries to hold the line against the infiltration of theatre by cinema, as well as vice versa. In the theatre, not only can the spectator not change his angle of vision but, unlike movies, "the settings of the stage cannot change during one act (except for such incidentals as rising moons or gathering clouds and such illegitimate reborrowings from film as turning wings or gliding backdrops)." Were we to assent to this, the ideal play would be *No Exit,* the ideal set a realistic living room or a blank stage.

No less dogmatic is the complementary dictum about what is illegitimate in films—according to which, since films are "a visual experience," all components must be demonstrably subordinate to the image. Thus, Panofsky asserts: "Wherever a poetic emotion, a musical outburst, or a literary conceit (even, I am grieved to say, some of the wisecracks of Groucho Marx) entirely lose contact with visible movement, they strike the sensitive spectator as, literally, out of place." What, then, of the films of Bresson and Godard, with their allusive, densely thoughtful texts and their characteristic refusal to be visually beautiful? How could one explain the extraordinary rightness of Ozu's relatively immobilized camera?

The decline in average quality of films in the early sound period (compared with the level reached by films in the 1920's) is undeniable. Although it would be facile to call the sheer uninterestingness of most films of this period simply a regression to theatre, it is a fact that film-makers did turn more frequently to plays in the 1930's than they had in the preceding decade. Countless stage successes like *Outward Bound, Dinner at Eight, Blithe Spirit, Faisons un Rêve, Twentieth Century, Boudu Sauvé des Eaux, She Done Him Wrong, Anna Christie, Marius, Animal Crackers, The Petrified Forest,* were filmed. The success of movie versions of plays is measured by the extent to which the script rearranges and displaces the action and deals less than respectfully with the spoken text—as do certain films of plays by Wilde and Shaw, the Olivier Shakespeare films (at least *Henry V*), and Sjöberg's *Miss Julie*. But the basic disapproval of films which betray their origins in plays remains. A recent example: the outright hostility which greeted Dreyer's latest film, *Gertrud*. Not only does *Gertrud*, which I believe to be a minor masterpiece, follow a turn-of-the-century play that has characters conversing at length and quite formally, but it is filmed almost entirely in middle-shot.

Some of the films I have just mentioned are negligible as art; several are first-rate. (The same for the plays, though no correlation between the merits of the movies and those of the "original" plays can be established.) However, their virtues and faults cannot be sorted out as a cinematic versus a theatrical element. Whether derived from plays or not, films with complex or formal dialogue, films in which the camera is static or in which the action stays indoors, are not necessarily theatrical. *Per contra*, it is no more part of the putative "essence" of movies that the camera must rove over a large physical area, than it is that movies ought to be silent. Though most of the action of Kurosawa's *The Lower Depths*, a fairly faithful transcription of Gorki's play, is confined to one large room, it is as cinematic as the same director's *Throne of Blood*, a very free and laconic adaptation of *Macbeth*. The quality of Melville's claustrophobic *Les Enfants Terribles* is as peculiar to the movies as Ford's *The Searchers* or a train journey in Cinerama.

What does make a film theatrical in an invidious sense is when the narration becomes coy or self-conscious: compare Autant-Lara's *Occupe-Toi d'Amélie,* a brilliant cinematic use of the conventions and materials of theatricality, with Ophuls' clumsy use of similar conventions and materials in *La Ronde*.

Allardyce Nicoll, in his book *Film and Theatre* (1936), argues that the difference may be understood as a difference in kinds of characters. "Practically all effectively drawn stage characters are types [while] in the cinema we demand individualization and impute greater power of independent life to the figures on the screen." (Panofsky, it might be mentioned, makes exactly the opposite point: that the nature of films, in contrast to plays, requires flat or stock characters.)

Nicoll's thesis is not as arbitrary as it may at first appear. I would relate it to the fact that often the indelible moments of a film, and the most potent elements of characterization, are precisely the "irrelevant" or unfunctional details. (A random example: the ping-pong ball the schoolmaster toys with in Ivory's *Shakespeare Wallah*.) Movies thrive on the narrative equivalent of a technique familiar from painting and photography, off-centering. It is this that creates the pleasing disunity of fragmentariness (what Nicoll means by "individualization"?) of the characters of many of the greatest films. In contrast, linear "coherence" of detail (the gun on the wall in the first act that must go off by the end of the third) is the rule in Occidental narrative theatre, and gives rise to the sense of the unity of the characters (a unity that may appear like the statement of a "type").

But even with these adjustments, Nicoll's thesis seems less than appealing when one perceives that it rests on the idea that "When we go to the theatre, we expect theatre and nothing else." What is this theatre-and-nothing-else? It is the old notion of artifice. (As if art were ever anything else. As if some arts were artificial but others not.) According to Nicoll, when we are in a theatre "in every way the 'falsity' of a theatrical production is borne in upon us, so that we are prepared to demand nothing save a theatrical truth." In the cinema, however, every member of the audience, no matter how sophisticated, is on essentially the same level; we all believe that the camera cannot lie. As the film actor and his role are identical, so the image cannot be dissociated from what is imaged. Cinema, therefore, gives us what is experienced as the truth of life.

Couldn't theatre dissolve the distinction between the truth of artifice and the truth of life? Isn't that just what the theatre as ritual seeks to do? Isn't that what is being sought when theatre is conceived as an *exchange* with an audience?—something that films can never be.

If an irreducible distinction between theatre and cinema does exist, it may be this. Theatre is confined to a logical or *continuous* use of space. Cinema (through editing, that is, through the change of shot—which is the basic unit of film construction) has access to an alogical or *discontinuous* use of space. In the theatre, people are either in the stage space or "off." When "on," they are always visible or visualizable in contiguity with each other. In the cinema, no such relation is necessarily visible or even visualizable. (Example: the last shot of Paradjanov's *In the Shadows of Our Ancestors*.) Some films considered objectionably theatrical are those which seem to emphasize spatial continuities, like Hitchcock's virtuoso *Rope* or the daringly anachronistic *Gertrud*. But closer analysis of both these films would show how complex their treatment of space is. The longer and longer "takes" toward which sound films have been moving are, in themselves, neither more nor less cinematic than the short "takes" characteristic of silents.

Thus, cinematic virtue does not reside in the fluidity of the positioning of the camera nor in the mere frequency of the change of shot. It consists in the arrangement of screen images and (now) of sounds. Méliès, for example, though he didn't get beyond the static positioning of his camera, had a very striking conception of how to link screen images. He grasped that editing offered an equivalent to the magician's sleight of hand—thereby suggesting that one of the features of film (as distinct from theatre) is that *anything* can happen, that there is nothing that can't be represented convincingly. Through editing, Méliès presents discontinuities of physical substance and behavior. In his films, the discontinuities are, so to speak, practical, functional; they accomplish a transformation of ordinary reality. But the continuous *re*invention of space (as well as the option of temporal indeterminacy) peculiar to film narration does not pertain only to the cinema's ability to fabricate "visions," to show us a radically altered world. The most "realistic" use of the motion-picture camera also involves a discontinuous account of space.

Film narration has a "syntax," composed of the rhythm of associations and disjunctions. As Cocteau has written, "My primary concern in a film is to prevent the images from flowing, to oppose them to each other, to anchor them and join them without destroying their relief." (But does such a conception of film syntax entail, as Cocteau thinks, our disavowal of movies as "mere entertainment instead of a vehicle for thought"?)

In drawing a line of demarcation between theatre and films, the issue of the continuity of space seems to me more fundamental than the difference that might be pointed out between theatre as an organization of movement in three-dimensional space (like dance) versus cinema as an organization of plane space (like painting). The theatre's capacities for manipulating space and time are, simply, much cruder and more labored than film's. Theatre cannot equal the cinema's facilities for the strictly-controlled repetition of images, for the duplication or matching of word and image, and for the juxtaposition and over-lapping of images. (Through advanced lighting techniques, one can now "dissolve" on the stage. But as yet there is no equivalent, not even through the most adept use of scrim, of the "lap dissolve.")

Theatre has been described as a mediated art, presumably because it usually consists of a pre-existent play mediated by a particular performance which offers one of many possible interpretations of the play. Film, in contrast, is regarded as unmediated—because of its larger-than-life scale and more unrefusable impact on the eye, and because (in Panofsky's words) "the medium of the movies is physical reality as such" and the characters in a movie "have no aesthetic existence outside the actors." But there is an equally valid sense which shows movies to be the mediated art and theatre the unmediated one. We see what happens on the stage with our own eyes. We see on the screen what the camera sees. In the cinema, narration proceeds by ellipsis (the "cut" or change of shot); the camera eye is a unified point of view that continually displaces itself. But the change of shot can provoke questions, the simplest of which is: from *whose* point of view is the shot seen? And the ambiguity of point of view latent in all cinematic narration has no equivalent in the theatre.

Indeed, one should not neglect to emphasize the aesthetically positive role of disorientation in the cinema. Examples: Busby Berkeley dollying back from an ordinary-looking stage already established as some thirty feet deep to disclose a stage area three hundred feet square. Resnais panning from character X's point of view a full 360°, to come to rest upon X's face.

Much may be made of the fact that, in its concrete existence, cinema is an *object* (a *product,* even) while theatre is a *performance.* Is this so important? In a way, no. Whether objects (like films or paintings) or performances (like music or theatre), all art is first a mental act, a fact of consciousness. The object aspect of film, the performance aspect of theatre are merely means—means to the experience, which is not only "of" but "through" the film and the theatre-event. Each subject of an aesthetic experience shapes it to his own measure. With respect to any *single* experience, it hardly matters that a film is usually identical from one projection of it to another while theatre performances are highly mutable.

The difference between object-art and performance-art lies behind Panofsky's observation that "the screenplay, in contrast to the theatre play, has no aesthetic existence independent of its performance," and characters in movies *are* the stars who enact them. It is because the film is an object, a totality that is set, that movie roles are identical with the actors' performances; while in the theatre (in the West, an additive rather than an organic art?) only the written play is "fixed," an object and therefore existing apart from any staging of it. Yet this dichotomy is not beyond dispute. Just as movies needn't necessarily be designed to be shown in theatres at all (they can be intended for more continuous and casual looking), a movie *may* be altered from one projection to the next. Harry Smith, when he runs off his own films, makes each projection an unrepeatable performance. And, again, it is not true that all theatre is only about written plays which may be given a good or a bad production. In Happenings and other recent theatre-events, we are precisely being offered "plays" identical with their productions in the same sense as the screenplay is identical with the film.

Yet, a difference remains. Because the film is an object, it is totally manipulable, totally calculable. A film is like a book, another portable art-object; making a film, like writing a book, means constructing an inanimate thing, every element of which is determinate. Indeed, in films, this determinacy has or can have a quasi-mathematical form, like music. (A shot lasts a certain number of seconds, a change of angle of so many degrees is required to "match" two shots.) Given the total determinacy of the result on celluloid (whatever the extent of the director's conscious intervention), it was inevitable that some film directors would want to devise schemas to make their intentions more exact. Thus, it was neither perverse nor primitive of Busby Berkeley to have used only one camera to shoot the whole of each of his mammoth dance numbers. Every "set-up" was designed to be shot from only one exactly calculated angle. Bresson, working on a far more self-conscious level of artistry, has declared that, for him, the director's task is to find the single correct way of doing each shot. An image cannot be justified in itself, according to Bresson; it has an exactly specifiable relation to the temporally adjacent images, which relation constitutes its "meaning."

But the theatre allows only the loosest approximation to this sort of formal concern. (And responsibility. Justly, French critics speak of the director of a film as its "author.") Because they are performances, something always "live," theatre-events are not subject to a comparable degree of control, do not admit a comparably exact integration of effects.

It would be foolish to conclude that the best films are those which arise from the greatest amount of conscious planning; the plan may be faulty; and with some directors, instinct works better than any plan. Besides, there is an impressive body of "improvised" cinema. (To be distinguished from the work of some film-makers, notably Godard, who have become fascinated with the "look" of improvised cinema.) Nevertheless, it seems indisputable that cinema, not only potentially but by its nature, is a more rigorous art than theatre.

Thus, not merely a failure of nerve accounts for the fact that theatre, this seasoned art, occupied since antiquity with all sorts of local offices—enacting sacred rites, reinforcing communal loyalty, guiding morals, provoking the therapeutic discharge of violent emotions, conferring social status, giving practical instruction, affording entertainment, dignifying celebrations, subverting established authority—is now on the defensive before movies, this brash art with its huge, amorphous, passive audience. Meanwhile, movies continue to maintain their astonishing pace of formal articulation. (Take the commercial cinema of Europe, Japan, and the United States simply since 1960, and consider what audiences have become habituated to in the way of increasingly elliptical story-telling and visualization.)

But note: this youngest of the arts is also the one most heavily burdened with memory. Cinema is a time machine. Movies preserve the past, while theatres—no matter how devoted to the classics, to old plays—can only "modernize." Movies resurrect the beautiful dead; present intact vanished or ruined environments; employ, without irony, styles and fashions that seem funny today; solemnly ponder irrelevant or naïve problems. The historical flavor of anything registered on celluloid is so vivid that practically all films older than two years or so are saturated with a kind of pathos. (The pathos I am describing, which overtakes animated cartoons and drawn, abstract films as well as ordinary movies, is not simply that of old photographs.) Films age (being objects) as no theatre-event does (being always new). There is no pathos of mortality in theatre's "reality" as such, nothing in our response to a good performance of a Mayakovsky play comparable to the aesthetic role the emotion of nostalgia has when we see a film by Pudovkin.

Also worth noting: compared with the theatre, innovations in cinema seem to be assimilated more efficiently, seem altogether to be more shareable—and not only because new films are quickly and widely circulated. Also, partly because virtually the entire body of accomplishment in film can be consulted in the present, most film-makers are more knowledgeable about the history of their art than most theatre directors are about the recent past of theirs.

The key word in many discussions of cinema is "possibility." A merely classifying use of the word occurs, as in Panofsky's engaging judgment that, "within their self-imposed limitations the earlier Disney films . . . represent, as it were, a chemically pure distillation of cinematic possibilities." But behind this relatively neutral sense lurks a more polemical sense of cinema's "possibility." What is regularly intimated is the obsolescence of theatre, its supercession by films.

Thus, Panofsky describes the mediation of the camera eye as opening "up a world of possibility of which the stage can never dream." Artaud, earlier, thought that motion pictures may have made the theatre obsolete. Movies "possess a sort of virtual power which probes into the mind and uncovers undreamt of possibilities. . . . When this art's exhilaration has been blended in the right proportions with the psychic ingredient it commands, it will leave the theatre far behind and we will relegate the latter to the attic of our memories."

Meyerhold, facing the challenge head on, thought the only hope for theatre lay in a wholesale emulation of the cinema. "Let us 'cinematify' the theatre," he urged. The staging of plays must be "industrialized," theatres must accommodate audiences in the tens of thousands rather than in the hundreds, etc. Meyerhold also seemed to find some relief in the idea that the coming of sound signalled the downfall of movies. Believing that their international appeal depended entirely on the fact that screen actors didn't speak any particular language, he couldn't imagine in

1930 that, even if that were so, technology (dubbing, sub-titling) could solve the problem.

Is cinema the successor, the rival, or the revivifier of the theatre?

Art forms *have* been abandoned. (Whether because they became obsolete is another question.) One can't be sure that theatre is not in a state of irremediable decline, spurts of local vitality notwithstanding. But why should it be rendered obsolete by movies? It's worth remembering that predictions of obsolescence amount to declaring that a something has one peculiar task (which another something may do as well or better). Has theatre one peculiar task or aptitude?

Those who predict the demise of the theatre, assuming that cinema has engulfed its function, tend to impute a relation between films and theatre reminiscent of what was once said about photography and painting. If the painter's job had been no more than fabricating likenesses, the invention of the camera might indeed have made painting obsolete. But painting is hardly just "pictures," any more than cinema is just theatre for the masses, available in portable standard units.

In the naïve tale of photography and painting, painting was reprieved when it claimed a new task, abstraction. As the superior realism of photography was supposed to have liberated painting, allowing it to go abstract, cinema's superior power to represent (not merely to stimulate) the imagination may appear to have emboldened the theatre in a similar fashion, inviting the gradual obliteration of the conventional "plot."

Actually, painting and photography evidence parallel developments rather than a rivalry or a supercession. And, at least in principle, so have theatre and film. The possibilities for theatre that lie in going beyond psychological realism, in seeking greater abstractness, are not less germane to the future of narrative films. Conversely, the notion of movies as witness to real life, testimony rather than invention, the treatment of collective situations rather than the depiction of personal "dramas," is equally relevant to the stage. Not surprisingly, what follows some years after the rise of *cinema verité,* the sophisticated heir of documentary films, is a documentary theatre, the "theatre of fact." (Cf. Hochhuth, Weiss's *The Investigation,* recent projects of the Royal Shakespeare Company in London.)

The influence of the theatre upon films in the early years is well known. According to Kracauer, the distinctive lighting of *Dr. Caligari* (and of many subsequent German silents) can be traced to an experiment with lighting Max Reinhardt made shortly before, in his production of Sorge's play, *The Beggar.* Even in this period, however, the impact was reciprocal. The accomplishments of the "Expressionist film" were immediately absorbed by the Expressionist theatre. Stimulated by the cinematic technique of the "iris-in," stage lighting took to singling out a lone player, or some segment of the scene, masking out the rest of the stage. Rotating sets tried to approximate the instantaneous displacement of the camera eye. (More recently, reports have come of ingenious lighting techniques used by the Gorki Theatre in Leningrad, directed since 1956 by Georgi Tovstonogov, which allow for incredibly rapid scene changes taking place behind a horizontal curtain of light.)

Today traffic seems, with few exceptions, entirely one way: film to theatre. Particularly in France and in Central and Eastern Europe, the staging of many plays is inspired by the movies. The aim of adapting neo-cinematic devices for the stage (I exclude the outright use of films within the theatre production) seems mainly to tighten up the theatrical experience, to approximate the cinema's absolute control of the flow and location of the audience's attention. But the conception can be even more directly cinematic. Example: Josef Svoboda's production of *The Insect Play* by the Capek brothers at the Czech National Theatre in Prague (recently seen in London) which frankly attempted to install a mediated vision upon the stage, equivalent to the discontinuous intensifications of the camera eye. According to a London critic's account, "the set consisted of two huge, faceted mirrors slung at an angle to the stage, so that they reflect whatever happens there defracted as if through a decanter stopper or the colossally magnified eye of a fly. Any figure placed at the base of their angle becomes multiplied from floor to proscenium; farther out, and you find yourself viewing it not only face to face but from overhead, the vantage point of a camera slung to a bird or a helicopter."

Perhaps the first to propose the use of film itself as *one* element in a theatre experience was Marinetti. Writing between 1910 and 1914, he envisaged the theatre as a final synthesis of all the arts; and as such it had to use the newest art form movies. No doubt the cinema also recommended itself for inclusion because of the priority Marinetti gave to the use of existing forms of popular entertainment, such as the variety theatre and the *café-chantant*. (He called his projected art form "the Futurist Variety Theatre.") And cinema, at that time, was not considered as anything other than a vulgar art.

Soon after, the idea begins to occur frequently. In the total-theatre projects of the Bauhaus group in the 1920's (Gropius, Piscator, etc.), film had a regular place. Meyerhold insisted on its use in the theatre. (He described his program as fulfilling Wagner's once "wholly utopian" proposals to "use all means available from the other arts.") Film's actual employment has by now a fairly long history, which includes "the living newspaper," "epic theatre," and "happenings." This year marked the introduction of a film sequence into Broadway-type theatre. In two highly successful musicals, London's *Come Spy with Me* and New York's *Superman,* both parodic in tone, the action is interrupted to lower a screen and run off a movie showing the pop-art hero's exploits.

Thus far, the use of film within live theatre-events has tended to be stereotyped. Film is employed as *document,* supportive of or redundant to the live stage events (as in Brecht's productions in East Berlin). Or else it is employed as *hallucinant;* recent examples are Bob Whitman's Happenings, and a new kind of nightclub situation, the mixed-media discothèque (Andy Warhol's The Plastic Inevitable, Murray the K's World). The interpolation of film into the theatre-experience may be enlarging from the point of view of theatre. But in terms of what film is capable of, it seems a reductive, monotonous use of film.

Every interesting aesthetic tendency now is a species of radicalism. The question each artist must ask is: What is *my* radicalism, the one dictated by *my* gifts and temperament? This doesn't mean all contemporary artists believe that art progresses. A radical position isn't necessarily a forward-looking position.

Consider the two principal radical positions in the arts today. One recommends the breaking down of distinctions between genres: the arts would eventuate in one art, consisting of many different kinds of behavior going on at the same time, a vast behavioral magma or synaesthesis. The other position recommends the maintaining and clarifying of barriers between the arts, by the intensification of what each art distinctively is; painting must use only those means which pertain to painting, music only those which are musical, novels those which pertain to the novel and to no other literary form, etc.

The two positions are, in a sense, irreconcilable. Except that both are invoked to support a perennial modern quest—the quest for the definitive art form. An art may be proposed as definitive because it is considered the most rigorous, or most fundamental. For these reasons, Schopenhauer suggested and Pater asserted that all art aspires to the condition of music. More recently, the thesis that all the arts are leading toward one art has been advanced by enthusiasts of the cinema. The candidacy of film is founded on its being so exact and, potentially, so complex—a rigorous combination of music, literature, and the image.

Or, an art may be proposed as definitive because it is the most inclusive. This is the basis of the destiny for theatre held out by Wagner, Marinetti, Artaud, John Cage—all of whom envisage theatre as nothing less than a total art, potentially conscripting all the arts into its service. And as the ideas of synaesthesia continue to proliferate among painters, sculptors, architects, and composers, theatre remains the favored candidate for the role of summative art. So conceived, of course, theatre's claims do contradict those of cinema. Partisans of theatre would argue that while music, painting, dance, cinema, the speaking of words, etc. can all converge on a "stage," the film-object can only become bigger (multiple screens, 360° projection, etc.) or longer in duration or more internally articulated and complex. Theatre can be anything, everything; in the end, films can only be more of what they specifically (that is to say, cinematically) are.

Underlying the competing apocalyptic expectations for both arts, one detects a common animus. In 1923 Béla Balázs, anticipating in great detail the thesis of Marshall McLuhan, described movies as the herald of a new "visual culture" that will give us back our bodies, and particularly our faces, which have been rendered illegible, soulless, unexpressive by the centuries-old ascendancy of "print." An animus against literature, against "the printing press" and its "culture of concepts," also informs most of the interesting thinking about the theatre in our time.

What's important is that no definition or characterization of theatre and cinema, even the most self-evident, be taken for granted.

For instance: both cinema and theatre are temporal arts. Like music (and unlike painting), everything is *not* present all at once.

Could this be modified? The allure of mixed-media forms in theatre suggests not only a more elongated and more complex "drama" (like Wagnerian opera) but also a more compact theatre-experience which approaches the condition of painting. This prospect of increased compactness is broached by Marinetti; he calls it simultaneity, a leading idea of Futurist aesthetics. In becoming a final synthesis of all the arts, says Marinetti, theatre "would use the new twentieth-century devices of electricity and the cinema; this would enable plays to be extremely short, since all these technical means would enable the theatrical synthesis to be achieved in the shortest possible space of time, as all the elements could be presented simultaneously."

A pervasive notion in both advanced cinema and theatre is the idea of art as an act of violence. Its source is to be found in the aesthetics of Futurism and of Surrealism; its principal "texts" are, for theatre, the writings of Artaud and, for cinema, the two classic films of Luis Buñuel, *L'Age d'Or* and *Un Chien Andalou.* (More recent examples: the early plays of Ionesco, at least as conceived; the "cinema of cruelty" of Hitchcock, Clouzot, Franju, Robert Aldrich, Polanski; work by the Living Theatre; some of the neocinematic lighting techniques used in experimental theatres; the sound of late Cage and LaMonte Young.) The relation of art to an audience understood to be passive, inert, surfeited, can only be assault. Art becomes identical with aggression.

This theory of art as assault on the audience—like the complementary notion of art as ritual—is understandable, and precious. Still, one must not neglect to question it, particularly in the theatre. For it can become as much a convention as anything else; and end, like all theatrical conventions, by reinforcing the deadness of the audience. (As Wagner's ideology of a total theatre played its role in confirming the stupidity and bestiality of German culture.)

Moreover, the depth of the assault must be assessed honestly. In the theatre, this entails not "diluting" Artaud. Artaud's writings represent the demand for a totally open (therefore, flayed, self-cruel) consciousness of which theatre would be *one* adjunct or instrument. No work in the theatre has yet amounted to this. Thus, Peter Brook has astutely and forthrightly disclaimed that his company's work in London in the "Theatre of Cruelty," which culminated in his celebrated production of Weiss's *Marat/Sade,* is genuinely Artaudian. It is Artaudian, he says, in a trivial sense only. (Trivial from Artaud's point of view, not from ours.)

For some time, all useful ideas in art have been extremely sophisticated. Like the idea that everything is what it is, and not another thing. A painting is a painting. Sculpture is sculpture. A poem is a poem, not prose. Etcetera. And the complementary idea: a painting can be "literary" or sculptural, a poem can be prose, theatre can emulate and incorporate cinema, cinema can be theatrical.

We need a new idea. It will probably be a very simple one. Will we be able to recognize it?

1966

ANDRÉ BAZIN
FROM WHAT IS CINEMA?

THEATRE AND CINEMA

The leitmotiv of those who despise filmed theatre, their final and apparently insuperable argument, continues to be the unparalleled pleasure that accompanies the presence of the actor. "What is specific to theater," writes Henri Gouhier, in *The Essence of Theater,* "is the impossibility of separating off action and actor." Elsewhere he says "the stage welcomes every illusion except that of presence; the actor is there is disguise, with the soul and voice of another, but he is nevertheless there and by the same token space calls out for him and for the solidity of his presence. On the other hand and inversely, the cinema accommodates every form of reality save one—the physical presence of the actor." If it is here that the essence of theater lies then undoubtedly the cinema can in no way pretend to any parallel with it. If the writing, the style, and the dramatic structure are, as they should be, rigorously conceived as the receptacle for the soul and being of the flesh-and-blood actor, any attempt to substitute the shadow and reflection of a man on the screen for the man himself is a completely vain enterprise. There is no answer to this argument. The successes of Laurence Olivier, of Welles, or of Cocteau can only be challenged—here you need to be in bad faith—or considered inexplicable. They are a challenge both to critics and philosophers. Alternatively one can only explain them by casting doubts on that commonplace of theatrical criticism "the irreplaceable presence of the actor."

THE CONCEPT OF PRESENCE

At this point certain comments seem called for concerning the concept of "presence," since it would appear that it is this concept, as understood prior to the appearance of photography, that the cinema challenges.

Can the photographic image, especially the cinematographic image, be likened to other images and in common with them be regarded as having an existence dis-

375

tinct from the object? Presence, naturally, is defined in terms of time and space. "To be in the presence of someone" is to recognize him as existing contemporaneously with us and to note that he comes within the actual range of our senses—in the case of cinema of our sight and in radio of our hearing. Before the arrival of photography and later of cinema, the plastic arts (especially portraiture) were the only intermediaries between actual physical presence and absence. Their justification was their resemblance which stirs the imagination and helps the memory. But photography is something else again. In no sense is it the image of an object or person, more correctly it is its tracing. Its automatic genesis distinguishes it radically from the other techniques of reproduction. The photograph proceeds by means of the lens to the taking of a veritable luminous impression in light—to a mold. As such it carries with it more than mere resemblance, namely a kind of identity—the card we call by that name being only conceivable in an age of photography. But photography is a feeble technique in the sense that its instantaneity compels it to capture time only piecemeal. The cinema does something strangely paradoxical. It makes a molding of the object as it exists in time and, furthermore, makes an imprint of the duration of the object.

The nineteenth century with its objective techniques of visual and sound reproduction gave birth to a new category of images, and relation of which to the reality from which they proceed requires very strict definition. Even apart from the fact that the resulting aesthetic problems cannot be satisfactorily raised without this introductory philosophical inquiry, it would not be sound to treat the old aesthetic questions as if the categories with which they deal had in no way been modified by the appearance of completely new phenomena. Common sense—perhaps the best philosophical guide in this case—has clearly understood this and has invented an expression for the presence of an actor, by adding to the placards announcing his appearance the phrase "in flesh and blood." This means that for the man in the street the word "presence," today, can be ambiguous, and thus an apparent redundancy is not out of place in this age of cinema. Hence it is no longer as certain as it was that there is no middle stage between presence and absence. It is likewise at the ontological level that the effectiveness of the cinema has its source. It is false to say that the screen is incapable of putting us "in the presence of" the actor. It does so in the same way as a mirror—one must agree that the mirror relays the presence of the person reflected in it—but it is a mirror with a delayed reflection, the tin foil of which retains the image.* It is true that in the theater Molière can die on the stage

---

*Television naturally adds a new variant to the "pseudopresences" resulting from the scientific techniques for reproduction created by photography. On the little screen during live television the actor is actually present in space and time. But the reciprocal actor-spectator relationship is incomplete in one direction. The spectator sees without being seen. There is no return flow. Televised theater, therefore, seems to share something both of theater and of cinema: of theater because the actor is present to the viewer, of cinema because the spectator is not present to the actor. Nevertheless, this state of not being present is not truly an absence. The television actor has a sense of the millions of ears and eyes virtually present and represented by the electronic camera. This abstract presence is most noticeable when the actor fluffs his lines. Painful enough in the theater, it is intolerable on television since the spectator who can do nothing to help him is aware of the unnatural solitude of the actor. In the theater in similar circumstances a sort of understanding exists with the audience, which is a help to an actor in trouble. This kind of reciprocal relationship is impossible on television.

and that we have the privilege of living in the biographical time of the actor. In the film about Manolete however we are present at the actual death of the famous matador and while our emotion may not be as deep as if we were actually present in the arena at that historic moment, its nature is the same. What we lose by way of direct witness do we not recapture thanks to the artificial proximity provided by photographic enlargement? Everything takes place as if in the time-space perimeter which is the definition of presence. The cinema offers us effectively only a measure of duration, reduced but not to zero, while the increase in the space factor reestablishes the equilibrium of the psychological equation.

OPPOSITION AND IDENTIFICATION

An honest appraisal of the respective pleasures derived from theater and cinema, at least as to what is less intellectual and more direct about them, forces us to admit that the delight we experience at the end of a play has a more uplifting, a nobler, one might perhaps say a more moral, effect than the satisfaction which follows a good film. We seem to come away with a better conscience. In a certain sense it is as if for the man in the audience all theater is "Corneillian." From this point of view one could say that in the best films something is missing. It is as if a certain inevitable lowering of the voltage, some mysterious aesthetic short circuit, deprived us in the cinema of a certain tension which is a definite part of theater. No matter how slight this difference it undoubtedly exists, even between the worst charity production in the theater and the most brilliant of Olivier's film adaptations. There is nothing banal about this observation and the survival of the theater after fifty years of cinema, and the prophecies of Marcel Pagnol, is practical proof enough. At the source of the disenchantment which follows the film one could doubtless detect a process of depersonalization of the spectator. As Rosenkrantz wrote in 1937, in *Esprit,* in an article profoundly original for its period, "The characters on the screen are quite naturally objects of identification, while those on the stage are, rather, objects of mental opposition because their real presence gives them an objective reality and to transpose them into beings in an imaginary world the will of the spectator has to intervene actively, that is to say, to will to transform their physical reality into an abstraction. This abstraction being the result of a process of the intelligence that we can only ask of a person who is fully conscious." A member of a film audience tends to identify himself with the film's hero by a psychological process, the result of which is to turn the audience into a "mass" and to render emotion uniform. Just as in algebra if two numbers equal a third, then they are equal to one another, so here we can say, if two individuals identify themselves with a third, they identify themselves with one another. Let us compare chorus girls on the stage and on the screen. On the screen they satisfy an unconscious sexual desire and when the hero joins them he satisfies the desire of the spectator in the proportion to which the latter has identified himself with the hero. On the stage the girls excite the onlooker as they would in real life. The result is that there is no identification with the hero. He becomes instead an object of jealousy and envy. In other words, Tarzan is only possible on the screen. The cinema calms the spectator, the theater excites him. Even when it appeals to the lowest instincts, the theater up to a certain point stands in the way of the creation of a mass mentality.* It stands in the way of any collective representation in the psychological sense, since theater calls for an active individual consciousness while the film requires only a passive adhesion.

These views shed a new light on the problem of the actor. They transfer him from the ontological to the psychological level. It is to the extent to which the cinema encourages identification with the hero that it conflicts with the theater. Put this way the problem is no longer basically insoluble, for it is a fact that the cinema has at its disposal means which favor a passive position or on the other hand, means which to a greater or lesser degree stimulate the consciousness of the spectator. Inversely the theater can find ways of lessening the psychological tension between spectator and actor. Thus theater and cinema will no longer be separated off by an unbridgeable aesthetic moat, they would simply tend to give rise to two attitudes of mind over which the director maintains a wide control.

Examined at close quarters, the pleasure derived from the theater not only differs from that of the cinema but also from that of the novel. The reader of a novel, physically alone like the man in the dark movie house, identifies himself with the character. That is why after reading for a long while he also feels the same intoxication of an illusory intimacy with the hero. Incontestably, there is in the pleasure derived from cinema and novel a self-satisfaction, a concession to solitude, a sort of betrayal of action by a refusal of social responsibility.

The analysis of this phenomenon might indeed be undertaken from a psychoanalytic point of view. Is it not significant that the psychiatrists took the term catharsis from Aristotle? Modern pedagogic research on psychodrama seems to have provided fruitful insights into the cathartic process of theater. The ambiguity existing in the child's mind between play and reality is used to get him to free himself by way of improvised theater from the repressions from which he suffers. This technique amounts to creating a kind of vague theater in which the play is of a serious nature and the actor is his own audience. The action that develops on these occasions is not one that is divided off by footlights, which are undoubtedly the architectural symbol of the censor that separates us from the stage. We delegate Oedipus to act in our guise and place him on the other side of a wall of fire—that fiery frontier between fantasy and reality which gives rein to Dionysiac monsters while protecting us from them. These sacred beasts will not cross this barrier of light beyond which they seem out of place and even sacrilegious—witness the disturbing atmosphere of awe which surrounds an actor still made up, like a phosphorescent light, when we visit him in his dressing room. There is no point to the argument that the theater did not always have footlights. These are only a symbol and there were others before them from the cothurnus and mask onwards. In the seventeenth century the fact that young nobles sat up on the stage is no denial of the role of the footlights, on the contrary, it confirms it, by way of a privileged violation so to speak, just as when today Orson Welles scatters actors around the auditorium to fire on the audience with revolvers. He does not do away with the footlights, he just

---

*Crowd and solitude are not antinomies: the audience in a movie house is made up of solitary individuals. Crowd should be taken here to mean the opposite of an organic community freely assembled.

crosses them. The rules of the game are also made to be broken. One expects some players to cheat.* With regard to the objection based on presence and on that alone, the theater and the cinema are not basically in conflict. What is really in dispute are two psychological modalities of a performance. The theater is indeed based on the reciprocal awareness of the presence of audience and actor, but only as related to a performance. The theater acts on us by virtue of our participation in a theatrical action across the footlights and as it were under the protection of their censorship. The opposite is true in the cinema. Alone, hidden in a dark room, we watch through half-open blinds a spectacle that is unaware of our existence and which is part of the universe. There is nothing to prevent us from identifying ourselves in imagination with the moving world before us, which becomes *the* world. It is no longer on the phenomenon of the actor as a person physically present that we should concentrate our analysis, but rather on the ensemble of conditions that constitute the theatrical play and deprive the spectator of active participation. We shall see that it is much less a question of actor and presence than of man and his relation to the decor.

BEHIND THE DECOR

The human being is all-important in the theater. The drama on the screen can exist without actors. A banging door, a leaf in the wind, waves beating on the shore can heighten the dramatic effect. Some film masterpieces use man only as an accessory, like an extra, or in counterpoint to nature which is the true leading character. Even when, as in *Nanook* and *Man of Aran,* the subject is man's struggle with nature, it cannot be compared to a theatrical action. The mainspring of the action is not in man but nature. As Jean-Paul Sartre, I think it was, said, in the theater the drama proceeds from the actor, in the cinema it goes from the decor to man. This reversal of the dramatic flow is of decisive importance. It is bound up with the very essence of the *mise-en-scène*. One must see here one of the consequences of photographic realism. Obviously, if the cinema makes use of nature it is because it is able to. The camera puts at the disposal of the director all the resources of the telescope and the microscope. The last strand of a rope about to snap or an entire army making an assault on a hill are within our reach. Dramatic causes and effects have no longer any material limits to the eye of the camera. Drama is freed by the camera from all contingencies of time and space. But this freeing of tangible dramatic powers is still only a secondary aesthetic cause, and does not basically explain the rever-

---

*Here is a final example proving that presence does not constitute theater except in so far as it is a matter of a performance. Everyone either at his own or someone else's expense has known the embarrassment of being watched without knowing it or in spite of knowing it. Lovers who kiss on public benches offer a spectacle to the passerby, but they do not care. My concierge who has a feeling for the *mot juste* says, when she sees them, that is like being at the movies. Each of us has sometimes found himself forced to his annoyance to do something absurd before other people. On those occasions we experience a sense of angry shame which is the very opposite of theatrical exhibitionism. Someone who looks through a keyhole is not at the theater; Cocteau has rightly demonstrated in *Le sang d'un poète* that he was already at the cinema. And nevertheless there are such things as "shows," when the protagonists are present to us in flesh and blood but one of the two parties is ignorant of the fact or goes through with it reluctantly. This is not "play" in the theatrical sense.

sal of value between the actor and the decor. For sometimes it actually happens that the cinema deliberately deprives itself of the use of setting and of exterior nature—we have already seen a perfect instance of this in *Les Parents terribles*—while the theater in contrast uses a complex machinery to give a feeling of ubiquity to the audience. Is *La Passion de Jeanne d'Arc* by Carl Dreyer, shot entirely in close-up, in the virtually invisible and in fact theatrical settings by Jean Hugo, less cinematic than *Stagecoach?* It seems to me that quantity has nothing to do with it, nor the resemblance to certain theater techniques. The ideas of an art director for a room in *Les Dames aux camélias* would not noticeably differ whether for a film or a play. It's true that on the screen you would doubtless have some close-ups of the blood-stained handkerchief, but a skillful stage production would also know how to make some play with the cough and the handkerchief. All the close-ups in *Les Parents terribles* are taken directly from the theater where our attention would spontaneously isolate them. If film direction only differed from theater direction because it allows us a closer view of the scenery and makes a more reasonable use of it, there would really be no reason to continue with the theater and Pagnol would be a true prophet. For it is obvious that the few square yards of the decor of Vilar's *La Danse de la mort* contributed as much to the drama as the island on which Marcel Cravene shot his excellent film. The fact is that the problem lies not in the decor itself but in its nature and function. We must therefore throw some light on an essentially theatrical notion, that of the dramatic place.

There can be no theater without architecture, whether it be the cathedral square, the arena of Nîmes, the palace of the Popes, the trestle stage on a fairground, the semicircle of the theater of Vicenza that looks as if it were decorated by Bérard in a delirium, or the rococo amphitheaters on the boulevard houses. Whether as a performance or a celebration, theater of its very essence must not be confused with nature under penalty of being absorbed by her and ceasing to be. Founded on the reciprocal awareness of those taking part and present to one another, it must be in contrast to the rest of the world in the same way that play and reality are opposed, or concern and indifference, or liturgy and the common use of things. Costume, mask, or make-up, the style of the language, the footlights, all contribute to this distinction, but the clearest sign of all is the stage, the architecture of which has varied from time to time without ever ceasing to mark out a privileged spot actually or virtually distinct from nature. It is precisely in virtue of this *locus dramaticus* that decor exists. It serves in greater or less degree to set the place apart, to specify. Whatever it is, the decor constitutes the walls of this three-sided box opening onto the auditorium, which we call the stage. These false perspectives, these façades, these arbors, have another side which is cloth and nails and wood. Everyone knows that when the actor "retires to his apartment" from the yard or from the garden, he is actually going to his dressing room to take off his make-up. These few square feet of light and illusion are surrounded by machinery and flanked by wings, the hidden labyrinths of which do not interfere one bit with the pleasure of the spectator who is playing the game of theater. Because it is only part of the architecture of the stage, the decor of the theater is thus an area materially enclosed, limited, circumscribed, the only discoveries of which are those of our collusive imagination.

Theater in Cinema. Jean Marais, Yvonne de Bray, Gabrielle Dorziat, Marcel André, and Josette Day in *Les Parents Terribles* (1948). It "deliberately deprives itself of the use of setting and of exterior nature" (BAZIN, page 380). Anna Magnani onstage in the *commedia dell'arte* of *The Golden Coach* (1952). Renoir incorporates the artifice of the theater into the cinema without destroying "that realism of space without which moving pictures do not constitute cinema" (BAZIN, page 386).

Its appearances are turned inward facing the public and the footlights. It exists by virtue of its reverse side and of anything beyond, as the painting exists by virtue of its frame. Just as the picture is not to be confounded with the scene it represents and is not a window in a wall. The stage and the decor where the action unfolds constitute an aesthetic microcosm inserted perforce into the universe but essentially distinct from the Nature which surrounds it.

It is not the same with cinema, the basic principle of which is a denial of any frontiers to action.

The idea of a *locus dramaticus* is not only alien to, it is essentially a contradiction of the concept of the screen. The screen is not a frame like that of a picture but a mask which allows only a part of the action to be seen. When a character moves off screen, we accept the fact that he is out of sight, but he continues to exist in his own capacity at some other place in the decor which is hidden from us. There are no wings to the screen. There could not be without destroying its specific illusion, which is to make of a revolver or of a face the very center of the universe. In contrast to the stage the space of the screen is centrifugal. It is because that infinity which the theater demands cannot be spatial that its area can be none other than the human soul. Enclosed in this space the actor is at the focus of a two-fold concave mirror. From the auditorium and from the decor there converge on him the dim lights of conscious human beings and of the footlights themselves. But the fire with which he burns is at once that of his inner passion and of that focal point at which he stands. He lights up in each member of his audience an accomplice flame. Like the ocean in a sea shell the dramatic infinities of the human heart moan and beat between the enclosing walls of the theatrical sphere. This is why this dramaturgy is in its essence human. Man is at once its cause and its subject.

On the screen man is no longer the focus of the drama, but will become eventually the center of the universe. The impact of his action may there set in motion an infinitude of waves. The decor that surrounds him is part of the solidity of the world. For this reason the actor as such can be absent from it, because man in the world enjoys no a priori privilege over animals and things. However there is no reason why he should not be the mainspring of the drama, as in Dreyer's *Jeanne d'Arc,* and in this respect the cinema may very well impose itself upon the theater. As actions *Phèdre* or *King Lear* are no less cinematographic than theatrical, and the visible death of a rabbit in *La Règle du jeu* affects us just as deeply as that of Agnès' little cat about which we are merely told.

But if Racine, Shakespeare, or Molière cannot be brought to the cinema by just placing them before the camera and the microphone, it is because the handling of the action and the style of the dialogue were conceived as echoing through the architecture of the auditorium. What is specifically theatrical about these tragedies is not their action so much as the human, that is to say the verbal, priority given to their dramatic structure. The problem of filmed theater at least where the classics are concerned does not consist so much in transposing an action from the stage to the screen as in transposing a text written for one dramaturgical system into another while at the same time retaining its effectiveness. It is not therefore essentially the action of a play which resists film adaptation, but above and beyond the phases of the intrigue (which it would be easy enough to adapt to the realism of the screen) it is the verbal form which aesthetic contingencies or cultural prejudices oblige us to respect. It is this which refuses to let itself be captured in the window of the screen. "The theater," says Baudelaire," is a crystal chandelier." If one were called upon to offer in comparison a symbol other than this artificial crystal-like object, brilliant, intricate, and circular, which refracts the light which plays around its center and holds us prisoners of its aureole, we might say of the cinema that it is the little flashlight of the usher, moving like an uncertain comet across the night of our waking dream, the diffuse space without shape or frontiers that surrounds the screen.

The story of the failures and recent successes of theater on film will be found to be that of the ability of directors to retain the dramatic force of the play in a medium that reflects it or, at least, the ability to give this dramatic force enough resonance to permit a film audience to perceive it. In other words, it is a matter of an aesthetic that is not concerned with the actor but with decor and editing. Henceforth it is clear that filmed theater is basically destined to fail whenever it tends in any manner to become simply the photographing of scenic representation even and perhaps most of all when the camera is used to try and make us forget the footlights and the backstage area. The dramatic force of the text, instead of being gathered up in the actor, dissolves without echo into the cinematic ether. This is why a filmed play can show due respect to the text, be well acted in likely settings, and yet be completely worthless. This is what happened, to take a convenient example, to *Le Voyageur sans baggages*. The play lies there before us apparently true to itself yet drained of every ounce of energy, like a battery dead from an unknown short. But over and beyond the aesthetic of the decor we see clearly both on the screen and on the stage that in the last analysis the problem before us is that of realism. This is the problem we always end up with when we are dealing with cinema.

THE SCREEN AND THE REALISM OF SPACE

The realism of the cinema follows directly from its photographic nature. Not only does some marvel or some fantastic thing on the screen not undermine the reality of the image, on the contrary it is its most valid justification. Illusion in the cinema is not based as it is in the theater on convention tacitly accepted by the general public; rather, contrariwise, it is based on the inalienable realism of that which is shown. All trick work must be perfect in all material respects on the screen. The "invisible man" must wear pyjamas and smoke a cigarette.

Must we conclude from this that the cinema is dedicated entirely to the representation if not of natural reality at least of a plausible reality of which the spectator admits the identity with nature as he knows it? The comparative failure of German expressionism would seem to confirm this hypothesis, since it is evident that *Caligari* attempted to depart from realistic decor under the influence of the theater and painting. But this would be to offer an oversimplified explanation for a problem that calls for more subtle answers. We are prepared to admit that the screen opens upon an artificial world provided there exists a common denominator between the cinematographic image and the world we live in. Our experience of space is the structural basis for our concept of the universe. We may say in fact, adapting Henri Gouhier's formula, "The stage welcomes every illusion except the illusion of presence," that "the cinematographic image can be emptied of all reality save one—the reality of space."

It is perhaps an overstatement to say "all reality" because it is difficult to imagine a reconstruction of space devoid of all reference to nature. The world of the screen and our world cannot be juxtaposed. The screen of necessity substitutes for it since the very concept of universe is spatially exclusive. For a time, a film is the Universe, the world, or if you like, Nature. We will see how the films that have attempted to substitute a fabricated nature and an artificial world for the world of experience have not all equally succeeded. Admitting the failure of *Caligari* and *Die Nibelungen* we then ask ourselves how we explain the undoubted success of *Nosferatu* and *La Passion de Jeanne d'Arc,* the criterion of success being that these films have never aged. Yet it would seem at first sight that the methods of direction belong to the same aesthetic family, and that viewing the varieties of temperament and period, one could group these four films together as expressionist as distinct from realist. However, if we examine them more closely we see that there are certain basic differences between them. It is clear in the case of R. Wiene and Murnau. *Nosferatu* plays, for the greater part of the time, against natural settings whereas the fantastic qualities of *Caligari* are derived from deformities of lighting and decor. The case of Dreyer's *Jeanne d'Arc* is a little more subtle since at first sight nature plays a nonexistent role. To put it more directly, the decor by Jean Hugo is no whit less artificial and theatrical than the settings of *Caligari;* the systematic use of close-ups and unusual angles is well calculated to destroy any sense of space. Regular cinéclub goers know that the film is unfailingly introduced with the famous story of how the hair of Falconetti was actually cut in the interest of the film and likewise, the actors, we are told, wore no make-up. These references to history ordinarily have no more than gossip value. In this case, they seem to me to hold the aesthetic secret of the film; the very thing to which it owes its continued survival. It is precisely because of them that the work of Dreyer ceases to have anything in common with the theater, and indeed one might say, with man. The greater recourse Dreyer has exclusively to the human "expression," the more he has to reconvert it again into Nature. Let there be no mistake, that prodigious fresco of heads is the very opposite of an actor's film. It is a documentary of faces. It is not important how well the actors play, whereas the pockmarks on Bishop Cauchon's face and the red patches of Jean d'Yd are an integral part of the action. In this drama-through-the-microscope the whole of nature palpitates beneath every pore. The movement of a wrinkle, the pursing of a lip are seismic shocks and the flow of tides, the flux and reflux of this human epidermis. But for me Dreyer's brilliant sense of cinema is evidenced in the exterior scene which every other director would assuredly have shot in the studio. The decor as built evoked a Middle Ages of the theater and of miniatures. In one sense, nothing is less realistic than this tribunal in the cemetery or this drawbridge, but the whole is lit by the light of the sun and the gravedigger throws a spadeful of real earth into the hole.*

It is these "secondary" details, apparently aesthetically at odds with the rest of the work, which give it its truly cinematic quality.

If the paradox of the cinema is rooted in the dialectic of concrete and abstract, if cinema is committed to communicate only by way of what is real, it becomes all the more important to discern those elements in filming which confirm our sense of natural reality and those which destroy that feeling. On the other hand, it certainly argues a lack of perception to derive one's sense of reality from these accumulations of factual detail. It is possible to argue that *Les Dames du Bois de Boulogne* is an eminently realistic film, though everything about it is stylized. Everything, except for the rarely noticeable sound of a windshield-wiper, the murmur of a waterfall, or the rushing sound of soil escaping from a broken vase. These are the noises, chosen precisely for their "indifference" to the action, that guarantee its reality.

The cinema being of its essence a dramaturgy of Nature, there can be no cinema without the setting up of an open space in place of the universe rather than as part of it. The screen cannot give us the illusion of this feeling of space without calling on certain natural guarantees. But it is less a question of set construction or of architecture or of immensity than of isolating the aesthetic catalyst, which it is sufficient to introduce in an infinitesimal dose, to have it immediately take on the reality of nature.

The concrete forest of *Die Nibelungen* may well pretend to be an infinite expanse. We do not believe it to be so, whereas the trembling of just one branch in the wind, and the sunlight, would be enough to conjure up all the forests of the world.

If this analysis be well founded, then we see that the basic aesthetic problem of filmed theater is indeed that of the decor. The trump card that the director must hold is the reconversion into a window onto the world of a space oriented toward an interior dimension only, namely the closed and conventional area of the theatrical play.

It is not in Laurence Olivier's *Hamlet* that the text seems to be rendered superfluous or its strength diminished by directorial interpretations, still less in Welles' *Macbeth,* but paradoxically in the stage productions of Gaston Baty, to the precise extent that they go out of their way to create a cinematographic space on the stage; to deny that the settings have a reverse side, thus reducing the sonority of the text simply to the vibration of the voice of the actor who is left without his "resonance box" like a violin that is nothing else but strings. One would never deny that the essential thing in the theater is the text. The latter conceived for the anthropocentric expression proper to the stage and having as its function to bring nature to it cannot, without losing its raison d'être, be used in a space transparent as glass. The problem

---

*This is why I consider the graveyard scene in *Hamlet* and the death of Ophelia bad mistakes on Olivier's part. He had here a chance to introduce sun and soil by way of counterpoint to the setting of Elsinore. Does the actual shot of the sea during the soliloquy of Hamlet show that he had sensed the need for this? The idea, excellent in itself, is not well handled technically.

then that faces the filmmaker is to give his decor a dramatic opaqueness while at the same time reflecting its natural realism. Once this paradox of space has been dealt with, the director, so far from hesitating to bring theatrical conventions and faithfulness to the text to the screen will find himself now, on the contrary, completely free to rely on them. From that point on it is no longer a matter of running away from those things which "make theater" but in the long run to acknowledge their existence by rejecting the resources of the cinema, as Cocteau did in *Les Parents terribles* and Welles in *Macbeth,* or by putting them in quotation marks as Laurence Olivier did in *Henry V.* The evidence of a return to filmed theater that we have had during the last ten years belongs essentially to the history of decor and editing. It is a conquest of realism—not, certainly, the realism of subject matter or realism of expression but that realism of space without which moving pictures do not constitute cinema.

1951

LEO BRAUDY
FROM THE WORLD IN A FRAME

ACTING: STAGE VS. SCREEN

Acting in Europe and America has been historically defined by the varying interplay of the heightened and the normal, the theatrical and the nonchalant, in the conception of the role. Until the Renaissance, there was little attempt to place any special value on the absorption of the rhythm, themes, and gestures of everyday life into drama or acting style. Aristotle had taught that the most intense feelings possible in drama were those in tragedy, when the characters and the acting style were on a much higher plane than the normal life of the audience. Everyday life, where the characters and the way they behave tend to be on the same or lower social levels than the audience, was primarily a source of stylized comedy. The stage was raised above the audience in part because the characters and their impersonators were not to be considered as individually as the audience might assess each other. In Greek, Roman, and medieval society, actors therefore tended to portray beings purer than the audience, the somber figures of myth and the caricatures of comedy—a division of acting labor not unlike that of the silent screen.

Shakespeare helped make an enormous change in this relation between the audience and the actors by elaborating the analogies possible between the world and the stage. He began the European theater's effort to absorb and reflect the life of the audience as much as to bring the audience out of itself into another world. Comedy could therefore become more serious because it was no longer necessary to involve emotions lower than the grand style of tragedy. More intimate theaters and better lighting permitted a more nuanced acting style. By the mid-eighteenth century David Garrick had become the first to attempt historical authenticity in costuming, once again asserting the need to ground the play and the style of acting in some possible and plausible setting rather than a special world of theater. The "fourth wall" theories of the latter nineteenth century further defined theatrical space and dramatic acting as an extension of the world of the audience. Stylized acting did not disappear, of course. The broader styles remained in opera, ballet, and popular comedy, as well as revivals of classics, symbolic and proletarian drama, and the experiments with ritual theater from the end of World War Two to the present.

Acting on stage had necessarily developed a tradition of naturalness as well. In the eighteenth century Diderot had argued that the paradox of acting is that an actor must be cold and tranquil in order to project emotion. Actors who play from the soul, he said, are mediocre and uneven. We are not moved by the man of violence, but by the man who possesses himself. In the early twentieth century, Konstantin Stanislavsky turned Diderot's view of the actor self-possessed in passion into a whole style. He rejected theories of acting based on imitation and emphasized instead an actor's inner life as the source of energy and authenticity for his characterizations. More "mechanical" and expressionist styles of stage acting implicitly attacked Stanislavsky's methods by their emphasis on the intensity of emotion and the visual coherence of the stage ensemble. Minglings of the two traditions produced such hybrids as the Group Theater, in which the interplay between ensemble and individual produced a thematic tension often missing from Eisenstein's productions, whether on stage or in film. Elia Kazan's film style, for example, with its mixture of expressionistic, closed directorial style and open, naturalistic acting, is a direct descendant of this tradition.*

Our ability to learn what films can tell us about human character has suffered not only from preconceptions derived from the novel of psychological realism, but also from assumptions about acting that are drawn from the stage. We know much better what our attitude should be toward characters in fiction and drama. Unlike those forms, films emphasize acting and character, often at the expense of forms and language. Films add what is impossible in the group situation of the stage or the omniscient world of the novel: a sense of the mystery inside character, the strange core of connection with the face and body the audience comes to know so well, the sense of an individuality that can never be totally expressed in words or action. The stage cannot have this effect because the audience is constantly aware of the actor's impersonation. Character in film generally is more like character as we perceive it everyday than it is in any other representational art. The heightened style of silent film acting could be considered an extension of stage acting, but the more personal style allowed by sound film paradoxically both increased the appeal of films and lowered their intellectual status. The artistic was the timeless, Garbo not Dietrich, Valentino not Gable.

But character in sound film especially was not so much deficient as it was elusive. Films can be less didactic about character because the film frame is less confining than the fictional narrative or the theatrical proscenium. Sound films especially can explore the tension between the "real person" playing the role and the image projected on the screen. The line between film actor and part is much more difficult to draw than that between stage actor and role, and the social dimension of "role"

---

*Diderot's *Paradoxe sur le comédien* was not published until 1930, although it was written in the late 1760s. A later printing in 1902 may have had an influence on Stanislavsky's theories.

contrasts appropriately with the personal dimension of "part." Film acting is less impersonation than personation, part of personality but not identifiable with it. "Can Ingrid Bergman commit murder?" ask the advertisements for *Murder on the Orient Express* (Sidney Lumet, 1975); the casual substitution of actress for character crudely makes an assertion that better films explore more subtly. Unlike the stage actor, the film actor cannot get over the footlights. Although this technical necessity may seem to make him less "real" than the stage actor, it makes his relation to the character he plays much more real. Audiences demand to hear more about the private life of the film actor than the stage actor because film creates character by tantalizing the audience with the promise of the secret self, always just out of the grasp of final articulation and meaning. The other life of a stage character is the real life of the person who plays him. But the other life of a film character is the continuity in other films of the career of the actor who plays him. In plays the unrevealed self tends to be a reduced, meaner version of the displayed self; in films it is almost always a complex enhancement. Within the film a character may have a limited meaning. But the actor who plays him can potentially be a presence larger than that one part, at once more intimate and more distant than is ever possible on stage.*

Film preserves a performance that is superior to the script, whereas stage performances and plays are separate realities, with the performance often considered second best. The stage actor is performing a role: he may be the best, one of the best, the only, or one of many to play that role. But the role and its potentials will exist long after he has ceased to play it, to be interested in it, to be alive. The film actor does not so much perform a role as he creates a kind of life, playing between his characterization in a particular film and his potential escape from that character, outside the film and perhaps into other films. The stage actor memorizes an entire role in proper order, putting it on like a costume, while the film actor learns his part in pieces, often out of chronological order, using his personality as a kind of armature, or as painters will let canvas show through to become part of the total effect. If the movie is remade and another actor plays the part, there is little sense of the competition between actors that characterizes revivals on stage. "Revival" is a stage word and "remake" is a film word. Hamlet remains beyond Booth's or Olivier's or Gielgud's performance, but Alan Ladd as Gatsby and Robert Redford as Gatsby exist in different worlds.

Filmmaking is a discontinuous process, in which the order of filming is influenced more by economics than by aesthetics. Film actors must therefore either have stronger personalities than stage actors or draw upon the resources of personality much more than stage actors do. Strong film actors can never do anything out of character. Their presence defines their character and the audience is always ready for them to reveal more. Even though studio heads like Louis Mayer forced actors

---

*In these remarks, I am obviously talking not so much about the craft of acting as about the effects of acting on the audience. I would hope, however, that what I say has implications for craft and method as well, at least in terms of a test of effectiveness beyond the pleasures of theory.

Marlene Dietrich and John Lodge in Josef von Sternberg's *The Scarlet Empress* (1934). "Films add what is impossible in the group situation of the stage or the omniscient world of the novel: a sense of the mystery inside character, the strange core of connection with the face and body the audience comes to know so well, the sense of an individuality that can never be totally expressed in words or action" (BRAUDY, page 388).

and actresses to appear "in character" offscreen as well, we sense and accept potential and variety from the greatest movie actors, while we may reject less flamboyant fictional characters as "unreal" or refer to the woodenness of stage characterization. Continuity in stage acting is thematic continuity: "Watch in happiness someone whom you will soon see in sorrow" is one of the fatalistic possibilities. But the discontinuities of film acting allow the actor to concentrate on every moment as if it were the only reality that existed. No matter how conventionalized the plot, the film actor can disregard its clichés and trust instead to the force and continuity of his projected personality to satisfy beyond the more obvious forms of theme and incident. Because he must present his play in straightforward time, a stage director will work with the actor to get a "line" or a "concept" of the character that will permeate every scene. But movie acting, bound in time to the shooting schedule and the editing table, must use what is left out as well as what is expressed. The greatest difference between a film and a stage version of the same work is less in the "opening" of space that films usually emphasize than in the different sense of the inner life of the characters we get. . . .

Movies therefore stand between the strongly social emphasis of theater and the strongly individual emphasis of novels, incorporating elements of both. At a play we are always outside the group, at the footlights. But at a film we move between inside and outside, individual and social perspectives. Movie acting can therefore include stage acting better than stage acting can include movie acting. George C. Scott, for example, is essentially a stage actor who also can come across very well in film. When he was making *Patton* (Franklin Schaffner, 1970), he insisted that he repeat his entire first speech eight times to allow for the different camera angles; he refused to repeat only the sections that corresponded to the rephotographing. His sense of the character was therefore what I have been describing as a stage sense of character, in which the continuity is linear and spelled out. The performance is excellent and effective, but Scott's way of doing it tells us nothing of the differences in stage and film acting. It may have a touch of the New York stage actor's almost traditional hostility to films. At best, it is only another example of the way a newer art can more comfortably embrace the methods of an older art than the other way around. In fact, virtuosity in films tends to be a characteristic of second leads or medium minor characters, not stars, and the Academy Awards perpetuate the stage-derived standards by giving so many awards to actors and actresses cast against type, that is, for stage-style "virtuosity."

The film actor emphasizes display, while the stage actor explores disguise. But stage acting is still popularly considered to be superior to film acting. An actor who does a good job disappears into his role, while the bad (read "film") actor is only playing himself. The true actor, the professional craftsman, may use his own experience to strengthen his interpretation. But the audience should always feel that he has properly distanced and understood that experience; it is another tool in his professional workchest. The false actor, the amateur actor, the film actor, on the other hand, works on his self-image, carries it from part to part, constantly projecting the same thing—"himself." Such a belief is rooted in an accurate perception; but it is a false interpretation of that perception. The stage actor does project a sense of holding back, of discipline and understanding, the influence of head over feelings, while the film actor projects effortlessness, nonchalance, immediacy, the seemingly unpremeditated response. Thus, when stage actors attack film actors, they attack in some puritanical way the lack of perceptible hard work, obvious professional craft, in the film actor's performance. Like many nonprofessionals in their audience, such stage actors assume that naïveté, spontaneity, "being yourself," are self-images that anyone in front of a camera can achieve. A frequent Actors Studio exercise, for example, is "Private Moment," in which the student is asked to act out before the group something he or she ordinarily does alone that would be very embarrassing if someone happened to see. Private self-indulgences and private games are thereby mined for their exposable, group potential. But the concentration of film, its ability to isolate the individual, makes every moment that way, and so the problem of the film actor may be to scale down intimacy rather than discover and exaggerate it.

How do we know the "themselves" film actors play except through the residue of their playing? How much do film actors, as opposed to stage actors, model their offscreen selves to continue or contrast with their screen images? To accuse an actor of "playing himself" implies that we have seen and compared the "real" and "false" selves of the actor and reached a conclusion. Film acting deposits a residual self that snowballs from film to film, creating an image with which the actor, the scriptwriter, and the director can play as they wish. Donald Richie has recorded that the Japanese director Yasujiro Ozu said: "I could no more write, not knowing who the actor was to be, than an artist could paint, not knowing what color he was using." Ozu's remark indicates how a director takes advantage of a previously developed image in order to create a better film. But the stage actor in a sense ceases to exist from play to play; we experience only the accumulation of his talent, his versatility. In our minds the stage actor stays within the architectures he has inhabited, while the film actor exists in between as well, forever immediate to our minds and eyes, escaping the momentary enclosures that the individual films have placed around him.

"Playing yourself" involves one's interpretation of what is most successful and appealing in one's own nature and then heightening it. Film actors play their roles the way we play ourselves in the world. Audiences may now get sustenance from films and from film acting because they no longer are so interested in the social possibilities of the self that has been the metaphysic of stage acting since Shakespeare and the Renaissance, the place of role-playing in the life of the audience. The Shakespearean films of Laurence Olivier and Orson Welles clearly express the contrast. The tendency in stage acting is to subordinate oneself to the character, while the great film actor is generally more important than the character he plays. Our sense of Olivier, in his Shakespearean roles is one of distance and disguise: the purified patriotism of Henry V, in which all the play's negative hints about his character have been removed; the blond wig he uses to play Hamlet, so that, as he has said, no one will associate him with the part; the bent back, twisted fingers, and long black hair of Richard III. But Welles assimilates the roles to himself. Costume for Welles is less a disguise than a generation from within and so he presented it in various television appearances of the 1950s, gradually making up for his part while he explained the play to the audience, until he turned full face into the camera and spoke the lines. In theater we experience the gap between actor and role as expertise; in film it may be described as a kind of self-irony. The great stage actor combats the superiority of the text, its preexistence, by choosing his roles: Olivier will play Hamlet; Olivier will play a music-hall comic. The great film actor, assured that his image absorbs and makes real the script, may allow himself to be cast in unpromising roles, if only for visibility. In the audience we feel Welles's character to be part of his role, whereas we perceive not Olivier's character but his intelligence and his ability to immerse himself in a role. Olivier is putting on a great performance, but Welles feels superior enough to the Shakespearean text to cut, reorganize, and invent. Olivier is a great interpreter; Welles is an equal combatant. For both, Shakespeare is like a genre, similar to the western, that offers materials for a contemporary statement. But Olivier sticks closely to the language and form of the play itself. We judge Olivier finally by Shakespeare, but we judge Welles by other films. Both choose those Shakespearean plays that emphasize a central character. But Olivier's willingness to allow Shakespeare the last word frees him for the more assertive political roles, whereas Welles stays with the more domestic or even isolated figures of Macbeth and Othello. Olivier began his Shakespearean film career with the heroic self-confidence of Henry V, while Welles, at least for the moment, has ended his with Falstaff—the choice of the ironic imagination of film over the theatrical assertion of social power.

These distinctions between stage acting and film acting are, of course, not absolute but points on a slippery continuum. Marlon Brando's career, for example, is a constant conflict between his desire to be versatile—to do different kinds of films, use different accents, wear different costumes—and the demand of his audience that he elaborate his residual cinematic personality. Brando tries to get into his roles, and often sinks them in the process, while Cary Grant pumps them up like a balloon and watches them float off into the sky. The main trouble that Chaplin has in *A Countess from Hong Kong* (1967) is taking two actors (Brando and Sophia Loren), whose own sense of their craft emphasizes naturalistic, historically defined character, and placing them within a film world where they would best exist as masks and stereotypes. Their efforts to ground their characters destroys the film. It may be funny if Chaplin or Cary Grant vomited out a porthole, but it's not funny when Brando does it. Brando can be funny in films only as a counterpoint to our sense of "Brando," for example in *Bedtime Story* (Ralph Levy, 1964). When he is acting someone else, the ironic sense of self-image that is natural to a film actor does not exist. We share Cary Grant's sense of distance from his roles, whether they are comic, melodramatic, or whatever, because it corresponds to our sense of personal distance from our daily roles in life. The sense of "putting it on" that we get from Brando's greatest roles—*A Streetcar Named Desire, Viva Zapata!, The Wild One, On the Waterfront*—stands in paradoxical relation to Method theories of submergence in the role. Brando's willingness to cooperate with Bernardo Bertolucci in the commentary on and mockery of his screen image that forms so much of the interest of *Last Tango in Paris* may indicate that he no longer holds to the theatrical definition of great acting. His progenitor role in *The Godfather* seems to have released him to create the paradox of the self-revealed inner life of a screen image elaborated by *Last Tango*. In the films of the 1970s, character, and therefore acting as well, has taken on the central importance in film. And the stage actor in film finds that his virtuosity is more a parlor trick than a technique of emotional and artistic power. Films make us fall in love with, admire, even hate human beings who may actually in the moment we watch them be dead and dust. But that is the grandeur of films as well: the preservation of human transience, the significance not so much of social roles as of fragile, fleeting feelings.

1976

SERGEI EISENSTEIN
FROM FILM FORM

DICKENS, GRIFFITH, AND THE FILM TODAY

The most thrilling figure was Griffith, for it was in his works that the cinema made itself felt as more than an entertainment or pastime. The brilliant new methods of the American cinema were united in him with a profound emotion of story, with human acting, with laughter and tears, and all this was done with an astonishing ability to preserve all that gleam of a filmically dynamic holiday, which had been captured in *The Gray Shadow* and *The Mark of Zorro* and *The House of Hate.* That the cinema could be incomparably greater, and that this was to be the basic task of the budding Soviet cinema—these were sketched for us in Griffith's creative work, and found ever new confirmation in his films.

Our heightened curiosity of those years in *construction and method* swiftly discerned wherein lay the most powerful affective factors in this great American's films. This was in a hitherto unfamiliar province, bearing a name that was familiar to us, not in the field of art, but in that of engineering and electrical apparatus, first touching art in its most advanced section—in cinematography. This province, this method, this principle of building and construction was *montage.*

This was the montage whose foundations had been laid by American film-culture, but whose full, completed, conscious use and world recognition was established by our films. Montage, the rise of which will be forever linked with the name of Griffith. Montage, which played a most vital rôle in the creative work of Griffith and brought him his most glorious successes.

Griffith arrived at it through the method of parallel action. And, essentially, it was on this that he came to a standstill. But we mustn't run ahead. Let us examine the question of how montage came to Griffith or—how Griffith came to montage.

Griffith arrived at montage through the method of parallel action, and he was led to the idea of parallel action by—Dickens! . . .

What were the novels of Dickens for his contemporaries, for his readers? There is one answer: they bore the same relation to them that the film bears to the same strata in our time. They compelled the reader to live with the same passions. They appealed to the same good and sentimental elements as does the film (at least on the surface); they alike shudder before vice, they alike mill the extraordinary, the unusual, the fantastic, from boring, prosaic and everyday existence. And they clothe this common and prosaic existence in their special vision.

Illumined by this light, refracted from the land of fiction back to life, this commonness took on a romantic air, and bored people were grateful to the author for giving them the countenances of potentially romantic figures.

This partially accounts for the close attachment to the novels of Dickens and, similarly, to films. . . .

Perhaps the secret lies in Dickens's (as well as cinema's) creation of an extraordinary plasticity. The observation in the novels is extraordinary—as is their optical quality. The characters of Dickens are rounded with means as plastic and slightly exaggerated as are the screen heroes of today. The screen's heroes are engraved on the senses of the spectator with clearly visible traits, its villians are remembered by certain facial expressions, and all are saturated in the peculiar, slightly unnatural radiant gleam thrown over them by the screen.

It is absolutely thus that Dickens draws his characters—this is the faultlessly plastically grasped and pitilessly sharply sketched gallery of immortal Pickwicks, Dombeys, Fagins, Tackletons, and others. . . .

Analogies and resemblances cannot be pursued too far—they lose conviction and charm. They begin to take on the air of machination or card-tricks. I should be very sorry to lose the conviction of the affinity between Dickens and Griffith, allowing this abundance of common traits to slide into a game of anecdotal semblance of tokens.

All the more that such a gleaning from Dickens goes beyond the limits of interest in Griffith's individual cinematic craftsmanship and widens into a concern with film-craftsmanship in general. This is why I dig more and more deeply into the film-indications of Dickens, revealing them through Griffith—for the use of future film-exponents. So I must be excused, in leafing through Dickens, for having found in him even—a "dissolve." . . .

However, let us turn to the basic montage structure, whose rudiment in Dickens's work was developed into the elements of film composition in Griffith's work. Lifting a corner of the veil over these riches, these hitherto unused experiences, let us look into *Oliver Twist*. Open it at the twenty-first chapter. Let's read its beginning:

CHAPTER XXI*

1. It was a cheerless morning when they got into the street; blowing and raining hard; and the clouds looking dull and stormy.
The night had been very wet: for large pools of water had collected in the road: and the kennels were overflowing.

---

*For demonstration purposes I have broken this beginning of the chapter into smaller pieces than did its author; the numbering is, of course, also mine.

There was a faint glimmering of the coming day in the sky; but it rather aggravated than relieved the gloom of the scene: the sombre light only serving to pale that which the street lamps afforded, without shedding any warmer or brighter tints upon the wet housetops, and dreary streets.

There appeared to be nobody stirring in that quarter of the town; for the windows of the houses were all closely shut; and the streets through which they passed, were noiseless and empty.

2. By the time they had turned into the Bethnal Green Road, the day had fairly begun to break. Many of the lamps were already extinguished;

a few country waggons were slowly toiling on, towards London;

and now and then, a stage-coach, covered with mud, rattled briskly by:

the driver bestowing, as he passed, an admonitory lash upon the heavy waggoner who, by keeping on the wrong side of the road, had endangered his arriving at the office, a quarter of a minute after his time.

The public-houses, with gas-lights burning inside, were already open.

By degrees, other shops began to be unclosed; and a few scattered people were met with.

Then, came straggling groups of labourers going to their work;

then, men and women with fish-baskets on their heads;

donkey-carts laden with vegetables;

chaise-carts filled with live-stock or whole carcasses of meat;

milk-women with pails;

and an unbroken concourse of people, trudging out with various supplies to the eastern suburbs of the town.

3. As they approached the City, the noise and traffic gradually increased;

and when they threaded the streets between Shoreditch and Smithfield, it had swelled into a roar of sound and bustle.

It was as light as it was likely to be, till night came on again; and the busy morning of half the London population had begun. . . .

4. It was market-morning.

The ground was covered, nearly ankle-deep, with filth and mire;

and a thick steam, perpetually rising from the reeking bodies of the cattle,

and mingling with the fog,

which seemed to rest upon the chimney-tops, hung heavily above. . . .

Countrymen,

butchers,

drovers,

hawkers,

boys,

thieves,

idlers,

and vagabonds of every low grade,

were mingled together in a dense mass;

5. the whistling of drovers,

the barking of dogs,

the bellowing and plunging of oxen,

the bleating of sheep,

the grunting and squeaking of pigs;

the cries of hawkers,

the shouts, oaths and quarelling on all sides;

the ringing of bells

and roar of voices, that issued from every public-house;

the crowding, pushing, driving, beating,
whooping and yelling;
the hideous and discordant din that resounded from every corner of the market;
and the unwashed, unshaven, squalid, and dirty figures constantly running to and fro,
and bursting in and out of the throng; rendered it a stunning and bewildering scene,
which quite confounded the senses.

How often have we encountered just such a structure in the work of Griffith? This austere accumulation and quickening tempo, this gradual play of light: from burning street-lamps, to their being extinguished; from night, to dawn; from dawn, to the full radiance of day *(It was as light as it was likely to be, till night came on again);* this calculated transition from purely visual elements to an interweaving of them with aural elements: at first as an indefinite rumble, coming from afar at the second stage of increasing light, so that the rumble may grow into a roar, transferring us to a purely aural structure, now concrete and objective (section 5 of our breakdown); with such scenes, picked up *en passant,* and intercut into the whole—like the driver, hastening towards his office; and, finally, these magnificently typical details, the reeking bodies of the cattle, from which the steam rises and mingles with the overall cloud of morning fog, or the close-up of the legs in the almost ankle-deep filth and mire, all this gives the fullest cinematic sensation of the panorama of a market. . . .

If in the above-cited examples we have encountered prototypes of characteristics for Griffith's *montage exposition,* then it would pay us to read further in *Oliver Twist,* where we can find another montage method typical for Griffith—the method of a *montage progression of parallel scenes, intercut into each other.*

For this let us turn to that group of scenes in which is set forth the familiar episode of how Mr. Brownlow, to show faith in Oliver in spite of his pick-pocket reputation, sends him to return books to the book-seller, and of how Oliver again falls into the clutches of the thief Sikes, his sweetheart Nancy, and old Fagin.

These scenes are unrolled absolutely à la Griffith: both in their inner emotional line, as well as in the unusual sculptural relief and delineation of the characters; in the uncommon full-bloodedness of the dramatic as well as the humorous traits in them; finally, also in the typical Griffith-esque montage of parallel interlocking of all the links of the separate episodes. Let us give particular attention to this last peculiarity, just as unexpected, one would think, in Dickens, as it is characteristic for Griffith!

CHAPTER XIV

COMPRISING FURTHER PARTICULARS OF OLIVER'S STAY AT MR. BROWNLOW'S, WITH THE REMARKABLE PREDICTION WHICH ONE MR. GRIMWIG UTTERED CONCERNING HIM, WHEN HE WENT OUT ON AN ERRAND.

. . . "Dear me, I am very sorry for that," exclaimed Mr. Brownlow; "I particularly wished those books to be returned tonight."

"Send Oliver with them," said Mr. Grimwig, with an ironical smile; "he will be sure to deliver them safely, you know."

"Yes; do let me take them, if you please, Sir," said Oliver. "I'll run all the way, Sir."

The old gentleman was just going to say that Oliver should not go out on any account;

when a most malicious cough from Mr. Grimwig determined him that he should; and that, by his prompt discharge of the commission, he should prove to him the injustice of his suspicions: on this head at least: at once.

[Oliver is prepared for the errand to the bookstall-keeper.]

"I won't be ten minutes, Sir," replied Oliver, eagerly.

[Mrs. Bedwin, Mr. Brownlow's housekeeper, gives Oliver the directions, and sends him off.]

"Bless his sweet face!" said the old lady, looking after him. "I can't bear, somehow, to let him go out of my sight."

At this moment, Oliver looked gaily round, and nodded before he turned the corner. The old lady smilingly returned his salutation, and, closing the door, went back to her own room.

"Let me see; he'll be back in twenty minutes, at the longest," said Mr. Brownlow, pulling out his watch, and placing it on the table. "It will be dark by that time."

"Oh! you really expect him to come back, do you?" inquired Mr. Grimwig.

"Don't you?" asked Mr. Brownlow, smiling.

The spirit of contradiction was strong in Mr. Grimwig's breast, at the moment; and it was rendered stronger by his friend's confident smile.

"No," he said, smiting the table with his fist, "I do not. The boy has a new suit of clothes on his back; a set of valuable books under his arm; and a five-pound note in his pocket. He'll join his old friends the thieves, and laugh at you. If ever that boy returns to this house, Sir, I'll eat my head."

With these words he drew his chair closer to the table; and there the two friends sat, in silent expression, with the watch between them.

This is followed by a short "interruption" in the form of a digression:

It is worthy of remark, as illustrating the importance we attach to our own judgments, and the pride with which we put forth our most rash and hasty conclusions, that, although Mr. Grimwig was not by any means a bad-hearted man, and though he would have been unfeignedly sorry to see his respected friend duped and deceived, he really did most earnestly and strongly hope, at that moment, that Oliver Twist might not come back.

And again a return to the two old gentlemen:

It grew so dark, that the figures on the dial-plate were scarcely discernible; but there the two old gentlemen continued to sit, in silence: with the watch between them.

Twilight shows that only a little time has passed, but the *close-up* of the watch, *already twice* shown lying between the old gentlemen, says that a great deal of time has passed already. But just then, as in the game of "will he come? won't he come?", involving not only the two old men, but also the kind-hearted reader, the worse fears and vague forebodings of the old housekeeper are justified by the cut to the new scene—Chapter XV. This begins with a short scene in the public-house, with the bandit Sikes and his dog, old Fagin and Miss Nancy, who has been obliged to discover the whereabouts of Oliver.

"You are on the scent, are you, Nancy?" inquired Sikes, proffering the glass.

"Yes, I am, Bill," replied the young lady, disposing of its contents; "and tired enough of it I am, too. . . ."

Then, one of the best scenes in the whole novel—at least one that since childhood has been perfectly preserved, along with the evil figure of Fagin—the scene in which Oliver, marching along with the books, is suddenly startled by a young woman screaming out very loud, "Oh, my dear brother!" And he had hardly looked up, to see what the matter was, when he was stopped by having a pair of arms thrown tight round his neck.

With this cunning maneuver Nancy, with the sympathies of the whole street, takes the desperately pulling Oliver, as her "prodigal brother," back into the bosom of Fagin's gang of thieves. This fifteenth chapter closes on the now familiar montage phrase:

> The gas-lamps were lighted; Mrs. Bedwin was waiting anxiously at the open door; the servant had run up the street twenty times to see if there were any traces of Oliver; and still the two old gentlemen sat, perseveringly, in the dark parlour: with the watch between them.

In Chapter XVI Oliver, once again in the clutches of the gang, is subjected to mockery. Nancy rescues him from a beating:

> "I won't stand by and see it done, Fagin," cried the girl. "You've got the boy, and what more would you have? Let him be—let him be, or I shall put that mark on some of you, that will bring me to the gallows before my time."

By the way, it is characteristic for both Dickens and Griffith to have these sudden flashes of goodness in "morally degraded" characters and, though these sentimental images verge on hokum, they are so faultlessly done that they work on the most skeptical readers and spectators!

At the end of this chapter, Oliver, sick and weary, falls "sound asleep." Here the physical time unity is interrupted— an evening and night, crowded with events; but the montage unity of the episode is not interrupted, tying Oliver to Mr. Brownlow on one side, and to Fagin's gang on the other.

Following, in Chapter XVIII, is the arrival of the parish beadle, Mr. Bumble, in response to an inquiry about the lost boy, and the appearance of Bumble at Mr. Brownlow's, again in Grimwig's company. The content and reason for their conversation is revealed by the very title of the chapter: OLIVER'S DESTINY CONTINUING UNPROPITIOUS, BRINGS A GREAT MAN TO LONDON TO INJURE HIS REPUTATION . . .

> "I fear it is all too true," said the old gentleman sorrowfully, after looking over the papers. "This is not much for your intelligence; but I would gladly have given you treble the money, if it had been favourable to the boy."
> It is not at all improbable that if Mr. Bumble had been possessed of this information at an earlier period of the interview, he might have imparted a very different coloring to his little history. It was too late to do it now, however; so he shook his head gravely; and, pocketing the five guineas, withdrew. . . .
> "Mrs. Bedwin," said Mr. Brownlow, when the housekeeper appeared; "that boy, Oliver, is an impostor."
> "It can't be, Sir. It cannot be," said the old lady energetically. . . . "I never will believe it, Sir. . . . Never!"
> "You old women never believe anything but quack-doctors, and lying story-books," growled Mr. Grimwig. "I knew it all along. . . ."
> "He was a dear, grateful, gentle child, Sir," retorted Mrs. Bedwin, indignantly. "I know what children are, Sir; and have done these forty years; and people who can't say the same, shouldn't say anything about them. That's my opinion!"
> This was a hard hit at Mr. Grimwig, who was a bachelor. As it extorted nothing from

that gentleman but a smile, the old lady tossed her head, and smoothed down her apron preparatory to another speech, when she was stopped by Mr. Brownlow.

"Silence!" said the old gentleman, feigning an anger he was far from feeling. "Never let me hear the boy's name again. I rang to tell you that. Never. Never, on any pretence, mind! You may leave the room, Mrs. Bedwin. Remember! I am in earnest."

And the entire intricate montage complex of this episode is concluded with the sentence:

There were sad hearts in Mr. Brownlow's that night.

It was not by accident that I have allowed myself such full extracts, in regard not only to the composition of the scenes, but also to the delineation of the characters, for in their very modeling, in their characteristics, in their behavior, there is much typical of Griffith's manner. This equally concerns also his "Dickens-esque" distressed, defenseless creatures (recalling Lillian Gish and Richard Barthelmess in *Broken Blossoms* or the Gish sisters in *Orphans of the Storm*), and is no less typical for his characters like the two old gentlemen and Mrs. Bedwin; and finally, it is entirely characteristic of him to have such figures as are in the gang of "the merry old Jew" Fagin.

In regard to the immediate task of our example of Dickens's montage progression of the story composition, we can present the results of it in the following table:

1. *The old gentlemen.*
2. Departure of Oliver.
3. *The old gentlemen and the watch. It is still light.*
4. Digression on the character of Mr. Grimwig.
5. *The old gentlemen and the watch. Gathering twilight.*
6. Fagin, Sikes, and Nancy in the public-house.
7. Scene on the street.
8. *The old gentlemen and the watch. The gas-lamps have been lit.*
9. Oliver is dragged back to Fagin.
10. Digression at the beginning of Chapter XVII.
11. The journey of Mr. Bumble.
12. *The old gentlemen* and Mr. Brownlow's command to forget Oliver forever.

As we can see, we have before us a typical and, for Griffith, a model of parallel montage of two story lines, where one (the waiting gentlemen) emotionally heightens the tension and drama of the other (the capture of Oliver). It is in "rescuers" rushing along to save the "suffering heroine" that Griffith has, with the aid of parallel montage, earned his most glorious laurels!

Most curious of all is that in the *very center* of our breakdown of the episode, is wedged another "interruption"—a whole digression at the beginning of Chapter XVII, on which we have been purposely silent. What is remarkable about this digression? It is Dickens's own "treatise" on the principles of this montage construction of the story which he carries out so fascinatingly, and which passed into the style of Griffith. Here it is:

It is the custom on the stage, in all good murderous melodramas, to present the tragic and the comic scenes, in as regular alternation, as the layers of red and white in a side of streaky well-cured bacon. The hero sinks upon his straw bed, weighed down by fetters and misfortunes; and, in the next scene, his faithful but unconscious squire regales the audience with a comic song. We behold, with throbbing bosoms, the heroine in the grasp of a proud and ruthless baron: her virtue and her life alike in danger; drawing forth her dagger to preserve the one at the cost of the other; and just as our expectations are wrought up to the highest pitch, a whistle is heard: and we are straightway transported to the great hall of the castle: where a grey-headed seneschal sings a funny chorus with a funnier body of vassals, who are free of all sorts of places from church vaults to palaces, and roam about in company, carolling perpetually.

Such changes appear absurd; but they are not so unnatural as they would seem at first sight. The transitions in real life from well-spread boards to death-beds, and from mourning-weeds to holiday garments, are not a whit less startling; only, there, we are busy actors, instead of passive lookers-on; which makes a vast difference. The actors in the mimic life of the theatre, are blind to violent transitions and abrupt impulses of passion of feeling, which, presented before the eyes of mere spectators, are at once condemned as outrageous and preposterous.

As sudden shiftings of the scene, and rapid changes of time and place, are not only sanctioned in books by long usage, but are by many considered as the great art of authorship: an author's skill in his craft being, by such critics, chiefly estimated with relation to the dilemmas in which he leaves his characters at the end of every chapter: this brief introduction to the present one may perhaps be deemed unnecessary. . . .

There is another interesting thing in this treatise: in his own words, Dickens (a life-long amateur actor) defines his direct relation to the theater melodrama. This is as if Dickens had placed himself in the position of a connecting link between the future, unforeseen art of the cinema, and the not so distant (for Dickens) past—the traditions of "good murderous melodramas."

This "treatise," of course, could not have escaped the eye of the patriarch of the American film, and very often his structure seems to follow the wise advice, handed down to the great film-maker of the twentieth century by the great novelist of the nineteenth. And Griffith, hiding nothing, has more than once acknowledged his debt to Dickens's memory. . . .

I don't know how my readers feel about this, but for me personally it is always pleasing to recognize again and again the fact that our cinema is not altogether without parents and without pedigree, without a past, without the traditions and rich cultural heritage of the past epochs. It is only very thoughtless and presumptuous people who can erect laws and an esthetic for cinema, proceeding from premises of some incredible virgin-birth of this art!

Let Dickens and the whole ancestral array, going back as far as the Greeks and Shakespeare, be superfluous reminders that both Griffith and our cinema prove our origins to be not solely as of Edison and his fellow inventors, but as based on an enormous cultured past; each part of this past in its own moment of world history has moved forward the great art of cinematography. Let this past be a reproach to those thoughtless people who have displayed arrogance in reference to literature, which has contributed so much to this apparently unprecedented art and is, in the first and most important place: the art of viewing—not only the *eye,* but *viewing*—both meanings being embraced in this term. . . .

1944

SEYMOUR CHATMAN
WHAT NOVELS CAN DO THAT FILMS CAN'T (AND VICE VERSA)

The study of narrative has become so popular that the French have honored it with a term—*la narratologie*. Given the escalating and sophisticated literature on the subject, its English counterpart, "narratology," may not be as risible as it sounds. Modern narratology combines two powerful intellectual trends: the Anglo-American inheritance of Henry James, Percy Lubbock, E. M. Forster, and Wayne Booth; and the mingling of Russian formalist (Viktor Shklovsky, Boris Eichenbaum, Roman Jakobson, and Vladimir Propp) with French structuralist approaches (Claude Lévi-Strauss, Roland Barthes, Gérard Genette, and Tzvetan Todorov). It's not accidental that narratology has developed during a period in which linguistics and cinema theory have also flourished. Linguistics, of course, is one basis for the field now called semiotics—the study of all meaning systems, not only natural language. Another basis is the work of the philosopher Charles S. Peirce and his continuator, Charles W. Morris. These trees have borne elegant fruit: we read fascinating semiotic analyses of facial communication, body language, fashion, the circus, architecture, and gastronomy. The most vigorous, if controversial, branch of cinema studies, the work of Christian Metz, is also semiotically based.

One of the most important observations to come out of narratology is that narrative itself is a deep structure quite independent of its medium. In other words, narrative is basically a kind of text organization, and that organization, that schema, needs to be actualized: in written words, as in stories and novels; in spoken words combined with the movements of actors imitating characters against sets which imitate places, as in plays and films; in drawings; in comic strips; in dance movements, as in narrative ballet and in mime; and even in music, at least in program music of the order of *Till Eulenspiegel* and *Peter and the Wolf*.

403

A salient property of narrative is double time structuring. That is, all narratives, in whatever medium, combine the time sequence of plot events, the time of the *histoire* ("story-time") with the time of the presentation of those events in the text, which we call "discourse-time." What is fundamental to narrative, regardless of medium, is that these two time orders are independent. In realistic narratives, the time of the story is fixed, following the ordinary course of a life: a person is born, grows from childhood to maturity and old age, and then dies. But the discourse-time order may be completely different: it may start with the person's deathbed, then "flashback" to childhood; or it may start with childhood, "flashforward" to death, then end with adult life. This independence of discourse-time is precisely and only possible because of the subsumed story-time. Now of course *all* texts pass through time: it takes x number of hours to read an essay, a legal brief, or a sermon. But the internal structures of these *non*-narrative texts are not temporal but logical, so that their discourse-time is irrelevant, just as the viewing time of a painting is irrelevant. We may spend half an hour in front of a Titian, but the aesthetic effect is as if we were taking in the whole painting at a glance. In narratives, on the other hand, the dual time orders function independently. This is true in any medium: flashbacks are just as possible in ballet or mime or opera as they are in a film or novel. Thus, in theory at least, any narrative can be actualized by any medium which can communicate the two time orders.

Narratologists immediately observed an important consequence of this property of narrative texts, namely, the translatability of a given narrative from one medium to another: *Cinderella* as verbal tale, as ballet, as opera, as film, as comic strip, as pantomime, and so on. This observation was so interesting, so much in keeping with structuralist theory, and so productive of further work in narrative analysis that it tended to concentrate attention exclusively on the constancies in narrative structure across the different media at the expense of interesting differences. But now the study of narrative has reached a point where the differences can emerge as objects of independent interest.

In the course of studying and teaching film, I have been struck by the sorts of changes typically introduced by screen adaptation (and vice versa in that strange new process "novelization," which transforms already exhibited films into novels). Close study of film and novel versions of the same narrative reveals with great clarity the peculiar powers of the two media. Once we grasp those peculiarities, the reasons for the differences in form, content, and impact of the two versions strikingly emerge. Many features of these narratives could be chosen for comparison, but I will limit myself to only two: description and point of view.

Critics have long recognized that descriptive passages in novels are different somehow in textual *kind* from the narrative proper. They have spoken of "blocks" or "islands" or "chunks" of description in early fiction and have noted that modern novels shy away from blatantly purple descriptive passages. Joseph Conrad and Ford Madox Ford formulated theories of what they called "distributed" exposition and description, in which the described elements were insinuated, so to speak, into the running narrative line. What has not emerged very clearly until recently, however, is a genuine theoretical explanation of novelistic description. The emphasis has been on the pictorial, the imaged. We read in typical handbooks like Thrall and

Hibbard: "Description . . . has as its purpose the picturing of a scene or setting." But that is only part of the story; such a definition eliminates *inter alia* the description of an abstract state of affairs, or of a character's mental posture, or, indeed, of anything not strictly visual or visualizable. Narratologists argue that a more correct and comprehensive account of description rests on temporal structure. As we have already noted, narrative proper requires a double and independent time ordering, that of the time line of the story and that of the time line of the discourse. Now what happens in description is that the time line of the story is interrupted and frozen. Events are stopped, though our reading or discourse-time continues, and we look at the characters and the setting elements as at a *tableau vivant.*

As an example of this process, consider a bit of the short story which underlies a film by Jean Renoir, Maupassant's "Une Partie de campagne" [A Country Excursion].* The story opens with a summary of events which clearly establishes story-time: "For five months they had been talking of going to lunch at some country restaurant. . . . They had risen very early that morning. Monsieur Dufour had borrowed the milkman's cart, and drove himself [on avait projeté depuis cinq mois d'aller déjeuner aux environs de Paris. . . . Aussi . . . s'était-on levé de fort bonne heure ce matin-là. M. Dufour, ayant emprunté la voiture du latier, conduisait lui-même]" (p. 63). There are three events, and, as we note from the use of the past perfect with "had," they predate the opening moment of the story proper, the moment of story-now, so to speak, which is the moment named by the expression "and drove himself." The story proper begins with the family *en voyage,* already in the midst of their excursion. The story sequence is *naturally* ordered: at some point in that past before the story proper began, someone first mentioned going to lunch in the country (let's call that event A); the family continued this discussion, thus event A was iterated (let's call that A sub-n since we don't know how many times the topic came up during those five months); next, Monsieur Dufour borrowed the milkman's cart, presumably the Saturday night before the trip (event B); then they arose early on Sunday morning (event C); and finally, here they are, driving along the road (event D). Notice, incidentally, the disparity between the story order and discourse order: story order is A, B, C, D; discourse order is A, C, B, D.

This first sentence, then, is straight narration which takes us out of the expository past into the narrative present. Now the very next sentence is clearly of a different order: ". . . it [the cart] had a roof supported by four iron posts to which were attached curtains, which had been raised so that they could see the countryside [. . . elle avait un toit supporté par quatre montants de fer où s'attachaient les rideaux qu'on avait relevés pour voir le paysage]" (p. 63). This is, of course, unadulterated description. Story-time stops as the narrator characterizes a story object, a prop. The sentence reflects the static character of the passage. The verb "to have" is clearly equivalent to the typical copula of description: it is not a verb of action and communicates no sense of an event but simply evokes the quality of an object or state of affairs. Maupassant could have—and more recent writers probably would have—avoided direct description by writing something like "The cart, its

---

*Guy de Maupassant, "Une Partie de campagne," *Boule de Suif* (Paris, n.d.), pp. 63–78; all further references will be cited parenthetically in the text; my translations.

roof supported by four iron posts, rolled merrily down the road." This active syntax would have kept story-time going and would have eased in the characterization of the cart. Maupassant's prose provokes, rather, the start-and-stop effect customary to early fiction, a fashion now somewhat dated. Not that the surface verb, the verb in the actual verbal medium, *needs* to be the copula "to be." It could be a perfectly active verb in the strict grammatical sense and still evoke the descriptive copula at the deep narrative level, as in the sentence that immediately follows: "The curtain at the back . . . fluttered in the breeze like a flag [celui de derrière, seul, flottait au vent, comme un drapeau]." "Fluttered" is an active verb, but from the textual point of view, the sentence is pure description; it is not tied into the event chain. The sentence could as easily be phrased, "In the back there *was* a curtain fluttering in the breeze like a flag."

The paragraph continues with a brief description of Mme Dufour and makes references to the grandmother, to Henriette, and to a yellow-haired youth who later becomes Henriette's husband. Paragraphs immediately thereafter continue the narrative by citing events: the passing of the fortifications at Porte Maillot; the reaching of the bridge of Neuilly; the pronouncement by M. Dufour that at last they have reached the country, and so on.

Let's consider the opening scene of Jean Renoir's 1936 film version of this story, also entitled *Une Partie de campagne.* (Ideally, you would watch the film as you read this essay, but something of the effect, I hope, can be communicated by the following illustrations.) The whole sequence introducing the Dufours takes only a minute of viewing time, so we don't have much time to remark on the details of their borrowed cart. But looking at a single frame enables us to examine it at our leisure (fig. 1).

We note, for instance, that the cart is absurdly small, has only two wheels, bears the name of the owner, "Ch. Gervais," painted on the side, and has a railing on the roof. There is no flapping curtain at the back but instead some kind of sun shield, and so on. Now these details are apparently of the same order as those in the story—remember the reference to the roof, the four iron posts, and the rolled up curtains. But there are some vital differences. For one thing, the number of details in Maupassant's sentence is limited to three. In other words, the selection among the possible number of details evoked was absolutely determined: the author, through his narrator, "selected" and named precisely three. Thus the reader learns only those three and can only expand the picture imaginatively. But in the film representation, the number of details is indeterminate, since what this version gives us is a simulacrum of a French carriage of a certain era, provenance, and so on. Thus the number of details that we could note is potentially large, even vast. In practice, however, we do not register many details. The film is going by too fast, and we are too preoccupied with the meaning of this cart, with what is going to happen next, to dwell upon its physical details. We simply label: we say to ourselves, "Aha, a cart with some people in it." We react that way because of a technical property of film texts: the details are not asserted as such by a narrator but simply presented, so we tend, in a pragmatic way, to contemplate only those that seem salient to the plot as it unrolls in our minds (in what Roland Barthes calls a "hermeneutic" inquiry). Now if you think about it, this is a rather odd aesthetic situation. Film narrative possesses a plenitude of visual details, an excessive particularity compared to the verbal version, a plenitude aptly called by certain aestheticians visual "over-specification" *überbestimmtheit),* a property that it shares, of course, with the other visual arts. But unlike those arts, unlike painting or sculpture, narrative films do not usually allow us time to dwell on plenteous details. Pressure from the narrative component is too great. Events move too fast. The contemplation of beautiful framing or color or lighting is a pleasure limited to those who can see the film many times or who are fortunate enough to have access to equipment which will allow them to stop the frame. But watching a movie under normal circumstances in a cinema is not at all like being in a gallery or art museum. The management wants us up and out of the theater so that the 10:30 patrons can take our seats. And even sophisticated moviegoers who call a film "beautiful" are more likely to be referring to literary than to visual components. Indeed, there are movies (like Terence Malick's recent *Days of Heaven*) which are criticized because their visual effects are too striking for the narrative line to support. Narrative pressure is so great that the interpretation of even non-narrative films is sometimes affected by it—at least for a time, until the audience gets its bearings. For example, there is a film which presents a sequence of frozen frames, on the basis of which the audience is prompted to construct a story. Then, after the last frame, the camera pulls away to reveal that the frames were all merely part of a collage of photographs organized randomly. This last shot "denarrativizes" the film.

Narrative pressure similarly affects the genre of film that André Bazin writes about in his essay "Painting and Cinema," the kind in which the camera moves around close-up details of a single painting. An example of this genre is Alain Resnais' film on Picasso's *Guernica.* No less a personage than the Inspector General of Drawing of the French Department of Education complained: "However you look at it the film is not true to the painting. Its dramatic and logical unity establishes relationships that are chronologically false." The inspector was speaking about the relationships and chronology in the implied narrative of Picasso's development as an artist, but he might as well have been speaking of the relationships and chronology implicit in a narrative hypothecated on the visual deaths of *Guernica* itself. By controlling the viewer's order and duration of perceiving, a film scanning a painting might imply the double time structure of narrative texts. For example, if the camera wandering over *Guernica* were first focused on the head and lantern-bearing arm sweeping in through the window, then shifted to the screaming horse, then to the body on the ground with the broken sword and flower in its hand, the audience might read into the painting a story sequence which Picasso did not intend: first the alarm was heard, then the horse whinnied as the bombs fell, then one victim died.

The key word in my account of the different ways that visual details are presented by novels and films is "assert." I wish to communicate by that word the force it has in ordinary rhetoric: an "assertion" is a statement, usually an independent sentence or clause, that something is in fact the case, that it is a certain sort of thing, that it does in fact have certain properties or enter into certain relations, namely, those listed. Opposed to asserting there is mere "naming." When I say, "The cart was tiny; it came onto the bridge," I am asserting that certain property of the cart of being small in size and that certain relation of arriving at the bridge. However, when I say "The green cart came onto the bridge," I am asserting nothing more than its arrival at the bridge; the greenness of the cart is not asserted but slipped in without syntactic fuss. It is only named. Textually, it emerges by the way. Now, most film narratives seem to be of the latter textual order: it requires special effort for films to assert a property or relation. The dominant mode is presentational, not assertive. A film doesn't say, "This *is* the state of affairs," it merely shows you that state of affairs. Of course, there could be a character or a voice-over commentator asserting a property or relation; but then the film would be using its sound track in much the same way as fiction uses assertive syntax. It is not cinematic description but merely description by literary assertion transferred to film. Filmmakers and critics traditionally show disdain for verbal commentary because it explicates what, they feel, should be implicated visually. So in its essential visual mode, film does not describe at all but merely presents; or better, it *depicts,* in the original etymological sense of that word: renders in pictorial form. I don't think that this is mere purism or a die-hard adherence to silent films. Film attracts that component of our perceptual apparatus which we tend to favor over the other senses. Seeing is, after all, believing.

That the camera depicts but does not describe seems confirmed by a term often used by literary critics to characterize neutral, "non-narrated" Hemingwayesque fiction—the *camera eye* style. The implication of "camera eye" is that no one recounts the events of, for example, "The Killers": they are just *revealed,* as if some instrument—some cross between a video tape recorder and speech synthesizer—had recorded visually and then translated those visuals into the most neutral kind of language.

Now, someone might counterargue: "You're forgetting obvious cinematic devices whose intention is arguably descriptive. What about the telling close-up? What about establishing shots?" But the close-ups that come immediately to mind seem introduced for plot unraveling, for hermeneutic purposes. Think of Hitchcock's famous close-ups: the villian's amputated little finger in *The Thirty-Nine Steps;* the poisoned coffee cup in *Notorious;* Janet Leigh's horribly open eye in the bloody shower in *Psycho.* For all their capacity to arrest our attention, these close-ups in no way invite aesthetic contemplation; on the contrary, they function as extremely powerful components in the structure of the suspense. They present, in the most dramatic fashion, that abiding narrative–hermeneutic question: "My God," they cry out, "what next?" Of course, a real description in a novel may also serve to build suspense. We curse Dickens for stopping the action at a critical moment to describe something. "Keep still," shouts the sudden, terrifying figure to Pip at the beginning of *Great Expectations,* "or I'll cut your throat." And then, as we dangle in suspense, a whole paragraph describes the man: the iron on his leg, his broken shoes, the rag tied around his head, and so on. Yes, we curse Dickens—and love every second of it. But in the movie version, the sense of continuing action could not stop. Even if there were a long pause to give us a chance to take in the fearsome details of Magwitch's person, we would still feel that the clock of story-time was ticking away, that that pause was *included* in the story and not just an interval as we perused the discourse. We might very well infer that the delay means something, perhaps that Magwitch was trying to decide what to do with Pip, or, in a supersophisticated "psychological" version, that Pip's own time scale had somehow been stretched out because of his great terror. In either case, the feeling that we were sharing time passage with a character would be a sure clue that not only our discourse-time but their story-time was continuing to roll. And if it is the case that story-time necessarily continues to roll in films, and if description entails precisely the arrest of story-time, then it is reasonable to argue that films do not and cannot describe.

Then what about establishing shots? An establishing shot, if you're not up on movie jargon, is defined as follows (in Ernest Lindgren's *The Art of the Film*): "A long shot introduced at the beginning of a scene to establish the interrelationship of details to be shown subsequently in nearer shots." Standard examples are the bird's-eye shots that open *The Lady Vanishes* and *Psycho*. In *The Lady Vanishes,* the camera starts high above a Swiss ski resort, then moves down, and in the next shot we're inside the crowded hotel; in *Psycho,* the camera starts high above Phoenix, then glides down into a room where a couple are making love. It is true that both of these shots are in a certain sense descriptive or at least evocative of place; but they seem to enjoy that status only because they occur at the very beginning of the films, that is to say, before any characters have been introduced. Now narrative in its usual definition is a causal chain of events, and since "narrative event" means an "action performed by or at least of some relevance to a character," we can see why precisely the absence of characters endows establishing shots with a descriptive quality. It is not that story-time has been arrested. It is just that it has not yet begun. For when the same kind of shot occurs in the middle of a film, it does not seem to entail an arrest or abeyance of story-time. For example, recall the scene in the middle of *Notorious* just at the moment when Cary Grant and Ingrid Bergman are flying into Rio de Janeiro. We see shots of the city from the air, typical street scenes, and so on. Yet our sense is not of a hiatus in the story-time but rather that Rio is down there waiting for Cary and Ingrid to arrive. All that street activity is felt to be transpiring while the two go about their business, the business of the plot, which because of its momentarily mundane character—landing, clearing customs, and so on—is allowed to happen off screen.

Even the literal arrest of the picture, the so-called freeze-frame, where the image is reduced to a projected still photograph, does not automatically convey a description. It was popular a dozen years ago to end films that way, *in medias res.* Remember how Truffaut's young hero Antoine Doinel was frozen on the beach in *The Four Hundred Blows?* Truffaut has continued to follow the Doinel character in an interesting way, as the actor Jean-Pierre Léaud has himself aged, but I for one had no idea when I originally saw *The Four Hundred Blows* that there would be sequels; for me the sense of the frozen ending was that Doinel was trapped in a fugitive way of life. I perceived not a description but a kind of congealed iteration of future behavior.

Why is it that the force of plot, with its ongoing march of events, its ticking away of story-time, is so hard to dispel in the movies? That's an interesting question, but a psychologist or psychologically oriented aesthetician will have to answer it. I can only hazard a guess. The answer may have something to do with the medium itself. Whereas in novels, movements and hence events are at best constructions imaged by the reader out of words, that is, abstract symbols which are different from them in kind, the movements on the screen are so iconic, so like the real life movements they imitate, that the illusion of time passage simply cannot be divorced from them. Once that illusory story-time is established in a film, even dead moments, moments when nothing moves, will be felt to be part of the temporal whole, just as the taxi meter continues to run as we sit fidgeting in a traffic jam.

Let's try these ideas out on a longer and more challenging passage of Maupassant's story, the third paragraph:

[1] Mademoiselle Dufour was trying to swing herself standing up, but she could not succeed in getting a start. [2] She was a pretty girl of about eighteen; [3] one of those women who suddenly excite your desire when you meet them in the street, and who leave you with a vague feeling of uneasiness and of excited senses. [4] She was tall, had a small waist and large hips, with a dark skin, very large eyes, and very black hair. [5] Her dress clearly marked the outlines of her firm, full figure, which was accentuated by the motion of her hips as she tried to swing herself higher. [6] Her arms were stretched over her head to hold the rope, so that her bosom rose at every movement she made. Her hat, which a gust of wind had blown off, was hanging behind her, [7] and as the swing gradually rose higher and higher, she showed her delicate limbs up to the knees at each time. . . . [p. 66]*

The first narrative unit, "Mademoiselle Dufour was trying to swing herself" and so on, refers to an event. The second, "She was a pretty girl of about eighteen," seems on the face of it a straightforward description; but look at it from the point of view of a filmmaker. For one thing, "pretty" is not only descriptive but evaluative: one person's "pretty" may be another person's "beautiful" and still a third person's "plain." There will be some interesting variations in the faces selected by directors across cultures and even across time periods: Mary Pickford might be just the face for the teens and twenties, while Tuesday Weld may best represent the sixties. Renoir chose the face of Sylvie Bataille. The interesting theoretical point to be made about evaluative descriptions in verbal narrative is that they can invoke visual elaboration in the reader's mind. If he or she requires one, each reader will provide just the mental image to suit his or her own notions of prettiness. But the best a film (or theater) director can hope for is some degree of consensus with the spectator's ideal of prettiness. Even with the luckiest choice, some patrons will mutter, "I didn't think she was pretty at all." A similar point could be made about age; Sylvie Bataille's Henriette seems closer to thirty than eighteen, but that may be because of the costume she's wearing. The more serious point is that visual appearance is only a rough sign of age. Again the author's task is easier: correct attribution can be

---

*"Mlle Dufour essayait de se balancer debout, toute seule, sans parvenir à se donner un élan suffisant. C'était une belle fille de dix-huit à vingt ans; une de ces femmes dont la recontre dans la rue vous fouette d'un désir subit, et vous laisse jusqu'à la nuit une inquiétude vague et un soulèvement des sens. Grande, mince de taille et large des hanches, elle avait la peau très brune, les yeux très grands, les cheveux très noirs. Sa robe dessinait nettement les plénitudes fermes de sa chair qu'accentuaient encore les efforts des reins qu'elle faisait pour s'enlever. Ses bras tendus tenaient les cordes au-dessus de sa tête, de sorte que sa poitrine se dressait, sans une secousse, à chaque impulsion qu'elle donnait. Son chapeau, emporté par un coup de vent, était tombé derrière elle; et l'escarpolette peu à peu se lançait, montrant à chaque retour ses jambes fines jusqu'au genou. . . ."

insured by simply naming the attribute. The filmmaker, on the other hand, has to depend on the audience's agreement to the justice of the visual clues.

Still another point to be made about this piece of description concerns the word "about" and the whole of the next descriptive bit in the third unit. These not only refine and add to the description but also make salient the voice of a narrator. "*About* eighteen" stresses that the narrator himself is guessing. And, "one of those women who suddenly excite your desire" tells us even more: the narrator is a man responsive to female charms, perhaps a *roué,* at least a man-about-town. Such is the character of speech: it usually tells us something about the speaker. Long ago I. A. Richards labeled this function "tone." The camera, poor thing, is powerless to invoke tone, though it can present some alternatives to it. In this case, as we shall see, Renoir's sense of the need to show Henriette's innocent seductiveness seems to have prompted several amusing reaction shots which compensate for the camera's sexless objectivity.

The adjectives in our fourth segment are easier for film to handle: height, girth, skin, and hair color are features that film can communicate reliably. (The communication, of course, is always comparative, scalar: a character is tall relative to other people and objects in the film.) The motion of her hips bears a double function: the movement itself is an event, but it also contributes to the description of a part of Henriette's anatomy that the narrator finds quite absorbing. The same double role is played by the bosom and falling hat in segment six. As movements, these of course are simple for the film to convey; Henriette's voluptuousness, however, is not asserted but only suggestively depicted.

In the seventh segment, an odd ambiguity is introduced. The text says that as the swing rose, "she showed her delicate limbs up to the knees [montrant à chaque retour ses jambes fines jusqu'au genou]." The camera is certainly capable of presenting the requisite portion of anatomy. But what about the implications of "showed"? In both story and film, Henriette is generally represented as innocent; conscious exhibitionism does not go with her character, her family situation, or the times. The answer is perhaps an equivoque on the verb "to show": the definition of that word neither excludes nor includes conscious intention. And it is precisely an ambiguity that would go with the coquetry of a nineteenth-century maiden: to show but not *necessarily* to be conscious of showing. The camera, again, would seem unable to translate that verbal innuendo.

But see what Renoir makes of this problem. He elects to present Henriette first from the point of view of one of the two young boat men—not Henri, who is later to fall in love with her, but his comrade, Rodolphe. The term "point of view" means several things, but here I am using it in the strictly perceptual sense. Because the camera is behind Rodolphe's back as he looks out onto the garden through the window he's just opened, the camera, and hence the narrative point of view, identifies with him. It conspires, and invites us to conspire, with his voyeurism. Point of view is a complex matter worthy of a whole other discussion, but one theoretical observation is worth making here. The fact that most novels and short stories come to us through the voice of a narrator gives authors a greater range and flexibility than filmmakers. For one thing, the visual point of view in a film is always *there:* it is fixed and determinate precisely because the camera always need to be placed *some-*

where. But in verbal fiction, the narrator may or may not give us a visual bearing. He may let us peer over a character's shoulder, or he may represent something from a generalized perspective, commenting indifferently on the front, sides, and back of the object, disregarding how it is possible to see all these parts in the same glance. He doesn't have to account for his physical position at all. Further, he can enter solid bodies and tell what things are like inside, and so on. In the present case, Maupassant's narrator gives us a largely frontal view of Henriette on the swing, but he also casually makes observations about her posterior. And, of course, he could as easily have described the secret contents of her heart. The filmmaker, with his bulky camera, lights, tracks, and other machinery, suffers restrictions. But the very limitations, as Rudolf Arnheim has shown so eloquently, encourage interesting artistic solutions. Renoir uses precisely the camera's need for placement to engage the problem of communicating the innocent yet seductive quality of Henriette's charms. Since sedutiveness, like beauty, is in the eye of a beholder, Renoir requisitions Rodolphe's point of view to convey it. It is not Henriette so much as Rodolphe's reaction to Henriette, even on first seeing her, that shall establish her seductiveness and not only in his mind but in ours, because we cannot help but look on with him. Small plot changes help to make the scene plausible. Henri, disgusted with the Parisians invading his fishing sanctuary, does not even care to see what this latest horde looks like. It is Rodolphe who opens the window, flooding sunlight into the gloomy dining room and making a little stage in the deep background against which Henriette and her mother move like cute white puppets (fig. 2).

At this range, we can't see anything very clearly except the waving of Henriette's skirt in the wind, but the way that Rodolphe lowers his back and settles his body clearly communicates his intention to gaze, and we become his accomplices. After all, what is a stage except a space to gaze at? (Renoir often used stagelike frames in his films to suggest several planes of action; one of his more delightful later films is called *Le Petit Théâtre de Jean Renoir*.) Notice that the swing is so placed that Henriette's to-and-fro movement is toward Rodolphe's window, quite as if she were performing for him, although, of course, she is quite innocent of his existence. Here we begin to get something equivalent to the ambiguity of the word "show" that we found in the story: Henriette will display herself without being aware of it, she will reveal, yet *malgré elle*. And as if clearly to establish her innocence in the matter, Renoir's next shot (fig. 3) is very different: it is a homely, mundane view of her *en famille*, the black figure of her granny on the right and her father and fiancé, Anatole, talking to each other on the left. This is followed by a discussion with the *patron* M. Poulain (played by Renoir himself) about what and where to eat. The whole effect of this shot is to background Henriette, to make her again just a bourgeois daughter and not the inducer of vague feelings of uneasiness and excited senses.

There follows a shot of Henriette's joyous face (fig. 4). The shot is from below, and it wonderfully communicates her lightheartedness and euphoria at being aloft. Suddenly we are very much identified with Henriette's feelings: Rodolphe's voyeurism is forgotten. This identification also entails "point of view" but now in a transferred or even metaphorical sense of the term: it is not Henriette's perceptual point of view that the camera identifies with, since she is looking toward it. Rather, her movements and the infectious joy on her face incite us to share her emotional point of view; we empathize with her. For this effect I offer the term "interest" point of view.* We become identified with the fate of a character, and even if we don't see things or even think about them from his or her literal perspective, it still makes sense to say that we share the character's point of view. Renoir brilliantly communicates the effect by swaying the camera to and fro in rhythm with the to-and-fro motions of the swing.

The contrast with the banalities of the previous and following shots enhances the difference between the buoyant fresh girl, a product of nature, and the ponderous and torpid family, especially the father, who seems rooted to the ground by his heavy black jacket, absurd tie, and gross belly bulging out of checkered trousers (fig. 5). It would be ludicrous to see such a man swinging aloft among the trees. The mother is in a middle position: though a woman of some beauty, she has become too heavy and maladroit to get her swing going on her own. She has lost the young girl's powers to fly, though she still has inclinations (which she later ends up showing in a delicious bacchanal with Rodolphe).

Now we get one of my favorite shots in the film (fig. 6). It starts out as another and rather uninteresting view of mother and daughter on the swings. But then there is a long pan over the apparently empty space of the garden, past granny and some trees. Suddenly, completely unexpected figures appear—a column of young seminarians shepherded by their teachers. Heads are down until one of them spots Henriette and alerts his friend (fig. 7). Momentarily we're in their perceptual point of view, watching Henriette from their angle and distance. The shepherd prods the black sheep to cast his eyes down again to avoid the sins of the flesh but manages to sneak a glance of his own (fig. 8). There follows another shot of exhilarated Henriette, enjoying her swing and totally oblivious to this new set of eyes watching her. To clinch the point, Renoir then points the camera at a third set of voyeurs (fig. 9), five precocious boys behind a hedge who exchange knowing glances. Another shot to and fro of Henriette swinging up and down, and we cut back to the boat men, but now seen from *outside* their window (fig. 10). By this time, Henriette's innocent movements have been clearly established as the provocation for Rodolphe's libidinous thoughts.

Rodolphe's voyeurism becomes explicit in an intercut sequence. First there is a shot of Henriette from Rodolphe's angle and distance; the comment in the subtitle, "Wonderful invention—swings!," is, of course, Rodolphe's (fig. 11). The distance preserves the illusion that it is through Rodolphe's vantage that we see Henriette. She unconsciously grants his wish that she sit down so that he can see her legs better (fig. 12). So the camera moves in for a closer view (fig. 13), as if Rodolphe's erotic imagination has given him extra optical magnification. We are carried along and risk being implicated further in his gaze at that wondrous flurry of petticoats, though Henri comments that nothing really can be seen. At this flourish, Rodolphe is shown in an amusing reaction close-up, stroking his mustache and looking rather sheepish (fig. 14).

---

[2]See my *Story and Discourse: Narrative Structure in Fiction and Film* (Ithaca, N.Y. and London, 1978).

A sequence from Jean Renoir's *Une Partie de Campagne* (1946), a film adaptation of Guy de Maupassant's short story. "Close study of film and novel versions of the same narrative reveals with great clarity the peculiar powers of the two media. Once we grasp those peculiarities, the reasons for the differences in form, content, and impact of the two versions strikingly emerge" (CHATMAN, p. 404).

and wine.

Wonderful invention – swings!

So even though Renoir had no direct way of communicating the ambivalences in the expression "showed her legs," he created a sequence in which it can be argued that Henriette is at once innocent and seductive. The sequence is a little masterpiece of reaction editing, not only communicating the essential plot information but also providing a light commentary on French mores and the joys of youth and life, on the birth, amid sunshine and trees, of the sexual impulse. But notice that the sequence illustrates the point I was trying to make at the outset. No member of the audience will formulate in so many words that Henriette was tall, had a small waist and large hips, and so on. We may have a profound sense of Henriette's presence as incarnated by Sylvie Bataille but not of the *assertion* of those details as such. The erotic effect of her appearance explicitly described by the narrator of Maupassant's story is only implicitly depicted in the film by the reaction shots. Something of her appeal is caught by the looks on the faces of four ages of gazing men—the pubescent peekers in the hedge, the seminarians, Rodolphe, and the older priest leading his students.

One final difference between the film and the story: the features of Henriette's appearance that Maupassant's narrator asserts are given an order. First he mentions her height, then her shape, her skin, eyes, hair, then her shape again, her arms, her bosom, her hat, and finally her legs. The order itself seems at once clinical and caressing, going up and down her body, confirming our impression of the narrator as a sensualist. There is no such implication in Renoir's shots. The camera *could* have scanned her body in a cliché shot in the Hollywood mode accompanied by an offscreen wolf whistle. Renoir elected not to compromise the camera: it would have spoiled the whole effect of unconsciously seductive innocence. The camera is not required to share its viewpoint with Rodolphe and the three other groups of voyeurs. It maintains a clear distinction between shots from Rodolphe's point of view and those from a neutral point of view.*

---

*Several participants in the narrative conference objected to my analysis of the point of view situation at this moment in Renoir's film. I hope I am correct in reporting their complaints: the chief objection was to the assumption that female members of the audience would identify with Rodolphe's voyeurism. Such identification, it was contended, would have to be limited to men—and only sexist men at that. The objection seemed to be not about the voyeurism itself but about the willingness of members of an audience to go along with it. (I hope I'm not simplifying the issue by using terms like "identify" and "going along with it"; if I am, I would welcome further clarification from interested readers.)

My response appeals largely and familiarly to the distinction, crucial to interpretation, as I see it, between aesthetics and ethics. The kind of identification that I was discussing is of course purely aesthetic. A reader must obviously be able to participate imaginatively in a character's set of mind, even if that character is a nineteenth-century lecher. One would think the days long gone in which we needed to apologize for donning the perceptual and conceptual clothing of objectionable fictional characters or unreliable narrators—Raskolnikovs or Verlocs or Jason Compsons or one of Celine's "hero" narrators. Imaginative participation in the point of view of fictional characters (need one say again?) in no way implies moral endorsement. It is simply the way we make sense—the way implied authors enable us to become implied readers that make sense—out of unusual or even downright alien viewpoints. We don't compromise our right thinking by engaging in that kind of participation; we don't condone the character's outlook. Why should female members of Renoir's audience have any more difficulty participating in Rodolphe's lecherous point of view

So writer, filmmaker, comic strip artist, choreographer—each finds his or her own ways to evoke the sense of what the objects of the narrative look like. Each medium has its own properties, for better and worse usage, and intelligent film viewing and criticism, like intelligent reading, needs to understand and respect both the limitations these create and also the triumphs they invite.

1980

---

than male members have in participating in the point of view of Molly Bloom? How responsible is an ideology which accuses critics of promulgating characters' viewpoints which they merely wish to analyze? Does a herpetologist become a snake by dissecting a snake? I cannot see how it can be denied that Renoir's presentation of four ages of voyeurs establishes a textual intention to show Henriette as a woman eminently worth looking at, albeit with lust in some men's hearts. For a woman to participate in a male character's doing so requires no greater act of imagination than for a man to participate in Scarlett O'Hara's lust for Rhett Butler. To deny that Renoir intended to communicate voyeurism (because that would make a classic film sexist) seems critically naive. Of course Maupassant and Renoir—or more properly the implied authors of these works—are sexist by modern standards. That doesn't mean that we become sexist by reading, studying, and, yes, even enjoying them.

A comment by Roy Schafer was more useful. Schafer argued that the close-up of Henriette on the swing conveyed to him something of *her* sexual pleasure. It is not difficult to agree that swinging is easily allied to sexuality. The attribution goes along perfectly with other motifs of innocent, pre-conscious sexuality, of "showing her limbs," and of the vague feelings of longing for even the tiny things that move under the leaves and grass that Henriette expresses to her mother a bit later in the film. I think Schafer is right: the point of view could also be attributed to Henriette. But that causes no theoretical problem. Two points of view can exist concurrently in a single shot. It is an interesting property of cinematic narrative that we can see through one character's eyes and feel through another's heart. The camera adopts a position, an angle, and a distance which by convention associates itself with the position, angle, and distance of a character's vision. But so great is its capacity to inspire identification with characters' thinking, feeling, and general situation that we tend to identify even when the character appears to us in a completely frontal view. This sympathetic or "interest" point of view (as I call it) is particularly strong in film narratives and can easily combine with the more conventionally marked perceptual point of view.

DUDLEY ANDREW
FROM CONCEPTS IN FILM THEORY

ADAPTATION

THE SOURCES OF FILMS

Frequently the most narrow and provincial area of film theory, discourse about adaptation is potentially as far-reaching as you like. Its distinctive feature, the matching of the cinematic sign system to prior achievement in some other system, can be shown to be distinctive of all representational cinema.

Let us begin with an example, *A Day in the Country.* Jean Renoir set himself the task of putting his knowledge, his troupe, and his artistry at the service of a tale by Guy de Maupassant. No matter how we judge the process or success of the film, its "being" owes something to the tale that was its inspiration and potentially its measure. That tale, "A Country Excursion," bears a transcendent relation to any and all films that adapt it, for it is itself an artistic sign with a given shape and value, if not a finished meaning. A new artistic sign will then feature this original sign as either its signified or its referent. Adaptations claiming fidelity bear the original as a signified, whereas those inspired by or derived from an earlier text stand in a relation of referring to the original.

The notion of a transcendent order to which the system of the cinema is beholden in its practice goes well beyond this limited case of adaptation.[1] What is a city symphony, for example, if not an adaptation of a concept by the cinema?[2] A definite notion of Berlin preexisted Walter Ruttman's 1927 treatment of that city. What is any documentary for that matter except the signification by the cinema of some

---

[1] For this idea I am indebted to a paper written by Dana Benelli in a class at the University of Iowa, autumn term 1979.

[2] The "city symphony" is a genre of the 1920s which includes up to fifteen films all built on formal or abstract principles, yet dedicated to the presentation of a single city, be it Berlin, Paris, Nice, Moscow, or the like.

prior whole, some concept of person, place, event, or situation. If we take seriously the arguments of Marxist and other social theorists that our consciousness is not open to the world but filters the world according to the shape of its ideology, then every cinematic rendering will exist in relation to some prior whole lodged unquestioned in the personal or public system of experience. In other words, no filmmaker and no film (at least in the representational mode) responds immediately to reality itself, or to its own inner vision. Every representational film *adapts* a prior conception. Indeed the very term "representation" suggests the existence of a model. Adaptation delimits representation by insisting on the cultural status of the model, on its existence in the mode of the text or the already textualized. In the case of those texts explicitly termed "adaptations," the cultural model which the cinema represents is already treasured as a representation in another sign system.

The broader notion of the process of adaptation has much in common with interpretation theory, for in a strong sense adaptation is the appropriation of a meaning from a prior text. The hermeneutic circle, central to interpretation theory, preaches that an explication of a text occurs only after a prior understanding of it, yet that prior understanding is justified by the careful explication it allows.* In other words, before we can go about discussing and analyzing a text we must have a global conception of its meaning. Adaptation is similarly both a leap and a process. It can put into play the intricate mechanism of its signifiers only in response to a general understanding of the signified it aspires to have constructed at the end of its process. While all representational films function this way (as interpretations of a person, place, situation, event, and so forth), we reserve a special place for those films which foreground this relation by announcing themselves as versions of some standard whole. A standard whole can only be a text. A version of it is an adaptation in the narrow sense.

Although these speculations may encourage a hopelessly broad view of adaptation, there is no question that the restricted view of adaptation from known texts in other art forms offers a privileged locus for analysis. I do not say that such texts are themselves privileged. Indeed, the thrust of my earlier remarks suggests quite the opposite. Nevertheless, the explicit, foregrounded relation of a cinematic text to a well-constructed original text from which it derives and in some sense strives to reconstruct provides the analyst with a clear and useful "laboratory" condition which should not be neglected.

The making of film out of an earlier text is virtually as old as the machinery of cinema itself. Well over half of all commercial films have come from literary originals—though by no means all of these originals are revered or respected. If we confine ourselves to those cases where the adaptation process is foregrounded, that is, where the original is held up as a worthy source or goal, there are still several possible modes of relation between the film and the text. These modes can, for convenience, be reduced to three: borrowing, intersection, and fidelity of transformation.

---

*In the theory of interpretation this is generally attributed to Wilhelm Dilthey, although Martin Heidegger has made much of it in our century.

BORROWING, INTERSECTING, AND TRANSFORMING SOURCES

In the history of the arts, surely "borrowing" is the most frequent mode of adaptation. Here the artist employs, more or less extensively, the material, idea, or form of an earlier, generally successful text. Medieval paintings featuring biblical iconography and miracle plays based on Bible stories drew on an exceptional text whose power they borrowed. In a later, secular age the artworks of an earlier generation might be used as sacred in their own right. The many types of adaptations from Shakespeare come readily to mind. Doubtless in these cases, the adaptation hopes to win an audience by the prestige of its borrowed title or subject. But at the same time it seeks to gain a certain respectability, if not aesthetic value, as a dividend in the transaction. Adaptations from literature to music, opera, or paintings are of this nature. There is no question of the replication of the original in Strauss's *Don Quixote.* Instead the audience is expected to enjoy basking in a certain preestablished presence and to call up new or especially powerful aspects of a cherished work.

To study this mode of adaptation, the analyst needs to probe the source of power in the original by examining the use made of it in adaptation. Here the main concern is the generality of the original, its potential for wide and varied appeal; in short, its existence as a continuing form or archetype in culture. This is especially true of that adapted material which, because of its frequent reappearance, claims the status of myth: *Tristan and Isolde* for certain, and *A Midsummer Night's Dream* possibly. The success of adaptations of this sort rests on the issue of their fertility not their fidelity. Frank McConnell's ingenious *Storytelling and Mythmaking* catalogues the garden of culture by examining borrowing as the history of grafting and transplantation in the fashion of Northrop Frye or even Carl Jung.[1] This direction of study will always elevate film by demonstrating its participation in a cultural enterprise whose value is outside film and, for Jung and others, outside texts altogether. Adaptation is the name of this cultural venture at its most explicit, though McConnell, Frye, and Jung would all immediately want to extend their theories of artistic fertility to "original" texts which upon inspection show their dependence on the great fructifying symbols and mythic patterns of civilization.

This vast and airy mode of borrowing finds its opposite in that attitude toward adaptation I choose to call "intersecting." Here the uniqueness of the original text is preserved to such an extent that it is intentionally left unassimilated in adaptation. The cinema, as a separate mechanism, records its confrontation with an ultimately intransigent text. Undoubtedly the key film exhibiting this relation is Robert Bresson's *Diary of a Country Priest.* André Bazin, championing this film and this mode,[2] claimed that in this instance we are presented not with an adaptation so much as a refraction of the original. Because Bresson featured the writing of the diary and because he went out of his way to avoid "opening up" or in any other

[1]Frank McConnell, *Storytelling and Mythmaking* (New York: Oxford University Press, 1979).
[2]André Bazin, *What Is Cinema?* (Berkeley: University of California Press, 1968), p. 142.

way cinematizing the original, Bazin claims that the film *is* the novel as seen by cinema. To extend one of his most elaborate metaphors,* the original artwork can be likened to a crystal chandelier whose formal beauty is a product of its intricate but fully artificial arrangement of parts while the cinema would be a crude flashlight interesting not for its own shape or the quality of its light but for what it makes appear in this or that dark corner. The intersection of Bresson's flashlight and the chandelier of Bernanos's novel produces an experience of the original modulated by the peculiar beam of the cinema. Naturally a great deal of Bernanos fails to be lit up, but what is lit up is only Bernanos, Bernanos however as seen by the cinema.

The modern cinema is increasingly interested in just this sort of intersecting. Bresson, naturally, has given us his Joan of Arc from court records and his *Mouchette* once again from Bernanos. Straub has filmed Corneille's *Othon* and *The Chronicle of Anna Magdalena Bach.* Pasolini audaciously confronted Matthew's gospel with many later texts (musical, pictorial, and cinematic) which it inspired. His later *Medea, Canterbury Tales,* and *Decameron* are also adaptational events in the intersecting mode. All such works fear or refuse to adapt. Instead they present the otherness and distinctiveness of the original text, initiating a dialectical interplay between the aesthetic forms of one period with the cinematic forms of our own period. In direct contrast to the manner scholars have treated the mode of "borrowing," such intersecting insists that the analyst attend to the *specificity* of the original within the *specificity* of the cinema. An original is allowed its life, its own life, in the cinema. The consequences of this method, despite its apparent forthrightness, are neither innocent nor simple. The disjunct experience such intersecting promotes is consonant with the aesthetics of modernism in all the arts. This mode refutes the commonplace that adaptations support only a conservative film aesthetics.

Unquestionably the most frequent and most tiresome discussion of adaptation (and of film and literature relations as well) concerns fidelity and transformation. Here it is assumed that the task of adaptation is the reproduction in cinema of something essential about an original text. Here we have a clear-cut case of film trying to measure up to a literary work, or of an audience expecting to make such a comparison. Fidelity of adaptation is conventionally treated in relation to the "letter" and to the "spirit" of the text, as though adaptation were the rendering of an interpretation of a legal precedent. The letter would appear to be within the reach of cinema for it can be emulated in mechanical fashion. It includes aspects of fiction generally elaborated in any film script: the characters and their inter-relation, the geographical, sociological, and cultural information providing the fiction's context, and the basic narrational aspects that determine the point of view of the narrator (tense, degree of participation, and knowledge of the storyteller, and so on). Ultimately, and this was Bazin's complaint about faithful transformations, the literary work can readily become a scenario written in typical scenario form. The skeleton of the original can, more or less thoroughly, become the skeleton of a film.

More difficult is fidelity to the spirit, to the original's tone, values, imagery, and rhythm, since finding stylistic equivalents in film for these intangible aspects is the

---

*Bazin, p. 107.

opposite of a mechanical process. The cinéaste presumably must intuit and reproduce the feeling of the original. It has been argued variously that this is frankly
impossible, or that it involves the systematic replacement of verbal signifiers by cinematic signifiers, or that it is the product of artistic intuition, as when Bazin found
the pervasive snowy decor in *Symphonie Pastorale* (1946) to reproduce adequately
the simple past tense which Gide's verbs all bear in that tale.[1]

It is at this point that the specificity of these two signifying systems is at stake.
Generally film is found to work from perception toward signification, from external
facts to interior motivations and consequences, from the givenness of a world to the
meaning of a story cut out of that world. Literary fiction works oppositely. It begins
with signs (graphemes and words) building to propositions which attempt to
develop perception. As a product of human language it naturally treats human
motivation and values, seeking to throw them out onto the external world, elaborating a world out of a story.

George Bluestone, Jean Mitry, and a host of others find this opposition to be
most graphic in adaptation.[2] Therefore they take pleasure in scrutinizing this practice even while ultimately condemning it to the realm of the impossible. Since signs
name the inviolate relation of signifier to signified, how is translation of poetic texts
conceivable from one language to another (where signifiers belong to diffferent systems); much less how is it possible to transform the signifiers of one material (verbal) to signifiers of another material (images and sounds)? It would appear that one
must presume the global signified of the original to be separable from its text if one
believes it can be approximated by other sign clusters. Can we attempt to reproduce
the meaning of the *Mona Lisa* in a poem, or of a poem in a musical phrase, or even
of a musical phrase in an aroma? If one accepts this possibility, at the very least one
is forced to discount the primary articulations of the relevant language systems. One
would have to hold that while the material of literature (graphemes, words, and sentences) may be of a different nature from the materials of cinema (projected light
and shadows, identifiable sounds and forms, and represented actions), both systems
may construct in their own way, and at higher levels, scenes and narratives that are
indeed commensurable.

The strident and often futile arguments over these issues can be made sharper
and more consequential in the language of E. H. Gombrich or the even more systematic language of semiotics. Gombrich finds that all discussion of adaptation
introduces the category of "matching."[3] First of all, like Bazin he feels one cannot
dismiss adaptation since it is a fact of human practice. We can and do correctly
match items from different systems all the time: a tuba sound is more like a rock
than like a piece of string; it is more like a bear than like a bird; more like a romanesque church than a baroque one. We are able to make these distinctions and insist
on their public character because we are matching equivalents. In the system of

---

[1]Bazin, p. 67.

[2]George Bluestone, *Novels into Film* (Berkeley: University of California Press, 1957), and Jean
Mitry, "Remarks on the Problem of Cinematic Adaptation," *Bulletin of the Midwest Modern Language Association* 4, no. 1 (Spring 1971): 1–9.

[3]E. H. Gombrich, *Art and Illusion* (Princeton: Princeton University Press, 1960).

musical instruments the tuba occupies an equivalent position to that enjoyed by the romanesque in its system of architectural styles. Nelson Goodman has treated this issue at length in *Languages of Art* pointing to the equivalence not of elements but of the position elements occupy vis-à-vis their different domains.[1] Names of properties of colors may thus metaphorically, but correctly, describe aspects of the world of sound (a blue note, a somber or bright tone). Adaptation would then become a matter of searching two systems of communication for elements of equivalent position in the systems capable of eliciting a signified at a given level of pertinence, for example, the description of a narrative action. For Gombrich adaptation is possible, though never perfect, because every artwork is a construct of elements built out of a traditional use of a system. Since humans have the general capacity to adapt to new systems with different traditions in achieving a like goal or construct, artistic adaptation poses no insurmountable obstacles. Nevertheless attention to such "proportional consistencies" demands that the study of adaptation include the study of both art forms in their proper *historic* context.

Gombrich and Goodman anticipated the more fashionable vocabulary of semiotics in their clarification of these issues. In *Film and Fiction, The Dynamics of Exchange,* Keith Cohen tries to justify this new, nearly scientific approach to questions of relations between these arts; he writes, citing Metz:

> A basic assumption I make is that both words and images are sets of signs that belong to systems and that, at a certain level of abstraction, these systems bear resemblances to one another. More specifically, within each such system there are many different codes (perceptual, referential, symbolic). What makes possible, then, a study of the relation between two separate sign systems, like novel and film, is the fact that the same codes may reappear in more than one system. . . . The very mechanisms of language systems can thus be seen to carry on diverse and complex interrelations: "one function, among others, of language is to name the units segmented by vision (but also to help segment them), and . . . one function, among others, of vision is to inspire semantic configurations (but also to be inspired by them)."[2]

Cohen, like Metz before him, suggests that despite their very different material character, despite even the different ways we process them at the primary level, verbal and cinematic signs share a common fate: that of being condemned to connotation. This is especially true in their fictional use where every signifier identifies a signified but also elicits a chain reaction of other relations which permits the elaboration of the fictional world. Thus, for example, imagery functions equivalently in films and novels. This mechanism of implication among signs leads Cohen to conclude that "narrativity is the most solid median link between novel and cinema, the most pervasive tendency of both verbal and visual languages. In both novel and cinema, groups of signs, be they literary or visual signs, are apprehended consecutively through time; and this consecutiveness gives rise to an unfolding structure,

---

[1] Nelson Goodman, *Languages of Art,* esp. pp. 143–48 (Indianapolis: Bobbs-Merrill, 1968).
[2] Keith Cohen, *Film and Fiction: The Dynamics of Exchange* (New Haven: Yale University Press, 1979), p. 4. Cohen's citation from Metz comes from Christian Metz, *Langage et cinéma* (Paris: Larçosse, 1971).

the diegetic whole that is never fully *present* in any one group yet always *implied* in each such group."[1]

Narrative codes, then, always function at the level of implication or connotation. Hence they are potentially comparable in a novel and a film. The story can be the same if the narrative units (characters, events, motivations, consequences, context, viewpoint, imagery, and so on) are produced equally in two works. Now this production is, by definition, a process of connotation and implication. The analysis of adaptation then must point to the achievement of equivalent narrative units in the absolutely different semiotic systems of film and language. Narrative itself is a semiotic system available to both and derivable from both. If a novel's story is judged in some way comparable to its filmic adaptation, then the strictly separate but equivalent processes of implication which produced the narrative units of that story through words and audio-visual signs, respectively, must be studied. Here semiotics coincides with Gombrich's intuition: such a study is not comparative between the arts but is instead intensive within each art. And since the implicative power of literary language and of cinematic signs is a function of its use as well as of its system, adaptation analysis ultimately leads to an investigation of film styles and periods in relation to literary styles of different periods.

We have come round the other side of the argument now to find once more that the study of adaptation is logically tantamount to the study of the cinema as a whole. The system by which film involves us in fictions and the history of that system are ultimately the questions we face even when starting with the simple observation of an equivalent tale told by novel and film. This is not to my mind a discouraging arrival for it drops adaptation and all studies of film and literation out of the realm of eternal principle and airy generalization, and onto the uneven but solid ground of artistic history, practice, and discourse.

THE SOCIOLOGY AND AESTHETICS OF ADAPTATION

It is time for adaptation studies to take a sociological turn. How does adaptation serve the cinema? What conditions exist in film style and film culture to warrant or demand the use of literary prototypes? Although adaptation may be calculated as a relatively constant volume in the history of cinema, its particular function in any moment is far from constant. The choices of the mode of adaptation and of prototypes suggest a great deal about the cinema's sense of its role and aspirations from decade to decade. Moreover, the stylistic strategies developed to achieve the proportional equivalences necessary to construct matching stories not only are symptomatic of a period's style but may crucially alter that style.

Bazin pointed to an important instance of this in the immediate post-war era when adaptations from the stage by Cocteau, Welles, Olivier, Wyler, and others not only developed new ways for the cinema to be adequate to serious theater, but also developed a kind of discipline in *mise-en-scène* whose consequences go far beyond the production of *Macbeth, Les Parents terribles, The Little Foxes,* and *Henry V.*[2]

---

[1]Cohen, p. 92.
[2]Bazin, *What Is Cinema?*, p. 76.

Cocteau's film, to take one example, derives its style from Welles's use of interior shooting in *Kane* and *Ambersons,* thus responding to a new conception of dramatic space; but at the same time his film helped solidify a shooting style that would leave its mark on Alexandre Astruc and André Michel among others. Furthermore his particular cinematic *écriture* would allow Truffaut to set him against the cinema of quality in the famous 1954 diatribe.[1] It is instructive to note that while Truffaut railed against the status quo for its literariness and especially for its method of adaptation, the directors he praised were also working with literary originals: Bresson adapting Bernanos, Ophuls adapting Maupassant and Schnitzler, and Cocteau adapting his own theater pieces. Like Bazin, Truffaut looked upon adaptation not as a monolithic practice to be avoided but as an instructive barometer for the age. The cinema *d'auteur* which he advocated was not to be pitted against a cinema of adaptation; rather one method of adaptation would be pitted against another. In this instance adaptation was the battleground even while it prepared the way for a stylistic revolution, the New Wave, which would for the most part avoid famous literary sources.

To take another sort of example, particular literary fashions have at times exercised enormous power over the cinema and, consequently, over the general direction of its stylistic evolution. The Romantic fiction of Hugo, Dickens, Dumas, and countless lesser figures originally set the stylistic requirements of American and mainstream French cinema at the end of the silent era. Similarly Zola and Maupassant, always of interest to French cinéastes, helped Jean Renoir muscularly reorient the style of world cinema in the 1930's. Not only that, through Luchino Visconti this naturalist impulse directly developed one strain of neorealism in his adaptations of Giovanni Verga *(La Terra Trema)* and James M. Cain *(Ossessione).*

This latter case forces us to recall that the "dynamics of exchange," as Cohen calls it, go both ways between film and fiction. Naturalist fiction helped cinema develop its interest in squalid subjects and a hard-hitting style. This in turn affected American hard-boiled novelists like Cain and Hammett, eventually returning to Europe in the film style of Visconti, Carné, Clouzot, and others. This general trading between film and literature in the currency of naturalism had some remarkable individual incidents associated with it. Renoir's adaptation of *The Lower Depths* can serve as an example. In 1881 Zola had cried out for a naturalist theater[2] and had described twenty years before the time precisely the sort of drama Gorki would write in *The Lower Depths:* a collection of real types thrown together without a domineering plot, the drama driven by the natural rhythms of little incidents and facts exposing the general quality of life in an era. Naturalism here coincided with a political need, with Gorki's play preceding the great uprisings in Russia by only a few years.

In another era and in response to a different political need, Renoir leapt at the chance to adapt the Gorki work. This was 1935, the year of the ascendancy of the

[1]François Truffaut, "A Certain Tendency in French Cinema," in Bill Nichols, *Movies and Methods,* I (Berkeley: University of California Press, 1976), pp. 224–36.

[2]Emile Zola, "Naturalism and the Theater," in *The Experimental Novel and Other Essays,* tr. by Belle Sherman (New York: Haskell House, 1964).

Popular Front, and Renoir's treatment of the original is clearly marked by the pressures and aspirations of that moment. The film negotiates the mixture of classes which the play only hints at. Louis Jouvet as the Baron dominates the film, descending into the social depths and helping organize a collective undoing of Kastylylov, the capitalist landlord. Despite the gloomy theme, the murder, jailing, deaths by sickness and suicide, Renoir's version overflows with a general warmth evident in the airy setting by the Marne and the relaxed direction of actors who breathe languidly between their lines.

Did Gorki mind such an interpretation? We can never know, since he died a few months before its premier. But he did give Renoir his imprimatur and looked forward to seeing the completed version, this despite the fact that in 1932 he declared that the play was useless, out of date, and unperformable in socialist Russia. Perhaps these statements were the insincere self-criticism which that important year elicited from many Russian artists. I prefer, however, to take Gorki at his word. More far-sighted than most theorists, let alone most authors, he realized that *The Lower Depths* in 1932 Russia was by no means the same artwork as *The Lower Depths* in the France of the Popular Front. This is why he put no strictures on Renoir assuming that the cinéaste would deal with his play as he felt necessary. Necessity is, among other things, a product of the specific place and epoch of the adaptation, both historically and stylistically. The naturalist attitude of 1902, fleshing out the original plans of Zola, gave way to a new historic and stylistic moment, and fed that style that Renoir had begun elaborating ever since *La Chienne* in 1931, and that despite its alleged looseness and airiness in comparison to the Gorki, would help lead European cinema onto the naturalist path.

This sketch of a few examples from the sociology of adaptation has rapidly taken us into the complex interchange between eras, styles, nations, and subjects. This is as it should be, for adaptation, while a tantalizing keyhole for theorists, nevertheless partakes of the univeral situation of film practice, dependent as it is on the aesthetic system of the cinema in a particular era and on that era's cultural needs and pressures. Filmmaking, in other words, is always an event in which a system is used and altered in discourse. Adaptation is a peculiar form of discourse but not an unthinkable one. Let us use it not to fight battles over the essence of the media or the inviolability of individual art works. Let us use it as we use all cultural practices, to understand the world from which it comes and the one toward which it points. The elaboration of these worlds will demand, therefore, historical labor and critical acumen. The job of theory in all this is to keep the questions clear and in order. It will no longer do to let theorists settle things with a priori arguments. We need to study the films themselves as acts of discourse. We need to be sensitive to that discourse and to the forces that motivate it.

1984

V

Film Genres

The study of artistic genres is as old as Aristotle, and at least one of his generic terms, "comedy," has been regularly applied to films. (Significantly, tragedy has not established itself as a film genre.) The generic approach to art has frequently been attacked, however, for its terms are often imprecise and its methods of categorization unclear. What, precisely, is a documentary film or a screwball comedy? Are films to be classified by their physical properties (silent, color), by their subject matter (gangster, western), or by their purpose or effect (comic, educational)? Further, are these categories legitimate? Of what interest is a category like the "educational" film? In any case, is it even proper to arrange works of art in classes, viewing them as instances of types? Benedetto Croce, the influential Italian philosopher and critic, argued that generic criticism was necessarily incompatible with an aesthetic point of view, which always treats works of art as individual and unique. Croce's views have not prevailed, however, and the concept of genre continues to be employed in film theory and criticism, as it is in all art theory and criticism, and with important results.

The most familiar system by which films are generically classified distinguishes between the different kinds of fictional narrative (almost inevitably American) feature films: westerns, gangster films, newspaper pictures, detective dramas, screwball comedies, courtroom dramas, *films noirs,* musicals, war films, spy films, prison films, horror films, science fictions, fantasies, thrillers. An obvious difficulty with such commonly used categories is that they overlap; a film might combine gangsters, detectives, newspapermen, a courtroom, a prison, suspense, and a bleak, *"noir"* atmosphere; a film might combine screwball comedy, newspapermen, and prisons (as *His Girl Friday* does), or screwball comedy, the western, and the musical (as *Calamity Jane* and *Annie Get Your Gun* do). In classifying such a film one would have to rely on a judgment about what is important. Or one might decide to employ a compound category. But this sort of adjustment does not present genre criticism with an insoluble difficulty, for to be able to speak of a compound genre at all implies that elemental genres exist in order to be compounded.

Another problem of classifying fictional narrative films in this way arises when we ask if such categories have any impact on either the making of films or our responses to films. Are they critical and commercial conveniences, designed merely to help market a film or to describe a film for those who have not seen it? How conscious are filmmakers of their use of generic conventions? How conscious are audiences of these conventions? How do we recognize that a film does indeed represent a particular genre? How do the conventions of a genre evolve over the history of film? Are such evolutions the result of changing artistic conventions in films, of developing cultural standards in society, or both? Despite these questions, there can be no doubt that treating a film as a representative of a familiar and perceptively formulated genre is often essential to a proper understanding of it.

For Leo Braudy the concept of genre must first be rescued from the presumption that it can only describe a debased and degraded kind of art. "Genre films offend our most common definition of artistic excellence: the uniqueness of the art object, whose value can in part be defined by its desire to be uncaused and unfamiliar, as much as possible unindebted to any tradition, popular or otherwise." After tracing this critical prejudice to its roots in the aesthetic and literary theories of the Romantic Era, Braudy posits the two kinds of connection which genre films achieve. First, genre films forge a deliberate connection between each new instance of the genre and its past tradition and manifestations. Second, genre films, because of their popularity and familiarity, have a more powerful impact on their audience—and a highly democratic one—converting that audience into a unified cultural force: "Genre films strike beneath our intellectual appreciation of high art and make us one with a large mass audience, often despite our more articulate and elitist views." His specific look at musicals of the 1930s and 1940s demonstrates the way that the genre, especially as embodied in the contrast between Fred Astaire and Gene Kelly, sought to interject energy and spontaneity into the repetitiveness of everyday social reality, either by Astaire's escape into the perfect world of dance or by Kelly's making the imperfect world more perfect by making it dance.

Robert Warshow, the influential American analyst of the popular arts in the era just after World War II, would agree with Braudy's observation that the popular genre film makes connections both with its filmic past and with the temperaments of its contemporary viewers. Although he would be less willing to grant the general artistic excellence and importance to genre films that Braudy does, he does consider the gangster and the westerner as the two most important creations of American movies. The power of both genres derives from their concern with the problem of violence. The hero of the western asserts his honor and demonstrates the possibility of "style" in the face of inevitable defeat. He asserts that even in killing and being killed we are not freed from the necessity of establishing an admirable mode of behavior. Because the pattern of the classical western is so firmly fixed, our pleasure is that of the connoisseur. We must appreciate minor variations in the characteristics of the actors who play the hero's role, and it is only in virtue of the film's ability to record such variations that these films can remain interesting to us. Any attempt to break the set pattern (to violate the "rules" of the genre), either by turning the western into a "social drama" (as in *The Ox-Bow Incident*) or by aestheticizing it (as in *Shane*), destroys its power. According to Warshow, part of our pleasure in this kind of complete and self-contained art derives precisely from its contrast with the more complex, uncertain, and self-conscious creations of modernism. The art of the western is not an art that precedes modernism (as it is for Stanley Cavell), but one that is contemporary with it and draws strength from the contrast.

In the face of those who would dismiss genre films as a lower form of art, Warshow tries to salvage their importance by emphasizing their invariable and almost ritual qualities. His argument is countered by critics, Braudy among them, who contend that a central aspect of all great genre art is its ability to serve as a barometer of the social and cultural concerns of its audience. As Jean-Loup Bourget argues about the genre film, "its conventionality is the very paradoxical reason for its creativity." Bourget focuses particularly on melodrama and musical forms that have both been adapted by film from their incarnations on the popular stage. Although he emphasizes that genre films can raise basic questions about social reality, his more pervasive view is that these subversive possibilities are realized only rarely by genre directors and that the audience leaves a genre film "with a clear conscience and a dim consciousness."

Bourget's argument thus assumes the essentially conservative nature of popular art (of which genre film is the prime example) and the passivity of its audience. It reflects the influence of Marxist ideas prevalent since the 1930s that revise Marx's famous dictum about religion to say that it is popular culture that is the opium of the people. Robin Wood looks at the genre question from a quite different Marxist angle, which considers the meaning of genre films to be much less clear, because it is rooted in ideological contradictions. Unlike those who would create a taxonomy that distinguishes and separates individual genres, Wood considers them all to be connected but "different strategies for dealing with the same ideological tensions."

A prime characteristic of the "high" or "classic" art to which genre is so often negatively compared is its creation by a great artist. Genre art, in this account, can never reach the heights of greatness because its creators are too tied to artistic precedents and are therefore not "original." The countervailing argument asserts that genre creativity is defined by exactly that manipulation of past motifs to create a new work. Drawing upon the legacy of the auteur controversy over who should receive the creative "credit" for filmmaking (see Section VI, especially the articles by Sarris and Wollen), Wood continues his argument by focusing especially on the way in which Frank Capra and Alfred Hitchcock embed genre themes and motifs in their films.

Both Braudy and Bourget emphasize the musical as a genre that crucially involves questions of social organization and cooperation. Jane Feuer, in contrast, looks in detail at the "deceptions" of the idealizing process that is at the heart of so many musicals. Drawing on Claude Lévi-Strauss's view of myth as a way of mediating contradictions, she focuses on the self-congratulatory side of musicals, how they have been created by studio organizations whose own production processes are thereby praised as natural rather than artificial. Like Bourget, she also ultimately considers the genre (and perhaps all genre) to be essentially conservative. Even that prime characteristic of modernist art, its self-consciousness and reflexivity, in the Hollywood musical serves only "to perpetuate rather than to deconstruct the codes of the genre."

John Cawelti's essay on the private-eye, detective film takes a longer historical view of the evolution of the codes of a particular genre back to its roots. For Cawelti, the generic categories of American studio films have their analogues and ancestors in American popular fictions. On the other hand, he notes a new attitude toward genre that has dominated many American films of the past decade, particularly the most interesting and important ones—the generic transformation. This deliberately self-conscious metamorphosis of familiar film genres might be seen as an American compromise between the modernist art-films of post-war Europe and the traditional American tendency toward generic plots and characters. Cawelti sees these contemporary generic transformations, though manifestations of a single spirit, as having four emphases. The film can parody a familiar genre (as Mel Brooks's films do), can nostalgically evoke a familiar genre (as a film like *Farewell, My Lovely* does), can demythologize the familiar genre (as *Chinatown* and Arthur Penn's films do), or can recognize its artificiality but deliberately choose to sustain the myth of the familiar genre (as Sam Peckinpah's films do). Of these four transformations, Cawelti finds the demythologizing film the richest, most complex, and most challenging to its audience's values and responses, approaching the complexity of response required for European art-films. Considering the virtual collapse of the detective genre after *Chinatown,* one might be tempted to ask if the achievement of such a complex view of the genre may be the precondition for its disappearance.

Thomas Elsaesser looks at melodrama, a particularly long-lived genre, with an intricate literary and theatrical history before it emerges into film. Unlike Bourget and Feuer's assumption of the basic conservatism of the genre work and the passivity of the genre audience, Elsaesser's richly detailed account emphasizes the "radical ambiguity" of melodrama, especially film melodrama, which "would appear to function either subversively or as escapism—categories that are always relative to the given historical and social context." The melodrama, he argues, is particularly important to an understanding of popular culture because it is the quintessence of the way in which popular forms process social change in terms of private and emotional effects. In the melodrama, the failure to act is paramount, while in genres like the western, it is action that is stressed. The melodrama thus highlights the victim's point of view, "reproducing more directly than other genres the patterns of domination and exploitation existing in a given society. . . ."

Tania Modleski also takes up the issue of melodrama as a film genre, but emphasizes instead genre distinctions that derive from or coincide with gender distinctions, in both the characters and the audience. Through her focus on Max Ophuls's *Letter from an Unknown Woman,* Modleski criticizes Elsaesser among others for further ignoring the gender component in their efforts to define melodrama. Noting how the feminine voice has often been repressed in Hollywood films, especially those that define their worlds through male action (like the gangster film and the western), she points out that women have traditionally been considered the prime audience for melodrama because of its alliance with emotional states and situations. The appeal of melodrama for both men and women she finds is in its dramatization of a sense of loss that can be only partially explained by recourse to traditional psychological categories.

In contrast to Bourget and Feuer's almost exclusive emphasis on the social context of genre, Bruce Kawin, like Modleski, emphasizes how particular genre forms—in his essay, the horror and science fiction film—appeal psychologically to their audiences. Grounding his argument in the influential studies of Frazer, Freud, and Jung, he first defines the audience's experience with horror and science fiction in terms of myths and dreams: "One goes to the horror film in order to have a nightmare . . . a dream whose undercurrent of anxiety both presents and masks the desire to fulfill and be punished for certain conventionally unacceptable impulses." A horror film like *The Wolf Man,* for example, is a "transparently Oedipal . . . playing out of castration anxiety." Second, Kawin draws a careful distinction between science fiction films and horror films, arguing that these appeal to different mental activities: "Science fiction appeals to consciousness, horror to the unconscious."

Kawin's exploration of the psychological grounding of the horror genre is finally deployed to help make distinctions between two otherwise closely related genres. Linda Williams approaches horror from an equally psychological point of view, but one more allied to the concerns with the gender distinctions that animate Modleski's essay. In the voyeurism and look of victimization that characterizes much of the horror genre, Williams sees an intriguing intensification of the feminist preoccupation with the "gaze" (see Section VII, especially the essays by Mulvey, Doane, and Studlar). The horror film, she argues, connects the experience of terror with the acknowledgment of woman's sexual power, usually absent from film, which is first celebrated then punished, in both the performer and the spectator. Williams's analysis demonstrates the genre's development from early silent films down to the recent past not so much in terms of a specific historical and social context, but as a psychological history of male and female in America represented by the different versions of the horror motifs.

LEO BRAUDY
FROM THE WORLD IN A FRAME

GENRE: THE CONVENTIONS OF CONNECTION

Actually I do not think that there are any wrong reasons for liking a statue or a picture . . . There are wrong reasons for disliking a work of art.

E. H. GOMBRICH,
The Story of Art

No part of the film experience has been more consistently cited as a barrier to serious critical interest than the existence of forms and conventions, whether in such details as the stereotyped character, the familiar setting, and the happy ending, or in those films that share common characteristics—westerns, musicals, detective films, horror films, escape films, spy films—in short, what have been called *genre* films. Films in general have been criticized for their popular and commercial appeal, seemingly designed primarily for entertainment and escape rather than enlightenment. Genre films especially are criticized because they seem to appeal to a preexisting audience, while the film "classic" creates its own special audience through the unique power of the filmmaking artist's personal creative sensibility. Too often in genre films the creator seems gone and only the audience is present, to be attacked for its bad taste and worse politics for even appreciating this debased art.

The critical understanding of genre films therefore becomes a special case of the problem of understanding films in general. Genre films offend our most common definition of artistic excellence: the uniqueness of the art object, whose value can in part be defined by its desire to be uncaused and unfamiliar, as much as possible unindebted to any tradition, popular or otherwise. The pure image, the clear personal style, the intellectually respectable content are contrasted with the impurities of convention, the repetitions of character and plot. We undervalue their attractions and inner dynamics because there seems to be no critical vocabulary with which to talk about them without condescending, and therefore no aesthetic criteria by which to judge them, no way of understanding why one horror film scares us and another leaves us cold, why one musical is a symphony of style and another a clashing disarray.

Critics have ignored genre films because of their prejudice for the unique. But why should art be restricted only to works of self-contained intensity, while many other kinds of artistic experience are relegated to the closet of aesthetic pleasure, unfit for the daylight? Genre films, in fact, arouse and complicate feelings about the self and society that more serious films, because of their bias toward the unique, may rarely touch. Within film the pleasures of originality and the pleasures of familiarity are at least equally important. Following Marcel Duchamp and Antonin Artaud, Andy Warhol in the early 1960s announced "no more classics." In painting and sculpture this meant an attack on the canonization of museum art and the acceptance of previously unacceptable, often popular, forms. For films, the problem has usually been the other way around. "No more classics" for film might mean no more films defined as separate from the popular forms that are the great energy of film, artistically as well as thematically.

The modern prejudice against genre in art can be traced to the aesthetic theories of the Romantic period. In the later eighteenth century the older idea of poetic inspiration began to be expanded into a major literary theory by works like Edward Young's *Conjectures on Original Composition* (1759). Poetic "imitation," the building of creativity on the achievements of the past, began to fade as the standard of personal vision became more important. Only conventions that could be understood liberally survived, and the eighteenth-century unwillingness to accord imaginative sympathy to convention received its most famous expression in Samuel Johnson's attack on John Milton's *Lycidas,* a poem in the form of a pastoral elegy, which drew upon a tradition of lament that went back to Theocritus and Vergil. The English and German Romantic writers consolidated this trend by establishing originality not only as a criterion of art, but, in their crudest statements, the *only* criterion of art. Art could owe nothing to tradition or the past because that debt qualified the power and originality of the individual creator. The poet was inspired by what he saw and experienced, and the intervention of any prior categories for that experience doomed the work to secondary value unless the forms that intervened were primitive forms—the folktale or the ballad—that had none of the hated sophistication of the art of the previous age. Any use of genre and convention as such necessarily debarred a work and its author from the status of true art. If poetry were defined as the spontaneous outpouring of strong feelings, how could a work that employed stock characters and stock situations, stock images and stock resolutions, have any art or originality in it? Folk art or popular art could be used because it was generally assumed that serious art was the purity of which popular art was the degeneracy, and that purity necessarily precedes degeneracy.* Poetic inspiration and self-sufficiency occupied the higher peaks of art, while hack work

---

*Ballad-collectors like Bishop Percy or Sir Walter Scott could therefore argue that their rewritings were an effort to restore the ballads to the form in which the "Bard" originally created them, before they were passed on to the fumbling brains of the folk. Pop Art has revived this theory in a somewhat different form. Ostensibly making us look at the common objects of the world with new intensity, Pop Art also conveys the idea that serious art and artists make popular themes and motifs worthy (read "self-conscious") by putting them into museum settings and charging high prices. Warhol may have first done this to satirize the whole elitist-popular division, but the joke seems to have run thin.

and despised formulas inhabited the more populated and bourgeois valleys. Genre and convention were the fare of the multitudes, while originality and storming self-assertion, without a past, without any controls, was the caviar of the truly aware audience.

Until the eighteenth century, artists had generally been distinguished by their class, their education, and their patrons. But, with the growth of a mass society and a mass culture, the hierarchy shifted from distinctions in genealogy to distinctions in sensibility. Almost all of the great eighteenth-century English novelists and essayists had spent some time in Grub Street, that world created to serve the new hunger for the printed word. But the Romantic sensibility turned Grub Street into a synonym for the convention-ridden enemies of art. The true artist was noncommercial, struggling on the fringes of human existence, with neither society nor companions (and hardly any publishers), alone with his indomitable self. Only Byron, the most eighteenth-century of the Romantics, could have said, "I awoke to find myself famous" (on the publication of *Childe Harold*); such an obvious interest in the approval of a book-buying public was disdained in the Romantics' image of their calling. And Byron himself preoccupied much of his writing with the depiction of solitary heroes, striding mountainsides to challenge gloomy fates. The Romantic artist tried to make his work unique to escape from the dead hand of traditional form. The only serious use of the past was the contemplation of vanished greatness, to raise the artist out of what he believed to be an uncultured present and establish for himself a continuity with what has been best before the triumph of modern degeneracy. Like T. S. Eliot in *The Wasteland,* the serious, unpopular artist was the only one in a corrupt age who could summon up the artistic Eden of the past and collect its fragments into some coherence.

Such absolute creativity is finally a fraud because all art must exist in some relation to the forms of the past, whether in contrast or continuation. Both the generic work and the more self-contained work expand our sense of the possibilities of art. But the nineteenth-century stress on literary originality and freedom has inhibited our responses, both intellectual and emotional, to works that try to complicate our appreciation of tradition and form, works that may in fact embody a more radical critique of the past than those which ignore it. More people dislike westerns or musicals because such film genres outrage their inherited and unexamined sense of what art *should* be than because the films are offensive in theme, characterization, style, or other artistic quality. Every lover of musicals, for example, has heard the complaint that musicals are unrealistic and the viewer gets embarrassed when people start singing or dancing. But the relationship between realism and stylization is a central issue in musicals, not an absurd convention. When auteur critics applaud the studio director for triumphing over his material and point to the glimmers of original style shining through the genre assignment, they may awaken us to the merits of an individual artist. But they also fall into the Romantic trap of searching for only what is obviously original and personal in a work. In auteur theory, genre directors with large popular audiences become transformed into embattled Romantic artists trying to establish their personal visions in the face of an assembly-line commercialism. Frank Capra has pointed out the opposite possibility: in the days of big studio monopoly, there was a great deal of freedom to experiment because every film had guaranteed distribution, whereas now, with increased independent production, films have become more uniform and compromised, because each has to justify itself financially. Underground and avant-garde films with their emphasis on the individual creative sensibility above all, are naturally enough the most hostile to genre. But the bulk of films fall between pure personal expression and pure studio exploitation, mingling the demands of art and culture, creativity and talent. By their involvement in collective creativity, film directors have, at least practically, moved away from the image of the isolated Romantic artist, no matter how they may indulge that image in their public statements.

Instead of dismissing genre films from the realm of art, we should therefore examine what they accomplish. Genre in films can be the equivalent of conscious reference to tradition in the other arts—the invocation of past works that has been so important a part of the history of literature, drama, and painting. Miró's use of Vermeer, Picasso's use of Delacroix are efforts to distinguish their view of the proper ends of painting. Eliot's use of Spenser or Pynchon's of Joyce make similar assertions of continuity and difference. The methods of the western, the musical, the detective film, or the science-fiction film are also reminiscent of the way Shakespeare infuses old stories with new characters to express the tension between past and present. All pay homage to past works even while they vary their elements and comment on their meaning.

Perhaps the main difference between genre films and classic films is the way that genre films invoke past forms while classic films spend time denying them. The joy in genre is to see what can be dared in the creation of a new form or the creative destruction and complication of an old one. The ongoing genre subject therefore always involves a complex relation between the compulsions of the past and the freedoms of the present, an essential part of the film experience. The single, unique work tries to be unforgettable by solving the whole world at once. The genre work, because of its commitment to pre-existing forms, explores the world more slowly. Its hallmark is less the flash of inspiration than the deep exploration of craft. Like Ford's *Stagecoach* or Aldrich's *Ulzana's Raid* (1972) it can exist both in itself and as the latest in a line of works like it, picking and choosing among possible conventions, refusing one story or motif to indulge another, avoiding one "cliché" in order to show a self-conscious mastery of the cliché that has been avoided. After all, the reason that an artistic element becomes a cliché is that it answers so well to the experience, intelligence, and feelings of the audience. Subsequent artists, perceiving the same aptness, want to exercise its power themselves, even in a potentially hostile new context, to discover if all the possibilities of the form have thoroughly been explored. The only test is its continuing relevance, and a genre will remain vital, as the western has, and the musical has not, so long as its conventions still express themes and conflicts that preoccupy its audience. When either minority or majority art loses contact with its audience, it becomes a mere signpost in history, an aesthetic rather than an art.

Genre films affect their audience especially by their ability to express the warring traditions in society and the social importance of understanding convention. When Irene Dunne, in *The Awful Truth* (Leo McCarey, 1937), disguises herself as Cary Grant's (fictitious) sister and arrives drunk and raucous at a society gathering where

Grant is trying to establish himself, we can open a critical trapdoor and say that the other people at the party, who already know her, don't recognize her in her flimsy disguise because of the necessities of plot and comic form. But we must go on to say that this particular convention, used with all its force, allows McCarey, without dropping the general humorous tone, to point out that she is unrecognized because the upper classes base their estimates and knowledge of character on dress, voice, and manners—a theme supported by the rest of the film as well. The conflict between desire and etiquette can define both a social comedy like *The Awful Truth* and even a more obviously stylized genre work like *Dr. Jekyll and Mr. Hyde* (Rouben Mamoulian, 1932); it parallels in the plot the aesthetic contrast between the individual film and the conventions to which it plays a complex homage.

Genre demands that we know the dynamics of proper audience response and may often require a special audience because of the need to refer the latest instance to previous versions. But response is never invariable. Convention isn't only whatever we don't have to pay attention to. Explaining Shakespeare's use of soliloquies by observing that the practice was an Elizabethan dramatic convention tells us as little as saying that Picasso used blue because it was cheap or that Edward Everett Horton appeared in so many Fred Astaire-Ginger Rogers films because comic relief was needed. Why a soliloquy *now*? What does Horton's presence mean *here*? The possibility exists in all art that convention and comment coexist, that overlapping and even contradictory assumptions and conventions may be brought into play to test their power and make the audience reflect on why they were assumed. The genre film lures its audience into a seemingly familiar world, filled with reassuring stereotypes of character, action, and plot. But the world may actually be not so lulling, and, in some cases, acquiescence in convention will turn out to be bad judgment or even a moral flaw—the basic theme of such Hitchcock films as *Blackmail* (1929), *Rear Window* (1954), and *Psycho*. While avant-garde and original works congratulate the audience by implying it has the capacity to understand them, genre films can exploit the automatic conventions of response for the purposes of pulling the rug out from under their viewers. The very relaxing of the critical intelligence of the audience, the relief that we need not make decisions—aesthetic, moral, metaphysical—about the film, allows the genre film to use our expectations against themselves, and, in the process, reveal to us expectations and assumptions that we may never have thought we had. They can potentially criticize the present, because it too automatically *accepts* the standards of the past, to build subversion within received forms and thereby to criticize the forms instead of only setting up an alternate vision.*

---

*The three main American critics who appreciated such films before the New Wave popularized them critically—Otis Ferguson, James Agee, and Manny Farber—were less interested in them for their formal qualities than for their action and unpretentiousness, aspects of energy related to their formal self-consciousness. But both Agee and Farber (and Pauline Kael is their true heir in this) wanted to protect at all costs their beloved movies from any charge of art. As far as the definition of art they were attacking goes, they were right. But to continue such attacks now confuses where it once illuminated. One virtue of the French New Wave critics was that they didn't have to defend themselves simultaneously against pompous ideas of high art, the myth of the American tough guy artist, and the specter of Hollywood commercialism.

Through a constant interplay between the latest instance and the history of a particular form, genre films can call upon a potential of aesthetic complexity that would be denied if the art defined itself only in terms of its greatest and most inimitable works. Because of the existence of generic expectations—how a plot "should" work, what a stereotyped character "should" do, what a gesture, a location, an allusion, a line of dialogue "should" mean—the genre film can step beyond the moment of its existence and play against its own aesthetic history. Through genre, movies have drawn upon their own tradition and been able to reflect a rich heritage unavailable to the "high" arts of the twentieth century which are so often intent upon denying the past and creating themselves totally anew each time out. Within the world of genre films one finds battles, equivalent to those in the history of literature, drama, and painting, between artists who are willing to reproduce a tradition through their own vision because they believe it still has the ability to evoke the emotional response that made it a satisfying artistic form to begin with, and those who believe the form has dried up and needs an injection, usually of "realism." Poets, for example, may contrast the city and the country because that opposition answers to some real beliefs in their audience and because the choice of the rural virtues of the country satisfactorily resolves the conflict. Others might question the authenticity of the traditional materials: did shepherds really play their pipes in singing contests? isn't the elaborate language untrue to rural idioms? or, to extend the analogy, did cowboys really respect law and justice so much? do people really break into dances on the street when they're happy, and does the neighborhood automatically join in? The later generations may feel an emotional pull in the form, but they might want to destylize it and make it more real. The directors of the "adult" western of the 1950s accepted the vitality of the western but thought that a more realistic treatment would strengthen its inherent virtues. If controversy were part of film tradition, we might have an argument between John Ford and Fred Zinnemann on the essence of the western like that between Alexander Pope and Ambrose Phillips on the pastoral, Ford and Pope arguing for the value of form and style, while Zinnemann and Phillips press the need to make the characters of art as close as possible to the real persons who live or lived in that place.

Genre films share many of the characteristics of the closed films I have described in the previous chapter. But, instead of being framed visually, genre films are primarily *closed by convention.* Of course, they may be visually enclosed as well, as, for example, are horror films and 1930s musicals; but the more important enclosure is the frame of pre-existing motifs, plot turns, actors, and situations—in short everything that makes the film a special place with its own rules, a respite from the more confusing and complicated worlds outside. The frame of genre, the existence of expectations to be used in whatever way the intelligence of the filmmaker is capable, allows freedoms within the form that more original films cannot have because they are so committed to a parallel between form and content. The typical genre situation is a contrast between form and content. With the expectations of stock characters, situations, or narrative rhythms, the director can choose areas of free aesthetic play within. In genre films the most obvious focus of interest is neither complex characterization nor intricate visual style, but pure story. Think about the novel we can't put down. That rare experience in literature is the common experience in film, where we stay only because we want to, where we often must be intrigued by the first five minutes or not at all, and where we know that once we leave the spell is broken. Like fairy tales or classical myths, genre films concentrate on large contrasts and juxtapositions. Genre plots are usually dismissed with a snide synopsis (a process that is never very kind to drama that employs conventions, like Shakespeare's plays). But, amid the conventions and expectations of plot, other kinds of emphasis can flourish. To the unsympathetic eye, the pleasures of variation are usually invisible, whether they appear in the medieval morality play, the Renaissance sonnet, the Restoration comedy, the eighteenth-century portrait, the Chopinesque étude, the horror film, the romantic comedy, the musical, or the western. When we can perceive the function of vampire-film conventions in *Persona* or boxing-film conventions in *On the Waterfront* as clearly as we note the debt of Kurosawa's samurai films to American westerns, or that of the New Wave films to American crime films of the 1950s, then we will be able to appreciate more fully the way in which films can break down the old visions between elite and popular art to establish, almost unbeknown to aesthetics and criticism, a vital interplay between them. . . .*

The epic sweep of the early westerns could be conveyed by the silent screen, but musicals necessarily begin their real film career with sound (and sound films begin, appropriate enough, with *The Jazz Singer*). The Charleston sequences of the silent *Our Dancing Daughters* (Harry Beaumont, 1928) look oddly impersonal and detached today, hardly more real than the bunny-costumed Rockettes. Sound not only individualizes the performer, but also provides a bridge of music between otherwise separate visual moments, a continuity against which the image can play, potentially freeing the film from a strict adherence to a one-to-one relation between sight and sound. Once sound frees image from the necessity to appear logical and casual, the director can experiment with different kinds of nonlogical, noncausal narrative. But, after the first years of sound and such experiments with the new form as René Clair's *Under the Roofs of Paris* (1929), Lang's *M* (1931), Renoir's *Boudu Saved from Drowning* (1932), and Ernst Lubitsch's *Trouble in Paradise* (1932), primarily musicals explored its possibilities. The western may be self-conscious about its myths, but the musical is self-conscious about its stylization, the heightened reality that is its norm. The games with continuous narrative that Busby Berkeley plays in the musical numbers of *Footlight Parade* (1933), *42nd Street* (1933), or *Gold Diggers of 1935* are hardly attempted by nonmusical directors until the jumpcutting achronicity of the New Wave.

Berkeley's films show how the stylistic self-consciousness of musicals directly concerns the relation of their art to the everyday world outside the confines of the

---

*The way in which television "cannibalizes" material therefore has less to do with its constant demand than with the speed with which such material becomes outdated. When the audience accepts material as generic and ritualistic—situation comedy, talk shows, sports, news, weather—the form can include an infinite variety of nuance. But when the paradigms are no longer emotionally appealing, formal variety will do no good and there arises a desperate, cannibalizing, attempt to discover the new form of audience solace, whether the subject matter is Dick Cavett or the Vietnam War. Thus the whole process of cultural history is speeded up through successive purgations of used-up subject matter and style.

film. His camera presses relentlessly forward, through impossible stages that open up endlessly, expanding the inner space of film and affirming the capacity of the world of style to mock the narrowness of the "real" world outside the theater walls, populated by bland tenors, greedy producers, and harried directors. Ford uses theater in *Liberty Valance* to purify his genre vision. But Berkeley uses theater, the impossible theater available to film artifice, to give a sense of exuberance and potential. Playing with space, Berkeley in *Footlight Parade* creates an incredible extravaganza supposedly taking place in miniature within a waterfall, with pyramids of swimming girls, diving cameras, and fifty-foot fountains.

Berkeley's real problem, however, is his concentration on the production number and the spectacle. The sense of play and opulence he brought to the musical, his effort to make its stage artifice a source of strength, was, if we look back upon the direction the musical took, a minor stream in its history. His influence appears in the show business biography (*A Star Is Born,* 1937; *The Jolson Story,* 1946; *Funny Girl,* 1968), the production story (*Summer Stock,* 1950; *The Band Wagon,* 1953), and that great amalgam of realized style and stylized realism, *Singin' in the Rain* (1952). There is also a darker side apparent in a film like *All About Eve* (1950), in which the urge to theater is considered to be manipulative, a reduction of the self rather than an expansion. The dark side may be the truer side of Berkeley's inheritance, because his musicals lack any sense of the individual. The strange melancholy of the "Lullaby of Broadway" number from *Gold Diggers of 1935,* in which, after some elaborately uplifting production numbers, an unsuccessful showgirl commits suicide, combines comedy and the tragedy of sentimental realism in a way that only penetrated serious films in the late 1940s. It presages the urbane tragedies of fatality in a theatrical setting that mark the late films of Julien Duvivier (*Flesh and Fantasy,* 1943) and Max Ophuls (*La Ronde,* 1950; *Lola Montès,* 1955). The showgirl commits suicide in "Lullaby of Broadway" in part because the Berkeley ensemble of faceless dancers holds no place for her at all, perhaps because of her lack of talent, but more clearly because her individuality is contrary to the demands of the uniform musical group. Like Eisenstein or the Lang of *Metropolis,* Berkeley magisterially juxtaposes sequences and articulates crowds with ritual symmetry. Berkeley's attitude toward individuals is that of a silent film director, iconographic and symmetric. The community of the Berkeley girls is cold and anonymous, like Lang's workers, a community created by a nonparticipating choreographer-director. But the kind of musical that had the greatest popular strength, spawned the largest number of descendants, and historically defined the American musical film, is the musical in which the dancer-choreographer himself was a participant, in which an individual man danced with an individual woman, and in which the theme of the individual energy of the dance, the relation of the dancer to his own body, became the main theme of the film. Obviously I am referring to the films of Fred Astaire and Ginger Rogers.*

---

*Rouben Mamoulian in *Love Me Tonight* (1932, songs by Rodgers and Hart) focuses on individuals (Jeanette MacDonald and Maurice Chevalier), but the style of the film is still one of directional control rather than a performer's energy. The most impressive song settings are those in which parts of the song are sung and played by people in isolated places, visually linked by the director's wit and style (for example, "Isn't It Romantic?").

Shall We Dance (1937, songs by George and Ira Gershwin), the last film of the basic Astaire-Rogers series, is a model of their films, perhaps not least because it contains a final sequence that seems to be an implicit attack against the Berkeley emphasis on anonymous spectacle. Astaire plays the Great Petrov, star of the Russian ballet, who is in reality Peter P. Peters, from Philadelphia. The basic conflict of the film is established in the first scene, when Petrov's manager Jeff (Edward Everett Horton) comes into his rehearsal room to find Petrov improvising a dance to a jazz record. "The Great Petrov doesn't dance for fun," he tells him, emphasizing that ballet is a serious business to which the artist must devote his full time. "But I do," responds Astaire. "Remember me? Pete Peters from Philadelpha, P.A.?" Horton points to the taps on Astaire's ballet shoes and continues his insistence that whatever Astaire is doing, it's not art. "Maybe it's just the Philadelphia in me," says Astaire, and begins dancing again. The forces have been set in motion: the dancing that Astaire likes to do when he is alone directly expresses his personal emotions as well as his real identity—the American tap dancer under the high-culture disguise of the Russian ballet dancer. Horton, as he usually does in these films, comically combines a commitment to high culture (and high society) with a definite antagonism to emotion and feeling. When Astaire falls in love with Linda Keene (Ginger Rogers), a nightclub dancer, after seeing a series of movie-like flip cards of her dancing, Horton speaks darkly of the danger to Astaire's "serious" career and the need to be personally pure (i.e., nonsexual and nonemotional) for art. Like so many musicals, *Shall We Dance* contrasts the emotionally detached and formal patterns of high art with the involved and spontaneous forms of popular art. (Vincente Minnelli's *Meet Me in St. Louis,* 1944, for example, establishes the same relationship between serious music and popular music, and many musicals include parodies of serious theater by vaudevillians.) The 1930s musical may have its historical roots in the silent-film urge to the respectablity of theater, the importation of theatrical performers both to give the young industry tone and to banish the generally lower-class associations that film had from its vaudeville beginnings. But the sound musical—like so many genres of the 1930s, comedies and horror films included—begins to mock this respect for older forms just as it parodies the upper class in general. Tap dancing is superior to ballet as movies are superior to drama, not merely because they are more popular, but because they contain more life and possibility. The flip-card stills that turn into a sequence of Rogers dancing present her as a creature of the film, not the stage. Like Astaire in the film, Rogers is also an American, but more proudly: she doesn't like the "hand-kissing heel-clickers of Paris" and rejects Peters when he attempts to impress her by coming on as the formal Petrov. Berkeley attacks theater in favor of film and dance by destroying the limits of theatrical space. But Astaire and Rogers (and their directors, especially Mark Sandrich and choreographer Hermes Pan) attack all high art in favor of the new dancing forms of spontaneity, American style. The Berkeleyan world spawns the myth of show-business biography that success on stage buys only unhappiness in one's personal life. But the silvery world of Astaire and Rogers celebrates the ability of individual energy to break away from the dead hand of society, class and art as well. The open space of the western that offers a chance to build becomes in the musical the endless inner energy released in dance.

Shall We Dance is defined by the collision between the forces of inertia and stasis and the forces of vitality, between Astaire as Petrov—the commitment to high art and personal repression—and Astaire as Peters—the commitment to an art that attempts to structure individual energy instead of excluding it. Musical comedy therefore also attacks any theories of acting in which character comes from the past. Character in musical comedy is physiological and external: the ability to dance and the way dancing functions in specific situations becomes a direct expression of the tensions within the self. In the first scene Astaire dances along at the proper speed; and then, when the machine needs to be wound up again, he slows down as the record itself slows down. On the ship that takes him and Rogers back to America, he descends into the engine room and dances there in time to the pistons while black members of the crew who are taking a musical break play for him. In both sequences the energy of the dance—the personal emphasis in the first, the relation to jazz and black music in the second ("Slap That Bass")—draws upon the analogy between body and machine. But here, unlike literary attacks against the machine, the film, true to its mechanical and technological origins, celebrates the machine as a possible element in the liberation of the individual rather than in his enslavement (similar to the ambivalence about machines that characterizes *Metropolis*). Machines are outside class, purifiers of movement. The real threat to individual energy and exuberance is not the machine, but the forces of society and respectability—the impresario Jeff, the rich suitor Jim with the weak chin (William Brisbane), who wants to take Rogers away from show business, and the punctilious hotel manager Cecil Flintridge (Eric Blore). Here they are comic, but they nevertheless play the same repressive roles as they would in the more melodramatic world of the western.*

At the end of *Shall We Dance,* the comically hostile forces (including an outside world of publicity and gossip) are reconciled by Astaire's typical process of self-realization—the search for the perfect partner. The perfect partner is always a dancing partner, since it is within the world of dance that true communication and complementarity can be achieved: the male-female dance duo is a model of male-female relationship in general. Dancing isn't a euphemism for sex; in Astaire-Rogers films at least, dancing is much better. Two sequences in *Shall We Dance* constitute the dance of courtship and they appear after the first dancing sequences, which establish the separate personalities of Astaire and Rogers. In the first, "They All Laughed," Astaire begins with ballet-like steps while Rogers stands still. Then she begins to tap, and he responds, first with a ballet version of the tapping, then a straight tap. In the second such number, "Let's Call the Whole Thing Off," the importance of the dancing situation to their relationship is further underlined. They are taking a walk in a stage-set Central Park and decide to go skating, even though neither of them has skated in a long time. They begin very haltingly, with frequent stumbles. But, as soon as the music starts, they skate perfectly together.

---

*The positive interpretation of the machine analogy to the body is a constant theme in musicals, most recently expressed in the Ken Russell film of *Tommy* (1975, words and music by Peter Townshend and The Who), in which the deaf, dumb, and blind boy first discovers his real nature through his symbiotic relation with pinball machines.

Then, at the end of the song, as the music ends, they hit the grass outside the skating rink and fall down. Once the magic world of dance and its ability to idealize personal energy into a model of relationship has vanished, Astaire and Rogers again become separate and even bickering individuals. "Let's Call the Whole Thing Off" memorializes their differences, even while it provides a context for their relationship. The next musical number, "They Can't Take That Away from Me," contains no dancing. It takes place at night on a ferry between New Jersey and New York and emphasizes the problems of their relationship, especially the seeming conflict between their real feelings, which can be expressed at night, and the public and social demands on them that the daylight world of the rest of the film exerts. Like Astaire and Rogers themselves, who feel the pressure to continue their successful film partnership despite their own wishes, Peter Peters and Linda Keene have been forced into marriage primarily so they can get divorced. The publicity generated by their managers is meant to connect them, but it succeeds only in driving them apart, as aesthetic as well as emotional partners.

Astaire solves the conflict and rejoins Rogers in the remarkable final sequence. In a theatrical setting reminiscent of the roof of the Winter Garden, an open space within the city, Astaire stages a show that summarizes the main elements of the film. In the early sequences Astaire plays a Russian ballet dancer; Rogers appears; he loses her. Meanwhile, the real Rogers, the comic Claudius in this mousetrap, sits in a box, part of the audience, but separate from it. Astaire reprises "You Can't Take That Away from Me" to lead into a sequence in which a whole group of dancing partners appear—all wearing a mask with Rogers' face on it. The song then becomes ironic, since the memory of her uniqueness that it celebrates has been confused in the many Rogers of the present. Ruby Keeler is obviously pleased to be multiplied into many images for the adoration of Dick Powell in Berkeley's *Dames* (1934), but the Ginger Rogers in the audience of *Shall We Dance* cannot take this anonymous crowd of Busby Berkeley chorus girls all wearing her face. Astaire's message makes the same plea: deliver me from the life of a single man amid innumerable faceless girls by asserting the perfection of our relationship. Rogers goes backstage and puts on one of the masks. She comes onstage, briefly reveals herself to Astaire, and then glides back into the anonymity of the many Rogers. Which is the real Rogers among the false, the reality and energy of the individual beneath the generalized artifice of the image? Astaire finds her and together they sing and dance the final song, "Shall We Dance," an invitation to let the dancing, emotional energetic self out, to reject depression and the forms of society, and to accept the frame of theater that allows one, through the exuberance of dance, to be free.

The figure of Fred Astaire implies that dance is the perfect form, the articulation of motion that allows the self the most freedom at the same time that it includes the most energy. The figure of Gene Kelly implies that the true end of dance is to destroy excess and attack the pretensions of all forms in order to achieve some new synthesis. Kelly the sailor teaching Jerry the Mouse to dance in *Anchors Aweigh* (George Sidney, 1945) stands next to Bill Robinson teaching Shirley Temple to dance in *The Little Colonel* (David Butler, 1935). Astaire may move dance away from the more formal orders of the ballet, but Kelly emphasizes its appeal to the somewhat recalcitrant, not quite socialized part of the self, where the emotions are

Fred Astaire among the many masks or Ginger Rogers in *Shall We Dance* (1937). "Which is the real Rogers among the false, the reality and energy of the individual beneath the generalized artifice of the image? Astaire finds her and together they sing and dance, 'Shall We Dance', an invitation to let the dancing, emotional energetic self out . . ." (BRAUDY, page 445). Gene Kelly and cast at the end of the "Gotta Dance" production number in *Singing' in the Rain* (1952). "The musical, technically the most complex type of film produced in Hollywood, paradoxically has always been the genre that attempts to give the greatest illusion of spontaneity and effortlessness" (FEUER, page 491).

hidden. Astaire and Kelly are part of the same continuum of themes and motifs in musicals (an interesting study could be done of the interaction of their images in the 1940s and 1950s). There are many contrasts that can be made between the way they use dance and the way they appear in their films, but the basic fact of their continuity should be remembered. The question of personal energy, which I have characterized as the musical's basic theme, once again appears centrally. The social world against which Astaire defined himself in the 1930s no longer had the same attraction to movie audiences in the 1940s; it was a hangover from the early days of film and their simultaneous fascination with the 1920s high life and the higher seriousness of theater, in a double effort both to imitate and to mock. Astaire is the consummate theatrical dancer, while Kelly is more interested in the life outside the proscenium. The energy that Astaire defines within a theatrical and socially formal framework Kelly takes outside, into a world somewhat more "real" (that is, similar to the world of the audience) and therefore more recalcitrant. Kelly's whole presence is therefore more rugged and less ethereal than Astaire's. Both Astaire and Kelly resemble Buster Keaton, their prime ancestor in dancing's paean to the freedom and confinement of the body. But Astaire is the spiritual Keaton while Kelly is the combative, energetic Keaton, compounded with the glee of Douglas Fairbanks. Kelly has more obvious physical presence than Astaire, who hides his well-trained body in clothes that give the impression he has nothing so disruptive as muscles, so that the form of his dancing is even more an ideal and a mystery. Astaire often wears suits and tuxedos, while Kelly generally wears open-collared shirts, slacks, white socks, and loafers—a studied picture of informality as opposed to Astaire's generally more formal dress. Astaire wears the purified Art Deco makeup of the 1930s, but Kelly keeps the scar on his cheek visible—an emblem of the interplay between formal style and disruptive realism in his definition of the movie musical.*

Astaire may mock social forms for their rigidity, but Kelly tries to explode them. Astaire purifies the relation between individual energy and stylized form, whereas Kelly tries to find a new form that will give his energy more play. Astaire dances onstage or in a room, expanding but still maintaining the idea of enclosure and theater; Kelly dances on streets, on the roofs of cars, on tables, in general bringing the power of dance to bear on a world that would ordinarily seem to exclude it. (Astaire absorbs this ability of Kelly's to reorganize normal space and integrates it with his own lighter-than-air quality in the dancing on the walls sequence in *Royal Wedding,* 1951, directed by Kelly's favorite collaborator Stanley Donen.) Astaire usually plays a professional dancer; Kelly sometimes does and sometimes does not, although he is usually an artist of some kind, often, as in *The Pirate,* a popular artist, or, as in *Summer Stock,* a director, associated with the stage but not totally inside

---

*I have been using Astaire and Kelly to represent the change in the movie musical as much as I have been describing what they do themselves. A full account would also have to include a close consideration of Eleanor Powell, whose fantastic exuberance and bodily freedom often threatened to destroy the generally theatrical plots in which she was encased. The most important film for these purposes might be *Broadway Melody of 1940* (Normal Taurog), in which she and Astaire dance together with an equality of feeling and ability that presages the teaming of Kelly and Judy Garland.

it. Kelly therefore merges the director emphasis of Berkeley with the performer emphasis of Astaire. To complement the distance from theatrical form Kelly maintains, his whole style of acting is self-mocking, while Astaire's is almost always serious and heartfelt, at far as comedy will allow. Because the film attitude toward serious art is less defensive in the 1940s than in the 1930s, Kelly can include ballet and modern dance in his films, although always in a specifically theatrical setting (the pirate dream ballet in *The Pirate,* the gangster ballet in *Les Girls*). Theater and style in Astaire's films reconcile the conflict between personal life and social pressures, and allow the self to repair and renovate its energy. Many of his films have more or less autobiographical elements in them, not the autobiography of Astaire's private life, but the autobiography of Astaire's professional life: the effect to get a new partner after Ginger Rogers decided to do dramatic films instead (*Easter Parade,* Charles Walters, 1948, with Judy Garland), the celebration of Rogers' return to dance after several "serious" films (*The Barkleys of Broadway,* Charles Walters, 1949). Kelly, however, far from taking refuge in theater, wants to make theater take over daily life. His films are hardly ever autobiographical; unlike Astaire's, they have stories in which Kelly plays a role. Astaire may dance by himself, with a partner, or with a company of dancers. Kelly wants to galvanize a community of nondancers as well. Astaire and his partner are professionals; Kelly and his partner are often amateurs, but everyone they meet knows the steps to their dances and the words to their songs.[1]

A Kelly film that highlights the differences and similarities between the two great definers of the American musical comedy is Vincent Minnelli's *The Pirate* (1948, songs by Cole Porter, story by Frances Goodrich and Albert Hackett). In the beginning of *The Pirate,* Manuela (Judy Garland), the poor niece of a wealthy family on an eighteenth-century Caribbean island, is leafing through a book detailing the highly romanticized adventures of the pirate Macoco. She dreamily desires the embraces of Macoco but is realistically resigned to marrying the unromantic, fat town mayor (Walter Slezak), who courts her with propriety and respect. One of her companions tells her that the life of Macoco is pure fantasy and she responds by expressing the sense of separate worlds she feels within her: "I realize there's a practical world and a dream world. I won't mix them"[2] Enter Serafin (Gene Kelly), the head of a traveling company of players. He flirts with Manuela, and falls in love with her. By accidental hypnosis the reserved Manuela changes into a manic performer, and she and Serafin dance and sing together in a funny scene in which Serafin thinks he's tricked this pretty girl into dancing with him, while the exuberance released in Manuela by the hypnosis threatens to knock him off the stage. Horrified

---

[1]It is worth mentioning that Astaire and Kelly are appropriately enough the two supreme examples of Hollywood stars who never really gave their private lives in any way over to the fan magazines or the mechanism of offscreen publicity, since their screen presences are personal enough.

[2]Observers of Vincente Minnelli have often pointed out the constant interest in the clash of reality and dream in his films. Here, of course, I am considering these themes in terms of the larger issue of the history of musicals as a genre. The way specific directors, with their own thematic and stylistic preoccupations, interact with pre-existing conventions to change those conventions and clarify their own interests at the same time is a topic that requires much more minute examination than I can give it here.

at what she's done, Manuela leaves for her hometown away from the big city to prepare for her marriage to the mayor. Serafin follows her and recognizes the mayor as the real Macoco. He threatens to expose him unless the mayor allows Serafin to pretend that he is Macoco, since Serafin knows of Manuela's hero-worship. The mayor agrees, until he sees that Manuela's attraction to Serafin is increased by the impersonation. The mayor then arrests Serafin and is about to hang him when Serafin, asking for the opportunity to do a last act on stage, plays a scene with Manuela that reveals to the mayor her actual love for Macoco the Pirate. Unaware of the game, the mayor announces that he is the real Macoco and therefore Manuela should love him. He is arrested, and the united Kelly and Garland appear in the last scene as stage partners singing "Be a Clown" to the audience.

Through the personalities of Garland and Kelly, *The Pirate* explores the theme of identity I have discussed in Astaire's films in a very different way. Serafin's courtship of Manuela reveals that her desire for Macoco is a desire for a romantic individualism outside society—a theme made especially strong by setting the film in an eighteenth-century Spanish Roman Catholic country with all its elaborate social forms and ceremonies. Kelly hypnotizes her with a spinning mirror—an image of the many possible selves. The Manuela that is released, the self below the social surface, is a singing, dancing self. Her exuberance indicates that Serafin has in fact released more than he expects or may want. He is a professional artist. But she gets her art directly from her inner life, untamed by society or by learned craft. Garland is perfect for this kind of role because she projects so clearly the image of a restrained, almost mouse-like person until she begins to sing and dance. (Her first important film, *The Wizard of Oz,* Victor Fleming, 1939, solidified this tension in Garland between the acceptance of daily life in a world of drabness and moral boredom, and the possibility of escape to an exuberant singing, dancing world of dream. It appeared as well in *Meet Me in St. Louis,* 1944, another Minnelli film, where the pattern of stability and release is more parallel to that of *The Pirate.*)

Serafin is the alternative to Macoco in more ways than one. The real pirate has changed from an antisocial adventurer to a socially dictatorial mayor, thus rejecting the Macoco side of himself to become almost the opposite. But Kelly instead tries to mediate individuality and community. His first song in the film is "Niña," a typical Kelly dance in a street fair, where he sings and dances with half the surprised people there to weave together a kind of community of otherwise isolated individuals and objects through the catalyst of his own personality and artistic ability. The song relates how he calls every girl he meets "niña," that is, little girl. At the end of the song Garland appears and the amazed Kelly asks her what her name is. Like Rogers at the end of *Shall We Dance,* she stands apart from communal anonymity. Serafin is the articulate adventurer, the popular artist, who sees his art to be part of a creation of community; she is the individual artist, whose art is less craft than a swelling sense of herself from within. We admire and feel friendly to him because he includes us in his dance. But we identify with her, for she, like us, is not professional, even in the loose sense in which Serafin is professional. Serafin realizes this and therefore pretends to be Macoco to win her. In the climactic moment, when he is plotting to get the real Macoco to reveal himself and brings out the mirror to rehypnotize Garland, Slezak breaks the mirror. But it doesn't matter. Manuela is willing to go along with Serafin's plot, as Garland accepts Kelly's choreography and control. Her energy, once released, can be controlled, especially within the context of love and theater. *The Pirate* is therefore a next step from the themes of the Astaire-Rogers films. Kelly makes the perfect couple the center of an ideal community created by dance, a world of harmony where everyone on the street not only sympathizes with the exuberance you feel because you're in love, but also knows all the words and dance steps that express your feelings.

The context of the ideal, the place where the true self can be revealed, is still theatrical space. The final song, "Be a Clown," emphasizes the responsible escape of art, especially popular art, in a way very reminiscent of the title song at the end of *Shall We Dance.* But the inclusion of the Garland figure—the nonprofessional dancer from the heart—indicates the direction that Kelly has taken the musical, as does the fact that Kelly and Garland are not elegant in their world of theater, but clownish and self-mocking, more willing than Astaire and Rogers to include the potential disruptiveness of the world outside them and the world within. Astaire and Rogers dance for us, looking at each other primarily to integrate their dancing. Kelly and Garland convey a much friendlier and more personal relationship. We may watch Astaire and Rogers. But we empathize with Kelly and Garland.*

Kelly in *The Pirate* is an entertainer. But the emphasis of the film is less on his dancing and singing than on the world that dance and theater can create together. The stylization and historical setting of *The Pirate* emphasize the release from the stultifying social self dance allows; the contemporary setting of most other Kelly films further highlights Kelly's effort to bring his dancing out of the enclosed world of theater and make the whole world a theater, responsive to and changed by his energy. Astaire's dances define a world of perfect form, while Kelly's often reach out to include improvisation, spontaneity, and happenstance. The scene that contrasts best with Astaire's imitation of the record player and the machines in *Shall We Dance* is Kelly's marvelous interweaving of a creaky board and a piece of paper left on the stage in *Summer Stock* (1950). Kelly's self-mocking smile reflects the way most of his films continue the attack of Astaire's films against artistic pretension. Embodying the catalytic possibilities of dance to create a new coherence for the nontheatrical world, Kelly journeys through parody and realism, attacking formal excesses on the one hand and transforming everyday reality on the other.

Singin' in the Rain (Kelly and Stanley Donen, 1952), is one aspect of his effort and *On the Town* (Kelly and Stanley Donen, 1949) is the other. The frame of *Singin' in the Rain* is a full-scale parody of the early days of sound film (an appropriate subject for the musical), complete with an attack on artistic high seriousness in favor of the comic exuberance of popular art. The essential scene is Donald

---

*The strength of Minnelli's own vision obviously has its place in understanding *The Pirate* (1948), although the comparative visual stasis and the commitment to the values of stability that characterize *Meet Me in St. Louis* (1944) indicate the importance of Kelly in changing his style and his ideas. Minnelli's musicals may try to celebrate the triumph of the individual through art, but just as often (for example, in *The Band Wagon,* 1953) they catch a tint of gloom from his more melancholic nonmusical films, which often deal with artistic compromise and disintegration, either in the context of the world of film (*The Bad and the Beautiful,* 1952; *Two Weeks in Another Town,* 1962) or the other arts (*Lust for Life,* 1956; *Some Came Running,* 1958). Only in the pure world of the musical can art and individuality succeed without compromise.

O'Connor's incredible acrobatic dance "Make 'Em Laugh" (unfortunately often cut for television), like "Be a Clown" a description of the popular artist's relation to his audience. But this time, instead of being on a stage, the number is done amid a welter of different film sets depicting different worlds, with stagehands moving through the scene. O'Connor's partner for a while is a featureless, uncostumed dummy that he makes seem alive (a reminiscence of the Ginger Rogers dummy in *Shall We Dance*), and for a finale he starts walking up the set walls and finally jumps right through them. In the early scenes of the film, Kelly, the phony silent-screen lover, needs to set up a sound stage and props before he can tell Debbie Reynolds he loves her and sings "You Were Meant for Me." But the declaration becomes acceptable as real emotion only when, in the next scene, he and Donald O'Connor parody the demands of their diction coach in "Moses Supposes." By this time, to parallel his change from form to substance, Kelly has left his suits and tuxedoes behind and dresses in the more familiar open-collared shirt and loafers. Once again, the scar on his cheek is an emblem of the reality that will emerge. In *Singin' in the Rain* silent films are artificial in their stylized actions and hoked-up emotions; only sound is real. The discovery of communication with an audience changes clearly from "Shall We Dance" to "Be a Clown" to "Make 'Em Laugh," with an increasing emphasis on the place of informality and personal style. The solution of the plot of *Singin' in the Rain* is to make the bad serious film into the parodic musical; almost all the dances in the film contain parodies of earlier dances and dancers, in the same somewhat mocking homage that characterizes the attitude to Impressionism in *An American in Paris* (Minnelli, 1951). This is the essence of the kind of energy Kelly's film embodies: theater, like the ability to dance, is a manner of inner perspective on the world outside. The reality of sound film that Kelly discovers follows his own curve of increased dancing in the film until the great set piece of "Gotta Dance," another statement of Kelly's belief that dancing is a compulsion from within more authentic than the forms imposed from without. The final scene, in which Debbie Reynolds is revealed as the voice of Jean Hagen from behind the curtain, repeats on still another level the basic theme of outer form and inner reality. Music and dance are the real spirit of film in the same way they are the real soul and energy of New York in *On the Town*, or Paris in *An American in Paris*.

Kelly's dancing tries not to be the aesthetic escape of Astaire's. It is more utopian because it aims to bring the world together. Astaire's films often imply that dance and therefore energy itself can be a refuge from a stuffy world of social forms; Kelly's films imply that dance and the individual can change the world. The three sailors on leave in *On the Town*—Kelly, Frank Sinatra, and Jules Munshin—are searching for the perfect partner and all find their girls, not in a purified world of dance, but in a real New York (the first musical made on location) that embraces both their dancing and their search. The women—Vera-Ellen, Ann Miller, and Betty Garrett—are all at least the equals of the men in exuberance, energy, and wit. They make their own space in a public world, like Kelly in the "Singin' in the Rain" sequence, splashing through puddles of chance and nature. The great pretenders in *On the Town* are Kelly and Vera-Ellen, the small-town kids who come on to each other as sophisticates. The moral is that of almost all Kelly films: don't worry about the true self; it will turn out to be better than the one you're pretending to be. Kelly's kind of musical doesn't retreat from reality. It tries to subvert reality through its new energy, an energy available to everyone in the audience through Kelly's insistence on the nonprofessional character, the musical self that wells from inside instead of being imposed from without, whether by training, tradition, or society. . . .

1976

ROBERT WARSHOW
MOVIE CHRONICLE: THE WESTERNER

They that have power to hurt and will do none,
That do not do the thing they most do show,
Who, moving others, are themselves as stone,
Unmoved, cold, and to temptation slow;
They rightly do inherit heaven's graces,
And husband nature's riches from expense;
They are the lords and owners of their faces,
Others but stewards of their excellence.

The two most successful creations of American movies are the gangster and the Westerner: men with guns. Guns as physical objects, and the postures associated with their use, form the visual and emotional center of both types of films. I suppose this reflects the importance of guns in the fantasy life of Americans; but that is a less illuminating point than it appears to be.

The gangster movie, which no longer exists in its "classical" form, is a story of enterprise and success ending in precipitate failure. Success is conceived as an increasing power to work injury, it belongs to the city, and it is of course a form of evil (though the gangster's death, presented usually as "punishment," is perceived simply as defeat). The peculiarity of the gangster is his unceasing, nervous activity. The exact nature of his enterprises may remain vague, but his commitment to enterprise is always clear, and all the more clear because he operates outside the field of utility. He is without culture, without manners, without leisure, or at any rate his leisure is likely to be spent in debauchery so compulsively aggressive as to seem only another aspect of his "work." But he is graceful, moving like a dancer among the crowded dangers of the city.

Like other tycoons, the gangster is crude in conceiving his ends but by no means inarticulate; on the contrary, he is usually expansive and noisy (the introspective gangster is a fairly recent development), and can state definitely what he wants: to take over the North Side, to own a hundred suits, to be Number One. But new "frontiers" will present themselves infinitely, and by a rigid convention it is understood that as soon as he wishes to rest on his gains, he is on the way to destruction.

The gangster is lonely and melancholy, and can give the impression of a profound worldly wisdom. He appeals most to adolescents with their impatience and their feeling of being outsiders, but more generally he appeals to that side of all of us which refuses to believe in the "normal" possibilities of happiness and achievement; the gangster is the "no" to that great American "yes" which is stamped so big over our official culture and yet has so little to do with the way we really feel about our lives. But the gangster's loneliness and melancholy are not "authentic"; like everything else that belongs to him, they are not honestly come by: he is lonely and melancholy not because life ultimately demands such feelings but because he has put himself in a position where everybody wants to kill him and eventually somebody will. He is wide open and defenseless, incomplete because unable to accept any limits or come to terms with his own nature, fearful, loveless. And the story of his career is a nightmare inversion of the values of ambition and opportunity. From the window of Scarface's bulletproof apartment can be seen an electric sign proclaiming: "The World Is Yours," and, if I remember, this sign is the last thing we see after Scarface lies dead in the street. In the end it is the gangster's weakness as much as his power and freedom that appeals to us; the world is not ours, but it is not his either, and in his death he "pays" for our fantasies, releasing us momentarily both from the concept of success, which he denies by caricaturing it, and from the need to succeed, which he shows to be dangerous.

The Western hero, by contrast, is a figure of repose. He resembles the gangster in being lonely and to some degree melancholy. But his melancholy comes from the "simple" recognition that life is unavoidably serious, not from the disproportions of his own temperament. And his loneliness is organic, not imposed on him by his situation but belonging to him intimately and testifying to his completeness. The gangster must reject others violently or draw them violently to him. The Westerner is not thus compelled to seek love; he is prepared to accept it, perhaps, but he never asks of it more than it can give, and we see him constantly in situations where love is at best an irrelevance. If there is a woman he loves, she is usually unable to understand his motives; she is against killing and being killed, and he finds it impossible to explain to her that there is no point in being "against" these things: they belong to his world.

Very often this woman is from the East and her failure to understand represents a clash of cultures. In the American mind, refinement, virtue, civilization, Christianity itself, are seen as feminine, and therefore women are often portrayed as possessing some kind of deeper wisdom, while the men, for all their apparent self-assurance, are fundamentally childish. But the West, lacking the graces of civilization, is the place "where men are men"; in Western movies, men have the deeper wisdom and the women are children. Those women in the Western movies who share the hero's understanding of life are prostitutes (or, as they are usually presented, barroom entertainers)—women, that is, who have come to understand in the most practical way how love can be an irrelevance, and therefore "fallen" women. The gangster, too, associates with prostitutes, but for him the important things about a prostitute are her passive availability and her costliness: she is part of his winnings. In Western movies, the important thing about a prostitute is her quasi-masculine independence: nobody owns her, nothing has to be explained to her, and she is not, like a virtuous woman, a "value" that demands to be protected. When the Westerner leaves the prostitute for a virtuous woman—for love—he is in fact forsaking a way of life, though the point of the choice is often obscured by having the prostitute killed by getting into the line of fire.

The Westerner is *par excellence* a man of leisure. Even when he wears the badge of a marshal or, more rarely, owns a ranch, he appears to be unemployed. We see him standing at a bar, or playing poker—a game which expresses perfectly his talent for remaining relaxed in the midst of tension—or perhaps camping out on the plains on some extraordinary errand. If he does own a ranch, it is in the background; we are not actually aware that he owns anything except his horse, his guns, and the one worn suit of clothing which is likely to remain unchanged all through the movie. It comes as a surprise to see him take money from his pocket or an extra shirt from his saddlebags. As a rule we do not even know where he sleeps at night and don't think of asking. Yet it never occurs to us that he is a poor man; there is no poverty in Western movies, and really no wealth either: those great cattle domains and shipments of gold which figure so largely in the plots are moral and not material quantities, not the objects of contention but only its occasion. Possessions too are irrelevant.

Employment of some kind—usually unproductive—is always open to the Westerner, but when he accepts it, it is not because he needs to make a living, much less from any idea of "getting ahead." Where could he want to "get ahead" to? By the time we see him, he is already "there": he can ride a horse faultlessly, keep his countenance in the face of death, and draw his gun a little faster and shoot it a little straighter than anyone he is likely to meet. These are sharply defined acquirements, giving to the figure of the Westerner an apparent moral clarity which corresponds to the clarity of his physical image against his bare landscape; initially, at any rate, the Western movie presents itself as being without mystery, its whole universe comprehended in what we see on the screen.

Much of this apparent simplicity arises directly from those "cinematic" elements which have long been understood to give the Western theme its special appropriateness for the movies: the wide expanses of land, the free movement of men on horses. As guns constitute the visible moral center of the Western movie, suggesting continually the possibility of violence, so land and horses represent the movie's material basis, its sphere of action. But the land and the horses have also a moral significance: the physical freedom they represent belongs to the moral "openness" of the West—corresponding to the fact that guns are carried where they can be seen. (And, as we shall see, the character of land and horses changes as the Western film becomes more complex.)

The gangster's world is less open, and his arts not so easily identifiable as the Westerner's. Perhaps he too can keep his countenance, but the mask he wears is really no mask: its purpose is precisely to make evident the fact that he desperately

Easterners and Westerners. Paul Muni in *Scarface* (1932); John Carradine, Andy Devine, Chris Martin, George Bancroft, Louise Platt, Donald Meek, Claire Trevor, and John Wayne in *Stagecoach* (1939). "The two most successful creations of American movies are the gangster and the Westerner: men with guns . . . . The land and the horses have . . . a moral significance: the physical freedom they represent belongs to the moral 'openness' of the West—corresponding to the fact that guns are carried where they can be seen . . . . The gangster's world is less open . . ." (WARSHOW, pages 453, 455).

wants to "get ahead" and will stop at nothing. Where the Westerner imposes himself by the appearance of unshakable control, the gangster's pre-eminence lies in the suggestion that he may at any moment lose control; his strength is not in being able to shoot faster or straighter than others, but in being more willing to shoot. "Do it first," says Scarface expounding his mode of operation, "and keep doing it!" With the Westerner, it is a crucial point of honor *not* to "do it first"; his gun remains in its holster until the moment of combat.

There is no suggestion, however, that he draws the gun reluctantly. The Westerner could not fulfill himself if the moment did not finally come when he can shoot his enemy down. But because that moment is so thoroughly the expression of his being, it must be kept pure. He will not violate the accepted forms of combat though by doing so he could save a city. And he can wait. "When you call me that—smile!"—the villain smiles weakly, soon he is laughing with horrible joviality, and the crisis is past. But it is allowed to pass because it must come again: sooner or later Trampas will "make his play," and the Virginian will be ready for him.

What does the Westerner fight for? We know he is on the side of justice and order, and of course it can be said he fights for these things. But such broad aims never correspond exactly to his real motives; they only offer him his opportunity. The Westerner himself, when an explanation is asked of him (usually by a woman), is likely to say that he does what he "has to do." If justice and order did not continually demand his protection, he would be without a calling. Indeed, we come upon him often in just that situation, as the reign of law settles over the West and he is forced to see that his day is over; those are the pictures which end with his death or with his departure for some more remote frontier. What he defends, at bottom, is the purity of his own image—in fact his honor. This is what makes him invulnerable. When the gangster is killed, his whole life is shown to have been a mistake, but the image the Westerner seeks to maintain can be presented as clearly in defeat as in victory: he fights not for advantage and not for the right, but to state what he is, and he must live in a world which permits that statement. The Westerner is the last gentleman, and the movies which over and over again tell his story are probably the last art form in which the concept of honor retains its strength.

Of course I do not mean to say that ideas of virtue and justice and courage have gone out of culture. Honor is more than these things: it is a style, concerned with harmonious appearances as much as with desirable consequences, and tending therefore toward the denial of life in favor of art. "Who hath it? he that dies o' Wednesday." On the whole, a world that leans to Falstaff's view is a more civilized and even, finally, a more graceful world. It is just the march of civilization that forces the Westerner to move on; and if we actually had to confront the question it might turn out that the woman who refuses to understand him is right as often as she is wrong. But we do not confront the question. Where the Westerner lives it is always about 1870—not the real 1870, either, or the real West—and he is killed or goes away when his position becomes problematical. The fact that he continues to hold our attention is evidence enough that, in his proper frame, he presents an image of personal nobility that is still real for us.

Clearly, this image easily becomes ridiculous: we need only look at William S. Hart or Tom Mix, who in the wooden absoluteness of their virtue represented little that an adult could take seriously; and doubtless such figures as Gene Autry or Roy Rogers are no better, though I confess I have seen none of their movies. Some film enthusiasts claim to find in the early, unsophisticated Westerns a "cinematic purity" that has since been lost; this idea is as valid, and finally as misleading, as T. S. Eliot's statement that *Everyman* is the only play in English that stays within the limitations of art. The truth is that the Westerner comes into the field of serious art only when his moral code, without ceasing to be compelling, is seen also to be imperfect. The Westerner at his best exhibits a moral ambiguity which darkens his image and saves him from absurdity; this ambiguity arises from the fact that, whatever his justifications, he is a a killer of men.

In *The Virginian,* which is an archetypal Western movie as *Scarface* or *Little Caesar* are archetypal gangster movies, there is a lynching in which the hero (Gary Cooper), as leader of a posse, must supervise the hanging of his best friend for stealing cattle. With the growth of American "social consciousness," it is no longer possible to present a lynching in the movies unless the point is the illegality and injustice of the lynching itself; *The Ox-Bow Incident,* made in 1943, explicitly puts forward the newer point of view and can be regarded as a kind of "anti-Western." But in 1929, when *The Virginian* was made, the present inhibition about lynching was not yet in force; the justice, and therefore the necessity, of the hanging is never questioned—except by the school-teacher from the East, whose refusal to understand serves as usual to set forth more sharply the deeper seriousness of the West. The Virginian is thus in a tragic dilemma where one moral absolute conflicts with another and the choice of either must leave a moral stain. If he had chosen to save his friend, he would have violated the image of himself that he had made essential to his existence, and the movie would have had to end with his death, for only by his death could the image have been restored. Having chosen instead to sacrifice his friend to the higher demands of the "code"—the only choice worthy of him, as even the friend understands—he is none the less stained by the killing, but what is needed now to set accounts straight is not his death but the death of the villain Trampas, the leader of the cattle thieves, who had escaped the posse and abandoned the Virginian's friend to his fate. Again the woman intervenes: Why must there be *more* killing? If the hero really loved her, he would leave town, refusing Trampas's challenge. What good will it be if Trampas should kill him? But the Virginian does once more what he "has to do," and in avenging his friend's death wipes out the stain on his own honor. Yet his victory cannot be complete: no death can be paid for and no stain truly wiped out; the movie is still a tragedy, for though the hero escapes with his life, he has been forced to confront the ultimate limits of his moral ideas.

This mature sense of limitation and unavoidable guilt is what gives the Westerner a "right" to his melancholy. It is true that the gangster's story is also a tragedy—in certain formal ways more clearly a tragedy than the Westerner's—but it is a romantic tragedy, based on a hero whose defeat springs with almost mechanical inevitability from the outrageous presumption of his demands: the gangster is *bound* to go on until he is killed. The Westerner is a more classical figure, self-contained and limited to begin with, seeking not to extend his dominion but only to assert his personal value, and his tragedy lies in the fact that even this circumscribed demand cannot be fully realized. Since the Westerner is not a murderer but (most of the time) a man of virtue, and since he is always prepared for defeat, he retains his inner invulnerability and his story need not end with his death (and usually does not); but what we finally respond to is not his victory but his defeat.

Up to a point, it is plain that the deeper seriousness of the good Western films comes from the introduction of a realism, both physical and psychological, that was missing with Tom Mix and William S. Hart. As lines of age have come into Gary Cooper's face since *The Virginian,* so the outlines of the Western movie in general have become less smooth, its background more drab. The sun still beats upon the town, but the camera is likely now to take advantage of this illumination to seek out more closely the shabbiness of buildings and furniture, the loose, worn hang of clothing, the wrinkles and dirt of the faces. Once it has been discovered that the true theme of the Western movie is not the freedom and expansiveness of frontier life, but its limitations, its material bareness, the pressures of obligation, then even the landscape itself ceases to be quite the arena of free movement it once was, but becomes instead a great empty waste, cutting down more often than it exaggerates the stature of the horseman who rides across it. We are more likely now to see the Westerner struggling against the obstacles of the physical world (as in the wonderful scenes on the desert and among the rocks in *The Last Posse*) then carelessly sur-mounting them. Even the horses, no longer the "friends" of man or the inspired chargers of knight-errantry, have lost much of the moral significance that once seemed to belong to them in their careering across the screen. It seems to me the horses grow tired and stumble more often than they did, and that we see them less frequently at the gallop.

In *The Gunfighter,* a remarkable film of a couple of years ago, the landscape has virtually disappeared. Most of the action takes place indoors, in a cheerless saloon where a tired "bad man" (Gregory Peck) contemplates the waste of his life, to be senselessly killed at the end by a vicious youngster setting off on the same futile path. The movie is done in cold, quiet tones of gray, and every object in it—faces, cloth-ing, a table, the hero's heavy mustache—is given an air of uncompromising authen-ticity, suggesting those dim photographs of the nineteenth-century West in which Wyatt Earp, say, turns out to be a blank untidy figure posing awkwardly before some uninteresting building. This "authenticity," to be sure, is only aesthetic; the chief fact about nineteenth-century photographs, to my eyes at any rate, is how stonily they refuse to yield up the truth. But that limitation is just what is needed: by preserving some hint of the rigidity of archaic photography (only in tone and décor, never in composition), *The Gunfighter* can permit us to feel that we are look-ing at a more "real" West than the one the movies have accustomed us to—harder, duller, less "romantic"—and yet without forcing us outside the boundaries which give the Western movie its validity.

We come upon the hero of *The Gunfighter* at the end of a career in which he has never upheld justice and order, and has been at times, apparently, an actual crim-inal; in this case, it is clear that the hero has been wrong and the woman who has rejected his way of life has been right. He is thus without any of the larger justifi-cations, and knows himself a ruined man. There can be no question of his "redeem-ing" himself in any socially constructive way. He is too much the victim of his own reputation to turn marshal as one of his old friends has done, and he is not offered

The aging Westerner—Gary Cooper (with Mary Brian) in *The Virginian* (1929) and (with Grace Kelly) in *High Noon* (1952). "As lines of age have come into Gary Cooper's face since *The Virginian,* so the outlines of the Western movie in general have become less smooth, its background more drab . . . . In *High Noon* we find Gary Cooper still the upholder of order that he was in *The Virginian,* but twenty-four years older, stooped, slower moving . . . the flesh sagging . . ." (WARSHOW, pages 459, 462).

the sentimental solution of a chance to give up his life for some good end; the whole point is that he exists outside the field of social value. Indeed, if we were once allowed to see him in the days of his "success," he might become a figure like the gangster, for his career has been aggressively "anti-social" and the practical problem he faces is the gangster's problem: there will always be somebody trying to kill him. Yet it is obviously absurd to speak of him as "anti-social," not only because we do not see him acting as a criminal, but more fundamentally because we do not see his milieu as a society. Of course it has its "social problems" and a kind of static history: civilization is always just at the point of driving out the old freedom; there are women and children to represent the possiblity of a settled life; and there is the marshal, a bad man turned good, determined to keep at least his area of jurisdiction at peace. But these elements are not, in fact, a part of the film's "realism," even though they come out of the real history of the West; they belong to the conventions of the form, to that accepted framework which makes the film possible in the first place, and they exist not to provide a standard by which the gunfighter can be judged, but only to set him off. The true "civilization" of the Western movie is always embodied in an individual, good or bad is more a matter of personal bearing than of social consequences, and the conflict of good and bad is a duel between two men. Deeply troubled and obviously doomed, the gunfighter is the Western hero still, perhaps all the more because his value must express itself entirely in his own being—in his presence, the way he holds our eyes—and in contradiction to the facts. No matter what he has done, he *looks* right, and he remains invulnerable because, without acknowledging anyone else's right to judge him, he has judged his own failure and has already assimilated it, understanding—as no one else understands except the marshal and the barroom girl—that he can do nothing but play out the drama of the gun fight again and again until the time comes when it will be he who gets killed. What "redeems" him is that he no longer believes in this drama and nevertheless will continue to play his role perfectly: the pattern is all.

The proper function of realism in the Western movie can only be to deepen the lines of that pattern. It is an art form for connoisseurs, where the spectator derives his pleasure from the appreciation of minor variations within the working out of a pre-established order. One does not want too much novelty: it comes as a shock, for instance, when the hero is made to operate without a gun, as has been done in several pictures (e.g., *Destry Rides Again*), and our uneasiness is allayed only when he is finally compelled to put his "pacifism" aside. If the hero can be shown to be troubled, complex, fallible, even eccentric, or the villain given some psychological taint or, better, some evocative physical mannerism, to shade the colors of his villainy, that is all to the good. Indeed, that kind of variation is absolutely necessary to keep the type from becoming sterile; we do not want to see the same movie over and over again, only the same form. But when the impulse toward realism is extended into a "reinterpretation" of the West as a developed society, drawing our eyes away from the hero if only to the extent of showing him as the one dominant figure in a complex social order, then the pattern is broken and the West itself begins to be uninteresting. If the "social problems" of the frontier are to be the movie's chief concern, there is no longer any point in reexamining these problems twenty times a year; they have been solved, and the people for whom they once were real are dead. Moreover, the hero himself, still the film's central figure, now tends to become its one unassimilable element, since he is the most "unreal."

The *Ox-Bow Incident,* by denying the convention of the lynching, presents us with a modern "social drama" and evokes a corresponding response, but in doing so it almost makes the Western setting irrelevant, a mere backdrop of beautiful scenery. (It is significant that *The Ox-Bow Incident* has no hero; a hero would have to stop the lynching or be killed in trying to stop it, and then the "problem" of lynching would no longer be central.) Even in *The Gunfighter* the women and children are a little too much in evidence, threatening constantly to become a real focus of concern instead of simply part of the given framework; and the young tough who kills the hero has too much the air of juvenile criminality: the hero himself could never have been like that, and the idea of a cycle being repeated therefore loses its sharpness. But the most striking example of the confusion created by a too conscientious "social" realism is in the celebrated *High Noon.*

In *High Noon* we find Gary Cooper still the upholder of order that he was in *The Virginian,* but twenty-four years older, stooped, slower moving, awkward, his face lined, the flesh sagging, a less beautiful and weaker figure, but with the suggestion of greater depth that belongs almost automatically to age. Like the hero of *The Gunfighter,* he no longer has to assert his character and is no longer interested in the drama of combat; it is hard to imagine that he might once have been so youthful as to say, "When you call me that—smile!" In fact, when we come upon him he is hanging up his guns and his marshal's badge in order to begin a new, peaceful life with his bride, who is a Quaker. But then the news comes that a man he had sent to prison has been pardoned and will get to town on the noon train; three friends of this man have come to wait for him at the station, and when the freed convict arrives the four of them will come to kill the marshal. He is thus trapped; the bride will object, the hero himself will waver much more than he would have done twenty-four years ago, but in the end he will play out the drama because it is what he "has to do." All this belongs to the established form (there is even the "fallen woman" who understands the marshal's position as his wife does not). Leaving aside the crudity of building up suspense by means of the clock, the actual Western drama of *High Noon* is well handled and forms a good companion piece to *The Virginian,* showing in both conception and technique the ways in which the Western movie has naturally developed.

But there is a second drama along with the first. As the marshal sets out to find deputies to help him deal with the four gunmen, we are taken through the various social strata of the town, each group in turn refusing its assistance out of cowardice, malice, irresponsibilty, or venality. With this we are in the field of "social drama"— of a very low order, incidentally, altogether unconvincing and displaying a vulgar anti-populism that has marred some other movies of Stanley Kramer's. But the falsity of the "social drama" is less important than the fact that it does not belong in the movie to begin with. The technical problem was to make it necessary for the marshal to face his enemies alone; to explain *why* the other townspeople are not at his side is to raise a question which does not exist in the proper frame of the Western movie, where the hero is "naturally" alone and it is only necessary to contrive the physical absence of those who might be his allies, if any contrivance is needed at all.

In addition, though the hero of *High Noon* proves himself a better man than all around him, the actual effect of this contrast is to lessen his stature: he becomes only a rejected man of virtue. In our final glimpse of him, as he rides away through the town where he has spent most of his life without really imposing himself on it, he is a pathetic rather than a tragic figure. And his departure has another meaning as well; the "social drama" has no place for him.

But there is also a different way of violating the Western form. This is to yield entirely to its static quality as legend and to the "cinematic" temptations of its landscape, the horses, the quiet men. John Ford's famous *Stagecoach* (1938) had much of this unhappy preoccupation with style, and the same director's *My Darling Clementine* (1946), a soft and beautiful movie about Wyatt Earp, goes further along the same path, offering indeed a superficial accuracy of historical reconstruction, but so loving in execution as to destroy the outlines of the Western legend, assimilating it to the more sentimental legend of rural America and making the hero a more dangerous Mr. Deeds. (*Powder River,* a recent "routine" Western shamelessly copied from *My Darling Clementine,* is in most ways a better film; lacking the benefit of a serious director, it is necessarily more concerned with drama than with style.)

The highest expression of this aestheticizing tendency is in George Stevens' *Shane,* where the legend of the West is virtually reduced to its essentials and then fixed in the dreamy clarity of a fairy tale. There never was so broad and bare and lovely a landscape as Stevens puts before us, or so unimaginably comfortless a "town" as the little group of buildings on the prairie to which the settlers must come for their supplies and to buy a drink. The mere physical progress of the film, following the style of *A Place in the Sun,* is so deliberately graceful that everything seems to be happening at the bottom of a clear lake. The hero (Alan Ladd) is hardly a man at all, but something like the Spirit of the West, beautiful in fringed buckskins. He emerges mysteriously from the plains, breathing sweetness and a melancholy which is no longer simply the Westerner's natural response to experience but has taken on spirituality; and when he has accomplished his mission, meeting and destroying in the black figure of Jack Palance a Spirit of Evil just as metaphysical as his own embodiment of virtue, he fades away again into the more distant West, a man whose "day is over," leaving behind the wondering little boy who might have imagined the whole story. The choice of Alan Ladd to play the leading role is alone an indication of this film's tendency. Actors like Gary Cooper or Gregory Peck are in themselves, as material objects, "realistic," seeming to bear in their bodies and their faces mortality, limitation, the knowledge of good and evil. Ladd is a more "aesthetic" object, with some of the "universality" of a piece of sculpture; his special quality is in his physical smoothness and serenity, unworldly and yet not innocent, but suggesting that no experience can really touch him. Stevens has tried to freeze the Western myth once and for all in the immobility of Alan Ladd's countenance. If *Shane* were "right," and fully successful, it might be possible to say there was no point in making any more Western movies; once the hero is apotheosized, variation and development are closed off.

Shane is not "right," but it is still true that the possibiities of fruitful variation in the Western movie are limited. The form can keep its freshness through endless

The lawyer from the East learns the law of the West: John Wayne and James Stewart in John Ford's *The Man Who Shot Liberty Valance* (1962). "Ford's . . . preoccupation with style" has the tendency "to destroy the outlines of the Western legend, assimilating it to the more sentimental legend of rural America and making the hero a more dangerous Mr. Deeds . . ." (WARSHOW, page 463).

repetitions only because of the special character of the film medium, where the physical difference between one object and another—above all, between one actor and another—is of such enormous importance, serving the function that is served by the variety of language in the perpetuation of literary types. In this sense, the "vocabulary" of films is much larger than that of literature and falls more readily into pleasing and significant arrangements. (That may explain why the middle levels of excellence are more easily reached in the movies than in literary forms, and perhaps also why the status of the movies as art is constantly being called into question.) But the advantage of this almost automatic particularity belongs to all films alike. Why does the Western movie especially have such a hold on our imagination?

Chiefly, I think, because it offers a serious orientation to the problem of violence such as can be found almost nowhere else in our culture. One of the well-known peculiarities of modern civilized opinion is its refusal to acknowledge the value of violence. This refusal is a virtue, but like many virtues it involves a certain willful blindness and it encourages hypocrisy. We train ourselves to be shocked or bored by cultural images of violence, and our very concept of heroism tends to be a passive one: we are less drawn to the brave young men who kill large numbers of our enemies than to the heroic prisoners who endure torture without capitulating. In art, though we may still be able to understand and participate in the values of the Iliad, a modern writer like Ernest Hemingway we find somewhat embarrassing: there is no doubt that he stirs us, but we cannot help recognizing also that he is a little childish. And in the criticism of popular culture, where the educated observer is usually under the illusion that he has nothing at stake, the presence of images of violence is often assumed to be in itself a sufficient ground for condemnation.

These attitudes, however, have not reduced the element of violence in our culture but, if anything, have helped to free it from moral control by letting it take on the aura of "emancipation." The celebration of acts of violence is left more and more to the irresponsible: on the higher cultural levels to writers like Céline, and lower down to Mickey Spillane or Horace McCoy, or to the comic books, television, and the movies. The gangster movie, with its numerous variations, belongs to this cultural "underground" which sets forth the attractions of violence in the face of all our higher social attitudes. It is a more "modern" genre than the Western, perhaps even more profound, because it confronts industrial society on its own ground— the city—and because, like much of our advanced art, it gains its effects by a gross insistence on its own narrow logic. But it is anti-social, resting on fantasies of irresponsible freedom. If we are brought finally to acquiesce in the denial of these fantasies, it is only because they have been shown to be dangerous, not because they have given way to a better vision of behavior.*

In war movies, to be sure, it is possible to present the uses of violence within a framework of responsibility. But there is the disadvantage that modern war is a co-

---

*I am not concerned here with the actual social consequences of gangster movies, though I suspect they could not have been so pernicious as they were thought to be. Some of the compromises introduced to avoid the supposed bad effects of the old gangster movies may be, if anything, more dangerous, for the sadistic violence that once belonged only to the gangster is now commonly enlisted on the side of the law and thus goes undefeated, allowing us (if we wish) to find in the movies a sort of "confirmation" of our fantasies.

operative enterprise; its violence is largely impersonal, and heroism belongs to the group more than to the individual. The hero of a war movie is most often simply a leader, and his superiority is likely to be expressed in a denial of the heroic: you are not supposed to be brave, you are supposed to get the job done and stay alive (this too, of course, is a kind of heroic posture, but a new—and "practical"—one). At its best, the war movie may represent a more civilized point of view than the Western, and if it were not continually marred by ideological sentimentality we might hope to find it developing into a higher form of drama. But it cannot supply the values we seek in the Western.

Those values are in the image of a single man who wears a gun on his thigh. The gun tells us that he lives in a world of violence, and even that he "believes in violence." But the drama is one of self-restraint: the moment of violence must come in its own time and according to its special laws, or else it is valueless. There is little cruelty in Western movies, and little sentimentality; our eyes are not focused on the sufferings of the defeated but on the deportment of the hero. Really, it is not violence at all which is the "point" of the Western movie, but a certain image of man, a style, which expresses itself most clearly in violence. Watch a child with his toy guns and you will see: what most interests him is not (as we so much fear) the fantasy of hurting others, but to work out how a man might look when he shoots or is shot. A hero is one who looks like a hero.

Whatever the limitations of such an idea in experience, it has always been valid in art, and has a special validity in an art where appearances are everything. The Western hero is necessarily an archaic figure; we do not really believe in him and would not have him step out of his rigidly conventionalized background. But his archaicism does not take away from his power; on the contrary, it adds to it by keeping him just a little beyond the reach both of common sense and of absolutized emotion, the two usual impulses of our art. And he has, after all, his own kind of relevance. He is there to remind us of the possibility of style in an age which has put on itself the burden of pretending that style has no meaning, and, in the midst of our anxieties over the problem of violence, to suggest that even in killing or being killed we are not freed from the necessity of establishing satisfactory modes of behavior. Above all, the movies in which the Westerner plays out his role preserve for us the pleasures of a complete and self-contained drama—and one which still effortlessly crosses the boundaries which divide our culture—in a time when other, more consciously serious art forms are increasingly complex, uncertain, and ill-defined.

1954

JEAN-LOUP BOURGET
SOCIAL IMPLICATIONS IN THE HOLLYWOOD GENRES

From the outset, the cinema has been characterized by a certain tension, even a certain conflict, between an apparent content, derived from popular literature, and a number of autonomous stylistic devices (the various uses of actors, sets, camera movements, montage). Strictures traditionally passed on the Hollywood film fail to take into account the basic fact that its conventionality is the very paradoxical reason for its creativity. Conventions inherited from literature have added themselves to social pressures, such as the necessity for self-censorship, and to commercial imperatives, and may well have badly hampered the explicit content and meaning of movies—plot and characterization frequently tending to become stereotyped. But in many instances the newness of the medium made it possible, even mandatory, to resort to a language both visual and aural, whose implicit meaning was far removed from what the mere script might convey. Here are two brief examples. In Griffith's films, we find a tension between the conventional Victorian moralizing of the plot and titles, and the much more subtle meanings of sets, lighting, close-ups of actresses' faces, camera movements, and editing. In Josef von Sternberg's films, there is an open, unresolved conflict between the stereotypes of the plot and dialogue and the "pure poetry" of the visual elements.

Another point that should be borne in mind is that, whenever an art form is highly conventional, the opportunity for subtle irony or distanciation presents itself all the more readily. The director's (that is to say, the camera's) point of view need not coincide with the hero's point of view; or again, and more generally, since a film represents a superposition of texts, it is not surprising that large segments of an audience (notably including literary-minded critics) should decipher only one of these texts and therefore misread the sum total of the various texts. European directors working in Hollywood developed a technique for telling stories with implicit ironical meanings. For example, Ernst Lubitsch's *Trouble in Paradise* (1932) presents a coherent view of contemporary society under the neat gloss of the sophisticated comedy: thieves are capitalists; capitalists are thieves. Similarly, *To Be or Not to Be* (Lubitsch, 1942) is not just a farce: it makes the not altogether frivolous point that the historical Nazis were worse actors than the fictitious bad actors of the Polish underground. The point was completely missed by the contemporary audience, who regarded the film as being in very bad taste. The same remark applies to most of Douglas Sirk's American films. Thus *All That Heaven Allows* (1956) is not a "weepie," but a sharp satire of small-town America; *Written on the Wind* (1957) is not about the glamor of American high society, but about its corruption; *Imitation of Life* (1959) is superficially naïve and optimistic, but profoundly bitter and anti-racist.

The conflict between the movie's pre-text (the script, the source of the adaptation) and its text (all the evidence on the screen and sound track) provides us with an analytic tool, because it allows for a reconciliation of two apparently antagonistic approaches: the auteur theory, which claims that a film is the work of one creative individual, and the iconological approach, which assumes that a film is a sequence of images whose real meaning may well be unconscious on the part of its makers. Elsewhere I have tried to show that the original version of *Back Street* (John M. Stahl, 1932), while apparently describing a woman's noble and sad sacrifice, is in fact a melodrama with profound social and feministic implications.* I also stated that "melodrama" in its traditional sense was born at the time of the French Revolution and reflected social unrest in a troubled historical period. In the context of the description of society, we may therefore distinguish between melodramas such as *Back Street,* which express a certain state of society, depicting its relative stability and the occasions of potential conflict, and melodramas such as *Orphans of the Storm* (D. W. Griffith, 1922) and *Anthony Adverse* (Mervyn LeRoy, 1936), which comment on actual turmoil. It would probably be possible to give a survey of other popular genres in search of similar examples of these alternative approaches: description of an operative system, description of the breaking up of a given structure.

In the first category—films describing how a given social structure operates—we find many movies belonging to genres that are often dismissed as escapist and alienating. While this may well be true in a majority of cases, it nevertheless remains that escapism can also be used as a device for criticizing reality and the present state of society. A utopian world that calls itself a utopia is not escapist in the derogatory sense of the word; rather, it calls the viewer's attention to the fact that his or her own society is far removed from such an ideal condition. Many films by such Rousseauistic directors as Allan Dwan and Delmar Daves belong to this category; they might best be described as "South Seas adventure dramas"—see Allan Dwan's

---

*Jean-Loup Bourget, "Aspects du mélodrame américain," *Positif,* no. 131 (October 1971): 31–43; for the English version, see *"Back Street* (Reconsidered)," *Take One* 3, no. 2 (November–December 1970): 33–34. The implicit significance of Stahl's *Back Street* is due not to the Fannie Hurst story itself, but to its treatment by Stahl. A confirmation will be found in a comparison with the latest version of the same story (retold by David Miller in 1961), where the meaning is altered, reduced both to its mawkish pretext and to very few fulgurant images listlessly "borrowed" from films by Douglas Sirk.

adaptation of Melville's *Typee* (*Enchanted Island,* 1958) and Delmer Daves's *Bird of Paradise* (1951), *Treasure of the Golden Condor* (1953), and his western *Broken Arrow* (1950). Some of these films suffer from a stylistic incompetence that somewhat forces the implicit meaning back out of the film itself, into the director's generous but unrealized intentions. More to the point are perhaps two films by John Ford, *The Hurricane* (1937) and *Donovan's Reef* (1963). The first film implicitly contrasts Raymond Massey, who embodies the oppressive law, with the Lincoln of other John Ford films, Lincoln being an incarnation of the law which gives life and freedom. In *Donovan's Reef,* a brief scene located in Boston supplies the key to implicit meaning as we are allowed to glimpse a caricatural reality of America opposed to the idealized vision of the Pacific island.

In contradistinction to the legend that in all traditional westerns "the only good Indian is a dead Indian," a closer look at early Hollywood westerns reveals surprising conflicts between explicit and implicit meanings. Thus in DeMille's *The Squawman,* a subject obviously dear to him since he treated it on three different occasions (1913, 1918, 1931), an Englishman who has settled in America is seduced by the "primitive" and therefore "immoral" beauty of an Indian woman drying her naked body by the fire. He lives with her without marrying her, and she bears him a child. Years later, the Englishman's relatives look him up and insist on taking his child to England in order to give him a proper education. Because of her "primitive" mind (as the man puts it), the Indian woman does not understand why her son should be taken away from her, and she commits suicide. Earlier on, she had already been rejected by the child, who had preferred an electric train to the crude wooden horse that she had carved for him. In its treatment of the story, DeMille's point of view is sympathetic to the Indian woman rather than to the Europeans. To him, she is morally superior. This is made clear less by the plot than by the lyricism of the sequences devoted to Lupe Velez "seducing" the Englishman or carving the wooden toy. At the same time, because of its tragic conclusion, the film could hardly be accused of being escapist or naively optimistic. In a much more subtle way, the indictment of white pseudo-civilization is as harsh as in Arthur Penn's *Little Big Man* of 1970. But these cultural tensions remain implicit and unresolved. Obviously, the "deconstruction" of ironical analysis is not synonymous with "destruction." Is this failure to resolve tensions due to weakness in the creative act or rather to the capitalistic mode of film production? In Hollywood, the director's work, however conscious it may be of social alienation, is bound by the same alienation.

Ironical implications of a social breakdown can be embedded in the most highly conventional and least realistic films. Such a movie is *Heidi* (Allan Dwan, 1937), starring Shirley Temple, where kitsch, as is usual, verges on parody. Only in a kitsch film or in a comedy could servants be emblematically described as holding a feather duster. The kitsch movie is often located in Central Europe, and the ideal society it tends to refer to is that of the Hapsburg Empire. There we find a static hierarchical society where everybody is defined by a social function rather than by individual traits. But the providential architecture of this social system is so exaggerated that (whether consciously or unconsciously on the part of the filmmakers) the effect produced is, in the last analysis, satirical. Stylistically, social functions are indicted by emblems (folkloric costumes, pointed helmets, plumes), which look slightly ridiculous. For example, in *Zoo in Budapest* (Rowland V. Lee, 1933), society is neatly divided between the haves and the have-nots, between those with some parcel of authority and those without any. On the other hand, we find certain aristocratic visitors to the zoo and a multitude of characters in quasi-military uniforms: wardens, policemen, bus drivers. On the other hand, we have the peasant visitors in colorful garb, the girls from an orphanage, and the unsociable hero who seeks the company of animals rather than that of men. This amounts to the description of a society so alienated that, in order to be free, one has to live behind bars in a zoo! The last part of the film bursts into nightmare, as all the wild beasts escape from their cages—a suggestion that this neatly organized society is no less prone to explosions and revolutions, notwithstanding the literally incredible ending, which claims to reconcile the feudal system and the individual's happiness.*

Similarly, a turn-of-the-century setting seems to be very popular in a variety of genres, from the literary adaptation (*The Picture of Dorian Gray,* Albert Lewin, 1945) to the horror film (*Hangover Square,* John Brahm, 1945), from the romantic drama (*Letter from an Unknown Woman,* Max Ophuls, 1948) to the musical (*Meet Me in St. Louis,* Vincente Minnelli, 1944; *Gigi,* Minnelli, 1958; *My Fair Lady,* George Cukor, 1964). There are probably two reasons for this popularity. For one thing, such a setting has stylistic qualities that readily lend themselves to artistic effects. For another thing, it refers to Western society—usually but not necessarily European—at its most sophisticated, on the eve of the First World War and of the economic collapse of Europe. This presumably accounts for the success of the Viennese film, a genre that has often been wrongly explained in naively biographical and nostalgic terms. The satirical element that is obvious in von Stroheim's films is implicit in the works of other European directors. Josef von Sternberg's *Dishonoured* (1931) contrasts Marlene Dietrich's *amour fou* with the sense of decadence and the collapse of empires, Austrian and Russian. In Anatole Litvak's *Mayerling* (1936), the lovers are doomed, not by fate but by the ominous sign of the Hapsburg Empire, the oppressive Eagle of *raison d'état:* the ball scene in particular opens with the camera seemingly tracking through a glass eagle and ends with the same movement in reverse. In many "Viennese" films, both European and American, Ophuls uses the device of a duel, which points out the way in which a particular class of society goes about solving its private problems when they cannot be kept private any longer.

Such films therefore enable us to put forward a tentative definition of melodrama as opposed to tragedy: in melodrama, fate is not metaphysical but rather social or political. Thus melodrama is bourgeois tragedy, dependent upon an awareness of the existence of society. This echoes Benjamin Constant's own definition of the new tragedy: "Social order, the action of society on the individual, in different phases and at different epochs, this network of institutions and conventions in which we are caught from our birth and which does not break until we die, these are the main-

---

*In *Zoo in Budapest,* Gene Raymond and Loretta Young first find happiness in a bear's den overlooking the town, the outside world. Their situation recalls that of Borzage's heroes in *Seventh Heaven* (1927): the "little man" lives in a garret, close to the stars, which allows him symbolic "overlooking" of a world that crushes him in every other way.

springs of tragedy. One only has to know how to use them. They are absolutely equivalent to the Fatum of the Ancients."[1]

In several respects, the musical is close to the cinematic melodrama, both having developed from forms of spectacle associated with the conventions of the popular stage. In order to express an implicit meaning, they both have to rely almost exclusively on stylization, at once visual and musical (melodrama is etymologically "drama with music"), for they are both removed from the convention of realism.[2] In the hands of creative individual directors, musicals therefore lend themselves to statements that will pass unnoticed by the majority of the entertainment-seeking audience and by critics who judge the explicit content. Unsurprisingly, some directors have excelled in both genres—above all, Minnelli. *Brigadoon* (1954) is an excellent example of what is meant here: the musical is set against the motif of bustling New York, and the meaning of the supposedly escapist part of the movie can only be induced from the satirized madness of the everyday setting toward the end of the film.

An allegory frequent in the musical is that of Pygmalion, of a member of respectable society raising a girl of the lower classes to his own level of civilized sophistication. It is the particular failure of *My Fair Lady* (George Cukor, 1964) to have used Audrey Hepburn in such a part, because the actress is evidently an extremely sophisticated one. Thus the parable rings false; in order to make it convincing, Cukor should have used an actress of a completely different type, Shirley MacLaine, for example, and have her look like a lady by the end of the film. For the implication should be that there is nothing in high society that a good actor or dancer should not be capable of achieving through imitation. Again, it should suggest a reversal of the apparent roles and functions similar to the one found in Lubitsch's *Trouble in Paradise:* if dancers are ladies, ladies cannot be far different from dancers. The whole oeuvre of such directors as Minnelli and Cukor is based on this underlying assumption, which, hidden behind a playful guise, is both a satire of actual social solidity and an indication of possible social fluidity (see Cukor's films starring Judy Holliday and Minnelli's films starring Judy Garland).

Easter Parade (Charles Walters, 1948) tells a story similar to that of *My Fair Lady,* with Fred Astaire and Judy Garland in roles similar to those of Rex Harrison and Audrey Hepburn. But there the allegory works, and goes farther, because it has serious bearings on woman's status in society. At the end of the film, Judy Garland,

---

[1]Benjamin Constant, *Oeuvres* (Paris: Bibl. de la Pléiade, 1957), p. 952, translation mine. Obviously, many cinematic melodramas still pretend to rely on the device of superhuman fate; it is only an analysis of their implicit meanings, of their subtext, which makes it possible to unmask such fate and give it its actual name of social necessity.

[2]In fact, what is variously termed "romantic drama," "soap opera," "sudser," "woman's film," etc., spans all the gamut from the operatic formalism of Dietrich's films and Garbo's *Queen Christina* (Rouben Mamoulian, 1933) to the drab realism of the kitchen-sink drama. There are some successful examples of fairly "realistic" melodramas, notably John Cromwell's *Made for Each Other* and *In Name Only* (both 1939). Nevertheless, even such films are highly unrealistic in their catastrophic situations and providential endings. The impression of realism is largely due to the actors (Carole Lombard as opposed to, say, Joan Crawford) rather than to the verisimilitude of plot and setting. As a rule, both the musical and the melodrama are more openly formalized and ritualized than the realistic guise normally allows. This is due to their common theatrical origin and to their disregard of subtle, novelistic psychological analysis.

tired of waiting to be proposed to, decides that there is no reason why she should not in fact woo Fred Astaire. She adopts the man's traditional role, sends numerous gifts to the object of her thoughts, and compliments him on his beautiful clothes. The musical, like a court jester, is allowed a saturnalian freedom because it is not a "serious" genre. Its self-eulogy ("Be a Clown" in Minnelli's *The Pirate,* 1948; "Make 'Em Laugh" in Donen and Kelly's *Singin' in the Rain,* 1952; and "That's Entertainment" in Minnelli's *The Band Wagon,* 1953) shows its understandable reluctance to part with such a liberty.

Another category of films is not content with describing a system, but portrays its collapse. (Screwball comedies and Busby Berkeley musicals, connected with the Depression, can be mentioned in passing.)* The implicit meaning may be more difficult to assert in historical films and epics because they often refer to revolutions or civil wars whose pattern is given as fact and thus not susceptible to an interpretation. Yet a coherent explanation is sometimes to be found hidden behind the historical or adventurous plot. *Anthony Adverse,* referred to earlier, is located in the time of the French Revolution and of the First Empire. It is critical of both the former aristocracy and of the new classes, depicted as a ruthless mob aping the former nobility. The only solution is found in leaving a doomed continent and sailing for the new land and the democratic society of America. A somewhat similar point of view is expressed in *A Tale of Two Cities* (Jack Conway, 1935), where the French Revolution must be shown as almost simultaneously profoundly justified and profoundly unjust. This is achieved in a very interesting way. The first part of the film is, despite a few hints, rather sympathetic to the idea of a revolution, which is shown as inevitable. Even more committed are the sequences of the revolution proper (the storming of the Bastille), which were directed by a different team—Jacques Tourneur and Val Lewton. They are absolutely Eisensteinlike in their depiction of blatant injustice and spontaneous union, Sovietlike, of people and army. From there on, it is impossible to think of any adequate transition; the trick consists in skipping over the transition, in reverting to a title, a pre-text, which claim that the spirit of liberty had been betrayed even before it had triumphed. But such is not the evidence on the screen, and the film embodies a strange, unresolved discrepancy between the sequences directed by Jack Conway (pleasant but traditional in style, faithful to the source of the adaptation) and those by Jacques Tourneur, formally very original, unambiguous in their meaning, and telling a tale of their own.

Conversely, a perfectly coherent film about the French Revolution is *Marie Antionette* (Woody S. Van Dyke, 1937)—coherent, that is, from a reactionary point of view. Yet, even in this case, we see a tension at work between the explicit argument of the film as signified by the title (a woman's picture, the sad, dignified story of Marie Antoinette) and the implicit political message, according to which the hero/victim is King Louis XVI rather than Marie Antoinette. In the light of the film, she is not much more than a pleasure-loving girl, but he is portrayed as a man of good will who was betrayed by a conspiracy of Freemasons and the Duke of Orleans.

---

*See Jean-Loup Bourget, "Capra et la screwball comedy," *Positif,* no. 133 (December 1971): 47–53.

A subgenre of the adventure film that almost inevitably acclaims a pattern of social unrest and revolution (always successful in this case, because it is far removed in time and space, and therefore with no apparent direct bearings on present society) is the swashbuckler, the pirate film. The most "democratic" examples of the genre include two films by Michael Curtiz, *Captain Blood* (1935) and *The Sea Hawk* (1940). In both, an apolitical man is charged with sedition and actually becomes a rebel (cf. a similar parable in John Ford's *Prisoner of Shark Island,* 1936). Both films describe the way a colonial system rests on political oppression, slavery, and torture; they both advocate violent revolution as the only means of destroying such a system. The evidence of the genre therefore conflicts with the evidence of colonial films set in the twentieth century—for example, in British India or in French North Africa—where it is the outlaw who is supposedly guilty of savagery. It might be illuminating to show to what extent a contemporary, politically committed filmmaker like Gillo Pontecorvo has relied on the traditional Hollywood and Cinecittà genre of the pirate film in his 1968 film *Quemada* (*Burn!* in English).

As pointed out before, the danger of certain explicit statements about Robin Hood and pirate figures in distant times or remote places is that the remoteness can be emphasized rather than played down. In historical films about outlaws, the viewer is allowed to walk out with a clear conscience and a dim consciousness. This danger was realized and pointed out by directors more sophisticated than Michael Curtiz. In *Sullivan's Travels* (1942), Preston Sturges satirized the conventions of the social-problem genre that had flourished at Warners under the guidance of Mervyn LeRoy, among others. The bittersweet conclusion of Sturges's film was that directors should not go beyond the camera, that they should not make social statements when they have but the vaguest notions about the condition of society, and should rather devote their time and energy to the making of comedies. But his own film showed that he could somehow do both at the same time: entertain and make valid comments. Similarly, Minnelli's *The Pirate* underlies the conventions of the swashbuckler. It adds another dimension to the meaning of the pirate film. Judy Garland, the governor's daughter, falls in love with Gene Kelly, an actor who parades as Macoco, the fierce pirate. The point is, first, that to make a "revolutionary" and "democratic" pirate film is partly to base the argument on Errol Flynn's— or Gene Kelly's—sex appeal. But this is only the first layer of meaning. The actor, not the pirate, turns out to be the "revolutionary" individual who is going to achieve social change, for he unmasks Walter Slezak (Judy Garland's fiancé), the real Macoco who parades as a respectable citizen. The lesson is therefore that piracy can be identified with respectable bourgeois society, and that the artist (whether an actor or a Hollywood director) emerges as the one person with both a sense of individual freedom and the refusal to oppress others.

Thus the freedom of Hollywood directors is not measured by what they can openly do within the Hollywood system, but rather by what they can imply about American society in general and about the Hollywood system in particular. They can describe in extensive detail how a given social structure operates, but cannot do so openly unless the society in question is remote in time or space; if they describe the breakdown of a social system, they must somehow end on a hopeful note and show that both order and happiness are eventually restored. However, the interplay of implicit meanings, either subtly different from or actually clashing with the conventional self-gratification, allows the Hollywood director to make valid comments about contemporary American society in an indirect way, by "bending" the explicit meaning (Sirk's phrase). Genre conventions can be either used as an alibi (the implicit meaning is to be found elsewhere in the film) or turned upside down (irony underlines the conventionality of the convention). The implicit subtext of genre films makes it possible for the director to ask the inevitable (but unanswerable) question: Must American society be like this? Must the Hollywood system function like this?

1973

ROBIN WOOD
IDEOLOGY, GENRE, AUTEUR

The truth lies not in one dream but in many.

Arabian Nights (PIER PAOLO PASOLINI, 1974)

Each theory of film so far has insisted on its own particular polarization. Montage theory enthrones editing as the essential creative act at the expense of other aspects of film; Bazin's realist theory, seeking to right the balance, merely substitutes its own imbalance, downgrading montage and artifice; the revolutionary theory centered in Britain in *Screen* (but today very widespread) rejects—or at any rate seeks to "deconstruct"—realist art in favor of the so-called open text. Auteur theory, in its heyday, concentrated attention exclusively on the fingerprints, thematic or stylistic, of the individual artist; recent attempts to discuss the complete "filmic text" have tended to throw out ideas of personal authorship altogether. Each theory has, given its underlying position, its own validity—the validity being dependent upon and restricted by the position. Each can offer insights into different areas of cinema and different aspects of a single film.

I have suggested elsewhere* the desirability for critics—whose aim should always be to see the work as wholly as possible, as it is—to be able to draw on the discoveries and particular perceptions of each theory, each position, without committing themselves exclusively to any one. The ideal will not be easy to attain, and even the attempt raises all kinds of problems, the chief of which is the validity of evaluative criteria that are not supported by a particular system. For what, then, *do* they receive support? No critic, obviously, can be free from a structure of values, nor can he or she afford to withdraw from the struggles and tensions of living to some posi-

---

*Robin Wood, "Old Wine, New Bottles: Structuralism or Humanism?" *Film Comment* 12, no. 6 (November–December 1976): 22–25.

475

tion of "aesthetic" contemplation. Every critic who is worth reading has been, on the contrary, very much caught up in the effort to define values beyond purely aesthetic ones (if indeed such things exist). Yet to "live historically" need not entail commitment to a system or a cause; rather, it can involve being alive to the opposing pulls, the tensions, of one's world.

The past two decades have seen a number of advances in terms of the opening up of critical possibilities, of areas of relevance, especially with regard to Hollywood: the elaboration of auteur theory in its various manifestations; the interest in genre; the interest in ideology. I want here tentatively to explore some of the ways in which these disparate approaches to Hollywood movies might interpenetrate, producing the kind of synthetic criticism I have suggested might now be practicable.

In order to create a context within which to discuss *It's a Wonderful Life* (Frank Capra, 1946) and *Shadow of a Doubt* (Alfred Hitchcock, 1943), I want to attempt (at risk of obviousness) a definition of what we mean by American capitalist ideology—or, more specifically, the values and assumptions so insistently embodied in and reinforced by the classical Hollywood cinema. The following list of components is not intended to be exhaustive or profound, but simply to make conscious, prior to a discussion of the films, concepts with which we are all perfectly familiar:

1. Capitalism, the right of ownership, private enterprise, personal initiative; the settling of the land.

2. The work ethic: the notion that "honest toil" is in itself and for itself morally admirable, this and concept 1 both validating and reinforcing each other. The moral excellence of work is also bound up with the necessary subjugation or sublimation of the libido: "the Devil finds work for idle hands." The relationship is beautifully epitomized in the zoo-cleaner's song in *Cat People* (Jacques Tourneur, 1942):

> Nothing else to do,
> Nothing else to do,
> I strayed, went a-courting
> 'cause I'd nothing else to do.

3. Marriage (legalized heterosexual monogamy) and family—at once the further validation of concepts 1 and 2 (the homestead is built for the woman, whose function is to embody civilized values and guarantee their continuance through her children) and an extension of the ownership principle to personal relationships ("*My* house, *my* wife, *my* children") in a male-dominated society.

4a. Nature as agrarianism; the virgin land as Garden of Eden. A concept into which, in the western, concept 3 tends to become curiously assimilated (ideology's function being to "naturalize" cultural assumptions): for example, the treatment of the family in *Drums along the Mohawk* (John Ford, 1939).

4b. Nature as the wilderness, the Indians, on whose subjugation civilization is built; hence by extension the libido, of which in many westerns the Indians seem an extension or embodiment, as in *The Searchers* (Ford, 1956).

5. Progress, technology, the city ("New York, New York, it's a wonderful town").

6. Success and wealth—a value of which Hollywood ideology is also deeply ashamed, so that, while hundreds of films play on its allure, very few can allow themselves openly to extol it. Thus its ideological "shadow" is produced.

7. The Rosebud syndrome. Money isn't everything; money corrupts; the poor are happier. A very convenient assumption for capitalist ideology; the more oppressed you are, the happier you are, as exemplified by the singing "darkies" of *A Day at the Races* (Sam Wood, 1937).

8. America as the land where everyone is or can be happy; hence the land where all problems are solvable within the existing system (which may need a bit of reform here and there but no *radical* change). Subversive systems are assimilated wherever possible to serve the dominant ideology. Andrew Britton, in a characteristically brilliant article on Hitchcock's *Spellbound* (1945), argues that there even Freudian psychoanalysis becomes an instrument of ideological repression.[1] Above all, this assumption gives us that most striking and persistent of all classical Hollywood phenomena, the happy ending: often a mere "emergency exit" (Sirk's phrase)[2] for the spectator, a barely plausible pretense that the problems the film has raised are now resolved. *Hilda Crane* (Philip Dunne, 1950) offers a suitably blatant example among the hundreds possible.

Out of this list logically emerge two ideal figures:

9. The ideal male: the virile adventurer, the potent, untrammeled man of action.

10. The ideal female: wife and mother, perfect companion, the endlessly dependable mainstay of hearth and home.

Since these combine into an ideal couple of quite staggering incompatibility, each has his or her shadow:

11. The settled husband/father, dependable but dull.

12. The erotic woman (adventuress, gambling lady, saloon "entertainer"), fascinating but dangerous, liable to betray the hero or turn into a black panther.

The most striking fact about this list is that it presents an ideology that, far from being monolithic, is *inherently* riddled with hopeless contradictions and unresolvable tensions. The work that has been done so far on genre has tended to take the various genres as "given" and discrete, defining them in terms of motifs, iconography, conventions, and themes. What we need to ask, if genre theory is ever to be productive, is less *what* than *why*. We are so used to the genres that the peculiarity of the phenomenon itself has been too little noted. The idea I wish to put forward is that the development of the genres is rooted in the sort of ideological contradictions my list of concepts suggests. One impulse may be the attempt to deny such

---

[1] Andrew Britton, "Hitchcock's *Spellbound:* Text and Counter-Text," *Cine-Action!* no. 3/4 (January 1986): 72–83.

[2] See *Sirk on Sirk,* edited by Jon Halliday (London: Secker & Warburg/British Film Institute, 1971).

contradiction by eliminating one of the opposed terms, or at least by a process of simplification.

Robert Warshow's seminal essays on the gangster hero and the westerner (still fruitfully suggestive, despite the obvious objection that he took too little into account) might be adduced here. The opposition of gangster film and western is only one of many possibilities. *All* the genres can be profitably examined in terms of ideological oppositions, forming a complex interlocking pattern: small-town family comedy/sophisticated city comedy; city comedy/film noir; film noir/small-town comedy, and so on. It is probable that a genre is ideologically "pure" (i.e., safe) only in its simplest, most archetypal, most aesthetically deprived and intellectually contemptible form—such as the Hopalong Cassidy films or Andy Hardy comedies.

The Hopalong Cassidy films (in which Indians, always a potentially disruptive force in ideological as well as dramatic terms, are, in general, significantly absent), for example, seem to depend on two strategies for their perfect ideological security: the strict division of characters into good and evil, with no "grays"; and Hoppy's sexlessness (he never becomes emotionally entangled). Hence the possibility of evading all the wandering/settling tensions on which aesthetically interesting westerns are generally structured. (An intriguing alternative: the ideal American family of Roy Rogers/Dale Evans/Trigger.) *Shane* (George Stevens, 1953) is especially interesting in this connection. A deliberate attempt to create an "archetypal" western, it also represents an effort to resolve the major ideological tensions harmoniously.

One of the greatest obstacles to any fruitful theory of genre has been the tendency to treat the genres as discrete. An ideological approach might suggest why they can't be, however hard they may appear to try: at best, they represent different strategies for dealing with the same ideological tensions. For example, the small-town movie with a contemporary setting should never be divorced from its historical correlative, the western. In the classical Hollywood cinema motifs cross repeatedly from genre to genre, as can be made clear by a few examples. The home/wandering opposition that Peter Wollen rightly sees as central to Ford* is not central only to Ford or even to the western; it structures a remarkably large number of American films covering all genres, from *Out of the Past* (Tourneur, 1947) to *There's No Business Like Show Business* (Walter Lang, 1954). The explicit comparison of women to cats connects screwball comedy (*Bringing Up Baby,* Howard Hawks, 1938), horror film (*Cat People*), melodrama (*Rampage,* Phil Karlson, 1963), and psychological thriller (*Marnie,* Hitchcock, 1964). Another example brings us to this essay's specific topic: notice the way in which the potent male adventurer, when he enters the family circle, immediately displaces his "shadow," the settled husband/father, in both *The Searchers* and *Shadow of a Doubt.*

Before we attempt to apply these ideas to specific films, however, one more point needs to be especially emphasized: the presence of ideological tensions in a movie, though it may give it an interest beyond Hopalong Cassidy, is not in itself a reliable evaluative criterion. It seems probable that artistic value has always been dependent

---

*Peter Wollen, *Signs and Meaning in the Cinema,* 3d. ed. (Bloomington and London: Indiana University Press, 1972), pp. 94–101.

on the presence—somewhere, at some stage—of an individual artist, whatever the function of art in the particular society and even when (as with the Chartres cathedral) one no longer knows who the individual artists were. It is only through the medium of the individual that ideological tensions come into particular focus, hence become of aesthetic as well as sociological interest. It can perhaps be argued that works are of especial interest when the defined particularities of an auteur interact with specific ideological tensions and when the film is fed from more than one generic source.

The same basic ideological tensions operate in both *It's a Wonderful Life* and *Shadow of a Doubt*. They furnish further reminders that the home/wandering antinomy is by no means the exclusive preserve of the western. Bedford Falls and Santa Rosa can be seen as the frontier town seventy or so years on; they embody the development of the civilization whose establishment was celebrated around the same time by Ford in *My Darling Clementine* (1946). With this relationship to the western in the background (but in Capra's film made succinctly explicit), the central tension in both films can be described in terms of genre: the disturbing influx of film noir into the world of small-town domestic comedy. (It is a tension clearly present in *Clementine* as well: the opposition between the daytime and nighttime Tombstones.)

The strong contrast presented by the two films testifies to the decisive effect of the intervention of a clearly defined artistic personality in an ideological-generic structure. Both films have as a central ideological project the reaffirmation of family and small-town values that the action has called into question. In Capra's film this reaffirmation is magnificently convincing (but with full acknowledgment of the suppressions on which it depends and, consequently, of its precariousness); in Hitchcock's it is completely hollow. The very different emotional effects of the films—the satisfying catharsis and emotional fullness of Capra's, the "bitter taste" (on which so many have commented) of Hitchcock's—are very deeply rooted not only in our response to two opposed directorial personalities but in our own ideological structuring.

One of the main ideological and thematic tensions of *It's a Wonderful Life* is beautifully encapsulated in the scene in which George Bailey (James Stewart) and Mary (Donna Reed) smash windows in a derelict house as a preface to making wishes. George's wish is to get the money to leave Bedford Falls, which he sees as humdrum and constricting, and travel about the world; Mary's wish (not expressed in words, but in its subsequent fulfillment—confirming her belief that wishes don't come true if you speak them) is that she and George will marry, settle down, and raise a family in the same derelict house, a ruined shell that marriage-and-family restores to life.

This tension is developed through the extended sequence in which George is manipulated into marrying Mary. His brother's return home with a wife and a new job traps George into staying in Bedford Falls to take over the family business. With the homecoming celebrations continuing inside the house in the background, George sits disconsolately on the front porch; we hear an off-screen train whistle, to which he reacts. His mother (the indispensable Beulah Bondi) comes out and begins "suggesting" that he visit Mary; he appears to go off in her direction, physically pointed that way by his mother, then reappears and walks away past the mother—in the opposite direction.

This leads him, with perfect ideological/generic logic, to Violet (Gloria Grahame). The Violet/Mary opposition is an archetypally clear rending of that central Hollywood female opposition that crosses all generic boundaries—as with Susan (Katherine Hepburn) and Alice (Virginia Walker) in *Bringing Up Baby*, Irene (Simone Simon) and Alice (Jane Randolph) in *Cat People*, Chihuahua (Linda Darnell) and Clementine (Cathy Downs) in *My Darling Clementine*, Debby (Gloria Grahame) and Katie (Jocelyn Brando) in *The Big Heat* (Fritz Lang, 1953). But Violet (in front of an amused audience) rejects his poetic invitation to a barefoot ramble over the hills in the moonlight; the good-time gal offers no more solution to the hero's wanderlust than the wife-mother figure.

So back to Mary, whom he brings to the window by beating a stick aggressively against the fence of the neat, enclosed front garden—a beautifully precise expression of his ambivalent state of mind: desire to attract Mary's attention warring with bitter resentment of his growing entrapment in domesticity. Mary is expecting him; his mother has phoned her, knowing that George would end up at her house. Two ideological premises combine here: the notion that the "good" mother always knows, precisely and with absolute certitude, the workings of her son's mind; and the notion that the female principle is central to the continuity of civilization, that the "weaker sex" is compensated with a sacred rightness.

Indoors, Mary shows George a cartoon she has drawn of George, in cowboy denims, lassoing the moon. The moment is rich in contradictory connotations. It explicitly evokes the western and the figure of the adventurer-hero to which George aspires. Earlier, it was for Mary that George wanted to "lasso the moon," the adventurer's exploits motivated by a desire to make happy the woman who will finally entrap him in domesticity. From Mary's point of view, the picture is at once affectionate (acknowledging the hero's aspirations), mocking (reducing them to caricature), and possessive (reducing George to an image she creates and holds within her hands).

The most overtly presented of the film's structural oppositions is that between the two faces of capitalism, benign and malignant. On the one hand, there are the Baileys (father and son) and their building and loan company, its business practice based on a sense of human needs and a belief in human goodness; on the other, there is Potter (Lionel Barrymore), described explicitly as a spider, motivated by greed, egotism, and miserliness, with no faith in human nature. Potter belongs to a very deeply rooted tradition. He derives most obviously from Dickens's Scrooge (the film is set at Christmas)—a Scrooge disturbingly unrepentant and irredeemable—but his more distant antecedents are in the ogres of fairy tales.

The opposition gives us not only two attitudes to money and property but two father images (Bailey, Sr., and Potter), each of whom gives his name to the land (Bailey Park, in small-town Bedford Falls, and Pottersville, the town's dark alternative). Most interestingly, the two figures (representing American choices, American tendencies) find their vivid ideological extensions in Hollywood genres: the happy, sunny world of small-town comedy (Bedford Falls is seen mostly in the daytime) and the world of film noir, the dark underside of Hollywood ideology.

Pottersville—the vision of the town as it would have been if George had never existed, shown him by his guardian angel (Henry Travers)—is just as "real" as (or no more stylized than) Bedford Falls. The iconography of small-town comedy is exchanged, unmistakably, for that of film noir, with police sirens, shooting in the streets, darkness, vicious dives, alcoholism, burlesque shows, strip clubs, and the glitter and shadows of noir lighting. George's mother, embittered and malevolent, runs a seedy boardinghouse; the good-time gal/wife-mother opposition, translated into noir terms, becomes an opposition of prostitute and repressed spinster-librarian. The towns emerge as equally valid images of America—validated by their generic familiarity.

Beside *Shadow of a Doubt, It's a Wonderful Life* manages a convincing and moving affirmation of the values (and value) of bourgeois family life. Yet what is revealed, when disaster releases George's suppressed tensions, is the intensity of his resentment of the family and desire to destroy it—and with it, in significant relationship, his work (his culminating action is furiously to overthrow the drawing board with his plans for more small-town houses). The film recognizes explicitly that behind every Bedford Falls lurks a Pottersville, and implicitly that within every George Bailey lurks an Ethan Edwards of *The Searchers.* Potter, tempting George, is given the devil's insights into his suppressed desires. His remark, "You once called me a warped, frustrated old man—now you're a warped, frustrated *young* man," is amply supported by the evidence the film supplies. What is finally striking about the film's affirmation is the extreme precariousness of its basis; and Potter survives without remorse, his crime unexposed and unpunished. It may well be Capra's masterpiece, but it is more than that. Like all the greatest American films— fed by a complex generic tradition and, beyond that, by the fears and aspirations of a whole culture—it at once transcends its director and would be inconceivable without him.

Shadow of a Doubt has always been among the most popular of Hitchcock's middle-period films, with critics and public alike, but it has been perceived in very different, almost diametrically opposed ways. On its appearance it was greeted by British critics as the film marking Hitchcock's coming to terms with America; his British films were praised for their humor and "social criticism" as much as for their suspense, and the early American films, notably *Rebecca* (1940) and *Suspicion* (1941), seemed like attempts artificially to reconstruct England in Hollywood. In *Shadow of a Doubt* Hitchcock (with the aid of Thornton Wilder and Sally Benson) at last brought to American middle-class society the shrewd, satirical, affectionate gaze previously bestowed on the British. A later generation of French critics (notably Rohmer and Chabrol in their Hitchcock book) praised the film for very different reasons, establishing its strict formalism (Truffaut's "un film fondé sur le chiffre 2") and seeing it as one of the keys to a consistent Catholic interpretation of Hitchcock, a rigorous working out of themes of original sin, the loss of innocence, the fallen world, the exchange (or interchangeability) of guilt.* The French noted the family comedy beloved of British critics, if at all, as a mildly annoying distraction.

---

*See Eric Rohmer and Claude Chabrol, *Hitchcock: The First Forty-Four Films,* translated by Stanley Hochman (New York: Ungar, 1979), p. 72.

That both these views correspond to important elements in the film and throw light on certain aspects of it is beyond doubt; both, however, now appear false and partial, dependent upon the abstracting of elements from the whole. If the film is, in a sense, completely dominated by Hitchcock (nothing in it is unmarked by his artistic personality), a complete reading would need to see the small-town-family elements and the Catholic elements are threads weaving through a complex fabric in which, again, ideological and generic determinants are crucial.

The kind of "synthetic" analysis I have suggested (going beyond an interest in the individual auteur) reveals *It's a Wonderful Life* as a far more potentially subversive film than has been generally recognized, but its subversive elements are, in the end, successfully contained. In *Shadow of a Doubt* the Hollywood ideology I have sketched is shattered beyond convincing recuperation. One can, however, trace through the film its attempts to impose itself and render things "safe." What is in jeopardy is above all the family—but, given the family's central ideological significance, once that is in jeopardy, everything is. The small town (still rooted in the agrarian dream, in ideals of the virgin land as a garden of innocence) and the united happy family are regarded as the real sound heart of American civilization; the ideological project is to acknowledge the existence of sickness and evil but preserve the family from their contamination.

A number of strategies can be discerned here: the attempt to insist on a separation of Uncle Charlie from Santa Rosa; his death at the end of the film as the definitive purging of evil; the production of the young detective (the healthy, wholesome, small-town male) as a marriage partner for Young Charlie so that the family may be perpetuated; above all, the attribution of Uncle Charlie's sexual pathology to a childhood accident as a means of exonerating the family of the charge of producing a monster, a possibility the American popular cinema, with the contemporary overturning of traditional values, can now envisage—for example, *It's Alive* (Larry Cohen, 1974).

The famous opening, with its parallel introductions of Uncle Charlie and Young Charlie, insists on the city and the small town as *opposed,* sickness and evil being of the city. As with Bedford Falls/Pottersville, the film draws lavishly on the iconography of usually discrete genres. Six shots (with all movement and direction—the bridges, the panning, the editing—consistently rightward) leading up to the first interior of Uncle Charlie's room give us urban technology, wreckage both human (the down-and-outs) and material (the dumped cars by the sign "No Dumping Allowed"), children playing in the street, the number 13 on the lodging-house door. Six shots (movement and direction consistently left) leading to the first interior of Young Charlie's room give us sunny streets with no street games (Santa Rosa evidently has parks), an orderly town with a smiling, paternal policemen presiding over traffic and pedestrians.

In Catholic terms, this is the fallen world against a world of apparent prelapsarian innocence; but it is just as valid to interpret the images, as in *It's a Wonderful Life,* in terms of the two faces of American capitalism. Uncle Charlie has money (the fruits of his crimes and his aberrant sexuality) littered in disorder over table and floor; the Santa Rosa policeman has behind him the Bank of America. The detailed paralleling of uncle and niece can of course be read as comparison as much as contrast, and the opposition that of two sides of the same coin. The point is clearest in that crucial, profoundly disturbing scene where film noir erupts into Santa Rosa itself: the visit to the Til Two bar, where Young Charlie is confronted with her alter ego Louise the waitress, her former classmate. The scene equally invites Catholic and Marxist commentaries; its force arises from the revelation of the fallen world/ capitalist-corruption-and-deprivation at the heart of the American small town. The close juxtaposition of genres has implications that reach throughout the whole generic structure of the classical Hollywood cinema.

The subversion of ideology within the film is everywhere traceable to Hitchcock's presence, to the skepticism and nihilism that lurk just behind the jocular facade of his public image. His Catholicism is in reality the lingering on in his work of the darker aspects of Catholic mythology: hell without heaven. The traces are clear enough. Young Charlie wants a "miracle"; she thinks of her uncle as "the one who can save us" (and her mother immediately asks, "What do you mean, *save* us?"); when she finds his telegram, in the very act of sending hers, her reaction is an ecstatic "He heard me, he heard me!" Hitchcock cuts at once to a low-angle shot of Uncle Charlie's train rushing toward Santa Rosa, underlining the effect with an ominous crashing chord on the sound track.

Uncle Charlie is one of the supreme embodiments of the key Hitchcock figure: ambiguously devil and lost soul. When he reaches Santa Rosa, the image is blackened by its smoke. From his first appearance, Charlie is associated consistently with a cigar (its phallic connotations evident from the outset, in the scene with the landlady) and repeatedly shown with a wreath of smoke curling around his head (no one else in the film smokes except Joe, the displaced father, who has a paternal pipe, usually unlit). Several incidents (the escape from the policemen at the beginning, the garage door slammed as by remote control) invest him with a quasi-supernatural power. Rather than restrict the film to a Catholic reading, it seems logical to connect these marks with others: the thread of superstition that runs through the film (the number 13; the hat on the bed; "Sing at table and you'll marry a crazy husband"; the irrational dread of the utterance, however innocent, of the forbidden words "Merry Widow") and the telepathy motif (the telegrams, the tune "jumping from head to head")—the whole Hitchcockian sense of life at the mercy of terrible, unpredictable forces that have to be kept down.

The Hitchcockian dread of repressed forces is characteristically accompanied by a sense of the emptiness of the surface world that represses them, and this crucially affects the presentation of the American small-town family in *Shadow of a Doubt*. The warmth and togetherness, the mutual responsiveness and affection that Capra so beautifully creates in the Bailey families, senior and junior, of *It's a Wonderful Life* are here almost entirely lacking—and this despite the fact, in itself of great ideological interest, that the treatment of the family in *Shadow of a Doubt* has generally been perceived (even, one guesses, by Hitchcock himself) as affectionate.

The most striking characteristic of the Spencers is the separateness of each member; the recurring point of the celebrated overlapping dialogue is that no one ever listens to what anyone else is saying. Each is locked in a separate fantasy world: Emmy in the past, Joe in crime, Anne in books that are read apparently less for pleasure than as a means of amassing knowledge with which she has little emotional contact (though she also believes that everything she reads is "true"). The parents are trapped in a petty materialism (both respond to Young Charlie's dissatisfaction with the assumption that she's talking about money) and reliance on "honest toil" as the means of using up energies. In *Shadow of a Doubt* the ideological image of the small-town happy family becomes the flimsiest facade. That so many are nonetheless deceived by it testifies only to the strength of the ideology—one of whose functions is of course to inhibit the imagining of radical alternatives.

I have argued elsewhere that the key to Hitchcock's films is less suspense than sexuality (or, alternatively, that his "suspense" always carries a sexual charge in ways sometimes obvious, sometimes esoteric); and that sexual relationships in his work are inevitably based on power, the obsession with power and dread of impotence being as central to his method as to his thematic. In *Shadow of a Doubt* it is above all sexuality that cracks apart the family facade. As far as the Hays Code permitted, a double incest theme runs through the film: Uncle Charlie and Emmy, Uncle Charlie and Young Charlie. Necessarily, this is expressed through images and motifs, never becoming verbally explicit; certain of the images depend on a suppressed verbal play for their significance.

For the reunion of brother and sister, Hitchcock gives us an image (Emmy poised left of screen, arrested in mid-movement, Charlie right, under trees and sunshine) that iconographically evokes the reunion of lovers (Charlie wants to see Emmy again as she was when she was "the prettiest girl on the block"). And Emmy's breakdown, in front of her embarrassed friends and neighbors, at the news of Charlie's imminent departure is eloquent. As for uncle and niece, they are introduced symmetrically lying on beds, Uncle Charlie fondling his phallic cigar, Young Charlie, prone, hands behind head. When Uncle Charlie gets off the train he is bent over a stick, pretending to be ill; as soon as he sees Young Charlie, he "comes erect," flourishing the stick. One of his first actions on taking over her bedroom is to pluck a rose for his buttonhole ("deflowering"). More obviously, there is the business with the ring, which, as a symbolic token of engagement, not only links Charlie sexually with her uncle, but also links her, through its previous ownership, to his succession of merry widows. The film shows sexual pathology at the heart of the American family, the necessary product of its repressions and sublimations.

As for the "accident"—that old critical stumbling block—it presents no problem at all, provided one is ready to acknowledge the validity of a psychoanalytical reading of movies. Indeed, it provides a rather beautiful example of the way in which ideology, in seeking to impose itself, succeeds merely in confirming its own subversion. The "accident" (Charlie was "riding a bicycle" for the first time, which results in a "collision") can be read as an elementary Freudian metaphor for the trauma of premature sexual awakening (after which Charlie was "never the same again"). The smothering sexual/possessive devotion of a doting older sister may be left to provide a clue to the sexual motivation behind the merry-widow murders; Charlie isn't interested in money. Indeed, Emmy is connected to the merry widows by an associative chain in which important links are her own practical widowhood (her ineffectual husband is largely ignored), her ladies' club, and its leading light, Mrs. Potter, Uncle Charlie's potential next-in-line.

A fuller analysis would need to dwell on the limitations of Hitchcock's vision, nearer the nihilistic than the tragic; on his inability to conceive of repressed energies as other than evil and the surface world that represses them as other than shallow and unfulfilling. This explains why there can be no heaven corresponding to Hitchcock's hell, for every vision of heaven that is not merely negative is rooted in a concept of the liberation of the instincts, the resurrection of the body, which Hitchcock must always deny. But my final stress is less on the evaluation of a particular film or director than on the implications for a criticism of the Hollywood cinema of the notions of interaction and multiple determinacy I have been employing. Its roots in the Hollywood genres, and in the very ideological structure it so disturbingly subverts, make *Shadow of a Doubt* so much more suggestive and significant a work than Hitchcock the bourgeois entertainer could ever have guessed.

1977

JANE FEUER
THE SELF-REFLEXIVE MUSICAL AND THE MYTH OF ENTERTAINMENT

Within the musical film the most persistent subgenre has involved kids (or adults) "getting together and putting on a show." *The Jazz Singer* (Alan Crosland, 1927) featured a show-business story, and during the talkie boom that followed (1929–1930), a large percentage of the early musicals took for their subjects the world of entertainment: Broadway, vaudeville, the Ziegfeld Follies, burlesque, night clubs, the circus, Tin Pan Alley, and, to a lesser extent, mass entertainment media in the form of radio or Hollywood itself. Warner Brothers' *Forty-Second Street* (Lloyd Bacon, 1933) precipitated a second cycle of musicals. The *Forty-Second Street* spinoffs tended to feature a narrative strategy typical of the backstage musical: musical interludes, usually in the form of rehearsal sequences detailing the maturation of the show, would be interspersed with parallel dramatic scenes detailing maturation of the off-stage love affairs. Even a radio story such as *Twenty Million Sweethearts* (Ray Enright, 1934) took its narrative structure from this paradigm. Perhaps these "art" musicals fulfilled a need for verisimilitude; perhaps the audience felt more comfortable viewing musical numbers within the context of a show than seeing fairy-tale queens and princes suddenly feel a song coming on in the royal boudoir. Whatever the explanation of its origins, the backstage pattern was always central to the genre. Incorporated into the structure of the art musical was the very type of popular entertainment represented by the musical film itself. The art musical is thus a self-referential form.

All art musicals are self-referential in this loose sense. But given such an opportunity, some musicals have exhibited a greater degree of self-consciousness than others. *Dames* (Enright, 1934) climaxes its show-within-the-film with an apology for its own mode of entertainment, appropriately entitled "Dames." Moreover, the "Dames" number resolves a narrative in which the forces of Puritanism do battle with the forces of entertainment. It is the victory of what might be termed the "pru-

486

rient ethic" over the Puritan ethic that the final show celebrates within the film and that the "Dames" number celebrates within that show. In similar fashion, the Fred Astaire–Ginger Rogers cycle at RKO (1933–1939) began to reflect upon the legends created in its dancing stars.[1]

Shall We Dance (Mark Sandrich, 1937) culminates in a show merging popular dancing with ballet. Yet that merger consists not in an equal union but rather in the lending of youth, rhythm, and vitality to the stiff, formal, classical art of ballet. Once again, a musical film has affirmed its own value for the popular audience.

Dames and *Shall We Dance* are early examples of musicals that are *self-reflective* beyond their given self-referentiality. Historically, the art musical has evolved toward increasingly greater degrees of self-reflectivity. By the late forties and into the early fifties, a series of musicals produced by the Freed unit at MGM used the backstage format to present sustained reflections upon, and affirmations of, the musical genre itself. Three of these apologies for the musical (all scripted by Betty Comden and Adolph Green), *The Barkleys of Broadway* (Charles Walters, 1949), *Singin' in the Rain* (Stanley Donen and Gene Kelly, 1952), and *The Band Wagon* (Vincente Minnelli, 1953) involve contrasts between performances that fail to please audiences and performances that are immediately audience-pleasing.[2] Performances in these films are not restricted to onstage numbers. Multiple levels of performance and consequent multiple levels of audience combine to create a myth about musical entertainment permeating ordinary life. Through the work of these filmic texts all successful performances, both in art and in life, are condensed into the MGM musical.

To say that entertainment is "mythified" is to institute a triple play upon conventional meanings of the word "myth." Most simply, it means that entertainment is shown as having greater value than it actually does. In this sense musicals are ideological products; they are full of deceptions. As students of mythology have demonstrated, however, these deceptions are willingly suffered by the audience. In *American Vaudeville as Ritual,* Albert F. McLean attempts to explain this contradiction in his definition of myth as "a constellation of images and symbols, whether objectively real or imaginary, which brings focus and a degree of order to the psychic (largely unconscious) processes of a group or society and in so doing endows a magical potency upon the circumstances of persons involved."[3] McLean's notion of myth as "aura" occupies a pole opposite that of myth as "untruth" in constituting the myth of entertainment.

---

[1] See Leo Braudy, *The World in a Frame* (New York: Anchor Press/Doubleday, 1976), pp. 143–147, for a discussion of self-consciousness in *Shall We Dance.*

[2] *The Barkleys of Broadway* presents Josh and Dinah Barkley (Fred Astaire and Ginger Rogers) as the Lunts of musical comedy. Dinah leaves musical comedy to do a serious play ("Young Sarah"), and finally learns the lesson that there's no difference between serious acting and musical comedy acting. She returns to do a musical at the end of the film. *Singin' in the Rain* depicts the coming of sound to Hollywood. An early talkie that fails ("The Dueling Cavalier") is remade as a musical that succeeds ("The Dancing Cavalier"). *The Band Wagon* also involves a second production of a show that flops (a musical version of the Faust story called "The Band Wagon") into a musical revue that succeeds (again called "The Band Wagon").

[3] Albert F. McLean, *American Vaudeville as Ritual* (Lexington: University of Kentucky Press, 1965), p. 223.

According to Claude Lévi-Strauss, the seemingly random surface structure of a myth masks contradictions that are real and therefore unresolvable.[1] Art musicals are structurally similar to myths, seeking to mediate contradictions in the nature of popular entertainment. The myth of entertainment is constituted by an oscillation between demystification and remythicization.[2] Musicals, like myths, exhibit a stratified structure. The ostensible or surface function of these musicals is to give pleasure to the audience by revealing what goes on behind the scenes in the theater or Hollywood—that is, to demystify the production of entertainment. But the films remythicize at another level that which they set out to expose. Only unsuccessful performances are demystified. The musical desires an ultimate valorization of entertainment; to destroy the aura, reduce the illusion, would be to destroy the myth of entertainment as well.[3] For the purpose of analysis, the myth of entertainment can be subdivided into three categories: the myth of spontaneity, the myth of integration, and the myth of the audience. In the films, however, the myth makes its impact through combination and repetition. Thus, a single musical number can be highly overdetermined and may be discussed under all three categories.

THE MYTH OF SPONTANEITY

Perhaps the primary positive quality associated with musical performance is its spontaneous emergence out of a joyous and responsive attitude toward life. The musical buffs' parlor game that attempts to distinguish Fred Astaire's screen persona from Gene Kelly's ignores the overriding similarities in both dancers' spontaneous stances.[4] *The Barkleys of Broadway, Singin' in the Rain,* and *The Band Wagon* contrast the spontaneity of Astaire or Kelly with the prepackaged or calculated behavior of other performers.

In *Singin' in the Rain,* spontaneous talent distinguishes Don, Cosmo, and Kathy from Lina Lamont. Lina's laborious attempts to master basic English are followed by Don Lockwood's elocution lesson. Don and Cosmo seize upon the tongue-twister to turn the lesson into a spontaneous, anarchic dance routine, "Moses Supposes." Spontaneous self-expression through song and dance characterizes the three positive performers: Cosmo in "Make 'Em Laugh," Don in "Singin' in the Rain," and all three in "Good Mornin'," which evolves out of their collective solution to the problems of "The Dueling Cavalier."

---

[1] Claude Lévi-Strauss, "The Structural Study of Myth," in *Structural Anthropology* (New York: Basic Books, 1963), p. 220. I am also indebted to Lévi-Strauss for other ideas contained in the same essay: first, that a myth works itself out through repetition in a number of texts; second, that myth works through the mediation of binary oppositions.

[2] These terms are taken from Paul Ricoeur, *Freud and Philosophy* (New Haven: Yale University Press, 1970), p. 54. Ricoeur uses them to refer to two schools of hermeneutics that nevertheless constitute "a profound unity." I find them equally applicable to texts that seek to interpret themselves.

[3] The inseparability of demystification from its opposite (remythicization) is best illustrated by *A Star Is Born* (George Cukor, 1954), at once the last bearer of the studio's myth of entertainment and the first of the antimusicals. Even the supposedly Brechtian antimusical *Cabaret* (Bob Fosse, 1972) merely inverts the backstage paradigm while maintaining its narrative strategy.

[4] See Braudy, *The World in a Frame,* pp. 147–155, for a discussion of the function of spontaneity in the Astaire and Kelly personas.

In addition, the impression of spontaneity in these numbers stems from a type of *bricolage;* the performers make use of props at hand—curtains, movie paraphernalia, umbrellas, furniture—to create the imaginary world of the musical performance. This *bricolage,* a hallmark of the post–Gene Kelly MGM musical, creates yet another contradiction: an effect of spontaneous realism is achieved through simulation.

The Barkleys of Broadway opposes strained, artificial "serious" performances to spontaneous and natural musical comedy performances. Dinah Barkley's sparkling costume and demeanor in the title sequence with Astaire ("Swing Trot") contrasts with her subdued garb and sullen demeanor as a dramatic actress. Early in the film we see Dinah truncating her understudy's carefully calculated audition, doing a brief warm-up, and going into a perfectly executed rehearsal of a tap routine with her husband. The rehearsals of "Young Sarah" (a play about Sarah Bernhardt's *struggle* to become an actress) are quite the opposite. Josh (Astaire), the musical comedy director-performer, is always spontaneous and natural. In the parallel sequence to Dinah's labors over "Young Sarah," we see Josh doing a completed number from his new show. "Shoes with Wings On" presents musical comedy dancing as an involuntary response, like breathing. Dancing is so spontaneous for Josh that animated shoes pull him into performance. The Astaire character never changes; he is presented as an utterly seamless monument of naturalness and spontaneity. Others must adapt to his style. Dinah can succeed as a performer only in a musical setting with Josh. Even their offstage performances stem from a spontaneous responsiveness to ordinary life, as when their dance to "You'd Be Hard to Replace" evolves out of the natural movements of putting on robes.

Similar oppositions between spontaneous and canned performers structure *Singin' in the Rain* and *The Band Wagon.* Astaire's trademark, "reflex" dancing, has its counterpart in the "Gotta Dance" motif that informs Kelly's "Broadway Ballet," part of the ultimately successful film-within-the-film. *The Band Wagon* cuts from Tony Hunter's (Astaire's) spontaneous eruption into song and dance at the penny arcade to Jeffrey Cordova in *Oedipus Rex.* The moaning sounds in the background of this production are later associated with the reactions of an audience to Cordova's laborious musical version of *Faust.* We are shown Cordova from the point of view of Tony and the Martons in the wings (almost always a demystifying camera position), as he segues from his curtain calls as Oedipus into his offstage pomposity. Although Cordova's *Oedipus* is said to be successful with audiences in the film, the extent to which it is demystified for us undercuts its status as a successful show. Cordova is characterized throughout the first half of the film by the mechanical nature of his actions and utterances. He continually gives rehearsed speeches such as the one about Bill Shakespeare's immortal lines and Bill Robinson's immortal feet. On the first day of rehearsals, Cordova tells the cast exactly what will happen to them before the show opens. Not until he dances with Astaire (and in Astaire's style) in the top hat, white tie, and tails soft-shoe number in the second "Band Wagon" does Cordova achieve true spontaneity as a performer.

Almost every spontaneous performance in *The Band Wagon* has a matched segment that parodies the lack of spontaneity of the high art world. Tony drops Gaby while attempting a lift during the rehearsal of a ballet number for the first show;

later in "The Girl Hunt," a jazz ballet, he lifts her effortlessly. Tony and Gaby's relaxed offstage rehearsal of a dance to "You and the Night and the Music" literally explodes onstage at the dress rehearsal. A prepackaged orchestra rendition of "Something to Remember You By" at the official New Haven cast party dissolves into a vocal version of the same song spontaneously performed by the "kids" at the chorus party. Spontaneity thus emerges as the hallmark of a successful performance.

The myth of spontaneity operates through what we are shown of the work of production of the respective shows as well as how we are shown it. In *Singin' in the Rain,* we see the technical difficulties involved with filming and projecting "The Dueling Cavalier," including Lina's battle with the microphone and the failure of the film when its technological base is revealed to the preview audience. "The Dancing Cavalier," in contrast, springs to life effortlessly. The film shows an awareness of this opposition between the foregrounding of technology in "The Dueling Cavalier" and the invisibility of technology in "The Dancing Cavalier." "The Broadway Ballet" is presented in the context of an idea for a production number, and one of the biggest jokes in the film concerns the producer's inability to visualize what we have just been shown, elaborate and complete. Yet at many other points in *Singin' in the Rain* this awareness is masked, often in quite complex ways.* In "You Were Meant for Me" the exposure of the wind machine figures prominently in the demystification of romantic musical numbers. Yet in a dialogue scene outside the soundstage just prior to this number, Kathy's scarf had blown to the breeze of an invisible wind machine. Even after we are shown the tools of illusion at the beginning of the number, the camera arcs around and comes in for a tighter shot of the performing couple, thereby remasking the exposed technology and making the duet just another example of the type of number whose illusions it exposes. Demystification is countered by the reassertion of the spontaneous evolution of musical films. Perhaps the ultimate in spontaneous evolution of a musical number occurs in *The Barkleys of Broadway.* At the end of the film, the couple decides to do another musical. Josh describes a dance routine which, unlike "Young Sarah," will have *tempo,* and the couple goes into a dance, framed to the right of a curtain in their living room. As they spin, there is a dissolve to the same step as part of an elaborate production number in the new show.

In *The Band Wagon* the labor of producing the first show eclipses the performances. Never do we see a completed number from the first show. Technical or personal problems prevent the completion of every number shown in rehearsal, as when Tony walks out or when Cordova is levitated by the revolving stage. It is not because high art (ballet) and popular art (musical comedy) are inherently mutually exclusive that Cordova's show fails. After all, it is Tony's impressionist paintings that pay for the successful show. Rather, the film suggests that Cordova fails because he has been unable to render invisible the technology of production in order to

---

*See David Lusted, "Film as Industrial Product—Teaching a Reflexive Movie," *Screen Education* 16 (Autumn 1975): 26–30, for detailed examples of the mystification–demystification dynamic in *Singin' in the Rain.*

achieve the effect of effortlessness by which all entertainment succeeds in winning its audience.

Of course spontaneous performances that mask their technology have been calculated, too—not for audiences within the films but for audiences *of* the film. The musical, technically the most complex type of film produced in Hollywood, paradoxically has always been the genre that attempts to give the greatest illusion of spontaneity and effortlessness. It is as if engineering were to affirm *bricolage* as the ultimate approach to scientific thought. The self-reflective musical is aware of this in attempting to promulgate the myth of spontaneity. The heavily value-laden oppositions set up in the self-reflective films promote the mode of expression of the film musical itself as spontaneous and natural rather than calculated and technological. Musical entertainment thus takes on a natural relatedness to life processes and to the lives of its audiences. Musical entertainment claims for its own all natural and joyous performances in art and in life. The myth of spontaneity operates (to borrow Lévi-Strauss's terminology) to make musical performance, which is actually part of culture, appear to be part of nature.

THE MYTH OF INTEGRATION

Earlier musicals sometimes demonstrated ambiguous attitudes toward the world of musical theater, perceiving conflicts between success on the stage and success in the performers' personal lives. In *Ziegfeld Girl* (Robert C. Leonard, 1941), Lana Turner is destroyed when she forsakes the simple life in Brooklyn for the glamour of the Follies. In *Cain and Mabel* (Lloyd Bacon, 1936), Marion Davies has to be physically dragged onto the stage after deciding to retire to a garage in Jersey with prize-fighter beau Clark Gable. But the self-reflective musical asserts the integrative effect of musical performance. Successful performances are intimately bound up with success in love, with the integration of the individual into a community or a group, and even with the merger of high art with popular art.

In *Singin' in the Rain,* the success of the musical film brings about the final union of Don and Kathy. This consummation takes place on the stage at the premiere in front of a live audience and in the form of a duet. The music is carried over to a shot of the lovers embracing in front of a billboard of Don and Kathy's images. But the successful show on the billboard is no longer "The Dancing Cavalier"; it is *Singin' in the Rain,* that is, the film itself. This hall-of-mirrors effect emphasizes the unity-giving function of the musical both for the couples and audiences *in* the film and for the audience *of* the film. In *The Barkleys of Broadway,* Josh and Dinah are reunited when she realizes she wants "nothing but fun set to music," that is, the type of performance associated with the MGM musical. Gaby, in *The Band Wagon,* learns the value of popular entertainment as she learns to love Tony. "Dancing in the Dark" imitates the form of a sexual act as it merges two kinds of dancing previously set in conflict. The number combines the ballet movements associated with Gaby and her choreographer beau Paul Byrd with the ballroom dancing associated with Astaire. At the end of the film the long run of their successful show is used by Gaby as a metaphor for her relationship with Tony.

The right kind of musical performance also integrates the individual into a unified group just as the wrong kind alienates. *The Band Wagon* traces Tony's repeated movements from isolation to the joy of being part of a group. At the beginning of the film, Tony sings "By Myself" isolated by the tracking camera; as he enters the crowded terminal, the camera stops moving to frame him against the crowd, a mass that becomes an audience for Tony's antics with the Martons. The arcade sequence repeats this opening movement. Once again Tony overcomes his sense of isolation by reestablishing contact with an audience through spontaneous musical performance. The "?" machine at the arcade symbolizes the problem/solution format of the narrative. When Tony answers the question of how to make a comeback by dancing with a shoeshine man, the machine bursts open and his audience rushes to congratulate him. Another such movement occurs when, after the failure of the first show, Tony finds himself the only guest at the official cast party. "I Love Louisa" marks his renewal of contact with yet another audience—this time the common folk of the theater itself. At the end of the film, Tony moves from a reprise of "By Myself" into the final integration—a symbolic marriage to Gaby and to the rank and file of the theater. The myth of integration makes itself felt through the repetitive structure of the film.

Paralleling Tony's movement from isolation to integration and also paralleling the integration of the couple is Gaby's integration into the populist world of musical theater from the elitist world of high art. We first see Gaby in a ballet performance in which she functions as prima ballerina backed by the corps. At Cordova's, the two worlds are spatially isolated as the representatives of high art (Gabrielle and Paul) and those of popular art (Tony and the Martons) occupy separate rooms. The possibility of movement between the two worlds is stressed by the precisely parallel actions taking place in each room as well as by Cordova's role as mediator between the two rooms (worlds). Cordova prevents a terminal clash between Tony and Gaby by rushing into the neutral space of the front hall and drawing the representatives of both worlds back into his own central space.

Gabrielle begins her integration into the world of popular art through a renewal of contact with the common folk in Central Park, a process which culminates in "I Love Louisa" with Gaby serving as part of the chorus. Paul Byrd draws Gaby away from the group into an isolated space symbolic of the old world of ballet; the camera frames the couple apart from the mass. The colors of their isolated space—subdued shades of brown and white—contrast with the vibrant colors of the chorus's costumes, which have just filled the frame. In leaving this isolated space to return to the group, Gaby has taken the side of the collective effort that will produce the successful musical. "New Sun in the Sky," the first number in the new show, again finds Gaby backed up by a chorus, but this time the mood is celebratory—the bright golds and reds as well as the lyrics of the song emphasize Gaby's rebirth. Even the musical arrangement of the song, upbeat and jazzy, contrasts with the more sedate balletic arrangement we heard in that rehearsal for the Faustian *Band Wagon* in which Tony dropped Gaby. At the end of the film, Gaby expresses her feelings for Tony by speaking for the group, the chorus framed in back of her as she speaks.

Everyone knows that the musical film was a mass art produced by a tiny elite for a vast and amorphous consuming public; the self-reflective musical attempts to overcome this division through the myth of integration. It offers a vision of musical performance originating in the folk, generating love and a cooperative spirit that includes everyone in its grasp and that can conquer all obstacles. By promoting audience identification with the collectively produced shows, the myth of integration seeks to give the audience a sense of participation in the creation of the film itself. The musical film becomes a mass art that aspires to the condition of a folk art—produced and consumed by the same integrated community.

THE MYTH OF THE AUDIENCE

It follows that successful performances will be those in which the performer is sensitive to the needs of the audience and which give the audience a sense of participation in the performance. Josh Barkley berates Dinah for her participation in the performance in the subway scene because "the audience wants to cry there and you won't let them." Cordova is more concerned with the revolving stage than with delivering audience-pleasing performances; his canned speeches of solidarity with the cast are undercut by his delivering them with his back to the group, oblivious to their response. Tony Hunter, on the other hand, is willing to leave the self-enclosed world of the theater to regain contact with the folk who make up his audience. "Dancing in the Dark" is precipitated by observing ordinary people dancing in Central Park.

The insensitive performer also attempts to manipulate the audience. Cordova wants to control the timing of the curtain, the actress's exit pace, and the placing of an amber spot in *Oedipus*. Lina Lamont masks the fact that she is unable to speak for herself either onstage or onscreen.

Yet while setting up an association between success and lack of audience manipulation, the musicals themselves exert continuous control over the responses of their audiences. The film musical profits rhetorically by displacing to the theater the myth of a privileged relationship between musical entertainment and its audience. Popular theater can achieve a fluidity and immediacy in this respect that the film medium lacks. The out-of-town tryout, the interpolation of new material after each performance, the instantaneous modulation of performer-to-audience response—none of these common theatrical practices is possible for film. Hollywood had only the limited adaptations made possible by the preview system and the genre system itself, which accommodated audience response by making (or not making) other films of the same type. The backstage musical, however, manages to incorporate the immediate performer-audience relationship into films, thus gaining all the advantages of both media. Musical numbers can be shot from the point of view of a front-row theatrical spectator and then move into filmic space—combining the immediate contact of the theater with the mobility of perspective of the camera. Numbers that begin within theatrical space merge, often quite imperceptibly, into filmic space. Extended musical sequences such as "Shoes with Wings On" and "The Girl-Hunt Ballet" start within a proscenium frame and then become fully edited filmic sequences, in a tradition stemming from the early Berkeley musicals.

The Band Wagon uses this double perspective to manipulate the film audience's point of view. In "That's Entertainment," Cordova and the Martons try to convince Tony that all successful art is entertainment. The number takes place on the stage of an empty theater with the first refrain of the song shot from camera positions that approximate the point of view of a spectator *on* the stage (angles available only to the cinema). Midway through the number, at the point where Tony is convinced, the action shifts to the performing area of the stage and the point of view shifts to that of a spectator in the theater. The film audience sees, from the point of view of a theater audience, the number performed in the empty theater becoming a direct address to the film's audience. The effort to convince Tony has become an effort to convince *us*. In the reprise of "That's Entertainment" at the film's finale, the point of view shifts from over-the-shoulder shots to frame the performers directly in front of the camera as they ask us to celebrate once again the merging of all art into entertainment, this time in the form of the film *The Band Wagon* itself (an effect quite like that of the billboard at the end of *Singin' in the Rain*). "Make 'Em Laugh" is much more subtle in shifting point of view. Starting from a subjective shot over Don's shoulder, the number begins as an affirmation of the value of entertainment as Cosmo attempts to cheer up his friend; however, the point of view quickly shifts so that the message is addressed to the film's audience. We quickly lose track of Don's point of view, and the number never returns to it.

The use of theatrical audiences *in* the films provides a point of identification for audiences *of* the film. Even *Singin' in the Rain* emphasizes the responses of live audiences at previews and premieres. Although inserted shots of applauding audiences can be used as a trick similar to television's use of canned laughter, self-reflective musicals tend to use audiences within the film more subtly. In *The Barkleys of Broadway,* Astaire and Rogers dance "Swing Trot," a routine designed to arouse nostalgia for the famous team, under the film's titles. At the end of the number there is a cut to a side angle, and we see the couple taking a bow before a live audience. The audience in the film is there to express the adulation the number itself sought to arouse from the film's audience.

MGM musicals make use of natural, spontaneous audiences that form around offstage performances.* "Shine on Your Shoes" in *The Band Wagon* demonstrates Astaire's ability to adapt his dancing to any occasion and any audience as well. In "I Love Louisa" the chorus serves first as an audience for Tony and the Martons' clowning, and then participates in the dance, providing a vicarious sense of participation for the film audience. Audiences in the films suggest a contagious spirit inherent in musical performance, related to the suggestion that the MGM musical is folk art; the audience must be shown as participating in the production of entertainment.

Intertextuality and star iconography can be a means of manipulating audience

---

*Other good examples of "natural audiences" in the MGM musical include "By Strauss," "I Got Rhythm," and "'S Wonderful" in *An American in Paris* (Minnelli, 1951); "Nina" in *The Pirate* (Minnelli, 1948); and "I Like Myself," Gene Kelly's dance on roller skates in *It's Always Fair Weather* (Kelly, 1955). The history of this device in the musical film may be traced from Jolson to Chevalier to Astaire to Kelly and back to Astaire, spontaneity of performance providing the link among the major male musical stars.

response. Many of the later MGM musicals play upon the audience's memories of earlier musicals. *The Barkleys of Broadway* plays on the Astaire-Rogers legend from its first shot of the couple's feet, which echoes the title sequence of *Top Hat* (Sandrich, 1935). The couple's reunion performance to "You Can't Take That Away from Me" harks back to *Shall We Dance,* with the dance itself reminiscent of one of their old routines. Such attempts to evoke nostalgia play on the star system's desire to erase the boundaries between star persona and character, between onscreen and offscreen personalities. *The Barkleys of Broadway* thus celebrates the return of Ginger Rogers to musical comedy after a series of straight dramatic films, suggesting that the only way she can succeed with an audience is by dancing with Astaire in musicals.*

Other self-reflective musicals make use of audience response to songs from previous stage musicals or films. Most of the songs in *Singin' in the Rain* were written for the earliest MGM film musicals. *The Band Wagon* takes its music from stage reviews of the same period, the late twenties to early thirties. In the interim many of these songs had become standards, and the films were able to play upon the audience's familiarity with the lyric. "Dancing in the Dark," for example, is used only in instrumental arrangement, thus inviting the audience to participate by supplying the lyric. Two related practices of the Freed unit—biopics fashioned around a composer's hit songs and the purchase of a song catalog around which to construct an original musical—depended upon audience familiarity (through both filmic and nonfilmic intertexts) for their effectiveness.

CONCLUSION

Self-reflective musicals mediate a contradiction between live performance in the theater and the frozen form of cinema by implying that the MGM musical *is* theater, possessing the same immediate and active relationship to its audience. Both the myth of integration and the myth of the audience suggest that the MGM musical is really a folk art, that the audience participates in the creation of musical entertainment. The myth of integration suggests that the achievement of personal fulfillment goes hand in hand with the enjoyment of entertainment. And the myth of spontaneity suggests that the MGM musical is not artificial but rather completely natural. Performance is no longer defined as something professionals do on stage; instead, it permeates the lives of professional and nonprofessional singers and dancers. Entertainment, the myth implies, can break down the barriers between art and life.

The myth of entertainment, in its entirety, cannot be celebrated in a single text or even across three texts. Different aspects of the myth achieve prominence in different films, but the myth is carried by the genre as a whole. The notion of breaking down barriers between art and life, for example, is more prominent in Vincente

---

*The extreme example of this phenomenon is *A Star is Born,* the signification of which depends upon the audience's knowledge of Judy Garland's offscreen life as the negation of her MGM onscreen image.

Minnelli's *The Pirate* than in any of the films discussed here. It might be said that the elements of the myth of entertainment constitute a paradigm that generates the syntax of individual texts.

Ultimately, one might wonder why these films go to such lengths to justify the notion that all life should aspire to the conditions of a musical performance. That is, why expend so much effort to celebrate mythic elements the audience is likely to accept anyway? Answering this question involves an awareness both of the function of ritual and of the ritual function of the musical. All ritual involves the celebration of shared values and beliefs; the ritual function of the musical is to reaffirm and articulate the place that entertainment occupies in its audience's psychic lives. Self-reflective musicals are then able to celebrate myths created by the genre as a whole.

Yet the extremes of affirmation in *The Band Wagon* need further justification in terms of its function for MGM as well as for the popular audience. At a time when the studio could no longer be certain of the allegiance of its traditional mass audience, *The Band Wagon,* in ritual fashion, served to reaffirm the traditional relationship. For the musical was always the quintessential Hollywood product: all Hollywood films manipulated audience response, but the musical could incorporate that response into the film itself; all Hollywood films sought to be entertaining, but the musical could incorporate a myth of entertainment into its aesthetic discourse. As Thomas Elsaesser says, "The world of the musical becomes a kind of ideal image of the [film] medium itself."*

Nowhere is Lévi-Strauss's notion of myth more applicable to the musical than in the relationship of the genre to the studio system that produced it. Faced with declining attendance due to competition from television, the studio could suggest, through *Singin' in the Rain,* that making musicals can provide a solution to any crisis of technological change. Faced with charges of infantilism from the citadels of high art, the studio could suggest, through *The Barkleys of Broadway,* that all successful performances are musical performances. Faced with the threat of changing patterns of audience consumption, the studio could suggest, through *The Band Wagon,* that the MGM musical can adapt to any audience. *The Band Wagon* ends where *That's Entertainment* (Jack Haley, Jr., 1974) and *That's Entertainment, Part 2* (Gene Kelly, 1976) commence, in an attempt to recapture the aura of the "Golden Age" of the Freed/MGM musicals. It is not surprising that the "That's Entertainment" number from *The Band Wagon* should have been inserted into the contemporary sequences of the nostalgia compilations. For the ending of *The Band Wagon* already marked the genre's celebration of its own (and Hollywood's) economic death and ritual rebirth.

Self-reflectivity as a critical category has been associated with films, such as those of Godard, which call attention to the codes constituting their own signifying practices. The term has been applied to aesthetically or politically radical films that react against so-called classical narrative cinema by interrogating their own narrativity. Thus we tend to associate reflexivity with the notion of deconstruction within film-

---

*Thomas Elsaesser, "The American Musical," *Brighton Film Review* 15 (December 1969): 13.

making practice. The MGM musical, however, uses reflexivity to perpetuate rather than to deconstruct the codes of the genre. Self-reflective musicals are conservative texts in every sense. MGM musicals have continued to function both in the popular consciousness and within international film culture as representatives of the Hollywood product at its best. I hope to have shown that this was the very task these texts sought to accomplish.

1977

JOHN G. CAWELTI
CHINATOWN AND GENERIC TRANSFORMATION IN RECENT AMERICAN FILMS

One of the fascinating things about Roman Polanski's *Chinatown* is that it invokes in so many ways the American popular genre of the hard-boiled detective story. Most of us, I suppose, associate this tradition particularly with two films, both of which starred Humphrey Bogart: John Huston's *The Maltese Falcon* (1941) and Howard Hawks' *The Big Sleep* (1946). But these are only the two most-remembered and perhaps the most memorable versions of a narrative formula which has been replicated in hundreds of novels, films, and television programs. Next to the western, the hard-boiled detective story is America's most distinctive contribution to the world's stock of action-adventure stories, our contemporaneous embodiment of the drama of heroic quest which has appeared in so many different cultures in so many different guises. Unlike the western—heroic quest on the frontier—which can perhaps be traced back as far as the Indian captivity narratives of the late seventeenth century, and certainly to Cooper's Leatherstocking saga of the early nineteenth century, the hard-boiled detective story is of quite recent origin. It developed in the twenties through the medium of short action stories in pulp magazines like the famous *Black Mask*. By 1929, Dashiell Hammett had produced in *Red Harvest* the first hard-boiled detective novel. Before retiring into literary silence in the mid-thirties, Hammett had created a basic core of hard-boiled adventure in his Continental Op stories and his novels—*The Maltese Falcon* (1930), *The Dain Curse* (1929), *The Glass Key* (1931) and *The Thin Man* (1934). In very short order, the hard-boiled detective made the transition from novel to film. *The Maltese Falcon* appeared in two film versions in the early 30s, before John Huston made the definitive version in 1941. *The Glass Key* was produced in the early 30s and in the 40s; *The Thin Man* became one of the great movie successes of the later 30s, so popular that it led to a number of invented sequels. And while the hard-boiled

498

detective flourished in film, Hammett's example was followed in novels by writers whose literary approach ranged from the subtlety and depth of Raymond Chandler and Ross Macdonald to the sensational—and bestselling—crudity of Mickey Spillane. Radio and television, too, made many series based on the figure of the hard-boiled detective and his quest for justice through the ambiguous landscape of the modern American city. If a myth can be defined as a pattern of narrative known throughout the culture and presented in many different versions by many different tellers, then the hard-boiled detective story is in that sense an important American myth.

Chinatown invokes this myth in many different ways. Its setting in Los Angeles in the 1930s is very much the archetypal "hard-boiled" setting, the place and time of Hammett's and Chandler's novels. While it is true that many hard-boiled novels and films are set in different places and times—Mickey Spillane's Mike Hammer stories in New York City, John D. Macdonald's Travis McGee saga in Florida— the California city setting of Hammett and Chandler and the approximate time of their stories, memorialized in the period furnishings, visual icons, and style of the great hard-boiled films of the 1940s, have become for us the look and the temporal-spatial aura of the hard-boiled myth. It is this aura which Polanski generates, though there is something not quite right, something disturbingly off about it. In this case, it is the color. The world of the hard-boiled myth is preeminently a world of black and white. Its ambience is that compound of angular light and shadow enmeshed in webs of fog which grew out of the visual legacy of German expressionism in drama and film, transformed into what is now usually called *film noir* by its adjustment to American locales and stories. Polanski carefully controls his spectrum of hue and tone in order to give it the feel of *film noir,* but it is nonetheless color with occasional moments of rich golden light—as in the scene in the dry riverbed. These moments of warm color often relate to scenes that are outside the usual setting or thematic content—for example, scenes in the natural landscape outside the city— which are themselves generally outside the world of the hard-boiled detective story. The invocation of many other traditional elements of the hard-boiled myth, the *film noir* tone and the 1930s setting cue us to expect the traditional mythical world of the private eye hero. But the presence of color, along with increasing deviations from established patterns of plot, motive and character give us an eerie feeling of one myth colliding with and beginning to give way to others.

Let us begin by examining *Chinatown*'s relation to the traditional myth of the hard-boiled detective. The established narrative formula of the hard-boiled story has as its protagonist a private investigator who occupies a marginal position with respect to the official social institutions of criminal justice. The private eye is licensed by the state, but though he may be a former member of a police force or district attorney's staff, he is not now connected with such an organization. In the course of the story, he is very likely to come into conflict with representatives of the official machinery, though he may also have friends who are police officers. His position on the edge of the law is very important, because one of the central themes of the hard-boiled myth is the ambiguity between institutionalized law enforcement and true justice. The story shows us that the police and the courts are incapable of effectively protecting the innocent and bringing the guilty to appropriate justice.

Only the individual of integrity who exists on the margins of society can solve the crime and bring about a true justice.

The marginal character of the private eye hero is thus crucial to his role in the myth. It is also central to his characterization. We see him not only as a figure outside the institutionalized process of law enforcement, but as the paradoxical combination of a man of character who is also a failure. The private eye is a relatively poor man who operates out of a seedy office and never seems to make very much money by his exploits; he is the most marginal sort of lower-middle class quasi-professional. Yet unlike the usual stereotype of this social class, he is a man of honor and integrity who cannot be made to give up his quest for true justice. He is a compelling American hero type, clearly related to the traditional western hero who manifests many of the same characteristics and conditions of marginality.

The story begins when the hard-boiled hero is given a mission by a client. It is typical that this initial mission is a deceptive one. Either the client is lying, as Brigid O'Shaughnessy lies to Sam Spade in *The Maltese Falcon,* or the client has himself been deceived and does not understand what is really at stake when he gives the detective his case, as with General Sternwood in *The Big Sleep.* Often the detective is being used as a pawn in some larger plot of the client's. Whatever his initial impetus to action, the detective soon finds himself enmeshed in a very complex conspiracy involving a number of people from different spheres of society. The ratiocinative English detective in authors like Dorothy Sayers, Agatha Christie, or Ngaio Marsh, investigates crimes by examining clues, questioning witnesses and then using his intellectual powers of insight and deduction to arrive at the solution. The hard-boiled detective investigates through movement and encounter; he collides with the web of conspiracy until he has exposed its outlines. The crime solved by the ratiocinative detective is usually that of a single individual. With this individual's means and motives for the criminal act rationally established he can be turned over to the law for prosecution. But the hard-boiled detective encounters a linked series of criminal acts and responsibilities; he discovers not a single guilty individual, but a corrupt society in which wealthy and respectable people are linked with gangsters and crooked politicians. Because it is society and not just a single individual which is corrupt, the official machinery of law enforcement is unable to bring the guilty to justice. The hard-boiled detective must decide for himself what kind of justice can be accomplished in the ambiguous urban world of modern America, and he must, in many instances, undertake to see this justice through, himself. There have always been two different tendencies within the hard-boiled myth. Some writers, like Mickey Spillane and his many current followers, place their emphasis on the hero as private vigilante avenger. Their stories climax with the hero playing the role of executioner as well as detective and judge. More complex and artistic writers, like Hammett, Chandler and Ross Macdonald, develop instead the theme of the hero's own relationship to the mythical role of lawman-outside-the-law. Their versions of the story rarely end with the detective's execution of the criminal; they prefer instead either to arrange for the criminal's self-destruction as in Chandler's *Farewell, My Lovely,* or simply to bring about the criminal's exposure and confession, as in *The Maltese Falcon.* But this latter trend, though it has produced greater literature, is perhaps best understood as a humane avoidance of the true thrust of the myth which is, I think, essentially toward the marginal hero becoming righteous judge and executioner, culture-hero for a society which has profoundly ambiguous conflicts in choosing between its commitment to legality and its belief that only individual actions are ultimately moral and just.

One further element of the hard-boiled myth needs to be particularly noted: the role of the feminine antagonist. In almost every case, the hard-boiled hero encounters a beautiful and dangerous woman in the course of his investigations and he finds himself very much drawn toward her, even to the point of falling in love. Sometimes the woman is his client, sometimes a figure in the conspiracy. In a surprising number of cases (*The Maltese Falcon, The Big Sleep, Farewell, My Lovely, I, The Jury,* and many others) the woman turns out to be the murderess, and, in Spillane at least, is killed by her detective-lover. This murky treatment of the "romance" between detective and dangerous female is occasionally resolved happily as in the Bogart-Bacall relationship at the end of the film version of *The Big Sleep* (in the novel this romantic culmination does not take place). However, such an outcome is rare. Even if the beautiful woman does not turn out to be a murderess, the detective usually separates from her at the end to return to his marginal situation, basically unchanged by what has happened to him and ready to perform more acts of justice when the occasion arises.

We can see from this brief resumé of the hard-boiled formula how close a resemblance *Chinatown* bears to it. But the film deviates increasingly from the myth until, by the end of the story, the film arrives at an ending almost contrary to that of the myth. Instead of bringing justice to a corrupt society, the detective's actions leave the basic source of corruption untouched. Instead of protecting the innocent, his investigation leads to the death of one victim and the deeper moral destruction of another. Instead of surmounting the web of conspiracy with honor and integrity intact, the detective is overwhelmed by what has happened to him.

True, the action of *Chinatown* increasingly departs from the traditional hard-boiled formula as the story progresses; however, there are, from the very beginning, a number of significant departures from the standard pattern. The choice of Jack Nicholson and Faye Dunaway as leading actors is a good instance of this. Nicholson and Dunaway have certain physical and stylistic resemblances to Bogart and Bacall and these are obviously played up through costume, makeup and gesture. Indeed, there is one early scene in a restaurant between them which is almost eerily reminiscent of the famous horse-racing interchange between Bogart and Bacall in *The Big Sleep*. But much as they echo the archetypal hard-boiled duo in a superficial way, Nicholson and Dunaway play characters which are very different. Dunaway has a neurotic fragility, an underlying quality of desperation which becomes even more apparent as her true situation is revealed. She never generates the sense of independence and courage that Bacall brought to her hard-boiled roles; her qualities of wit and sophistication—those characteristics which made Bacall such an appropriate romantic partner for the hard-boiled detective—are quickly seen to be a veneer covering depths of anguish and ambiguity. Nicholson also portrays, at least early on, a character who is not quite what he seems. His attempt to be the tough, cynical, and humorous private eye is undercut on all sides; he is terribly inept as a wit, as his attempt to tell his assistants the Chinese joke makes clear. Nor is he the tough, marginal man of professional honor he pretends to be at the beginning; actually, he is a successful small businessman who has made a good thing out of exploiting the more sordid needs of his fellowmen. One of the most deeply symbolic clichés of the traditional hard-boiled formula is the hero's refusal to do divorce business, in fact one of the primary functions of the private detective. By this choice the traditional private-eye of the myth established both his personal sense of honor and his transcendent vocation, distinguishing himself from the typical private investigator. However, from the beginning of *Chinatown,* it is clear that the accumulation of evidence of marital infidelity is Jake Gittes' primary business. He is, indeed, drawn into the affairs of Noah Cross, his daughter, and her husband by a commission to document a supposedly clandestine affair between the latter and a much younger woman. The name, J. J. Gittes, which Polanski and Robert Towne, the screenwriter, chose for their protagonist is a good indication of this aspect of his character. Think of the names of the traditional hard-boiled detectives: Sam Spade, with its implication of hardness and digging beneath the surface; Philip Marlowe with its aura of knightliness and chivalry; Lew Archer with its mythical overtones. Gittes, or "Gits" as Noah Cross ironically keeps pronouncing it, connotes selfishness and grasping and has, in addition, a kind of ethnic echo very different from the pure Anglo of Spade, Marlowe and Archer.

Yet, qualified and even "anti-heroic" as he is, Gittes is swept up into the traditional hard-boiled action. His initial and deceptive charge involves him in the investigation of a murder, which in turn leads him to evidence of a large-scale conspiracy involving big business, politics, crime and the whole underlying social and environmental structure of Los Angeles. Like the traditional hard-boiled detective, Gittes begins as a marginal individual, but gradually finds himself becoming a moral agent with a mission. At the same time he becomes romantically involved with a character deeply implicated in the web of conspiracy, the mysterious widow of the man who has been murdered. By the middle of the film Gittes is determined to expose the political conspiracy which he senses beneath the surface, and also to resolve the question of the guilt or innocence of the woman to whom he has been so strongly attracted. Thus far, the situation closely resembles that of *The Maltese Falcon* and *The Big Sleep.* It is at this point, however, that the action again takes a vast departure from that of the traditional hard-boiled story. Instead of demonstrating his ability to expose and punish the guilty, Gittes steadily finds himself confronting a depth of evil and chaos so great that he is unable to control it. In relation to the social and personal depravity represented by Noah Cross and the world in which he can so successfully operate, the toughness, moral concern, and professional skill of Gittes not only seem ineffectual, but lead to ends that are the very opposite of those intended. At the end of the film, Noah Cross is free to continue his rapacious depredations on the land, the city and the body of his own daughter-granddaughter; and the one person who might have effectively brought Cross to some form of justice—his daughter-mistress—has been destroyed. Gittes' confrontation with a depth of depravity beyond the capacity of the hard-boiled ethos of individualistic justice is, I think, the essential significance of the Chinatown motif in the film. Chinatown becomes a symbol of life's deeper moral enigmas, those unintended consequences of action that are past understanding and control. Gittes has been there before. In another case his attempts at individual moral action had led to the death of a woman he cared for. It is apparently this tragedy that motivated him to leave the police force and set up as a private investigator. Now he has been drawn back into moral action, and it is again, in Chinatown, that his attempt to live out the myth of individualistic justice collides with the power of evil and chance in the world. The result is not heroic confrontation and the triumph of justice, but tragic catastrophe and the destruction of the innocent.

Chinatown places the hard-boiled detective story within a view of the world that is deeper and more catastrophic, more enigmatic in its evil, more sudden and inexplicable in its outbreaks of violent chance. In the end, the image of heroic, moral action embedded in the traditional private-eye myth turns out to be totally inadequate to overcome the destructive realities revealed in the course of this story. This revelation of depths beneath depths is made increasingly evident in the film's relentless movement toward Chinatown, the symbolic locus of darkness, strangeness and catastrophe; but it also appears in the film's manipulation of action and image. The themes of water and drought, which weave through the action, not only reveal the scope of Noah Cross's conspiracy to dominate a city by manipulating its water supply, but create a texture of allusion which resonates with the mythical meanings traditionally associated with water and drought. Polanski's version of Los Angeles in the 1930s reveals the transcendent mythical world of the sterile kingdom, the dying king and the drowned man beneath it—the world, for example, of Eliot's *Wasteland* and before that of the cyclical myths of traditional cultures. Another of the film's motifs, its revelation of the rape-incest by which Noah Cross has fathered a daughter on his own daughter and is apparently intending to continue this method of establishing a progeny through the agency of his daughter-granddaughter, is another of the ways in which the hard-boiled myth is thrust into depths beyond itself. Though traditionally an erotically potent figure, the private eye's sexuality seems gentility itself when confronted with the potent perversity embodied in the figure of Noah Cross. Cross is reminiscent of the primal father imagined by Freud in *Totem and Taboo,* but against his overpowering sexual, political and economic power, our hero-Oedipus in the form of J. J. Gittes proves to be tragically impotent, an impotence symbolized earlier in the film by the slashing of his nose and the large comic bandage he wears throughout much of the action.

In its manipulation of a traditional American popular myth and the revelation of the tragic inadequacy of this myth when it collides with a universe that is deeper and more enigmatic in its evil and destructive force, *Chinatown* is one of the richest and most artistically powerful instances of a type of film of which we have seen many striking instances in the last decade. It is difficult to know just what to call this type of film. On one level, it relates to the traditional literary mode of burlesque or parody in which a well-established set of conventions or a style is subjected to some form of ironic or humorous exploitation. Indeed, many of the most striking and successful films of the period have been out and out burlesques of traditional popular genres such as Mel Brooks' *Blazing Saddles* (westerns), *Young Frankenstein* (the Frankenstein horror cycle), and *High Anxiety* (Hitchcock's psychological suspense films). However, burlesque and parody embody a basically humorous thrust, and many of the most powerful generic variations of the last decade or so—

films like *Bonnie and Clyde, The Wild Bunch, The Godfather* and *Nashville*—tend more toward tragedy than comedy in their overall structures. It seem odd to speak of a tragic parody or a doomed burlesque. Therefore, one is at first tempted to conclude that the connection between *Blazing Saddles* and *The Wild Bunch,* or *The Black Bird* and *The Long Goodbye* is only superficial. Yet it is clear that in many of these films the line between comedy and tragedy is not so simply drawn. What, for example, of the extraordinary combination of Keystone Cops chase scenes and tragic carnage in *Bonnie and Clyde,* or the interweaving of sophomoric high jinks and terrible violence in Altman's *MASH?* This puzzling combination of humorous burlesque and high seriousness seems to be a mode of expression characteristic of our period, not only in film, but in other literary forms. It is at the root of much that is commonly described as the literature of the absurd, or of so-called "Black humor," and is, as well, characteristic of the style of major contemporary novelists like Thomas Pynchon. By adopting this mode, American movies have, in a sense, become a more integral part of the mainstream of postmodernist literature, just as, through their frequent allusion to the narrative conventions of American film, contemporary novelists and dramatists have created a new kind of relationship between themselves and the traditions of popular culture.

The linkage between these many different kinds of contemporary literary, dramatic and cinematic expression is their use of the conventions of traditional popular genres. Basically, they do in different ways what Polanski does in *Chinatown:* set the elements of a conventional popular genre in an altered context, thereby making us perceive these traditional forms and images in a new way. It appears to me that we can classify the various relationships between traditional generic elements and altered contexts into four major modes.

First, there is the burlesque proper. In this mode, elements of a conventional formula or style are situated in contexts so incongruous or exaggerated that the result is laughter. There are many different ways in which this can be done. The formulaic elements can be acted out in so extreme a fashion that they come into conflict with our sense of reality forcing us to see these aspects of plot and character as fantastic contrivances. A good example of this is the burlesque image of the gunfighter in *Cat Ballou.* In this film we are shown how, by putting on his gunfighter costume, a process that involves strapping himself into a corset within which he can barely move, an old drunk can become the terror of the bad guys. Or, in a closely related type of altered context, a situation that we are ordinarily accustomed to seeing in rather romanticized terms can be suddenly invested with a sense of reality. This is how the famous campfire scene in *Blazing Saddles* operates. The cowboys sit around a blazing campfire at night, a scene in which we are accustomed to hearing mournful and lyrical cowboy ballads performed by such groups as the Sons of the Pioneers. Instead we are treated to an escalating barrage of flatulence. Anyone who knows the usual effect of canned wilderness fare is likely to be delighted at this sudden exposure of the sham involved in the traditional western campfire scene. Sam Peckinpah's *Ride the High Country* offers another instance of the humorous effect of a sudden penetration of reality into a fantasy when one of his aging heroes attempts to spring gracefully into the saddle and is suddenly halted by a twinge of rheumatism.

Roy Jenson and John Huston threaten Jack Nicholson in a scene from *Chinatown* (1974) that is "outside the usual setting or thematic content—for example, scenes in the natural landscape outside the city—which are themselves outside the world of the hardboiled detective story." (CAWELTI, page 499). The Sheriff (Cleavon Little) encounters the Count Basie band on the prairie in *Blazing Saddles* (1972). "Many of the most striking and successful films of the period have been out and out burlesques of traditional popular genres such as Mel Brooks' *Blazing Saddles* . . ." (CAWELTI, page 503).

In addition to these sudden confrontations with "reality" conventional patterns can be turned into laughter by inverting them. A good example of this is the device of turning a character who shows all the marks of a hero into a coward, or vice versa. A favorite manifestation of this in recent films and novels is what might be called the hard-boiled schlemiehl, the private detective who turns out to be totally unable to solve a crime or resist villains except by accident. This type of burlesque is even more effective when the inverted presentation actually seems to bring out some latent meanings which were lurking all the time in the original convention. Mel Brooks is a particular master of this kind of burlesque. In his *Young Frankenstein,* the monster attacks Frankenstein's fiancee Elizabeth—a moment of tragic violence in the original novel—and the result is complete sexual satisfaction on both sides, something most of us had suspected all along.

These two primary techniques of burlesque, the breaking of convention by the intrusion of reality and the inversion of expected implications, have frequently appeared in the history of literature as a response to highly conventionalized genres. Just as the Greek tragedies gave rise to their burlesque counterparts in the plays of Aristophanes, the western, one of our most formally distinctive genres, has been the inspiration of parody and burlesque throughout its history from Twain and Harte's assaults on James Fenimore Cooper to Brooks' send-up of *Shane* and *High Noon.* Thus, there is nothing particularly new in the penchant toward humorous burlesque so evident in recent films. What is more striking in the films of the last decade is their use of these techniques of generic parody for ultimately serious purposes.

The second major mode of generic transformation is the cultivation of nostalgia. In this mode, traditional generic features of plot, character, setting and style are deployed to recreate the aura of a past time. The power of nostalgia lies especially in its capacity to evoke a sense of warm reassurance by bringing before our mind's eye images from a time when things seemed more secure and full of promise and possibility. Though one can, of course, evoke nostalgia simply by viewing films of the past, a contemporary nostalgia film cannot simply duplicate the past experience, but must make us aware in some fashion of the relationship between past and present. Attempts to evoke nostalgia merely by imitating past forms, as was the case with the television series *City of Angels,* do not generally work because they seem simply obsolescent. A truly successful nostalgia film—like Fred Zinneman's *True Grit,* one of the last highly popular westerns—succeeds because it set its highly traditional generic content in a slightly different context, thereby giving us both a sense of contemporaneity and of pastness. In *True Grit,* this was done in a number of ways. First of all, the central character played by Kim Darby represented an extremely contemporary image of adolescent girlhood. She was independent, aggressive and full of initiative, a shrewd horsetrader and a self-confident, insistent moralist, unlike the shy desert rose of the traditional western. John Wayne, aging and paunchy, did not attempt to cover up the ravages of the years and reaffirm without change the vigorous manhood of his earlier films. Instead, with eyepatch, unshaven face and sagging flesh, he fully enacted his aging. Similarly, the film's images of the western landscape were in many ways deromanticized. But out of this context of contemporaneity there sprang the same old story of adventure and heroism culminating in an exhuberant shootout which seemed to embody everybody's best dreams of Saturday matinees. The same quality of nostalgic reinvocation of the past played an even more powerful role in Peckinpah's *Ride the High Country* in which two tired, aging and obsolescent heroes ride again, and in Dick Richard's recent version of Raymond Chandler's *Farewell, My Lovely* where a sagging Robert Mitchum moves out of the malaise of modernity and reenacts once more the ambiguous heroic quest of the hard-boiled detective of the 1930s and 1940s.

The difference between nostalgic reincarnation of an earlier genre like *Farewell, My Lovely* and the more complex ironies of *Chinatown* and Robert Altman's *The Long Goodbye* is considerable. It is a difference similar to the one between *True Grit* and neo-westerns like Altman's *McCabe and Mrs. Miller* or Arthur Penn's *Little Big Man.* In the former case, nostalgia is the end result of the film. In the latter nostalgia is often powerfully evoked, but as a means of undercutting or ironically commenting upon the generic experience itself. This brings us to the third and, in many respects, the most powerful mode of generic transformation in recent films: the use of traditional generic structures as a means of demythologization. A film like *Chinatown* deliberately invokes the basic characteristics of a traditional genre in order to bring its audience to see that genre as the embodiment of an inadequate and destructive myth. We have seen how this process of demythologization operates in *Chinatown* by setting the traditional model of the hard-boiled detective's quest for justice and integrity over and against Polanski's sense of a universe so steeped in ambiguity, corruption and evil that such individualistic moral enterprises are doomed by their innocent naiveté to end in tragedy and self-destruction.

The work of Arthur Penn has also explored the ironic and tragic aspects of the myths implicit in traditional genres. His *Night Moves,* a transformation of the detective story, was, like *Chinatown,* the ambiguous enactment of a reluctant quest for the truth about a series of crimes. As the detective approaches a solution to the crimes, he becomes morally and emotionally involved in the quest, making it more and more difficult for him to integrate truth, feeling, and morality. In the end, like Polanski's Jake Gittes, he is more dazed than fulfilled by the catastrophe his investigation has brought about.

In other films, such as *The Left-Handed Gun, Bonnie and Clyde* and *Little Big Man,* Penn created a version of the western or the gangster film in which traditional meanings were inverted, but the effect was tragic rather than humorous. In *Little Big Man,* for example, the conventional western opposition between Indians and pioneers serves as the basis of the plot, which embodies two of the most powerful of our western myths, the Indian captivity and the massacre. However, the conventional renderings of these myths pit the humanely civilizing thrust of the pioneers against the savage ferocity and eroticism of the Indians and thereby justify the conquest of the West. Penn reverses these implications. In his film it is the Indians who are humane and civilized, while the pioneers are violent, corrupt, sexually repressed and madly ambitious. By the end, when Custer's cavalry rides forward to attack the Indian villages, our sympathies are all with the Indians. From this perspective, the conquest of the West is demythologized from the triumph of civilization into a historical tragedy of the destruction of a rich and vital human culture.

Despite its many virtues, the film version of *Little Big Man* was less artistically successful than Thomas Berger's novel on which it was based, primarily because as the film proceeds, Penn loses the ironic detachment which Berger successfully maintains throughout the novel. Penn's portrayal of Custer as a lunatic symbol of aggressive American imperialism is overstated, and toward the end the cinematic *Little Big Man* tends to fall back from the serious exploration of mythical meanings into melodramatic burlesque. This is an artistic problem common to films in the mode of demythologization of traditional genres. Penn was far more successful in *Bonnie and Clyde,* which will remain one of the major masterpieces of recent American film. Taking off from the traditional gangster film with its opposition between the outlaw and society, *Bonnie and Clyde* establishes a dialectic between conventional and inverted meanings which is far richer and more powerfully sustained throughout the film. In the traditional gangster film, a powerful individual, frustrated by the limitations of his lower-class origin, is driven to a life of crime. Initially the audience is inclined to sympathize and identify with this character, but as he becomes involved in criminal actions, he overreaches himself and becomes a vicious killer who must be tracked down and destroyed by the representatives of society. The underlying myth of this genre affirms the limits of individual aggression in a society which tolerates and even encourages a high degree of personal enterprise and violence. The gangster becomes a tragic figure not because he is inherently evil, but because he fails to recognize these limits. The myth assures us that society is not repressive or violent; instead it shows how criminal violence evokes its own inevitable doom.

It is this comforting myth of proper and improper violence that Penn demythologizes in *Bonnie and Clyde.* As in *Little Big Man,* meanings become inverted. Instead of representing a limit to aggression and violence, society is portrayed as its fountainhead, while the outlaw protagonists are seen as victims of society's bloodlust. Throughout the film, we are shown a society of depression and chaos which yearns for action, and which projects this yearning into a vicarious excitement about the robberies and murders of the Barrow gang. Penn effectively develops this theme through his representation of the newspapers which so avidly report the gang's adventures and by the reactions of witnesses to the gang's attacks on banks. Finally, its lust for the hunt aroused, society itself takes up the pursuit in packs and posses and, in a final ambush which set a new level in explicit screen violence, the doomed Bonnie and Clyde are shot to pieces. But the inversion of generic meanings is still more complex, for Penn refuses to make the opposition between gangster and society a simple reversal of traditional generic meanings as he does in *Little Big Man.* The protagonists of *Bonnie and Clyde* are not simply victims of society. They are themselves very much a part of the society they are attacking. They share its basic aspirations and confusions and they yearn above all to be reintegrated with it. In many respects, their actions reflect a desperate and misconceived attempt to achieve some measure of the status, security and belongingness which ought to be among the basic gifts of a society to its members. Instead of simply reversing the meanings conventionally ascribed to the opposing forces of criminal and society in the gangster genre, *Bonnie and Clyde* expressed a more complex and dark awareness that this basic opposition was itself a mythical simplification, and showed us the deeper and more difficult irony of the twisted and inseparable fates of individuals and their society. This was in its way a recognition of that skein of ambiguous inevitability which Polanski summed up in the symbol of Chinatown, and which Francis Ford Coppola developed through the fateful intertwining of individuals, "families" and society in *The Godfather.*

Though the demythologization of traditional genres has been primarily evident in the work of younger directors, it has also had some influence on the later work of some of the classic filmmakers, most noticeably perhaps in the later westerns of John Ford, particularly *The Searchers, Cheyenne Autumn* and *The Man who Shot Liberty Valance.* Indeed, in the latter film, Ford symbolized the conquest of the West through a story in which the territory's last major outlaw was killed in a shootout by a man destined to lead the territory into the blessings of civilization. In fact, the legend of Senator Stoddard's heroic deed was a myth, the actual shooting of Liberty Valance having been done by another man. Toward the end of the film, the newspaper editor to whom Senator Stoddard confesses the truth about his past makes the famous and ambiguous comment "when the legend becomes a fact, print the legend." But is this an ironic comment on the falsity of legends and newspapers alike, or is it some kind of affirmation of the significance of myth in spite of its unreality? Ford was apparently inclined to the latter interpretation, for he once told Peter Bogdanovich, "We've had a lot of people who were supposed to be great heroes and you know damn well they weren't. But it's good for the country to have heroes to look up to."*

This brings us to a fourth and final mode of generic transformation which might be described as the affirmation of myth for its own sake. In films in this mode, a traditional genre and its myth are probed and shown to be unreal, but then the myth itself is at least partially affirmed as a reflection of authentic human aspirations and needs. This is the element which becomes dominant in Ford's later westerns in which he seems to see the heroic ethos of the West in critical terms and becomes more and more sympathetic with the Indian victims of the Westward movement. Yet, at the same time that he became more cynical about the reality of the West, he seemed to feel even more strongly the need to affirm its heroic ideals. Thus, in his powerful late film *The Searchers,* Ford turns to the old western theme of Indian captivity, portraying the mad obsessive hatred with which a White man pursues a band of Indians who have captured and adopted his niece. Yet Ford also accepted a change in the ending of the original novel, where this mad Indian hater was finally destroyed by his obsession, in order to reaffirm at the end the heroism and self-sacrifice of this obsessive quest. *The Searchers* is a powerful and beautiful film, yet one feels uncomfortable at the end, as if the gap between Ford's sense of historical reality and his feelings about genre and myth have come into collision.

Sam Peckinpah's *The Wild Bunch,* for all its ugliness and violence, is a more coherent example of the destruction and reaffirmation of myth. Throughout the film, Peckinpah points up the gap between the conventional western's heroic struggle between pioneers and outlaws. His pioneer lawmen are despicable bounty hunters in the employ of the railroad and they kill the guilty and the innocent indiscriminately. His outlaws are not much better; they are brutal, coarse, and quite capable

---

*Quoted in Jon Tuska, *The Filming of the West.* (Garden City, N.Y.: Doubleday and Co., 1976, p. 519.)

of leaving a wounded comrade behind. Moreover, their type of criminal operation has become absurdly obsolescent in the early twentieth-century West of the film. In the end, Peckinpah's outlaw protagonists are drawn in to a ridiculously destructive shootout with an entire Mexican village full of troops and are completely wiped out in the process. Yet the film also leaves us with a sense that through their hopeless action these coarse and vicious outlaws have somehow transcended themselves and become embodiments of a myth of heroism that men need in spite of the realities of their world.

While I have separated the four modes of generic transformation—humorous burlesque, evocation of nostalgia, demythologization of generic myth, and the affirmation of myth as myth—into separate categories in order to define them more clearly, it should be clear that most films which employ one of these modes are likely to use another at some point. Probably the best films based on generic transformation employ some combination of several of these modes in the service of one overriding artistic purpose; *Chinatown* uses both humorous burlesque and nostalgic evocation as a basis for its devastating exploration of the genre of the hard-boiled detective and his myth. Some directors seem to have a primary predilection for one of these modes; Brooks is primarily oriented toward burlesque, Bogdanovich toward nostalgia, Penn toward demythologization and Peckinpah toward reaffirmation. Some directors—Robert Altman springs particularly to mind—have, in their best films, worked out a rich and fascinating dialectic between different modes of generic transformation. In films like *McCabe and Mrs. Miller, The Long Goodbye, Thieves Like Us,* and *Nashville* it is quite difficult to decide at the end whether Altman is attacking or reaffirming the genre on which he has based each particular work. In fact, until the last two or three years, Altman's filmography looks almost as if he had planned a systematic voyage through the major traditional film genres. That generic transformation has been so important a source of artistic energy to the most vital younger directors suggests that it is a central key to the current state of the American film.

There are probably many reasons for the importance of these modes of filmmaking in the last decade, but in conclusion, I will comment briefly on what seem to me the most important factors involved in the proliferation of this kind of film. I think it is not primarily the competition of television. Though television has been somewhat more conservative in its use of generic transformation than film, the same modes seem to be turning up with increasing frequency in television series. Instead I would point to the tendency of genres to exhaust themselves, to our growing historical awareness of modern popular culture, and finally, to the decline of the underlying mythology on which traditional genres have been based since the late nineteenth century. Generic exhaustion is a common phenomenon in the history of culture. One can almost make out a lifecycle characteristic of genres as they move from an initial period of articulation and discovery, through a phase of conscious self-awareness on the part of both creators and audiences, to a time when the generic patterns have become so well-known that people become tired of their predictability. It is at this point that parodic and satiric treatments proliferate and new genres gradually arise. Our major traditional genres—the western, the detective story, the musical, the domestic comedy—have, after all, been around for a considerable period of time and it may be they have simply reached a point of creative exhaustion.

In our time, the awareness of the persistence of genres has been intensified by an increasing historical awareness of film. A younger generation of directors has a sense of film history quite different from many of their predecessors who, like Ford and Hawks, were involved with the art of film almost from its beginnings. Similarly, audiences have a kind of sophistication about the history of genres different from earlier film publics because of the tremendous number of past films now regularly shown on television and by college film societies.

But I am inclined to think that there is more to it than that. The present significance of generic transformation as a creative mode reflects the feeling that not only the traditional genres, but the cultural myths they once embodied, are no longer fully adequate to the imaginative needs of our time. It will require another essay to explain and justify this assertion, but if I may hazard a final prediction, I think we will begin to see emerging out of this period of generic transformation a new set of generic constructs more directly related to the imaginative landscape of the second half of the twentieth century. Thus, the present period of American filmmaking will seem in retrospect an important time of artistic and cultural transition. Like many transition periods, it may also turn out to be a time of the highest artistic accomplishment.

1978

THOMAS ELSAESSER
TALES OF SOUND AND FURY: OBSERVATIONS ON THE FAMILY MELODRAMA

Asked about the color in *Written on the Wind* (1957), Douglas Sirk replied: "Almost throughout the picture I used deep-focus lenses which have the effect of giving a harshness to the objects and a kind of enamelled, hard surface to the colours. I wanted this to bring out the inner violence, the energy of the characters which is all inside them and can't break through." It would be difficult to think of a better way of describing what this particular movie and indeed most of the best melodramas of the fifties and early sixties are about. Or, for that matter, how closely this film style and technique are related to theme.

I want to pursue an elusive subject in two directions: first, to indicate the development of what one might call the melodramatic imagination across different artistic forms and in different epochs; second, prompted by Sirk's remark, to look for some structural and stylistic constants in one medium during one particular period (the Hollywood family melodrama between roughly 1940 and 1963) and to speculate on the cultural and psychological context that this form of melodrama so manifestly reflected and helped to articulate. Nonetheless, this isn't an historical study in any strict sense, nor a *catalogue raisonné* of names and titles, for reasons that have something to do with my general method as well as with the obvious limitations imposed on film research by the unavailability of most of the movies. Thus I lean rather heavily on half a dozen films, notably *Written on the Wind,* to develop my points. This said, it is difficult to see how references to twenty more movies would make the argument any truer. For better or worse, what I have to say should at this stage be taken to be provocative rather than proven.

HOW TO MAKE STONES WEEP

Bearing in mind that everybody has some idea of what is meant by "melodramatic" (whatever one's scruples about an exact definition), any discussion of the melodrama as a specific cinematic mode of expression has to start from its antecedents—the novel and certain types of "entertainment" drama—from which scriptwriters and directors have borrowed their models.

The first thing one notices is that the media and literary forms that have habitually embodied melodramatic situations have changed considerably in the course of history and, further, that they differ from country to country. In England it has mainly been the novel and the literary gothic where melodramatic motifs persistently crop up (though the Victorian stage, especially in the 1880s and 1890s, knew an unprecedented vogue for the melodramas of R. Buchanan and G. R. Sims, plays in which "a footbridge over a torrent breaks under the steps of the villain; a piece of wall comes down to shatter him; a boiler bursts, and blows him to smithereens").* In France, it is the costume drama and historical novel; in Germany, "high" drama and the ballad, as well as more popular forms like *Moritat* (street songs); finally, in Italy the opera rather than the novel reached the highest degree of sophistication in the handling of melodramatic situations.

Two currents make up the genealogy. One leads from the late medieval morality play, the popular *gestes,* and other forms of oral narrative and drama, like fairy tales and folk songs, to their romantic revival and the cult of the picturesque in Scott, Byron, Heine, and Hugo, which has its lowbrow echo in barrel-organ songs, music-hall drama, and what in Germany is known as *Bänkellied,* the latter coming to late literary honors through Brecht in his songs and musical plays, *The Threepenny Opera* or *Mahagonny.* The characteristic features for our present purposes in this tradition are not so much the emotional shock tactics and the blatant playing on the audience's known sympathies and antipathies, but rather the nonpsychological conception of the dramatis personae, who figure less as autonomous individuals than to transmit the action and link the various locales within a total constellation. In this respect, melodramas have a myth-making function, insofar as their significance lies in the structure and articulation of the action, not in any psychologically motivated correspondence with individualized experience.

Yet what particularly marks the ballad or the *Bänkellied* (i.e., narratives accompanied by music) is that the moral/moralistic pattern which furnishes the primary content (crimes of passion bloodily revenged, murderers driven mad by guilt and drowning themselves, villains snatching children from their careless mothers, servants killing their unjust masters) is overlaid not only with a proliferation of "realistic" homely detail, but also "parodied" or relativized by the heavily repetitive

---

*Pierre Marie Augustin Filon, *The English Stage,* translated by Frederic Whyte (1897; reprint Port Washington, N.Y.: Kennikat Press, 1970), p. 195. Filon also offers an interesting definition of melodrama: "When dealing with Irving, I asked the question, so often discussed, whether we go to the theatre to see a representation of life, or to forget life and seek relief from it. Melodrama solves this question and shows that both theories are right, by giving satisfaction to both desires, in that it offers the extreme of realism in scenery and language together with the most uncommon sentiments and events" (p. 196).

verse form or the mechanical up-and-down rhythms of the barrel organ, to which the voice of the singer adapts itself (consciously or not), thereby producing a vocal parallelism that has a distancing or ironic effect, to the extent of often crisscrossing the moral of the story by a "false" or unexpected emphasis. Sirk's most successful German melodrama, *Zu neuen Ufern* (To New Shores, 1937), makes excellent use of the street ballad to bring out the tragic irony in the courtroom scene, and the tune which Walter Brennan keeps playing on the harmonica in King Vidor's *Ruby Gentry* (1952) works in a very similar way. A variation on this is the use of fairgrounds and carousels in films like *Some Came Running* (Vincente Minnelli, 1958) and *The Tarnished Angels* (Sirk, 1957), or more self-consciously by Hitchcock in *Strangers on a Train* and *Stage Fright* (both 1951) and Welles in *Lady from Shanghai* and *The Stranger* (both 1946) to underscore the main action and at the same time "ease" the melodramatic impact by providing an ironic parallelism. Sirk uses the motif repeatedly, as, for instance, in *A Scandal in Paris* (1946) and *Take Me to Town* (1952). What such devices point to is that in the melodrama the *rhythm* of experience often establishes itself against its value (moral, intellectual).

Perhaps the current that leads more directly to the sophisticated family melodrama of the 1940s and 1950s, though, is derived from the romantic drama which had its heydey after the French Revolution and subsequently furnished many of the plots for operas, but which is itself unthinkable without the eighteenth-century sentimental novel and the emphasis put on private feelings and interiorized (puritan, pietist) codes of morality and conscience. Historically, one of the interesting facts about this tradition is that its height of popularity seems to coincide (and this remains true throughout the nineteenth century) with periods of intense social and ideological crisis. The prerevolutionary sentimental novel—Richardson's *Clarissa* or Rousseau's *Nouvelle Héloïse,* for example—go out of their way to make a case for extreme forms of behavior and feeling by depicting very explicitly certain external constraints and pressures bearing upon the characters, and by showing up the quasi-totalitarian violence perpetrated by (agents of) the "system." (Lovelace tries everything, from bribing her family to hiring pimps, prostitutes, and kidnappers in order to get Clarissa to become his wife, only to have to rape her after all.) The same pattern is to be found in the bourgeois tragedies of Lessing (*Emilia Galotti,* 1768) and the early Schiller (*Kabale und Liebe,* 1776), both deriving their dramatic force from the conflict between an extreme and highly individualized form of moral idealism in the heroes (again, nonpsychological on the level of motivation) and a thoroughly corrupt yet seemingly omnipotent social class (made up of feudal princes and petty state functionaries). The melodramatic elements are clearly visible in the plots, which revolve around family relationships, star-crossed lovers, and forced marriages. The villains (often of noble birth) demonstrate their superior political and economic power invariably by sexual aggression and attempted rape, leaving the heroine no other way than to commit suicide or take poison in the company of her lover. The ideological "message" of these tragedies, as in the case of *Clarissa,* is transparent: they record the struggle of a morally and emotionally emancipated bourgeois consciousness against the remnants of feudalism. They pose the problem in political terms and concentrate on the complex interplay of ethical principles, religious-metaphysical polarities, and the idealist aspirations typical of the bourgeoisie in its militant phase, as the protagonists come to grief in a maze of economic necessities, realpolitik, family loyalties, and through the abuse of aristocratic privilege from a still divinely ordained and therefore doubly depraved absolutist authority.

Although these plays and novels, because they use the melodramatic–emotional plot only as their most rudimentary structure of meaning, belong to the more intellectually demanding forms of melodrama, the element of interiorization and personalization of what are primarily ideological conflicts, together with the metaphorical interpretation of class conflict as sexual exploitation and rape, is important in all subsequent forms of melodrama, including that of the cinema. (The latter in America, of course, is a stock theme of novels and movies with a "Southern" setting.)

Paradoxically, the French Revolution failed to produce a new form of social drama or tragedy. The restoration stage (when theaters in Paris were specially licensed to play melodramas) trivialized the form by using melodramatic plots in exotic settings and by providing escapist entertainment with little social relevance. The plays warmed up the standard motif of eighteenth-century French fiction and drama, that of innocence persecuted and virtue rewarded, and the conventions of melodrama functioned in their most barren form as the mechanics of pure suspense.

What before the revolution had served to focus on suffering and victimization—the claims of the individual in an absolutist society—was reduced to ground glass in the porridge, poisoned handkerchiefs, and last-minute rescues from the dungeon. The sudden reversals of fortune, the intrusion of chance and coincidence, had originally pointed to the arbitrary way feudal institutions could ruin the individual unprotected by civil rights and liberties. The system stood accused of greed, willfulness, and irrationality through the Christlike suffering of the pure virgin and the selfless heroism of the right-minded in the midst of court intrigues and callous indifference. Now, with the bourgeoisie triumphant, this form of drama lost its subversive charge and functioned more as a means of consolidating an as yet weak and incoherent ideological position. Whereas the prerevolutionary melodramas had often ended tragically, those of the Restoration had happy endings; they reconciled the suffering individual to his or her social position by affirming an "open" society where everything was possible. Over and over again, the victory of the "good" citizen over "evil" aristocrats, lecherous clergymen, and the even more conventional villains drawn from the lumpenproletariat was reenacted in sentimental spectacles full of tears and high moral tones. Complex social processes were simplified either by blaming the evil disposition of individuals or by manipulating the plots and engineering coincidences and other dei ex machina, such as the instant conversion of the villain, moved by the plight of his victim, or suddenly struck by divine grace on the steps of Notre Dame.

Since the overtly "conformist" strategy of such drama is quite evident, what is interesting is certainly not the plot structure, but whether the conventions allowed authors to dramatize in their episodes actual contradictions in society and genuine clashes of interests in the characters. Already during the Revolution plays such as Monvel's *Les Victimes cloîtrées* or Laya's *L'Ami des lois,* though working with very stereotyped plots, conveyed quite definite political sympathies (the second, for instance, backed the Girondist moderates in the trial of Louis XVI against the Jacobites) and were understood as such by their public.[1]

Even if the form might act to reinforce attitudes of submission, the actual working out of the scenes could nonetheless present fundamental social evils. Many of the pieces also flattered popular sympathies by giving the villains the funniest lines, just as Victorian drama playing east of Drury Lane was often enlivened by low-comedy burlesque put on as curtain-raisers and by the servants' farces during the intermission.

All this is to say that there seems a radical ambiguity attached to the melodrama, which holds even more for the film melodrama. Depending on whether the emphasis fell on the odyssey of suffering or the happy ending, on the place and context of rupture (moral conversion of the villain, unexpected appearance of a benevolent Capucine monk throwing off his pimp's disguise), that is to say, depending on what dramatic mileage was got out of the heroine's perils before the ending (and one only has to think of Sade's Justine to see what could be done with the theme of innocence unprotected), melodrama would appear to function either subversively or as escapism—categories that are always relative to the given historical and social context.[2]

In the cinema, Griffith is a good example. Using identical dramatic devices and cinematic techniques, he could create, with *Intolerance* (1916), *Way Down East* (1920), or *Broken Blossoms* (1919), if not exactly subversive, at any rate socially committed melodramas, whereas *Birth of a Nation* (1915) or *Orphans of the Storm* (1921) are classic examples of how melodramatic effects can successfully shift explicit political themes onto a personalized plane. In both cases, Griffith tailored ideological conflicts into emotionally charged family situations.

The persistence of the melodrama might indicate the ways in which popular culture has not only taken note of social crises and the fact that the losers are not always those who deserve it most, but has also resolutely refused to understand social change in other than private contexts and emotional terms. In this, there is obviously a healthy distrust of intellectualization and abstract social theory—insisting that other structures of experience (those of suffering, for instance) are more in

---

[1]See Jean Duvignaud, *Sociologie du théâtre* (Paris: Presses Universitaires du France, 1965), 4, no. 3, "Théâtre sans révolution, révolution sans théâtre."

[2]About the ideological function of nineteenth-century Victorian melodrama, see Maurice Willson Disher, *Blood and Thunder: Mid-Victorian Melodrama and Its Origins* (London: F. Muller, 1949): "Even in gaffs and saloons, melodrama so strongly insisted on the sure reward to be bestowed in this life upon the law-abiding that sociologists now see in this a Machiavellian plot to keep democracy servile to Church and State. . . . There is no parting the two strains, moral and political, in the imagination of the nineteenth-century masses. They are hopelessly entangled. Democracy shaped its own entertainments at a time when the vogue of Virtue Triumphant was at its height and they took their pattern from it. . . . Here are Virtue Triumphant's attendant errors: confusion between sacred and profane, between worldly and spiritual advancement, between self-interest and self-sacrifice" (pp. 13–14). However, it ought to be remembered that there are melodramatic traditions outside the puritan-democratic world view: Catholic countries, such as Spain and Mexico (cf. Buñuel's Mexican films) have a very strong line in melodramas, based on the themes of atonement and redemption. Japanese melodramas have been "high-brow" since the Monogatari stories of the sixteenth century, and in Mizoguchi's films *(O Haru, Shinheike Monogatari)* they reach a transcendence and stylistic sublimation rivalled only by the very best Hollywood melodramas.

keeping with reality. But it has also meant ignorance of the properly social and political dimensions of these changes and their causality, and consequently it has encouraged increasingly escapist forms of mass entertainment.

However, this ambivalence about the "structures" of experience, endemic in the melodramatic mode, has served artists throughout the nineteenth century for the depiction of a variety of themes and social phenomena while remaining within the popular idiom. Industrialization, urbanization, and nascent entrepreneurial capitalism have found their most telling literary embodiment in a type of novel clearly indebted to the melodrama, and the national liberals in Italy during the Risorgimento, for example, saw their political aspirations reflected in Verdi's operas (as in the opening of Luchino Visconti's *Senso* [1954]). In England, Dickens, Collins, and Reade relied heavily on melodramatic plots to sharpen social conflicts and portray an urban environment where chance encounters, coincidences, and the side-by-side existence of extreme social and moral contrasts were the natural products of the very conditions of existence—crowded tenement houses, narrow streets backing up to the better residential property, and other facts of urban demography of the time. Dickens in particular uses the element of chance, the dream/waking, horror/bliss switches in *Oliver Twist* or *Tale of Two Cities,* partly to feel his way toward a portrayal of existential insecurity and moral anguish that fiction had previously not encompassed, but also to explore deep psychological phenomena for which the melodrama—as Freud was later to confirm—has supplied the dynamic motifs and the emotional-pictorial decor. What seems to me important in this form of melodrama (and one comes across a similar conception in the sophisticated Hollywood melodramas) is the emphasis Dickens places on discontinuity, on the evidence of fissures and ruptures in the fabric of experience, and the appeal to a reality of the psyche—to which the notions of sudden change, reversal, and excess lend a symbolic plausibility.

In France it is the works of Sue, Hugo, and Balzac that reflect most closely the relation of melodrama to social upheaval. Sue, for example, uses the timeworn trapdoor devices of cloak-and-dagger stage melodrama for an explicitly sensationalist, yet committed journalism. In a popular form and rendered politically palatable by the fictionalized treatment, his *Mystères de Paris* were intended to crusade on such issues as public health, prostitution, overcrowding and slum housing, sanitation, black-market racketeering, corruption in government circles, opium smoking, and gambling. Sue exploited a "reactionary" form for reformist ends, and his success, both literary and practical, proved him right. Twenty years later Victor Hugo, who had learnt as much from Sue as Sue had picked up from *Nôtre-Dame de Paris,* produced with *Les Misérables* a supermelodrama spectacular that must stand as the crowning achievement of the genre in the novel. The career of Jean Valjean, from convict and galley slave to factory owner and capitalist, his fall and literal emergence from the sewers of Paris to become a somewhat unwilling activist in the 1848 revolution, is staged with the help of mistaken identities, orphans suddenly discovering their noble birth, inconvenient reappearance of people long thought dead, hair-breadth escapes and rescues, multiple disguises, long-suffering females dying of consumption or wandering for days through the streets in search of their child— and yet, through all this Hugo expresses a hallucinating vision of the anxiety, the moral confusion, the emotional demands, in short, the metaphysics of social change and urban life between the time of Waterloo and 1848. Hugo evidently wanted to bring together in a popular form subjective experiences of crises while keeping track of the grand lines of France's history, and he succeeds singularly well in reproducing the ways in which individuals with different social backgrounds, levels of awareness, and imaginations respond to objective changes in the social fabric of their lives. For this, the melodrama, with its shifts in mood, its different *tempi,* and the mixing of stylistic levels, is ideally suited: *Les Misérables,* even more so than the novels of Dickens, lets through a symbolic dimension of psychic truth, with the hero in turn representing very nearly the id, the superego, and finally the sacrificed ego of a repressed and paranoid society.

Balzac, on the other hand, uses melodramatic plots to a rather different end. Many of his novels deal with the dynamics of early capitalist economics. The good/ evil dichotomy has almost disappeared, and the Manichaean conflicts have shifted away from questions of morality to the paradoxes of psychology and economics. What we see is a Schopenhauerian struggle of the will: the ruthlessness of industrial entrepreneurs and bankers; the spectacle of an uprooted, "decadent" aristocracy still holding tremendous political power; the sudden twists of fortune with no-good parasites becoming millionaires overnight (or vice versa) through speculation and the stock exchange; the antics of hangers-on, parvenus, and cynical artist-intellectuals; the demonic, spellbinding potency of money and capital; the contrasts between abysmal poverty and unheard-of affluence and waste, which characterized the "anarchic" phase of industrialization and high finance. All were experienced by Balzac as both vital and melodramatic. His work reflects this more in plot and style than through direct comment.

To sum up, these writers understood the melodrama as a form that carried its own values and already embodied its own significant content: it served as the literary equivalent of a particular historically and socially conditioned mode of experience. Even if the situations and sentiments defied all categories of verisimilitude and were totally unlike anything in real life, the structure had a truth and a life of its own, which artists could make part of their material. This meant that those who consciously adopted melodramatic techniques of presentation did not necessarily do so out of incompetence or always from a cynical distance, but, by turning a body of techniques into a stylistic principle that carried the distinct overtones of spiritual crisis, they could put the finger on the texture of their social and human material while still being free to shape this material dramatically. For there is little doubt that the whole conception of life in nineteenth-century Europe and England and especially the spiritual problems of the age were often viewed in categories we would today call melodramatic—one can see this in painting, architecture, the ornamentation of gadgets and furniture, the domestic and public mise-en-scène of events and occasions, the oratory in parliament, and the tractarian rhetoric from the pulpit as well as the more private manifestations of religious sentiment. Similarly, the timeless themes that Dostoyevsky brings up again and again in his novels—guilt, redemption, justice, innocence, freedom—are made specific and historically real not least because he was a great writer of melodramatic scenes and confrontations, and they more than anything else define that powerful irrational logic in the motivation and moral outlook of, say, Raskolnikov, Ivan Karamasov, or Kirilov. Finally, how different Kafka's novels would be if they did not contain those melodramatic family situations, pushed to the point where they reveal a dimension at once comic and tragically absurd—perhaps the existential undertow of all genuine melodrama.

PUTTING MELOS INTO DRAMA

In its dictionary sense, melodrama is a dramatic narrative in which musical accompaniment marks the emotional effects. This is still perhaps the most useful definition, because it allows melodramatic elements to be seen as constituents of a system of punctuation, giving expressive color and chromatic contrast to the story line, by orchestrating the emotional ups and downs of the intrigue. The advantage of this approach is that it formulates the problems of melodrama as problems of style and articulation.

Music in melodrama, for example, as a device among others to dramatize a given narrative, is subjective and programmatic. But because it is also a form of punctuation in the above sense, it is both functional (i.e., of structural significance) and thematic (i.e., belonging to the expressive content) in formulating certain moods—sorrow, violence, dread, suspense, happiness. The syntactic function of music has, as is well known, survived into the sound film, and the experiments conducted by Hanns Eisler and T. W. Adorno are highly instructive in this respect.[1] A more practical demonstration of the problem can be gleaned from the almost farcical account that Lillian Ross gives of Gottfried Reinhardt and Dore Shary reediting John Huston's *Red Badge of Courage* (1951) to give the narrative a smoother dramatic shape by a musical build-up to the dramatic climaxes, which is exactly what Huston had wanted to avoid when he shot it.[2]

Because it had to rely on piano accompaniment for punctuation, all silent film drama—from *True Heart Susie* (Griffith, 1919) to *Foolish Wives* (Erich von Stroheim, 1922) or *The Lodger* (Alfred Hitchcock, 1926)—is "melodramatic." It meant that directors had to develop an extremely subtle and yet precise formal language (of lighting, staging, decor, acting, close-up, montage, and camera movement), because they were deliberately looking for ways to compensate for the expressiveness, range of inflection and tonality, rhythmic emphasis, and tension normally present in the spoken word. Having had to replace that part of language which is sound, directors like Murnau, Renoir, Hitchcock, Mizoguchi, Hawks, Lang, and Sternberg achieved in their films a high degree (well recognized at the time) of plasticity in the modulation of optical planes and spatial masses, which Panofsky rightly identified as a "dynamization of space."[3]

Among less gifted directors this sensitivity in the deployment of expressive means was partly lost with the advent of direct sound, since it seemed no longer necessary

---

[1] Hanns Eisler, *Composing for Film* (London: Dobson, 1981).
[2] Lillian Ross, *Picture* (London: Penguin, 1958).
[3] Erwin Panofsky, "Style and Medium in the Motion Pictures," in *Film: An Anthology,* ed. Daniel Talbot (Berkeley: University of California Press, 1969), p. 18.

in a strictly technical sense—pictures "worked" on audiences through their dialogue, and the semantic force of language drowned out and overshadowed the more sophisticated pictorial effects and architectural values. This perhaps helps to explain why some major technical innovations, such as color, wide-angle and deep-focus lenses, crane and dolly, have in fact encouraged a new form of sophisticated melodrama. Directors (quite a sizeable proportion of whom came during the 1930s from Germany, and others were clearly indebted to German expressionism and Max Reinhardt's methods of theatrical mise-en-scène) began showing a similar degree of visual culture as the masters of silent film-drama: Ophüls, Lubitsch, Sirk, Preminger, Welles, Losey, Ray, Minnelli, Cukor.

Considered as an expressive code, melodrama might therefore be described as a particular form of dramatic mise-en-scène, characterized by a dynamic use of spatial and musical categories, as opposed to intellectual or literary ones. Dramatic situations are given an orchestration that will allow for complex aesthetic patterns: indeed, orchestration is fundamental to the American cinema as a whole (being essentially a dramatic cinema, spectacular, and based on a broad appeal) because it has drawn the aesthetic consequences of having the spoken word more as an additional "melodic" dimension than as an autonomous semantic discourse. Sound, whether musical or verbal, acts first of all to give the illusion of depth to the moving image, and by helping to create the third dimension of the spectacle, dialogue becomes a scenic element, along with more directly visual means of the mise-en-scène. Anyone who has ever had the bad luck of watching a Hollywood movie dubbed into French or German will know how important diction is to the emotional resonance and dramatic continuity. Dubbing makes the best picture seem visually flat and dramatically out of sync: it destroys the flow on which the coherence of the illusionist spectacle is built.

That the plasticity of the human voice is quite consciously employed by directors for what are often thematic ends is known: Hawks trained Lauren Bacall's voice so that she could be given "male" lines in *To Have and Have Not* (1944), an effect that Sternberg anticipated when he took great care to cultivate Marlene Dietrich's diction, and it is hard to miss the psychological significance of Robert Stack's voice in *Written on the Wind,* sounding as if every word had to be painfully pumped up from the bottom of one of his oil wells.

If it is true that speech and dialogue in the American cinema lose some of their semantic importance in favor of their aspects as sound, then conversely lighting, composition, and decor increase their semantic and syntactic contribution to the aesthetic effect. They become functional and integral elements in the construction of meaning. This is the justification for giving critical importance to the mise-en-scène over intellectual content or story value. It is also the reason why the domestic melodrama in color and wide screen, as it appeared in the 1940s and 1950s, is perhaps the most highly elaborated, complex mode of cinematic signification that the American cinema has ever produced, because of the restricted scope for external action determined by the subject, and because everything, as Sirk said, happens "inside." To the "sublimation" of the action picture and the Busby Berkeley/Lloyd Bacon musical into domestic and family melodrama corresponded a sublimation of dramatic conflict into decor, color, gesture, and composition of frame, which in the best melodrama is perfectly thematized in terms of the characters' emotional and psychological predicaments.

For example, when in ordinary language we call something melodramatic, what we often mean is an exaggerated rise-and-fall pattern in human actions and emotional responses, a from-the-sublime-to-the-ridiculous movement, a foreshortening of lived time in favor of intensity—all of which produces a graph of much greater fluctuation, a quicker swing from one extreme to the other than is considered natural, realistic, or in conformity with literary standards of verisimilitude: in the novel we like to sip our pleasures rather than gulp them. But if we look at, say, Minnelli, who had adapted some of his best melodramas—*The Cobweb* (1955), *Some Came Running, Home from the Hill* (1960), *Two Weeks in Another Town* (1962), *The Four Horsemen of the Apocalypse* (1962)—from extremely long, circumstantially detailed popular novels by James Jones, Irving Shaw, and others, it is easy to see how in the process of having to reduce seven to nine hours of reading matter to ninety-odd minutes or so, a more violent "melodramatic" graph almost inevitably produces itself, short of the narrative becoming incoherent. Whereas in novels, especially when they are staple pulp fare, size connotes solid emotional involvement for the reader, the specific values of the cinema lie in its concentrated visual metaphors and dramatic acceleration rather than in the fictional techniques of dilation. The commercial necessity of compression (being also a formal one) is taken by Minnelli into the films themselves and developed as a theme—that of a pervasive psychological pressure on the characters. An acute sense of claustrophobia in decor and locale translates itself into a restless and yet suppressed energy surfacing sporadically in the actions and the behavior of the protagonists—a dialectic that is part of the subject of a film like *Two Weeks in Another Town,* with hysteria bubbling all the time just below the surface. The feeling that there is always more to tell than can be said leads to very consciously elliptical narratives, proceeding often by visually condensing the characters' motivation into nonessential sequences of images, seemingly lyrical interludes not advancing the plot. The shot of the Trevi fountain at the end of a complex scene where Kirk Douglas is making up his mind in *Two Weeks* is such a metaphoric condensation, and so is the silent sequence, consisting entirely of what might appear to be merely impressionistic dissolves, in the *Four Horsemen,* when Glenn Ford and Ingrid Thulin go for a ride to Versailles, but which in fact tells and foretells the whole trajectory of their relationship.

Sirk, too, often constructs his films in this way: the restlessness of *Written on the Wind* is not unconnected with the fact that he almost always cuts on movement. His visual metaphors ought to have a chapter to themselves: a yellow sportscar drawing up the gravelled driveway to stop in front of a pair of shining white doric columns outside the Hadley mansion is not only a powerful piece of American iconography, especially when taken in a plunging high-angle shot, but the contrary associations of imperial splendor and vulgar materials (polished chrome plate and stucco plaster) create a tension of correspondences and dissimilarities in the same image, which perfectly crystallizes the decadent affluence and melancholy energy that give the film its uncanny fascination. Sirk has a peculiarly vivid eye for the contrasting emotional qualities of textures and materials, and he combines them or makes them clash to very striking effect, especially when they occur in a nondramatic sequence: again in *Written on the Wind,* after the funeral of Hadley, Sr., a black servant is seen taking an oleander wreath off the front gate. A black silk ribbon gets unstuck and is blown by the wind along the concrete path. The camera follows the movement, dissolves, and dollies in on a window, where Lauren Bacall, in an oleander-green dress, is just about to disappear behind the curtains. The scene has no plot significance whatsoever. But the color parallels black/black, green/green, white concrete/white lace curtains provide an extremely strong emotional resonance in which the contrast of soft silk blown along the hard concrete is registered the more forcefully as a disquieting visual association. The desolation of the scene transfers itself onto the Bacall character, and the traditional fatalistic association of the wind reminds us of the futility implied in the movie's title.

These effects, of course, require a highly self-conscious stylist, but they are by no means rare. The fact that commercial necessities, political censorship, and the various morality codes have restricted directors in what they could tackle as a subject has entailed a different awareness of what constituted a worthwhile subject, a change in orientation from which sophisticated melodrama benefited perhaps most. Not only did they provide a defined thematic parameter, but they encouraged a conscious use of style-as-meaning, the mark of a modernist sensibility working in popular culture. To take another example from Minnelli: his theme of a character trying to construct the world in the image of an inner self, only to discover that this world has become uninhabitable because it is both frighteningly suffocating and intolerably lonely (as in *The Long, Long Trailer* [1954] and *The Cobweb*) is transformed and given social significance in the recurrent melodrama plot of the woman who, having failed to make it in the big city, comes back to the small-town home in the hope of finding her true place at last, but who is made miserable by meanmindedness and bigotry and then suffocated by the sheer weight of her none-too-glorious, still-raw-in-the-memory past (*Hilda Crane* [Philip Dunne, 1956], *Beyond the Forest* [King Vidor, 1949], *All I Desire* [Sirk, 1953].* But in Minnelli, it becomes an opportunity to explore in concrete circumstances the more philosophical questions of freedom and determinism, especially as they touch the aesthetic problem of how to depict characters who are not constantly externalizing themselves into action, without thereby trapping them in an environment of ready-made symbolism.

Similarly, when Robert Stack shows Lauren Bacall her hotel suite in *Written on the Wind,* where everything from flowers and pictures on the wall to underwear, nail polish, and handbag is provided, Sirk is not only characterizing a rich man wanting to take over the woman he fancies body and soul or showing the oppressive nature of an unwanted gift. He is also making a direct comment on the Hollywood stylistic technique that "creates" a character out of the elements of the decor and that prefers actors who provide as blank a facial surface and as little of a personality as possible.

Everyone who has at all thought about the Hollywood aesthetic wants to for-

---

*The impact of *Madame Bovary* via Willa Cather on the American cinema and the popular imagination would deserve a closer look.

mulate one of its peculiar qualities: that of direct emotional involvement—whether one calls it "giving resonance to dramatic situations" or "fleshing out the cliché" or whether, more abstractly, one talks in terms of identification patterns, empathy, and catharsis. Since the American cinema, determined as it is by an ideology of the spectacle and the spectacular, is essentially dramatic (as opposed to lyrical—i.e., concerned with mood or the inner self) and not conceptual (dealing with ideas and the structures of cognition and perception), the creation or reenactment of situations that the spectator can identify with and recognize (whether this recognition is on the conscious or unconscious level is another matter) depends to a large extent on the aptness of the iconography (the "visualization") and on the quality (complexity, subtlety, ambiguity) of the orchestration for what are transindividual, popular mythological (and therefore generally considered culturally "lowbrow") experiences and plot structures. In other words, this type of cinema depends on the ways "melos" is given to "drama" by means of lighting, montage, visual rhythm, decor, style of acting, music—that is, on the ways the mise-en-scène translates character into action (not unlike the pre-Jamesian novel) and action into gesture and dynamic space (comparable to nineteenth-century opera and ballet).

This granted, there seems to be a further problem that has some bearing on the question of melodrama: although the techniques of audience orientation and the possibility of psychic projection on the part of the spectator are as much in evidence in a melodrama like *Home from the Hill* or *Splendor in the Grass* (Elia Kazan, 1961) as they are in a western or adventure picture, the difference of setting and milieu affects the dynamics of the action. In the western, especially, the assumption of "open" spaces is virtually axiomatic; it is indeed one of the constants that makes the form perennially attractive to a largely urban audience. Yet this openness becomes problematic in films that deal with potential melodrama themes and family situations. The complex father-son relationships in *The Left-Handed Gun* (Arthur Penn, 1958), the Cain-Abel themes of Mann's *Winchester 73* (1950) and *Bend of the River* (1952), the conflict of virility and mother-fixation in Jacques Tourneur's *Great Day in the Morning* (1956) and *Wichita* (1955), or the search for the mother (-country) in Fuller's *Run of the Arrow* (1957) seem to find resolution because the hero can act positively on the changing situations where and when they present themselves. In Raoul Walsh's adventure pictures, as Peter Lloyd has shown,* identity comes in an often paradoxical process of self-confirmation and overreaching, but always through direct action, while the momentum generated by the conflicts pushes the protagonists forward in an unrelentingly linear course.

The family melodrama, by contrast, though dealing largely with the same Oedipal themes of emotional and moral identity, more often records the failure of the protagonist to act in a way that could shape the events and influence the emotional environment, let alone change the stifling social milieu. The world is closed, and the characters are acted upon. Melodrama confers on them a negative identity through suffering, and the progressive self-immolation and disillusionment gener-

*Peter Lloyd, "Raoul Walsh," *Brighton Film Review,* no. 14 (November 1969): 9; "Raoul Walsh: The Hero," ibid., no. 15 (December 1969): 8–12; "Raoul Walsh," ibid., no. 21 (June 1970): 20–21.

ally end in resignation: they emerge as lesser human beings for having become wise and acquiescent to the ways of the world.

The difference can be put in another way. In one case, the drama moves toward its resolution by having the central conflicts successively externalized and projected into direct action. A jail break, a bank robbery, a western chase or cavalry charge, and even a criminal investigation all lend themselves to psychologized, thematized representations of the heroes' inner dilemmas and frequently appear that way, as in Walsh's *White Heat* (1949) or *They Died with Their Boots On* (1941), Losey's *The Criminal* (1960), Preminger's *Where the Sidewalk Ends* (1950). The same is true of the melodrama in the *série noire* tradition, where the hero is egged on or blackmailed by the femme fatale—the smell of honeysuckle and death in *Double Indemnity* (Billy Wilder, 1944), *Out of the Past* (Jacques Tourneur, 1947), or *Detour* (Edgar G. Ulmer, 1946)—into a course of action that pushes him farther and farther in one direction, opening a narrowing wedge of equally ineluctible consequences that usually lead the hero to wishing his own death as the ultimate act of liberation, but where the mechanism of fate at least allows him to express his existential revolt in strong and strongly antisocial behavior.

Not so in the domestic melodrama. The social pressures are such, the frame of respectability so sharply defined, that the range of "strong" actions is limited. The tellingly impotent gesture, the social gaffe, the hysterical outburst replaces any more directly liberating or self-annihilating action, and the cathartic violence of a shoot-out or a chase becomes an inner violence, often one that the characters turn against themselves. The dramatic configuration, the pattern of the plot, makes them, regardless of attempt to break free, constantly look inward, at each other and themselves. The characters are, so to speak, each others' sole referent; there is no world outside to be acted on, no reality that could be defined or assumed unambiguously. In Sirk, of course, they are locked into a universe of real and metaphoric mirrors, but quite generally what is typical of this form of melodrama is that the characters' behavior is often pathetically at variance with the real objectives they want to achieve. A sequence of substitute actions creates a kind of vicious circle in which the close nexus of cause and effect is somehow broken and—in an often overtly Freudian sense—displaced. James Dean in *East of Eden* (Elia Kazan, 1955) thinks up a method of cold storage for lettuce, grows beans to sell to the army, falls in love with Julie Harris, not to make a pile of money and live happily with a beautiful wife, but in order to win the love of his father and oust his brother—neither of which he achieves. Although very much on the surface of Kazan's film, this is a conjunction of puritan capitalist ethic and psychoanalysis that is sufficiently pertinent to the American melodrama to remain exemplary.

The melodramas of Ray, Sirk, or Minnelli do not deal with this displacement-by-substitution directly, but by what one might call an intensified symbolization of everyday actions, the heightening of the ordinary gesture and a use of setting and decor so as to reflect the characters' fetishist fixations. Violent feelings are given vent on "over-determined" objects (James Dean kicking his father's portrait as he storms out of the house in *Rebel without a Cause* [Ray, 1955]), and aggressiveness is worked out by proxy. In such films, the plots have a quite noticeable propensity to form a circular pattern, which in Ray involves an almost geometrical variation of triangle into circle and vice versa,[1] whereas Sirk *(nomen est omen)* often suggests in his circles the possibility of a tangent detaching itself—the full-circle construction of *Written on the Wind* with its linear coda of the Hudson-Bacall relationship at the end, or even more visually apparent, the circular race around the pylons in *The Tarnished Angels* broken when Dorothy Malone's plane in the last image soars past the fatal pylon into an unlimited sky.

It is perhaps not too fanciful to suggest that the structural changes from linear externalization of action to a sublimation of dramatic values into more complex forms of symbolization, and which I take to be a central characteristic of the melodramatic tradition in the American cinema, can be followed through on a more general level where it reflects a change in the history of dramatic forms and the articulation of energy in the American cinema as a whole.

As I have tried to show in an earlier article,[2] one of the typical features of the classical Hollywood move has been that the hero was defined dynamically, as the center of a continuous movement, often both from sequence to sequence as well as within the individual shot. Perceptually, in order to get its bearing, the eye adjusts almost automatically to whatever moves, and movement, together with sound, completes the realistic illusion. It was on the basis of sheer physical movement, for example, that the musicals of the 1930s (Lloyd Bacon's *Forty-Second Street* [1933] being perhaps the most spectacular example), the gangster movie, and the B thriller of the 1940s and early 1950s could subsist with the flimsiest of plots, an almost total absence of individual characterization, and rarely any big stars. These deficiencies were made up by focusing to the point of exaggeration on the drive, the obsession, the *idée fixe*—that is to say, by a concentration on the purely kinetic-mechanical elements of human motivation. The pattern is most evident in the gangster genre, where the single-minded pursuit of money and power is followed by the equally single-minded and peremptory pursuit of physical survival, ending in the hero's apotheosis through violent death. This curve of rise and fall—a wholly stylized and external pattern that takes on a moral significance—can be seen in movies like *Underworld* (Josef von Sternberg, 1927), *Little Caesar* (Mervyn LeRoy, 1930), *The Roaring Twenties* (Raoul Walsh, 1939), and *The Rise and Fall of Legs Diamond* (Budd Boetticher, 1960) and depends essentially on narrative pace, though it permits interesting variations and complexities, as in Fuller's *Underworld USA* (1961). A sophisticated director, such as Hawks, has used speed of delivery and the pulsating urgency of action to comic effect (*Scarface* [1932], *Twentieth Century* [1934]) and has even applied it to films whose dramatic structure did not naturally demand such a treatment (notably *His Girl Friday* [1940]). In parenthesis, Hawks's reputed stoicism is itself a dramaturgical device, whereby sentimentality and cynicism are played so close together and played so fast that the result is an emotional hot-cold shower that is apt to numb the spectator's sensibility into feeling a sustained moral

---

[1]I have not seen *A Woman's Secret* (1949) or *Born to Be Bad* (1950), either of which might include Ray in this category, and the Ida Lupino character in *On Dangerous Ground* (1952)—blind, living with a homicidal brother—is distinctly reminiscent of this masochistic strain in Hollywood feminism.

[2]Thomas Elsaesser, "Nicholas Ray (Part 1)," *Brighton Film Review,* no. 19 (April 1970): 13–16: "Nicholas Ray (Part 2)," ibid., no. 20 (May 1970): 15–16.

charge, where there is more often simply a very skilled switchboard manipulation of the same basic voltage. I am thinking especially of films like *Only Angels Have Wings* (1939).

This unrelenting internal combustion engine of physical and psychic energy, generically exemplified by the hard-boiled, crackling aggressiveness of the screwball comedy, but which Walsh diagnosed in his Cagney heroes as psychotic *(White Heat)* and a vehicle for extreme redneck republicanism (*A Lion Is in the Streets* [1953]), shows signs of a definite slowing down in the 1950s and early 1960s, where raucous vitality and instinctual "lust for life" is deepened psychologically to intimate neuroses and adolescent or not so adolescent maladjustments of a wider social significance. Individual initiative is perceived as problematic in explicitly political terms, as in *All the King's Men* (Robert Rossen, 1949), after having previously been merely stoically and heroically antisocial, as in the film noir. The external world is more and more riddled with obstacles that oppose themselves to personal ambition and are not simply overcome by the hero's assertion of a brawny or brainy libido. In Mann's westerns the madness at the heart of the James Stewart character only occasionally breaks through an otherwise calm and controlled surface, like a strong subterranean current suddenly appearing above ground as an inhuman and yet somehow poetically apt thirst for vengeance and primitive biblical justice, where the will to survive is linked to certain old-fashioned cultural and moral values of dignity, honor, and respect. In the films of Sirk, an uncompromising, fundamentally innocent energy is gradually turned away from simple, direct fulfillment by the emergence of a conscience, a sense of guilt and responsibility, or the awareness of moral complexity, as in *Magnificent Obsession* (1953), *Sign of the Pagan* (1954), *All That Heaven Allows* (1955), and even *Interlude* (1957)—a theme that in Sirk is always interpreted in terms of cultural decadence.

WHERE FREUD LEFT HIS MARX IN THE AMERICAN HOME

There can be little doubt that the postwar popularity of the family melodrama in Hollywood is partly connected with the fact that in those years America discovered Freud. This is not the place to analyze why the United States should have become the country in which his theories found their most enthusiastic reception anywhere or why they became such a decisive influence on American culture, but the connections of Freud with melodrama are as complex as they are undeniable. An interesting fact, for example, is that Hollywood tackled Freudian themes in a particularly "romantic" or gothic guise, through a cycle of movies inaugurated possibly by Hitchcock's first big American success, *Rebecca* (1940). Relating his Victorianism to the Crawford-Stanwyck-Davis type of "women's picture," which for obvious reasons became a major studio concern during the war years and found its apotheosis in such movies as John Cromwell's *Since You Went Away* (1944) (to the Front, that is), Hitchcock infused his film, and several others, with an oblique intimation of female frigidity producing strange fantasies of persecution, rape, and death—masochistic reveries and nightmares that cast the husband into the role of the sadistic murderer. This projection of sexual anxiety and its mechanisms of displacement and transfer is translated into a whole string of movies often involving hypnosis and playing on the ambiguity and suspense of whether the wife is merely imagining it or whether her husband really does have murderous designs on her. Hitchcock's *Notorious* (1946) and *Suspicion* (1941), Minnelli's *Undercurrent* (1946), Cukor's *Gaslight* (1944), Sirk's *Sleep, My Love* (1947), Tourneur's *Experiment Perilous* (1944), and Lang's *Secret beyond the Door* (1948) all belong in this category, as does Preminger's *Whirlpool* (1949) and in a wider sense Renoir's *Woman on the Beach* (1946). What strikes one about this list is not only the high number of European émigrés entrusted with such projects, but that virtually all of the major directors of family melodramas (except Ray) in the fifties had a (usually not entirely successful) crack at the Freudian feminist melodrama in the forties.

More challenging, and difficult to prove, is the speculation that certain stylistic and structural features of the sophisticated melodrama may involve principles of symbolization and coding that Freud conceptualized in his analysis of dreams and later also applied in his *Psychopathology of Everyday Life*. I am thinking less of the prevalence of what Freud called "Symptomhandlungen" or "Fehlhandlungen," that is, when slips of the tongue project inner states into interpretable overt behavior. This is a way of symbolizing and signaling attitudes common to the American cinema in virtually every genre and perhaps more directly attributable to the metonymic use of detail in the realist novel rather than to any Freudian influence. However, there is a certain refinement of this in the melodrama—it becomes part of the composition of the frame, more subliminally and unobtrusively transmitted to the spectator. When Minnelli's characters find themselves in an emotionally precarious or contradictory situation, it often affects the balance of the visual composition; wine glasses, a piece of china, or a tray full of drinks emphasizes the fragility of their situation—e.g., Judy Garland over breakfast in *The Clock* (1945), Richard Widmark in *The Cobweb,* explaining himself to Gloria Grahame, or Gregory Peck trying to make his girlfriend see why he married someone else in *Designing Woman* (1957). When Robert Stack in *Written on the Wind,* standing by the window he has just opened to get some fresh air into an extremely heavy family atmosphere, hears of Lauren Bacall expecting a baby, his misery becomes eloquent by the way he squeezes himself into the frame of the half-open window, every word his wife says to him bringing torment to his lacerated soul and racked body.

Along similar lines, I have in mind the kind of condensation of motivation into metaphoric images or sequences of images mentioned earlier, the relation that exists in Freudian dream work between manifest dream material and latent dream content. Just as in dreams certain gestures and incidents mean something by their structure and sequence rather than by what they literally represent, the melodrama often works, as I have tried to show, by a displaced emphasis, by substitute acts, by parallel situations and metaphoric connections. In dreams one tends to "use" as dream material incidents and circumstances from one's waking experience during the previous day, in order to "code" them, while nevertheless keeping a kind of emotional logic going, and even condensing their images into what, during the dream at least, seems an inevitable sequence. Melodramas often use middle-class American society, its iconography, and the family experience in just this way as their manifest material, but "displace" it into quite different patterns, juxtaposing stereotyped situations in strange configurations and provoking clashes and ruptures that not only open up new associations but also redistribute the emotional energies that suspense and tensions have accumulated in disturbingly different directions. American movies, for example, often manipulate very shrewdly situations of extreme embarrassment (a blocking of emotional energy) and acts or gestures of violence (direct or indirect release) in order to create patterns of aesthetic significance that only a musical vocabulary might be able to describe accurately and for which psychoanalysis or anthropology might offer some explanation.

One of the principles involved is that of continuity and discontinuity. What Sirk has called the "rhythm of the plot" is what makes a movie hang together. This, it seems to me, is a particularly complex aspect of the sophisticated melodrama. A typical situation in 1950s American melodramas occurs where the plot builds up to an evidently catastrophic collision of counterrunning sentiments, but a string of delays gets the greatest possible effect from the clash when it does come. In Minnelli's *The Bad and the Beautiful* (1952) Lana Turner plays an alcoholic actress who has been "rescued" by producer Kirk Douglas, giving her a new start in the movies. After their premiere, flushed with success, self-confident for the first time in years, and in happy anticipation of celebrating with Douglas, with whom she has fallen in love, she drives to his home armed with a bottle of champagne. However, we already know that Douglas isn't emotionally interested in her ("I need an actress, not a wife," he later tells her) and is spending the evening with a broad in his bedroom. Turner, suspecting nothing, is met by Douglas at the foot of the stairs. At first too engrossed in herself to notice how cool he is, she is stunned when the other woman suddenly appears at the top of the stairs in Douglas's dressing gown. Her nervous breakdown is signaled by the car headlights flashing against her windshield like a barrage of footlights and arc lamps as she drives home.

Letting the emotions rise and then bringing them suddenly down with a thump is an extreme example of dramatic discontinuity, and a similar, vertiginous drop in the emotional temperature punctuates a good many melodramas—almost invariably played out against the vertical axis of a staircase.* In one of the most paroxysmic montage sequences that the American cinema has known, Sirk has Dorothy Malone in *Written on the Wind* dance like some doomed goddess from a Dionysian mystery while her father is collapsing on the stairs and dying from a heart attack. Again, in *Imitation of Life* (1959), John Gavin gets the brush-off from Lana Turner as they are going downstains, and in *All I Desire* Barbara Stanwyck has to disappoint her daughter about not taking her to New York to become an actress, after the girl has rushed downstairs to tell her father the good news. Ray's use of the staircase for similar emotional effects is well known and most spectacular in *Bigger*

---

*As a principle of mise-en-scène the dramatic use of staircases recalls the famous *Jessner-treppe* of German theater. The thematic conjunction of family and height/depth symbolism is nicely described by Max Tessier: "Le héros ou l'héroïne sont ballotés dans un véritable scenic-railway social, ou les classes sont rigoureusement compartimentées. Leur ambition est de quitter à jamais un milieu moralement dépravé, physiquement éprouvant, pour accéder au Nirvana de la grande bourgeoisie. . . . Pas de famille, pas de mélo! Pour qu'il y ait mélo il faut avant tout qu'il y ait faute, péché, transgression sociale. Or, quel est le milieu idéal pour que se développe (cette gangrène, sinon cette cellule familiale, liée à une conception hiérarchique de la société)?" (*Cinéma 71*, no. 161, p. 46).

Than Life (1956). In Henry King's *Margie* (1946), a film following rather closely Minnelli's *Meet Me in St. Louis* (1944), the heroine, Jeanne Crain, about to be taken to the graduation ball by a blind date (whom we know to be her father) since her poetry-loving bespectacled steady has caught a cold, comes tearing down from her bedroom when she hears the French master, on whom she has a crush, has dropped in. She virtually rips the bouquet of flowers out of his hands and is overwhelmed by joy. With some embarrassment, the poor man has to explain that he is taking someone else to the ball, that he has only come to return her papers. Margie, mortified, humiliated, and cringing with shame, has just enough time to get back upstairs before she dissolves in tears.

All this may not sound terribly profound on paper, but the orchestration of such a scene can produce strong emotional effects, and the strategy of building up to a climax so as to throttle it the more abruptly is a form of dramatic reversal by which Hollywood directors have consistently criticized the streak of incurably naive moral and emotional idealism in the American psyche, first by showing it to be often indistinguishable from the grossest kind of illusion and self-delusion and then by forcing a confrontation when it is most wounding and contradictory. The emotional extremes are played off in such a way that they reveal an inherent dialect, and the undeniable psychic energy contained in this seemingly vulnerable sentimentality is utilized to furnish its own antidote, to bring home the discontinuities in the structures of emotional experience that give a kind of realism and toughness rare if not unthinkable in the European cinema.

What makes these discontinuities in the melodrama so effective is that they occur, as it were, under pressure. Although the kinetics of the American cinema are generally directed toward creating pressure and manipulating it (as suspense, for example), the melodrama presents in some ways a special case. In the western or the thriller, suspense is generated by the linear organization of the plot and the action, together with the kind of "pressure" that spectators bring to the film by way of anticipation and a priori expectations of what they hope to see; melodrama, however, has to accommodate the latter type of pressure, as already indicated, in what amounts to a relatively closed world.

This is emphasized by the function of the decor and the symbolization of objects: the setting of the family melodrama is almost by definition the middle-class home, filled with objects, which in a film like Philip Dunne's *Hilda Crane,* typical of the genre in this respect, surround the heroine in a hierarchy of apparent order that becomes increasingly suffocating. From Father's armchair in the living room and Mother's knitting, to the upstairs bedroom, where after five years' absence dolls and teddies are still neatly arranged on the bedspread, home not only overwhelms Hilda with images of parental oppression and a repressed past (which indirectly provoke her explosive outbursts that sustain the action), it also brings out the characteristic attempt of the bourgeois household to make time stand still, immobilize life, and fix forever domestic property relations as the model of social life and a bulwark against the more disturbing sides in human nature. The theme has a particular poignancy in the many films about the victimization and enforced passivity of women—women waiting at home, standing by the window, caught in a world of objects into which they are expected to invest their feelings. Cromwell's *Since You*

Went Away has a telling sequence in which Claudette Colbert, having just taken her husband to the troop train at the station, returns home to clear up after the morning's rush. Everything she looks at or touches—dressing gown, pipe, wedding picture, breakfast cup, slippers, shaving brush, the dog—reminds her of her husband, until she cannot bear the strain and falls on her bed sobbing. The banality of the objects, combined with the repressed anxieties and emotions, forces a contrast that makes the scene almost epitomize the relation of decor to characters in the melodrama: the more the setting is filled with objects to which the plot gives symbolic significance, the more the characters are enclosed in seemingly ineluctable situations. Pressure is generated by things crowding in on them, life becomes increasingly complicated because it is cluttered with obstacles and objects that invade the characters' personalities, take them over, stand for them, become more real than the human relations or emotions they were intended to symbolize.

It is again an instance of Hollywood stylistic devices supporting the themes or commenting on each other. Melodrama is iconographically fixed by the claustrophobic atmosphere of the bourgeois home and/or the small-town setting; its emotional pattern is that of panic and latent hysteria, reinforced stylistically by a complex handling of space in interiors (Sirk, Ray, and Losey particularly excel in this) to the point where the world seems totally predetermined and pervaded by "meaning" and interpretable signs.

This marks another recurrent feature, already touched on: that of desire focusing on the unobtainable object. The mechanisms of displacement and transfer, in an enclosed field of pressure, open a highly dynamic, yet discontinuous cycle of nonfulfillment, where discontinuity creates a universe of powerfully emotional but obliquely related fixations. In melodrama, violence, the strong action, the dynamic movement, the full articulation, and the fleshed-out emotions so characteristic of the American cinema become the very signs of the characters' alienation and thus serve to formulate a devastating critique of the ideology that supports it.

Minnelli and Sirk are exceptional directors in this respect, not least because they handle stories with four, five, or sometimes six characters all tied up in a single configuration, and yet give each of them an even thematic emphasis and an independent point of view. Such skill involves a particularly "musical" gift and a very sensitive awareness of the harmonizing potential contained in contrasting material and the structural implications of different characters' motives. Films like *Home from the Hill, The Cobweb, The Tarnished Angels,* or *Written on the Wind* strike one as "objective" films, since they do not have a central hero (though there may be a gravitational pull toward one of the protagonists). Nonetheless they cohere, mainly because each of the characters' predicaments is made plausible in terms that relate to the problems of the others. The films are built architecturally, by a combination of structural tensions and articulated parts, and the overall design appears only retrospectively, as it were, when with the final coda of appeasement the edifice is complete and the spectator can stand back and look at the pattern. But there is, especially in the Minnelli movies, also a wholly "subjective" dimension. Because the parts are so closely organized around a central theme or dilemma, the films can be interpreted as emanating from a single consciousness, which is testing or experiencing in dramatic form the various options and possibilities flowing from an initially outlined moral or existential contradiction. In *The Cobweb* John Kerr wants both total self-expression and a defined human framework in which such freedom is meaningful, and George Hamilton in *Home from the Hill* wants to assume adult responsibilities while at the same time he rejects the standards of adulthood implied in his father's aggressive masculinity. In the latter the drama ends with a "Freudian" resolution of the father being eliminated at the very point when he has resigned himself to his loss of supremacy, but this is underpinned by a "biblical" one which fuses the mythology of Cain and Abel with that of Abraham blessing his firstborn. The interweaving of motifs is achieved by a series of parallels and contrasts. Set in the South, the story concerns the relations of a mother's boy with his tough father, played by Robert Mitchum, whose wife so resents his having a bastard son (George Peppard) that she won't sleep with him. The plot progresses through all the possible permutations of the basic situation: lawful son/natural son, sensitive George Hamilton/hypochondriac mother, tough George Peppard/tough Robert Mitchum, both boys fancy the same girl, Hamilton gets her pregnant. Peppard marries her, the girl's father turns nasty against the lawful son because of the notorious sex life of his father, etc. However, because the plot is structured as a series of mirror reflections on the theme of fathers and sons, blood ties and natural affinities, Minnelli's film is a psychoanalytical portrait of the sensitive adolescent—but placed in a definite ideological and social context. The boy's consciousness, we realize, is made up of what are external forces and circumstances, his dilemma the result of his social position as heir to his father's estate, unwanted because felt to be undeserved, and an upbringing deliberately exploited by his mother in order to get even with his father, whose own position as a Texas landowner and local big-shot forces him to compensate for his wife's frigidity by proving his virility with other women. Melodrama here becomes the vehicle for diagnosing a single individual in ideological terms and objective categories, while the blow-by-blow emotional drama creates the second level, where the subjective aspect (the immediate and necessarily unreflected experience of the characters) is left intact. The hero's identity, one the other hand, emerges as a kind of picture puzzle from the various pieces of dramatic action.

Home from the Hill is also a perfect example of the principle of substitute acts, mentioned earlier, which is Hollywood's way of portraying the dynamics of alienation. The story is sustained by pressure that is applied indirectly and by desires that always chase unattainable goals: Mitchum forces George Hamilton to "become a man" though he is temperamentally his mother's son, while Mitchum's "real" son in terms of attitudes and character is George Peppard, whom he cannot acknowledge for social reasons. Likewise, Eleanor Parker puts pressure on her son in order to get at Mitchum, and Everett Sloane (the girl's father) takes out on George Hamilton the sexual hatred he feels against Mitchum. Finally, after his daughter has become pregnant he goes to see Mitchum to put pressure on him to get his son to marry the girl, only to break down when Mitchum turns the tables and accuses him of blackmail. It is a pattern that in an even purer form appears in *Written on the Wind:* Dorothy Malone wants Rock Hudson, who wants Lauren Bacall, who wants Robert Stack, who just wants to die. *Le Ronde à l'américaine.* The point is that the melodramatic dynamism of these situations is used by both Sirk and Minnelli to make the emotional impact carry over into the very subdued, apparently neutral, sequences of images that so often round off a scene and that thereby have a strong lyrical quality.

One of the characteristic features of melodramas in general is that they concentrate on the point of view of the victim: what makes the films mentioned above exceptional is the way they manage to present *all* the characters convincingly as victims. The critique—the questions of "evil," of responsibility—is firmly placed on a social and existential level, away from the arbitrary and finally obtuse logic of private motives and individualized psychology. This is why the melodrama, at its most accomplished, seems capable of reproducing more directly than other genres the patterns of domination and exploitation existing in a given society, especially the relation between psychology, morality, and class consciousness, by emphasizing so clearly an emotional dynamic whose social correlative is a network of external forces directed oppressingly inward and with which the characters themselves unwittingly collude to become their agents. In Minnelli, Sirk, Ray, Cukor, and others, alienation is recognized as a basic condition, fate is secularized into the prison of social conformity and psychological neurosis, and the linear trajectory of self-fulfilment so potent in American ideology is twisted into the downward spiral of a self-destructive urge seemingly possessing a whole social class.

This typical masochism of melodrama, with its incessant acts of inner violation, its mechanism of frustration and overcompensation, is perhaps brought most into the open in characters who have a drinking problem (*Written on the Wind, Hilda Crane, Days of Wine and Roses* [Blake Edwards, 1963]). Although alcoholism is too common an emblem in films and too typical of middle-class America to deserve a close thematic analysis, drink does become interesting in movies where its dynamic significance is developed and its qualities as a visual metaphor recognized: wherever characters are seen swallowing and gulping their drinks as if they were swallowing their humiliations along with their pride, vitality and the life force have become palpably destructive, and a phony libido has turned into real anxiety. *Written on the Wind* is perhaps the movie that most consistently builds on the metaphoric possibilities of alcohol (liquidity, potency, the phallic shape of bottles). Not only is its theme an emotional drought that no amount of alcohol, oil pumped by the derricks, or petrol in fast cars and planes can mitigate, it also has Robert Stack compensate for his sexual impotence and childhood guilt feelings by hugging a bottle of raw corn every time he feels suicidal, which he proceeds to smash in disgust against the paternal mansion. In one scene, Stack makes unmistakable gestures with an empty martini bottle in the direction of his wife, and an unconsummated relationship is visually underscored when two brimful glasses remain untouched on the table, as Dorothy Malone does her best to seduce an unresponsive Rock Hudson at the family party, having previously poured her whiskey into the flower vase of her rival, Lauren Bacall.

Melodrama is often used to describe tragedy that doesn't quite come off: either because the characters think of themselves too self-consciously as tragic or because the predicament is too evidently fabricated on the level of plot and dramaturgy to carry the kind of conviction normally termed "inner necessity." In some American family melodramas inadequacy of the characters' responses to their predicament becomes itself part of the subject. In Cukor's *The Chapman Report* (1962) and Minnelli's *The Cobweb*—two movies explicitly concerned with the impact of Freudian notions on American society—the protagonists' self-understanding as well as the doctors' attempts at analysis and therapy are shown to be either tragically or comically inadequate to the situations that the characters are supposed to cope with in everyday life. Pocket-size tragic heroes and heroines, they are blindly grappling with a fate real enough to cause intense human anguish, which as the spectator can see, however, is compounded by social prejudice, ignorance, and insensitivity on top of bogus claims to scientific objectivity by the doctors. Claire Bloom's nymphomania and Jane Fonda's frigidity in the Cukor movie are seen to be two different but equally hysterical reactions to the heavy ideological pressures that American society exerts on the relations between the sexes. *The Chapman Report,* despite having apparently been cut by Darryl F. Zanuck, Jr., remains an extremely important film partly because it treats its theme both in the tragic and the comic mode without breaking apart, underlining thereby the ambiguous springs of the discrepancy between displaying intense feelings and the circumstances to which they are inadequate—usually a comic motif but tragic in its emotional implications.

Both Cukor and Minnelli, however, focus on how ideological contradictions are reflected in the characters' seemingly spontaneous behavior—the way self-pity and self-hatred alternate with a violent urge toward some form of liberating action, which inevitably fails to resolve the conflict. The characters experience as a shamefully personal stigma what the spectator (because of the parallelisms between the different episodes in *The Chapman Report* as well as the analogies in the fates of the seven principal figures of *The Cobweb*) is forced to recognize as belonging to a wider social dilemma. The poverty of the intellectual resources in some of the characters is starkly contrasted with a corresponding abundance of emotional resources, and as one sees them helplessly struggling inside their emotional prisons with no hope of realizing to what degree they are the victims of their society, one gets a clear picture of how a certain individualism reinforces social and emotional alienation, and of how the economics of the psyche are as vulnerable to manipulation and exploitation as is a person's labor.

The point is that this inadequacy has a name, relevant to the melodrama as a form: irony or pathos, which both in tragedy and melodrama is the response to the recognition of different levels of awareness. Irony privileges the spectator vis-à-vis the protagonists, for he or she registers the difference from a superior position of knowledge. Pathos results from noncommunication or silence made eloquent—people talking at cross-purposes (Lauren Bacall telling Robert Stack she's pregnant in *Written on the Wind*), a mother watching her daughter's wedding from afar (Barbara Stanwyck in *Stella Dallas* [King Vidor, 1937]), or a woman returning unnoticed to her family, watching them through the window (Barbara Stanwyck in *All I Desire*). These highly emotional situations are underplayed to present an ironic discontinuity of feeling or a qualitative difference in intensity, usually visualized in terms of spatial distance and separation.

Such archetypal melodramatic situations activate very strongly an audience's participation, for there is a desire to make up for the emotional deficiency, to impart the different awareness, which in other genres is systematically frustrated to produce suspense: the primitive desire to warn the heroine of the perils looming visibly

over her in the shape of the villain's shadow. But in the more sophisticated melodramas this pathos is most acutely produced through a "liberal" mise-en-scène
which balances different points of view, so that the spectator is in a position of seeing and evaluating contrasting attitudes within a given thematic framework—a
framework which is the result of the total configuration and therefore inaccessible
to the protagonists themselves. The spectator, say in Otto Preminger's *Daisy Kenyon* (1947) or a Nicholas Ray movie, is made aware of the slightest qualitative
imbalance in a relationship and also sensitized to the tragic implications that a radical misunderstanding or a misconception of motives might have, even when this
is not played out in terms of a tragic ending.

If pathos is the result of a skillfully displaced emotional emphasis, it is frequently
used in melodramas to explore psychological and sexual repression, usually in conjunction with the theme of inferiority; inadequacy of response in the American cinema often has an explicitly sexual code. Male impotence and female frigidity is a
subject that allows for thematization in various directions, not only to indicate the
kinds of psychological anxiety and social pressures that generally make people sexually unresponsive, but as metaphors of a lack of freedom (Hitchcock's frigid heroines) or as a quasi-metaphysical "overreaching" (as in Ray's *Bigger Than Life*). In
Sirk, where the theme has an exemplary status, it is treated as a problem of decadence—where intention, awareness, and yearning outstrip sexual, social, and
moral performance. From the Willi Birgel character in *Zu neuen Ufern* onward,
Sirk's most impressive characters are never up to the demands that their lives make
on them, though some are sufficiently sensitive, alive, and intelligent to feel and
know about this inadequacy of gesture and response. It gives their pathos a tragic
ring, because they take on suffering and moral anguish knowingly, as the just price
for having glimpsed a better world and having failed to live it. A tragic self-awareness is called upon to compensate for lost spontaneity and energy, and in films like
All I Desire or *There's Always Tomorrow* (Sirk, 1956), where as so often, the fundamental irony is in the titles themselves, this theme which has haunted the European imagination at least since Nietzsche, is absorbed into an American small-town
atmosphere, often revolving around the questions of dignity and responsibility, of
how to step down, how to yield when confronted with true talent and true vitality—
in short, those qualities that dignity is called upon to make up for.

In Hollywood melodrama characters made for operettas play out the human
tragedies (which is how they experience the contradictions of American civilization). Small wonder they are constantly baffled and amazed, as Lana Turner is in
Imitation of Life, about what is going on around them and within them. The tensions of seeming and being, of intention and result, register as a perplexing frustration, and an ever-increasing gap opens between the emotions and the reality they
seek to reach. What strikes one as the true pathos is the very mediocrity of the
human beings involved, putting such high demands upon themselves, trying to live
up to an exalted vision of the human being, but instead living out the impossible
contradictions that have turned the American dream into its proverbial nightmare.
It makes the best American melodramas of the fifties not only critical social docu-
ments but genuine tragedies, despite or rather because of the happy ending: they

record some of the agonies that have accompanied the demise of the "affirmative culture." Spawned by liberal idealism, they advocated with open, conscious irony that the remedy is to apply more of the same idealism. But even without the national disasters that were to overtake America in the late sixties, this irony, too, almost seems now to belong to a different age.

                                                                    1972

TANIA MODLESKI
TIME AND DESIRE IN THE
WOMAN'S FILM

Max Ophuls' 1948 film, *Letter from an Unknown Woman,* which is set in turn-of-the-century Vienna, begins late at night with the hero of the story, Stefan, returning by coach to his home and promising to fight a duel at dawn. That his attitude toward the situation is utterly frivolous is obvious from his remark as he steps out of the coach: "Gentlemen, I don't so much mind being killed, but you know how I hate to get up in the morning." Reaching his home, he tells his mute servant, John, that they should prepare for immediate departure since he does not intend to fight the duel. At stake here is a man's word. "A man's word is his honor," and, as Adrienne Rich observes, this notion of honor usually has "something to do with killing."* The terms of the drama seem already to have been posed with utter clarity. Stefan lives a life of ease, indulgence, and irresponsibility, unwilling to accept the values of duty and sacrifice espoused by his patriarchal society.

We might suspect, then, that the film's movement will involve Stefan's coming to repudiate the former childishness of his ways and to acknowledge the sway of patriarchal law. And indeed the final sequence of the film shows Stefan bravely setting off to keep his word and get himself killed. Thus, though the body of the film concerns the story of Lisa, the woman referred to in the title, it would appear that her story is really a story of and for the man, and, looked at this way, the film seems to provide exceptionally strong support for those critics who contend that there *is* no such thing as a woman's film, that Hollywood films are always dramas of and for the male.

When Stefan enters the house, he is given a letter which begins, "By the time you

---

*Adrienne Rich, *On Lies, Secrets, and Silence: Selected Prose 1966–1978* (New York: Norton, 1979), 186.

read this, I may be dead." It is the letter from the unknown woman who has indeed lived her life in and for Stefan, has even had a child by him, and yet has remained silent about her life-long devotion until her words, written in death's shadow, can no longer possibly bring her any benefit. At stake, then, is not only a man's word, but a woman's silence. At one point in the film, Lisa explains her radical refusal to speak about her own and their son's existence; "I wanted to be the one woman you had known who never asked you for anything." As Lisa perceives it, to speak as a woman would mean losing herself and becoming an object like the many other women in Stefan's life. However, when her own impending death releases her from her vow of silence, she only reveals how little of herself there is to know, so thoroughly has she become one with the man. Lisa's is the classic dilemma of what psychoanalysis calls the hysterical woman, caught between two equally alienating alternatives: either identifying with the man or being an object of his desire.

"Silence is the mark of hysteria," writes Hélène Cixous. "The great hysterics have lost speech, they are aphonic, and at times they have lost more than speech. They are pushed to the point of choking, nothing gets through."[1] It seems fair to say that many of the classic film melodramas from the 30s through the 50s are peopled by great, or near-great hysterics—women possessed by an overwhelming desire to express themselves, to make themselves known, but continually confronting the difficulty, if not the impossibility of realizing this desire. In the various film versions of *Madame X* (another title signalling the woman's anonymity), the heroine's son is defending her from criminal charges, unaware that the woman is his mother. Though she longs to reveal herself to her son, she refuses to speak, for fear of ruining his status and career. In *The Old Maid,* Bette Davis's character, who has had a child out of wedlock, masquerades as the old maid aunt to her own daughter so that the daughter may marry a suitable—rich, upper-class—man. And Stella Dallas, on becoming aware of her hopelessly lower-class life style, pretends to be interested in having a sexual affair in order to provoke her daughter to leave her. The central truth about Stella's feelings—that she loves her daughter to the exclusion of all else—remains unexpressed to the end.

In a short but illuminating article on film melodrama, Geoffrey Nowell-Smith has theorized a close connection between melodrama and conversion hysteria. He claims that castration is always at issue in Hollywood melodrama because "melodrama is fundamentally concerned with the child's problems of growing up into a sexual identity within the family, under the aegis of a symbolic law which the Father incarnates."[2] Now this applies to all the aforementioned films, and perhaps most obviously to *Letter from an Unknown Woman,* in which the duel may be understood as the castration Stefan finally comes to accept. But, Nowell-Smith argues, acceptance of castration never occurs without repression, and in melodrama, what is repressed at the level of the *story* often returns through the music or the mise-en-scène. Hence melodrama's resemblance to conversion hysteria, in which "the energy attached to an idea that has been repressed returns converted into a bodily

[1]Hélène Cixous, "Castration or Decapitation?" trans. Annette Kuhn, *Signs: Journal of Women in Culture and Society* 7, no. 1 (Autumn 1981): 49.
[2]Geoffrey Nowell-Smith, "Minnelli and Melodrama," *Screen* 18 (Summer 1977): 116.

symptom."[1] Although Nowell-Smith's argument is persuasive, he never notes that traditionally medical science and psychoanalysis have labeled *women* hysterics.[2] Yet surely we find here a clue as to why for a large period of film history melodrama and the "woman's film" have been virtually synonymous terms. If women are hysterics in patriarchal culture because, according to the feminist argument, their voice has been silenced or repressed, and if melodrama deals with the return of the repressed through a kind of conversion hysteria, perhaps women have been attached to the genre because it provides an outlet for the repressed feminine voice.

Peter Brooks argues in his book on nineteenth-century stage melodrama that melodrama may even be *defined* as a genre which works to overcome all repression in order to achieve full expressivity. In the nineteenth century, it was the beauty of moral virtue that continually sought expression over whatever attempted to silence, bury, or negate it. Often this beauty would be conveyed in *visual* terms, in the form, say, of a tableau. Nevertheless, melodrama is *not* primarily about the problems of sight and insight—the problems, that is, of tragedy. Brooks makes this point nicely in his discussion of the special place of the mute in many melodramatic plays:

> One is tempted to speculate that the different kinds of drama have their corresponding sense deprivations: for tragedy, blindness, since tragedy is about insight and illumination; for comedy, deafness, since comedy is concerned with problems in communication, misunderstandings and their consequences; and for melodrama, muteness, since melodrama is about expression.[3]

One need only point to the importance of the mute servant John in *Letter from an Unknown Woman* to demonstrate the force of Brooks's remarks. John is melodrama's equivalent to the figure of blind Tiresias in tragedy. He is, finally, the only character who is able to recognize Lisa and to name her, filling in the signature she herself has not been able to complete at the end of her letter.

It is this essentially melodramatic preoccupation with expression and muteness that Stephen Heath misses when he characterizes the entire problem of *Letter from an Unknown Woman* and of narrative cinema in general as one of *"seeing and knowing."*[4] In effect, Heath is collapsing all genres into one quintessentially masculine genre: tragedy, the paradigmatic example of which is *Oedipus,* with its privileging of sight and insight. For Heath, the project of the film is to present the woman "as a desired and untouchable image, an endless *vision.*"[5] And indeed a crucial moment of the drama occurs when Stefan, on his way to fight the duel, glances back over his shoulder and sees Lisa standing behind the glass door where he first saw her years ago. The image of the woman, forever silenced, is presented as the lost object whom Stefan may mourn and incorporate, thereby successfully

---

[1]Ibid., 117.

[2]A point made in passing by Griselda Pollock in her "Report on the Weekend School," which appears in the same issue of *Screen,* 109.

[3]Peter Brooks, *The Melodramatic Imagination: Balzac, Henry James, Melodrama, and the Mode of Excess* (New Haven: Yale University Press, 1976), 56–57.

[4]Stephen Heath, "The Question Oshima," in *Questions of Cinema* (Bloomington: Indiana University Press, 1981), 148.

[5]Ibid., 146.

taking up castration. He can now assume his place in patriarchal culture, and Lisa's image disappears from the screen.

But though Heath deplores the repression of the woman effected by turning her into a sight whose only meaning is the insight it offers the man into his life, he himself may be said to maintain this repression. As Brooks points out, melodrama cannot be fully grasped by analyzing it solely in terms of seeing and knowing. To continue relying on these terms is to obliterate what may be seeking expression through the woman in the films; and it is also to contribute to the hystericization of the female *spectator,* who is offered the limited choice between identifying with the man in his active desire or identifying with the passive, apparently mute object of that desire.

But how are we to begin attempting to locate a feminine voice in texts which repress it and which, as we saw in *Letter from an Unknown Woman,* grant possession of the Word only to men? Nowell-Smith, we have seen, suggests that the repressed aspects of the script reside in the mise-en-scène. Thomas Elsaesser, in an essay on film melodrama and its historical antecedents, argues that melodrama may best be understood in terms of "spatial and musical categories" rather than "intellectual or literary ones."[1] Melodrama is, after all, a hybrid form which traditionally combines music and drama. In a brief discussion of the use of fairgrounds and carousels in film melodrama, Elsaesser claims that these motifs "underscore the main action" and at the same time take on an independent significance. "What such devices point to," Elsaesser concludes, "is that in melodrama the *rhythm* of experience often establishes itself against its value (moral, intellectual)."[2] As wide-ranging as Elsaesser's essay is, tracing the development of melodrama cross-culturally through many centuries, he does not address himself to women's particular attraction to the genre. However, it is possible to appropriate his insight for our purposes, and so we will begin by looking at melodrama's rhythm for meanings which are opposed to the male Word.

In *Letter from an Unknown Woman,* Lisa and Stefan enjoy one night together, and this episode occurs in the middle of the film. They dine, dance, ride in a coach, and visit an amusement park where they sit in a stationary train while on a painted backdrop the scenery of the world revolves around them. Carousel music plays as they discuss the pleasures of travel. When they run out of countries to visit, Stefan pays the attendant to begin again, saying, "We will revisit the scenes of our youth." For Lisa these words are prophetic: after losing Stefan for many years and finding him again, she revisits the scenes of their youth in her quest to be reunited with him—returning to the place where they had dinner, buying flowers from a vendor as they had years ago, and going back to his apartments where they once made love. Most painful of all, she revisits the train station where Stefan departed from her so many years before, and this time sends her son away from her—to his death, as it turns out. This excessive repetition characterizes many film melodramas, and per-

---

[1] Thomas Elsaesser, "Tales of Sound and Fury: Observations on the Family Melodrama," *Monograph* 4 (1973): 6.

[2] Ibid., 3.

haps reaches its apotheosis in the 1932 film *Back Street*. At the end of this film the heroine, about to die, revisits in fantasy the scene of her youth when she missed meeting her lover and his mother in the park. As a result of this lost opportunity, she was not able to marry the hero and instead became his mistress, forced to reside in the back street of his life. Her final thoughts materialize on the screen as she pictures herself walking in the dazzling sunlight of the park toward the mother and son who welcome her into their family.

Unlike most Hollywood narratives, which give the impression of a progressive movement toward an end that is significantly different from the beginning, much melodrama gives the impression of a ceaseless returning to a prior state. Perhaps the effect may be compared to sitting in a train watching the world move by, and each time you reach a destination, you discover that it is the place you never really left. In this respect melodrama appears to be quite closely linked to an hysterical experience of time and place. The hysteric, in Freud's famous formulation, suffers from reminiscences. In melodrama, the important moments of the narrative are often felt as eruptions of involuntary memory, to the point where sometimes the *only* major events are repetitions of former ones. In *The Old Maid,* for example, four weddings occurring among two generations comprise the large units of the film, huge gaps in time separating some of these units. Melodrama, then, tends to be concerned with what Julia Kristeva calls the "anterior temporal modalities," these modalities being stereotypically linked with female subjectivity in general (with the "cycles, gestation, the eternal recurrence of a biological rhythm which conforms to that of nature").[1] As Kristeva notes, this conception of time is indissociable from space and is opposed to the idea of time most commonly recognized in Western thought: "time as project, teleology, linear and prospective, unfolding; time as departure, progression, and arrival—in other words, the time of history."[2] The train which first carries Stefan away from Lisa and then takes her son to his death is a train that departs, progresses, and arrives, whereas the train on which Lisa prefers to travel is one which, like the woman, always stays in its place. And as the world turns, visiting inevitably becomes a revisiting.

Two conceptions of time here seem unalterably opposed: the time repetition, which for Lisa means never entering history, but forever remaining childlike, fixated on the scenes of her youth. And the time of history which Stefan definitively enters at the end of the film when he takes his journey by coach to meet Lisa's husband and his own death. For Stefan this means, as we have already observed, that he must put away childish things and repudiate the self-indulgent life he has been leading in order to become a responsible adult. It is no mere coincidence that Stefan's entry into historical time and adulthood occurs simultaneously with his coming to accept the binding power of the word and the sway of death. For to quote Kristeva, this "linear time is that of language considered as the enunciation of sentences . . . and . . . this time rests on its own stumbling block, which is also the stum-

---

[1]Julia Kristeva, "Women's Time," trans. Alice Jardine and Harry Blake, *Signs: Journal of Women in Culture and Society* 7, no. 1 (Autumn 1981): 16.
[2]Ibid., 17.

bling block of that enunciation—death.''* And with the entry into historical time and language occurs the birth of desire: Stefan looks back at Lisa with recognition and longing only when the possibility of possessing her is forever lost. In accepting his place in language and history, he must assume a certain relation to desire: one based on an expectation destined to remain eternally unfulfilled.

But I have been a bit disingenuous in considering the antinomy between "hysterical time" and what Kristeva calls "obsessional time" to be based on sexual difference. Superficially it appears that in the film woman's time is hysterical time and man's time is obsessional time. Closer analysis, however, reveals that Stefan is the hysteric until the last few moments of the film, whereas Lisa adopts an altogether different relationship to time and desire which points beyond this deadly antinomy. For Stefan is the one who truly suffers from reminiscences. He cannot remember the name or the face of the woman who is the mother of his child and who is also, as the film implies, his muse. In a way, he has had a family, a career, and an entire life and never known it: the woman has lived it for him. When he sees Lisa, he struggles to overcome his forgetting and, in anguish, speaks of something which lies just over the edge of his memory. Unable to remember the woman who alone gives his life significance, Stefan is doomed to an existence of meaningless repetition, especially in relation to women, who become virtually indistinguishable to him. Moreover, it might plausibly be argued that insofar as Lisa is forced to keep repeating events, she is to a certain extent enacting *his* compulsion, for she herself has not forgotten a single moment with him.

That men may be hysterics too is an important point for feminism. Perhaps we have too quickly and unreservedly accepted theories of feminine hysteria. For if it can be said, as Lisa herself does say, that she has had no life apart from the moment with Stefan and his son, it is equally true that Stefan has had no life except the one Lisa has lived on his behalf. She has undergone all the joys and sorrows attendant on loving, possessing and losing a family while he, the father of that family, has remained oblivious. The woman and her emotional life is what Stefan has repressed and, like John Marcher in Henry James's "The Beast in the Jungle," he is doomed to keep suffering his fate without ever having known it.

Intuitively, of course, we ally melodrama with the feminine insofar as it is a genre quintessentially concerned with emotional expression. Women in melodrama almost always suffer the pains of love and even death (as in *Dark Victory*) while husbands, lovers, and children remain partly or totally unaware of their experience. Women carry the burden of feeling for everyone. *Letter from an Unknown Woman* simply takes this situation to its furthest extreme and shows that though women are hysterics with respect to male desire, men may be hysterics with respect to feminine "emotion"; unable to experience it directly, they gain access to it only at second hand.

Lisa's letter might be said to perform the "talking cure" for Stefan. If women are traditionally considered hysterics because, in Catherine Clément's concise formulation, they feel in the body what comes from outside the body, we can again see

---

*Kristeva, 17.

how Stefan is placed in the position of hysteric, as throughout the long night it takes to read the letter the disembodied feminine voice is repeatedly shown to be speaking through the mute Stefan.[1] And just as Freud said that the hysteric is a visual type of person whose cure consists in making a "'picture' vanish 'like a ghost that has been laid to rest,' . . . getting rid of it by turning it into words," so too is Stefan cured when after reading Lisa's letter, he looks back at her image behind the glass door, and looks back again to find that the picture has vanished.[2] The ghost of femininity—that spectre that haunts cinema—has been laid to rest.

Stefan's trajectory represents an interesting variant on that which Laura Mulvey claims is typical of one strain of melodrama. In her "Afterthoughts on 'Visual Pleasure and Narrative Cinema,'" she suggests that there is a kind of film in which "a woman central protagonist is shown to be unable to achieve a stable sexual identity, torn between the deep blue sea of passive femininity and the devil of regressive masculinity."[3] Mulvey points to Freud's theories of femininity, according to which the young girl first goes through an active masculine phase before attaining the "correct" feminine position. In *Letter from an Unknown Woman,* it is the man who first goes through a feminine phase before reaching the active, phallic phase and thus achieving a stable sexual identity. It is possible that Stefan's experience is analogous to that undergone by the male spectator of melodrama. For it may be that insofar as films like this are appealing to men (and there is plenty of evidence to suggest that *Letter from an Unknown Woman* strongly appeals to male critics), it is because these films provide them with a vicarious, hysterical, experience of femininity which can be more definitively laid to rest for having been "worked through."

And it may be that one of the appeals of such a film for women is precisely its tendency to feminize the man, to complicate and destabilize his identity. There is a moment in *Letter from an Unknown Woman* when confusion in sexual identity reigns supreme—the moment when after years of separation Lisa sees Stefan again at the opera. Briefly we see a close-up of Stefan through a soft focus filter, the device typically used in filming beautiful women. The image appears against a gray background which renders its diegetic status uncertain. The cutting from Lisa to Stefan further enhances this uncertainty, as it is unclear how each is placed in relation to the other and who is looking at whom. Finally, ambiguity reaches almost vertiginous extremes when over the image of Stefan, which is strongly coded to connote what Mulvey calls "to-be-looked-at-ness," Lisa's voice says in some panic, "Somewhere out there were your eyes and I knew I couldn't escape them."[4] Nowell-Smith argues that often the "'hysterical' moment of a text [that is, the moment when the repressed element returns to find expression in a bodily symptom] can be identified as the point at which the realist representative convention breaks down."[5] Here we

---

[1]Catherine Clément, "Enslaved Enclave," in *New French Feminisms,* ed. Elaine Marks and Isabelle de Courtivron (Amherst: University of Massachusetts Press, 1980), 134.

[2]Quoted in Joan Copjec, *"Flavit et Dissipati Sunt," October,* 18 (Fall 1981): 21.

[3]Laura Mulvey, "Afterthoughts on 'Visual Pleasure and Narrative Cinema' Inspired by 'Duel in the Sun,'" *Framework,* nos. 15/16/17 (1981): 12.

[4]Laura Mulvey, "Visual Pleasure and Narrative Cinema," in *Women and the Cinema,* ed. Karyn Kay and Gerald Peary (New York: Dutton, 1977), 418.

[5]Nowell-Smith, "Minnelli and Melodrama," 117.

Joan Fontaine (Lisa) gazes adoringly at Louis Jourdan (Stefan) in Max Ophuls' *Letter from an Unknown Woman* (1948). "Lisa's father strikingly resembles the pre-oedipal, imaginary father Julia Kristeva has theorized . . . . he represents a potential escape from the two neurotic modes of existence in which Stefan is successively trapped: the hysterical and the obsessional. If Stefan, who could be a great pianist, were to heed the message given him by Lisa through the imagining father, he would no longer be forced to choose between a sensuous but meaningless and repetitive existence and a life given over to duty and sacrifice." (MODLESKI, page 546).

Barbara Stanwyck (Stella) watches her daughter's wedding at the end of *Stella Dallas* (1937). "The association of tears and 'wet wasted afternoons' (in Molly Haskell's words) with genres specified as feminine (the soap opera, the 'woman's picture') points very precisely to the type of over-identification, this abolition of distance, in short, this inability to fetishise. The woman is constructed differently in relation to processes of looking." (DOANE, p. 764).

find a classic example of an hysterical moment in which the possibility of feminine desire being actively aimed at the passive, eroticized male is briefly glimpsed while being explicitly denied at the verbal level. Interestingly, in Heath's discussion of this scene, he for once listens only to the words, which articulate woman's traditional position as object of the look, and completely misses the subversive element of feminine desire which is struggling for expression in the body of the text.[1]

Partly because the erotic is conventionally equated with the feminine, it is paradoxically not the virile, masculinized male, the so-called "man's man," who elicits woman's desire in many of these films, but the feminine man: the attractive, cosmopolitan type (John Boles in *Stella Dallas, Only Yesterday,* and the first version of *Back Street*) or the well-bred, charming foreigner (Charles Boyer in the second version of *Back Street;* Louis Jourdan in *Letter from an Unknown Woman*). Moreover, the man with "feminine" attributes frequently functions as a figure upon whom feminine desires for freedom from patriarchal authority may be projected. Here I disagree with Mulvey who claims that in classic women's films like *Stella Dallas* the masculine figure enables the heroine to postpone the power of patriarchy.[2] *Stella Dallas,* in fact, provides a clear example to the contrary.

At the beginning of the film, Stephen Dallas, played by John Boles, is the son of a failed patriarch. His father, having gone bankrupt, has committed suicide, and Stephen has retreated from the world to take a management position in a rural factory. He is frequently figured as the rather lovely though unwitting object of Stella's desirous gaze as she watches him from behind her white picket fence or stares at his photograph in a newspaper clipping. He seems to be in all ways the antithesis of Stella's harsh and repressive father, and on him Stella pins her hope of escape from this patriarch. In a stunning sequence which ends the opening section of the film, Stella's father discovers that Stella has not been home all night. He sits with his back to the camera in the foreground of the picture and bangs his fist on the table shouting that Stella must never come home again. The mother cowers in the background and Stella's brother stands arguing with his father in the middle ground. This is a scene straight out of a nineteenth-century melodrama in which the stern patriarch prepares to exile his fallen daughter into the cold, cruel world. The sound of Stella's voice interrupts the argument, and the brother opens the door to Stella and Stephen who are coming up the porch stairs announcing their marriage. As the son runs back into the house, the screen door bangs shut on the couple, still outside, and the image fades. Patriarchy and its cruelties and excesses seem to be abruptly left behind, and the next scene shows Stella, now living in the city, returning from the hospital with her new-born daughter. However, the power of patriarchy has merely been postponed, since Stephen proves to be more domineering than Stella can bear. So she relinquishes her desire for men altogether and transfers it exclusively to her daughter.

The feminized man is attractive, then, because of the freedom he seems to offer the woman: freedom to get in touch with and to act upon her own desire and freedom to reject patriarchal power. The latter point is made forcefully in *Letter from*

---

[1]Heath, *Questions of Cinema,* 148.
[2]Mulvey, "Afterthoughts," 15.

an Unknown Woman, whose family romance involves two sets of fathers: the true fathers and the false fathers.[1] The false fathers—representative of patriarchal values and attitudes—are, firstly, Lisa's stepfather, a man attached to the military who takes Lisa away from Vienna and attempts to marry her off to a stiff, boring young lieutenant; and, secondly, the stepfather of Lisa's son, a military man always prating about duty, sacrifice, and responsibility. This is the man with whom Stefan is destined to fight the duel. Stefan, the father of Lisa's child, is one of the true fathers. Although he is a womanizer, this activity paradoxically womanizes *him,* for it immerses him in a sensuous existence stereotypically associated with the feminine and running counter to the life of self-denial espoused by Lisa's husband. And then there is Lisa's real father, who, though dead, is very much alive in Lisa's imagination. On the train in the amusement park Lisa tells Stefan of all the make-believe journeys she and her father took when she was a little girl, vividly evoking the pleasures and pains encountered in various climates. Lisa's father strikingly resembles the pre-oedipal, imaginary father Julia Kristeva has theorized.[2] He is the spokesman for creativity and play and as such he represents a potential escape from the two neurotic modes of existence in which Stefan is successively trapped: the hysterical and the obsessional. If Stefan, who could be a great pianist, were to heed the message given him by Lisa through the imaginary father, he would no longer be forced to choose between a sensuous but meaningless and repetitive existence and a life given over to duty and sacrifice.

The "pre-oedipal" father is, I would argue, another manifestation of the feminized male who helps the woman reject the repressive father by authorizing her own desire. For while Lisa appears here to be doubly an hysteric, invoking the words and activities of one man for the benefit of another, she is actually articulating a relation to the world that in the film is uniquely her own. On the train and elsewhere Lisa demonstrates an allegiance to the imagination which she considers superior to lived experience.[3] Clearly this applies to her entire existence, since she has had only one brief interlude with Stefan in a lifetime of desiring him. Like the voyages she took with her father, her journey with Stefan has gone nowhere, has been an adventure mainly of consciousness.

But that it has *been* conscious makes all the difference. We have seen that *Letter from an Unknown Woman* enacts a process of mourning for the man. Stefan has forgotten everything he has had and never realized what he could have had, and therefore in reading the letter he must work through the pain of loss and nonfulfillment in order to "lay the ghost to rest." Lisa, however, has remained fully aware of what was and what might have been; and having buried nothing she has no need to mourn. Hélène Cixous finds in the question of mourning a difference between

---

[1]Nowell-Smith discusses the way melodrama "enacts, often with uncanny literalness, the 'family romance' described by Freud—that is to say the imaginary scenario played out by children in relation to their paternity, the asking and answering of the question: whose child am I (or would I like to be)?" See 116.

[2]Julia Kristeva, "Woes of Love," lecture given at the Center for Twentieth Century Studies, University of Wisconsin-Milwaukee, Milwaukee, Wisconsin, November 2, 1982.

[3]For example, on the way to the amusement park, Stefan remarks that he only visits it in the winter, never in the spring when it is so much more beautiful. Lisa replies that perhaps he prefers to imagine its beauties rather than to experience them.

men and women. I would like to quote her at length because her words open up the possibility of a new way of thinking about women's experience in melodrama and women's response *to* melodrama:

> Man cannot live without resigning himself to loss. He has to mourn. It's his way of withstanding castration. He goes through castration, that is, and by sublimation incorporates the lost object. Mourning, resigning oneself to loss, means not losing. When you've lost something and the loss is a dangerous one, you refuse to admit that something of yourself might be lost in the lost object. So you "mourn," you make haste to recover the investment made in the lost object. But I believe women *do not mourn,* and this is where the pain lies. When you've mourned it's all over after a year, there's no more suffering. Woman, though, does not mourn, does not resign herself to loss. She basically *takes up the challenge of loss . . .* , seizing it, living it. Leaping. This goes with not withholding; she does not withhold. She does not withhold, hence the impression of constant return evoked by this lack of withholding. It's like a kind of open memory that ceaselessly makes way. And in the end, she will write this not withholding, this not writing: she writes of not writing, not happening.*

On the train which goes nowhere, Lisa describes journeys which did not happen, and the exquisite enjoyment they occasioned. In doing so, she articulates one of the basic pleasures of melodrama, which is also fundamentally about events that do not happen: the wedding that did not occur; the meeting in the park that was missed; and, above all, the word that was not spoken. Not speaking is very different from *keeping* one's word—the very phrase suggests the withholding and the resistance to loss which Cixous attributes to masculinity. Lisa resists speech not out of a need to hoard the word and not only because she wants to be different from Stefan's other women. Rather, she refuses to hold on to a man who has forgotten her, and what's more important, refuses to *hold him to* an obligation. Not seeing the relationship in terms of an investment or debt—that is, in terms of the property relations which, according to Cixous, structure masculine sexuality—she will not make him pay. So she takes up the challenge of loss and lives it. And from one point of view this challenge is more radical than the one Stefan takes up at the end of the film, resigning himself to his loss and the fate which consequently awaits him.

Cixous's words invite us to look deeper into the experience of loss which is at the heart of melodrama. After all, what lingers on in our memories long after the films have ended are just those moments when the heroine relinquishes all that has mattered in her life: Lisa saying goodbye to her son at the train station, where he promises, like his father before him, to see her in two weeks; Stella Dallas standing behind an iron fence watching her daughter's wedding through the window; Bette Davis's heroine in *Dark Victory* waiting in a darkened room for death to overtake her, having cheerfully sent her husband off to a medical convention. Cixous, in a rather poetic manner, suggests that in order to understand woman's experience of loss, we must go beyond the traditional psychoanalytic model based on the male's castration anxiety and his relation to the lost object. Nor do we gain in understanding by relegating woman to the position of hysteric, where film critics and theorists have been eager to place her. For though I began this paper by indicating that Lisa, the

---

*Cixous, "Castration or Decapitation?" 54.

archetypal melodramatic heroine, seems to fit neatly into the psychoanalytic category of hysteric, I would now like to point to the inadequacy of this model for understanding the position of woman in the woman's film.

The experience Lisa attempts to articulate on the train to nowhere is neither obsessional nor hysterical. It is not obsessional, for it does not entail moving forward through time and space toward an ever-receding goal until one reaches the stumbling block of death. She shows that one can *be moved* without moving. And it is only superficially the experience of an hysteric. According to Freud, the hysteric, who suffers from reminiscences, is "linked to place."[1] Now, this would seem accurately to characterize Lisa as she sits in a train that stays in place and reminisces about past journeys with her father. But the point is that Lisa does not *suffer* from reminiscences, as Stefan does. She voluntarily and even joyfully evokes them, here as elsewhere ceaselessly gives way to them, demonstrating the possession of the "open memory" Cixous describes. Hence the impression of constant return, which in her case has nothing compulsive about it. In his discussion of the film, Stephen Heath remarks, "Repetition is the return to the same in order to abolish the difficult time of desire, and the resurgence in that very moment of inescapable difference."[2] This is only partly true: it is true of Stefan, who, because he does not recognize the object of his desire, makes his experience with Lisa a mere repetition of those he has had with other women. For Lisa, however, and perhaps for all the women in melodrama constantly revisiting the scenes of their youth, repetition and return are manifestations of *another* relationship to time and space, desire and memory, and it is of this difference that the text speaks to me.[3]

1984

---

[1]Quoted in Kristeva, "Women's Time," 15.
[2]Heath, *Questions of Cinema,* 156.
[3]I would like to thank Kathleen Woodward and the Center for Twentieth Century Studies for generously providing me with a fellowship which enabled me to research and write this essay.

BRUCE KAWIN
THE MUMMY'S POOL

Helen: Have I been asleep? I had—strange dreams. Dreams of ancient Egypt, I think. There was someone like you in them.
Ardeth Bey: My pool is sometimes troubled. One sees strange fantasies in the water. But they pass, like dreams.

The Mummy

Sir John Talbot: All astronomers are amateurs. When it comes to the heavens, there's only one professional.

The Wolf Man

Karl Freund's *The Mummy* (1932), George Waggner's *The Wolf Man* (1941), Reginald LeBorg's *The Mummy's Ghost* (1944), and Peter Weir's *The Last Wave* (1978) each point to some very interesting connections among horror films, nightmares, and prophetic dreams—connections that might help explain what horror films do and why they remain interesting to viewers who probably stopped believing in Dracula along with Santa Claus. To clarify some of these points—such as the relations between displacement and reflexivity, prophecy and the attractions of being the "first victim," catharsis and the Land of the Dead, reincarnation and repression—it is necessary to define the elementary ways in which films are like dreams and the broad characteristics of horror film as a genre.

Watching a film and having a dream are both passive and active events. The dreamer/audience is physically cushioned in a darkened room, most of his movements restricted to slight shifts of position in a bed or chair, and mentally in various degrees of alertness, watching a visual process that often tells a story and often masks/presents some type of thought. In both cases the eyes move and the mind exercises creative attention. The dreamer might be considered more creative since

549

the dream manifests his own thought processes, but the role of the film audience is also an active one since the viewer creates his own experience of the work: we all have different interpretations of *Persona* not because the film is difficult, but because we interact with the signs in the generation of meaning and because our attention is selective. Although the dreamer is completely responsible for the dream, he usually avoids this awareness and casts himself in the role of participant or spectator; although the filmmakers are responsible for the movie, the viewer decides which film to attend and so chooses the general content of his experience. Thus dreamer and filmgoer approach a middle ground of pseudo-responsibility for what is watched. Both dreams and films include verbal and visual information but are effectively dominated by the limits of pictorialization. Film is primarily a visual medium, and the stories and symbols in dreams are subject not only to condensation, displacement, and secondary revision, but also to translation into pictorial and concrete representability, according to Freud.[1] In *Mindscreen*[2] I have attempted to show how the visual fields of film and dream are analogous, particularly in the ways each field indicates the "offscreen" activity of a consciousness. In a film this "narrating" mind may be that of the artist, of a character within the fiction, or of the work's self-awareness; "mindscreen" generally refers to the visual and sometimes aural field of such a consciousness, as opposed for instance to "subjective camera," which imitates the visual field of the physical eye of a character. A dream is the mindscreen of its dreamer, as the color section of *The Wizard of Oz* is the mindscreen of Dorothy and as *Persona* is the mindscreen of its own systemic self-consciousness. A film like Wise's *The Curse of the Cat People* plays with the question of whether the ghost is "real" or an aspect of the mindscreen of the child.

One goes to a horror film in order to have a nightmare—not simply a frightening dream, but a dream whose undercurrent of anxiety both presents and masks the desire to fulfill and be punished for certain conventionally unacceptable impulses. This may be a matter of unconscious wish fulfillment, following Freud; of confronting a hidden evil in the culture, as in *Alien* or *The Stepford Wives;* or of voyaging through the Land of the Dead and indulging a nostalgia for ritual, as we shall see when we turn to Frazer. Horror films function as nightmares for the individual viewer, as diagnostic eruptions for repressive societies, and as exorcistic or transcendent pagan rituals for supposedly post-pagan cultures. They can be analyzed in all these ways because they represent a unique juncture of personal, social, and mythic structure and because each of these structures has a conscious/official and an unconscious/repressed dualism, whose dialectic finds expression in the act of masking.

The clearest way to define the horror film genre is to compare it with that of science fiction, since the two are regularly confused with each other and often draw on the same materials (*Alien,* for instance, is a monster movie set in outer space). In what may seem like an unnecessarily long digression, I would like to show how

---

[1]Sigmund Freud, *The Interpretation of Dreams,* in *The Basic Writings of Sigmund Freud,* ed. A. A. Brill (N.Y.: Random House/Modern Library, 1938), pp. 319–68.

[2]Bruce Kawin, *Mindscreen: Bergman, Godard, and First-Person Film* (Princeton: Princeton Univ. Press, 1978).

horror and science fiction tend to present radically opposite interpretations of what may look like comparable situations, because the closed-system world view of horror may be a key to its personal and societal dreamwork.

Genres are determined not by plot-elements so much as of attitudes toward plot-elements. Horror and science fiction are different because of their attitudes toward curiosity and the openness of systems, and comparable in that both tend to organize themselves around some confrontation between an unknown and a would-be knower. To lay to rest the usual assumption that a film is science fiction if it has scientists in it and horror if it has monsters, let us look quickly at a science fiction film, *The Day the Earth Stood Still*, and a horror film, *The Thing*, both of which are 1951 Cold War American studio films about flying saucers with highly intelligent pilots.

The Day the Earth Stood Still (directed by Robert Wise) is the story of a space-man, Klaatu (Michael Rennie), who sets down his flying saucer in Washington, D.C. with the intention of putting Earth on notice: anything resembling nuclear violence will be punished by the obliteration of the planet, courtesy of a race of interstellar robot police. The spaceman has three forces to contend with: the army, which wants to destroy him; the scientists, who are willing to listen to him; and a woman (Patricia Neal) who understands and helps him. The central scientist (Sam Jaffe) is a kooky but open-minded and serious figure. Although it is suggested that earthlings understand violence better than most kinds of communication, they do respond to a nonviolent demonstration of Klaatu's power, and he does manage to deliver his message—perhaps at the expense of his life. The film's bias is in favor of open-minded communication, personal integrity, nonviolence, science, and friendship. The major villain (Hugh Marlowe) is a man who values personal fame and power more than integrity and love; he is willing to turn Klaatu over to the army, which shoots first and asks questions later—even if it means losing Neal, his fiancee.

The Thing From Another World (directed by Christian Nyby with considerable assistance from the producer, Howard Hawks) is deliberately formulaic, and so it is particularly valuable as a key to the genre. It is the story of a team of military men sent to an Arctic station at the request of its scientists, to investigate what turns out to be the crash of a flying saucer. The saucer's pilot (James Arness) is a blood-sucking vegetable that is described as intelligent but spends most of its time yelling and killing and leaving evidence of plans for conquest. The minor villain is a scientist (Robert Cornthwaite) who wants to communicate with the Thing rather than destroy it and who admires the alien race for its lack of sexual emotion. The Thing, however, has no interest in the scientist; and the human community (from which the scientist wishes to exclude himself), led by an efficient, hard-headed, and sexually active Captain (Kenneth Tobey), manages to electrocute the "super carrot." The film's bias is in favor of that friendly, witty, sexy, and professionally effective— Hawksian—human community, and opposed to the dark forces that lurk outside (the Thing as *Beowulf*'s Grendel). The film also opposes the lack of a balanced professionalism (the scientist who becomes indifferent to the human community and whose professionalism approaches the fanatical, as opposed to the effective Captain and the klutzy but less seriously flawed reporter), and what was meant in that paranoid time by the term Communism (we are all one big vegetable or zombie with each cell equally conscious).

This is how the oppositions between these two movies stack up:

1. *Army vs. Scientists.* In both films the army and the scientists are in conflict with each other. The army sees the alien as a threatening invader to be defended against and, if necessary or possible, destroyed. The scientists see the alien as a visitor with superior knowledge, to be learned from and, if possible, joined. In *The Thing* the army is right and the scientist is an obsessive visionary who gets in the way of what obviously needs to be done. In *The Day* the scientists are right and the army is an impulsive force that is almost responsible for the end of the world (hardly a far-fetched perspective).

2. *Violence vs. Intelligence.* The Thing is nonverbal and destructive; Klaatu is articulate and would prefer to be nonviolent. The army, which meets violence with violence, is correct in *The Thing* and wrong in *The Day* because of the nature of the alien; but what I am suggesting here is that the alien has its nature because of each genre's implicit attitude toward the unknown. The curious scientist is a positive force in *The Day* and a negative force in *The Thing,* for the same reasons.

3. *Closing vs. Opening.* Both horror and science fiction open our sense of the possible (mummies can live, men can turn into wolves, Martians can visit) especially in terms of community (the Creature walks among us). Most horror films are oriented toward the restoration of the status quo rather than toward any permanent opening. *The Day* is about man's opportunity to join an interstellar political system; it opens the community's boundaries and leaves them open. *The Thing* is about the expulsion of an intruder and ends with a warning to "watch the skies" in case more monsters show up; in other words, the community is opened against its will and attempts to reclose. What the horrified community has generally learned from the opening is to be on guard and that chaos can be repressed.

4. *Inhuman vs. Human.* Science fiction is open to the potential value of the inhuman; one can learn from it, take a trip with it *(Close Encounters),* include it in a larger sense of what is. Horror is fascinated by transmutations between human and inhuman (wolfmen, etc.), but the inhuman characteristics decisively mandate destruction. This can be rephrased as Uncivilized vs. Civilized or as Id vs. Superego, suggesting the way a horror film allows forbidden desire to find masked expression before it is destroyed by more decisive repression. The Id attempts to include itself in the wholeness of the dream-picture but is perceived as a threat and expelled from the community of what is human.

It is not too heavy a borrowing from *The Republic* to observe that the Gestalts of an artwork, a person, and a society are comparable. *The Wolf Man* expresses and exorcises the Id-force of uncontrolled aggression in its own system (the werewolf), in Larry Talbot (his werewolf phases), and in the community (the destabilizing forces of rape, murder, gypsy liminality, and aristocratic privilege—Talbot often behaves as if he had *droit du seigneur* when courting the engaged Gwen). In *The Invasion of the Body Snatchers* the egoless emotionless attitude of the "pods" is as undesirable in Becky as it is in the culture.

5. *Communication vs. Silence.* This links most of the above. The Thing doesn't talk; Klaatu does. (Or: Romero's Living Dead are completely nonverbal, while the

climax of *Close Encounters* is an exchange of languages.) What one can talk with, one can generally deal with. Communication is vital in *The Day,* absurd in *The Thing.* The opened community can be curious about and learn from the outsiders, while the closed community talks only among itself. Horror emphasizes the dread of knowing, the danger of curiosity, while science fiction emphasizes the danger and irresponsibility of the closed mind. Science fiction appeals to consciousness, horror to the unconscious.

In Gestalt terms, any dream (or fantasy or artwork) involves the projection of aspects of the self and the arrangement or interplay of those projections in a structure that corresponds to the whole self; the therapist's task is to help the dreamer re-own the projections. If I dream that I am walking in the desert and see a flower, a therapist might have me speak in the voice of the flower and then in the voice of the desert, to help me realize that they are as much myself as that image of the wandering observer and that the whole scene is a display of my wholeness. In this sense the science fiction Gestalt features a split-off creative hope that, once re-owned, can lead to an open, growthful, positive system. The horror Gestalt features a split-off destructive element that will be feared until it is re-owned, at which point the system can become stable. In most horror films, however, the negative projection is not re-owned but rejected and repressed: the Blob is frozen but can never be killed, the Mummy is burned but reappears in sequel, and in *Alien* the monster is destroyed but the corporate evil survives. Repression solves nothing, but (coupled with the momentary wish-fulfillment) gives a temporary sense of relief. Henry Frankenstein (leaving the novel out of this) may attempt to reverse the Original Sin and re-enter the community by acquiescing to the horror cliché that "there are things we are not meant to know"—except that his initial hubristic motive was not just to figure out eternity but to create life without the help of any Eve (he wants to "be as God" in a double sense) and when in the sequel he manages to get married it is a sure bet that some Dr. Praetorius will "force" him into an all-male effort to create a bride for the monster, Henry's split-off rejected/rejecting child-self.

In the dreamworld of movies, horror films come under two headings: in the Freudian sense, they are anxiety dreams or nightmares; anthropologically they express a nostalgia for contact with the spirit world. In his *Introductory Lectures on Psycho-Analysis,* Freud observed that "the attitude of the dreamer towards his wishes is a peculiar one; he rejects them, censors them, in short, he will have none of them. Their fulfillment, then, can afford him no pleasure, rather the opposite, and here experience shows that this 'opposite,' which has still to be explained, takes the form of *anxiety.*"*

In *The Wolf Man* this process is extremely clear. Larry Talbot (Lon Chaney Jr.) is a big Americanized engineer who is being groomed by his short and controlling father, Sir John (Claude Rains) to take over Talbot castle and the role of village Baron. Larry meets Gwen (Evelyn Ankers) and comes on like a "wolf," despite her being engaged to his father's gamekeeper (a model of controlled animal aggression, who is suited for the civilized institution of marriage). After he is bitten by a gypsy werewolf (Bela Lugosi) Larry splits into a wolf and a man. The man experiences

---

The Interpretation of Dreams, p. 520n.

pain and anxiety at the prospect of acting out his unconscious desires; at the climax the wolf begins to attack Gwen and then abandons her for more pressing game, Sir John. Larry insures he will be punished for this, for although he has given Gwen his own protective medallion, he has given his father the silver-headed wolf cane that can kill him. *The Wolf Man* is a transparently Oedipal nightmare, a full playing out of castration anxiety, and a clear example of how some horror films are analogous to one kind of dream. Although it can be said that *The Wolf Man* is the dream of the screenwriter (Curt Siodmak, who went on to dream the similar *Bride of the Gorilla*), it could also be analyzed as Larry's dramatized dreamworld—or, taking a cue from *Beauty and the Beast,* as Gwen's projection of the two sides of her sexuality, werewolf and gamekeeper; but it is also obviously the dream of the audience, which has decided to let its own unconscious desires find as-if expression, with the scariness of the film carrying the dream's anxiety quotient and the killing of the beast appearing to vindicate repression.

There is yet another side to all this. Sir John (a prize-winning researcher) believes in God, the universal "professional"; his religious sense is conventionally patriarchal, and Larry's Oedipal rebellion includes his participation in an erupting/repressed religion, gypsy superstition. (Recall the scene where Larry is too upset to join his father in church.) Whereas Sir John believes that all this is in Larry's mind and that werewolfery can be explained as a split between "the good and evil in a man's soul," with the evil finding expression in a fantasy of animality, the film attempts to prove him wrong. Sir John finds that all this is *not* a dream, that the wolf he has killed is his son. In this sense the horror film asserts the survival of "paganism" (the gypsies are right) and the inadequacy of science ("all astronomers are amateurs," a theme recognizable in *The Thing*)—a return to magic. Judaeo-Christianity represses, in this sense, the mystical unconscious that the horror-system allows to be expressed. (All this opens the possibility of a Jungian reading as well.) We may recall Van Helsing's pronouncement in *Dracula* that "the strength of the vampire is that people will *not* believe in him."

In *The Golden Bough* Frazer observed that dreams are often considered instances of contact with the spirits of the dead and that such dreams may serve as keys to the future and (through the symbolism of mistletoe, placed under pillows to induce prophetic dreams[1] and, as "the golden bough," an illuminating open-sesame) to the Underworld. Freud too mentions the ancient concept of "true and valuable dreams which were sent to the dreamer as warnings, or to foretell future events,"[2] and there is a considerable surviving literature of dreaming as genuine out-of-body travel, usually on the astral plane.[3] A medieval poem like *Pearl* (in which the poet mourns the death of his daughter and then has a dream of her full-grown in heaven) can be Electra-cuted by any number of Freudian readings, but its appeal and point are clearly in the way it presents itself as a genuine visionary experience.

Horror films appeal to this kind of dreaming through the figures of seer and "first

---

[1]Sir James George Frazer, *The Golden Bough* (N.Y.: Macmillan, 1963), pp. 818–19.

[2]*The Interpretation of Dreams,* p. 184.

[3]For an interesting and unusual approach to the question of night travel, see John-Roger, *Dreams* (N.Y.: Baraka Press, 1976.)

victim," and thus to the audience's desire to glimpse the truth, no matter how horrible. (A Freudian might translate this into the desire to learn about sex and be punished for it, which is often a legitimate reading.) In science fiction the visionary is usually rewarded; in horror, punished. Peter Weir's *The Last Wave* is the story of an Australian lawyer named David (Richard Chamberlain) who defends a group of aborigines involved in a ritual murder, one of whom (Gulpilil) begins to appear in his dreams. These dreams put him in touch with a parallel world ("the other side," in Western terminology) and remind him of his childhood experiences of night travel and prophetic dreaming. Eventually David discovers that he is a member of a race of priests and that the aborigines expect and may even have summoned up a great wave to destroy the intruding white civilization. As soon as he accepts his true vocation, David sees the wave and becomes its first victim. The wish such a horror film fulfills is that of *seeing,* and the world view it confirms is that "the other side" is real. In other words, David is a surrogate for the audience's desire to have, through watching a horror film, a spiritual vision. The satisfaction of being "first victim" is that one knows the hidden truth.

In the greatest of all horror films, Dreyer's *Vampyr,* the world and "the other side" continuously overlap, a dream within this dreamworld reveals to the hero the identity of the vampire. It is within this dream—of nearly being buried in a coffin whose window is clearly a reference to the frame of the movie-screen, so that the audience is cast as the victim/dreamer of the film-as-horror-object—that the hero is most in danger. The survival of Dreyer's dreamer and the death of Weir's visionary show that the crucial issue is not the destruction of the seer, but the threat of victimization. They also show that, although the more common impulse in the horror film is to exorcise the demon and save the community (*Vampyr, Jaws, The Thing, Tarantula, The Blob, Frankenstein,* etc.), there is a parallel track in which the community is rightfully destroyed *(The Last Wave, Dawn of the Dead, Dr. Strangelove).*

"The other side" may be a parallel spirit-world or it may be the Underworld, the Land of the Dead; in horror films these are usually comparable. At the climax of *The Last Wave,* David finds that he is a reincarnated priest, in a sense his own ghost. In *Apocalypse Now* (which advertises its indebtedness to *The Golden Bough*) the possibility of the community's being restored by the exorcism of Kurtz is overwhelmingly ironic, since the truths of the Underworld have more integrity than the lies of the conscious Establishment and the transfigured seer can never rejoin "their fucking army." So although there are many horror films that play on the dangerous attractions of prophecy and spirit-contact, the cathartic journey into the Land of the Dead presents itself as the larger category and as the key to all the patterns observed so far, especially if no one makes the link between death and the rigidity of unconscious fixations. Freud's work on the relations between compulsive repetition and the death instinct *(Beyond the Pleasure Principle)* is very useful here, but the more luminous juncture is that between the Mummy films and *The Golden Bough.*

The Mummy opens with the best "first victim" scene I know of. An expedition has discovered a mummy, Imhotep (Boris Karloff), and with him a sealed casket bearing a formidable curse. While two senior Egyptologists (one a straight scientist, one superstitious) discuss whether to open the box, the junior researcher, left alone, opens it and finds the Scroll of Thoth. Mouthing an impromptu translation under his breath, he inadvertently raises the Mummy from the dead. Imhotep takes the scroll and exits, leaving a terminal madman in his wake. Here the desire to discover what is forbidden is related to the thrills of danger and self-destruction that are part of the cathartic masochism of attending horror films and having nightmares; and the mechanism of releasing an unconscious deathless force is tied into the legend of Isis and Osiris.

According to Frazer, the spell of Thoth was first used by Isis to raise her son Horus from the dead. When her brother/husband Osiris was murdered and dismembered, Isis had the aid of several gods and relatives in reassembling the body-parts (except for his genitals) and raising him from the dead. Revived, Osiris became the King of the Underworld, Lord of Eternity, and Ruler of the Dead. The rituals Isis practiced were imitated in Egyptian burial ceremonies so that the deceased might be born again in the Underworld (although Osiris, the first mummy, was supposed to have been revived in this world too).* In Freund's film, this is condensed into Isis' using the Scroll of Thoth to revive Osiris from the dead. The story is that Imhotep had tried to read the scroll over the body of his beloved Anckesenamon, a priestess of Isis and daughter of the Pharoah; for this attempted sacrilege, Imhotep had been buried alive along with the scroll, which could thus never again be used. Revived and in possession of the scroll, however, Imhotep (now calling himself Ardeth Bey) sets out to find the reincarnation of Anckesenamon, who turns out to be Helen Grosvener (Zita Johann). He nearly convinces her to die and be reborn as a living mummy like himself, but at the last moment Helen decides to live rather than to let her ancient identity dominate her (i.e., she chooses health over neurosis) and appeals to Isis to teach her again the spells she has forgotten over the ages. The statue of Isis responds to the spells and kills the Mummy; this implies it was not enough for Helen simply to reject Imhotep, that she had to integrate her Helen and her Anckesenamon aspects in order to come into her full power. This is very similar to what Imhotep wanted her to do, except that he would have had her proceed from that integration to a fuller Anckesenamon rather than to a fuller Helen. What this shows is that there is no safety in ignoring the Id/Underworld/monster (the attitude of the ineffectual patsy in most horror films, e.g., the mayor in *Jaws* and Helen's modern boyfriend [David Manners] in *The Mummy*) but that there is considerable strength in confronting the danger and surviving that deeply acknowledged contact—in other words, re-owning the projection. In this sense horror films are valuable and cathartic, for they may offer the possibility of participating in the acting-out of an unacknowledged wish or fear in a context of resolution rather than of repression. This is of course what happens to Helen and not to the Mummy. He is a walking repetition compulsion, determined to complete his frustrated sacrilege and consummate his romance (the sexist aspects of all this are quite blatant in the film). He would have her "go through moments of horror for an eternity of love," but what he means by love is the insatiability of unconscious drives (which are, to

---

The Golden Bough, pp. 422–26.

be fair, often involved in fantasies of eternal romance). There is value, then, not in being Imhotep but in, like Helen and like the audience, *almost* being Imhotep.

We are now back to Osiris and Frazer. One of the major points of *The Golden Bough* is that the agricultural year and the sacred year are closely related in a great many cultures, and that the myth of the death and resurrection of Osiris (like that of Jesus, whose death and resurrection occur in the spring) may have served the Egyptians as an explanation or prompter (through ritual re-enactment) of the land's return to life in the spring after its death in the winter. The parallel with horror films should be immediately obvious: one enters the Land of the Dead, gives death temporary dominion, in order to emerge reborn and refreshed. Horror films are the Land of the Dead, the visionary/ghost-world where shades and demons have power, one goes to the theatre as to the Underworld, becomes Imhotep or Helen on an as-if basis, undergoes a catharsis, and steps back into the light of day (if it happens to be a matinee, which is how most children see horror films and form lasting impressions of the paradigmatic content of the experience). For Osiris, this transit left him in a position of power over the Underworld, and it will be remembered that Jesus too harrowed Hell when he died; thus for the community, the benefits include an assured sense of the existence of divinity and a reborn economy, and for the god, the benefits include life and power. But not all dreams, not all winters, and not all horror films have such happy resolutions. The stories of Osiris and Jesus do not depend on repression. A Freudian dream solves little or nothing until it is understood in analysis, simply to allow the unconscious wish to find masked fulfillment does not remodel the psyche. Left to his own devices, the Mummy will simply repeat his compulsive and insatiable project in sequel after sequel, like an incarnation of neurosis itself. So it is valuable to have a character within the film who can, like Helen, acknowledge the unconscious drive and go on from there into an integrated life, or a dreamer who can re-own projections and live a free, healthy, flexible future.

This reduces itself to a question of audience intention, since even a film like *The Thing* or *The Wolf Man* in which the horror object is simply repressed/killed and the community reasserts its boundaries can serve its audience as a visit to the Land of the Dead. The overall structure of such a visit may be cathartic in the same way that to dream may promote psychic health regardless of dream content. One could, in any case, go to *The Wolf Man* because one would enjoy participating in a fantasy of uncontrolled aggression and victimization (which is why most people went to *Jaws* and *Alien* and *The Texas Chainsaw Massacre*). But once there, one has the option of feeling that one's private beast has been purged and will require no further playground, or of enjoying the punishment and anxiety that attend unconscious wish-fulfillment and planning to attend another horror film the next time one feels in conflict about such desires. The latter is clearly more in line with Freud's reading of dreamwork, and with my outline of closed-system behavior, and it is doubtless the more common experience of horror films. Yet the former response is possible and legitimate, and it strikes me as being encouraged in those films that call the viewer's attention to the fact that he is watching a horror film and pretending to believe it, much as the analyst may attempt to engage the patient's ego while interpreting a dream. This is the method of *Vampyr* and of the bizarre, neglected, wonderful *Mummy's Ghost.*

The intervening sequels—*The Mummy's Hand* (1940) and *The Mummy's Tomb* (1942)—changed many of the terms of the story. The Mummy, Kharis, is now presented as having tried to raise the Princess Ananka by giving her the fluid from nine tana leaves; his tongue is torn out (Kharis is silent, unlike Ardeth Bey), and he is buried with a box of the leaves and charged with guarding her tomb for eternity. The Banning expedition discovers Ananka and ships her mummy back to the Scripps Museum in America, despite considerable interference from Kharis, who has been revived by a cult of priests (led by George Zucco). Kharis' motives are to keep the dead Ananka with him (neurotic possessiveness) and to defend the integrity of the Ancient Gods (against whom he rebelled in the first place). Therefore in these two films he is fulfilling the curse made against himself and has no strategy for reviving Ananka. The climax of these films comes when the priest (George Zucco in *Hand,* Turhan Bey in *Tomb*) decides to administer tana fluid to himself and the nearest heroine (who is never Ananka), but is foiled or killed, after which the Mummy is burned and the community of Americans restored. So if Kharis represents anything here, it is the deathless persistence of compulsive fixation that may have begun in sexual desire but has become only an undead, rigid, destructive, rejecting anger.

The Mummy's Ghost may be a brilliant parody of the series, a self-deconstructing masterpiece, or simply what used to be called a really good bad movie. It exploits every formula it can, turning them against themselves, right up to the climax where the monster, for once, gets the girl. It begins in the tombs of Arkham (a reference to Lovecraft?), where Zucco explains his role to the new priest, Yusef Bey (John Carradine). When told of his mission, Yusef Bey says incredulously, "Kharis—still *lives?*" His "you've got to be putting me on" tone puts the film in sync with the audience immediately, as the sequel declares its awareness of being a formulaic sequel or its worldly equivalent. Next we see Professor Norman explaining to his college students the legend of Kharis, who was supposedly destroyed in their own town, Mapleton. A student argues that, "Maybe it was a man made up as a mummy, to keep the legend alive." The student is of course right in a way he could not guess but the audience can. The professor, however, insists that he saw the monster (i.e., this is a horror-film-like world and these dangers are real). This scientist is of course the first victim.

The romantic lead, Tom Harvey (Robert Lowery), has a crush on an Egyptian, Amina Monzouri (Ramsay Ames) who is working on the college staff; he also has a little dog named Peanuts. Whenever Amina thinks of Egypt, she gets a chill, but Tom insists that Egypt is just like any other modern country. Tom is the all-time ineffectual patsy of the formula, blindly confident in the status quo of modern America and uncomplicated marriage, while Amina is in conflict about her destiny, which is called Egypt but means sex and death—"forbidden love." When Kharis is on his way to kill Professor Norman, his shadow crosses her sleeping face and Amina walks in a trance to the site of the murder. When she is found in the morning, her wrist bears the birthmark of Ananka and her hair has a white streak. The next evening, Tom manages to convince Amina to neck with him in his car; while they kiss, Kharis' shadow crosses her face again.

By this time Yusef Bey has brought Kharis to the museum. Downstairs a guard prepares to relax, hanging his hat on a realistic statue of a woman (i.e., he doesn't believe art is real), opening a crime magazine, and turning on the radio ("This is *The Hour of Death*. The forces of evil stand at the threshold. A man shall die tonight ... Did you ever meet a killer, my friend? You will tonight—"). The guard is a surrogate for the horror audience, who enjoys pretending that horrors exist, and a play on and against the suspension of disbelief—because the lies on the radio describe the truth of his situation. The reflexivity of this picture allows it to disarm the audience completely, since it continually calls attention to the fact that it is just a ghost story and just as continually presents its horrors as *real anyway.*

Upstairs Kharis finally touches the mummy of Ananka; there is a straight cut to Amina in bed, waking and screaming; straight cut back to a collapsed pile of wrappings. Ananka's soul has been reborn in Amina, again to seek its salvation. (This would frustrate the curse—for in this version of the story, Ananka and Kharis are equally culpable for their forbidden love, and the priests' motives include keeping either of them from working out their karma through reincarnation.) The site of Amina's joining her repressed Ananka is, as usual, implicitly sexual. A friend reassures her that she "must have been having a nightmare." Back at the museum, Kharis kills the guard ("gunshots—crash—" the radio had said; the guard shoots Kharis and then is smashed against a glass door before being strangled).

Kharis finds Amina in bed and takes her away, unconscious, to a shack where Yusef Bey waits. Yusef Bey soon tells her that she is Ananka, and points to Kharis as an example of eternal unfilfillment and restlessness; she faints, and in her sleep her hair turns completely white. Then Yusef Bey decides to give her and himself the tana fluid—the most blatant instance of formula (or compulsive role-playing) in the whole film, coming absolutely out of nowhere—and Kharis kills him. Peanuts has led Tom to the scene, and Kharis knocks him out; then he carries Amina into the swamp (in New England?—again, more formula than "reality"). Tom is joined by the sheriff's posse (which has been digging a pit for the Mummy and burning tana leaves—another fakeout, since the Mummy transcends his compulsive desire for the fluid and walks on with his romantic burden; i.e., the fixed pattern of his sexual desire is stronger than the fixed pattern of the movie's formula; this pit business would have served as a typical solution in many films of the period). A formulaic rush to the rescue ensues—reminiscent of the torchlight parades in *Frankenstein* and *The Mummy's Tomb*—with Peanuts and Tom and the posse all chasing the Mummy. Such crosscut chase scenes have signified climax and resolution since Griffith, and aside from the St. Bartholomew's Day Massacre sequence of *Intolerance* there are very few examples of failed climactic chases in the whole history of film. One of the most troubling closes *The Mummy's Ghost.*

Because the chase does fail, and in a masterful way. As Kharis carries her, Amina becomes entirely Ananka: her flesh dries, her frame contracts, but she is still alive. Imhotep's project has been fulfilled (Kharis too has returned to his origins): the two lovers are united as living mummies. This rare moment of absolute fulfillment of forbidden love, which Amina has been shrinking from and growing toward and which Kharis has been yearning after for 3000 years, is immediately succeeded by their deaths—they drown in the swamp. The posse stands there looking beaten; Tom (who has seen Ananka's face) is a wreck; Peanuts is alone on the swampbank cocking his puzzled head. There is a sudden feeling of "what happened!" Suddenly a real horror has asserted itself—Amina has given herself over to her unconscious drives; the Mummy has abducted her and gotten away with it; all the formulas have failed at once. And at this point a George Zucco voice-over intones the curse: "The fate of those who defy the will of the Ancient Gods will be a cruel and violent death." (This is what Derrida would recognize as a good place to begin deconstructing the film, except that the film has already done it for us.) Although it seems that Ananka has repeated her sin rather than sought her salvation, and therefore is properly punished (Freud again), there is no denying the satisfactions of romantic apotheosis. Except if one views it from a feminist perspective, whereby Amina could be seen as surrendering to the deadly obsessions of her abductor, utterly identifying with her state of victimization; the horror of her no-win situation is that her only alternative to Kharis, in this culture, would be to play the role of Tom's wife. Whether Amina is seen as joining her demon lover or as the victim of a cosmic rape, it is still clear that the curse, as formulated, is not in control, and that horror has triumphed.

Behaving according to formula is one aspect of repetition compulsion and of neurosis. In this film the force of Kharis and Ananka's unconscious desires is so strong that they at least balance and perhaps make irrelevant the repressive curse. (To say that Amina has these "desires" is to say that she behaves like a Freudian construct of masochistic femininity; if one abandons the feminist reading, one is left with the less complex observation that she allows the aspects of her sexuality that frighten her to find complete expression.) Kharis is so compulsive that he wins, even if briefly, and the formulaic aspects of the genre are turned against themselves; the community is not restored. The audience is unable to take comfort from the expected formulaic resolution and has been made aware of the presence of formula all along: so the possibility exists that this film educates its audience (engages the ego in self-consciousness) rather than encouraging it only to participate in unconscious wish fulfillment (while, as usual, having it both ways and fulfilling the wish completely). As it reminds the audience that it is a formulaic film, *The Mummy's Ghost* is like a dream, one of whose major strategies has been undermined—since one of the basic functions of displacement and secondary revision is not just to mask the desire but to keep the dreamer asleep, to keep the dreamer from realizing what these masked desires are, and that they are his own. Like the most intense nightmares, *The Mummy's Ghost* awakens the audience in a moment of anxious clarity and fulfillment. It may be, to reverse the phrase, that the sleep of monsters breeds reason.

1981

LINDA WILLIAMS
WHEN THE WOMAN LOOKS

Whenever the movie screen holds a particularly effective image of terror, little boys and grown men make it a point of honor to look, while little girls and grown women cover their eyes or hide behind the shoulders of their dates. There are excellent reasons for this refusal of the woman to look, not the least of which is that she is often asked to bear witness to her own powerlessness in the face of rape, mutilation, and murder. Another excellent reason for the refusal to look is the fact that women are given so little to identify with on the screen. Laura Mulvey's extremely influential article on visual pleasure in narrative cinema has best defined this problem in terms of a dominant male look at the woman that leaves no place for the woman's own pleasure in seeing: she exists only to be looked at.[1]

Like the female spectator, the female protagonist often fails to look, to return the gaze of the male who desires her. In the classical narrative cinema, to see is to desire. It comes as no surprise, then, that many of the "good girl" heroines of the silent screen were often figuratively, or even literally, blind.[2] Blindness in this context signifies a perfect absence of desire, allowing the look of the male protagonist to regard the woman at the requisite safe distance necessary to the voyeur's pleasure, with no

---

[1] Laura Mulvey, "Visual Pleasure and Narrative Cinema," *Screen,* vol. 16, no. 3 (Autumn 1975), pp. 6–18. See also John Berger's description of the different "social presence" of the woman in western painting and advertisement, in *Ways of Seeing* (London: Penguin Books, 1978), pp. 46–47. Berger argues that where the man in such works simply "surveys" the woman before acting toward her, the woman is split into a "surveyor" and a "surveyed." In other words, she is constantly aware of being looked at, even as she herself looks. Mary Ann Doane similarly notes the woman's status as spectacle rather than spectator and goes on to make a useful distinction between primary and secondary identifications within these structures of seeing in "Misrecognition and Identity," *Ciné-Tracts,* vol. 3, no. 3 (Fall 1980), pp. 25–31.

[2] The pathetic blind heroine is a cliché of melodrama from D. W. Griffith's *Orphans of the Storm* to Chaplin's *City Lights* to Guy Green's *A Patch of Blue.*

danger that she will return that look and in so doing express desires of her own. The relay of looks within the film thus duplicates the voyeuristic pleasure of the cinematic apparatus itself—a pleasure that Christian Metz and Laura Mulvey have suggested to be one of the primary pleasures of film viewing: the impression of looking in on a private world unaware of the spectator's own existence.[1]

But even when the heroine is not literally blind, the failure and frustration of her vision can be the most important mark of her sexual purity. An illuminating example of this failed vision occurs in D. W. Griffith's 1911 two-reeler, *Enoch Arden*.[2] A remarkable illustration of the pleasures of voyeurism the cinema could offer audiences of that time, the film is entirely structured as a series of romantic or domestic scenes which are spied upon by two successive male voyeurs.

In a small fishing village Enoch Arden and Phillip Ray are rivals for Annie Lee's affections. After separate shots which introduce each of them, Enoch in the background spies upon what he presumes to be the happy love of Phillip and Annie Lee. Soon after the shot is repeated, but this time with Phillip as the outsider spying on Annie Lee and Enoch. A title provides Tennyson's lines, "Phillip looked, and in their eyes and faces read his doom."[3] The decision as to which of these rivals "gets" the girl is based on the abdication of an unseen onlooker who believes he "reads" the true desires of the couple. But since Enoch and Phillip have each read the same desire in the couple which excludes them, it becomes apparent that what matters is not so much the desire of the couple but the sad and jealous look of the outsider-voyeur who imagines—and thus constitutes—a happiness that must exclude him. Through this process Enoch wins Annie.

After some years of marriage, Enoch is forced to leave his happy home and family to go to sea. Annie Lee stands on the beach waving to Enoch's ship as it disappears in the distance, watching "to the last dip of the vanishing sail." The frustration of her look is emphasized by the spyglass she brings with her and through which she vainly peers for the next twenty years as she awaits Enoch's return.[4]

What Annie strains to see but cannot, Griffith's parallel editing permits us to see clearly: Enoch's shipwreck and long vigil on a desert island, scanning the horizon for the ship that will bring him home. Throughout their long separation Griffith is careful to maintain consistent screen direction in both Enoch and Annie Lee's looks "off." Annie always looks screen left, Enoch on his island looks screen right, thus preserving the spectator's hope that their gazes, and their paths, might one day meet. This is especially acute when Enoch is on the ship transporting him home.

[1]Mulvey, "Visual Pleasure." Also Christian Metz, "The Imaginary Signifier," *Screen*, vol. 16, no. 2 (Summer 1975), pp. 14–76.

[2]*Enoch Arden* (1911) is a two-reel remake of Griffith's earlier one-reeler entitled *After Many Years* (1908). Both are adaptations of Tennyson's 1864 poem "Enoch Arden." The earlier version is often cited as Griffith's first integrative use of the close-up and as his first radical use of spatial discontinuity. The 1911 version is usually cited as his first expansion into the two-reel length. Lewis Jacobs, *The Rise of the American Film* (New York: Teachers College Press, 1967), pp. 103–104.

[3]The intertitle is quoted verbatim from Tennyson's poem.

[4]In Tennyson's poem Annie Lee fails to catch even this last sight of Enoch. Enoch had assured her that she could prolong their farewell by looking at him through a spyglass—the same spyglass that Griffith uses to emphasize her inability to see in subsequent scenes. In the poem Annie fails to operate the glass properly and thus misses her last look at Enoch.

Throughout his long absence Annie has steadfastly resisted Phillip's renewed advances. Although she finally gives in to his offer of marriage "for the children's sake," she still refuses his embrace and remains loyal to Enoch by continuing to look out her window in the "correct" direction—away from Phillip and toward the absent Enoch.

But just as parallel editing informs us that Enoch is about to arrive home, an intertitle, for which we have had no visual preparation, informs us that "when her new baby came, then Phillip was her all and all." Given the visual evidence of Annie's rejection of Phillip's advances and her persistent watch out the window for Enoch, this baby comes as rather a surprise. It does not seem possible for it to have arisen out of any sexual desire for Phillip on Annie Lee's part. Griffith uses this baby, which will soon become the visual proof of Annie's happiness with Phillip *in Enoch's eyes,* as the proper maternal justification of Annie finally turning *her* eyes from the window and toward her new family now headed by Phillip. The baby thus functions as cause, rather than effect, of Annie's desire for Phillip. This remarkable reversal of the usual logic of cause and effect allows the narrative to deny Annie a look of desire in *both* directions—at both Enoch and Phillip. The film ends as it began, with the look of the male voyeur (this time a literal voyeur) as the long-lost Enoch creeps up to the window to spy on the happy family scene from which he is now excluded. Once again he "reads" their happiness and his own "doom."

Let us take *Enoch Arden* as one paradigm for the frustration of the woman's "look" in the silent melodrama. It is a frustration necessary for the male regime of voyeuristic desire already clearly articulated by 1911. Given this paradigm we can go on to examine the exceptions to it: those moments (still in the silent film) when the woman in the text not only tries to look, but actually sees.

The bold, smouldering dark eyes of the silent screen vamp offer an obvious example of a powerful female look.[1] But the dubious moral status of such heroines, and the fact that they must be punished in the end, undermine the legitimacy and authentic subjectivity of this look, frequently turning it into a mere parody of the male look.[2] More instructive are those moments when the "good girl" heroines are granted the power of the look, whether in the woman's film, as discussed by Mary Ann Doane,[3] or in the horror film as discussed below. In both cases, as Doane suggests, "the woman's exercise of an active investigating gaze can only be simultaneous with her own victimization."[4] The woman's gaze is punished, in other words, by narrative processes that transform curiosity and desire into masochistic fantasy.

---

[1] It could very well be that the tradition of the fair-haired virgin and the dark-haired vamp rests more upon this difference in the lightness or darkness of the eyes than in hair color. The uncanny light eyes of many of Griffith's most affecting heroines—Mae Marsh, Lillian Gish and even his wife Linda Arvidson, who plays Annie Lee—contribute to an effect of innocent blindness in many of his films. Light eyes seem transparent, unfocused, easy to penetrate, incapable of penetration themselves, while dark eyes are quite the reverse.

[2] Mae West is, of course, one "master" of such reversals.

[3] Mary Ann Doane, "The 'Woman's Film': Possession and Address," *Re-vision: Essays in Feminist Film Criticism,* eds. Mary Ann Doane, Patricia Mellencamp, and Linda Williams (Frederick, Md.: University Publications of America 1984).

[4] Ibid., p. 72.

The horror film offers a particularly interesting example of this punishment in the woman's terrified look at the horrible body of the monster. In what follows I will examine the various ways the woman is punished for looking in both the classic horror film and in the more recent "psychopathic" forms of the genre. I hope to reveal not only the process of punishment but a surprising (and at times subversive) affinity between monster and woman, the sense in which her look at the monster recognizes their similar status within patriarchal structures of seeing.

In F. W. Murnau's *Nosferatu* (1922), for example, Nina's ambiguous vigil by the sea is finally rewarded, not by the sight of her returning husband who arrives by land in a carriage, but by the vampire's ship toward which a wide-eyed Nina in a trance-like state reaches out her arms.* Later, from the windows of facing houses, Nina and the vampire stare at one another until she finally opens the window. When the vampire's shadow approaches, she again stares at him in wide-eyed terror until he attacks.

There are several initial distinctions to be made between what I have character-ized above as the desiring look of the male-voyeur-subject and the woman's look of horror typified by Nina's trancelike fascination. First, Nina's look at the vampire fails to maintain the distance between observer and observed so essential to the "pleasure" of the voyeur. For where the (male) voyeur's properly distanced look safely masters the potential threat of the (female) body it views, the woman's look of horror paralyzes her in such a way that distance is overcome; the monster or the freak's own spectacular appearance holds her originally active, curious look in a trancelike passivity that allows him to master her through *her* look. At the same time, this look momentarily shifts the iconic center of the spectacle away from the woman to the monster.

Rupert Julian's 1925 version of *The Phantom of the Opera,* starring Lon Chaney and Mary Philbin, offers another classic example of the woman's look in the horror film. Christine, an aspiring young opera singer, is seduced by the voice of the Phan-tom speaking to her through the walls of her dressing room at the Paris Opera. She follows "her master's voice" by stepping through the mirror of her dressing room. Her first glimpse of the masked Phantom occurs as she turns to respond to the touch of his hand on her shoulder. Thus her look occurs *after* the film audience has had its own chance to see him—they are framed in a two-shot that has him standing slightly behind her; only when she turns does she see his masked face.

Similarly, in the famous unmasking scene, Christine first thrills to the sound of the organ music the Phantom plays ("Don Juan Triumphant"), then sneaks up behind him and hesitates several times before finally pulling the string that will drop his mask. Since both he and Christine face the camera in a two-shot (with Christine situated behind him) we again see the Phantom's face, this time unmasked, before

---

*Miriam White points out that the film's visuals suggest that Nina is really awaiting the Count, not her husband, even though the film's intertitles construe Nina's behavior only in relation to her husband: "Narrative Semantic Deviation: Duck-Rabbit Texts of Weimar Cinema." (Paper deliv-ered at the Center for Twentieth Century Studies conference on Cinema and Language, University of Wisconsin-Milwaukee, March 1979.)

The Terror of the Monster's Eyes: Max Shreck as Nosferatu in F. W. Murnau's *Nosferatu, the Vampire* (1929). "... where the (male) voyeur's properly distanced look safely masters the potential threat of the (female) body it views, the woman's look of horror paralyzes her in such a way that distance is overcome; the monster or the freak's own spectacular appearance holds her originally active, curious look in a trancelike passivity that allows him to master her through *her* look." (WILLIAMS, p. 564)

The Terror of the Camera Eye: Anna Massey in Michael Powell's *Peeping Tom* (1959). "*Peeping Tom* . . . lays bare the voyeuristic structure of cinema and that structure's dependence on the woman's acceptance of her role as narcissist." (WILLIAMS, p. 572)

Christine does. The audience thus receives the first shock of the horror even while it can still see the curiosity and desire *to see* on Christine's face.*

Everything conspires here to condemn the desire and curiosity of the woman's look. Our prior knowledge of what she will see encourages us to judge her look as a violation of the Phantom's privacy. Her unmasking of his face reveals the very wounds, the very lack, that the Phantom had hoped her blind love would heal. It is as if she has become responsible for the horror that her look reveals, and is punished by not being allowed the safe distance that ensures the voyeur's pleasure of looking. "Feast your eyes, glut your soul, on my accursed ugliness!" cries the Phantom as he holds her face up close to his.

When the men in this film look at the Phantom, the audience first sees the man looking, then adopts his point of view to see what he sees. The audience's belated adoption of the woman's point of view undermines the usual audience identification and sympathy with the look of the cinematic character. But it may also permit a different form of identification and sympathy to take place, not between the audience and the character who looks, but between the two objects of the cinematic spectacle who encounter one another in this look—the woman and the monster.

In *The Phantom of the Opera* Christine walks through her mirror to encounter a monster whose face lacks the flesh to cover its features. Lon Chaney's incarnation of the Phantom's nose, for example, gives the effect of two large holes; the lips fail to cover a gaping mouth. Early in the film women dancers from the corps de ballet argue excitedly about his nose: "He had no nose!" "Yes he did, it was enormous!" The terms of the argument suggest that the monster's body is perceived as freakish in its possession of too much or too little. Either the monster is symbolically castrated, pathetically lacking what Christine's handsome lover Raoul possesses ("He had no nose!"), or he is overly endowed and potent ("Yes he did, it was enormous!"). Yet it is a truism of the horror genre that sexual interest resides most often in the monster and not the bland ostensible heroes like Raoul who often prove powerless at the crucial moment. (*The Phantom of the Opera* is no exception. Raoul passes out when most needed and Christine's rescue is accomplished by her accidental fall from the Phantom's racing carriage.)

Clearly the monster's power is one of sexual difference from the normal male. In this difference he is remarkably like the woman in the eyes of the traumatized male: a biological freak with impossible and threatening appetites that suggest a frightening potency precisely where the normal male would perceive a lack. In fact, the Phantom's last act of the film is to restage the drama of the lack he represents to others. Cornered by a crowd more bestial than he has ever been, a crowd that wants to tear him apart, the Phantom pulls back his hand as if threatening to detonate an explosive device. The crowd freezes, the Phantom laughs and opens his hand to reveal that it contains . . . nothing at all.

It is this absence, this nothing at all so dramatically brandished by the Phantom,

---

*I am indebted to Bruce Kawin for pointing out to me the way in which the audience receives the first shock of this look at the Phantom.

that haunts a great many horror films and often seems the most effective element of their horror. It may very well be, then, that the power and potency of the monster body in many classic horror films—*Nosferatu, The Phantom of the Opera, Vampyr, Dracula, Freaks, Dr. Jekyll and Mr. Hyde, King Kong, Beauty and the Beast*— should not be interpreted as an eruption of the normally repressed animal sexuality of the civilized male (the monster as double for the male viewer and characters in the film), but as the feared power and potency of a different kind of sexuality (the monster as double for the women).

As we have seen, one result of this equation seems to be the difference between the look of horror of the man and of the woman. The male look expresses conventional fear at that which differs from itself. The female look—a look given preeminent position in the horror film—shares the male fear of the monster's freakishness, but also recognizes the sense in which this freakishness is similar to her own difference. For she too has been constituted as an exhibitionist-object by the desiring look of the male. There is not that much difference between an object of desire and an object of horror as far as the male look is concerned. (In one brand of horror film this difference may simply lie in the age of its female stars. The Bette Davises and the Joan Crawfords considered too old to continue as spectacle-objects nevertheless persevere as horror objects in films like *Whatever Happened to Baby Jane?* and *Hush Hush Sweet Charlotte.*) The strange sympathy and affinity that often develops between the monster and the girl may thus be less an expression of sexual desire (as in *King Kong, Beauty and the Beast*) and more a flash of sympathetic identification.

In Carson McCullers' *The Member of the Wedding,* Frankie fears that the carnival freaks look at her differently, secretly connecting their eyes with hers, saying with their look "We know you. We are you!"[1] Similarly, in *The Phantom of the Opera,* when Christine walks through a mirror that ceases to reflect her, it could very well be that she does so because she knows she will encounter a truer mirror in the freak of the Phantom on the other side. In other words, in the rare instance when the cinema permits the woman's look, she not only sees a monster, she sees a monster that offers a distorted reflection of her own image. The monster is thus a particularly insidious form of the many mirrors patriarchal structures of seeing hold up to the woman. But there are many kinds of mirrors; and in this case it may be useful to make a distinction between beauty and the beast in the horror film.

Laura Mulvey has shown that the male look at the woman in the cinema involves two forms of mastery over the threat of castration posed by her "lack" of a penis: a sadistic voyeurism which punishes or endangers the woman through the agency of an active and powerful male character; and fetishistic overvaluation, which masters the threat of castration by investing the woman's body with an excess of aesthetic perfection.[2]

Stephen Heath, summarizing the unspoken other side of Mulvey's formulation,

---

[1] Leslie Fiedler refers to this passage in *Freaks: Myths and Images of the Secret Self* (New York: Simon and Schuster, 1978), p. 17.

[2] Mulvey, pp. 10–16.

suggests that the woman's look can only function to entrap her further within these patriarchal structures of seeing:

> If the woman looks, the spectacle provokes, castration is in the air, the Medusa's head is not far off; thus, she must not look, is absorbed herself on the side of the seen, seeing herself seeing herself, Lacan's femininity.[1]

In other words, her look even here becomes a form of not seeing anything more than the castration she so exclusively represents for the male.

If this were so, then what the woman "sees" would only be the mutilation of her own body displaced onto that of the monster. The destruction of the monster that concludes so many horror films could therefore be interpreted as yet another way of disavowing and mastering the castration her body represents. But here I think it may be helpful to introduce a distinction into Mulvey's, Heath's, and ultimately Freud's, notion of the supposed "mutilation" of the "castrated" woman that may clarify the precise meaning of the woman's encounter with a horror version of her own body.

A key moment in many horror films occurs when the monster displaces the woman as site of the spectacle. In *King Kong,* Kong is literally placed on stage to "perform" before awed and fearful audiences. In *The Phantom of the Opera,* the Phantom makes a dramatic, show-stopping entrance at the Masked Ball as the Masque of the Red Death, wearing a mask modeled on the absences of his own face beneath. Count Dracula, in both the Murnau and the Browning versions, makes similarly show-stopping performances. Tod Browning's *Freaks* begins and ends with the side-show display of the woman who has been transformed by the freaks into part bird, part woman. These spectacular moments displaying the freakish difference of the monster's body elicit reactions of fear and awe in audiences that can be compared to the Freudian hypothesis of the reaction of the male child in his first encounter with the "mutilated" body of his mother.

In her essay, "Pornography and the Dread of Woman," Susan Lurie offers a significant challenge to the traditional Freudian notion that the sight of the mother's body suggests to the male child that she has herself undergone castration. According to Lurie, the real trauma for the young boy is not that the mother is castrated but that she *isn't:* she is obviously *not* mutilated the way he would be if his penis were taken from him. The notion of the woman as a castrated version of a man is, according to Lurie, a comforting, wishful fantasy intended to combat the child's imagined dread of what his mother's very real power could do to him. This protective fantasy is aimed at convincing himself that "women are what men would be if they had no penises—bereft of sexuality, helpless, incapable."[2]

I suggest that the monster in the horror film is feared by the "normal" males of

---

[1]Stephen Heath, "Difference," *Screen,* vol. 19, no. 3 (Autumn 1978), p. 92

[2]Susan Lurie, "Pornography and the Dread of Woman," in *Take Back the Night,* ed. Laura Lederer (New York: William Morrow, 1980), pp. 159–173. Melanie Klein, in *Psycho-Analysis of Children* (London: Hogarth Press, 1932), has written extensively of the child's terror of being devoured, torn up, and destroyed by the mother, although for Klein these fears derive from a pre-oedipal stage and apply to both male and female infants.

such films in ways very similar to Lurie's notion of the male child's fear of this mother's power-in-difference. For, looked at from the woman's perspective, the monster is not so much lacking as he is powerful in a different way. The vampire film offers a clear example of the threat this different form of sexuality represents to the male. The vampiric act of sucking blood, sapping the life fluid of a victim so that the victim in turn becomes a vampire, is similar to the female role of milking the sperm of the male during intercourse.* What the vampire seems to represent then is a sexual power whose threat lies in its difference from a phallic "norm." The vampire's power to make its victim resemble itself is a very real mutilation of the once human victim (teeth marks, blood loss), but the vampire itself, like the mother in Lurie's formulation, is not perceived as mutilated, just different.

Thus what is feared in the monster (whether vampire or simply a creature whose difference gives him power over others) is similar to what Lurie says is feared in the mother: not her own mutilation, but the power to mutilate and transform the vulnerable male. The vampire's insatiable need for blood seems a particularly apt analogue for what must seem to the man to be an insatiable sexual appetite—yet another threat to his potency. So there is a sense in which the woman's look at the monster is more than simply a punishment for looking, or a narcissistic fascination with the distortion of her own image in the mirror that patriarchy holds up to her; it is also a recognition of their similar status as potent threats to a vulnerable male power. This would help explain the often vindictive destruction of the monster in the horror film and the fact that this destruction generates the frequent sympathy of the women characters, who seem to sense the extent to which the monster's death is an exorcism of the power of their own sexuality. It also helps to explain the conventional weakness of the male heroes of so many horror films (e.g., David Manners in *Dracula,* Colin Clive in *Frankenstein*) and the extreme excitement and surplus danger when the monster and the woman get together.

Thus I suggest that, in the classic horror film, the woman's look at the monster offers at least a potentially subversive recognition of the power and potency of a non-phallic sexuality. Precisely because this look is so threatening to male power, it is violently punished. In what follows I would like to look closely at a different kind of horror film that offers a particularly self-conscious and illuminating version of the significance of the woman's look in the horror genre. And then, lest we get carried away with enthusiasm, I shall look at two other, more typically exploitative, examples of the recent evolution of the genre.

Michael Powell's *Peeping Tom* (1959) is a self-conscious meditation on the relations between a sadistic voyeur-subject and the exhibitionist objects he murders. Along with *Psycho* (also 1960), it marked a significant break in the structure of the classic horror film, inaugurating a new form of psychological horror. In these two films, a physically normal but psychologically deranged monster becomes the central figure of the narrative. For better or worse (we will see later just how bad it can

---

*According to Stan Brakhage the word "nosferatu" itself means "splashed with milk" in Transylvanian. A Rumanian legend tells how a servant woman frightened by Count Dracula spilled a pitcher of milk on him. Brakhage thus suggests that the word connotes a homosexual allusion of "sucking for milk." (*Film Biographies* [Berkeley, CA: Turtle Island, 1977], p. 256)

be) the audience is now asked to identify with the monster's point of view, and even to sympathize with the childhood traumas that produced his deranged behavior. In *Peeping Tom,* the first images we see are through the lens of Mark's 16mm camera as he murders a prostitute with a knife concealed in a leg of his tripod. We learn in the opening credits that Mark is a killer whose only apparent sexual gratification comes while watching from the womblike safety of his dark projection room the murders he commits in his own movies.

Peeping Tom suggests that Mark's obsession evolved as a protection against his father's voyeuristic experimentation upon him as young child. We see home movies showing the young Mark terrified by lizards placed in his bed, probed with lights and coldly spied upon by his father's camera. It becomes clear that Mark's only defense was to master the very system that had turned him into an exhibitionist object of scientific spectacle. In one of the home movies we see Mark receive a camera from his father and turn it, weaponlike, back upon the world, mastering his own victimization by gaining the means to victimize others.

Where Mark's father represents the sadistic power of the voyeur-scientist to scrutinize his subjects safe from any involvement with them, Mark's own manipulation is on a different level: he is the voyeur as romantic artist. His home movies are a desperate attempt to capture on film the perfect expression of the terror of his victims—a terror that might match his own. A classic voyeur, any actual contact with his victims disrupts the distance so necessary to his sadistic pleasure. It is precisely this distance that Helen, an artist herself (she has a book of stories about a "magic camera" that she wants Mark to illustrate) disrupts. Helen intrudes upon the inner sanctum of his screening room, looks herself at the home movies of Mark as a child, demands an explanation ("I like to understand what I'm shown!"), and eventually switches on the projector to view his latest murder. Her own autonomous looking, her ambitious sense of herself as a creator of images in her own right, and her instinctive distrust of Mark's dependence on his camera to avoid contact with the world, force him to see her not as another victim, but as a subject with her own power of vision. All of his other victims, a prostitute, a movie stand-in, and a pornographer's model, have willingly accepted their positions as exhibitionist spectacles for his camera.

Helen's power of vision becomes dramatically evident in her ability to refuse the mirror-snare that ultimately gives this film its greatest horror. For Mark not only films his victims as he stabs them, the artist in him wants to perfect this image of their terror. To do this, he holds up before them, while filming and stabbing, a concave mirror that reflects the hideous distortion of their faces. Thus what Mark films is his victim at the moment of death looking at her own distorted reflection and not, as in the conventional look of horror, back at the monster. Our own awareness of this mirror is withheld until near the end when Mark finally turns the apparatus on himself, running on the knife as he looks into the distorting mirror, uniting voyeur and exhibitionist in a one-man movie of which he is both director and star.

In the classic horror film, the woman encountered a monster whose deformed features suggested a distorted mirror-reflection of her own putative lack in the eyes of patriarchy, although this supposed lack could also be construed as a recognition of the threat both beauty and the beast presented to this patriarchy. In *Peeping*

Tom, however, the woman's look is literally caught up in a mirror reflection that does not simply suggest an affinity with the monster in the eyes of patriarchy, but attempts to lure her into the false belief that she *is* the monster. Mark's self-reflective cinematic apparatus uses its mirror-effect to haunt the woman with her own image, to trap her in an attitude of exhibitionism and narcissism that has traditionally been offered as the "natural" complement to the voyeur's sadistic pleasure.

The point of the film, of course, is to show that the woman is *not* the monster. Mark's attempt to convince her that she is, is simply a way of alienating her from her own look, of forcing her into a perverse reenactment of his own traumatic experience of being looked at. In making his films (the *mise-en-scène* of which is murder) Mark assumes the role of his sadistic father, mastering his own terror by becoming the victimizer himself. Then in watching his films he can relive his original experience of terror at a safe distance, identify with his own victims, and repossess his own look of terror from a safer aesthetic distance.

Throughout the film we are invited to equate the art and technology of movie making with the sadist-voyeur's misuse of the female body. Mark lures the women he kills into exhibitionist performances—the prostitute's come-on, the stand-in's frenetic jazz dance, the pornographic model's pose—which he captures with his camera-mirror-weapon and then punishes. Yet this punishment is clearly only a substitute for the revenge on his dead father that he can never accomplish. Ultimately he will turn the weapon back on himself and exult in his own terror as he dies before the distorting mirror.

Mark's regression to his original position of victim occurs when Helen refuses to occupy that same position herself. Helen is not transfixed by the mirror Mark holds up to her; she sees it for the distortion it is and has the power to turn away, to reject the image of woman as terrified victim and monster proferred by the male artist.

Helen's refusal of the mirror marks an important moment in the history of the woman's look in the horror film: in a rare instance her look both sees and understands the structure of seeing that would entrap her; her look is not paralyzed by the recognition of the horror she represents, and she therefore refuses the oppressive lie of the narcissistic mirror that the cinematic apparatus holds up to her.

Peeping Tom thus lays bare the voyeuristic structure of cinema and that structure's dependence on the woman's acceptance of her role as narcissist. Both Mark and his victims are trapped in a perverse structure of seeing that is equated throughout the film with the art of making "true-to-life" movies. Yet it is also true that Helen's ability to refuse the mirror is simply a result of her status as a non-sexual "good girl." As played by Anna Massey, Helen is the stereotypical "girl next door." She mothers Mark, feeds him, tells him not to work so hard and gives him a chaste goodnight kiss which he later, and much more erotically, transfers to the lens of his camera.

Helen's refusal of narcissism also turns out to be a refusal of the only way patriarchal cinema has of representing woman's desire. If she has the power to recognize and refuse the mirror-trap, it is because she is portrayed as ignorant of sexual desire altogether. She is like the one virginal babysitter who survives the attacks of the monster in *Halloween* (John Carpenter, 1978), or like Lila, Marion Crane's "good girl" sister in *Psycho,* who survives Norman Bates's final attack, or even like Helen's blind mother in *Peeping Tom* who immediately "sees"—in the tradition of the blind seer—the turbulence in Mark's soul. In other words, in most horror films, the tradition of the power of the woman "pure of heart" is still going strong: the woman's power to resist the monster is directly proportional to her absence of sexual desire.[1] Clarity of vision, it would seem, can only exist in this absence.

If *Peeping Tom* can be privileged as a progressive horror film, not so much for sparing the life of its "good girl" heroine as for exposing the perverse structures of seeing that operate in the genre, then we might compare two much more popular horror films in the same mode: Alfred Hitchcock's *Psycho* (made in the same year as *Peeping Tom*) and Brian De Palma's *Psycho*-inspired *Dressed to Kill* (1980). Both films offer insidious and much more typical forms of the narcissistic trap that frustrates the woman's look of desire.

Psycho has been the model for the new form of the "psycho at large" horror films that began to emerge in the early 1960s and which now dominate the market. There is no more convincing proof of the influence of this model than De Palma's flagrant imitation of it in *Dressed to Kill*. In both *Psycho* and *Dressed to Kill*, the primary female stars are killed off early by knife-wielding murderers who appear, to both their victims and the audience, to be female. In both films the snooping of a second heroine, who is similarly endangered but not killed, corrects the original vision: the attacking she is a he. But also in both films, the psychoanalytic voice of reason revises this vision as well: although the body of the attacker might appear to be male, it is really the woman in this man who kills.

In other words, both films offer yet another form of the look of recognition between the woman and the monster. The monster who attacks both looks like and, in some sense, *is* a woman. But unlike *Peeping Tom*, which exposes the lie of the female victim's encounter with her own horror in the mirror image that Mark holds up to her, *Psycho* and *Dressed to Kill* perpetuate this lie, asking us to believe that the woman is both victim and monster.[2]

In *Psycho* we learn that the mother did it. As the psychiatrist explains at the end of the film, Norman Bates had been dominated by his demanding and clinging mother whom he eventually killed. Not able to bear the crime of matricide, he maintains the fiction that she lives by dressing in her clothes and speaking in her voice. Each time he feels sexual desire for a woman, the mother he has killed rises up in him to murder the cause of this betrayal of her son's affections. Thus Norman, the matricide and killer of several other women, is judged the victim of the very mother he has killed.

Marion Crane is punished for sexual desires which put her in the wrong place at the wrong time. Yet her decision to return the money and go back to face the consequences of her theft makes her subsequent murder seem all the more gratuitous. One of the more insidious changes in Brian De Palma's reworking of the *Psycho* plot in *Dressed to Kill* is that Kate, the Angie Dickinson character who replaces

---

[1] *The Book of the Vampires*, as quoted in Murnau's *Nosferatu*, states that only a woman "pure in heart," who will keep the vampire by her side until the first cock crows, can break his spell.

[2] Henry Herrings' as yet unpublished comparison of these two films, "The Endurance of Misogyny: *Psycho* and *Dressed to Kill*," points out the way in which the woman is both cause and perpetrator of the violence against her in both films.

Janet Leigh's Marion, is a sexually frustrated middle-aged woman whose desperate search for satisfaction leads directly to her death. Not only does a "woman" commit the crime but the female victim asks for it.[1]

In this and other ways De Palma's film *Dressed to Kill* extends *Psycho*'s premise by holding the woman responsible for the horror that destroys her. Here too the psychiatrist explains at the end that it was the woman in the man who killed—in this case the female, "Bobbie," half of Kate's schizophrenic therapist, Dr. Elliot. Bobbie wants the doctor to undergo a sex change operation so that "she" will become dominant. Bobbie kills Kate when she discovers that Kate's sexual desires have aroused the very penis that Bobbie would like to eradicate. But this time the murder is clearly meant to be seen as the fault of the sex-hungry victim who, in the words of the detective who solves the case, was "*looking* to get killed."

The film begins with a form of interior "looking" with Kate's violent sexual fantasy of being attacked in the shower. This fantasy, which begins with the blurring of Kate's vision by the steam of the shower, condenses Hitchcock's illicit love-in-a-motel-room scene with the famous shower sequence, encouraging us to believe that Kate's desire is to be the victim of male aggression. The rest of the film will give her what she "wants."

A second instance of Kate's desiring look occurs during a therapy session with Dr. Elliot. She discusses her sexual frustrations with her husband and her unwillingness to confess her lack of satisfaction: "I moaned with pleasure at his touch, isn't that what every man wants?" The doctor assures her that the problem must lie in her husband's technique; she is perfectly attractive so there could be nothing wrong with *her*. The film thus assumes that sexual satisfaction must be given by the aggressive man to the passive and sufficiently attractive woman; there is no route to achieving it herself. This lesson is borne out by Kate's very next act; her aggressive proposition to Dr. Elliot leads not to sexual satisfaction but to humiliation and death.

Proof follows in an elaborate cat-and-mouse chase in the labyrinthine art museum where Kate tentatively pursues a strange man.[2] Throughout the sequence Kate's look and pursuit of the man is continually frustrated and outmaneuvered by his look and pursuit of her. It is as if the game for him consists in hiding from her look in order to surprise her with his.

Once again the camera adopts Kate's subjective point of view only to demonstrate her failure to see, while the objective shots reveal the many times she fails to look in the right direction to see the lurking figure of the man she seeks and whom we so easily see. Repeatedly, her look of expectation encounters thin air. She only

---

[1] Andrew Sarris, one of the few critics to call the film on this issue, writes: "In De Palma's perhaps wishful world, women do not just ask for it, they are willing to run track meets for it" (*Village Voice,* 17 September 1980, p. 44).

[2] This is another of De Palma's Hitchcock allusions—this one to *Vertigo*—in which the Kim Novak character sits pretending to be entranced before the portrait of her supposedly dead former self. Sarris correctly points out with respect to such borrowings that De Palma "steals Hitchcock's most privileged moments without performing the drudgery of building up to these moments as thoroughly earned climaxes." (Ibid.)

encounters him when vision can give her no warning, as when she turns at the sudden touch of his hand, wearing her dropped glove; or outside the museum when he waves her lost glove, symbol of his triumph, at her from a cab.

When she thanks him for the glove he pulls her into the cab, aggressively undresses her and performs cunnilingus. Her ectasy is mixed with the humiliation of watching the cab driver adjust his rear-view mirror to get a better view. Later, in the stranger's apartment, she encounters a second humiliating punishment for the dubious pleasure she has just received: a public health record attesting to the fact that the stranger has venereal disease. But these humiliations are only teases for the real punishment to come: the revenge of Bobbie, the tall blond in sunglasses, who slashes her to pieces in the elevator, spoiling her pretty white suit.

Bobbie wreaks her revenge on Kate as a substitute for the castration she has not yet been able to have performed on her male half. The film stresses the gory details of the transexual operation in no uncertain terms when Liz the hooker explains to Peter, Kate's son, just how a "penectomy" is performed. In *Psycho* the dead mother-villain was guilty of an excessive domination that figuratively castrated her son, eventually turning him into her entirely. In *Dressed to Kill* this figurative castration by the woman in the man becomes a literal possibility, and the desiring look of the female victim becomes a direct cause of the sexual crisis that precipitates her own death.

"If the woman looks, the spectacle provokes, castration is in the air."* Kate's crime is having tried to look, having actively sought the satisfaction of her desires. The film teaches that such satisfaction cannot be actively sought; it must be received, like rape, as a gift from the gods. And if Kate dies while Liz, the hooker and ostensibly promiscuous woman, survives (much as Marion Crane's "good girl" sister survives in *Psycho*) it is because Kate's desires have made disturbing demands on the male that Liz does not make.

Thus, although the film gives the impression of reversing the conventions by which the "good girls" are saved and the promiscuous ones punished, it actually reinforces the convention by redefining the "good girl" as the professional sex machine who knows how to satisfy but makes no demands of her own.

The film leaves us with one last, nagging "insight" as to the nature of woman's desire: Liz's dream of the return of Bobbie to murder her as she steps out of the shower that was the scene of Kate's original fantasy. She awakens from the dream and is comforted by Peter as the film ends. But there can be no comfort for the female spectator, who has been asked to accept the truth of a masochistic female imagination that envisions its own punishment at the hands of the sick man whose very illness lies in the fact that he wants to become a woman.

In the 22 years since *Psycho* and *Peeping Tom* began the new horror tradition of the psychopathic hero, one of the most significant changes in the genre has been the deepening of the woman's responsibility for the horror that endangers her. We have seen that in the classic horror film the woman's sexually charged look at the monster encounters a horror version of her own body. The monster is thus one of many

---

*Heath, p. 92.

mirrors held up to her by patriarchy. But, as I have tried to suggest, she also encounters in this mirror at least the possibility of a power located in her very difference from the male.

In the more recent psychopathic horror films, however, the identification between woman and monster becomes greater, the nature of the identification is more negatively charged, and women are increasingly punished for the threatening nature of their sexuality. *Peeping Tom* is both exception and rule to this in its self-conscious exploration of the male monster's need to shift responsibility for her victimization to the woman. For *Peeping Tom* exposes the male aggressor's need to believe that his female victims are terrified by their own distorted image. It thus reveals the process by which films themselves ask women to believe that they have asked for it.

Much more typical are *Psycho, Dressed to Kill* and a host of vastly inferior exploitation films—what Roger Ebert calls the new brand of "woman-in-danger" films—including *He Knows You're Alone, Prom Night, Terror Train, Friday the 13th.*[1] Ebert points out that in these films we rarely see the psychopathic murderer whose point of view the audience nevertheless adopts. This "non-specific male killing force" thus displaces what was once the subjective point of view of the female victim onto an audience that is now asked to view the body of the woman victim as the only visible monster in the film. In other words, in these films the recognition and affinity between woman and monster of the classic horror film gives way to pure identity: she *is* the monster, her mutilated body is the only visible horror.

These films are capitalizations—and vulgarizations—of currently popular formulae begun with *Psycho* and *Peeping Tom.* There are, of course, obvious differences of technical and aesthetic quality between these exploitative women-in-danger films and a film like *Dressed to Kill.* Ebert suggests that the distinction lies in the "artistry . . . and inventive directional point-of-view" of such films as *Halloween, Dressed to Kill, The Texas Chainsaw Massacre* over *Friday the 13th* and the rest. The former films endow their villains with characters, while in the exploitative films they are faceless non-characters whose point of view the audience is forced to adopt.[2]

Although we must be deeply indebted to Ebert for identifying and condemning the onslaught of these offensive films (and for doing so on public television), the argument that the greater artistry and characterization of the more "artistic" films exonerate them from the charge of gratuitously punishing their female heroines rings false. The real issue (to continue the argument in Ebert's terms of false or non-existent characterization) is that the *women* in these films are non-existent fantasies. *Dressed to Kill* is a male horror fantasy in drag; the film attributes a whole slew of inauthentic fantasies to an ostensible female subject who is never really there in the first place. While supposedly about Bobbie's desire to castrate her male half, what the film actually shows is not this mutilation but another: the slow motion slashing of Kate's body as substitute for the castration Bobbie cannot yet perform on Elliot.

---

[1]Roger Ebert, "Why Movie Audiences Aren't Safe Any More," *American Film,* vol. 6, no. 5 (March 1981), pp. 54–56.
[2]Ibid., p. 56.

In this light, Bobbie's vengeance on Kate can be viewed not as the act of a jealous woman eliminating her rival, but as acting out the *male* fantasy that woman is castrated, mutilated, "what men would be if they had no penises—bereft of sexuality, helpless, incapable."* Thus the mutilation of Kate should be properly viewed as a form of symbolic castration on a body that is frightening to the male precisely because it cannot be castrated, has none of his own vulnerability. The problem, in other words, is that she is not castrated; the fantasy solution of the male psychopath and the film itself is symbolically to prove that she is.

It is crucial for women spectators to realize the important change that is taking place before our very eyes, but which habits of viewing, not to mention habits of *not* viewing, of closing our eyes to violence and horror in general, may keep us from seeing. We are so used to sympathizing, in traditional cringing ways, with the female victims of horror that we are likely not to notice the change, to assume that films such as these have maintained this sympathy while simply escalating the doses of violence and sex. What we need to see is that in fact the sexual "freedom" of such films, the titillating attention given to the expression of women's desires, is directly proportional to the violence perpetrated against women. The horror film may be a rare example of a genre that permits the expression of women's sexual potency and desire, and which associates this desire with the autonomous act of looking, but it does so in these more recent examples only to punish her for this very act, only to demonstrate how monstrous female desire can be.

1984

(

---

*Lurie, p. 166.

VI

The Film Artist

The infant American film business grew into a multi-million-dollar industry in the first decade of the twentieth century. By the mid-1910s, in the years during and just after World War I, that industry organized itself according to what came to be called the Hollywood studio system (although, in fact, the final power of the system resided not in the Hollywood studios where the films were made but in the New York business offices where they were financed and distributed). Consolidated at the same time as Henry Ford's automobile assembly plant, the Hollywood studio also resembled a factory where goods—motion picture entertainments—were manufactured for a mass audience. The films rolled down the assembly line, like one of Henry Ford's Model A's, through story departments, past departments of scenic and costume design, and onto the set where technicians (scenic and make-up craftsmen, camera and lighting crews) and actors united to help shape the final product. Then it continued down the line to the cutting and release departments, until it was shipped to the company's showrooms—whether the small-town Bijous or the big-city Movie Palaces.

From its beginnings, this industrialized studio system provoked a predictable question: how can a work of art result from such varied intentions and collective labors? For years, most American critics argued (or simply assumed) that, whatever the product of this mechanized assembly of disparate talents was, it was not art. They considered it to be, instead, mere commercial entertainment that could not be compared to the "art films" of Europe or the "underground" films of the personal, experimental filmmaker. Ford's assembly line may have made the luxury of automobile ownership possible for a majority of Americans. But when Hollywood similarly brought drama and comedy into the lives of millions, the result, according to such critics, was not the expansion of art but its debasement.

One early reply to this argument was to deny that a purely aesthetic intention or the vision of a single artist is necessary to create a work of art. Panofsky specifically compares the making of a film to the building of a cathedral, for the cathedral was built for the greater glory of God and was the result of the collective labor of as many specialists as a Hollywood film. François Truffaut, beginning in 1954 with his *Cahiers du cinéma* essay, "On a Certain Tendency of the French Cinema," took the opposite tack and argued instead for a theory of film art that drew upon older ideas of aesthetic creation. His *"politique des auteurs"* defended the Hollywood studio film by maintaining that, although unappreciated or even unnoticed, the work of an author, an *auteur,* could be seen in many Hollywood films. This *auteur* was not the film's scriptwriter, however, but the film's director whose "signature" could be discerned by the sensitive critic who bothered to look for it. Truffaut's aim in this and succeeding articles, along with that of his follow-*auteuristes* at *Cahiers du Cinéma,* was somewhere between a theory of film creation and a theory of film taste. He was reacting against mainstream French film criticism, which had emphasized the "tradition of quality," extolling the polished literary adaptations of such scenarists as Jean Aurenche and Pierre Bost *(La Symphonie Pastorale, The Red and the Black, The Idiot)* at the expense of the genuinely cinematic thinking of Jacques Tati, Jean Renoir, or Robert Bresson.

According to what has become known as the *"auteur* theory," the director's "style" or his "basic motifs," as Peter Wollen calls them, can be discerned by viewing his work as a whole—for these marks of directorial authorship will manifest themselves in all of a true *auteur*'s films, even as he works with different writers, cinematographers, and stars. Andrew Sarris, the primary American spokesman for the *auteur* theory, suggests not only that the distinguishable personality of the director is a criterion of value, but also that the "meaning" which he is able to impose on the material with which he must work is the "ultimate" glory of the cinema. This observation raises a problem, however, concerning Wollen's two key terms— "style" and "basic motifs." Does Sarris mean that the "ultimate" glory is a director's imposition of "style" (e.g., the use of deep-focus photography) on a film's given "basic motifs" (e.g., domestic melodrama) or does he mean that the glory is the director's imposition of "style" that elicits new "basic motifs" (i.e., the meaning of love) from the melodrama? If the latter, does Sarris realize that the same can be said of any artist (say, Shakespeare in *King Lear* or *Othello*)? If the former, does Sarris mean that a director whose films deal with trash stylishly is an artist worthy of our attention? In a fierce reply to Sarris's formulation, Pauline Kael remarked that there is something perverse about admiring an artist for managing to make an artistic silk purse out of the sow's ear of Hollywood trash. Isn't the true artist responsible for the choice of his materials and for finding an appropriate form for his chosen subject?

Sarris, like Kael, is a working film critic required to write on many films a year. To a great extent, both his desire to categorize films in terms of their directors, as well as the attack on his views by Kael and others, spring from their similar need to find evaluative standards more general than the vagaries of their own taste. Those who originally proposed the *auteur* theory, however, were not simply arguing that an artist's personality will manifest itself in his works. They were seeking to establish that there was, indeed, an artist at work where many had never seen one. In doing so, they unquestionably helped to establish or re-establish the reputations of certain directors who worked within the Hollywood system, directors who did not exert much more control over the total project than many studio hacks, but who managed to make the kind of personal, significant statement that John Ford or (as Peter Wollen shows) Howard Hawks did. But Sarris's insistence on the sheer value of an artist's triumphing over the limitations of his material seems a mistake, even from Sarris's own point of view. This is a useful strategy for rescuing some Hollywood reputations, but it lays the wrong groundwork for demonstrating the merits of the directors that Sarris (and almost everyone else) most admires. Directors such as Lubitsch, Renoir, Chaplin, Welles, and Keaton in fact enjoyed a large measure of individual control over scripts, shooting, and cutting.

Peter Wollen, later a scriptwriter and filmmaker himself, combines the *auteur* theory's emphasis on the individual creator with a structuralist and semiotic account of film meaning. For Wollen, the *auteur* theory allows "an operation of decipherment" that distinguishes between *auteur* films in which the meaning is not just conveyed through style but is "deeply within" and *metteur-en-scène* films in which the meaning is merely cinematically translated from the script or another medium. His prime example is Howard Hawks, who worked in the studio system and yet was able to create a personal set of attitudes and motifs that permeate his films whatever their ostensible genre or subject matter. In a series of afterthoughts added to a second edition of *Signs and Meanings in the Cinema,* Wollen expands his basic effort to detach the *auteur* theory from any adulation of the creative personality as such, or any search for the creator behind (rather than in) the work.

If the signature of an *auteur* director can be recognized by a careful examination of all his works, this is equally true of other film artists. Richard Corliss, in a formulation that clearly owes its format to Sarris's idea of the "pantheon" of directors, makes equally strong claims for the creative importance of the scriptwriter. He argues, for instance, that a film whose script is by a Norman Krasna or a Jules Furthman (who also wrote frequently for Howard Hawks) will more likely display their personalities than that of its director.

As Peter Wollen insists, the essential role of the critic is to show that the film, which appears so directly to us, is not a transparent text, but one that requires interpretive work. With film scholarship looking more closely at all the works of the past, rather than the small number of designated classics, critics and historians have been able to describe the special contributions of those in charge of lighting, sound, and set decoration, while more polemic writers have argued the crucial importance of cinematographers and composers for determining the overall effect of a film.

The most serious challenge for any theory that stresses the central importance of one or another of these invisible filmmakers is the visible presence of the star on the screen in front of us. Many stars have made the most decisive contributions to the films in which they appear, and their unique "presence," like that of the director, scriptwriter, etc., can also be determined by viewing the totality of their works. In *The World Viewed* Stanley Cavell remarks how surprising he found the *auteur* theory, for it never previously occurred to him that anyone *made* a Hollywood film. For Cavell, the world of film revolved about, and was determined by, the star.

Yet in much film theory, especially that influenced by the montage emphasis of

Pudovkin and Eisenstein, the star and the star's performance has been undervalued in favor of the greater expressive meaning of editing (and the greater creative importance of the director and the editor). In an almost legendary experiment, the same shot of an actor's face was juxtaposed with that of a plate of soup, a coffin, and a little girl playing. The audience response, according to Pudovkin, was to ascribe hunger, sorrow, and joy respectively to what was in fact an unchanging expression. Similarly, in many formalist theories of film, the performer, if mentioned at all, becomes almost indistinguishable from other patterns generated by the film medium. The semiotic perspective of Roland Barthes straddles these two possibilities by implying that Greta Garbo's "face" is both the main object of interest and the main conveyor of meaning in most of the films in which she appears.

Another response to arguments against the significance of stars and performance has been first to stress the importance of performance in general to the fabric of film, and then to make a distinction—akin to Wollen's between *metteurs-en-scène* and *auteurs*—between the cinematic performer and the star who might reasonably be considered a creative force. Richard Dyer takes up these two issues, discussing the nature of film performance and then focusing on the special characteristics of those stars who could be considered authors, at least of their own images and perhaps of the films in which they appear. Reflecting Braudy's formulation in *The World in a Frame* that film acting employs an "aesthetics of omission," John Ellis emphasizes not only the star within the film and within a series of films, but also the star as existing in other formats—fan magazines, studio publicity, radio and television appearances, etc.—outside the film. These corollary aspects of the star image enhance the way in which the audience experiences the star as both present and absent, ordinary and extraordinary, at the same time.

In a return to the question of the interplay of creative forces within a film, Molly Haskell points out the way in which many films of the 1940s, especially those of Howard Hawks, find their shape through the presence of strong female stars. Such actresses often in themselves constitute a "point of view" that their casting brings into the story, even in some contrast or resistance to what the script and perhaps the director demand from them. Unlike Garbo, whose face is a palimpsest of audience projections, Bette Davis, says Haskell, deliberately plays against easy audience sympathy, while Rosalind Russell and Katharine Hepburn similarly upset expectations of pat or traditional distinctions between male and female traits.

Even more complicated is the film star who does not merely perform in the scripts of others, like Garbo, but who writes her own scripts and whose characters on screen seek goals which very much resemble her own off screen. According to Joan Mellen, Mae West was such a star, not merely a performer but an *auteur* who wrote her own films, wrote the plays on which many of them were based, wrote the songs she sang, and portrayed screen characters who, like West herself, were professional entertainers seeking self-sufficiency and independence in a world dominated by men. For Mellen, West herself is the most interesting thing about any of her films, not only for her artistry but for the social issues which the West persona both generated and avoided. Mellen sees West as a deeply paradoxical figure who simultaneously reduced herself to a sexual object, pandering to the prevailing sexist notions of her era, yet who simultaneously manipulated those notions as the only means to achieve self-sufficient control over her own life.

Finally, Thomas Schatz points out that the *auteur* theory has essentially distorted at least American film history by emphasizing the works and careers of a "few dozen heroic directors." In fact, the studio system makes it impossible to designate any particular individual as the sole creative force. Instead, Schatz argues that it is the producer, who has both the authority and power to make final decisions, whose role ought to be investigated if we are truly to understand the special interplay between individual artistry and collective organization that defines the Hollywood film. Such social issues indicate that the study of film art and the film artist cannot be isolated from the functions of that art and artist in the society as a whole—an issue which will become a concern of this volume's final section.

ANDREW SARRIS
NOTES ON THE AUTEUR THEORY
IN 1962

... As far as I know, there is no definition of the *auteur* theory in the English language, that is, by any American or British critic. Truffaut has recently gone to great pains to emphasize that the *auteur* theory was merely a polemical weapon for a given time and a given place, and I am willing to take him at his word. But, lest I be accused of misappropriating a theory no one wants anymore, I will give the *Cahiers* critics full credit for the original formulation of an idea that reshaped my thinking on the cinema. First of all, how does the *auteur* theory differ from a straightforward theory of directors. Ian Cameron's article "Films, Directors, and Critics," in *Movie* of September, 1962, makes an interesting comment on this issue: "The assumption that underlies all the writing in *Movie* is that the director is the author of a film, the person who gives it any distinctive quality. There are quite large exceptions, with which I shall deal later." So far, so good, at least for the *auteur* theory, which even allows for exceptions. However, Cameron continues: "On the whole, we accept the cinema of directors, although without going to the farthest-out extremes of the *la politique des auteurs,* which makes it difficult to think of a bad director making a good film and almost impossible to think of a good director making a bad one." We are back to Bazin again, although Cameron naturally uses different examples. That three otherwise divergent critics like Bazin, Roud, and Cameron make essentially the same point about the *auteur* theory suggests a common fear of its abuses. I believe there is a misunderstanding here about what the *auteur* theory actually claims, particularly since the theory itself is so vague at the present time.

First of all, the *auteur* theory, at least as I understand it and now intend to express it, claims neither the gift of prophecy nor the option of extracinematic perception. Directors, even *auteurs,* do not always run true to form, and the critic can never assume that a bad director will always make a bad film. No, not always, but almost always, and that is the point. What is a bad director, but a director who has made many bad films? What is the problem then? Simply this: The badness of a director is not necessarily considered the badness of a film. If Joseph Pevney directed Garbo, Cherkassov, Olivier, Belmondo, and Harriet Andersson in *The Cherry Orchard,* the resulting spectacle might not be entirely devoid of merit with so many subsidiary *auteurs* to cover up for Joe. In fact, with this cast and this literary property, a Lumet might be safer than a Welles. The realities of casting apply to directors as well as to actors, but the *auteur* theory would demand the gamble with Welles, if he were willing.

Marlon Brando has shown us that a film can be made without a director. Indeed, *One-Eyed Jacks* is more entertaining than many films with directors. A director-conscious critic would find it difficult to say anything good or bad about direction that is nonexistent. One can talk here about photography, editing, acting, but not direction. The film even has personality, but, like *The Longest Day* and *Mutiny on the Bounty,* it is a cipher directorially. Obviously, the *auteur* theory cannot possibly cover every vagrant charm of the cinema. Nevertheless, the first premise of the *auteur* theory is the technical competence of a director as a criterion of value. A badly directed or an undirected film has no importance in a critical scale of values, but one can make interesting conversation about the subject, the script, the acting, the color, the photography, the editing, the music, the costumes, the decor, and so forth. That is the nature of the medium. You always get more for your money than mere art. Now, by the *auteur* theory, if a director has no technical competence, no elementary flair for the cinema, he is automatically cast out from the pantheon of directors. A great director has to be at least a good director. This is true in any art. What constitutes directorial talent is more difficult to define abstractly. There is less disagreement, however, on this first level of the *auteur* theory than there will be later.

The second premise of the *auteur* theory is the distinguishable personality of the director as a criterion of value. Over a group of films, a director must exhibit certain recurrent characteristics of style, which serve as his signature. The way a film looks and moves should have some relationship to the way a director thinks and feels. This is an area where American directors are generally superior to foreign directors. Because so much of the American cinema is commissioned, a director is forced to express his personality through the visual treatment of material rather than through the literary content of the material. A Cukor, who works with all sorts of projects, has a more developed abstract style than a Bergman, who is free to develop his own scripts. Not that Bergman lacks personality, but his work has declined with the depletion of his ideas largely because his technique never equaled his sensibility. Joseph L. Mankiewicz and Billy Wilder are other examples of writer-directors without adequate technical mastery. By contrast, Douglas Sirk and Otto Preminger have moved up the scale because their miscellaneous projects reveal a stylistic consistency.

The third and ultimate premise of the *auteur* theory is concerned with interior meaning, the ultimate glory of the cinema as an art. Interior meaning is extrapolated from the tension between a director's personality and his material. This conception of interior meaning comes close to what Astruc defines as *mise en scène,* but not quite. It is not quite the vision of the world a director projects nor quite his attitude toward life. It is ambiguous, in any literary sense, because part of it is imbedded in the stuff of the cinema and cannot be rendered in noncinematic terms. Truffaut has called it the temperature of the director on the set, and that is a close approximation of its professional aspect. Dare I come out and say what I think it to be is an *élan* of the soul?

Lest I seem unduly mystical, let me hasten to add that all I mean by "soul" is that intangible difference between one personality and another, all other things being equal. Sometimes, this difference is expressed by no more than a beat's hesitation in the rhythm of a film. In one sequence of *La Règle du Jeu,* Renoir gallops up the stairs, turns to his right with a lurching movement, stops in hoplike uncertainty when his name is called by a coquettish maid, and, then, with marvelous postreflex continuity, resumes his bearishly shambling journey to the heroine's boudoir. If I could describe the musical grace note of that momentary suspension, and I can't, I might be able to provide a more precise definition of the *auteur* theory. As it is, all I can do is point at the specific beauties of interior meaning on the screen and, later, catalogue the moments of recognition.

The three premises of the *auteur* theory may be visualized as three concentric circles: the outer circle as technique; the middle circle, personal style; and the inner circle, interior meaning. The corresponding roles of the director may be designated as those of a technician, a stylist, and an *auteur.* There is no prescribed course by which a director passes through the three circles. Godard once remarked that Visconti had evolved from a *metteur en scène* to an *auteur,* whereas Rossellini had evolved from an *auteur* to a *metteur en scène.* From opposite directions, they emerged with comparable status. Minnelli began and remained in the second circle as a stylist; Buñuel was an *auteur* even before he had assembled the technique of the first circle. Technique is simply the ability to put a film together with some clarity and coherence. Nowadays, it is possible to become a director without knowing too much about the technical side, even the crucial functions of photography and editing. An expert production crew could probably cover up for a chimpanzee in the director's chair. How do you tell the genuine director from the quasichimpanzee? After a given number of films, a pattern is established.

In fact, the *auteur* theory itself is a pattern theory in constant flux. I would never endorse a Ptolemaic constellation of directors in a fixed orbit. At the moment, my list of *auteurs* runs something like this through the first twenty: Ophuls, Renoir, Mizoguchi, Hitchcock, Chaplin, Ford, Welles, Dreyer, Rossellini, Murnau, Griffith, Sternberg, Eisenstein, von Stroheim, Buñuel, Bresson, Hawks, Lang, Flaherty, Vigo. This list is somewhat weighted toward seniority and established reputations. In time, some of these *auteurs* will rise, some will fall, and some will be displaced either by new directors or rediscovered ancients. Again, the exact order is less important than the specific definitions of these and as many as two hundred other potential *auteurs.* I would hardly expect any other critic in the world fully to endorse this list, especially on faith. Only after thousands of films have been reevaluated, will any personal pantheon have a reasonably objective validity. The task of validating the *auteur* theory is an enormous one, and the end will never be in sight. Meanwhile, the *auteur* habit of collecting random films in directorial bundles will serve posterity with at least a tentative classification.

Although the *auteur* theory emphasizes the body of a director's work rather than isolated masterpieces, it is expected of great directors that they make great films every so often. The only possible exception to this rule I can think of is Abel Gance, whose greatness is largely a function of his aspiration. Even with Gance, *La Roue* is as close to being a great film as any single work of Flaherty's. Not that single works matter that much. As Renoir has observed, a director spends his life on variations of the same film.

Two recent films—*Boccaccio '70* and *The Seven Capital Sins*—unwittingly reinforced the *auteur* theory by confirming the relative standing of the many directors involved. If I had not seen either film, I would have anticipated that the order of merit in *Boccaccio '70* would be Visconti, Fellini, and De Sica, and in *The Seven Capital Sins* Godard, Chabrol, Demy, Vadim, De Broca, Molinaro. (Dhomme, Ionesco's stage director and an unknown quantity in advance, turned out to be the worse of the lot.) There might be some argument about the relative badness of De Broca and Molinaro, but, otherwise, the directors ran true to form by almost any objective criterion of value. However, the main point here is that even in these frothy, ultracommercial servings of entertainment, the contribution of each director had less in common stylistically with the work of other directors on the project than with his own previous work.

Sometimes, a great deal of corn must be husked to yield a few kernels of internal meaning. I recently saw *Every Night at Eight,* one of the many maddeningly routine films Raoul Walsh has directed in his long career. This 1935 effort featured George Raft, Alice Faye, Frances Langford, and Patsy Kelly in one of those familiar plots about radio shows of the period. The film keeps moving along in the pleasantly unpretentious manner one would expect of Walsh until one incongruously intense scene with George Raft thrashing about in his sleep, revealing his inner fears in mumbling dream-talk. The girl he loves comes into the room in the midst of his unconscious avowals of feeling and listens sympathetically. This unusual scene was later amplified in *High Sierra* with Humphrey Bogart and Ida Lupino. The point is that one of the screen's most virile directors employed an essentially feminine narrative device to dramatize the emotional vulnerability of his heroes. If I had not been aware of Walsh in *Every Night at Eight,* the crucial link to *High Sierra* would have passed unnoticed. Such are the joys of the *auteur* theory.

1962

PETER WOLLEN
FROM SIGNS AND MEANING IN
THE CINEMA

THE AUTEUR THEORY

The *politique des auteurs*—the *auteur* theory, as Andrew Sarris calls it—was developed by the loosely knit group of critics who wrote for *Cahiers du Cinéma* and made it the leading film magazine in the world. It sprang from the conviction that the American cinema was worth studying in depth, that masterpieces were made not only by a small upper crust of directors, the cultured gilt on the commercial gingerbread, but by a whole range of authors, whose work had previously been dismissed and consigned to oblivion. There were special conditions in Paris which made this conviction possible. Firstly, there was the fact that American films were banned from France under the Vichy government and the German Occupation. Consequently, when they reappeared after the Liberation they came with a force— and an emotional impact—which was necessarily missing in the Anglo-Saxon countries themselves. And, secondly, there was a thriving ciné-club movement, due in part to the close connections there had always been in France between the cinema and the intelligentsia: witness the example of Jean Cocteau or André Malraux. Connected with this ciné-club movement was the magnificent Paris *Cinémathèque,* the work of Henri Langlois, a great *auteur,* as Jean-Luc Godard described him. The policy of the *Cinémathèque* was to show the maximum number of films, to plough back the production of the past in order to produce the culture in which the cinema of the future could thrive. It gave French *cinéphiles* an unmatched perception of the historical dimensions of Hollywood and the careers of individual directors.

The *auteur* theory grew up rather haphazardly; it was never elaborated in programmatic terms, in a manifesto or collective statement. As a result, it could be interpreted and applied on rather broad lines; different critics developed somewhat different methods within a loose framework of common attitudes. This looseness and diffuseness of the theory has allowed flagrant misunderstandings to take root, particularly among critics in Britain and the United States. Ignorance has been compounded by a vein of hostility to foreign ideas and a taste for travesty and caricature. However, the fruitfulness of the *auteur* approach has been such that it has made headway even on the most unfavorable terrain. For instance, a recent straw poll of British critics, conducted in conjunction with a Don Siegel Retrospective at the National Film Theatre, revealed that, among American directors most admired, a group consisting of Budd Boetticher, Samuel Fuller and Howard Hawks ran immediately behind Ford, Hitchcock and Welles, who topped the poll, but ahead of Billy Wilder, Josef Von Sternberg and Preston Sturges.

Of course, some individual directors have always been recognised as outstanding: Charles Chaplin, John Ford, Orson Welles. The *auteur* theory does not limit itself to acclaiming the director as the main author of a film. It implies an operation of decipherment; it reveals authors where none had been seen before. For years, the model of an author in the cinema was that of the European director, with open artistic aspirations and full control over his films. This model still lingers on; it lies behind the existential distinction between art films and popular films. Directors who built their reputations in Europe were dismissed after they crossed the Atlantic, reduced to anonymity. American Hitchcock was contrasted unfavourably with English Hitchcock, American Renoir with French Renoir, American Fritz Lang with German Fritz Lang. The *auteur* theory has led to the revaluation of the second, Hollywood careers of these and other European directors; without it, masterpieces such as *Scarlet Street* or *Vertigo* would never have been perceived. Conversely, the *auteur* theory has been sceptical when offered an American director whose salvation has been exile to Europe. It is difficult now to argue that *Brute Force* has ever been excelled by Jules Dassin or that Joseph Losey's recent work is markedly superior to, say, *The Prowler*.

In time, owing to the diffuseness of the original theory, two main schools of *auteur* critics grew up: those who insisted on revealing a core of meanings, of thematic motifs, and those who stressed style and *mise en scène*. There is an important distinction here, which I shall return to later. The work of the *auteur* has a semantic dimension, it is not purely formal; the work of the *metteur en scène,* on the other hand, does not go beyond the realm of performance, of transposing into the special complex of cinematic codes and channels a pre-existing text: a scenario, a book or a play. As we shall see, the meaning of the films of an *auteur* is constructed *a posteriori;* the meaning—semantic, rather than stylistic or expressive—of the films of a *metteur en scène* exists *a priori.* In concrete cases, of course, this distinction is not always clear-cut. There is controversy over whether some directors should be seen as *auteurs* or *metteurs en scène.* For example, though it is possible to make intuitive ascriptions, there have been no really persuasive accounts as yet of Raoul Walsh or William Wyler as *auteurs,* to take two very different directors. Opinions might differ about Don Siegel or George Cukor. Because of the difficulty of fixing the distinction in these concrete cases, it has often become blurred; indeed, some French critics have tended to value the *metteur en scène* above the *auteur.* MacMahonism sprang up, with its cult of Walsh, Lang, Losey and Preminger, its fascination with violence and its notorious text: "Charlton Heston is an axiom of the cinema." What André Bazin called "aesthetic cults of personality" began to be formed. Minor directors were acclaimed before they had, in any real sense, been identified and defined.

Yet the *auteur* theory has survived despite all the hallucinating critical extravaganzas which it has fathered. It has survived because it is indispensable. Geoffrey Nowell-Smith has summed up the *auteur* theory as it is normally presented today:

> One essential corollary of the theory as it has been developed is the discovery that the defining characteristics of an author's work are not necessarily those which are most readily apparent. The purpose of criticism thus becomes to uncover behind the superficial contrasts of subject and treatment a hard core of basic and often recondite motifs. The pattern formed by these motifs . . . is what gives an author's work its particular structure, both defining it internally and distinguishing one body of work from another.

It is this "structural approach," as Nowell-Smith calls it, which is indispensable for the critic.

The test case for the *auteur* theory is provided by the work of Howard Hawks. Why Hawks, rather than, say, Frank Borzage or King Vidor? Firstly, Hawks is a director who has worked for years within the Hollywood system. His first film, *Road to Glory,* was made in 1926. Yet throughout his long career he has only once received general critical acclaim, for his wartime film, *Sergeant York,* which closer inspections reveals to be eccentric and atypical of the main *corpus* of Hawks's films. Secondly, Hawks has worked in almost every genre. He has made westerns, *(Rio Bravo),* gangsters *(Scarface),* war films *(Air Force),* thrillers *(The Big Sleep),* science fiction *(The Thing from Another World),* musicals *(Gentlemen Prefer Blondes),* comedies *(Bringing up Baby),* even a Biblical epic *(Land of the Pharaohs).* Yet all of these films (except perhaps *Land of the Pharaohs,* which he himself was not happy about) exhibit the same thematic preoccupations, the same recurring motifs and incidents, the same visual style and tempo. In the same way that Roland Barthes constructed a species of *homo racinianus,* the critic can construct a *homo hawksianus,* the protagonist of Hawksian values in the problematic Hawksian world.

Hawks achieved this by reducing the genres to two basic types: the adventure drama and the crazy comedy. These two types express inverse views of the world, the positive and negative poles of the Hawksian vision. Hawks stands opposed, on the one hand, to John Ford and, on the other hand, to Budd Boetticher. All these directors are concerned with the problem of heroism. For the hero, as an individual, death is an absolute limit which cannot be transcended: it renders the life which preceded it meaningless, absurb. How then can there be any meaningful individual action during life? How can individual action have any value—be heroic—if it cannot have transcendent value, because of the absolutely devaluing limit of death? John Ford finds the answer to this question by placing and situating the individual within society and within history, specifically within American history. Ford finds transcendent values in the historic vocation of America as a nation, to bring civilisation to a savage land, the garden to the wilderness. At the same time, Ford also sees these values themselves as problematic; he begins to question the movement of American history itself. Boetticher, on the contrary, insists on a radical individualism. "I am not interested in making films about mass feelings. I am for the individual." He looks for values in the encounter with death itself: the underlying metaphor is always that of the bull-fighter in the arena. The hero enters a group of companions, but there is no possibility of group solidarity. Boetticher's hero acts by dissolving groups and collectives of any kind into their constituent individuals, so that he confronts each person face-to-face; the films develop, in Andrew Sarris's words, into "floating poker games, where every character takes turns at bluffing about his hand until the final showdown." Hawks, unlike Boetticher, seeks transcendent values beyond the individual, in solidarity with others. But, unlike Ford, he does not give his heroes any historical dimension, any destiny in time.

For Hawks the highest human emotion is the camaraderie of the exclusive, self-sufficient, all-male group. Hawk's heroes are cattlemen, marlin-fishermen, racing-drivers, pilots, big-game hunters, habituated to danger and living apart from society, actually cut off from it physically by dense forest, sea, snow or desert. Their aerodromes are fog-bound; the radio has cracked up; the next mail-coach or packet-boat does not leave for a week. The *élite* group strictly preserves its exclusivity. It is necessary to pass a test of ability and courage to win admittance. The group's only internal tensions come when one member lets the other down (the drunk deputy in *Rio Bravo*, the panicky pilot in *Only Angels Have Wings*) and must redeem himself by some act of exceptional bravery, or occasionally when too much 'individualism' threatens to disrupt the close-knit circle (the rivalry between drivers in *Red Line 7000*, the fighter pilot among the bomber crew in *Air Force*). The group's security is the first commandment: "You get a stunt team in acrobatics in the air—if one of them is no good, then they're all in trouble. If someone loses his nerve catching animals, then the whole bunch can be in trouble." The group members are bound together by rituals (in *Hatari!* blood is exchanged by transfusion) and express themselves univocally in communal sing-songs. There is a famous example of this in *Rio Bravo*. In *Dawn Patrol* the camaraderie of the pilots stretches even across the enemy lines: a captured German ace is immediately drafted into the group and joins in the sing-song; in *Hatari!* hunters of different nationality and in different places join together in a song over an intercom radio system.

Hawks's heroes pride themselves on their professionalism. They ask: "How good is he? He'd better be good." They expect no praise for doing their job well. Indeed, none is given except: 'The boys did all right.' When they die, they leave behind them only the most meagre personal belongings, perhaps a handful of medals. Hawks himself has summed up this desolate and barren view of life:

> It's just a calm acceptance of a fact. In *Only Angels Have Wings,* after Joe dies, Cary Grant says: "He just wasn't good enough." Well, that's the only thing that keeps people going. They just have to say: "Joe wasn't good enough, and I'm better than Joe, so I go ahead and do it." And they find out they're not any better than Joe, but then it's too late, you see.

In Ford films, death is celebrated by funeral services, an impromptu prayer, a few staves of "Shall we gather at the river?"—it is inserted into an ongoing system of ritual institutions, along with the wedding, the dance, the parade. But for Hawks it is enough that the routine of the group's life goes on, a routine whose only relieving features are "danger *(Hatari!)* and "fun." Danger gives existence pungency: "Every time you get real action, then you have danger. And the question, 'Are you living or not living?' is probably the biggest drama we have." This nihilism, in which 'living' means no more than being in danger of losing your life—a danger entered into quite gratuitously—is augmented by the Hawksian concept of having "fun." The word "fun" crops up constantly in Hawks's interviews and scripts. It masks his despair.

When one of Hawks's *élite* is asked, usually by a woman, why he risks his life, he replies: "No reason I can think of makes any sense. I guess we're just crazy." Or Feathers, sardonically, to Colorado in *Rio Bravo:* "You haven't even the excuse I have. We're all fools." By "crazy" Hawks does not mean psychopathic: none of his characters are like Turkey in Peckinpah's *The Deadly Companions* or Billy the Kid in Penn's *The Left-Handed Gun.* Nor is there the sense of the absurdity of life which we sometimes find in Boetticher's films: death, as we have seen, is for Hawks simply a routine occurrence, not a *grotesquerie,* as in *The Tall T* ('Pretty soon that well's going to be chock-a-block') or *The Rise and Fall of Legs Diamond.* For Hawks "craziness" implies difference, a sense of apartness from the ordinary, everyday, social world. At the same time, Hawks sees the ordinary world as being "crazy" in a much more fundamental sense, because devoid of any meaning or values. "I mean crazy reactions—I don't think they're crazy, I think they're normal—but according to bad habits we've fallen into they seemed crazy." Which is the normal, which the abnormal? Hawks recognises, inchoately, that to most people his heroes, far from embodying rational values, are only a dwindling band of eccentrics. Hawks's 'kind of men' have no place in the world.

The Hawksian heroes, who exclude others from their own *élite* group, are themselves excluded from society, exiled to the African bush or to the Arctic. Outsiders, other people in general, are perceived by the group as an undifferentiated crowd. Their role is to gape at the deeds of the heroes whom, at the same time, they hate. The crowd assembles to watch the showdown in *Rio Bravo,* to see the cars spin off the track in *The Crowd Roars.* The gulf between the outsider and the heroes transcends enmities among the *élite:* witness *Dawn Patrol* or Nelse in *El Dorado.* Most dehumanised of all is the crowd in *Land of the Pharaohs,* employed in building the Pyramids. Originally the film was to have been about Chinese labourers building a "magnificent airfield" for the American army, but the victory of the Chinese Revolution forced Hawks to change his plans. ("Then I thought of the building of the Pyramids; I thought it was the same kind of story.") But the presence of the crowd, of external society, is a constant covert threat to the Hawksian *élite,* who retaliate by having "fun." In the crazy comedies ordinary citizens are turned into comic butts, lampooned and tormented: the most obvious target is the insurance salesman in *His Girl Friday.* Often Hawks's revenge becomes grim and macabre. In *Sergeant York* it is "fun" to shoot Germans "like turkeys"; in *Air Force* it is "fun" to blow up the Japanese fleet. In *Rio Bravo* the geligniting of the badmen "was very funny." It is at these moments that the *élite* turns against the world outside and takes the opportunity to be brutal and destructive.

Besides the covert pressure of the crowd outside, there is also an overt force which threatens: woman. Man is woman's "prey." Women are admitted to the male group only after much disquiet and a long ritual courtship, phased round the offer-

ing, lighting and exchange of cigarettes, during which they prove themselves worthy
of entry. Often they perform minor feats of valour. Even then though they are never
really full members. A typical dialogue sums up their position:

Woman: You love him, don't you?

Man (embarrassed): Yes . . . I guess so. . . .

Woman: How can I love him like you?

Man: Just stick around.

The undercurrent of homosexuality in Hawks's films is never crystallised, though
in *The Big Sky,* for example, it runs very close to the surface. And he himself
described *A Girl in Every Port* as "really a love story between two men." For Hawks
men are equals, within the group at least, whereas there is a clear identification
between women and the animal world, most explicit in *Bringing Up Baby, Gentlemen Prefer Blondes* and *Hatari!* Man must strive to maintain his mastery. It is also
worth noting that, in Hawks's adventure dramas and even in many of his comedies,
there is no married life. Often the heroes were married or at least intimately committed, to a woman at some time in the distant past but have suffered an unspecified
trauma, with the result that they have been suspicious of women ever since. Their
attitude is "Once bitten, twice shy." This is in contrast to the films of Ford, which
almost always include domestic scenes. Woman is not a threat to Ford's heroes; she
falls into her allotted social place as wife and mother, bringing up the children,
cooking, sewing, a life of service, drudgery and subordination. She is repaid for this
by being sentimentalised. Boetticher, on the other hand, has no obvious place for
women at all; they are phantoms, who provoke action, are pretexts for male modes
of conduct, but have no authentic significance in themselves. "In herself, the
woman has not the slightest importance."

Hawks sees the all-male community as an ultimate; obviously it is very retrograde. His Spartan heroes are, in fact, cruelly stunted. Hawks would be a lesser
director if he was unaffected by this, if his adventure dramas were the sum total of
his work. His real claim as an author lies in the presence, together with the dramas,
of their inverse, the crazy comedies. They are the agonised exposure of the underlying tensions of the heroic dramas. There are two principal themes, zones of tension. The first is the theme of regression: of regression to childhood, infantilism, as
in *Monkey Business,* or regression to savagery: witness the repeated scene of the
adult about to be scalped by painted children, in *Monkey Business* and in *The Ransom of Red Chief.* With brilliant insight, Robin Wood has shown how *Scarface*
should be categorised among the comedies rather than the dramas: Camonte is perceived as savage, child-like, subhuman. The second principal comedy theme is that
of sex-reversal and role-reversal. *I Was A Male War Bride* is the most extreme
example. Many of Hawks's comedies are centred round domineering women and
timid, pliable men: *Bringing Up Baby* and *Man's Favourite Sport,* for example.
There are often scenes of male sexual humiliation, such as the trousers being pulled
off the hapless private eye in *Gentlemen Prefer Blondes.* In the same film, the Olympic Team of athletes are reduced to passive objects in an extraordinary Jane Russell
song number; big-game hunting is lampooned, like fishing in *Man's Favourite
Sport;* the theme of infantilism crops up again: "The child was the most mature one
on board the ship, and I think he was a lot of fun."

Howard Hawks's battle between the sexes. Carole Lombard and John Barrymore in *Twentieth Century* (1934), Cary Grant and Katharine Hepburn in *Bringing Up Baby* (1938). "Besides the covert pressure of the crowd outside, there is also an overt force which threatens: woman. Man is woman's prey" (WOLLEN, page 593).

Whereas the dramas show the mastery of man over nature, over woman, over the animal and childish; the comedies show his humiliation, his regression. The heroes become victims; society, instead of being excluded and despised, breaks in with irruptions of monstrous farce. It could well be argued that Hawks's outlook, the alternative world which he constructs in the cinema, the Hawksian heterocosm, is not one imbued with particular intellectual subtlety or sophistication. This does not detract from its force. Hawks first attracted attention because he was regarded naïvely as an action director. Later, the thematic content which I have outlined was detected and revealed. Beyond the stylemes, semantemes were found to exist; the films were anchored in an objective stratum of meaning, a plerematic stratum, as the Danish linguist Hjelmslev would put it. Thus the stylistic expressiveness of Hawks's films was shown to be not purely contingent, but grounded in significance.

Something further needs to be said about the theoretical basis of the kind of schematic exposition of Hawks's work which I have outlined. The 'structural approach' which underlies it, the definition of a core of repeated motifs, has evident affinities with methods which have been developed for the study of folklore and mythology. In the work of Olrik and others, it was noted that in different folk-tales the same motifs reappeared time and time again. It became possible to build up a lexicon of these motifs. Eventually Propp showed how a whole cycle of Russian fairy-tales could be analysed into variations of a very limited set of basic motifs (or moves, as he called them). Underlying the different, individual tales was an archi-tale, of which they were all variants. One important point needs to be made about this type of structural analysis. There is a danger, as Lévi-Strauss has pointed out, that by simply noting and mapping resemblances, all the texts which are studied (whether Russian fairy-tales or American movies) will be reduced to one, abstract and impoverished. There must be a moment of synthesis as well as a moment of analysis: otherwise, the method is formalist, rather than truly structuralist. Structuralist criticism cannot rest at the perception of resemblances or repetitions (redundancies, in fact), but must also comprehend a system of differences and oppositions. In this way, texts can be studied not only in their universality (what they all have in common) but also in their singularity (what differentiates them from each other). This means of course that the test of a structural analysis lies not in the orthodox canon of a director's work, where resemblances are clustered, but in films which at first sight may seem eccentricities.

In the films of Howard Hawks a systematic series of oppositions can be seen very near the surface, in the contrast between the adventure dramas and the crazy comedies. If we take the adventure dramas alone it would seem that Hawks's work is flaccid, lacking in dynamism; it is only when we consider the crazy comedies that it becomes rich, begins to ferment: alongside every dramatic hero we are aware of a phantom, stripped of mastery, humiliated, inverted. With other directors, the system of oppositions is much more complex: instead of there being two broad strata of films there are a whole series of shifting variations. In these cases, we need to analyse the roles of the protagonists themselves, rather than simply the worlds in which they operate. The protagonists of fairy-tales or myths, as Lévi-Strauss has pointed out, can be dissolved into bundles of differential elements, pairs of opposites. Thus the difference between the prince and the goose-girl can be reduced to two antinomic pairs: one natural, male versus female, and the other cultural, high versus low. We can proceed with the same kind of operation in the study of films, though, as we shall see, we shall find them more complex than fairy tales. . . .

It is instructive, for example, to consider three films of John Ford and compare their heroes: Wyatt Earp in *My Darling Clementine,* Ethan Edwards in *The Searchers* and Tom Doniphon in *The Man Who Shot Liberty Valance.* They all act within the recognizable Ford world, governed by a set of oppositions, but their *loci* within that world are very different. The relevant pairs of opposites overlap; different pairs are foregrounded in different movies. The most relevant are garden versus wilderness, plough-share versus sabre, settler versus nomad, European versus Indian, civilised versus savage, book versus gun, married versus unmarried, East versus West. These antimonies can often be broken down further. The East, for instance, can be defined either as Boston or Washington and, in *The Last Hurrah,* Boston itself is broken down into the antipodes of Irish immigrants versus Plymouth Club, themselves bundles of such differential elements as Celtic versus Anglo-Saxon, poor versus rich, Catholic versus Protestant, Democrat versus Republican, and so on. At first sight, it might seem that the oppositions listed above overlap to the extent that they become practically synonymous, but this is by no means the case. As we shall see, part of the development of Ford's career has been the shift from an identity between civilised versus savage and European versus Indian to their separation and final reversal, so that in *Cheyenne Autumn* it is the Europeans who are savage, the victims who are heroes.

The master antinomy in Ford's films is that between the wilderness and the garden. As Henry Nash Smith has demonstrated, in his magisterial book *Virgin Land,* the contrast between the image of America as a desert and as a garden is one which has dominated American thought and literature, recurring in countless novels, tracts, political speeches, and magazine stories. In Ford's films it is crystallised in a number of striking images. *The Man Who Shot Liberty Valance,* for instance, contains the image of the cactus rose, which encapsulates the antinomy between desert and garden which pervades the whole film. Compare with this the famous scene in *My Darling Clementine,* after Wyatt Earp has gone to the barber (who civilises the unkempt), where the scent of honeysuckle is twice remarked upon: an artificial perfume, cultural rather than natural. This moment marks the turning-point in Wyatt Earp's transition from wandering cowboy, nomadic, savage, bent on personal revenge, unmarried, to married man, settled, civilised, the sheriff who administers the law.

Earp, in *My Darling Clementine,* is structurally the most simple of the three protagonists I have mentioned: his progress is an uncomplicated passage from nature to culture, from the wilderness left in the past to the garden anticipated in the future. Ethan Edwards, in *The Searchers,* is more complex. He must be defined not in terms of past versus future or wilderness versus garden compounded in himself, but in relation to two other protagonists: Scar, the Indian chief, and the family of homesteaders. Ethan Edwards, unlike Earp, remains a nomad throughout the film. At the start, he rides in from the desert to enter the log-house; at the end, with perfect symmetry, he leaves the house again to return to the desert, to vagrancy. In many respects, he is similar to Scar; he is a wanderer, a savage, outside the law: he scalps his enemy. But, like the homesteaders, of course, he is a European, the mortal foe of the Indian. Thus Edwards is ambiguous; the antinomies invade the personality of the protagonist himself. The oppositions tear Edwards in two; he is a tragic hero. His companion, Martin Pawley, however, is able to resolve the duality; for him, the period of nomadism is only an episode, which has meaning as the restitution of the family, a necessary link between his old home and his new home.

Ethan Edwards's wandering is, like that of many other Ford protagonists, a quest, a search. A number of Ford films are built round the theme of the quest for the Promised Land, an American re-enactment of the biblical exodus, the journey through the desert to the land of milk and honey, the New Jerusalem. This theme is built on the combination of the two pairs: wilderness versus garden and nomad versus settler; the first pair precedes the second in time. Thus, in *Wagonmaster,* the Mormons cross the desert in search of their future home; in *How Green Was My Valley* and *The Informer,* the protagonists want to cross the Atlantic to a future home in the United States. But, during Ford's career, the situation of home is reversed in time. In *Cheyenne Autumn* the Indians journey in search of the home they once had in the past; in *The Quiet Man,* the American Sean Thornton returns to his ancestral home in Ireland. Ethan Edwards's journey is a kind of parody of this theme: his object is not constructive, to found a home, but destructive, to find and scalp Scar. Nevertheless, the weight of the film remains orientated to the future: Scar has burned down the home of the settlers, but it is replaced and we are confident that the homesteader's wife, Mrs Jorgensen, is right when she says: 'Some day this country's going to be a fine place to live.' The wilderness will, in the end, be turned into a garden.

The Man Who Shot Liberty Valance has many similarities with *The Searchers.* We may note three: the wilderness becomes a garden—this is made quite explicit, for Senator Stoddart has wrung from Washington the funds necessary to build a dam which will irrigate the desert and bring real roses, not cactus roses; Tom Doniphon shoots Liberty Valance as Ethan Edwards scalped Scar; a log-home is burned to the ground. But the differences are equally clear: the log-home is burned after the death of Liberty Valance; it is destroyed by Doniphon himself; it is his own home. The burning marks the realisation that he will never enter the Promised Land, that to him it means nothing; that he has doomed himself to be a creature of the past, insignificant in the world of the future. By shooting Liberty Valance he has destroyed the only world in which he himself can exist, the world of the gun rather than the book; it is as though Ethan Edwards has perceived that by scalping Scar, he was in reality committing suicide. It might be mentioned too that, in *The Man Who Shot Liberty Valance,* the woman who loves Doniphon marries Senator Stoddart. Doniphon when he destroys his log-house (his last words before doing so are 'Home, sweet home!') also destroys the possibility of marriage.

The themes of *The Man Who Shot Liberty Valance* can be expressed in another way. Ransom Stoddart represents rational-legal authority, Tom Doniphon represents charismatic authority. Doniphon abandons his charisma and cedes it, under what amounts to false pretences, to Stoddart. In this way charismatic and rational-legal authority are combined in the person of Stoddart and stability thus assured.

In *The Searchers* this transfer does not take place; the two kinds of authority remain separated. In *My Darling Clementine* they are combined naturally in Wyatt Earp, without any transfer being necessary. In many of Ford's late films—*The Quiet Man, Cheyenne Autumn, Donovan's Reef*—the accent is placed on traditional authority. The island of Ailakaowa, in *Donovan's Reef*, a kind of Valhalla for the homeless heroes of *The Man Who Shot Liberty Valance*, is actually a monarchy, though complete with the Boston girl, wooden church, and saloon made familiar by *My Darling Clementine*. In fact, the character of Chihuahua, Doc Holliday's girl in *My Darling Clementine*, is split into two: Miss Lafleur and Lelani, the native princess. One represents the saloon entertainer, the other the non-American in opposition to the respectable Bostonians, Amelia Sarah Dedham and Clementine Carter. In a broad sense, this is a part of a general movement which can be detected in Ford's work to equate the Irish, Indians, and Polynesians as traditional communities, set in the past, counterposed to the march forward to the American future, as it has turned out in reality, but assimilating the values of the American future as it was once dreamed.

It would be possible, I have no doubt, to elaborate on Ford's career, as defined by pairs of contrasts and similarities, in very great detail, though—as always with film criticism—the impossibility of quotation is a severe handicap. My own view is that Ford's work is much richer than that of Hawks and that this is revealed by a structural analysis; it is the richness of the shifting relations between antinomies in Ford's work that makes him a great artist, beyond being simply an undoubted *auteur*. Moreover, the *auteur* theory enables us to reveal a whole complex of meaning in films such as *Donovan's Reef*, which a recent filmography sums up as just 'a couple of Navy men who have retired to a South Sea island now spend most of their time raising hell.' Similarly, it throws a completely new light on a film like *Wings of Eagles*, which revolves, like *The Searchers*, round the vagrancy versus home antinomy, with the difference that when the hero does come home, after flying round the world, he trips over a child's toy, falls down the stairs and is completely paralysed so that he cannot move at all, not even his toes. This is the macabre *reductio ad absurdum* of the settled.

Perhaps it would be true to say that it is the lesser *auteurs* who can be defined, as Nowell-Smith put it, by a core of basic motifs which remain constant, without variation. The great directors must be defined in terms of shifting relations, in their singularity as well as their uniformity. Renoir once remarked that a director spends his whole life making one film; this film, which it is the task of the critic to construct, consists not only of the typical features of its variants, which are merely its redundancies, but of the principle of variation which governs it, that is its esoteric structure, which can only manifest itself or 'seep to the surface', in Lévi-Strauss's phrase, 'through the repetition process'. Thus Renoir's 'film' is in reality a 'kind of permutation group, the two variants placed at the far ends being in a symmetrical, though inverted, relationship to each other.' In practice, we will not find perfect symmetry, though as we have seen, in the case of Ford, some antinomies are completely reversed. Instead, there will be a kind of torsion within the permutation group, within the matrix, a kind of exploration of certain possibilities, in which some antinomies are foregrounded, discarded, or even inverted, whereas others remain stable and constant. The important thing to stress, however, is that it is only the analysis of the whole *corpus* which permits the moment of synthesis when the critic returns to the individual film.

Of course, the director does not have full control over his work; this explains why the *auteur* theory involves a kind of decipherment, decryptment. A great many features of films analysed have to be dismissed as indecipherable because of 'noise' from the producer, the cameraman, or even the actors. This concept of 'noise' needs further elaboration. It is often said that a film is the result of a multiplicity of factors, the sum total of a number of different contributions. The contribution of the director—the 'directorial factor', as it were—is only one of these, though perhaps the one which carries the most weight. I do not need to emphasize that this view is quite the contrary of the *auteur* theory and has nothing in common with it at all. What the *auteur* theory does is to take a group of films—the work of one director—and analyse their structure. Everything irrelevant to this, everything non-pertinent, is considered logically secondary, contingent, to be discarded. Of course, it is possible to approach films by studying some other feature; by an effort of critical ascesis we could see films, as Von Sternberg sometimes urged, as abstract light-show or as histrionic feasts. Sometimes these separate texts—those of the cameraman or the actors—may force themselves into prominence so that the film becomes an indecipherable palimpsest. This does not mean, of course, that it ceases to exist or to sway us or please us or intrigue us; it simply means that it is inaccessible to criticism. We can merely record our momentary and subjective impressions.

Myths, as Lévi-Strauss has pointed out, exist independently of style, the syntax of the sentence, or musical sound, euphony or cacophony. The myth functions 'on an especially high level where meaning succeeds practically in *"taking off"* from the linguistic ground on which it keeps rolling.' *Mutatis mutandis,* the same is true of the *auteur* film. 'When a mythical schema is transmitted from one population to another, and there exist differences of language, social organization, or way of life which make the myth difficult to communicate, it begins to become impoverished and confused.' The same kind of impoverishment and confusion takes place in the film studio, where difficulties of communication abound. But none the less the film can usually be discerned, even if it was a quickie made in a fortnight without the actors or the crews that the director might have liked, with an intrusive producer and even, perhaps a censor's scissors cutting away vital sequences. It is as though a film is a musical composition rather than a musical performance, although, whereas a musical composition exists *a priori* (like a scenario), an *auteur* film is constructed *a posteriori.* Imagine the situation if the critic had to construct a musical composition from a number of fragmentary, distorted versions of it, all with improvised passages or passages missing. . . .

What the *auteur* theory demonstrates is that the director is not simply in command of a performance of a pre-existing text; he is not, or need not be, only a *metteur en scène.* Don Siegel was asked on television what he took from Hemingway's short story for his film, *The Killers;* Siegel replied that 'the only thing taken from it was the catalyst that a man has been killed by somebody and he did not try to run away.' The word Siegel chose—'catalyst'—could not be bettered. Incidents and episodes in the original screenplay or novel can act as catalysts; they are the agents which are introduced into the mind (conscious or unconscious) of the *auteur* and react there with the motifs and themes characteristic of his work. The director does not subordinate himself to another author; his source is only a pretext, which provides catalysts, scenes which fuse with his own preoccupations to produce a radically new work. Thus the manifest process of performance, the treatment of a subject, conceals the latent production of a quite new text, the production of the director as an *auteur*.

Of course, it is possible to value performances as such, to agree with André Bazin that Olivier's *Henry V* was a great film, a great rendering, transposition into the cinema, of Shakespeare's original play. The great *metteurs en scène* should not be discounted simply because they are not *auteurs:* Vincente Minnelli, perhaps, or Stanley Donen. And, further than that, the same kind of process can take place that occurred in painting: the director can deliberately concentrate entirely on the stylistic and expressive dimensions of the cinema. He can say, as Josef Von Sternberg did about *Morocco,* that he purposely chose a fatuous story so that people would not be distracted from the play of light and shade in the photography. Some of Busby Berkeley's extraordinary sequences are equally detached from any kind of dependence on the screenplay: indeed, more often than not, some other director was entrusted with the job of putting the actors through the plot and dialogue. Moreover, there is no doubt that the greatest films will be not simply *auteur* films but marvellous expressively and stylistically as well: *Lola Montès, Shinheike Monogatari, La Règle du Jeu, La Signora di Tutti, Sansho Dayu, Le Carrosse d'Or.*

The *auteur* theory leaves us, as every theory does, with possibilities and questions. We need to develop much further a theory of performance, of the stylistic, of graded rather than coded modes of communication. We need to investigate and define, to construct critically the work of enormous numbers of directors who up to now have only been incompletely comprehended. We need to begin the task of comparing author with author. There are any number of specific problems which stand out: Donen's relationship to Kelly and Arthur Freed, Boetticher's films outside the Ranown cycle. Welles's relationship to Toland (and—perhaps more important—Wyler's), Sirk's films outside the Ross Hunter cycle, the exact identity of Walsh or Wellman, the decipherment of Anthony Mann. Moreover there is no reason why the *auteur* theory should not be applied to the English cinema, which is still utterly amorphous, unclassified, unperceived. We need not two or three books on Hitchcock and Ford, but many, many more. We need comparisons with authors in the other arts: Ford with Fenimore Cooper, for example, or Hawks with Faulkner. The task which the critics of *Cahiers du Cinéma* embarked on is still far from completed.

1969

. . . At this point, it is necessary to say something about the *auteur* theory since this has often been seen as a way of introducing the idea of the creative personality into the Hollywood cinema. Indeed, it is true that many protagonists of the *auteur* theory do argue in this way. However, I do not hold this view and I think it is important to detach the *auteur* theory from any suspicion that it simply represents a 'cult of personality' or apotheosis of the director. To my mind, the *auteur* theory actually represents a radical break with the idea of an 'art' cinema, not the transplant of traditional ideas about 'art' into Hollywood. The 'art' cinema is rooted in the idea of creativity and the film as the expression of an individual vision. What the *auteur* theory argues is that any film, certainly a Hollywood film, is a network of different statements, crossing and contradicting each other, elaborated into a final 'coherent' version. Like a dream, the film the spectator sees is, so to speak, the 'film façade', the end-product of 'secondary revision', which hides and masks the process which remains latent in the film 'unconscious'. Sometimes this 'façade' is so worked over, so smoothed out, or else so clotted with disparate elements, that it is impossible to see beyond it, or rather to see anything in it except the characters, the dialogue, the plot, and so on. But in other cases, by a process of comparison with other films, it is possible to decipher, not a coherent message or world-view, but a structure which underlies the film and shapes it, gives it a certain pattern of energy cathexis. It is this structure which *auteur* analysis disengages from the film.

The structure is associated with a single director, an individual, not because he has played the role of artist, expressing himself or his own vision in the film, but because it is through the force of his preoccupations that an unconscious, unintended meaning can be decoded in the film, usually to the surprise of the individual involved. The film is not a communication, but an artefact which is unconsciously structured in a certain way. *Auteur* analysis does not consist of retracing a film to its origins, to its creative source. It consists of tracing a structure (not a message) within the work, which can then *post factum* be assigned to an individual, the director, on empirical grounds. It is wrong, in the name of a denial of the traditional idea of creative subjectivity, to deny any status to individuals at all. But Fuller or Hawks or Hitchcock, the directors, are quite separate from 'Fuller' or 'Hawks' or 'Hitchcock', the structures named after them, and should not be methodologically confused. There can be no doubt that the presence of a structure in the text can often be connected with the presence of a director on the set, but the situation in the cinema, where the director's primary task is often one of coordination and rationalisation, is very different from that in the other arts, where there is a much more direct relationship between artist and work. It is in this sense that it is possible to speak of a film *auteur* as an unconscious catalyst.

However, the structures discerned in the text are often attacked in another way. Robin Wood, for example, has argued that the *'auteur'* film is something like a Platonic Idea. It posits a 'real' film, of which the actual film is only a flawed transcript, while the archi-film itself exists only in the mind of the critic. This attack rests on a misunderstanding. The main point about the Platonic Idea is that it predates the empirical reality, as an archetype. But the *'auteur'* film (or structure) is not an archi-film at all in this sense. It is an explanatory device which specifies partially how any individual film works. Some films it can say nothing or next-to-nothing about at all. *Auteur* theory cannot simply be applied indiscriminately. Nor does an *auteur* analysis exhaust what can be said about any single film. It does no more than provide one way of decoding a film, by specifying what its mechanics are at one level. There are other kinds of code which could be proposed, and whether they are of any value or not will have to be settled by reference to the text, to the films in question.

Underlying the anti-Platonic argument, however, there is often a hostility towards any kind of explanation which involves a degree of distancing from the 'lived experience' of watching the film itself. Yet clearly any kind of serious critical work—I would say scientific, though I know this drives some people into transports of rage—must involve a distance, a gap between the film and the criticism, the text and the meta-text. It is as though meteorologists were reproached for getting away from the 'lived experience' of walking in the rain or sunbathing. Once again, we are back with the myth of transparency, the idea that the mark of a good film is that it conveys a rich meaning, an important truth, in a way which can be grasped immediately. If this is the case, then clearly all the critic has to do is to describe the experience of watching the film, reception of a signal, in such a way as to clear up any little confusions or enigmas which still remain. The most that the critic can do is to put the spectator on the right wavelength so that he can see for himself as clearly as the critic, who is already tuned in.

The *auteur* theory, as I conceive it, insists that the spectator has to work at reading the text. With some films this work is wasted, unproductive. But with others it is not. In these cases, in a certain sense, the film changes, it becomes another film—as far as experience of it is concerned. It is no longer possible to look at it 'with the same eyes'. There is no integral, genuine experience which the critic enjoys and which he tries to guide others towards. Above all, the critic's experience is not essentially grounded in or guaranteed by the essence of the film itself. The critic is not at the heart of the matter. The critic is someone who persists in learning to see the film differently and is able to specify the mechanisms which make this possible. This is not a question of 'reading in' or projecting the critic's own concerns in to the film; any reading of a film has to be justified by an explanation of how the film itself works to make this reading possible. Nor is it the single reading, the one which gives us the true meaning of the film; it is simply a reading which produces more meaning.

Again, it is necessary to insist that since there is no true, essential meaning there can therefore be no exhaustive criticism, which settles the interpretation of a film once and for all. Moreover, since the meaning is not contained integrally in any film, any decoding may not apply over the whole area of it. Traditional criticism is always seeking for the comprehensive code which will give the complete interpretation, covering every detail. This is a wild goose chase, in the cinema, above all, which is a collective form. Both Classical and Romantic aesthetics hold to the belief that every detail should have a meaning—Classical aesthetics because of its belief in a common, universal code; Romantic aesthetics because of its belief in an organic unity in which every detail reflects the essence of the whole. The *auteur* theory argues that any single decoding has to compete, certainly in the cinema, with noise from signals coded differently. Beyond that, it is an illusion to think of any work as complete in itself, an isolated unity whose intercourse with other films, other texts, is carefully controlled to avoid contamination. Different codes may run across the frontiers of texts at liberty, meet and conflict within them. This is how language itself is structured, and the failure of linguistics, for instance, to deal with the problem of semantics, is exemplified in the idea that to the unitary code of grammar (the syntactic component of language) there must correspond a unitary semantic code, which would give a correct semantic interpretation of any sentence. Thus the idea of 'grammaticality' is wrongly extended to include a quite false notion of 'semanticity'. In fact, no headway can be made in semantics until this myth is dispelled.

The *auteur* theory has important implications for the problem of evaluation. Orthodox aesthetics sees the problem in predictable terms. The 'good' work is one which has both a rich meaning and a correspondingly complex form, wedded together in a unity (Romantic) or isomorphic with each other (Classical). Thus the critic, to demonstrate the value of a work, must be able to identify the 'content', establish its truth, profundity, and so forth, and then demonstrate how it is expressed with minimum loss or leakage in the signals of the text iself, which are patterned in a way which gives coherence to the work as a whole. 'Truth' of content is not envisaged as being like scientific truth, but more like 'human' truth, a distillation of the world of human experience, particularly interpersonal experience. The world itself is an untidy place, full of loose ends, but the artefact can tie all these loose ends together and thus convey to us a meaningful truth, an insight, which enables us to go back to the real world with a reordered and recycled experience which will enable us to cope better, live more fully, and so on. In this way art is given a humanistic function, which guarantees its value.

All this is overthrown when we begin to see loose ends in works of art, to refuse to acknowledge organic unity or integral content. Moreover, we have to revise our whole idea of criteria, of judgement. The notion behind criteria is that they are timeless and universal. They are then applied to a particular work and it is judged accordingly. This rigid view is varied to the extent that different criteria may apply to different kinds of works or that slightly different criteria may reflect different points of view or kinds of experience, though all are rooted in a common humanity. But almost all current theories of evaluation depend on identifying the work first and then confronting it with criteria. The work is then criticised for falling short on one score or another. It is blemished in some way. Evidently, if we reject the idea of an exhaustive interpretation, we have to reject this kind of evaluation. Instead, we should concentrate on the *productivity* of the work. This is what the 'modern movement' is about. The text, in Octavio Paz's words, is something like a machine for producing meaning. Moreover, its meaning is not neutral, something to be simply absorbed by the consumer.

The meaning of texts can be destructive—of the codes used in other texts, which may be the codes used by the spectator or the reader, who thus finds his own habitual codes threatened, the battle opening up in his own reading. In one sense, everybody knows this. We know that *Ulysses* or *Finnegans Wake* are destructive of the nineteenth-century novel. But it seems difficult to admit this destructiveness into court when judgements are to be made. We have to. To go to the cinema, to read books, or to listen to music is to be a partisan. Evaluation cannot be impartial. We cannot divorce the problem of codes from the problem of criteria. We cannot be passive consumers of films who then stand back to make judgements from above the fray. Judgements are made in the process of looking or reading. There is a sense in which to reject something as unintelligible is to make a judgement. It is to refuse to use a code. This may be right or wrong, but it is not the same thing as decoding a work before applying criteria. A valuable work, a powerful work at least, is one which challenges codes, overthrows established ways of reading or looking, not simply to establish new ones, but to compel an unending dialogue, not at random but productively. . . .

1972

RICHARD CORLISS
THE HOLLYWOOD
SCREENWRITER

Eight years ago, when popular movie criticism consisted mainly of plot summaries and star-gazing, and Bosley Crowther of *The New York Times* was scorning Godard and ignoring Ford and Hawks, *Film Culture* magazine published two articles by Andrew Sarris that were to revolutionize film criticism in the United States. In the first article, "Notes on the Auteur Theory in 1962," Sarris proposed an Americanization of the *politique des auteurs,* which held that the director is the author of a film and that visual style is the key to assessing a director's standing as an *auteur.* In *The American Cinema,* he evaluated—indeed, he rated—106 American directors (and seven foreigners) in categories ranging from the "Pantheon" to "Oddities and One Shots."

It took some time for the importance of Sarris' work to become evident to the community of film scholars. Hadn't Pauline Kael demolished his stratified silliness for good in a *Film Quarterly* polemic read by far more people than Sarris' original articles? Hadn't Dwight Macdonald resigned his regular column in *Film Quarterly* because Sarris was invited to contribute, and hadn't he done so with a venom that suggested an angry redneck burning a cross on the lawn of his new Negro neighbor's house? Hadn't Richard Dyer MacCann conspicuously omitted Sarris' writing (or any *auteur* criticism) from his anthology, *Film: A Montage of Theories,* which did include a piece by Kael the theory-baiter?

It's a pity that Academia didn't notice what Sarris had going for him: an engaging prose style that ranged from entertainingly analytical to deliriously lyrical; a popular, hip publication *(The Village Voice)* just right for reaching the young intellectuals for whom film was the most exciting art; a subject matter (the Hollywood sound film) that he knew almost viscerally, and whose product was bound to interest his readers more than the "serious" European films praised by his detractors;

and a burgeoning group of articulate acolytes (like Roger Greenspun and James Stoller) who could spread the faith without his losing face.

Came the Revolution, which coincided with the growing number of film courses and monographs. Sarris' thoughtful and well-timed challenge to the near-monopoly of social-realist criticism was adopted by most of the younger critics, and even adapted by some of the less secure older ones. It was refreshing to examine films as the creations of artists rather than of social forces, and to be able to do so in a manner that was serious without being solemn. Americans could finally admit that their movies weren't sinful just because they were entertaining, and that the films deserved to be judged by the same artistic standards applicable to any film.

By 1969, when Sarris expanded *The American Cinema* to book length, the critical attitude that had begun as a reaction to the party line was in serious danger of hardening into the Gospel According to St. Andrew. *The New York Times* had been converted into a veritable *auteur* shrine; its first- and second-string critics adhered closely to Sarris' tastes and standards, and its Almanac welcomed the word *auteur* into the English language, along with *acid, activist* and *Afro*. Film societies mounted ambitious retropectives of directors, from John Ford and Jean Renoir to Sam Fuller and Russ Meyer. Publishers commissioned extended studies of Fritz Lang (who has made forty-three films) and Roman Polanski (who has made five). The Revolution was victorious.

In some respects, however, the anarchists show tendencies of close-minded classicism. They put the spotlight on the once-despised Hollywood movie system and sprinkled a little cultural respectability on the industry's "hack" directors—fine. But in doing so they retarded investigation of other, equally vital film crafts, especially that of the screenwriter, who creates (or creatively adapts) a film's plot, characters, dialogue and theme.

The director *is* right in the middle of things. At the very least, he's on the sound stage while the director of photography is lighting the set that the art director has designed and, later, while the actors are speaking the lines that the screenwriter wrote. Quite often, he steers all these factors—story, actors, camera—in the right *direction*. So why not just say it's his film, that he is the author? Simply because the director is almost always an interpretive artist, not a creative one, and because the Hollywood film is a corporate art, not an individual one. This doesn't diminish the importance of the director, or the validity of the Hollywood film as an art. Both Chartres and *Charade* were the work of a number of individuals who contributed their unique talents to a corporate enterprise, but this fact doesn't necessarily make either work less appropriate for serious study than, say, the Mona Lisa or *Mothlight*. It just makes it more difficult for the critic to assign sole authorship to the work— and why should he waste time on a Name Game like this?

In the same way, both Stanley Donen and Stan Brakhage may be called film artists, but Donen is an interpretive artist while Brakhage is a creative one; Donen is a conductor and Brakhage is a composer. Donen is a film *director* who collaborates with his writers, actors and technicians in a completely different way than Brakhage, the film*maker,* collaborates with his film strips and viewer. The case can be made that Donen is a better film director than Brakhage is a filmmaker; they work in separate but equal film traditions, and it is possible that Donen succeeds in his genre, whereas Brakhage may fail in his. The theory used to be that the solitary, creative artist produced Art, and the corporate, interpretive craftsman produced Entertainment—a prejudice that kept people from examining the Hollywood movie. The *auteur* theory says, in effect, "What you thought was just Entertainment is really Art, because it is the work of an individual creator—an *auteur*. Therefore the Hollywood movie is worthy to be examined."

Many films are indeed dominated by the personality of the director, although not, perhaps, in the way the auteurists mean. The phrase "directorial personality" makes more sense if taken quite literally. The good director is usually a man with a strong, persuasive personality. He has to be a combination of tough guy, to make the technicians respond to his commands, and best friend, to coax a good performance out of a sensitive actress. Whether he directs with a riding crop (Stroheim), an icy stare (Sternberg), or a few soft-spoken words (Cukor), his personality is often crucial to the success of a film. The importance of a director's personal—or even visual—style is not questioned here, only the assumption that he creates a style out of thin air (with his collaborating craftsmen acting merely as paint, canvas, bowl of fruit, and patron), instead of adapting it to the equally important styles of the story and performers. The same literal meaning can apply to a director's "authority," which accurately describes his function on the set.

But the director need not be the only dominant force in a successful film. Often the actor is the *auteur*. Keaton and Chaplin may be fine directors, but it is their screen personalities that we especially cherish. Who would trade Keaton the actor for Keaton the director? And who would prefer analyzing the directorial styles of James W. Horne, Donald Crisp, Edward Sedgwick or Charles F. Reisner to savoring that sublime bodily mechanism that Buster controls so beautifully? The unique cinema personae of W. C. Fields, Mae West and Laurel and Hardy also flourished with little regard to the director of record, and can be defined without much reference to him—although, quite naturally, the combination of the comedians with different scripts and directors produced varying results. The same can be said of such incandescent performers as Greta Garbo, Katharine Hepburn and Cary Grant. Just as one can be drawn to an exercise in visual style like Blake Edwards' *Darling Lili* without finding it a completely successful film, so can one delight in the way Garbo dignifies and illuminates a rickety melodrama like *Mata Hari* with her beauty, her passion, and her ironic acceptance of an innate and tragic superiority.

It's instructive—indeed, it's often fun—to see a great actor transcend a ridiculous script and unfeeling direction; it's interesting to watch a fine director play around with an incredible story and poor performers. But the real joy in movies comes from seeing the fortuitous communion of forces (story, script, direction, acting, lighting, editing, design, scoring) that results in a great Hollywood film. *Frankenstein, Scarface, Love Me Tonight, Camille, Holiday, Mr. Smith Goes to Washington, His Girl Friday, Citizen Kane, Penny Serenade, Casablanca, Double Indemnity, Body and Soul, Rachel and the Stranger, Born Yesterday, Seven Brides for Seven Brothers, The Searchers, Invasion of the Body Snatchers, Psycho, The Manchurian Candidate, Charade* and *Planet of the Apes* are just a few examples of collaborative moviemaking at its best. Intelligent appreciation of films like these, and not scholastic disputes over the validity of individual signatures, should be our first critical concern.

The cry *"cherchez l' auteur"* can lead unwary film scholars astray when the *auteur* happens to be the author—or rather, when the script is the basis for a film's success. More often than not, when a fine film is signed by a mediocre director, the film's distinctive qualities can be traced to the screenwriter. There's no need to rescue Mitchell Leisen, Garson Kanin, Sam Wood and William D. Russell from the underworld of neglected directors simply because they were each fortunate enough to direct a comedy written by Norman Krasna *(Hands Across the Table, Bachelor Mother, The Devil and Miss Jones,* and *Dear Ruth,* respectively). The direction of these films is usually adroit and sensitive, and the presence of charming comediennes enhances them even further; but the delightfully dominant personality behind the screen is undoubtedly Krasna's. Similarly, the team of Sydney Gilliatt and Frank Launder constructed the frame—and contributed most of the furnishings—for two witty thrillers of the Thirties, Alfred Hitchcock's *The Lady Vanishes* and Carol Reed's *Night Train.* With the credits and Hitchcock's cameo cut from the films (but with the Gilliatt and Launder figures, in the puckish persons of Naunton Wayne and Basil Radford, left in), even an auteurist might have trouble determining which director was responsible for which film. That is because the authorship, and thus the responsibility, belonged to the two writers.

Body and Soul, written by Abraham Polonsky and directed by Robert Rossen, fits securely into Polonsky's very personal urban Hellmouth, with its Breughelesque, subway-at-rush-hour density, its stylized but fiercely realistic dialogue, and its cheeky characters who seem to carry both a chip and an albatross on their shoulders. His authorship of *Body and Soul* can be certified, if need be, by a look at his next film, the malignant *Force of Evil,* which he also directed, and which extends and enriches the penny-ante pessimism of *Body and Soul.* Waldo Salt's adaptations of *Rachel and the Stranger* (1948) and *Midnight Cowboy* (1969) are both graced by intelligent empathy for some very unusual characters, and by the gentle humor he evokes from the most improbable situations. Ring Lardner Jr.'s penchant for bantering, overlapping dialogue distinguishes *Woman of the Year* (1942) and *M*A*S*H* (1970), although most of his other assignments during those three decades offered him little chance to display his talent. Paul Mazursky and Larry Tucker, not director Hy Averback, are surely the authors of *I Love You, Alice B. Toklas;* its successor, *Bob & Carol & Ted & Alice,* evinced the same social concerns and behavioral absurdities, while Averback has loped further into obscurity with each new film. (Significantly, now that Mazursky is a director, he tends to ignore the contribution of his writing partner.)

It's clear that some method of classification and evaluation is necessary, both to identify and to assess the contributions of the over-paid but underrated *genus* known as the screenwriter. But that is a game that conceals even more perils than Sarris' Hit Parade of Directors. Once the *auteur* scholar accepts the myth of the omnipotent director, his game is won: he can Pass Kael and Collect $200. Indeed, even an adherent of the *politique des collaborateurs* can be fairly sure that the director of record is the man who hollered "Action!" and "Cut!"—though his importance in controlling what went on between those two commands may be disputed. But the size of a screenwriter's contribution to any given film is often far more difficult to ascertain. A writer may have received screen credit for work he didn't do (such as Sidney Buchman on *Holiday*) or for a few minor suggestions (Orson Welles on *Citizen Kane*). More likely, his name may not appear on the screen even if he has written virtually the entire script. Ben Hecht was responsible for far more of *Gone with the Wind's* dialogue than Sidney Howard, who had merely written a treatment of the Margaret Mitchell novel for producer David O. Selznick. But it was Howard who received sole screen credit, as well as a posthumous Oscar—for Hecht's work. Michael Wilson wrote the screenplay for *Friendly Persuasion* and co-scripted *The Bridge on the River Kwai*. But the Hollywood Blacklist kept his name off both films, and the writing Oscar for *Kwai* was awarded to Pierre Boulle, who had nothing to do with the film adapted from his novel.

A more subtle problem is appraising the work of a screenwriter who specializes in adaptations. Few screenwriters can boast a more impressive list of credits than Donald Ogden Stewart. As with George Cukor, the director for whom he produced his finest scripts, Stewart's "filmography is his most eloquent defense." Both Stewart and Cukor, however, had the good luck to be assigned adaptations of some of the wittiest and most actable theatre pieces of their time—*Holiday, The Women* (for which Stewart received no screen credit), *The Philadelphia Story,* and *Edward, My Son,* among others—and Stewart adhered closely to both in spirit and letter. Stewart's achievement should not be degraded; many screenwriters failed at the delicate craft he mastered. But, as with directors, one can distinguish several levels of screenwriting: the indifferent work of a mediocre writer, whether an original script or an adaptation (which we may call procrustean); the gem polishing of a gifted adaptor like Stewart (protean); and the creation of a superior original script, like Herman J. Mankiewicz's *Citizen Kane* or Polonsky's *Body and Soul* (promethean). When faced with the career of a Stewart, the critic who has discarded the convenience of the *auteur* theory must compare Stewart's adaptation with the source work, in hopes of detecting such changes as plot compression or expansion, bowdlerization, addition or deletion of dialogue, and differences in theme and tone. At worst, this research will exhaust and discourage the critic; at best, it will convince him that the creation of a Hollywood movie involves a complex weave of talents, properties, and personalities.

When a screenwriter, like Preston Sturges or George Axelrod, has a distinctive style, his contributions to films with multiple script credits can usually be discerned. But the hallmark of many of the best screenwriters is versatility, not consistency. Subject matter dictates style. Given the chameleon-like quality of these writers, how are we to know which part of the *Casablanca* script is the work of the sophisticated but self-effacing Howard Koch, and which part was written by Warners' prolific Epstein brothers? Luckily, Koch himself has told the *Casablanca* production story, and revealed that the Epsteins fabricated a plot around the name of a saloon—Rick's—they had found in an unproduced play, and that, when the brothers moved on to another assignment, Koch developed the strands of their story into a full-blooded screenplay that reads as well as it plays. We don't have many of these memoirs, though, and since most Hollywood egos are about as large as the Graf Zeppelin, the accounts of screenwriters may be taken with the same pillar of salt we keep handy for directors' interviews and actors' autobiographies.

Nevertheless, a screenwriter's work should, and can, be judged by considering his entire career, as is done with a director. If a writer has been associated with a number of favorite films, if we can distinguish a common style in films with different directors and actors, and if he has received sole writing credit on several films, an authorial personality begins to appear. The high polish and excitement of Koch's other work, for example (he wrote *Invasion from Mars,* better known as *War of the Worlds,* for the Orson Welles Mercury Theatre, and his film scripts include *The Letter, Sergeant York, Three Strangers, Letter from an Unknown Woman,* and *The Thirteenth Letter*), and his fulfillment of the three conditions mentioned above, give credence to his account of the writing of *Casablanca.* In fact, most of the best screenwriters were the sole authors of a substantial number of scripts.

The paucity of critical and historical literature makes all screenwriters "Subjects for Further Research." The cavalier group-headings on the following lists are meant only to emphasize the tentative nature of the classifications. As more films are seen from a screenwriter's point of view, names will be shuffled from one list to another. Ultimately, each of these fine screenwriters, and a hundred more, should have an artistic identity clear enough so that such capricious classifications will be unnecessary. Until that enlightened time comes to pass, we must make do with an Acropolis of Screenwriters something like the one which follows. (To make matters even more delphic, the screenwriter's work is defined simply by three of his finest films.)

The men and women so honored, by adapting their conspicuous talents to the byzantine demands of the trade, developed the most successful screenwriting techniques. Success usually begat power, and power begat authority. By authority is meant the right to complete your own script without being forced to surrender it to the next fellow on the assembly line, the right to consult with any actor or director who wants changes, and the right to fight for your film through the taffy pull of front-office politics, pressure groups, and publicists. The power of the most important screenwriters often resulted in superior films, in which the distinctive contributions of writer and director can be analyzed with greater assurance. Inevitably, some writers had literary pretensions, not only for themselves but for the cinemah, and when these men achieved some measure of autonomy, the cheerful cynicism of their earlier, more successful scripts was replaced by sesquipedalian platitudes on The Brotherhood of Man Through World Government. Thus, the most famous screenwriters, such as Dudley Nichols, Dalton Trumbo and, of late, Buck Henry, are not necessarily the best. Nichols' thoughtful articles on the need for sparse, realistic dialogue were not often matched by his actual scripts, which tend to talk the characters into the ground with palaver and pontification. Dalton Trumbo's private letters (now published in book form) reveal an easy-going but pungent wit that was concealed by his attempts to radicalize bourgeois movie melodrama. The pomp currently surrounding Buck Henry derives largely from the fortuitous circumstance of his visible connection with Mike Nichols and *The Graduate,* a film whose dialogue was lifted, almost word for word, from Charles Webb's novel. When on his own (in *The Troublemaker* and *Candy*), Henry's humor is decidedly undergraduate, even sophomoric.

ACROPOLIS

PARTHENON	ERECHTHEION	BRAURONION	PANDROSEION
Sidney Buchman	**George Axelrod**	**W. R. Burnett**	**Charles Brackett**
Mr. Smith Goes	The Manchurian Candidate	High Sierra	Midnight
to Washington	How to Murder Your Wife	The Asphalt Jungle	To Each His Own
Theodora Goes Wild	Lord Love a Duck	The Great Escape	The Model and the Marriage
Here Comes Mr. Jordan	**Borden Chase**	**John Huston**	Broker
Jules Furthman	Red River	The African Queen	**Delmer Daves**
Rio Bravo	Winchester 73	Jezebel	An Affair to Remember
The Big Sleep	The Far Country	The Maltese Falcon	Dark Passage
Shanghai Express	**Garson Kanin**	**Nunnally Johnson**	Professor Beware
Ben Hecht	Born Yesterday	Jesse James	**Philip Dunne**
Scarface	Pat and Mike	Prisoner of Shark Island	How Green Was My Valley
Gone With the Wind	Adam's Rib	The Dirty Dozen	The Ghost and Mrs. Muir
The Scoundrel	**Charles Lederer**	**John Lee Mahin**	Hilda Crane
Howard Koch	His Girl Friday	North to Alaska	**Frances Goodrich and**
Casablanca	The Thing	Red Dust	**Albert Hackett**
Letter from	The Front Page	The Horse Soldiers	The Thin Man
an Unknown Woman	**Anita Loos**	**Joseph L. Mankiewicz**	Seven Brides
The Letter	Reaching for the Moon	All About Eve	for Seven Brothers
Norman Krasna	Hold Your Man	A Letter to Three Wives	It's a Wonderful Life
Bachelor Mother	Down to Earth	Million Dollar Legs	**Casey Robinson**
Hands Across the Table	**Daniel Mainwearing**	**Seton I. Miller**	Now Voyager
The Devil and Miss Jones	Invasion of the	The Criminal Code	Dark Victory
Frances Marion	Body Snatchers	Ministry of Fear	Captain Blood
Camille [1936]	Out of the Past	The Dawn Patrol [1930]	**Charles Schnee**
Stella Maris	The Tall Target	**Dudley Nichols**	The Bad and The Beautiful
The Scarlet Letter	**Herman J. Mankiewicz**	Judge Priest	They Live By Night
Frank S. Nugent	Citizen Kane	Sister Kenny	I Walk Alone
The Searchers	Citizen Kane	Swamp Water	**R. C. Sheriff**
Wagonmaster	Citizen Kane	**Abraham Polonsky**	The Invisible Man
Two Rode Together	**Robert Riskin**	Force of Evil	Odd Man Out
Samson Raphaelson	It Happened One Night	Body and Soul	The Old Dark House
Trouble in Paradise	Platinum Blonde	Madigan	**Frank Tashlin**
Suspicion	The Whole Town's Talking	**Morrie Ryskind**	Will Success Spoil
The Shop Around	**Donald Ogden Stewart**	Penny Serenade	Rock Hunter?
the Corner	Holiday	A Night at the Opera	The Paleface
Preston Sturges	Love Affair	Stage Door	Bachelor Flat
The Lady Eve	Edward My Son	**Jo Swerling**	**Anthony Veiller**
Sullivan's Travels	**Michael Wilson**	Leave Her to Heaven	The Killers
Easy Living	Five Fingers	Lifeboat	The List of
Billy Wilder	Lawrence of Arabia	Man's Castle	Adrian Messenger
Ninotchka	A Place in the Sun		The Stranger
Sunset Boulevard			**Phillip Yordan**
Some Like It Hot			The Man From Laramie
			The Fall of the
			Roman Empire
			Johnny Guitar [disputed by
			the authors of *Trente Ans*
			du Cinema Americain who
			contend that Ben Maddow
			is the film's
			sole screenwriter.]

Unfortunately, the best screenwriters are likely to be ignored by film critics and historians. It's a minor scandal that film students are aware of Don Siegel's montages for *Casablanca* but not of Howard Koch's script; that Jules Furthman is trampled under foot in the mad rush to canonize Hawks and Sternberg; that film buffs, who can trace Gregg Toland's deep-focus work from *Wuthering Heights* through *Citizen Kane,* don't know, and probably don't care, that Herman Mankiewicz wrote *Citizen Kane* with only nominal assistance from Orson Welles. "In my opinion," Welles said twenty years ago, "the writer should have the first and last word in filmmaking, the only better alternative being the writer-director, but with the stress on the first word."

Perhaps the day of the hyphenate, the writer-director, has already dawned, and the screenwriter will become just another high-priced artifact in that great Hollywood auction in the sky. Perhaps not. Some of the most successful and popular films of the Right-Now Generation have been close adaptations of novels, with tight, efficient scripts (such as *The Graduate, Rosemary's Baby* and *Midnight Cowboy*). It's also encouraging to note the return to prominence of veteran screenwriters who have learned to meet the demands of a youth market while doing work that an adult can be proud of: Waldo Salt with *Midnight Cowboy,* Ring Lardner Jr. with *M*A*S*H,* Abraham Polonsky with *Tell Them Willie Boy is Here,* and Albert Maltz with *Two Mules for Sister Sara.* But whether these trends are heralding the screenwriter's second wind or portending his last gasp, the first forty years of the American commercial sound film cannot be evaluated without considering the crucial role he has played. The best screenwriters were talented and tenacious enough to assure that their visions and countless revisions would be realized on the screen. Now it is time for them to be remembered in film history.

                                                                    1970

JOHN ELLIS
FROM VISIBLE FICTIONS

STARS AS A CINEMATIC PHENOMENON

Stars have a similar function in the film industry to the creation of a 'narrative image': they provide a foreknowledge of the fiction, an invitation to cinema. Stars are incomplete images outside the cinema: the performance of the film is the moment of completion of images in subsidiary circulation, in newspapers, fanzines, and so on. Further, a paradox is present in these subsidiary forms. The star is at once ordinary and extraordinary, available for desire and unattainable. This paradox is repeated and intensified in cinema by the regime of presence-yet-absence that is the filmic image. Further, the star's particular performance in a film is always more than the culmination of the star images in subsidiary circulation: it is a balancing act between fiction and cultism. It may well be that a similar creation of stars is impossible for broadcast TV (which fosters 'personalities'), but does take place in the rock music industry.

The basic definition of a star is that of a performer in a particular medium whose figure enters into subsidiary forms of circulation, and then feeds back into future performances. Hence the tradition of the 'star' stretches back beyond cinema, into theatre, and especially into opera. The discovery of stars by cinema is a well-documented legend. The 'Trust', the MPPC set up by the manufacturers of equipment in 1908 to muscle in on the profits of the nickelodeon boom, had a primitive concept of marketing. They relied on selling the experience of cinema (and the newer experience of cinema fiction) alone: all films were treated as fundamentally similar. However, exhibitors realised that some performers had a greater value than others, and some producers began to offer them in roles with the same name: Little Mary, Bronco Bill, etc. The Trust could see perfectly well where this would lead, but other independent producers decided that they were willing to take the risk, so they offered some hitherto anonymous performers a billing with the film's title, subsidiary publicity, and substantially more pay. The Trust were indeed correct in their

614

supposition that inflation in salaries to performers would result. Amongst a small group it was astronomic. Some (Chaplin, Pickford, Fairbanks) pricing themselves out of the market entirely (hence United Artists). However, the star became very quickly a standard item of marketing: so much so that films like DeMille's post-1918 'scandal + haute couture' specials were billed as 'all-star' productions (i.e., no-star productions).

The star arrived as a marketing strategy in American cinema at the point at which the initial expansion of cinema had taken place. The nickelodeon boom was over: basic patterns had been established (centralised production, distribution by rental, atomised exhibition) which were to last almost to the 1920s. Marketing of films began to develop. Films needed to be distinguished from each other so that they could be recognisable to exhibitors and audiences, so that they could attract their particular fragments of the mass audience. Increasingly, narrative forms settled into genres, recognisable from posters, reviews, and gossip, if not named by a specific label. Increasingly, the supposed personality of the performer became a means of describing or specifying a particular film. The performer's supposed personality was not the ostensible subject of many films, however. It was discussed and promoted elsewhere, in other media, and very quickly it became one of the staple functions of the film industry to supply 'appropriate' material to those other media. The 'image' of the star began to become a major part of the creation of narrative images. The importance of the star image in the creation of narrative images is that the star is also an incomplete and paradoxical phenomenon.

There is always a temptation to think of a 'star image' as some kind of fixed repertory of fixed meanings (Joan Crawford = tough, independent, ruthless, threateningly sexy, etc.). However, this seems to simplify the process, and to misstate the role of the star in producing meanings in films and beyond films. Star images are paradoxical. They are composed of elements which do not cohere, of contradictory tendencies. They are composed of clues rather than complete meanings, of representations that are less complete, less stunning, than those offered by cinema. The star image is an *incoherent* image. It shows the star both as an ordinary person and as an extraordinary person. It is also an *incomplete* image. It offers only the face, only the voice, only the still photo, where cinema offers the synthesis of voice, body, and motion. The star image is paradoxical and incomplete so that it functions as an invitation to cinema, like the narrative image. It proposes cinema as the completion of its lacks, the synthesis of its separate fragments.

The relationship is not, however, only that of star-image = incomplete: film performance = completion. It is also one where the process of the star image echoes, repeats, and develops a fundamental aspect of cinema itself. The star image rests on the paradox that the star is ordinary and extraordinary at the same time. The cinematic image (and the film performance) rests on the photo effect, the paradox that the photograph presents an absence that is present. In this sense, the star image is not completed by the film performance, because they both rest on the same paradox. Instead the star image promises cinema. It restates the terms of the photo effect, renews the desire to experience this very particular sense of present-absence. So the star image is incomplete and paradoxical. It has a double relationship to the film performance: it proposes that the film performance will be more complete than the star image; and it echoes and promotes the photo effect which is fundamental to cinema as a regime of representation.

The process of circulation of a star image has been broadly the same whether it has been undertaken by a centralised studio agency (the form of classic Hollywood) or by a specialised enterprise contracted by the star themselves (the current form). The star's activities are presented in a number of media, some associated quite directly with the film industry, others using the film industry as one raw material amongst many. In the classic period of Hollywood, stars would 'feature' both in newspapers and magazines of general interest, and in magazines associated with cinema, fan magazines (or as we can now call them, fanzines). They appeared in advertisements, endorsing products. They appeared on radio, both in news, chat-shows, and fiction. At certain points, they appeared directly as products and merchandise effects. The first star to do so was (probably) Mickey Mouse. In all of these media, the star appears directly as face, body, and voice; and as a figure constructed by writing. There are photographs of the star; there are written descriptions of the star's activities; there are the voices of stars speaking (or singing) on the radio, from the mid-1920s onward. Each of these forms of appearance is less than that offered by sound cinema, which will present the animated, talking figure of the star. So on the simplest level, through the presentation of the star in photos, writing, and radio, the elements of the star's person are offered to the public, but in discrete bits and without movement. The promise of these various presentations is that the film performance will present the completeness of the star, the real mystery at which these only hint. Hence the presentation of Marlene Dietrich to the American audience. Already a star in Europe because of *The Blue Angel* (1930), a film not then released in America, she arrived to film *Morocco* (1930). Her image (photographic and written) appeared in the press; she had already 'proved' herself in another unavailable film; her mystery was well cultivated. So *Morocco* appeared, its narrative multiply punning on that of *The Blue Angel,* and its publicity announced: 'Now you can see . . .'. The film revealed what the star image in its subsidiary circulation could only hint at or describe in a veiled meta-language.

The particular nature of the copy, the photos, and the broadcasts made by/from stars reveals the other side of the star image's relation to the cinema. The stars are presented both as stars and as ordinary people: as very special beings, and as beings just like the readers. This seems to be the case both for male and for female stars, but sexual difference inevitably colours what kinds of roles are shown. Thus we have Bette Davis's recipes but Tyrone Power's baseball achievements; Audrey Hepburn's affinity for Givenchy clothes but Errol Flynn's big game hunting. Photographs similarly will show stars in the most mundane of postures, feeding babies, or just relaxing in old clothes; and then in the most exotic, performing stunts at a lavish party or meeting the King of England. These are the general rules that govern the specific coverage given to stars: there are two aspects, one the ordinariness of the star and the other the totally exceptional nature of the star, endowed with some special talent and position.

These general characteristics of the coverage are inflected in different ways by the different kinds of publications which make use of stars. It could be said that mass circulation daily and Sunday newspapers tend to use stars as a kind of moral barometer, whereas fanzines push the paradoxical constitution of the star image to its limits. Mass newspapers use stars for their own ends: they can be the occasion of scandals, and they provide a repertory of figures who are in the public eye, yet have no political power. Stars provide newspapers with the vehicle for discussion of sexuality, of the domain of the personal and the familial. This is relatively absent from public political life, so the stars perform a valuable function in newspapers: they provide the dimension of the personal. This dimension is that which is inhabited by most of their readers, yet is not that of the events portrayed in the news. Stars have a soldering function: they hold the news and the personal together by being both public and intimate, by being news only in so far as they are persons.

Fanzines are a different kind of publication, very much more directly linked in to the industry itself. They emphasise stars-as-workers much more than other publications, with details of the punishing studio schedules, the indignities of make-up and costume for some parts, the hard training for dancing and stunts, even the lousy facilities offered by studios. Yet at the same time they can present the extraordinary aspects of the star as well, because they are generally high-quality printing jobs with glossy, high-definition full-page photos. These photos present both male and female stars with all the sophisticated techniques that are available. These are images of faces (sometimes bodies as well) in all their impossibility: smooth, free of blemishes, clear-eyed, every feature perfect. Often, the two aspects cross over each other in the same feature: pieces about the hard work of rehearsal dive into sentences which stress 'nevertheless' the exceptional talent of the performer.

Perhaps the living and dynamic paradox that is the star image was captured in Ophuls's *Caught* (1948): we are shown a page of a fanzine covered by a photo of a luxurious mansion with pool, accompanied by the headline: "Would you be happy in these surroundings? *We would.*' The photo is then animated into a moving picture, the camera dollies in to reveal Barbara Bel Geddes a former shopgirl who, having married into this luxury, is indeed miserable, and for very good reasons. *Caught* constantly plays on the paradox in the star image that it can oscillate between two opposing poles. A desperately attractive James Mason is cast as the ordinary doctor in a poor district with whom Bel Geddes falls in love. Mason, the matinee idol, is meant to incarnate the ordinary and the honest against Robert Ryan's neurotic millionaire. The film multiplies the indications of ordinariness around him, spectacularly since this is an Ophuls film. Yet it only succeeds in intensifying the paradox of the star image, perhaps expressed by the melodrama's audience as 'if only *my* boss was like James Mason.'

The star image functions in two ways. First it is the invitation to cinema, posing cinema as synthesising all the disparate and scattered elements of the star image. Second, it repeats the cinematic experience by presenting an impossible paradox: people who are both ordinary and extraordinary. This is the same paradox as the photo effect. The oscillation between the ordinariness and the extraordinariness of the star implies a whole series of features which echo the photo effect. The star is ordinary, and hence leads a life like other people, is close to them, shares their hopes and fears: in short, the star is present in the same social universe as the potential film viewer. At the same time the star is extraordinary, removed from the life of mere mortals, has rarified and magnified emotions, is separate from the world of the potential film viewer. The circulation of the contradictory star image therefore operates a kind of summary or reminder of the photo effect of cinema. Yet it is more than that as well. The figure of the star crystallises the equivocal relationship to the viewer's desire that can be said to be produced by the photo effect.

By presenting a present-absence, by making statements in the impossible mode of 'this is was', the photo effect awakens a series of psychic mechanisms which involve various impossible images: the narcissistic experience of the mirror phase; the masculine fetishistic refusal (yet acknowledgment) of the fact of sexual differ-ence; and at the same time, a particular variant of the voyeuristic contract. The photo effect can be said to be involved with a series of psychic mechanisms which participate in the construction of the polyvalent desires of both male and female viewers. The star is an impossible image, like the cinematic image. The star is tan-talisingly close and similar, yet at the same time remote and dissimilar. Further, the star is a legitimate object for the desire of the viewer in so far as the star is like the viewer, and an impossible object for the desire of the viewer in so far as the star is extraordinary, unlike the viewer. There is a complicated game of desires that plays around the figure of the star: every feature in it is counteracted by another feature. The male and female star can be desired by either sex, yet that desire has access to its object only on condition that its object is presented as absent. Desire is both per-mitted and encouraged, yet knows it cannot achieve any tangible form of satisfac-tion, except the satisfactions of looking. The phenomenon of stardom relies on the photo effect for its full expression; it is equally a summary of the photo effect, mak-ing explicit the relationship between the photographic and the realm of desire. Con-stituted by a central paradox, the star system is both a promise of cinema ('this is the photo effect'), and an invitation to cinema ('these are clues; cinema synthesises them'). The film performance of a star both animates the desire that plays around the star's published image, yet holds that desire in place by the operations of the fiction. The use of the fiction always exceeds the star's image and the star's presence in a film, except at that single point where the fiction is suspended in favour of the pure performance: the 'fetishistic' moment.

The star's performances in individual films have a particular relationship with the images in subsidiary circulation. In the period of classic Hollywood at least, each star's figure was around all the time in subsidiary forms of circulation, but was seen in the cinema only occasionally: in two or three films a year. The film performance was therefore rare; the subsidiary circulation was commonplace. The film perfor-mance was a special event. The film performance of a star also involved a large degree of overt fiction, which the star in circulation outside the cinema did not. The construction of a star's image in subsidiary circulation must have routinely involved forms of fiction, but these were offered as though they were true facts. The fictional element of a star's film performance is acknowledged by all concerned, performers, filmmakers, and audiences alike. These two features of the film perfor-mance, its comparative rarity and its explicit use of fiction, mark it as a rather sep-arate phenomenon from the circulation of star images in other areas.

The film performance of the star takes up and furthers the star image from other media. The relation between the figure of the star and the desire of the spectator is animated and intensified. The play between the possibility and impossibility of the star as an object of desire is intensified by the photo effect of presence-absence. The star finally appears as a physical figure observable over an extended period by the film audience: no longer a disembodied radio voice, a frozen photo image, or a character in a piece of journalistic writing. Introduced here is a whole new dimension of the star: not just the star-in-movement, but also the incidental aspects of that movement. The star's performance in a film reveals to the viewer all those small gestures, particular aspects of movement and expression, unexpected similarities to acquaintances or even to self. Acres of writing have been produced to celebrate this or that phenomenon in such or such a star: Garbo's laugh, Cary Grant's eyes, the way Rock Hudson bites his lip in *All That Heaven Allows* (1955). . . . The journalistic apotheosis of these moments witnesses the feeling that the star is caught unawares in them. They are things, it seems, that could hardly have been planned or foreseen. They mark the absorption of the star into the fictional character. The star seems to be feeling the emotion of the role at that point as his or her own emotion. The star is not performing here, so much as 'being'. In other words, what the film performance permits is moments of pure voyeurism for the spectator, the sense of overlooking something which is not designed for the onlooker but passively allows itself to be seen. This is different from the star's image in other forms of circulation, where the elements of intentionality are very marked. The fanzine photo is obviously constructed for the look; the magazine interview or the radio broadcast participate in forms of direct address where the star is present as an intentional 'I'.

This sense of overlooking the incidental and the unmotivated aspects of the star's figure has two consequences which tend to outrun the film-as-fiction. First, it pushes the photo effect to its limits, especially with a star who is dead. This effect is an epidemic with stars like Garland or Monroe, whose presence on the screen brings with it the widespread myths of their tragic lives, the stories of their absence. It also radically compromises the stoic strength of Agnes Moorehead or the shrill complaints of Gloria Grahame. Less spectacular tragedies, both of these: the tragedies of women who always inhabited the films of others, whose careers never provided them with a definitive role. In both cases, the combination of the extra-filmic circulation of a star's tragic story with their film performance promotes a voyeuristic relation to the performance. Rather than identifying the role in the fiction with the life of the star (a comparatively rare possibility), the incidental moments are promoted to the forefront of attention. These 'poignant' moments thus become the only remaining route to the truth or the essence of the star's personality. The incidental moments of the star caught unawares seem to provide a glimpse of the secret personality that disappeared (or destroyed itself) leaving behind the perpetual, unresolvable paradox of the star image. The film photograph constructs the possibility of a voyeuristic effect of catching the star unawares. The paradox of the star's image (especially Monroe's) exacerbates this effect, sending the desiring viewer off to the film itself as the only remaining physical manifestation of the star amid the welter of photo sessions, TV and film biographies, memoirs of associates both would-be and real. The viewer glimpses something, perhaps only a trick of the light. But it is only glimpsed during the film performance. Then the circuit begins again: more consumption of forms of subsidiary circulation, the desire to see more films, and even films-that-never-were: the out-takes, the screen-tests and so on. . . .

The star performance in the fiction can have three kinds of relation to the star image in subsidiary circulation. The fiction can content itself with performing the image in those rare cases where the star's image outside of cinema is fairly stable. This is perhaps more possible for male stars, whose characters can be defined by their activities. Such is the case perhaps with Errol Flynn, whose roles seem to a large extent the kind of exploit for which he became famous. The second, more usual, relation is that in which the fiction exceeds the circulated image. At its limits, the fictional figure can go against the grain of the circulated image, creating a specific tension in the film. Such is the case with Hitchcock's *Suspicion* (1941) where Cary Grant is cast as the likely murderer and swindler. The whole film is constructed on this dislocation in order to render Joan Fontaine's suspicions incongruous at first, and then increasingly irrefutable even to the most incredulous audience as the 'evidence' mounts. Despite the reconciliatory ending, this film represents something more than 'casting against type'. *Suspicion* needs the star image of Cary Grant in order to function at all. Its effect would have been totally different with Reginald Denny.

More usually, the fictional figure is 'to one side' of the star's general image, where this can be established. Certain elements of the publicly circulated star image complex are used by the film, other elements are refused, further elements are added. Doris Day's films display her in a much wider range of characters than her image would suggest. Certain elements of her image are always present (sometimes her pervasive ordinariness or directness of approach to people), but they are not always the same elements. Further characteristics are accumulated to her fictional personas that have little or nothing to do with her star images. Yet the star image continues in circulation, feeding off the films where it can, trying to ignore aspects of her past as well as aspects of her fictional roles. The importance of Doris Day as a star phenomenon is the way in which her star images have obliterated the memory of her films. Doris Day's fictional roles are very much 'to one side' of her circulated images. It is possible that the circulated images are unperformable in a film: they provided so little scope for any dramatic action that there were few attempts to narrativise them. However, they provided acceptable and 'useful' themes in other, less narrative, less fictional, forms of circulation. Hence the endurance of 'Doris Day' as a touchstone of respectability, moral probity, young Americanicity, unrestrained enthusiasm, and other characteristics that play around her figure without constituting a fixed identity.

The star's place in a film thus seems to be a difficult one. The film is constructed by the process of the star image as the point at which the paradox of the image will be explicated, and the disparate elements of the image will come together. The star performance thus animates the star image, and animates the desire which circulates in it. In doing so, the performance exceeds the circulated image in two usually mutually compensating ways. First, the performance is fictional, placing the star in a role whose characteristics have to be fairly stable. This role can have a number of different relationships to the circulated image: it can resemble it to a large degree; it can contradict it; it can be to one side of it. In most cases, the fictional context of the star's performance is enough to hold in check or to balance a second way in which the star's performance exceeds the star's circulated image. This second excess is the way in which desire is animated toward the performing figure. The performance produces the effect that, in its incidental rather than intended moments, it reveals something of the essence of the star's personality. Occasionally, effects either from within the film (Von Sternberg) or from beyond the film (Monroe) foster this effect and allow it to escape the effects of the fiction. The result is a cultism, of an inquisitive voyeuristic kind, or a fascinated fetishistic type.

For the star him- or herself, two options for performance are offered by this regime. One is that of drastically underperforming in comparison to the 'unknown' section of the cast; and the other is to overperform in order to emphasise the work of acting. Underperformance is not a question of restraint or lack of histrionics. It is a question of producing the effect of behaving rather than performing. This is always a comparative effect, generated by a disparity within any one film between the styles of acting of the star-group and the supporting group. The supporting group have to produce emphases in their gestures, delivery of lines, and expression simply in order to signify the required meanings. For the star, it is different. The star has the attention of the audience and is a recognised figure, with a recognised voice, face, and figure, even if no stable meanings accumulate to those features in the star image. Having the audience's attention, (and the camera's, and the fiction's), anything that the star does becomes significant. Hence the star is permitted to underact, compared to the supporting cast, and this underacting produces the effect that the star behaves rather than acts. However, some stars have been dissatisfied with this state of affairs and the whispered remarks that it produces ('so-and-so can't act', etc.). So a certain section of the star firmament at any one time will be seeking to reverse this tendency toward underacting in order to produce an effect of 'performance'. Some stars produce a very explicit regime of expression which is again divergent from that of the supporting cast. In Hollywood, it has often been those actors who are most concerned with the artistic nature of their work (Bette Davis, for instance). More recently, a craft approach has been adopted to performance under the influence of the Method Acting theory. Examples are the antics of Marlon Brando or the disguises of Peter Sellers. Finally, a more traditional overacting is characteristic of certain stars, especially those from the British stage: Glenda Jackson for instance. All of these stars tend to offer a supplementary signification: they are there as star; they are there as fictional role; but they are also there as actor, saying, 'Look at me, I can perform.'

1982

RICHARD DYER
FROM STARS

PERFORMANCE SIGNS

Performance is what the performer does in addition to the actions/functions she or he performs in the plot and the lines she or he is given to say. Performance is how the action/function is done, how the lines are said.

The signs of performance are: facial expression; voice; gestures (principally of hands and arms, but also of any limb, e.g., neck, leg); body posture (how someone is standing or sitting); body movement (movement of the whole body, including how someone stands up or sits down, how they walk, run, etc.). Of these the first is often held to be the most important, on analogy with its primary importance in interpersonal communication in everyday life. Yet just as its importance may be the greatest, so too is its ambiguity. Shaffer points out that we hold, despite arguments to the contrary, to the illusion that the face is supremely expressive of personality:

> A face that looks 'lived in' is a face that *seems* to comprise (or reprise) its past in any of its momentary expressions. Fredric March's sensibility did not somehow 'inform' his features osmotically . . . And yet that was the illusion.

At the same time, when it comes to deciphering facial expression we are at a considerable loss. Aside from films that use this ambiguity in the service of the notion of the eternal ineffability of the face as the window to the soul, most films do, through the use of codes discussed below, narrow down the range of meanings that a facial expression considered in isolation may have. Nonetheless ambiguity is seldom totally eliminated.

This ambiguity needs to be understood in terms of the relation between the performer and the audience in film. This can be considered by comparing the character of Maurice (Montgomery Clift) in *The Heiress* with the same character in the novel the film is based on, *Washington Square* by Henry James. In the latter, we are clearly told from the word go that Maurice is deceitful. In the film, however, we are in the same position as Catherine (Olivia de Havilland) in this regard; we have to work out from our observation of him whether he is sincere or not. This is further complicated by the particular relation we have to Clift as a star. In these ways, film and especially performance in film fabricates a relationship to, rather than a telling about, the characters. . . . A star will have a particular performance style that through its familiarity will inform the performance she or he gives in any particular film. The specific repertoire of gestures, intonations, and so on that a star establishes over a number of films carries the meaning of her or his image just as much as the 'inert' element of appearance, the particular sound of her/his voice or dress style.

An example is provided by G. Hill who quotes from a reviewer of *The War Wagon:* 'it is worth seeing to watch John Wayne wrap his horse's reins round a hitch post!' It is not only that it happens to be Wayne doing it or that the action is always redolent of meaning, but that the particular way Wayne habitually does it sums up a particular aspect of his image. (The relish with which men tell me of this example suggests that what it sums up above all is Wayne's easy and confident masculinity.)

Part of the business of studying stars is to establish what these recurrent features of performance are and what they signify in terms of the star's image. They will usually only sum up an aspect of that image. The example just given does not remind us of everything about Wayne—in particular its joyous appeal operates because he is in the saddle in the West, not in Vietnam, not with a woman. . . .

One of the few debates about film performance that has recurred in film theory is the degree to which performance may be considered an expressive element of any significance. While everyday critical talking about film tends to concentrate on performance (e.g., 'What was so-and-so like in the film you just saw?'), an important tradition in film theory has tended to deny that performance has any expressive value: what you read into the performer, you read in by virtue of signs *other than* performance signs. . . .

[T]he most famous instance of this is probably the final shot of Garbo in *Queen Christina.* She stands on the prow of the boat taking her away from Sweden and after the death of her lover. She stares ahead and into the wind which ruffles her hair. Much can be read into this shot—of resignation, melancholy, profound feeling. Yet it is well known that the director, Rouben Mamoulian, told Garbo to do nothing for this scene, and she did as she was told. (In itself, one should say, a considerable feat of performance.) The meaning of her face in this shot thus derives entirely from its place in the film's narrative, the way it is shot, and the resonances of Garbo's image carried by her face. . . .

Let us consider John Wayne in relation to the last point. Wayne is a performer commonly credited without acting abilities. The assumption is that he is just there, and just by being there a statement is made. In so far as any other meaning can be attributed to him in a particular film, it has to come from montage, mise-en-scène, what is said,—or so runs the argument. This in fact was my view of him. However, an analysis of his performance in the scene in *Fort Apache* where he, as Captain York, and Colonel Thursday (Henry Fonda) go with a cavalry troop to meet Cochise, proved me wrong.

Let it be stressed that this has nothing to do with evaluation (I am not remotely interested in vindicating Wayne as a 'good' actor) nor with (Wayne's) 'authorship'. Performance is defined as what the performer does, and whether s/he, the director, or some other person is authorially responsible for this is a different question altogether. What is of interest here is whether performance—what Wayne does—contributes to the construction of Wayne/York or whether that construction is achieved purely by other means. (The latter include Wayne as an already-signifying star image, but not Wayne as performing.)

Near the beginning of this scene, there is a single take in which Wayne/York (hereinafter, W/Y), having been summoned from the rear of the cavalry column by Fonda/Thursday (hereinafter F/T), comes up to discuss with the latter where they are to meet Cochise. F/T is placed right (as we look at it); he is rigidly uptight against the sky. W/Y is placed left, lower on the screen than F/T, only partially against the sky; he moves in the saddle. In the course of the conversation, F/T announces his plans to deploy his men. W/Y tells him these are inappropriate to the actual position of the Indians, which he (W/Y) knows because he has been following the dust swirls. He points off screen. The shot ends here, and there is a cut to a shot of Indians riding up *en masse* over the brow of a hill (through 'creative geography' where W/Y has pointed) with threatening music over.

Clearly mise en scène and montage are important vis-à-vis W/Y here. The placing of him in relation to F/T not only expresses their relative positions in the military hierarchy, but also contrasts F/T's self-styled epic aspirations with W/Y's more down-to-earth/natural (but still in fact 'epic') qualities. (This reading depends of course on knowledge of the elaboration of this contrast throughout the film.) The cut to the Indians confirms the 'truth' of what W/Y has said, and hence stamps him with the mark of authenticity (allied to the fact that he knows this truth through his understanding of 'nature'—the dust swirls).

However, performance *also* signifies. The contrast between F/T's rigidity and W/Y's movement suggests the greater 'relaxedness' of the latter, thus picking up on another aspect of the film's opposition between them, namely, his immediate, intuitive, at-homeness with military life as compared to F/T's bookish approach. (This has class connotations that are explicitly presented in the film in a displaced aristocratic/populist opposition.) When F/T announces that he will be deploying two troops to the North, the placing means that he has only to make a slight turn of his head to the left (of the screen), whereas W/Y has to turn the whole of his body round in the saddle. This he does very swiftly and easily. The placing demands the larger movement, but this performance of the movement both suggests a sense of urgency (F/T is making a disastrous decision) and, because it is so easily done, signifies again W/Y's total at-homeness in the saddle.

Later in this scene, the Spanish interpreter repeats Cochise's extremely derogatory descriptions of the gun-runner Meecham. There is a reaction shot, showing Meecham and F/T seated and the other men standing behind, W/Y to the rear and slightly to the right of F/T. W/Y expresses 'amusement' at Cochise's words by the following performance: his eyes look slightly left, slightly heavenward, there is a faint smile on his face, he moves his right leg and upper body just a little, keeping his arms behind his back. (This performance ends with him casting a contemptuous look at Meacham.) Three points are of interest for our purposes about this: (1) nothing in mise en scène or montage constructs for the character the response 'amusement'; it resides in performance alone; (2) it fits with what we know of the character—we can read it in terms of relaxedness, and so on; (3) its more specific signification, beyond 'amusement', is not clear. On the one hand, its subtlety and relative unusualness (i.e., it's not just a grin) suggest 'meaningfulness', yet what that meaning is one would have to select from 'translations' such as 'This proves me right', 'Cochise is cute', 'This puts Thursday on the spot', and so forth. (Arguably, it expresses all these fleeting thoughts.)

This sort of exercise is useful not only as part of the business of putting performance signs in their determinate context, but also:

(1) to distinguish between different modes of articulation of character in film; (e.g. to test Braudy's distinction between 'closed' and 'open' films.)
(2) to distinguish between films in which performance fits with other signs of character (the case, as far as I have gone with it, with Wayne in *Fort Apache*) and those in which the fit is more contradictory;
(3) following from that, to test the possibility of stars resisting their material not only by what they inescapably signify (= miscasting), but also through performance. . . .

STARS AS AUTHORS

The study of stars as themselves authors belongs essentially to the study of the Hollywood production situation. It is certainly possible to establish, as 'auteur theory' enjoins us, continuities, contradictions, and transformations either in the totality of a star's image or in discrete elements such as dress or performance style, roles, publicity, iconography. However, the relationship between these and the star always has to be established by examination of what sources there are concerning the actual making of the image and films. That is to say that a star, in films, publicity, and promotion, is a semiotic construction and the fact that that construction exhibits continuities does not prove that the star as person is responsible for them. S/he may be, but also may not be.

In his study of James Cagney, *Cagney, the Actor as Auteur,* Patrick McGilligan makes this point very clearly:

The auteur theory can be revised and reproposed with actors in mind: under certain circumstances, an actor may influence a film as much as a writer, director or producer; some actors are more influential than others; and there are certain rare few performers whose acting capabilities and screen personas are so powerful that they embody and define the very essence of their films. If an actor is responsible only for acting but is not involved in any of the artistic decisions of film-making, then it is accurate surely to refer to the actor as a semi-passive icon, a symbol that is manipulated by writers and directors. But actors who not only influence artistic decisions (casting, writing, directing, etc.) but demand certain limitations on the basis of their screen personas, may justly be regarded as 'auteurs.' When the performer becomes so important to a production that he or she changes lines, adlibs, shifts meaning, influences the narrative and style of a film and altogether signifies something clear-cut to audiences despite the intent of writ-

ers and directors, then the acting of that person assumes the force, style and integrity of
an auteur.

He then proceeds to argue that Cagney does fit the category of actor-auteur, drawing on interviews with him and those he worked with, as well as observing how, for
instance, Cagney's films made with directors such as Lloyd Bacon, William Keighley, Roy Del Ruth are all very similar to each other, and more like Cagney's other
films than films by those directors with different stars. (Unfortunately this last point
lacks the precision of most of McGilligan's study; one needs the specific aspects of
performance, characterisation, narrative structure, and so forth, pinpointed in the
way that one would expect from auteurist analyses of directors and not the vague
references to 'spontaneity' (Bacon), 'a polished emphasis on action and dialogue'
(Keighley), and 'urbanity' (Del Ruth).)

McGilligan's aim is to demonstrate that Cagney is *the* author of his films, the
classic auteurist position. However, any of the models of authorship outlined above
might apply to given stars. In considering this, we must first distinguish between on
the one hand authorship of the star image and/or performance, and on the other
hand authorship of films.

In the case of images and/or performance, there may be stars who totally controlled this (Fred Astaire, Joan Crawford), or only contributed to it (Marlene Dietrich, Robert Mitchum), as part of a collective team (John Wayne) or just one disparate voice among many (Marilyn Monroe, Marlon Brando); alternatively there
will be others who were almost totally the product of the studio/Hollywood
machine (Lana Turner). (The names in parentheses are guesses only and require
further research to confirm or disprove.) The fact that the person of the star coincides with a text (the star image, the character, the performance) in the construction
of which s/he was only a collaborator or even a mere vehicle should warn us not to
elide the star-as-person with the star-as-text and assume that the former is the
author of the latter. Although I find it hard to conceive of a star having no power in
the decisions made about her/his image or performance, just how much power
s/he had and how s/he exercised it has to be determined by looking at specific cases.

In the case of stars as authors of the films they starred in, we must begin by excepting those cases where stars directed (or scripted) themselves in films: for instance,
Charlie Chaplin, Buster Keaton, Mae West (scripts), Ida Lupino, Jerry Lewis, John
Wayne, Clint Eastwood. In these cases, we have to make a theoretical distinction
between their role as star and their other role in the production.

The number of cases on which the totality of a film can be laid at the door of the
star must be very few indeed. (Candidates include Greta Garbo and *Queen Christina,* Ellen Burstyn and *Alice Doesn't Live Here Any More,* and most persuasively
Barbra Streisand and *A Star is Born.*) However, the star as one of the 'voices' in a
film (always remembering any voice can only be returned to its author as the point
of decision-making in production, not that of unmediated expressivity) is surely
very common. This 'voice' is not necessarily confined to matters of performance,
dress, etc., but may affect almost any aspect of the film, depending upon how the
star exercised his/her power. . . .

This notion of the star and the director mutually bringing something out in each other informs much auteurist criticism. This approach does usually privilege the director over the star in their collaborative interaction, and examples are usually confined to a few paragraphs within broader considerations of a director's work. In *Horizons West,* Jim Kitses notes the Mann-Stewart, Budd Boetticher–Randolph Scott collaborations, while John Baxter in his *The Cinema of John Ford* writes of Ford's different views of the hero according to whether he is using John Wayne, James Stewart, or Henry Fonda. Other less satisfactory examples of this approach include Stanley Solomon's discussion in *The Film Idea* of the use made of Cary Grant by Stanley Donen and Alfred Hitchcock and Gary Carey's article 'The Lady and the Director' dealing with Bette Davis and William Wyler.

One need not, as Perkins, Kitses, and Baxter are, be concerned to find a perfect fit between star image and directorial pattern. Disjunctions between them may be just as interesting, especially from an ideological point of view, since they may correspond to, or at any rate suggest, ideological contradictions. I would cite here Monroe v. Hawks in *Gentlemen Prefer Blondes.* Lorelei, as Anita Loos wrote her, is the hero* of the film, and she is the hero by her deliberate use of her (socially constructed) femininity. In Hawks' films such a character (e.g., Rita Hayworth in *Only Angels Have Wings*) is not so sympathetic, or central. Thus he submits her here to humiliation (trapped in a porthole up to her hips, themselves part of her sexual armoury) and send-up (Jane Russell's impersonation of her in the court scene), while constructing the Russell character as a warm, practical buddy-woman comparable to other 'Hawksian' women (cf. Jean Arthur in *Only Angels Have Wings*). In this context, Monroe's construction of Lorelei as innocently, utterly but not manipulatively, sexual, a construction stemming from the basic pattern of Monroe's image and at variance with Loos' Lorelei, confuses Hawks' division of the female world into manipulative feminine women and likeable masculine (or non-feminine) ones. There is reason for Hawks to deride Loos' Lorelei, but not Monroe's—but this then throws us back to the problem of just what place the 'feminine' has in Hawks' films, and, more importantly, in Hollywood and in patriarchy generally. 'Femininity' is primarily a social construction and, moreover, a construction made by men. Yet it is a construction men often find hard to cope with—it is the category onto which they project more fundamental fears about gender, which one can conceive psycho-analytically in terms of castration or socio-historically in terms of men's power over women and simultaneous dependence on them. Hawks' films, like most films, legitimate this fear. They say, in effect, that women, especially 'feminine' women, really should be feared by men; in other words, they take what is a projection from men and claim that it really emanates from women. Monroe as Lorelei, however, disturbs this pattern, because Lorelei, as Monroe's image has already constructed her and as she plays her, is both extremely feminine and not evil or castrating. Monroe as Lorelei refuses to corroborate this male construction of the female.

1979

---

*I use the term 'hero' here, not 'heroine', partly to stress that Lorelei for Loos is 'heroic', admirable, a winner, and partly because the term 'heroine' implies a structural position in narratives in relation to a male protagonist—as the object of his quest or his love.

ROLAND BARTHES
THE FACE OF GARBO

Garbo still belongs to that moment in cinema when capturing the human face still plunged audiences into the deepest ecstasy, when one literally lost oneself in a human image as one would in a philtre, when the face represented a kind of absolute state of the flesh, which could be neither reached nor renounced. A few years earlier the face of Valentino was causing suicides; that of Garbo still partakes of the same rule of Courtly Love, where the flesh gives rise to mystical feelings of perdition.

It is indeed an admirable face-object. In *Queen Christina,* a film which has again been shown in Paris in the last few years, the make-up has the snowy thickness of a mask: it is not a painted face, but one set in plaster, protected by the surface of the colour, not by its lineaments. Amid all this snow at once fragile and compact, the eyes alone, black like strange soft flesh, but not in the least expressive, are two faintly tremulous wounds. In spite of its extreme beauty, this face, not drawn but sculpted in something smooth and friable, that is, at once perfect and ephemeral, comes to resemble the flour-white complexion of Charlie Chaplin, the dark vegetation of his eyes, his totem-like countenance.

Now the temptation of the absolute mask (the mask of antiquity, for instance) perhaps implies less the theme of the secret (as is the case with Italian half mask) than that of an archetype of the human face. Garbo offered to one's gaze a sort of Platonic Idea of the human creature, which explains why her face is almost sexually undefined, without however leaving one in doubt. It is true that this film (in which Queen Christina is by turns a woman and a young cavalier) lends itself to this lack of differentiation; but Garbo does not perform in it any feat of transvestism; she is always herself, and carries without pretence, under her crown or her wide-brimmed hats, the same snowy solitary face. The name given to her, *the Divine,* probably aimed to convey less a superlative state of beauty than the essence of her corporeal

Greta Garbo in *Love* (1927). "Garbo still belongs to that moment in cinema when capturing the human face still plunged audiences into the deepest ecstasy . . ." (BARTHES, page 628).

Greta Garbo in *Anna Christie* (1930) ". . . where she could ensconce herself, most of the time, in mute or monosyllabic sullenness . . ." (PANOFSKY, page 242). "Garbo's face represents this fragile moment when the cinema is about to draw an existential from an essential beauty, when the archetype leans towards the fascination of mortal faces . . ." (BARTHES, page 631).

person, descended from a heaven where all things are formed and perfected in the clearest light. She herself knew this: how many actresses have consented to let the crowd see the ominous maturing of their beauty. Not she, however; the essence was not to be degraded, her face was not to have any reality except that of its perfection, which was intellectual even more than formal. The Essence became gradually obscured, progressively veiled with dark glasses, broad hats and exiles: but it never deteriorated.

And yet, in this deified face, something sharper than a mask is looming: a kind of voluntary and therefore human relation between the curve of the nostrils and the arch of the eyebrows; a rare, individual function relating two regions of the face. A mask is but a sum of lines; a face, on the contrary, is above all their thematic harmony. Garbo's face represents this fragile moment when the cinema is about to draw an existential from an essential beauty, when the archetype leans towards the fascination of mortal faces, when the clarity of the flesh as essence yields its place to a lyricism of Woman.

Viewed as a transition the face of Garbo reconciles two iconographic ages, it assures the passage from awe to charm. As is well known, we are today at the other pole of this evolution: the face of Audrey Hepburn, for instance, is individualized, not only because of its peculiar thematics (woman as child, woman as kitten) but also because of her person, of an almost unique specification of the face, which has nothing of the essence left in it, but is constituted by an infinite complexity of morphological functions. As a language, Garbo's singularity was of the order of the concept, that of Audrey Hepburn is of the order of the substance. The face of Garbo is an Idea, that of Hepburn, an Event.

1957

MOLLY HASKELL
FROM FROM REVERENCE TO RAPE

FEMALE STARS OF THE 1940S

The preoccupation of most movies of the forties, particularly the "masculine" genres, is with man's soul and salvation, rather than with woman's. It is man's prerogative to follow the path from blindness to discovery, which is the principal movement of fiction. In the bad-girl films like *Gilda* and *Out of the Past,* it is the man who is being corrupted, his soul which is in jeopardy. Women are not fit to be the battleground for Lucifer and the angels; they are something already decided, simple, of a piece. Donna Reed finally refused to make any more movies with Alan Ladd because he always had a scene (it was in his contract) in which he would leave the little woman in the outer office, or some equivalent, while he went off to deal with the Big Problem that only a man could handle. Even the musicals of the forties—the Donen–Kelly collaborations—concentrate on man's quest, on his rather than her story.

In the penumbral world of the detective story, based on the virile and existentially skeptical work of writers like Hammett, Chandler, Cain, and David Goodis (which found its way into crime films like *Dark Passage, The Blue Dahlia, Farewell My Lovely, Double Indemnity, I Wake Up Screaming,* and *The Big Sleep*), the proliferation of women—broads, dames, and ladies in as many shapes and flavors, hard and soft centers as a Whitman's sampler—was a way of not having to concentrate on a single woman, and again, of reducing woman's stature by siphoning her qualities off into separate women.

Although Howard Hawks would seem to fall into this tradition with *The Big Sleep,* in which he actually increases the number of women from the Chandler novel, there is something in the women and in Hawks' conception of them that suggests a real, if not entirely articulated, sense of a woman's point of view (or at least an antisexist point of view) that will become increasingly apparent in the work of this supposed "man's director." In contrast to most crime melodramas, where plot and its unraveling are all, the plot of *The Big Sleep* is next to incomprehensible, and the women are what it is all about: Lauren Bacall's sleek feline lead, Martha Vickers' spoiled, strung-out younger sister, Dorothy Malone's deceptively dignified bookstore clerk, Peggy Knudsen's petulant gangster's moll, and an unbilled woman taxi driver. Their lechery is as playful as the plot, and they are not stock figures of good and evil but surprisingly mixed and vivid, some of them in roles lasting only a few moments.

By including women in traditionally male settings (the newspaper office in *His Girl Friday,* the trapping party in *The Big Sky,* the big-game hunters in *Hatari!*), Hawks reveals the tension that other directors conceal or avoid by omitting women or by relegating them to the home. Many of Ford's thirties' and forties' films have no women in them at all, whereas even in Hawks' most rough-and-tumble, male-oriented films, the men are generally seen in relation to women, and women are the point of reference and exposition.

Hawks is both a product of sexual puritanism and male supremacy, and, in the evolution of his films and the alternation-compensation between tragedy and comedy, a critic of it. In the group experience of filmmaking, he lives out the homoerotic themes of American life, literature, and his own films. Thus, the John Wayne older-man figure in *Rio Bravo* and its companion westerns seems finally to have developed into a "complete" man, to the point where he is able to go it alone, to find his self-esteem within himself rather than from the admiration of his friends, and to greet a "complete" woman on her own terms. Like most American men, Hawks and Ford and their protagonists become more at ease with women as they grow older. In his early adventure films, in which the women repeatedly break up male friendships and the men do little to resist what filmwriter Robin Wood has called the "lure of irresponsibility," Hawks betrays the sensibility of an arrested adolescent. His fear of woman is twofold: (1) as the emotional and "unmanly" side of human nature, and (2) as its progenitor. He is like the young boy who, in recoiling from his mother's kiss, refuses to acknowledge his debt of birth to her and who simultaneously fears revealing his own feelings of love and dependency.

In *Only Angels Have Wings,* Jean Arthur provides an alternative to the all-male world of stoical camaraderie on the one hand, and to the destructive femininity represented by Rita Hayworth on the other, but what an alternative! A man dies trying to land a plane in a storm in time for a date with her, she breaks down in defiance of the prevailing stiff-upper-lip ethic, and thereafter she hangs around like a puppy dog waiting for Cary Grant to fall in love with her. For female Hawksians, this is the film most difficult to accept, more difficult than the early films in which women figure only as devils *ex machina.* Although the relationship Jean Arthur offers Grant seems to have been conceived as something "different but equal," women feel it (as Hawks seems to have felt it) as second best. In the all-male community of civil aviators Grant heads up, the central relationship is the tacit, mutual devotion between Grant and Thomas Mitchell. In a milieu of constant, physical danger and sublimated feelings, Arthur's emotionalism is a threat—but it is also, or it is meant to be, a release. The trouble is that Arthur, deprived of the pepperiness and sense of purpose she has in her other thirties' and forties' films (or the sweetly misplaced glamour of *Easy Living*), becomes a sobbing stone around the collective

neck of civil aviation; and she doesn't have the easy come–easy go sexual confidence with which Lauren Bacall and Angie Dickinson invest Slim and Feathers,
Hawks' most sensually aggressive, European-style heroines. Still, technically, *Only
Angels Have Wings* is a transition film. When Mitchell dies, Arthur takes his place,
marking the progression of woman from second to first string.

   Ball of Fire is a perfect fusion of Hawks' dialectics and those of Brackett, and
Wilder, who wrote the screenplay. When Barbara Stanwyck as a fast-talking gangster's moll invades the sanctuary of a group of lexicographers headed by Gary Cooper, it is as if Hawks had recognized the sclerotic danger of male camaraderie—and
was resisting it. But Sugarpuss O'Shea is as much a Wilder–Brackett creation, a
worldly, romantic sensualist who shakes up a group of typically American fuddy-
duddies and "regenerates" them. Stanwyck is as emotionally responsive as Jean
Arthur, but tougher; she brings her own world of jive and street talk with her, and
manages to "corrupt" the ivory-tower purity of the scholars—and expand their
vision. Her humanizing influence paves the way for the rapprochement of the sexes
that occurs in Hawks' subsequent films, particularly in the Bogart–Bacall melodramas, and in the John Wayne–Angie Dickinson relationship in *Rio Bravo.* If the
highest tribute Hawks can pay a woman is to tell her she has performed like a man
(Bogey's "You're good, you're awful good"), isn't that, at least partly, what the
American woman has always wanted to be told? Hasn't she always wanted to join
the action, to be appreciated for her achievements rather than for her sex? But one
often seems to have been gained at the expense of the other, the performing excellence at the cost of the "womanly" awareness. Hawks' sensitivity to the American
girl's anxiety, to her shame at "being a girl," expresses itself later in such fifties' characters as Charlene Holt in *Red Line 7000,* and Paula Prentiss in *Man's Favorite
Sport?* As actresses, and as characters, they lack the usual coordinates of "sex
appeal"; both their athletic ability and their anxiety bespeak a lack of sexual confidence that is disturbingly real. In *Man's Favorite Sport?* it is Paula Prentiss who
makes Rock Hudson take the plunge into the sport (fishing, or, on an allegorical
level, sex) on which he is supposed to be an authority. He was written a "how to"
book without ever having gotten his feet wet.

   In Hawks' best films, there is a sense of playacting for real, of men and women
thrusting themselves ironically at each other, auditioning for acceptance but finding
out in the process who they really are. In *To Have and Have Not,* Bacall combines
intelligence and sensuality, pride and submission. She holds her own. She is a singer
and is as surrounded by her "musical world" as Bogart is by his underground one,
and she combines with him to create one of the great perfectly balanced couples, as
highly defined by fantasy and wit as Millamant and Mirabell in *The Way of the
World,* or as Emma Woodhouse and Mr. Knightley in *Emma.* For the Hawks' heroine, the vocal quality, the facial and bodily gestures are the equivalent of the literary heroine's words, and with these she engages in a thrust-and-parry as highly
inflected and intricate as the great love duels of literature.

   The fable of *To Have and Have Not,* like so many of the action melodramas during the forties (for example, *Casablanca*) is that of the tough guy who "doesn't
believe in" patriotic action or sticking his neck out, and who eventually sticks his
neck out farther and more heroically than anyone else. In *To Have and Have Not,*

it is Bogart's willingness to risk death, pshawing all the while, to bring a French Resistance fighter into Martinique, under the eyes of the Vichy government. But there is an additional, and even more important, meaning to the idea of involvement in Hawks, the involvement of a man with a woman, a scarier and deeper risk of oneself, perhaps, than death.

Typically, a man (in *Only Angels Have Wings, To Have and Have Not,* and *Rio Bravo*) is avoiding women like the plague. He has been badly burned and he doesn't want to get involved. But he, we are entitled to think, doth protest too much. Like the woman's child obsession in the woman's film, which conceals a secret desire to be rid of her offspring, the single man's retreat from marriage conceals a contrary desire. Otherwise, why would he leave so many strings for her to seize upon? (There are very few such "strings," and little sense of heterosexual need, in the action films of the sixties and seventies, which is one of the differences between then and now, and between Hawks and his colleagues and successors.) But it is the woman who has to bring the man around to seeing and claiming the invisible ties (in *To Have and Have Not,* Bacall asks Bogey to walk around her, and then says, "See? No strings," while he is tripping over them without realizing it). The man backs off, using as a pretext or real motive his disapproval of the woman's past. They exchange roles: The woman "proves herself" by playing it his way, by showing her physical courage or competence. And through a respect for her, first on his own terms, then on hers, he is brought around to a more "feminine" point of view.

Because proving themselves to each other is so fundaemntally important for the action here, and for Hawks' men, a woman who is (behaves, thinks) like a man is the transitional step to heterosexual love. In some ways this tribute to love means more coming from a "man's director" than if it had come from a "woman's director." *To Have and Have Not* is so far from the machismo mold of the Hemingway original that the Resistance Frenchman's courage is not in being willing to die, but in having brought along the woman whose presence "weakened" him, by making him concerned for her safety. His heroism, for which he will win no medals, is to have accepted the consequences of heterosexual love. And she, as a spoiled, destructive girl, redeems herself when she understands this. *To Have and Have Not* ultimately contradicts the mystique of those forties' films that, in pretending to deprecate heroics, are most infatuated with them as judged by and performed for men themselves. In the end of *Casablanca,* it is with Claude Rains that Bogart walks off into the Moroccan mist, the equivalent of the lovers' sunset; in *To Have and Have Not,* it is with Lauren Bacall. *Casablanca* reaps the conventional glory for an act— rejection—that is easiest; *To Have and Have Not,* opting for the love that is least honored in the virility ethic, is more truly glorious.

Under Hawks' supervision (being forced, the story goes, to yell at the top of her lungs on a mountaintop, to deepen her voice), Lauren Bacall's Slim is one of film's richly superior heroines and a rare example of a woman holding her own in a man's world. Her characters in *The Big Sleep* and *To Have and Have Not* are romantic paragons, women who have been conceived in what remains, essentially, a "man's world." But in the forties, certain movie stars emerged with distinctive, highly intelligent points of view (strong women like Davis, Crawford, Hepburn, and Russell), which they imposed openly or surreptitiously on the films they made. In this, either as stars or in the parts they played, they corresponded to certain kinds of women that literature had abstracted, over the years, from life. Because society dictated the proper, and severely restricted, domain for women, those who didn't "fit"—the "extraordinary women"—were tortured and frustrated; hence, the "neurotic woman." Finding no outlet for her brains or talent except as wife and mother, she dissipates her energies, diverts them, or goes outside society. Of such women, literature gives us two basic types, one European, the other Anglo-Saxon.

The first, and basically European model, is the "superfemale"—a woman who, while exceedingly "feminine" and flirtatious, is too ambitious and intelligent for the docile role society has decreed she play. She is uncomfortable, but not uncomfortable enough to rebel completely; her circumstances are too pleasurable. She remains within traditional society, but having no worthwhile project for her creative energies, turns them onto the only available material—the people around her—with demonic results. Hedda Gabler, Emma Bovary, and Emma Woodhouse are literary superfemales of the first order.

The other type is the "superwoman"—a woman who, like the "superfemale," has a high degree of intelligence or imagination, but instead of exploiting her femininity, adopts male characteristics in order to enjoy male prerogatives, or merely to survive. In this category are the transsexual impersonators (Shakespeare's Rosalind and Viola) who arrogate male freedoms along with their clothes, as well as the Shavian heroines who assume "male logic" and ideology to influence people—and who lose friends and, most triumphantly, make enemies in the process.

Scarlett and Jezebel, Vivien Leigh and Bette Davis, are superfemales. Sylvia Scarlett and Vienna, Joan Crawford and (often) Katharine Hepburn, are superwomen. The southern heroine, because of her conditioning and background, is a natural superfemale. Like the European woman, she is treated by men and her society with something close to veneration, a position she is not entirely willing to abandon for the barricades. Rather than rebel and lose her status, she plays on her assets, becomes a self-exploiter, uses her sex (without ever surrendering it) to gain power over men. Romantically attractive, even magnetic, she is not sexual (though more so than her northern counterpart, hence the incongruity, even neurosis, in the New England Davis' southern belle performances); she is repressed more from Victorianism than puritanism, and instinctively resists any situation in which she might lose her self-control. (The distinction between North and South obtains in the literary "superfemales" as well; the "Northern European" types, Hedda Gabler and Emma Woodhouse, suggest respectively sexual frigidity and apathy; Mme Bovary, being more Mediterranean, is more likely to have found sexual satisfaction.)

Bette Davis, superfemale and sometime southern belle, was not born in the South at all, but in Lowell, Massachusetts, of an old, respectable Protestant family. The only clue in her background to the seething polarities of toughness and vulnerability expressed in her roles was the trauma (glossed over in her autobiography) of her father's desertion of the family when she was only a child. She was supported in her theatrical career by her mother, Ruthie, who was also her lifelong friend, even as she progressed (or regressed) from the guardian of her struggling daughter to the spoiled charge of her successful one. All this might or might not explain the conflicting impulses of the Davis persona (in tandem or from film to film): the quicksilver shifts between distrust and loyalty, the darting, fearful eyes, and the bravura, the quick wit of the abruptly terminated sentences, the defensiveness, and the throttled passion.

She was the wicked girl who sometimes was, sometimes wasn't, so bad underneath, while Crawford was the self-made gracious lady with ice water for blood. At some point (Crawford in *Rain* and *A Woman's Face*) each of them was bisected by the puritan ethic into two mutually exclusive extremes of good and evil. But even in her double role in *A Stolen Life,* when she played Katy, the sweet-and-passive sister and her bitch twin Pat, Davis did not really draw a radical distinction between the two (as de Haviland did in *The Dark Mirror*), thus suggesting the interdependence of the two halves.

In the beginning of her career, Davis was just plain Katy ("the cake," as Glenn Ford describes her, in contrast to Pat, "without the frosting"). In her first picture, *Bad Sister,* reportedly one of the worst films ever made, Davis was not the eponymous hellion (that was Zasu Pitts) but her simpering, virtuous sibling. "Embarrassment always made me have a one-sided smile," she recounts in her autobiography, "and since I was constantly embarrassed in front of a camera, I constantly smiled in a one-sided manner."

She was universally considered unsexy, not to say unusable: still, when her contract expired she managed to hang on until she was taken up by Warners. Her lack of success or star status became an asset, as she was able to take parts—like Mildred in *Of Human Bondage*—that nobody else would touch. This was her first villainess, and her enthusiasm extended to the makeup, which she persuaded director John Cromwell to let her apply herself. In so doing, she thus gained the upper hand, which she would use whenever she could (and not always to her own advantage), and demonstrated that feeling for greasepaint grotesque that only she could get away with, and sometimes even she could not.

She determined to make it very clear "that Mildred was not going to die of a dread disease looking as if a deb had missed her noon nap. The last stages of consumption, poverty and neglect are not pretty and I intended to be convincing-looking. We pulled no punches and Mildred emerged as a reality—as immediate as a newsreel and as starkly real as a pestilence." (Actually, Davis' notions of feminine vanity and excesses, daring as they often are, have led her into those parodies of womanhood that are closer to Grand Guignol than newsreel, and that have surrounded her with camp followers whose image of her obliterates her real strengths.)

From then on, she was one of the few actresses willing—even eager—to play against audience sympathy. In her southern belle phase, she managed to combine the vanity of the "deb" with the venality of Mildred. Even in her superfemale roles, the charm has a cutting edge—the taunting Julie Marsden of *Jezebel* (the consolation role for missing out on Scarlett); the "jinx" actress, Joyce Heath, patterned on Jeanne Eagels, in *Dangerous* (for which she won the consolation Academy Awared denied her for *Of Human Bondage*); the mortally ill socialite, Judith Traherne, in *Dark Victory;* and the frivolous Fanny Trellis of *Mr. Skeffington.*

The superfemale is an actress by nature; what is flirtation, after all, but role-playing? Coquetry is an art, and Davis exulted in the artistry. In *Jezebel,* she captivates her beaux but with less natural effervescence than Scarlett. Davis is more neurotic than Vivien Leigh, less cool. When coolness is called for, Davis gives us a cold chill: when warmth, a barely suppressed passion. Her charm, like her beauty, is something willed into being. It is not a question of whether she is inside or outside the part (for curiously she is both) but of the intensity of her conviction, a sense of character in the old-fashioned sense of "moral fiber." Through sheer, driving guts she turns herself into a flower of the Old South, and in that one determined gesture reveals the bedrock toughness of the superfemale that we discover only by degrees in Scarlett.

Davis' reputation is based on a career composed of equal parts art, three-star trash, and garbage, sometimes all in the same film—which makes fine critical distinctions difficult. Warners gave her a hard time, and she reciprocated. (She even brought a lawsuit against them once, which she lost, but in so doing, she paved the way for future action on actors' behalf.) William Wyler was her toughest and best director—on *Jezebel, The Letter,* and *The Little Foxes*—but she broke with him over *The Little Foxes.* She was in an invisible competition with Tallulah Bankhead, who had played Regina brilliantly on Broadway, and from whom she also inherited (and probably improved upon) *Jezebel* and *Dark Victory.* Surely none of these films was a "betrayal" of the original stage play, and as to who outshone whom, only those who have witnessed both can decide—and even they, given the fierce, partisan loyalties these two women inspire, are not entirely trustworthy.

For all her enmities, Davis really was a friend to other actresses, content to take the back seat and let them run with the showy parts. (Actually, some of her "backseat" parts—the sweet-tempered but strong girl in *The Great Lie*—are some of her most appealing and underrated roles.) Mary Astor tells the story of how she and Davis built her—Mary's—part in *The Great Lie* into an Academy Award-winning performance. Every day before shooting they added material to the screen play, to make Mary look good as well as to enliven the movie, and between them (and with the sympathetic direction of Edmund Goulding) they created one of the most complex women's relationships in a woman's film. They are cast as stereotypes: Astor, the sophisticated and selfish concert pianist who wants George Brent more than his baby; Davis, Brent's Baltimore bride, who makes a deal with Astor for the baby when they think Brent is dead. Their relationship during Astor's delivery alternates between tenderness and spite, love and hate, as Davis plays the "father" (in jodhpurs, pacing the floor) to Astor's mother.

Part of Davis' greatness lies in the sheer, galvanic force she brought to the most outrageous and unlikely roles, giving an intensity that saved them, usually, from camp. Even when she is "outside" a part (through its, or her, unsuitability), she is dynamic. As the harridan housewife of *Beyond the Forest,* she surveys her despised domestic kingdom and says "What a dump!" and we are with her. By the time Martha in *Who's Afraid of Virginia Woolf?* says the same line, it has already been consecrated as camp. In spite of the fact that the only way we can think of Davis as a *femme fatale* is if she contemplates murder or literally kills somebody *(The Letter, The Little Foxes),* she makes us accept her as a girl men fight duels over and die for. She is constantly being cast against type as a heartbreaker, and then made to pick up the pieces when foolish hearts shatter. As the actress "witch" *(Dangerous)* whose stage presence has caused suicides and inspired epiphanies, she is made to do penance, for the rest of her life, with her Milquetoast husband. But if we look closely, here and elsewhere, it is not she but others who insist on her supernatural evil, who throw up a smoke screen of illusions, who invoke mystical catchwords to explain her "magic" or her "jinx," why she is "different" from other women.

In her film career, Davis casts a cold eye, and not a few dampening remarks, on sentimentality. When Claude Rains, as the doting Mr. Skeffington, tells her "A woman is beautiful only when she is love," Davis, miserable over the discovery of her pregnancy, replies, "A woman is beautiful if she has eight hours of sleep and goes to the beauty parlor every day. And bone structure has a lot to do with it."

In King Vidor's *Beyond the Forest,* her wildest and most uncompromising film, one she herself dislikes, she plays the evil Rosa Moline, married to Joseph Cotton's small-town doctor. He is seen as "good" because he goes without, and makes his wife go without, so his impecunious patients won't have to pay their bills—and will "love" the good doctor. His "virtue" succeeds in driving his wife into further malice. One of the earliest discontented housewives on record, Rosa sashays around wearing a long black wig, like her surly housekeeper, Dona Drake, who is a dark-skinned lower-class parody of her. Davis' obsession is to go to Chicago, and to this end she wrecks everyone's lives. In one of the film's most modern, *angst*-ridden scenes, she wanders the back streets of Chicago, staggering through the rain (having been turned out of a bar where women '"without escorts" are not allowed), looking like another star who would later claim her influence—Jeanne Moreau in *La Notte.*

"I don't want people to love me," Rosa says—one of the most difficult things for a woman to bring herself to say, ever, and one of the most important. It is something Davis the actress must have said. Thus, does the superfemale become the superwoman, by taking life into her own hands, her own way.

Davis' performance in *Beyond the Forest,* as a kind of female W. C. Fields, and Vidor's commitment to her, are astonishing. Even though she is contrasted with a "good woman" (Ruth Roman) to show that she is the exception, that all women are not like that (a moralistic pressure that Hollywood is not the only one to exercise—the French government made Godard change the title of *The Married Woman* to *A Married Woman*), the Ruth Roman character has little moral weight or value. As Rosa Moline, Davis creates her own norms, and is driven by motives not likely to appeal to the average audience. She is ready and eager to give up husband, position, security, children (most easily, children), even lover; for what? Not for anything so noble as "independence" in terms of a job, profession, or higher calling, but to be rich and fancy in Chicago! And here is Davis, not beautiful, not sexy, not even young, convincing us that she is all these things—by the vividness of her own self-image, by the vision of herself she projects so fiercely that we have no choice but to accept it. She is smart, though, smarter than everyone around her. She says it for all smart dames when David Brian tells her he no longer loves her, that he's found the "pure" woman of his dreams. "She's a book with none of the pages cut," he says.

"Yeah," Davis replies, "and nothing on them!"

Since she began as a belle and emerged as a tough (in *Beyond the Forest* she is a crack shot and huntress), Davis' evolution from superfemale to superwoman was the most dramatic, but she was by no means the only actress in the forties to undergo such a transformation.* Perhaps reflecting the increased number of working women during the war and their heightened career inclinations, other stars made the transition from figurative hoop skirts to functional shoulder pads, and gained authority without necessarily losing their feminity.

The war was *the* major turning point in the pattern and attitudes of (and toward) working women. From 1900 to 1940, women in the labor force had been mostly young, unmarried women in their early twenties who were biding their time until marriage. Suddenly, to fill men's places and aid in the expanded war industries, older, married women were recruited, and from that time to the present (when the typical working woman is forty and married) the median age rose with the percentage of women in the labor force. A poll of working women taken during the war came up with the startling fact that 80 percent wanted to keep their jobs after it was over. After a sharp drop-off following the end of the war—when women were fired with no regard for seniority—married women *did* go back to work, although as late as 1949 it was still frowned upon. This, of course, is the source of the tremendous tension in films of the time, which tried, by ridicule, intimidation, or persuasion, to get women out of the office and back to the home, to get rid of the superwoman and bring back the superfemale.

Rosalind Russell came out of the superfemale closet into superwoman roles fairly early in her career. But in *Craig's Wife,* an adaptation of the George Kelly play, she is not only a superfemale but the definitive superfemale, the housewife who becomes obsessive about her home, the perfectionist housekeeper for whom, finally, nothing else exists. It would be comforting to look upon this film, directed by Dorothy Arzner, as a protest against the mindlessness of housewifery, but, like *The Women,* of which the same claim has been made, it is not so much a satire as an extension, in high relief, of the tics and intellectual tremors of a familiar American type. In *The Women,* as the malicious (and funny and stylish) Mrs. Fowler, Russell is the superfemale par excellence; but in *His Girl Friday,* as the newspaper reporter, in *My Sister Eileen,* as the short-story writer, and in *Take a Letter, Darling,* as the business executive, she begins pulling her own weight in a man's world, risks making enemies and losing lovers, becomes, that is, a superwoman.

In *Take a Letter, Darling,* she is the partner in an advertising firm where she began as a secretary. She runs the operation while Robert Benchley, the titular head of the firm, plays miniature golf in his office. He is, to Russell, the kind of benign father figure that Charles Coburn was to Jean Arthur and Irene Dunne. Not in the least bitter at Russell's success, he is quite happy to have been "kicked upstairs"

---

*In a characteristically perverse fashion, Ida Lupino went in the opposite direction, from the superwoman matriarch of *The Man I Love* and *The Hard Way* (1942), in which she channels all of her ambitions into promoting her younger sister, to *The Bigamist* (1953), which she herself directed, and in which she plays Edmund O'Brien's mousy, submissive mistress against Joan Fontaine's aggressive career woman. Although Lupino takes the standard anti-career woman position in her treatment of Fontaine, the film presents a positive case for bigamy, or at least suggests that the binary system—one man, one woman, married for life without loopholes—is not the most flexible or realistic arrangement.

and gives her support and advice whenever she comes to him. At one point, he complains that her competitors—all men, of course—don't understand her:

"They don't know the difference between a woman and a . . ."
"A what?" Russell asks.
"I don't know," Benchley replies, "there's no name for you."

In *My Sister Eileen,* Russell plays the writer-sister trying to sell her stories to a prestigious national magazine. Although the stories concern the escapades of her pretty and popular sister, Russell steals the show as the cerebral one, and gets editor Brian Aherne, too. (The difference in attitudes between the forties and fifties can be seen in the shift of emphasis in the musical remake of *My Sister Eileen* in 1955, in which Betty Garrett retains little dignity as the intellectual sister, but is overshadowed—and shamed—by the popularity of the sister played by Janet Leigh.)*

Katharine Hepburn made the transition from superfemale to superwoman most easily and most successfully of all—perhaps because she was already halfway there to begin with. In her second film, Dorothy Arzner's *Christopher Strong,* she played an aviatrix torn between her profession and her man. Flying presents an appropriately extreme metaphor for the freedom of the single woman that has to be surrendered once the idea of a family becomes a concrete reality. Torn apart by these conflicting pulls, Hepburn finally dies in a plane crash—that is, she propels herself, like the dancer in *The Red Shoes,* into the abyss between love and career. In both cases, the ending is not just a cautionary warning to deflect women from careers, but a true reflection of the dynamics of the situation: A woman has only so much energy, so much "self" to give; is there enough for profession (especially if it is a dangerous or demanding one), lover, and children? *Christopher Strong* raises these questions, but doesn't really pursue them, and as a consequence it is a less interesting film than it should be, less interesting than Arzner's more "feminist" film, *Dance, Girl, Dance.* But, for all its weaknesses, *Christopher Strong* leaves us with a blazingly electric image of Katharine Hepburn unlike that of any other film: a woman in a silver lamé body-stocking which covers everything but her face—and suggests the chrysalis of the superwoman of the future.

Hepburn, like most tomboy actresses, played Jo in *Little Women,* and shortly thereafter played the eponymous "transvestite" of *Sylvia Scarlett,* one of George Cukor's most enchanting and least-known films. Disguised as a boy, she accompanies her father, a crook on the lam, through the hills of Cornwall. They join forces with a troupe of wandering actors, led by Cary Grant, and embark on a free, magical, oneiric adventure, giving plays in the moonlight. Cukor's feeling for the conventions of theater, where he began his career, leads him into a world halfway between theater and life, a world in which disguises are often worn more easily and more "honestly" than native hues. The milieu and the story of *Sylvia Scarlett* have a Shakespearian feel to them, harking back to an age and a theatrical convention in which sex-exchange was permissible. This is Cukor's first film (and last for a while)

---

*If Columbia had used the Bernstein musical, with Rosalind Russell retaining her stage role, the move might have been better but no less sexist, with its rousing point-by-point denunciation of feminism: "100 Ways to Lose a Man."

in which he dared to challenge, in a lyrical stage whisper, our traditional assumptions about male-female roles.

The delicate equilibrium between a man and a woman and between a woman's need to distinguish herself and the social demands on her become the explicit theme of Cukor's great films of the late forties and early fifties, specifically the Judy Holliday films and Hepburn-Tracy vehicles written by the husband-and-wife team of Ruth Gordon and Garson Kanin. Gordon and Kanin wrote a series of seven screenplays for Cukor, three of which dealt, comically and sublimely, with the problems and the chemistry of individuals.

Almost as a parody of the extraordinary individuals represented by Hepburn and Tracy in *Adam's Rib* and *Pat and Mike,* Aldo Ray and Judy Holliday were a typical, dumb, middle-class, well-meaning, ordinary married couple in Cukor's *The Marrying Kind.* Almost a parody, but not quite. For it is one of the glories of the film that the two characters, without ever being patronized and at the same time without ever being lifted above the class and the cliché in which they are rooted, are intensely moving. Ray and Holliday, on the brink of divorce, have come to a woman judge (who, in her relationship with her male assistant, shows both authority and warmth). Through a series of flashbacks reconstructing their marriage we, and they, come to realize that together they are something they never were apart: a unit, a whole. Two ordinary, less-than-complete individuals who have grown into each other to the point where they can be defined only by the word "couple" have no right to divorce. Separately, they are two more swallowers of the American myth, two more victims of its fraudulence: but together, with their children, they add up to something full and affirmative. In losing their child, they are at first destroyed—their "meaning" evaporates. But in that nothingness, old roles dissolve and they must rediscover themselves. Cukor, Gordon, and Kanin are very much aware of the sexual insecurities that arise from too rigid a concept of male-female roles, and suggest, in the visual and verbal motifs of these "companion" films, that through some kind of "merger" of identities, through a free exchange of traits (as when Holliday, in defiance of the law whereby it is the man who "storms out" of the house in a fight, throws herself into the night), a truer sense of the self may emerge.

In the growing isolation of the New York cultural elite from the rest of America in the sixties, this is the side of marriage and the middle class that has been lost to us. We seem to be able to approach middle-America only through giggles of derision *(The Graduate, Sticks and Bones,* "All in the Family"): and, in dismissing the housewife as a lower form of life, women's lib confirms that the real gap is cultural and economic rather than sexual. In the difference between the couples in *The Marrying Kind* and *Adam's Rib,* Cukor and company acknowledge the most fundamental intellectual, spiritual, and economic inequality between the educated elite and the less privileged and less imaginative members of lower-middle-class America; but they never deprive them of their dignity, or deny them joys and sorrows and a capacity to feel as great as the poets of the earth. The true emotional oppression—the oppression of blacks by whites, of housewives by working women, is pity. For in such lessons in life as we get from suffering, degrees are granted without reference to class or sex. Finally, most honestly, Holliday's Florence and Ray's Chet are the sheep of the world rather than its shepherds: They are the victims of emotions they haven't the words to express, the tools of a mechanical-industrial society they haven't the knowledge to resist. Their greatest defense against its monolithic oppressiveness, against being overwhelmed by routine, inhumanity, and their "proletarian" identity, is each other, is their identity as a couple. In the final, quite noble strength we feel in them as a couple, they confirm the theory Cukor, Gordon, and Kanin seem to be endorsing: that marriage is an institution ideally suited to the people at both the bottom and the top—the truly ordinary and the truly extraordinary, those who are preserved and protected by it, and those who can bend it to their will.

Hepburn and Tracy were nothing if not extraordinary. While preserving their individuality, they united to form a whole greater than the sum of its parts. As Tracy says to Hepburn in *Pat and Mike,* in a line that could have been written by Kanin-Gordon, Cukor, or Tracy himself and that finally tapers off into infinity, "What's good for you is good for me is good for you. . . ."

This was true of them professionally. They came together at a time when their careers were foundering: misfits in the Hollywood mold, they were not in any way typical romantic leads. Hepburn had grown older, the face that once blushed in gracious concession to femininity now betrayed in no uncertain terms the recalcitrant New England spirit. And Tracy, too short and dumpy for conventional leading roles, hadn't found the woman who could lure him from the rugged, masculine world he inhabited. Out of their complementary incongruities, they created one of the most romantic couples the cinema has ever known. His virility acts as a buffer to her intelligence: she is tempered by him just as he is sharpened by her, and their self-confidence is increased, rather than eroded, by their need for each other.

Adam's Rib, that *rara avis,* a commercial "feminist" film, was many years ahead of its time when it appeared in 1949, and, alas, still is. Even the slightly coy happy ending testifies to the fact that the film strikes deeper into the question of sexual roles than its comic surface would indicate and raises more questions than it can possible answer.

Tracy and Hepburn play a couple of married lawyers who find themselves on opposite sides of a case: he is the prosecuting attorney, and she, seizing upon the crime and its implications, takes it upon herself to defend the accused. A dopey young wife—Judy Holliday, in her first major movie role—has shot, but not killed, her husband (Tom Ewell) over another woman. Hepburn, reading an account in the newspaper, is outraged by the certainty that the woman will be dealt with harshly while a man in that position would be acquitted by the courts and vindicated by society. Hepburn goes to visit Holliday at the woman's prison, and, in a long, lovely single-take scene, Holliday spills out her story, revealing, comically and pathetically, her exceptionally low consciousness. Once of the constant and most relevant sources of comedy in the film is the lack of rapport between Hepburn's militant lawyer, constructing her case on feminist principles, and Holliday's housewife, contrite and idiotically eager to accept guilt. The film raises the means-and-end dilemma which has long been the philosophical thorn in the side of our thinking about the rights and reparations of minority groups. Hepburn marshals evidence of women's accomplishments to prove their equality with men, even to the point of having a lady wrestler lift Tracy onto her shoulders and make a laughingstock of him. She goes *too* far and humiliates him, while he remains a gentleman. She stoops to unscrupulous methods while he maintains strict honor and decorum. But, then, he can afford to, since the law was created by and for him.

Even down to his animal magnetism, Tracy wears the spoiled complacency of the man, but Hepburn, ambitious and intelligent, scrapes the nerves of male authority. An acute sense of the way male supremacy is institutionalized in the "games people play" occurs in two contrasting situations of one-upmanship: Hepburn, fiery about the case she is about to take, is describing it to Tracy on the telephone: Tracy, in a familiar male (or marital) riposte, effectively cuts her off by teasing, "I love you when you get caus-y." This is greeted with delight by audiences, who usually disapprove of Hepburn's "emasculation" of Tracy in court, a more obvious but perhaps a less damaging tactic of bad faith. Cukor gives Hepburn an ally in the Cole Porter-type composer played by David Wayne, a character who seems to stand, at least partially, for Cukor himself. He identifies with Hepburn and, in marital feuds, takes her side against the virile, meat-and-potatoes "straight" played by Tracy. Thus the neutral or homosexual character, when he is sympathetic, can help to restore some of the balance in the woman's favor. But as soon as the Hepburn–Wayne collusion becomes devious or bitchy, the balance shifts, and our sympathy goes, as it should, to Tracy.

The film brilliantly counterpoints and reconciles two basic assumptions: (1) that there are certain "male" qualities—stability, stoicism, fairness, dullness—possessed by Tracy, and that there are certain "female" qualities—volatility, brilliance, intuition, duplicity—possessed by Hepburn; and (2) that each can, and must, exchange these qualities like trading cards. It is important for Hepburn to be ethical, just as it is important for Tracy to be able to concede defeat gracefully, and if she can be a bastard, he can fake tears. If each can do everything the other can do, just where, we begin to wonder, are the boundaries between male and female? The question mark is established most pointedly and uncomfortably when, during the courtroom session, the faces of Holliday and Ewell are transposed, each becoming the other.

But Hepburn and Tracy are not quite so interchangeable, and the success of their union derives from the preservation of their individuality, not rigidly but through a fluctuating balance of concession and assertion. Tracy can be humiliated and still rebound without (too much) loss of ego. Hepburn occasionally can defer to him and still not lose her identity. A purely political-feminist logic would demand that she be given Tracy's head, in unqualified triumph (an ending that some small part of us would like to see), rather than make an equivocal, "feminine" concession to his masculinity. But marriage and love do not flourish according to such logic. Their love is the admission of their incompleteness, of their need and willingness to listen to each other, and their marriage is the certification—indeed, the celebration—of that compromise.

This finally is the greatness of Hepburn's superwoman, and Davis' and Russell's too—that she is able to achieve her ends in a man's world, to insist on her intelligence, to insist on using it, and yet be able to "dwindle," like Millamant in *The Way of the World,* "into marriage," but only after an equal bargain has been struck of conditions mutually agreed on. It is with just such a bargain, and a contract, that Cukor's great Tracy-Hepburn film of the fifties, *Pat and Mike,* is concerned.

For the most part, the superwoman, with her angular personality and acute, even abrasive, intelligence, begins to disappear in the fifties. The bad-girl is whitewashed, or blown up into some pneumatic technicolor parody of herself. Breast fetishism, a wartime fixation of the G.I.'s, came in in the fifties. (Its screen vogue was possibly retarded by the delay in releasing Howard Hughes' *The Outlaw,* introducing Jane Russell's pair to the world.) But even amidst the mostly vulgar fumblings toward sensuality, Cukor was there—with Ava Gardner in *Bhowani Junction* and Sophia Loren in *Heller in Pink Tights*—to give some dignity to the sex goddesses and, in films like *The Actress* and *Born Yesterday,* to pay tribute to the enterprising woman.

1974

JOAN MELLEN
FROM WOMEN AND THEIR SEXUALITY IN THE NEW FILM

THE MAE WEST NOBODY KNOWS

In my long and colorful career, one thing stands out; I have been misunderstood.

MAE WEST

The Mae West of legend has long excited men and infuriated women. Her voluptuous image, exploited by the Hollywood dream machine, appears to women as a mockery. West as sex queen and manipulator of weak, drooling men represents a liberation in reverse. Aggressively flaunting herself, Mae West thinks she thereby transcends the sexual role of passive and fawning object set for women. In reality, she compounds the injury. While scorning passivity, the image of woman as bestower of sexual favors seems to be perpetuated by Mae West unrelentingly. Her belief that liberation and frankness about the risqué are synonymous is, of course, outdated, and sexuality in Mae West has been made a repository for abundant energies directed by more liberated women to activities providing satisfaction beyond the physical. The stereotyped image thus draws upon a partial truth.

But there are two sides to Mae West. In most of her films she reduces herself to a sexual object in quest of economic security while she is, simultaneously, defiant and self-sufficient, seeking mastery over her life. It is the latter aspect of the West personality that is revolutionary. It projects a uniquely free image of woman rare for Hollywood during the 1930's, or now.

Mae West understands the fact that in our culture women have obtained acceptance primarily by offering their bodies in contract, although the pattern has been surrounded by legitimacy to conceal its meaning. Hence, submissive coyness has been approved, excessive forwardness not. The exception is when the sexual aggressiveness of women is part of a condemned subculture, the prostitute or the burlesque queen solicited and stigmatized. In this sense Mae West fulfills the canons of our culture where women are concerned, but frequently for the purpose of sub-

646

verting them. Often her license, bawdy humor, sexual explicitness and bravado are invested with a challenge to those who disapprove. It is true that Mae West, no social revolutionary, does not project new values. But within the existing structure of attitudes defining the appropriate responses of men and women, West turns the tables. It is she who is superior and achieved, she for whom sexual command affirms feminine strength.

This reversal often renders her men uncomfortable and off-balance, her first victory. They approach her expecting to enhance their masculine pride and sexual self-esteem—at her expense. West reverses the roles. It is true that men often become *her* sexual objects, leaving us with the old pattern of exploiter-exploited that has long distorted relations between men and women. But West also transforms sexual allure on the part of women into an item of pride, power and autonomy. She transcends the cultural meaning of sexual availability in women because she separates it from servility and servitude.

Despite her moments approaching the licentious, if West uses her sensuality to entice, she is also the polar opposite of the simpering coquette or the manipulative subordinate. West looks over the field, reduces and discards, takes lovers at will, but never surrenders freedom or control. Although her example is difficult to imitate successfully, she takes a first step toward challenge of the expected female role; she arrogates to herself all the insolent privilege, haughtiness and self-esteem which our culture had until her time in the film granted the male alone.

Mae West thus deploys her own brand of sexism to create an image of a liberated woman—and Hollywood is her vehicle. At her best moments, we forget the reversal of a repugnant sexual politics to relish the free spirit of the West *persona*. It is the common thread of *She Done Him Wrong* (based on West's own Broadway play, *Diamond Lil*), *I'm No Angel*, *Klondike Annie*, *Belle of The Nineties*, *My Little Chickadee*, *Go West Young Man*, *Goin' To Town* and *The Heat's On*. What has been cited as her narcissism was hardly a liberated response; but West's endless filing of her fingernails, bored by all, or examining herself in multiple mirrors, are also devices she employs as foils for shrewd observations into a petty, ambitious and hypocritical society where women have always had to conceal their intelligence and remain on guard. When West masks her intellectuality, it is of course a measure of continued enslavement. That she can act upon her own insights shows her on the path to liberation.

It could be said that the elaborate facade West presents of rejecting dominance in men is retrograde because it conceals her unconscious fear of them, or, her longing for that man against whom she would not pre-emptively have to defend so fiercely. But such a psychologism, although it may entail a prescient guess about West's interaction with her much admired, strong and brawling father, misses the point. It is precisely because our culture recreates for women the situation of the paternal male figure who would dominate as a price for approval and love that West's response is so liberating and true to the common experience. And West's *persona* actually merges with the real woman. Mae West married only once, as an adolescent to a husband as young as she. Regretting her decision, she refused to set up house with him and was separated so quickly that her indulgent parents were unaware that a marriage had occurred.

In her own life West's energy was directed as much toward the hard work of writing as toward romantic attachments. She wrote a series of successful Broadway plays followed by novels, and finally by the screenplays and the dialogue for virtually all her films. (An exception like *The Heat's On* suffers accordingly in loss of verve and intelligence). "All my life," West writes in her autobiography, "I would not conform to the old-fashioned limits they had set on a woman's freedom of action. Or the myth of a woman's need of male wisdom and protection."

Mae West on screen always retains the decision about whether to commit herself to a man for an extended time; and she is wary about choosing one partner for life. "Ever meet a man that could make you happy?" she is asked. "Sure, lots of times," is her reply. In *I'm No Angel* a fortune teller promises West, "a man in your life," to the swift retort, "what, only one?" It is no wonder that even Adolph Zukor, who would have insisted otherwise had she not enriched the coffers of Paramount Pictures, called her "the strong, confident woman, always in command."

She Done Him Wrong pictures West as a "gold digger" named Lady Lou attached to a saloon whose owner is involved in the white slave trade, in which Lou takes no part. Lou prefers the poor Salvation Army "Captain" Cummings (Cary Grant), a poor detective in disguise. Accidentally murdering the slave trade proprietess, Lady Lou faces arrest. Yet when she is tempted by detective Grant to marry him and escape punishment, she refuses to submit. The last line of the film gives an impenitent West the sentiment usually implicit in the male's attitude to his conquest. "I always knew you could be had," she tells her leading man. Captain Cummings wants to be "her jailer for a long, long time." But Lady Lou's ironic view of marriage was conveyed when she said earlier of Cummings that "he'd be the kind a woman would have to marry to get rid of." Lou would remain free in the event she were to marry, even as some men do, rejecting the hint of a double standard.

The West character, despite her sexism, will neither acknowledge nor accede to the superior wisdom of any man. Interestingly, the characterizations of males which she creates in her films are often of personalities rich in talents of their own, i.e., the inventor in *Go West Young Man* (Randolph Scott) and the successful executive in *I'm No Angel* (Cary Grant). It is in relation to men of talent and not merely the inadequate male that she makes it clear that their qualities could never oblige relinquishment of her judgment for theirs. In this sense the West character is far more liberated than the women of an overtly feminist writer like Doris Lessing, whose male characters are weak, whining and tiresome.

Contrary to popular belief, the image of West is only partially that of a woman soliciting by wiles the support of a man or his gifts. In all her films West earns her own way, making hard work appear easy. In most of the films West plays a professional entertainer, one of the few arenas for economic independence open to a woman of her limited resources and education, especially during the depression era when her films were made. Thus even as Diamond Lil she is primarily supported by her work. This undercuts and renders ambivalent the image of the West character as reliant for luxuries upon her physical attributes, as indeed she also is.

Frequently she assumes professions normally available to men alone, and she is never unequal to them. *I'm No Angel* has West as a lion tamer who sues Grant for breach of promise. The circus owner, fearful of losing his star to marriage, had planted a "lover" in West's room, the discovery of whom causes Grant to break their engagement. West conducts her own defense at the trial, exposing with panache the lies of witness after witness, while simultaneously flirting with an unnerved, if spellbound, judge and jury. Again we are presented with the two sides of Mae West, attorney and coquette, the liberated woman and the tease, a character not yet strong enough to transcend the old values completely.

This theme is enlarged upon in other films. In *Goin' To Town* she is a rich "widow" whose "husband" dies before the wedding. She proceeds to manage his oil wells and a huge cattle ranch with skill and ease while at the same time searching for and pursuing her next husband! In *Klondike Annie* West as the "San Francisco Doll" (again the sex queen) escapes with great daring from an infamous saloon in San Francisco and proceeds by ship to Nome, Alaska. There she transforms an abandoned settlement house into a financially thriving center of activity. Disguised as "sister Annie," a Salvation Army worker who dies aboard ship, West relates religious platitudes to the deeply felt needs of lonely miners. Underlying her toughness is a demonstrated sympathy for those who are disadvantaged. The miners are indeed enticed by her sexual allure, barely concealed in Salvation Army garb, but she uses it not for sexual encounters, but to win an audience for the meeting house.

West's independence and strength of will are epitomized in the lion taming sequence of *I'm No Angel.* The head trainer was absent from the set because he had been attacked by one of the lions that morning. West actually went in among the lions for the shooting. No trembling Hollywood ingenue, she enjoyed the experience which expresses again the two sides of her personality: independent woman and seeker of revenge and power over the male. She places her head in the lion's mouth and wisecracks, "remember my contract, baby . . . speak up for yourself or you'll end up as a rug!" "Every man wants to protect me," says Mae West disingenuously in *My Little Chickadee,* "I can't figure out what from."

In *My Little Chickadee,* a Western with a female hero, Flower Belle (West) is run out of her home town for behavior unbecoming a proper young lady (she has been "kidnapped" by her lover, the "masked bandit"). On the train bound for a neighboring village, Flower Belle single-handedly routs an army of attacking Indians. Presented later with the opportunity to teach a class of wild and unruly boys, she wins and tames them (like the lions) through wit and bravado, despite sparse knowledge. "Two and two are four, and five will get you ten if you know how to work it" becomes part of their arithmetic lesson. When she is jailed for collusion with the "masked bandit," Flower Belle escapes through cunning, if also through the use of her charms, in time to rescue W. C. Fields from imminent hanging as the "real" bandit. If her sexuality is always presented as an enticement, her boldness and self-possession present another focus to her film character.

Another side of West's rejection of passivity which goes beyond sexism is a refusal to wait for events to turn in her direction. She appears ever ready for the unexpected, and the quick response is her trademark. At the end of *My Little Chickadee,* when a departing Fields asks West to "come up and see me sometime," it is West who calls *him* "my little Chickadee," emphasizing that such an appellation, contrary to custom, may just as easily be attached to a male. During the film two attractive men, the masked bandit (the saloon owner in disguise) and the local newspaper editor pursue her, but Flower Belle will marry neither, keeping both at bay with "maybe tomorrow, maybe never." She can return to her home town only when she is "respectable and married." Rather than capitulate to the norms of a society that would not acknowledge her existence in terms other than marriage and family, West prefers to live elsewhere.

The hostile view of Mae West which notes, simplistically, only her vulgarity, also regards her as selfish and hard-boiled, but this too cannot survive close examination. There is self-irony in her portrayals and her characters display generosity and a sense of justice which are understated if omnipresent. When it appears that she may implicate the man she loves, Klondike Annie returns from Nome to San Francisco to face murder charges. Cleo Borden in *Goin' To Town* is generous toward a weak aristocrat, although, regressing, she married him in the first place for his name and social position. In *She Done Him Wrong,* Lady Lou warmly takes under her wing the "fallen" girl Sally and persuades her that "betrayal" by a man does not mean her life is over: "When women go wrong, men go right after them!" If the content of the advice does not free woman from her traditional role, its spirit redresses the balance. West shields the local Runyonesque characters from police bullies and befriends all whom she finds in need. Flower Belle *(Chickadee),* for example, saves the obnoxious Fields not because she has any feeling for him, but because he has been falsely accused. Free of the stereotype of woman as weak or in need of man as protector, West's values transcend her sexual role. A sense of fair play is the complement to her indefatigable spirit.

Sex itself for the West *persona* is always a matter of *her own* pleasure. The men she invites to "come up and see me sometime" are only those who appeal to her. If her aggressive personality attracted the label of "predatory," West was well aware that this would be the social response to any woman bold enough to take sexual initiatives. It should be remembered as well that men were most often the predators of the kind of woman West portrayed in her films—and for whom she has sympathy—poor, uneducated women living on the margins of a hostile society by singing in saloons. And it is in response to such treatment that West advises these women to "take all you can, and give as little as possible." The context is one of unceasing struggle against potential and actual victimization, although this advice also replaces men with women as victimizers.

There is another facet to West's rebellion against sexual orthodoxy. She is relaxed about sex, not faintly hysterical, as Hollywood custom usually required. She treats her adventures with bountiful humor and her exaggerated "sexy" walk is at once a sexist ploy and a mockery of the sexual signals assumed to bind men to women. She is also ironic when men assume that her sexuality is an invitation to easy usage. Lady Lou, admiring a nude portrait of herself, wishes only that it were not "hung up over the free lunch!"

"When I was fourteen," Mae West said in a recent interview, "I resented men having all the freedom of sex and from then on I thought women should have it too." Such remarks about "free lunch," the lurid and mercenary side of this character, should not obscure the irony and rebellion which are continually present as well. And West's response to the very different virtues of each of her lovers, from Victor McLaglen *(Klondike Annie)* to Gilbert Roland *(She Done Him Wrong)* to

Mae West with her adoring servants—with Louise Beavers in *She Done Him Wrong* and Soo Yong in *Klondike Annie*. "There are aspects of her films that pander to the most corrupt values of the Hollywood of her day; the black maids named Beulah or Pearl, invariably fat and childish, the racist portrayals of sinister Chinese, such as the infamous Chan Lo of *Klondike Annie's* San Francisco Chinatown, the "savage" Indian horde which Flower Belle overwhelms and such salty, questionable ballads as "I'm an Occidental Woman in an Oriental Mood for Love'" (MELLEN, page 652).

Cary Grant *(She Done Him Wrong, I'm No Angel)* belies the allegation that men are only faceless objects to her. "A man's kiss is his signature," she declares, stressing her respect for the uniqueness of her lovers, in contrast to the image of a woman who would turn men solely into objects. There is far more discrimination and less promiscuity in West's approach than that accorded, for example, to intellectual women by men on the Hollywood screen. "There's something about every man," says West. "A man may be short, dumpy and rapidly getting bald—but if he has *fire,* women will like him." West may celebrate promiscuity in her sexual encounters, but generosity and kindness are important to her as well. Klondike Annie is genuinely moved when the ship captain (McLaglen) is prepared to risk his life and career for her. "Your love is terrific," Annie tells him. A good heart is matched by West in kind and there is considerable pride and self-esteem even in her prurience.

There are aspects of her films that pander to the most corrupt values of the Hollywood of her day: the black maids named Beulah or Pearl, invariably fat and childish, the racist portrayals of sinister Chinese, such as the infamous Chan Lo of *Klondike Annie's* San Francisco Chinatown, the "savage" Indian horde which Flower Belle overwhelms and such salty, questionable ballads as "I'm An Occidental Woman In An Oriental Mood For Love." And the Hollywood of the 1930's delighted in Mae West because her screen personality fit in so well with the American myth that with enough energy, drive and initiative, any deprived person might achieve riches and status. The dream machine must especially have welcomed this theme in 1932 when Mae West first went to Hollywood. Made during the depression, most of West's films are set in an earlier period, usually the gay nineties, when the myth that fortunes could be made overnight seemed more credible.

West as free spirit constantly combines with West as sexist. At her worst, she equates the subtle with prudery. Her seeming freedom from men, her refusal to commit herself completely even in marriage, may be seen as fear of anything beyond the casual relationship and the one night stand. It is as if West, doubting her sexual capacity, were driven to exaggerate her prowess. Her need for a steady stream of men coming up to "see me sometime" makes her the equivalent of the Don Juan who, fearing impotence, must forever make new conquests. The Mae West who at 77 appears in *Myra Breckinridge* as a lascivious Hollywood agent collecting well-endowed young boys, like the West who appears at interviews with a collection of studs, is embarrassing when she does not offend. To qualify, each young man must possess not only the standard "six feet," but also a required "seven inches." "I don't care about your credits," she adds to an aspiring young actor, "as long as you're oversexed." The irony is gone. The heroic side of West is besmirched, suggesting that her interest all long has been in the exploitation of sex, at its best daring for its day, but no mark of emancipation. *Myra Breckinridge* shows us West as merely a distortion of the female, a travesty of self-parody which convinces us of the truth of its opposite, that compulsive sex is neither desirable nor pleasureable, that despite her bravura, West did women less a favor than a disservice.

In *Myra Breckinridge* and at the worst moments of all the flims, West is the least liberated creature imaginable, retaining no portion of herself beyond the sexual. Her abundant self-confidence becomes no more than a concealment of the retrograde. It is this West which, making virtue of necessity (woman's enslavement), deploys style to conceal what it would have been far more liberating to expose. Those who applaud West's performances at the re-run houses on St. Marks Place do not differentiate the Mae West of *She Done Him Wrong* from the West of *Myra Breckinridge*. She is cheered there primarily by some men perhaps because she seems to them to represent the ultimate of sexual degradation in a woman. In her aggressiveness West imparts at times an aura of the transvestite, making a mockery of female sexuality by flaunting what are no more than ordinary female attributes.

Yet there is also the Mae West whose appeal as a new woman approaches the universality of Chaplin. "What would you do without me?" a producer asks Mae in *The Heat's On*. "Much better," is the reply and she goes on to prove it. West was the *auteur* of films redolent with wit in which the punchline always went to the woman. It should not be forgotten that she worked in a medium devoted to glorifying male prowess and female incapacity. And it took a courage heroic in its time (she was jailed for "indecency" as the author of one of her plays) to present Hollywood with a reversal of roles and a manifest contempt for the culture which had for so long demeaned the capacities of women.

1973

THOMAS SCHATZ
FROM THE GENIUS OF THE
SYSTEM

"THE WHOLE EQUATION OF PICTURES"

Walking at dawn in the deserted Hollywood streets in 1951 with David [Selznick], I
listened to my favorite movie boss topple the town he had helped to build. The movies,
said David, were over and done with. Hollywood was already a ghost town making foolish
efforts to seem alive. . . .

But now that the tumult was gone, what had Hollywood been?

BEN HECHT, 1954

. . . The collapse of the studio system was bound to provoke questions like Ben
Hecht's—"What had Hollywood been?"—and the answers have been plentiful but
less than adequate. Hecht himself answered as so many of his industry colleagues
did, with an anecdotal, self-serving memoir laced with venom for the "system" and
for the "Philistines" who controlled it—and who paid Hecht up to $5,000 a week
for his services as a screenwriter. Hecht was an essential part of that system, of
course, though he hardly saw things that way, and his reminiscence was less revealing of Hollywood filmmaking than of the attitudes of eastern-bred writers toward
the priorities and the power structure in the movie industry. Hecht's answer did
provide yet another piece of evidence to be factored in, along with countless other
interviews and autobiographies, critical studies, and economic analyses. But the
accumulated evidence scarcely adds up, and our sense of what Hollywood had been
remained a vague impression, fragmented and contradictory, more mythology than
history.

Promising to change all that, a cadre of critics and historians in the 1960s and
1970s cultivated a "theory of film history" based on the notion of directorial
authorship. As the New Hollywood emerged from the ashes of the studio era, pro-
ponents of the "auteur theory" proclaimed that what the Old Hollywood had been
was a director's cinema. They proclaimed, too, that the only film directors worthy

of canonization as author-artists were those whose personal style emerged from a certain antagonism toward the studio system at large—the dehumanizing, formulaic, profit-hungry machinery of Hollywood's studio-factories. The auteurist's chief proponent was Andrew Sarris, who in his landmark study, *The American Cinema: Directors and Directions, 1929–1968,* cast the studio boss as the heavy in Hollywood's epic struggle and reduced American film history to the careers of a few dozen heroic directors. Keying on an observation by director George Stevens that as the industry took shape, "the filmmaker became the employee, and the man who had time to attend to the business details became the head of the studio," Sarris developed a simplistic theory of his own, celebrating the director as the sole purveyor of Film Art in an industry overrun with hacks and profitmongers. The closing words of his introduction said it all: "He [the director] would not be worth bothering with if he were not capable now and then of a sublimity of expression almost miraculously extracted from his money-oriented environment."

Auteurism itself would not be worth bothering with if it hadn't been so influential, effectively stalling film history and criticism in a prolonged stage of adolescent romanticism. But the closer we look at Hollywood's relations of power and hierarchy of authority during the studio era, at its division of labor and assembly-line production process, the less sense it makes to assess filmmaking or film style in terms of the individual director—or *any* individual, for that matter. The key issues here are style and authority—creative expression and creative control—and there were indeed a number of Hollywood directors who had an unusual degree of authority and a certain style. John Ford, Howard Hawks, Frank Capra, and Alfred Hitchcock are good examples, but it's worth noting that their privileged status— particularly their control over script development, casting, and editing—was more a function of their role as producers than as directors. Such authority came only with commercial success and was won by filmmakers who proved not just that they had talent but that they could work profitably within the system. These filmmakers were often "difficult" for a studio to handle, perhaps, but no more so than its top stars or writers. And ultimately they got along, doing what Ford called "a job of work" and moving on to the next project. In fact, they did their best and most consistent work on calculated star vehicles for one particular studio, invariably in symbiosis with an authoritative studio boss.

Consider Ford's work with Darryl Zanuck at Twentieth Century-Fox on a succession of Henry Fonda pictures: *Young Mr. Lincoln, Drums Along the Mohawk,* and *The Grapes of Wrath.* Or Alfred Hitchcock doing *Spellbound* and *Notorious,* two psychological dramas scripted by Ben Hecht and prepared by David Selznick for his European discovery, Ingrid Bergman. Or Howard Hawks working for Jack Warner on *To Have and Have Not* and *The Big Sleep,* two hard-boiled thrillers with Bogart and Bacall that were steeped in the Warners style. These were first-rate Hollywood films, but they were no more distinctive than other star-genre formulations turned out by routine contract directors; Universal's horror films with Boris Karloff directed by James Whale, for instance, or the Paul Muni biopics directed by William Dieterle for Warners. Whale and Dieterle are rarely singled out for their style or artistry, and each would have been lost without the studio's resources and regimented production process. But that doesn't diminish the integrity of films like

Frankenstein, The Old Dark House, and *The Bride of Frankenstein,* or *The Story of Louis Pasteur* and *The Life of Emile Zola.*

The quality and artistry of all these films were the product not simply of individual human expression, but of a melding of institutional forces. In each case the "style" of a writer, director, star—or even a cinematographer, art director, or costume designer—fused with the studio's production operations and management structure, its resources and talent pool, its narrative traditions and market strategy. And ultimately any individual's style was no more than an inflection on an established studio style. Think of Jimmy Cagney in *Public Enemy,* staggering down that dark, rain-drenched street after a climactic shoot-out with rival gangsters, gazing just past the camera and muttering "I ain't so tough," then falling face-down into the gutter. That was a signature Warner Bros. moment, a narrative-cinematic epiphany when star and genre and technique coalesced into an ideal expression of studio style, vintage 1931. Other studios had equally distinctive styles and signature moments, involving different stars and story types and a different "way of seeing" in both a technical and an ideological sense. On a darkened, rain-drenched street at MGM, for instance, we might expect to find a glossy, upbeat celebration of life and love—Mickey Rooney in another Andy Hardy installment, struggling to get the top up on his old jalopy while his date gets soaked, or Gene Kelly dancing through puddles and singin' in the rain. Over at Universal a late-night storm was likely to signal something more macabre: Count Dracula on the prowl, perhaps, or Dr. Frankenstein harnessing a bolt of lightning for some horrific experiment.

These are isolated glimpses of a larger design, both on screen and off. Each top studio developed a repertoire of contract stars and story formulas that were refined and continually recirculated through the marketplace. Warners in the 1930s, for example, cranked out urban crime films with Cagney and Edward G. Robinson, crusading biopics with Paul Muni, backstage musicals with Dick Powell and Ruby Keeler, epic swashbucklers with Errol Flynn and Olivia de Haviland, and in a curious counter to the studio's male ethos, a succession of "women's pictures" starring Bette Davis. These stars and genres were the key markers in Warners' Depression-era style, the organizing principles for its entire operation from the New York office to the studio-factory across the continent. They were a means of stabilizing marketing and sales, of bringing efficiency and economy into the production of some fifty feature films per year, and of distinguishing Warners' collective output from that of its competitors.

The chief architects of a studio's style were its executives, which any number of Hollywood chroniclers observed at the time. Among the more astute chroniclers was Leo Rosten, who put it this way in *Hollywood: The Movie Colony,* an in-depth study published in 1940:

> Each studio has a personality; each studio's product shows special emphases and values. And, in the final analysis, the sum total of a studio's personality, the aggregate pattern of its choices and its tastes, may be traced to its producers. For it is the producers who establish the preferences, the prejudices, and the predispositions of the organization and, therefore, of the movies which it turns out.

Rosten was not referring to the "supervisors" and "associated producers" who monitored individual productions, nor to the pioneering "movie moguls" who controlled economic policy from New York. He was referring to studio production executives like Louis B. Mayer and Irving Thalberg at MGM, Jack Warner and Hal Wallis at Warner Bros., Darryl Zanuck at Twentieth Century-Fox, Harry Cohn at Columbia, and major independent producers like David Selznick and Sam Goldwyn. These men—and they were always men—translated an annual budget handed down by the New York office into a program of specific pictures. They coordinated the operations of the entire plant, conducted contract negotiations, developed stories and scripts, screened "dailies" as pictures were being shot, and supervised editing until a picture was ready for shipment to New York for release. These were the men Frank Capra railed against in an open letter to *The New York Times* in April 1939, complaining that "about six producers today pass on about 90 percent of the scripts and edit 90 percent of the pictures." And these were the men that F. Scott Fitzgerald described on the opening page of *The Last Tycoon*, the Hollywood novel he was writing at the time of his death, in 1940. "You can take Hollywood for granted like I did," wrote Fitzgerald, "or you can dismiss it with the contempt we reserve for what we don't understand. It can be understood too, but only dimly and in flashes. Not a half dozen men have been able to keep the whole equation of pictures in their heads."

Fitzgerald was thinking of Irving Thalberg when he wrote that passage, and it would be difficult to find a more apt description of Thalberg's role at MGM. Nor could we find a clearer and more concise statement of our objective here: to calculate the whole equation of pictures, to get down on paper what Thalberg and Zanuck and Selznick and a very few others carried in their heads. After digging through several tons of archival materials from various studios and production companies, I have developed a strong conviction that these producers and studio executives have been the most misunderstood and undervalued figures in American film history. So in a sense this is an effort to reconsider their contributions to Hollywood filmmaking; but I don't want to overstate their case or misstate my own. Hollywood's division of labor extended well into the executive and management ranks, and isolating the producer or anyone else as artist or visionary gets us nowhere. We would do well, in fact, to recall French film critic André Bazin's admonition to the early auterists, who were transforming film history into a cult of personality. "The American cinema is a classical art," wrote Bazin in 1957, "so why not then admire in it what is most admirable—i.e., not only the talent of this or that filmmaker, but the genius of the system."

It's taken us a quarter-century to appreciate that insight, to consider the "classical Hollywood" as precisely that: a period when various social, industrial, technological, economic, and aesthetic forces struck a delicate balance. That balance was conflicted and ever shifting but stable enough through four decades to provide a consistent system of production and consumption, a set of formalized creative practices and constraints, and thus a body of work with a uniform style—a standard way of telling stories, from camera work and cutting to plot structure and thematics. It was the studio system at large that held those various forces in equilibrium; indeed, the "studio era" and the classical Hollywood describe the same industrial and historical phenomenon. The sites of convergence for those forces were the studios themselves, each one a distinct variation on Hollywood's classical style. . . .

The movies were a "vertical" industry in that the ultimate authority belonged to the owners and top corporate officers in New York. But the New York office couldn't make movies, nor could it dictate audience interest and public taste. And whatever the efforts to regulate production and marketing, moviemaking remained a competitive and creative enterprise. In the overall scheme of things, the West Coast management team was the key to studio operations, integrating the company's economic and creative resources, translating fiscal policy into filmmaking practice. This demanded close contact with New York and a feel for the company's market skew, but also an acute awareness of the studio's resources and heavy interaction with the top filmmakers on the lot, particularly the directors, writers, and stars.

Because of the different stakes involved for each of these key players, studio filmmaking was less a process of collaboration than of negotiation and struggle—occasionally approaching armed conflict. But somehow it worked, and it worked well. What's most remarkable about the classical Hollywood, finally, is that such varied and contradictory forces were held in equilibrium for so long. The New Hollywood and commercial television indicate all too clearly what happens when that balance is lost, reminding us what a productive, efficient, and creative system was lost back in the 1950s. There was a special genius to the studio system, and perhaps when we understand that we will learn, at long last, what Hollywood had been.

1988

VII

Film: Psychology, Society, and Ideology

What are the nature and sources of film's psychological and political power? Is there something special about the film medium that confers this power? Is this power repressive or liberating? Can it be criticized and controlled? Questions of this sort have always been asked about cinema, but in recent years film studies have focused on them with unusual intensity. Many of these studies have relied on the Marxist notions of superstructure and ideology and on Freudian ideas about the development and constitution of the self. Writers in this tradition have been committed to exposing the ideological biases of classic narrative film and, in the writings of feminist authors, to revealing its sexist procedures and assumptions. Earlier sections have included essays that apply these perspectives to such perennial issues as the nature of film reality, the film medium, and film genre. In this section the reader will find some of the most arresting recent writing on the psychological and social bases of film, as well as essays by important precursors of present thinking such as Walter Benjamin and Parker Tyler.

In his classic paper, the pre-war Marxist critic, Walter Benjamin, reflects on alterations in the artistic superstructure that the capitalist mode of production produces. In the past, art works have been unique objects, possessing "aura" and traditional "authority." They played a ritual role, contemplated by men who kept a "natural" distance from them. But the contemporary masses want to see things closer, spatially and humanly. They overcame the uniqueness of the work of art by accepting a mechanical reproduction of it as an equivalent. These reproductions are no longer hallowed cult objects but consumer goods sold on the market; rather than absorbing their beholders, they are absorbed by them. Reactions to these "works of art" are rarely personal and are almost completely determined by the mass audience to which the individual is subordinated. Indeed, films have now become one of the most powerful agents of mass political movements—in them the mass has for the first time come face to face with itself. In Benjamin's view, the film and the audience's relation to it are so different from all that has gone before that he is inclined to think that photography has transformed the very nature of art.

The editors of *Cahiers du cinéma* were, in the period subsequent to the student uprisings in Paris in 1968, central to the discussions represented in this section. In their Marxist view film produced in the West today has two aspects. On the one hand, it is a commodity produced by labor and exchanged according to the laws of the market. On the other hand, it is part of the ideological superstructure determined by the capitalist economic system. One assumption of the prevailing ideological system is that cinema "reproduces" reality but, in fact, it only reproduces the world of the dominant ideology. As Louis Althusser formulates it, men express in their ideologies not their actual relation to the conditions of their existence, but their reactions to it. The filmmaker's primary task is, therefore, to expose the cinema's alleged "depiction of reality." If the filmmaker can do this, there is some chance that we will be able to disrupt and sever the connection between cinema and its ideological function.

Some filmmakers are simply imbued with the dominant ideology and reflect it in both the form and content of their works. The task of the film critic, in these cases, is to exhibit the film's blindness to the ideology it presents. Other films attack their ideological assimilation on two levels. On the level of the signified they engage in direct political action while on the level of the signifier they try to break down the traditional way of depicting reality. These levels, which it is the critics task to display, are indissolubly linked.

Another category of film appears to be completely within the dominant ideology yet can be shown to be so only in an ambiguous manner. John Ford's *Young Mr. Lincoln* is a film of this type and is the subject of a famous analysis by the editors of *Cahiers*. They urge that the film attempts to suppress the realities of politics by presenting Lincoln's career as one based on an idealist morality superior to mere politics. Yet Ford, who is consciously sympathetic to that ideology, nevertheless shows us a Lincoln characterized by a violence which displays his truly repressive character. According to J. P. Oudart this shows the distance Ford, in his "writing," keeps between himself and the idealist propositions he deploys.

Investigations of the logical effects of the cinematic apparatus plainly raise questions concerning the psychology of the spectator. Not surprisingly, the cinema spectator has been compared with both the reader of a novel and the viewer of a play. Like the reader of a novel, the viewer of a film, sitting in a darkened hall, enjoys a degree of solitude. Like the viewer of a play, the movie-goer sits in a public place and reacts to humanly significant events in the company of other human beings. André Bazin, who distinguished between the "community" that views a play and the "mass" that watches a film, tries to hold both of these features in balance. But most theorists emphasize one or the other.

As we have seen, for Stanley Cavell watching a film preserves the modern sense of privacy, offering the viewer both invisibility and an absence of responsibility. The experience is essentially voyeuristic and even pornographic. Parker Tyler's view of the film experience is even more explicitly sexual and psychological. For him, the "dark-enshrouded" passivity of the movie house encourages "the daylight dream."

In this state, the movie screen transcends its role as a mirror of nature, and the viewer's unconscious mind can read the film's images symbolically. Tyler realizes that the Hollywood film (as opposed to the European film) cannot meet the standards of high art. But the resonant images of a Hollywood film mirror mythic cultural values and evoke primitive responses in the mass audience. Modern movie stars, "the gods and goddesses of Hollywood," are vestiges of the old Greek divinities and they gratify our deepest sexual fantasies. Comparative mythology and psychoanalysis have made us aware of the persistence of deep psychic needs, and the Hollywood film responds to these needs in a way that contemporary popular religions fail to do.

Like Parker Tyler, Jean-Louis Baudry compares the experience of film to that of dream. He attempts, in doing so, to account for the "impression of reality," that "more than real" experience created by film. Baudry observes that many features of the film spectator's situation—features, that is, of the cinematic apparatus—resemble the dream. The spectator's movements are inhibited; he sits in a darkened room and is unable to engage in reality testing. The distinction between perception and representation does not operate. The images he views are projected on a screen (in the dreamer's case the mother's breast, what Bertram Lewin calls the dream screen); the intense images are more-than-real. According to psychoanalytic theory, the dream is endowed with this quality of heightened reality because it occasions a regression to the stage of primitive narcissism. Given the many similarities between the film experience and the dream experience, we can infer that the more-than-real experience of the film spectator is attributable to a similar regression. The desire for this regressive experience explains the history and creation of the cinematic apparatus and can be traced all the way back to its frequently invoked precursor, Plato's myth of the cave. According to Baudry, the prisoner in Plato's cave bears a striking analogy both to the dreamer and to the film spectator.

Noël Carroll challenges every significant feature of Baudry's analogy between the film spectator and the dreamer. In his view, the film spectator does not suffer motor inhibition but can get up and even have a smoke. Unlike dreams, film images are publicly accessible, but reality testing in Baudry's sense is in fact inapplicable to them. The dreamer may be (or may not be) in a darkened room, but this is not, in any case, part of the dream experience. Dreams are not, in fact, typically projected on (white) breasts, and, insofar as one can work with the vague concept of the "more-than-real" this notion applies more typically to dreams than to film. To be sure, some films provide a heightened experience of this sort but, when they do, this should be attributed more to particular features of their internal structure than to the projection situation or the cinematic apparatus itself. Carroll doubts the utility of the dream analogy to the understanding of film since we understand film better than we understand dreams. And he is highly critical of what he regards as a literary and impressionistic approach to questions that require scientific evidence and analytic precision.

In his more recent work, Christian Metz, like Baudry, also looks to psychoanalysis for an explanation of cinema's power. He applies ideas of Lacanian psychoanalysis to an examination of the ideology of specularization. For Metz, the uniqueness of the cinema lies in the duality of its signifier. Cinema is capable of an unprecedented range of perceptions (it is a machine of the visible), but these perceptions are stamped with unreality to an unusual degree because the cinematic apparatus does not succeed in identifying the visible with the real. What is perceived is not really the object, which is not really present, but rather its absence, its phantom, its double, its *replica* in a new kind of mirror. But this mirror differs from the primordial mirror of Lacanian analysis. In the Lacanian mirror, which the mother holds before the child, the child perceives its own image and its ego is formed by its identification with this likeness. In the cinema, the spectator identifies with himself as a pure act of perception. He identifies, that is, with the camera. But what makes the spectator's absence from the screen possible is the fact that the spectator has already experienced the primordial mirror. The experience of the mirror phase makes the film experience possible.

For the spectator, film unfolds in that definitively inaccessible "elsewhere" in which the child sees the amorous play of the parental couple, who, like the actors in a film, are similarly ignorant of the voyeur or spectator and leave him alone. The filmic spectator is a privileged onlooker whose participation in the scene he witnesses is impossible. In this sense, the cinematic signifier is not only "psychoanalytic"; it is more precisely Oedipal. The cinema retains some of the prohibitions peculiar to the vision of the primal scene. But the institutionalization of the cinema legalized this practice, making it socially permissible. Going to the cinema is one lawful activity among others. Still, it constitutes a peephole opening on to something slightly more crazy, slightly less acceptable, than what one does the rest of the time.

Laura Mulvey uses psychoanalysis to help explain the pleasure and unpleasure offered by narrative film. In her essay "Visual Pleasure and Narrative Cinema," she argues that narrative film provides what Freud calls "scopophilic" pleasure, the pleasure of viewing another as an erotic object. In a narrative film, this activity characteristically takes the form of looking at women as erotic objects. But narrative film, echoing the experience of the child at Lacan's mirror, also provides the contrasting narcissistic pleasure of identification with the projected images, in particular with that of the male character, who makes things happen and controls them. Woman is, however, also a source of unpleasure since she represents the threat of castration and, in so being, motivates the voyeuristic and fetishistic mechanisms that attempt to circumvent her threat. (Mulvey studies their operation in the films of Sternberg and Hitchcock.)

None of these mechanisms is, however, intrinsic to film, and the pleasures of mainstream film can be challenged by breaking down the cinematic codes and the formative external structures that support them. Indeed, radical filmmakers have already begun to undermine the ideologically inspired illusion of three-dimensional space in which the spectator's surrogate performs and in which the look of the spectator is denied intrinsic force. This deconstruction is accomplished by freeing the look of the camera into its materiality in space and time and by transforming the scopophilic gaze of the audience into a detached and dialectical one. These changes destroy the pleasures and privilege of the "invisible guest" and highlight the ways film has depended on voyeuristic mechanisms. Women, whose images have continually been stolen and used for this purpose, cannot view the decline of traditional film with anything more than sentimental regret.

According to Mulvey's analysis, the spectator's point of view in the case of classical narrative film is a masculine one. Mary Ann Doane offers a further account of the female's eviction from a discourse that is, at the same time, about her. To assume the voyeuristic or fetishistic position characteristic of the masculine spectator requires keeping the distance that is presupposed by desire. Indeed, it requires that Metzian absence, which is absolute and irrecoverable. However, because of woman's inability to separate from the maternal body, because of the overwhelming presence of the female body to itself, women cannot achieve that distance from their bodily images that men can. This overidentification with the female image, this inability to fetishize, explains the female spectator's affinity with genres such as the woman's picture and the soap opera, genres which occasion Molly Haskell's "wet, wasted afternoons." Unless the female spectator engages in transvestitism and identifies with the male spectator she is given untenable alternatives: the masochism of overidentification with the female object of the spectator's gaze or the narcissism of becoming one's own object of desire. Neither of these positions provides the distance required for an adequate reading of the film's image. But the spectator's position so described is not an ahistorical essence. Rather, it is a place which is culturally assigned and reflects relations of power. The value of accurately analyzing the repression of femininity and the female gaze is the opportunity this provides for revising and relocating them.

Gaylyn Studlar proposes replacing the model of cinematic spectatorial pleasure, represented by Laura Mulvey and Mary Ann Doane, a model based on the work of Freud, Lacan, and Metz, with a model suggested by Gilles Deleuze's *Masochism: An Interpretation of Coldness and Cruelty*. In Mulvey's theory the male spectator, for whose pleasure the narrative film is created, escapes the castration anxiety the female evokes either by an act of voyeurism, which sadistically demystifies the female, or by a fetishistic response, which turns the female into a signifier of the absent phallus. But, according to Studlar, cinematic pleasure is much closer to the submissive, scopic pleasure of masochism than it is to the sadistic, controlling pleasure Mulvey and Metz describe. And, because of the political nature of her argument against phallocentrism, it has been suggested that Mulvey cannot admit that the masculine look contains passive elements and is capable of signifying submission to, rather than possession of, the female. Like Mulvey, Studlar studies Sternberg's films, but she notices that in them Dietrich, in response to the male gaze, looks back—or even initiates the look.

On the masochistic model, the female no longer signifies simply the possibility of castration. Instead of being apprehended as lacking the male symbol of power, she is seen as powerful in her own right because she possesses what the male lacks, the womb and the breast. And, as we recall, Baudry analogizes the cinematic apparatus to Lewin's dream screen of the mother's breast. The masochistic fantasy is characterized by oral pleasure, the desire to return to the undifferentiated body state of the mother-child. These wishes are recapitulated by the film spectator who becomes a child again in response to the dream screen of cinema. In this state the cinematic spectator re-experiences the primary identification with the mother and enjoys the pleasures of gender mobility. Identification with one's sex does not preclude identification with the other. The polarities of the Freudian model, and the exclusive and excluding position of the male spectator, can therefore be overcome. It is no longer necessary to regard film spectatorship or "libidinalized looking" as a problem for the female spectator. Rather it is an opportunity available to both sexes.

WALTER BENJAMIN
THE WORK OF ART IN THE AGE OF MECHANICAL REPRODUCTION

"Our fine arts were developed, their types and uses were established, in times very different from the present, by men whose power of action upon things was insignificant in comparison with ours. But the amazing growth of our techniques, the adaptability and precision they have attained, the ideas and habits they are creating, make it a certainty that profound changes are impending in the ancient craft of the Beautiful. In all the arts there is a physical component which can no longer be considered or treated as it used to be, which cannot remain unaffected by our modern knowledge and power. For the last twenty years neither matter nor space nor time has been what it was from time immemorial. We must expect great innovations to transform the entire technique of the arts, thereby affecting artistic invention itself and perhaps even bringing about an amazing change in our very notion of art."

Paul Valéry, PIÈCES SUR L'ART,
"La Conquète de l'ubiquité," Paris.

PREFACE

When Marx undertook his critique of the capitalistic mode of production, this mode was in its infancy. Marx directed his efforts in such a way as to give them prognostic value. He went back to the basic conditions underlying capitalistic production and through his presentation showed what could be expected of capitalism in the future. The result was that one could expect it not only to exploit the proletariat with increasing intensity, but ultimately to create conditions which would make it possible to abolish capitalism itself.

The transformation of the superstructure, which takes place far more slowly than that of the substructure, has taken more than half a century to manifest in all areas of culture the change in the conditions of production. Only today can it be indicated what form this has taken. Certain prognostic requirements should be met by these statements. However, theses about the art of the proletariat after its assumption of power or about the art of a classless society would have less bearing on these demands than theses about the developmental tendencies of art under present conditions of production. Their dialectic is no less noticeable in the superstructure than in the economy. It would therefore be wrong to underestimate the value of such theses as a weapon. They brush aside a number of outmoded concepts, such as creativity and genius, eternal value and mystery—concepts whose uncontrolled (and at present almost uncontrollable) application would lead to a processing of data in the Fascist sense. The concepts which are introduced into the theory of art in what follows differ from the more familiar terms in that they are completely useless for the purposes of Fascism. They are, on the other hand, useful for the formulation of revolutionary demands in the politics of art.

I

In principle a work of art has always been reproducible. Man-made artifacts could always be imitated by men. Replicas were made by pupils in practice of their craft, by masters for diffusing their works, and, finally, by third parties in the pursuit of gain. Mechanical reproduction of a work of art, however, represents something new. Historically, it advanced intermittently and in leaps at long intervals, but with accelerated intensity. The Greeks knew only two procedures of technically reproducing works of art: founding and stamping. Bronzes, terra cottas, and coins were the only art works which they could produce in quantity. All others were unique and could not be mechanically reproduced. With the woodcut graphic art became mechanically reproducible for the first time, long before script became reproducible by print. The enormous changes which printing, the mechanical reproduction of writing, has brought about in literature are a familiar story. However, within the phenomenon which we are here examining from the perspective of world history, print is merely a special, though particularly important, case. During the Middle Ages engraving and etching were added to the woodcut; at the beginning of the nineteenth century lithography made its appearance.

With lithography the technique of reproduction reached an essentially new stage. This much more direct process was distinguished by the tracing of the design on a stone rather than its incision on a block of wood or its etching on a copperplate and permitted graphic art for the first time to put its products on the market, not only in large numbers as hitherto, but also in daily changing forms. Lithography enabled graphic art to illustrate everyday life, and it began to keep pace with printing. But only a few decades after its invention, lithography was surpassed by photography. For the first time in the process of pictorial reproduction, photography freed the hand of the most important artistic functions which henceforth devolved only upon the eye looking into a lens. Since the eye perceives more swiftly than the hand can draw, the process of pictorial reproduction was accelerated so enormously that it could keep pace with speech. A film operator shooting a scene in the studio captures the images at the speed of an actor's speech. Just as lithography virtually implied the illustrated newspaper, so did photography foreshadow the sound film. The technical reproduction of sound was tackled at the end of the last century. These convergent endeavors made predictable a situation which Paul Valéry pointed up in this sentence: "Just as water, gas, and electricity are brought into our houses from far off to satisfy our needs in response to a minimal effort, so we shall be supplied with visual or auditory images, which will appear and disappear at a simple movement of the hand, hardly more than a sign." Around 1900 technical reproduction had reached a standard that not only permitted it to reproduce all transmitted works of art and thus to cause the most profound change in their impact upon the public; it also had captured a place of its own among the artistic processes. For the study of this standard nothing is more revealing than the nature of the repercussions that these two different manifestations—the reproduction of works of art and the art of the film—have had on art in its traditional form.

II

Even the most perfect reproduction of a work of art is lacking in one element: its presence in time and space, its unique existence at the place where it happens to be. This unique existence of the work of art determined the history to which it was subject throughout the time of its existence. This includes the changes which it may have suffered in physical condition over the years as well as the various changes in its ownership. The traces of the first can be revealed only by chemical or physical analyses which it is impossible to perform on a reproduction; changes of ownership are subject to a tradition which must be traced from the situation of the original.

The presence of the original is the prerequisite to the concept of authenticity. Chemical analyses of the patina of a bronze can help to establish this, as does the proof that a given manuscript of the Middle Ages stems from an archive of the fifteenth century. The whole sphere of authenticity is outside technical—and, of course, not only technical—reproducibility. Confronted with its manual reproduction, which was usually branded as a forgery, the original preserved all its authority; not so *vis à vis* technical reproduction. The reason is twofold. First, process reproduction is more independent of the original than manual reproduction. For example, in photography, process reproduction can bring out those aspects of the original that are unattainable to the naked eye yet accessible to the lens, which is adjustable and chooses its angle at will. And photographic reproduction, with the aid of certain processes, such as enlargement or slow motion, can capture images which escape natural vision. Secondly, technical reproduction can put the copy of the original into situations which would be out of reach for the original itself. Above all, it enables the original to meet the beholder halfway, be it in the form of a photograph or a phonograph record. The cathedral leaves its locale to be received in the studio of a lover of art; the choral production, performed in an auditorium or in the open air, resounds in the drawing room.

The situations into which the product of mechanical reproduction can be brought may not touch the actual work of art, yet the quality of its presence is always depreciated. This holds not only for the art work but also, for instance, for a landscape which passes in review before the spectator in a movie. In the case of the art object, a most sensitive nucleus—namely, its authenticity—is interfered with whereas no natural object is vulnerable on that score. The authenticity of a thing is the essence of all that is transmissible from its beginning, ranging from its substantive duration to its testimony to the history which it has experienced. Since the historical testimony rests on the authenticity, the former, too, is jeopardized by reproduction when substantive duration ceases to matter. And what is really jeopardized when the historical testimony is affected is the authority of the object.

One might subsume the eliminated element in the term "aura" and go on to say: that which withers in the age of mechanical reproduction is the aura of the work of art. This is a symptomatic process whose significance points beyond the realm of art. One might generalize by saying: the technique of reproduction detaches the reproduced object from the domain of tradition. By making many reproductions it substitutes a plurality of copies for a unique existence. And in permitting the reproduction to meet the beholder or listener in his own particular situation, it reactivates the object reproduced. These two processes lead to a tremendous shattering of tradition which is the obverse of the contemporary crisis and renewal of mankind. Both processes are intimately connected with the contemporary mass movements. Their most powerful agent is the film. Its social significance, particularly in its most positive form, is inconceivable without its destructive, cathartic aspect, that is, the liquidation of the traditional value of the cultural heritage. This phenomenon is most palpable in the great historical films. It extends to ever new positions. In 1927 Abel Gance exclaimed enthusiastically: "Shakespeare, Rembrandt, Beethoven will make films . . . all legends, all mythologies and all myths, all founders of religion, and the very religions . . . await their exposed resurrection, and the heroes crowd each other at the gate." Presumably without intending it, he issued an invitation to a far-reaching liquidation.

III

During long periods of history, the mode of human sense perception changes with humanity's entire mode of existence. The manner in which human sense perception is organized, the medium in which it is accomplished, is determined not only by nature but by historical circumstances as well. The fifth century, with its great shifts of population, saw the birth of the late Roman art industry and the Vienna Genesis, and there developed not only an art different from that of antiquity but also a new kind of perception. The scholars of the Viennese school, Riegl and Wickhoff, who resisted the weight of classical tradition under which these later art forms had been buried, were the first to draw conclusions from them concerning the organization of perception at the time. However far-reaching their insight, these scholars limited themselves to showing the significant, formal hallmark which characterized perception in late Roman times. They did not attempt—and, perhaps, saw no way—to show the social transformations expressed by these changes of perception. The conditions for an analogous insight are more favorable in the present. And if changes in the medium of contemporary perception can be comprehended as decay of the aura, it is possible to show its social causes.

The concept of aura which was proposed above with reference to historical objects may usefully be illustrated with reference to the aura of natural ones. We define the aura of the latter as the unique phenomenon of a distance, however close it may be. If, while resting on a summer afternoon, you follow with your eyes a mountain range on the horizon or a branch which casts its shadow over you, you experience the aura of those mountains, of that branch. This image makes it easy to comprehend the social bases of the contemporary decay of the aura. It rests on two circumstances, both of which are related to the increasing significance of the masses in contemporary life. Namely, the desire of contemporary masses to bring things "closer" spatially and humanly, which is just as ardent as their bent toward overcoming the uniqueness of every reality by accepting its reproduction. Every day the urge grows stronger to get hold of an object at very close range by way of its likeness, its reproduction. Unmistakably, reproduction as offered by picture magazines and newsreels differs from the image seen by the unarmed eye. Uniqueness and permanence are as closely linked in the latter as are transitoriness and reproducibility in the former. To pry an object from its shell, to destroy its aura, is the mark of a perception whose "sense of the universal equality of things" has increased to such a degree that it extracts it even from a unique object by means of reproduction. Thus is manifested in the field of perception what in the theoretical sphere is noticeable in the increasing importance of statistics. The adjustment of reality to the masses and of the masses to reality is a process of unlimited scope, as much for thinking as for perception.

IV

The uniqueness of a work of art is inseparable from its being imbedded in the fabric of tradition. This tradition itself is thoroughly alive and extremely changeable. An ancient statue of Venus, for example, stood in a different traditional context with the Greeks, who made it an object of veneration, than with the clerics of the Middle Ages, who viewed it as an ominous idol. Both of them, however, were equally confronted with its uniqueness, that is, its aura. Originally the contextual integration of art in tradition found its expression in the cult. We know that the earliest art works originated in the service of a ritual—first the magical, then the religious kind. It is significant that the existence of the work of art with reference to its aura is never entirely separated from its ritual function. In other words, the unique value of the "authentic" work of art has its basis in ritual, the location of its original use value. This ritualistic basis, however remote, is still recognizable as secularized ritual even in the most profane forms of the cult of beauty. The secular cult of beauty, developed during the Renaissance and prevailing for three centuries, clearly showed that ritualistic basis in its decline and the first deep crisis which befell it. With the advent of the first truly revolutionary means of reproduction, photography, simultaneously with the rise of socialism, art sensed the approaching crisis which has become evident a century later. At the time, art reacted with the doctrine of *l'art pour l'art,* that is, with a theology of art. This gave rise to what might be called a negative theology in the form of the idea of "pure" art, which not only denied any social function of art but also any categorizing by subject matter. (In poetry, Mallarmé was the first to take this position.)

An analysis of art in the age of mechanical reproduction must do justice to these relationships, for they lead us to an all-important insight: for the first time in world history, mechanical reproduction emancipates the work of art from its parasitical dependence on ritual. To an ever greater degree the work of art reproduced becomes the work of art designed for reproducibility. From a photographic negative, for example, one can make any number of prints; to ask for the "authentic" print makes no sense. But the instant the criterion of authenticity ceases to be applicable to artistic production, the total function of art is reversed. Instead of being based on ritual, it begins to be based on another practice—politics.

V

Works of art are received and valued on different planes. Two polar types stand out: with one, the accent is on the cult value; with the other, on the exhibition value of the work. Artistic production begins with ceremonial objects destined to serve in a cult. One may assume that what mattered was their existence, not their being on view. The elk portrayed by the man of the Stone Age on the walls of his cave was an instrument of magic. He did expose it to his fellow men, but in the main it was meant for the spirits. Today the cult value would seem to demand that the work of art remain hidden. Certain statues of gods are accessible only to the priest in the cella; certain Madonnas remain covered nearly all year round; certain sculptures on medieval cathedrals are invisible to the spectator on ground level. With the emancipation of the various art practices from ritual go increasing opportunities for the exhibition of their products. It is easier to exhibit a portrait bust that can be sent here and there than to exhibit the statue of a divinity that has its fixed place in the interior of a temple. The same holds for the painting as against the mosaic or fresco that preceded it. And even though the public presentability of a mass originally may have been just as great as that of a symphony, the latter originated at the moment when its public presentability promised to surpass that of the mass.

With the different methods of technical reproduction of a work of art, its fitness for exhibition increased to such an extent that the quantitative shift between its two poles turned into a qualitative transformation of its nature. This is comparable to the situation of the work of art in prehistoric times when, by the absolute emphasis on its cult value, it was, first and foremost, an instrument of magic. Only later did it come to be recognized as a work of art. In the same way today, by the absolute emphasis on its exhibition value the work of art becomes a creation with entirely new functions, among which the one we are conscious of, the artistic function, later may be recognized as incidental. This much is certain: today photography and the film are the most serviceable exemplifications of this new function.

VI

In photography, exhibition value begins to displace cult value all along the line. But cult value does not give way without resistance. It retires into an ultimate retrenchment: the human countenance. It is no accident that the portrait was the focal point of early photography. The cult of remembrance of loved ones, absent or dead, offers a last refuse for the cult value of the picture. For the last time the aura emanates from the early photographs in the fleeting expression of a human face. This is what constitutes their melancholy, incomparable beauty. But as man withdraws from the photographic image, the exhibition value for the first time shows its superiority to the ritual value. To have pinpointed this new stage constitutes the incomparable significance of Atget, who, around 1900, took photographs of deserted Paris streets. It has quite justly been said of him that he photographed them like scenes of crime. The scene of a crime, too, is deserted; it is photographed for the purpose of establishing evidence. With Atget, photographs become standard evidence for historical occurrences, and acquire a hidden political significance. They demand a specific kind of approach; free-floating contemplation is not appropriate to them. They stir the viewer; he feels challenged by them in a new way. At the same time picture magazines begin to put up signposts for him, right ones or wrong ones, no matter. For the first time, captions have become obligatory. And it is clear that they have an altogether different character than the title of a painting. The directives which the captions give to those looking at pictures in illustrated magazines soon become even more explicit and more imperative in the film where the meaning of each single picture appears to be prescribed by the sequence of all preceding ones.

VII

The nineteenth-century dispute as to the artistic value of painting versus photography today seems devious and confused. This does not diminish its importance, however; if anything, it underlines it. The dispute was in fact the symptom of a historical transformation the universal impact of which was not realized by either of the rivals. When the age of mechanical reproduction separated art from its basis in cult, the semblance of its autonomy disappeared forever. The resulting change in the function of art transcended the perspective of the century; for a long time it even escaped that of the twentieth century, which experienced the development of the film.

Earlier much futile thought had been devoted to the question of whether photography is an art. The primary question—whether the very invention of photography had not transformed the entire nature of art—was not raised. Soon the film theoreticians asked the same ill-considered question with regard to the film. But the difficulties which photography caused traditional aesthetics were mere child's play as compared to those raised by the film. Whence the insensitive and forced character of early theories of the film. Abel Gance, for instance, compares the film with hieroglyphs: "Here, by a remarkable regression, we have come back to the level of expression of the Egyptians. . . . Pictorial language has not yet matured because our eyes have not yet adjusted to it. There is as yet insufficient respect for, insufficient cult of, what it expresses." Or, in the words of Séverin-Mars: "What art has been granted a dream more poetical and more real at the same time! Approached in this fashion the film might represent an incomparable means of expression. Only the most high-minded persons, in the most perfect and mysterious moments of their lives, should be allowed to enter its ambience." Alexandre Arnoux concludes his fantasy about the silent film with the question: "Do not all the bold descriptions we have given amount to the definition of prayer?" It is instructive to note how their desire to class the film among the "arts" forces these theoreticians to read ritual elements into it—with a striking lack of discretion. Yet when these speculations were published, films like L'Opinion publique and The Gold Rush had already appeared. This, however, did not keep Abel Gance from adducing hieroglyphs for purposes of comparison, nor Séverin-Mars from speaking of the film as one might speak of paintings by Fra Angelico. Characteristically, even today ultrareactionary authors give the film a similar contextual significance—if not an outright sacred one, then at least a supernatural one. Commenting on Max Reinhardt's film version of *A Midsummer Night's Dream,* Werfel states that undoubtedly it was the sterile copying of the exterior world with its streets, interiors, railroad stations, restaurants, motorcars, and beaches which until now had obstructed the elevation of the film to the realm of art. "The film has not yet realized its true meaning, its real possibilities . . . these consist in its unique faculty to express by natural means and with incomparable persuasiveness all that is fairylike, marvelous, supernatural."

VIII

The artistic performance of a stage actor is definitely presented to the public by the actor in person; that of the screen actor, however, is presented by a camera, with a twofold consequence. The camera that presents the performance of the film actor to the public need not respect the performance as an integral whole. Guided by the cameraman, the camera continually changes its position with respect to the performance. The sequence of positional views which the editor composes from the material supplied him constitutes the completed film. It comprises certain factors of movement which are in reality those of the camera, not to mention special camera angles, close-ups, etc. Hence, the performance of the actor is subjected to a series of optical tests. This is the first consequence of the fact that the actor's performance is presented by means of a camera. Also, the film actor lacks the opportunity of the stage actor to adjust to the audience during his performance, since he does not present his performance to the audience in person. This permits the audience to take the position of a critic, without experiencing any personal contact with the actor. The audience's identification with the actor is really an identification with the camera. Consequently the audience takes the position of the camera; its approach is that of testing. This is not the approach to which cult values may be exposed.

IX

For the film, what matters primarily is that the actor represents himself to the public before the camera, rather than representing someone else. One of the first to sense the actor's metamorphosis by this form of testing was Pirandello. Though his remarks on the subject in his novel *Si Gira* were limited to the negative aspects of the question and to the silent film only, this hardly impairs their validity. For in this respect, the sound film did not change anything essential. What matters is that the part is acted not for an audience but for a mechanical contrivance—in the case of the sound film, for two of them. "The film actor," wrote Pirandello, "feels as if in exile—exiled not only from the stage but also from himself. With a vague sense of discomfort he feels inexplicable emptiness: his body loses its corporeality, it evaporates, it is deprived of reality, life, voice, and the noises caused by his moving about, in order to be changed into a mute image, flickering an instant on the screen, then vanishing into silence. . . . The projector will play with his shadow before the public, and he himself must be content to play before the camera." This situation might also be characterized as follows: for the first time—and this is the effect of the film—man has to operate with his whole living person, yet forgoing its aura. For aura is tied to his presence; there can be no replica of it. The aura which, on the stage, emanates from Macbeth, cannot be separated for the spectators from that of the actor. However, the singularity of the shot in the studio is that the camera is substituted for the public. Consequently, the aura that envelops the actor vanishes, and with it the aura of the figure he portrays.

It is not surprising that it should be a dramatist such as Pirandello who, in characterizing the film, inadvertently touches on the very crisis in which we see the theater. Any thorough study proves that there is indeed no greater contrast than that of the stage play to a work of art that is completely subject to or, like the film, founded in, mechanical reproduction. Experts have long recognized that in the film "the greatest effects are almost always obtained by 'acting' as little as possible. . . ." In 1932 Rudolf Arnheim saw "the latest trend . . . in treating the actor as a stage prop chosen for its characteristics and . . . inserted at the proper place." With this idea something else is closely connected. The stage actor identifies himself with the character of his role. The film actor very often is denied this opportunity. His creation is by no means all of a piece; it is composed of many separate performances. Besides certain fortuitous considerations, such as cost of studio, availability of fellow players, décor, etc., there are elementary necessities of equipment that split the actor's work into a series of mountable episodes. In particular, lighting and its installation require the presentation of an event that, on the screen, unfolds as a rapid and unified scene, in a sequence of separate shootings which may take hours at the studio; not to mention more obvious montage. Thus a jump from the window can be shot in the studio as a jump from a scaffold, and the ensuing flight, if need be, can be shot weeks later when outdoor scenes are taken. Far more paradoxical cases can easily be construed. Let us assume that an actor is supposed to be startled by a knock at the door. If his reaction is not satisfactory, the director can resort to an expedient: when the actor happens to be at the studio again he has a shot fired behind him without his being forewarned of it. The frightened reaction can be shot now and be cut into the screen version. Nothing more strikingly shows that art has left the realm of the "beautiful semblance" which, so far, had been taken to be the only sphere where art could thrive.

X

The feeling of strangeness that overcomes the actor before the camera, as Pirandello describes it, is basically of the same kind as the estrangement felt before one's own image in the mirror. But now the reflected image has become separable, transportable. And where is it transported? Before the public. Never for a moment does the screen actor cease to be conscious of this fact. While facing the camera he knows that ultimately he will face the public, the consumers who constitute the market. This market, where he offers not only his labor but also his whole self, his heart and soul, is beyond his reach. During the shooting he has as little contact with it as any article made in a factory. This may contribute to that oppression, that new anxiety which, according to Pirandello, grips the actor before the camera. The film responds to the shriveling of the aura with an artificial build-up of the "personality" outside the studio. The cult of the movie star, fostered by the money of the film industry, preserves not the unique aura of the person but the "spell of the personality," the phony spell of a commodity. So long as the movie-makers' capital sets the fashion, as a rule no other revolutionary merit can be accredited to today's film than the promotion of a revolutionary criticism of traditional concepts of art. We do not deny that in some cases today's films can also promote revolutionary criticism of social conditions, even of the distribution of property. However, our present study is no more specifically concerned with this than is the film production of Western Europe.

It is inherent in the technique of the film as well as that of sports that everybody who witnesses its accomplishments is somewhat of an expert. This is obvious to anyone listening to a group of newspaper boys leaning on their bicycles and discussing the outcome of a bicycle race. It is not for nothing that newspaper publishers arrange races for their delivery boys. These arouse great interest among the participants, for the victor has an opportunity to rise from delivery boy to professional racer. Similarly, the newsreel offers everyone the opportunity to rise from passerby to movie extra. In this way any man might even find himself part of a work of art, as witness Vertoff's *Three Songs About Lenin* or Iven's *Borinage*. Any man today can lay claim to being filmed. This claim can best be elucidated by a comparative look at the historical situation of contemporary literature.

For centuries a small number of writers were confronted by many thousands of readers. This changed toward the end of the last century. With the increasing extension of the press, which kept placing new political, religious, scientific, professional, and local organs before the readers, an increasing number of readers became writers—at first, occasional ones. It began with the daily press opening to its readers space for "letters to the editor." And today there is hardly a gainfully employed European who could not, in principle, find an opportunity to publish somewhere or other comments on his work, grievances, documentary reports, or that sort of thing. Thus, the distinction between author and public is about to lose its basic character. The difference becomes merely functional; it may vary from case to case. At any moment the reader is ready to turn into a writer. As expert, which he had to become willy-nilly in an extremely specialized work process, even if only in some minor respect, the reader gains access to authorship. In the Soviet Union work itself is given a voice. To present it verbally is part of a man's ability to perform the work. Literary license is now founded on polytechnic rather than specialized training and thus becomes common property.

All this can easily be applied to the film, where transitions that in literature took centuries have come about in a decade. In cinematic practice, particularly in Russia, this change-over has partially become established reality. Some of the players whom we meet in Russian films are not actors in our sense but people who portray *themselves*—and primarily in their own work process. In Western Europe the capitalistic exploitation of the film denies consideration to modern man's legitimate claim to being reproduced. Under these circumstances the film industry is trying hard to spur the interest of the masses through illusion-promoting spectacles and dubious speculations.

XI

The shooting of a film, especially of a sound film, affords a spectacle unimaginable anywhere at any time before this. It presents a process in which it is impossible to assign to a spectator a viewpoint which would exclude from the actual scene such extraneous accessories as camera equipment, lighting machinery, staff assistants, etc.—unless his eye were on a line parallel with the lens. This circumstance, more than any other, renders superficial and insignificant any possible similarity between a scene in the studio and one on the stage. In the theater one is well aware of the place from which the play cannot immediately be detected as illusionary. There is no such place for the movie scene that is being shot. Its illusionary nature is that of the second degree, the result of cutting. That is to say, in the studio the mechanical equipment has penetrated so deeply into reality that its pure aspect freed from the foreign substance of equipment is the result of a special procedure, namely, the shooting by the specially adjusted camera and the mounting of the shot together with other similar ones. The equipment-free aspect of reality here has become the height of artifice; the sight of immediate reality has become an orchid in the land of technology.

Even more revealing is the comparison of these circumstances, which differ so much from those of the theater, with the situation in painting. Here the question is: How does the cameraman compare with the painter? To answer this we take recourse to an analogy with a surgical operation. The surgeon represents the polar opposite of the magician. The magician heals a sick person by the laying on of hands; the surgeon cuts into the patient's body. The magician maintains the natural distance between the patient and himself; though he reduces it very slightly by the laying on of hands, he greatly increases it by virtue of his authority. The surgeon does exactly the reverse; he greatly diminishes the distance between himself and the patient by penetrating into the patient's body, and increases it but little by the caution with which his hand moves among the organs. In short, in contrast to the magician—who is still hidden in the medical practitioner—the surgeon at the decisive moment abstains from facing the patient man to man; rather, it is through the operation that he penetrates into him.

Magician and surgeon compare to painter and cameraman. The painter maintains in his work a natural distance from reality, the cameraman penetrates deeply into its web. There is a tremendous difference between the pictures they obtain. That of the painter is a total one, that of the cameraman consists of multiple fragments which are assembled under a new law. Thus, for contemporary man the representation of reality by the film is incomparably more significant than that of the painter, since it offers, precisely because of the thoroughgoing permeation of reality with mechanical equipment, an aspect of reality which is free of all equipment. And that is what one is entitled to ask from a work of art.

XII

Mechanical reproduction of art changes the reaction of the masses toward art. The reactionary attitude toward a Picasso painting changes into the progressive reaction toward a Chaplin movie. The progressive reaction is characterized by the direct, intimate fusion of visual and emotional enjoyment with the orientation of the expert. Such fusion is of great social significance. The greater the decrease in the social significance of an art form, the sharper the distinction between criticism and enjoyment by the public. The conventional is uncritically enjoyed, and the truly new is criticized with aversion. With regard to the screen, the critical and the receptive attitudes of the public coincide. The decisive reason for this is that individual reactions are predetermined by the mass audience response they are about to produce, and this is nowhere more pronounced than in the film. The moment these responses become manifest they control each other. Again, the comparison with painting is fruitful. A painting has always had an excellent chance to be viewed by one person or by a few. The simultaneous contemplation of paintings by a large public, such as developed in the nineteenth century, is an early symptom of the crisis of painting, a crisis which was by no means occasioned exclusively by photography but rather in a relatively independent manner by the appeal of art works to the masses.

Painting simply is in no position to present an object for simultaneous collective experience, as it was possible for architecture at all times, for the epic poem in the past, and for the movie today. Although this circumstance in itself should not lead one to conclusions about the social role of painting, it does constitute a serious threat as soon as painting, under special conditions and, as it were, against its nature, is confronted directly by the masses. In the churches and monasteries of the Middle Ages and at the princely courts up to the end of the eighteenth century, a collective reception of paintings did not occur simultaneously, but by graduated and hierarchized mediation. The change that has come about is an expression of the particular conflict in which painting was implicated by the mechanical reproducibility of paintings. Although paintings began to be publicly exhibited in galleries and salons, there was no way for the masses to organize and control themselves in their reception. Thus the same public which responds in a progressive manner toward a grotesque film is bound to respond in a reactionary manner to surrealism.

XIII

The characteristics of the film lie not only in the manner in which man presents himself to mechanical equipment but also in the manner in which, by means of this apparatus, man can represent his environment. A glance at occupational psychology illustrates the testing capacity of the equipment. Psychoanalysis illustrates it in a different perspective. The film has enriched our field of perception with methods which can be illustrated by those of Freudian theory. Fifty years ago, a slip of the tongue passed more or less unnoticed. Only exceptionally may such a slip have revealed dimensions of depth in a conversation which had seemed to be taking its course on the surface. Since the *Psychopathology of Everyday Life* things have changed. This book isolated and made analyzable things which had heretofore floated along unnoticed in the broad stream of perception. For the entire spectrum of optical, and now also acoustical, perception the film has brought about a similar deepening of apperception. It is only an obverse of this fact that behavior items shown in a movie can be analyzed much more precisely and from more points of view than those presented on paintings or on the stage. As compared with painting, filmed behavior lends itself more readily to analysis because of its incomparably more precise statements of the situation. In comparison with the stage scene, the filmed behavior item lends itself more readily to analysis because it can be isolated more easily. This circumstance derives its chief importance from its tendency to promote the mutual penetration of art and science. Actually, of a screened behavior item which is neatly brought out in a certain situation, like a muscle of a body, it is difficult to say which is more fascinating, its artistic value or its value for science To demonstrate the identity of the artistic and scientific uses of photography which heretofore usually were separated will be one of the revolutionary functions of the film.

By close-ups of the things around us, by focusing on hidden details of familiar objects, by exploring common place milieus under the ingenious guidance of the camera, the film, on the one hand, extends our comprehension of the necessities which rule our lives; on the other hand, it manages to assure us of an immense and unexpected field of action. Our taverns and our metropolitan streets, our offices and furnished rooms, our railroad stations and our factories appeared to have us locked up hopelessly. Then came the film and burst this prison-world asunder by the dynamite of the tenth of a second, so that now, in the midst of its far-flung ruins and debris, we calmly and adventurously go traveling. With the close-up, space expands; with slow motion, movement is extended. The enlargement of a snapshot does not simply render more precise what in any case was visible, though unclear: it reveals entirely new structural formations of the subject. So, too, slow motion not only presents familiar qualities of movement but reveals in them entirely unknown ones "which, far from looking like retarded rapid movements, give the effect of singularly gliding, floating, supernatural motions." Evidently a different nature opens itself to the camera than opens to the naked eye—if only because an unconsciously penetrated space is substituted for a space consciously explored by man. Even if one has a general knowledge of the way people walk, one knows nothing of a person's posture during the fractional second of a stride. The act of reaching for a lighter or a spoon is familiar routine, yet we hardly know what really goes on between hand and metal, not to mention how this fluctuates with our moods. Here the camera intervenes with the resources of its lowerings and liftings, its interruptions and isolations, it extensions and accelerations, its enlargements and reductions. The camera introduces us to unconscious optics as does psychoanalysis to unconscious impulses.

XIV

One of the foremost tasks of art has always been the creation of a demand which could be fully satisfied only later. The history of every art form shows critical epochs in which a certain art form aspires to effects which could be fully obtained only with a changed technical standard, that is to say, in a new art form. The extravagances and crudities of art which thus appear, particularly in the so-called decadent epochs, actually arise from the nucleus of its richest historical energies. In recent years, such barbarisms were abundant in Dadaism. It is only now that its impulse becomes discernible: Dadaism attempted to create by pictorial—and literary—means the effects which the public today seeks in the film.

Every fundamentally new, pioneering creation of demands will carry beyond its goal. Dadaism did so to the extent that it sacrificed the market values which are so characteristic of the film in favor of higher ambitions—though of course it was not conscious of such intentions as here described. The Dadaists attached much less importance to the sales value of their work than to its usefulness for contemplative immersion. The studied degradation of their material was not the least of their means to achieve this uselessness. Their poems are "word salad" containing obscenities and every imaginable waste product of language. The same is true of their paintings, on which they mounted buttons and tickets. What they intended and achieved was a relentless destruction of the aura of their creations, which they branded as reproductions with the very means of production. Before a painting of Arp's or a poem by August Stramm it is impossible to take time for contemplation and evaluation as one would before a canvas of Derain's or a poem by Rilke. In the decline of middle-class society, contemplation became a school for asocial behavior; it was countered by distraction as a variant of social conduct. Dadaistic activities actually assured a rather vehement distraction by making works of art the center of scandal. One requirement was foremost: to outrage the public.

From an alluring appearance or persuasive structure of sound the work of art of the Dadaists became an instrument of ballistics. It hit the spectator like a bullet, it happened to him, thus acquiring a tactile quality. It promoted a demand for the film, the distracting element of which is also primarily tactile, being based on changes of place and focus which periodically assail the spectator. Let us compare the screen on which a film unfolds with the canvas of a painting. The painting invites the spectator to contemplation; before it the spectator can abandon himself to his associations. Before the movie frame he cannot do so. No sooner has his eye grasped a scene than it is already changed. It cannot be arrested. Duhamel, who detests the film and knows nothing of its significance, though something of its structure, notes this circumstance as follows: "I can no longer think what I want to think. My thoughts have been replaced by moving images." The spectator's process of association in view of these images is indeed interrupted by their constant, sudden change. This constitutes the shock effect of the film, which, like all shocks, should be cushioned by heightened presence of mind. By means of its technical structure, the film has taken the physical shock effect out of the wrappers in which Dadaism had, as it were, kept it inside the moral shock effect.

xv

The mass is a matrix from which all traditional behavior toward works of art issues today in a new form. Quantity has been transmuted into quality. The greatly increased mass of participants has produced a change in the mode of participation. The fact that the new mode of participation first appeared in a disreputable form must not confuse the spectator. Yet some people have launched spirited attacks against precisely this superficial aspect. Among these, Duhamel has expressed himself in the most radical manner. What he objects to most is the kind of participation which the movie elicits from the masses. Duhamel calls the movie "a pastime for helots, a diversion for uneducated, wretched, worn-out creatures who are consumed by their worries . . . , a spectacle which requires no concentration and presupposes no intelligence . . . , which kindles no light in the heart and awakens no hope other than the ridiculous one of someday becoming a 'star' in Los Angeles." Clearly, this is at bottom the same ancient lament that the masses seek distraction whereas art demands concentration from the spectator. That is a commonplace.

The question remains whether it provides a platform for the analysis of the film. A closer look is needed here. Distraction and concentration form polar opposites which may be stated as follows: A man who concentrates before a work of art is absorbed by it. He enters into this work of art the way legend tells of the Chinese painter when he viewed his finished painting. In contrast, the distracted mass absorbs the work of art. This is most obvious with regard to buildings. Architecture has always represented the prototype of a work of art the reception of which is consummated by a collectivity in a state of distraction. The laws of its reception are most instructive.

Buildings have been man's companions since primeval times. Many art forms have developed and perished. Tragedy begins with the Greeks, is extinguished with them, and after centuries its "rules" only are revived. The epic poem, which had its origin in the youth of nations, expires in Europe at the end of the Renaissance. Panel painting is a creation of the Middle Ages, and nothing guarantees its uninterrupted existence. But the human need for shelter is lasting. Architecture has never been idle. Its history is more ancient than that of any other art, and its claim to being a living force has significance in every attempt to comprehend the relationship of the masses to art. Buildings are appropriated in a twofold manner: by use and by perception—or rather, by touch and sight. Such appropriation cannot be understood in terms of the attentive concentration of a tourist before a famous building. On the tactile side there is no counterpart to contemplation on the optical side. Tactile appropriation is accomplished not so much by attention as by habit. As regards architecture, habit determines to a large extent even optical reception. The latter, too, occurs much less through rapt attention than by noticing the object in incidental fashion. This mode of appropriation, developed with reference to architecture, in certain circumstances acquires canonical value. For the tasks which face the human apparatus of perception at the turning points of history cannot be solved by optical means, that is, by contemplation, alone. They are mastered gradually by habit, under the guidance of tactile appropriation.

The distracted person, too, can form habits. More, the ability to master certain tasks in a state of distraction proves that their solution has become a matter of habit. Distraction as provided by art presents a covert control of the extent to which new tasks have become soluble by apperception. Since, moreover, individuals are tempted to avoid such tasks, art will tackle the most difficult and most important ones where it is able to mobilize the masses. Today it does so in the film. Reception in a state of distraction, which is increasing noticeably in all fields of art and is symptomatic of profound changes in apperception, finds in the film its true means of exercise. The film with its shock effect meets this mode of reception halfway. The film makes the cult value recede into the background not only by putting the public in the position of the critic, but also by the fact that at the movies this position requires no attention. The public is an examiner, but an absent-minded one.

EPILOGUE

The growing proletarianization of modern man and the increasing formation of masses are two aspects of the same process. Fascism attempts to organize the newly created proletarian masses without affecting the property structure which the masses strive to eliminate. Fascism sees its salvation in giving these masses not their right, but instead a chance to express themselves. The masses have a right to change property relations; Fascism seeks to give them an expression while preserving property. The logical result of Fascism is the introduction of aesthetics into political life. The violation of the masses, whom Fascism, with its *Führer* cult, forces to their knees, has its counterpart in the violation of an apparatus which is pressed into the production of ritual values.

All efforts to render politics aesthetic culminate in one thing: war. War and war only can set a goal for mass movements on the largest scale while respecting the traditional property system. This is the political formula for the situation. The technological formula may be stated as follows: Only war makes it possible to mobilize all of today's technical resources while maintaining the property system. It goes without saying that the Fascist apotheosis of war does not employ such arguments. Still, Marinetti says in his manifesto on the Ethiopian colonial war: "For twenty-seven years we Futurists have rebelled against the branding of war as antiaesthetic. . . . Accordingly we state: . . . War is beautiful because it establishes man's dominion over the subjugated machinery by means of gas masks, terrifying megaphones, flame throwers, and small tanks. War is beautiful because it initiates the dreamt-of metalization of the human body. War is beautiful because it enriches a flowering meadow with the fiery orchids of machine guns. War is beautiful because it combines the gunfire, the cannonades, the cease-fire, the scents, and the stench of putrefaction into a symphony. War is beautiful because it creates new architecture, like that of the big tanks, the geometrical formation flights, the smoke spirals from burning villages, and many others. . . . Poets and artists of Futurism! . . . remember these principles of an aesthetics of war so that your struggle for a new literature and a new graphic art . . . may be illumined by them!"

This manifesto has the virtue of clarity. Its formulations deserve to be accepted by dialecticians. To the latter, the aesthetics of today's war appears as follows: If the natural utilization of productive forces is impeded by the property system, the increase in technical devices, in speed, and in the sources of energy will press for an unnatural utilization, and this is found in war. The destructiveness of war furnishes proof that society has not been mature enough to incorporate technology as its organ, that technology has not been sufficiently developed to cope with the elemental forces of society. The horrible features of imperialistic warfare are attributable to the discrepancy between the tremendous means of production and their inadequate utilization in the process of production—in other words, to unemployment and the lack of markets. Imperialistic war is a rebellion of technology which collects, in the form of "human material," the claims to which society has denied its natural material. Instead of draining rivers, society directs a human stream into a bed of trenches; instead of dropping seeds from airplanes, it drops incendiary bombs over cities; and through gas warfare the aura is abolished in a new way.

"Fiat ars—pereat mundus," says Fascism, and, as Marinetti admits, expects war to supply the artistic gratification of a sense perception that has been changed by technology. This is evidently the consummation of *"l'art pour l'art."* Mankind,

which in Homer's time was an object of contemplation for the Olympian gods, now is one for itself. Its self-alienation has reached such a degree that it can experience its own destruction as an aesthetic pleasure of the first order. This is the situation of politics which Fascism is rendering aesthetic. Communism responds by politicizing art.

1935

JEAN-LUC COMOLLI AND JEAN NARBONI
CINEMA/IDEOLOGY/CRITICISM

Scientific criticism has an obligation to define its field and methods. This implies awareness of its own historical and social situation, a rigorous analysis of the proposed field of study, the conditions which make the work necessary and those which make it possible, and the special function it intends to fulfill.

It is essential that we at *Cahiers du Cinéma* should now undertake just such a global analysis of our position and aims. Not that we are starting entirely from zero. Fragments of such an analysis have been coming out of material we have published recently (articles, editorials, debates, answers to readers' letters) but in an imprecise form and as if by accident. They are an indication that our readers, just as much as we ourselves, feel the need for a clear theoretical base to which to relate our critical practice and its field, taking the two to be indivisible. 'Programmes' and 'revolutionary' plans and declarations tend to become an end in themselves. This is a trap we intend to avoid. Our objective is not to reflect upon what we 'want' (would like) to do, but upon what we *are* doing and what we *can* do, and this is impossible without an analysis of the present situation.

WHERE?

(a) First, our situation. *Cahiers* is a group of people working together; one of the results of our work appearing as a magazine.* A magazine, that is to say, a particular product, involving a particular amount of work (on the part of those who write it, those who produce it and, indeed, those who read it). We do not close our eyes to the fact that a product of this nature is situated fairly and squarely inside the economic system of capitalist publishing (modes of production, spheres of circulation, etc.). In any case it is difficult to see how it could be otherwise today, unless one is

---

*Others include distribution, screening, and discussion of films in the provinces and the suburbs, sessions of theoretical work.

led astray by Utopian ideas of working 'parallel' to the system. The first step in the latter approach is always the paradoxical one of setting up a false front, a 'neo-system' alongside the system from which one is attempting to escape, in the fond belief that it will be able to negate the system. In fact all it can do is reject it (idealist purism) and consequently it is very soon jeopardized by the enemy upon which it modelled itself.[1] This 'parallelism' works from one direction only. It touches only one side of the wound, whereas we believe that both sides have to be worked upon. And the danger of the parallels meeting all too speedily in infinity seems to us sufficient to argue that we had better stay in the finite and allow them to remain apart.

This assumed, the question is: what is our attitude to our situation? In France the majority of films, like the majority of books and magazines, are produced and distributed by the capitalist economic system and within the dominant ideology. Indeed, strictly speaking all are, whatever expedient they adopt to try and get around it. This being so, the question we have to ask is: which films, books, and magazines allow the ideology a free, unhampered passage, transmit it with crystal clarity, serve as its chosen language? And which attempt to make it turn back and reflect itself, intercept it, make it visible by revealing its mechanisms, by blocking them?

(b) For the situation in which we are *acting* is the field of cinema (*Cahiers* is a film magazine),[2] and the precise object of our study is the history of a film: how it is produced, manufactured, distributed,[3] understood.

What is the film today? This is the relevant question; not, as it possibly once was: what is the cinema? We shall not be able to ask that again until a body of knowledge, of theory, has been evolved (a process to which we certainly intend to contribute) to inform what is at present an empty term, with a concept. For a film magazine the question is also: what work is to be done in the field constituted by films? And for *Cahiers* in particular: what is our specific function in this field? What is to distinguish us from other 'film magazines'?

THE FILMS

What is a film? On the one hand it is a particular product, manufactured within a given system of economic relations, and involving labour (which appears to the capitalist as money) to produce—a condition to which even 'independent' film-makers and the 'new cinema' are subject—assembling a certain number of workers for this purpose (even the director, whether he is Moullet or Oury, is in the last

---

[1] Or tolerated, and jeopardized by this very toleration. Is there any need to stress that it is the tried tactic of covertly repressive systems not to harass the protesting fringe? They go out of their way to take no notice of them, with the double effect of making one half of the opposition careful not to try their patience too far and the other half complacent in the knowledge that their activities are unobserved.

[2] We do not intend to suggest by this that we want to erect a corporatist fence round our own field, and neglect the infinitely larger field where so much is obviously at stake politically. Simply, we are concentrating on that precise point of the spectrum of social activity in this article, in response to precise operational needs.

[3] A more and more pressing problem. It would be inviting confusion to allow it to be tackled in bits and pieces and obviously we have to make a unified attempt to pose it theoretically later on. For the moment we leave it aside.

analysis only a film worker). It becomes transformed into a commodity, possessing exchange value, which is realized by the sale of tickets and contracts, and governed by the laws of the market. On the other hand, as a result of being a material product of the system, it is also an ideological product of the system, which in France means capitalism.*

No filmmaker can, by his own individual efforts, change the economic relations governing the manufacture and distribution of his films. (It cannot be pointed out too often that even filmmakers who set out to be 'revolutionary' on the level of message and form cannot effect any swift or radical change in the economic system—deform it, yes, deflect it, but not negate it or seriously upset its structure. Godard's recent statement to the effect that he wants to stop working in the 'system' takes no account of the fact that any other system is bound to be a reflection of the one he wishes to avoid. The money no longer comes from the Champs-Elysées but from London, Rome, or New York. The film may not be marketed by the distribution monopolies but it is shot on film stock from another monopoly—Kodak.) Because every film is part of the economic system it is also a part of the ideological system, for 'cinema' and 'art' are branches of ideology. None can escape, somewhere, like pieces in a jigsaw, all have their own allotted place. The system is blind to its own nature, but in spite of that, indeed because of that, when all the pieces are fitted together they give a very clear picture. But this does not mean that every filmmaker plays a similar role. Reactions differ.

It is the job of criticism to see where they differ, and slowly, patiently, not expecting any magical transformations to take place at the wave of a slogan, to help change the ideology which conditions them.

A few points, which we shall return to in greater detail later: *every film is political,* inasmuch as it is determined by the ideology which produces it (or within which it is produced, which stems from the same thing). The cinema is all the more thoroughly and completely determined because unlike other arts or ideological systems its very manufacture mobilizes powerful economic forces in a way that the production of literature (which becomes the commodity 'books', does not—though once we reach the level of distribution, publicity, and sale, the two are in rather the same position).

Clearly, the cinema 'reproduces' reality: this is what a camera and film stock are

---

*Capitalist ideology. This term expresses our meaning perfectly, but as we are going to use it without further definition in this article, we should point out that we are not under any illusion that it has some kind of 'abstract essence'. We know that it is historically and socially determined, and that it has multiple forms at any given place and time, and varies from historical period to historical period. Like the whole category of 'militant' cinema, which is totally vague and undefined at present. We must (a) rigorously define the function attributed to it, its aims, its side effects (information, arousal, critical reflection, provocation 'which always has *some* effect' . . .); (b) define the exact political line governing the making and screening of these films—'revolutionary' is too much of a blanket term to serve any useful purpose here; and (c) state whether the supporters of militant cinema are in fact proposing a line of action in which the cinema would become the poor relation, in the illusion that the less the cinematic aspect is worked on, the greater the strength and clarity of the 'militant' effect will be. This would be a way of avoiding the contradictions of 'parallel' cinema and getting embroiled in the problem of deciding whether 'underground' films should be included in the category, on the pretext that their relationship to drugs and sex, their preoccupation with form, might possibly establish new relationships between film and audience.

for—so says the ideology. But the tools and techniques of filmmaking are a part of 'reality' themselves, and furthermore 'reality' is nothing but an expression of the prevailing ideology. Seen in this light, the classic theory of cinema that the camera is an impartial instrument which grasps, or rather is impregnated by, the world in its 'concrete reality' is an eminently reactionary one. What the camera in fact registers is the vague, unformulated, untheorized, unthought-out world of the dominant ideology. Cinema is one of the languages through which the world communicates itself to itself. They constitute its ideology for they reproduce the world as it is experienced when filtered through the ideology. (As Althusser defines it, more precisely: 'Ideologies are perceived-accepted-suffered cultural objects, which work fundamentally on men by a process they do not understand. What men express in their ideologies is not their true relation to their conditions of existence, but how they react to their conditions of existence; which presupposes a real relationship and an imaginary relationship.') So, when we set out to make a film, from the very first shot, we are encumbered by the necessity of reproducing things not as they really are but as they appear when refracted through the ideology. This includes every stage in the process of production: subjects, 'styles', forms, meanings, narrative traditions; all underline the general ideological discourse. The film is ideology presenting itself to itself, talking to itself, learning about itself. Once we realize that it is the nature of the system to turn the cinema into an instrument of ideology, we can see that the filmmaker's first task is to show up the cinema's so-called 'depiction of reality'. If he can do so there is a chance that we will be able to disrupt or possibly even sever the connection between the cinema and its ideological function.

The vital distinction between films today is whether they do this or whether they do not.

a. The first and largest category comprises those films which are imbued through and through with the dominant ideology in pure and unadulterated form, and give no indication that their makers were even aware of the fact. We are not just talking about so-called 'commercial' films. The *majority* of films in all categories are the unconscious instruments of the ideology which produces them. Whether the film is 'commercial' or 'ambitious', 'modern' or 'traditional', whether it is the type that gets shown in art houses, or in smart cinemas, whether it belongs to the 'old' cinema or the 'young' cinema, it is most likely to be a re-hash of the same old ideology. For all films are commodities and therefore objects of trade, even those whose discourse is explicitly political—which is why a rigorous definition of what constitutes 'political' cinema is called for at this moment when it is being widely promoted. This merging of ideology and film is reflected in the first instance by the fact that audience demand and economic response have also been reduced to one and the same thing. In direct continuity with political practice, ideological practice reformulates the social need and backs it up with a discourse. This is not a hypothesis, but a scientifically established fact. The ideology is talking to itself; it has all the answers ready before it asks the questions. Certainly there is such a thing as public demand, but 'what the public wants' means 'what the dominant ideology wants'. The notion of a public and its tastes was created by the ideology to justify and perpetuate itself. And this public can only express itself via the thought-patterns of the ideology. The whole thing is a closed circuit, endlessly repeating the same illusion.

The situation is the same at the level of artistic form. These films totally accept the established system of depicting reality: 'bourgeois realism' and the whole conservative box of tricks: blind faith in 'life', 'humanism', 'common sense', etc. A blissful ignorance that there might be something wrong with this whole concept of 'depiction' appears to have reigned at every stage in their production, so much so, that to us it appears a more accurate gauge of pictures in the 'commercial' category than box-office returns. Nothing in these films jars against the ideology or the audience's mystification by it. They are very reassuring for audiences for there is no difference between the ideology they meet every day and the ideology on the screen. It would be a useful complementary task for film critics to look into the way the ideological system and its products merge at all levels: to study the phenomenon whereby a film being shown to an audience becomes a monologue, in which the ideology talks to itself, by examining the success of films by, for instance, Melville, Oury, and Lelouch.

(b) A second category is that of films which attack their ideological assimilation on two fronts. Firstly, by direct political action, on the level of the 'signified', that is, they deal with a directly political subject. 'Deal with' is here intended in an active sense: they do not just discuss an issue, reiterate it, paraphrase it, but use it to attack the ideology (this presupposes a theoretical activity which is the direct opposite of the ideological one). This act only becomes politically effective if it is linked with a breaking down of the traditional way of depicting reality. On the level of form, *Unreconciled, The Edge* and *Earth in Revolt* all challenge the concept of 'depiction' and mark a break with the tradition embodying it.

We would stress that only action on both fronts, 'signified' and 'signifiers'[1] has any hope of operating against the prevailing ideology. Economic/political and formal action have to be indissolubly wedded.

(c) There is another category in which the same double action operates, but 'against the grain'. The content is not explicitly political, but in some way becomes so through the criticism practised on it through its form.[2] To this category belong

---

[1] We are not shutting our eyes to the fact that it is an oversimplification (employed here because operationally easier) to make such a sharp distinction between the two terms. This is particularly so in the case of the cinema, where the signified is more often than not a product of the permutations of the signifiers, and the sign has dominance over the meaning.

[2] This is not a magical doorway out of the system of 'depiction' (which is particularly dominant in the cinema) but rather a rigorous, detailed, large-scale work on this system—what conditions make it possible, what mechanisms render it innocuous. The method is to draw attention to the system so that it can be seen for what it is, to make it serve one's own ends, condemn itself out of its own mouth. Tactics employed may include 'turning cinematic syntax upside-down' but it cannot be just that. Any old film nowadays can upset the normal chronological order in the interests of looking vaguely 'modern'. But *The Exterminating Angel* and *The Diary of Anna Magdalena Bach* (though we would not wish to set them up as a model) are rigorously chronological without ceasing to be subversive in the way we have been describing, whereas in many a film the mixed-up time sequence simply covers up a basically naturalistic conception. In the same way, perceptual confusion (avowed intent to act on the unconscious mind, changes in the texture of the film, etc.) are not sufficient in themselves to get beyond the traditional way of depicting 'reality'. To realize this, one has only to remember the unsuccessful attempts there have been of the 'lettriste' or 'zacum' type to give back its infinity to language by using nonsense words or new kinds of onomatopoeia. In the one and the other case only the most superficial level of language is touched. They create a new code, which operates on the level of the impossible, and has to be rejected on any other, and is therefore not in a position to transgress the normal.

Méditerranée, The Bellboy, Persona. . . . For *Cahiers* these films (b and c) constitute the essential in the cinema, and should be the chief subject of the magazine.

(d) Fourth case: those films, increasingly numerous today, which have an explicitly political content (*Z* is not the best example as its presentation of politics is unremittingly ideological from first to last; a better example would be *Le Temps de Vivre*) but which do not effectively criticize the ideological system in which they are embedded because they unquestioningly adopt its language and its imagery.

This makes it important for critics to examine the effectiveness of the political criticism intended by these films. Do they express, reinforce, strengthen the very thing they set out to denounce? Are they caught in the system they wish to break down . . .? (see a)

(e) Five: films which seem at first sight to belong firmly within the ideology and to be completely under its sway, but which turn out to be so only in an ambiguous manner. For though they start from a nonprogressive standpoint, ranging from the frankly reactionary through the conciliatory to the mildly critical, they have been worked upon, and work, in such a real way that there is a noticeable gap, a dislocation, between the starting point and the finished product. We disregard here the inconsistent—and unimportant—sector of films in which the director makes a *conscious* use of the prevailing ideology, but leaves it absolutely straight. The films we are talking about throw up obstacles in the way of the ideology, causing it to swerve and get off course. The cinematic framework lets us see it, but also shows it up and denounces it. Looking at the framework one can see two moments in it: one holding it back within certain limits, one transgressing them. An internal criticism is taking place which cracks the film apart at the seams. If one reads the film obliquely, looking for symptoms; if one looks beyond its apparent formal coherence, one can see that it is riddled with cracks: it is splitting under an internal tension which is simply not there in an ideologically innocuous film. The ideology thus becomes subordinate to the text. It no longer has an independent existence: It is *presented* by the film. This is the case in many Hollywood films, for example, which while being completely integrated in the system and the ideology end up by partially dismantling the system from within. We must find out what makes it possible for a filmmaker to corrode the ideology by restating it in the terms of his film: if he sees his film simply as a blow in favour of liberalism, it will be recuperated instantly by the ideology; if on the other hand, he conceives and realizes it on the deeper level of imagery, there is a chance that it will turn out to be more disruptive. Not, of course, that he will be able to break the ideology itself, but simply its reflection in his film. (The films of Ford, Dreyer, Rossellini, for example.)

Our position with regard to this category of films is: that we have absolutely no intention of joining the current witch-hunt against them. They are the mythology of their own myths. They criticize themselves, even if no such intention is written into the script, and it is irrelevant and impertinent to do so for them. All we want to do is to show the process in action.

(f) Films of the 'live cinema' *(cinéma direct)* variety, group one (the larger of the two groups). These are films arising out of political (or, it would probably be more exact to say: social) events or reflections, but which make no clear differentiation between themselves and the nonpolitical cinema because they do not challenge the cinema's traditional, ideologically conditioned method of 'depiction'. For instance a miner's strike will be filmed in the same style as *Les Grandes Familles*. The makers of these films suffer under the primary and fundamental illusion that if they once break off the ideological filter of narrative traditions (dramaturgy, construction, domination of the component parts by a central idea, emphasis on formal beauty) reality will then yield itself up in its true form. The fact is that by doing so they only break off one filter, and not the most important one at that. For reality holds within itself no hidden kernel of self-understanding, of theory, of truth, like a stone inside a fruit. We have to manufacture those. (Marxism is very clear on this point, in its distinction between 'real' and 'perceived' objects.) Compare *Chiefs* (Leacock) and a good number of the May films.

This is why supporters of *cinéma direct* resort to the same idealist terminology to express its role and justify its successes as others use about products of the greatest artifice: 'accuracy', 'a sense of lived experience', 'flashes of intense truth', 'moments caught live', 'abolition of all sense that we are watching a film' and finally: fascination. It is that magical notion of 'seeing is understanding': ideology goes on display to prevent itself from being shown up for what it really is, contemplates itself but does not criticize itself.

(g) The other kind of 'live cinema'. Here the director is not satisfied with the idea of the camera 'seeing through appearances', but attacks the basic problem of depiction by giving an active role to the concrete stuff of his film. It then becomes productive of meaning and is not just a passive receptacle for meaning produced outside it (in the ideology): *La Règne du Jour, La Rentrée des Usines Wonder*.

CRITICAL FUNCTION

Such, then, is the field of our critical activity: these films, within the ideology, and their different relations to it. From this precisely defined field spring four functions: (1) in the case of the films in category (a): show what they are blind to; how they are totally determined, moulded, by the ideology; (2) in the case of those in categories (b), (c) and (g), read them on two levels, showing how the films operate critically on the level of signified and signifiers; (3) in the case of those of types (d) and (f), show how the signified (political subject matter) is always weakened, rendered harmless, by the absence of technical/theoretical work on the signifiers; (4) in the case of those in group (e) point out the gap produced between film and ideology by the way the films work, and show how they work.

There can be no room in our critical practice either for speculation (commentary, interpretation, de-coding even) or for specious raving (of the film-columnist variety). It must be a rigidly factual analysis of what governs the production of a film (economic circumstances, ideology, demand, and response) and the meanings and forms appearing in it, which are equally tangible.

The tradition of frivolous and evanescent writing on the cinema is as tenacious as it is prolific, and film analysis today is still massively predetermined by idealistic presuppositions. It wanders farther abroad today, but its method is still basically empirical. It has been through a necessary stage of going back to the material elements of a film, its signifying structures, its formal organization. The first steps here were undeniably taken by André Bazin, despite the contradictions that can be picked out in his articles. Then followed the approach based on structural linguistics (in which there are two basic traps, which we fell into—phenomenological positivism and mechanistic materialism). As surely as criticism had to go through this stage, it has to go beyond. To us, the only possible line of advance seems to be to use the theoretical writing of the Russian filmmakers of the twenties (Eisenstein above all) to elaborate and apply a critical theory of the cinema, a specific method of apprehending rigorously defined objects, in direct reference to the method of dialectical materialism.

It is hardly necessary to point out that we know that the 'policy' of a magazine cannot—indeed, should not—be corrected by magic overnight. We have to do it patiently, month by month, being careful in our own field to avoid the general error of putting faith in spontaneous change, or attempting to rush into a 'revolution' without the preparation to support it. To start proclaiming at this stage that the truth has been revealed to us would be like talking about 'miracles' or 'conversion'. All we should do is to state what work is already in progress and publish articles which relate to it, either explicitly or implicitly.

We should indicate briefly how the various elements in the magazine fit into this perspective. The essential part of the work obviously takes place in the theoretical articles and the criticisms. There is coming to be less and less of a difference between the two, because it is not our concern to add up the merits and defects of current films in the interests of topicality, nor, as one humorous article put it 'to crack up the product'. The interviews, on the other hand, and also the 'diary' columns and the list of films, with the dossiers and supplementary material for possible discussion later, are often stronger on information than theory. It is up to the reader to decide whether these pieces take up any critical stance, and if so, what.

1969

JEAN-LOUIS BAUDRY
THE APPARATUS:
METAPSYCHOLOGICAL
APPROACHES TO THE
IMPRESSION OF REALITY IN THE
CINEMA

One constantly returns to the scene of the cave: real effect or impression of reality. Copy, simulacrum, and even simulacrum of simulacrum. Impression of the real, more-than-the-real? From Plato to Freud, the perspective is reversed; the procedure is inverted—so it seems. The former comes out of the cave, examines what is intelligible, contemplates its source, and, when he goes back, it is to denounce to the prisoners the apparatus which oppresses them, and to persuade them to leave, to get out of that dim space. The latter (on the contrary—no, for it is not a matter of simple opposition, or of a simplifying symmetry) is more interested in making them go back there precisely where they are; where they didn't know how to find themselves, for they thought themselves outside, and it is true they had been contemplating the good, the true, and the beautiful for a long time. But at what price and as a result of what ignorance; failure to recognize or repress, compromise, defense, sublimation? Like Plato, he urges them to consider the apparatus to overcome their resistances, to look a little more closely at what is coming into focus on the screen, the other scene. The other scene? What brings the two together and separates them? For both, as in the theater, a left side, a right side, the master's lodge, the valet's orchestra. But the first scene would seem to be the second's other scene. It is a question of truth in the final analysis, or else: "the failure to recognize has moved to the other side." Both distinguish between two scenes, or two places, opposing or confronting one another, one dominating the other. These aren't the same places; they don't respond point by point, although, in many respects, we who come after Freud would not be unjustified in superimposing more or less grossly the solar scene where the philosopher is at first dazzled, blinded by the good, on the scene of the conscious and its well-meaning exploits—we who, as a result of this very discovery of the unconscious, or of the other scene, could be induced to interpret the move, the exit, ascension, an initial blinding of the philosopher in a totally different manner. "Suppose one of them were set free and forced suddenly to stand up, turn his head, and walk with eyes lifted to the light; all these movements would be painful, and he would be too dazzled to make out the objects. . . . And if he were forced to look at the firelight itself, would not his eyes ache, so that he would try to escape and turn back to the things which he could see distinctly?" But the philosopher's cave could certainly not be superimposed onto that other scene, the scene of the unconscious! That remains to be seen. For we are dealing here with an apparatus, with a metaphorical relationship between places or a relationship between metaphorical places, with a topography, the knowledge of which defines for both philosopher and analyst the degree of relationship to truth or to description, or to illusion, and the need for an ethical point of view.

So you see, we return to the real or, for the experiencing subject (I could say, for the subject who is felt or who is acted), the impression of reality. And one could naively wonder why, some two and half thousand years later, it is by means of an optical metaphor—of an optical construct which signals term for term the cinematographic apparatus—that the philosopher exposes man's condition and the distance that separates him from "true reality"; and why it is again precisely by means of an optical metaphor that Freud, at the beginning and at the end of his writings, tries to account for the arrangement of the physical apparatus, for the functioning of the Unconscious and for the rapport/rupture Conscious-Unconscious. Chapter 7 of the *Traumdeutung:*

> What is presented to us in these words is the idea of a *psychical locality.* I shall entirely disregard the fact that the mental apparatus with which we are concerned is also known to us in the form of an anatomical preparation, and I shall carefully avoid the temptation to determine psychical locality in an anatomical fashion. I shall remain upon psychological ground, and I propose simply to follow the suggestion that we should picture the instrument which carries out our mental functions as resembling a compound microscope or a photographic apparatus, or something of the kind. On that basis, psychical locality will correspond to a point inside the apparatus at which one of the preliminary stages of an image comes into being. In the microscope and telescope, as we know, these occur in part at ideal points, regions in which no tangible component to the apparatus is situated. I see no necessity to apologize for the imperfections of this or of any similar imagery.*

However imperfect this comparison may be, Freud takes it up again forty years later at the very beginning of the *Abriss:* "We admit that psychical life is the function of an apparatus to which we attribute a spatial extension which is made up of several parts. We imagine it like a kind of telescope, or microscope or some similar device." Freud doesn't mention cinema. But this is because cinema is already too technologically determined an apparatus for describing the psychical apparatus as a whole. In 1913, however, Lou Andréas Salomé remarked: "Why is it that cinema has been of no use to us [analysts]? To the numerous arguments that could be advanced to save face for this Cinderella of the artistic conception of art, several psychological considerations should be added. First, that the cinematographic technique is the only one that makes possible a succession of images rapid enough to

---

*Sigmund Freud, *The Interpretation of Dreams* (New York: Avon, 1965), pp. 574–75.

roughly correspond to our faculty for producing mental images. Furthermore," she concludes "this provides food for reflection about the impact film could have in the future for our psychical make-up." Clearly Salomé seems to envision a very enigmatic track, unless we have misunderstood her. Does she mean that film may bear some sort of likeness to the psychical apparatus, that, for this reason, it could be of interest to those who, because of its direct relation to their practice, are immediately affected by a theorization of psychical operation linked to the discovery of the Unconscious? And is it not the apparatus, the cinematographic process itself rather than the content of images—that is, the film—which is under scrutiny here? She only points out that there might be correspondences between cinematographic technique and our ability to produce mental images. But there are many aspects of film technique, many different connections, from the recording of the images to their reproduction—an entire process which we have named elsewhere the *basic cinematographic apparatus.* And certainly such a technical construct—if only as examples and metaphor—should have interested Freud, since the major purpose of metapsychological research is to comprehend and to theoretically construct devices capable of recording traces, memory traces, and of restoring them in the form of representation. He admits: the concept of the "magic writing pad" (which he substitutes for the optical metaphor to which he later returns) is missing something: the possibility of restoring inscribed traces by using specific memory mechanisms which are exclusively constituted by living matter but which a certain number of technical inventions of the time already mimic: the phonograph and cinema, precisely. The advantage of the magic writing pad is that since the external surface doesn't retain any trace of the inscriptions, it is best suited to illustrate the system Perception-Conscious; in addition, the waxy substance inside preserves, superimposed and to some extent associated, the different traces which have inscribed themselves throughout time, preserves them from what could be called historical accidents. Obviously, nothing prevents the same thing from applying to the material of the record or to the film stock of the film if not that such reproduction would be confusing and indecipherable to us: the inscription follows other tracks, which are organized according to other principles than those of inanimate matter.

Yet, there is something there which should capture our attention: the double place of the subject (constituted on the one hand by the system perception = Conscious characterized by the transcience, successiveness, and mobility of perceptions and representations; on the other by Unconscious system traces/inscriptions characterized by permanence) finds itself once more within an idealist perspective considerably displaced with respect to the unconscious in Plato. But as we have learned from Marx, there is often a truth hidden from or in idealism, a truth which belongs to materialism, but which materialism can only discover after many detours and delays—a hidden or disguised truth. In Plato, something haunts the subject; something belabors him and determines his condition (could it be the pressure of the "Ideas"?) As for Freud, the subject which Plato describes, the prisoner in the cave, is deceived (this whole theme of the mistaken subject which runs through the history of philosophy!); he is the prey of illusions, and, as for Freud, these illusions are but distortions and symptoms (gradations, the idealist would say—and admit this changes everything) of what is happening somewhere else. Even though Ideas take the place of the Unconscious for him, Plato confronts a problem equivalent to that which at first preoccupies Freud in his metapsychological research and which, precisely, the cave myth is presumed to resolve: the transfer, the access from one place to another, along with the ensuing distortions. Plato's prisoner is the victim of an illusion of reality, that is, of precisely what is known as a hallucination, if one is awake, as a dream, if asleep; he is the prey of an impression, of *an impression of reality*. As I have said, Plato's *topos* does not and could not possibly correspond exactly to Freud's and surely, although it may be interesting to show what displacement occurs from one *topos* to the other (the location of reality for Plato obviously doesn't correspond to what is real for Freud), it is still more important to determine what is at work on the idealist philosopher's discourse unknown to him, the truth which proclaims, very different yet contained within the one he consciously articulates.

As a matter of fact, isn't it curious that Plato, in order to explain the transfer, the access from one place to another and to demonstrate, reveal, and make understood what sort of illusion underlies our direct contact with the real, would imagine or resort to an apparatus that doesn't merely evoke, but quite precisely describes in its mode of operation the cinematographic apparatus* and the spectator's place in relation to it.

It is worth rereading the description of the cave from this perspective.

First, the space: "a kind of cavernous underground chamber with an entrance open to the light" but too small to light it up. As Plato points out farther on: "a dim space." He emphasizes the effect of the surrounding darkness on the philosopher after his sojourn in the outside world. To his companions he will at first appear blind, his eyesight ruined; and his clumsiness will make them laugh. They will not be able to have confidence in him. In the cave, the prisoner-spectators are seated, still, prisoners because immobilized: unable to move—constraint or paralysis? It is true that they are chained, but, freed, they would still refuse to leave the place where they are; and so obstinately would they resist that they might put to death anyone trying to lead them out. In other words, this first constraint, against their will, this deprivation of movement which was imposed on them initially, this motor inhibition which affected so much their future dispositions, conditions them to the point that they prefer to stay where they are and to perpetuate this immobility rather than leave. Initial constraint which seems in this way to turn itself into a kind of spite or at least to inscribe the compulsion to repeat, the return to a former condition. There are things like that in Plato? It is not unnecessary to insist on this point as we reread the Platonic myth from the special perspective of the cinematographic apparatus. Forced immobility is undoubtedly a valuable argument for the dem-

---

*In a general way, we distinguish the *basic cinematographic apparatus* [*l'appareil de base*], which concerns the ensemble of the equipment and operations necessary to the production of a film and its projection, from the apparatus [*le dispositif*] discussed in this article, which solely concerns projection and which includes the subject to whom the projection is addressed. Thus the *basic cinematographic apparatus* involves the film stock, the camera, developing, montage considered in its technical aspects, etc., as well as the apparatus [*dispositif*] of projection. The basic cinematographic apparatus is a long way from being the camera by itself, to which some have wanted to say I limit it (one wonders what bad arguments this can serve).

onstration/description that Plato makes of the human condition: the coincidence of religious and idealist conceptions; but the initial immobility was not invented by Plato; it can also refer to the forced immobility of the child who is without motor resources at birth, and to the forced immobility of the sleeper who we know repeats the postnatal state and even interuterine existence; but this is also the immobility that the visitor to the dim space rediscovers, leaning back into his chair. It might even be added that the spectators' immobility is characteristic of the filmic apparatus as a whole. The prisoner's shackles correspond to an actual reality in the individual's evolution, and Plato even draws the conclusion that it could have an influence on his future behavior, and would be a determining factor in the prisoner's resistance to breaking away from the state of illusion. "He might be required once more to deliver his opinion on those shadows, in competition with the prisoners who had never been released. . . . If they could lay hands on the man who was trying to set them free and lead them up, they would kill him." Does he mean that immobility constitutes a necessary if not sufficient condition for the prisoner's credulity, that it constitutes one of the causes of the state of confusion into which they have been thrown and which makes them take images and shadows for the real? I don't want to stretch Plato's argument too far, even if I am trying to make his myth mean more than it actually says. But note: "In this underground chamber they have been *from childhood,* chained by the leg and also by the neck, so that they cannot move and can see only what is in front of them, because the chains will not let them turn their heads" [my emphasis]. Thus it is their motor paralysis, their inability to move about that, making the reality test impractical for them, reinforces their error and makes them inclined to take for real that which takes its place, perhaps its figuration or its projection onto the wall/screen of the cavern in front of them and from which they cannot detach their eyes and turn away. They are bound, shackled to the screen, tied and related—relation, extension between it and them due to their inability to move in relation to it, the last sight before falling asleep.

Plato says nothing about the quality of the images: is two-dimensional space suited to the representation of depth produced by the images of objects? Admittedly, they are flat shadows, but their movements, crossings over, superimpositions, and displacements allow us perhaps to assume that they are moving along different planes. However, Plato calls the projector to mind. He doesn't feel a need for making use of natural light; but it is also important to him to preserve and protect that light from an impure usage: idealism makes the technician. Plato is satisfied with a fire burning behind them "at some distance higher up." As a necessary precaution, let us examine Plato's accuracy in assembling his apparatus. He is well aware that, placed otherwise, the fire would transmit the reflections of the prisoners themselves most prominently onto the screen. The "operators," the "machinists" are similarly kept out of the prisoners' sight, hidden by "a parapet, like the screen at a puppet-show, which hides the performers while they show their puppets over the top." For, undoubtedly, by associating themselves with the objects that they are moving back and forth before the fire, they would project a heterogeneous image capable of canceling the reality effect they want to produce: they would awake the prisoner's suspicions; they would awake the prisoners.

Here is the strangest thing about the whole apparatus. Instead of projecting images of natural/real objects, of living people, etc. onto the wall/screen of the cave as it would seem only natural to do for simple shadow plays, Plato feels the need, by creating a kind of conversion in the reference to reality, to show the prisoners not direct images and shadows of reality but, even at this point, a simulacrum of it. One might easily recognize the idealist's prudence, the calculated progress of the philosopher who prefers pushing the real back another notch and multiplying the steps leading to it, lest excessive haste lead his listener again to trust his senses too much. In any case, for this reason (or for another), he is led to place and to suppose between the projector, the fire, and the screen something which is itself a mere prop of reality, which is merely its image, its copy, its simulacrum: "figures of men and animals in wood or stone or other materials" suggestive of studio objects of papier mâché decor, were it not for the more striking impression created by their passing in front of the fire like a film.

All that is missing is the sound, in effect much more difficult to reproduce. Not only this: more difficult to copy, to employ like an image in the visible world; as if hearing, as opposed to sight, resisted being caught up in simulacra. Real voices, then, they would emanate from the bearers, the machinists, and the marionette players (a step is skipped in the reference to reality) but nevertheless, given over to the apparatus, integrated with it since it requires a total effect for fear of exposing the illusion. But voice that does not allow representation as do artificial objects—stone and wooden animals, and statues—will still give itself over to the apparatus thanks to its reverberation. "And suppose their prison had an echo from the wall facing them?" "When one of the people crossing behind them spoke, they could only suppose that the sound came from the shadow passing before their eyes." If a link is missing in the chain that connects us back to reality, the apparatus corrects this, by taking over the voice's echo, by integrating into itself these excessively real voices. And it is true that in cinema—as in the case of all talking machines—one does not hear an image of the sounds but the sounds themselves. Even if the procedures for recording the sounds and playing them back deforms them, they are reproduced and not copied. Only their source of emission may partake of illusion; their reality cannot. Hence, no doubt one of the basic reasons for the privileged status of voice in idealist philosophy and in religion: voice does not lend itself to games of illusion, or confusion, between the real and its figurativity (because voice cannot be represented figuratively) to which sight seems particularly liable. Music and singing differ qualitatively from painting in their relation to reality.

As we have seen, Plato constructs an apparatus very much like sound cinema. But, precisely because he has to resort to sound, he anticipates an ambiguity which was to be characteristic of cinema. This ambiguity has to do with the impression of reality: with the means used to create it, and with the confusion and lack of awareness surrounding its origin, from which result the inventions which mark the history of cinema. Plato effectively helps us to recognize this ambiguity. For, on the one hand, he is careful to emphasize the artificial aspect of reproduced reality. It is the apparatus that creates the illusion, and not the degree of fidelity with the Real: here *the prisoners have been chained since childhood,* and it will therefore not be the reproduction of this or that specific aspect of that reality, which they do not know, which will lead them to attribute a greater degree of reality to the illusion to which they are subject (and we have seen that Plato was already careful to insert artifice, and that already what was projected was deception). On the other hand, by introducing voice, by reconstructing a talking machine, by complementing the projection with sound, by illustrating, as it were, the need to affect as many sense faculties as possible, at any rate the two most important, he certainly seems to comply with a necessity to duplicate reality in the most exact manner and to make his artifice as good a likeness as can be made. Plato's myth evidently functions as a metaphor for an analogy on which he himself insists before dealing with the myth: namely, that what can be known through the senses is in the same relationship to that which can be known through the intellect as projection in the cave is to experience (that is, to ordinary reality). Besides that, isn't it remarkable that Plato should have been forced to resort to such a procedure and that, in his attempt to explain the position, the locus of that which can be known through the intellect, he was led to take off, so to speak, toward "illusion"; he was led to construct an apparatus which will make it possible, that it is capable of producing a special effect through the impression of reality it communicates to the spectator.

Here I must add something which may be of importance: in the scene taking place inside the cave, voices, words, "[these echoes which] they could only suppose that the sound came from the shadow passing before their eyes," do not have a discursive or conceptual role; they do not communicate a message; they belong to ordinary reality which is as immediate to the prisoners as are images; they cannot be separated from the latter; they are characterized according to the same mode of existence and in effect treated in the same way as words in a dream "fragments of discourse *really* spoken or heard, *detached from their context*" (my emphasis), and functioning like other kinds of dream representation.

But there is another way to state the problem. What desire was aroused, more than two thousand years before the actual invention of cinema, what urge in need of fulfillment would be satisifed by *a montage, rationalized into an idealist perspective precisely in order to show that it rests primarily on an impression of reality?* The impression of reality is central to Plato's demonstration. That his entire argument is developed in order to prove that this impression is deceptive abundantly demonstrates its existence. As we have already noted, something haunts Plato's text: the prisoners' fascination (how better to convey the condition that keeps them chained up, those fetters that prevent them from moving their heads and necks), their reluctance to leave, and even their willingness to resort to violence. But isn't it principally the need to construct another scene apart from the world, underground, in short to construct it as if it existed, or as if this construction also satisfied a desire to objectify a similar scene—an apparatus capable precisely of fabricating an impression of reality. This would appear to satisfy and replace the nostalgia for a lost impression which can be seen as running through the idealist movement and eating away at it from inside, and setting it in motion. That the real in Plato's text is at an equal distance from or in a homologous relationship to the "intelligibly real"—the world of Ideas—and "reality-subject"—"the impression of reality" produced by the apparatus in the cave should moreover be sufficient to make us aware of the real meaning of the world of Ideas and of the field of desire on which it has been built (a world which, as we know, "exists outside of time," and which, after numerous encounters, the conscious subject can rediscover in himself).

Cave, grotto, "sort of cavernous chamber underground," people have not failed to see in it a representation of the maternal womb, of the matrix into which we are supposed to wish to return. Granted, but only the place is taken into account by this interpretation and not the apparatus as a whole; and if this apparatus really produces images, it first of all produces an effect of specific subjects—to the extent that a subject is intrinsically part of the apparatus; once the cinema has been technically perfected, it produces this same effect defined by the words "impression of reality" (words that may be confusing but which nevertheless need to be clarified). This impression of reality appears as if—just as if—it were known to Plato. At the very least, it seems that Plato ingeniously attempts and succeeds in fixing up a machine capable of reproducing "something" that he must have known, and that has less to do with its capacity for repeating the real (and this is where the Idealist is of great help to us by sufficiently emphasizing the artifice he employs to make his machine work) than with reproduction and repetition of a particular condition, and the representation of a particular place on which this condition depends.

Of course, from the analytic perspective we have chosen, by asking cinema about the wish it expresses, we are aware of having distorted the allegory of the cave by making it reveal, from a considerable historic distance, the approximate construct of the cinematographic apparatus. In other words, a same apparatus was responsible for the invention of the cinema and was already present in Plato. The text of the cave may well express a desire inherent to a participatory effect deliberately produced, sought for, and expressed by cinema (and the philosopher is first of all a spokesman of desire before becoming its great "channeler," which shows why it is far from useless to bring an analytic ear to bear on him despite or because of his rationalizations, even though he would deny it as tolerable suspicion, even and especially though he complains, rightly from his point of view, of our having distorted his text). We can thus propose that the allegory of the cave is the text of a signifier of desire which haunts the invention of cinema and the history of its invention.

You see why historians of cinema, in order to unearth its first ancestor, never leave off dredging a prehistory which is becoming increasingly cluttered. From the magic lantern to the praxinoscope and the optical theater up to the *camera obscura,* as the booty piles up, the excavations grow: new objects and all kinds of inventions—one can feel the disarray increasing. But if cinema was really the answer to a desire inherent in our psychical structure, how can we date its first beginnings? Would it be too risky to propose that painting, like theater, for lack of suitable technological and economic conditions, were dry runs in the approximation not only of the world of representation but of what might result from a certain aspect of its functioning and which only the cinema is in a position to implement? These attempts have obviously produced their own specificity and their own history, but their existence has at its origin a psychical source equivalent to the one which stimulated the invention of cinema.

It is very possible that there was never any first invention of cinema. Before being

the outcome of technical considerations and of a certain state of society's development (necessary to its realization and to its completion), it was primarily the target of a desire which, moreover, its immediate success as well as the interest which
its ancestors had aroused has demonstrated clearly enough. A desire, to be sure, a
form of lost satisfaction which its apparatus would be aimed at rediscovering in one
way or another (even to the point of simulation) and to which the impression of
reality would seem to be the key.

I would now like to look more closely at what the impression of reality and the
desire objectified in its entails by surveying certain analytical texts.

And since I have already mentioned the cave, "a kind of cavernous underground
chamber," as Plato says, I went back to the *Interpretation of Dreams* and discovered
a remark of Freud's that could guide our search. This remark is to be found in the
passage dedicated to examples of dream work. Freud examines the kinds of figuration that occur during analysis. After having shown how the treatment gets itself
represented, Freud comes to the unconscious, "If the unconscious, insofar as it
belongs to waking thought, needs to be represented in dreams, it is represented in
them in underground places." Freud adds the following which, because of the
above, is very interesting: "Outside of analytic treatment, these representations
would have symbolized the woman's body or the womb." If the world of Ideas offers
numerous concepts which correspond to those which Freud discovered in the
Unconscious (the permanence of traces, the ignorance of time), that is, if the philosophical edifice can be envisaged as a rationalization of the Unconscious's thrust,
of its suspected but rejected existence, then we can ask whether it is not the Unconscious or certain of its mechanisms that are figured, that represent themselves in the
apparatus of the cave. In any case, paraphrasing Fechner, we could propose that the
scene of the cave (and of cinema) is perhaps quite different from that of the activity
of representation in a state of wakefulness. In order to learn a little more about that
other scene, it might be useful to linger a while before the dream scene.

A parallel between dream and cinema had often been noticed: common sense
perceived it right away. The cinematographic projection is reminiscent of dream,
would appear to be a kind of dream, really a dream,* a parallelism often noticed by
the dreamer when, about to describe his dream, he is compelled to say "It was like
in a movie . . ." At this point, it seems useful to follow Freud closely in his meta-
physchological analysis of dream. Once the role and function of dream as a protector of sleep and as fulfillment of a wish has been recognized as well as its nature and
the elaboration of which it is the result, and after the material, the translation of the
manifest content into dream thoughts, has been studied, one must still determine
the conditions of dream formation, the reasons that give dream a specific qualita-

---

*A close relationship which has led filmmakers to believe that cinema was the instrument finally
suited for the representation of dreams. The failure of their attempt still reamins to be understood.
Is it not that the representation of dreams in cinema would not function like the representation of
dreams in dreams, precisely destroying the impression of reality in the same way as the thought
that one is dreaming intervenes in dream as a defense mechanism against the "mashing" desire of
dream. The displacement of dream in the projection results unavoidably in sending the spectator
back to his consciousness; it imposes a distance which denounces the artifice (and is there anything
more ridiculous than those soft focus clouds, supposedly dreamlike representations) and it destroys
completely the *impression of reality* which precisely also defines dream.

tive nature in the whole of the psychical life, the specific "dream effect" that it determines. This is the subject of chapter 7 of *The Interpretations of Dreams* and the *Supplement to the Theory of Dreams* fifteen years later. In the latter text, Freud at first seems concerned with understanding why dream manifests itself to the dreamer's consciousness in the form of what might be called the "specific mode of dream," a feature of reality which should more properly belong to the perception of the external world. What are the determining factors of a necessarily metapsychological order, that is, involving the construction and operation of the psychical apparatus, which makes it possible for dream to pass itself off for reality to the dreamer. Freud begins with sleep: dream is the psychical activity of the dreamer. Sleep, he tells us, "from a somatic viewpoint is *a revivescence of one's stay in the body of the mother, certain conditions of which it recreates: the rest position, warmth, and isolation which protects him from excitement*" [emphasis added]. This makes possible a first form of regression: *temporal regression,* which follows two paths—regression of the libido back to a previous period of hallucinatory satisfaction of desire; and regression in the development of the self back to a primitive narcissism which results in what has been defined as the totally egotistical nature of dream: *"the person who plays the main part in dream scenes is always the dreamer himself."* Sleep favors the appearance of another form of regression which is extremely important for the manifestation of the dream effect: by deactivating equally the Cs, Pcs, and Ucs systems, that is, by allowing an easier communication between them, sleep leaves open the regressive path which the cathetic representations will follow as far as perception. *Topical regression* and *temporal regression* combine to reach the edge of dream.

I do not want to insist excessively on Freud's analysis. We need only note that the dream wish is formed from daytime residues in the Proconscious system which are reinforced by drives emanating from the Unconscious. Topical regression first allows the transformation of the dream thoughts into images. It is through the intermediary of regression that word representations belonging to the Preconscious system are translated into thing representations which dominate the Unconscious system.* "Thoughts are transposed into images—mostly visual ones—thus the representations of words are reduced to representations of objects corresponding to them as if, throughout the whole system, considerations of representability overwhelmed the whole process." So much so that a dream wish can be turned into a dream fantasy. Once again, it is regression which gives dream its definitive shape. "The completion of the dream process is also marked by the fact that the content of thought, transformed by regression and reshaped into a fantasy of desire, comes into consciousness as a sensory perception and then undergoes the secondary elaboration which affects any perceptual content. We are saying that the dream wish is hallucinated and finds, in the guise of hallucination a belief in the reality of its fulfillment." Dream is "an hallucinatory psychosis of desire"—that is, a state in which

---

*In *The Ego and the Id,* Freud adds comments which allow him to assert that "visual thought is closer to the unconscious processes than verbal thought, and older than the latter, from the phylogenetic as well as from the ontogenetic standpoints. Verbal representations all belong to the Pcs, while the unconscious only relies on visual ones."

mental perceptions are taken for perceptions of reality. Moreover, Freud hypothesized that the satisfaction resulting from hallucination is a kind of satisfaction which we knew at the beginning of our psychical life when perception and representation could not be differentiated, when the different systems were confused, that is, when the system of Consciousness-Perception had not differentiated itself. The object of desire (the object of need), if it happens to be lacking, can at this point be hallucinated. It is precisely the repeated failure offered by this form of satisfaction which results in the differentiation between perception and representation through the creation of the reality test. A perception which can be eliminated by an action is recognized as exterior. The reality test is dependent on "motoricity." Once "motoricity" has been interrupted, as during sleep, the reality test can no longer function. The suspension of "motoricity," its being set apart, would indeed favor regression. But it is also because sleep determines a withdrawal of cathexis in the Cs, Ucs, and Pcs systems that the fantasies of the dream wish follow the original path which differentiate them from fantasies produced during the waking state.* Like daytime fantasies, they could have become conscious without nevertheless being taken for real or completed; but, having taken the path of regression, not only are they capable of taking over consciousness but, because of the subject's inability to rely upon the reality test, they are marked by the very character of perception and appear as reality. The processes of dream formation succeed well in presenting dream as real.

The transformations accomplished by sleep in the psychical apparatus: withdrawal of cathexis, instability of the different systems, return to narcissism, loss of motoricity (because of the impossibility of applying the reality test), contribute to produce features which are specific to dream: its capacity for figuration, translation of thought into images, reality extended to representations. One might even add that we are dealing with a *more-than-real* in order to differentiate it from the impression of the real which reality produces in the normal waking situation: the more-than-real translating the cohesion of the subject with his perceived representations, the submersion of the subject in his representations, the near impossibility for him to escape their influence and which is dissimilar if not incompatible with the impression resulting from any direct relation to reality. There appears to be an ambiguity in the words poorly expressing the difference between the relationship of the subject to his representations experienced as perceived and his relation to reality.

Dream, Freud also tells us, is a projection, and, in the context in which he uses the word, projection evokes at once the analytic use of the defense mechanism which consists in referring and attributing to the exterior representations and affects

---

*This is why it is not by paying attention to the content of images that one is able to account for the impression of reality but by questioning the apparatus. The differentiation between fantasies and dream is due to the transformation of the psychical apparatus during the transition from the state of being awake to sleep. Sleep will make necessary the work of figuration the economy of which can be created by daytime fantasies; in addition, daytime fantasies do not accompany the belief in reality of the fulfillment which characterizes dream. This is why in attempting to understand the cinema effect—the impression of reality—we have to go through the intermediary of dream and not daytime fantasies.

which the subject refuses to acknowledge as his own, and it also evokes a distinctly cinematographic use since it involves images which, once projected, come back to the subject as a reality perceived from the outside.

That dream is a projection reminiscent of the cimematographic apparatus is indeed what seems to come out of Lewin's discovery of the *dream screen,* the hypothesis for which was suggested to him by his patients' enigmatic dreams. One young woman's dream, for example: "I had my dream all ready for you, but while I was lying here looking at it, it began to move in circles far from me, wrapped up on itself, again and again, like two acrobats." This dream shows that the screen, which can appear by itself, like a white surface, is not exclusively a representation, a content—in which case it would not be necessary to privilege it among other elements of the dream content; but, rather, it would present itself in all dreams as the indispensable support for the projection of images. It would seem to pertain to the dream apparatus. "The dream screen is a surface on which a dream seems to be projected. It is the 'blank background' (empty basic surface) which is present in dream although it is not necessarily seen; the manifest content of dream ordinarily perceived takes place over it, or in front of it." "Theoretically it can be part of the latent content or of the manifest content, but the distinction is academic. The dream screen is not often noticed by analysts, and, in the practice of dream interpretation, the analyst does not need to deal with it." It is cinema which suggested the term to Lewin because, in the same way as its analog in the cinematographic apparatus, the dream screen is either ignored by the dreamer (the dreaming spectator) or unrelated to the interest resulting from the images and the action.* Lewin adds nevertheless (and this remark reminds us of a modern use of the screen in cinema) that in some circumstances, the screen does play a part of its own and becomes discernible. According to Lewin's hypothesis, the dream screen is the dream's hallucinatory representation of the mother's breast on which the child used to fall asleep after nursing. In this way, it expresses a state of complete satisfaction while repeating the original condition of the oral phase in which the body did not have limits of its own, but was extended undifferentiated from the breast. Thus, the dream screen would correspond to the desire to sleep: archetype and prototype of any dream. Lewin adds another hypothesis: the dream itself, the visual representations which are projected upon it, would correspond to the desire to be awake. "A visual dream repeats the child's early impression of being awake. His eyes are open and he sees. For him, to see is to be awake." Actually, Lewin insists on Freud's explanation of the predominance of visual elements in dream: that latent thoughts in a dream are to a large extent shaped by unconscious mnemic traces which can only exist as a visual representation—the repetition of a formal element from the child's earliest experience. It is evident that the dream screen is a residue from the most archaic mnemic traces. But, additionally, and this is at least as important, one might assume that it provides an opening for understanding the dreamer's "primal scene" which establishes itself during the oral phase. The hallucinatory factor, the

---

*Bertram Lewin, "Sleep, the Mouth and the Dream Screen," *Psychoanalytic Quarterly* (1946), 15:419–43, "Inferences from the Dream Screen," *International Journal of Psychoanalysis* (1948). 29:224–431.

lack of distinction between representation and perception—representation taken as perception which makes for our belief in the reality of dream—would correspond to the lack of distinction between active and passive, between acting and suffering experience, undifferentiation between the limits of the body (body/breast), between eating and being eaten, etc., characteristics of the oral phase and borne out by the envelopment of the subject by the screen. For the same reasons, we would find ourselves in a position to understand the specific mode in which the dreamer identifies with his dream, a mode which is anterior to the mirror stage, to the formation of the self, and therefore founded on a permeability, a fusion of the interior with the exterior.

On the other hand, if the dream itself, in its visual content, is likely to represent the desire to stay awake, the combination dream screen/projected images would manifest a conflict between contradictory motions, a state in effect of undistinction between a hallucinatory wish, sign of satisfaction, and desire for perception, of contact with the real. It is therefore conceivable that something of a desire in dream unifying perception and representation—whether representation passes itself for perception, in which case we would be closer to hallucination, or whether perception passes itself for perceived representation, that is, acquires as perception the mode of existence which is proper to hallucination—takes on the character of specific reality which reality does not impart, but which hallucination provokes: *a more-than-real* that dream precisely, considered as apparatus and as the repetition of a particular state which defines the oral phase, would, on its own, be able to bring to it. Dream alone?

Lewin's hypothesis, which complements and extends Freud's ideas on the formation of dream in relation to the feeling of reality which is linked to it, presents, in my opinion, the advantage of offering a kind of formation stage, of dream constitution, which might be construed as operative in the cinema effect. Impression of reality and that which we have defined as the desire of cinema, as cinema in its general apparatus would recall, would mime a form of archaic satisfaction experienced by the subject by reproducing the scene of it.

Of course, there is no question of identifying mental image, filmic image, mental representation, and cinematographic representation. The fact that the same terms are used, however, does reveal the very workings of desire in cinema, that is, at the same time the desire to rediscover archaic forms of desire which in fact structure any form of desire, and the desire to stage for the subject, to put in the form of representation, what might recall its own operation.

In any case, this deviation through the "metapsychological fiction" of dream could enlighten us about the effect specific to cinema, "the impression of reality," which, as is well known, is different from the usual impression which we receive from reality, but which has precisely this characteristic of being more than real which we have detected in dream.

Actually, cinema is a simulation apparatus. This much was immediately recognized, but, from the positivist viewpoint of scientific rationality which was predominant at the time of its invention, the interest was directed toward the simulation of reality inherent to the moving image with the unexpected effects which could be derived from it, without finding it necessary to examine the fact that the cinematographic apparatus was initially directed toward the subject and that *simulation could be applied to states or subject effects before being directed toward the reproduction of the real.* It is nevertheless curious that in spite of the development of analytic theory, the problem should have remained unsolved or barely considered since that period. Almost exclusively, it is the technique and content of film which have retained attention: characteristics of the image, depth of field, offscreen space, shot, single-shot sequence, montage, etc.; the key to the impression of reality has been sought in the structuring of image and movement, in complete ignorance of the fact that the impression of reality is dependent first of all on a subject effect and that it might be necessary to examine the position of the subject facing the image in order to determine the raison d'être for the cinema effect. Instead of considering cinema as an ideologically neutral apparatus, as it has been rather stupidly called, the impact of which would be entirely determined by the content of the film (a consideration which leaves unsolved the whole question of its persuasive power and of the reason for which it revealed itself to be an instrument particularly well suited to exert ideological influence), in order to explain the cinema effect, it is necessary to consider it from the viewpoint of the apparatus that it constitutes, apparatus which in its totality includes the subject. And first of all, the subject of the unconscious. The difficulties met by the theoreticians of cinema in their attempt to account for the impression of reality are proportionate to the persisting resistance to really recognizing the unconscious. Although nominally accepted, its existence has nevertheless been left out of the theoretical research. If psychoanalysis has finally permeated the content of certain films, as a complement to the classic psychology of character's action and as a new type of narrative spring, it has remained practically absent from the problematics raised by the relation of the projection to the subject. The problem is nevertheless to determine the extent to which the cinematographic apparatus plays an important part in this subject which Lacan after Freud defines as an apparatus,* and the way in which the structuring of the unconscious, the modalities of the subject's development throughout the different strata deposited by the various phases of drives, the differentiation between the Cs, Pcs, and Ucs systems and their relations, the distinction between primary and secondary processes, make it possible to isolate the effect which is specific to cinema.

Consequently, I will only propose several hypotheses.

First of all, that taking into account the darkness of the movie theater, the relative passivity of the situation, the forced immobility of the cine-subject, and the effects which result from the projection of images, moving images, the cinematographic apparatus brings about a state of artificial regression. It artificially leads back to an anterior phase of his development—a phase which is barely hidden, as dream and certain pathological forms of our mental life have shown. It is the desire, unrecognized as such by the subject, to return to this phase, an early state of development with its own forms of satisfaction which may play a determining role in his desire for cinema and the pleasure he finds in it. Return toward a relative narcissism, and

---

*"The subject is an apparatus. This apparatus is lacunary, and it is within this lacuna that the subject sets up the function of an object as lost object." Jacques Lacan, *Les Quatres Concepts fondamenteux de la psychanalyse* (Paris: Le Seuil, 1973).

even more toward a mode of relating to reality which could be defined as enveloping and in which the separation between one's own body and the exterior world is not well defined. Following this line of reasoning, one may then be able to understand the reasons for the intensity of the subject's attachment to the images and the process of identification created by cinema. A return to a primitive narcissism by the regression of the libido, Freud tells us, noting that the dreamer occupies the entire field of the dream scene; the absence of delimitation of the body; the transfusion of the interior out into the exterior, added Lewin (other works, notably Melanie Klein's could also be mentioned); without excluding other processes of identification which derive from the specular regime of the ego, from its constitution as "Imaginary." These do not, however, strictly pertain to the cinema effect, although the screen, the focalization produced by the basic apparatus, as I indicated in my earlier paper,* could effectively produce mirror effects and cause specular phenomena to intervene directly in the viewing experience. In any case, the usual forms of identification, already supported by the apparatus, would be reinforced by a more archaic mode of identification, which has to do with the lack of differentiation between the subject and his environment, a dream scene model which we find in the baby/breast-screen relationship.

In order to understand the particular status of cinema, it is necessary to underline the partial elimination of the reality test. Undoubtedly, the means of cinematographic projection would keep the reality test intact when compared to dreams and hallucination. The subject has always the choice to close his eyes, to withdraw from the spectacle, or to leave, but no more than in dream does he have means to act in any way upon the object of his perception, change his viewpoint as he would like. There is no doubt that in dealing with images, and the unfolding of images, the rhythm of vision and movement are imposed on him in the same way as images in dream and hallucination. His relative motor inhibition which brings him closer to the state of the dreamer, in the same way as the particular status of the reality he perceives (a reality made up of images) would seem to favor the simulation of the regressive state, and would play a determining role in the subject effect of the impression of reality, this more-than-real of the impression of reality, which as we have seen is characteristic not of the relation of the subject to reality, but precisely of dreams and hallucinations.

One must therefore start to analyze the impression of reality by differentiating between perception and representation. The cinematographic apparatus is unique in that *it offers the subject perceptions "of a reality" whose status seems similar to that of representations experienced as perception.* It should also be noted in this connection that if the confusion between representation and perception is characteristic of the primary process which is governed by the pleasure principle, and which is the basic condition for the satisfaction produced by hallucination, the cinematographic apparatus appears to succeed in suspending the secondary process and anything having to do with the principle of reality without eliminating it com-

---

*Jean-Louis Baudry, "Cinéma: Effets idéologiques produits par l'appareil de base," *Cinéthique* (1970) nos. 7–8, pp. 1–8. Published in an English translation by Alan Williams in *Film Quarterly* (Winter 1974–75), 28(2):39–47.

pletely. This would then lead us to propose the following paradoxical formula: the more-than-real, that is, the specific characteristic (whatever is specific) of what is meant by the expression "impression of reality," consists in keeping apart (toning down, so that they remain present but as background) the secondary process and the reality principle. Perception of the image passing for perception: one might assume that it is precisely here that one might find the key to the impression of reality, that which would at once approximate and differentiate the cinematographic effect and the dream. Return effect, repetition of a phase of the subject's development during which representation and perception were not yet differentiated, and the desire to return to that state along with the kind of satisfaction associated to it, undoubtedly an archetype for all that which seeks to connect with the multiple paths of the subject's desire. It is indeed desire as such, that is, desire of desire, the nostalgia for a state in which desire has been satisfied through the transfer of a perception to a formation resembling hallucination, which seems to be activated by the cinematographic apparatus. According to Freud: "To desire initially must have been a hallucinatory cathexis of the memory of satisfaction."* Survival and insistence of bygone periods, an irrepressible backward movement. Freud never ceased to remind us that in its formal constitution, dream was a vestige of the subject's phylogenetic past, and the expression of a wish to have again the very form of existence associated with this experience. "Dream which fulfills its wish by the short-cut of regression does nothing but conserve a type of primary operation of the psychical apparatus which had been eliminated because of its inefficiency." It is also the same survival and the same wish which are at work in some hallucinatory psychoses. Cinema, like dream, would seem to correspond to a temporary form of regression, but whereas dream, according to Freud, is merely a "normal hallucinatory psychosis," cinema offers an artificial psychosis without offering the dreamer the possibility of exercising any kind of immediate control. What I am really saying is that for such a regression to be possible, it is necessary for anterior phases to survive, but that it be cathected by a wish, as is proven by the existence of dream. This wish is remarkably precise, and consists in obtaining, from reality a position, a condition in which what is perceived would no longer be distinguished from representations. It can be assumed that it is this wish which prepares the long history of cinema: the wish to construct a simulation machine capable of offering the subject perceptions which are really representations mistaken for perceptions. Cinema offers a simulation of regressive movement which is characteristic of

---

*It may seem peculiar that desire which constituted the cine-effect is rooted in the oral structure of the subject. The conditions of projection do evoke the dialectics internal/external, swallowing/swallowed, eating/being eaten, which is characteristic of what is being structured during the oral phase. But, in the case of the cinematographic situation, the visual orifice has replaced the buccal orifice: the absorption of images is at the same time the absorption of the subject in the image, prepared, predigested by his very entering the dark theater. The relationship visual orifice/buccal orifice acts at the same time as analogy and differentiation, but also points to the relation of consecution between oral satisfaction, sleep, white screen of the dream on which dream images will be projected, beginning of the dream. On the importance of sight during the oral phase, see Spitz's remarks in The Yes and the No. In the same order of ideas, it may be useful to reintroduce Melanie Klein's hypothesis on the oral phase, her extremely complex dialectics between the inside and the outside which refer to reciprocal forms of development.

dream—the transformation of thoughts by means of figuration. The withdrawal of cathexis of all the systems Cs, Pcs, Ucs during sleep causes the representations cathected by dream during the dream work to determine a sensory activity; the operation of dream can be crudely represented by a diagram.

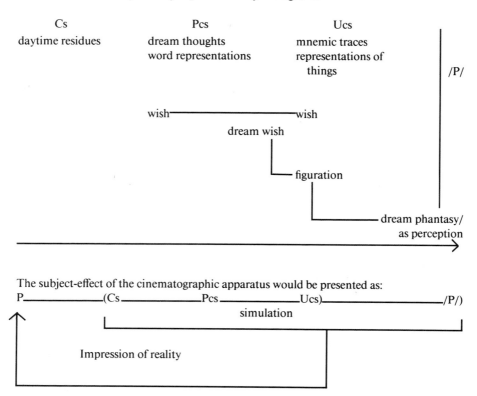

The subject-effect of the cinematographic apparatus would be presented as:

The simulation apparatus therefore consists in transforming a perception into a quasi-hallucination endowed with a reality effect which cannot be compared to that which results from ordinary perception. The cinematographic apparatus reproduces the psychical apparatus during sleep: separation from the outside world, inhibition of motoricity; in sleep, these conditions causing an overcathexis of representation can penetrate the system of perception as sensory stimuli; in cinema, the images perceived (very likely reinforced by the setup of the psychical apparatus) will be overcathected and thus acquire a status which will be the same as that of the sensory images of dream.

One cannot hesitate to insist on the *artificial* character of the cine-subject. It is precisely this artificiality which differentiates it from dream or hallucinations. There is, between cinema and these psychical states, the same distance as between a real object and its simulacrum, with this additional factor that dream and hallucination are already states of simulation (something passing itself off for something else, representation for perception). One might even argue that it is this embedded structure which makes it so difficult to deal with the subject effect. While, in dreams and hallucinations, representations appear in the guise of perceived reality, a real perception takes place in cinema, if not an ordinary perception of reality. It would appear that it is this slight displacement which has misled the theoreticians of cinema, when analyzing the impression of reality. In dream and hallucination, representations are taken as reality in the absence of perception; in cinema, images are taken for reality but require the mediation of perception. This is why, on the one hand, for the realists, cinema is thought of as a duplicate of reality—and on the other cinema is taken as an equivalent of dream—but the comparison stops there, leaving unresolved the problem raised by the impression of reality. It is evident that cinema is not dream: but it reproduces an impression of reality, it unlocks, releases a cinema effect which is comparable to the impression of reality caused by dream. The entire cinematographic apparatus is activated in order to provoke this simulation: it is indeed a simulation of a condition of the subject, a position of the subject, a subject and not reality.

Desire for a real that would have the status of hallucination or of a representation taken for a perception—one might wonder whether cinema is not doubled by another wish, complementary to the one that is at work in the subject and which we have presumed to be at work in Plato's cave apparatus.

For, if dream really opens onto another scene by way of a regressive track, one might suppose that the existence of an unconscious where the subject's early mode of functioning, defined by the primary process, persists, the unconscious, constantly denied, rejected, excluded, never ceases requiring of the subject and proposing to him, by multiple detours (even if only through artistic practice), representations of his own scene. In other words, without his always suspecting it, the subject is induced to produce machines which would not only complement or supplement the workings of the secondary process but which could represent his own overall functioning to him: he is led to produce mechanisms mimicking, simulating the apparatus which is no other than himself. The presence of the unconscious also makes itself felt through the pressure it exerts in seeking to get itself represented by a subject who is still unaware of the fact that he is representing to himself the very scene of the unconscious where he is.

1975

NOËL CARROLL
FROM MYSTIFYING MOVIES

JEAN-LOUIS BAUDRY AND "THE APPARATUS"

A major reason, given by contemporary film theorists, for their shift from a semiological framework of study to a psychoanalytic one, is that the semiological model is too narrow. It concerns itself with the structure of the cinematic sign but does not, according to many contemporary film theorists, pay sufficient attention to the effects of cinema upon the spectator. The semiological model, at least in the ways it was employed in the late sixties and early seventies, was felt to be myopically object-oriented. In order to remedy this putative shortcoming, film theorists resorted to psychoanalysis.

Jean-Louis Baudry's essay "The Apparatus" was a seminal essay in the turn to psychoanalysis. In this essay, he attempts to account for the impression of reality that cinema is said to impart to spectators. He intends to use psychoanalysis, that is, to analyze what he takes to be a paramount effect of cinema on audiences. However, though the phrase "impression of reality" recurs frequently in "The Apparatus," one must be careful in that which one identifies as the phenomenon with which Baudry is concerned. For Baudry does not contend that the impression of reality caused by cinema is equivalent to our everyday encounters with the world; cinema is not a replication of our ordinary impressions of reality. Rather, cinema is said to deliver an impression of reality that is more-than-real. That is, less paradoxically stated, Baudry wishes to deploy psychoanalysis to explain cinema's intense effect on spectators; he wants to analyze the peculiarly charged relationship we have with the screen when we attend movies.

Moreover, Baudry does not search for this effect by scrutinizing the content of the images or the stories of particular films or even of particular kinds of films. Instead he sees this effect as the product of what he calls "the apparatus," a network which includes the screen, the spectator, and the projector. That is, Baudry seeks the origin of the impression-of-reality effect in the projection situation itself, irrespective of what is being screened.

Baudry's basic procedure for discovering the origin of the impression-of-reality effect is to draw a series of analogies between dreams and the projection context, or, as he prefers to call the latter, the apparatus. He is motivated in this by a belief that dreams like film engender an impression of reality that is highly charged, that is, an impression of what Baudry thinks of as the more-than-real effect. Thus, Baudry hopes to extrapolate the psychoanalytic explanation of the charged impression of reality in dreams into an explanation of the impression of reality in cinema.

Though Baudry does not set out his case in a logically rigorous fashion, his analysis implicitly takes the form of an inductive argument by logical analogy. For example, he notes that the film viewer and the dreamer share the property of having their movements inhibited, that both inhabit darkened rooms, and that both film and dream impart an impression of reality. Dream, in turn, is said to have this consequence insofar as it induces regression to an earlier psychosexual stage, that of primitive narcissism where the self is supposedly not differentiated from the other nor is perception differentiated from representation. On the basis of the similar conditions and effects, respectively, of film and dream, Baudry infers that the impression of reality in film is brought about by a regressive mechanism similar to that operative in dream.

Though arguments by analogy are not absolutely conclusive—they are, after all, inductive rather than deductive—and though they are often abused, they are a respectable form of reasoning. We use them all the time. For example, if you have a 1964 Saab and I have a 1964 Saab, and both cars are the same model, both engines are in exactly the same condition and state of repair, both carry the same weight, use the same fuel, and have been serviced in the same way by the same mechanic, and my Saab can go 55 mph, then we infer that (probably) your car can go 55 mph. Stated formally, this type of argument takes the following pattern: If we have items A and B, and they are similar in a number of relevant respects, say in terms of properties $p1$ through $px-1$, and item B also has property px, then we infer that (probably) A has px. That is,

1. Item A has properties $p1 \ldots px-1$ (e.g., A is a 1964 Saab).
2. Item B has properties $p1 \ldots px-1$.
3. Item B also has property px (e.g., B can go 55 mph).
4. Therefore, (probably) Item A also has property px.

Premises 1 and 2 set out the analogy; if more items are being analogized more premises will be added here. Once the analogy is set out, these premises can be combined with premise 3, which states a property known to be possessed by B (but not observed to be a property of A), in order to license the probable conclusion stated in 4. Obviously such arguments gain strength when the number of items and/or the number of relevant properties cited are multiplied. Inversely, the argument loses force as either data base for the analogy is diminished. This can be done by:

A. showing that the analogies cited fail (for example, your car is really a 1921 Ford, not a 1964 Saab).

B. demonstrating that the analogies cited are irrelevant to what is at issue (for example, that both cars are green).

C. noting relevant disanalogies between items A, B . . . in order to challenge the purported similarity of the cases under comparison (for example, that your Saab has no wheels).

With this sketch of the logic of Baudry's approach, we can go on to fill in the details and evaluate the persuasiveness of his account of the psychic mechanism that he believes causes cinema's characteristic impression of reality.

As we have already noted, Baudry holds that the conditions of reception of film and dream are analogous; both involve a darkened room and the inhibition of movement. The film viewer sits in his seat; the dreamer lies abed. Inhibited motoricity is also a feature of the infantile state to which the dreamer is said to regress. Connected to this inhibition of motoricity is another feature: the lack of the means to test reality. Baudry writes:

> In order to understand the particular status of cinema, it is necessary to underline the partial elimination of the reality test. Undoubtedly, the means of cinematographic projection would keep the reality test intact when compared to dreams and hallucination. The subject always has the choice to close his eyes, to withdraw from the spectacle or to leave but no more than dreams does he have means to act in any way upon the object of his perception, change his viewpoint as he would like. . . . His relative motor inhibition which brings him closer to the state of the dreamer, in the same way as the particular status of the reality he perceives (a reality made up of images) would seem to favor the simulation of the regressive state, and would play a determining role in the subject effect of the impression of reality, this more-than-real of the impression of reality, which as we have seen is characteristic not of the relation of the subject to reality, but precisely of dreams and hallucinations.*

Here, Baudry notes that there is only a partial analogy in regard to reality testing between film and dream. But he thinks this similarity is important because along with inhibited motoricity, and perhaps because of it, the lack of reality testing reproduces the conditions of the infantile state of primitive narcissism that explains the impression-of-reality effect that the cinematic apparatus is said to induce. Also, in this passage, Baudry alludes to two other analogies between film and dreams: both traffic in the medium of images and both deliver a more-than-real impression of reality.

So far five analogies between film and dream have been noted: inhibited motoricity in the subject; lack of reality testing; darkened rooms; the medium of images; the more-than-real impression of reality. Are there other analogies?

For Baudry, following the psychoanalyst Bertram Lewin, dreams, like the cinematic apparatus, have screens. That is, Baudry argues that dreams are projections onto dream screens in a way that is analogous to film projection. Baudry writes:

> That dream is a projection reminiscent of the cinematographic apparatus is indeed what seems to come out of Lewin's discovery of the *dream screen,* the hypothesis for which

---

*Jean-Louis Baudry, "The Apparatus: Metapsychological Approaches to the Impression of Reality in the Cinema" [see this edition, p. 704.]

was suggested to him by his patients' enigmatic dreams. One young woman's dream, for example: "I had my dream all ready for you, but while I was lying here looking at it, it began to move in circles far from me, wrapped up on itself, again and again like two acrobats." This dream shows that the screen, which can appear by itself, like a white surface, is not exclusively a representation, a content—in which case it would not be necessary to privilege it among other elements of the dream content; but, rather, it would present itself in all dreams as the indispensable support for the projection of images. It would seem to pertain to the dream apparatus. "The dream screen is a surface on which a dream seems to be projected. It is the 'blank background' (empty basic surface) which is present in the dream although it is not necessarily seen; the manifest content of dream ordinarily perceived takes place over it, or in front of it."[1]

Baudry also points out that people often describe their dreams as being like movies.

The dream screen/film screen, dream apparatus/film apparatus analogy is particularly crucial for Baudry. For Lewin has a psychoanalytic account of the dream screen that is pertinent to the effect dreams have upon us. And Baudry intends to extend that account to cinema.

> According to Lewin's hypothesis, the dream screen is the dream's hallucinatory representation of the mother's breast on which the child used to fall asleep after nursing. In this way, it expresses a state of complete satisfaction while repeating the original condition of the oral phase in which the body did not have limits of its own, but was extended undifferentiated from the breast.[2]

Thus, via the dream screen, the dreamer regresses to and relives a stage in our psychosexual development marked by primitive narcissism, a stage where self and environment are said to merge and where perception and representation are believed to be undifferentiated. Moreover, this regression satisfies a desire, a desire to return to that sense of undifferentiated wholeness. It is this desire in turn which gives the dream imagery its special charge and which accounts for the intensity with which we regard it.

Insofar as the cinematic apparatus mirrors relevant aspects of the dream apparatus—inhibited motoricity, lack of reality testing, visual imagery, the more-than-real impression of reality, projection, and a screen support—Baudry feels warranted in adopting Lewin's hypothesis about the causation of dream and the dream effect as an explanation of our animating desire for and our experience of the cinematic apparatus. That is, a regressive mechanism seeking to revive the experience of primitive narcissism in what draws us to movies while satisfaction of that desire is what renders that experience more-than-real. So, by postulating the return to primitive narcissism as the operative agency in film spectators, Baudry thinks he has isolated the cause of the cinematic effect while also, in the process, supplying an account of why the movie experience is desirable to us. . . . From Baudry's perspective, the answer seems to be to relive that stage of primitive narcissism where all-is-one, including a conflation of perception and representation. Indeed, for Baudry, the cinematic apparatus incarnates a wish for a simulation machine "capable of offering the subject perceptions which are really representations mistaken for

---

[1]Baudry, p. 701.
[2]Ibid., p. 701.

perceptions,"* thereby recalling the dream state which itself derives from a regression to an archaic state where perception and representation are not differentiated. Summarizing Baudry's case so far, his argument looks like this:

1. The dream apparatus has the following features: inhibition of movement; lack of reality testing; an imagistic medium; a dark room; projection; a screen; a more-than-real impression of reality; a tendency to efface the distinction between perception and representation.
2. The cinematic apparatus has exactly the same features noted in premise 1.
3. A significant animating force behind the dream apparatus is the desire for and regression to primitive narcissism which enactment causes the charged experience of dreams.
4. Therefore it is probable that a significant animating force behind the cinematic apparatus is the desire for and regression to primitive narcissism which enactment causes the charged experience of cinema.

Baudry, of course, does not hold that films are mistaken for dreams. He rather construes them as simulations of dreams. For this reason he might want to say that the regression encountered in cinema is less intense than that of dreams. Nevertheless, he would appear to hold that to whatever degree the more-than-real impression of reality of film approximates the analogous effect of dreams, it is a function of the process of some measure of regression to the all-is-one state of primitive oral narcissism.

Because of the emphasis Baudry places on the cinematic apparatus as a simulation of unconscious phenomena, specifically of the hallucinatory aura of dreams, one might offer a slightly different interpretation of Baudry's argument than the one just presented. That is, one might take Baudry to be saying that since film replicates the most significant conditions of dreaming—for example, motor inhibition, lack of reality testing, and so on—it triggers the same effect—regression to primitive narcissism. On this interpretation of Baudry's strategy, the argument rides on the principle: same conditons, same effects. However, whether one chooses this interpretation or the interpretation of the analysis as an inductive argument by analogy is logically indifferent for the purposes of evaluating Baudry's central claims. For in either case Baudry's central assertions stand or fall on the basis of the adequacy of the correlations he draws between cinema and dreams.

Baudry concludes his essay by asserting that the unconscious has an instinctual desire to manifest itself to consciousness. This suggests that cinema is one means for fulfilling this instinctual desire. For in simulating dream, cinema satisfies the desire of the unconscious for acknowledgment. This somewhat resembles a claim that Metz makes to the effect that by combining elements of night dream and day-dream film causes pleasure by externalizing what is usually experienced as internal. But this claim of Baudry's can only be accepted if cinema is a suitable simulation of dreams, that is, if the analogies Baudry draws between film and dream are fitting and if they are not outweighed by significant disanalogies.

However, before turning to an assessment of Baudry's central thesis, it is impor-

---

*Baudry, p. 705.

tant to take notice of an elaborate complication in the text which has not been remarked upon so far. Baudry not only analogizes film and dream but he also compares both with the description of the circumstances of the prisoners in Plato's myth of the cave.[1] Those prisoners are chained in a darkened vault. Behind and above them, fires burn. As passersby walk between the prisoners and the flames, the strollers' ambulating shadows are cast upon the wall of the cave. The prisoners see these moving shadows and take them for reality. Through this allegory, Plato sets forth his disparaging estimation of the ordinary person's "knowledge" of the world. It is based on illusion; it is nought but shadowy deception.

Baudry calls attention to the ways in which Plato's cave resembles the cinematic apparatus. The cave is analogous to the apparatus in obvious respects: the motoricity of the prisoners is inhibited as is their capacity to test reality. The cave, like the movie theater, is a dim space. The shadows in Plato's cave might be thought of as projections and the wall of the cave is a screen of sorts. Moreover, the projecting device is above and behind the prisoners and is, so to speak, hidden from them. The imagery in both Plato's cave and the cinema is a matter of shadows or reflections caused by passing something before a light. And in both cases, one can designate the play of "two scenes": first, the scene in the world that gives rise to the "shadows" and second, the scene comprised of the shadows themselves. These analogies lead Baudry to conclude that Plato's myth of the cave "doesn't merely evoke, but quite precisely describes in its mode of operation the cinematographic apparatus and the spectator's place in relation to it."[2]

Now the question immediately arises as to what logical purpose the analogies between Plato's cave and the cinematic apparatus serve in the context of Baudry's overall analysis of film in terms of regression to primitive narcissism. For these added cave analogies do not function logically to enhance Baudry's argument concerning film and dream. The conclusion of that argument is that regression is the motor of the cinematic apparatus just as it is the motor of the dream apparatus. For the analogies with Plato's cave to film and dream to bolster this conclusion— namely, that regression to primitive narcissism is the motor of the cinematic apparatus—we would have to have reason to claim antecedent knowledge to the effect that Plato's myth was generated by the type of regressive mechanism that the argument wants to attribute to the cinematic apparatus. But we do not have such knowledge. Whether Plato's myth of the cave derives from a regressive desire remains to be proved to the same degree that the cinematic apparatus' origin in such a desire does. That is, the psychoanalytic cause of Plato's myth is not known prior to Baudry's argument and in that sense is logically in the same boat as whatever the animating force behind the cinematic apparatus turns out to be. Thus, adding the analogies of Plato's cave, since the cause of that myth cannot be supplied as a premise of the argument (but, at best, as a corollary conclusion), does not strengthen the argument by analogy between the cinematic apparatus and the dream apparatus. So the question remains as to the point of Baudry's ornate rendition of Plato's myth.

---

[1]Plato *Republic* 7.514.
[2]Baudry, "The Apparatus," p. 693.

Baudry, of course, has no wish to endorse Plato's epistemological position which he, Baudry, misidentifies as idealism, a label more apt for a post-Cartesian such as Berkeley (that is, Plato does not believe that all that exists is mental and, indeed, the mental/physical distinction relevant to the formation of an idealist philosophy does not appear to have been historically available to Plato). Rather, Baudry tears the myth of the cave out of the context in which it functions as an allegory, and he treats it as a fantasy ripe for psychoanalysis. Among other things, Baudry claims that it is a proto-cinematic wish, that is, a deep-seated wish for something very much like cinema before the invention of cinema. Baudry sees evidence for similar proto-cinematic wishes throughout history: the camera obscura, the magic lantern, the praxinoscope. What Baudry seems to conclude from the existence of a proto-cinema stretching from Plato's cave to the praxinoscope is that it supplies evidence for a transhistorical, psychical, or instinctual source of desire behind the invention of the cinematic apparatus and its prefigurations.[1] And, of course, if the compelling force behind cinema is instinctual, that may supply prima facie grounds for approaching it psychoanalytically. Thus, I take it that the point of Baudry's use of Plato's cave in "The Apparatus" is not to enhance the central argument about the causal relevance of regression to film, but rather to mount a coordinated but independent argument to persuade us that the recent invention of cinema is really a manifestation of a long-standing, transhistorical, or instinctual desire of the sort that psychoanalysis is fitted to examine. That is, the discussion of Plato's cave is meant to convince us of the appropriateness of psychoanalyzing cinema and it is not, properly speaking, part of the argument by analogy that concludes with the assertion of regression as key to the cinematic apparatus.

Of course, in speaking this way I am offering an interpretation of Baudry's essay, one guided by the logical requirements of the type of argument Baudry appears to advance. I admit that at points Baudry himself writes as though the analysis of the allegory of the cave were an essential part of the film/dream argument. Not only does this fly in the face of the logical point made earlier, but it also promotes many extravagant and confusing, free-associative leaps as Baudry attempts to forge connections simultaneously between Plato's cave, film, and dream. For example, Plato's cave correlates with the darkened room of the movie theater. What connection does this have with dreams? Baudry says that the dreamwork often represents the unconscious by means of underground places.[2] Now even if this has some connection with Plato's cave, what is its relevance to the cinematic apparatus? Films are not characteristically viewed in caves or underground places. The effects of such whimsical flights of fancy can be minimized if we restrict our attention to the central argument that analogizes film and dream which, anyway, is the logical fulcrum of Baudry's case. Thus, a sense of interpretive charity leads me to regard the film/dream argument and the analysis of Plato's cave as making separate though coordinated points.

Undoubtedly, Baudry's essay also attempts to show that the "apparatus" of Plato's cave has the same regressive mechanism behind it as does the dream "appara-

---

[1]Baudry, p. 697.
[2]Ibid., p. 698.

tus." And Baudry's way of showing this is ostensibly an argument by analogy like that concerning the cinematic apparatus. But this is, logically, a parallel argument to the film/dream argument, one that neither supports nor derives support from the speculations on film and dream. That is, the cave/dream argument concluding with regression as the motor behind Plato's myth is an induction to be pursued independently of the film/dream argument. Indeed, Baudry's discussion of Plato is only relevant to film theorists—as opposed to historians of philosophy—insofar as the myth of the cave can be demonstrated to be proto-cinematic. Thus, I will restrict comment upon Baudry's cave/dream analogies to those points that are relevant to establishing the existence of a proto-cinematic wish.

Baudry's "The Apparatus," then, contains at least two major arguments for film theorists: that the apparatus of cinema importantly involves regression to primitive narcissism and that the archaic wish underlying cinema is atavistic, reaching as far back in history as Plato's myth of the cave. Of these two arguments the former seems to me of greater moment because, if it is true, it is what gives the claim about a proto-cinematic wish precise substance, and also because it would supply an interesting and substantial insight even if the claims about proto-cinematic wishes were false, that is, if the invention of cinema responded to a historically recent wish rather than to an ancient longing of the human race.

The argument that the cinematic apparatus involves regression to a period of primitive narcissism where self is not differentiated from the environment is an inductive argument by analogy and, therefore, its conclusions are only probable. This is not problematic for most of what we value as knowledge is at best probable. The degree of warrantability in such an argument, however, depends on the strength of the analogies cited in the premises and on the presumption that there are not significant disanalogies, in this case between film and dream, which would neutralize or outweigh the persuasiveness of the analogies advanced. Thus, to assess Baudry's thesis we must consider whether his analogies are apt and compelling, and whether or not there are profound disanalogies between film and dream which render Baudry's analogies fledgling.

The two analogies that Baudry repeatedly stresses involve the inhibition of movement and the absence of reality testing, features purportedly shared by the cinematic apparatus and dream. Supposing that these are features of dreams, are they also features of film viewing? The dreamer is asleep; insofar as he is not a somnambulist, his literal movement is restricted to tossing and turning. Of course, his movement capacities as a character in his own dream can be quite expansive. But insofar as he is asleep, the movement of his physical body is involuntary. But what of the cinema viewer?

Conventionally we sit in our seats, moving our heads, arms, and so on within a small perimeter of activity. But is our movement inhibited in a way that is significantly analogous to the inertness of sleep? First of all, a key reason for speaking of motor inhibition, both in terms of sleep and in terms of the infantile state of primitive narcissism, is that in those cases the lack of mobility, for different reasons, is involuntary. However, no matter how sedentary our film viewing is, we are not involuntary prisoners in our seats.

Of course, Baudry speaks of this lack of motoricity not only in respect to film viewing and dreaming, but also with reference to Plato's prisoners whose constraint is involuntary. So the dream state and that of the prisoners correlate along the dimension of involuntary motor inhibition. And movie viewers are supposed to resemble the prisoners. But from this one cannot surmise that it is correct to claim corresponding motor inhibition for movie spectators since movie spectators resemble the prisoners only in such respects as being viewers of reflection and not in terms of involuntariness. Unlike Plato's prisoners, the film viewer can move her head voluntarily, attending to this part of the screen and then the next. What she sees comes under her control, unlike the dreamer or the prisoner, in large measure because of her capacity to move her head and her eyes. And, the film viewer, as Baudry admits, can leave the theater, change her seat, or go into the lobby for a smoke.

Though Baudry does not make this move, a proponent of the inhibition analogy might claim that when a film spectator adopts the convention of sitting before the movie screen, she adopts the pretense of having her motor capacities inhibited. But there is no evidence that such a game of make-believe is occurring. A more likely description of what the spectator does when adopting the convention of taking a seat is that she opts for the easiest method of attending to the film. Literally, her motoricity is not inhibited, nor does she feel it or pretend it to be. If we are willing to describe film viewing as involving motor inhibition, we should be equally willing to describe witnessing baseball games and listening to political speeches as involving motor inhibition. And to the extent that such descriptions of baseball and speeches is inaccurate, so is a description of movie viewing as movement inhibited inaccurate. Moreover, even if there is a sense in which we might say that movement in all these cases is "inhibited," it is certainly not a matter of motor inhibition, but a voluntary inhibition promoted by respect for conventional decorum.

Of course, the point that sitting at movies is a social convention is central. Movies can be watched *with no loss of effect* while standing; people frequently walk to the rear of the theater and watch, stand in the aisles while they grab a smoke or relax their bottoms. Nor are such standing filmgoers necessarily stationary; if one watches the film while pacing across a side aisle, the impression the film imparts need not be lost. Baudry connects the putative impression of reality imparted by film to inhibited motoricity. Given this, one would predict that that impression would not occur if the spectator watched while also moving voluntarily. If there is such a phenomenon as the impression of reality, then it should be an empirical matter to establish whether it disappears when the spectator is in movement. In my own case, I have found that I can back out of a movie theater while watching the screen or return to my seat from the beverage bar with no discernible difference in the impressions I derive from the screen than when I am seated. I know I'm walking in one case and sitting in the other, but these are proprioceptive impressions and not screen impressions.

Perhaps Baudry would admit that the film viewer's movement is not literally inhibited, but would attempt to save his analogy by saying that the film viewer *feels* inhibited. Phenomenologically, I have never had such an experience. But even if others do have such experiences, this will not help the analogy that Baudry wishes to draw. Why? Well, if we shift to a phenomenological register, then the dreamer often *feels* in motion when dreaming, for instance, when one dreams one is falling or being pursued by a three-headed ogre. That is, the dreamer often feels in motion when he is not, whereas the film viewer does not ordinarily take himself to be literally in motion when he is not.* Of course, Baudry may say that the inhibited movement which is attributed to the movie spectator is really metaphorical. But why should a correlation between his metaphorical description of the film viewer and the literal motor inhibition of the sleeper count as anything more than an entertaining but fanciful piece of equivocation?

Baudry's second key analogy between the cinematic apparatus and dream hinges on the claim that both involve an absence of reality testing. Of course, in one sense, the film viewer is fully capable of indulging in reality testing. He can go up to the screen and touch it; he can shift his view of the screen, noting that the contours around the objects do not alter, and, thereby, he can surmise that the projected array is two dimensional. Also, things like coke bottles and cabbages can be and have been thrown at movies, a dramatic measure for revealing the nature of the screen. Baudry is aware of this; when he speaks of an absence of reality testing in film viewing, his reference is not to an incapacity the viewer has in relation to objects, such as screens, in the actual world; rather Baudry has in mind that the viewer lacks the ability to test reality within the world of the film. That is, the movie viewer cannot enter the visual array onscreen in order to ascertain whether the buildings in *Siegfried* are concrete or merely cardboard.

Baudry also connects lack of reality testing with the inhibition of movement. Plato's prisoners, and the preambulatory infants at the stage of primitive narcissism cannot test reality at a distance because they are immobile. But the same correlation between motor inhibition and absence of reality testing cannot, as Baudry suggests, be extrapolated to film viewing and dreaming. For if there is an absence of reality testing in both these cases, then that is a function of the fact that, *loosely speaking, there is no reality to be tested in* the world of the film and the world of the dream (where "reality" is understood as the foil of "representation"). So if the correlation based on absence of reality due to inhibited movement is key to aligning film and dream with the infantile state of primitive narcissism, the analogy is inaccurate.

We may also wish to know whether it is really appropriate to hold that the film viewer has no means for testing reality inside the world of the film. Certainly it is true that we cannot walk into the world of *Casablanca* in order to determine whether the characters are really drinking whiskey. But at the same time, I think that it pays to recall a really overwhelming disanalogy between film viewing and dreaming. Namely, films are publicly accessible; they can be viewed by more than one person. Moreover, they can be repeated; we can see the same film again and again, and we can fall back on all sorts of evidence—production and distribution records, the testimony of other viewers and of the filmmakers, the existence of similar prints, and so on—to warrant the claim that the film we just saw, say *Captain Blood,* is the same film we saw in the past. This is a radical disanalogy with dreaming. Neither the analyst nor anyone but the dreamer has access to the dream. And

---

*"Ordinarily" here is meant to acknowledge that there are certain tricks which, as in Cinerama, can induce the impression of, say, plummeting. But these are extraordinary moments of cinema, and not the sort of evidence to be adduced in an account of the customary effects of film.

no one, including the dreamer, can be sure that his report of a dream is accurate; there is no interpersonal validation available. Even with a "recurring" dream, we have little reason to be confident that the dreamer experienced exactly the same dream from night to night. What does this epistemic disanalogy have to do with reality testing? Simply that with films there is a way in which we can "test reality," that is, corroborate our experience of a movie. We can ask someone else if she saw what we saw. Nor is this something we do only after a film is over. During *Lifeforce* I leaned over to my neighbor and asked "Did I really just see a vampire-nun?" to which she replied "I saw her too."

There are, in short, means to test the veracity of our experience of films. We cannot plunge into the image, but we can corroborate what we see there, which is the sort of reality testing that is appropriate to visual fictions (as opposed to what might be called ordinary visual "realities"). Moreover, if we are worried about testing the fidelity of documentaries to their subjects, that is also possible. My point here is simply that it seems to me inappropriate to describe the film viewer as lacking the means for testing reality. And if I am right in this matter, this short-circuits Baudry's second key analogy between film and dream. However, if I am wrong and the analogy is acceptable, the considerations I have just raised present another problem for Baudry. For even if in some sense his analogy works, I have also pointed to a major disanalogy between film and dream: namely, that film experiences are open to interpersonal verification. This appears to me to be important enough to outweigh analogies between film and quasi-solipsistic phenomena, since it establishes that film viewing has an objective dimension and is not purely subjective.

Films are a visual medium and so are dreams. Is this a significant analogy between the external and internal phenomena under comparison? Not really. For memories are also often visual. Why not analogize film to memories as certain film realists might propose? Here, it might be argued that dream is the appropriate analog—that we know to eliminate memory as a viable candidate—because of the earlier analogies that correlate film with dream rather than memory. But as I hope I have shown, those earlier analogies are not so sturdy, nor, I might add, is the film theorist under any imperative to identify *any* mental correlate for film.

However, there is also an important disanalogy between film imagery and dream imagery which indicates that the two are not congruent. The single film image is ordinarily complete, by which I mean that, typically, it is visually articulated throughout. Dream images, on the other hand, tend to be incomplete, foregrounds without backgrounds or figures in a void. This can be simulated in film as can the "noise" of the dreamwork; note Brakhage's films. However, the ordinary film image does not "look like" the ordinary dream image. That is, even if film and dream are imagistic, they are radically dissimilar imagistic media. They are too unlike to be treated as cognate phenomena. . . . Metz notices further, crucial dissimilarities between film and dream,* which added to the disanalogies I adduce render Baudry's argument even more unlikely.

Baudry's analogy between film and dream in respect of darkened rooms is also

---

*In Christian Metz, "The Fiction Film and its Spectator," *New Literary History* (Fall 1976).

problematic. One can, of course, fall asleep mid-day on the beach. And movies can be viewed in well-lit circumstances. I expect that Baudry is probably right in asserting that most of the time we dream and view films in the dark. But there is still something strange about this correlation. The film viewer is not only objectively in a darkened room; she is experientially aware of being in a darkened room. But even if the dreamer is objectively in a darkened room, she is unaware of it. Indeed, she may believe that she is on a blistering, sun-baked desert. That is, though there is a possible objective analogy between the film viewer and the dreamer, their experiences are disanalogous. Now if a film is supposed to simulate dreams or trigger the same kind of response or mechanism in the subject, wouldn't it seem more likely that what the viewer experiences be key to the dream analogy rather than the objective, physical conditions of reception? That is, the dreamer does not have the same experiential awareness of a darkened room that the film viewer does. So why would the film viewer's awareness of a darkened room remind one of dreaming or simulate dreaming for the unconscious? In this case, Baudry seems to overvalue the significance of correlations between the objective, physical conditions of film viewing and dreaming while forgetting the crucial, phenomenological disanalogies between the film experience and dream experience. We saw that there was a similar problem with his treatment of inhibited motoricity, where he ignored the fact that objectively, physically leaden sleepers often feel in vigorous motion.

Another analogy that Baudry proposes between film and dream is that both impart what he refers to as a more-than-real impression of reality. Part of the problem with evaluating this claim is the vagueness of the notion of a more-than-real impression of reality. That is, even if film and dream impart such broadly describable impressions, are their respective impressions the same in analytically revealing respects? Both quartz and lemurs can be described as matter but they are matter of such different sorts that the observation does not tell us much that is useful. Are the respective more-than-real impressions proffered by film and dream very alike or very unalike?

Answering this question is difficult since Baudry tells us next to nothing about the phenomena to which he wants us to refer. However, if the impressions he has in mind are a matter of imagery charged with affect, we can remark that dream imagery is, if not just more vividly charged, it is at least more invariantly charged than movie imagery. The reason for this, which Metz notes,* is that the affect that attaches to dream imagery originates in the dreamer and her personal associations whereas the affect derivable from film imagery comes from an external source—such as the imaginations of screenwriters and directors—which may or may not correspond to the film viewer's emotive life. Thus, if the more-than-real impression of reality of films and dreams is identified with a constant correlation of imagery and affect, then the film apparatus and dream are very different. Moreover, if the more-than-real impression of reality is not a matter of a constant coincidence of affect and imagery, what is it? Merely occasionally exciting imagery? But isn't that enough to correlate a televised chess game to dreams?

---

*Ibid.

But there is another way to probe the problems with Baudry's use of the notion of the more-than-real impression of reality. In dream, this impression appears to refer to imagery charged with affect. In film, we are told that this impression is one that diverges from our ordinary encounters with mundane life. And, admittedly, the events we witness on film are most often more exciting, more expressively characterized, and more emotionally arresting than those of quotidian existence. However, it is important to note that films of this sort, though common, are also very special. They are, in the majority of cases, fiction films or they are films otherwise designed explicitly to promote intense affective responses. A film like *Greed,* or *Sunrise,* or *Potemkin,* or *The Passion of Joan of Arc,* may leave an impression that is, as they say, "larger than life." But this sort of impression is not a function of simply throwing an image on the screen. It is the internal structure of these films that accounts for their effect, not the fact that they are projected. Not all films bestow comparable affective results. Home movies, or bank surveillance footage, especially of persons unknown to us, may appear affectless, flat, and lackadaisical. That is, many films are projected, but few are chosen. Now this is an important point against Baudry. For he claims that the more-than-real impression of which he writes is a consequence of the cinematic apparatus, a claim tantamount to predicting that whatever is projected onscreen will be swathed in affect. But this is downright false; just recall Warhol's *Empire.*

Another major analogy between film and dream that Baudry produces asserts that both have screens, or projection supports. It seems reasonable, barring the complications of TV, to agree that films are *normally* projected onto screens. But frankly the claim seems shaky in regard to dreams. The evidence appears to be that some of Lewin's patients reported dream screens in their nightly reveries. I have no reason to question their reports. However, does this amount to evidence that something like a dream screen is an essential or normal element in all dreams? Perhaps Lewin's patients had personal associations with movie screens and this accounts for the appearance of screens in *their* dreams. Why suppose that a screen element is a characteristic feature of all dreams? Were there visions of screens in dreams before there were screened entertainments? Were there visions of screens in cultures without screened entertainments? And, furthermore, what general criteria are there for establishing that phenomena, like the appearance of a screen in a dream, are organic ingredients of dreaming rather than the associative imagery of given dreams? Until these questions can be satisfactorily answered the dream screen/film screen correspondence—and with it the dream/film apparatus analogy—appear extremely dubious. Of course, as I have already admitted, dream imagery is often incomplete; but where the dream "picture" is unarticulated it is not necessarily the case that the dreamer apprehends a screen, white, silver, or otherwise. There is rather just a void.

So far Baudry's argument by analogy has been attacked by showing that his analogies are hardly compelling and by remarking upon salient disanalogies between film and dream. The accumulated force of these objections shows that Baudry's argument by analogy is without substantial warrant. I think the previously cited disanalogies are enough to swamp his case. But also the premises that set out the analogies between film and dream are virtually without support.[1] Thus, Baudry's argument fails to go through.[2]

Of course, questions, as well, might be raised not only about Baudry's analogies but also about the crucial premise that asserts that the underlying mechanism in dream is regression to primitive, oral narcissism. This is a psychoanalytic claim, not a film theoretical one, and, as such, we should probably not pursue this issue in depth here. Yet, it pays to remember that the Lewin-Baudry hypothesis about regression is extremely controversial.

The regression hypothesis appears to ride upon the postulation of a dream screen which, in turn, can be associated with a mother's breast. The evidence for a dream screen as an organic, essential, or merely characteristic element of dreaming has already been challenged. Insofar as the dream screen serves as a linchpin for the inference of regression, and insofar as the dream screen phenomenon is not generic, then there is no evidence for a generic regressive mechanism, of the specificity Baudry claims, in dreaming.

Also one must at least question the purported screen/breast association. What is its basis? And how extensive is it? Maybe some white people envision breasts as white and then go on to associate the latter with white screens. But not everyone is white. And I even wonder if many whites associate breasts and screens. Certainly it is not an intuitively straightforward association like that between guns and penises. For example, screens are flat; and lactating breasts are not. A screen is, ideally, uniform in color and texture; but a breast has a nipple. Nor will the association work if it is put forward by saying that breasts are, for the infant in the state of oral regression, targets of projections as are screens. For according to the theory of primitive narcissism, the mother's breasts are part of an undifferentiated, all-is-one experience, and, therefore, could not have been recognized way back then by the primitive narcissist, and, thus, cannot be recalled now to be targets of projection. For primitive narcissism admits no distinctions between targets of projections, projections, and projectionists.

I do not deny that there may be some people who associate screens and breasts, thereby at least suggesting the hypothesis of oral regression in those cases. After all, it is probably psychologically possible to associate anything with anything else. But even if some people associate breasts and screens, that does not provide enough evidence to claim a general pattern of association between breasts and screens such as might support a theory about all dreaming. And if oral regression is not the general causal force energizing the dream, then it cannot be extrapolated by analogy as the causal force behind the cinema apparatus.

Baudry's central argument in "The Apparatus" is beset by problems at every turn. Do his subsidiary arguments fare any better? By analogical reasoning, he links

---

[1]A film/dream analogy of Baudry's that I have not touched upon is the assertion that, in film and dream, representation is taken as perception. I reject the notion that film spectators mistake cinematic representations as perceptions and, therefore, reject the basis of this analogy.

[2]Moreover, if Baudry's analogies between film and dream are groundless, then it is hard to see how film could simulate dream, nor is it easy to see how film could trigger the same sort of regression that dreams do.

Plato's myth of the cave with dreaming, and also with filmgoing, inferring that all three can be explicated by reference to regression. Plato's cave, furthermore, is identified as proto-cinematic, indicating to Baudry, that the instinctual desire that propels filmgoing is ancient.

The analogies between Plato's prisoners and dreamers are rather weak, often in ways reminiscent of the problems with Baudry's film/dream analogies. Both prisoners and dreamers are said to be immobile, in a darkened place, bombarded with visual imagery, and unable to test reality. Contra Baudry, we must note again, with reference to darkened places, that people can sleep and dream in broad daylight, while the "world of the dream" need not be dark. And, as was pointed out earlier, the dreamer as a character in a dream need not be immobile, while the sleeper, unlike Plato's prisoners, is unaware of being immobile. Also, what Plato's prisoners see differs radically from the dreamer's imagery—that is, Plato's prisoners see uniformly black figures whose only features are shadowy contours rather than internally articulated figures with eyes and moustaches. And, of course, Plato's prisoners are awake while dreamers are not, which reminds us that Plato's prisoners do literally see something—even if they misinterpret it—and this indicates that they can objectively correct each other about the look of the shadows before them, a type of reality testing not available to the dreamer. One could go on at length discounting Baudry's dream analysis of Plato, but this appears to be more of an issue for historians of philosophy, if it is an issue for anyone, than for film theorists. So let the preceding, hurried refutation of Baudry's version of Plato's cave suffice.

Baudry also claims that Plato's myth of the cave is a prefiguration of cinema. Needless to say this ignores the philosophical purposes Plato designed the myth to serve. But Baudry believes that the myth evinces a myth deeper than Plato was aware of. Baudry holds that Plato's cave is proto-cinematic, which leads him to claim that cinema answers a desire of ancient, instinctual origins. Many, more historically minded, film theorists might wish to question the existence of transhistorical, transcultural desires of the sort Baudry postulates. Nor is the existence of such a transcultural desire absolutely integral to the project of psychoanalyzing the cinematic apparatus. For cinema might be the answer to culturally specific desires of the nineteenth and twentieth centuries.

Baudry's analogies between the cinematic apparatus and Plato's cave are underwhelming. Both, purportedly, involve projection from behind the spectator. But films are often rear-projected and early Japanese cinemas positioned their audiences at right angles to the projection apparatus (not to mention the possibility of projecting films via large video screens). Are either of these practices uncinematic or do audiences at, for example, rear-projected movies have different film experiences than those at cinemas with projectors behind the audience. Baudry speaks of the projection in the cave and in cinema as hidden. But film projection is not always hidden. One can set up a projector in one's living room or in a classroom or boardroom, for all to see, and still have a typical film experience. We have already noted the film viewer is not necessarily immobile. Plato's prisoners are shackled at the neck; even the seated film viewer can move her head. Furthermore, the images of film are immensely different than Plato's shadows. The prisoners see solid black blotches on the wall while film viewers see internally articulated pictures. How, for example, could Plato's prisoner see the eyes of one of the people who cast the shadows on their wall? And isn't this disanalogy far more striking than the analogies that Baudry defends?

Plato's prisoners cannot enter the world of the shadows for purposes of reality testing and neither can viewers of *Casablanca* belly up to Rick's bar for a fast Scotch. But, on the other hand, film viewers can touch the screen, and what is more important, they are aware that there is a screen, and that they are watching a movie. Thus, their status, epistemologically, is exactly opposite that of Plato's prisoners. Also, I think we would agree that one could see a film that portrayed the world accurately whereas Plato's shadow representations are putatively always deceptive. There are surely some surface resemblances between Plato's prisoners and film viewers—they both see projections. But this is hardly sufficient for supporting the claim that both film and the myth of the cave address the same psychic need and mobilize the same psychic mechanism.

Baudry believes that Plato's cave is part of the prehistory of cinema. Apart from the inductive weakness of the analogies he draws, there is also something strained in Baudry's use of the notion of the prehistory of cinema. Is every instance and/or report of shadow projection, prior to 1895, to be considered part of the prehistory of cinema? What criteria determine that which we are to count as legitimately and four-squaredly part of the prehistory of cinema? The camera obscura, Marey's repeating camera, the praxinoscope, and Muybridge's battery of cameras are clear-cut examples of what people include in the prehistory of cinema. And it is easy to see that what these devices have in common is that they can figure in causal accounts of the invention of cinema. But there is no historical argument in sight to show that Plato's myth of the cave literally played a role in the invention of cinema. Thus, even if Baudry's analogies were more convincing, it is not clear that it would be appropriate to consider Plato's cave as part of the prehistory of cinema.

The central argument, as well as the subsidiary ones, in "The Apparatus" appear, upon scrutiny, to be utterly groundless. Undoubtedly, some readers may complain that my methods of examining Baudry's hypotheses are not suitable and perhaps even boorish. For, in my account, Baudry is making a series of literal, logical, scientific claims about a causal process. Thus, Baudry's conclusions are assessed with the rigor one would apply to any scientific hypothesis. However, many contemporary film theorists might object that Baudry is doing something more "interesting" or "important" than pedestrian science.

Personally, I find it difficult to see why a claim about the isolation of a causal mechanism (in this case, regression as a motor force behind cinema) should not be treated as a scientific hypothesis. And so treated, Baudry's arguments by analogy are woefully inept; he fails to consider significant disanalogies, while the analogies he presents are loose and superficial. But many contemporary film theorists, especially those with backgrounds in literature, may counter that that which I call "loose" and "superficial" is really graceful, imaginative, and ingenious. They admire Baudry, as they admire Barthes, for his supposed expertise in belles lettres. But however seductive to some literary sensibilities "The Apparatus" may be, contemporary belles lettres does not afford the means to defend causal claims about the processes underlying cinema. Film theorists with backgrounds in literature may bewail this fact; but it is unavoidable. Moreover, as we shall see, the confusion of belles lettres, on the one hand, with scientific and philosophical reasoning, on the other, is one of the most egregious problems in contemporary film theory. Indeed, the extremely detailed, literal-minded, and argumentive style of this chapter . . . is mandated by my conviction that contemporary film theorists, with their penchant for belletristic expression, including slippery analogies and metaphors, must be shown that they are using the wrong tools for the tasks at hand.

1988

PARKER TYLER
FROM MAGIC AND MYTH OF THE MOVIES

PREFACE

That the movies offer nothing but entertainment is a myth in a sense never used or implied in the following pages. I am not denying that millions of America's movie fans succeed in finding only entertainment in the nation's theaters. Aside from the newsreels and the documentaries given impetus by the war, entertainment remains all that is consciously demanded by those paying rising prices at movie box offices. . . . Patrons of all art media may get more than they demand as well as less, and since the surplus is not precisely expected, it may register vaguely, obliquely, unconsciously. Especially is this true of the movie audience, if only because as a large mass it is critically inarticulate. I hope that my efforts may succeed in giving it some voice on the positive side—movie reviewers take care of its voice on the negative side—and I hope also that for the benefit of students and those hitherto indifferent to the "folk" art of cinema I may further demonstrate that Hollywood is a vital, interesting phenomenon, at least as important to the spiritual climate as daily weather to the physical climate. A myth foisted specifically on the movies proper rather than on the reaction of audiences is furnished by devotees of both stage and novel who scorn movies as below the serious level—as standing in relation to true art somewhat as the circus does to the legitimate stage. But unfortunately these judges, unaware of the ritual importance of the screen, its baroque energy and protean symbolism, are unwarrantably summary, basically uneducated in the movie medium.

. . . The true field of the movies is not *art* but *myth,* between which—in the sense "myth" is invariably used here—there is a perhaps unsuspectedly wide difference. Assuredly a myth is a fiction, and this is its bare link with art, but a myth is specifically a free, unharnessed fiction, a basic, prototypic pattern capable of many variations and distortions, many betrayals and disguises, even though it remains *imaginative* truth. It has one degraded function connected with the idea of entertainment I discussed above, as when the word itself becomes adjectival and is deliberately attached to that pseudonymous Baltic kingdom having no existence saving in fifth-rate novels and in the movies. It is unsound to make a fact such as the existence of the very nation where a story occurs into a fiction, for it is like taking the props out from under a building and assuming it will still stand. No matter how fantastic an action, its background must be firm. It is the status of background that determines the strength of a myth, the status of its perspective in human history.

Essentially the *scene* of imaginative truth, or art, is the mind itself, but in some manner this truth must be objective, capable of projection onto the screen of the world. In a sense man *is* his past, the past of his race, and all the beliefs he ever held. Reality cannot be made up from the material facts of his existence, his immediate sensory reactions; nor can it be fundamentally a world that never was. Certainly man has ceased to believe much he used to believe. "Oh, that is a myth," we say, meaning that even if significant, it is an ideal or an illusion, a thing that has no substance. But psychology has taught us the strange reality of chimeras, their symbolic validity; and comparative mythology has revealed the great persistence of psychic patterns, with special reference to the supernatural, whose continuity in human belief is sometimes surprisingly self-evident. At one time men believed the earth was flat. Today this is a purely ornamental myth; it has died because imagining the earth is flat has no relation to our desires or employments. At one time the pagans believed in Diana as goddess of the moon and the hunt. Today this also might be considered a decorative myth, something in the fairy-tale class. Yet like so many legends it holds a mesmeric appeal for the mind; Diana represents, as a matter of fact, a certain sexual type—the vigorous virgin, the woman resistant to love; and yet according to the legend Endymion made her lose her heart; that is, the man lived who could break down her defenses merely through his physical image. Obviously this sexual pattern is repeated today. The modern belief that the earth is round corresponds to the conditions of our planetary existence insofar as, proceeding on this premise, our astronomical calculations work out. The belief is consistent with *all the facts*. Today the fact that Diana once had for the pagans a reality she does not have for us means merely that the myth lives in another form. It is an ideal archetype, a part of human experience that has its home in the imagination. And yet . . . that which was once true once may become true again. What was symbolized by the Diana myth in actual human experience is a permanent legacy of the race. So the essence of myth also has the status of permanent possibility . . . in short, *desires* may have the same power over the mind and behavior, indeed a much greater power, than *facts*.

In the following pages I have occasion to refer specifically to the great researches made in ancient magic by Sir James Frazer. That there are anthropological assumptions contradictory to various of Frazer's own premises is of no importance to the point I am making. In order to explain a single phenomenon, the priest cult of the King of the Wood at Nemi, Frazer accumulated into one work a prodigious array of ancient primitive beliefs and customs suggesting the limitless lineage of the relatively recent cult at Nemi. At this moment, as when his book was written, nobody is a devotee of his cult; nobody believes in the magic of the golden bough that had to be plucked by the aspirant to Diana's priesthood before he was empowered to kill in single combat the incumbent priest. And yet those who do not profoundly know anthroplogy might be astonished to learn how much of our personal lives is influenced by all the ancient magical and religious beliefs connected with this one cult. The whole history of the decay and fall of gods, the extermination of divine hierarchies, could be told with just the Nemian cult as basis. In discussing in later pages the male comics of the screen who entertained troops all over the world during the war, I show how they may be considered modern medicine men or primitive priests, scapegoats who transferred to themselves the inner fears of the soldier striving to be brave and made cowardice and bravery alike into a kind of joke. Consequently in relation to my argument the myth is not, as a psychological or historical nucleus of fact, necessarily to be judged as true or false, illusory or real, according to its specfic labels, its historic status, its literal beliefs. Essentially myths are not factual but symbolic. I assume that movies are essentially likewise.

   . . . Briefly movies, similar to much else in life, are seldom what they seem. In this sense—being, to begin with, fiction—movies are dreamlike and fantastic, their fantasy and examples of this are the folk myths of the absent-minded professor, of the efficiency expert, and of the eccentricity of genius. . . .

   Naturally when I ally myth with superstition I am taking not only Frazier's view of the profound interrelatedness of myths but also Freud's view that beneath the upper levels of the mind lies a vast human capacity to think in terms of frantic passions and above all in terms of symbols. Even ten years ago it would have been thought impossible by movie moguls that a surrealist artist, Salvador Dali, should be employed to devise images to portray movie dreams, which in turn are subjected to psychoanalysis, a clinical process that provides the solution of the plot. . . .

   The fundamental eye trickery that is a genius of the camera—you see the object, yet it isn't there—came to the fore in the movies and ever since then has mocked with its dynamic plasticity the very form from which it developed, the still camera. Today the movie has all the flexibility of the novel as well as the vision and speech of the stage. In striving through imaginative works to create the illusion of reality the movie screen must constantly transcend its own mirror nature of literal reflection. Camera trickery is really camera magic, for illusion can be freely created by the movie camera with more mathematical accuracy and shock value than by sleight-of-hand magic or stage illusion. The very homogeneity of cinema illusion— the images of the actors themselves are illusive, their corporal bodies absent—creates a throwback in the mood of the spectator to the vestiges of those ancient beliefs that I discuss in detail later in the chapter on supernaturalism, such as beliefs in ghosts, secret forces, telepathy, etc.

   Moreover, the movie-theater rite corresponds directly to the profoundly primitive responses of the audience; the auditorium is dark, the spectator is relaxed, the movie in front of him requires less sheer mental attention than would a novel or stage play—less attention because all movement seems to exist on the screen; even the background changes easily, quickly; the whole world moves around the spectator, who is a still point. From the capacity of the screen for trick illusion, plus the dark-enshrouded passivity of the spectator, issues a state of daydream, which I termed in my previous book "the daylight dream" because it occurs in the dark: the screen is the focus of light, while the spectator is conscious in a darkness of the bedroom. It is in daydreams that magic seems to operate, in daydreams that things begin to seem rather than to be. "The movie theater," to quote directly from my previous book, "is the psychoanalytic clinic of the average worker's daylight dream." It is likewise in the process of psychoanalysis, where the *part,* truly recognized as symbol, transforms the meaning of the whole. The movie process is a complex myth of sheer synecdoche. People go to the movies merely to see a favorite player, or for the locale or period, or for the genre, or because they are bored almost to death. How, under these conditions, can anyone hope to appreciate the *whole* movie, especially since, to begin with, the movie can hardly be considered a whole?

No longer does man believe in myth or magic. No! For magic has been sifted and reorganized into science and governs only his material world, not the realm of his spirit, while comparative mythology and anthropology merely comprise school subjects. The sects of Christian religion have organized Western man's spiritual beliefs under one heading: the myth of Christ. Yet Christ's myth too can be related to pagan myths. The very fact that for children the Bible itself is but another series of fairy tales, weighted but little by a sense of historical fact, alone demonstrates my point as to the basic importance of myth with regard to popular or folk art. Our imaginary lives as children survive in us as adults and enrich our subsequent natures. So the fairy-tale lives of primitive races, our ancient antecedents, survive in the religions we formally believe in today as well as among those tribes still unassimiated to modern civilization. I do not claim any absolute value for the myth and magic of Hollywood or for those modern vestiges of the old Greek divinities I have dubbed "the gods and goddesses of Holywood." On the contrary the principle I mean is one of relativity and metamorphosis rather than absolutism and changelessness: just as a word has synonyms and antonyms—so has a myth. In psychoanalytical symbolism, the deepest symbolism of the mind, the identity of objects is established by a complex frame of reference in which an image may represent one of three objects or all three objects at once. If, then, I say that the actors of Hollywood are an enlarged personnel of the realistically anthropomorphic deities of ancient Greece, I do not indulge in a mere bit of verbal humor, satiric or otherwise; on the other hand neither am I proposing or assuming the existence of an unconscious cult of supernatural worship. I feel I am but calling attention to the fact that the glamour actors and actresses of the movie realm are fulfilling an ancient need, unsatisifed by popular religions of contemporary times. Those men and women who perform for us are human, as we are; they have homes, children, love affairs; they suffer and die. And yet a magic barrier cuts across the texture of our mutual humanity; somehow their wealth, fame, and beauty, their apparently unlimited field of worldy pleasure—these conditions tinge them with the supernatural, render them immune to the bitterness of ordinary frustrations. It does not matter if this thought is a mythological exaggeration. It is a *tendency* of the popular imagination. The secret of the power of Hollywood gods and goddesses is that they seem to do everything anyone else does except that when they die—in movies—they die over and over; when they love, they love over and over. Even as the gods do, they undergo continual metamorphoses, never losing their identities, being Rita Hayworth or Glenn Ford no matter what their movie aliases. And like Jupiter in the modern comedy, *Amphitryon 38,* they can condescend, even be ridiculous. All that the public demands is what it always gets—the power to make and break stars—but gods have always had basically mortal lives.

Lastly, in this and my previous book, do I have *a method?* Not in the sense that I am selling ideas, nor above all, is mine a method by which one can test the high or low esthetic content of a given movie. . . . If my method is worthy of a label, it is "psychoanalyticmythological," often socially angled. I have invented little or nothing. I have merely applied it to new material and formulated in accordance with the reapplication. That I speak metaphorically, in dream symbols, and . . . in terms of my own "hallucination," is a fact I wish not only to admit but to proclaim. Yes, I have made up a collective myth of my own, and I confess that in so doing I have plagiarized Hollywood exhaustively. If I have interpreted many things as dreams are interpreted, I cite as belated authorities recent movies of psychoanalytical themes and dream-symbol material. Indirectly, however, I have only been obeying Hollywood's own law of fluidity, of open and ingenious invention. If I have formulated an element of moviedom to be known as "the supernatural hush" and interpreted it as applicable at once to the hush of a cathedral, the hush of a psychiatrist's clinic, the hush of an isolated lovers' session on Riverside Drive, and the hush of the studio while Jennifer Jones does a scene in *The Song of Bernadette,* I feel that I am defining a quality of the movies as one would classify an acidic combination in the laboratory. And if in one of the magic-lantern metamorphoses internal movie meanings are discussed in terms of doubting the evidence of the senses, I am merely following the technique of psychoanalysis as well as paralleling legal criticism of circumstantial evidence of crimes: *things are not always what they seem.* I hope to have revealed a deeper sort of truth than that to be found on surfaces and at the same time to have assembled here a little mythology, a kind of concordance, showing the frequently unconscious magic employed by Hollywood—a magic of dream creation that far transcends its literal messages.

1947

CHRISTIAN METZ
FROM THE IMAGINARY SIGNIFIER

IDENTIFICATION, MIRROR

"What contribution can Freudian psychoanalysis make to the knowledge of the cinematic signifier?": that was the question-dream I posed (the scientific imaginary wishing to be symbolised), and it seems to me that I have now more or less *unwound* it; unwound but no more; I have not given it an answer. I have simply paid attention to what it was I wished to say (one never knows this until one has written it down), I have only questioned my question: this unanswered character is one that has to be deliberately accepted, it is constitutive of any epistemological procedure.

Since I have wished to mark the places (as empty boxes some of which are beginning to fill without waiting for me, and so much the better), the places of different directions of work, and particularly of the last, the psychoanalytic exploration of the signifier, which concerns me especially, I must now begin to inscribe something in this last box; must take further, and more plainly in the direction of the unconscious, the analysis of the investigator's desire that makes me write. And to start with, of course, this means asking a new question: among the specific features of the cinematic signifier that distinguish the cinema from literature, painting, etc. which ones by nature call most directly on the type of knowledge that psychoanalysis alone can provide?

Perception, Imaginary

The cinema's signifier is *perceptual* (visual and auditory). So is that of literature, since the written chain has to be *read,* but it involves a more restricted perceptual register: only graphemes, writing. So too are those of painting, sculpture, architecture, photography, but still within limits, and different ones: absence of auditory

730

perception, absence in the visual itself of certain important dimensions such as time and movement (obviously there is the time of the look, but the object looked at is not inscribed in a precise and ordered time sequence forced on the spectator from outside). Music's signifier is perceptual as well, but, like the others, less "extensive" than that of the cinema: here it is vision which is absent, and even in the auditory, extended speech (except in song). What first strikes one then is that the cinema is *more perceptual,* if the phrase is allowable, than many other means of expression; it mobilises a larger number of the axes of perception. (That is why the cinema has sometimes been presented as a "synthesis of all the arts"; which does not mean very much, but if we restrict ourselves to the quantitative tally of the registers of perception, it is true that the cinema contains within itself the signifiers of other arts: it can present pictures to us, make us hear music, it is made of photographs, etc.)

Nevertheless, this as it were numerical "superiority" disappears if the cinema is compared with the theatre, the opera and other spectacles of the same type. The latter too involve sight and hearing simultaneously, linguistic audition and nonlinguistic audition, movement, real temporal progression. Their difference from the cinema lies elsewhere: they do not consist of *images,* the perceptions they offer to the eye and the ear are inscribed in a true space (not a photographed one), the same one as that occupied by the public during the performance; everything the audience hear and see is actively produced in their presence, by human beings or props which are themselves present. This is not the problem of fiction but that of the definitional characteristics of the signifier: whether or not the theatrical play mimes a fable, its *action,* if need be mimetic, is still managed by real persons evolving in real time and space, *on the same stage or "scene" as the public.* The "other scene," which is precisely not so called, is the cinematic screen (closer to phantasy from the outset): what unfolds there may, as before, be more or less fictional, but the unfolding itself is fictive: the actor, the "décor," the words one hears are all absent, everything is *recorded* (as a memory trace which is immediately so, without having been something else before), and this is still true if what is recorded is not a "story" and does not aim for the fictional illusion proper. For it is the signifier itself, and as a whole, that is recorded, that is absence: a little rolled up perforated strip which "contains" vast landscapes, fixed battles, the melting of the ice on the River Neva, and whole life-times, and yet can be enclosed in the familiar round metal tin, of modest dimensions, clear proof that it does not "really" contain all that.

At the theatre, Sarah Bernhardt may tell me she is Phèdre or, if the play were from another period and rejected the figurative regime, she might say, as in a type of modern theatre, that she is Sarah Bernhardt. But at any rate, I should see Sarah Bernhardt. At the cinema, she could make the same two kinds of speeches too, but it would be her shadow that would be offering them to me (or she would be offering them in her own absence). Every film is a fiction film.

What is at issue is not just the actor. Today there are a theatre and a cinema without actors, or in which they have at least ceased to take on the full and exclusive function which characterises them in classical spectacles. But what is true of Sarah Bernhardt is just as true of an object, a prop, a chair for example. On the theatre stage, this chair may, as in Chekhov, pretend to be the chair in which the melancholy Russian nobleman sits every evening; on the contrary (in Ionesco), it can explain to me that it is a theatre chair. But when all is said and done it is a chair. In the cinema, it will similarly have to choose between two attitudes (and many other intermediate or more tricky ones), but it will not be there when the spectators see it, when they have to recognise the choice; it will have delegated its reflection to them.

What is characteristic of the cinema is not the imaginary that it may happen to represent, but the imaginary that it *is* from the start, the imaginary that constitutes it as a signifier (the two are not unrelated; it is so well able to represent it because it is it; however it is it even when it no longer represents it). The (possible) reduplication inaugurating the intention of fiction is preceded in the cinema by a first reduplication, always-already achieved, which inaugurates the signifier. The imaginary, by definition, combines within it a certain presence and a certain absence. In the cinema it is not just the fictional signified, if there is one, that is thus made present in the mode of absence, it is from the outset the signifier.

Thus the cinema, "more perceptual" than certain arts according to the list of its sensory registers, is also "less perceptual" than others once the status of these perceptions is envisaged rather than their number or diversity; for its perceptions are all in a sense "false." Or rather, the activity of perception which it involves is real (the cinema is not a phantasy), but the perceived is not really the object, it is its shade, its phantom, its double, its *replica* in a new kind of mirror. It will be said that literature, after all, is itself only made of replicas (written words, presenting absent objects). But at least it does not present them to us with all the really perceived detail that the screen does (giving more and taking as much, i.e., taking more). The unique position of the cinema lies in this dual character of its signifier: unaccustomed perceptual wealth, but at the same time stamped with unreality to an unusual degree, and from the very outset. More than the other arts, or in a more unique way, the cinema involves us in the imaginary: it drums up all perception, but to switch it immediately over into its own absence, which is nonetheless the only signifier present.

The All-Perceiving Subject

Thus film is like the mirror. But it differs from the primordial mirror in one essential point: although, as in the latter, everything may come to be projected, there is one thing and one thing only that is never reflected in it: the spectator's own body. In a certain emplacement, the mirror suddenly becomes clear glass.

In the mirror the child perceives the familiar household objects, and also its object par excellence, its mother, who holds it up in her arms to the glass. But above all it perceives its own image. This is where primary identification (the formation of the ego) gets certain of its main characteristics: the child sees itself as an other, and beside another. This other other is its guarantee that the first is really it: by her authority, her sanction, in the register of the symbolic, subsequently by the resemblance between her mirror image and the child's (both have a human form). Thus the child's ego is formed by identification with its like, and this in two senses simultaneously, metonymically and metaphorically: the other human being who is in the glass, the own reflection which is and is not the body, which is like it. The child identifies with itself as an object.

In the cinema, the object remains: fiction or no, there is always something on the screen. But the reflection of the own body has disappeared. The cinema spectator is not a child and the child really at the mirror stage (from around six to around eighteen months) would certainly be incapable of "following" the simplest of films. Thus, what *makes possible* the spectator's absence from the screen—or rather the intelligible unfolding of the film despite that absence—is the fact that the spectator has already known the experience of the mirror (of the true mirror), and is thus able to constitute a world of objects without having first to recognise himself within it. In this respect, the cinema is already on the side of the symbolic (which is only to be expected): the spectator knows that objects exist, that he himself exists as a subject, that he becomes an object for others: he knows himself and he knows his like: it is no longer necessary that this similarity be literally *depicted* for him on the screen, as it was in the mirror of his childhood. Like every other broadly "secondary" activity, the practice of the cinema presupposes that the primitive undifferentiation of the ego and the non-ego has been overcome.

But *with what*, then, does the spectator identify during the projection of the film? For he certainly has to identify: identification in its primoral form has ceased to be a current necessity for him, but he continues, in the cinema—if he did not the film would become incomprehensible, considerably more incomprehensible than the most incomprehensible films—to depend on that permanent play of identification without which there would be no social life (thus, the simplest conversation presupposes the alternation of the *I* and the *you*, hence the aptitude of the two interlocutors for a mutual and reversible identification). What form does this *continued* identification, whose essential role Lacan has demonstrated even in the most abstract reasoning and which constituted the "social sentiment" for Freud (= the sublimation of a homosexual libido, itself a reaction to the aggressive rivalry of the members of a single generation after the murder of the father), take in the special case of one social practice among others, cinematic projection?

Obviously the spectator has the opportunity to identify with the *character* of the fiction. But there still has to be one. This is thus only valid for the narrative-representational film, and not for the psychoanalytic constitution of the signifier of the cinema as such. The spectator can also identify with the actor, in more or less "a-fictional" films in which the latter is represented as an actor, not a character, but is still offered thereby as a human being (as a perceived human being) and thus allows identification. However this factor (even added to the previous one and thus covering a very large number of films) cannot suffice. It only designates secondary identification in certain of its forms (secondary in the cinematic process itself, since in any other sense all identification except that of the mirror can be regarded as secondary).

An insufficient explanation, and for two reasons, the first of which is only the intermittent, anecdotal and superficial consequence of the second (but for that reason more visible, and that is why I call it the first). The cinema deviates from the theatre on an important point that has often been emphasised: it often presents us with long sequences that can (literally) be called "inhuman"—the familiar theme of cinematic "cosmo-morphism" developed by many film theorists—sequences in which only inanimate objects, landscapes, etc. appear and which for minutes at a time offer no human form for spectator identification: yet the latter must be supposed to remain intact in its deep structure, since at such moments the film *works* just as well as it does at others, and whole films (geographical documentaries, for example) unfold intelligibly in such conditions. The second, more radical reason is that identification with the human form appearing on the screen, even when it occurs, still tells us nothing about the *place of the spectator's ego* in the inauguration of the signifier. As I have just pointed out, this ego is already formed. But since it exists, the question arises precisely of *where it is* during the projection of the film (the true primary identification, that of the mirror, forms the ego, but all other identifications presuppose, on the contrary, that it has been formed and can be "exchanged" for the object or the fellow subject). Thus when I "recognise" my like on the screen, and even more when I do not recognise it, where am I? Where is that someone who is capable of self-recognition when need be?

It is not enough to answer that the cinema, like every social practice, demands that the psychical apparatus of its participants be fully constituted, and that the question is thus the concern of general psychoanalytic theory and not that of the cinema proper. For my *where is it?* does not claim to go so far, or more precisely tried to go slightly further: it is a question of the *point* occupied by this already constituted ego, occupied during the cinema showing and not in social life in general.

The spectator is absent from the screen: contrary to the child in the mirror, he cannot identify with himself as an object, but only with objects which are there without him. In this sense the screen is not a mirror. The perceived, this time, is entirely on the side of the object, and there is no longer any equivalent of the own image, of that unique mix of perceived and subject (of other and I) which was precisely the figure necessary to disengage the one from the other. At the cinema, it is always the other who is on the screen; as for me, I am there to look at him. I take no part in the perceived, on the contrary, I am *all-perceiving.* All-perceiving as one says all-powerful (this is the famous gift of "ubiquity" the film makes its spectator); all-perceiving, too, because I am entirely on the side of the perceiving instance: absent from the screen, but certainly present in the auditorium, a great eye and ear without which the perceived would have no one to perceive it, the instance, in other words, which *constitutes* the cinema signifier (it is I who make the film). If the most extravagant spectacles and sounds or the most unlikely combination of them, the combination furthest removed from any real experience, do not prevent the constitution of meaning (and to begin with do not *astonish* the spectator, do not really astonish him, not intellectually: he simply judges the film as strange), that is because he knows he is at the cinema.

In the cinema the *subject's knowledge* takes a very precise form without which no film would be possible. This knowledge is dual (but unique). I know I am perceiving something imaginary (and that is why its absurdities, even if they are extreme, do not seriously disturb me), and I know that it is I who am perceiving it. This second knowledge divides in turn: I know that I am really perceiving, that my sense organs are physically affected, that I am not phantasising, that the fourth wall of the auditorium (the screen) is really different form the other three, that there is a projector facing it (and thus it is not I who am projecting, or at least not all alone), and I also know that it is I who am perceiving all this, that this perceived-imaginary material is deposited in me as if on a second screen, that it is in me that it forms up into an organised sequence, that therefore I am myself the place where this really perceived imaginary accedes to the symbolic by its inauguration as the signifier of a certain type of institutionalised social activity called the "cinema."

In other words, the spectator *identifies with himself*, with himself as a pure act of perception (as wakefulness, alertness): as the condition of possibility of the perceived and hence as a kind of transcendental subject, which comes before every *there is*.

A strange mirror, then, very like that of childhood, and very different. Very like, as Jean-Louis Baudry has emphasized, because during the showing we are, like the child, in a sub-motor and hyper-perceptive state; because, like the child again, we are prey to the imaginary, the double, and are so paradoxically through a real perception. Very different, because this mirror returns us everything but ourselves, because we are wholly outside it, whereas the child is both in it and in front of it. As an *arrangement* (and in a very topographical sense of the word), the cinema is more involved on the flank of the symbolic, and hence of secondariness, than is the mirror of childhood. This is not surprising, since it comes long after it, but what is more important to me is the fact that it is inscribed in its wake with an incidence at once so direct and so oblique, which has no precise equivalent in other apparatuses of signification.

Identification With the Camera

The preceding analysis coincides in places with others which have already been proposed and which I shall not repeat: analyses of *quattrocento* painting or of the cinema itself which insist on the role of monocular perspective (hence of the *camera*) and the "vanishing point" that inscribes an empty emplacement for the spectator-subject, an all-powerful position which is that of God himself, or more broadly of some ultimate signified. And it is true that as he identifies with himself as look, the spectator can do no other than identify with the camera, too, which has looked before him at what he is now looking at and whose stationing (= framing) determines the vanishing point. During the projection this camera is absent, but it has a representative consisting of another apparatus, called precisely a "projector." An apparatus the spectator has behind him, *at the back of his head*, that is, precisely where phantasy locates the "focus" of all vision. All of us have experienced our own look, even outside the so-called *salles obscures* [= cinemas], as a kind of searchlight turning on the axis of our own necks (like a pan) and shifting when we shift (a tracking shot now): as a cone of light (without the microscopic dust scattered through it and streaking it in the cinema) whose vicariousness draws successive and variable slices of obscurity from nothingness wherever and whenever it comes to rest. (And in a sense that is what perception and consciousness are, a *light*, as Freud put it, in the double sense of an illumination and an opening, as in the arrangement of the cinema, which contains both, a limited and wandering light that only attains a small part of the real, but on the other hand possesses the gift of casting light on it.) Without this identification with the camera certain facts could not be understood, though they are constant ones: the fact, for example, that the spectator is not amazed when the image "rotates" (= a pan) and yet he knows he has not turned his head. The explanation is that he has no need to turn it really, he has turned it in his all-seeing capacity, his identification with the movement of the camera being that of a transcendental, not an empirical subject.

All vision consists of a double movement: projective (the "sweeping" searchlight) and introjective: consciousness as a sensitive recording surface (as a screen). I have the impression at once that, to use a common expression, I am "casting" my eyes on things, and that the latter, thus illuminated, come to be deposited within me (we then declared that it is these things that have been "projected," on to my retina, say). A sort of stream called the look, and explaining all the myths of magnetism, must be sent out over the world, so that objects can come back up this stream in the opposite direction (but using it to find their way), arriving at last at our perception, which is now soft wax and no longer an emitting source.

The technology of photography carefully conforms to this (banal) phantasy accompanying perception. The camera is "trained" on the object like a fire-arm (= projection) and the object arrives to make an imprint, a trace, on the receptive surface of the film-strip (= introjection). The spectator himself does not escape these pincers, for he is part of the apparatus, and also because pincers, on the imaginary plane (Melanie Klein), mark our relation to the world as a whole and are rooted in the primary figures of orality. During the performance the spectator is the searchlight I have described, duplicating the projector, which itself duplicates the camera, and he is also the sensitive surface duplicating the screen, which itself duplicates the film-strip. There are two cones in the auditorium: one ending on the screen and starting both in the projection box and in the spectator's vision insofar as it is projective, and one starting from the screen and "deposited" in the spectator's perception insofar as it is introjective (on the retina, a second screen). When I say that "I see" the film, I mean thereby a unique mixture of two contrary currents; the film is what I receive, and it is also what I release, since it does not pre-exist my entering the auditorium and I only need close my eyes to suppress it. Releasing it, I am the projector, receiving it, I am the screen; in both these figures together, I am the camera, which points and yet which records.

Thus the constitution of the signifier in the cinema depends on a series of mirror-effects organised in a chain, and not on a single reduplication. In this the cinema as a topography resembles that other "space," the technical equipment (camera, projector, film-strip, screen, etc.), the objective precondition of the whole institution: as we know, the apparatuses too contain a series of mirrors, lenses, apertures and shutters, ground glasses, through which the cone of light passes: a further reduplication in which the equipment becomes a metaphor (as well as the real source) for the mental process instituted. Further on we shall see that it is also its fetish.

In the cinema, as elsewhere, the constitution of the symbolic is only achieved through and above the play of the imaginary: projection-introjection, presence-absence, phantasies accompanying perception, etc. Even when acquired, the ego still depends in its underside on the fabulous figures thanks to which it has been acquired and which have marked it lastingly with the stamp of the lure. The secondary process does no more than "cover" (and not always hermetically) the primary process which is still constantly present and conditions the very possibility of what covers it.

Chain of many mirrors, the cinema is at once a weak and a robust mechanism: like the human body, like a precision tool, like a social institution. And the fact is that it is really all of these at the same time.

And I, at this moment, what am I doing if not to add to all these reduplications one more whereby theory is attempting to set itself up? Am I not looking at myself looking at the film? This *passion for seeing* (and also hearing), the foundation of the whole edifice, am I not turning it, too, on (against) that edifice? Am I not still the voyeur I was in front of the screen, now that it is this voyeur who is being seen, thus postulating a second voyeur, the one writing at present, myself again?

On the Idealist Theory of the Cinema

The place of the ego in the institution of the signifier, as transcendental yet radically deluded subject, since it is the institution (and even the equipment) that give it this place, surely provides us with an appreciable opportunity the better to understand and judge the precise epistemological import of the idealist theory of the cinema which culminates in the remarkable works of André Bazin. Before thinking directly about their validity, but simply reading texts of this kind, one cannot but be struck by the great precision, the acute and immediately sensitive intelligence that they often demonstrate; at the same time they give the diffuse impression of a permanent ill foundedness (which affects nothing and yet affects everything), they suggest that somewhere they contain something like a weak point at which the whole might be overturned.

It is certainly no accident that the main form of idealism in cinematic theory has been phenomenology. Bazin and other writers of the same period explicitly acknowledged their debt to it, and more implicitly (but in a more generalised fashion) all conceptions of the cinema as a mystical revelation, as "truth" or "reality" unfolding by right, as the apparition of what is [*l'ètant*], as an epiphany, derive from it. We all know that the cinema has the gift of sending some of its lovers into prophetic trances. However, these cosmophanic conceptions (which are not always expressed in an extreme form) register rather well the "feeling" of the *deluded ego* of the spectator, they often give us excellent descriptions of this feeling and to this extent there is something scientific about them and they have advanced our knowledge of the cinema. But the *lure of the ego* is their blind spot. These theories are still of great interest, but they have, so to speak, to be put the other way round, like the optical image of the film.

For it is true that the topographical apparatus of the cinema resembles the conceptual apparatus of phenomenology, with the result that the latter can cast light on the former. (Besides, in any domain, a phenomenology of the object to be understood, a "receptive" description of its appearances, must be the starting-point; only afterwards can *criticism* begin; psychoanalysts, it should be remembered, have their own phenomenology.) The *"there is"* of phenomenology proper (philosophical phenomenology) as an ontic revelation referring to a perceiving-subject (= "perceptual *cogito*"), to a subject for which alone there can be anything, has close and precise affinities with the installation of the cinema signifier in the ego as I have tried to define it, with the spectator withdrawing into himself as a pure instance of perception, the whole of the perceived being "out there." To this extent the cinema really is the "phenomenological art" it has often been called, by Merleau-Ponty himself, for example. But it can only be so because its objective determinations make it so. The ego's position in the cinema does not derive from a miraculous resemblance between the cinema and the natural characteristics of all perception; on the contrary, it is foreseen and marked in advance by the institution (the equipment, the disposition of the auditorium, the mental system that internalises the two), and also by more general characteristics of the psychical apparatus (such as projection, the mirror structure, etc.), which although they are less strictly dependent on a period of social history and a technology, do not therefore express the sovereignty of a "human vocation," but inversely are themselves shaped by certain specific features of man as an animal (as the only animal that is not an animal): his primitive *Hilflosigkeit,* his dependence on another's care (the lasting source of the imaginary, of object relations, of the great oral figures of feeding), the motor prematurity of the child which condemns it to an initial self-recognition by sight (hence outside itself) anticipating a muscular unity it does not yet possess.

In other words, phenomenology can contribute to knowledge of the cinema (and it has done so) insofar as it happens to be like it, and yet it is on the cinema *and* phenomenology in their common illusion of *perceptual mastery* that light must be cast by the real conditions of society and man.

On Some Sub-Codes of Identification

The play of identification defines the cinematic situation in its generality, i.e. *the* code. But it also allows more specific and less permanent configurations, "variations" on it, as it were; they intervene in certain coded figures which occupy precise segments of precise films.

What I have said about identification so far amounts to the statement that the spectator is absent from the screen *as perceived,* but also (the two things inevitably go together) present there and even "all-present" as *perceiver.* At every moment I am in the film by my look's caress. This presence often remains diffuse, geographically undifferentiated, evenly distributed over the whole surface of the screen; or more precisely *hovering,* like the psychoanalyst's listening, ready to catch on preferentially to some motif in the film, according to the force of that motif and according to my own phantasies as a spectator, without the cinematic code itself intervening to govern this anchorage and impose it on the whole audience. But in other cases, certain articles of the cinematic codes or sub-codes (which I shall not try to survey completely here) are made responsible for suggesting to the spectator the vector along which his permanent identificiaton with his own look should be extended temporarily inside the film (the perceived) itself. Here we meet various classic problems of cinematic theory, or at least certain aspects of them: subjective images, out-of-frame space, looks (looks and no longer the look, but the former are articulated to the latter).

There are various sorts of subjective image and I have tried elsewhere (following Jean Mitry) to distinguish between them. Only one of them will detain me for the moment, the one which "expresses the viewpoint of the film-maker" in the standard formula (and not the viewpoint of a character, another traditional sub-case of the subjective image): unusual framings, uncommon shot-angles, etc. as for example in one of the sketches which make up Julien Duvivier's film *Carnet de bal* (the sketch with Pierre Blanchar, shot continuously in tilted framings). In the standard definitions one thing strikes me: I do not see why these uncommon angles should express the viewpoint of the film-maker any more than perfectly ordinary angles, closer to the horizontal. However, the definition is comprehensible even in its inaccuracy: precisely because it is uncommon, the uncommon angle makes us more aware of what we had merely forgotten to some extent in its absence: an identification with the camera (with "the author's viewpoint"). The ordinary framings are finally felt to be non-framings: I espouse the film-maker's look (without which no cinema would be possible), but my consciousness is not too aware of it. The uncommon angle reawakens me and (like the cure) teaches me what I already knew. And then, it obliges my look to stop wandering freely over the screen for the moment and to scan it along more precise lines of force which are imposed on me. Thus for a moment I became directly aware of the *emplacement* of my own presence-absence in the film simply because it has changed.

Now for looks. In a fiction film, the characters look at one another. It can happen (and this is already another "notch" in the chain of identifications) that a character looks at another who is momentarily out-of-frame, or else is looked at by him. If we have gone one notch further, this is because everything out-of-frame *brings us closer to the spectator,* since it is the peculiarity of the latter to be out-of-frame (the out-of-frame character thus has a point in common with him: he is looking at the screen). In certain cases the out-of-frame character's look is "reinforced" by recourse to another variant of the subjective image, generally christened the "character's point of view": the framing of the scene corresponds precisely to the angle from which the out-of-frame character looks at the screen. (The two figures are dissociable moreover: we often know that the scene is being looked at by someone other than ourselves, by a character, but it is the logic of the plot, or an element of the dialogue, or a previous image that tells us so, not the position of the camera, which may be far from the presumed emplacement of the out-of-frame onlooker.)
  In all sequences of this kind, the identification that founds the signifier is *twice relayed,* doubly duplicated in a circuit that leads it to the heart of the film along a line which is no longer hovering, which follows the inclination of the looks and is therefore governed by the film itself: the spectator's look (= the basic identification), before dispersing all over the surface of the screen in a variety of intersecting

lines (= looks of the characters in the frame = second duplication), must first "go through"—as one goes through a town on a journey, or a mountain pass—the look of the character out-of-frame (= first duplication), himself a spectator and hence the first delegate of the true spectator, but not to be confused with the latter since he is inside, if not the frame, then at least the fiction. This invisible character, supposed (like the spectator) to be seeing, will collide obliquely with the latter's look and play the part of an obligatory intermediary. By offering himself as a crossing for the spectator, he inflects the circuit followed by the sequence of identifications and it is only in this sense that he is himself seen: as we see through him, we see ourselves not seeing him.

Examples of this kind are much more numerous and each of them is much more complex than I have suggested here. At this point textual analysis of precise film sequences is an indispensable instrument of knowledge. I just wished to show that in the end there is no break in continuity between the child's game with the mirror and, at the other extreme, certain localised figures of the cinematic codes. The mirror is the site of primary identification. Identification with one's own look is secondary with respect to the mirror, i.e. for a general theory of adult activities, but it is the foundation of the cinema and hence primary when the latter is under discussion: it is *primary cinematic identification* proper ("primary identification" would be inaccurate from the psychoanalytic point of view; "secondary identification," more accurate in this respect, would be ambiguous for a cinematic psychoanalysis). As for identifications with characters, with their own different levels (out-of-frame character, etc.), they are secondary, tertiary cinematic identifications, etc.; taken as a whole in opposition to the identification of the spectator with his own look, they constitute secondary cinematic identification in the singular.

"Seeing a Film"

Freud noted, *vis-à-vis* the sexual act, that the most ordinary practices depend on a large number of psychical functions which are distinct but work consecutively, so that all of them must be intact if what is regarded as a normal performance is to be possible (it is because neurosis and psychosis dissociate them and put some of them out of court that a kind of commutation is made possible whereby they can be listed retrospectively by the analyst). The apparently very simple act of *seeing a film* is no exception to this rule. As soon as it is subjected to analysis it reveals to us a complex, multiply interconnected imbrication of the functions of the imaginary, the real and the symbolic, which is also required in one form or another for every procedure of social life, but whose cinematic manifestation is especially impressive since it is played out on a small surface. (To this extent the theory of the cinema may some day contribute something to psychoanalysis, even if, through force of circumstances, this "reciprocation" remains very limited at the moment, the two disciplines being very unevenly developed.)

In order to understand the fiction film, I must both "take myself" for the character (= an imaginary procedure) so that he benefits, by analogical projection, from all the schemata of intelligibility that I have within me, and not take myself for him

(= the return to the real) so that the fiction can be established as such (= as symbolic): this is *seeming-real*. Similarly, in order to understand the film (at all), I must perceive the photographed object as absent, its photograph as present, and the presence of this absence as signifying. The imaginary of the cinema presupposes the symbolic, for the spectator must first of all have known the primordial mirror. But as the latter instituted the ego very largely in the imaginary, the second mirror of the screen, a symbolic apparatus, itself in turn depends on reflection and lack. However, it is not phantasy, a "purely" symbolic-imaginary site, for the absence of the object and the codes of that absence are really produced in it by the *physis* of an equipment: the cinema is a body (a *corpus* for the semiologist), a fetish that can be loved.

THE PASSION FOR PERCEIVING

The practice of the cinema is only possible through the perceptual passions: the desire to see (= scopic drive, scopophilia, voyeurism), which was alone engaged in the art of the silent film, the desire to hear which has been added to it in the sound cinema (this is the *"pulsion invocante,"* the invocatory drive, one of the four main sexual drives for Lacan; it is well known that Freud isolated it less clearly and hardly deals with it as such).

These two sexual drives are distinguished from the others in that they are more dependent on a lack, or at least dependent on it in a more precise, more unique manner, which marks them from the outset, even more than the others, as being on the side of the imaginary.

However, this characteristic is to a greater or lesser degree proper to all the sexual drives insofar as they differ from purely organic instincts or needs (Lacan), or in Freud from the self-preservation drives (the "ego drives" which he tended subsequently to annex to narcissism, a tendency he could never quite bring himself to pursue to its conclusion). The sexual drive does not have so stable and strong a relationship with its "object" as do for example hunger and thirst. Hunger can only be satisfied by food, but food is quite certain to satisfy it; thus instincts are simultaneously more and less difficult to satisfy than drives; they depend on a perfectly real object for which there is no substitute, but they depend on nothing else. Drives, on the contrary, can be satisfied up to a point outside their objects (this is sublimation, or else, in another way, masturbation) and are initially capable of doing without them without putting the organism into immediate danger (hence repression). The needs of self-preservation can neither be repressed nor sublimated; the sexual drives are more labile and more accommodating, as Freud insisted (more radically perverse, says Lacan). Inversely, they always remain more or less unsatisfied, even when their object has been attained; desire is very quickly reborn after the brief vertigo of its apparent extinction, it is largely sustained by itself as desire, it has its own rhythms, often quite independent of those of the pleasure obtained (which seemed nonetheless its specific aim); the lack is what it wishes to fill, and at the same time what it is always careful to leave gaping, in order to survive as desire. In the end it has no object, at any rate no real object; through real objects which are all substitutes (and all the more numerous and interchangeable for that), it pursues an imaginary object (a "lost object") which is its truest object, an object that has always been lost and is always desired as such.

How, then, can one say that the visual and auditory drives have a stronger or more special relationship with the absence of their object, with the infinite pursuit of the imaginary? Because, as opposed to other sexual drives, the "perceiving drive"—combining into one the scopic drive and the invocatory drive—*concretely represents the absence of its object* in the distance at which it maintains it and which is part of its very definition: distance of the look, distance of listening. Psychophysiology makes a classic distinction between the "senses at a distance" (sight and hearing) and the others all which involve immediate proximity and which it calls the "senses of contact" (Pradines): touch, taste, smell, cœnaesthetic sense, etc. Freud notes that voyeurism, like sadism in this respect, always keeps apart the *object*. (Here the object looked at) and the *source* of the drive, i.e. the generating organ (the eye); the voyeur does not look at his eye. With orality and anality, on the contrary, the exercise of the drive inaugurates a certain degree of partial fusion, a coincidence (= contact, tendential abolition of distance) of source and aim, for the aim is to obtain pleasure at the level of the source organ (= "organ pleasure"): e.g. what is called "pleasure of the mouth."

It is no accident that the main socially acceptable arts are based on the senses at a distance, and that those which depend on the senses of contact are often regarded as "minor" arts (e.g. the culinary arts, the art of perfumes, etc.). Nor is it an accident that the visual or auditory imaginaries have played a much more important part in the histories of societies than the tactile or olfactory imaginaries.

The voyeur is very careful to maintain a gulf, an empty space, between the object and the eye, the object and his own body: his look fastens the object at the right distance, as with those cinema spectators who take care to avoid being too close to or too far from the screen. The voyeur represents in space the fracture which forever separates him from the object; he represents his very dissatisfaction (which is precisely what he needs as a voyeur), and thus also his "satisfaction" insofar as it is of a specifically voyeuristic type. To fill in this distance would threaten to overwhelm the subject, to lead him to consume the object (the object which is now too close so that he cannot see it any more), to bring him to orgasm and the pleasure of his own body, hence to the exercise of other drives, mobilising the senses of contact and putting an end to the scopic arrangement. *Retention* is fully part of perceptual pleasure, which is thereby often coloured with anality. Orgasm is the object rediscoverd in a state of momentary illusion; it is the phantasy suppression of the gap between object and subject (hence the amorous myths of "fusion"). The looking drive, except when it is exceptionally well developed, is less directly related to orgasm than are the other component drives; it favours it by its excitatory action, but it is not generally sufficient to produce it by its figures alone, which thus belong to the realm of "preparatives." In it we do not find that illusion, however brief, of a lack filled, of a non-imaginary, of a full relation to the object, better established in other drives. If it is true of all desire that it depends on the infinite pursuit of its absent object, voyeuristic desire, along with certain forms of sadism, is the only desire whose principle of distance symbolically and spatially evokes this fundamental rent.

The same could be said, making the necessary modifications of course, about the invocatory (auditory) drive, less closely studied by psychoanalysis hitherto, with the exception of writers like Lacan and Guy Rosolato. I shall merely recall that of all hallucinations—and what reveals the dissociation of desire and real object better than the hallucination?—the main ones by far are visual and auditory hallucinations, those of the senses at a distance (this is also true of the dream, another form of hallucination).

The Scopic Regime of the Cinema

However, although this set of features seems to me to be important, it does not yet characterise the signifier of the cinema proper, but rather that of all means of expression based on sight or hearing, and hence, among other "languages," that of practically all the arts (painting, sculpture, architecture, music, opera, theatre, etc.). What distinguishes the cinema is an extra reduplication, a supplementary and specific turn of the screw bolting desire to the lack. First because the spectacles and sounds the cinema "offers" us (offers us at a distance, hence as much *steal* from us) are especially rich and varied: a mere difference of degree, but already one that counts: the screen presents to our apprehension, but absents from our grasp, more "things." (The mechanism of the perceiving drive is identical for the moment but its object is more endowed with matter; this is one of the reasons why the cinema is very suited to handling "erotic scenes" which depend on direct, non-sublimated voyeurism.) In the second place (and more decisively), the specific affinity between the cinematic signifier and the imaginary persists when film is compared with arts such as the theatre in which the audio-visual given is as rich as it is on the screen in the number of perceptual axes involved. Indeed, the theatre really does "give" this given, or at least slightly more really: it is physically present, in the same space as the spectator. The cinema only gives it in effigy, inaccessible from the outset, in a primordial *elsewhere,* infinitely desirable (= never possessible), on another scene which is that of absence and which nonetheless represents the absent in detail, thus making it very present, but by a different itinerary. Not only am I at a distance from the object, as in the theatre, but what remains in that distance is now no longer the object itself, it is a delegate it has sent me while itself withdrawing. A double withdrawal.

What defines the specifically cinematic *scopic regime* is not so much the distance kept, the "keeping" itself (first figure of the lack, common to all voyeurism), as the absence of the object seen. Here the cinema is profoundly different from the theatre as also from more intimate voyeuristic activities with a specifically erotic aim (there are intermediate genres, moreover: certain cabaret acts, strip-tease, etc.): cases where voyeurism remains linked to exhibitionism, where the two faces, active and passive, of the component drive are by no means so dissociated; where the object seen is present and hence presumably complicit; where the perverse activity—aided if need be by a certain dose of bad faith and happy illusion, varying from case to case, moreover, and sometimes reducible to very little, as in true perverse couples—

is rehabilitated and reconciled with itself by being as it were undividedly taken in charge by two actors assuming its constitutive poles (the corresponding phantasies, in the absence of the actions, thus becoming interchangeable and shared by the play of reciprocal identification). In the theatre, as in domestic voyeurism, the passive actor (the one seen), simply because he is bodily present, because he does not go away, is presumed to consent, to cooperate deliberately. It may be that he really does, as exhibitionists in the clinical sense do, or as, in a sublimated fashion, does that oft noted triumphant exhibitionism characteristic of theatrical acting, coun- terposed even by Bazin to cinematic representation. It may also be that the object seen has only accepted this condition (thus becoming an "object" in the ordinary sense of the word, and no longer only in the Freudian sense) under the pressure of more or less powerful external constraints, economic ones for example with certain poor strippers. (However, they must have consented at some point; rarely is the degree of acceptance zero, except in the case of *victimisation,* e.g. when a fascist militia strips its prisoners; the specific characteristics of the scopic arrangement are then distorted by the overpowering intervention of another element, sadism.) Voy- eurism which is not too sadistic (there is none which is not so at all) rests on a kind of *fiction,* more or less justified in the order of the real, sometimes institutionalised as in the theatre or strip-tease, a fiction that stipulates that the object "agrees," that it is therefore exhibitionist. Or more precisely, what is necessary in this fiction for the establishment of potency and desire is presumed to be sufficiently guaranteed by the physical presence of the object: "Since it is there, it must like it," such, hypo- critical or no, deluded or no, is the retrenchment needed by the voyeur so long as sadistic infiltrations are insufficient to make the object's refusal and constraint necesary to him. Thus, despite the distance instituted by the look—which trans- forms the object into a *picture* (a *"tableau vivant"*) and thus tips it over into the imaginary, even in its real presence—that presence, which persists, and the active consent which is its real or mythical correlate (but always real as myth) re-establish in the scopic space, momentarily at least, the illusion of a fullness of the object rela- tion, of a state of desire which is not just imaginary.

It is this last recess that is attacked by the cinema signifier, it is in its precise emplacement (*in its place,* in both senses of the word) that it installs a new figure of the lack, the physical absence of the object seen. In the theatre, actors and spectators are present at the same time and in the same location, hence present one to another, as the two protagonists of an authentic perverse couple. But in the cinema, the actor was present when the spectator was not (= shooting), and the spectator is present when the actor is no longer (= projection): a failure to meet of the voyeur and the exhibitionist whose approaches no longer coincide (they have "missed" one another). The cinema's voyeurism must (of necessity) do without any very clear mark of consent on the part of the object. There is no equivalent here of the theatre actors' final "bow." And then the latter could see their voyeurs, the game was less unilateral, slightly better distributed. In the darkened hall, the voyeur is rally left alone (or with other voyeurs, which is worse), deprived of his other half in the myth- ical hermaphrodite (a hermaphrodite not necessarily constituted by the distribu- tion of the sexes but rather by that of the active and passive poles in the exercise of the drive). Yet still a voyeur, since there is something to see, called the film, but something in whose definition there is a great deal of "flight": not precisely something that hides, rather something that *lets* itself be seen without *presenting* itself to be seen, which has gone out of the room before leaving only its trace visible there. This is the origin in particular of that "recipe" of the classical cinema which said that the actor should never look directly at the audience (= the camera).

Thus deprived of rehabilitatory agreement, of a real or supposed consensus with the other (which was also the Other, for it had the status of a sanction on the plane of the symbolic), cinematic voyeurism, *unauthorised* scopophilia, is from the outset more strongly established than that of the theater in direct line from the primal scene. Certain precise features of the institution contribute to this affinity: the obscurity surrounding the onlooker, the aperture of the screen with its inevitable keyhole effect. But the affinity is more profound. It lies first in the spectator's solitude in the cinema: those attending a cinematic projection do not, as in the theatre, constitute a true "audience," a temporary collectivity; they are an accumulation of individuals who, despite appearances, more closely resemble the fragmented group of readers of a novel. It lies on the other hand in the fact that the filmic spectacle, the object seen, is more radically ignorant of its spectator, since he is not there, than the theatrical spectacle can ever be. A third factor, closely linked to the other two, also plays a part: the *segregation of spaces* that characterises a cinema performance and not a theatrical one. The "stage" and the auditorium are no longer two areas set up in opposition to each other within a single space; the space of the film, represented by the screen, is utterly heterogeneous, it no longer communicates with that of the auditorium: one is real, the other perspective: a stronger break than any line of footlights. For its spectator the film unfolds in that simultaneously very close and definitively inaccessible "elsewhere" in which the child *sees* the amorous play of the parental couple, who are similarly ignorant of it and leave it alone, a pure onlooker whose participation is inconceivable. In this respect the cinematic signifier is not only "psychoanalytic"; it is more precisely Oedipal in type. . . .

1975

LAURA MULVEY
VISUAL PLEASURE AND
NARRATIVE CINEMA

I. INTRODUCTION

A. A Political Use of Psychoanalysis

This paper intends to use psychoanalysis to discover where and how the fascination of film is reinforced by pre-existing patterns of fascination already at work within the individual subject and the social formations that have moulded him. It takes as starting point the way film reflects, reveals and even plays on the straight, socially established interpretation of sexual difference which controls images, erotic ways of looking and spectacle. It is helpful to understand what the cinema has been, how its magic has worked in the past, while attempting a theory and a practice which will challenge this cinema of the past. Psychoanalytic theory is thus appropriate here as a political weapon, demonstrating the way the unconscious of patriarchal society has structured film form.

The paradox of phallocentrism in all its manifestations is that it depends on the image of the castrated woman to give order and meaning to its world. An idea of woman stands as lynch pin to the system: it is her lack that produces the phallus as a symbolic presence, it is her desire to make good the lack that the phallus signifies. Recent writing in *Screen* about psychoanalysis and the cinema has not sufficiently brought out the importance of the representation of the female form in a symbolic order in which, in the last resort, it speaks castration and nothing else. To summarise briefly: the function of woman in forming the patriarchal unconscious is two-fold, she first symbolises the castration threat by her real absence of a penis and second thereby raises her child into the symbolic. Once this has been achieved, her meaning in the process is at an end, it does not last into the world of law and language except as a memory which oscillates between memory of maternal plenitude and memory of lack. Both are posited on nature (or on anatomy in Freud's famous phrase). Woman's desire is subjected to her image as bearer of the bleeding wound, she can exist only in relation to castration and cannot transcend it. She turns her child into the signifier of her own desire to possess a penis (the condition, she imagines, of entry into the symbolic). Either she must gracefully give way to the word, the Name of the Father and the Law, or else struggle to keep her child down with her in the half-light of the imaginary. Woman then stands in patriarchal culture as signifier for the male other, bound by a symbolic order in which man can live out his phantasies and obsessions through linguistic command by imposing them on the silent image of woman still tied to her place as bearer of meaning, not maker of meaning.

There is an obvious interest in this analysis for feminists, a beauty in its exact rendering of the frustration experienced under the phallocentric order. It gets us nearer to the roots of our oppression, it brings an articulation of the problem closer, it faces us with the ultimate challenge: how to fight the unconscious structured like a language (formed critically at the moment of arrival of language) while still caught within the language of the patriarchy. There is no way in which we an produce an alternative out of the blue, but we can begin to make a break by examining patriarchy with the tools it provides, of which psychoanalysis is not the only but an important one. We are still separated by a great gap from important issues for the female unconscious which are scarcely relevant to phallocentric theory: the sexing of the female infant and her relationship to the symbolic, the sexually mature woman as non-mother, maternity outside the signification of the phallus, the vagina. . . . But, at this point, psychoanalytic theory as it now stands can at least advance our understanding of the status quo, of the patriarchal order in which we are caught.

B. Destruction of Pleasure is a Radical Weapon

As an advanced representation system, the cinema poses questions of the ways the unconscious (formed by the dominant order) structure ways of seeing and pleasure in looking. Cinema has changed over the last few decades. It is no longer the monolithic system based on large capital investment exemplified at its best by Hollywood in the 1930's, 1940's and 1950's. Technological advances (16mm, etc.) have changed the economic conditions of cinematic production, which can now be artisanal as well as capitalist. Thus it has been possible for an alternative cinema to develop. However self-conscious and ironic Hollywood managed to be, it always restricted itself to a formal mise-en-scène reflecting the dominant ideological concept of the cinema. The alternative cinema provides a space for a cinema to be born which is radical in both a political and an aesthetic sense and challenges the basic assumptions of the mainstream film. This is not to reject the latter moralistically, but to highlight the ways in which its formal preoccupations reflect the psychical obsessions of the society which produced it, and, further, to stress that the alternative cinema must start specifically by reacting against these obsessions and assumptions. A politically and aesthetically avant-garde cinema is now possible, but it can still only exist as a counterpoint.

The magic of the Hollywood style at its best (and of all the cinema which fell within its sphere of influence) arose, not exclusively, but in one important aspect, from its skilled and satisfying manipulation of visual pleasure. Unchallenged, mainstream film coded the erotic into the language of the dominant patriarchal order. In the highly developed Hollywood cinema it was only through these codes that the alienated subject, torn in his imaginary memory by a sense of loss, by the terror of potential lack in phantasy, came near to finding a glimpse of satisfaction: through its formal beauty and its play on his own formative obsessions. This article will discuss the interweaving of that erotic pleasure in film, its meaning, and in particular the central place of the image of woman. It is said that analysing pleasure, or beauty, destroys it. That is the intention of this article. The satisfaction and reinforcement of the ego that represent the high point of film history hitherto must be attacked. Not in favour of a reconstructed new pleasure, which cannot exist in the abstract, nor of intellectualised unpleasure, but to make way for a total negation of the ease and plenitude of the narrative fiction film. The alternative is the thrill that comes from leaving the past behind without rejecting it, transcending outworn or oppressive forms, or daring to break with normal pleasurable expectations in order to conceive a new language of desire.

II. PLEASURE IN LOOKING/FASCINATION WITH THE HUMAN FORM

A. The cinema offers a number of possible pleasures. One is scopophilia. There are circumstances in which looking itself is a source of pleasure, just as, in the reverse formation, there is pleasure in being looked at. Originally, in his *Three Essays on Sexuality,* Freud isolated scopophilia as one of the component instincts of sexuality which exist as drives quite independently of the erotogenic zones. At this point he associated scopophilia with taking other people as objects, subjecting them to a controlling and curious gaze. His particular examples centre around the voyeuristic activities of children, their desire to see and make sure of the private and the forbidden (curiosity about other people's genital and bodily functions, about the presence or absence of the penis and, retrospectively, about the primal scene). In this analysis scopophilia is essentially active. (Later, in *Instincts and their Vicissitudes,* Freud developed his theory of scopophilia further, attaching it initially to pre-genital auto-eroticism, after which the pleasure of the look is transferred to others by analogy. There is a close working here of the relationship between the active instinct and its further development in a narcissistic form.) Although the instinct is modified by other factors, in particular the constitution of the ego, it continues to exist as the erotic basis for pleasure in looking at another person as object. At the extreme, it can become fixated into a perversion, producing obsessive voyeurs and Peeping Toms, whose only sexual satisfaction can come from watching, in an active controlling sense, an objectified other.

At first glance, the cinema would seem to be remote from the undercover world of the surreptitious observation of an unknowing and unwilling victim. What is seen of the screen is so manifestly shown. But the mass of mainstream film, and the conventions within which it has consciously evolved, portray a hermetically sealed world which unwinds magically, indifferent to the presence of the audience, producing for them a sense of separation and playing on their voyeuristic phantasy. Morover, the extreme contrast between the darkness in the auditorium (which also isolates the spectators from one another) and the brilliance of the shifting patterns of light and shade on the screen helps to promote the illusion of voyeuristic separation. Although the film is really being shown, is there to be seen, conditions of screening and narrative conventions give the spectator an illusion of looking in on a private world. Among other things, the position of the spectators in the cinema is blatantly one of repression of their exhibitionism and projection of the repressed desire on to the performer.

B. The cinema satisfies a primordial wish for pleasurable looking, but it also goes further, developing scopophilia in its narcissistic aspect. The conventions of mainstream film focus attention on the human form. Scale, space, stories are all anthropomorphic. Here, curiosity and the wish to look intermingle with a fascination with likeness and recognition: the human face, the human body, the relationship between the human form and its surroundings, the visible presence of the person in the world. Jacques Lacan has described how the moment when a child recognises its own image in the mirror is crucial for the constitution of the ego. Several aspects of this analysis are relevant here. The mirror phase occurs at a time when the child's physical ambitions outstrip his motor capacity, with the result that his recognition of himself is joyous in that he imagines his mirror image to be more complete, more perfect than he experiences his own body. Recognition is thus overlaid with mis-recognition: the image recognised is conceived as the reflected body of the self, but its misrecognition as superior projects this body outside itself as an ideal ego, the alienated subject, which, re-introjected as an ego ideal, gives rise to the future generation of identification with others. This mirror-moment predates language for the child.

Important for this article is the fact that it is an image that constitutes the matrix of the imaginary, of recognition/misrecognition and identification, and hence of the first articulation of the "I," of subjectivity. This is a moment when an older fascination with looking (at the mother's face, for an obvious example) collides with the initial inklings of self-awareness. Hence it is the birth of the long love affair/despair between image and self-image which has found such intensity of expression in film and such joyous recognition in the cinema audience. Quite apart from the extraneous similarities between screen and mirror (the framing of the human form in its surroundings, for instance), the cinema has structures of fascination strong enough to allow temporary loss of ego while simultaneously reinforcing the ego. The sense of forgetting the world as the ego has subsequently come to perceive it (I forgot who I am and where I was) is nostalgically reminiscent of that pre-subjective moment of image recogntiion. At the same time the cinema has distinguished itself in the production of ego ideals as expressed in particular in the star system, the stars centering both screen presence and screen story as they act out a complex proccess of likeness and difference (the glamorous impersonates the ordinary).

C. Sections II. A and B have set out two contradictory aspects of the pleasurable structures of looking in the conventional cinematic situation. The first, scopophilic, arises from pleasure in using another person as an object of sexual stimulation through sight. The second, developed through narcissism and the constitution of the ego, comes from identification with the image seen. Thus, in film terms, one implies a separation of the erotic identity of the subject from the object on the screen (active scopophilia), the other demands identification of the ego with the object on the screen through the spectator's fascination with and recognition of his like. The first is a function of the sexual instincts, the second of ego libido. This dichotomy was crucial for Freud. Although he saw the two as interacting and over-laying each other, the tension between instinctual drives and self-preservation con-tinues to be a dramatic polarisation in terms of pleasure. Both are formative struc-tures, mechanisms not meaning. In themselves they have no signification, they have to be attached to an idealisation. Both pursue aims in indifference to percep-tual reality, creating the imagised, eroticised concept of the world that forms the perception of the subject and makes a mockery of empirical objectivity.

During its history, the cinema seems to have evolved a particular illusion of real-ity in which this contradiction between libido and ego has found a beautifully com-plementary phantasy world. In *reality* the phantasy world of the screen is subject to the law which produces it. Sexual instincts and identification processes have a meaning within the symbolic order which articulates desire. Desire, born with lan-guage, allows the possibility of transcending the instinctual and the imaginary, but its point of reference continually returns to the traumatic moment of its birth: the castration complex. Hence the look, pleasurable in form, can be threatening in con-tent, and it is woman as representation/image that crystallises this paradox.

III. WOMAN AS IMAGE, MAN AS BEARER OF THE LOOK

A. In a world ordered by sexual imbalance, pleasure in looking has been split between active/male and passive/female. The determining male gaze projects its phantasy on to the female figure which is styled accordingly. In their traditional exhibitionist role women are simultaneously looked at and displayed, with their appearance coded for strong visual and erotic impact so that they can be said to connote *to-be-looked-at-ness*. Women displayed as sexual object is the leit-motiff of erotic spectacle: from pin-ups to strip-tease, from Ziegfeld to Busby Berkeley, she holds the look, plays to and signifies male desire. Mainstream film neatly combined spectacle and narrative. (Note, however, how in the musical song-and-dance num-bers break the flow of the diegesis.) The presence of woman is an indispensible ele-ment of spectacle in normal narrative film, yet her visual presence tends to work against the development of a story line, to freeze the flow of action in moments of erotic contemplation. This alien presence then has to be integrated into cohesion with the narrative. As Budd Boetticher has put it:

> What counts is what the heroine provokes, or rather what she represents. She is the one, or rather the love or fear she inspires in the hero, or else the concern he feels for her, who makes him act the way he does. In herself the woman has not the slightest impor-tance.

(A recent tendency in narrative film has been to dispense with this problem altogether; hence the development of what Molly Haskell has called the "buddy movie," in which the active homosexual eroticism of the central male figures can carry the story without distraction.) Traditionally, the woman displayed has functioned on two levels: as erotic object for the characters within the screen story, and as erotic object for the spectator within the auditorium, with a shifting tension between the looks on either side of the screen. For instance, the device of the showgirl allows the two looks to be unified technically without any apparent break in the diegesis. A woman performs within the narrative, the gaze of the spectator and that of the male characters in the film are neatly combined without breaking narrative verisimilitude. For a moment the sexual impact of the performing woman takes the film into a no-man's-land outside its own time and space. Thus Marilyn Monroe's first appearance in *The River of No Return* and Lauren Bacall's songs in *To Have or Have Not*. Similarly, conventional close-ups of legs (Dietrich, for instance) or a face (Garbo) integrate into the narrative a different mode of eroticism. One part of a fragmented body destroys the Renaissance space, the illusion of depth demanded by the narrative, it gives flatness, the quality of a cut-out or icon rather than verisimilitude to the screen.

B. An active/passive heterosexual division of labour has similarly controlled narrative structure. According to the principles of the ruling ideology and the psychical structures that back it up, the male figure cannot bear the burden of sexual objectification. Man is reluctant to gaze at his exhibitionist like. Hence the split between spectacle and narrative supports the man's role as the active one of forwarding the story, making things happen. The man controls the film phantasy and also emerges as the representative of power in a further sense: as the bearer of the look of the spectator, transferring it behind the screen to neutralise the extra-diegetic tendencies represented by woman as spectacle. This is made possible through the processes set in motion by structuring the film around a main controlling figure with whom the spectator can identify. As the spectator identifies with the main male* protagonist, he projects his look on to that of his like, his screen surrogate, so that the power of the male protagonist as he controls events coincides with the active power of the erotic look, both giving a satisfying sense of omnipotence. A male movie star's glamourous characteristics are thus not those of the erotic object of the gaze, but those of the more perfect, more complete, more powerful ideal ego conceived in the original moment of recognition in front of the mirror. The character in the story can make things happen and control events better than the subject/spectator, just as the image in the mirror was more in control of motor coordination. In contrast to woman as icon, the active male figure (the ego ideal of the identification process) demands a three-dimensional space corresponding to that of the mirror-recognition in which the alienated subject internalised his own representation of this

---

*There are films with a woman as main protagonist, of course. To analyse this phenomenon seriously here would take me too far afield. Pam Cook and Claire Johnston's study of *The Revolt of Mamie Stover* in Phil Hardy, ed.: *Raoul Walsh,* Edinburgh 1974, shows in a striking case how the strength of this female protagonist is more apparent than real.

Marlene Dietrich playing blind man's bluff in Josef von Sternberg's *The Scarlet Empress* (1934). "As the spectator identifies with the main male protagonist, he projects his look on to that of his like, his screen surrogate, so that the power of the male protagonist as he controls events coincides with the active power of the erotic look, both giving a satisfying sense of omnipotence" (MULVEY, p. 751). "With their submissive male masochist, the oral mother embodied in the ambivalent, alluring presence of Marlene Dietrich, and their ambiguous sexuality that has often been linked to 'sado-masochism' and 'degradation,' the von Sternberg/Dietrich collaborations offer themselves as a prime case study of the masochistic aesthetic in film" (STUDLAR, p. 778)."

imaginary existence. He is a figure in a landscape. Here the function of film is to reproduce as accurately as possible the so-called natural conditions of human perception. Camera technology (as exemplified by deep focus in particular) and camera movements (determined by the action of the protagonist), combined with invisible editing (demanded by realism) all tend to blur the limits of screen space. The male protagonist is free to command the stage, a stage of spatial illusion in which he articulates the look and creates the action.

C.1 Sections III. A and B have set out a tension between a mode of representation of woman in film and conventions surrounding the diegesis. Each is associated with a look: that of the spectator in direct scopophilic contact with the female form displayed for his enjoyment (connoting male phantasy) and that of the spectator fascinated with the image of his like set in an illusion of natural space, and through him gaining control and possession of the woman within the diegesis. (This tension and the shift from one pole to the other can structure a single text. Thus both in *Only Angels Have Wings* and in *To Have and Have Not,* the film opens with the woman as object of the combined gaze of spectator and all the male protagonists in the film. She is isolated, glamourous, on display, sexualised. But as the narrative progresses she falls in love with the main male protagonist and becomes his property, losing her outward glamorous characteristics, her generalised sexuality, her show-girl connotations; her eroticism is subjected to the male star alone. By means of identification with him, through participation in his power, the spectator can indirectly possess her too.)

But in psychoanalytic terms, the female figure poses a deeper problem. She also connotes something that the look continually circles around but disavows: her lack of penis, implying a threat of castration and hence unpleasure. Ultimately, the meaning of woman is sexual difference, the absence of the penis as visually ascertainable, the material evidence on which is based the castration complex essential for the organisation of entrance to the symbolic order and the law of the father. Thus the woman as icon, displayed for the gaze and enjoyment of men, the active controllers of the look, always threatens to evoke the anxiety it originally signified. The male unconscious has two avenues of escape from this castration anxiety: preoccupation with the re-enactment of the original trauma (investigating the woman, demystifying her mystery), counterbalanced by the devaluation, punishment or saving of the guilty object (an avenue typified by the concerns of the *film noir*); or else complete disavowal of castration by the substitution of a fetish object or turning the represented figure itself into a fetish so that it becomes reassuring rather than dangerous (hence over-valuation, the cult of the female star). This second avenue, fetishistic scopophilia, builds up the physical beauty of the object, transforming it into something satisfying in itself. The first avenue, voyeurism, on the contrary, has associations with sadism: pleasure lies in ascertaining guilt (immediately associated with castration), asserting control and subjecting the guilty person through punishment or forgiveness. This sadistic side fits in well with narrative. Sadism demands a story, depends on making something happen, forcing a change in another person, a battle of will and strength, victory/defeat, all occurring in a linear time with a beginning and an end. Fetishistic scopophilia, on the other hand, can exist outside linear time as the erotic instinct is focussed on the look alone. These contradictions and ambiguities can be illustrated more simply by using works by Hitchcock and Sternberg, both of whom take the look almost as the content or subject matter of many of their films. Hitchcock is the more complex, as he uses both mechanisms. Sternberg's work, on the other hand, provides many pure examples of fetishistic scopophilia.

C.2 It is well known that Sternberg once said he would welcome his films being projected upside down so that story and character involvement would not interfere with the specator's undiluted appreciation of the screen image. This statement is revealing but ingenuous. Ingenuous in that his films do demand that the figure of the woman (Dietrich, in the cycle of films with her, as the ultimate example) should be identifiable. But revealing in that it emphasises the fact that for him the pictorial space enclosed by the frame is paramount rather than narrative or identification processes. While Hitchcock goes into the investigative side of voyeurism, Sternberg produces the ultimate fetish, taking it to the point where the powerful look of the male protagonist (characteristic of traditional narrative film) is broken in favour of the image in direct erotic rapport with the spectator. The beauty of the woman as object and the screen space coalesce; she is no longer the bearer of guilt but a perfect product, whose body, stylised and fragmented by close-ups, is the content of the film, and the direct recipient of the spectator's look. Sternberg plays down the illusion of screen depth; his screen tends to be one-dimensional, as light and shade, lace, steam, foliage, net, streamers, etc, reduce the visual field. There is little or no mediation of the look through the eyes of the main male protagonist. On the contrary, shadowy presences like La Bessière in *Morocco* act as surrogates for the director, detached as they are from audience identification. Despite Sternberg's insistence that his stories are irrelevant, it is significant that they are concerned with situation, not suspense, and cyclical rather than linear time, while plot complications revolve around misunderstanding rather than conflict. The most important absence is that of the controlling male gaze within the screen scene. The high point of emotional drama in the most typical Dietrich films, her supreme moments of erotic meaning, take place in the absence of the man she loves in the fiction. There are other witnesses, other spectators watching her on the screen, their gaze is one with, not standing in for, that of the audience. At the end of *Morocco,* Tom Brown has already disappeared into the desert when Amy Jolly kicks off her gold sandals and walks after him. At the end of *Dishonoured,* Kranau is indifferent to the fate of Magda. In both cases, the erotic impact, sanctified by death, is displayed as a spectacle for the audience. The male hero misunderstands and, above all, does not see.

In Hitchcock, by contrast, the male hero does see precisely what the audience sees. However, in the films I shall discuss here, he takes fascination with an image through scopophilic eroticism as the subject of the film. Moreover, in these cases the hero portrays the contradictions and tensions experienced by the spectator. In *Vertigo* in particular, but also in *Marnie* and *Rear Window,* the look is central to the plot, oscillating between voyeurism and fetishistic fascination. As a twist, a further manipulation of the normal viewing process which in some sense reveals it, Hitchcock uses the process of identification normally associated with ideological correctness and the recognition of established morality and shows up its perverted side. Hitchcock has never concealed his interest in voyeurism, cinematic and non-cinematic. His heroes are exemplary of the symbolic order and the law—a police-man *(Vertigo)*, a dominant male possessing money and power *(Marnie)*—but their erotic drives lead them into compromised situations. The power to subject another person to the will sadistically or to the gaze voyeuristically is turned on to the woman as the object of both. Power is backed by a certainty of legal right and the established guilt of the woman (evoking castration, psychoanalytically speaking). True perversion is barely concealed under a shallow mask of ideological correct-ness—the man is on the right side of the law, the woman on the wrong. Hitchcock's skilful use of identification processes and liberal use of subjective camera from the point of view of the male protagonist draw the spectators deeply into his position, making them share his uneasy gaze. The audience is absorbed into a voyeuristic situation within the screen scene and diegesis which parodies his own in the cinema. In his analysis of *Rear Window,* Douchet takes the film as a metaphor for the cin-ema. Jeffries is the audience, the events in the apartment block opposite correspond to the screen. As he watches, an erotic dimension is added to his look, a central image to the drama. His girlfriend Lisa had been of little sexual interest to him, more or less a drag, so long as she remained on the spectator side. When she crosses the barrier between his room and the block opposite, their relationship is re-born erotically. He does not merely watch her through his lens, as a distant meaningful image, he also sees her as a guilty intruder exposed by a dangerous man threatening her with punishment, and thus finally saves her. Lisa's exhibitionism has already been established by her obsessive interest in dress and style, in being a passive image of visual perfection: Jeffries' voyeurism and activity have also been established through his work as a photo-journalist, a maker of stories and captor of images. However, his enforced inactivity, binding him to his seat as a spectator, puts him squarely in the phantasy position of the cinema audience.

In *Vertigo,* subjective camera predominates. apart from one flash-back from Judy's point of view, the narrative is woven around what Scottie sees or fails to see. The audience follows the growth of his erotic obsession and subsequent despair pre-cisely from his point of view. Scottie's voyeurism is blatant: he falls in love with a woman he follows and spies on without speaking to. Its sadistic side is equally bla-tant: he has chosen (and freely chosen, for he had been a successful lawyer) to be a policeman, with all the attendant possibilities of pursuit and investigation. As a result, he follows, watches and falls in love with a perfect image of female beauty and mystery. Once he actually confronts her, his erotic drive is to break her down and force her to tell by persistent cross-questioning. Then, in the second part of the film, he re-enacts his obsessive involvement with the image he loved to watch secretly. He reconstructs Judy as Madeleine, forces her to conform in every detail to the actual physical appearance of his fetish. Her exhibitionism, her masochism, make her an ideal passive counterpart to Scottie's active sadistic voyeurism. She knows her part is to perform, and only by playing it through and then replaying it can she keep Scottie's erotic interest. But in the repetition he does break her down and succeeds in exposing her guilt. His curiosity wins through and she is punished. In *Vertigo,* erotic involvement with the look is disorientating: the spectator's fascination is turned against him as the narrative carries him through and entwines him with the processes that he is himself exercising. The Hitchcock hero here is firmly placed within the symbolic order, in narrative terms. He has all the attributes of the patriarchal super-ego. Hence the spectator, lulled into a false sense of security by the apparent legality of his surrogate, sees through his look and finds himself exposed as complicit, caught in the moral ambiguity of looking. Far from being simply an aside on the perversion of the police, *Vertigo* focuses on the implications of the active/looking, passive/looked-at split in terms of sexual difference and the power of the male symbolic encapsulated in the hero. Marnie, too, performs for Mark Rutland's gaze and masquerades as the perfect to-be-looked-at image. He, too, is on the side of the law until, drawn in by obsession with her guilt, her secret, he longs to see her in the act of committing a crime, make her confess and thus save her. So he, too, becomes complicit as he acts out the implications of his power. He controls money and words, he can have his cake and eat it.

IV. SUMMARY

The psychoanalytic background that has been discussed in this article is relevant to the pleasure and unpleasure offered by traditional narrative film. The scopophilic instinct (pleasure in looking at another person as an erotic object), and, in contradistinction, ego libido (forming identification processes) act as formations, mechanisms, which this cinema has played on. The image of woman as (passive) raw material for the (active) gaze of man takes the argument a step further into the structure of representation, adding a further layer demanded by the ideology of the patriarchal order as it is worked out in its favourite cinematic form—illusionistic narrative film. The argument turns again to the psychoanalytic background in that woman as representation signifies castration, inducing voyeuristic or fetishistic mechanisms to circumvent her threat. None of these interacting layers is intrinsic to film, but it is only in the film form that they can reach a perfect and beautiful contradiction, thanks to the possibility in the cinema of shifting the emphasis of the look. It is the place of the look that defines cinema, the possibility of varying it and exposing it. This is what makes cinema quite different in its voyeuristic potential from, say, strip-tease, theatre, shows, etc. Going far beyond highlighting a woman's to-be-looked-at-ness, cinema builds the way she is to be looked at into the spectacle itself. Playing on the tension between film as controlling the dimension of time (editing, narrative) and film as controlling the dimension of space (changes in distance, editing), cinematic codes create a gaze, a world, and an object, thereby producing an illusion cut to the measure of desire. It is these cinematic codes and their relationship to formative external structures that must be broken down before mainstream film and the pleasure it provides can be challenged.

To begin with (as an ending), the voyeuristic-scopophilic look that is a crucial part of traditional filmic pleasure can itself be broken down. There are three different looks associated with cinema: that of the camera as it records the pro-filmic event, that of the audience as it watches the final product, and that of the characters at each other within the screen illusion. The conventions of narrative film deny the first two and subordinate them to the third, the conscious aim being always to eliminate intrusive camera presence and prevent a distancing awareness in the audience. Without these two absences (the material existence of the recording process, the critical reading of the spectator), fictional drama cannot achieve reality, obviousness and truth. Nevertheless, as this article has argued, the structure of looking in narrative fiction film contains a contradiction in its own premises: the female image as a castration threat constantly endangers the unity of the diegesis and bursts through the world of illusion as an intrusive, static, one-dimensional fetish. Thus the two looks materially present in time and space are obsessively subordinated to the neurotic needs of the male ego. The camera becomes the mechanism for producing an illusion of Renaissance space, flowing movements compatible with the human eye, an ideology of representation that revolves round the perception of the subject; the camera's look is disavowed in order to create a convincing world in which the spectator's surrogate can perform with verisimilitude. Simultaneously, the look of the audience is denied an intrinsic force: as soon as fetishistic representation of the female image threatens to break the spell of illusion, and the erotic image on the screen appears directly (wthout mediation) to the spectator, the fact of fetishisation, concealing as it does castration fear, freezes the look, fixates the spectator and prevents him from acheiving any distance from the image in front of him.

This complex interaction of looks is specific to film. The first blow against the monolithic accumulation of traditional film conventions (already undertaken by radical film-makers) is to free the look of the camera into its materiality in time and space and the look of the audience into dialectics, passionate detachment. There is no doubt that this destroys the satisfaction, pleasure and privilege of the 'invisible guest', and highlights how film has depended on voyeuristic active/passive mechanisms. Women, whose image has continually been stolen and used for this end, cannot view the decline of the traditional film form with anything much more than sentimental regret.*

1975

---

*This article is a reworked version of a paper given in the French Department of the University of Wisconsin, Madison, in the Spring of 1973.

MARY ANN DOANE
FILM AND THE MASQUERADE: THEORISING THE FEMALE SPECTATOR

HEADS IN HIEROGLYPHIC BONNETS

In his lecture on "Femininity', Freud forcefully inscribes the absence of the female spectator of theory in his notorious statement, '. . . to those of you who are women this will not apply—you are yourselves the problem . . .'.[1] Simultaneous with this exclusion operated upon the female members of his audience, he invokes, as a rather strange prop, a poem by Heine. Introduced by Freud's claim concerning the importance and elusiveness of his topic—'Throughout history people have knocked their heads against the riddle of the nature of femininity . . .'—are four lines of Heine's poem:

> Heads in hieroglyphic bonnets,
> Heads in turbans and black birettas,
> Heads in wigs and thousand other
> Wretched, sweating heads of humans . . .[2]

The effects of the appeal to this poem are subject to the work of over-determination Freud isolated in the text of the dream. The sheer proliferation of heads and hats (and hence, through a metonymic slippage, minds), which are presumed to have confronted this intimidating riddle before Freud, confers on his discourse the weight of an intellectual history, of a tradition of interrogation. Furthermore, the image of hieroglyphics strengthens the association made between femininity and

---

[1] Sigmund Freud, "Femininity," *The Standard Edition of the Complete Psychological Works of Sigmund Freud,* ed. James Strachey, (London: The Hogarth Press and the Institute of Psycho-analysis, 1961), p. 113.

[2] This is the translation given in a footnote in *The Standard Edition,* p. 113.

the enigmatic, the undecipherable, that which is 'other'. And yet Freud practices a slight deception here, concealing what is elided by removing the lines from their context, castrating, as it were, the stanza. For the question over which Heine's heads brood is not the same as Freud's—it is not 'What is Woman?', but instead, '. . . what signifies Man?' The quote is taken from the seventh section (entitled 'Questions') of the second cycle of *The North Sea*. The full stanza, presented as the words of 'a young man,/His breast full of sorrow, his head full of doubt', reads as follows:

> O solve me the riddle of life,
> The teasingly time-old riddle,
> Over which many heads already have brooded,
> Heads in hats of hieroglyphics,
> Turbaned heads and heads in black skull-caps,
> Heads in perrukes and a thousand other
> Poor, perspiring human heads—
> Tell me, what signifies Man?
> Whence does he come? Whither does he go?
> Who lives up there upon golden stars?*

The question in Freud's text is thus a disguise and a displacement of that other question, which in the pretext is both humanistic and theological. The claim to investigate an otherness is a pretense, haunted by the mirror-effect by means of which the question of the woman reflects only the man's own ontological doubts. Yet what interests me most in this intertextual misrepresentation is that the riddle of femininity is initiated from the beginning in Freud's text as a question in masquerade. But I will return to the issue of masquerade later.

More pertinently, as far as the cinema is concerned, it is not accidental that Freud's eviction of the female spectator/auditor is co-present with the invocation of a hieroglyphic language. The woman, the enigma, the hieroglyphic, the picture, the image—the metonymic chain connects with another: the cinema, the theatre of pictures, a writing in images of the woman but not *for* her. For she *is* the problem. The semantic valence attributed to a hieroglyphic language is two-edged. In fact, there is a sense in which the term is inhabited by a contradiction. On the one hand, the hieroglyphic is summoned, particularly when it merges with a discourse on the woman, to connote an indecipherable language, a signifying system which denies its own function by failing to signify anything to the uninitiated, to those who do not hold the key. In this sense, the hieroglyphic, like the woman, harbours a mystery, an inaccessible though desirable otherness. On the other hand, the hieroglyphic is the most readable of languages. Its immediacy, its accessibility are functions of its status as a *pictorial* language, a writing in images. For the image is theorised in terms of a certain *closeness*, the lack of a distance or gap between sign and referent. Given its iconic characteristics, the relationship between signifier and signified is understood as less arbitrary in imagistic systems of representation than in language 'proper'. The intimacy of signifier and signified in the iconic sign

---

*Heinrich Heine, *The North Sea*, trans. Vernon Watkins (New York: New Direction Books, 1951), p 77.

negates the distance which defines phonetic language. And it is the absence of this crucial distance or gap which also, simultaneously, specifies both the hieroglyphic and the female. This is precisely why Freud evicted the woman from his lecture on femininity. Too close to herself, entangled in her own enigma, she could not step back, could not achieve the necessary distance of a second look.[1]

Thus, while the hieroglyphic is an indecipherable or at least enigmatic language, it is also and at the same time potentially the most universally understandable, comprehensible, appropriable of signs.[2] And the woman shares this contradictory status. But it is here that the analogy slips. For hieroglyphic languages are *not* perfectly iconic. They would not achieve the status of languages if they were—due to what Todorov and Ducrot refer to as a certain non-generalisability of the iconic sign:

> Now it is the impossibility of generalizing this principle of representation that has introduced even into fundamentally morphemographic writing systems such as Chinese, Egyptian, and Sumerian, the phonographic principle. We might almost conclude that every logography [the graphic system of language notation] grows out of *the impossibility of a generalized iconic representation;* proper nouns and abstract notions (including inflections) are then the ones that will be noted phonetically.[3]

The iconic system of representation is inherently deficient—it cannot disengage itself from the 'real', from the concrete; it lacks the gap necessary for generalisability (for Saussure, this is the idea that, 'Signs which are arbitrary realise better than others the ideal of the semiotic process.'). The woman, too, is defined by such an insufficiency. My insistence upon the congruence between certain theories of the image and theories of femininity is an attempt to dissect the *episteme* which assigns to the woman a special place in cinematic representation while denying her access to that system.

The cinematic apparatus inherits a theory of the image which is not conceived outside of sexual specifications. And historically, there has always been a certain imbrication of the cinematic image and the representation of the woman. The woman's relation to the camera and the scopic regime is quite different from that of the male. As Noël Burch points out, the early silent cinema, through its insistent inscription of scenarios of voyeurism, conceives of its spectator's viewing pleasure in terms of that of the Peeping Tom, behind the screen, reduplicating the spectator's position in relation to the woman as screen.[4] Spectatorial desire, in contemporary film theory, is generally delineated as either voyeurism or fetishism, as precisely a

---

[1] In other words, the woman can never ask her own ontological question. The absurdity of such a situation within traditional discursive conventions can be demonstrated by substituting a 'young woman' for the 'young man' of Heine's poem.

[2] As Oswald Ducrot and Tzvetan Todorov point out in *Encyclopedic Dictionary of the Science of Language,* trans. Catherine Porter (Baltimore and London: Johns Hopkins University Press, 1979), p. 195, the potentially universal understandability of the hieroglyphic is highly theoretical and can only be thought as the unattainable ideal of an imagistic system: 'It is important of course not to exaggerate either the resemblance of the image with the object—the design is stylized very rapidly—or the "natural" and "universal" character of the signs: Sumerian, Chinese, Egyptian, and Hittite hieroglyphics for the same object have nothing in common.'

[3] Ibid., p. 194. Emphasis mine.

[4] See Noël Burch's film, *Correction Please, or How We Got Into Pictures.*

pleasure in seeing what is prohibited in relation to the female body. The image orchestrates a gaze, a limit, and its pleasurable transgression. The woman's beauty, her very desirability, becomes a function of certain practices of imaging—framing, lighting, camera movement, angle. She is thus, as Laura Mulvey has pointed out, more closely associated with the surface of the image than its illusory depths, its constructed three-dimensional space which the man is destined to inhabit and hence control.[1] In *Now Voyager,* for instance, a single image signals the momentous transformation of the Bette Davis character from ugly spinster aunt to glamorous single woman. Charles Affron describes the specifically cinematic aspect of this operation as a 'stroke of genius':

> The radical shadow bisecting the face in white/dark/white strata creates a visual phenomenon quite distinct from the makeup transformation of lipstick and plucked eyebrows. . . . This shot does not reveal what we commonly call acting, especially after the most recent exhibition of that activity, but the sense of face belongs to a plastique pertinent to the camera. The viewer is allowed a different perceptual referent, a chance to come down from the nerve-jarring, first sequence and to use his eyes anew.[2]

A 'plastique pertinent to the camera' constitutes the woman not only as the image of desire but as the desirous image—one which the devoted cinéphile can cherish and embrace. To 'have' the cinema is, in some sense, to 'have' the woman. But *Now Voyager* is, in Affron's terms, a 'tear-jerker', in others, a 'woman's picture', that is, a film purportedly produced for a female audience. What, then, of the female spectator? What can one say about her desire in relation to this process of imaging? It would seem that what the cinematic institution has in common with Freud's gesture is the eviction of the female spectator from a discourse purportedly about her (the cinema, psychoanalysis)—one which, in fact, narrativises her again and again.

A LASS BUT NOT A LACK

Theories of female spectatorship are thus rare, and when they are produced, seem inevitably to confront certain blockages in conceptualisation. The difficulties in thinking female spectatorship demand consideration. After all, even if it is admitted that the woman is frequently the object of the voyeuristic or fetishistic gaze in the cinema, what is there to prevent her from reversing the relation and appropriating the gaze for her own pleasure? Precisely the fact that the reversal itself remains locked within the same logic. The male striptease, the gigolo—both inevitably signify the mechanism of reversal itself, constituting themselves as aberrations whose acknowledgment simply reinforces the dominant system of aligning sexual difference with a subject/object dichotomy. And an essential attribute of that dominant system is the matching of male subjectivity with the agency of the look.

The supportive binary opposition at work here is not only that utilised by Laura Mulvey—an opposition between passivity and activity, but perhaps more impor-

[1]Laura Mulvey, "Visual Pleasure and Narrative Cinema," *Screen* (Autumn 1975), vol. 16, no. 3, pp. 12–13. [See also this volume—Eds]
[2]Charles Affron, *Star Acting: Gish, Garbo, Davis* (New York, E. P. Dutton, 1977, pp. 281–282.

tantly, an opposition between proximity and distance in relation to the image.[1] It is in this sense that the very logic behind the structure of the gaze demands a sexual division. While the distance between image and signified (or even referent) is theorised as minimal, if not non-existent, that between the film and the spectator must be maintained, even measured. One need only think of Noël Burch's mapping of spectatorship as a perfect distance from the screen (two times the width of the image)—a point in space from which the filmic discourse is most accessible.[2]

But the most explicit representation of this opposition between proximity and distance is contained in Christian Metz's analysis of voyeuristic desire in terms of a kind of social hierarchy of the senses: 'It is no accident that the main socially acceptable arts are based on the senses at a distance, and that those which depend on the senses of contact are often regarded as "minor" arts (= culinary arts, art of perfumes, etc.).'[3] The voyeur, according to Metz, must maintain a distance between himself and the image—the cinéphile *needs* the gap which represents for him the very distance between desire and its object. In this sense, voyeurism is theorised as a type of meta-desire:

> If it is true of all desire that it depends on the infinite pursuit of its absent object, voyeuristic desire, along with certain forms of sadism, is the only desire whose principle of distance symbolically and spatially evokes this fundamental rent.[4]

Yet even this status as meta-desire does not fully characterise the cinema for it is a feature shared by other arts as well (painting, theatre, opera, etc.). Metz thus adds another reinscription of this necessary distance. What specifies the cinema is a further re-duplication of the lack which prompts desire. The cinema is characterised by an illusory sensory plenitude (there is 'so much to see') and yet haunted by the absence of those very objects which are there to be seen. Absence is an absolute and irrecoverable distance. In other words, Noël Burch is quite right in aligning spectatorial desire with a certain spatial configuration. The viewer must not sit either too close or too far from the screen. The result of both would be the same—he would lose the image of his desire.

It is precisely this opposition between proximity and distance, control of the image and its loss, which locates the possibilities of spectatorship within the problematic of sexual difference. For the female spectator there is a certain overpresence of the image—she *is* the image. Given the closeness of this relationship, the female spectator's desire can be described only in terms of a kind of narcissism—the female look demands a becoming. It thus appears to negate the very distance or gap spec-

---

[1]This argument focuses on the image to the exclusion of any consideration of the soundtrack primarily because it is the process of imaging which seems to constitute the major difficulty in theorising female spectatorship. The image is also popularly understood as metonymic signifier for the cinema as a whole and for good reason: historically, sound has been subordinate to the image within the dominant classical system. For more on the image/sound distinction in relation to sexual difference see my article, "The Voice in the Cinema: The Articulation of Body and Space," *Yale French Studies,* no. 60, pp. 33–50.

[2]Noël Burch, *Theory of Film Practice,* trans. Helen R. Lane (New York and Washington: Praeger Publishers, 1973), p. 35.

[3]Christian Metz, "The Imaginary Signifier," *Screen* (Summer 1975), vol. 16, no. 2, p. 60. [See also this volume.]

[4]Ibid., p. 61.

ified by Metz and Burch as the essential precondition for voyeurism. From this perspective, it is important to note the constant recurrence of the motif of proximity in feminist theoriest (especially those labelled 'new French feminisms') which purport to describe a feminine specificity. For Luce Irigaray, female anatomy is readable as a constant relation of the self to itself, as an autoeroticism based on the embrace of the two lips which allow the woman to touch herself without mediation. Furthermore, the very notion of property, and hence possession of something which can be constituted as other, is antithetical to the woman: '*Nearness* however, is not foreign to woman, a nearness so close that any identification of one or the other, and therefore any form of property, is impossible. Woman enjoys a closeness with the other that is *so near she cannot possess it any more than she can possess herself*.'[1] Or, in the case of female madness or delirium, '. . . women do not manage to articulate their madness: they suffer it directly in their body . . .'.[2] The distance necessary to detach the signifiers of madness from the body in the construction of even a discourse which exceeds the boundaries of sense is lacking. In the words of Hélène Cixous, 'More so than men who are coaxed toward social success, toward sublimation, women are body.'[3]

This theme of the overwhelming presence-to-itself of the female body is elaborated by Sarah Kofman and Michèle Montrelay as well. Kofman describes how Freudian psychoanalysis outlines a scenario whereby the subject's passage from the mother to the father is simultaneous with a passage from the senses to reason, nostalgia for the mother henceforth signifying a longing for a different positioning in relation to the sensory or the somatic, and the degree of civilization measured by the very distance from the body.[4] Similarly, Montrelay argues that while the male has the possibility of displacing the first object of desire (the mother), the female must become that object of desire:

> Recovering herself as maternal body (and also as phallus), the woman can no longer repress, 'lose,' the first stake of representation. . . . From now on, anxiety, tied to the presence of this body, can only be insistent, continuous. This body, so close, which she has to occupy, is an object in excess which must be 'lost,' that is to say, repressed, in order to be symbolised.[5]

This body so close, so excessive, prevents the woman from assuming a position similar to the man's in relation to signifying systems. For she is haunted by the loss of a loss, the lack of that lack so essential for the realisation of the ideals of semiotic systems.

Female specificity is thus theorised in terms of spatial proximity. In opposition to this 'closeness' to the body, a spatial distance in the male's relation to his body rapidly becomes a temporal distance in the service of knowledge. This is presented quite explicitly in Freud's analysis of the construction of the 'subject supposed to know'. The knowledge involved here is a knowledge of sexual difference as it is

---

[1] Luce Irigaray, "This Sex Which Is Not One," *New French Feminisms,* ed. Elaine Marks and Isabelle de Courtivron (Amherst: University of Massachusetts Press, 1980), pp. 104–105.

[2] Irigaray, "Women's Exile," *Ideology and Consciousness,* no. 1 (May 1977), p. 74.

[3] Hélène Cixous, "The Laugh of the Medusa," *New French Feminisms,* p. 257.

[4] Sarah Kofman, "Ex: The Woman's Enigma" *Enclitic* 4, no. 2 (Fall 1980), p. 20.

[5] Michèle Montrelay, "Inquiry into Femininity," *m/f,* no. 1 (1978), pp. 91–92.

organised in relation to the structure of the look, turning on the visibility of the penis. For the little girl in Freud's description, seeing and knowing are simultaneous—there is no temporal gap between them. In 'Some Psychological Consequences of the Anatomical Distinction Between the Sexes', Freud claims that the girl, upon seeing the penis for the first time, 'makes her judgement and her decision in a flash. She has seen it and knows that she is without it and wants to have it.'[1] In the lecture on 'Femininity' Freud repeats this gesture, merging perception and intellection: 'They [girls] at once notice the difference and, it must be admitted, its significance too.'[2]

The little boy, on the other hand, does not share this immediacy of understanding. When he first sees the woman's genitals he 'begins by showing irresolution and lack of interest; he sees nothing or disowns what he has seen, he softens it down or looks about for expedients for bringing it into line with his expectations'.[3] A second event, the threat of castration, is necessary to prompt a rereading of the image, endowing it with a meaning in relation to the boy's own subjectivity. It is in the distance between the look and the threat that the boy's relation to knowledge of sexual difference is formulated. The boy, unlike the girl in Freud's description, is capable of a revision of earlier events, a retrospective understanding which invests the events with a significance which is in no way linked to an immediacy of sight. This gap between the visible and the knowable, the very possibility of disowning what is seen, prepares the ground for fetishism. In a sense, the male spectator is destined to be a fetishist, balancing knowledge and belief.

The female, on the other hand, must find it extremely difficult, if not impossible, to assume the position of fetishist. That body which is so close continually reminds her of the castration which cannot be 'fetishised away'. The lack of a distance between seeing and understanding, the mode of judging 'in a flash', is conducive to what might be termed as 'overidentification' with the image. The association of tears and 'wet wasted afternoons' (in Molly Haskell's words)[4] with genres specified as feminine (the soap opera, the "woman's picture') points very precisely to this type of overidentification, this abolition of a distance, in short, this inability to fetishise. The woman is constructed differently in relation to processes of looking. For Irigaray, this dichotomy between distance and proximity is described as the fact that:

The masculine can partly look at itself, speculate about itself, represent itself and describe itself for what it is, whilst the feminine can try to speak to itself through a new language, but cannot describe itself from outside or in formal terms, except by identifying itself with the masculine, thus by losing itself.[5]

---

[1]Freud, "Some Psychological Consequences of the Anatomical Distinction Between the Sexes," *Sexuality and the Psychology of Love,* ed. Philip Rieff (New York: Collier Books, 1963), pp. 187–188.

[2]Freud, "Femininity," p. 125.

[3]Freud, "Some Psychological Consequences," p. 187.

[4]Molly Haskell, *From Reverence to Rape* (Baltimore: Penguin Books, 1974), p. 154.

[5]Irigaray, "Women's Exile," p. 65.

Irigaray goes even further: the woman always has a problematic relation to the visible, to form, to structures of seeing. She is much more comfortable with, closer to, the sense of touch.

The pervasiveness, in theories of the feminine, of descriptions of such a claustrophobic closeness, a deficiency in relation to structures of seeing and the visible, must clearly have consequences for attempts to theorise female spectatorship. And, in fact, the result is a tendency to view the female spectator as the site of an oscillation between a feminine position and a masculine position, invoking the metaphor of the transvestite. Given the structures of cinematic narrative, the woman who identifies with a female character must adopt a passive or masochistic position, while identification with the active hero necessarily entails an acceptance of what Laura Mulvey refers to as a certain 'masculinisation' of spectatorship.

> . . . as desire is given cultural materiality in a text, for women (from childhood onwards) trans-sex identification is a *habit* that very easily becomes *second Nature.* However, this Nature does not sit easily and shifts restlessly in its borrowed transvestite clothes.*

The transvestite wears clothes which signify a different sexuality, a sexuality which, for the woman, allows a mastery over the image and the very possibility of attaching the gaze to desire. Clothes make the man, as they say. Perhaps this explains the ease with which women can slip into male clothing. As both Freud and Cixous point out, the woman seems to be *more* bisexual than the man. A scene from Cukor's *Adam's Rib* graphically demonstrates this ease of female transvestism. As Katharine Hepburn asks the jury to imagine the sex role reversal of the three major characters involved in the case, there are three dissolves linking each of the characters successively to shots in which they are dressed in the clothes of the opposite sex. What characterises the sequence is the marked facility of the transformation of the two women into men in contradistinction to a certain resistance in the case of the man. The acceptability of the female reversal is quite distinctly opposed to the male reversal which seems capable of representation only in terms of farce. Male transvestism is an occasion for laughter; female transvestism only another occasion for desire.

Thus, while the male is locked into sexual identity, the female can at least pretend that she is other—in fact, sexual mobility would seem to be a distinguishing feature of femininity in its cultural construction. Hence, transvestism would be fully recuperable. The idea seems to be this: it is understandable that women would want to be men, for everyone wants to be elsewhere than in the feminine position. What is not understandable within the given terms is why a woman might flaunt her femininity, produce herself as an excess of femininity, in other words, foreground the masquerade. Masquerade is not as recuperable as transvestism precisely because it constitutes an acknowledgement that it is femininity itself which is constructed as mask—as the decorative layer which conceals a non-identity. For Joan Riviere, the first to theorise the concept, the masquerade of femininity is a kind of reaction-formation against the woman's trans-sex identification, her transvestism. After

---

*Mulvey, "Afterthoughts . . . inspired by Duel in the Sun," *Framework* (Summer 1981), p. 13.

assuming the position of the subject of discourse rather than its object, the intellectual woman whom Riviere analyses felt compelled to compensate for this theft of masculinity by overdoing the gestures of feminine flirtation.

> Womanliness therefore could be assumed and worn as a mask, both to hide the possession of masculinity and to avert the reprisals expected if she was found to possess it—much as a thief will turn out his pockets and ask to be searched to prove that he has not the stolen goods. The reader may now ask how I define womanliness or where I draw the line between genuine womanliness and the masquerade. My suggestion is not, however, that there is any such difference; whether radical or superficial, they are the same thing.[1]

The masquerade, in flaunting femininity, holds it at a distance. Womanliness is a mask which can be worn or removed. The masquerade's resistance to patriarchal positioning would therefore lie in its denial of the production of femininity as closeness, as presence-to-itself, as, precisely, imagistic. The transvestite adopts the sexuality of the other—the woman becomes a man in order to attain the necessary distance from the image. Masquerade, on the other hand, involves a realignment of femininity, the recovery, or more accurately, simulation, of the missing gap or distance. To masquerade is to manufacture a lack in the form of a certain distance between oneself and one's image. If, as Moustafa Safouan points out, '. . . to wish to include in oneself as an object the cause of the desire of the Other is a formula for the structure of hysteria',[2] then masquerade is anti-hysterical for its works to effect a separation between the cause of desire and oneself. In Montrelay's words, 'the woman uses her own body as a disguise.'[3]

The very fact that we can speak of a woman 'using' her sex or 'using' her body for particular gains is highly significant—it is not that a man cannot use his body; in this way but that he doesn't have to. The masquerade doubles representation; it is constituted by a hyperbolisation of the accoutrements of femininity. A propos of a recent performance by Marlene Dietrich, Sylvia Bovenschen claims, '. . . we are watching a woman demonstrate the representation of a woman's body.'[4] This type of masquerade, an excess of feminity, is aligned with the *femme fatale* and, as Montrelay explains, is necessarily regarded by men as evil incarnate: 'It is this evil which scandalises whenever woman plays out her sex in order to evade the word and the law. Each time she subverts a law or a word which relies on the predominantly masculine structure of the look.'[5] By destabilising the image, the masquerade confounds this masculine structure of the look. It effects a defamiliarisation of female iconog-

---

[1]Joan Riviere, "Womanliness as a Masquerade," *Psychoanalysis and Female Sexuality,* ed. Hendrik M. Ruitenbeek (New Haven: College and University Press, 1966), p. 213. My analysis of the concept of masquerade differs markedly from that of Luce Irigaray. See *Ce sexe qui n'en est pas un* (Paris: Les Éditions de Minuit, 1977), pp. 131–132. It also diverges to a great extent from the very important analysis of masquerade presented by Claire Johnston in "Femininity and the Masquerade: Anne of the Indies," *Jacques Tourneur* (London: British Film Institute, 1975), pp. 36–44. I am indebted to her for the reference to Riviere's article.
[2]Moustala Safouan, "Is the Oedipus Complex Universal?" *m/f,* nos. 5–6 (1981), pp. 84–85.
[3]Montrelay, "Inquiry into Femininity," p. 93.
[4]Silvia Bovenschen, "Is There a Feminine Aesthetic?" *New German Critique,* no. 10 (Winter 1977), p. 129.
[5]Montrelay, p. 93.

raphy. Nevertheless, the preceding account simply specifies masquerade as a type of representation which carries a threat, disarticulating male systems of viewing. Yet, it specifies nothing with respect to female spectatorship. What might it mean to masquerade as spectator? To assume the mask in order to see in a different way?

'MEN SELDOM MAKE PASSES AT GIRLS WHO WEAR GLASSES'

The first scene in *Now Voyager* depicts the Bette Davis character as repressed, unattractive, and undesirable or, in her own words, as the spinster aunt of the family. ('Every family has one.') She has heavy eyebrows, keeps her hair bound tightly in a bun, and wears glasses, a drab dress, and heavy shoes. By the time of the shot discussed earlier, signalling her transformation into beauty, the glasses have disappeared, along with the other signifiers of unattractiveness. Between these two moments there is a scene in which the doctor who cures her actually confiscates her glasses (as a part of the cure). The woman who wears glasses constitutes one of the most intense visual clichés of the cinema. The image is a heavily marked condensation of motifs concerned with repressed sexuality, knowledge, visibility and vision, intellectuality, and desire. The woman with glasses signifies simultaneously intellectuality and undesirability; but the moment she removes her glasses (a moment which, it seems, must almost always be *shown* and which is itself linked with a certain sensual quality), she is transformed into spectacle, the very picture of desire. Now, it must be remembered that the cliché is a heavily loaded moment of signification, a social knot of meaning. It is characterised by an effect of ease and naturalness. Yet, the cliché has a binding power so strong that it indicates a precise moment of ideological danger or threat—in this case, the woman's appropriation of the gaze. Glasses worn by a woman in the cinema do not generally signify a deficiency in seeing but an active looking, or even simply the fact of seeing as opposed to being seen. The intellectual woman looks and analyses, and in usurping the gaze she poses a threat to an entire system of representation. It is as if the woman had forcefully moved to the other side of the specular. The overdetermination of the image of the woman with glasses, its status as a cliché, is a crucial aspect of the cinematic alignment of structures of seeing and being seen with sexual difference. The cliché, in assuming an immediacy of understanding, acts as a mechanism for the naturalisation of sexual difference.

But the figure of the woman with glasses is only an extreme moment of a more generalised logic. There is always a certain excessiveness, a difficulty associated with women who appropriate the gaze, who insist upon looking. Linda Williams has demonstrated how, in the genre of the horror film, the woman's active looking is ultimately punished. And what she sees, the monster, is only a mirror of herself—both woman and monster are freakish in their difference—defined by either 'too much' or 'too little'.* Just as the dominant narrative cinema repetitively inscribes

---

*Linda Williams, "When the Woman Looks . . . ," in *Revision: Feminist Essays in Film Analysis,* ed. Mary Ann Doane, Pat Mellencamp, and Linda Williams (Frederick, Md.: AFI-University Publications, 1984). [See also this volume.—Eds.]

scenarios of voyeurism, internalising or narrativising the film-spectator relationship (in films like *Psycho, Rear Window, Peeping Tom*), taboos in seeing are insistently formulated in relation to the female spectator as well. The man with binoculars is countered by the woman with glasses. The gaze must be dissociated from mastery. In *Leave Her to Heaven* (John Stahl, 1945), the female protagonist's (Gene Tierney's) excessive desire and overpossessiveness are signalled from the very beginning of the film by her intense and sustained stare at the major male character, a stranger she first encounters on a train. The discomfort her look causes is graphically depicted. The Gene Tierney character is ultimately revealed to be the epitome of evil—killing her husband's crippled younger brother, her unborn child, and ultimately herself in an attempt to brand her cousin as a murderess in order to ensure her husband's future fidelity. In *Humoresque* (Jean Negulesco, 1946), Joan Crawford's problematic status is a result of her continual attempts to assume the position of spectator—fixing John Garfield with her gaze. Her transformation from spectator to spectacle is signified repetitively by the gesture of removing her glasses. Rosa, the character played by Bette Davis in *Beyond the Forest* (King Vidor, 1949), walks to the station every day simply to *watch* the train departing for Chicago. Her fascination with the train is a fascination with its phallic power to transport her to 'another place'. This character is also specified as having a 'good eye'—she can shoot, both pool and guns. In all three films the woman is constructed as the site of an excessive and dangerous desire. This desire mobilises extreme efforts of containment and unveils the sadistic aspect of narrative. In all three films the woman dies. As Claire Johnston points out, death is the "location of all impossible signs',* and films demonstrate that the woman as subject of the gaze is clearly an impossible sign. There is a perverse rewriting of this logic of the gaze in *Dark Victory* (Edmund Goulding, 1939), where the woman's story achieves heroic and tragic proportions not only in blindness, but in a blindness which mimes sight—when the woman pretends to be able to see.

OUT OF THE CINEMA AND INTO THE STREETS: THE CENSORSHIP OF THE FEMALE GAZE

This process of narrativising the negation of the female gaze in the classical Hollywood cinema finds its perfect encapsulation in a still photograph taken in 1948 by Robert Doisneau, *Un Regard Oblique*. Just as the Hollywood narratives discussed above purport to centre a female protagonist, the photograph appears to give a certain prominence to a woman's look. Yet, both the title of the photograph and its organisation of space indicate that the real site of scopophiliac power is on the margins of the frame. The man is not centred; in fact, he occupies a very narrow space on the extreme right of the picture. Nevertheless, it is his gaze which defines the problematic of the photographs: it is his gaze which effectively erases that of the woman. Indeed, as subject of the gaze, the woman looks intently. But not only is the object of her look concealed from the spectator, her gaze is encased by the two poles defining the masculine axis of vision. Fascinated by nothing visible—a blank-

---

*Johnston, "Femininity and the Masquerade," p. 40.

Un Regard Oblique by Robert Doisneau. "The feminine presence in the photograph, despite a diegetic centering of the female subject of the gaze, is taken over by the picture as object .... The spectator's pleasure is thus produced through the framing negation of the female gaze. The woman is there as the butt of a joke—a 'dirty joke' which as Freud has demonstrated, is always constructed at the expense woman" (DOANE, page 770).

ness or void for the spectator—unanchored by a 'sight' (there is nothing 'proper' to her vision—save, perhaps, the mirror), the female gaze is left free-floating, vulnerable to subjection. The faint reflection in the shop window of only the frame of the picture at which she is looking serves merely to rearticulate, *en abŷme,* the emptiness of her gaze, the absence of her desire in representation.

On the other hand, the object of the male gaze is fully present, *there* for the spectator. The fetishistic representation of the nude female body, fully in view, insures a masculinisation of the spectatorial position. The woman's look is literally outside the triangle which traces a complicity between the man, the nude, and the spectator. The feminine presence in the photograph, despite a diegetic centring of the female subject of the gaze, is taken over by the picture as object. And, as if to doubly 'frame' her in the act of looking, the painting situates its female figure as a spectator (although it is not clear whether she is looking at herself in a mirror or peering through a door or window). While this drama of seeing is played out at the surface of the photograph, its deep space is activated by several young boys, out-of-focus, in front of a belt shop. The opposition out-of-focus/in-focus reinforces the supposed clarity accorded to the representation of the woman's 'non-vision'. Furthermore, since this out-of-focus area constitutes the precise literal centre of the image, it also demonstrates how the photograph makes figurative the operation of centring—draining the actual centre point of significance in order to deposit meaning on the margins. The male gaze is centred, in control—although it is exercised from the periphery.

The spectator's pleasure is thus produced through the framing/negation of the female gaze. The woman is there as the butt of a joke—a 'dirty joke' which, as Freud has demonstrated, is always constructed at the expense of a woman. In order for a dirty joke to emerge in its specificity in Freud's description, the object of desire—the woman—must be absent and a third person (another man) must be present as witness to the joke—'so that gradually, in place of the woman, the onlooker, now the listener, becomes the person to whom the smut is addressed . . .'[1] The terms of the photograph's address as joke once again ensure a masculinisation of the place of the spectator. The operation of the dirty joke is also inextricably linked by Freud to scopophilia and the exposure of the female body:

> Smut is like an exposure of the sexually different person to whom it is directed. By the utterance of the obscene words it compels the person who is assailed to imagine the part of the body or the procedure in question and shows her that the assailant is himself imagining it. It cannot be doubted that the desire to see what is sexual exposed is the original motive of smut.[2]

From this perspective, the photograph lays bare the very mechanics of the joke through its depiction of sexual exposure and a surreptitious act of seeing (and desiring). Freud's description of the joke-work appears to constitute a perfect analysis of the photograph's orchestration of the gaze. There is a 'voice-off' of the photographic discourse, however—a component of the image which is beyond the frame of this

---

[1] Freud, *Jokes and Their Relation to the Unconscious,* trans. James Strachey (New York: W. W. Norton, 1960), p. 99.

[2] Ibid., p. 98.

little scenario of voyeurism. On the far left-hand side of the photograph, behind the wall holding the painting of the nude, is the barely detectable painting of a woman imaged differently, in darkness—*out of sight* for the male, blocked by his fetish. Yet, to point to this almost invisible alternative in imaging is also only to reveal once again the analyst's own perpetual desire to find a not-seen that might break the hold of representation. Or to laugh last.

There is a sense in which the photograph's delineation of a sexual politics of looking is almost uncanny. But, to counteract the very possibility of such a perception, the language of the art critic effects a naturalisation of this joke on the woman. The art-critical reception of the picture emphasizes a natural but at the same time 'imaginative' relation between photography and life, ultimately subordinating any formal relations to a referential ground: 'Doisneau's lines move from right to left, directed by the man's glance; the woman's gaze creates a line of energy like a hole in space. . . . The creation of these relationships from life itself is imagination in photography.'[1] 'Life itself', then, presents the material for an 'artistic' organisation of vision along the lines of sexual difference. Furthermore, the critic would have us believe that chance events and arbitrary clicks of the shutter cannot be the agents of a generalised sexism because they are particular, unique—'Kertesz and Doisneau depend entirely upon our recognition that they were present at the instant of the unique intersection of events.'[2] Realism seems always to reside in the streets and, indeed, the out-of-focus boys across the street, at the centre of the photograph, appears to act as a guarantee of the 'chance' nature of the event, its arbitrariness, in short—its realism. Thus, in the discourse of the art critic the photograph, in capturing a moment, does not construct it; the camera finds a naturally given series of subject and object positions. What the critic does not consider are the conditions of reception of photography as an art form, its situation within a much larger network of representation. What is it that makes the photograph not only readable but pleasurable—at the expense of the woman? The critic does not ask what makes the photograph a negotiable item in a market of signification.

THE MISSING LOOK

The photograph displays insistently, in microcosm, the structure of the cinematic inscription of a sexual differentiation in modes of looking. Its process of framing the female gaze repeats that of the cinematic narratives described above, from *Leave Her to Heaven* to *Dark Victory*. Films play out scenarios of looking in order to outline the terms of their own understanding. And given the divergence between masculine and feminine scenarios, those terms would seem to be explicitly negotiated as markers of sexual difference. Both the theory of the image and its apparatus, the cinema, produce a position for the female spectator—a position which is ultimately untenable because it lacks the attribute of distance so necessary for an adequate reading of the image. The entire elaboration of femininity as a closeness,

---

[1]Weston J. Naef, *Counterparts: Form and Emotion in Photographs* (New York: E. P. Dutton and the Metropolitan Museum of Art, 1982), pp. 48–49.
[2]Ibid.

a nearness, as present-to-itself is not the definition of an essence but the delineation of a *place* culturally assigned to the woman. Above and beyond a simple adoption of the masculine position in relation to the cinematic sign, the female spectator is given two options: the masochism of overidentification or the narcissism entailed in becoming one's own object of desire, in assuming the image in the most radical way. The effectivity of masquerade lies precisely in its potential to manufacture a distance from the image, to generate a problematic within which the image is manipulable, producible, and readable by the woman. Doisneau's photograph is not readable by the female spectator—it can give her pleasure only in masochism. In order to 'get' the joke, she must once again assume the position of transvestite.

It is quite tempting to foreclose entirely the possibility of female spectatorship, to repeat at the level of theory the gesture of the photograph, given the history of a cinema which relies so heavily on voyeurism, fetishism, and identification with an ego ideal conceivable only in masculine terms. And, in fact, there has been a tendency to theorise femininity and hence the feminine gaze as repressed, and in its repression somehow irretrievable, the enigma constituted by Freud's question. Yet, as Michel Foucault has demonstrated, the repressive hypothesis on its own entails a very limited and simplistic notion of the working of power.* The 'no' of the father, the prohibition, is its only technique. In theories of repression there is no sense of the productiveness and positivity of power. Femininity is produced very precisely as a position within a network of power relations. And the growing insistence upon the elaboration of a theory of female spectatorship is indicative of the crucial necessity of understanding that position in order to dislocate it.

1982

---

*Michel Foucault, *The History of Sexuality,* trans. Robert Hurley (New York: Pantheon Books, 1978).

GAYLYN STUDLAR
MASOCHISM AND THE PERVERSE
PLEASURES OF THE CINEMA

This study offers an alternative model to the current discourse that emphasizes voyeurism aligned with sadism, the male controlling gaze as the only position of spectatorial pleasure, and a polarized notion of sexual difference with the female regarded as "lack." In 1978, Christine Gledhill wrote of the need to broaden the focus of feminist film theory, to question guiding theoretical assumptions, and to confront the complexity of "woman's place" within patriarchal culture.[1] In the context of feminist-psychoanalytic approaches to film, the hegemony of the Freudian-Lacanian-Metzian model has, unfortunately, reduced rather than enlarged the field of questions that feminist theory has asked about specific forms of enunciation in classic narrative cinema and the possibilities of subject positioning. While I do not assume to displace the dominant model, there is, I believe, an obvious call to question some of the assumptions that have shaped current trends.

My alternative model is derived from Gilles Deleuze's *Masochism: An Interpretation of Coldness and Cruelty.*[2] Deleuze employs a psychoanalytic-literary approach to the novels of Leopold von Sacher-Masoch, the namesake of masochism, to challenge basic Freudian tenets regarding the sado-masochistic duality and the etiology of masochism as a response to the father and castration fear. If the qualitative differences between sadism and masochism are disregarded and only the pain/pleasure content is considered, then the two perversions might well be considered to be complementary as Freud maintained, but Deleuze shows that only when

---

[1]Christine Gledhill, "Recent Developments in Feminist Criticism," *Quarterly Review of Film Studies* 3 (Fall 1978), pp. 457–93. In her 1984 revision of this article for *Re-Vision: Essays in Feminist Film Criticism* (Frederick, Md.: AFI-University Publications of America, 1984), Gledhill rearticulates her original critique.
[2]Gilles Deleuze, *Masochism: An Interpretation of Coldness and Cruelty* (New York: George Braziller, 1971); Leopold von Sacher-Masoch, "Venus in Furs," trans. Jean McNeil, in Deleuze.

773

masochism's formal patterns are recognized as reflections of a unique underlying psychoanalytic structure can the perversion be correctly defined as a distinct clinical entity or as an aesthetic:

> Masochism is above all formal and dramatic: this means that its peculiar pleasure-pain complex is determined by a particular kind of formalism, and its experience of guilt by a specific story.[1]

Deleuze considers masochism to be a phenomenology of experience that reaches far beyond the limited definition of a perverse sexuality. Similarly, the masochistic aesthetic extends beyond the purely clinical realm into the arena of artistic form, language, and production of pleasure through a text.

Comparing Masoch's and Sade's novels, Deleuze concludes that Sade's intentions, formal techniques, and language are completely at odds with those of Masoch. These differences are but a reflection of differing psychoanalytic determinants. The Sadian discourse—denotative, scientific, unblinkingly direct in its obscene imperatives and descriptions—creates a fantastically cruel heterocosm based exclusively on the rule of reason. The governing sadistic fantasy expressed in Sade's work exalts the father "beyond all laws," says Deleuze, and negates the mother.[2] In contrast, Masoch's fictive world is mythical, persuasive, aesthetically oriented, and centered around the idealizing, mystical exaltation of love for the punishing woman. In her ideal form as representative of the powerful oral mother, the female in the masochistic scenario is not sadistic, but must inflict cruelty in love to fulfill her role in the mutually agreed upon masochistic scheme. Masoch writes in a typical passage from his most famous novel, "Venus in Furs":

> To love and be loved, what joy! And yet how this splendour pales in comparison with the blissful torment of worshipping a woman who treats one as a plaything, of being the slave of a beautiful tyrant who mercilessly tramples one underfoot.[3]

As Deleuze notes, the paradox of the masochistic alliance as exemplified in Masoch's work is the subversion of the expected patriarchal positions of power/powerlessness, master/slave, with the ultimate paradox being the slave's (the male's) willingness to confer power to the female.[4]

An excerpt from Sade's *One Hundred and Twenty Days of Sodom* illustrates the blatant absurdity of equating sadism and masochism on a literary level, and, as Deleuze shows, on a psychoanalytic level as well:

> This libertine requires a dozen women, six young, six old and if 'tis possible, six of them should be mothers and the other six daughters. He pumps out their cunts, asses, and mouths; when applying his lips to the cunt, he wants copious urine; when at the mouth, much saliva; when at the ass, abundant farts.[5]

---

[1]Deleuze, p. 95.
[2]Deleuze, p. 52.
[3]Sacher-Masoch, p. 129
[4]Deleuze, p. 80.
[5]Donatien Alphonse Francois de Sade, *The 120 Days of Sodom and Other Writings,* trans. and ed. Austryn Wainhouse and Richard Seaver (New York: Grove Press, 1966), p. 577.

Even when Sade chooses a woman as "heroine," she still acts out the criminally misogynistic impulse that is not satisfied with merely objectifying or demystifying women but must destroy them. In the masochistic text, the female is not one of a countless number of discarded objects but an idealized, powerful figure, both dangerous and comforting. Fetishization, fantasy, and idealizing disavowal replace the frenzied Sadian destruction of the female. While Sade's incessantly active libertines challenge the limits of human endurance and evil in endlessly repeated cycles of sex and violence, the masochistic world barely suggests sexual activity or violence. Deleuze remarks: "Of Masoch it can be said, as it cannot be of Sade, that no one has ever been so far with so little offence to decency."[1] In the masochistic aesthetic, dramatic suspense replaced Sadian accelerating repetition of action, intimacy between mutually chosen partners replaces the impersonality of masses of libertines and victims, idealized eroticism replaces the obscenity that threatens to burst the limits of conventional language in an attempt to match the unattainable, destructive Idea of Evil.[2] If Sade's writing is "structurally linked to crime and sex" as Roland Barthes has said,[3] then the work of Masoch reveals a formal and narrative pattern structurally linked to self-abasement and pre-Oedipal desire.

The formal structures of the masochistic aesthetic—fantasy, disavowal, fetishism, and suspense—overlap with the primary structures that enable classic narrative cinema to produce visual pleasure. These similarities raise fundamental questions about the relationship of cinematic pleasure to masochism, sexual differentiation, processes of identification, the representation of the female in film, and other issues in which a model derived from Deleuze's theory offers a radical alternative to those Freudian assumptions that have been adopted by most of psychoanalytic film theory.

The key question is: Why replace the line of thought represented by Christian Metz and Laura Mulvey, with its stress on the similarity between the structures of sadism and visual pleasure, with an emphasis on masochism's relationship to visual pleasure? What are the advantages?

By focusing on the pregenital period in the development of desire and sexual identity rather than on the phallic phase emphasized in Freud's studies, a consideration of the masochistic aesthetic and film shifts attention to a stage of psychosexual life that has been an overlooked determinant in the "sadistic" model of cinematic spectatorship. The "masochistic model" rejects a stance that has emphasized the phallic phase and the pleasure of control or mastery and therefore offers an alternative to strict Freudian models that have proven to be a dead end for feminist-psychoanalytic theory. In trying to come to terms with patriarchal society and the cinema as a construct of that society, current theoretical discourse has often inadvertently reduced the psychoanalytic complexity of spectatorship through a regressive phallocentrism that ignores a wider range of psychological influences on visual pleasure.

---

[1]Deleuze, p. 31.
[2]Deleuze, pp. 16–19. See also Roland Barthes, *Sade/Loyola/Fourier,* trans. Richard Miller (New York: Hill & Wang, 1976), pp. 31–37.
[3]Barthes, p. 34.

The approach presented here brings together two lines of theoretical work previously separated: (1) the analogy between the cinematic apparatus and the dream screen of the oral period of infancy pursued by Jean-Louis Baudry and Robert Eberwein,[1] and (2) the consideration of representation of the female, identification, and sexually differentiated spectatorship in the theories of Laura Mulvey, Claire Johnston, Mary Ann Doane, and others.[2] The "masochistic model" could be viewed as an attempt to use the former approach to address the concerns of the latter.

Freud dealt with the question of masochism in several essays; his views on the perversion changed over the years, but he was consistent in his belief that Oedipal conflict was the cause of the perversion. Guilt and fear of castration by the father led the male child to assume a passive position in order to placate the father and win his love. Being beaten by the father (or the female who provides the father's disguise in the conscious fantasy) was "not only the punishment for the forbidden genital relation with the mother, but also a regressive substitute for it." The punishment acquired "libidinal excitation," and "here," Freud declared, "we have the essence of masochism."[3] Freud developed a theory of masochism as a primary drive expressing the Death Instinct but was continually drawn into reaffirming the complementary status of masochism and sadism. He stated that, in the former, the heightened sadism of the superego was retained in the libido with the ego as "victim." In sadism, the Death Instinct was deflected outward.[4]

Deleuze believes the superego/ego activities of sadism and masochism are completely different, but, more important to a study of masochism and film, he makes the mother the primary determinant in the structure of the masochistic fantasy and in the etiology of the perversion.[5] Both love object and controlling agent for the helpless child, the mother is viewed as an ambivalent figure during the oral period. Whether due to the child's experience of real trauma, as Bernhard Berliner asserts, or due to the narcissistic infant's own insatiability of demand, the pleasure associ-

---

[1]Jean-Louis Baudry, "The Apparatus," *Camera Obscura* 1 (Fall 1976), pp. 105–26; Robert Eberwein, "Reflections on the Breast," *Wide Angle* 4, 3 (1981), pp. 48–53.

[2]Laura Mulvey, "Visual Pleasure and Narrative Cinema," *Screen* 16 (Autumn 1975), pp. 6–18, reprinted here. Claire Johnston, *Notes on Women's Cinema* (London: Society for Education in Film and Television, 1973), pp. 2–4; Mary Ann Doane, "Misrecognition and Identity," *Cine-Tracts* 11 (Fall 1980), pp. 28–30; Doane, "Film and the Masquerade: Theorising the Female Spectator," *Screen* 23 (September–October 1982), pp. 74–87.

[3]Sigmund Freud, "A Child Is Being Beaten" (1919), in *Sexuality and the Psychology of Love,* ed. Philip Rieff (New York: Macmillan, Collier Books, 1963), p. 117. See "The Economic Problem in Masochism," in *General Psychological Theory: Papers on Metapsychology,* ed. Philip Rieff (New York: Macmillan, Collier Books, 1963), pp. 190–93, for Freud's first essay to use the Death Instinct theory as an approach to the clinical and theoretical dilemmas. See also "Instincts and Their Vicissitudes" (1915) in *General Psychological Theory,* p. 25 and "Three Essays on the Theory of Sexuality," *Standard Edition of the Complete Psychological Works,* ed. James Strachey (London: Hogarth Press, 1953–66) vol. 7, pp. 159–61.

[4]Freud, "The Economic Problem in Masochism," pp. 190–91.

[5]Deleuze, pp. 50–54. See also Bernhard Berliner, "On Some Psychodynamics of Masochism," *Psychoanalytic Quarterly* 16 (1947), pp. 459–71; Gustav Bychowski, "Some Aspects of Masochistic Involvement," *Journal of the American Psychoanalytic Association* 7 (April 1959), pp. 248–73; E. Bergler, *The Basic Neurosis* (New York: Grune and Stration, 1949) for other views that locate masochism's genesis in the mother/child relationship. See Deleuze, pp. 111–12, on superego/ego.

ated with the oral mother is joined in masochism with the need for pain.[1] The masochistic fantasy cannot by its very nature fulfill its most primal desire— "dual unity and the complete symbiosis between child and mother"—except in the imagination.[2] As a consequence, death becomes the fantasy solution to masochistic desire.

The mother assumes her authority in masochism on the basis of her own importance to the child, not, as Freud maintained, because the father figure must be "hidden" behind her in order to deflect the homosexual implications of the male subject's fantasy. Roy Schafer identifies the child's fear of losing the mother as the primary source of her authority.[3] Rooted in the fear of being abandoned by the mother, masochism obsessively recreates the movement between concealment and revelation, disappearance and appearance, seduction and rejection. Posited as "lacking nothing," the mother is allied with the child in the disavowal of the destruction of the superego. Deleuze maintains that the father's punishing superego and genital sexuality are symbolically punished in the son, who must expiate his likeness to the father. Pain symbolically expels the father and "fools" the superego. It is not the son who is guilty, as in Freud's theory, but the father who attempts to come between mother and child.[4] In Deleuze's view, fear of the castrating father and Oedipal guilt cannot account for masochism's paradoxical pain/pleasure structure. His denial of the importance of castration anxiety to the perversion's formation constitutes a revision of Freudian theory that stands in agreement with Michael de M'Uzan and Theodore Reik. M'Uzan deduces from clinical observation that the masochist "fears nothing, not even castration."[5] In his lengthy study *Masochism in Modern Man,* in which he details the social rather than sexual manifestations of masochism, Reik parallels M'Uzan's assessment: castration anxiety is not of major significance in the etiology of the perversion.[6]

It should be noted that Deleuze positions the male as the fantasizing subject of

---

[1]Berliner, "Libido and Reality in Masochism," *Psychoanalytic Quarterly* 9 (1940), pp. 323–26, 333. Deleuze believes that the oral mother of masochism is the good mother who takes on the functions of the two "bad mothers of masochism," the uterine mother and the Oedipal mother. In the process, the functions are idealized and, as Deleuze explains, "This concentration of functions in the person of the good oral mother is one of the ways in which the father is cancelled out" (p. 55).

[2]Bychowski, p. 260. The issue of why pain is necessary to masochism's dynamic of pleasure is still one of the most controversial in psychoanalysis. See Abram Kardiner, Aaron Karush, and Lionel Ovesey, "A Methodological Study of Freudian Theory III: Narcissism, Bisexuality, and the Dual Instinct Theory," *Journal of Nervous and Mental Disorders* 129 (1959), pp. 215–22. See also Deleuze, pp. 108–9.

[3]Roy Schafer, "The Idea of Resistance," *International Journal of Psycho-Analysis* 54 (1973), p. 278.

[4]Deleuze, p. 95. "Again, while the sense of guilt has great importance in masochism, it acts only as a cover, as the humorous outcome of a guilt that has already been subverted; for it is no longer the guilt of the child towards the father, but that of the father himself, and of his likeness in the child . . . When guilt is experienced 'masochistically,' it is already distorted, artificial and ostentatious" (p. 95). Deleuze's theory—that the father is the guilty one—is not as unusual as it might first appear. See Claude Lévi-Strauss, *The Raw and the Cooked,* trans. Johan and Doreen Weightman (New York: Harper & Row, 1969), p. 48.

[5]Michael de M'Uzan, "A Case of Masochistic Perversion and an Outline of a Theory," *International Journal of Psycho-Analysis* 54 (1973), p. 462.

[6]Theodore Reik, *Masochism in Modern Man,* trans. M. H. Beigel and G. M. Kruth (New York: Farrar, Straus, 1941), p. 428.

his construct. In this respect, his model might be regarded as sexist, although he notes that the female child can take the same position in relation to the oral mother.[1] Deleuze's model may also be approached from another perspective that makes it more applicable to a consideration of spectatorial response to film. The masochistic fantasy may be viewed as a situation in which the subject (male or female) assumes the position of the child who desires to be controlled *within* the dynamics of the fantasy. The sadistic fantasy (while not a simple reversal of instinct or aim) is one in which the subject takes the position of the controlling parent, who is not allied with the child (object) in a mutually agreed upon pact of pleasure/pain but who exercises (within the fantasy) a sadistic power over an unwilling victim.[2]

Masochism subverts traditional psychoanalytic notions regarding the origins of human desire and the mother's and father's roles in the child's psychic development. A theory of masochism that emphasizes pre-Oedipal conflicts and pleasures invites consideration of responses to film by spectators of both sexes that may conflict with conscious cultural assumptions about sexual difference, gender identity, and the separation of identification from object cathexis. A theory of masochistic desire also questions the complicity of most psychoanalytic film theory with phallocentrism as a formative instance in structuring identity and scopic pleasure. It also questions the pre-eminence of a pleasure based on a position of control rather than submission. In suggesting that the oral mother could be the primary figure of identification and power in clinical and aesthetic manifestations of masochism, Deleuze's theory of masochistic desire challenges the notion that male scopic pleasure must center around control—never identification with or submission to the female.

This article is derived from a book-length study of the films of Josef Von Sternberg that uses practical criticism to examine the masochistic aesthetic in film and the relationship between the formal elements of the aesthetic, the films' psychodynamics, and the specific forms of visual pleasure. With their submissive male masochist, the oral mother embodied in the ambivalent, alluring presence of Marlene Dietrich, and their ambiguous sexuality that has often been linked to "sadomasochism" and "degradation,"[3] the Von Sternberg/Dietrich collaborations offer themselves as a prime case study of the masochistic aesthetic in film.

Within the context of the post-modernist critique of realism, Von Sternberg's films have become the center of increasing interest. They are creations of sublime visual beauty and sensuality; dreamlike chiaroscuro and stifling decorative excess form the backdrop for melodrama pervaded by a diffuse sexuality. As many critics have remarked, the films are poetic but not symbolic, melodramatic and even tragic, but marked by a detached, ironic humor. In these narratives dominated by

---

[1]Deleuze, pp. 59–60.

[2]See Victor Smirnoff, "The Masochistic Contract," *International Journal of Psycho-Analysis* 50 (1969), pp. 666–71, for an analysis of masochism heavily indebted to Deleuze's work, but which discounts the role of pain and emphasizes the role of the contractual alliance in the perversion. I must acknowledge my own debt to Marsha Kinder for suggesting this expansion of Deleuze's model.

[3]Robin Wood, "Venus de Marlene," *Film Comment* 14 (March–April 1978), p. 60.

passion, even passion takes on a curiously distancing coldness. The films featuring Marlene Dietrich add the paradox of the dazzling yet androgynous female who is simultaneously moral and amoral, eminently proper yet irredeemably decadent.

As a result of their multiple layers of paradox, fascinating ambiguity of emotion, and almost transcendental visual beauty, Von Sternberg's films have again and again inspired attempts to explain their structure and meaning. They have just as frequently served as examples in theoretical treatises dealing with the representation of the female in narrative cinema or questions concerning the unconscious determinants of visual pleasure. Among the most important of these is Laura Mulvey's use of Von Sternberg's films to illustrate the concept of fetishistic scopophilia in her milestone article, "Visual Pleasure and Narrative Cinema." To her, Von Sternberg's *Morocco* typifies the kind of visual style and narrative structure which traps the female into a position of "to-be-looked-at-ness," of passive exhibitionism that oppresses women for the sake of the patriarchy's fetishistic aims. Mulvey regards such a female fetish as "reassuring rather than dangerous."[1] Although subscribing to Mulvey's thesis, Mary Ann Doane has referred to Dietrich's image as exemplifying the "excess of femininity . . . aligned with the *femme fatale* . . . and . . . necessarily regarded by men as evil incarnate."[2] Contrary to Doane, it is Dietrich's androgynous quality that is most often noted, and Carole Zucker has argued (with justification) that Dietrich's morality is "impossibly exalted" in the von Sternberg films.[3] Adding to the controversy is Robin Wood's attempt to counter Mulvey's analysis of the role of the female in the films' narrative strategy and visual style. He argues that Von Sternberg is "fully aware" of the female's position as object for the male gaze and uses this as "an articulated theme" in *Blonde Venus* rather than an end product.[4] He has not, however, countered Mulvey's fundamental premise: that visual pleasure in classic narrative cinema is based on the workings of the castration complex.

Rather than develop a detailed textual analysis, this examination of the masochistic aesthetic and film explores the wider theoretical implications of masochism to cinematic pleasure. I will very briefly examine these implications in regard to five crucial issues: (1) the female defined as lack, (2) the male gaze defined by control,

---

[1]Mulvey, p. 14.

[2]Doane, "Film and the Masquerade: Theorising the Female Spectator," p. 82. Doane refers to Dietrich's image as a stage performer. She takes Silvia Bovenschen's comments in "Is There a Feminine Aesthetic?" *New German Critique* 11 (Winter 1977), p. 130, and uses them to support her remarks on excess femininity. Bovenschen actually associates Dietrich with an "intellectual understatement" and refers to her becoming a "myth" despite "her subtle disdain for men." The complexity of Dietrich's images as discussed by Bovenschen does not support Doane's use of her statements to associate Dietrich with "an excess of femininity." David Davidson has placed Dietrich's Lola character in *The Blue Angel* within the tradition of the "amoral woman." He makes some interesting remarks on the "threatening" sexuality of these female characters in relation to Mulvey's theory.

[3]Carole Zucker, "Some Observations on Sternberg and Dietrich," *Cinema Journal* 19 (Spring 1980), p. 21. Masochism's ambivalent stance toward the female ensures her alternation between coldness and warmth, sacrifice and torture, but, as Deleuze points out, the female in the masochistic scenario is not sadistic, she "incarnates instead the element of 'inflicting pain' in an exclusively masochistic situation" (p. 38). It is rarely the sexualized female who is judged guilty in Von Sternberg's films, but the representative of the superego and the father.

[4]Wood, p. 61.

(3) the cause and function of disavowal and fetishism, (4) the dream screen, and (5) identification, particularly identification with the opposite sex.

THE FEMALE AS LACK

The female as cinematic image is often considered to be an ambivalent spectatorial pleasure for the male because she signifies the possibility of castration. She represents difference, nonphallus, lack. Undoubtably, the tension between attraction and fear is an ambivalence underlying much of cinema's representation of the female, but it is an oversimplification to collapse the entire signification of woman to phallic meaning.[1]

Within masochism, the mother is not defined as lack nor as "phallic" in respect to a simple transference of the male's symbol of power. She is powerful in her own right because she possesses what the male lacks—the breast and the womb.[2] Active nurturer, first source of love and object of desire, first environment and agent of control, the oral mother of masochism assumes all symbolic functions. Parallel to her idealization is a degrading disavowal of the father. "The father is nothing," says Deleuze, "he is deprived of all symbolic function."[3]

The infant's fantasy goal of re-fusion, of complete symbiosis with the mother is necessarily informed by ambivalence. The promise of blissful reincorporation into the mother's body and re-fusion of the child's narcissistic ego with the mother as ideal ego is also a threat. Only death can hold the final mystical solution to the expiation of the father and symbiotic reunion with the idealized maternal rule. The masochist imagines the final triumph of a parthenogenetic rebirth from the mother.[4]

Deleuze associates the good oral mother of masochism with the "ideal of coldness, solicitude, and death," the mythic extremes that crystallize her ambivalence.[5] The female reflects the fantasy of the desiring infant who regards the mother as both sacred and profane, loving and rejecting, frustratingly mobile yet the essence of rhythmic stability and stillness. In the masochist's suspension of the final "gratification" of death, the obsessive return to the moment of separation from the oral mother must be reenacted continuously as the masochistic *fort/da* game of desire

---

[1]Claire Pajaczkowska discusses this point in "The Heterosexual Presumption: A Contribution to the Debate on Pornography," *Screen* 22 (1981), p. 86.

[2]Deleuze, p. 56. Although the mothering agent might be considered to be a socially determined role rather than a strictly biological one, this alternative definition does not seem appropriate to this particular application of Deleuze and pregenital research. Interestingly, it has been suggested that in the pregenital stage, sexual difference is not an issue to the child except in terms of breast/nonbreast.

[3]Deleuze, p. 56.

[4]Deleuze, pp. 80–81; Bychowski, p. 260.

[5]Deleuze, p. 49. The female in the masochistic scenario is a *femme fatale,* but a very specific kind. Her danger supersedes her portrayal as an "amoral," sexualized female who threatens social control. The "mystery" of the *femme fatale* of masochism is the mystery of the womb, rebirth, and the child's symbiotic bond with the mother. She represents the dialectical unity between liberation and death, the bonding of Eros with Thanatos that places the former in the service of the latter.

that is the meeting point between fantasy and action.[1] Masochistic repetition sustains the paradoxical pain/pleasure structure of the perversion's psychodynamics and reflects the careful control of desire so necessary to sustaining the masochistic scenario even as it expresses the compulsive aspect of the fixation in infantile sexuality. Overriding the demands of the incest taboo, the castration complex, and progress into genital sexuality, masochism is a "subversive" desire that affirms the compelling power of the pre-Oedipal mother as a stronger attraction than the "normalizing" force of the father who threatens the alliance of mother and child.

The repetition of loss, of suffering, does not deter or confuse masochistic desire but inflames it, as graphically demonstrated in Von Sternberg's *The Devil Is a Woman*. His health broken, his career ruined by his involvement with "the most dangerous woman alive," Don Pasquale protests that he gains "no pleasure" in telling his friend Antonio about his road to ruin. It becomes obvious that he not only enjoys telling his story, but the retelling itself is the impetus for a new round robin in Don Pasquale's masochistic pursuit of Concha Perez. He allows himself to be shot in a duel to satisfy Concha's desire for another man (Antonio). Lying on his deathbed, he attains what he desires most, Concha and Death, one in the same, both still suspended, promised, but withheld. The eternal masochistic attitude of waiting and suspended suffering is maintained in all its tragedy and comic absurdity to the very end of this, the last Von Sternberg/Dietrich collaboration.

The ambivalence of separation/union from the mother, formalized in masochistic repetition and suspension, is an ambivalence shared by all human beings. Contrary to the Freudian view of familial dynamics, in which the mother has little psychological impact on her children's development, Deleuze, Schafer, Robert Stoller, Nancy Chodorow, and Janine Chasseguet-Smirgel regard the mother's influence and her *authority* as major factors in the child's development. The child's view of the powerful, loved, but threatening female during the pre-Oedipal stage is not obliterated by later stages of life—including the male's passage through the castration complex.[2] Hans Loewald suggests that, while the identification with the powerful pre-Oedipal mother is fundamental to the individual's organization of ego-reality, this same identification is the "source of the deepest dread."[3] Janine Chas-

---

[1] See Kaja Silverman, "Masochism and Subjectivity," *Framework* 12 (1980), p. 2. Silverman's discussion of the masochistic use of the *fort/da* game is most valuable; however, I cannot agree with her generalizations about cultural pleasure/instinctual unpleasure or with her reading of Freud (especially concerning transference of drive expression to a contrary drive). She also approaches the idea that fetishism is related to identification (p. 6), a notion worth exploring in detail.

[2] Schafer, p. 278. See also Robert Stoller, *Sexual Excitement* (New York: Simon and Schuster, 1979); Nancy Chodorow, *The Reproduction of Mothering: Psychoanalysis and the Sociology of Gender* (Berkeley: University of California Press, 1978); *Mothering: Essays in Feminist Theory,* ed. Joyce Trebilcot (Totowa, N.J.: Rowman & Allanheld, 1984). While my brief consideration of Freud in this article necessitates a generalization about his stance on women, it should be noted that he did consider the influence of the mother, but, as demonstrated in his theories on masochism and various other symptomatologies, the father, penis envy, castration fear, and the emphasis on the phallic stage (and corresponding disinterest in pre-Oedipal or pregenital stages) effectively displace the mother from his work. See Viola Klein, *The Feminine Character: History of an Ideology* (New York: International Universities Press, 1949).

[3] Hans Loewald, *Papers on Psychoanalysis* (New Haven: Yale University Press, 1980), p. 165.

seguet-Smirgel goes so far as to suggest that the contempt for women Freud believed was an inevitable male reaction to the perception of female "castration" is actually a pathological and defensive response to maternal power.[1]

In returning to the fantasies originating in the oral stage of development, the masochistic aesthetic opens the entirety of film to the existence of spectatorial pleasures divorced from issues of castration, sexual difference, and female lack. Current theory ignores the pleasure in submission that is phylogenetically older than the pleasure of mastery—for both sexes. In masochism, as in the infantile stage of helpless dependence that marks its genesis, pleasure does not involve mastery of the female but submission to her. This pleasure applies to the infant, the masochist, and the film spectator as well. Psychoanalytic film theory must reintegrate the powerful maternal image that is viewed as a complex, pleasurable "screen memory" by both male and female spectators, even in the patriarchal society.[2] As Janine Chasseguet-Smirgel asserts:

Now the woman as she is depicted in Freudian theory is exactly the opposite of the primal maternal image as she is revealed in the clinical material of both sexes . . . the contradictions . . . throughout Freud's work on the problem of sexual phallic monism and its consequences, force us to take a closer notice of this opposition between the woman, as she is described by Freud, and the mother as she is known to the Unconscious. . . . If we underestimate the importance of our earliest relations and our cathexis of the maternal image, this means we allow paternal law to predominate and are in flight from our infantile dependence.[3]

Castration fear and the perception of sexual differences have no importance in forming the masochistic desire for complete symbiosis with the mother. The polarities of female lack/male phallus and the narrow view that the female in film can only function as the object of a sadistic male spectatorial possession must yield to other considerations.

The female in the masochistic aesthetic is more than the passive object of the male's desire for possession. She is also a figure of identification, the mother of plenitude whose gaze meets the infant's as it asserts her presence and her power. Von Sternberg's expression of the masochistic aesthetic in film offers a complex image of the female in which she is the object of the look but also the holder of a "controlling" gaze that turns the male into an object of "to-be-looked-at-ness." In *Morocco*, Private Tom Brown (Gary Cooper), a notorious "ladykiller," is reduced to the passive "feminine" position as object of Amy Jolly's appraising, steady gaze.

---

[1]Janine Chasseguet-Smirgel, "Freud and Female Sexuality: The Consideration of Some Blind Spots in the Exploration of the Dark Continent," *International Journal of Psycho-Analysis* 57 (1976), p. 196.

[2]Robert Dickes discusses the fetish as "screen memory" in "Fetishistic Behavior: A Contribution to Its Complex Development and Significance," *Journal of the American Psychoanalytic Association* 11 (1963), pp. 324–30. See also Anneliese Riess, "The Mother's Eye: For Better and for Worse," *The Psychoanalytic Study of the Child* 33 (1978), pp. 381–405.

[3]Chasseguet-Smirgel, p. 281. Ethel Spector Person has suggested that infantile dependence may be the key to power relations in sexuality: "The limitations to sexual 'liberation,' meaning liberation from power contaminants, do not reside in the biological nature of sexuality, or in cultural or political arrangements, and certainly not in the sex difference, but may lie in the universal condition of infantile dependence" (p. 627). See "Sexuality as the Mainstay of Identity: Psychoanalytic Perspective," *Signs* 5 (Summer 1980).

Amy throws him a rose, which Brown then wears behind his ear. Operating within the limitations of the patriarchy, the Dietrich character in these films displays her ability to fascinate in confirmation of what Michel Foucault has called "power asserting itself in the pleasure of showing off, scandalizing, or resisting."[1] In response to the male gaze, Dietrich looks back or initiates the look. This simple fact contains the potential for questioning her objectification.

THE GAZE

While the pleasures of the cinematic apparatus as dream screen have been associated with oral phase pleasure by Jean-Louis Baudry and Robert Eberwein, the pleasures of viewing the female image in film have consistently been linked to the phallic phase, the castration complex, and the resulting physiological "needs" of the male spectator.

The structure of the look is one of the most important elements in defining visual pleasure. According to Laura Mulvey, narrative film is made for the pleasure of the male spectator alone, who "indirectly" possesses the female through the look, or rather the relay of looks created by the camera, the male star's gaze, and the spectator's own gaze. The woman is the bearer of the "burden of male desire," which is "born with language." She crystallizes the paradox of "the traumatic moment" of desire's birth—the castration complex, because she represents sexual difference. The male spectator escapes the castration anxiety the female image evokes either by a sadistic voyeurism (demystifying the female) or through fetishistic scopophilia. The latter, a "complete disavowal of castration," turns the female into a fetish, the signifier of the absent phallus.[2]

Mulvey's deterministic, polarized model leads to a crucial "blind spot" in her theory of visual pleasure, which has been noted by D. N. Rodowick. In "The Difficulty of Difference," Rodowick argues that Mulvey avoids the logical conclusion of her own theory that would necessitate pairing masochism, the passive submission to the object, with fetishistic scopophilia. Because of the "political nature of her argument," Rodowick concludes, Mulvey cannot admit that the masculine look contains passive elements and can signify *submission to* rather than *possession of* the female.[3]

In eliding a possible male spectatorial position informed by masochism, Mulvey is forced to limit the male gaze to one that only views the female as a signifier of castration and an object for possession. In reducing spectatorial pleasure to the workings of the castration complex, Mulvey also ignores the existence of pre-Oedipal desires and ambivalences that play a part in the genesis of scopophilia and fetishism as well as masochism. In Mulvey's construct of immutable polarities, the female "can exist only in relation to castration"; she is either the "bearer of guilt" or the "perfect product."[4]

---

[1]Michel Foucault, *The History of Sexuality Vol. 1: An Introduction,* trans. Robert Hurley (New York: Pantheon Books, 1978), pp. 108–9.

[2]Mulvey, pp. 13–14.

[3]D. N. Rodowick, "The Difficulty of Difference," *Wide Angle* 5, 1 (1982), pp. 7–9.

[4]Mulvey, pp. 11, 14.

Cinematic pleasure is much closer to masochistic scopic pleasure than to a sadistic, controlling pleasure privileged by Mulvey and also by Christian Metz. In Metz's *The Imaginary Signifier,* the voyeuristic separation of subject/screen object is used to align the spectator with sadism. "Voyeuristic desire, along with certain forms of sadism," says Metz, "is the only desire whose principle of distance symbolically and spatially evokes this fundamental rent." Metz believes that all voyeurism is sadistic to a degree and compares cinematic voyeurism to "unauthorized scopophilia" and its prototype, the child viewing the primal scene.[1]

Contrary to Metz, Jean Laplanche has shown how the spectatorial position in the primal gaze is aligned with masochism, not sadism. Laplanche considers masochism to be the "fundamental fantasy." He compares the infant's position to that of "Odysseus tied to the mast or Tantalus, on whom is imposed the spectacle of parental intercourse." Corresponding to the perturbation of pain is the "sympathetic excitation . . . the passive position of the child . . . [that] is not simply a passivity in relation to adult activity, but passivity in relation to adult fantasy intruding within him."[2] Parallel to Laplanche's description of the primal scene is Masoch's "A Childhood Memory and Reflection on the Novel." Ten-year-old Leopold von Sacher-Masoch, hiding in his aunt's bedroom closet, hears his aunt welcome her lover: "I did not understand what they were saying, still less what they were doing, but my heart began to pound, for I was acutely aware of my situation. . . ." The husband interrupts the lovers' rendezvous. Madame Zenobia begins to beat him. She then discovers Leopold and whips *him.* "I must admit," Masoch writes, "while I writhed under my aunt's cruel blows, I experienced acute pleasure."[3] Not surprisingly, Von Sternberg's films also contain many scenes that evoke the situation of the child witnessing or overhearing parental intercourse. In *Shanghai Express,* Doc Harvey eavesdrops on the "negotiations" between Lily and the nefarious General Chang. Like the passive child who sees/overhears the primal scene and fantasizes both discovery and punishment, Doc is threatened with punishment for his curiosity and his desire: General Chang decides to blind him. In *The Scarlet Empress,* Alexei loves Catherine but is forced by her to prepare the royal bedchamber for the arrival of her lover, General Orloff. Alexei assumes the role of the child-spectator.

If Sade's novels are taken as the prototype of sadistic object relations, then it is obvious that the sadist is driven to consume or destroy the object in order to bring about the directly experienced pleasure of orgasm for himself. This negation cannot be exercised merely through the sadistic "look"—the active gaze. Orgasm is not the goal of the masochist, who is bound to the regime of pregenital sexuality. Masoch's heroes are forever swooning into a faint before the blissful moment of consummation. Closing the gap between the desiring masochistic subject and the object actually threatens the narcissistic gratification of the masochist who "gives noth-

---

[1] Christian Metz, *The Imaginary Signifier,* trans. Celia Britton, Annwyl Williams, Ben Brewster, Alfred Guzzetti (Bloomington: Indiana University Press, 1982), pp. 59–63.

[2] Jean Laplanche, *Life and Death in Psychoanalysis,* trans. Jeffrey Mehlman (Baltimore: Johns Hopkins University Press, 1976), p. 102.

[3] Leopold von Sacher-Masoch, "A Childhood Memory and Reflection on the Novel," Appendix I in Deleuze, pp. 232–33.

ing" and cannot endure the "anxiety [of giving] that must accompany orgasm."[1] Masochistic desire depends on separation to guarantee the structure of its ambivalent desire. To close the gap, to overcome separation from the mother, to fulfill desire, to achieve orgasm means death. The contracted, mutual alliance of the masochistic relationship guarantees distance/separation. Unlike sadism, which depends upon action and immediate gratification, masochism savors suspense and distance.

The spectator at the cinematic dream screen regresses to a similar state of orality as the masochist and also experiences a loss of ego-body boundary. Spectatorial pleasure is a limited one like the infantile, extragenital sexual pleasure that defines the masochist. Like the masochist, but unlike the sadist, to remain within the confines of normal spectatorship and not become, as Stephen Heath says, "a true voyeur,"[2] the spectator must avoid the orgasmic release that would effectively destroy the boundaries of disavowal and disrupt the magical thinking that defines his/her oral, infantile, and narcissistic use of the cinematic object. The spectator's narcissistic omnipotence is like the narcissistic, infantile omnipotence of the masochist, who ultimately cannot control the active partner. Immobile, surrounded in darkness, the spectator becomes the passive receiving object who is also subject. The spectator must comprehend the images, but the images cannot be controlled. On this level of pleasure, the spectator receives, but no object-related demands are made.

FETISHISM AND DISAVOWAL

The masochistic aesthetic appears to be a major site for developing a critique of theories of visual pleasure that hinge on the role of castration fear in the formation of male spectatorial pleasure. Masochism is not associated with castration fear, yet fetishism is an integral part of its dynamic. Disavowal and fetishism, the two common matrices of masochism and cinematic spectatorial pleasure, do not always reflect the psychic trauma of the castration and sexual difference defined as feminine lack.

Recent psychoanalytic research into the pre-Oedipal period indicates that disavowal and fetishism are operative much, much earlier than the phallic stage and are not necessarily used as a defense against castration anxiety. Of particular importance to the study of visual pleasure and masochism is the view that fetishism and masochism evidence the prolonged need for primary identification with the "almighty pre-Oedipal mother."[3] If the mother/infant relationship is disturbed when the child's body boundaries are not well established, fetishism based on the

---

[1]Sylvan Keiser, "Body Ego During Orgasm," *Psychoanalytic Quarterly* 21 (April 1952), pp. 160, 193.

[2]Stephen Heath, *Questions of Cinema* (Bloomington: Indiana University Press, 1981), p. 189.

[3]P. J. Van der Leeuw, "The Preoedipal Phase of the Male," *The Psychoanalytic Study of the Child* 13 (1958), p. 369. See also Robert C. Bak, "Fetishism," *Journal of the American Psychoanalytic Association* 1 (1953), p. 291.

disavowal of her loss may develop as a defensive maneuver to restore the mother's body, permit passive infant satisfaction, and protect primary identification.[1]

In summarizing various findings, Robert Dickes states that most pregenital research stands in direct opposition to Freud, for example, that "the fetish represents more than the female phallus."[2] Dickes believes that the traditional view of the fetish as "a talisman in relieving phallic castration anxiety" is a "late stage of the development . . . ordinarily . . . never reached."[3] Most children, regardless of sex, use transitional objects to soothe the separation from the mother. If the child cannot accommodate itself to this separation, the transitional object may be retained and lead to fetishism. While Socarides believes fetishism "may have no etiological connection with phallic or genital sexuality," Wulff concludes that the fetish "represents a substitute for the mother's breast and the mother's body."[4]

Fetishism and disavowal are not exclusively male psychoanalytic manifestations, but males may be much more likely to develop such perversions because of problems in resolving gender identity (crossing over from primary to same-sex identification) unrelated to the existence of any sexually differentiated scopic drive.[5] Female perversion does exist; however, the extreme forms, in particular, are less "visible" than the male version because the female can "hide" impaired sexual function.[6] As a result, females may, as Charles Socarides believes, tend to exhibit "forms of fetishism not obviously associated with genital functioning," for example, ritualistic preparations for intercourse.[7] Although it is naive to assume that the identification of female scopophilia or fetishism would open a gap for the female spectator within dominant cinema, the pregenital origin of these manifestations

---

[1] Van der Leeuw, pp. 352–74; Charles Socarides, "The Development of a Fetishistic Perversion: The Contribution of Preoedipal Phase Conflict," *Journal of the American Psychoanalytic Association* 8 (April 1960), pp. 307–9; Bak, p. 291. Bak maintains that the normal male child thinks it is possible to identify with the mother and emulate her positive power (i.e., bear a child) while also repairing the separation from her (through fetishism) without endangering phallic integrity (p. 286). Joseph Solomon, "Transitional Phenomena and Obsessive-Compulsive States," in *Between Reality and Fantasy: Transitional Objects and Phenomena,* Simon A. Grolnick, Leonard Barkin, and Werner Muensterberger, eds. (New York: Jason Aronson, 1978), pp. 250–51, associates fetishism with the child's sense of body intactness derived from the mother.

[2] Dickes, p. 320.

[3] Dickes, p. 327.

[4] M. Wulff, "Fetishism and Object Choice in Early Childhood," *Psychoanalytic Quarterly* 15 (1945), pp. 465–70. Socarides, p. 309. Brunswick, Lampl-de Groot, Jacobson, Kestenberg, Socarides, and a number of others link fetishistic perversion to the pre-Oedipal period. Most conclude that fetishism has little connection to the phallic period or genital sexuality in its formation, but this does not mean that a fetish cannot represent the phallus. Wulff qualifies the link between childhood fetishism and adult fetishism by noting the inconsistences in their relationship and the need for further research. Griselda Pollock has pointed out in "What's Wrong with Images of Women," *Screen Education* 24 (Autumn 1977), pp. 25–33, that Freud's theory of fetishism (as adopted by Mulvey in particular) cannot account for vaginal imagery in pornography.

[5] Ralph Greenson, "Dis-Identifying from Mother: Its Special Importance for the Boy," *International Journal of Psycho-Analysis* 49 (1968), pp. 370–74; see also Nancy Chodorow, "Family Structure and Feminine Personality," in *Woman, Culture, and Society,* S. Rosaldo and L. Lamphere, eds. (Stanford, Calif.: Stanford University Press, 1978), p. 50; Chasseguet-Smirgel, pp. 281–84. In "Film and the Masquerade," Doane insists that the female is "constructed differently in relation to processes of looking" (p. 80).

[6] Socarides, p. 304. See also Stoller, *Sexual Excitement,* pp. 7–13; Freud, "The Psychogenesis of a Case of Homosexuality in a Woman," in *Sexuality and the Psychology of Love,* pp. 133–59.

[7] Socarides, p. 304.

calls into question the views that use them to exclude the female from the fundamental structures of cinematic pleasure or even from the possibility of libidinalized looking.

DREAM SCREEN

Masochistic fantasy is dominated by oral pleasure, the desire to return to the non-differentiated body state of the mother/child, and the fear of abandonment (the state of nonbreast, nonplenitude). In a sense, these same wishes are duplicated by the film spectator who becomes a child again in response to the dream screen of cinema. This dream screen affords spectatorial pleasure in recreating the first fetish—the mother as nurturing environment. The spectator at the cinematic dream screen regresses to a state that Baudry says is analogous to the oral period.[1] Like the fetish objects that follow, the dream screen restores the sense of wholeness of the first symbiotic relationship as it restores the unity of the undifferentiated ego/ego ideal. It functions like a "good blanket" reuniting the spectator/child with the earliest object of desire that lessens the anxiety of the ego loosened from body boundaries.[2]

In restoring the first sleep environment of the dream screen, the cinematic apparatus re-establishes the fluid boundaries to self. In "The Unrememberable and the Unforgettable: The Passive Primal Repression," Alvan Frank discusses the psychic benefits of hallucinatory screen/breast experiences that create an absence of ego boundaries and permit the regression to earlier perceptual modes.[3] The cinema may also offer this type of psychic reparation in the re-creation of a screen phenomenon that gives access to the unremembered "memories" of earliest childhood experience.

The dream screen as the first hallucination of gratification is an essential notion to considering cinematic pleasure. Through imagination the child creates the mother and the breast. Just as the fantasized breast cannot offer real nourishment or interaction with the mother, the cinematic apparatus cannot provide intimacy or fusion with real objects. The spectator must disavow an absence: the dream screen offers only partial gratification of the symbiotic wish. The object/screen/images cannot be physically possessed or controlled by the spectator. The spectator's "misapprehension" of control over cinematic images is less a misapprehension than it is a disavowal of the loss of ego autonomy over image formation.

---

[1] Baudry, p. 125. "It may seem peculiar that desire which constituted the cine-effect is rooted in the oral structure of the subject. The conditions of projection do evoke the dialectics internal/external, swallowing/swallowed, eating/being eaten, which is characteristic of what is being structured during the oral phase . . . The relationship visual orifice/buccal orifice acts at the same time as analogy and differentiation, but also points to the relation of consecution between oral satisfaction, sleep, white screen of the dream on which dream images will be projected, beginning of the dream."

[2] Judith S. Kestenberg and Joan Weinstock, "Transitional Objects and Body-Image Formation," in *Between Reality and Fantasy,* p. 82.

[3] Alvan Frank, "The Unrememberable and the Unforgettable," *The Psychoanalytic Study of the Child* 24 (1969), p. 56. See also Ernst Kris, "On Preconscious Mental Processes," in *Organization and Pathology of Thought,* ed. David Rapaport (New York: Columbia University Press, 1951), p. 493.

IDENTIFICATION

In restoring the pre-ego of primary narcissism, the cinema encourages a regression characterized by all the possibilities of identification and projection resembling the infantile mechanisms operative in perversions. The pleasures of perversion depend directly on a splitting kind of ego defense to solidify identity.[1] By satisfying the compulsion to repeat archaic stages of life, the artificial regression of the cinema enlarges and reintegrates the ego through different forms of ego-reality.[2] The cinematic spectator experiences infantile forms of object cathexis and identification normally repressed. Among the most important aspects of the release of repressed material are the pleasures of re-experiencing the primary identification with the mother and the pleasurable possibilities of gender mobility through identification. Leowald regards identification with the mother as essential to ego formation and the structuring of the personality:

> ... the primary narcissistic identity with the mother forever constitutes the deepest unconscious origin and structural layer of the ego and reality, and the motive force for the ego's "remarkable striving toward unification, synthesis."[3]

While the male's pre-Oedipal identification with the mother is repressed in adult life, for both male and female, same-sex identification does not totally exclude opposite-sex identification.[4] The wish to be both sexes—to *overcome* sexual difference—remains.

Although Freud recognized the bisexuality of every human being, he continually returned to an emphasis on the polarity between masculine and feminine—a polarity that has infiltrated feminist-psychoanalytic approaches to film. Recent research has revealed the vital importance of psychic androgyny (bisexuality) to understanding sexuality, identity, and the search for pleasure. In his study, "The Drive to Become Both Sexes," Lawrence Kubie details two prominent aspects of bisexuality: (1) the reverse of penis envy, and (2) the urge to become both sexes:

> Overlooked is the importance of the reverse and complementary envy of the male for the woman's breast, for nursing as well as his envy for the woman's ability to conceive and to bring forth babies ... from childhood and throughout life, on conscious, preconscious, and unconscious levels, in varying proportions and emphases, the human goal seems almost invariably to be *both* sexes, with the inescapable consequence that we are always attempting in every moment and every act both to affirm and deny our gender identities.[5]

---

[1]W. Gillespie, "Notes on the Analysis of Sexual Perversion," *International Journal of Psychoanalysis* (1952), p. 397. See also Loewald, pp. 268–69, 401–2. See Chodorow, *Mothering,* on the splitting technique of ego defense, primary identification, and the oral stage, p. 60.

[2]Loewald, pp. 16–17.

[3]Loewald, p. 17.

[4]Freud, "A Child Is Being Beaten," p. 129; Robert Stoller, "Facts and Fancies: An Examination of Freud's Concept of Bisexuality," in *Women and Analysis,* ed. Jean Strouse (New York: Grossman, 1974), pp. 357–60.

[5]Lawrence Kubie, "The Drive to Become Both Sexes," in *Symbols and Neurosis,* ed. Herbert J. Schlesinger (New York: International Universities Press, 1978), pp. 195, 202. See also Zilboorg and Kittay.

Socarides, Zilboorg, and others have linked the male's fetishization of the female to this same urge to restore the wholeness of bisexuality—of having both male and female sexual characteristics. In Socarides's view, the male's identification with the pre-Oedipal mother expresses itself in "the wish for female genitalia, the wish for a child, and the wish to undo the separation from the mother."[1] Cathexis and identification are simultaneous in the dual aim of the bisexual urge.[2] The ability to simultaneously desire and also identify with the opposite sex has important implications for film spectatorship. When opposite-sex identification has been considered, it has most often been regarded as a problem for the female spectator rather than as a potential pleasure available to both sexes. The "masculinization" of the feminine spectator has been discussed by Mary Ann Doane and Laura Mulvey in terms of the female spectator's identification with the male position. In their view, this trans-sex identification is the result of the female's lack of a spectatorial position of her own other than a masochistic–female/object identification.[3] Neglected are the possibilities of male identification with the female (even as an ideal ego) or his identification with a "feminized" masculine character.

Like the wish and counterwish for fusion with and separation from the mother, the wish to change gender identity, the "attempt to identify with and to become both parents," cannot be fulfilled in "reality."[4] Laplanche has stated that fantasy is one means of achieving the goal of reintegrating opposite-sex identification.[5] Otto Fenichel believed that scopophilic pleasure was dependent on taking the position, not of the observed same-sex participant in intercourse, but the opposite sex.[6] Through the mobility of multiple, fluid identifications, the cinema provides an enunciative apparatus that functions as a protective guise like fantasy or dream to permit the temporary satisfaction of what Kubie regards as "one of the deepest tendencies in human nature."[7]

Because pleasure in looking and, especially, looking at the dream screen of cinema and the female involves pregenital pleasures and ambivalences, the role and reaction of the sexually differentiated spectator must be approached in a completely different light. The pregenital pleasures of perversion are not limited to the enjoyment of the male spectator, nor available to the female only if she abandons masochistic identification with the "female object" and then identifies with a male spectatorial position defined only by control.

Prompted by the need to delineate the relationship of masochism and its formal

---

[1]Socarides, p. 307; Gregory Zilboorg, "Masculine and Feminine: Some Biological and Cultural Aspects," *Psychiatry* 7 (1944), pp. 257–96; Eva Feder Kittay, "Womb Envy: An Explanatory Concept," in *Mothering,* pp. 94–128.

[2]Bruno Bettelheim, *Symbolic Wounds* (Glencoe, Ill.: The Free Press, 1954), p. 260.

[3]Doane, "Film and the Masquerade," pp. 74–88; Laura Mulvey "Afterthoughts on 'Visual Pleasure and Narrative Cinema' Inspired by *Duel in the Sun*," *Framework* 15/16/17 (Summer 1981), pp. 12–15.

[4]Kubie, p. 211. See also Loewald, pp. 268–69.

[5]Jean Laplanche and J. B. Pontalis, *The Language of Psychoanalysis* (New York: W. W. Norton, 1973), pp. 243–46.

[6]Otto Fenichel, "Scopophilic Instinct and Identification," in *Collected Papers of Otto Fenichel: First Series* (New York: W. W. Norton, 1953), p. 377.

[7]Kubie, p. 211.

structures to current psychoanalysis, a reconsideration of the role of pregenital states of psychic development holds great promise for opening new areas of exploration in the study of spectatorial pleasure. Many of the assumptions adopted by film theorists from Freudian metapsychology or Lacan seem inadequate in accounting for cinematic pleasure. To understand the structure of looking, visual pleasure must be connected to its earliest manifestations in infancy. As Edith Jacobson's work implies, as well as that of Stoller, Bak, Loewald, and others, the visual pleasure experienced in archaic stages is not automatically negated by later stages of the child's development.* The close resemblance of the cinematic apparatus to the structures of perversion and, specifically, to masochism warrants further investigation beyond the limitations imposed by current theoretical discourse if the nature of cinematic pleasure is to be understood in its full complexity and psychological significance.

1985

---

*Edith Jacobson, *The Self and the Object World* (New York: International Universities Press, 1964).

BIBLIOGRAPHY

Affron, Charles. *Star Acting.* New York: Dutton, 1977.
———. *Cinema and Sentiment.* Chicago: University of Chicago Press, 1982.
Agee, James. *Agee on Film: Reviews and Comments.* Boston: Beacon Press, 1964.
Agel, Henri. *Le Cinéma et la sacré.* Paris: Editions du Cerf, 1961.
———. *Poétique du cinéma.* Paris: Editions du Signe, 1973.
Allen, Robert C., and Douglas Gomery. *Film History: Theory and Practice.* New York: Knopf, 1985.
Altman, Rick, ed. *Genre: The Musical.* (BFI Series) London: Routledge and Kegan Paul, 1981.
———. *The American Film Musical.* Bloomington: Indiana University Press, 1987.
Andrew, J. Dudley. *The Major Film Theories.* New York: Oxford University Press, 1976.
———. *André Bazin.* New York: Oxford University Press, 1978.
———. *Concepts in Film Theory.* New York: Oxford University Press, 1984.
Arnheim, Rudolf. *Art and Visual Perception.* Berkeley and Los Angeles: University of California Press, 1954.
———. *Film as Art.* Berkeley and Los Angeles: University of California Press, 1966.
———. *Visual Thinking.* Berkeley and Los Angeles: University of California Press, 1969.
Ayfre, Amédée. *Le Cinéma et sa vérité.* Paris: Editions du Cerf, 1964.
———. *Conversion aux images?* Paris: Editions du Cerf, 1964.
———. *Cinéma et mystère.* Paris: Editions du Cerf, 1969.
Balázs, Béla. *Theory of the Film: Character and Growth of a New Art.* New York: Dover Publications, 1970.
Balio, Tino, ed. *The American Film Industry,* rev. ed. Madison: University of Wisconsin Press, 1985.
Barnouw, Eric. *Documentary: A History of Non-Fiction Film.* New York: Oxford University Press, 1974.
Barr, Charles. "CinemaScope: Before and After." *Film Quarterly 16,* no. 4, Summer 1963.
Barsam, Richard Meran. *Nonfiction Film: A Critical History.* New York: Dutton, 1972.
———. *Nonfiction Film: Theory and Criticism.* New York: Dutton, 1975.
Barthes, Roland. *Elements of Semiology,* tr. Annette Laversy and Colin Smith. New York: Hill and Wang, 1967.

————. *Mythologies,* ed. Annette Laversy. New York: Hill and Wang, 1972.

————. *Image-Music-Text,* tr. Stephen Heath. New York: Hill and Wang, 1977.

Battcock, Gregory, ed. *The New American Cinema.* New York: Dutton, 1967.

Bazin, André. *What is Cinema?* Vol. 1. Berkeley and Los Angeles: University of California Press, 1971.

————. *What is Cinema?* Vol. 2. Berkeley and Los Angeles: University of California Press, 1971.

Benjamin, Walter. *Illuminations,* ed. and intro. Hannah Arendt. New York: Harcourt Brace, 1968.

Bergman, Andrew. *We're in the Money.* New York: Harper Colophon, 1972.

Bergson, Henri. "Laughter," in *Comedy,* ed. Wylie Sypher. Garden City, N.Y.: Doubleday Anchor, 1956.

Bluestone, George. *Novels into Film.* Berkeley and Los Angeles: University of California Press, 1966.

Bobker, Lee R. *Elements of Film.* New York: Harcourt Brace, 1969.

Bordwell, David. *Narration in the Fiction Film.* Madison: University of Wisconsin Press, 1985.

————, and Kristin Thompson. *Film Art: An Introduction.* Reading, Mass.: Addison and Wesley, 1979.

————, Janet Staiger, and Kristin Thompson. *The Classical Hollywood Cinema: Film Style and Mode of Production to 1960.* New York: Columbia University Press, 1985.

Brakhage, Stan. "Metaphors on Vision." *Film Culture,* no. 30, Fall 1963.

Branigan, Edward. *Point of View in the Cinema.* The Hague: Mouton, 1984.

Braudy, Leo. *The World in a Frame.* Garden City, N.Y.: Anchor Press, 1976; 2d ed., Chicago: University of Chicago Press, 1984.

————, and Morris Dickstein, eds. *Great Film Directors: A Critical Anthology.* New York: Oxford University Press, 1978.

Browne, Nick. *The Rhetoric of Film Narrative.* Ann Arbor: UMI, 1982.

Burch, Noël. *Theory of Film Practice,* tr. Helen R. Lane, intro. Annette Michelson. New York: Praeger, 1973.

Carroll, Noël. "Address to the Heathens." *October* no. 23 (Winter 1982), 89–163.

————. *Mystifying Movies: Fads and Fallacies in Contemporary Film Theory.* New York: Columbia University Press, 1988.

————. *Philosophical Problems of Classical Film Theory.* Princeton: Princeton University Press, 1988.

Caughie, John, ed. *Theories of Authorship.* (BFI Series) London: Routledge and Kegan Paul, 1981.

Cavell, Stanley. *The World Viewed: Reflections on the Ontology of Film.* New York: Viking, 1971; 2d ed., 1979.

————. *Pursuits of Happiness: The Hollywood Comedy of Remarriage.* Cambridge: Harvard University Press, 1981.

Cawelti, John. *The Six-Gun Mystique.* Bowling Green, Ohio: Bowling Green Popular Press, 1971.

————. *Adventure, Mystery and Romance: Formula Stories as Art and Popular Culture.* Chicago: University of Chicago Press, 1976.

Chatman, Seymour. *Coming to Terms: The Rhetoric of Narrative in Fiction and Film.* Ithaca: Cornell University Press, 1990.

————. *Story and Discourse: Narrative Structures in Fiction and Film.* Ithaca: Cornell University Press, 1978.

Clarens, Carlos. *An Illustrated History of the Horror Film.* New York: Capricorn Books, 1968.

Cocteau, Jean. *Cocteau on the Film,* tr. Vera Triall. New York: Roy Publishers, 1954.

Cohen, Keith. *Film and Fiction: The Dynamics of Exchange.* New Haven: Yale University Press, 1979.

Cohen-Séat, Gilbert. *Essai sur les principes d'une philosophie due cinéma.* Paris: Presses Universitaires de France, 1958.

———. *Problèmes du cinéma et de l'information visuelle.* Paris: Presses Universitaires de France, 1961.

Corliss, Richard. *Talking Pictures: Screenwriters in the American Cinema.* New York: Overlook Press, 1974.

Cripps, Thomas. *Slow Fade to Black: The Negro in American Film, 1900–42.* New York: Oxford University Press, 1977.

Croce, Arlene. *The Fred Astaire and Ginger Rogers Book.* New York: Vintage Books, 1972.

DeLauretis, Teresa. *Alice Doesn't: Feminism, Semiotics, Cinema.* Bloomington: Indiana University Press, 1984.

———. *Technologies of Gender.* Bloomington: Indiana University Press, 1987.

———, and Stephen Heath, eds. *The Cinematic Apparatus.* New York: St. Martin's Press, 1980.

Derrida, Jacques. *Writing and Difference.* Chicago: University of Chicago Press, 1978.

Doane, Mary Ann. *Femmes Fatales: Feminism, Film Theory, Psychoanalysis.* New York: Routledge, 1991.

———. *The Desire to Desire: The Woman's Film of the 1940s.* Bloomington: Indiana University Press, 1987.

———, Patricia Mellencamp, and Linda Williams, eds. *Re-Vision: Essays in Feminist Film Criticism.* Frederick, Md.: University Publications of America, Inc. and the American Film Institute, 1984.

Doesburg, Theo van. "Film as Pure Form." *Form* (Cambridge), no. 1, Summer 1966.

Durgnat, Raymond. *Films and Feelings.* Cambridge, Mass.: The M.I.T. Press, 1967.

Dyer, Richard. *Stars.* London: British Film Institute, 1979.

Earle, William. "Revolt Against Realism in the Films." *The Journal of Aesthetics and Art Criticism 27,* no. 2, Winter 1968.

Eco, Umberto. *A Theory of Semiotics.* Bloomington: Indiana University Press, 1976.

Eisentein, Sergei M. *Film Form,* ed. and tr. Jay Leyda. New York: Harcourt Brace, 1949.

———. *The Film Sense,* ed. and tr. Jay Leyda. New York: Harcourt Brace, n.d.

Ellis, John. *Visible Fictions.* London: Routledge and Kegan Paul, 1982.

Farber, Manny. *Negative Space.* New York: Praeger Publishers, 1971.

Faure, Élie. *The Art of Cineplastics.* Boston: Four Seas Company, 1923.

Fell, John. *Film and the Narrative Tradition.* Berkeley: University of California Press, 1974.

Fenin, George N., and William K. Everson. *The Western.* New York: Grossman, 1973.

Ferguson, Otis. *The Film Criticism of Otis Ferguson,* ed., with preface by Robert Wilson, foreword by Andrew Sarris. Philadelphia: Temple University Press, 1971.

Feuer, Jane. *The Hollywood Musical.* Bloomington: Indiana University Press, 1982.

Film Comment. "Hollywood Screenwriters" (Special Issue), *6,* no. 4, Winter 1970–71.

———. "The Men with the Movie Cameras" (Special Issue). *8,* no. 2, Summer 1972.

Fischer, Lucy. *Shot/Countershot: Film Tradition and Women's Cinema.* Princeton: Princeton University Press, 1989.

Fredericksen, Donald L. *The Aesthetic of Isolation in Film Theory: Hugo Münsterberg.* New York: Arno Press, 1977.

Gabler, Neal. *An Empire of Their Own: How the Jews Invented Hollywood.* New York: Doubleday, 1988.

Geduld, Harry. *Film Makers on Film Making.* Bloomington: Indiana University Press, 1981.

Gessner, Robert. *The Moving Image: A Guide to Cinematic Literacy.* New York: Dutton, 1968.

Gomery, Douglas. *The Hollywood Studio System.* London: Macmillan, 1986.

Gouhier, Henri. *L'essence du théâtre.* Paris: Plon, 1948.

———. *Le théâtre et l'existence.* Paris: Auber, 1952.

Grant, Barry Keith, ed. *Film Genre Reader.* Austin: University of Texas Press, 1986.

Grierson, John. *Grierson on Documentary,* ed. Forsyth Hardy. New York: Harcourt Brace, 1947.

Harrington, John. *The Rhetoric of Film.* New York: Holt, Rinehart, and Winston, 1973.

Harvey, Sylvia. *May Sixty-Eight and Film Culture.* (BFI Series) New York: New York Zoetrope, 1980.

Haskell, Molly. *From Reverence to Rape: The Treatment of Women in the Movies.* New York: Holt, Rinehart, and Winston, 1974.

Hauser, Arnold. *The Social History of Art,* 2 vols. New York: Knopf, 1951.

Heath, Stephen. *Questions of Cinema.* Bloomington: Indiana University Press, 1981.

———. "Le Père Noël." *October* 26 (1983), 63–115.

Henderson, Brian. *A Critique of Film Theory.* New York: Dutton, 1980.

Hjelmslev, Louis. *Essais linguistiques.* Copenhagen: Nordisk Sprog-og kulturforlag, 1959.

———. *Prolegomena to a Theory of Language.* Bloomington: Indiana University Publications in Anthropology and Linguistics, 1953.

Houston, Beverle, and Marsha Kinder. *Self and Cinema.* Pleasantville, N.Y.: Redgrave Publishing Company, 1980.

Huss, Roy, and Norman Silverstein. *The Film Experience: Elements of Motion Picture Art.* New York: Harper and Row, 1968.

Jacobs, Lewis. *The Rise of the American Film: A Critical History.* New York: Teachers College Press, 1967.

Jarvie, I. C. *Movies and Society.* New York: Basic Books, 1970.

Jowett, Garth. *Film: The Democratic Art.* Boston: Little, Brown, 1976.

Kael, Pauline. *I Lost It at the Movies.* Boston: Little, Brown, 1965.

Kaplan, E. Ann, ed. *Women in Film Noir.* (BFI Series) New York: New York Zoetrope, 1980.

———. *Women and Film: Both Sides of the Camera.* New York: Methuen, 1983.

Kauffmann, Stanley. "Notes on Theater-and-Film." *Performance* 1, no. 4, October 1972.

———, with B. Henstell. *American Film Criticism.* New York: Liveright, 1972.

Kawin, Bruce F. *Mindscreen: Bergman, Godard and First-Person Film.* Princeton: Princeton University Press, 1978.

Kelman, Ken. "The Reality of New Cinema," in *The New American Cinema,* ed. Gregory Battcock. New York: Dutton, 1967.

Kinder, Marsha, and Beverle Houston. *Close Up: A Critical Perspective on Film.* New York: Harcourt, Brace, Jovanovich, 1972.

Kitses, Jim. *Horizons West.* Bloomington: Indiana University Press, 1970.

Kozarski, Richard. *Hollywood Directors, 1914–1940.* New York: Oxford University Press, 1976.

Kracauer, Siegfried. *From Caligari to Hitler: A Psychological History of the German Film.* Princeton: Princeton University Press, 1947.

———. *Theory of Film: The Redemption of Physical Reality.* London, Oxford, New York: Oxford University Press, 1960.

Kuhn, Annette. *Women's Pictures: Feminism and Cinema.* London: Routledge and Kegan Paul, 1982.

Kuleshov, Lev. *Kuleshov on Film.* Berkeley: University of California Press, 1974.

Lacan, Jacques. *Écrits: A Selection.* New York: W. W. Norton, 1977.

Langer, Susanne, K. *Feeling and Form.* New York: Scribner's, 1953.

Lawder, Standish D. *The Cubist Cinema.* New York: New York University Press, 1975.

Lawson, John Howard. *The Creative Process.* New York: Hill and Wang, 1964.

Lessing, Gotthold Ephraim. *Laocoön: An Essay Upon the Limits of Painting and Poetry.* Baltimore: John Hopkins University Press, 1984.

Lévi-Strauss, Claude. "Structural Analysis in Linguistics and in Anthropology," in *Structural Anthropology.* New York: Basic Books, 1963.

Leyda, Jay. *Kino, A History of Russian and Soviet Film.* New York: Macmillan, 1960.

Lindgren, Ernest. *The Art of the Film,* rev. ed. London: Allen and Unwin, 1963.

Lindsay, Vachel. *The Art of the Moving Picture,* rev. ed. New York: Macmillan, 1922.

Lotman, Jurij. *Semiotics of the Cinema,* tr. Mark E. Suino. Ann Arbor: University of Michigan Press, 1976.

Lovell, Terry. *Pictures of Reality: Aesthetics, Politics, Pleasure.* (BFI Series) New York: New York Zoetrope, 1980.

Macbean, James Roy. *Film and Revolution.* Bloomington: University of Indiana Press, 1975.

MacCabe, Colin. *Tracking the Signifier: Theoretical Essays.* Minneapolis: University of Minnesota Press, 1985.

McCann, Richard Dyer. *Film: A Montage of Theories.* New York: Dutton, 1966.

McConnell, Frank. *Storytelling and Mythmaking: Images from Film and Literature.* New York: Oxford University Press, 1970.

Manvell, Roger. *Film.* London: Penguin Books, 1946.

———. *Shakespeare and the Film.* New York: Praeger, 1971.

Marinetti, Filippo T. *Selected Writings,* tr. Arthur A. Coppotelli and R. W. Flint. New York: Noonday, 1972.

Martin, Marcel. *Le langage cinématographique.* Paris: Editions du Cerf, 1955.

Martinet, André. *Elements of General Linguistics,* tr. Elisabeth Palmer. London: Faber and Faber, 1960.

Mast, Gerald. *The Comic Mind: Comedy and the Movies.* New York: Bobbs-Merrill, 1973.

———. *Film/Cinema/Movie: A Theory of Experience.* New York: Harper and Row, 1977.

Mellen, Joan. *Big Bad Wolves: Masculinity in American Films.* New York: Pantheon Books, 1978.

Merleau-Ponty, Maurice. "The Film and the New Psychology," in *Sense and Non-sense,* tr. Hubert L. and Patricia A. Dreyfus. Evanston, Ill.: Northwestern University Press, 1964.

Metz, Christian. *Film Language: A Semiotics of the Cinema,* tr. Michael Taylor. New York: Oxford University Press, 1974.

———. *Language and Cinema,* tr. Donna Jean Umiker-Seboek. The Hague: Mouton, 1974.

———. *The Imaginary Signifier: Psychoanalysis and the Cinema,* tr. Celia Britton et al. Bloomington: Indiana University Press, 1982.

Meyerhold, Vsevolod. *Meyerhold on Theater,* ed. Edward Braun. New York: Hill and Wang, 1969.

Mitry, Jean. *Esthétique et psychologie du cinéma,* 2 vols. Paris: Éditions Universitaires, 1963–65.

Modleski, Tania. *Loving with a Vengeance: Mass-Produced Fantasies for Women.* London and New York: Methuen, 1984.

———. *The Women Who Knew Too Much: Hitchcock and Feminist Theory.* New York: Methuen, 1988.

Moholy-Nagy, Lâszló. *Vision in Motion.* Chicago: University of Chicago Press, 1947.

Monaco, James. *How to Read a Film.* New York: Oxford University Press, 1981.

Montagu, Ivor. *Film World.* Baltimore: Penguin, 1964.

Morin, Edgar. *Le Cinéma ou l'homme imaginaire.* Paris: Editions de Minuit, 1956.

———. *The Stars,* tr. Richard Howard. New York: Grove Press, 1960.

Münsterberg, Hugo. *The Film: A Psychological Study.* New York: Dover, 1969.

Naremore, James. *Acting in the Cinema.* Berkeley: University of California Press, 1988.

Newcomb, Horace, ed. *Television: The Critical View,* 3rd ed. New York: Oxford University Press, 1982.

Nichols, Bill. *Ideology and Image.* Bloomington: Indiana University Press, 1981.

———, ed. *Movies and Methods.* Berkeley and Los Angeles: University of California Press, 1976.

———, ed. *Movies and Methods, Volume 2.* Berkeley, Los Angeles, London: University of California Press, 1985.

Nicoll, Allardyce. *Film and Theatre.* New York: Thomas Y. Crowell, 1937.

Olson, Elder. *The Theory of Comedy.* Bloomington and London: Indiana University Press, 1968.

Orwell, George. "Boys' Weeklies," in *Essays.* New York: Doubleday, 1954.

Panofsky, Erwin. "Style and Medium in the Motion Pictures." *Critique* 1, no. 3, January–February 1947.

Penley, Constance. *Feminism and Film Theory.* New York: Routledge, 1988.

Perkins, V. F. *Film as Film: Understanding and Judging Movies.* Baltimore: Penguin, 1972.

Polan, Dana. *The Political Language of Film and the Avant-garde.* Ann Arbor: UMI, 1985.

———. *Power and Paranoia: History, Narrative, and the American Cinema.* New York: Columbia University Press, 1986.

Powdermaker, Hortense. *Hollywood, the Dream Factory.* Boston: Little Brown, 1960.

Pudovkin, Vsevolod I. *Film Technique and Film Acting,* ed. and tr. Ivor Montagu. New York: Grove Press, 1960.

Quarterly Review of Film Studies. "Interdisciplinary Approaches to Film Study" (Special Issue). *1*, no. 2, Summer 1976.

———. "Film and Semiotics" (Special Issue). *2*, no. 1, Winter 1977.

Ray, Robert. *A Certain Tendency of the Hollywood Cinema, 1930–1980.* Princeton: Princeton University Press, 1985.

Reisz, Karel. *The Technique of Film Editing.* New York: Hastings House, 1968.

Renan, Sheldon. *An Introduction to the American Underground Film.* New York: Dutton, 1967.

Richie, Donald. *The Japanese Movie,* rev. ed. Tokyo: Kodansha International Ltd., 1982.

Richter, Hans, "The Film as an Original Art Form." *Film Culture* 1, no. 1, January 1955.

Rosen, Philip, ed. *Narrative, Apparatus, Ideology: A Film Theory Reader.* New York: Columbia University Press, 1986.

Rotha, Paul, Road Sinclair, and Richard Griffith. *Documentary Film.* London: Faber and Faber, 1966.

Rothman, William. *Hitchcock: The Murderous Gaze.* Cambridge, Mass.: Harvard University Press, 1982.

Russo, Vito. *The Celluloid Closet: Homosexuality in the Movies.* New York: Harper and Row, 1981.

Sadoul, Georges. *Histoire générale du cinéma,* 5 vols. Paris: Editions Denoël, 1946–54.

Salt, Barry. *Film Style and Technology: History and Analysis.* London: Starwood, 1983.

Sarris, Andrew. *The American Cinema: Directors and Directions 1929–1968.* New York: Dutton, 1969.

———. "Notes on the *Auteur* Theory in 1962," in *Film Culture Reader,* ed. P. Adams Sitney. New York: Praeger, 1970.

———. "Notes on the *Auteur* Theory in 1970." *Film Comment 6,* no. 3, Fall 1970.

———. "Film Criticism in the Seventies." *Film Comment 14,* no. 1, January 1978.

de Saussure, Ferdinand. *Course in General Linguistics,* tr. Wade Baskin. New York: McGraw-Hill, 1966.

Schatz, Thomas. *Hollywood Genres: Formulas, Filmmaking, and the Studio System.* New York: Random House, 1981.

———. *The Genius of the System: Hollywood Filmmaking in the Studio Era.* New York: Pantheon, 1988.

Schnitzer, Luda, and Jean and Marcel Martin, eds. *Cinema in Revolution: The Heroic Age of the Soviet Film.* New York: Hill and Wang, 1973.

Seldes, Gilbert. *The Movies Come From America.* New York: Scribner's, 1937.

———. *The Great Audience.* New York: Viking, 1950.

———. *The Public Arts.* New York: Simon and Schuster, 1956.

Silverman, Kaja. *The Subject of Semiotics.* New York: Oxford University Press, 1983.

———. *The Acoustic Mirror: The Female Voice in Psychoanalysis and Cinema.* Bloomington: Indiana University Press, 1988.

Sitney, P. Adams, ed. *Film Culture Reader.* New York: Praeger, 1970.

———. *Visionary Film: The American Avant-Garde.* New York: Oxford University Press, 1974.

———, ed. *The Essential Cinema: Essays on the Films in the Collection of Anthology Film Archives.* New York: Anthology Film Archives and New York University Press, 1975.

————, ed. *The Avant Garde Film, A Reader of Theory and Criticism*. New York: New York University Press, 1978.

Sklar, Robert. *Movie-Made America*. New York: Random House, 1975.

Slusser, George E., and Eric S. Rabkin. *Shadows of the Magic Lamp: Fantasy and Science Fiction in Film*. Carbondale: Southern Illinois University Press, 1985.

Sontag, Susan. *Against Interpretation*. New York: Farrar, Straus & Giroux, 1966.

————. *Styles of Radical Will*. New York: Farrar, Straus & Giroux, 1966.

————. *On Photography*. New York: Farrar, Straus & Giroux, 1977.

Spottiswoode, Raymond. *A Grammar of the Film*. Berkeley and Los Angeles: University of California Press, 1950.

Stephenson, Ralph, and J. R. Debrix. *The Cinema as Art*. Baltimore: Penguin, 1965.

Studlar, Gaylyn. *In the Realm of Pleasure: Von Sternberg, Dietrich, and the Masochistic Aesthetic*. Urbana: University of Illinois Press, 1988.

Taylor, John Russell, and Arthur Jackson. *The Hollywood Musical*. New York: McGraw-Hill, 1971.

Thompson, Kristin. *Breaking the Glass Armor: Neoformalist Film Analysis*. Princeton: Princeton University Press, 1988.

Todd, Janet, ed. *Women and Film*. New York: Holmes and Meier, 1988.

Tudor, Andrew. *Theories of Film*. New York: Viking, 1973.

Tyler, Parker. *The Hollywood Hallucination*. New York: Simon and Schuster, 1970.

————. *Magic and Myth of the Movies*. New York: Simon and Schuster, 1970.

————. *Sex Psyche Etcetera in the Film*. Baltimore: Penguin, 1971.

Warshow, Robert. *The Immediate Experience*. New York: Doubleday Anchor, 1964.

Weis, Elizabeth, and John Belton, eds. *Film Sound: Theory and Practice*. New York: Columbia University Press, 1985.

Williams, Christopher, ed. *Realism and the Cinema: A Reader*. London: Routledge and Kegan Paul, 1980.

Williams, Linda. *Figures of Desire: A Theory and Analysis of Surrealist Film*. Urbana: University of Illinois Press, 1981.

————. *Hard Core: Power, Pleasure, and the "Frenzy of the Visible."* Berkeley: University of California Press, 1989.

Wilson, George. *Narration in Light: Studies in Cinematic Point of View*. Baltimore: Johns Hopkins University Press, 1986.

Wolfenstein, Martha, and Nathan Leites. *Movies, a Psychological Study*. Glencoe, Illinois: The Free Press, 1950.

Wollen, Peter. *Signs and Meaning in the Cinema*, new and enlarged ed. Bloomington: Indiana University Press, 1972.

Wood, Michael. *America at the Movies*. New York: Basic Books, 1975; 2d ed., Columbia University Press, 1990.

Wood, Robin. *Hollywood from Vietnam to Reagan*. New York: Columbia University Press, 1986.

Youngblood, Gene. *Expanded Cinema*. New York: Dutton, 1970.